TOOLS

OF

DOMINION

The case laws of Exodus? What are case laws, anyway? What have they got to do with anything in the modern world? What have they got to do with the church of Jesus Christ?

Case laws are the specific applications of one or more of God's Ten Commandments in specific areas of life. Case laws are where "the rubber meets the road" for those who claim that they are doing their best to obey the Ten Commandments. Will our political leaders encourage us to honor the Ten Commandments by honoring the case laws, or will they encourage us to break the Ten Commandments by ignoring the case laws?

For over three centuries, American Christians and humanists alike have agreed: there is no need to enforce the case laws. At most, only the "moral laws" of the Bible should be enforced. What are these "moral laws"? In practice, they are whatever laws the voters are familiar with and satisfied with. People baptize the status quo with the designation, "moral laws of God."

God is not mocked. Societies that think they are being progressive by ignoring the specifics of God's law discover that they cannot provide justice. Individuals find themselves at the mercy of unjust rules. They pursue freedom from God and gain bondage under men.

Today, abortion on demand is legal. Christians suspect that there is something wrong with this, but they don't know what. They have not been told that abortion is prohibited by the case laws of Exodus.

Today, drunk drivers are issued traffic citations and are back on the highways in a few hours. If the case laws of Exodus were enforced, drunk drivers would receive capital-impairing fines, and the death penalty would be imposed on them in cases of so-called "manslaughter." There are no "accidents" for drunk drivers.

Today, criminals are rarely convicted, and those who are convicted receive suspended sentences. Only hard-core criminals are likely to be sent to jail for a few years, leaving their victims even poorer

e case laws of Exodus
d be required to make

one hand from local
d from federal bureau-
siness by accusing it
virtually no scientific
Exodus were enforced,
he pollution level they
reby keep local busi-

central bank inflates
ncy on its own author-
s accelerate this proc-
hen recessions. If the
orced, there could be
te mass inflation or

vs of Exodus are dis-
. "A modern society
v code of a primitive
. And who assures us?
t we need more politi-
re of our government

for 3,400 years, but
it in favor of the crea-
y have pursued their
sions, and they have
Exodus. They have
s, that all we need to
ourselves in order to
n society. Christians
hy rather than to the
ustice. But they have
e ancient Greeks.
r. Gary North exam-
e case laws. How did
What moral and judi-
h of them? How did
ify them? How could

ribes in great detail
to work in God's his-
evealed law. It shows
uired by God to dis-
e promises that God
honor His word.

is also a warning. It
ls and societies that
d daily by ignoring
varns of the negative
brings against all
on His precepts. He
ut He also brings

(continued on back flap)

TOOLS OF DOMINION

Other books by Gary North

Marx's Religion of Revolution, 1968 [1988]
An Introduction to Christian Economics, 1973
Unconditional Surrender, 1981 [1988]
Successful Investing in an Age of Envy, 1981
The Dominion Covenant: Genesis, 1982 [1988]
Government By Emergency, 1983
The Last Train Out, 1983
Backward, Christian Soldiers?, 1984
75 Bible Questions Your Instructors Pray You Won't Ask, 1984 [1988]
Coined Freedom: Gold in the Age of the Bureaucrats, 1984
Moses and Pharaoh: Dominion Religion Versus Power Religion, 1985
Negatrends, 1985
The Sinai Strategy: Economics and the Ten Commandments, 1986
Conspiracy: A Biblical View, 1986
Unholy Spirits: Occultism and New Age Humanism, 1986
Honest Money, 1986
Fighting Chance, 1986 [with Arthur Robinson]
Dominion and Common Grace, 1987
Inherit the Earth, 1987
The Pirate Economy, 1987
Liberating Planet Earth, 1987
Healer of the Nations, 1987
Is the World Running Down?, 1988
Puritan Economic Experiments, 1988
Trespassing for Dear Life, 1989
When Justice Is Aborted, 1989
Political Polytheism: The Myth of Pluralism, 1989

Books edited by Gary North

Foundations of Christian Scholarship, 1976
Tactics of Christian Resistance, 1983
The Theology of Christian Resistance, 1983
Editor, *Journal of Christian Reconstruction* (1974-1981)

TOOLS OF DOMINION

The Case Laws of Exodus

Gary North

Institute for Christian Economics
Tyler, Texas

Copyright © 1990
Gary North

Published by
The Institute for Christian Economics,
P.O. Box 8000, Tyler, Texas 75711

Typesetting by Thoburn Press,
P.O. Box 2459, Reston, Virginia 22090

Library of Congress Cataloging-in-Publication Data

North, Gary.
    Tools of Dominion : the case laws of Exodus / Gary North.
        p.   cm.
    Includes bibliographical references.
    ISBN 0-930464-10-9 (alk. paper) : $29.95
    1. Bible. O.T.   Exodus XXI-XL — Commentaries.
2. Dominion theology. 3. Economics in the Bible. 4. Jewish
law. 5. Economics — Religious aspects — Christianity. 6. Law
(Theology) 7. Church and state — Biblical teaching.
I. Institute for Christian Economics. II. Title.
BS1245.3.N59   1990
261.8'5 — dc20   90-4054
                                                              CIP

This book is dedicated to

James Dobson

whose rhetorical question (p. 360)
deserved an exegetical response.

TABLE OF CONTENTS

INTRODUCTION

This is he [Moses], that was in the church in the wilderness with the angel which spake to him in the mount Sina, and with our fathers: who received the lively oracles to give unto us: To whom our fathers would not obey, but thrust him from them, and in their hearts turned back again into Egypt (Acts 7:38-39).

We are witnessing today a recapitulation of Moses' experience with the Jews of his day. Protestant fundamentalist Christians have their eyes on the sky, their heads in the clouds, their hearts in Egypt, and their children in the government's schools. So, for that matter, do most of the other Christian groups. The handful of Christian Reconstructionist authors who are serving as modern-day Stephens with respect to defending the continuing validity of biblical law have experienced a response from the various ecclesiastical Sanhedrins of our day somewhat analogous to the response that Stephen's testimony produced: verbal stones. (Prior to 1986, we received mostly stony silence.)

If the modern church were honest, it would rewrite one of the popular hymns of our day: "O, how hate I thy law, O, how hate I thy law. It is my consternation all the day." But the modern church, hating God's revealed law with all its Egyptian heart, is inherently dishonest. It is self-deceived, having no permanent ethical standards to use as an honest mirror. The hearer of the word who refuses to obey, James says, is like a man who beholds his face in a looking glass, walks away, "and straightway forgetteth what manner of man he was" (James 1:24b). The modern Christian refuses even to pick up the mirror of God's law and look.

Tools of Dominion is the final volume of my economic commentary on the Book of Exodus. This multi-volume commentary on Exodus constitutes the second installment of my general series, *The Dominion Covenant*, also titled "An Economic Commentary on the Bible." No

1

doubt these multiple names will drive future graduate students crazy as they try to footnote each volume. I had hoped to see Exodus published someday as a two-volume hardback set, but the size of this third volume precludes such a venture. The first volume of the general series, on Genesis, was published in 1982.[1] The first Exodus volume, *Moses and Pharaoh*, covers Exodus 1-18.[2] The second volume, *The Sinai Strategy*, covers Exodus 20.[3] (I have found nothing with specifically economic content in Exodus 19. Given the costs of typesetting and the difficulty of re-indexing, I hope I never do.)

Fat Books and Social Transformation

This is a fat book. I have no illusions about its becoming a bestseller. But I hold to what I call the fat book theory of social transformation. Most of the major turning points in Western history have had fat books at their center. The Bible is certainly a fat book. Augustine's *City of God* is a fat book, and by adhering to the biblical worldview, it restructured Western civilization's concept of history.[4] Thomas Aquinas' *Summa Theologica* is a fat book, and it gave the medieval West the crucial synthesis of scholastic philosophy, an intellectual tradition still defended by a handful of Roman Catholic conservatives and (implicitly, at least) by most contemporary Protestant fundamentalist philosophers. John Calvin's *Institutes of the Christian Religion* is a fat book, and it structured a large segment of Reformation theology.

Christians have not been the only social transformationists who have written fat books that have changed Western civilization. Thomas Hobbes' *Leviathan* is a fat book, and it launched the long tradition of social contract political theory. Immanuel Kant's *Critique of Pure Reason* is a fat book, and you just about have to take his *Critique of Practical Reason* as its companion volume. This set restructured modern philosophy, and in the twentieth century, theology (by way of Karl Barth and Emil Brunner).[5] William Blackstone's *Commen-*

---

1. *The Dominion Covenant: Genesis* (Tyler, Texas: Institute for Christian Economics, 1982). Reprinted with additions, 1987.

2. *Moses and Pharaoh: Dominion Religion vs. Power Religion* (Tyler, Texas: Institute for Christian Economics, 1985).

3. *The Sinai Strategy: Economics and the Ten Commandments* (Tyler, Texas: Institute for Christian Economics, 1986).

4. Karl Löwith, *Meaning in History* (University of Chicago Press, 1949), ch. 9.

5. Cornelius Van Til, *The New Modernism* (Philadelphia: Presbyterian & Reformed, 1947).

taries on the Laws of England is a four-volume fat book, yet it was read by just about every lawyer in the British colonies after 1765. *The Federalist* is fat. (Of course, it had its greatest initial effect as a series of newspaper articles, 1787-88, during the debate over the ratification of the U.S. Constitution, which gives us some comparative indication of the recent effects of humanist public school programs to achieve universal literacy in the United States. Try to get the average American newspaper reader to read, digest, and comment on *The Federalist*.)

A decade after Blackstone's *Commentaries*, came Adam Smith's *Wealth of Nations*, a fat book. Karl Marx's *Das Kapital* is a fat book; if you include the two posthumous volumes, it is a very fat book. If you include his posthumous multi-volume *Theories of Surplus Value*, it is positively obese. All these fat books have sat on library shelves and have intimidated people, generation after generation. And a handful of influential people actually went to the effort to read them, subsequently believed them, and then wrote more books in terms of them.

Exceptions to the Rule

There are exceptions to my fat book theory. Machiavelli's *The Prince* is a thin book. So is his *Discourses*. John Locke's *Second Treatise of Government* is a thin book. Jean Jacques Rousseau's *Social Contract* is thin. So is Edmund Burke's *Reflections on the Revolution in France*.

Then there are medium-sized books. The first edition of Charles Darwin's *Origin of Species* was a medium-sized book. John Maynard Keynes' *General Theory of Employment, Interest, and Money* is a medium-sized book. So is F. A. Hayek's *Road to Serfdom*. (But when he wrote it, Hayek's bookshelf contained Eugen von Böhm-Bawerk's three-volume *Capital and Interest* and Ludwig von Mises' *Theory of Money and Credit, Socialism*, and *Nationalökonomie [Human Action]*, all of which are fat books.)

Thin and medium-sized books have their rightful place in initiating social transformations. But to maintain such a transformation, there had better be some fat back-up books on the shelf. "What should we do now?" the initially victorious revolutionaries inescapably ask. Fat books provide answers. More than this: *if fat books with believable answers are not already on the shelf, there will not be a successful social transformation.* Men will not draw others into their revolutionary cause unless the potential recruits become persuaded that the promoters have answers to specific real-world problems — problems that contemporary society is not dealing with successfully.

Producing a true revolution requires the support of many kinds of printed materials, from pamphlets to thick, technical volumes. Those in the midst of a revolution seldom have time to think through every aspect of the changes their slogans and actions are producing, but the revolution's leaders need to know that the basic theoretical work has been done, that workable, principled, and consistent answers to specific historical problems are in reserve, and that after the dust settles, the heirs of the revolution will be able steadily to restructure society in ways that are consistent with the ideals of the revolution. This faith has been misplaced on many past occasions, the obvious example being Communists' faith in Marx's *Das Kapital*, which had been inaccurate economics in theory, and which could not be applied successfully in any Communist nation without destroying the productivity of that economy. But it was necessary that at least the first volume of *Das Kapital* be on the shelves of the revolutionaries (the three subsequent volumes were not published in the lifetime of either Marx or Engels). Its very presence gave confidence to those who were launching the Communist revolution. The book was fat and unreadable, but that was an advantage; men's faith in Marx's solutions was not shattered by ever having read it.

The wise social strategist writes fat books and thin books and books in between, not knowing which will work. Augustine and Aquinas wrote all sorts of books. So did Kant, whose brief *Universal Natural History and Theory of the Heavens* first proposed the idea of galactic evolution. Darwin kept fattening up *Origin*, and then added *The Descent of Man*. Marx wrote the *Communist Manifesto*, plus endless journalism pieces, some of which constituted books. He also was in partnership with Frederick Engels, who was smart enough to extract and separately publish *Socialism: Utopian and Scientific* from the stillborn *Herr Eugen Dühring's Revolution in Science*. Lenin wrote materials of all sizes, decade after decade. I, too, have written my share of thin and medium-sized books. (Well, mostly the latter.)

Why So Fat?

This book is fat, but it is not unreadable. It may sit on many shelves for many years, but those who open it will be able to find specific answers to real-world economic problems — answers that are self-consciously structured in terms of the revealed word of God. If my answers were not detailed, if my logic were not spelled out, and if my sources were not cited in full, then this book could no more serve as a reliable guide to economic reconstruction than some fat polemical tract published by the Maryknoll Order or written by a sociology professor at Wheaton College.

Tools of Dominion is a commentary, not a novel; it is a reference work, not a catechism. It tries to accomplish a great deal: exegete verses, describe how they applied in the Old Testament era, explain why they should be applied today, and offer examples of how they might be applied in practice. It is large because I want it to serve for many years (preferably centuries) as one of the two key reference works on specific applications of biblical law in economics and jurisprudence; the other is not yet written: my commentary on Deuteronomy. I have decided to extract from this book separate sections that deal with narrower problems, which I intend to publish under separate titles: *Clean Living: A Biblical View of Pollution*, *Victim's Rights: A Biblical View of Jurisprudence*, and *Slavery: A Biblical View*. Nevertheless, I have retained the same information in this volume, simply because not every library will have the other three books plus this one on its shelves. I want to make certain that readers of this comprehensive volume have all of my arguments in front of them.

In some ways, I wish I could imitate Moses Maimonides, the late-twelfth-century Jewish scholar. In defending the style of the enormous output of his life's literary work (he was also a full-time physician to the Sultan in Cairo), including his monumental fourteen-volume *Code* (the *Mishneh Torah*), he wrote: "All our works are concise and to the point. We have no intention of writing bulky books nor of spending time on that which is useless. Hence when we explain anything, we explain only what is necessary and only in the measure required to understand it, and whatever we write is in summary form. . . . Were I able to condense the entire Talmud into a single chapter, I would not do so in two."[6] The problem with his concise style is this: when we go to his *Code* (which is not a detailed commentary, despite its huge length), time and again we cannot follow his reasoning. It is not simply because we are gentiles living many centuries later; learned contemporary rabbinical correspondents expressed this same dissatisfaction to him.[7] It takes considerable expla-

---

6. Cited in Isadore Twersky, *Introduction to the Code of Maimonides (Mishneh Torah)* (New Haven, Connecticut: Yale University Press, 1980), p. 45.

7. See, for example, his lengthy reply to Rabbi Phinehas ben Meshullam, judge in Alexandria: *ibid.*, pp. 30-37. Twersky cites Rabbi Joseph Karo, the sixteenth-century scholar and Kabbalist: "The generations that followed him could not understand his works well . . . for the source of every decision is concealed from them. . . ." Twersky then remarks: "To this day [1980], the quest for *Mishneh Torah* sources in unknown Midrashim and Geonic responsa, variant readings, etc., continues unabated as one of the main forms of Rabbinic scholarship." *Ibid.*, p. 106.

nation, plus running debates in footnotes, to clarify scholarly points. Better to write a long book that can be digested in a series of bite-sized portions than a highly condensed book that takes enormous intellectual energy and vast background knowledge in order to decipher.

I had to make this book long in order to make each section coherent. Writing which is highly condensed is too difficult to read, too easy to skip over key parts in some argument, and therefore too easy to misinterpret. On the other hand, long, involved arguments are difficult to follow and remember. Therefore, I have broken up long arguments into manageable portions by adopting a liberal use of subsections and sub-subsections, plus summaries at the end of each chapter, and in my lengthy chapter on pollution (Chapter 18), at the end of each major section. I strongly recommend that whenever you see a bold-faced subhead, you should pay attention to it; the same goes for the italicized sub-subheads. They are there to help you get through each argument, as well as for convenient reviewing.

This book is supposed to be consumed in bite-sized portions; I have therefore done my best to make every mouthful both tasty and nourishing. To keep readers in their chairs and turning the pages of this book, I have done my best to put useful information on every page. There is no fluff in this book. The extended footnotes are also filled with all sorts of choice tidbits that would otherwise be quite difficult to locate. I also use footnotes for running debates that do not belong in the main text. I sometimes settle scores with my critics in the footnotes. Footnotes can be fun!

Why an Economic Commentary?

I have explained in the Introduction to my economic commentary on Genesis why I began this project in 1973.[8] I presented there my case for the whole idea of a specifically economic commentary. Basically, my reason is this: the Bible presents mankind with a God-mandated set of social, economic, educational, political, and legal principles that God expects His people to use as permanent blueprints for the total reconstruction of every society on earth. *The Dominion Covenant* provides a model of what kind of exegetical materials can and must be produced in every academic field if Christians are successfully to press the claims of Christ on the world. Since the publication of the first two commentaries on Exodus, I have also edited

---

8. Initial presentations of my economic commentary on the Pentateuch appeared monthly in the *Chalcedon Report*, from 1973 until 1981.

and published a ten-volume set of books that I call the Biblical Blueprints Series, four of which I wrote.[9]

What I want to stress from the outset is that writing this economic commentary has been very nearly a bootstrap operation. For almost two thousand years, Bible commentators — Jews and gentiles — have simply not taken seriously the specific details of Old Testament law. Despite the fact that John Calvin did preach about two hundred sermons on the Book of Deuteronomy, including its case laws,[10] and that the Puritans, especially the New England Puritans, did take biblical law seriously,[11] they did not write detailed expositions showing how these laws can be applied institutionally in New Testament times.

I found only two exegetical books repeatedly useful in writing this volume: R. J. Rushdoony's *Institutes of Biblical Law* (1973) and James Jordan's *Law of the Covenant* (1984). Both are recent studies, and both are written by people who share my view of how the Old Testament case laws should be read, interpreted, and applied in New Testament times. This exegetical approach is unquestionably new, especially when coupled with Cornelius Van Til's presuppositional apologetics. This is why the Christian Reconstruction movement does represent a major break with recent church history. On this point — and just about only on this one — Reconstructionism's critics are correct. We represent a discontinuity in church history.[12] Christian Reconstructionists alone have gone to the Bible's legal passages in search of permanent authoritative guidelines ("blueprints") for what society ought to do and be. In this sense, we Reconstructionists are theological revolutionaries. If our view of biblical law continues to spread to the Christian community at large, as we expect it to do, there will eventually be a social revolution — hopefully nonviolent change, but unquestionably revolutionary. Why revolutionary? Because one of the primary manifestations of the rev-

---

9. Published by Dominion Press, Ft. Worth, Texas, 1986-87. I wrote the books on monetary theory, economic theory, foreign policy, and the introductory volume on biblical liberation.

10. John Calvin, *Sermons on Deuteronomy* (Edinburgh: Banner of Truth Trust, [1683, 1685] 1987).

11. Symposium on Puritanism and Law, *Journal of Christian Reconstruction*, V (Winter 1978-79).

12. I hope that it will be regarded by future church historians as a discontinuity analogous to the appearance of the Wycliffe movement or the advent of the Reformation rather than that other bold discontinuity, the introduction around the year 1000 of the doctrine of transubstantiation.

olutionary character of this change will be a radical and comprehensive alteration of the West's legal order.

This commentary is the foundation of my attempt to reconstruct the entire field of economics in terms of the Bible. If I did not have total confidence in the Bible, I would not even attempt such an outlandish task. It involves too great a break with the past, as well as a break with the fundamental presuppositions of the most methodologically rigorous of all the social sciences, economics. To attempt such a project, a man has to be confident. To do so as part of a movement which seeks to reconstruct every other field also requires confidence.

The Question of Confidence

This "Reconstructionist confidence" is frequently misunderstood. Our numerous critics view it as arrogance. Those who accuse theonomists of arrogance miss the point: *we are totally confident in biblical law.* We are also totally confident that without biblical law, there is no way to create a self-consistent intellectual system or academic discipline. On the other hand, we are not totally confident in our specific applications of the law to real-world problems. Thus, while we acknowledge that we may be wrong in our particular interpretations, there is no possibility that we are wrong in our general intellectual strategy. King David said it well: he was wiser than his enemies, his teachers, and the ancients because of his commitment to, and continual study of, the law of God (Ps. 119:98-100). So am I, for the same reason. David had many enemies because of this confidence; so do I. So do Reconstructionists in general. But understand: *ours is not self-confidence; ours is confidence in the law.* However inferior our minds or intellectual skills may be in comparison to the giants of the age, or even of the past, Christians have the one thing that none of them possessed: covenant theology. The more we understand God's revealed law, the greater our advantage over those who do not understand it. It is not primarily a matter of intellect; it is primarily a matter of ethics.

The task we Christian Reconstructionists have set for ourselves — the reconstruction of every intellectual discipline in terms of the Bible — has always been the task of the church as *ekklesia.* The more that Christians have deferred to the humanists in intellectual affairs, the more pressing this task of reconstruction has become. Philosopher Alvin Plantinga is correct: our enemies have established the operating presuppositions in every academic field. "In each of these areas the fundamental and often unexpressed presuppositions that govern and direct the discipline are not religiously neutral; they are often antithetic to a Christian perspective. In these areas, then, as in philosophy, it is up to Christians who practice the relevant discipline to develop the right alternatives."[13] What he neglected to mention is that when Christians within the discipline fail to develop the right alternatives—or, in the case of economics, any alternatives—then someone outside the field has to attempt it.[14]

Conflicting Hermeneutics

Because of our commitment to the Old Testament case laws, Christian Reconstructionists' intentions are frequently misinterpreted. For example, Robert M. Bowman, Jr. complains: "One distressing application of theonomy by the Reconstructionists is their charge that all who reject any aspect of theonomy are 'antinomian' (against the law) and are pursuing 'autonomy' (self-law). According to Reconstructionists, it is either autonomy or theonomy; there apparently is no middle ground."[15] He is correct with respect to the "either/or" assertion by theonomists, but incorrect regarding our concern over the acceptance of specific laws. Those who have written the major Reconstructionists books do not argue that "all who reject any aspect of theonomy are 'antinomian' (against the law) and are pursuing 'autonomy' (self-law)." Serious Bible students can, do, and will continue to disagree regarding the proper application of specific Old Testament laws, both in ancient Israel and in the present New Covenant era. Our criterion of antinomianism is the acceptance of the principle of biblical interpretation (hermeneutic) which says, in Bowman's correct description of dispensationalism, that "the com-

---

13. Alvin Plantinga, "Advice to Christian Philosophers (With a special preface for Christian thinkers from different disciplines)," *Truth*, I (1985), p. 11.

14. Thomas Kuhn, in his influential book, *The Structure of Scientific Revolutions* (2nd ed.; University of Chicago Press, 1970), argues that the major paradigm shifts in any discipline are inaugurated by younger researchers who are either very young or very new to the field (pp. 89-90). These breakthroughs are often made by two types of researchers: skilled amateurs operating outside the guild's disciplinary system and obscure professionals laboring on the fringes of the academic discipline. For example, Darwin was an unknown amateur naturalist who had been laboring for almost three decades outside any academic setting when *Origin of Species* appeared. He had come to his insights as a young man, but had not had the courage or incentive to publish his thesis until much later. Einstein was an obscure clerk in the Swiss patent office when he made his major breakthroughs in physics.

15. Robert M. Bowman, Jr., "The New Puritanism: A Preliminary Assessment of Reconstructionism," *Christian Research Journal*, X (Winter/Spring 1988), p. 26.

mands of the Law are presumed to be no longer binding except where the New Testament repeats or ratifies them."[16] We would agree with Bowman when he concludes that "dispensationalism, technically speaking, is antinomian, though more in theory than practice; . . ."[17]

This is precisely the Reconstructionists' point: most of our opponents are antinomian in theory, though not necessarily in practice (i.e., in the specific details of personal ethics).[18] It is not the details of the personal ethics of our critics that concern Reconstructionists theologically; rather, it is our opponents' governing principle of interpretation regarding Old Testament law in New Testament times. Our primary theological distinctives as a movement are judicial and cultural. We do not ignore the question of personal ethics, but *personal ethical issues must inevitably be dealt with intellectually on the basis of some general principle of biblical interpretation.* Our principle of biblical interpretation is explicit (theonomy); that of our opponents is generally implicit (antinomianism). Our hermeneutical explicitness is now forcing our critics to respond explicitly, and this pressure bothers them. They resent it. They must give up either their antinomianism or their claims to cultural relevance as Christians. They do not want to give up either position, but they no longer have any intellectual choice. They do not like to admit this, however. It disturbs them. But if they had an answer, someone in the evangelical world would provide at least an outline of a comprehensive Christian social theory based neither on biblical case laws nor natural law theory. We are still waiting. It has been 1,900 years.

Their silence in this time of escalating international crises, in every area of life, in the decades immediately preceding the third millennium after Christ, is an important reason for the growing influence of Christian Reconstructionism. Their silence is costing them heavily, but so will any attempt to respond to us without offering a biblically plausible alternative worldview. You cannot beat something with nothing.

---

16. *Ibid.*, p. 25.

17. *Ibid.*, p. 26.

18. Given the sexual scandals of television evangelists Jim Bakker in 1987 and Jimmy Swaggart in 1988, we Reconstructionists are sorely tempted to conclude that dispensationalism tends toward antinomianism in practice, too.

Dispensationalism by Any Other Name

Dispensationalists have in the past been ethically explicit, denying God's revealed law in the New Covenant era. They have been self-conscious theological antinomians. They have argued for decades that a person can be saved eternally by accepting Jesus as Savior but not as Lord, a radically antinomian and widely accepted opinion which one of their number has recently criticized quite eloquently.[19] Nevertheless, most of the leading intellectual targets of our theological criticisms have publicly disassociated themselves from dispensationalism. They deeply resent being tarred and feathered by us with dispensationalism's antinomian brush, yet when they reply to our accusations, they adopt the hermeneutic of dispensationalism regarding the Old Testament case laws. This poses continuing intellectual problems for them.[20]

Their original reaction was stony silence. It took two decades for Christian Reconstructionists to gain even a hostile public reception; until the mid-1980's, our theological opponents usually played the children's game of "let's pretend": "Let's pretend that the Reconstructionists are not here, and maybe they will go away soon!" Finally, when they correctly concluded that we were not going away, some of them started their public attacks.[21] Prior to this, most of them had been content with murmuring, plus spreading an occasional nasty rumor.

They adopted the second strategy: publishing hostile but brief reviews. It was too late; by 1985 we had too many books in print and too many names on our computerized mailing lists. The theological paradigm shift was too far advanced, not to mention the paradigm itself. To call attention to us publicly has become increasingly risky, given the voluminous quantity of our books. Too many bright young Christian scholars and activists are already being alerted to our existence, and we are enlisting many of them. Yet not calling attention to us publicly made it appear as though the critics had no coherent answers.

There has been a third strategy: attacking a brief outline or caricature of a few of the ideas of the Reconstruction movement but

---

19. John F. MacArthur, Jr., *The Gospel According to Jesus* (Grand Rapids, Michigan: Zondervan, 1988).

20. Cf. Gary North, *Political Polytheism: The Myth of Pluralism* (Tyler, Texas: Institute for Christian Economics, 1989).

21. I include the various academic Sanhedrins in this observation. Try to find as many as five book reviews of Christian Reconstructionist books in either *Bibliotheca Sacra* or the *Westminster Theological Journal*, 1963-88.

without naming its leaders or any of our books. This will not work either, although it does delay the day of ideological reckoning. I call this strategy "hide and don't seek." The critic hides all specific references to our books, and hopes that his followers will not locate the unmentioned original sources.[22]

Our critics would much prefer to live in a world where they are not forced to deal with public issues in terms of a specific definition of Christian ethics, meaning *specific Old Testament civil laws with their accompanying public sanctions*. They wish that theonomists would go away and leave them in their ethical slumber. We won't. That is what the 1980's demonstrated: theonomists will not go away. We will not shut up. Our critics can ignore us no longer and still remain intellectually respectable. We have written too much, and we continue to write. Fifteen years after the publication of R. J. Rushdoony's *Institutes of Biblical Law* (1973), over a decade after the publication of Greg L. Bahnsen's *Theonomy in Christian Ethics* (1977), there was still only one brief book-length academic reply from any critic in any theological camp: Walter Chantry's.[23] It has become apparent that the professional theologians have been playing a game of "hide and go sleep." This tactic was adopted for a decade and a half, from 1973 to mid-1988. It did not work. We are still here. But to change this tactic at this late date, our critics must now respond to one hundred volumes of books and scholarly journals, not to mention newsletters. They are unwilling to do this. It would be too much work. What now? More silence.

---

22. An example of this tactic is found in Charles Colson's defense of pluralism and ethical dualism, *Kingdoms in Conflict*, co-published by William Morrow (secular humanist) and Zondervan (fundamentalist) in 1987. He mentions the theonomist movement, but never names any of these "utopians," as he calls us (pp. 117-18). Why not name us? If the targets of your attack are "doomed to failure" (p. 117), why not at least identify us? If we are dead, then give us a decent Christian burial!

23. In late 1988, two critical books appeared: Dave Hunt, *Whatever Happened to Heaven?* (Eugene, Oregon: Harvest House), and H. Wayne House and Thomas Ice, *Dominion Theology: Blessing or Curse?* (Portland, Oregon: Multnomah Press), to which Greg Bahnsen and Kenneth Gentry wrote a reply: *House Divided: The Break-Up of Dispensational Theology* (Tyler, Texas: Institute for Christian Economics, 1989). A third critique appeared in 1989: Hal Lindsey, *The Road to Holocaust* (New York: Bantam), refuted by Gary DeMar and Peter J. Leithart, *The Legacy of Hatred Continues* (Tyler, Texas: Institute for Christian Economics, 1989). Gary DeMar already has co-authored one book replying to earlier criticisms by Hunt: *The Reduction of Christianity* (Ft. Worth, Texas: Dominion Press, 1988). A second book replies to issues raised in the April, 1988, debate: Hunt and Ice vs. DeMar and North: Gary DeMar, *The Debate Over Christian Reconstruction* (Ft. Worth, Texas: Dominion Press, 1988). A third book by DeMar, which replies to numerous specific criticisms of Christian Reconstruction, is *You Have Heard It Said* (Tyler, Texas: Institute for Christian Economics), forthcoming.

The Silence is Deafening

Those few critics who have gone into print against us have generally been amateur theologians and imitation scholars.[24] They have read a few of our newsletters and a couple of our books (if that), and then have invented the rest. They have refuted stick men of their own creation. They forget that stick men burn easily, setting aflame those who rely heavily on them. This makes it easy for us to refute them. We cite them word for word, we show that they are either deliberately lying or have failed to read more than a tiny fraction of what we have written, and then we wait for the next willing victim.[25] If a critic cannot accurately summarize what his opponents have said, with direct citations from original sources to prove his point, and then refute what his opponents have said by showing that they are inconsistent, ignorant, or intellectually dishonest, the critic is in no position to go into print. Yet this is what our critics have done. It has been amateur night at the critics' typewriters for the last ten years. (They resent it when I say so in print repeatedly.)

Meanwhile, we keep publishing. The longer a competent critic waits to produce a comprehensive, detailed attack on us, the more difficult his job becomes. No intelligent critic wants to become a sacrificial lamb who is subsequently exposed publicly as someone who failed to do his homework. This is why time is on our side. This is also why we are so confident in our theological paradigm. After fifteen years of either silence or intellectually third-rate published criticisms of our work, we are increasingly persuaded that we have the theological goods, while our critics are holding empty theological bags. This confidence on our part is occasionally visible, and it makes our critics hopping mad, so they rush into print with yet another third-rate, easily answered criticism. The prudent ones still keep their mouths shut and wait for us to go away.

---

24. The exception is Westminster Seminary's Meredith G. Kline, who made the intellectually fatal mistake of attacking in print Greg Bahnsen's *Theonomy* in the Fall 1978 issue of the *Westminster Theological Journal*. Bahnsen's devastating reply has silenced Kline for almost a decade. Kline got his academic head handed to him on a platter. See Greg L. Bahnsen, "M. G. Kline on Theonomic Politics: An Evaluation of His Reply," *Journal of Christian Reconstruction*, VI (Winter 1979-80), pp. 195-221.

25. See, for example, my reply to Rodney Clapp's article, "Democracy as Heresy," *Christianity Today* (Feb. 20, 1987): "Honest Reporting as Heresy: My Response to *Christianity Today*" (Tyler, Texas: Institute for Christian Economics, 1987).

Do not misunderstand me. Far be it from me to say that our critics should remain silent. I have waited for a long time to see a well-thought-out, detailed critical analysis from someone, an analysis that does not rely on lists of ideas that we do not believe and sometimes have specifically attacked (e.g., "Reconstructionists believe that the world will be transformed through political action"). A wise innovator knows the weak points in his own system. There is no man-made system without weak points. If a critic ever appears who can zero in on the weak points of Christian Reconstructionism, he will receive my respect. Better to sharpen one's skills by arguing the basic points with a competent critic than bludgeoning a long series of amateurs. What I am saying, however, is that we have yet to see even one critic who understands our system well enough to go for the theological jugular. In short, we have done our homework; our published critics have not. ("If that be arrogance, make the best of it!")

What Christian Reconstructionists argue is that virtually all schools of biblical interpretation today, and too often in the past (excepting only the Puritans), have been far closer to dispensationalism's hermeneutic principle — "the commands of the Law are presumed to be no longer binding except where the New Testament repeats or ratifies them" — than to the theonomists' hermeneutical principle, also correctly summarized by Bowman: "[T]he commands of the Law are presumed to be binding today except where the New Testament modifies them or sets them aside in some manner."[26] This is why Christian Reconstructionism does represent a break with traditional Protestant theology, not in the details of theology — our distinguishing theological beliefs have all been preached before within orthodox circles — but in *our packaging of a unique, comprehensive system*: predestination, covenant theology, biblical law, Cornelius Van Til's presuppositional apologetics,[27] and postmillennialism.

Beating Something With Something Better

It is my opinion, stated repeatedly, that you cannot beat something with nothing. This is the strategic and tactical problem facing Christians today whenever they seek to challenge apostate humanism in any sphere of life. This inescapable fact of political life is the

---

26. Bowman, *op. cit.*, p. 25.

27. If there is one major break with traditional Christianity, it is here — apologetics — which is a philosophical break, not a discontinuity in theology proper. Van Til's apologetic method is unquestionably radical, for it refutes natural law theory.

major stumbling stone for non-theonomic Christian activists. Christian pietists who self-consciously, religiously, and confidently deny that Christians should ever get involved in any form of public confrontation with humanism, for any reason, have recognized this weakness on the part of antinomian Christian activists. They never tire of telling the activists that they are wasting their time in some "eschatologically futile reform program." Such activism is a moral affront to the pietists. Those of us who have repeatedly marched in picket lines in front of an abortionist's office have from time to time been confronted by some outraged Christian pietist who is clearly far more incensed by the sight of Christians in a picket line than the thought of infanticide in the nearby office. "Who do you think you are?" we are asked. "Why are you out here making a scene when you could be working in an adoption center or unwed mothers' home?" (These same two questions seem equally appropriate for the pietist critic. Who does he think *he* is, and why isn't *he* spending his time working in an adoption center or an unwed mothers' home?)

Pietists implicitly and occasionally explicitly recognize that *the vast majority of today's implicitly antinomian Christian activists possess no biblical blueprint for building a comprehensive alternative to the kingdom of humanism.* The pietistic critics of activism also understand that in any direct confrontation, Christians risk getting the stuffings—or their tax exemptions—knocked out of them. They implicitly recognize that a frontal assault on entrenched humanism is futile and dangerous if you have nothing better to offer, since you cannot legitimately expect to beat something with nothing. They implicitly recognize that neither modern fundamentalism nor modern antinomian evangelicalism has any such blueprint, and therefore neither movement has anything better to offer, i.e., nothing biblically sanctioned by God for use in New Testament times (the so-called Church Age). Fundamentalism and evangelicalism deny the legitimacy of any such blueprint, for blueprints inescapably require civil law and civil sanctions. Fundamentalists have for a century chanted, "We're under grace, not law!" They have forgotten (or never understood) that this statement inescapably means: "We're therefore under humanist culture, not Christianity." When reminded of this, they take one of three approaches: 1) abandon their fundamentalism in favor of Christian Reconstructionism, 2) abandon their activism, or 3) refuse to answer.[28]

---

28. Gary North, "The Intellectual Schizophrenia of the New Christian Right," *Christianity and Civilization*, No. 1 (1982), pp. 1-40.

The Hatred of Biblical Law

Worse, those scholars who have accepted the intellectual burden of defending the Christian faith have generally had an abiding hatred for God's revealed law. "Hatred" is the proper word. "Indifference" misses the point. "Ignorance" would be misleadingly gentle. *There can be no neutrality regarding God's revealed law, any more than there can be neutrality regarding God's revelation of Himself.* You either accept His authority over you or you reject it. You either accept His law's authority over you or you reject it.

God's authority over mankind is manifested ethically by His law, and it is manifested judicially by His law's sanctions. You either affirm God's law in its specifics, especially its sanctions, or you deny it, especially its sanctions. You either accept the 119th psalm or you reject it. "I will delight myself in thy statutes: I will not forget thy word" (Ps. 119:16). There is no middle ground. Middle ground with respect to anything in the Bible is always deception: either self-deception or self-conscious deception of others.

The general attitude of the modern fundamentalist world — and really, of the whole evangelical world — regarding the authority of God's law today was stated plainly in 1963 by then-Professor S. Lewis Johnson of Dallas Theological Seminary, in the seminary's scholarly journal, *Bibliotheca Sacra*: "At the heart of the problem of legalism is pride, a pride that refuses to admit spiritual bankruptcy. That is why the doctrines of grace stir up so much animosity. Donald Grey Barnhouse, a giant of a man in free grace, wrote: 'It was a tragic hour when the Reformation churches wrote the Ten Commandments into their creeds and catechisms and sought to bring Gentile believers into bondage to Jewish law, which was never intended either for the Gentile nations or for the church.'[29] He was right, too."[30] Operationally, all denominations believe this today, but it took Presbyterian Barnhouse and independent fundamentalist Johnson to state the position plainly.

Dispensationalist Roy L. Aldrich also did not flinch from the same conclusion: ". . . the entire Mosaic system — including the Ten Commandments — is done away."[31] Again, "the Mosaic ten laws can-

---

29. He cites Barnhouse, *God's Freedom*, p. 134.

30. S. Lewis Johnson, "The Paralysis of Legalism," *Bibliotheca Sacra*, Vol. 120 (April/June 1963), p. 109.

31. Roy L. Aldrich, "Has the Mosaic Law Been Abolished?" *ibid.*, Vol. 116 (Oct. 1959), p. 326.

not apply to the Christian," although he hastened to affirm that "the New Testament believer is not without the highest moral obligations."[32] Problem: these supposedly high obligations are unaccompanied by specific biblical content or specific biblical sanctions. That is to say, the Christian is on his own, making up his own rules as he goes along, at best illuminated by the mystical whisperings of the Holy Spirit. (If anyone wonders why Dallas Seminary has experienced continual student outbreaks of antinomian versions of Pentecostalism, which Dallas' dispensational "no signs in the Church Age" theology explicitly rejects, and even outbreaks within its own faculty,[33] he need search no farther than Dallas Seminary's antinomian theology. If God does not direct Christians through His law, then only mysticism, antinomian intuition, and inner voices remain to provide uniquely "Christian" guidance.)

This hostility to Old Testament law is also why dispensationalism has always had an unstated working alliance with modern humanism: they both share an antinomian theology that seeks to "liberate" man and the State from the restraints of God's revealed law and its sanctions. Their agreement has been simple: Christians should stay out of politics as Christians. This explicit antinomianism is also why dispensationalism has never developed an explicitly Christian social theory. If it could have, it would have, especially in the crucial years of protest, 1965-71. The silence of dispensational leaders and scholars in those years indicated that the movement was incapable of responding to real-world problems. In that era, dispensationalism committed intellectual suicide. Intellectual rigor mortis has now visibly begun to set in.[34]

---

32. *Ibid.*, p. 331.

33. Two Dallas Seminary professors resigned and one was fired in 1987 because of their commitment to the legitimacy of the gifts of physical healing in the "Church Age." See *Christianity Today* (Feb. 5, 1988), p. 52; Jack Deere (one of the dismissed professors), "Being Right Isn't Enough," in Kevin Springer (ed.), *Power Encounters* (New York: Harper & Row, 1988), ch. 8.

34. The fact is, Talbot Seminary in California has quietly departed from dispensationalism, and Dallas Seminary is now staffed by a faculty that pays little or no attention to the theological system of C. I. Scofield, Lewis Sperry Chafer, John Walvoord, Dwight Pentecost, and Charles Ryrie (who has long since departed). The "new, revisionist dispensationalism" taught by Prof. Wayne House and others is in fact the repudiation of key dispensational tenets, though not the pre-tribulational Rapture doctrine. Only the faithful donors who no longer read *Bibliotheca Sacra* remain unaware of what has happened. House's *Dominion Theology: Blessing or Curse?* is as far from Scofield as John MacArthur's *The Gospel According to Jesus.*

Natural Law Philosophy and Antinomianism

Some variation of the dispensational hermeneutic has long been adopted by theologians who officially claim they reject the idea of an ultimate ethical dualism between the Old Testament and New Testament. A good example is the statement by Robert Dabney, the Calvinist Presbyterian of the late-nineteenth-century American South. He assures us that the Ten Commandments provide universal ethical standards. "Although the Ten Commandments were given along with the civil and ceremonial laws of the Hebrews, we do not include them along with the latter, because the Decalogue was, unlike them, given for all men and all dispensations."[35] The Ten Commandments were basically the Hebrews' version of natural law. "It is a solemn repetition of the sum of those duties founded in the natures of man and of God, and on their relations, enjoined on all ages alike."[36]

Dabney's primary presumption is obvious: the whole of the Old Testament civil legal order is a dead letter because the case laws are no longer judicially binding. His secondary presumption is also obvious: the case laws were not covenantally connected to the Decalogue. They were merely temporary injunctions. Not so the Ten Commandments. "Hence, all the principles of right stated or implied in this Decalogue, are valid, not for Hebrews only, but for all men and ages. They rise wholly above the temporary and positive precepts, which were only binding while they were expressly enjoined."[37] He even argued that Christ's words in Matthew 5:18 applied only to the Ten Commandments: "Till heaven and earth pass, one jot or one tittle of this law shall not pass away."[38]

This has been the ethical argument of Christian commentators almost from the beginning. Without exception, such a dispensationalist ethical argument rests either implicitly or explicitly on some version of *natural law philosophy*. If you abandon the continuing judicial authority of the Old Testament case laws *and their sanctions*, you must actively adopt or at least passively accept some other civil law structure to serve as the judicial basis of society. There are no judicial vacuums. *Either God's revealed law is sovereign in society or else autonomous man's declared law is sovereign.* There is no third choice. When a

---

35. Robert L. Dabney, *A Defence of Virginia [And Through Her, of the South]* (New York: Negro University Press, [1867] 1969), p. 122.
36. *Idem.*
37. *Ibid.*, p. 123.
38. *Idem.*

Christian denies the unbreakable connection between the case laws and the Ten Commandments, he must then seek to apply the "general moral principles" of the Decalogue to his own society in order to provide legitimacy to the "common legal order." Yet he is then forced by his theory of natural law to defend the Decalogue's highly general principles in terms of their common status among all "right thinking" people.

There is a major problem here: *there have been so many wrong-thinking tyrants and societies in history.* Christians have suffered under many of them, usually in silence, for they have been taught that there are no specific legal standards of righteousness on which to base a legitimate appeal to God (for example, by corporately praying the imprecatory psalms, such as Psalm 83). Nevertheless, Christians again and again have proclaimed their nearly unqualified allegiance to this or that humanist alternative to biblical social order. They base their allegiance on the supposed "natural conformity" to the Decalogue of their societies' legal order. Natural law theory then becomes an all-purpose smoke screen for the Christians' passive (or even active) acceptance of specific social evils.

The Problem of Social Reform

The acceptance of natural law philosophy inevitably leads to two possible and recurring evils. First, it paralyzes the Christians' legitimate efforts to reform society, for it denies that there are specific biblical blueprints for social reform. This is the curse of the pietistic *escape religion* on Christianity. Second, it enables humanist reformers to enlist Christians in this or that reform effort that is wrapped in the language of the Ten Commandments but which is in fact inspired by covenant-breakers and designed to further their aims. This is the curse of the *power religion* on Christianity.

In American history, no better example exists of both of these processes than the Unitarians' successful enlisting of evangelical Christians in the State-centralizing abolitionist movement.[39] The fact is, the Quakers had pioneered the theory of abolitionism in the 1755-75 period, decades before the Unitarian Church even existed. The unwillingness of trinitarian American Christians to obey the New Testament teachings with regard to the illegitimacy of lifetime chattel slavery allowed the Unitarians to capture the Quakers' issue

---

39. Otto Scott, *The Secret Six: John Brown and the Abolitionist Movement* (New York: Times Books, 1979), reprinted by the Foundation for American Education; Bertram Wyatt-Brown, *Lewis Tappan and the Evangelical War Against Slavery* (Cleveland, Ohio: Case Western Reserve University Press, 1969).

and fan the evangelicals' moral fervor, 1820-65, which in turn allowed them to capture the whole country for the Unitarian worldview from the 1860's onward.[40] In short, American Christians ignored their social responsibilities by ignoring the Quakers' moral challenge regarding chattel slavery (1760-1820), for they did not recognize or acknowledge the judicial authority of the New Testament on this question.[41] As a result, they became institutionally and intellectually subordinate to those who hated Christianity (1820-1865).

Simultaneously, a parallel phenomenon took place with the rise of the state school systems, another Unitarian reform in the United States. Funded by Christian taxpayers, the schools have been operated in terms of an alien worldview.[42] *The escape religion led to the triumph of the power religion.* It always does. Dominion religion invariably suffers. This defeat of dominion religion is the temporal goal of the power religionists and the escape religionists, of Pharaoh and the enslaved Israelites. They always want Moses to go away and take his laws with him.

These two evil consequences of natural law theory — retreat from social concerns and the co-opting of Christians by non-Christian social reformers — have been the curse of natural law theory for almost two millennia. Dabney could have protested until kingdom come — or until Sherman's army came — against the anti-Constitution agenda of the northern Abolitionists,[43] but his own commitment to natural law philosophy undercut his theological defense. He did not understand that when a law-abiding Christian adopts a hostile attitude toward the case laws of the Old Testament, he necessarily also adopts an attitude favorable to natural law theory, which is inescapably philosophical humanism: common-ground philosophy, common-ground ethics, and the autonomy of man.[44] Dispensationalist theologian and natural law philosopher Norman Geisler is simply more forthright regarding this necessary two-fold commitment: anti-Old

---

40. R. J. Rushdoony, *The Nature of the American System* (Fairfax, Virginia: Thoburn Press, [1965] 1978), ch. 6: "The Religion of Humanity."

41. See Chapter 4: "A Biblical Theology of Slavery."

42. R. J. Rushdoony, *The Messianic Character of American Education* (Nutley, New Jersey: Craig Press, 1963).

43. *Defence of Virginia*, Conclusion.

44. Archie P. Jones, "Natural Law and Christian Resistance to Tyranny," *Christianity and Civilization*, No. 2 (1983), pp. 94-132.

Testament law and pro-natural law philosophy.[45] (It is unfortunate that both Cornelius Van Til and Francis Schaeffer were inconsistent in this regard: they ignored or denied biblical law, yet also officially denied natural law philosophy. This has produced great confusion among their respective followers.)[46]

For two centuries, humanists in the United States have been enlisting Christian evangelicals into a seemingly endless stream of "save the world" programs. The humanists cry out, "Baptize us! Baptize us! . . . and please take up a compulsory collection for us." For two centuries, well-meaning Christians have been digging deep into their wallets in order to supply the tax collectors with funds to finance a series of supposedly religiously neutral social reform programs that have been created by the messianic State and staffed by humanist bureaucrats. Taxpayer-funded, evolution-teaching government schools have been the most persistent, effective, and representative example of this continuing delusion. Without the spurious supporting doctrine of morally and intellectually neutral natural law, it would not be possible for the humanists to wrap these anti-Christian programs in the ragged swaddling clothes of common morality.

---

45. Norman Geisler, "A Premillennial View of Law and Government," in J. I. Packer (ed.), *The Best in Theology* (Carol Stream, Illinois: Christianity Today/Word, 1986). Writes the *Fundamentalist Journal* (Sept. 1988): "Geisler credits [Thomas] Aquinas with 'having the most influence on my life,' and says that if his house were burning he would grab his wife, his Bible, and the *Summa Theologiae* by Aquinas" (p. 20). It is hardly surprising that he should be a professor of philosophy at Baptist fundamentalist Liberty University. The anabaptists, who possess no separate philosophical tradition of their own, have always relied on the philosophy of medieval Roman Catholic scholasticism to defend their cause.

46. See North, *Political Polytheism*, chapter 2: "Halfway Covenant Ethics," and chapter 3: "Halfway Covenant Social Criticism." Van Til's self-conscious rejection of both dispensationalism and natural law theory left him without any concept of social law or social justice, for he also rejected the continuing authority of the Old Testament case laws—by silence in his published writings and explicitly in private communications. Thus, his system was always incomplete, hanging timelessly in the air like a ripe fruit that has just begun its fall to the ground. That the fruit was grabbed by R. J. Rushdoony in the early 1960's did not please Van Til, but there was not much that he could politely do about it. He had to remain silent, for his system is inherently ethically silent: it rejects both forms of law, natural and biblical, which is why he explicitly denied ethical cause and effect in history, and why he implicitly adopted the humanists' version of ethical cause and effect: the good guys lose in history, and the bad guys win.

"Normal Science"

Our critics can legitimately reply, "All right, let's see if you can make sense of the case laws. Let's see how you would apply them to today's problems. Put up or shut up." Since I do not intend to shut up, I am hereby "putting up." This book is a detailed study of the economic applications of the case laws of Exodus. It offers no grand hypothesis, no major breakthrough in biblical hermeneutics. It is an example of what someone can accomplish if he is willing to spend a lot of time thinking about the specifics of biblical law, comparing his conclusions with contemporary scholarship in several areas. To write this book, I have made a detailed study of modern economics, plus at least a cursory examination of the relatively new academic discipline of law and economics, plus studies of Jewish jurisprudence (Mishnah and Talmud), modern criminology, the history of slavery, and ecology. This effort I regard as basic intellectual trench work, or what Thomas Kuhn calls "normal science."[47] It is not in the same league with a breakthrough book like Rushdoony's *Institutes of Biblical Law*,[48] with its innovative insight that each of the case laws of the Bible can be subsumed under one of the Ten Commandments (even if the thesis is overstated),[49] and which surveys a wide array of topics — academic, cultural, historical, and contemporary. *Tools of Dominion* has neither the precision nor the relentlessness of Greg Bahnsen's apologetic defense of biblical law in *Theonomy in Christian Ethics*. It does not have the organizational power of Ray Sutton's five-point covenant model.[50] It does not have the innovative insights into biblical meaning that James Jordan's "maximal" hermeneutic offers.[51] It just plugs along, trying to make economic sense out of the details of the case laws.

A Theonomic Strategy

Despite these limitations, this book still is part of my overall publishing strategy. If a reader is impressed with my conclusions regard-

---

47. Thomas Kuhn, *The Structure of Scientific Revolutions, op. cit.* Kuhn distinguishes normal science from a scientific revolution that produces a major paradigm shift.

48. R. J. Rushdoony, *The Institutes of Biblical Law* (Nutley, New Jersey: Craig Press, 1973).

49. James B. Jordan, *The Law of the Covenant: An Exposition of Exodus 21-23* (Tyler, Texas: Institute for Christian Economics, 1984), pp. 22-23.

50. Ray R. Sutton, *That You May Prosper: Dominion By Covenant* (Tyler, Texas: Institute for Christian Economics, 1987).

51. James B. Jordan, *Judges: God's War Against Humanism* (Tyler, Texas: Geneva Ministries, 1985).

ing both the wisdom and the benefits that the case laws of Exodus offer, he will be pulled in the direction of the Christian Reconstructionists' paradigm. If he rejects the paradigm, he will then find himself asking: "Why do the case laws seem to be workable? Why have previous Christian theologians ignored the case laws? What was it in their theological paradigms that kept them from seeing how relevant the case laws are?" When a person starts asking himself such questions, he is approaching a personal paradigm shift.

Unless a whole series of studies like this one come into print, the brilliance of the previously mentioned paradigm-shifting theonomic books will fail to capture the minds of future generations of Christians. The proof of the pudding is in the eating, says an old slogan; similarly, the proof of theonomy is in its judicial applications. If what this book insists regarding the case laws of Exodus is not true—if they cannot in fact be applied productively in New Testament societies—then the brilliance of the theonomic paradigm is like the brilliance of a burning bush that is soon consumed by the fire. The paradigm is wood, hay, and stubble. So, while this book is not intended to be paradigm-shifting, it is unquestionably designed to be paradigm-confirming and paradigm-luring. If the reviewers do anything except pan this book, they will have aided the theonomists' cause, but if they pan it without having effectively discredited the case laws themselves, they will have identified themselves to their more perceptive readers as intellectual lightweights.

This is why I do not expect the book to be widely reviewed. This, plus its size. A reviewer cannot fake a review of a book on the case laws. The subject matter is just too complex. Reviewers will actually have to read the book before reviewing it negatively, something our critics so far have been unwilling to do with our previous books. I expect the silence to continue. This, too, is now in our favor. The word is spreading: our critics have no answers to our paradigm.

Yes, this is a fat book. But like Volume I of Rushdoony's *Institutes of Biblical Law*, this book is divided into bite-sized portions: compact chapter sections and subsections. To make things as easy as possible for the reader, I have structured it for easy preliminary scanning and easy review. You deal with it as you would eat an elephant: one bite at a time. Chew well; it is occasionally tough.

A Final Note to Readers and Critics

Richard Baxter, in 1678, listed seven highly predictable objections to his *Christian Directory*. I feel compelled to list the first three again, though not his specific answers. (I have also dropped his italics.) I too have heard variations of these objections repeatedly.

Objection I: "You have written too many Books already: Who do you think hath so little to do as to read them all?"

Objection II: "Your Writings differing from the common judgment have already caused offence to the godly."

Objection III: "You should take more leisure, and take other mens judgement of your Writings before you thrust them out so hastily."[52]

And in response, I can do no better than to close with Baxter's summary comments. Indeed, if I were to issue a challenge to the critics of me in particular and Christian Reconstruction in general, this would be it:

In summ, to my quarrelsome Brethren I have two requests, 1. That instead of their unconscionable, and yet unreformed custome of backbiting, they would tell me to my face of my offences by convincing evidence, and not tempt the hearers to think them envious: and 2. That what I do amiss, they would do better: and not be such as will neither laboriously serve the Church themselves, not suffer others: and that they will not be guilty of Idleness themselves, nor tempt me to be a slothful servant, who have so little time to spend: For I dare not stand before God under that guilt: And that they will not joyn with the enemies and resisters of the publication of the Word of God.

And to the Readers my request is, 1. That whatever for Quantity or Quality in this Book is an impediment to their regular universal obedience, and to a truly holy life, they would neglect and cast away: 2. But that which is truly Instructing and Helpful, they would diligently Digest and Practice; And I encourage them by my testimony, that by long experience I am assured, that this PRACTICAL RELIGION will afford both to Church, State and Conscience, more certain and more solid Peace, than contending Disputers, with all their pretences of Orthodoxness and Zeal against Errors for the Truth, will ever bring, or did ever attain to.

I crave your pardon for this long Apology: It is an Age where the Objections are not feigned, and where our greatest and most costly services of God, are charged on us as our greatest sins; and where at once I am accused of Conscience for doing no more, and of men for doing so much: Being really

A most unworthy Servant of so good a Master.

---

52. Richard Baxter, *A Christian Directory: Or, A Summ of Practical Theologie, and Cases of Conscience* (London: Robert White for Nevil Simmons, [1673] 1678), unnumbered pages, in Advertisements.

Part I
PROLEGOMENA

THE RESTORATION OF BIBLICAL CASUISTRY

I have more understanding than all my teachers: for thy testimonies are my meditation. I understand more than the ancients, because I keep thy precepts (Psalm 119:99-100).

We need to take David's words seriously. He defines personal progress in history in terms of a better understanding of God's revealed laws. He can measure his progress beyond anything achieved by those who have preceded him, not in terms of better study techniques, or improved means of communication, or greater per capita wealth, but in terms of his mastery of God's precepts.

Modern man regards such an idea of historical progress as preposterous. Sad to say, so does the modern Christian. This is why modern society is headed either for an enormous series of disasters or an enormous and culturally comprehensive revival. God will not be mocked. His covenantal sanctions — blessings and cursings — still operate in history. This book deals with God's covenantal case laws from an economic point of view. This strategy is theologically appropriate in the late twentieth century, for modern man worships at his own shrine in the hope of achieving unbroken compound economic growth per capita.

Tools of Dominion is a work of casuistry: the application of conscience to moral decisions. The conscience needs a reliable guide: biblical law. Casuistry has not been a popular academic endeavor within Bible-believing Protestantism since the late seventeenth century. The only works I can think of that are anything like *The Dominion Covenant* in scope are Richard Baxter's enormous study, *A Christian Directory*, written in 1664-65 and first published in 1673, and Samuel Willard's equally massive commentary on the Westminster Shorter Catechism, *A Compleat Body of Divinity* (1726). Richard Baxter's goal was basically the same as mine: "I do especially desire you to observe, that the resolving of *practical Cases of Conscience*, and the reducing of Theological knowledge into *serious Christian Practice*, and promoting a *skilful facility* in the faithful exercise of universal obedience and Holiness of heart and life, is the great work of this Treatise; . . ."[1] Unlike Baxter, I had access to my library when I wrote my book; he did not, having been barred from his pulpit by the State (after the Restoration of Charles II in 1660), and having to write most of it from memory, only subsequently checking the original sources.

Ignoring the Case Laws

The major problem I had in writing this book is that there are very few books that even explain the case laws, let alone take them seriously. There are at least three approaches to (or, more accurately, justifications for the rejection of) the case laws.

1. The Case Laws as Annulled

This is the standard Christian view. It has been the common viewpoint almost from the beginning of the church. This is why theonomy appears to be a major break with broad church tradition. Basically, the position boils down to this: a compromise with late classical philosophy's natural law theory began in the early centuries of the church. Christian scholars appealed to universal human reason as the source of rational man's universal knowledge of civil law. This law was seen as natural, meaning that it is implicitly in the common possession of all rational men.

There was an early recognition on the part of church scholars and leaders that an appeal to Old Testament case laws could not be conformed intellectually to natural law theory. They understood the obvious question: "If these laws were universally binding on all men, then why did God have to reveal the specifics of His law to the Hebrews, and only to them?" This, in fact, is a very good Christian rhetorical answer to those who declare the universality of natural law. The answer is simple: *there is no such thing as a universal system of rational natural law which is accessible to fallen human reason.* But this answer was too radical to suit scholars and apologists in the early church, just as it has been too radical for Christians ever since. It involves a sharp break with the doctrine of natural law.

---

1. Richard Baxter, *A Christian Directory: Or, A Summ of Practical Theologie, and Cases of Conscience* (London: Robert White for Nevil Simmons, [1673] 1678), unnumbered page, but the second page of Advertisements.

The early commentators were sorely tempted to seek a way out of their common-ground apologetic difficulty by interpreting Paul's language regarding the annulment of the law's eternal death sentence against redeemed mankind to mean that the Old Covenant's legal order is in no way judicially binding on New Testament society. They abandoned the concept of God's historical sanctions as applicable in New Testament history. They lumped together Israel's civil case laws with the Old Covenant's laws of ritual cleanliness, and then they dismissed both varieties. This tradition lives on in modern conservative Christian theology.

2. The Case Laws as Antiquarian

Christian Bible commentators pass over these laws on the assumption that they are only of antiquarian interest. Commentators almost never attempt to explain how these laws might have worked in ancient Israel. They never discuss how they might be applied in the New Testament era. Also, the commentators are unfamiliar with even the rudiments of economic theory, so their comments on the economic implications of these verses are almost nonexistent. Their few brief observations are what the reader could readily have figured out for himself. Another major problem is that far too often, the commentators compare the biblical text with fragments of the legal texts of the surrounding Near Eastern cultures. This is not an evil practice in itself, but it is when they make the unproven assumption that Israel must have borrowed its legal code from these pagan cultures. They never discuss the possibility that Israel's law code preceded these pagan extracts, which once again raises the question of the need for the reconstruction of biblical and Near Eastern chronologies.[2]

3. The Case Laws as Mythical

Liberal humanist Bible scholars are so enamored with biblical "higher criticism" that they pay little attention to the meaning of the biblical texts. They prefer instead to spend their lives inventing multiple authors for each text, re-dating subsections in order to make the Book of Exodus appear to be a composite document written centuries after the exodus event (which many of them downplay any-

---

2. Gary North, *Moses and Pharaoh: Dominion Religion vs. Power Religion* (Tyler, Texas: Institute for Christian Economics, 1985), Appendix A: "The Reconstruction of Egypt's Chronology."

way).[3] When commentators believe that the oldest laws are remnants of some "primitive nomadism" or else imports from pagan law codes, they have no incentive to think through how these laws should be applied today. When they view most of the case laws as late developments that were inserted retroactively into older biblical texts for political reasons, they have little incentive to understand them as specific historical applications of permanent general principles. Jews and gentiles alike are afflicted with Bible scholarship that relies on the principles of higher criticism.

Useless Commentaries

The Dominion Covenant is not a typical Bible commentary. The typical Bible commentary judiciously avoids the really difficult questions, especially in the area of ethics. It also neglects all but the most obvious of the economic principles involved. It is hard to believe how little practical information is provided by the typical modern Bible commentary. It is understandable why people seldom use them after having bought them. Reality does not meet expectations when it comes to Bible commentaries. What is not understandable is that people continue to buy them. They sit unused on most pastors' book shelves. Maybe their primary use is decorative. I gave up on most Bible commentaries years ago. I use them mainly to keep myself from making major linguistic or textual errors. This is why you will find very few references to Bible commentaries in my footnotes. I long ago stopped wasting my time trying to find economic and judicial information in them. Or, as the economist would say, "the marginal return on each additional invested unit of my time spent in reading them was consistently below the marginal cost." In short, the information costs were too high per unit of relevant data.

Jewish Commentaries

If Christian commentaries are unhelpful, what about commentaries written by Jews? Not much better. I did not find the traditional Jewish commentaries useful in writing this commentary, including the Talmud. Until only about a century and a half ago,

---

3. In recent years, this has been changing to some degree. The arcane intricacies of the many rival textual reconstructions have led to such a cobweb of complexity that scholars prefer to avoid trying to untangle it. Thus, scholars are sorely tempted to do what was once considered a breach of faith: treat the text as a unit when searching for its meaning.

Jewish scholarship focused almost exclusively on the Talmud, which was completed around A.D. 500, parts of which extended back to several centuries before Christ in the form of oral tradition.[4] Traditional Jewish commentaries on ethics often deal with highly specific legal cases involving economic disputes between men, or academic disputes among the rabbis, but there is seldom an attempt to spell out the general economic principles guiding any decision of a Jewish court. At best, the rabbis may try to explain why certain forms of restitution are imposed in certain cases, but nothing beyond a kind of common-sense view of economic justice. Thus, Jewish religious scholars until very recently did not bring their great skills of erudition and detailed scholarship to bear on the modern world. "Secular" topics did not interest them, and even today, those Jews who have become illustrious academically in so many fields display little or no interest in the Talmud.

There is a very important reason why the writings of Jewish legal scholars and judges prove to be of little assistance: Jewish courts after the Bar Kokhba revolt of 135 A.D. were not allowed to impose specifically biblical sanctions. Very few gentiles are aware of this, and I suspect that few Jews are, either. When the Romans captured Jerusalem and burned the Temple in A.D. 70, the ancient official Sanhedrin court came to an end. The rabbis, under the leadership of Rabbi Johanan ben Zakkai, then took over many of the judicial functions of the Sanhedrin.[5] They established as a principle that every Jewish court must have at least one judge who had been ordained by the laying on of hands (*semikah*), and who could in principle trace his ordination back to Moses. This laying on of hands could take place only in the Holy Land. Legal scholar George Horowitz comments: "A court not thus qualified had no jurisdiction to impose the punishments prescribed in the Torah."[6] After the Bar Kokhba revolt, the Jews were scattered across the Roman Empire in the diaspora. "The Rabbis were compelled, therefore, in order to preserve the Torah and to maintain law and order, to enlarge the authority of Rabbinical tribunals. This they accomplished by emphasizing the distinction between Biblical penalties and Rabbinical penalties. Rabbinical courts after the second century had no authority to

---

4. See Appendix B: "Maimonides' *Code*: Is It Biblical?"

5. George Horowitz, *The Spirit of Jewish Law* (New York: Central Book Co., 1963), pp. 92-93.

6. *Ibid.*, p. 93.

impose Biblical punishments since they lacked *semikah;* but as regards penalties created by Rabbinical legislation, the Rabbis had of necessity, accordingly, a whole series of sanctions and penalties: excommunications, fines, physical punishment, use of the 'secular arm' in imitation of the Church, etc."[7] Thus, by the time of the Mishnah, which was Rabbi Judah the Prince's authoritative late-second-century compilation of rabbinical laws, Jewish courts had already abandoned Old Testament sanctions.

Thus tied intellectually and ethically to the Mishnah, to the massive Talmud (completed around A.D. 500), and to the literature produced in terms of this ancient tradition, Jewish commentators have never attempted to produce anything like the kind of Bible commentary that *The Dominion Covenant* represents. I am aware of no Jewish compilation of Old Testament case laws that is organized in terms of the Ten Commandments or any other biblical organizational principle (e.g., the covenant model) which is comparable to R. J. Rushdoony's *Institutes of Biblical Law,* and no apologetic comparable to Greg L. Bahnsen's *Theonomy in Christian Ethics.* Furthermore, despite the intellectual dominance of economists who are Jews,[8] there is as yet no body of scholarship known as Jewish economics.[9] This is in sharp contrast to the Islamic academic community, which has produced a growing body of self-consciously Islamic economic literature, especially since 1975.[10] With the exception only of Professor

---

7. *Idem.*

8. Murray Rothbard, an agnostic Jew and a defender of free market economics, once made the observation that "The fate of Western Civilization will be determined by whether our Jews beat their Jews." He presumably had in mind Ludwig von Mises, F. A. Hayek, and Milton Friedman (in his anti-regulatory writings) vs. Karl Marx, Paul Samuelson, Lawrence Klein, etc.

9. The two titles that might be offered as examples of such scholarship are quite recent: Aaron Levine, *Free Enterprise and Jewish Law* (New York: Ktav Publishing House, Yeshiva University Press, 1980); Meir Tamari, *"With All Your Possessions": Jewish Ethics and Economic Life* (New York: Free Press, 1987). Neither study is particularly theoretical or detailed in its practical applications. They are more like introductory surveys of a handful of themes in the Talmud that are related to economics.

10. See Muhammed Nejatullah Siddiqi, *Muslim Economic Thinking: A Survey of Contemporary Literature* (Leicester, England: Islamic Foundation, 1981); Muhammed Akram Khan, *Islamic Economics: Annotated Sources in English and Urdu* (Leicester, England: Islamic Foundation, 1983). A cursory list of English-language examples of this literature includes the following: Ibnul Hasan (ed.), *In Search of an Islamic Economic Model* (London: New Century Publishers, 1983); Afzal-Ur-Rahman, *Economic Doctrines of Islam,* 4 vols. (Lahore, Pakistan: Islamic Publications Limited, 1974-82); Muazzam Ali (ed.), *Islamic Banks and Strategies of Economic Cooperation* (London: New Century Publications, 1982); Mohammed Muslehuddin, *Insurance and Islamic Law*

Israel Kirzner, I can think of no contemporary academically recognized Jewish economist[11] who might agree with Rabbi Chajes' mid-nineteenth-century pronouncement: "Allegiance to the authority of the said [oral] rabbinic tradition is binding upon all sons of Israel, since these explanations and interpretations have come down to us by word of mouth from generation to generation, right from the time of Moses. They have been transmitted to us precise, correct, and unadulterated, and he who does not give his adherence to the un-written law and the rabbinic tradition has no right to share the heritage of Israel; he belongs to the Sadducees or the Karaites who severed connection to us long ago."[12]

Orthodox Judaism

During the last century in the West, Orthodox Judaism has almost disappeared from sight, so widespread has been the defection of millions of Jews who have been assimilated into modern society; by Chajes' definition, there are today few Jews remaining in the world, except in the State of Israel. Even the term "Orthodox Judaism" indicates the nature of the problem; it was originally a term of derision used by liberal Jews in the nineteenth century against their traditionalist opponents. Grunfeld writes: "The word 'Orthodoxy',

---

(Lahore, Pakistan: Islamic Publications, 1969); Muslehuddin, *Economics and Islam* (Lahore, Pakistan: Islamic Publications, 1974); Alhaj A. D. Ajijola, *The Islamic Concept of Social Justice* (Lahore, Pakistan: Islamic Publications, 1977); Muhammed Nejatullah Siddiqi, *Banking Without Interest* (Leicester, England: Islamic Foundation, 1983); Siddiqi, *Issues in Islamic Banking: Selected Papers* (Leicester, England: Islamic Foundation, 1983); Siddiqi, *Partnership and Profit-Sharing in Islamic Law* (Leicester, England: Islamic Foundation, 1985); M. Umer Chapra, *Towards a Just Monetary System* (Leicester, England: Islamic Foundation, 1985); Waqar Masood Khan, *Towards an Interest-Free Islamic Economic System* (Leicester, England: Islamic Foundation, 1985); Raquibuz M. Zaman, *Elimination of Interest from the Banking System in Pakistan* (Karachi: State Bank of Pakistan, 1985). I do not believe that Shaikh Mahmud Ahmad's book, *Economics of Islam* (Lahore, Pakistan: Ashraf Press, 1947), is representative of recent Islamic economic thought in general; the book is a socialist polemic in the name of Islam.

11. Kirzner is not a prominent academic figure, but he is the only "Austrian School" economist who has a reputation among academic economists. Kirzner's dual mastery of the Talmud and the works of Ludwig von Mises is not visible in his writings; the two fields are kept by Kirzner in hermetically sealed separate academic compartments. Few professional economists are aware that he is known as a rabbi in Orthodox Jewish circles. See Aaron Levine, *Free Enterprise and Jewish Law*, p. xi.

12. Z. H. Chajes, *The Student's Guide Through the Talmud* (London: East and West Library, 1952), p. 4. The Karaites were a sect of Judaism established in 767 A.D. by Jews in Babylon. They did not accept the Talmud or the idea of an oral tradition stretching back to Moses.

on the other hand, which was applied by the Reformers to what they called 'Old-Timers' or 'Old-Believers' (Altgläubige), was taken from the sphere of Christian theology and does not fit Judaism at all, in which the main stress is laid on action or law and not on 'faith', as the Greek term orthodox would express. Nevertheless, once the word 'Orthodoxy' had been thrown at Hirsch and his followers in a derogatory sense, he accepted the challenge with the intention of turning that word into a name of honour."[13] Notice his assertion regarding Judaism that "the main stress is laid on action or law and not on 'faith.' " This is indeed the main stress of orthodox Judaism, which nevertheless has an underlying theology: *salvation by law*. Writes Robert Goldenberg: "Classical Judaism, drawing indirectly on its biblical antecedents, tends to emphasize act over intention, behavior over thought. Righteousness is chiefly a matter of proper behavior, not correct belief or appropriate intention."[14] In contrast, Christianity stresses salvation by faith in Christ. But this faith means faith in Christ's *representative perfect obedience to God's perfect law*; Christian orthodoxy should never lead to a denial of the validity and moral authority of that perfect law which Christ obeyed perfectly.

Revolution and Law

I am convinced that both the West and the Far East are about to experience a major transformation. The pace of social change is already rapid and will get faster. The technological possibility of a successful Soviet nuclear strike against the United States grows daily;[15] so does the possibility of chemical and biological warfare;[16] so does the threat of an AIDS epidemic. None of these threats to civilization may prove in retrospect to be devastating, but they are certainly perceived today as threats. Added to these grim possibilities is

---

13. I. Grunfeld, "Samson Raphael Hirsch — The Man and His Mission," in *Judaism Eternal: Selected Essays from the Writings of Samson Raphael Hirsch* (London: Soncino Press, 1956), p. xlvii.

14. Robert Goldenberg, "Law and Spirit in Talmudic Religion," in Arthur Green (ed.), *Jewish Spirituality: From the Bible Through the Middle Ages* (New York: Crossroad, 1986), p. 232.

15. Angelo Codevilla, *While Others Build: The Commonsense Approach to the Strategic Defense Initiative* (New York: Free Press, 1988); Quentin Crommelin, Jr., and David S. Sullivan, *Soviet Military Supremacy* (Washington, D.C.: Citizens Foundation, 1985).

16. Joseph D. Douglas and Neil C. Livingstone, *America the Vulnerable: The Threat of Chemical and Biological Warfare* (Lexington, Massachusetts: Lexington Books, 1987).

the much more predictable threat of an international economic collapse as a result of the vast build-up of international debt; this in turn could produce domestic political transformations. Also possible is the spread of terrorism and Marxist revolution. Drug addiction is spreading like a plague. Changes in the weather as a result of the use of fossil fuels (the "greenhouse effect") are in the newspapers because of international drought. Agricultural output may be endangered, long term, by weather changes and also by soil erosion. We are not sure. What Christians should be certain of is this: *God has been plowing up the ethically erosion-prone world since World War I, and this process is accelerating.*

This has created a unique opportunity for Christian revival, but this time revival could lead to a broad-based cultural transformation. In short, revival could produce an international revolution: family by family, church by church, nation by nation. For a true social revolution to take place, there must be a transformation of the legal order. This transformation takes several generations, but without it, there has been no revolution, only a *coup d'état*.[17] There is today an international crisis in the Western legal tradition.[18] This, far more than the build-up of nuclear weapons or the appearance of AIDS, testifies to the likelihood of a comprehensive, international revolution—not necessarily violent, but a revolution nonetheless. The Holy Spirit could produce such a revolution without firing a shot or launching a missile. This is my prayer. It should be every Christian's prayer.

Harold Berman's point is correct: without a transformation of the legal system, there is no revolution. This is why I am devoting so much space to explaining the case laws of Exodus. It is these laws, and their amplification in the Book of Deuteronomy, that must serve as the foundation of any systematically, self-consciously Christian revolution. Natural law is a dead mule; it was always a sterile hybrid, and Darwinism has long-since killed the last known living specimens.[19] (Anti-theistic conservative philosophers and a handful

---

17. Harold J. Berman, *Law and Revolution: The Formation of the Western Legal Tradition* (Cambridge, Massachusetts: Harvard University Press, 1983), p. 20.

18. *Ibid.*, pp. 33-41.

19. R. J. Rushdoony writes: "Darwinism destroyed this faith in nature. The process of nature was now portrayed, not as a perfect working of law, but as a blind, unconscious energy working profligately to express itself. In the struggle for survival, the fittest survive by virtue of their own adaptations, not because of natural law. Nature produces many 'mistakes' which fail to survive and become extinct species and fossils. The destiny of the universe is extinction as its energy runs down." Rushdoony, *The Biblical Philosophy of History* (Nutley, New Jersey: Presbyterian & Reformed, 1969), p. 7.

of traditional Roman Catholic and Protestant college instructors and magazine columnists still visibly cling to one or another of these taxidermic specimens, each proclaiming that his specimen is still alive.) Thus, there is nowhere for Christians to turn for guidance in developing a believable social theory and workable social programs except to the case laws of the Old Testament. Once the myth of neutrality is abandoned — really abandoned, not just verbally admitted to be a myth — then the inevitable question arises: By what standard? Christians who have abandoned faith in the myth of neutrality have only one possible answer: "By *this* standard: biblical law."[20]

The Conflict Between Two Kingdoms

What I am attempting to do with my life is to publish Christian worldview materials that will lead to the steady replacement of the humanist intellectual foundations of modern civilization. The arena of conflict is nothing less than world civilization. The issue is the kingdom of God, both in heaven and on earth (Matt. 28:18). There are many books that deal with the kingdom of God, but my view of the kingdom of God as it is visibly manifested in history is simple: it is God's authorized and morally required *civilization*. It is simultaneously internal (world-and-life view), ethical (a moral law-order), and institutional (covenantal judicial relationships). Raymond Zorn begins his book on the Kingdom of God with these words: "In the broadest sense God's Kingdom refers to the most extended reaches of His sovereignty. As Psalm 103:19 puts it, 'The Lord hath prepared his throne in the heavens; and his kingdom ruleth over all.' "[21] The kingdom of God is all-encompassing, in the same sense that a civilization is all-encompassing.[22] I agree in principle with the Jewish

---

20. Greg L. Bahnsen, *By This Standard: The Authority of God's Law Today* (Tyler, Texas: Institute for Christian Economics, 1985).

21. Raymond O. Zorn, *Church and Kingdom* (Philadelphia: Presbyterian and Reformed, 1962), p. 1. Zorn, an amillennialist, stresses the kingdom as the reign of God rather than the sphere or domain of His rule (p. 1). Greg Bahnsen's response to this sort of argument is correct: it is ridiculous to speak of the reign of a king whose kingdom has few if any historical manifestations that are as comprehensive in scope as his self-proclaimed sovereignty. Such a limited definition of God's kingdom and kingship is in fact a denial of God's kingdom. Bahnsen, "The World and the Kingdom of God" (1981), reprinted as Appendix D in Gary DeMar and Peter J. Leithart, *The Reduction of Christianity: A Biblical Response to Dave Hunt* (Ft. Worth, Texas: Dominion Press, 1988).

22. The reader should not misinterpret what I am saying. I am not saying that the kingdom of God is the primary theme in the Bible, or in the message of Jesus. His primary theme is the same as the whole Bible's primary theme: *the glory of God*. I

scholar, I. Grunfeld, when he writes that "true religion and true civilisation are identical. It is the view of the Torah as the civilisation of the state of God—where Torah is coextensive with life in all its manifestations, personal, economic, political, national."[23]

Nothing less than this *comprehensive replacement* of humanism and occultism with Christianity will suffice to please God. We are called to work for the progressive replacement of humanist civilization by Christian civilization, a replacement that was definitively achieved with the death, resurrection, and ascension of Jesus Christ, and manifested by the coming of the Holy Spirit at Pentecost. We are to *replace* Satan's humanistic kingdoms. "Kingdom" is an inescapable concept. It is never a question of kingdom vs. no kingdom; it is always a question of *whose* kingdom. Rushdoony is correct in his evaluation of mankind's inevitable quest for utopia, the final order, which only God can inaugurate and bring to pass: "The church accordingly has never been alone in history but has rather faced a multiplicity of either anti-Christian or pseudo-Christian churches fiercely resentful of any challenge to their claim to represent the way, truth and life of that final order. The modern state, no less than the ancient empire, claims to be the vehicle and corporate body of that true estate of man. As the incarnation of that final order, it views family, church, school and every aspect of society as members and phases of its corporate life and subject to its general government. It

---

agree with Geerhardus Vos' statement: "While thus recognizing that the kingdom of God has an importance in our Lord's teaching second to that of no other subject, we should not go to the extreme into which some writers have fallen, of finding in it the only theme on which Jesus actually taught, which would imply that all other topics dealt with in his discourses were to his mind but so many corollaries or subdivisions of this one great truth. . . . Salvation with all it contains flows from the nature and subserves the glory of God. . . ." Geerhardus Vos, *The Teaching of Jesus Concerning the Kingdom and the Church* (Grand Rapids, Michigan: Eerdmans, 1958), p. 11. I am saying only that the kingdom of God is inherently all-encompassing culturally. In fact, I am convinced that the best biblical definition of "kingdom" is *civilization*. The kingdom of God is the civilization of God—internal, external, heavenly, earthly, historical, and eternal.

23. Grunfeld, "Samson Raphael Hirsch—the Man and His Mission," *Judaism Eternal*, I, p. xiv. Obviously, I do not agree with Grunfeld's next sentence: "This concept is applicable, of course, only when there is a Jewish State, or at least an autonomous Jewish Society, which can be entirely ruled by the Torah." This statement provides evidence of the accuracy of Vos' analysis of Jewish teaching concerning the Kingdom of heaven: "The emphasis was placed largely on what the expected state would bring for Israel in a national and temporal sense. Hence it was preferably thought of as the kingdom of Israel over the other nations." Vos, *Kingdom and the Church*, p. 19.

is in terms of this faith, therefore, that the state claims prior or ultimate jurisdiction over every sphere, and steadily encroaches on their
activity."[24]

Comprehensive Revival

Christian Reconstructionists are self-consciously attempting to
lay new intellectual foundations for a comprehensive moral and
therefore intellectual, social, political, and economic transformation
of the world. Not until at least the preliminary steps in this theological and intellectual transformation are accomplished can we expect
God to send worldwide revival. If the coming revival is not comprehensive in its effects, it will no more change the world permanently
than earlier revivals have changed it permanently. The regeneration
of people's souls is only the first step on the road to comprehensive
redemption. Christian philosopher Cornelius Van Til, who died in
1987, has issued a warning: "The temptation is very great for the believers in these times when the Church is in apostasy, and its conquest of the world for Christ seems to be losing out, that they shall
spend a great deal of their time in passive waiting instead of in active
service. Another danger that lurks at a time of apostasy is that the
few faithful ones give up the comprehensive ideal of the kingdom
and limit themselves to the saving of individual souls."[25] We need a
comprehensive revival that will produce comprehensive redemption.[26]

We must understand from the beginning that the message of the
kingdom of God rests on a concept of *salvation which is supernaturally
imparted*, not politically imparted. The kingdom of God is categorically not a narrow political program of social transformation; it is
rather a supernaturally imposed salvational program that inevitably
produces world-changing political, social, legal, and economic
effects. The amillennial theologian Geerhardus Vos was correct:
"The kingdom represents the specifically *evangelical* element in our
Lord's teaching. . . . Jesus' doctrine of the kingdom as both inward
and outward, coming first in the heart of man and afterwards in the
external world, upholds *the primacy of the spiritual and ethical* over the

---

24. R. J. Rushdoony, Foreword, in Zorn, *Church and Kingdom*, pp. xix-xx.
25. Cornelius Van Til, *Christian Theistic Ethics*, vol. III of *In Defense of Biblical
Christianity* (Phillipsburg, New Jersey: Presbyterian & Reformed, [1958] 1980), p. 122.
26. Gary North, "Comprehensive Redemption: A Theology for Social Action," in
North, *Is the World Running Down? Crisis in the Christian Worldview* (Tyler, Texas: Institute for Christian Economics, 1988), Appendix C.

physical. The invisible world of the inner religious life, the righteousness of the disposition, the sonship of God are in it made supreme, the essence of the kingdom, the ultimate realities to which everything else is subordinate. The inherently ethical character of the kingdom finds subjective expression in the demand for repentance."[27]

The primary need today, as always, is the need for widespread personal repentance before God. We therefore need a Holy Spirit-initiated Christian revival to extend the kingdom of God across the face of the earth. If we do not get this revival soon, my work and the work of those who are involved in the Biblical Blueprints project will remain curiosities, and then become antiquarian curiosities, until the revival comes.

Blueprints and Responsibility

Without a bottom-up religious transformation of civilization, the policies that we Christian Reconstructionists recommend will at best have only a peripheral influence on society. The reader should understand, however, that we expect the revival and this bottom-up transformation, if not in our own lifetimes, then eventually. The Bible's blueprints for society will eventually be universally adopted across the face of the earth as the waters cover the sea (Isa. 11:9).[28] Christian Reconstructionists regard this as historically inevitable. This confidence is what makes the theonomic postmillennial worldview so hard-nosed and uncompromising. We annoy almost every Christian who has doubts about the earthly triumph of God's kingdom, which means that we initially alienate just about everyone who reads our materials. Our antinomian Christian critics call us arrogant. Bear in mind that the word "arrogant" usually means "a confident assertion of something I don't approve of."

Christians who doubt the future earthly triumph of God's kingdom tend to be less confident and less sure about the practical reliability of the Bible's blueprints. Sometimes they even deny that the Bible offers such blueprints. If it does offer such blueprints, then evangelical Christians have major responsibilities outside the sanctuary and the family. This prospect of worldwide, culture-wide responsibility frightens millions of Christians. They have even adopted eschatologies that assure them that God does not hold them

---

27. Vos, *Kingdom and the Church*, pp. 102-3.
28. J. A. De Jong, *As the Waters Cover the Sea: Millennial Expectations in the Rise of Anglo-American Missions, 1640-1810* (Kampen, Netherlands: J. H. Kok, 1970).

responsible for anything so comprehensive as the transformation of today's sin-filled world. They do not believe that God offers to His church the tools, skills, and time necessary for such a generations-long project of social transformation. Therefore, they adopt the philosophy that says that Christians should not even try to reform society, for such efforts are futile, wasteful, and shift precious resources from the only legitimate tasks of the church: preaching individual salvation to the lost, and sustaining the converted spiritually in a time of inevitable cultural decline. They equate social reform programs with polishing brass on a sinking ship. As dispensationalist newsletter writer Peter Lalonde remarked concerning Christians who possess such a vision of God's world-transforming kingdom in history, "It's a question, 'Do you polish brass on a sinking ship?' And if they're working on setting up new institutions, instead of going out and winning the lost for Christ, then they're wasting the most valuable time on the planet earth right now, and that is the serious problem. . . ."[29]

Doubt vs. Dominion

Christians, paralyzed by their own versions of eschatological pessimism, have not taken advantage of the growing self-doubt that is progressively paralyzing their humanistic opponents. Christians should recognize the extent of the despair that has engulfed those who have rejected the idea that the Bible is the infallible word of God. An example of such despair is the following:

We live in a time in which old perspectives informing our understanding of the world have been seriously shaken by events of modern times. In many cases these old perspectives have collapsed; they no longer hold as our centers. . . . Against the backdrop of such events, an erosion of traditional values has taken place—an erosion which has left us feeling that we [are] adrift in a sea of relativity in which anything, including such evils as the holocaust or nuclear war might be rationalized as "necessary." It is with this experience that we know that the cultural foundations have been shaken. We know that we are no longer guided by a vision of coherence and relatedness concerning our individual existence. We know that we are no longer bound together by a set of values infused with a common sense of destiny. Our sense of destiny, if any, is dominated by an uneasiness and sense of foreboding about the future. The future itself is now feared by

29. Tape One, *Dominion: A Dangerous New Theology,* in *Dominion: The Word and the New World Order,* a 3-tape set distributed by the Omega-Latter, Ontario, Canada, 1987.

many as the ultimate danger to the fragile hold we have on whatever security we have achieved in the present. All of this has left some to question the meaning of their endeavors, while it has left many with a sense of isolation and loneliness. The irony is that this new sense of insecurity has come at a time when the material well-being of those in the advanced industrial nations has reached a height hitherto undreamed of.[30]

This is precisely what the Book of Deuteronomy predicts for a society that has covenanted with God, has been blessed with external wealth, and then has forgotten God in its humanistic confidence (Deut. 8:17): ". . . the LORD shall give thee there a trembling heart, and failing of eyes, and sorrow of mind: And thy life shall hang in doubt before thee; and thou shalt fear day and night, and shalt have none assurance of thy life" (Deut. 28:65b-66). This sort of widespread pessimism leads either to cultural collapse or military defeat, or else to revival. The first is taking place visibly, the second is a growing possibility,[31] and the third, revival, is also becoming more likely. Sociologist Robert Nisbet asks this question: "[W]hat is the future of the idea of progress? Any logical answer must be that the idea has no future whatever if we assume the indefinite, prolonged continuation of the kind of culture that has become almost universal in the West in the late twentieth century. If the roots are dying, as they would appear to be at the present time, how can there be shrub and foliage?"[32] But, he then asks, "is this contemporary Western culture likely to continue for long? The answer, it seems to me, must be in the negative—if we take any stock in the lessons of the human past." He makes no absolute prophecies—much of his academic career has been devoted to reminding us that such comprehensive cultural prophecies are always overturned by the facts of the future[33]—but he is correct when he says that "never in history have periods of culture such as our own lasted for very long." He sees "signs of the beginning of a religious renewal in Western civilization, notably in America."[34]

---

30. Howard J. Vogel, "A Survey and Commentary on the New Literature in Law and Religion," *Journal of Law and Religion*, I (1983), p. 151.

31. Arthur Robinson and Gary North, *Fighting Chance: Ten Feet to Survival* (Ft. Worth, Texas: American Bureau of Economic Research, 1986).

32. Robert A. Nisbet, *History of the Idea of Progress* (New York: Basic Books, 1980), p. 355-56.

33. Nisbet, "The Year 2000 And All That," *Commentary* (June 1968).

34. Nisbet, *History*, p. 356.

Guilt and Social Paralysis

This should not be a time for pessimism among Christians. Yet it is. They are missing an opportunity that has not been seen since the late eighteenth century, and possibly since the resurrection of Christ. A universal world civilization now exists for the first time since the Tower of Babel. It is disintegrating morally as it grows wealthy. It is ripe for the harvest.

A successful harvesting operation requires tools. To take advantage of this unique historical opportunity, Christians need tools of dominion — blueprints for the reconstruction of the world. But Christians today do not see that God has given them the tools of dominion, His revealed law. They agree with the humanists who in turn agree among themselves, above all, that the Bible offers society no specific legal standards for comprehensive reform and reconstruction. They agree with such statements as the one made by the editor of *The Journal of Law and Religion*, who is also a professor of Constitutional law at a Catholic law school:

> First, I assume that the Bible is not a detailed historical blueprint for American society, and that it does not contain much concrete guidance for the resolution of specific political conflicts or constitutional difficulties such as slavery and racism, sexism and equal opportunity to participate in society. The biblical traditions are not to be viewed as an arsenal of prooftexts for contemporary disputes. Contextual leaps from the situations in which the biblical authors wrote to the situations with which we find ourselves faced are likewise to be avoided. [35]

Notice that he raised the controversial issue of slavery. So does a professor of Hebrew scriptures at Notre Dame University in Indiana: "Then there is the larger hermeneutical issue of the *Christian* appropriation of Old Testament law and the binding nature of biblical norms and stipulations in general. Who today, for example, would be prepared to argue that laws concerning the conduct of war or slavery retain their binding authority for the Christian or for anyone else?"[36] Who would? I would, and so would those who call themselves Christian Reconstructionists. This is why Christian Recon-

---

35. Edward McGlynn Gaffney, Jr., "Of Covenants Ancient and New: The Influence of Secular Law on Biblical Religion," *Journal of Law and Religion*, II (1984), pp. 117-18.

36. Joseph Blenkinsopp, "Biblical Law and Hermeneutics: A Reply to Professor Gaffney," *ibid.*, IV (1986), p. 98.

struction represents a radical challenge to modern antinomian Christianity and modern humanism.

The enemies of God continue to bring up the issue of slavery in their war against Christianity. They seek to make Christians feel guilty regarding Christianity's theological and historical legacy. Christianity unquestionably condoned and even sanctioned chattel slavery until the nineteenth century. The enemies of Christianity then trace this judicial sanctioning of chattel slavery back to the Old Testament. In this way, they seek to create a sense of guilt and doubt in their targeted victims. They understand that guilt-ridden people are not effective opponents of the prevailing messianic social order. Rushdoony is correct when he says that "The reality of man apart from Christ is guilt and masochism. And guilt and masochism involve an unbreakable inner slavery which governs the total life of the non-Christian. The politics of the anti-Christian will thus inescapably be *the politics of guilt*. In the politics of guilt, man is perpetually drained in his social energy and cultural activity by his overriding sense of guilt and his masochistic activity. He will progressively demand of the state a redemptive role. What he cannot do personally, i.e., to save himself, he demands that the state do for him, so that the state, as man enlarged, becomes the human savior of man."[37]

That the Christians failed for many centuries to challenge chattel slavery is a black mark in the history of the church. But to lay the blame at the doorstep of the Bible is either a mistake or an ideological strategy, as I will prove in *Tools of Dominion*. If this book persuades Christians that this doubt-inducing accusation against the Bible regarding its supposed support of chattel slavery is false, then it will have achieved a major success.

Pietism vs. God's Law

What we find in our day is that Christians despise biblical law almost as much as secular humanists do. These Christians have begun to adopt arguments similar to those used by the English Deists. For example, they attack the very thought of stoning drunken, gluttonous sons — not young children, but adult sons who are living at home with their parents, debauching themselves — as some sort of "crime against humanity," when stoning them is specifically a civil sanction authorized by God (Deut. 21:18).[38] The very idea of execution

---

37. R. J. Rushdoony, *Politics of Guilt and Pity* (Fairfax, Virginia: Thoburn Press, [1970] 1978), p. 9.

38. Ed Dobson and Ed Hindson, "Apocalypse Now?", *Policy Review* (Fall 1986), p. 20.

by public stoning embarrasses Christians, despite the fact that public stoning is by far the most covenantally valid form of execution, for God's law requires the witnesses to cast the first stones, and it also requires representatives of the entire covenantal community to participate directly, rather than hiding the act in a sanitary room in some distant prison. The Bible is clear: "The hands of the witnesses shall be first upon him to put him to death, and afterward the hands of all the people. So thou shalt put the evil away from among you" (Deut. 17:7).

Stoning

Stoning was a communal activity, an aspect of the civil covenant: sanctions. It took place outside the town (Lev. 24:14; Num. 15:35-36; I Ki. 21:13). "If sentence was passed with the help of eye-witnesses, the witnesses had to begin the execution (Deut. 17:7). This was to discourage frivolous testimony in court."[39] Boecker argues that it was a form of excommunication, and that those stoned were not entitled to burial in the family plot, but he cites no Scriptural evidence. "For the ancients, the criminal was possessed of a real guilt which jeopardised the community. By covering the evil-doer with stones outside the town, the evil that he could spread was banished."[40] This argument is ridiculous, a liberal's self-conscious attempt to reinterpret the Bible's covenantal concepts as magical. The execution of the evil-doer was sufficient to stop the spread of his evil. The pile of stones was intended rather to serve as a covenantal reminder. Each pile of stones testified to the reality of covenant sanctions, a monument to God's judgment of cursing in history, just as the stones from the River Jordan were made into a memorial of God's judgment of the deliverance of Israel (Josh. 4:7-8).

Public stoning forces citizens to face the reality of the ultimate civil sanction, execution, which in turn points to God's ultimate sanction at judgment day. Stoning also faithfully images the promised judgment against Satan: the crushing of his head by the promised Seed (Gen. 3:15). Because most people, including Christians, do not want to think about God's final judgment, they prefer to assign to distant unknown executioners the grim task of carrying out God's judgment

---

39. Hans Jochen Boecker, *Law and the Administration of Justice in the Old Testament and Ancient East*, translated by Jeremy Moiser (Minneapolis, Minnesota: Augsburg, [1976] 1980), p. 40.

40. *Idem.*

in private. This privatization of execution is immoral; it is itself criminal. It is unjust to the convicted criminal,[41] and it is unjust to the surviving victims, who do not see God's justice done in public. The *systematic impersonalism of capital punishment* is the problem, not capital punishment as such. This deliberate impersonalism has corrupted the entire penal system today.[42]

The growth of impersonalism has been a problem for the West from the beginning. Even in the days of public executions, several centuries ago, the axeman wore a face mask. The Bible does not allow the establishment of a professional, taxpayer-financed guild of faceless executioners who, over time, inevitably either grow callous and impersonal toward their awful (full of awe) task, or else grow sadistic. Instead, the Bible imposes personal responsibility on members of society at large for enforcing this ultimate sanction. But people in the Christian West have always refused to accept this God-imposed personal responsibility. They prefer to make a lone executioner psychologically responsible for carrying out the sentence rather than participate in this covenantal responsibility, as God requires. This refusal to accept personal responsibility by citizens has led to a crisis in Western jurisprudence in the twentieth century. Decade by decade, the more consistent haters of God's law have become politically dominant. They have used the same kinds of arguments against capital punishment in general that embarrassed Christians had accepted in their rejection of public stoning. Step by step, society eliminates capital punishment. Men's hatred of God's law is steadily manifested covenantally in modern civil law.

---

41. Public stoning would allow a condemned man to confront the witnesses and his executioners. The idea of a private execution where the condemned person cannot have a final word to those who have condemned him is anything but liberal-minded. It was long considered a basic legal privilege in the West for a condemned person to have this final opportunity to speak his mind. The sign of the intolerance of the "liberal" French Revolutionaries was their unwillingness to allow King Louis XVI to speak to the crowd at his execution. The judges had ordered drummers to begin drumming the moment he began to speak, which they did. Leo Gershoy, *The French Revolution and Napoleon* (New York: Appleton-Century-Crofts, 1933), p. 238.

42. Whereas men used to be flogged in public or put in the stocks for a few days, we now put them in hidden jails that are filled with a professional criminal class (as well as with AIDS-carrying homosexual rapists). This impersonalism of punishment has been paralleled by a steady bureaucratization and institutionalization of the penal system. The guards in prisons tend to become as impersonal and callous as their prisoners. Bukovsky writes of Soviet prisons: "There's no real difference between the criminals and their guards. Except for the uniforms. The slang is the same, the manners, concepts, psychology. It's all the same criminal world, all joined by an unbreakable chain." Vladimir Bukovsky, *To Build a Castle — My Life as a Dissenter* (New York: Viking, 1978), p. 334.

Economic Restitution

A considerable percentage of this book is devoted to a defense of the biblical concept of penal restitution. *Convicted criminals are supposed to make restitution payments to their victims.* This "revolutionary" idea is at last being taken seriously by a few judges in the United States.[43] But behind the ability of today's civil courts to impose the sanction of restitution lies a greater threat to the criminal: *imprisonment.* This is the "dirty little secret" of those atheists, pietists, and antinomians who ridicule the biblical system of slavery: they have accepted the horror of unproductive imprisonment in place of the biblical institution of penal labor servitude, out of which an industrious slave could purchase his freedom. If the criminal in ancient Israel was financially unable to pay his victim, his sale to a slave-buyer was what provided the victim with his lawful restitution payment. The prison system has always been the Bible-hater's preferred substitute for the Old Testament's system of law-restricted labor servitude. In short, in order to enforce the Bible's principle of economic restitution to victims by criminals, there always has to be a more fearful support sanction in reserve: death, imprisonment, whipping, banishment, or indentured servitude. But only one of these reserve sanctions raises money for the victims: indentured servitude. The critics of biblical law just never seem to remember to mention this fact.

The Fear of God's Law

This hatred of God's law has affected millions of Christians who sing the old hymn, "O How Love I Thy Law." Even when they do not actively hate it (and most do), they are simply afraid of God's law. They have not studied it, and they have been beaten into intellectual submission by humanists, Christian antinomians, and those who fear personal and cultural responsibility.

A discouraging example of this is Dr. James Dobson, whose books, films, and daily radio broadcasts on Christian family issues have inspired millions of Americans, and who by 1988 had become the Protestant evangelical leader in the United States with the largest

---

43. For example, Lois G. Forer, *Criminals and Victims: A Trial Judge Reflects on Crime and Punishment* (New York: Norton, 1980).

and most dedicated following.[44] He has led the fight against abortion and pornography, and the fight for home schooling and the re-establishment of godly disciplining of children in the home. Yet in a pamphlet against abortion, he rejected as inapplicable the single most important passage in the Bible that deals with abortion, one which makes abortion a capital crime, Exodus 21:22-25. In response to a preposterous misinterpretation of this passage by a state-licensed, profit-seeking "Christian" murderer (a pro-abortion gynecologist), Dr. Dobson did not refute the misinterpretation, but instead dismissed the Old Testament case laws as inappropriate guides for contemporary Christian righteousness. He asked his critic rhetorically:

Do you agree that if a man beats his slave to death, he is to be considered guilty only if the individual dies instantly? If the slave lives a few days, the owner is considered not guilty (Exodus 21:20-21)[?] Do you believe that we should stone to death rebellious children (Deuteronomy 21:18-21)? Do you really believe we can draw subtle meaning about complex issues from Mosaic law, when even the obvious interpretation makes no sense to us today? We can hardly select what we will and will not apply now. If we accept the verses you cited, we are obligated to deal with every last jot and tittle.[45]

What we see here is an attempt to avoid dealing with "every last jot and tittle" of God's inspired word. Yet it was Jesus who warned His people: "Till heaven and earth pass, one jot or one tittle shall in no wise [way] pass from the law, till all be fulfilled" (Matt. 5:18). Are we to ignore this? Dr. Dobson does. Admittedly, it is possible to argue that "heaven and earth" here mean the Old Covenant order, and that the fall of Jerusalem did fulfil the law. It is also possible to argue, as James Jordan has argued, that the death of Christ buried the law, and that His resurrection restored it in a new form, with the various dietary and ritual cleansing laws fulfilled (and therefore annulled in history) by the resurrection (Acts 10; I Cor. 8). But this does not absolve us from the difficult task that so disturbs Dr. Dobson,

---

44. Pat Robertson, by resigning from the ministry and also from his "700 Club" television show in his quest for the Presidency in early 1988, inescapably exchanged his office of religious commentator for that of political activist. After his defeat in the Republican Party primaries, he returned to television, and he still has a large following, though smaller than when he left. His leadership role is probably perceived even by his most admiring followers as being different from what it had been before he entered politics.

45. James Dobson, "Dialogue on Abortion," in Dobson and Gary Bergel, *The Decision of Life* (Arcadia, California: Focus on the Family, 1986), p. 14.

namely, selecting "what we will and will not apply now." To retreat from this task of applied Christianity is to turn over the running of the world to pagan humanists and their theological allies, Christian antinomians. *It is to turn the medical world over to the God-hating abortionists who are opposed so vigorously by Dr. Dobson.* Yet this is precisely what every publicly visible Christian leader has done throughout the twentieth century, and what almost all of them did after the late seventeenth century. It is universally assumed by Christians that the case laws of Exodus are null and void, and *should* be. It is this assumption which this book is designed to challenge.

The tools of dominion, God's law, sit unused and generally unread by those who call themselves Christians. They are the best weapons that Christians possess for moral self-defense, since the best defense is a good offense, yet they steadfastly refuse to use them. To use God's revealed law effectively would require them to become intimately familiar with its many subtleties and complex applications, and even less appealing, to discipline themselves in terms of it. They prefer to let it sit unopened, either in their laps or on their shelves. Christians therefore continue to lose the war for civilization.

Tom Paine's Demon: The Bible

We know where antinomian (anti-God's law) theology has headed in the past: to Unitarianism, atheism, and bloody revolution. It winds up with the words of Tom Paine: that in consideration of "the obscene stories, the voluptuous debaucheries, the cruel and torturous executions, the unrelenting vindictiveness, with which more than half the Bible is filled, it would be more consistent that we called it the word of a demon, than the word of God."[46]

Is the Old Testament the word of a demon? If not, then why do antinomian Christians, liberals and conservatives, neo-evangelicals and fundamentalists, continue to ridicule Old Testament law? They stick their fists in the face of the God of Psalm 119, and shout in defiance of His law: "Is God really nothing more than the abstract, impersonal dispenser of equally abstract and impersonal laws?"[47]

---

46. *The Age of Reason*, Pt. I; cited by David Brion Davis, *The Problem of Slavery in the Age of Revolution, 1770-1823* (Ithaca, New York: Cornell University Press, 1975), p. 525.

47. Rodney Clapp, "Democracy as Heresy," *Christianity Today* (Feb. 20, 1987), p. 23.

Yes, He is *much* more than this. Among other things, He is the Eternal Slavemaster over those who rebel against Him, the dispenser not of abstract law but of personally experienced agony forever and ever. Hell is real. The lake of fire is real. God is therefore not to be mocked. But He has many mockers, and many of these mockers call themselves by His name. They do not fear Him. For now. But eventually God will stick His fist in their faces. People may choose to ignore God's law; they will not be able to ignore AIDS much longer.

Another major alternative to Paine's sort of outright apostasy is some variation of Marcion's second-century heresy of the two-gods theory of history: that an evil god operated in the Old Testament, but a nice god runs the world today. (For more details, see below: "The Continuing Heresy of Dualism.") Robert Davison is correct when he says that a "Marcionite tendency may be fairly traced in much modern discussion of Christian ethics, nor is this tendency confined to scholarly discussion."[48]

The third alternative is dispensationalism: God used the revealed laws of the Bible to govern people before the advent of Christ, but today we have new laws in operation, meaning vague, undefined personal laws, and no specifically New Testament cultural laws at all. The road to cultural impotence is paved with neat (and ultimately unworkable) solutions to difficult biblical problems. Slavery is one of these difficult problems.

What we must search for is the moral principle that undergirded each Old Testament law. When we find it, we can then begin to discuss how or to what extent God expects the civil government or some other government to enforce it today. Those who begin with the presupposition that a particular Old Testament law or God-required Hebrew practice was innately evil have already taken the first step toward Paine's view: that the Bible is the word of a demon.

Christians today are afraid of the laws in the Bible. They are actually embarrassed by them. They do not recognize that biblical law is a two-edged sword of God's judgment: blessing for the righteous, but cursing for the unrighteous (Rom. 13:1-7). They do not understand that *God's law-order for society is merciful.* For example, God allows the death penalty for kidnappers (Ex. 21:16). The death penalty

---

48. Robert Davison, "Some Aspects of the Old Testament Contribution to the Pattern of Christian Ethics," *Scottish Journal of Theology*, 12 (1959), p. 374; cited by Walter Kaiser, *Toward Old Testament Ethics* (Grand Rapids, Michigan: Zondervan Academie, 1983), p. 23.

used to be imposed on kidnappers in the United States, and kidnapping was rare. It is no longer imposed regularly, and kidnapping has become a blight. Kidnapping by terrorists in Europe is commonplace. Who says that God's law regarding kidnapping is too harsh? Harsher than kidnapping itself? So it is with *all* of God's civil laws. They are merciful compared with the effects of unpunished evil. The modern world is learning just how unmerciful a society can be that is not governed by biblical law.

"Theocraphobia": Fear of God's Rulership

When, in a court of law, the witness puts his hand on the Bible and swears to tell the truth, the whole truth, and nothing but the truth, so help him God, he thereby swears on the Word of God — the *whole* Word of God, and *nothing but* the Word of God. The Bible is a unit. It is a "package deal." The New Testament did not overturn the Old Testament; it is a *commentary* on the Old Testament. It tells us how to use the Old Testament properly in the period after the death and resurrection of Israel's messiah, God's Son.

Jesus said: "Think not that I am come to destroy the law, or the prophets: I am come not to destroy, but to fulfil. For verily I say unto you, Till heaven and earth pass, one jot or one tittle shall in no wise [way] pass from the law, till all be fulfilled. Whosoever therefore shall break one of these least commandments, and shall teach men so, he shall be called the least in the kingdom of heaven: but whosoever shall do and teach them, the same shall be called great in the kingdom of heaven" (Matt. 5:17-19). Christ took the Old Testament seriously enough to die for those condemned to the second death (Rev. 20:14) by its provisions. The Old Testament is not a discarded first draft of God's word. It is not "God's word (emeritus)."

If anything, the New Testament law is more stringent than the Mosaic law, not less stringent. Paul writes that an elder cannot have more than one wife (I Tim. 3:2). The king in the Old Testament was forbidden to have multiple wives (Deut. 17:17). This was not a general law, unless we interpret the prohibition of Leviticus 18:18 as applying to all additional wives, and not just to marrying a woman's sister, as ethicist John Murray interprets it.[49] If we attempt to inter-

---

49. John Murray, *Principles of Conduct* (Grand Rapids, Michigan: Eerdmans, 1957), Appendix B. Catholic theologian Angelo Tosato agrees with him: "The Law of Leviticus 18:18: A Reexamination," *Catholic Biblical Quarterly*, Vol. 46 (1984), pp. 199-214. They are not followed in this view by most Protestant commentators, nor by Nachmanides, who said that the verse applies only to a woman's sister: Rabbi Moshe ben Nachman [Ramban], *Commentary on the Torah: Leviticus* (New York: Shilo, [1267?] 1973), p. 255.

pret Leviticus 18:18 in Murray's fashion, the question arises: Why specify kings as being prohibited from becoming polygamists if the same law applied to all men anyway? Possibly to prohibit the system of political covenanting through marriage (Solomon is a good example here). Certainly, there is no equally clear-cut Old Testament prohibition against polygamy comparable to I Timothy 3:2, which indicates a tightening of the legal requirements for at least church officers. The New Testament appears to be more rigorous than the Old in this instance. Another alteration in marriage law that we find in the New Testament is the abolition of concubinage that resulted from Christ's fulfillment of the terms of the Old Testament's bride price system (see Chapter 6). There are no more second-class wives.

Dominion Christianity teaches that there are four covenants under God, meaning four kinds of *vows* under God: personal (individual), and the three institutional covenants: ecclesiastical, civil, and familial.[50] All other human institutions (business, educational, charitable, etc.) are to one degree or other under the jurisdiction of one or more of these four covenants. No single human covenant is absolute; therefore, no single human institution is all-powerful. Thus, Christian liberty is *liberty under God and God's law*, administered by plural legal authorities.

Biblical Pluralism

There is no doubt that Christianity teaches pluralism, but a very special kind of pluralism: *plural institutions* under God's single comprehensive law system. It does *not* teach a pluralism of law structures, or a pluralism of moralities, for this sort of hypothetical legal pluralism (as distinguished from *institutional* pluralism) is always either polytheistic or humanistic.[51] Christian people are required to take dominion over the earth by means of all three God-ordained institutions, not just the church, or just the State, or just the family. *The kingdom of God includes every human institution, and every aspect of life, for all of life is under God and is governed by His unchanging principles.* All of life is under God and God's law because God intends to *judge* all of life *in terms of* His law.[52]

---

50. Ray R. Sutton, *That You May Prosper: Dominion By Covenant* (Tyler, Texas: Institute for Christian Economics, 1987), ch. 4.

51. Gary DeMar, *Ruler of the Nations: The Biblical Blueprints for Government* (Ft. Worth, Texas: Dominion Press, 1987), ch. 3.

52. *Ibid.*, ch. 4.

In this structure of *plural governments*, the institutional churches
serve as *advisors* to the other institutions (the Levitical function), but
the churches can only pressure individual leaders through the threat
of excommunication. As a restraining factor on unwarranted church
authority, an excommunication by one local church or denomination
is always subject to review by another, if and when the excommunicated person seeks membership elsewhere. Thus, each of the three
covenantal institutions is to be run under God, as interpreted by its
lawfully elected or ordained leaders, with the advice of the churches,
not their compulsion.

All Christians are in principle theocrats. All Christians say that
God rules the universe. God (*theos*) rules (*kratos*). Theocracy means
simply that *God rules*. He rules in every area of life: church, State,
family, business, science, education, etc. There is no zone of neutrality. There is no "king's x" from God. Men are responsible for
everything they think, say, and do. God exercises total jurisdiction.
Jurisdiction means law (*juris*) and speaking (*diction*). God *speaks* His
word. It is a comprehensive word. Anyone who says that God's law
does not apply to some area of life is thereby saying that God does
not have jurisdiction in that area. "No law — no jurisdiction."

A Scare Word

The word "theocracy" is a scare word that humanists and fright-
ened Christians use to chase dedicated Christians away from areas
of their God-given responsibility. The critics focus on politics and
civil government as if God's rule in this area were somehow evil. Because almost all humanists today believe in salvation through legislation,[53] they necessarily believe that politics is the primary means of
social healing.[54] The Marxists are the most consistent defenders of
human transformation through political action: the religion of revolution.[55] Because Christians are today so used to thinking in these
humanistic terms, they seldom think to themselves: "Wait a minute.
I know that God rules the family, and the government of my family

---

53. The exceptions to this rule are classical liberals and free market economists
like F. A. Hayek and Milton Friedman, traditional conservatives like Russell Kirk
and William F. Buckley, neo-conservatives like Irving Kristol, and outright anarchists like Murray N. Rothbard.

54. R. J. Rushdoony, *The One and the Many: Studies in the Philosophy of Order and
Ultimacy* (Fairfax, Virginia: Thoburn Press, [1971] 1978), chaps. 2-5, 8, 9, 11.

55. Gary North, *Marx's Religion of Revolution: Regeneration Through Chaos* (rev. ed.;
Tyler, Texas: Institute for Christian Economics, 1989).

should reflect this fact. God also rules the church, and the government of my church is supposed to reflect this fact. I know that God
rules all civil governments, too. So why should it be evil for Christians to work hard to see to it that the civil government reflects this
fact, just as they do in their families, churches, and businesses?" In
short, why should politics be outside the realm of God-honoring
Christian action?[56]

Humanist critics present Christians with a kind of mental image:
a scarecrow that is locked in the stocks of Puritan New England.
Every time a Christian walks by this scarecrow, a tape recorded
message blares out: "Beware of theocracy! Beware of theocracy!" If
the critics meant, "Beware of ecclesiocracy," meaning civil rule by the
institutional church, they would have a valid point, but they mean
something different: "Beware of Christians in every area of life who
seek to exercise biblical dominion under God by obeying *and enforcing*
God's holy law."

What "Beware of theocracy!" really means is, "Beware of God's
righteous rule!"

The Dismantling of the Welfare-Warfare State

Those who reject the theocratic ideal are ready to accuse Calvinists of being tyrants. Historian Ronald Wells of Calvin College has
written an attack on Francis Schaeffer, which appears in a collection
of essays that is best described as a neo-evangelical tirade. He points
to the unfootnoted and unmentioned links between certain aspects of
Schaeffer's social thought and Christian Reconstructionism, and
then observes: "This tendency to promote one's own view by 'law'
has always been the dangerous part of Calvinism: one sees Calvinists in power as triumphal and dictatorial. . . . Calvinists in power
have wielded that power oppressively."[57]

I suspect that we Reconstructionists were Mr. Wells' target, for
we are the only Christians on earth calling for the building of a biblical theocracy. What I also suspect is that what really disturbs our
neo-evangelical academic critics is that we perceive this theocracy as
a system of decentralized power. We call for a vast purging of present-

---

56. George Grant, *The Changing of the Guard: The Biblical Blueprint for Politics* (Ft.
Worth, Texas: Dominion Press, 1987).

57. Ronald A. Wells, "Schaeffer on America," in Ronald W. Ruegsegger (ed.),
Reflections on Francis Schaeffer (Grand Rapids, Michigan: Zondervan Academie,
1986), p. 237.

day national power, both political and economic. We call for the dismantling of the welfare-warfare State, most notably every aspect of taxpayer-financing for education (except for the national military academies . . . maybe).[58] I have called for a reduction of aggregate taxes to the level required by I Samuel 8: where all levels of civil government *combined* are allowed to collect *less than 10 percent* of the *net increase* of annual private personal productivity.[59] I support the abolition of the local property tax, and all state and national direct taxation, which includes the graduated income tax, the Social Security tax, the corporate income tax, the capital gains tax, and all sales taxes. I recommend the abolition of all direct taxation by any agency of civil government above the local township or county; every other level of civil government would be forced to seek its revenues by taxing the level of civil government immediately below it. Civil governments above the most local would have to live off the revenues collected from other civil governments. This would decentralize power with a vengeance. The Reconstructionists' version of theocracy is a decentralized system of multiple competing governments in which the modern messianic State and its economic subsidies would be dismantled. By modern political standards, such a vision of the shrinking of the centralized power civil government is nothing short of utopian.

In short, if the Reconstructionists' version of theocracy were to be voted into operation, the tenured, subsidized intellectual class to which our academic critics belong would experience the end of its taxpayer-financed bonanza. An entire class would have to enter the competitive free market and seek productive employment. Consumers would reward former college professors in terms of what consumers want to buy, not what state legislatures want to buy. There would be no more compulsory education and no more tax support of existing schools. This fear, rather than the fear of tyranny, may well be the true underlying concern of our critics.

Majority Rule

The Bible does not allow the imposition of some sort of top-down bureaucratic tyranny in the name of Christ. The kingdom of God requires a bottom-up society. The bottom-up Christian society rests

---

58. Robert L. Thoburn, *The Children Trap: Biblical Blueprints for Education* (Ft. Worth, Texas: Dominion Press, 1986).

59. Gary North, *Healer of the Nations: Biblical Blueprints for International Relations* (Ft. Worth, Texas: Dominion Press, 1987), p. 61.

ultimately on the doctrine of *self*-government under God, with God's law as the publicly revealed standard of performance.[60] It is the humanists' view of society that promotes top-down bureaucratic power.

The basis for building a Christian society is evangelism and missions that lead to a widespread Christian revival, so that the great mass of earth's inhabitants will place themselves under Christ's protection, and voluntarily use His covenantal laws for self-government. Christian reconstruction begins with personal conversion to Christ and self-government under God's law, then it spreads to others through revival, and only later does it bring comprehensive changes in civil law, when the vast majority of voters voluntarily agree to live under biblical blueprints.

Let's get this straight: *Christian reconstruction depends on majority rule.* Of course, the leaders of the Christian Reconstruction movement expect a majority eventually to accept Christ as savior. We believe in postmillennialism.[61] Those who do not share our confidence concerning the future success of the gospel, as empowered by the Holy Spirit, believe that an earthly kingdom must be imposed by force from the top down (premillennialism),[62] or else they do not believe

---

60. DeMar, *Ruler of the Nations*, ch. 2.

61. David Chilton, *Paradise Restored: A Biblical Theology of Dominion* (Ft. Worth, Texas: Dominion Press, 1985); Roderick Campbell, *Israel and the New Covenant* (Tyler, Texas: Geneva Divinity School Press, [1954] 1981); R. J. Rushdoony, *Thy Kingdom Come: Studies in Daniel and Revelation* (Fairfax, Virginia: Thoburn Press, [1971] 1978).

62. Dave Hunt writes: "During His thousand-year reign, Christ will visibly rule the world in perfect righteousness from Jerusalem and will impose peace on all nations. Satan will be locked up, robbed of the power to tempt. Justice will be meted out swiftly." Hunt, *Beyond Seduction: A Return to Biblical Christianity* (Eugene, Oregon: Harvest House, 1987), p. 250. If Satan is unable to tempt mankind, then any evil that calls forth Christ's justice must be man-based evil. In a taped interview with Peter Lalonde, released in early 1987, Hunt said: "Christ himself is physically here. And He has us, the redeemed in our resurrection bodies, that nobody can kill us. And we are helping Him to maintain order. He is *forcing* this world to behave, and He gives a restoration of the Edenic state, so that the desert blossoms like a rose, and the lion lies down with the lamb, and you've got paradise on earth, once again, with Christ Himself maintaining it and, even better than the garden of Eden, Satan is locked up for a thousand years." *Dominion and the Cross*, Tape One of *Dominion: The Word and the New World Order, op. cit.*, 1987.

It should be pointed out that Hunt's argument that resurrected saints will return to rule with Jesus during the earthly millennium has long been rejected by dispensational theologians at Dallas Theological Seminary. Resurrected saints will be dwelling in a place called the heavenly Jerusalem, argues J. Dwight Pentecost: "The Relation between Living and Resurrected Saints in The Millennium," *Bibliotheca Sacra*, vol. 117 (October 1960), pp. 335-37. See also John F. Walvoord, *The Rapture Question* (rev. ed.; Grand Rapids, Michigan: Zondervan Academie, 1979), pp. 86-87.

in an earthly institutional kingdom at all (amillennialism).[63] Post-millennialists disagree, for several reasons.

Premillennialism and amillennialism both deny that the preaching of the gospel can ever bring a majority of people to faith in Christ, thereby bringing in the earthly kingdom of God in history on a voluntary basis, person by person, culture by culture. Premillennialist author Dave Hunt has gone so far as to argue that such a person-by-person extension of God's kingdom is literally impossible for God to achieve.[64] Thus, in order to produce universal peace on earth, premillennialists have always maintained, Jesus will have to impose a top-down bureaucracy when He comes to reign in person. In opposition to this view, amillennialists deny the premillennial doctrine that Jesus will ever physically return in history. They insist (as postmillennialism also insists) that Jesus will physically appear only at the end of history at the final judgment. They therefore deny (in contrast to postmillennialism) the possibility of an earthly manifestation of God's comprehensive kingdom of God in history.

Because of their denial of the widespread acceptance of the gospel at any point in history, premillennialists and amillennialists alike invariably associate the word "theocracy" with some sort of top-down, power-imposed, widely resisted rule that is imposed by an elite. Premillennialists accept this as a valid system of civil rule, but only if Christ personally and physically runs it from the top of the bureaucratic pyramid. Amillennialists deny that Christ will ever do this in history, so they deny bureaucratic theocracy's legitimacy at any point in the pre-final judgment future.

---

63. Oddly enough, Hunt also denies that there can ever be an earthly kingdom, even in the dispensational millennium. He says in his taped interview: "What happens at the end of this time, when Satan is loosed? He deceives the nations and like the sand of the seashore, so many — a multitude. They gather their armies and come against Christ in Jerusalem. And, of course, that is when they finally have to be banished from God's presence forever. I believe it's the final proof of the incorrigible nature of the human heart. So, Christ Himself cannot make humanity behave. He cannot by legislation, or by political or military or coercive means, establish this kingdom." *Ibid.*, Tape Two.

64. "In fact, dominion — taking dominion and setting up the kingdom for Christ — is an *impossibility*, even for God. The millennial reign of Christ, far from being the kingdom, is actually the final proof of the incorrigible nature of the human heart, because Christ Himself can't do what these people say they are going to do — New Agers or Manifested Sons." (Verbal emphasis in the original interview.) *Dominion*, Tape Two.

The Work of the Holy Spirit

First, we Calvinistic postmillennialists disagree with both groups concerning the supposed impotence of the gospel in history in changing whole societies, person by person. We believe that the Holy Spirit will *impose* His will on the recalcitrant hearts of huge numbers of people, just as He has always imposed His will on each recalcitrant heart every time He has saved anyone from his sins. God is utterly sovereign in election and salvation. He changes people's hearts, transforming them so that they can respond in faith to the free offer of the gospel. "The king's heart is in the hand of the LORD, as the rivers of water: he turneth it whithersoever he will" (Prov. 21:1). This is the only way anyone has ever been saved, for the natural man does not receive the things of the Spirit, for they are foolishness to him (I Cor. 2:14). The natural man does not partially receive the things of the Spirit in his unsaved state; he rejects the very idea that such a wrathful God exists. Thus, he needs to be transformed before he can accept the gospel.

Second, because we Calvinistic Christian Reconstructionists believe that the Holy Spirit forces hearts to change — the doctrine of irresistible grace — we also believe that human institutions are not allowed to seek to coerce men's hearts and minds. Such coercion of the human will — its transformation prior to the prior permission of the individual whose will is being transformed — is a monopoly that belongs exclusively to God. We must recognize that coercion is an inescapable concept in history. It is never a question of coercion vs. no coercion. It is always a question of *whose* coercion. We affirm the power of the Holy Spirit to change men's souls — to declare judicially that they are saved, and therefore possess Christ's righteousness — and to change them ethically at the point of their ethical transformation. Those who deny this exclusive power of the Spirit in transforming the lives of covenant-breakers instinctively expect to find coercion somewhere else: in human institutions — either humanist or "theocratic-bureaucratic" — or in a future personal kingdom ruled by Christ in Person.

Third, because we postmillennialists find it taught in the Bible that there will be a future outpouring of this soul-transforming Holy Spirit — the only possible basis of the Bible's prophesied millennial blessings — we disagree with premillennialists and amillennialists concerning the limited extent of the Spirit's work in the future. The kingdom will not be brought in by a bureaucratic theocratic regime,

but by the heart-transforming work of the Holy Spirit. We therefore
disagree with them concerning the supposed necessity of defining
theocracy as a top-down social transformation. God's kingdom rule
is always bottom-up: *self-government under God*. So, we do not call for a
theocratic bureaucracy, either now or in the future. Such a top-down
bureaucracy is not called for in the Bible, is impossible to maintain
without unlawful coercion, and is not necessary to impose to bring in
the kingdom. Christian Reconstructionists call instead for a decentralized, international, theocratic *republic*.[65] Such a republic is ethically necessary, now and in the future, and it will be historically possible in the future, when the Holy Spirit begins His visibly triumphant sweep of the nations.

If postmillennialism is incorrect, and the Holy Spirit does not act
to bring huge numbers of people to eternal life, then Christians must
be content with only partial social reconstruction, and only partial
external blessings from God. The earthly manifestations of God's
heavenly kingdom will necessarily be limited. When we pray, "Thy
kingdom come, thy will be done in earth, as it is in heaven," we
should expect God to answer this prayer. But many Christians teach
that God will *never* answer this prayer before Jesus comes again physically to rule the world in person. If they are correct, then we will not
see the pre-second coming advent of a holy commonwealth in which
God's laws are honored. We must content ourselves with less.

It is not possible to ramrod God's blessings from the top down,
unless you are God. Only humanists think that man is God. Christians are simply trying to get the ramrod away from them, and to
melt it down. This melted ramrod could then be used to make a
great grave marker for humanism: "The God That Failed."

The Continuing Heresy of Dualism

Dualism teaches that the world is inherently divided: spirit vs.
matter, or law vs. mercy, or mind vs. matter, or nature vs. grace.
What the Bible teaches is that this world is divided *ethically* and *personally*: Satan vs. God, right vs. wrong, freedom vs. tyranny. The
conflict between God and Satan will end at the final judgment.
Whenever Christians substitute some other form of dualism for ethical dualism, they fall into heresy and suffer the consequences. That

---

65. E. C. Wines, *The Hebrew Republic* (Rt. 1, Box 65-2, Wrightstown, New Jersey: American Presbyterian Press, 1980). This is a reprint of the late-nineteenth century book, *Commentary on the Laws of the Ancient Hebrews*, Book II.

is what has happened today. We are suffering from revived versions of ancient heresies.

Marcion's Dualism

The Old Testament was written by the same God who wrote the New Testament. There were not two Gods in history, meaning there was no dualism or radical split between the two testamental periods. There is only one God, in time and eternity.

This idea has had opposition throughout church history. An ancient two-gods heresy was first promoted in the church about a century after Christ's crucifixion, and the church has always regarded it as just that, a heresy. It was proposed by a man named Marcion. Basically, this heresy teaches that there are two completely different law systems in the Bible: Old Testament law and New Testament law (or non-law). But Marcion took the logic of his position all the way. He argued that two law systems means two gods. The god of wrath wrote the Old Testament, and the god of mercy wrote the New Testament. In short: "two laws-two gods."

You would be surprised how many Christians still believe something dangerously close to Marcionism: not a two-gods view, exactly, but a "God-who-changed-all-His-rules" sort of view. They begin with the accurate teaching that the ceremonial laws of the Old Testament were fulfilled by Christ, and therefore that the *unchanging principles* of worship are *applied differently* in the New Testament, but then they erroneously conclude that the whole Old Testament system of civil law was dropped by God, and *nothing biblical was put in its place*. In other words, God created a sort of vacuum for State law.

This idea turns civil law-making over to Satan. In our day, this means that civil law-making is turned over to humanism. *Christians have unwittingly become the philosophical allies of the humanists with respect to civil law.* With respect to their doctrine of the State, therefore, most Christians hold what is in effect a two-gods view of the Bible.

Gnostic Dualism

Another ancient heresy that is still with us is gnosticism. It became a major threat to the early church almost from the beginning. It was also a form of dualism, a theory of a radical split. The gnostics taught that the split is between evil matter and good spirit. Thus, their goal was to escape this material world through other-worldly exercises that punish the body. They believed in *retreat from the world* of human conflicts and responsibility. Some of these ideas got into the church, and people started doing ridiculous things. So-called "pillar saints" became temporarily popular in the fifth century, A.D. A "saint" would sit on a platform on top of a pole for several decades without coming down. This was considered very spiritual.[66] (Who fed them? Who cleaned up after them?)

Thus, many Christians came to view "the world" as something permanently outside the kingdom of God. They believed that this hostile, forever-evil world cannot be redeemed, reformed, and reconstructed. At best, it can be subdued by power (maybe). Jesus did not really die for it, and it cannot be healed. This dualistic view of the world vs. God's kingdom narrowly restricted any earthly manifestation of God's kingdom. Christians who were influenced by gnosticism concluded that God's kingdom refers only to the institutional church. They argued that the institutional church is the *only* manifestation of God's kingdom.

This led to two opposite and equally evil conclusions. First, power religionists who accepted this definition of God's kingdom tried to put the institutional church in charge of everything, since it is supposedly "the only manifestation of God's kingdom on earth." To subdue the supposedly unredeemable world, which is forever outside the kingdom, the institutional church has to rule with the sword. The institutional church must give orders to the State, and the State must enforce these orders with the sword. The institutional church must therefore concentrate political and economic power. *What then becomes of liberty?*

Second, escape religionists who also accepted this narrow definition of the kingdom sought refuge from the evil world of matter and politics by fleeing to hide inside the institutional church, an exclusively "spiritual kingdom," now narrowly defined. They abandoned the world to evil tyrants. *What then becomes of liberty?* What becomes of the idea of God's progressive restoration of all things under Jesus Christ? What, finally, becomes of the idea of biblical dominion?

When Christians improperly narrow their definition of the kingdom of God, the visible influence of this comprehensive kingdom (both spiritual and institutional at the same time) begins to shrivel up. The first heresy leads to tyranny *by* the church, and the second heresy leads to tyranny *over* the church. Both of these narrow defini-

---

66. Kenneth Scott Latourette, *A History of Christianity* (New York: Harper & Row, 1953), pp. 228, 298.

tions of God's kingdom destroy the liberty of the responsible Christian man, self-governed under God and God's law.

Manichaean Dualism

The last ancient pagan idea that still lives on is also a variant of dualism: matter vs. spirit. It teaches that God and Satan, good and evil, are forever locked in combat, and that good never triumphs over evil. The Persian religion of Zoroastrianism has held such a view for over 2,500 years. The incredibly popular "Star Wars" movies were based on this view of the world: the "dark" side of "the force" against its "light" side. In modern versions of this ancient dualism, the "force" is usually seen as itself impersonal: individuals personalize either the dark side or the light side by "plugging into" its power.

There are millions of Christians who have adopted a very pessimistic version of this dualism, though not in an impersonal form. God's kingdom is battling Satan's, and God's is losing. History is not going to get better. In fact, things are going to get a lot worse externally. Evil will visibly push good into the shadows. The church is like a band of soldiers who are surrounded by a huge army of Indians. "We can't win, boys, so hold the fort until Jesus and the angels come to rescue us!"

That does not sound like Abraham, Moses, Joshua, Gideon, and David, does it? Christians read to their children the children's favorite story, David and Goliath, yet in their own lives, millions of Christian parents really think that the Goliaths of this world are the unbeatable earthly winners. Christians have not even picked up a stone.

Until very recently.

Conclusion

We must not come to the Old Testament with a sense of fear and loathing. The Old Testament provides us with a vision of victory and the tools of dominion, namely, God's laws. These laws are not a threat to us as Christians; they are the foundation of our efforts to reconstruct society.

Christians have not wanted to think about God's law. It reminds them of their sins of commission. It also reminds them of their sins of omission. They have failed to press the claims of Jesus Christ in every area of life. They have failed to challenge the sins of this age.

They have refused to tell the world that God really does have specific answers for every area of life, including economics and politics. Christians have preferred to comfort themselves as they have sat in their rocking chairs in the shadows of history, rocking themselves back and forth, and saying over and over: "I am not a theocrat. I am not a theocrat."

What this phrase means is simple: *God does not rule, so neither will I.*

But what if God *does* rule? What if He has given us the unchanging laws by which He expects His people to rule? What if He has given us the tools of dominion, and we have left them in the rain to rust? What will He do with our generation?

Just what He did with Moses' generation: He will leave them behind to die in the wilderness.

2

WHAT IS COVENANT LAW?

Behold, I have taught you statutes and judgments, even as the LORD my God commanded me, that ye should do so in the land whither ye go to possess it. Keep therefore and do them; for this is your wisdom and your understanding in the sight of the nations, which shall hear all these statutes, and say, Surely this great nation is a wise and understanding people. For what nation is there so great, who hath God so nigh unto them, as the LORD our God is in all things that we call upon him for? And what nation is there so great, that hath statutes and judgments so righteous as all this law, which I set before you this day? (Deut. 4:5-8).

These verses teach clearly that the law of God is a tool of world-wide evangelism. The nations of the earth will recognize the justice that is provided by God's revealed law, as well as see the external blessings that inevitably come to any society that covenants itself to God, and subsequently adheres to the ethical terms of God's covenant. It is crucially important to maintain that these blessings will be visible (Deut. 28:1-14). The Bible is insistent: *there is an inescapable cause-and-effect relationship between national covenantal faithfulness and national prosperity.* Adherence to biblical law *inevitably* produces visible results that are universally regarded as beneficial. Why do covenant-breakers recognize this? Because all men have the work of God's law written on their hearts (Rom. 2:14-15), so they can and do perceive the blessings of God. This, God promised, would be the visible sign of Israel's wisdom, visible to the ends of the earth.

It is not remarkable that humanists deny the existence of this covenantal and historical cause-and-effect relationship, for such a relationship points beyond history to the existence of a sovereign Creator and Judge who will hold them eternally responsible on judgment day. They hold back the truth in unrighteousness (Rom. 1:18). What *is* remarkable, however, is that this view of revealed biblical

63

law as presently applicable to society is not widely believed by Christians. They believe that the cause-and-effect relationship between obedience to God's law and His positive blessings in history is just barely true within the socially and culturally narrow confines of the local church congregation and the Christian family. With respect to the authority of God's law in society, fundamentalist Christians deny it, neo-evangelical scholars deny it, and even traditional Reformed theologians deny it, and for the same reason: such a view of God's law makes Christians personally and corporately responsible for obeying God, for receiving the promised external blessings, and for using this real-world capital for the fulfillment of God's dominion covenant[1] — extending His kingdom (civilization) across the face of the earth.

In contrast, Christian Reconstructionists loudly affirm biblical law as a means of both evangelism and dominion. Indeed, *the affirmation of a long-term relationship between covenant-keeping and external blessings in history, as well as covenant-breaking and external cursings in history, is the heart and soul of the Christian Reconstructionist position on social theory, its theological identifying mark.*[2] This overwhelming confidence in the long-term historical efficacy of the biblical covenant is the reason why Christian Reconstructionists self-consciously claim to be the most consistent of all covenant theologians in history. It is also why we are confident that our view of the biblical covenant will eventually be triumphant in history. After all, God blesses covenant-keeping in history, and covenant-believing is surely an integral aspect of covenant-keeping. No doubt our confidence makes us insufferable in other theological circles, but such is always the effect of faith in God's covenant. Pharaoh found Moses insufferable, and he banished Moses from his presence (Ex. 10:28). The Hebrew leaders had earlier tried to do the same thing (Ex. 5:19-21). Bear in mind that Moses refused to leave Egypt until he took the people with him. Christian Reconstructionists have the same attitude.

God's Sanctions and Positive Feedback in History

God's visible, external covenantal blessings serve as a means of confirming His people's confidence in the reliability of His covenant. Christians are required to affirm the existence of a normative, cove-

---

1. Gary North, *The Dominion Covenant: Genesis* (2nd ed.; Tyler, Texas: Institute for Christian Economics, 1987).

2. There are other marks, of course, but this is its unique mark. No other theological movement proclaims this ethical cause-and-effect relationship in society. Indeed, all other Christian positions explicitly deny it.

nantal relationship of *positive feedback in history*. God intends His covenant to work this way: "But thou shalt remember the LORD thy God:
for it is he that giveth thee power to get wealth, *that he may establish his
covenant* which he sware unto thy fathers, as it is this day" (Deut.
8:18). In short: more obedience, more blessings; more blessings,
more confirmation; more confirmation, greater obedience. This is
covenantal positive feedback in history. This is Christianity's standard of ethical performance, both personally and corporately.[3] God
brings His sanctions in history, positive and negative, in terms of
men's public conformity to His revealed law.

We have read that the power to get wealth is one of God's positive
covenant sanctions in history.[4] This is a New Testament teaching,
too: "Every good gift and every perfect gift is from above, and cometh down from the Father of lights, with whom is no variableness,
neither shadow of turning" (James 1:17). How is this steadfastness of
God revealed in history? By the predictability of His historical sanctions in response to men's responses to the unchanging principles of
His covenant law. Conversely — much to the outrage of political liberals and most academic neo-evangelicals — long-run poverty is one
of God's negative sanctions in history.[5] Such a view of history is
unacceptable to the Christian world generally, and especially to university-trained Christian intellectuals. Why? Because such a view is
utterly hostile to the God-denying worldview of Darwinism, which
contemporary Christians have adopted far more than they are aware
of. Darwinism teaches that there is no supernatural force in history.
Until the advent of man, there was no direction to history, no morality, and no purpose. Only with the appearance of man in history
does cosmic personalism appear. Man proposes, and man disposes.[6]
Man extends dominion in the name of the human species. Man, and

---

3. These sanctions apply more clearly to corporate bodies than to individuals,
rather than the other way around, contrary to what pietism teaches. We know that
righteous individual covenant-keepers can suffer cursings in history, as the Book of
Job teaches. What the Bible teaches is that *in the aggregate* (corporately), and *in the long
run*, God's covenant sanctions are reliable and predictable.

4. Gary North, "Free Market Capitalism," in Robert G. Clouse (ed.), *Wealth and
Poverty: Four Christian Views on Economics* (Downers Grove, Illinois: InterVarsity
Press, 1984), pp. 27-65.

5. Gary North, *Unholy Spirits: Occultism and New Age Humanism* (Ft. Worth, Texas:
Dominion Press, 1986), ch. 8: "Magic, Envy, and Foreign Aid."

6. This was actually stated by Frederick Engels, the co-founder of Communism:
". . . man no longer merely proposes, but also disposes. . . ." Engels, *Herr Eugen
Dühring's Revolution in Science* (London: Lawrence & Wishart, [1878] 1934), p. 348.

only man, brings meaningful sanctions in history. Autonomous man is the sovereign judge in history, not God. This man-centered theology is the heart of Darwinism, not its technical discussions about genetic or environmental changes.[7]

This view of history is basic to all of modern scholarship, and the vast majority of those teaching social theory and social ethics in Christian colleges have adopted the basic anti-covenantal perspective of this worldview, at least with respect to New Testament era history. The assertion that nations remain poor because they are breaking the external terms of God's covenant outrages the modern Christian intellectual. It was not random that in its hatchet job on the Christian Reconstructionists, *Christianity Today* ran a clever (though a bit malicious) cartoon of me brandishing a giant dripping pen (blood rather than ink) with my statement nearby: "The so-called underdeveloped societies are underdeveloped because they are socialist, demonist, and cursed."[8] I really did say this, I have defended it in print,[9] and author Rodney Clapp cited it because he apparently regarded it as the most offensive statement that he could locate in his rather cursory examination of my writings. He recognized that the neo-evangelical audience of *Christianity Today* would take great offense at such a statement.[10]

What I am arguing here is simple: those people who truly believe that God's multi-institutional covenant is binding also necessarily believe that it is *historically and judicially* binding with respect to all three covenant (oath-bound)[11] institutions: family, church, and State. Conversely, if people do not believe that God's covenant is historically and judicially binding with respect to nations and local civil governments, then they have denied the relevance of Deuteronomy 4:5-6. They implicitly believe that the biblical doctrine of God's national

---

7. North, *Dominion Covenant: Genesis*, Appendix A: "From Cosmic Impersonalism to Humanistic Sovereignty."

8. Rodney Clapp, "Democracy as Heresy," *Christianity Today* (Feb. 20, 1987), p. 23.

9. North, *Unholy Spirits*, ch. 8. This chapter also appeared in the original version of this book, *None Dare Call It Witchcraft* (New Rochelle, New York: Arlington House, 1976).

10. Keynensian William Diehl took offense at this cause-and-effect explanation of *culture-wide* poverty, citing in response Jesus' denial of this relationship in the case on an *individual* blind man (John 9:1-3): "A Guided-Market Response," in Clouse (ed.), *Wealth and Poverty*, pp. 71-72. Art Gish was also upset: *ibid.*, p. 78.

11. Gary North, *The Sinai Strategy: Economics and the Ten Commandments* (Tyler, Texas: Institute for Christian Economics, 1986), ch. 3: "Oaths, Covenants, and Contracts."

covenant is some kind of New Testament theological "limiting concept," a kind of theoretical backdrop to history that no longer has any point of contact with the actual realm of historical cause and effect. Such a view of God's covenant I call *antinomian*: a denial of the law's effects in history. It reflects what I call halfway covenant thinking.

"Pro-nomianism" Defined

What do I mean by the term "antinomian"? To answer this, I need to offer a description of "pro-nomianism," meaning a defense of what God's law is and what it accomplishes, especially in history. I begin with a survey of Ray Sutton's discovery of the five-point biblical covenant model.[12] Sutton argues that the biblical covenant model has five parts:

> Transcendence (sovereignty), yet immanence (presence)
> Hierarchy/authority/representation
> Ethics/law/dominion
> Oath/judgment/sanctions (blessings, cursings)
> Succession/continuity/inheritance

While this terminology is slightly different from that which he adopted in his book, it is an accurate representation.[13] This model has become an integrating framework for the entire *Dominion Covenant* economic commentary.

I use this model to develop the "pro-nomianism" of Christian Reconstruction. It is the basis of my definition of anti-nomianism. I use the biblical covenant model as the source of definition because I have long maintained that language as well as everything else must be governed by the Bible. As I wrote in 1973, "Neutrality does not exist. Everything must be interpreted in terms of what God has revealed. The humanistic goal of neutral language (and therefore neutral law) was overturned at the Tower of Babel. Our *definitions* must be in terms of *biblical revelation*."[14]

As a representative example of the structure of the biblical covenant, I have selected Isaiah 45. From it we can get some sense of

---

12. Ray R. Sutton, *That You May Prosper: Dominion By Covenant* (Tyler, Texas: Institute for Christian Economics, 1987).

13. A correspondent to Sutton sent in the new version because it can be used to create an acronym: THEOS.

14. Gary North, "In Defense of Biblical Bribery," in R. J. Rushdoony, *The Institutes of Biblical Law* (Nutley, New Jersey: Craig Press, 1973), p. 843.

how the covenant works in history. We can also discuss the covenant's relation to biblical law.

1. Transcendence/Immanence

We must begin where the Bible does: the creation of all things by God (Gen. 1:1). We must maintain an absolute distinction between the Creator and the creature. God is the absolutely sovereign Master of all that comes to pass in history. Nothing takes place outside His sovereign decree. "I form the light, and create darkness: I make peace, and create evil: I the LORD do all these things" (Isa. 45:7).[15] "I have made the earth, and created man upon it: I, even my hands, have stretched out the heavens, and all their host have I commanded" (Isa. 45:12). "For thus saith the LORD that created the heavens; God himself that formed the earth and made it; he hath established it, he created it not in vain, he formed it to be inhabited: I am the Lord; and there is none else" (Isa. 45:18).

Isaiah uses the familiar (but extremely unpopular) biblical imagery of the potter and his clay: "Woe unto him that striveth with his Maker! Let the potsherd [strive] with the potsherds of the earth. Shall the clay say to him that fashioned it, What makest thou? Or thy work, He hath no hands? Woe unto him that saith unto his father, What begettest thou? Or to the woman, What hast thou brought forth?" (Isa. 45:9-10).[16] These words became the basis of Paul's argument regarding the absolute sovereignty of God in choosing to save one person and not another. It is the classic argument in the Bible for the doctrine of *election*. Paul says of Pharaoh: "For the scripture saith unto Pharaoh, Even for this same purpose have I raised thee up, that I might shew my power in thee, and that my name might be declared throughout all the earth" (Rom. 9:17). This explains the words in Exodus: "And he hardened Pharaoh's heart, that he hearkened not unto them; as the LORD had said" (Ex. 7:13). But this means that God keeps some men from responding positively to the universal offer of salvation. This keeps them from obeying His law.

The believer in free will (a degree of human autonomy outside of God's eternal decree) then asks: "How can any sinner therefore be

---

15. This does not mean that God is the author of sin. This verse speaks covenantally: God brings evil times to those who defy Him.

16. I have used brackets to indicate the italicized inserted words of the King James translators. Normally, I do not do this, preferring instead not to disrupt the flow of biblical language. But my arguments here are sufficiently controversial that I do not want critics saying that I relied on the translators to make my points.

personally responsible for his sin?" Paul well understood this line of reasoning, to which he replied:

> Therefore hath he mercy on whom he will [have mercy], and whom he will he hardeneth. Thou wilt say then unto me, Why doth he yet find fault? For who hath resisted his will? Nay but, O man, who art thou that repliest against God? Shall the thing formed say to him that formed [it], why hast thou made me thus? Hath not the potter power over the clay, of the same lump to make one vessel unto honor, and another unto dishonor? (Rom. 9:19-21).

Paul appealed directly to the biblical doctrine of creation — the imagery of the potter and the clay — in order to cut short every version of the free will (man's autonomy) argument. There is no area of chance or contingency in history. None. It is unlawful even to appeal to this line of reasoning, Paul said: "Who art thou that thou repliest against God?" The doctrine of the moral and legal responsibility of man before God must always be understood in terms of the absolute decree of God; it must never be defended in terms of the idea that man has a zone of uncontrolled decision-making at his disposal. Man's responsibility must be understood therefore in terms of the biblical doctrine of creation.

The biblical doctrine of creation teaches the sovereignty of God in electing some people to salvation. This is why so few Christians accept the biblical doctrine of the six-day creation, and why they are ready to compromise with this or that version of evolution. They want to affirm the partial sovereignty (partial autonomy) of man. They do so in terms of the pagan idea of *chance*: a realm of decision-making, of cause and effect, outside of God's absolute providential control and absolute predestination. They refuse to accept the words of Paul in Ephesians: "According as he hath chosen us in him before the foundation of the world, that we should be holy and without blame before him in love: Having predestinated us unto the adoption of children by Jesus Christ to himself, according to the good pleasure of his will" (Eph. 1:4-5).

The biblical doctrine of creation leads directly and inescapably to the biblical doctrine of the absolute providence of God. God creates and sustains all things in history. Speaking of Jesus Christ, Paul writes: "For by him were all things created, that are in heaven, and that are on earth, visible and invisible, whether [they be] thrones, or dominions, or principalities, or powers: all things were created by him, and for him: And he is before all things, and by him all things consist" (Col. 1:16-17). Nothing lies outside the sovereign providence of God. There is no area of contingency. There is no area of neutrality. There is no area that is outside the eternal decree of God or the law of God. This is the biblical doctrine of creation. Humanists hate it, and so do the vast majority of Christians today.

God as Creator brings all things to pass. When He says, "It shall come to pass," it comes to pass. "Declaring the end from the beginning, and from ancient times [the things] that are not [yet] done, saying, My counsel shall stand, and I will do all my pleasure" (Isa. 46:10). God does not simply know the future that He predicts; He causes the future to take place. There is no element of chance anywhere in the universe.

Consider the greatest crime in history: the betrayal and crucifixion of Jesus Christ. The act of betrayal by Judas was predetermined by God; nevertheless, Judas was still held fully responsible for this act. "And truly the Son of man goeth, as it was determined: but woe unto that man by whom he is betrayed!" (Luke 22:22). And what of those who unlawfully, defiantly condemned Jesus Christ to death? They were all predestined by God to do it.

The kings of the earth stood up, and the rulers were gathered together against the Lord, and against his Christ. For of a truth against thy holy child Jesus, whom thou hast anointed, both Herod, and Pontius Pilate, with the Gentiles, and the people of Israel, were gathered together. For to do whatsoever thy hand and thy counsel determined before to be done (Acts 4:26-28).

So, the Bible teaches man's personal responsibility and God's absolute predestination. If God was willing to predestinate the greatest crime in history, holding the criminals fully responsible, then surely He is willing to bring to pass all the other relatively minor crimes in history, also holding each criminal responsible. God's law touches everything, and each man is fully responsible for his thoughts and actions; he must obey the whole of God's law.

God did not create the world and then depart, leaving it to run by itself until the final judgment (Deism's god). He is present everywhere, but specially present with His people. He delivers them. But He also gives His law to them. He runs everything, yet men are made in His image, and they have the ability to understand the external world. They are responsible to God because God is totally sovereign. He has laid down the law, both moral and physical. His word governs all things. No appeal to the logic of autonomous man (free will) can change this.

2. Hierarchy/Authority/Representation

"Look unto me, and be ye saved, all the ends of the earth: for I am God, and [there is] none else. I have sworn by myself, the word is gone out of my mouth [in] righteousness, and shall not return, That unto me every knee shall bow, every tongue shall swear" (Isa. 45:22-23). In these verses we find four points of the covenant: sovereignty (point one), oath (point four), righteousness (point three), and hierarchy. Every knee shall bow. There is hierarchy in this world.

But knees shall also bow to Israel, if Israel remains faithful to God. "Thus saith the LORD, The labour of Egypt, and merchandise of Ethiopia and of the Sabeans, men of stature, shall come over unto thee, and they shall be thine: they shall come after thee; in chains they shall come over, and they shall fall down unto thee, they shall make supplication unto thee, saying, Surely God is in thee; and there is none else, there is no God" ["no other God": New King James Version] (Isa. 45:14). Israel represents God in history, and the nations will, *if Israel remains covenantally faithful*, become Israel's bond-servants.

This means that men who disobey God's law are required to do what they are told by those officers who declare God's law as His lawful covenantal representatives. These representatives speak in God's name through *covenantal institutions*. There is inescapable corporate responsibility in history. Nations will obey God and His representatives, said Isaiah, even if their citizens must be brought to judgment in chains.

In Israel, civil law was enforced hierarchically: a bottom-up appeals court system (Ex. 18). This is also true of church courts (Matt. 18:15-18). Thus, officers speak *representatively*: God's representatives before men, and men's representatives before God. This doctrine of representation is the basis of mankind's *corporate* dominion over nature (Gen. 1:26-28). Men are under God and God's law corporately; they are to exercise dominion corporately by bringing the whole earth under God's law. Thus, biblical law is a tool of dominion.

Hierarchical representation is also the basis of covenantal governments' *corporate* responsibility before God: church, State, and family. Collective units are given laws to enforce; God holds them responsible to Him through representatives. Sodom and Gomorrah were destroyed; Egypt and Babylon were destroyed. Israel and Judah were scattered. Classical Greece and Rome fell. There is both personal and corporate responsibility before God.

3. Ethics/Law/Dominion

"Drop down, ye heavens, from above, and let the skies pour down righteousness: let the earth open, and let them bring forth salvation, and let righteousness spring up together; I the LORD have created it" (Isa. 45:8). The whole cosmos is described here as being filled with righteousness. Righteousness is the basis of man's dominion over the earth.

But righteousness must be defined. This is what God's law does. It establishes *boundaries* to our lawful actions. The tree of the knowledge of good and evil was "hedged in" by God's law. Adam and Eve were not to eat from it, or as Eve properly interpreted, even touch it (Gen. 3:3).

These ethical boundaries are not exclusively personal; they are also corporate. There are biblical laws given by God that are to govern the actions of families, churches, and civil governments. Autonomous man would like to think that God's law has nothing to do with his institutions, especially civil government, but autonomous man is in rebellion. God's law is not restrained by autonomous man's preferred boundaries. It is not man who lawfully declares: "Fear ye not me? saith the LORD: will ye not tremble at my presence, which have placed the sand [for] the bound of the sea by a perpetual decree, that it cannot pass it: and though the waves thereof toss themselves, yet can they not prevail; though they roar, yet can they not pass over it? But this people hath a revolting and a rebellious heart; they are revolted and gone. Neither say they in their heart, Let us now fear the LORD our God, that giveth rain, both the former and the latter, in his season: he reserveth unto us the appointed weeks of the harvest" (Jer. 5:22-24).

Notice the development of God's argument, which is in fact a *covenant lawsuit* brought against Judah by His prophet, Jeremiah. God sets boundaries to the sea, the seasons, and the harvest. The implication is that He also sets *legal and moral boundaries* around people, both as individuals and nationally. Men are to fear this God who sets cosmic boundaries. How is this required fear to be acknowledged? The prophets answered this question over and over, generation after generation: *by obeying God's law.*

4. Oath/Judgment/Sanctions

"I have sworn by myself, the word is gone out of my mouth [in] righteousness, and shall not return, That unto me every knee shall bow, every tongue shall swear" (Isa. 45:23). His word is sufficient. He will not go back on His word. He has sworn by His own name. God has therefore taken a covenantal oath that in the future, every human knee shall bow, and every human tongue shall swear. There is no escape from God's authority; and therefore all mouths shall swear—they shall acknowledge His sovereignty, either on earth or in the afterlife. Even in the lake of fire, they must eternally swear that God is who He says He is.

God's law is our standard, both individually and corporately. There are covenantal institutions that are bound by the revealed law of God: church, State, and family. These are the three covenantal institutions that God has established to declare and enforce His law. All institutions must obey, but these are those that are exclusively governed by formal oaths before God.

What is an oath? It is the calling down on one's head the negative sanctions of God. If a person or covenanted institution disobeys the law of God, then God comes in wrath to punish the rebels. He comes in history. This was the warning of the Old Testament prophets. On the other hand, if men repent and obey, God is merciful and will bless them. "Your iniquities have turned away these [things]," Jeremiah warned Judah regarding the rain and the harvest, "and your sins have withholden good [things] from you" (Jer. 5:25). The prophets came in the name of God as covenantal representatives, calling individuals, as well as representative kings and priests, to repent, to turn back to God's law and thereby avoid God's negative sanctions in history.

The passage above all others in the Bible that describes the historical sanctions of God is Deuteronomy 28. Verses 1-14 describe the blessings (positive sanctions), and verses 15-68 describe the cursings (negative sanctions). Understand, these are *historical* sanctions. They are not appropriate sanctions for the final judgment. In this sense, they are *representative sanctions* of eternity's sanctions, what Paul called the "earnest" or *down payment* of God in history on what must inevitably come in eternity (Eph. 1:14).

5. Succession/Continuity/Inheritance

"In the LORD shall all the seed of Israel be justified, and shall glory" (Isa. 45:25). Because God is the Creator, His people will inherit the earth: "The earth is the LORD's, and the fulness thereof; the world, and they that dwell therein" (Ps. 24:1). (This is point one of the covenant.) Psalm 25:12-13 provides the covenantal promise:

What man [is] he that feareth the LORD? Him shall he teach in the way [that] he shall choose (v. 12).
His soul shall dwell at ease; and his seed shall inherit the earth (v. 13).

God is to be feared (point one). God teaches man (subordination: point two) the required way (point three). The man's soul shall dwell in ease (point four), and his heirs shall inherit (point five). These two brief verses set forth God's covenant model, and in these verses we can see the outline of God's plan of history for covenant-keepers. This is so simple that a child can grasp it. Unfortunately, as we shall see, very few theologians have.

My point is that these verses refer to history. The fear of God is historical. God's instruction to man is historical. The law applies in history. The man is spiritually blessed in history: his soul is at ease. His heirs shall inherit.

Some commentators might agree regarding the historical reference of points one through three, but object to my view of point four. Perhaps the focus of the verse is exclusively internal. After all, the covenant-keeper's soul is what is spoken of. Perhaps the blessings are not visible in history. My response is to ask a question: Why should point four — spiritual ease — be confined to only the inner person? If the inheritance is historical, then the spirit's ease must refer to contentment regarding the past, present, and future. Only if the inheritance will be post-historical could the ease of the soul be legitimately confined to the internal realm. The covenant-keeper is at ease in history because he is confident about the future success of those who share his faith. It is his *seed* that will inherit.

If the inheritance of the whole earth is merely symbolic of the inheritance of God's resurrected people, then why refer to the inheritance delivered to a man's seed? In eternity, this inheritance will be his, too. In short, the primary focus of the passage is on *history*, not eternity. Fear God *now*. Learn from God *now*. Obey God's law *now*. Experience spiritual contentment *now*. Why? Because your spiritual heirs will inherit in the *future*: in time and on earth.

Yet there are theologians, especially Calvinists in the Continental (Dutch) tradition, and all Lutherans, who insist that this promised inheritance is strictly limited to the post-final judgment world of eternity. The first point — the fear of God — is historical, but personal rather than corporate. The second — being taught by God — is historical, but personal rather than corporate. The third — obeying the law of God — applies in history, but is exclusively personal, familial, and ecclesiastical — never civil. The fourth — spiritual ease — is historical but exclusively internal. Why these restrictions on the first four points? Because the fifth — inheriting the earth — is seen as exclusively post-historical.

Summary

The definition of pro-nomianism must begin and end with the biblical concept of the covenant. All five points of the biblical covenant must be included in any valid definition of biblical law. We should not expect to be able to define biblical law without first considering the Bible's primary revelation of God's law: the structure of the various covenants God has made with men.

Thus, I define "pro-nomianism" in terms of God's covenant model:

The belief that God, the sovereign, predestinating Creator, has delegated to mankind the responsibility of obeying His Bible-revealed law-order, Old and New Testaments, and promises to bless or curse men in history, both individually and corporately, in terms of this law-order. This law-order and its historically applied sanctions are the basis of the progressive sanctification of covenant-keeping individuals and covenantal institutions — family, church, and State — over time, and they are also the basis of the progressive disinheritance of covenant-breakers.

This leads us to the question of the biblical definition of antinomianism, the antithesis of this definition.

"Antinomianism" Defined

We have seen that the biblical definition of God's law is governed by the structure of God's covenant. Thus, the biblical definition of antinomianism must also be governed by the structure of God's covenant. If being an antinomian means that you are against the law, then it must also mean that it is *God's law* that you are against, and God's law is always covenantal.

To understand what antinomianism is, we can do no better than to consider the first revelation in the Bible of the original antinomian: Satan. Satan came to Eve with a proposition: "Eat of the forbidden fruit, and you will become as God" (Gen. 3:5). "Run an experiment, and see if this isn't the case," he tempted Eve. "See whose word is authoritative, mine or God's." He offered her a covenantal argument, a perverse imitation of the biblical covenant:

1. God is not sovereign.
2. You need not obey Him.
3. His law is not authoritative.
4. The promised negative sanction will not come.
5. [implied:] You will keep the inheritance.

I choose to analyze the biblical definition of antinomianism in terms of Satan's temptation of Eve. This line of satanic reasoning is the heart of all antinomianism.

1. Transcendence/Immanence

Who is God? Satan was asking Eve to decide. Who lays down the law? Whose word is authoritative?

Obviously, the Creator is God. Then who is the true creator, man or God? This is what Satan was asking mankind, God's chronological and judicial *representatives*. If man answered anything but "God is the Creator, and His word alone is authoritative," then Satan would inherit the earth. Man would die unless, of course, God should later send His Son, the second Adam, to inherit it, but Satan chose either to ignore this possibility or to act against what he knew would happen in the future.

The first step in becoming an antinomian is to deny the absolute sovereignty of God. It usually begins with a denial, implicit or explicit, that God created the world. This usually begins with a softening of the doctrine of the six, literal, 24-hour-day creation. This is how the seeds of Darwinism were sown: denying the literal character of God's chronology in Genesis 1.[17]

The next step is to deny the obvious implication of the doctrine of Creation: that since God created the world, He also controls the world. In other words, men deny the absolute sovereignty of God or providence of God. They deny the doctrine of predestination.[18]

---

17. North, *Dominion Covenant: Genesis*, Appendix C: "Cosmologies in Conflict: Creation vs. Evolution."

18. Loraine Boettner, *The Reformed Doctrine of Predestination* (Philadelphia: Presbyterian & Reformed, [1932] 1965).

Why is a denial of predestination inherently antinomian? Because it means that events in history come to pass outside of God's decree. They are therefore *random* events in terms of His decree, what philosophers call *contingent* events. An element of contingency is thereby brought into the universe. If A takes place, B may not take place. It may or may not. It depends. On what? On something other than what God has decreed.

This means that there must be *gaps in historical causation*. These gaps are inherently contingent with respect to the decree of God. A providential cause is separated from its eternally decreed effect. God therefore does not bring all things to pass; man brings some things to pass. The more element of contingency there is in history, the greater man's autonomy from God's providential control of the universe. That modern science has steadily adopted chance events as the basis of modern quantum physics is not itself a random historical event.[19] This conclusion of quantum physics is the product of a humanistic worldview that denies any decree of God and His creation of the universe. That chaos has become the "hot new topic" of modern physical science is also not random.[20] The ethical rebellion of humanist man is increasing.

If God does not control everything that comes to pass, *then His word is not authoritative over everything that comes to pass*. This was the logic of Satan's temptation: to believe that a specific cause (eating the forbidden fruit) would not *inevitably* lead to a specific event (death). Somehow, Satan was arguing, there is contingency in this world. This is also the argument of all those who would use the concept of contingency to defend the idea of the free (semi-autonomous) will of man. This is why we are morally required to abandon any trace of the free will argument. Nevertheless, most Christians today hold to some version of the free will argument. Hence, *most Christians today are in principle antinomians*.

2. Hierarchy/Authority/Representation

Satan went to Eve first. He was implying that she, not her husband, was sovereign. God had spoken to her husband regarding the forbidden fruit. Presumably, he had told her, as God's representative. "Obey me, not your husband," Satan said. And by disobeying

---

19. Gary North, *Is the World Running Down? Crisis in the Christian Worldview* (Tyler, Texas: Institute for Christian Economics, 1988), ch. 1.

20. James Gleik, *Chaos: The Making of a New Science* (New York: Viking, 1987).

her husband, she disobeyed God. She ignored the hierarchy of authority over her. She ignored her representative before God: Adam. She acted autonomously.

Who must man obey, God or his own autonomous mind? This was Satan's implicit question. He asked Eve to disobey God, all in the name of a cosmic experiment. What would happen if she disobeyed? Good things, he promised.

"Trust me," Satan said. "Take my word for it." In other words, "I lay down the true law." Man thinks that he is disobeying God on his own account, in his own authority, but in fact, man must serve only one master. Ethically, he subordinates himself to Satan when he refuses to obey God. He comes under the hierarchical rule of another master. Man may think he is acting autonomously, but he in fact is simply shifting masters. God or Baal? This was Elijah's question (I Ki. 18:21). God or mammon? This was Jesus' question (Matt. 6:24).

But neither God nor Satan normally appears to an individual. Each sends human representatives. Men represent God in positions of corporate responsibility. God has established three monopolistic institutions: church, State, and family. The head of each can serve God or Satan, and those under him are sanctified (set apart) institutionally.

Soldiers live or die in terms of decisions made by their superiors. Nations rise and fall in terms of the decisions of their national leaders. An individual's success or failure in history cannot be discussed without reference to the institutional hierarchies above and below him, and their success or failure. Thus, to deny that God's law applies to your covenantal superior is another way of saying that it really does not apply to *you*. "I was just following orders!" says the subordinate who has sinned. In other words, "I was under someone else's authority—someone other than God."

Uriah the Hittite was a righteous man. He died because he was so righteous. Unrighteous King David told unrighteous General Joab to be sure that Uriah died in battle, and Joab carried out the order (II Sam. 12). In short, *covenantal hierarchy* is important.

David later decided to number the people. This was against God's law. Joab warned him about this, but David insisted, so Joab carried out the order. God's prophet then came to David and announced one of three judgments: seven years of famine, three months of David's fleeing before his enemies, or a three-day pestilence. Take your pick, the prophet said. David was too proud to accept the mild but personally humiliating second sanction, so he gave

God the choice. God sent the worst one, nationally speaking: a plague that killed 70,000 people (II Sam. 24). (Anyone who teaches that God does not send sickness to His people has a real problem in explaining this passage.) In short, *covenantal representation* is important.

There are theologians today who say that God's law applies only to individuals, that nations are not under God's law. They deny the very possibility of a national covenant in New Testament times. Such a covenant was only for ancient Israel. National leaders are not representatives of their subordinates before God, theologians insist, and national leaders are surely not God's representatives before their subordinates. God's law has nothing to do with politics, they insist. There is no hierarchy of appeal based on God's law. *There is no national covenant*: this is a basic philosophy of all modern secular political theory, and few Christian scholars disagree. And those few who are willing to affirm the legitimacy of a national covenant gag on the idea of a future international covenant. International covenants are unthinkable for them. Not so for Isaiah (19:18-25).[21]

3. Ethics/Law/Dominion

"Forget about the law against eating this fruit," Satan told Eve. "Go ahead and eat."

"Do what thou wilt shall be the whole of the law," announced the self-proclaimed early twentieth-century magician, Aleister Crowley, who also called himself the Beast and 666.[22] The ethical positions are the same. The results are also the same.

"We're under grace, not law." This is the fundamentalist Christians' version of the same ethical position. So is, "No creed but Christ, no law but love!" They do not mean what Paul meant: that Christians are no longer under the threat of the negative *eternal* sanctions of the law. They mean rather that God's law no longer applies in any of the five aspects of the covenant, eternally or historically.

Christian social thinkers, especially neo-evangelicals in the Wheaton College-InterVarsity Press-*Christianity Today* orbit, prefer to muddy the ethical waters by using fancier language than the fundamentalists use. Examples:

---

21. Gary North, *Healer of the Nations: Biblical Blueprints for International Relations* (Ft. Worth, Texas: Dominion Press, 1987).

22. Aleister Crowley, *Magick in Theory and Practice* (New York: Castle, n.d.), p. 193. A short biography of Crowley is Daniel P. Mannix, *The Beast* (New York: Ballentine, 1959).

The fact that our Scriptures can be used to support or condemn any economic philosophy suggests that the Bible is not intended to lay out an economic plan which will apply for all times and places. If we are to examine economic structures in the light of Christian teachings, we will have to do it in another way.[23]

Since koinonia includes the participation of everyone involved, there is no blueprint for what this would look like on a global scale. . . . We are talking about a process, not final answers.[24]

There is in Scripture no blueprint of the ideal state or the ideal economy. We cannot turn to chapters of the Bible and find in them a model to copy or a plan for building the ideal biblical state and national economy.[25]

"Blueprint" is the code word for biblical law for those who do not want to obey biblical law. Second, "God's principles" is the code phrase for fundamentalists who are nervous about appearing totally antinomian, but who are equally nervous about breaking openly with the teachings and language of dispensationalism, i.e., "we're under grace, not law." Finally, "God's moral law" is the code phrase for the evangelical and Reformed man who does not want to be branded an antinomian, but who also does not want to be bound by the case laws of the Old Testament. In all these cases, the speaker rejects the idea of the continuing authority of the case laws.

It all boils down to this: Satan's rhetorical question, "Hath God said?" (Gen. 3:1). The proper response is, "Yes, God hath said!" He is the sovereign Creator. He has laid down the law.

4. Oath/Judgment/Sanctions

There are two kinds of sanctions: blessings and cursings. God told Adam that in the very *day* he ate of the tree, he would surely die. ("Dying, you shall die": the familiar biblical pleonasm.)[26] This means a negative sanction in *history*. Satan told Eve that she would not surely die. Instead, she would know good and evil, as God does: a positive sanction. Which would it be? "To die or not to die, that is the question."

---

23. William Diehl, "The Guided-Market System," in Robert G. Clouse (ed.), *Wealth and Poverty, op. cit.*, p. 87.

24. Art Gish, "Decentralist Economics," *ibid.*, p. 154.

25. John Gladwin, "Centralist Economics," *ibid.*, p. 183.

26. See Chapter 7: "Victim's Rights."

Satan was a liar, but not so great a liar as to deny the idea of predictable sanctions in history. He simply denied God's negative sanction and promised Eve a positive one. Would that modern Christian theologians were as honest as Satan! Instead, they deny the very existence of predictable covenantal sanctions in New Testament times. They write such things as: "And meanwhile it [the common grace order] must run its course within the uncertainties of the mutually conditioning principles of common grace and common curse, prosperity and adversity being experienced in a manner largely unpredictable because of the inscrutable sovereignty of the divine will that dispenses them in mysterious ways."[27] This muddled prose matches an equally muddled concept of ethics and history. In English, this statement means simply that *there is no ethical cause-and-effect relationship in post-crucifixion history.*

Biblical case laws are still morally and judicially binding today. This is the thesis of *Tools of Dominion.* Kline's theology explicitly denies this. Second, Kline's argument also means the denial of God's sanctions — blessing and cursing — in New Testament history. It is the denial of any long-term cause-and-effect relationship between covenantal faithfulness and external blessings — positive feedback between covenant-keeping and *visible* blessings. It is also the denial of any long-term cause-and-effect relationship between covenantal unfaithfulness and external cursings. Thus, when I refer to "antinomianism," I have in mind the hostile attitude regarding ethical cause and effect in society — *social* antinomianism[28] — but also a deeper and more fundamental hostility: a denial, implicit or explicit, of the reliability of the covenantal promises (sanctions) of God in history.

5. Succession/Continuity/Inheritance

If you die, you do not inherit. If you die without children, someone else inherits. Who would inherit in history if Eve listened to the serpent and did what he recommended?

---

27. Meredith G. Kline, "Comments on the Old-New Error," *Westminster Theological Journal*, XLI (Fall 1978), p. 184.

28. Gary North, *The Sinai Strategy: Economics and the Ten Commandments* (Tyler, Texas: Institute for Christian Economics, 1986), Appendix C: "Social Antinomianism."

(I need to add something at this point. I believe that it really was a serpent who tempted Eve. He acted as a conscious, covenantal agent of Satan. He communicated in words. He brought God's curse on his posterity. Satan did not use him as a sort of hand puppet.)

If Satan was successful, he would inherit in history. Adam and Eve would die, as he well knew. He was a liar. He knew who is sovereign, whose word is law, and who will bring negative sanctions in history: God. Satan knew that he might inherit as a subordinate steward if Adam and Eve disobeyed God, or at the very least, this would keep Adam and his heirs from inheriting. He would thwart God's plan. This prospect was enough to please Satan.

But Satan's hopes were shattered by the second Adam, Jesus Christ, who bore the law's negative sanctions so that God's adopted children (John 1:12) might inherit the earth and gain eternal life as well. Rather than seeing Satan inherit the earth through his earthly representatives, God has created an inheritance system *governing history*: positive feedback for covenant-keepers and negative feedback for covenant-breakers. Notice that the question of the inheritance was clearly historical: Satan never had any possibility of inheriting heaven.

Antinomians deny the existence of this inheritance system in history. This antinomian viewpoint regarding the systematic long-term outworking of God's visible covenantal judgments in the Christian era leads directly to what F. N. Lee has termed *pessimillennialism*, referring to both premillennialism and amillennialism. Covenant-keeping people will not progressively inherit the earth before Christ comes again physically, we are told. In contrast, Christian Reconstructionists affirm God's visible sanctions in history. If there is predictable long-term positive feedback (external blessings) in history for covenant-keeping, which Deuteronomy 28:1-14 insists that there is, and if there is long-term negative feedback (external cursings) in history for covenant-breaking, which Deuteronomy 28:15-68 insists that there is, then those who obey God must *inevitably* extend their external dominion over time, while those who disobey God must *inevitably* have external dominion removed from them.

God's sanctions in history still exist. This was John Calvin's view,[29] but modern Calvinists have abandoned it. God's covenantal law-order *inevitably* leads to the *external cultural triumph* of God's cove-

---

29. John Calvin, *The Covenant Enforced: Sermons on Deuteronomy 27 and 28*, edited by James B. Jordan (Tyler, Texas: Institute for Christian Economics, 1989).

nantally faithful people. This, of course, is postmillennialism.[30] This combination of covenant sanctions in history and postmillennial eschatology is what distinguishes the Christian Reconstructionist worldview from all others today.[31]

Those who deny postmillennialism usually also deny the New Testament reality of God's law-governed historical sanctions. To this extent, premillennialists and amillennialists have generally been social antinomians. They have erred in the development of their view of God's law and its sanctions in history. They have allowed their eschatologies of historical defeat to shape their doctrine of law, i.e., making it impotent in its historical effects. This triumph of pessimistic eschatological views over biblical ethics is one of the most devastating theological problems that the modern church faces.

Thus, antinomianism is defined as that view of life which rejects one or more of the five points of the biblical covenant as they apply to God's revealed law in history. They deny that God, the sovereign, predestinating Creator, has delegated to mankind the responsibility of obeying His Bible-revealed law-order, Old and New Testaments, and promises to bless or curse men in history, both individually and corporately, in terms of this law-order. This law-order and its historically applied sanctions are the basis of the progressive sanctification of covenant-keeping individuals and covenantal institutions — family, church, and State — over time, and they are also the basis of the progressive disinheritance of covenant-breakers.

Definitions and Paradigms

Some readers may not accept my definition of *antinomian*, but every reader should at least understand how and why I am using the term. The biblical definition of God's law must include all five of the points of the biblical covenant model. Deny any one of these five doctrines, and you have thereby adopted an antinomian theology. Deny them, and you necessarily must also deny the continuing authority of Deuteronomy 28 in the New Testament era. Yet an im-

---

30. While Calvin did not see this as clearly as modern Reconstructionists do, there were still elements of postmillennialism in his theology. On this point, see Greg L. Bahnsen, "The *Prima Facie* Acceptance of Postmillennialism," *Journal of Christian Reconstruction*, III (Winter 1976-77), pp. 69-76. I argue that there were both amillennial and postmillennial arguments in Calvin's writings: "The Economic Thought of Luther and Calvin," *ibid.*, II (Summer 1975), pp. 102-6.

31. Postmillennial Puritans generally shared this view, which is why Reconstructionists regard themselves as neo-Puritans.

plicit and even explicit denial of these doctrines (and the relevance of Deuteronomy 28) has been a basic tactic of the vast majority of Christian theologians for over a millennium.[32] Thus, they have attempted to define away the case laws and historical sanctions. What I am saying is that it is theologically invalid to attempt to define away the continuing authority of Deuteronomy 28. I therefore see the inescapable theological necessity of restoring the biblical definition of biblical law and therefore anti-law.

I fully realize that my definition of *antinomian* is not the accepted usage. This common usage exists primarily because theological antinomians who have rejected one or more of the covenant model's five points have previously defined the word so that it conforms to their pessimistic historical outlook: the long-term cultural impotence of God's redeemed people in history. They argue that antinomianism is merely the denial of one's *personal* responsibility to obey God's moral law (undefined).[33] This deliberately restricted definition implicitly surrenders history to the devil. What I am saying is this: anyone who denies that there are cause-and-effect relationships *in history* between the application of biblical case laws and the success or failure of social institutions has also inevitably and *in principle* adopted the idea that the devil controls and will continue to control this world. Why? Because the devil's *representatives* are said to be able to maintain control over the social institutions of this world throughout history (point two of the covenant: representation). It does no good for a person to answer that he is not an antinomian just because he respects God's law in his personal life, family life, and church life. He is still saying that God's law is historically impotent in social affairs, that covenant-keeping or covenant-breaking offers rewards and curses only to individuals and only after the final judgment.

Yes, I am offering a more comprehensive definition of "antinomian." My major goal in life is to lay additional foundations for a major theological paradigm shift that has already begun. I am self-conscious about this task. Readers deserve to know this. One inescapable aspect of a new movement or new way of viewing the world is the creation of new terms (e.g., "theonomy"), and the redefining of

---

32. The major exceptions were the Puritans: *Journal of Christian Reconstruction*, V (Winter 1978-79): "Symposium on Puritanism and Law."

33. "It refers to the doctrine that the moral law is not binding upon Christians as a way of life." Alexander M. Renwick, "Antinomianism," in *Baker's Dictionary of Theology*, edited by Everett F. Harrison, Geoffrey W. Bromiley, and Carl F. H. Henry (Grand Rapids, Michigan: Baker, 1960), p. 48.

old terms. Einstein, for example, redefined several of the terms used by Newton.[34] Clearly, this is what the Barthians did with the vocabulary of trinitarian orthodoxy, or as Van Til remarked, they did it "under cover of an orthodox-sounding theology."[35] (Rushdoony has correctly identified Barth as an implicit polytheist.)[36] It is not wrong to redefine terms; it *is* wrong to define words or use them in any way other than the Bible defines and uses them.

Those who pioneer a new worldview must break the near-monopoly strangle hold over useful terms that existing intellectual guilds have gained for themselves. An objection to my definition of the word "antinomian" simply because it does not conform precisely to past usage is also to a large extent also an objection to the alternative worldview that I am proposing.[37] This implicit theological hostility is masked by an explicit appeal to supposedly neutral grammar. But Van Til has taught us well: *nothing is neutral.* "Every bit of supposedly impersonal and neutral investigation, even in the field of science, is the product of an attitude of spiritual hostility to the Christ through whom alone there is truth in any dimension."[38] This surely includes language. As I wrote in 1973, "Neutrality does not exist. Everything must be interpreted in terms of what God has revealed. The humanistic goal of neutral language (and therefore neutral law) was overturned at the Tower of Babel. Our *definitions* must be in terms of *biblical revelation.*"[39]

---

34. Thomas Kuhn, *The Structure of Scientific Revolutions* (2nd ed.; University of Chicago Press, 1970), pp. 101-2, 149. Kuhn writes: "Since new paradigms are born of old ones, they ordinarily incorporate much of the vocabulary and apparatus, both conceptual and manipulative, that the traditional paradigm had previously employed. But they seldom employ these borrowed elements in quite the traditional way." *Ibid.*, p. 149.

35. Van Til, *The New Modernism* (Philadelphia, Pennsylvania: Presbyterian & Reformed, 1947), p. 27. He later wrote: "It is at this point that the question of 'traditional phraseology' has its significance. The 'simple believer' is all too often given new wine in old bottles. It is our solemn duty to point out this fact to him. The matter is of basic importance and of the utmost urgency." Van Til, *Christianity and Barthianism* (Philadelphia, Pennsylvania: Presbyterian & Reformed, 1962), p. 2.

36. Rushdoony, *Institutes of Biblical Law*, p. 20.

37. By a new worldview, I mean a new packaging of theological doctrines that have always been accepted by representative segments of the orthodox church. But by adopting the five-point biblical covenant model to present these doctrines, I have been forced to reject existing theological systems which unsystematically and unselfconsciously reject this model by substituting other interpretations of one or more of the five points.

38. Van Til, *The Case for Calvinism* (Nutley, New Jersey: Craig Press, 1964), p. 145.

39. Gary North, "In Defense of Biblical Bribery," in Rushdoony, *Institutes of Biblical Law*, p. 843.

I am doing my best to help establish effective theological terminology for future use by those who have adopted a theonomic
worldview. Christian Reconstructionists need not be limited in our
critical analysis by the inherited vocabulary of our theological opponents. Besides, the winners in history get to write the dictionaries
as well as the textbooks. More to the point, dictionaries always reflect common usage after the paradigm shift. We are preparing for
this shift well in advance.

Antinomianism as I define it has been the ethical preference of
much of the church almost from its beginning. A philosophical
compromise with Greek categories of hypothetically neutral natural
law began in the second century,[40] and it still continues.[41] In politics,
this compromise is known in our day as pluralism. Just about every
Christian accepts the idea of pluralism, either implicitly or explicitly.
By defining antinomianism in terms of opposition to the Old Testament case laws, Christian Reconstructionists (theonomists) have
alienated Christians in all camps, for almost all Christian groups oppose the enforcement of Old Testament laws. No Christian likes to
be called an antinomian. Christians generally retaliate against such
an accusation with the counter-accusation, "Legalist!"

This book is designed to help answer the question: Who is an antinomian and who is a legalist, biblically defined?

Conclusion

I have offered a comprehensive view of what the pro-nomian
position teaches that biblical law is. We see biblical law as an integrated, unbreakable whole, an explicitly *covenantal* system of biblically
revealed law. Antinomianism is a denial of this integrated system,
yet in many cases, it offers as an alternative a perverse mirror image
of this system. Satan had to use the biblical covenant model in order
to refute it. He thereby honored the old political principle: "You can't
beat something with nothing."

The older definitions of "antinomian" were devised by those who,
if my version of God's law is correct, were themselves antinomians.
They did not adhere to all five points of the biblical covenant model.
They may or may not have denied all five points, but they refused to

---

40. Cornelius Van Til, *Christianity in Conflict* (mimeographed; Philadelphia: Westminster Theological Seminary, 1962).

41. Rex Downie, "Natural Law and God's Law: An Antithesis," *Journal of Christian Reconstruction*, V (Summer 1978), pp. 79-87.

affirm all five points, and then derive their definition of law and anti-law in terms of all five points.

So, for the sake of clarity, let me repeat my compact definition of pro-nomianism:

The belief that God, the sovereign, predestinating Creator, has delegated to mankind the responsibility of obeying His Bible-revealed law-order, Old and New Testaments, and promises to bless or curse men in history, both individually and corporately, in terms of this law-order. This law-order and its historically applied sanctions are the basis of the progressive sanctification of covenant-keeping individuals and covenantal institutions — family, church, and State — over time, and they are also the basis of the progressive disinheritance of covenant-breakers.

Deny this, and you are an antinomian.

3

WHAT ARE THE CASE LAWS?

For it is written in the law of Moses, Thou shalt not muzzle the mouth of the ox that treadeth out the corn. Doth God take care for oxen? Or saith he it altogether for our sakes? For our sakes, no doubt, this is written: that he that ploweth should plow in hope; and that he that thresheth in hope should be partaker of his hope. (I Cor. 9:9-10).

Let the elders that rule well be counted worthy of double honour, especially they who labour in the word and doctrine. For the scripture saith, Thou shalt not muzzle the ox that treadeth out the corn. And, The labourer is worthy of his reward (I Tim. 5:17-18).

This book is designed to press the case for biblical ethics, for it deals with a much-neglected portion of Scripture, the case laws of Exodus. These are the specific applications of the "lively oracles" that God gave to Moses (Acts 7:38). The case laws of Exodus appear in the chapters following the Ten Commandments of Exodus 20, especially in chapters 21-23. They are generally ignored today by Christian commentators, as surely as they were ignored in Moses' day. James Jordan's *Law of the Covenant* (1984)[1] is one of the rare exceptions to this established tradition of neglecting the case laws by Bible-believing scholars as well as liberal higher critics.

Christians are supposed to take the Old Testament's case laws seriously. As Paul's use of them indicates, they set forth in an encapsulated form fundamental principles of justice. They provide guidelines for the specific decisions of day-to-day life, and from them we are supposed to become skilled in discovering and then developing their underlying moral and judicial principles. The early church understood this, although the church's compromises with the pagan concept of natural law disguised the importance of biblical case laws

---

1. Tyler, Texas: Institute for Christian Economics.

in the compiling of early medieval law codes. These case law principles have long served as a major component of the judicial foundation of Western civilization. As Western civilization steadily departs
from the legal principles that the case laws set forth, we walk closer
toward the precipice of God's judgment, oblivious to the mortal
danger that faces us. Men have forgotten that God judges nations
and cultures in history. Biblical law warns them of this reality (Deut.
28:15-68), but Christians generally, not to mention the pagans who
dominate this civilization, pay no attention to biblical law, especially
its sanctions.

Case Laws and the Resurrection

It is with the case laws of Exodus that the Christian Reconstructionists' hermeneutical rubber inescapably meets the historical road.
It is here that the Old Testament first presents detailed social applications of the fundamental principles of the Mosaic law and, equally
important, the Mosaic law's required civil sanctions. Theonomists
argue that Christians cannot legitimately proclaim the continuing
moral validity of the Ten Commandments without also proclaiming
the continuing judicial validity of the Mosaic case laws. Furthermore, Christians cannot legitimately affirm the binding nature of the
Mosaic case laws apart from these laws' specified sanctions, unless
the New Testament has annulled these sanctions individually.[2]

What must be understood from the very beginning is the following theonomic principle of biblical interpretation: it was with the
death, resurrection, and ascension of Jesus Christ to the right hand
of God in heaven that the entire world was placed historically under
the full requirements of biblical law. From the creation, God placed
the *work* of the law in the hearts of all men (Rom. 2:14-15). God later
made a covenant with Noah, and this covenant necessarily involved
law as a tool of dominion (Gen. 9:1-17). He made a covenant with
Israel, and He gave laws to Israel that all nations would recognize as
being holy and just (Deut. 4:5-8). *But it was with the death, resurrection,
and ascension of Jesus Christ that biblical law burst the Old Covenant
wineskin of national Israel and flowed judicially across all nations.* It was not
the ministry of Moses that accomplished this; it was the ministry of
Jesus Christ.

---

2. This has been the case with the death penalty for sabbath-breaking: Gary
North, *The Sinai Strategy: Economics and the Ten Commandments* (Tyler, Texas: Institute
for Christian Economics, 1986), ch. 4, Appendix A.

This being our position, any attempt to refute the theonomic position by arguing that the Old Testament case laws were intended by God to apply only to Old Testament Israel misses a key theological point: *God's revealed law was resurrected to newness of life with Jesus.* Old Testament law, mediated and restored through Jesus Christ and preached by His church, has in New Testament times become judicially obligatory nationally on a worldwide basis. All nations will be judged finally in terms of God's law, as Jesus warned: "And before him shall be gathered all nations: and he shall separate them one from another, as a shepherd divideth his sheep from the goats" (Matt. 25:32). This means that the biblical case laws are now judicially obligatory for the nations, for where there is no binding law, there can be no valid sanctions.

Biblical Law and Civilization

Though it may seem strange to introduce the problems dealt with in this chapter with an extended citation from an Orthodox Jewish scholar, I have decided to do so anyway. Rarely has any commentator better understood the importance of biblical law for the full flowering of society than I. Grunfeld, the translator of Samson Raphael Hirsch's remarkable study, *Horeb* (1837). Grunfeld wrote in 1962:

Indeed, the leaders of Christian opinion in Europe, and their Jewish imitators, conscious or unconscious, have often 'hit the law of Moses with their fists'; but it seems that in doing so they have done more harm to European civilization than to the law of Moses.

The separation of law and religion has proved to be one of the greatest disasters in the history of human civilization. It has done untold harm to law and religion alike. It has robbed law of its sacred character and thereby of its strongest moral incentive; it has deprived religion of its legal element and, with that, of its influence over the greatest social movements of our time. Law alone can be the regulator of organized human life. The rejection of law as a religious discipline means, therefore, of necessity, the flight of religion from the world and its realities, a denial of the value of life and a state of detachment and capitulation on the part of religion. Hence originates the deplorably small influence which organized religion has wielded in the daily affairs of life, especially in its social and economic spheres, where religious activity should be at least as predominant as in the sphere of faith and morals. This aloofness of organized religion from the problems and difficulties of social life has alienated the best and noblest spirits among the social reformers and has paralysed the influence which organized religion could and should have had in the social and political advancement of the world.[3]

A study of the case laws of Exodus gives us legitimate grounds of belief in the intensely practical nature of biblical law in social and economic life. The asserted dualism between biblical law and society cannot be maintained without denying the continuing validity of the case laws of Exodus. It should not surprise anyone that these three chapters of the Book of Exodus have been ignored by biblical commentators for two centuries, because this era has been the age of philosophical dualism: the estrangement of religion from the "real world" of scientific cause and effect. The triumph of biblical "higher criticism,"[4] the triumph of the dualistic humanist philosophy of Immanuel Kant,[5] and the triumph of inward-looking, world-rejecting pietistic Christianity have been closely related events.

The Case Laws and Slavery

The case laws of Exodus begin with rules governing slavery (actually, temporary indentured servitude). This is appropriate, for two reasons. First, as I have written in my general introduction to this series,[6] the Pentateuch is structured in terms of the five-point biblical covenant model: transcendence, hierarchy, ethics, judgment, and inheritance.[7] Exodus, the second book, is concerned with the question of hierarchy. It asks this crucial question: *Which God should*

---

3. I. Grunfeld, "Religion, Law and Life: An Historical Vindication of the Horeb," in Samson Raphael Hirsch, *Horeb: A Philosophy of Jewish Laws and Observances* (New York: Soncino Press, 1962), pp. cxxxii-cxxxiii.

4. See Appendix C: "The Hoax of Higher Criticism."

5. Richard Kroner, *Kant's Weltanschauung*, translated by John E. Smith (University of Chicago Press, [1914] 1956). Kroner is correct when he writes that "No one before Kant had ever exalted man so much; no one had ever accorded him such a degree of metaphysical independence and self-dependence. Within himself man creates and preserves the supersensible as that excellence which distinguishes him from all other beings. The supersensible is precisely that trait which makes man what he is or rather what he ought to be. The idea of mankind and the idea of God are indeed so near to each other here that they almost coincide. Even God is dependent upon the moral law instead of the law being dependent upon him" (pp. 36-37).

6. Gary North, *The Dominion Covenant: Genesis* (2nd ed.; Tyler, Texas: Institute for Christian Economics, 1987), pp. x-xiii.

7. Ray R. Sutton, *That You May Prosper: Dominion By Covenant* (Tyler, Texas: Institute for Christian Economics, 1987). This five-point structure can be remembered by the mnemonic device, THEOS: transcendence, hierarchy, ethics, oath, and succession.

man serve? The Book of Exodus presents God as the God of history who delivers His people from oppression. In this sense, Meredith G. Kline's identification of the second point of the covenant is appropriate: historical prologue.[8] The breakdown of an older order inaugurates a new order. The breakdown of Egyptian political and military sovereignty led to the rise of Israel. But once God has identified Himself historically, along the lines of an ancient suzerain's covenant treaty, men's response becomes the central issue. They must then ask themselves this question: *Under whose hierarchical institutions should we operate?* This is the vassal's appropriate response after he hears of what the suzerain has done for him in the past. Ray Sutton's identification of the second point of the covenant as hierarchy correlates closely to man's response to God's historical prologue.[9]

The second reason why the case laws begin with laws governing bondservice is that the Israelites had just been delivered out of permanent slavery. They were ready to hear about laws governing servitude. We should recognize the obvious: civil laws making slavery as oppressive as the system that had governed them in Egypt would not have been laws imposed by the God of liberation on a nation that had suffered years of unjust oppression. Thus, we should recognize that these laws were a loosening of the bonds of servitude, not a tightening. Furthermore, as I argue later on, any attempt by antinomians, either Christian or anti-Christian, to ridicule the case laws of Exodus that govern bondservice is in effect a call for a return to Egyptian bondage, namely, bondage to the autonomous State. *Bondage is an inescapable concept.* It is never a question of "bondage vs. no bondage." It is a question of "bondage to whom."

Hierarchy

Let us begin with the first reason why the case laws begin with the laws of servitude: the biblical covenant model. The Book of Exodus occupies the second position in the Pentateuch, and is therefore best understood in terms of hierarchy, meaning the structure of covenantal authority. Exodus opens with the account of the subjection of the Israelites to a king who did not acknowledge the covenant that his royal predecessor had made with Joseph and his brothers (Ex.

---

8. Meredith G. Kline, *The Treaty of the Great King: The Covenant Structure of Deuteronomy* (Grand Rapids, Michigan: Eerdmans, 1963), pp. 52-61; cf. Kline, *The Structure of Biblical Authority* (rev. ed.; Grand Rapids, Michigan: Eerdmans, 1972), pp. 53-57.

9. Sutton, *That You May Prosper*, ch. 2.

1:8). He placed the Hebrews in permanent slavery. He attempted to replace the God of the Bible as the sovereign lord of the Hebrews. As a self-proclaimed divinity, Pharaoh asserted the right to rule over them without answering to the God of Abraham. Thus, the early chapters of Exodus are devoted to the story of God's subordination of Egypt to Himself through the judgment of cursing—plagues, death, and military defeat—and the subordination of Israel to Himself through the judgment of blessing: their deliverance from bondage.[10] The old order was marked by the Hebrews' enslavement by Pharaoh; the new order was to be marked by their service to God.

Exodus is the Bible's premier "book of the covenant" (Ex. 24:7). The Book of Exodus is itself structured in terms of the five-point covenant model. First, transcendence: Who is the *sovereign God* over nature and history, God or Pharaoh? Answer: the Creator God who delivered His people from Egypt (chapters 1-17). Second, hierarchy: What is the proper mode of *judicial organization* that reflects God's hierarchical chain of command over His people? Answer: a bottom-up appeals court structure (Ex. 18). Third, what are the *laws* by which God governs mankind and God's authorized representatives govern the covenantal institutions of family and civil government? Answer: the Ten Commandments (Ex. 20) and the case laws (Ex. 21-23:13). Fourth, how is the *covenantal oath* between God and His people manifested? Through a covenant meal (Ex. 23:14-19). What is the judgment that God brings on those who rebel against Him? National destruction: deliverance into the hands of the enemy (Ex. 23:20-33). Exodus 24 records the covenantal oath that Israel made with God. "And Moses came and told the people all the words of the LORD, and all the judgments: and all the people answered with one voice, and said, All the words which the LORD hath said will we do" (v. 3). Fifth, what is the *sign of inheritance* or continuity? Answer: the tabernacle that will go with them through the wilderness, and then into the promised land. Its blueprint appears in Exodus 25-31; its actual construction is described in Exodus 35-40.

Exodus 32-33 deals with Israel's rebellion with the golden calf and God's judgment of them, a recapitulation of Adam's Fall. In Exodus 34, God re-establishes Israel's covenant with Him, with Moses acting as the representative or intermediary in this hierarchy. Exodus 34 is therefore a section on *covenant renewal*, an aspect of historical continuity.

---

10. Gary North, *Moses and Pharaoh: Dominion Religion vs. Power Religion* (Tyler, Texas: Institute for Christian Economics, 1985).

The second reason why slavery becomes the initial focus of concern in the case laws is that the Israelites had just been delivered out of bondage. The whole book deals with the theme of deliverance from bondage into sabbath rest.[11] Thus, having just been delivered from slavery, God caught their attention by beginning the case law section with laws governing servitude. He confronts people "right where they are" in life. Where the Israelites were was in the wilderness, *in transition spiritually and culturally* from Pharaoh's slavery to God's servitude. Biblical servitude is one of God's authorized modes of transition from wrath to grace (blessing), both personally and culturally. Pagan slavery, in contrast, is one of God's ethically unauthorized but historically imposed modes of transition from grace to wrath (cursing) for His people: bondage in Egypt, Assyria, and Babylon. Becoming a slave-master over God's people is prohibited, yet God raises up such tyrants as a form of judgment against His people and the tyrants themselves (Jer. 25). What the New Testament says of Judas applies to slave-masters generally: "And truly the Son of man goeth, as it was determined: but woe unto that man by whom he is betrayed!" (Luke 22:22).

Liberals Protest

Because the case law section begins with bondservice, liberal scholars are immediately repulsed by it. In general, they react negatively to biblical law as a whole. It is not that they ignore the law. Liberal theologians have produced a large number of detailed studies of Old Testament law. What is notable about these academic studies is their almost self-conscious uselessness. Specialized scholarly journals in the field of Old Testament studies have been created by the dozens to serve as outlets for essays so narrow in focus, so irrelevant in conclusions, and so boring in style that not even publishers of scholarly books are willing to print them. The extent of the uselessness of these highly rarified, heavily footnoted studies cannot readily be appreciated by the average Christian, who reads his Bible, and then does his best to take its teachings seriously. Even in the world of formal academic scholarship, which specializes in the production of painstakingly documented irrelevance, Old Testament scholars are regarded by their colleagues as highly specialized, multi-lingual masters of useless historical details and even more

---

11. Jordan, *Law of the Covenant*, p. 75.

useless literary speculation. (If Old Testament higher criticism were pornographic, it could not be published in the United States, for in order to publish pornography legally, the publishers of such material must be capable of demonstrating in court that it has at least some socially redeeming value.)

Modern Bible scholarship has been governed by one overriding concern: to make the Old Testament seem archaic, irrelevant to the modern world, and in no way connected to man's final judgment by the God whose word the Old Testament is. Indeed, the bulk of all modern scholarship in every academic discipline has this as the primary goal: *to deny the biblical doctrine of final judgment.* This was the theological reason why Darwinism flourished so rapidly after its introduction in 1859,[12] and it is why it still flourishes today. People know that their deeds are evil, so they adopt an eschatology that conforms to their preferred eternal state, an eschatology without final judgment by a personal Creator God. Secular humanists therefore insist that mankind must be viewed as a randomly evolved being who is headed nowhere in particular, but especially not toward God's final judgment. Covenant-breakers seek substitutes for God's final judgment: either the heat death of the universe or the endless oscillating cycles of creative explosion, expansion, contraction, and cosmic crushing.[13] Either is deemed preferable to the eternal lake of fire, which is undoubtedly the place of residence for covenant-breakers.

A much better alternative is a return to covenant-keeping. This involves knowing what the ethical terms of the covenant are.

The Book of the Covenant

It has been my self-appointed task to study the "Book of the Covenant," Exodus 21-23, with the operating presupposition that these few pages of legal texts are consistent, coherent, sensible, and au-

---

12. Wrote liberal cleric Rev. James Maurice Wilson in 1925: "The evolution of man from lower forms of life was in itself a new and startling fact, and one that broke up the old theology. I and my contemporaries, however, accepted it as fact. The first and obvious result of this acceptance was that we were compelled to regard the Biblical story of the Fall as not historic, as it had long been believed to be. We were compelled to regard that story as a primitive attempt to account for the presence of sin and evil in the world. . . . But now, in the light of the fact of evolution, the Fall, as a historic event, already questioned on other grounds, was excluded and denied by science." Wilson, "The Religious Effect of the Idea of Evolution," in *Evolution in the Light of Modern Knowledge: A Collective Work* (London: Blackie & Son, 1925), pp. 497, 498.

13. Gary North, *Is the World Running Down? Crisis in the Christian Worldview* (Tyler, Texas: Institute for Christian Economics, 1988), ch. 2.

thoritative; and that they are judicially applicable as case laws to every culture in every era of history. These case laws deserve careful attention, not in order to discover why they are supposedly inapplicable today, but rather to discover how they *are* applicable today. These laws represent a significant portion of mankind's God-given and God-required tools of dominion. They are essential to a unique law-order that alone enables God's people to subdue the whole earth to His glory.

The case laws of Exodus constitute the second-longest passage in the Bible that deals with the specific laws of the civil government, the longest being Deuteronomy 13-27. (A considerable portion of Leviticus 18-21 is concerned with permanent judicial regulations, and not just the temporary laws of cleanliness.) Yet Exodus 21-23 is a brief section of the Bible. As the reader can see from the thickness of this book, a great deal of economic material can be gleaned from these three chapters; nevertheless, they fill only a few pages of the Bible. The implications of these case laws are wide-ranging; they constitute a major substantive foundation of Western law.[14] Thus, we must view them as part of an all-encompassing system of law.

James Jordan has made an incisive observation concerning the use of biblical law in Protestant theology: "Protestant theology has traditionally held to three uses of the Law of God. The use of the Law in justification is that it provides a legal indictment against fallen man, and drives him to Christ. The use of the Law in sanctification is that it provides a moral standard for the life of renewed man. The use of the Law in dominion is that it delineates the rule which is to be implemented by the adopted sons of God over His creation. In the past, theology has tended to neglect the dominical use of God's Law. . . ."[15] Such neglect has been debilitating for the church and also for civilization. It is the dominical aspect of biblical law that this commentary series, and specifically this volume, is intended to examine.

---

14. In terms of a formal foundation of Western law—case laws taken verbatim from the Old Testament—this statement would be more difficult to prove. An academic series of historical studies on these explicit references would be of great importance.

15. James B. Jordan, Slavery in Biblical Perspective, unpublished master's thesis, Westminster Theological Seminary, Philadelphia (April 1980), p. 4.

The Case Laws

What are case laws? How are we to understand them? Are Christians to work politically to get them enacted into civil law today? Even those scholars who believe in the Bible as the infallible word of God disagree over the answers to these questions. Greg L. Bahnsen devotes only two sentences to the case laws in a study of biblical law that is over 600 pages long: "The ten commandments cannot be understood and properly applied without the explanation given them throughout the case laws of the Older Testament. The case law illustrates the application or qualification of the principle laid down in the general commandment."[16] This is not what you would call a detailed study of the case laws. Rushdoony's two-volume *Institutes of Biblical Law* does not even have an entry in the index to "case laws" or "law, case," yet the combined work is over 1,600 pages. This does not mean that *Institutes* totally ignores the case laws, although a more detailed discussion would have been helpful. It means that the people who compiled the two indexes either did not notice the topic or else did not perceive its importance. The volumes' incomplete indexes makes it difficult for the reader to trace down this important aspect of biblical law.

Rushdoony breaks biblical law into three aspects: general law, case law, and prophetic commentary on the law. "*First*, certain broad premises or principles are declared. These are declarations of basic law. The Ten Commandments give us such declarations. The Ten Commandments are not therefore laws among laws, but are the basic laws, of which the various laws are specific examples."[17] Then there is "a *second* characteristic of Biblical law, namely, that the major portion of the law is *case law*, i.e., the illustration of the basic principle in terms of specific cases. These specific cases are often illustrations of the extent of the application of the law; that is, by citing a minimal type of case, the necessary jurisdictions of the law are revealed."[18]

The case laws are necessary in order to focus our concern on specific violations. The specific nature of the case laws is what keeps the Ten Commandments relevant in history. "Without case law, God's

---

16. Greg L. Bahnsen, *Theonomy in Christian Ethics* (2nd ed.; Phillipsburg, New Jersey: Presbyterian & Reformed, 1984), p. 313. His other brief references to the case laws only assert that they are still in force.

17. R. J. Rushdoony, *The Institutes of Biblical Law* (Nutley, New Jersey: Craig Press, 1973), p. 10.

18. *Ibid.*, p. 11.

law would soon be reduced to an extremely limited area of meaning. This, of course, is precisely what has happened. Those who deny the present validity of the law apart from the Ten Commandments have as a consequence a very limited definition of theft. Their definition usually follows the civil law of their country, is humanistic, and is not radically different from the definitions given by Moslems, Buddhists, and humanists."[19]

James Jordan speaks of four manifestations of biblical law. First, there is "the Greatest Commandment," as he calls it: "And thou shalt love the LORD thy God with all thine heart, and with all thy soul, and with all thy might" (Deut. 6:5; cf. Matt. 22:37). On this point, Rushdoony is in agreement, and he begins Chapter 1 of the *Institutes* with a discussion of Deuteronomy 6:5.[20] The command is: *love God.* Jordan says that this covenant has two sides: structural (submit to the law) and personal (willing acceptance). "This Greatest Commandment comprehends (includes) every other commandment."[21]

Second, there is the commandment to love our fellow man as we love ourselves (Lev. 19:18; Matt. 22:39). This commandment divides the Greatest Commandment into two parts: duty to God and duty to men. "We should notice that these two Great Commandments are not found in any special place in the Bible, but are placed among the 'small' particular laws of Leviticus and Deuteronomy."[22]

Third, there are the Ten Commandments, the Decalogue. "The Ten Commandments break the Greatest Commandment into ten parts. Each of the Ten Commandments relates to God, and each relates to our fellow men, but some relate more specifically to God and others relate more specifically to man."[23]

"*Fourth*, there are the case laws. The case laws of the Old and New Testaments break the Greatest Commandment into many parts. As we have seen, any given case law may be related to more than one of the Ten Commandments, and so it would be an error to try to pigeon-hole the case laws under one Commandment each. In reality the case law as a whole comes under the Ten Commandments as a whole. Some laws fit rather nicely under one or another of the Commandments, but most case laws seem to combine principles from several of the basic Ten."[24] This is a very important point. It

---

19. *Ibid.*, p. 12.
20. *Ibid.*, p. 16.
21. Jordan, *Law of the Covenant*, p. 21.
22. *Ibid.*, p. 22.
23. *Idem.*
24. *Ibid.*, pp. 22-23.

would be a mistake for us to seek to categorize each case law as being an application of one and only one of the Ten Commandments. The theologically innovative insight by Rushdoony that each of the case laws can be subsumed under a particular commandment in the Decalogue must not blind us to the fact that a case law may also be able to be subsumed under several of them.

Casuistry: The One and the Many

The case laws allow us to understand the scope of other fundamental laws in the Bible. They enable us to see how these fundamental principles are to be interpreted and applied in concrete cases. The case laws enable us to combine the *one* of general law with the *many* of historic circumstances. Every system of law possesses both features — general and specific, one and many[25] — but the Bible gives us reliable revelation concerning the proper balancing.

The case laws are specific applications of more general biblical legal principles. We are to use case laws as the Apostle Paul used the case law that prohibits the muzzling of an ox while it treads the grain in the field (Deut. 25:4). Paul derived two ecclesiastical applications from this case law: 1) that the Christian minister is worthy of his hire (I Cor. 9:9-14); and 2) that he is worthy of a double honor (I Tim. 5:17-18). These are both examples of the general principle to avoid stealing.[26] The case law, the general law, and the New Testament application of the law are all equally valid today, no less so than in the days of Moses. If this case law were no longer judicially binding today, then why would Paul cite it? If it is judicially binding, then on what basis can all other case laws be dismissed as inapplicable in New Testament times?

---

25. Writes legal scholar Max Rheinstein: "Even less irrational is judicial case law in the sense of judge-made law, as occurring particularly, but by no means solely, in the Common Law. Consistency, which indeed is the essence of rationality, is required by the very principle of *stare decisis* [legal precedent—G.N.]. As no case is ever completely identical with any other, we can never follow precedent in any way other than by trying to follow its *ratio decidendi*, i.e., the principle, broad or narrow, upon which we find, or believe, it to be based." Rheinstein, Introduction, Max Weber, *On Law in Economy and Society*, edited by Rheinstein (New York: Clarion, 1967), p. xlviii. He then adds this *obiter dictum*: "With much justification the judicial process of the Common Law has been characterized as reasoning by example in the Aristotelian sense." The judicial process in the pre-modern Common Law should rather be described as reasoning by example in the Mosaic sense.

26. Rushdoony, *Institutes*, pp. 11-12.

Any principle of biblical interpretation (hermeneutic) is dangerous which argues that unless an Old Testament case law is specifically repeated in the New Testament, it is automatically annulled in
New Testament times. Anyone who argues this way is going to run
into major problems. For example, bestiality is not specifically mentioned in the New Testament. In the Old Testament, it is listed as a
capital crime (Lev. 18:23). How are we to regard bestiality in the
New Testament? As a "victimless crime"? As an example of cruelty
to animals? As creative humanism's version of animal husbandry?
Or as a capital crime? If the act is still a moral crime in the New Testament (derived from, say, the law regarding adultery—unless the
interpreter has also abandoned John 8:1-11), is it also a matter for the
civil courts? If it is, is the death penalty still in force? Can you carry
over the Old Testament's definition of the act as criminal and yet not
carry over the Old Testament's penal sanction? On what hermeneutical basis? [27]

Homosexuality and God's Penal Sanctions

Homosexual behavior was a capital crime in the Old Testament
(Lev. 20:13). Is it still a capital crime today? Virtually all non-theonomic
interpreters draw back from this politically embarrassing (in 1989)
conclusion. The extent to which the Lord will not tolerate it is seen
in the HTLV-III lentivirus. This lentivirus (long-term virus) has
been identified as the source of AIDS, the immunity system-destroying
disease among homosexuals, first designated GRID: Gay Related
Immunodeficiency Disease. The well-organized homosexual community protested, and the Centers for Disease Control renamed it
AIDS (Acquired Immune Deficiency Syndrome). [28] The change in
its name in no way impaired its judgmental effectiveness biologically.

What is happening in our day is that *God is now applying His penal
sanctions to male homosexuals.* All of them are likely to be dead in the
year 2000, along with perhaps a hundred million of the rest of us. [29]

---

27. Gary North, *75 Bible Questions Your Instructors Pray You Won't Ask* (rev. ed.;
Tyler, Texas: Institute for Christian Economics, 1988), Question 26.

28. David A. Nobel, Wayne C. Lutton, and Paul Cameron, *AIDS: Acquired Immune Deficiency Syndrome: Special Report* (2nd ed.; Manitou Springs, Colorado: Summit Research Institute, 1987), p. 1.

29. One hundred million deaths, worldwide, has become the official estimate by
world health officials, as of early 1987. It is difficult to know whether this figure is
remotely accurate, or deliberately overestimated (to reduce political pressures to quarantine the carriers), or deliberately underestimated (to reduce the threat of panic).

What civil governments have refused to do, the HTLV-III lentivirus is doing with historically unprecedented efficiency. The plague has arrived.[30] The disease may now be spreading to the "straight" community, although there are journalists who think that it has not yet done so.[31] Therefore, God may be in the process of applying His penal sanctions to the entire civilization that refused to honor Leviticus 20:13. God will not be mocked, or even ignored. If AIDS continues to spread at today's officially admitted rates, Western Civilization will either topple or else be forced to rethink its first principles, repent, and pray for God to remove the scourge.

This is another reason why in the year 2000, the final year of the present millennium (but misunderstood by the public to be the first year of the next millennium), the Christian Reconstructionists' worldview will have begun to be taken seriously in the broader Christian community. People in general, let alone Christians, will no longer be able to pretend in comfortable safety that they can ignore God's laws with impunity. This is also why antinomian fundamentalists like Ed Dobson and Ed Hindson will not be sneering any longer.[32] They will no longer be able to write of Christian Reconstructionism in general and R. J. Rushdoony in particular, "Fortunately, we can say with confidence that he represents a very small

---

30. Gene Antonio, *The AIDS Cover-Up* (San Francisco: Ignatius Press, 1986).

31. Michael A. Fumento, "AIDS: Are Heterosexuals at Risk?" *Commentary* (Nov. 1987).

32. You can almost hear the sneer in the words of Ed Dobson (who until March of 1987 was vice president of student affairs at Jerry Falwell's Liberty University and who also served as editor of Falwell's *Fundamentalist Journal*) and Ed Hindson (professor of religion at Liberty University): "Some of Rushdoony's followers, in order to prepare the world for Christ's second coming, have called for laws mandating the death penalty for homosexuals and drunkards." They wrote this in a non-Christian magazine: "Apocalypse Now?", *Policy Review* (Fall 1986), p. 20. First, they would be hard-pressed to find any follower of Rushdoony who has called for the death penalty simply for drunkenness, nor do they mention anyone who has. This was a classic "cheap shot." The passage that they presumably are referring to, Deuteronomy 21:20, calls for the death penalty of rebellious sons, who manifest their rebellion as drunkards and gluttons, and whose parents are required by God to testify to this fact before the civil magistrates. Such sons are therefore rebels against lawfully constituted authority (parents), and are to receive the death penalty. Second, with respect to homosexual acts, the Bible clearly calls for the death penalty (Lev. 20:13), as these men surely know. Yet they try to trick their non-Christian audience into blaming unnamed followers of R. J. Rushdoony for this supposed embarrassment, rather than blaming its "shamefully unliberal" perpetrator, God. God's response to this antinomian embarrassment is AIDS. To say that such antinomian arguments by these biblical law-hating Christians are merely misleading is giving them far too much credit.

group with absolutely no chance of achieving their agenda."[33] AIDS
will eliminate their confidence, along with the self-confidence of fundamentalism's allies in the war against biblical law, the humanists.[34]

Which General Law?

The problem for biblical casuistry is that the case laws do not
always reveal to us which one (or more) of the fundamental ten laws
is directly involved. This is Jordan's point.[35] There is no simplistic
way to place every case law under one (and only one) of the Ten
Commandments. The search for a specific and primary principle
that undergirds any given case law can sometimes be frustrating. No
such principle may initially call attention to itself. This is why
human intuition, trained by long periods of Bible study and the discipline of *casuistry* (the application of general laws to specific cases),
coupled with regeneration by the Holy Spirit, is necessary for a
proper understanding of biblical law.

The art of Protestant biblical casuistry faded in the late seventeenth century, with the deaths of men like Jeremy Taylor, Richard
Baxter, and especially after the death of Samuel Willard in 1707.
After them, the secular vision of natural law once again overwhelmed Christian thinkers, as it had in the late Scholastic era, only
this time, the vision became more and more self-consciously autonomous from the Bible and religion. It has only been since 1973, with
the publication of Volume I of Rushdoony's *Institutes*,[36] that a handful of younger Protestant scholars began to publish preliminary exercises in the ancient discipline of casuistry, but without any reliance
on the quicksand of natural law theory. My specifically economic
commentary on the Bible, which I began in 1973 in the *Chalcedon
Report*, is an obvious example. This self-conscious break with natural
law theory was Cornelius Van Til's crucially important intellectual
legacy to the Christian Reconstructionists.[37]

By What Other Standard?

Are these case laws still in force? Bahnsen says yes: "Since the
case law's principles *define* the Decalogue, the case law's principles (in

---

33. *Idem.*
34. On the implicit alliance between fundamentalism and humanism, see my Introduction to *Moses and Pharaoh*, pp. 2-5.
35. Jordan, *Law of the Covenant*, pp. 22-23.
36. And also with the audio tapes that preceded the *Institutes* from about 1968.
37. For example, Cornelius Van Til, *A Christian Theory of Knowledge* (Nutley, New
Jersey: Presbyterian & Reformed, 1969), ch. 8: "Natural Theology and Scripture."

their full scope: personal and social, ecclesiastical and civil) are as *perpetual* as the Decalogue itself."[38] Others in the Christian Reconstruction "movement" agree: unless specifically abrogated through Christ's fulfillment of a specific case law in the New Testament (extremely rare), they are still morally and judicially binding.

There are many Christians who categorically deny this. They reject the judicially binding character of Old Testament laws. In response, Reconstructionists ask the question that served as the title of Rushdoony's first book: *By what standard?* What judicial standard is sovereign in New Testament times? More specifically, by what *other* standard than the word of God are men required by God to select and enforce civil laws? By some hypothetically universal natural law (which almost nobody believes in, including theoretical physicists, now that Darwinism is the reigning philosophy)?[39] By process philosophy, the shifting standard bequeathed by scientific Darwinism?[40] By existentialism's shifting standards?[41] By the shifting ethical standard of humanistic positive law (whatever the legislature this week says is law, *is* law)? *By what other standard?* Be specific. Prove your case. *And prove it in terms of the Bible, if you please.* Please cite chapter and verse.

Chapter and verse: no words anger the compromised Christian intellectual more than these. Chapter and verse: he is thrown back on the Bible as the ultimate judge of his speculations. Chapter and verse: this allows no autonomy for the mind of man. Chapter and verse: his humanistic colleagues will laugh at him. Worse than facing Almighty God on judgment day, the Christian antinomian intellectual fears ridicule by his humanistic peers. Chapter and verse: he *has* no chapters and verses. So he shouts his defiance of the laws of the Bible. He ridicules the laws of the Bible by ridiculing specific biblical law-based recommendations of the Christian Reconstruction movement. He sets himself up as the standard of interpretation. He clings to his 1968 (or 1948) classroom notes from the State University that granted him his advanced degree. "Here lies all truth, at

---

38. Greg L. Bahnsen, *By This Standard: The Authority of God's Law Today* (Tyler, Texas: Institute for Christian Economics, 1985), p. 318.

39. North, *Is the World Running Down?*, ch. 1.

40. Delwin Brown, Ralph E. James, Jr., and Gene Reeves (eds.), *Process Philosophy and Christian Thought* (Indianapolis, Indiana: Bobbs-Merrill, 1971); Ewert H. Cousins (ed.), *Process Theology: Basic Writings* (New York: Newman Press, 1971).

41. William Barrett, *Irrational Man: A Study in Existential Philosophy* (Garden City, New York: Doubleday Anchor, [1958] 1962).

least for the moment, and momentary truth is all we can hope to discover," he proclaims.

Not the Old Testament! Never, ever the Old Testament! After all, Christ has annulled the Old Testament. And even if He hasn't, State University has. This is the morally corrosive process that has been labeled so perceptively by Herbert Schlossberg, using a metaphor derived from the world of ruptured nuclear reactors: the evangelical meltdown.[42]

The Lack of Procedural Details

There is one problem that Christians need to recognize as a major problem to be solved in each society that attempts to rewrite civil legislation and jurisprudence in terms of the Old Testament case laws. This is the problem of legal procedure. The Bible is almost silent concerning civil and ecclesiastical judicial procedure.

J. J. Finkelstein made this observation in his fascinating monograph, *The Ox That Gored* (1981). (This is the single liberal source that proved really indispensable for this book — the fix that got me hooked again,[43] vainly hoping that some other liberal document would prove as useful. None ever did.) He spent many years of his life in a careful study of ancient Near Eastern legal texts. He found a crucial contrast between biblical texts and the compilations of law in rival Near Eastern societies: *the biblical texts reveal almost nothing about legal procedure.* "The contrast between the biblical and the Mesopotamian legal corpora is underscored even further by the almost total absence in the former of normative rules, that is, formulations of the proper procedures governing commerce and economic life in general. The legal sections of the Pentateuch betray what amounts to complete indifference to the formalities without which the most elementary social institutions could hardly be said to function. This silence applies not only to contracts and obligations, but also to the normative forms by which family life is ordered, such as marriage, family property rights, and inheritance. The Mesopotamian legal corpora dwell on these themes at great length; biblical law touches upon them only in the most cursory way, and then often within the framework of a narrative where it typically is a question of the unusual rather than the normative procedure. This is clearly illustrated by the petition of

---

42. Herbert Schlossberg, Review of David Chilton's *Paradise Restored*, in *American Spectator* (March 1987), p. 42.

43. See below: "A Lifelong Affliction," pp. 108-9.

the daughters of Zelophehad for inheritance rights in the absence of male heirs."[44]

He gives some good reasons for this contrast. One is that the climate of Palestine is inhospitable to the survival of parchment and papyrus. In contrast, Mesopotamian collections of tablets and sealed rolls have been found in profusion during archeological digs. "The bulk of the written remains from ancient Mesopotamia is accidental in the sense that all of it has been recovered by legitimate or illicit excavation."[45] It may be that attempts to impose coherence on the "incoherent assemblage of data of widely disparate dates" may be misleading. In the late 1970's, I heard a lecture by the editor of the *Biblical Archaeology Review*, David N. Freedman, who informed us that only about 10 percent of the tablets for any culture or archeological site are ever translated. There is always another discovery to catch the fancy of the archaeologists, and they eventually grow bored with the translation of seemingly similar commercial records and tax records. Furthermore, there are not that many specialists in the ancient languages, and fewer still who are social or legal theorists. They go on to new tablets instead of spending a lifetime interpreting the tablets they have already translated.

Finkelstein does not emphasize these more technical aspects of the differences between biblical and Near Eastern texts. The really important difference in the rate of survival, he says, was theological. "The Israelite nation was bound by an ancient and sacred pact with its deity to organize and conduct its life, both personally and institutionally, in accordance with the divinely ordained prescriptions. Directly or indirectly, whatever is included in the Old Testament by way of 'historical' information is meant to reinforce that central thesis; the vicissitudes of the people through the millennium embraced by the biblical time span serve as hardly more than a barometer of the nation's fidelity to, or perfidy against, its pact with Yahweh. Everything is subordinated to this overriding purpose, and whatever

---

44. J. J. Finkelstein, *The Ox That Gored* (Philadelphia: American Philosophical Society, 1981), p. 42. Boecker writes: "There are no OT 'rules of court.' We must remember above all that in its basic message the OT is not interested in conveying a picture of legal processes in Ancient Israel. Its concern lies elsewhere. Its purpose is to report God's activity in and with Israel and to demonstrate Israel's answer to this activity." Hans Jochen Boecker, *Law and the Administration of Justice in the Old Testament and Ancient East*, translated by Jeremy Moiser (Minneapolis, Minnesota: Augsburg, [1976] 1980), p. 28.

45. Finkelstein, *ibid.*, p. 44.

did not contribute to this 'transcendent' end was not considered for inclusion, no matter how fundamental it was to the pursuit of daily life. As a consequence norms and regulations governing trade, property, the crafts, family law, and the like—the institutions that constitute the very fabric of daily life—were of little concern to the biblical authors and redactors."[46]

I would add a third aspect of this structure of biblical revelation: the intention of God to provide a covenant document for all of human history rather than a temporary law code for professional use by Hebrew lawyers. The whole of God's revealed law had to be read every seventh year to all the residents of Israel (Deut. 31:10-13). Law had to be understandable by them. God's law was (and is) to be enforced primarily by *self-government under God*, not by formal agencies of government, whether civil or ecclesiastical. The law was (and is) to be *lived*, not broken into minute technical parts and rolled up in scrolls on lawyers' shelves. The inescapable technical and professional disputes of lawyers were peripheral to the fundamental point: *the restoration of the broken covenant of Adam.* God's revealed law was given to serve as a guide for the restoration of God's mandated kingdom, meaning the earthly, historical manifestation of God's cosmic civilization—"in earth, as it is in heaven." This meant (and still means) the restoration of God's law-order.[47] It was this law-order, not the technical terms of professional disputation within an elite guild of lawyers, that was the focus of concern in the Old Testament's texts relating to biblical law.

Formal Law and Ethics

Biblical law gives us God's fixed ethical standards. It also gives us warning: there will be a final judgment, eternal in its effects, awesome in its magnitude, and perfect in its casuistry. All the facts will be judged by all the law. Yet there is little said about how this final courtroom drama will be conducted. Any discussion of the technical details of God's formal legal procedure is irrelevant. We know only that there will be at least three witnesses against us, violation by violation: Father, Son, and Holy Ghost.[48]

---

46. *Ibid.*, p. 42.
47. Rushdoony, *Institutes*, p. 12.
48. Gary North, "Witnesses and Judges," *Biblical Economics Today*, VI (Aug./Sept. 1983). Reprinted as Appendix E in North, *Dominion Covenant: Genesis* (1987).

The quest for perfect earthly justice is socially debilitating. It is a demonic quest. Whenever lawyers dominate a society — usually during the society's final years — they steadily substitute formal procedure for ethics. (This is also true of many other academic guilds.) They adopt a theology of salvation by law, or at least continued employment by law. The practice of law replaces the law itself; "law" becomes case laws, precedents, and procedures, but without any thought or hope concerning an integrated law-order that provides meaning to the law in general. Law becomes what men say it is, and men do not agree. Humanism's implicit *judicial polytheism* then leads to the disintegration of civil law: jammed courts, endless litigation, plea bargaining, and all the other aspects of twentieth-century judicial tyranny that we have become numbed into accepting as normative.[49]

The Bible is concerned with ethics, not formal courtroom procedure. The New Testament's few rules for church courts (Matt. 18:15-18) are representative of the entire Bible's view of legal procedure. Without reliable ethical standards, formal procedure is the judicial equivalent of wood, hay, and stubble. Paul chastised the church at Corinth for having allowed its members to seek justice in the Roman courts of his day. Better, he said, to seek justice from the least esteemed member of the local church (I Cor. 6:4).

It is the mark of a culture in the process of disintegration that it substitutes procedure for ethics, the letter of its law for the spirit of its law. Even more important than the letter of the law is the *bureaucratic machinery* that defines the letter of the law. This is where the West is in the latter decades of the twentieth century. Techniques of judicial interpretation are considered more fundamental than the substance of the law. Such an attitude invariably transfers authority from the people to a self-certified elite, the interpreters. It creates a secular priesthood. This is the basis of modern education, where formal examinations and formal academic degrees have been substituted as standards of performance in place of performance on the job as evaluated by a master craftsman in a free market setting. Such bureaucratic formalism is the antithesis of the Reformation doctrine: every man a priest.

---

49. Macklin Fleming, *The Price of Perfect Justice* (New York: Basic Books, 1974); Carrol D. Kilgore, *Judicial Tyranny* (Nashville, Tennessee: Thomas Nelson, 1977).

A Lifelong Affliction

This book suffers from a deliberately imposed defect: the foot-noting of utterly irrelevant and/or utterly erroneous scholarly mate-rial. I attended seminary and graduate school, and I picked up some burdensome habits. One of the great weaknesses of modern Christi-anity is that prospective ministers are often required to attend semi-nary, and seminary students are often required by seminary pro-fessors to spend an inordinate amount of time reading the theological drivel produced by higher critics. In fact, this general rule governs seminary curricula: the better the seminary's academic reputation, the greater the quantity of assigned drivel. Higher criticism confuses students in conservative seminaries, forcing them to waste precious time that could otherwise be used in studying the Bible. It leads stu-dents into apostasy in liberal seminaries. Professors in conservative seminaries frequently structure their classes as if an important pas-toral task is to keep up with the latest theories of liberal theologians, so they train their students to become familiar with the defunct theories of long-forgotten German theologians. In the spring semester of 1964, I put this sign on my door at Westminster Sem-inary: "Help stamp out dead German theologians: Attend classes regularly."[50]

Conservative Bible scholars spend their lives shadow boxing with liberals, despite the fact that the liberals pay little or no attention to them, and are barely aware of their existence. (An exception was Cornelius Van Til's published criticisms of Karl Barth. "That man hates me!" Barth was once overheard to say when Van Til's name was mentioned. But Barth never responded to Van Til in print, any more than Ron Sider responded in print to David Chilton.[51] Liberals prefer not to expose their intellectual wounds in public, especially when these wounds are mortal.) In any case, liberals revise their theses so often that by the time the conservative has painstakingly refuted what had been the latest liberal fad, the fad is

---

50. The problem with the theological seminary is that it is an institution that is supported by donors primarily because they expect it to train ministers, when it is all too often a graduate school in theology staffed by men whose real interest is technical theology, and who have never themselves pastored churches. It is another example of procedure (formal academic certification) triumphing over substance (producing pastors).

51. Ron Sider, *Rich Christians in an Age of Hunger* (2nd ed.; Downers Grove, Il-linois: Inter-Varsity Press, 1984).

regarded by the liberals as ancient history.[52]

Nevertheless, this practice of citing liberal scholars, even if confined to footnotes only, is like a nasty habit picked up in one's youth; it is very difficult to overcome once you are afflicted. It usually becomes a lifelong addiction. You can spot the addict easily: as he reads the final manuscript version of his book, just before he sends it to the typesetter, he scans the footnotes, making sure that there are a sufficient number of German works cited, even if only in translation. If there are none, the author's hands begin to shake uncontrollably, like a heroin addict suffering withdrawal symptoms. He rushes back to make one more set of revisions, frantically scanning the latest theological journals in search of a handful of citations — any citations — just to make his book appear academically respectable. "One more fix; just one more fix! Then I'll quit forever!" But the pathetic addict knows he can't quit. Even when he is ashamed by his habit, he returns to the sins of his youth. He pretends that the drivel he reads in scholarly theological journals is significant. In time, he risks being remade in their image.

The works of modern theologians are overwhelmingly useless, yet occasionally one of them will randomly offer some vaguely useful insight, so the addicted scholar keeps plowing through their books, hoping for a footnote or two. *Tools of Dominion* displays occasional evidence of being the product of this bad habit picked up in my youth. But at least you will find no trace of ethical relativism in this book's thesis.

Conclusion

The case laws of Exodus provide us with fundamental legal principles that God has established in order to provide His people with a means of gaining His external, historical blessings. These case laws are mankind's God-given tools of dominion. Without them, and

---

52. A good example of such a fad was the "death of God" movement, which lasted from 1966 until (maybe) 1969. The "hot" theologians who promoted this short-lived fad were Gabriel Vahanian and Thomas J. J. Altizer. This is an affliction I call Altizer's disease: two years after people get it, they forget all about you. See Altizer, *The Gospel of Christian Atheism* (Philadelphia: Westminster Press, 1966). Altizer was teaching at Emory University, a Methodist school in Atlanta, Georgia; Westminster Press is mainline Presbyterian. See also Altizer and Hamilton, *Radical Theology and the Death of God* (New York: Bobbs-Merrill, 1966). Vahanian's book had been published half a decade earlier, but did not immediately catch on: *The Death of God: The Culture of Our Post-Christian Era* (New York: George Braziller, 1961).

without faith in the God who gave them, rebellious mankind cannot long sustain the external blessings of God.[53]

The modern world, including the Christian world, does not believe this. People think that they can have freedom without Christ, and prosperity without adherence to the external requirements of biblical law. They really do believe in the autonomy of man. They really do believe that "my power and the might of my hand hath gotten me this wealth" (Deut. 8:17). The problem is, God has warned us that when we say this, judgment is near (Deut. 8:18-20).

We find Christians who argue vehemently that "Christians can live under *any* economic or political system!" True, so we reply: "Even the Old Testament legal system?" And we are told emphatically, "*No!* Christians can live under any economic and political system *except* the Old Testament legal system." Anything is acceptable, therefore, except what God requires. So they reply, as Satan replied to Eve, "Hath God said?" Yes, God *hath* said!

Cornelius Van Til once wrote that if a covenant-breaking man could tune in his radio to only one station that did not testify of God to him, he would listen only to that station. No such station exists, Van Til says.[54] The whole creation testifies to the Creator (Rom. 1:18-23). We can extend this insight to social theory: if antinomian Christians could live under any system of politics and economics that did not testify to them of what God *really* requires, they would choose to live only under that system. They have said so repeatedly. But they cannot escape the voice of God. They cannot escape the requirements of Old Testament law. In short, they cannot escape the Bible. They are inevitably under the covenant's blessings and cursings.

It is time for Christians to place themselves consistently and forthrightly under the ethical terms of the covenant, and affirm the continuing judicial validity for all societies of the case laws. They can begin with the case laws of Exodus.

---

53. Gary North, *Dominion and Common Grace: The Biblical Basis of Progress* (Tyler, Texas: Institute for Christian Economics, 1987), ch. 6.

54. A variation of this analogy appears in *Common Grace and the Gospel* (Nutley, New Jersey: Presbyterian & Reformed, [1954] 1974). pp. 53-54.

4

A BIBLICAL THEOLOGY OF SLAVERY

The Spirit of the Lord is upon me, because he hath anointed me to preach the gospel to the poor; he hath sent me to heal the brokenhearted, to preach deliverance to the captives, and recovering of sight to the blind, to set at liberty them that are bruised, To preach the acceptable year of the Lord (Luke 4:18-19).

We know that the law is good if a man uses it properly. We also know that law is made not for good men but for lawbreakers and rebels, the ungodly and sinful, the unholy and irreligious; for those who kill their fathers or mothers, for murderers, for adulterers and perverts, for slave traders [kidnappers] and liars and perjurers . . . (I Tim. 1:8-10, NIV).

Without a proper understanding of the theological foundation and institutional functions of indentured servitude in the Old Testament, the reader will be baffled by several of the case laws of Exodus. Modern man's automatic negative reaction against the word "slavery" makes it imperative that the serious Bible student understand the biblical concept of servitude before he begins a study of Exodus 21; otherwise, he will be tempted to conclude in advance that these case laws do not apply today, that they were designed for use by "primitive desert tribes" rather than designed for use by all societies everywhere.

The principle of interpretation that I adopt in my economic commentaries is this: whenever we can discover it, we must begin with the theocentric principle that governs any particular biblical case law, for it is this theocentric relationship which is reflected by the person-to-person relationships established by any particular law. The theocentric principle that governs the Book of Exodus is *God's deliverance of His people in history.* We read at the beginning of Exodus 6, "Then the LORD said unto Moses, Now shalt thou see what I will do to Pharaoh: for with a strong hand he shall let them go, and with a strong hand shall he drive them out of his land" (Ex. 6:1). Israel was delivered out of Pharaoh's strong hand by God's far stronger hand.[1] Pharaoh and the Egyptians figuratively pushed them out of Egypt at the exodus (Ex. 12:31-36). The Book of Exodus is a book about covenant man's service to a powerful King. In Exodus 1, Israel was in slavery to the cruel Pharaoh. In Exodus 40, God descends to sit enthroned as Israel's King. Thus Exodus moves from the old hierarchy to the new, from *slavery to Pharaoh* to *bondservice to God*, which is the only basis of freedom. The Hebrews had learned first-hand what it means to be enslaved to a tyrant. God delivered His people from the strong hand of tyranny. Nevertheless, He did not deliver them out of servitude itself, for there can be no life outside of hierarchical service, meaning *the ethical and institutional subordination of man to his heavenly Master.*

The Book of Exodus is the second book of the Pentateuch (first five books of the Bible). We need to recognize also that this book corresponds to the second point of the five-point biblical covenant model: *authority/hierarchy.* The Pentateuch itself is structured in terms of this five-point model.[2] Thus, we find that the case laws of Exodus are primarily laws governing various hierarchical relationships among men, for these laws reflect the inherently hierarchical legal relationship between God and man.

Point Two of the Covenant: Man's Subordination

At this point, I need to clear up an area of confusion. Ray Sutton's adaptation of the five-point covenant model differs from Meredith G. Kline's with respect to the implications of point two and

---

1. Moses Maimonides' *Mishneh Torah*, "repetition of the law," completed about the year 1180, is usually called *The Code*, but it is also known in Jewish circles as "The Strong Hand": Jacob Schachter, "Talmudical Introductions Down to the Time of Chajes," in Z. H. Chajes, *The Student's Guide Through the Talmud* (London: East and West Library, 1952), p. 3 (footnote). Maimonides viewed Jewish law as God's strong hand. Rabbi Daniel Lapin pointed out to me that its fourteen volumes or sections correspond to the fourteen joints in the human hand. This is believable, given Maimonides' use of other physiological analogies as aids to memorization. For example, following the Talmud (*Makkot* 23b), Maimonides referred to the 613 laws of Judaism as follows: 248 are positive, "their mnemonic is the number of bones in the human body; 365 precepts are negative, and their mnemonic is the number of days in the solar year." Cited in Isadore Twersky, *Introduction to the Code of Maimonides (Mishneh Torah)* (New Haven, Connecticut: Yale University Press, 1980), p. 30. On the judicial teachings of Maimonides, see Appendix B: "Maimonides' *Code*: Is It Biblical?"

2. Gary North, *The Dominion Covenant: Genesis* (2nd ed.; Tyler, Texas: Institute for Christian Economics, 1987), pp. x-xiv.

point five.[3] Kline argues that the second point of the biblical covenant is "historical prologue." This is accurate with respect to what
God does in history. In the case of the exodus, God intervened in history and delivered His people out of bondage. But the primary focus
of the second point of the covenant is on *man's proper response* to the
God who has revealed Himself as the Lord of history. The proper
response is an oath of obedience (point four), man's affirmation of
the ethical terms of God's covenant (point three). *Man is to become
God's permanent vassal.* Kline implicitly recognizes this two-fold aspect
of point two: the king's description of his mighty historical deeds and
the vassal's required subordination. "Following the preamble in the
international suzerainty treaties there was an historical section, written in an I-thou style, which surveyed the previous relationships of
lord and vassal. Its purpose was to establish the historical justification for the lord's continuing reign."[4]

The second commandment is tied to point two: the prohibition of
idolatry, meaning subordination to false gods.[5] It is also significant
that the Book of Revelation is divided into five parts, and the second
section includes the letters to the seven churches that call them to
obey God and reject false idols. The focus is on the overcoming of
the world by Christians.[6] The issue is *authority.* The issue is therefore
also *dominion.*[7] David Chilton cites Revelation 2:26-27:

And he that overcometh, and keepeth my works unto the end, to him
will I give power over the nations: And he shall rule them with a rod of
iron; as the vessels of a potter shall they be broken to shivers: even as I received of my father.

His comments are important: "God the Son has been granted the
rule of all the world, and all nations will come under His messianic

---

3. I do not want to go into detail about the difference with respect to point five.
Kline, an amillennialist, calls it "succession arrangements," and ignores its implications for covenantal history. Sutton shows what this means in covenantal history: the
progressive inheritance of the world by covenant-keepers (Deut. 28:1-14), and the
progressive disinheritance by God of covenant-breakers (Deut. 28:15-68).

4. Meredith G. Kline, *Treaty of the Great King* (Grand Rapids, Michigan: Eerdmans, 1963), p. 52.

5. Gary North, *The Sinai Strategy: Economics and the Ten Commandments* (Tyler,
Texas: Institute for Christian Economics, 1986), ch. 2.

6. David Chilton, *The Days of Vengeance: An Exposition of the Book of Revelation* (Ft.
Worth: Dominion Press, 1987), ch. 2: "The Spirit Speaks to the Church: Overcome!"

7. *Ibid.*, ch. 3: "The Dominion Mandate."

kingship. . . . Whatever opposition is offered against His kingdom
will be crushed absolutely. . . . The point of the quotation here is
that the Christian overcomers, in this age, are promised a share in
the messianic reign of Jesus Christ, in time and on earth. In spite of
all opposition, God has set up His King over the nations (cf. Ps.
2:1-6). Those who are obedient to His commands will rule the world,
reconstructing it for His glory in terms of His laws. Psalm 2 shows
God laughing and sneering at the pitiful attempts of the wicked to
fight against and overthrow His Kingdom. . . . The nation that will
not serve us will perish (Isa. 60:12); all the peoples of the earth will
be subdued under our feet (Ps. 47:1-3) — promises made originally to
Israel, but now to be fulfilled in the New Israel, the Church."[8]

Chilton's *Days of Vengeance* is clearly a postmillennial and theonomic book. Kline totally rejects both positions. He has adopted
Mendenhall's theologically innocuous phrase, "historical prologue"
to describe this section of the covenant model. The phrase softens
the obvious hierarchical and dominical aspects of point two of the
biblical covenant. It was Sutton's lecture and preliminary essays on
the covenant model that persuaded Chilton to restructure his Revelation commentary into a five-point model. Thus, Chilton's self-
conscious adoption of Kline's phrase,[9] rather than Sutton's language
of hierarchy, is misleading; Chilton's terminology makes its appear
that *Days of Vengeance* is closer to Kline's theological use of point two
than to Sutton's, which is obviously not the case, as Kline will be the
first to admit. Sutton's *That You May Prosper* and Chilton's *Days of Vengeance* stand as eloquent refutations of Kline's amillennial rejection of
the God-enforced cause-and-effect relationship between ethics (biblical law) and temporal eschatology (postmillennialism). Sutton is
open about this difference of interpretation;[10] Chilton is not.

Old Testament Slavery Was Covenantal

"Man is born free; and everywhere he is in chains."[11] So begins
Rousseau's *Social Contract* (1762), perhaps the single most influential

---

8. *Ibid.*, p. 117.

9. Part Two: "Historical Prologue: The Letters to the Seven Churches," *ibid.*, p. 85.

10. Ray R. Sutton, *That You May Prosper: Dominion By Covenant* (Tyler, Texas:
Institute for Christian Economics, 1987), Appendix 7: "Meredith G. Kline: Yes and
No."

11. Jean Jacques Rousseau, *The Social Contract* (1762), ch. I. I am using the Cole
edition in Dent's Everyman's Library.

book of political philosophy in the modern West.[12] What Rousseau was struggling with was an apparent anomaly: the presence of slavery in a world that proclaims liberty. It was a variation of a theological dilemma that had plagued the early church fathers from the beginning: the existence of slavery in a world of people born equal in the eyes of God.[13] The early church pointed to sin as the cause of slavery, which it surely is. (This same explanation was familiar and widespread in all Protestant circles in seventeenth-century England.)[14] But this only pushes the problem back one step: What is the biblical meaning of equality? Is all inequality the product of sin? For example, is the subordination of the Second Person of the Trinity to the Father an aspect of sin? Is the subordination of the Holy Spirit to both Father and Son the product of sin? Obviously not. Then what is the meaning of equality?

Equality means the *equality of being*: within the Trinity, and within all of mankind. The three persons of the Trinity are of the same substance and majesty, co-eternal. Similarly, all men are made in God's image, and therefore are equally responsible before the Creator. In neither case is equality the equality of function, for *there is no equality of function*. Covenantal relationships are always hierarchical. This leads us inevitably to the two-fold doctrine of the Trinity: the *ontological* Trinity (equality of being) and the *economical* Trinity (subordination with respect to historical function).[15] Both doctrines must be affirmed in order to preserve Christian orthodoxy. Jesus said that anyone who has seen Him has seen the Father (John 14:9). "I and my Father are one" (John 10:30). Yet He was also a good and faithful *servant* of His Father, doing His Father's business (Luke 2:49), revealing everything that His Father had shown Him (John 6:28; 15:15b). There is equality of being but also functional subordination, even within the Godhead; how much more among men! There is always hierarchy.

---

12. Writes Robert Nisbet: "Plato may be the essential architect of this vision of community, but no one has equalled Rousseau's role in making it the single most attractive vision for modern man. Rousseau is the very archetype of the political modern, the embodiment of what might be called the modernist revolt in politics." Robert Nisbet, *The Social Philosophers: Community and Conflict in Western Thought* (New York: Crowell, 1973), p. 145.

13. R. W. Carlyle and A. J. Carlyle, *A History of Mediaeval Political Theory in the West*, 6 vols. (London: Blackwood, 1962), I, pp. 119-20.

14. Winthrop D. Jordan, *White Over Black: American Attitudes Toward the Negro, 1550-1812* (Chapel Hill: University of North Carolina Press, 1968), pp. 54-55.

15. Cornelius Van Til, *Apologetics* (Syllabus, Westminster Seminary, 1959), p. 8.

Biblically speaking, there can never be a release out of servitude as such, although there can be a release out of human slavery. Men serve one of two masters, God or mammon, meaning God or Satan. The great warfare in history between God and Satan is the war for the covenantal allegiance of men. Men's institutions reflect the nature of the servitude they have chosen: bondservice under God or slavery to Satan. Permanent slavery of man to man is the system that covenant-breaking man autonomously (self-law) establishes, thereby imitating Satan: a system of permanent tyranny. God publicly smashed this permanent slave system at the exodus. In contrast, hierarchical temporary bondservice of man to man under biblical law is the system that God has established for the reformation of covenant-breaking men, which in turn reflects His permanent covenantal rule. Indentured servitude always points to liberty, meaning covenant-keeping liberty under God. Covenant-keeping men are institutionally subordinated to God in terms of a law-order that progressively brings long-term prosperity and liberty (Deut. 28:1-14). Servitude is inescapable, but the forced system of bondage known as *indentured servitude* is used by God to bring self-discipline and maturity to His covenant people. This temporary legal servitude of man to man reflected God's judicial relationship to His people in the Old Covenant era, in which He delivered them from Egypt by placing them under His covenant, but one which was temporary. It would be replaced by a better covenant, Jeremiah announced:

Behold, the days come, saith the LORD, that I will make a new covenant with the house of Israel, and with the house of Judah: Not according to the covenant that I made with their fathers in the day that I took them by the hand to bring them out of the land of Egypt; which my covenant they brake, although I was an husband unto them, saith the LORD (Jer. 31:31-32).

The Hebrew phrase that the King James (and most) translators translated as, "although I was an husband unto them," is somewhat obscure. An alternative reading suggested in the New International Version is: "although I was their master." Jacob J. Rabinowitz has translated it: *although I had acquired ownership in them*. His comments on this passage are illuminating: "The phrase 'I took them by the hand' is used here in the sense of taking formal possession, such as one would take when acquiring ownership of a slave, and the phrase 'although I had acquired ownership in them' (*ba'alti bam*) refers to this formal act; see also Zech. 14:13. This is to be compared with *mancipium*—

the act of taking formal possession under Roman law — which, leading Romanists believe, originally applied only to slaves. . . . More striking perhaps is the parallel to the Roman *mancipium* in Isa. 41:9: *Thou whom I have taken hold of from the ends of the earth, and called thee from the uttermost parts thereof, and said unto thee: 'Thou art My servant,' I have chosen thee and not cast thee away.*"[16] When God delivered them out of Egyptian slavery, He did so by taking formal possession of them as a people. His relationship to them was visibly one of Master and servant. Covenantally, it still is: "No man can serve two masters: for either he will hate the one, and love the other; or else he will hold to the one, and despise the other. Ye cannot serve God and mammon" (Matt. 6:24).

Old Testament Slavery and Criminal Sanctions

The thief is always fully liable economically to make restitution for his criminal acts: ". . . if he have nothing, then he shall be sold for his theft" (Ex. 22:3b). It was the threat of compulsory labor servitude (bondservice) that reinforced the Old Testament's judicial sanction of economic restitution from criminals to their victims. If a poor man committed an economic crime against someone, he had to repay his victim; he did not pay restitution to the State, nor did the State pay restitution to his victims. The punishment therefore fit the crime, for the restitution payments were proportional to the losses that the crimes had inflicted. There was no respect of persons in biblical law: the same sanction applied to all, rich and poor. If the criminal was unable to pay his victim, he was sold into slavery in order to raise the money necessary for repayment. This sale for cash was possible only because a buyer expected to profit from the transaction. He expected to gain a net return from the future productivity of the slave. He was therefore willing to capitalize this expected future productivity by means of a cash payment to the victim.[17]

The criminal's term of service was limited in three ways. *First,* the extent of the damage he inflicted on his victims determined the amount of restitution that he owed to them. This established a ceil-

---

16. Jacob J. Rabinowitz, Introduction, Moses Maimonides, *The Book of Civil Laws*, vol. 13 of *The Code of Maimonides*, 14 vols. (New Haven, Connecticut: Yale University Press, 1949), p. xxi, footnote.

17. "Capitalize": pay a cash price for an expected stream of future net income, discounted by the prevailing rate of interest.

ing on the price the slave-buyer was asked to pay. The worse the damage, the higher this ceiling price. *Second*, the price that the victim received from the buyer was proportional to the time the criminal was expected to serve as a slave. He was allowed to buy his way back into freedom; thus, the lower the initial purchase price, the sooner he could become a free man with any given level of economic performance. *Third*, because he was allowed to redeem himself at any time by paying the owner the pro-rated value of his remaining term of service (Lev. 25:50-52), it follows that the more productive he became as a slave, the sooner he could become a free man. The length of the period of enslavement was inversely related to the ethical performance of the criminal: the better his performance, the shorter the sentence. The punishment fit both the crime and the program of rehabilitation through restitution.

The problem of sanctions faces modern jurisprudence. The punishment should fit the crime, we are told repeatedly — a principle of jurisprudence that is itself a secular manifestation of the biblical principle of jurisprudence. But private chattel slavery is illegal in the modern world (unlike slavery to the State, e.g., slave labor camps). There is no legal market for the labor services of convicted criminals.[18] Because a poor man today probably cannot afford to repay his victims, and he also cannot legally sell his long-term labor services to raise capital for making restitution, the humanist legal system adopts the sanction of prison. Humanism therefore refuses to allow richer criminals to repay their victims, since to allow this would be the economic equivalent of allowing rich criminals to "buy their way out of prison." The humanist believes that this would be judicially discriminatory, for the poor criminal today cannot afford to buy his way out. Therefore, every criminal, rich or poor, faces either prison or probation because of humanism's version of equality before the law ("no respect of persons"). The victims of crime are not allowed to be paid by rich criminals precisely because they cannot be repaid by poor criminals, given the absence of a legal slave market. Humanism's doctrine of equality before the law, *given the absence of legalized bondservice*, has led step by step to a system of law enforcement in which *victims are always the losers*. Because there is no longer a

---

18. Decades ago, prisons in the American South would rent collective labor services of inmates to private employers, but pressure from labor unions and humanitarians has generally ended this practice. In any case, the rent payments went to the prison system, not to the victims of crime.

legal market for the purchase of long-term labor services,[19] the civil courts have adopted imprisonment as the normal criminal sanction, a sanction in which the victim is not repaid. Furthermore, as a taxpayer who finances the prison system, the victim is subsequently forced to suffer additional economic losses.

The modern prison system is the product of the perverse logic of humanism. Humanists do not believe in making eternal restitution to the God of the Bible. They reject the doctrine of hell and the lake of fire. Nevertheless, the doctrine of hell is an inescapable concept. The question is: Who will impose it, man or God? The prison is the modern humanist State's equivalent of hell: an unproductive place of confinement from which the prisoner cannot legally buy his freedom. The prison is a widely acknowledged institutional failure,[20] but humanists cannot bring themselves to abandon it, because in order to do so, they might be forced to reconsider their denial of the biblical principle of restitution to victims, as well as its economic concomitant, legalized bondservice. They much prefer the slavery of unproductive, taxpayer-financed prison sentences to the Bible's system of bondservice — a bondservice which points all too clearly to God's eternal punishment of unrepentant rebels who refuse to accept God's exclusive system of restitution: the substitutionary atonement of Jesus Christ.

"Serving time" in prison is today preposterously referred to as "paying one's debt to society." In fact, the reverse is true: society (taxpayers) must finance the criminal's period of incarceration. Taxpayers and criminals alike pay a debt to the State, for it is the State's bureaucratic functionaries who become the recipients of the tax money. The State, as the operational god of this age, receives its restitution payment. But in today's humanistic theocracy, victims receive nothing except subpoenas to testify in court and bills from the tax collector. In the Old Testament, "serving time" meant *serving other men productively* in a compulsory employment system that benefited everyone: victims, slave-buyers, criminals who learned obedience and work skills, and society at large, which always needs sanctions

---

19. There are a few exceptions: voluntary enlistment into the monopoly armed services and labor contracts with large cash bonuses for prominent sports figures. Athletes are forbidden by law from selling their services to rival team owners until their contracts expire, although team owners are allowed to sell these contracts to other team owners.

20. Cf. Jessica Mitford, *Kind and Usual Punishment: The Prison Business* (New York: Knopf, 1973).

against criminals to protect itself. Today, the sanctions are themselves criminal: they penalize the victims a second time (tax bills for prisons). The victims are robbed twice. They are threatened with violence if they refuse to pay: first by the robber, then by the tax collector.

The perverse nature of the modern criminal justice system is slowly beginning to be recognized. A handful of judges are trying to impose a system of restitution by criminals to victims. But this attempt suffers greatly from the fact that there is no ready market for the capitalized value of the criminal's future stream of production because indentured servitude is illegal. The dilemma of the judge has been stated by Judge Lois Forer: "Most defendants I see are unemployed, often unemployable. A sentence of restitution or reparation may not be enforceable. On occasion it has spurred a defendant who has been on welfare for years to go out and get a job. It rarely produces adequate compensation to the victim. But the underlying principle seems to me to be valid. If people are to be held legally responsible for their acts, it follows that they should be responsible for the harm they have caused."[21] What the modern humanist dares not admit to himself or in public — and what embarrassed Christians also are fearful of admitting — is that the Bible's system of indentured servitude for criminals was *and still is* basic to the Bible's system of justice in which criminals are made legally *and economically* responsible for the harm they have caused.

Confusion Over Definitions: Slave and Bondservant

The Ten Commandments summarize for man the moral and legal foundations of a free society. Immediately following the presentation of these principles of freedom, God gives the laws regarding the freeing of indentured servants. A nation of former slaves could appreciate these laws. They had endured the trials of a slave society. If ever there were people who were ready, historically and environmentally, for a message of cultural liberation, they were the Hebrews of the exodus period. Therefore, before considering the specific implications of this verses governing slave marriages (Ex. 21:2-11), we need first to consider the role of slavery in the Old Testament period.

Before considering slavery in general, let us consider the use of the term in the Bible. This following fact may astound some readers;

---

21. Lois G. Forer, *Criminals and Victims: A Trial Judge Reflects on Crime and Punishment* (New York: Norton, 1980), p. 12.

it certainly astounded me. The word "slave" appears only once in the King James Bible: "Is Israel a servant? Is he a homeborn slave?" (Jer. 2:14a). The word "slaves" also appears only once, in reference to the wealth of mystery Babylon: ". . . horses, and chariots, and slaves, and souls of men" (Rev. 18:13b). The word "slavery" does not appear anywhere in the King James Version. The words "servant" and "servants" appear repeatedly throughout the King James Bible. The Hebrew and Greek terms do not distinguish grammatically or etymologically between indentured servitude and permanent slavery. We must therefore look at the various contexts in order to discover what information the Bible's authors intended to convey.

When English-speaking people use the word "slavery," they have in mind especially the West's Negro slave system, or perhaps some other system of permanent slavery. The word produces a kind of "knee-jerk" negative response. This is why it has been so difficult for Christians to discuss the Old Testament institution of slavery in a calm, analytical manner.[22] For example, in a hostile article attacking the Reconstruction movement, author Rodney Clapp warns his readers: "More startling than any degree of influence, however, is what Reconstructionists actually propose for society: the abolition of democracy and the reinstitution of slavery, for starters."[23] He never cites any evidence for his accusation. There is a reason for this gap in his documentation: Christian Reconstructionists *do* believe in democracy — meaning representative republican government, with Old Testament Israel as the model[24] — and they do *not* believe in slavery along the lines of Western Negro slavery.[25] What Christian Reconstructionists do accept is the continuing moral validity of the Old Testament's system of indentured servitude: for debt repayment (instead of nearly painless declarations of bankruptcy) and for restitution payments to victims by criminals.

Because of this confusion in terminology between indentured servitude and permanent slavery, any forthright discussion of slav-

22. David Chilton, *Productive Christians in an Age of Guilt-Manipulators: A Biblical Response to Ronald J. Sider* (4th ed.; Tyler, Texas: Institute for Christian Economics, 1986), pp. 59-66.

23. Rodney Clapp, "Democracy as Heresy," *Christianity Today* (Feb. 20, 1987), p. 17.

24. This was argued in the late nineteenth century by E. C. Wines in his book, *The Hebrew Republic*, which was reprinted in 1980 by the American Presbyterian Press, Rt. 1, Box 65-2, Wrightstown, NJ 08562.

25. See Gary North, "Honest Reporting As Heresy: My Response to *Christianity Today*" (1987), a report published by the Institute for Christian Economics.

ery in the Old Testament is likely to create many initial misunder-
standings. The only form of permanent slavery in the Old Testament was the enslavement of heathens: "Both thy bondmen, and thy
bondmaids, which thou shalt have, shall be of the heathen that are
round about you; of them shall ye buy bondmen and bondmaids.
Moreover of the children of the strangers that do sojourn among
you, of them shall ye buy, and of their families that are with you,
which they begat in your land: and they shall be your possession.
And ye shall take them as an inheritance for your children after you,
to inherit them for a possession; they shall be your bondmen for
ever: but over your brethren the children of Israel, ye shall not rule
over one another with rigour" (Lev. 25:44-46). I argue later in this
chapter that this slave law was abolished with the fulfillment of the
jubilee year by Jesus.

It was legal for the Israelites to make permanent slaves of defeated non-Canaanite enemies, but only of the women and children.
A distant non-Canaanite nation was always to be given an opportunity to surrender; if it did, its inhabitants were to become distant
tributaries, not household slaves. The Old Testament required the
total annihilation of all male opponents in a distant (non-Canaan)
war if the city had been offered terms of peace and had refused to
surrender (Deut. 20:10-13). Thus, a common means of gaining large
numbers of slaves—military conquest—was partially closed to
Israel. It was lawful to take captive only the women and children
(Deut. 20:14-15). Captured women were likely to become wives or
concubines, with their offspring becoming true family members in
the household, not a subclass of slaves. Furthermore, if a man married one of them and then grew tired of her, she had to be released as
a free woman (Deut. 21:10-14). Israel's policy regarding militarily defeated cities was a dual process of *adoption* (females and children) and
annihilation (adult males) through conquest. Men, as the heads of
households, either surrendered to the invading Israelites or else they
perished, but the system was not primarily one geared to permanent
enslavement.[26]

---

26. The fulfillment of the jubilee year by Christ would seem to have annulled
these wartime slave provisions: no more permanent heathen slaves. It may be that
this fulfillment is also the basis for annulling the requirement of the extermination of
foreign male enemies after a military victory. More likely, however, extermination is
annulled by the requirement to honor the universal extension of the gospel. Instead
of killing all the men, a victorious Christian nation would root out the defeated nation's public pagan religious practices, and then foster cooperation between churches

This was not only true of Israel; it was true of Mesopotamia in general. Military captives were primarily women and children; the men were executed, or, occasionally, placed into the king's personal bodyguard. Only the State could afford to make large numbers of captives into full-time slaves. I. J. Gelb writes: "Immediately upon their capture, POWs are slave property of the crown/state. As such, they are abused and exploited in the extreme. They may be worked to death on monumental projects of the crown."[27] In the New Assyrian period, captives were dispersed throughout the kingdom, turning them into free laborers. But full slavery based on the labor of military captives was not practical in the low-output agricultural kingdoms of Mesopotamia. The absence of Mesopotamian records of slave revolts, unlike Greece and Rome, indicates that slavery was not widespread there.[28]

In any case, such foreign wars would have been rare under biblical law, for Israel was prohibited from maintaining a standing army of any militarily significant size (Deut. 17:16).[29] Therefore, Exodus 21:2-4 does not deal with lifetime slavery of foreigners; it deals instead with temporary indentured servitude. Thus, what this chapter is intended to clarify is the system of *indentured servitude* in the Old Testament, and its possible applications in the modern world. I have chosen to use the King James terminology of servitude rather than slavery when referring to this Old Testament institution. The King James translators were being faithful to the meaning of the Hebrew words.

The Indentured Servitude of Hebrews

To understand properly the case laws of Exodus 21-23, we must first understand that God was placing the Hebrews under a form of

---

in the defeated nation and churches in the victorious nation, allowing churches in the defeated nation to call in missionaries from the victorious nation without resistance from the now-defeated anti-Christian leadership. Conquest today is to be primarily theological and cultural, not military: Gary North, *Healer of the Nations: Biblical Blueprints for International Relations* (Ft. Worth, Texas: Dominion Press, 1987). Cultural conquest is what the humanist U.S. imposed on defeated Japan, 1945-53, with remarkable success: having been forced by the Americans to abandon militarism, the Japanese economy subsequently outperformed the U.S. economy.

27. I. J. Gelb, "Prisoners of War in Early Mesopotamia," *Journal of Near Eastern Studies*, XXXII (1973), p. 95.

28. *Ibid.*, p. 96.

29. James B. Jordan, "The Israelite Militia in the Old Testament," in Morgan Norvel (ed.), *The Militia in 20th Century America* (Falls Church, Virginia: Gun Owners Foundation, 1985), pp. 23-40.

temporary indentured servitude, to test them, teach them, and provide them with the self-discipline necessary for spiritual and cultural maturity. *Wherever there is sin, there must remain some traces of the institution of indentured servitude,* although there is progressive release from the visible manifestations of this system as men and societies progressively conform themselves to the ethical terms of God's covenant (point three of the covenant model).[30]

At the beginning of Israel's release from Egyptian slavery, the people were not ready for full-scale dominion, for they were still suffering from the slave's mentality. That first generation was especially blinded by such an outlook, and they never ceased murmuring against Moses. They never ceased looking favorably back over their shoulders at the memory of Egyptian slavery (Ex. 16:3; Num. 11:5-6; 21:5; Ps. 106:7-25). Their heirs did not consistently perform significantly better, which is why God delivered them into foreign slavery again and again (Ps. 106:34-43). Thus, immediately following Exodus 20, in which God gives His people the Ten Commandments, we find a law that regulates the release of Hebrew bondservants. It stipulates that if a man marries during his period as a servant, his wife and children must remain with the master (Ex. 21:2-3).[31]

The modern reader, both Christian and non-Christian, is initially appalled by this law. It appears to condone chattel slavery: the ownership and control of human beings by other human beings. It also singles out wives of bondservants as second-class citizens who are not entitled to freedom; they are not allowed to go free with their husbands, or so the text indicates. Furthermore, no matter how much Christian commentators wriggle to get free, they cannot escape the fact that there is one passage in the Old Testament that unquestionably condones perpetual, or nearly perpetual, chattel slavery: Leviticus 25:44-46. The Creator and Sustainer of the universe, the Trinity, the Lord God Jehovah, unquestionably sanctioned slavery, at least for fourteen hundred years. Thus, at least for fourteen hundred years, slavery, *when regulated by God's law,* was not immoral. To have challenged its moral legitimacy and to have sought to abolish it during that period would have been an act of revolution against God. Whether or not modern Christian and Jewish commentators feel comfortable with this fact, it is nonetheless a fact.

---

30. Sutton, *That You May Prosper,* ch. 3.
31. See Chapter 5: "Servitude, Protection, and Marriage."

The Old Testament unquestionably authorized certain forms of slavery, and the New Testament does not explicitly alter these Old Testament institutions. Only an implicit change can be said to have resulted in the annulment of one form (and only one form) of Old Testament slavery, the perpetual enslavement of heathens: *Jesus Christ's fulfillment of the provisions of the jubilee year* (Luke 4:16-21). As far as I am aware, I am the first author to suggest this judicial application of Luke 4, so it has had no effect in the history of any Christian society's slave policies. (Even if I am not the first — and I am probably not — it has not been a familiar argument historically.) Perhaps it will have some impact on the future of slavery.

What God established for a certain class of Hebrew citizens was more like a system of indentured servitude, at least for the Israelites in their dealings with fellow believers.[32] Five forms of servitude for Hebrews existed in ancient Israel:

1. Debt bondservice for up to almost seven years
2. Becoming a permanent hired laborer for up to 49 years
3. Up to 49 years as a bondservant in a resident alien's household
4. Restitution bondservice for convicted criminals
5. Voluntary lifetime servitude in a Hebrew's household

1. Sabbath-Year-Release Bondservice

The first form of servitude was governed by the terms of the national sabbatical year. An individual Hebrew could ask his fellow Hebrew for a zero-interest charitable loan, and the potential lender was required by God to give it, if he could afford to. There were no negative civil sanctions associated with a refusal to lend a zero-interest charitable loan, but God did threaten historical sanctions: a refusal to provide positive blessings (Deut. 15:9-10). A failure to repay this loan on time could result in his temporary enslavement until the sabbatical year of release. In the sabbatical year, when all *charitable* debts were cancelled, Hebrew servants were to be released (Deut. 15).[33] In this form of servitude, bondage in ancient Israel was treated by the

---

32. J. J. Finkelstein, *The Ox That Gored* (Philadelphia: American Philosophical Society, 1981), p. 25.

33. The Code of Hammurabi limits to three years the debt bondage to a free person or person of higher standing; in the fourth year, he (and his wife and children) go free: CH, paragraph 117. "The Code of Hammurabi," trans. Theophile J. Meek, in *Ancient Near Eastern Texts Relating to the Old Testament*, edited by James B. Pritchard (3rd ed.; Princeton, New Jersey: Princeton University Press, 1969), pp. 170-71.

civil law as a form of debt, just as debt was treated as a form of servitude: the same year of release applied to both. A person could therefore keep from having to lease his land for a cash payment in advance, but to receive this morally mandatory, economically unsecured, zero-interest loan from his Hebrew neighbor, he had to become a bondservant until the next sabbatical year. An emergency might require this; also, failure to repay a debt might require this.

Hebrew servant-owners were not permitted to oppress their Hebrew servants. At the end of the term of bondage, the master was required to provide the departing servant with capital: "And when thou sendeth him out free from thee, thou shalt not let him go away empty: Thou shalt furnish him liberally out of thy flock, and out of thy floor, and out of thy winepress: of that wherewith the LORD thy God hath blessed thee thou shalt give unto him" (Deut. 15:13-14). By providing the ex-bondservant with capital, the master was encouraging the man to become economically independent. The man would not be forced back into servitude simply because he could not finance whatever skills he had developed during his years as a servant. He had capital; he had been given what was called in colonial American history his "freedom dues."[34] Therefore, the ex-bondservant

---

34. The customs governing indentured servitude in colonial America in the seventeenth and eighteenth centuries limited the term of service to a maximum of seven years, and required the master to provide the departing servant or apprentice with the tools of the trade he had learned. These "freedom dues" generally consisted of a suit or two of clothes, a set of tools, a rifle, and, prior to the mid-eighteenth century, sometimes 50 acres of land. See Oscar Theodore Barck, Jr. and Hugh Talmadge Lefler, *Colonial America* (New York: Macmillan, [1958] 1964), p. 297. John Van Der Zee reports that both Virginia and Maryland granted 50 acres of land to all immigrants, but the land-owners who paid the indentured servants' fare generally wound up as the owners. Between 1670 and 1680, of the 5,000 indentured servants entitled to receive 50 acres, only 1,300 actually collected, and of these 900 immediately sold their land. Only 241 took warrants for land. "In all, less than 4 percent of the people who entered the colony as servants finished out their time and settled as freeman." Van Der Zee, *Bound Over: Indentured Servitude and American Conscience* (New York: Simon & Schuster, 1985), p. 38. President James Madison's forefather, John Maddison, brought in indentured servants to Virginia and collected their land: 800 acres in 1657, 300 in 1662, 200 in 1664: *ibid.*, p. 40.

For a popular narrative history of indentured servitude, see Clifford Lindsey Alderman, *Colonists for Sale: The Story of Indentured Servants in America* (New York: Macmillan, 1975). He provides evidence that servants were not always rewarded with much upon their release: pp. 57-58, 74-75, 88-89. Cf. Warren B. Smith, *White Servitude in Colonial South Carolina* (Columbia: University of South Carolina Press, 1901); Cheeseman A. Herrick, *White Servitude in Pennsylvania* (Philadelphia: McVey, 1926); Abbott Emerson Smith, *Colonists in Bondage: White Servitude and Convict Labor in America, 1607-1776* (Chapel Hill: University of North Carolina Press, 1947).

would normally have had no excuse for a return to servitude except his own incompetence. It would not be his former master's fault. As James Jordan has said, "*The purpose of slavery . . . is to train irresponsible men into productive covenant members.*"[35]

It is important to understand that this grant of material capital was not the primary basis of the ex-servant's future economic independence. The major form of capital that he was to take from his place of former servitude was ethical and psychological. He then would return to his family inheritance, his land. He had learned to discipline himself under the threat of physical punishment, just as a child learns. He had been given an opportunity to lengthen his time perspective. He had been under the direction of a successful manager, someone who could afford to purchase a servant. Being managed by a good manager is one of the best ways to become a good manager. Also, those who serve others faithfully learn to lead others effectively. Cost-effective consumer-oriented service is the basis of economic success in a free society.[36] Thus, short-term indentured servitude was designed to produce long-term independence, just as slavery in Egypt was part of God's plan to make the Hebrews the conquerors of Canaan.

Anyone who argues that the sabbatical year of release only applied to the seventh year, and then the charity debt's obligation was reimposed in the eighth year, faces a very difficult exegetical problem: how to avoid the parallel conclusion, that indentured servitude also was reimposed in the eighth year. I see no way out: anyone who affirms the reimposition of the previous debt must also affirm the reimposition of previous indentured servitude. Only the jubilee year could therefore bring permanent release from the indentured servitude of the charitable loan. But if Jesus did away with the jubilee year by fulfilling it and then by transferring the kingdom to the international church (Matt. 21:43), as I argue, then what temporal limit, other than the death of the person in bondage, is placed on either debt or servitude? There is no indication that Jesus annulled the principle of the sabbatical year, but if the sabbatical year does not permanently release the debtor or the servant, and the jubilee year is gone, there appears to be less economic liberation in the New Testa-

---

35. James B. Jordan, *The Law of the Covenant: An Exposition of Exodus 21-23* (Tyler, Texas: Institute for Christian Economics, 1984), p. 77. Emphasis in the original.

36. Ludwig von Mises, *Human Action: A Treatise on Economics* (3rd ed.; Chicago: Regnery, 1966), pp. 269-72.

ment era than in the Old. I prefer not to follow this approach in describing the sabbatical year.

2. Jubilee-Release Bondservice

The second form of servitude was different. It applied to someone who had leased his land to another person, and who subsequently fell into poverty again. Let us consider the land lease first. A poor person could go to another person, Hebrew or resident alien, and offer him a long-term leasehold arrangement. The purchaser of the lease was able to make a cash payment to buy control over the first person's land. Such a purchase was temporally limited by the occurrence of the next jubilee year, the year following the seventh national sabbatical year. The individual could legally redeem the land at any time by paying to the leaseholder the pro-rated value remaining until the jubilee year. Also, his kinsman was allowed to repurchase the land for him on the same basis (Lev. 25:25-28). This transaction was strictly business; the potential purchaser was not told by God that he had any moral obligation to enter into such a transaction.

If a person without land fell into poverty again, he could lease himself in the same way that he had previously leased his land. He could seek an immediate cash payment in exchange for the promise of personal household service until the next jubilee year. This *capitalized sale of future labor services* also applied to a poor landless urban dweller. This transaction was also strictly business; the potential purchaser was not told by God that he had any moral obligation to enter into such a transaction.

Such a jubilee-release bondservant could not legally be treated as harshly as a sabbath-year-release bondservant could be. This was therefore a less rigorous form of servitude physically, but more extensive temporally (except in the final seven years prior to a jubilee year).

And if thy brother that dwelleth by thee be waxen poor, and be sold unto thee; thou shalt not compel him to serve as a bondservant: But as an hired servant, and as a sojourner, he shall be with thee, and shall serve thee unto the year of jubilee: And then he shall depart from thee, both he and his children with him, and shall return unto his own family, and unto the possession of his fathers shall he return (Lev. 25:39-41).

The master was warned: "Thou shalt not rule over him with rigour; but shall fear thy God" (Lev. 25:43).

The immediate question that must be answered is this: What did it mean to be a hired servant in ancient Israel? A hired servant was to be paid daily (Lev. 19:13). He was also free to leave his place of employment at any time. This made him a day laborer, or more precisely, a day-to-day laborer. Not so the bondservant, for obvious reasons. First, his wage payments had been capitalized in advance by the payment of the original purchase price. Second, he owed the master this money, or its pro-rated share until the jubilee year, before he could lawfully depart.

Did the master pay him daily wages in addition to the original capitalized payment? He had this option, of course, as a means of stimulating greater productivity from his bondservant. "Pay a man peanuts," says the old slogan, "and you've hired a monkey." The law does not say, however, that the master was required to pay a jubilee-release bondservant daily wages, since he had already paid the servant (or his creditor) the present discounted value of these wages when he purchased him. It must be understood that this capitalized value of future labor services was the economic and legal equivalent of the daily wages owed to a day laborer. Furthermore, the bondservant could not leave the employ of the master, as already mentioned. So, the only relevant context of the requirement that he be treated as a hired servant must refer to *corporal punishment*. The master would have suffered "eye for eye" civil penalties if he flogged the servant or in other ways abused him physically, unlike the owner of a sabbath-year-release bondservant, who could legally be subjected to corporal punishment (Ex. 21:20-21).

If the indentured laborer was not under the threat of the same sorts of physical compulsion that a debt bondservant was, then what kind of effective sanctions could the master lawfully impose on a reluctant servant? If the master had decided to pay him wages, he could then impose reduced wages, making it more difficult for the man to buy his way out of servitude. This would be the same penalty that could be imposed on any other unproductive hired laborer. But there was this difference: a hired laborer could leave his employer at will. Not so the indentured servant. He was legally bound to stay with his master until the purchase price was repaid. If he departed, this was the equivalent of theft of the principal sum. If convicted of theft, he could then have been sold into lifetime criminal servitude in order to repay the victimized original master. This was a highly feared sanction: the jubilee year would then no longer protect him.

This means that if the master had decided not to pay him any daily wages, the only visible sanction against his slothful behavior was his very position as a bondservant. But this was his condition whether he was slothful or not. Thus, the master needed additional sanctions—"sanctions at the margin"—to compel better service. Without them, the wage-less servant would have had no externally imposed incentives to obey. Biblical law does not say what additional sanctions could be lawfully imposed, but the law always allows the imposition of sanctions. A governing principle of biblical law is this: "Without sanctions, there is no law." (The sanctions sometimes are applied in history and eternity by God rather than by human governments in history—for example, the law against economic oppression [Ex. 22:21-24].)[37] Thus, I conclude from the law's very silence that the master could have taken a recalcitrant bondservant before the local civil magistrates. They were implicitly authorized to flog servants who violated the laws of the household. Surely this was the case, since they were required to try and then execute rebellious adult sons (Deut. 21:18-21). The implicit judicial restriction against corporal punishment—the requirement to treat all Hebrew jubilee-release bondservants as hired laborers—was placed on the master acting autonomously, but not on the magistrates acting corporately. Also, the master could sell a slothful servant to a resident alien, a publicly visible downward move by the latter on the Israelite social scale.

In summary, what this means is that a poor Hebrew could lawfully capitalize the expected future value of his family's land and also the expected future value of his family's labor services, although his children could escape this latter obligation at age 20, when they became legal adults. This is another way of saying that the poverty-stricken Hebrew could lawfully sell his future labor, including his family's future labor, for a *discounted cash price*.

The degree of servitude required by the Hebrew bondservant, as well as the appropriate level of pay (initial purchase price) he was entitled to, were both to be equivalent to what was owed from and to the hired day laborer. The hired servant was to be paid a daily wage (Lev. 19:13). Competitive market conditions would determine the appropriate pay scale. Thus, the imputed or estimated stream of future income (discounted by the prevailing market rate of interest) that was to be used by the purchaser in order to establish the capitalized price was this level of wages.

---

37. See Chapter 22: "Oppression, Omniscience, and Judgment."

As I said in the previous section, the Hebrew who was sold into slavery in order to repay a morally obligatory charitable loan (Deut. 15:12) was to be treated as a laborer worth twice as much as a hired servant. He was therefore to be sent away with capital at the end of his term of service (Deut. 15:13-14) because he was worth twice as much as a hired laborer (Deut. 15:18). He remained in bondage until the sabbatical year. In contrast, the Hebrew who was sold into slavery in order to repay a conventional, profit-seeking, non-compulsory personal or business loan came under the release provisions of the more distant jubilee year rather than the sabbatical year. He was said to be worth the same as a hired servant, but not twice as much. As I explain in the next section, the economic effect of the debt laws of Israel was to create a tendency for such insolvent and short-sighted people to wind up as long-term indentured servants in the households of heathen resident aliens.

3. Hebrew Bondservice in Resident Alien Households

The foreigner within the land of Israel could also buy a Hebrew to serve him until the next jubilee year. This period of servitude could be up to 49 years, although it would usually have been a shorter period. The person's next of kin, the kinsman-redeemer, had the responsibility of buying the indentured Hebrew out of bondage to the foreigner, if possible (Lev. 25:47-52). The price owed to the foreigner was pro-rated by the years remaining until the jubilee (vv. 51-52).

Why would a Hebrew sell himself to a resident alien instead of to another Hebrew? One reason is that the potential Hebrew purchaser of long-term labor services was under a prior economic restraint: he was morally obligated (though not judicially obligated) to lend to the destitute Hebrew neighbor under the terms of charitable (sabbath-year-release) bondservice. He did not tie up too much money in such transactions, since they were short-term loans, but there was a degree of risk. The risk of default increased as the year of release grew closer (Deut. 15:9), and the lender also had to provide the servant with capital in the year of release. Money available for buying long-term bondservants was supposed to be money left over after having made these charitable loans. If the charitably indebted Hebrew defaulted on his charitable loan, he could then be sold into short-term but judicially rigorous bondage to repay whatever principal was owed. This would have supplied a large percentage of Israel's indentured labor services.

Another reason why such demand for jubilee-release bondservants would have been reduced was the fact that a Hebrew who was
in the market for long-term servants could purchase heathen foreigners or the children of resident aliens as permanent slaves (Lev.
25:45-46). This purchase allowed him to gain ten generations of
bondservants for his family. So, there was presumably less demand
in Hebrew households for jubilee-release bondservants compared to
sabbath-year-release Hebrew bondservants and permanent heathen
bondservants.

The resident alien was under no moral obligation to make zero-
interest charitable loans to anyone. The Old Testament's laws of
debt did not compel him to lend. The Bible views the extension of
credit as a tool of dominion. It therefore does not require those outside the covenant to extend loans to those inside the covenant. But it
does not prohibit such loans. Old Testament law encouraged the
Hebrews to gain control over heathens in general by lending to
them: "For the LORD thy God blesseth thee, as he promised thee: and
thou shalt lend unto many nations, but thou shalt not borrow; and
thou shalt reign over many nations, but they shall not reign over
thee" (Deut. 15:6). This was a God-authorized means of dominion in
the Old Covenant era (cf. Isa. 45:14).

Resident aliens knew all about this law. The whole law was read
in the presence of the assembled nation every sabbatical year, and
this included resident aliens (Deut. 31:12). I presume, sin being what
it is and envy being what it is, that economically prosperous resident
aliens probably derived considerable pleasure in placing Hebrews in
long-term bondservice. God's law recognized this sinful tendency
and took advantage of it, as surely as God also took advantage of the
sinful intentions of heathen Empire-builders when He delivered
Israel into their hands temporarily. What we must understand is that
*the Old Testament laws regarding debt gave a competitive economic and legal
advantage to the resident alien who wanted to bring an improvident Hebrew
into long-term bondage.* That is to say, the debt laws placed at a covenantal disadvantage any landless Hebrew who was so improvident
that he needed a large loan. Why? Because to be in debt is in principle (and principal) the equivalent of servitude (Prov. 22:7). In order
to call this economic and psychological fact to the attention of covenant-keepers who were thinking about becoming debtors, biblical
law created economic incentives for the enemies of God to exercise

long-term authority over covenant-keeping but present-oriented debtors. Resident aliens became the local rods of God's displeasure with covenant-keepers who were economically and psychologically present-oriented, meaning people with high time-preference (high interest rates) — the Esaus of the world.[38] To become a permanent servant in the household of a resident alien was a visible reminder to all of Israel of the inevitable eternal fate of those who owe a payment to God, and who then default on judgment day.

A landless Hebrew who wanted to borrow a lot of money would probably have gone to a resident alien lender, since the heathen was in a competitive market position in relation to potential Hebrew purchases of Hebrew long-term bondservants. He could place the Hebrew and his family in long-term bondage if the Hebrew defaulted on his loan. In any case, no matter who made the initial loan, Hebrew or heathen, the person most likely to provide the creditor with cash to repay a defaulted loan would have been the resident alien. He was in a strong competitive position in the market for long-term Hebrew bondservants. High debt was therefore to be avoided; its potentially evil consequences pointed to a lifetime of servitude to a resident alien. This, of course, is exactly what God warned them about in the list of curses in Deuteronomy 28:

> The stranger that is within thee shall get up above thee very high; and thou shalt come down very low. He shall lend to thee, and thou shalt not lend to him: he shall be the head, and thou shalt be the tail. Moreover all these curses shall come upon thee, and shall pursue thee, and overtake thee, till thou be destroyed; because thou hearkenedst not unto the voice of the LORD thy God, to keep his commandments and his statutes which he commanded thee (vv. 43-45).

High debt was therefore a preliminary step toward the fulfillment of this curse. The debtor was the servant of the lender (Prov. 22:7); the reckless, present-oriented debtor was in principle already the servant of the foreign lender. *High debt testified to the moral evil that God promised to judge them for.* God established laws regulating servitude that made it easier for a resident alien to gain control over a big-spending Hebrew debtor than for a fellow Hebrew to gain control over him. High debt, in this sense, was treated as *near-apostasy* — potential subordination to uncircumcised aliens who were still in-

38. North, *Dominion Covenant: Genesis*, ch. 18.

fluenced by foreign household gods[39] — because personal bankruptcy could result in lifetime servitude in a resident alien's household.

A poor Hebrew without land could legally indenture himself to a Hebrew master, but if he could get no Hebrew to buy his long-term labor services, he would then have to go to a resident alien. Like the Hebrew master, the resident alien did not have to pay the Hebrew bondservant anything; he only had to feed, clothe, and shelter him. This was a disgraceful condition to be in: under the long-term domination of a covenant-breaker. Only one form of servitude had lower status: criminal bondservice.

4. Criminal Bondservice

The criminal who had stolen from someone owed restitution. Sometimes the criminal would not have had sufficient capital to repay the victim. He would then have been sold into servitude. The money would have gone to the victim or victims. There was no time limit on this form of servitude. There was also no guaranteed wage. A kinsman could redeem a criminal, but criminals were not under the release provisions of the sabbatical year or the jubilee year. He had become a covenantal stranger in Israel, and so did not gain the protection of the jubilee year. To interpret his situation differently would mean that as the year of jubilee approached, the declining sanctions chronologically would have acted as a subsidy to criminal behavior. The criminal might think: "Since I cannot be enslaved beyond the jubilee year, I cannot be compelled to make full restitution." This would have subsidized crime, which God's law is not intended to do. Also, it would have pointed symbolically to the idea of eternal punishment as temporally limited, despite a sinner's inability to make full restitution to God. This would have been an inaccurate symbol. The sinner is never released if he refuses the offer of freedom by man's kinsman-redeemer, Jesus Christ. The parable of the unjust debtor teaches that the sinner who owes God much is thrown into cosmic servitude, to be tormented forever, unable to repay (Matt. 18:34).

The criminal had broken the covenant, and he therefore had to remain a slave until his debt was paid. But this judicial infraction on

---

39. If Israel allowed aliens to bring their household gods into the land with them, and worship them in their homes, then the Hebrew servant was exposed to great evil. If, as seems likely, resident aliens were required to destroy their idols before permanently residing in the land, there would still have been occult cultural residues in their homes.

his part did not obligate his children to remain in slavery. He was not covenanted to a foreign god; he had simply broken the terms of God's covenant. The sins of the father did not obligate his adult sons (Deut. 24:16).

5. Lifetime Voluntary Bondservice

In Exodus 21:5-6, we find legal provisions whereby a servant in Israel was allowed to become a lifetime servant to a master.[40] It is repeated in Deuteronomy 15:16-17. No other law code in the ancient Near East has any similar provision.[41] A male Hebrew servant had the option of adopting a life of permanent servitude. (There is no indication that his adult children were under the terms of their father's personal covenant.) Such servitude was more like being adopted into a Hebrew household as a son, second-class. Nevertheless, the entrenched humanism of modern thought cannot tolerate the idea that a person would ever be given an opportunity to choose between personal independence and the lifetime covenantal bond of the family.[42] But such a lifetime bond is the very essence of the marriage covenant.[43] The Bible requires just such a choice under certain historical circumstances, the main one being the decision to marry.

A Hebrew could legitimately become a lifetime servant voluntarily (Ex. 21:5-6). He could also be put into lifetime bondage in order to make restitution for the crime of theft when he did not have sufficient assets to make restitution to the victim (Ex. 22:3). The institution of servitude in the Old Testament was quite properly understood as a legitimate one, *when governed by the Bible's laws concerning servitude*. The warning of Proverbs against debt used the example of the servant to convince men of its great dangers: "The rich ruleth over the poor, and the borrower is servant to the lender" (Prov. 22:7). While

---

40. Jordan, *The Law of the Covenant*, pp. 77-84.

41. Mendelsohn, *Slavery In the Ancient Near East* (New York: Oxford University Press, 1949), p. 18.

42. Libertarian theorist and economist Murray Rothbard writes: "Because a man's self-ownership over his will is inalienable, he cannot, on the unhampered market, be compelled to continue an arrangement whereby he submits his will to the orders of another, even though he might have agreed to this arrangement previously." Rothbard, *Man, Economy, and State* (New York: New York University Press, [1962] 1979), p. 142.

43. Rothbard understands this. He continues in a footnote: "This applies also to *marriage contracts*. Since human self-ownership cannot be alienated, a man or a woman, on a free market, could not be compelled to continue in marriage if he or she no longer desired to do so. This is regardless of any previous agreement." *Ibid.*, pp. 441-42.

there were legitimate reasons for going into indentured servitude, God's law informed the Hebrews, it was best to maintain one's freedom; the same was true of avoiding debt.

Servitude and Debt

Meir Tamari is probably the most influential Orthodox Jewish economist in the State of Israel. He serves as Chief Economist in the Office of the Governor of the Bank of Israel in Jerusalem and also as professor of economics in Bar Ilan University. In his important study of Jewish (meaning Talmudic) economic thought, he points out that "slavery in Judaism was primarily a means of punishing thieves or of providing a way for debtors to pay off their debts, since the penal system did not provide for any form of imprisonment for these 'crimes.' Slavery was, in effect, a system wherein a man sold the earnings arising out of his labor for a capital sum equal to that of either the debt or the theft."[44] He is correct in his statement that there is no evidence indicating that the economy of Old Testament Israel was based on labor by chattel slaves.

The Old Testament's system of indentured servitude stands in stark contrast to the system of permanent slavery in classical Greece. Those humanists who appeal to Greece as the supposed cradle of Western civilization, equal (and probably greater) in importance to Christianity, have a public relations problem with this fact. The city-states of Greece's "glorious" era after the seventh century B.C. allowed citizens to enslave each other permanently. They could sell their children into slavery in some cities (e.g., Thebes).[45] Socrates (according to Plato, who was the most successful ghost writer in Western history), complained against the practice of Greeks' enslaving other Greeks captured during wartime.[46] Not surprisingly, Socrates

---

44. Meir Tamari, *"With All Your Possessions": Jewish Ethics and Economic Life* (New York: Free Press, 1987), p. 62. His next sentence is far more difficult to defend: "Jewish law frowned heavily on men voluntarily selling themselves as slaves." In a footnote, he tries to defend this assertion by simultaneously arguing 1) that the high prices for slaves alluded to in Exodus 21:32 show how scarce they were in Israel, and 2) that the Bible's restrictions on the owners "made slave-owning an unattractive investment" (pp. 313-14). The obvious question is this: If slaves were such an unattractive investment, why did Hebrews pay high prices in capitalizing their labor? Furthermore, if slave-owning was so unattractive, how could the institution of indentured servitude have served as an effective means of compensating the victims of debtors and criminals?

45. William L. Westermann, *The Slave Systems of Greek and Roman Antiquity* (Philadelphia: American Philosophical Society, 1955), p. 44.

46. *Republic*, Book V, 469b-c. *The Republic of Plato*, translated by Alan Bloom (New York: Basic Books, 1968), p. 149; F. M. Cornford translation (New York: Oxford University Press, 1945), pp. 171-72.

was eventually executed by Athens as a troublemaker. Incredibly, Westermann attributes Greek slavery to the "greater maturity" of Greece's legal thought compared to the Semites.[47]

Servitude or Self-Government

Indentured servitude functioned in the Hebrew commonwealth as a means of dealing with men who were unwilling or unable to manage their own affairs. Indentured servitude provided tools, supervision, education, food, shelter, and some of the comforts of prosperity to those without capital. It also provided security. It was a way of building a capital base. Jacob served Laban for seven years in order to earn Rachel as his wife (Gen. 29:20). He became, in effect, an indentured servant. The point is, *he waited.* He was a future-oriented man. He was also an independent man who amassed a great deal of capital in his 20 years of service (7 + 7 + 6) to his corrupt uncle and father-in-law.

Rushdoony summarizes several aspects of the Old Testament's system of indentured servitude: "In the biblical form, slavery was rather a form of bond-service. The term 'servant' or 'slave' was used to describe anyone owing service to another, permanently or temporarily. Thus, David and Daniel described themselves as God's servants (Ps. 27:9; Dan. 9:17), and the virgin Mary described herself as 'the handmaiden of the Lord' (Luke 1:38). Biblical slavery was a form of feudal association and protection. The stealing of men for purposes of sale was strictly forbidden by law, so that what is popularly known as slavery was outlawed (Deut. 24:7), and Paul restated this condemnation and associated 'men-stealers' with 'whoremongers,' homosexuals, liars, perjurers, and heretics (I Tim. 1:10)."[48]

This is not to say that indentured servitude is morally wrong. It is simply an inferior way of life that should not be preferred by Christians. "From the biblical perspective, therefore, slavery is not

---

47. He writes: "One important fact seems to lie at the root of all the differences which are discernable between the pre-Greek and the Greek social responses to the institution of slavery. This is that the level of maturity attained in legal thought by the Greeks of the city-state period, as represented in their attitude toward slavery, was much higher than that reached by their predecessors in ancient Egypt and in the Semitic-speaking lands of Western Asia. This greater maturity expressed itself in a more logical recognition among the Greeks of the distinctions of status between the free and the unfree and a far greater semantic precision in the terms which expressed the gradations of social classification." Westermann, *Slave Systems*, p. 42.

48. R. J. Rushdoony, *Politics of Guilt and Pity* (Fairfax, Virginia: Thoburn Press, [1970] 1978), p. 23.

itself intrinsically evil; the failure to live as free men, the dependency or incompetence of a slave mind is, however, regarded as an inferior way. The believer cannot revolt against his situation, but he cannot become a slave in good conscience, voluntarily, for *any form* of slavery is an infringement of Christ's total rights over him (I Cor. 7:22, 23)."[49]

The Enslavement of Heathens

The question of heathen slavery then arises. Did this same ethical and cultural goal of personal independence govern the enslavement of the heathen in Israel? Were they also to become the beneficiaries of God's covenant blessings? Could they also find freedom in Israel? Was their enslavement permanent?

The Hebrews repeatedly violated God's requirement that they annihilate the Canaanites. Instead, the tribes made local Canaanites pay tribute to them, which was only legitimate in distant foreign wars (Deut. 20:11). The Canaanites of Ephraim's land paid tribute to them, but were not driven out (Josh. 16:10). The same was true of Manassah (Josh. 17:12-13; Jud. 1:28) and Zebulun (Jud. 1:30). The Hebrew tribes preferred to receive tribute rather than continue the war. The result, as God had predicted, was repeated apostasy. The Hebrews began to follow the gods of Canaan. For this sin, God repeatedly placed them in slavery to foreigners, whose societies were based on worshipping the demonic "first cousins" to the gods of Canaan.

Once the land was cleared of Canaanites, Israel was then supposed to use indentured servitude only to subdue evil "within the camp"—repayment for debt and criminal restitution—and, in the case of foreign slaves, to remove them from bondage to foreign gods and to place them under lifetime slavery *as a means of evangelism.* Foreign heathen adults and the children of resident aliens were to be *redeemed*—bought out of bondage to demons and placed under the authority of godly households (Lev. 25:44-46).

Permanent Slavery

The jubilee slave law unquestionably taught that it was legal for the Hebrews to import slaves from foreign lands. These outsiders were moral slaves because they were in subordination to foreign gods. They had been judged externally by God, having been sold to Hebrew families by their military conquerors or else by their nations'

---

49. *Ibid.*, p. 24.

own slave merchants. Resident aliens in Israel could legally sell themselves and their descendants into slavery. The jubilee legislation was emphatic:

Both thy bondmen, and thy bondmaids, which thou shalt have, shall be of the heathen that are round about you; of them shall ye buy bondmen and bondmaids. Moreover of the children of the strangers that do sojourn among you, of them shall ye buy, and of their families that are with you, which they begat in your land: and they shall be your possession. And ye shall take them as an inheritance for your children after you, to inherit them for a possession; they shall be your bondmen for ever: but over your brethren the children of Israel, ye shall not rule over one another with rigour (Lev. 25:44-46).

Because pagan slaves could be purchased for a lifetime of service, and because their children would become the property of the owner's heirs, they would have commanded higher purchase prices than Hebrew indentured servants. The present price of any asset is its expected net return over its expected term of service, discounted by the prevailing market rate of interest. The longer its expected net return, the higher the price. The pagan slave could legally produce a lifetime of service; his market price would have reflected this fact. Add to this the future value of his heirs' productivity, and we can safely conclude that pagan slaves would have commanded a higher market price than Hebrew indentured servants. An indentured servant could legally produce a stream of income for a much shorter period unless he voluntarily sold himself into permanent servitude (Ex. 21:5-6), something that the buyer could not have safely predicted at the time of purchase. There was no long-term market for non-criminal Hebrew servants. (Hebrew criminals could be purchased for price sufficiently high to pay their victims; thus, they could be placed into lifetime slavery, just as if they were pagan aliens. Still, there were greater risks associated with bringing a convicted criminal into a household. This would have depressed their prices somewhat.)

Robert L. Dabney, the Calvinist theologian of Virginia, appealed to the Levitical law of permanent heathen slavery in his defense of the South's slave system, published after the war.[50] "There was to be

---

50. Robert L. Dabney, *A Defence of Virginia [And Through Her, of the South]* (New York: Negro University Press, [1867] 1969), pp. 117-19. It had originally been written during the war. He had submitted the manuscript to the Confederate government.

no 'seventh year freedom here; there is no jubilee liberation.' So says the learned divine, Moses Stuart, of Andover, himself an anti-slavery man."[51] The question must be raised: Was heathen slavery designed by God to be permanent in the Old Testament era, as an initial reading of Leviticus 25:44-46 indicates that it was? What were the goals of this law? Was the goal to create a caste of permanent slaves?

Jubilee Redistribution vs. Permanent Slavery

The jubilee land tenure law, *when enforced*, made it impossible for any family to amass permanently large land holdings. It is usually assumed by commentators that the jubilee land law was never enforced, but this is debatable. The sabbatical year of rest for the land was clearly not enforced, which was the reason God gave for sending Israel into captivity (Jer. 50:34; I Chron. 36:21).[52] The jubilee land law was tied to the sabbatical year: it was to follow the seventh sabbatical year (Lev. 25:8-9). Nevertheless, the repeated unwillingness of Israelites to sell their land to those outside the family,[53] most notably

---

The government wanted it published in London, but commissioner A. T. Bledsoe, author of *Liberty and Slavery*, judged that it was too controversial, and so unilaterally killed the project. This disturbed the author: "Our failure to meet the Abolition charges squarely was viewed as a confession of our own guilt," he later wrote. Cited in Thomas Cary Johnson, *The Life and Letters of Robert Lewis Dabney* (Richmond, Virginia: Presbyterian Committee of Publication, 1903), p. 275. Dabney's book was published two years after the war ended. His biographer stated: "It was received with high appreciation by able men, North as well as South" (p. 275). He offers no supporting evidence. He then laments: "Then it was covered with the deluge of press output in praise of the victorious section, and the principles which prevailed in that section. The author saw the truths he had established discarded, and the slanders and sophistries he had refuted received by the world as truths of an indisputable character, and often by degenerate sons of the South, as well as by the multitudes of the North" (p. 275). Such language, published by the southern Presbyterian Church as late as 1903, indicates the extent of the deep-seated resentment of the defeated, and their unwillingness to rethink the antebellum theology of slavery. On the whole, however, such sentiments seldom came into print after 1865.

    51. *Ibid.*, p. 117.
    52. The sabbatical year was honored in the inter-testamental era. In 162 B.C., during his brief one-year reign, King Antiochus V (Eupator) "made peace with the people of Bethsura, who abandoned the town, having no more food there to withstand a siege, as it was a sabbatical year when the land was left fallow" (I Macc. 6:49, NEB).
    53. Archer Torrey cites Judges 11:2; 21:24; the Book of Ruth; I Samuel 8:10ff.; 22:7-8; and II Kings 19:29. Torrey, *The Land & Biblical Economics* (New York: Henry George Institute, [1979] 1985), pp. 9-11, 23. This booklet is a defense of the supposed continuation in the New Testament era of the jubilee land redistribution principle, and it ends with a reprint of Henry George's appeal to Pope Leo XIII to proclaim the principle of the single tax. Nevertheless, the booklet legitimately criticizes the

Naboth's refusal to sell his land to King Ahab (I Ki. 21),[54] indicates that the State must have enforced some sort of prohibition against the permanent sale of a family's land. What may have taken place was the continuing refusal of greedy owners to rest their land one year in seven, but also the insistence of heirs that the jubilee year be honored, at least with respect to the redistribution of family land. Both decisions are consistent with the assumption of land hunger in a predominantly agricultural economy.

A family could lease a neighboring piece of property for up to half a century, but then it reverted to the original family. We know that large families are a sign of God's covenantal blessing (Ps. 127:3-5). The larger that Israel's families grew in response to the nation's covenantal faithfulness to God, the smaller each family's inherited land holding would become. This made it economically impossible for any branch of a family to amass a large number of heathen slaves during periods of God's covenantal blessings, for it was illegal to amass permanently the large tracts of land that were necessary for the support of slaves.[55] Thus, at the beginning of each jubilee year, when all land holdings reverted to the heirs of the original land-owners, most heathen slaves would have been released by their owners, whether or not the law allowed them to retain ownership of them indefinitely. They were allowed to buy the land in these walled cities, where the jubilee land laws did not apply (Lev. 25:29-33). Those heathen who remained in slavery would have been parceled out among inheriting Hebrew children when the heirs

---

standard argument that the jubilee land tenure laws were never enforced in the Old Testament era.

Archer Torrey is the grandson of Reuben A. Torrey, who the grandson says did publicly endorse Henry George's teachings on economics. If he did, then this is one more example of an error-prone amateur economist leading an untrained Christian commentator into the swamps of pseudo-economics. Major Douglas' Social Credit movement is another such example. See my essay, "Gertrude Coogan and the Myth of Social Credit," in *An Introduction to Christian Economics* (Nutley, New Jersey: Craig Press, 1973), ch. 11. For a coherent critique of Georgist economics, see Murray N. Rothbard, *Power and Market: Government and the Economy* (Menlo Park, California: Institute for Humane Studies, 1970), pp. 91-100. Why Christians should become advocates of either system is something of a mystery. Neither movement was founded by a Christian, and the Bible speaks of neither a tax on land (Georgism) nor the necessity of State-issued fiat money or monetary inflation to keep pace with aggregate economic output (Social Credit). In fact, the Bible is opposed to both ideas. Yet each movement has its share of dedicated, if not fanatic, Christian supporters.

54. *Ibid.*, pp. 14-15.

55. Patrick Fairbairn, *The Revelation of Law in Scripture* (Grand Rapids, Michigan: Zondervan, [1868] 1957), p. 118.

returned to their share of the family's traditional lands, thereby reducing the possibility of large-scale slave gang labor. It would also have increased the likelihood of manumission: freedom for slaves whose economic productivity, without large land holdings, would have dropped sharply. In other words, by reducing Israel's per capita capital (land), the jubilee land tenure law would have reduced labor productivity for all those who remained in Israel. This was the whole idea: *to encourage covenantal dominion outside the land by encouraging Hebrew emigration.*

This economic link between the size of land holdings and the economic feasibility of large-scale gang slavery is the simplest explanation for God's inclusion of the heathen slave laws within the section of Leviticus that deals with the jubilee land tenure laws. One obvious reason why the Bible offers no example of the nation's honoring of the jubilee land distribution laws is that politically influential owners of large slave gangs no doubt recognized that the economic value of their slave holdings would be reduced drastically if they had to return their land to the original families. Thus, any significant increase of inter-generational slavery by heathens would have testified to a refusal by the judges to enforce the original jubilee land distribution agreement that had been agreed to by all the tribes prior to the conquest of Canaan. A growing population of permanent foreign slaves would therefore have been a visible warning to Israel that they were disobeying God's law. This was the same visible warning that God had given to Egypt (Ex. 1:12, 20).

Slavery very clearly was not supposed to become a major institution in Israel. Land and labor are complementary factors of production. The larger the population grew — a promised blessing of God — the more valuable land would become; the more valuable the land became, the less would be the return from net economic rents produced by slaves. Free laborers and tenants would be willing to work for low wages for as long as they remained in the land of Israel; slavery would offer no important economic advantages to rent-seekers. The primary economic goal in such a land-starved economy would have been to add to one's land holdings, not to one's supply of slaves.

Without cheap land, or increasingly productive land, permanent agricultural slavery is unlikely to be maintained long term.[56] Under circumstances of increasing land scarcity, the reasons for holding

---

56. Evsey D. Domar, "The Causes of Slavery or Serfdom: A Hypothesis," *Journal of Economic History*, XXX (1970), pp. 18-32.

slaves would then be more consumption-oriented than production-oriented: slaves as status symbols, i.e., consumer goods rather than producer goods.

(Because chattel slavery remained profitable in the American South prior to 1860, there is no need to resort to the thesis of slaves as merely status symbols. They were status symbols, surely, but they were also profitable. Where, then, was the South's cheap land, if this economic thesis is correct? There is evidence that it was the continuing development of the fertile lands in the West South Central region of the South—Alabama to Texas—that kept slave prices high throughout the South, since slave owners who owned less fertile lands could profitably export slaves to the region with more fertile lands.[57] But if cheap land is basic to profitable slavery, did the slave-owners in the British West Indies suffer losses when land became scarce? The tentative answer is yes, since it was only when new land could be brought under cultivation that the Caribbean economies grew.[58] The Genoveses write: "So long as land remained available at prices unthinkably low by European standards—so long as colonial settlers faced empty spaces or spaces that could be emptied by a controlled dose of genocide—resources would be shifted, and the grim wastefulness of the system as a whole would remain disguised."[59])

What we must understand from the beginning is that the whole economic thrust of the jubilee land tenure laws, when coupled with God's promise of population growth for national obedience, was to push the Israelites out of the land, and therefore outside the geo-

---

57. This was an important aspect of the argument by Alfred H. Conrad and John R. Meyer in their classic 1958 article, "The Economics of Slavery in the Antebellum South," Part III, *Journal of Economic History*, reprinted many times. There is not much debate about this: Stanley L. Engerman, "The Effects of Slavery upon the Southern Economy: A Review of the Recent Debate," in Hugh G. J. Aitkin (ed.), *Did Slavery Pay?* (Boston: Houghton Mifflin, 1971), pp. 318-20. Both essays are reprinted here, as they are in Robert W. Fogel and Stanley L. Engerman (eds.), *The Reinterpretation of American Economic History* (New York: Harper & Row, 1971).

58. "Thus, as early as the period 1670-90, overproduction plunged the sugar economies of Brazil and the Caribbean into crises that ruined both planters and their creditors. The pattern recurred many times. . . . When Caribbean sugar production ran afoul of market gluts, the ensuing crises led to a shift of resources to fresher land in newly developed colonies. Thus, one factor, 'land,' alone accounted for the regional economy's ability to survive the periodic purges of the market generated by the tendency toward overproduction." Elizabeth Fox-Genovese and Eugene D. Genovese, *Fruits of Merchant Capital: Slavery and Bourgeois Property in the Rise and Expansion of Capitalism* (New York: Oxford University Press, 1983), pp. 45-46.

59. *Ibid.*, p. 44.

graphical boundaries where the jubilee land law, including its slave
laws, operated. The jubilee law's goal was world missions and covenantal dominion, not the permanent enslavement of heathens inside
tiny Israel.[60]

Neither the Roman Republic nor the Roman Empire, as a pagan
society already in spiritual bondage, fell under the terms of the
jubilee land tenure law. That law applied to Israel because of the
specific terms of the *military spoils system* of land distribution that families had agreed to prior to Israel's invasion of Canaan (Num. 36).
Rome developed the latifundia, the huge family land holdings that
apparently supported the slave gang system. The Roman land
tenure system may not have produced slave gangs, if land holdings
were divided into smaller units within the latifundia. Scholars still
debate the issue. In any case, a legal order that permits the long-
term amassing of inheritable land, and does so through such restrictions on inheritance as *primogeniture* (eldest son inherits) and *entail*
(prohibition against the permanent sale of a family's land), makes
economically possible the creation of huge plantations.[61] Such permanent, inheritable land holdings, if accompanied by a legal order
that permits lifetime slavery, can lead to the creation of slave gangs
whenever market conditions make gang labor profitable. On the
other hand, whenever the legal principle of "all sons inherit" or "all
children inherit" is enforced, it becomes nearly impossible to create
an agricultural economy that is based on the widespread *family* ownership of large gangs of slaves. Such was to have been the case in
ancient Israel, for the eldest son was limited to an inheritance of only
a double portion of his father's assets (Deut. 21:17).

Jesus' Annulment of the Jubilee Land Laws

The fulfillment of the jubilee year by Jesus at the outset of His
ministry (Luke 4:17-21) made plain the liberating aspects of the rule
of Christ in history.[62] He announced His ministry with the reading
of Isaiah 61, "to preach delivery of the captives" (Luke 4:18). His intention was clearly the spiritual liberation of His people, and this
leads to progressive maturity in the faith, which in turn is supposed

---

60. Gary North, *Moses and Pharaoh: Dominion Religion vs. Power Religion* (Tyler,
Texas: Institute for Christian Economics, 1985), ch. 1.

61. So, for that matter, does corporate ownership of land, either by ecclesiastical
or State agencies, or by a corporate distribution of share ownership.

62. Gary North, *Liberating Planet Earth: An Introduction to Biblical Blueprints* (Ft.
Worth, Texas: Dominion Press, 1987).

to lead to liberation out of chattel slavery, *if offered by the owner* (I Cor. 7:21b). We have our "ears pierced" (Deut. 15:17) spiritually by Christ; we become permanent adopted sons of His household. Yet even in the case of Leviticus 25, God's goal was always liberation. These pagans were being purchased out of their covenantal slavery to demonic religion. They were being *redeemed* (bought back). They were being given an opportunity to hear the gospel and see it in operation in households covenanted to God. They were being given an opportunity to renounce paganism and thereby escape eternal slavery in the lake of fire.

Obviously, if the legal provision that allowed Hebrew families to retain the lifetime services of heathen slaves, as well as to transfer ownership of the heathens' children to the Hebrews' children, is severed from the jubilee land tenure law, then the economic possibility of establishing slave gangs becomes a reality. The legal restriction against the permanent amassing of land disappears. Thus, to argue that the lifetime slave-holding provisions of Leviticus 25 were not an integral part of the jubilee land tenure system is to argue that the history of chattel slavery in the West was in principle sanctioned by the Bible. I am arguing the opposite: *the lifetime slave-holding provisions of Leviticus 25 were an integral aspect of Israel's jubilee land tenure laws, and therefore when God annulled the latter, He also annulled the former.* By transferring legal title to His kingdom to the gentile world (Matt. 21:43), and by visibly annulling Israel's legal title to the land of Palestine at the time of the fall of Jerusalem in A.D. 70,[63] God thereby also annulled the Hebrew land tenure laws. What had been a God-approved spoils system for a unique historical situation — the military conquest of Canaan by Israel — became a dead letter of biblical law after the fall of Jerusalem.[64]

---

63. David Chilton, *The Days of Vengeance, op. cit.*, and *The Great Tribulation* (Ft. Worth, Texas: Dominion Press, 1987).

64. It is depressing to read essays and books by contemporary Christian writers who proclaim that the basic redistributionist principle of the jubilee land law still is applicable in the modern economy. Ronald Sider promoted this idea to liberation theologians and their hangers-on in the late 1970's: *Rich Christians in an Age of Hunger: A Biblical Study* (Downers Grove, Illinois: Inter-Varsity Press, 1977), pp. 88-90, 93-95, etc. He wanted the State to serve as the agent of compulsory wealth redistribution. Conservative Christians then picked up this jubilee theme, tying it to the so-called Kondratieff economic wave, with the free market as the enforcer rather than the State. Cf. David Knox Barker, *Jubilee on Wall Street: An Optimistic Look at the Coming Financial Crash* (Lafayette, Louisiana: Prescott Press, 1987).

The basic essay by Russian economist Nikolai Kondratieff was "Long Waves in

Constantine ruled in 315 that slaves who had been condemned to work in the mines or as gladiators were to be branded on the hands or legs, not on the face.[65] This act of comparative charity led the owners, who had formerly branded their slaves, to have metal collars put around their slaves' necks. Clearly, Constantine was no abolitionist. Later legislation under Christian rulers in Rome and Byzantium was not noted for any tendency toward abolitionism.

Because the Christian West did not honor God's abolition of permanent slavery through Christ's fulfillment of the jubilee year, the West later followed the example of the Roman Empire when the development of sugar plantations in the second half of the fourteenth century,[66] the Western hemisphere's plantations from the sixteenth century onward, and especially the American South in the nineteenth century, made slave gang agriculture profitable again. The church did not recognize that God no longer allows His people and those under His civil covenant the legal right to amass slaves and deed them to the next generation.

It was the creation of huge land grants in Virginia especially, but also in other southern colonies in the United States, from the late seventeenth century through the eighteenth, that initially made economically possible North American Negro slavery, with its extensive

Economic Life," *Review of Economic Statistics*, XVII (Nov. 1935). Several somewhat conventional economists who favor the existence of such a wave: W. W. Rostow, *The World Economy: History & Prospect* (Austin: University of Texas Press, 1978); Jay W. Forrester of the Massachusetts Institute of Technology: "New life for Kondratieff's gloomy cycle," *Business Week* (Sept. 10, 1979); and John D. Sterman, also of M.I.T.: "Debt, Default, and Long Waves: Is History Relevant?" *Bank Credit Analyst* (Nov. 1986); "Forecasters Who Are Expecting the Worst," *Business Week* (June 3, 1985).

Lester Thurow, also of the Sloan School of Management at M.I.T., offers this warning: the historical data are not good enough to prove the existence of such a cycle; cited by C. D. Bohon, "Hard Times Ahead?" *Auto Age* (Nov. 1986), p. 19. This is especially true in a world that no longer is disciplined by an international gold standard. See also G. Garvy, "Kondratieff's Theory of Long Cycles," *Review of Economic Statistics*, XXV (1943), pp. 203-20; C. Van Ewijk, "The Long Wave — A Real Phenomenon?" *The Economist* (Netherlands), vol. 129, No. 3 (1981); John A. Pugsley, "The Long Wave," *Common Sense Viewpoint*, VIII (Nov. 1982); a two-part article by Murray N. Rothbard, "The Kondratieff Cycle: Real or Fabricated?" *Investment Insights* (August and September, 1984); Solomos Solomou, "Non-Balanced Growth and Kondratieff Waves in the World Economy, 1850-1913," *Journal of Economic History*, XLVI (March 1986). I hope to reprint these and other essays in a paperback book, *The Kondratieff Wave: Myth or Reality?*

65. *Theodosian Code* 9:40:2; cited in Finley, *Ancient Slavery and Modern Ideology* (New York: Viking, 1980), p. 127.

66. David Brion Davis, *Slavery and Human Progress* (New York: Oxford University Press, 1984), pp. 59-66.

use of gang labor. The Virginia legislature repeatedly made land grants to politically favored families of many thousands of acres per family.[67] In New England, the towns did not make such huge land grants. They multiplied towns rather than allowing individual families to amass huge tracts of land.[68] Without large plantations, slave gang labor was not economically feasible. While New Englanders were involved in the slave trade, they were seldom owners of slaves.[69] In 1652, Rhode Island actually passed a law against Negro slavery, but there is no evidence that it was ever enforced. Newport, Rhode Island, became the center of the slave trade in the next century.[70]

Ten Generations to Freedom

The time restrictions placed on Hebrew servitude did not apply to non-Hebrew servants. They were the true slaves in Israel. Why were foreigners placed into slavery, generation after generation? The theological answer is clear: they were covenanted slaves to foreign gods. Their release from this covenantal bondage took ten generations of faithful service to a family or institution under God's covenant.

The foreigner or foreign nation that rejected God's older covenant faced judgment in history. One of these judgments in the Old Testament was to become a slave in Israel. "Thus saith the LORD, The labour of Egypt, and merchandise of Ethiopia and of the Sabeans, men of stature, shall come over unto thee, and they shall be thine: they shall come after thee; in chains they shall come over, and they shall fall down unto thee, they shall make supplication unto thee, saying, Surely God is in thee; and there is none else, there is no God" ["no other God": New King James Version] (Isa. 45:14). This was to be Israel's blessing and the foreigner's curse.

Yet with every curse in history there is a measure of blessing. Biblical servitude in the Old Testament was always intended to lead men to ethical reformation and spiritual freedom. What about

---

67. Leonard Woods Larabee, *Conservatism in Early American History* (Ithaca, New York: Cornell University Press Great Seal Books, [1948] 1962), pp. 32-36.

68. John W. Reps, *Town Planting in Frontier America* (Princeton, New Jersey: Princeton University Press, [1965] 1969), ch. 5; Sumner Chilton Powell, *Puritan Village: The Formation of a New England Town* (Garden City, New York: Doubleday Anchor, [1963] 1965), chaps. 2, 8, 9; Kenneth A. Lockridge, *A New England Town: The First Hundred Years* (New York: Norton, 1970), pp. 10-13, 70-72.

69. Jordan, *White Over Black*, pp. 66-71.

70. Charles M. Andrews, *The Colonial Period of American History*, 4 vols. (New Haven, Connecticut: Yale University Press, [1936] 1964), II, p. 30.

heathen slaves? Weren't they slaves "forever"? Leviticus 25:46 says, "they shall be your bondmen forever." Then in what way was heathen slavery a means of redemption in Israel? We know that in one crucial case, the word "forever" meant ten generations. Deuteronomy 23:3 specifies that it was to take ten generations for sojourners from Ammon and Moab, the "bastard" nations that were the sons of Lot's incestuous relationships with his daughters (Gen. 19:30-38), to enter the congregation, thereby becoming full citizens in Israel. But Nehemiah 13:1 reads: "On that day they read in the book of Moses in the audience of the people; and therein was found written, that the Ammonite and the Moabite should not come into the congregation of the LORD for ever." The Hebrews understood "forever" to mean ten consecutive generations of covenant membership (circumcision).

Why ten generations? This was the judicial curse imposed on bastards. There was also a ten-generation prohibition against a bastard's heirs' entering into the congregation of the Lord (Deut. 23:2). Judah and Tamar produced a bastard son, Pharez. David was symbolically[71] the tenth-generation son of this illicit union (Ruth 4:18-20). He then became the mightiest king in Israel's history. He "entered the congregation" as the supreme civil judge. As Rushdoony writes, "There is no reason to doubt that eunuchs, bastards, Ammonites, and Moabites regularly became believers and were faithful worshippers of God. *Congregation* has reference to the whole nation in its governmental function as God's covenant people."[72] Those who were the circumcised heirs of bastards had to wait patiently until their own heirs could regain legal access to the civil office of judge. Rushdoony continues: "The purpose of the commandment is here the protection of authority. Authority among God's people is *holy*; it does require a separateness. It does not belong to every man simply on the ground of his humanity."[73]

What about heathen slaves? Would they ever regain freedom? Yes: if they remained in the household for ten generations, they became full congregation members. At that point, they came under the laws that regulated Hebrew bondservants. At age 20, a Hebrew male became a legal adult, subject to military numbering (Ex.

---

71. See the subsection below: "The Incomplete Genealogy in Ruth 4," pp. 149-51.
72. R. J. Rushdoony, *The Institutes of Biblical Law* (Nutley, New Jersey: Craig Press, 1973), p. 85.
73. *Idem.*

30:14). It would have been illegal to keep such an adult, tenth-generation heathen slave in slavery after he reached age 20. Thus, it took ten generations of "circumcised service" to God and to the Hebrew household to escape slavery. But escape was legally possible for one's distant heirs. Better to serve as a slave in a Hebrew household than to be at ease in paganism outside of Zion. Pagans, then as now, went to hell if they were outside the household of faith. They then become eternal slaves under God, the Eternal Slave-Master. Thus, enslavement in ancient Israel was a means of potential liberation for the heathen.

Then what about the Gibeonites? The author of the Book of Joshua (possibly it was the prophet Samuel) says that they remained slaves, "even unto this day." The Gibeonites were still in bondage at least four centuries after they became slaves in the tabernacle, for Saul slew many of them, despite the fact they were under his covenantal protection as a separate people within the land (II Sam. 21:1-2).[74] Four centuries seems to be longer than ten generations, for the average lifespan of the Hebrews had shortened to 70 years by Moses' day (Ps. 90:10). This is comparable to today's lifespans, and one generation is classified as under 40 years — usually closer to 30 years.

The Incomplete Genealogy in Ruth 4

Could this 400-year time period of Gibeonite slavery have been less than ten generations after Joshua's covenant with them, in fact, a mere five generations? I ask this seemingly preposterous biological question because David is listed as the tenth generation after Tamar and Judah (Ruth 4:18-22), yet only five generations after the era of Joshua.[75] What are we to make of this evidence? Jephthah said that it had been 300 years from Joshua's conquest to his own day (Jud. 11:26). The only way to explain the genealogy of David — assuming that the genealogy of Ruth 4 is complete — is to assume that those born after Nahshon attained abnormally long lives, such as the 130 years of Jehoiada (II Chron. 24:15), and also to assume that they fathered the covenant-line sons remarkably late in life: close to age 100. These assumptions are highly improbable. It is therefore unlikely that this genealogy is complete.

---

74. I am dating the conquest of Canaan sometime close to 1400 B.C., and Saul's kingship sometime around 1080 B.C.

75. The listed line of Judah was Pharez, Hezron, Ram, Amminadab, and Nahshon. Nahshon was a contemporary of Moses (Num. 1:7). Thus, only four generations are listed in between Nahshon and David: Salmon, who married Rahab (Matt. 1:5), Boaz (who married Ruth), Obed, Jesse, and then David.

The Bible provides additional internal evidence that the genealogy is incomplete. First, Abraham was considered unique in having fathered a son at age 100, yet he lived centuries before the normal human lifespan had shortened to age 70 (Ps. 90:10). There is no mention of three consecutive abnormally long lifespans in the period of the judges (conquest to kingship). This silence is important evidence, though not conclusive, which testifies against the completeness of the genealogy of Ruth 4.

Second, the lifespans of those in the tribe of Judah had been comparatively short: five generations, Pharez to Nahshon, compared to four for the tribe of Levi: Levi to Moses (Ex. 6:16-26). Are we to believe that, without warning, every subsequent male in this family line fathered a child around age 100, while everyone else's lifespans had shortened to 70 years? This seems unlikely. If there had been such a return to pre-conquest lifespans in this single family line, why doesn't the Bible give us some reason for it? Caleb's strength at age 85 was a miracle, as he understood (Josh. 14:9-11): God's special sustaining of a faithful man because of God's promise to him 40 years earlier (Num. 14:30).

Third, Salmon was *at most* 59 when Jericho fell. Of the generation of the exodus, only Caleb and Joshua entered the land. This meant that at the time of the exodus, Salmon was not old enough to have been numbered as an adult. Since numbering of adult males took place at age 20 (Ex. 30:14), Salmon at most was 19 years old at the exodus. Add to this 40 years of wandering in the wilderness, and we get age 59. He married Rahab, who as a prostitute was probably at least 20 years old, and perhaps 30, at the time of the fall of Jericho. Did she give birth to Boaz forty years later (age 99 for Salmon)? How old was she if she did wait 40 years to bear Boaz? Sixty? Seventy? And if Salmon was under age 19 at the time of the exodus, and fathered Boaz around age 100, fifty or sixty years after the fall of Jericho, then Rahab would have been that much older. This seems extremely unlikely. It is therefore difficult to reject the conclusion that there were numerous unlisted generations in between Salmon and Boaz.

It would be emotionally convenient to believe in the long lifespan view, Salmon to Jesse, and therefore to accept the genealogy of Ruth 4 at face value, but the internal evidence from Scripture makes it difficult to accept. The highly specific revelation concerning the chronology of the judges (Jud. 11:26) is God's means of pointing to the literary nature of the post-Salmon genealogy. It would be difficult to argue that Jephthah erred by several centuries, when we are also told that there were 480 years between the exodus and the beginning of the construction of the temple (I Ki. 6:1), which began around 967 B.C.[76] Only by ignoring I Kings 6:1, and by dating the exodus centuries later than the mid-1400's — which so many compromising Christian authors have done[77] — could we shorten the period of the judges to such an extent that the lifespans of the final five generations of the Ruth 4 genealogy could be made to fit.

If the genealogy in Ruth 4 is incomplete, what explanation can we offer? I think it is because the author of Ruth wanted to emphasize the ethical basis of David's elevation to the throne: the liberating "tenth generation" after the covenantal mark of bastardy began. (This is additional indirect evidence for Samuel as the author of Ruth.) The shortened genealogy is a literary device pointing to a theological conclusion: *liberty and authority after ten generations.*[78] The genealogy's very incompleteness testifies to the importance of the tenth generation after the imposition of the covenantal curse. It points to the temporary nature of a curse in history that lasts "forever." It therefore points to God's grace to those who are patient in righteous living.

The Gibeonites: Whole Burnt Offerings

Then why were the Gibeonites still in bondage as a nation in Saul's day? One answer might be that they were Canaanites, and as such were entitled only to death. Their servitude was an alternative to death, and therefore they did not come under the slave laws of Leviticus 25. The Gibeonites had deliberately lied about their origins. They said that they were from a distant land (Josh. 9:9). Once the Israelites covenanted with them in terms of this lie, the Gibeonites came under the protection of the sanctuary. They became, in effect, whole burnt offerings before God — symbolic rather than literal. They became holy slaves who could not be ransomed

---

76. Merrill C. Tenney (ed.), *The Zondervan Pictorial Encyclopedia of the Bible*, 5 vols. (Grand Rapids, Michigan: Eerdmans, 1975), V, p. 627.

77. North, *Moses and Pharaoh*, Appendix A: "The Reconstruction of Egypt's Chronology."

78. Matthew's listing of fourteen generations from Abraham to David would therefore have to be explained as a similar literary device. His list of three successive sets of fourteen generations (Matt. 1:17) may have been related to the number seven: six sets of seven generations, or three sets of fourteen.

(Lev. 27:28-29). This is why Jephthah's daughter could not be ransomed; she had been devoted not as a servant but as a sacrifice.[79] The Gibeonites became servants of the *congregation*, meaning they were employed by the tabernacle (Josh. 9:27). This seems to be the basis of the prophecy of Zechariah 14, "and in that day there shall be no more the Canaanite in the house of the LORD of hosts" (Zech. 14:21b).[80]

The Gibeonites were still in bondage as a nation in Saul's day. They could have escaped bondage simply by leaving Israel, which God had intended them to do as an alternative to annihilation at the time of Joshua's invasion. Instead, they chose to remain permanent slaves in the tabernacle. The continuing bondage of the Gibeonites is therefore not sufficient evidence to refute the argument that "forever" meant ten generations. The goal of slavery in the Old Testament was spiritual and moral liberation, followed by judicial liberation. The Gibeonites would have been set free permanently at the time of the ultimate jubilee year, when Jesus Christ announced the fulfillment of the jubilee year principle (Luke 4).

Sabbath and Freedom

James Jordan argued in *The Law of the Covenant* that the central message of the Book of Exodus is tied closely the requirement in Exodus 21:2 of masters to release servants in the seventh (sabbatical) year.[81] Why the sabbatical year? *Because the Book of Exodus itself is a book about the sabbath.*[82] We need to understand this if we are to understand the Book of Exodus. The Hebrews were released from bondage in Egypt and brought to Mt. Sinai in order to worship God there (Ex. 3:12) and to gain spiritual rest. Thus, the ordinances (case laws) begin with sabbatical requirements and end with them (Ex. 23:10-19). Jordan writes: "The instructions for the design of the Tabernacle culminate in sabbath rules (31:12-17), and the procedure for

---

79. James B. Jordan, *Judges: God's War Against Humanism* (Tyler, Texas: Geneva Ministries, 1985), pp. 206-7.

80. My thanks to James Jordan for this insight.

81. Since the publication of Ray Sutton's *That You May Prosper*, Jordan has modified his thesis. He now thinks that the central message is transition: from one king to a new one; from one law-order to a new one, etc.

82. As the second book in the Pentateuch, Exodus corresponds most closely to point two of the covenant model. The commandment regarding the sabbath is number four. It pertains to covenant sanctions. It would normally be associated with Numbers, the fourth book of the Pentateuch. Nevertheless, deliverance from Egypt was a positive sanction for Israel and a negative sanction for Egypt, so the elements of subordination and sanctions are closely related.

building the Tabernacle commences with sabbath rules (35:1-3). The book closes with the definitive establishment of Old Covenant worship on the very first day of the new year. Thus, the book moves from the rigors of bondage to the sinful world order, to the glorious privilege of rest in the very throne room of God."[83]

This linear movement toward rest was governed by the hierarchical nature of Israel's relationship with God. Israel was subordinate to God; to the extent that the people confessed this fact of life, both metaphysical and ethical, they would move toward rest. Rest would be God's visible blessing on Israel in response to their covenantal faithfulness. But Israel did not achieve rest, either in the wilderness or in the promised land. The Hebrews' response to Moses over the next months and years indicated that *their problem was spiritual, not environmental.* They did not want freedom. Again and again, they complained about the burdens of freedom, and they looked backward toward the perceived benefits of Egypt's static social order.[84] Despite the tyranny they suffered at the hands of their Egyptian captors, *they preferred the illusion of institutional safety to the demanding moral and economic reality of personal freedom.* They did not understand that Egypt's static order had been definitively smashed by God during the exodus, that their former masters had become slaves themselves to invaders, the "Hyksos" rulers, who apparently were the Amalekites.[85] Their home would be either in Canaan or the wilderness; a return to bondage under the Pharaoh of Egypt had been closed to them by God.

The Hebrews had been delivered from empire. If they remained faithful to God, they would not again become the victims of empire, God promised them, for they would not suffer military defeats (Deut. 28:7). But if they turned away from God and again pursued foreign gods, they would be delivered back into captivity, for they would suffer military defeats (Deut. 28:25). Their external condition would reflect their internal condition, either as covenant-keepers or covenant-breakers. They could remain subordinate either to God or to some foreign deity; they could not escape ethical subordination.

---

83. Jordan, *The Law of the Covenant*, p. 75.

84. On the Egyptian social order, see North, *Moses and Pharaoh*, ch. 2: "Imperial Bureaucracy."

85. Immanuel Velikovsky, *Ages in Chaos*, vol. I, *From the Exodus to King Akhnaton* (Garden City, New York: Doubleday, 1952), ch. 2; Donovan Courville, *The Exodus Problem and Its Ramifications*, 2 vols. (Loma Linda, California: Challenge Books, 1971), I, pp. 229-41; North, *Moses and Pharaoh*, Appendix A.

They could live either as bondservants to God or slaves to some foreign nation; they could never achieve autonomy.

Would they serve the true God or foreign gods? To whom would they remain in covenantal bondage, God or Satan? If they covenanted with Satan through their worship of foreign deities, they would then be scattered, seeking rest but not finding it: "And among these nations shalt thou find no ease, neither shall the sole of thy foot have rest: but the LORD shall give thee there a trembling heart, and failing eyes, and sorrow of mind" (Deut. 28:65). Rest, both physical and psychological, is the product of spiritual faithfulness. Thus, to be delivered from institutional slavery is to be released symbolically from spiritual slavery; it is to receive the grace of God, for *freedom means deliverance into God's true rest*. Freedom is necessarily sabbatical. But it is also hierarchical.

In Bondage to Whom?

We must also be alert to another aspect of the story of the exodus. Jordan comments: ". . . the Exodus from Egypt was grounded not in a whim of God, but on a carefully worked out legal basis, which cannot be understood apart from the Biblical laws regarding slavery. Slavery thus forms one perspective from which the whole matter of salvation may be viewed. As Christ became the Slave (Servant) of God, so Christians also are slaves of God, delivered from bondage to sin and death."[86] We therefore need to understand the legal basis as well as the social and economic implications of the system of servitude outlined in biblical law.

If *Tools of Dominion* has a fundamental thesis regarding human servitude, it is this: *servitude is an inescapable concept*. It is never a question of servitude vs. no servitude. It is always a question of *servitude to whom or what*. As Jordan remarks, "man is still essentially a creature who needs an absolute reference point, a supreme master, to whom he can relate with absolute passivity. Man's rejection of the Creator as God does not result in his having no god at all, but in his having some false god. Man does not obliterate his psychological need for an absolute, he 'exchanges' it for a lie (Rom. 1:23). Thus, man may be said to have a 'slave drive' which ever seeks some god to submit to."[87] Even more clearly: "Man, *being* a slave, has a drive to *become*

---

86. Jordan, Slavery in Biblical Perspective, unpublished master's thesis, Westminster Theological Seminary, Philadelphia (April 1980), p. 5.
87. *Ibid.*, pp. 8-9.

what he is."[88] He is also correct in his observation: "The majority of people on the earth are presently enslaved to Babelic statist powers, owned in body and usually in soul as well by political masters. Moreover, even in the ostensibly free West, increasingly large numbers of persons forsake the dominion mandate and place themselves on the dole, crying out to the messianic state to become their sovereign provider. Scripture speaks to these matters, in the language of slavery."[89]

If men refuse to place themselves under God and God's required law-order for society, then they will inevitably place themselves in bondage to someone other than God, under laws that are different from God's. But only God is omniscient and omnipotent; only He can control men from the inside-out as well as from the outside-in.[90] To deny God's control over both body and soul is to surrender control to some other aspect of the fallen creation—a tyrant that will attempt to control both body and soul. Man cannot achieve freedom by rebelling against God and His law.

We must begin our journey on the road from serfdom by placing ourselves under covenantal bondage to the God of liberation.[91] We must seek to become passive toward God and active over His creation (Gen. 1:26-28). The only alternative to this unqualified ethical subordination to God is to become passive toward something or someone else—other men (tyranny), demonic spirits (occultism, mysticism), some aspect of nature (environmental determinism), the "cunning of history" (Hegel), "inevitable social forces" (Marx), the "unconscious" (Freud), alcohol or drugs, or even outright madness.[92] Second, becoming passive to something other than God, mankind then becomes either an active destroyer of both his environment and his own freedom (power religion) or else an essentially passive bystander who is subordinate to impersonal forces of nature or to some pantheist god (escape religion).

Slavery and Empire

Slavery in the ancient Near East was common, and the law codes of various Near Eastern societies provided rules that regulated the

---

88. *Ibid.*, p. 9.
89. *Ibid.*, pp. 4-5.
90. *Ibid.*, p. 20.
91. North, *Liberating Planet Earth, op. cit.*
92. Paul F. Stern, *In Praise of Madness* (New York: Dell, 1973).

institution. Nevertheless, from what we can discover from the presently known records, the economics of slavery seems to have militated against the private holding of large gangs of slaves. Slaves in Babylon during Hammurabi's reign seem to have cost somewhere in the range of three to four times what it would have cost to hire a free laborer for a year. In the era of Nebuchadnezzar and the Medo-Persians, there are at least some indications that a slave would have cost five or six times the cost of hiring a free laborer for a year. Isaac Mendelsohn's study of slavery in the ancient Near East concluded that it was generally cheaper to hire free laborers for the harvest than to own slaves. This is reflected in the relatively small number of slaves in the possession of private individuals throughout the long history of Ancient Mesopotamia. The average wealthy slave-owning family in Sumer owned only one or two slaves, although the households of the very rich, including state officials, might occasionally include as many as two dozen.[93] This is in stark contrast to the classical societies of Greece and Rome, in which, in the words of his-

---

93. Isaac Mendelsohn, *Slavery In the Ancient Near East*, p. 119. I rely heavily on Mendelsohn's relatively small book. There is not much else available. Even today, almost all the scholarly attention on slavery has been directed at Greece and Rome, not the ancient Near East, for only Greece and Rome are today regarded by most historians as the true slave societies of the ancient world: M. I. Finley, *Ancient Slavery and Modern Ideology*, p. 9.

What the reader may not be aware of is that there was very little detailed economic investigation of ancient slave societies until the 1950's. Writes David Brion Davis: "For reasons that deserve further study, scholarly interest in slavery and related forms of servitude languished from the First World War to the 1950s, a period that set new records for the mobilization, degradation, and extermination of millions of unfree workers." *Slavery and Human Progress*, p. 9. M. I. Finley agrees: "Apart from the single question of Christianity and slavery, the heat [of academic debate — G.N.] was generated by the larger question of the nature of the ancient economy, and the still larger one of stages in historical development, in which slavery was only a factor. The heat over slavery did not erupt until the 1950s, and then with little advance warning." *Ancient Slavery and Modern Ideology*, p. 55. The sharp ideological conflict did not break into the open until the International Historical Congress at Stockholm in 1960: *ibid.*, p. 56. Since then, the academic guild has tried to make up its long neglect of the topic through intense debates. "The volume and the polemical ferocity of work on the history of slavery are striking features of contemporary historiography." *Ibid.*, p. 11.

It is worth mentioning that the study of race relations was being rethought in the United States at precisely this point in history. Michael Banton, "1960: A Turning Point in the Study of Race Relations," *Daedalus* (Spring 1974). Furthermore, wrote historian Philip Curtin in 1974, "The serious study of African history in American and European universities began only in the 1950's, and detailed studies of African experience under colonialism are only now beginning to appear." Philip D. Curtin, "The Black Experience of Colonialism and Imperialism," *ibid.*, p. 17.

torian M. I. Finley, "there was no action or belief or institution in Graeco-Roman antiquity that was not one way or other affected by the possibility that someone involved [in a transaction] *might be* a slave."[94]

Moses lived a millennium before the Athens of Pericles, in which a third of the population was enslaved, a statistic that was repeated in ancient Rome.[95] Finley says that "In all Greek or Roman establishments larger than the family unit, whether on the land or in the city, the *permanent* work force was composed of slaves (or of other kinds of involuntary labour where that regime survived). . . . Not many generalizations about the ancient world can be substantiated with such certainty, with so few exceptions in the documentation."[96] There were always temporary employees available in the marketplace, but the permanent work force was enslaved. In short, "slaves dominated, and virtually monopolized, large-scale production in both the countryside and the urban sector. It follows that slaves provided the bulk of the immediate income from property (that is, income from other than political sources . . .) of the élites, economic, social and political."[97] The only exception was the slave who worked as an "independent" artisan or shopkeeper, which was probably a more common practice in Rome than in Greece. The slave was always "the basic source of élite income."[98]

(Those who follow the Enlightenment tradition of tracing modern freedom and culture back to classical Greece and Rome seldom come to grips with the economic foundation of classical civilization: slavery—a problem that Enlightenment *philosophes* never overcame with respect to either classical slavery or modern colonial slavery.[99] Finley is correct: "Anyone who clings to the cause of neo-classicism or classical humanism has little room for manoeuvre" on the subject

---

94. Finley, *Ancient Slavery*, p. 65.

95. This was also the percentage in the slave systems of the American South, Cuba, and Brazil during the mid-nineteenth century. *Ibid.*, p. 80. A. H. M. Jones agrees regarding this percentage as the maximum possible: one-third of the adult population of Athens. No census figures exist. To derive this percentage, he was forced to use data on total corn production and imports into Attica, as well as estimates regarding "normal" per capita corn consumption by free men and estimates of the size of Athens' free population. Economic historians are often forced into such makeshift proxies for nonexistent census figures. Jones, "Slavery in the Ancient World," *Economic History Review*, Second Series, IX (1956), p. 187.

96. *Ibid.*, p. 81.

97. *Ibid.*, p. 82.

98. *Idem.*

99. Writes historian David Brion Davis: ". . . the Enlightenment's actual verdict on colonial slavery was anything but clear-cut." Davis, *Slavery and Human Progress*, p. 131.

of slavery.[100] It was the late-medieval scholastic philosophers, specifically the School of Salamanca, which also pioneered free market economics,[101] who tried to check the evils of the new system of slavery and the wars of colonial conquest.[102])

The economic inefficiencies of slavery in the ancient Near East restrained slavery's development as a primary institution for private economic gain. It did not become a primary economic institution. Mendelsohn summarizes his findings: "With the exception of the state and the temple slaves, the proportion of the unfree population in every country and at almost any time was insignificant in relation to the free population. The number of slaves owned by private persons averaged from one to four. And it was for this reason that we often hear of individual escapes but never of organized slave revolts. The factors making for slave revolts — latifundia and mining industries where masses of slaves are employed — were nonexistent in the Near East."[103] The slave and his master labored side by side, whether in the field or the shop. "As a consequence the transition from freedom to slavery and vice versa was fluid."[104]

From what scanty evidence is available, the same is true of ancient Greece in Homeric times — the eighth century, B.C. William Westermann writes: "The number of the slaves owned, even by the wealthiest chieftains, was surprisingly limited; and the type of slavery was so mild that it is difficult to distinguish it at times from patriarchal clientage or serfdom."[105] All this was to change radically over the next three centuries, as Greece became a true slave society, and as power shifted from families to the city-state.

Even the case of the Hebrews in Egypt was not an exception. It was the Pharaoh who owned the Hebrews. They were put to work

---

100. Finley, *Ancient Slavery*, p. 64. See also Joseph Vogt, *Ancient Slavery and the Ideal of Man*, translated by Thomas Wiedemann (Oxford: Basil Blackwell, 1974), ch. 10: "Slavery and the Humanists." He writes: "In general, however, Humanist scholars continued to follow the judgements about slavery, and rarely dared to voice mild objections to Aristotle's doctrine of natural slavery. Barbarians and slaves remained excluded from the idea of man which the *studia humanitates* propagated" (p. 196).

101. Alejandro Antonio Chafuen, *Christians for Freedom: Late-Scholastic Economics* (San Francisco: Ignatius Press, 1986); Murray N. Rothbard, "Late Medieval Origins of Free Market Economic Thought," *Journal of Christian Reconstruction*, II (Summer 1975), pp. 62-75; Marjorie Grice-Hutchinson, *The School of Salamanca: Readings in Spanish Monetary Theory, 1544-1605* (Oxford: The Clarendon Press, 1952).

102. Vogt, *op. cit.*, pp. 197-98.

103. Mendelsohn, *Slavery In the Ancient Near East*, p. 121.

104. *Ibid.*, p. 122.

105. Westermann, *Slave Systems*, pp. 1-2.

on huge construction projects for the State. Mendelsohn is correct when he says that slavery alone was a suitable labor policy for the large public works projects of the ancient empires.[106]

Empire Economics: Turning Men Into Gold

The kings initially would get most of their slaves from the battlefield. To build an empire, a king had first to be successful on the battlefield. Then as now, empires are heavily reliant on military conquest. Nevertheless, only Greece and Rome became true slave societies, as far as the presently known records indicate. The empires of the ancient Near East found ways of integrating the captives into the conquering society. The Jews who were removed from Israel and Judah retained their religious nationality during their captivity, though it took God's intervention to save them on one occasion (Esther). What distinguished Greece and Rome was their use of military power to create a large subclass of permanent slaves. The State became part of the process of enslavement by allowing captives to be sold as slaves by victorious generals.

Soldiers on the march converted booty into gold; they had little use for slaves. Slave merchants followed the armies of the Greek city-states, harvesting human crops.[107] The same was true for Rome's armies.[108] The capitalization of expected future net income, so technical-sounding a phrase, became an acceptable way for soldiers and civil governments to convert humanity into capital, and therefore to make an expanding empire pay a substantial dividend to its promoters. In fact, the positive feedback relationship between the profits of slavery and the expansion of classical empire makes it difficult for the historian to distinguish the primary cause from the secondary. A plausible case can be made for either the demand for slaves promoting empire or the price effects of mass enslavement after a successful military campaign subsidizing those who dreamed of empire. There is no doubt that in the ancient world, enslavement and empire were aspects of a closely related reciprocal process.

Rome provides the best example of this process. As the Roman Republic expanded geographically, it established the economic and political foundations of the later Empire. The Romans enslaved

---

106. Mendelsohn, *Slavery in the Ancient Near East*, pp. 2, 92-96.
107. Westermann, *Slave Systems*, p. 26.
108. William I. Davisson and James E. Harper, *European Economic History*, vol. I, *The Ancient World* (New York: Appleton-Century-Crofts, 1972), p. 181.

others on a massive scale; as this process continued, the nation laid
the foundations of its own future enslavement. By the second century B.C., the slave system in Rome was in place.[109] From that time
forward, Roman citizens steadily lost their freedoms to the State.
The Roman Empire was based to a great extent on the legacy of
slavery from the Republic. The successful wars abroad became a
snare to Rome. In 262 B.C., Rome captured 25,000 Carthaginians
in the first of a series of mass enslavements during the Punic wars. A
generation earlier, in 296 B.C., as many as 40,000 people were taken
captive by Rome during the third Samnite war.[110] From 200 to 150
B.C., Rome may have taken prisoner as many as 250,000, although
many must have been ransomed back. At least 150,000 people were
enslaved from the 70 towns of Epirus in 167 B.C.[111] What is often ignored is the loss of life that these wars cost Rome.[112] In a sense, the
free peasantry was being replaced by slaves. This process continued
under the Empire, probably through accelerating debt bondage.[113]

Finley argues that military conquest led to the creation of large
agricultural estates in Rome,[114] but he denies that military conquest
has been the primary source of slaves historically. "Comparative evidence reveals that a necessary condition for an adequate supply of
slaves is not conquest but the existence, outside the society under
consideration, of a 'reservoir' of potential slave labour on which the
society can draw systematically. . . ."[115] This is an odd argument,
since the ability to inflict military defeats on a nation's enemies is
what creates the so-called reservoir. The victors begin to visualize
the defeated and the easy-to-defeat as potential sources of slaves.
Finley dismisses as "irrelevant" the fact that societies fight against
each other and then sell the captive losers to distant slave societies.
The key, in his view, is the existence of a market-driven slave trade
system. In short, "the demand for slaves precedes the supply."[116] He
neglects to ask what the economist always asks: Demand *at what
price?* A strong military reduces slave prices to the rich slave-buying
minority if the costs of financing military conquests are borne by a
broad base of taxpayers.

---

109. Finley, *Ancient Slavery*, p. 131.
110. *Ibid.*, p. 83.
111. Westermann, *Slave Systems*, p. 62.
112. *Ibid.*, p. 61.
113. Finley, *Ancient Slavery*, pp. 143-44.
114. *Ibid.*, p. 84.
115. *Ibid.*, p. 85.
116. *Ibid.*, p. 86.

A better argument would be that an expansionist empire fights fewer and fewer battles as it becomes visibly more powerful. Smaller city-states surrender to it without expensive conflicts. Slaves can be taken as a form of tribute. Also, as empires get rich from inanimate tribute, they may find it less expensive socially and politically to buy slaves from smaller, distant, mutually warring societies. This process was described by Strabo, the Roman Stoic author who was a contemporary of Jesus, who wrote about the growth of piracy in the region of the free port city of Delos. "The export trade in slaves was a major cause of all this criminal activity, as it had become extremely profitable. They were easy to capture, and the important and extremely wealthy centre of the trade was not very far away — the island of Delos, where tens of thousands of slaves could be received and dispatched again on the same day, so that there was a saying, 'Trader, dock here, unload, your cargo's already been sold.' The reason was that after the destruction of Carthage and Corinth, the Romans had become extremely rich and made use of large numbers of slaves; and as pirates could see how easy it was to make money in this way, they sprang up all over the place, and raided and traded in slaves themselves. The kings of Cyprus and Egypt co-operated with them because of their hostility to the Seleucids, and the Rhodians weren't friendly toward the Seleucids either, so that they had no help from anyone; and all the time the pirates pretended to be slave-dealers and carried on their activities unhindered."[117]

From Slave-Owner to Slave

Empires find that slavery easily becomes a way of life, first for the captives and then for the captors. Everyone wants to become a slave-owner; if this desire is not checked by law or circumstance, most people within slave societies eventually become slaves to the State. As Davisson and Harper summarize the demise of the institutions of the Roman Republic: "In a sense, then, the whole structure of Roman society worked for the exploitation of the Empire by a handful of families which had traditionally held high office. The desire of other citizens and of the allies — of every class with some political power — to share the profits of empire led to the great crisis of the Roman state."[118]

---

117. Extract from Strabo in Thomas Wiedemann, *Greek and Roman Slavery* (Baltimore, Maryland: Johns Hopkins University Press, 1981), p. 110.
118. Davisson and Harper, *Ancient World*, p. 186.

The State became an owner of slaves and the marketer of excess slaves. If the State had not become dependent on slaves, either as workers or as sources of revenue, slavery in the classical world would not have become a widespread phenomenon, for the land and the available technology could not easily support large concentrations of slaves. It took coercion by the State to mobilize the men and re- sources that made a true slave society possible, both militarily and economically. The State centralized political and economic power, but its power atrophied when men's faith in the future departed. Its wars of empire became defensive. In the case of Rome, slavery be- came serfdom; men were subsequently tied legally to the land, but not owned. Their productivity could no longer be capitalized through sale or purchase, except (rare) by sale or purchase of the land they tilled.

The case of the heathen peoples in Israel was not an exception to this rule of State-created slavery. Israel's State became the primary mobilizer of slaves during its brief era of slavery. A system of forced labor had been adopted by David: ". . . and Adoram was over the forced labor" (II Sam. 20:24, NASB). Solomon later forcibly drafted 153,000 resident Canaanites into service on his huge State con- struction projects, including the temple (II Chron. 2:18). These heathen peoples had remained as residents in Israel,[119] although they had originally been designated by God for annihilation. Solo- mon enslaved them, though only temporarily, to labor on his huge public works projects, including the construction of storage cities for his chariots and cavalry (I Ki. 6:19) — offensive weapons that violated God's law (Deut. 17:16). This paralleled his illegal multiplication of wives, also prohibited to a king, "that his heart not turn away" (Deut. 17:17). This terminology — turning away the heart — the Bible also uses with respect to Solomon's later years (I Ki. 11:2, 4). All of this was of a single piece: vast public works projects, a coerced heathen labor force, the multiplication of offensive weapons, the multiplication of wives, theological apostasy, and the subsequent judgment of God (I Ki. 11:11). This creation of an army of slaves was not the product of a free market economy.

In the generation after Solomon, the advisors to his son Rehoboam recommended policies that led to a revolt and the destruction of the kingdom (I Kgs. 12). Generally, this is explained as a tax revolt, but

---

119. Josh. 16:10; 17:12; Jud. 1:28, 30.

at least one specialist has argued that it was the Northern Kingdom's protest against Solomon's forced labor.[120] In any case, God put a check to the expansion of empire in Israel. The empire of Egypt invaded Judah, and this event brought Rehoboam to his theological senses (II Chron. 12:1-12). After the breakup of the united monarchy, there were no further examples of forced labor, except in the case of a national military emergency: fortifications (I Ki. 15:22).

Greece's descent into slavery to Rome, and Rome's subsequent descent into slavery to the State were both fitting. Free men of both societies had been unwilling to submit to the economic authority of other free men (i.e., the competitive free market). They eventually were compelled to submit to the State. Slaves served as high-level managers in both Greece and Rome. Why did these positions of great economic responsibility become the inheritance of slaves? A. H. M. Jones argues that the reason was the unwillingness of free men to work as employees of others. They refused to take orders from anyone. Freed slaves in Rome became the secretaries of the rich and powerful. The emperor's secretaries and accountants in Cicero's day became Rome's Secretaries of State and Ministers of Finance; "no Roman of standing would have demeaned himself by becoming the emperor's personal servant." Only in the first century A.D. did these offices become acceptable to the upper classes, though never to senators.[121] Men's arrogance led to their own enslavement.

Limited Slave Trade

It was possible in all ancient societies to purchase foreign slaves, but the evidence indicates that this form of commerce was limited. A separate class of slave traders did not develop in the ancient Near East, as far as the presently known records reveal.[122] This indicates that there was insufficient demand for imported foreign slaves. As Adam Smith said in *Wealth of Nations*, specialization is limited by the extent of the market.[123] The international market for slaves was not extensive.[124]

---

120. J. Alberto Soggin, "Compulsory Labor under David and Solomon," in Tomoo Ishida (ed.), *Studies in the Period of David and Solomon and other essays* (Winona Lake, Indiana: Eisenbrauns, 1982), p. 267.

121. Jones, "Slavery in the Ancient World," *Econ. Hist. Rev.*, p. 186.

122. Mendelsohn, *Slavery In the Ancient Near East*, p. 4.

123. Adam Smith, *An Inquiry into the Nature and Causes of the Wealth of Nations* (New York: Modern Library Edition, [1776] 1937), ch. 3.

124. It might be argued that all markets were limited in the ancient world. This in fact was the argument of Karl Polanyi, *The Livelihood of Man*, edited by Harry W. Peterson (New York: Academic Press, 1981), pp. 78-79, 146. This peculiar thesis is effectively refuted by Morris Silver, *Economic Structures of the Ancient Near East* (Totowa, New Jersey: Barnes & Noble, 1985), chaps. 5, 6.

What about the peacetime enslavement of a nation's citizens? There was household servitude, but on the whole it was the result of poverty or hard circumstances that befell individual families. Debt bondage would have been the most common reason for becoming an indentured servant. Another reason was the need for a criminal to raise the funds necessary to repay his victims.

If private, household servitude was relatively uncommon in the agriculture-based ancient Near East, why did God begin His case laws with laws governing household servitude? If the servitude laws were intended to govern only a minor area of Israel's social and economic life, why did God immediately focus the attention of His recently redeemed people on servitude? It was because God's concern is always theological, not simply social or economic. Their recent experiences in Egypt had been designed by God to teach them concerning the God-imposed relationship between covenant-keeping and liberty, and between covenant-breaking and permanent slavery. God's instructional purpose, as always, was covenantal.

Embarrassed by God

One thing every Christian reader should accept without question is this: *nothing in the Bible should be an embarrassment to any Christian.* We may not know for certain precisely how some biblical truth or historic event should be properly applied in our day, but every historic record, law, announcement, prophecy, judgment, and warning in the Bible is the very word of God, and is not to be flinched at by anyone who calls himself by Christ's name. We must never doubt that whatever God did in the Old Testament era, the Second Person of the Trinity also did. God's counsel and judgments are not divided. We must be careful not to regard Jesus Christ as a sort of "unindicted co-conspirator" when we read the Old Testament. "Whosoever therefore shall be ashamed of me and of my words in this adulterous and sinful generation; of him also shall the Son of man be ashamed, when he cometh in the glory of his Father with the holy angels" (Mark 8:38).

What we need to understand early in any serious discussion of the Old Testament is this: *most Christians today are embarrassed by God.* They are embarrassed by the very word of God. They are embarrassed by the ways that God dealt with people in the Old Testament. It makes them uncomfortable when they read the holy word of God when it says: "The righteous shall rejoice when he seeth the vengeance: he shall wash his feet in the blood of the wicked. So that a man shall say, Verily there is a reward for the righteous: verily he is a God that judgeth in the earth" (Ps. 58:10-11). They read to their children the stirring story of the fall of Jericho, seldom reflecting on the fact that the Hebrews had been ordered by God to kill every man, woman, and infant in Jericho without mercy, excepting only the household of Rahab. Moses warned the Israelites before their invasion of Canaan that they had to kill every last one of the people who dwelt in the land: "And when the LORD thy God shall deliver them before thee; thou shalt smite them, and utterly destroy them; thou shalt make no covenant with them, nor shew mercy unto them" (Deut. 7:2). No mercy? Not a speck of mercy. God hated the sin, and He also hated the sinners. He told His people to spare neither sin nor sinner in Canaan. The cup of their iniquity was at last historically full (Gen. 15:16).

Saul's Disobedience: Unauthorized Mercy

Saul lost his kingship because he showed mercy to the king and the animals of the Amalekites. He had been told by the prophet Samuel: "Thus saith the LORD of hosts, I remember that which Amalek did to Israel, how he laid wait for him in the way, when he came up from Egypt. Now go and smite Amalek, and utterly destroy all that they have, and spare them not; but slay both man and woman, infant and suckling, ox and sheep, camel and ass" (I Sam. 15:2-3). Saul mercifully spared the king, Agag—a king like himself—but destroyed all the people. He also saved the best of the sheep and oxen (I Sam. 15:8-9). "Then came the word of the LORD unto Samuel, saying, It repenteth me that I have set up Saul to be king: for he is turned back from following me, and hath not performed my commandments" (I Sam. 15:10-11a). *Following God's commandments*: this meant killing everyone and everything of Amalek. Samuel came to Saul and announced: "For rebellion is as the sin of witchcraft, and stubbornness is as iniquity and idolatry. Because thou hast rejected the word of the LORD, he hath also rejected thee from being king" (I Sam. 15:23). To emphasize his point, Samuel had Saul bring Agag before him, and Samuel hacked him to pieces before the Lord in Gilgal (I Sam. 15:33).

Gilgal was the first place where the Hebrews camped after entering Canaan. Each man was circumcised there, since they had not been circumcised during the forty years in the wilderness. Gilgal means "wheel"; [125] in the context of Joshua's invasion, it meant something very specific: "And the LORD said unto Joshua, This day have I *rolled away* the reproach of Egypt from off you. Wherefore the name of the place is called Gilgal unto this day" (Josh. 5:9). By hacking Agag to pieces, Samuel rolled from Israel the reproach to God of Saul's "merciful" disobedience regarding Agag and Amalek's animals.

While there is always a need for biblical disputations and clarifications regarding the proper New Testament application of any Old Testament text, there is no room for debate concerning the *innate morality of the total annihilation of the Canaanites* by the people of Israel, just as there is no debate regarding the morality of God's destruction of humanity by means of a great flood. This was morally required of them by God. To have done anything less would have been rebellion against God. Saul lost his kingship because he did less.

Why should this bother modern Christians? *Because they do not want to face the inescapable biblical reality of a God who has already sent to hell the vast majority of all people who have ever lived.* The doctrine of eternal damnation in the lake of fire (Rev. 20:14-15) embarrasses them, and they are also embarrassed by the far milder doctrine of God's historic judgments against nations. Such historic destruction is simply a minimal down payment by God to those who are eventually going to be ushered into the fires of eternal damnation.

Is there no mercy in hell? Not a speck. Was there no mercy for Canaanites? Only the mercy of perpetual slavery, and even this highly limited mercy was shown only to the Gibeonites, and only because they successfully tricked Joshua (Josh. 9). They should have been destroyed, but Joshua did not enquire of God before he made a covenant with them (Josh. 9:14-15).

Slavery and Hell

The doctrine of perpetual slavery is nothing special when compared to the doctrine of eternal damnation. In fact, perpetual slavery is an institutional testimony to the reality of eternal damnation. It should direct the slave's attention to the fate of his eternal soul. (It should also direct the master's attention to the same issue.) *Slavery was designed by God to be a means of evangelism in the Old Testament.* The question can therefore legitimately be raised: Is it a means of evangelism in New Testament times? For instance, why did Paul send

---

125. James Strong, "Hebrew and Chaldee Dictionary," in *The Exhaustive Concordance of the Bible* (New York: Abington, [1890] 1961), p. 27, Nos. 1534-37.

the runaway slave Onesimus back to his master Philemon (the Epistle to Philemon)? But anyone who dares raise this obvious question today faces the verbal wrath of Christian pietists and antinomians everywhere, not to mention secular humanists.

Slavery embarrasses Christians, yet earthly slavery can sometimes offer hope. Eternal slavery is hopelessness incarnate. Eternal slavery — without productivity, without hope of escape, and with perpetual pain — is a good description of hell. Is it any wonder that the doctrine of eternal damnation is de-emphasized in preaching today? Is it any wonder that God is spoken of mostly as a God of love, and seldom as the God of indescribable eternal wrath? D. L. Moody, the turn-of-the-century American evangelist, set the pattern by refusing to preach about hell. He made the preposterous statement that "Terror never brought a man in yet."[126] That a major evangelist could make such a theologically unsupported statement and expect anyone to take him seriously testifies to the theologically debased state of modern evangelicalism. It has gotten no better since he said it.

Consider the theological implications of Moody's statement. God created the place of eternal terror. He revealed His plans concerning final judgment in the New Testament, unlike the Old, which is very nearly silent concerning the details of hell and the lake of fire. If God does not intend that the terror of final judgment bring people to repentance, then hell is exclusively a means of God's vengeance, for supposedly it in no way brings anyone to repentance this side of death. Moody was implicitly arguing that there is no grace attached in history to the doctrine of hell; therefore, hell must be exclusively a means of punishment. But nothing in the creation is exclusively a means of punishment for those still living. There is grace to living men in every act of God and in every biblical doctrine. There *is* grace attached to the doctrine of hell; people sometimes *do* get scared into repentance. Any warning of imminent judgment before God's final judgment can serve as a means of personal or institutional restoration. All judgments in history are simply testimonies to the coming final judgment, and therefore all of God's temporal judgments offer both cursing and blessing.[127]

---

126. Cited by Stanley N. Gundry, *Love Them In: The Proclamation Theology of Dwight L. Moody* (Chicago, 1976), p. 99; cited in turn by George M. Marsden, *Fundamentalism and American Culture: The Shaping of Twentieth-Century Evangelicalism, 1870-1925* (New York: Oxford University Press, 1980), p. 35. Perhaps someone will cite me, making it three-stage faith in footnotes.

127. Sutton, *That You May Prosper*, ch. 4.

God punishes deceased covenant-breakers forever, not in order
to reform them, but because they refused to be reformed by God's
saving grace in history. Hell is not a reform school; it is a place of
eternal retribution.[128] God therefore holds ethical rebels in perpetual
slavery. God is in this sense *the Cosmic Slaveholder*. They do not work
in order to please this Cosmic Slaveholder; they are stripped of the
power to work, for labor is an aspect of dominion. They serve Him
exclusively as recipients of His incomparable wrath. We may not like
the idea, but this is what He says He has done and will do. No one
ever escapes God's eternal slave system if he departs from this life as
a moral slave to Satan rather than a moral bondservant to God.
There is no "underground railroad" out of slavery in hell. This is
why Christians offer the gospel of salvation to rebels against God: to
enable them to escape eternal punishment and eternal slavery to the
Sovereign Master of the eternal fiery whip.

In history, we are either involuntary slaves to God or voluntary
bondservants to God. Both conditions are permanent beyond the
grave. We either serve Him willingly in this lifetime, openly
acknowledging our status as unprofitable servants in His covenantal
household,[129] or else beyond this life we will experience perpetual
lashes from His judgmental whip as eternal slaves without hope.
There is no middle ground. There is no alternative scenario. Being a
bondservant to God is the essence of freedom. Being a slave to God
is the essence of hell. Choose this day which condition of servitude
you prefer.

Judgment: Eternal and Earthly

God has condemned Satan and his angelic followers to hell. Hell
was specifically designed for them (Matt. 25:41). No gospel of peace
and reconciliation was ever preached to them. No second chance
was ever offered to them. Does any Christian flinch or become in
any way embarrassed about God's condemnation of demons to the
eternal agony of fire? Of course not. No Christian ever worries that
"demons are God's creatures, too." So, why should we worry about

---

128. I have written in greater detail regarding the biblical doctrine of hell in my
Publisher's Epilogue to David Chilton's book, *The Great Tribulation*.

129. "So likewise ye, when ye shall have done all those things which are commanded you, say, We are unprofitable servants: we have done that which was our
duty to do" (Luke 17:10). See Gary North, "Unprofitable Servants," *Biblical Economics
Today*, VI (Feb./March 1983).

Satan's now-permanent followers, meaning eternally condemned sinners, either dead humans or fallen angels?[130]

Christians must openly acknowledge and gain courage from the fact that God's enemies are dealing with a God so powerful that He has already condemned to hell the vast majority of all those people who have died in the past. Christians know this; they have sent missionaries all over the world to help prevent a repetition of this; but they seldom like to think about it in its grim details. *God is presently torturing the vast majority of those who have ever lived, and He will continue to do so forever.*[131] Christians should never forget this, for it reflects in

---

130. One answer, based on biblical psychology, is that we are humans rather than angels. Our sympathies are instinctively with deceased humans. We may be occasionally tempted to worry about deceased friends or relatives who we are sure have died outside God's covenant. This is wasted worry. Once departed from this life, covenant-breakers retain none of their former personal gifts (restraints on evil) of God's common grace; they are now wholly self-consistent in their total rebellion against God. Their total depravity is now unrestrained. There is no longer anything left of them that is worth loving, caring about, or worrying about. Sentimentalism is legitimate regarding our memories of the common grace-blessed lives of now-deceased covenant-breakers during their stay on earth; it is a sinful denial of the faith when indulged in concerning their present condition or location. We are to take seriously in our own thinking the events of Ezekiel 9, God's sending of the faithful destroyers through the streets of Jerusalem, whom He instructed: ". . . let not your eye spare, neither have ye pity: slay utterly old and young, both maids, and little children, and women" (vv. 5b-6a). Mercy for covenant-breakers ends forever on the far side of death's door. For them, Christians cannot lawfully extend the false hope and judicially inappropriate blessing, "rest in peace."

131. The right to inflict torture on anyone is an exclusive prerogative of God in His office of cosmic Judge, which is why men and angels are not supposed to imitate Him in this practice. This is the theological basis of civil laws against torture, which was constantly denied in Christian Europe for centuries until the era of the French Revolution: John H. Langbein, *Torture and the Law of Proof: Europe and England in the Ancien Regime* (University of Chicago Press, 1977). It is also why God-denying, self-consistent Marxist societies use torture as a normal implement of social policy: they see the State as the agent of the Communist Party as having replaced God, including His office as Judge. For details, see Sidney Bloch and Peter Reddaway, *Psychiatric Terror; How Soviet Psychiatry Is Used to Suppress Dissent* (New York: Basic Books, 1977). Solzhenitsyn describes techniques of torture used by Soviet interrogators to force people to give up their gold in the late 1920's: Aleksandr Solzhenitsyn, *The Gulag Archipelago, 1918-1956*, pp. 53-54. Medvedev dates the beginning of torture as public policy with the collectivization of Soviet agriculture, which he dates as beginning in 1930. Roy A. Medvedev, *Let History Judge: The Origins and Consequences of Stalinism* (New York: Knopf, 1971), p. 398. Robert Conquest argues that torture became official policy in 1937 for gaining confessions out of accused Party members, although the great purge had begun in 1934: Conquest, *The Great Terror: Stalin's Purge of the Thirties* (New York: Collier, [1968] 1973), p. 195. Medvedev describes the practices used during the purge: *op. cit.*, ch. 8; cf. pp. 303, 476-77. For an account of more recent Communist torture, see the book by the Cuban refugee who spent over two decades in Cuban prisons, Armando Valladares, *Against All Hope* (New York: Knopf, 1986).

history the moral character of God the law-giver and Judge. Jesus
said that those who have been delivered from great wrath are more
thankful than those who have been delivered from less wrath (Luke
7:40-43). Christians should rejoice in their position as bondservants
to the Most High God because they understand the magnitude of the
wrath from which God has graciously delivered them.

This threat of eternal judgment now faces at least four to five billion people who are presently alive, which is why we need worldwide
revival now, in this generation. We need more evangelism. But our
enthusiasm for evangelism should be in part motivated by our confident knowledge that those souls that have already been condemned
by God now face eternal agony, without hope, without peace, and
without escape, forever and ever, amen. They have gone into eternal
slavery as people who are now and forever more under God's whip,
for they did not obey God when they had the option to do so. They
chose to remain unrighteous servants. They will be on God's whipping block forever.

Without the doctrine of hell, the meaning of Christ's gospel of
salvation becomes unclear. Without God's eternal judgment, His
eternal mercy has no comparable eternal significance. Without the
eternal fires of judgment as its background, the agony of Jesus Christ
on the cross was a mistake, a case of overkill. The threat of the lake of
fire is not the threat of mere annihilation; it is the threat of being tor-
tured forever by God Himself, who does everything perfectly.[132]

My point is simple enough: any *earthly* punishment that God has
brought, may bring, or wants His people to bring lawfully as His ordained agents of both mercy and condemnation, is minimal punishment when compared to the curse of eternal torment. Such earthly
cursings are hardly worth discussing, compared to the doctrine of

---

132. The doctrine of the annihilation of the soul in hell has generally been confined to the cults or borderline cults. This has begun to change in certain neo-
evangelical circles. The annihilationists argue that God does not punish the lost forever, but instead annihilates them. The most detailed defense of this position is
Seventh-Day Adventist Edward William Fudge's book, *The Fire That Consumes: A
Biblical and Historical Study of Final Punishment* (Houston, Texas: Providential Press,
1982). It is not surprising that this book should have changed the views of several
prominent neo-evangelical scholars, for ours is an age that is generally hostile to the
idea of God's covenantal cause and effect in history, let alone beyond history. God
the Judge is as disturbing to men as God the Law-giver and God the six-literal-day
Creator. Such a view of God does not conform to modern man's Darwinian view of
the universe. For a critique of Fudge, see Robert A. Morey, *Death and the Afterlife*
(Minneapolis, Minnesota: Bethany House, 1984), pp. 199-222.

the lake of fire. Yet the vast majority of today's Christians become embarrassed and begin to squirm uncomfortably when they are challenged by pagans (or Christian college professors in humanist-accredited liberal arts colleges) to explain and defend Old Testament stories of God's earthly cursings. Squirming should be the response of the covenant-breakers who hear of God's impending wrath, not the response of Christians who are seeking to obey the Bible.

The doctrine of the lake of fire should not embarrass any Bible-believing Christian; neither should anything else the Bible says that God did, does, or will do. God's warning to us is clear: "Wherefore, the LORD God of Israel saith, I said indeed that thy house, and the house of thy father, should walk before me forever: but now the LORD saith, Be it far from me; for them that honour me I will honour, and they that despise me shall be lightly esteemed" (I Sam. 2:30). Let us avoid being "lightly esteemed" by God; it is better to be despised by men—even by professors in fully accredited Christian colleges.[133]

If you have already accepted the doctrine of eternal punishment, then you have accepted the doctrine which above all other Christian doctrines outrages non-Christians. They do not want to think about it, which is understandable. The doctrine of eternal damnation is the ultimate offense of Christianity in the opinion of those who reject Christianity. This is why it is the first doctrine to be abandoned by covenant-breakers and heretics.[134] So, there is little reason for Christians to get embarrassed about other aspects of the Bible that the pagan world will taunt us with, since it is the doctrine of hell that really offends covenant-breakers, and we cannot give up this doctrine without accepting some version of an ancient heresy. In any case, ridicule by pagans is a temporary phenomenon; they will not be taunting us in eternity. They will be too busy being permanently offended by God in the lake of fire.

But if a Christian for some reason *is* embarrassed by the doctrine of hell, then he is not ready to get involved in the fight against humanism, or any other Bible-mandated fight. He must first know what he has been *delivered from* before he can bring the message of *sal-*

---

133. On the leftward drift into humanism by professors in neo-evangelical Christian colleges, and the theological liberalism and even apostasy that they produce in a significant percentage of their students, see James Davison Hunter, *Evangelicalism: The Coming Generation* (University of Chicago Press, 1987), pp. 165-80.

134. Cf. D. P. Walker, *The Decline of Hell: Seventeenth-Century Discussions of Eternal Torment* (University of Chicago Press, 1964), Part II.

vation to the lost. "Are you saved?" the Christian asks? We must get clear in our minds that *hell* is our first and most important answer to the question: "Saved from what?" Second, we are supposed to be saved from naive confidence in human institutions that have been captured by God-denying humanists and remade by them (frequently at our expense as taxpayers) in order to image hell. Because modern Christians are psychologically embarrassed by the doctrine of hell, and are therefore not quite sure just what it is they have been delivered from by the special grace of God, they find themselves increasingly impotent to bring a successful challenge to the humanist captors of the modern world. They even argue that God does not intend to deliver Christians from the temporal judgment of humanists, nor has He provided Christians with biblically legitimate and workable tools of dominion, this side of the Rapture.[135] They are embarrassed by the thought that Christians are required by God to work hard to reconstruct all human institutions in terms of biblical law by means of the Holy Spirit, in order that the earth might progressively image heaven and manifest the kingdom of God in history.[136] They have thereby reduced the gospel's message of comprehensive salvation.[137] As a result, they have long suffered under captured institutions that progressively image hell on earth, thereby manifesting the kingdom of Satan in history.[138] They labor as modern slaves in Egypt, for they are persuaded that there is no promised land in history during the so-called "Church Age."[139]

---

135. Dave Hunt and T. A. McMahon, *The Seduction of Christianity* (Eugene, Oregon: Harvest House, 1985); *Beyond Seduction: A Return to Biblical Christianity* (Harvest House, 1987). The "Biblical Christianity" that he refers to is premillennial dispensationalism, a theological system that can be traced back no earlier than 1830: Clarence B. Bass, *Backgrounds to Dispensationalism: Its Historical Genesis and Ecclesiastical Implications* (Grand Rapids, Michigan: Eerdmans, 1960), p. 129n. See also Dave MacPherson, *The Incredible Cover-up* (Medford, Oregon: Omega, 1975); *The Great Rapture Hoax* (Fletcher, North Carolina: New Puritan Library, 1983), ch. 3.

136. One such embarrassed Christian writer is former Richard Nixon aide Charles Colson (with Ellen Santilli Vaughn), *Kingdoms in Conflict* (New York: A Judith Markham Book, distributed by Zondervan Publishing House and William Morrow Co., 1987).

137. Gary DeMar and Peter Leithart, *The Reduction of Christianity: A Biblical Response to Dave Hunt* (Ft. Worth, Texas: Dominion Press, 1988).

138. Cf. Gary North, *Heaven or Hell on Earth: The Sociology of Final Judgment* (forthcoming).

139. Richard R. Reiter, Paul D. Feinberg, Gleason L. Archer, and Douglas J. Moo, *The Rapture: Pre-, Mid-, or Post-Tribulational?* (Grand Rapids, Michigan: Zondervan, 1984). For a book that shows that everything in history since A.D. 70 is post-tribulational, see David Chilton, *The Great Tribulation*.

Fishers of Men

In a clever use of this familiar New Testament phrase, economic historians Robert Paul Thomas and Richard Nelson Bean describe the profession of slave trading.[140] The New Testament condemns the profession: "We know that the law is good if a man uses it properly. We also know that law is made not for good men but for lawbreakers and rebels, the ungodly and sinful, the unholy and irreligious; for those who kill their fathers or mothers, for murderers, for adulterers and perverts, for slave traders [kidnappers] and liars and perjurers . . ." (I Tim. 1:8-10, NIV). Kidnappers are condemned, but the Greek word can easily be translated as slave traders.

In a very real sense, the slave trader did serve as a kind of perverse imitation of the New Testament evangelist: he harvested men's bodies, just as Christians are supposed to harvest both bodies and souls (John 4:35). The Old Testament allowed the importation of heathen slaves as a means of evangelism. With the gospel's breaking of national Israel's old wineskin, a new means of foreign evangelism began. New Testament evangelists are to go to foreign lands as servants, not as slave-masters or their economic agents, slave traders. They are to warn men and women to submit to God's rule voluntarily. God serves as the agent of cosmic coercion; Christians are to warn men of the true nature of slavery to sin, for it leads to the eternal cosmic whip. Christians are to bring the message of liberation which Jesus announced in Luke 4.

There is no explicit Old Testament condemnation of the slave trade, when that trade was confined to the importation of foreign slaves. It is clear, however, that the traders' services could be used only to import heathen slaves, never to sell Hebrew slaves to foreign nations (Ex. 21:8). The unstated implication is that *the heathen slave and his children were also protected from resale to heathen foreigners*, since the whole theological justification for enslaving a heathen was to bring him under God's visible covenantal rule. He had been made a part of a Hebrew family's household, even to the extent of being circumcised (Gen. 17:13). God was the owner of all Israel, including heathen slaves. Thus, to turn them out of the land, except as a civil sanction against a criminal act, was to symbolize God's casting men out of His covenantal jurisdiction, a most unlikely symbol. Richard

---

140. Thomas and Bean, "The Fishers of Men: The Profits of the Slave Trade," *Journal of Economic History*, XXXIV (1974), pp. 885-914.

Baxter recognized this redemption aspect of slavery in 1673, and he condemned anyone who would sell back a heathen slave to a heathen trader. The original purchase of slaves is a "heinous sin to buy them, unless it be in charity to deliver them." Thus, they may not be resold; rather, they are to be freed: "He that is bound to help to save a man, that is faln [fallen] into the hand of thieves by the High-way, if he should buy that man as a slave of the thieves, may not give him up to the thieves again."[141] He was quite clear: "Make it your chief end in buying and using slaves, to win them to Christ, and save their Souls."[142]

The slave trade had been condemned by a papal bull as early as 1425; Christian slave dealers were to be excommunicated.[143] This was seldom enforced, and traders ignored it. There is little doubt that the slave trade was regarded by English-speaking people as a socially very inferior occupation, despite the fact that the rich and upwardly mobile used the services of the traders. (There were very few English slave traders until 1660.)[144] There was a kind of residual awareness of the inherent immorality of the trade in New Testament times. But this residual awareness was insufficient to bring the judicial condemnation of slavery itself—a classic example of a deep-seated moral and intellectual schizophrenia that afflicted English Protestants for centuries.[145]

Thomas and Bean argue that the trade as a whole was not uniquely profitable because of nearly open entry and the impossibility of establishing property rights to the various markets. As is true in any profession or industry, individual slave traders reaped huge profits, but the trade as a whole did not. The slave-owners' profits from the slaves led to higher prices for slaves. Profits for the slave traders were eaten up by expenses in purchasing them and transporting them. Profits from the slave traders went to the black African "fishers of men." Step by step, the slave trade's profits eroded. Thomas and Bean conclude with the following remarkable but economically

---

141. Richard Baxter, *A Christian Directory* (London: Robert White for Nevil Simmons, 1678), Part II, *Christian Oeconomicks*, p. 73. The first edition appeared in 1673.

142. *Ibid.*, p. 74.

143. David Brion Davis, *The Problem of Slavery in Western Culture* (Ithaca, New York: Cornell University Press, 1966), p. 100.

144. Lester B. Scherer, *Slavery and the Churches in Early America, 1619-1819* (Grand Rapids, Michigan: Eerdmans, 1975), p. 20.

145. This same hostility to slave traders may have been present in other societies; I do not know one way or the other.

plausible conclusion, one which is appropriately ironic: "In Africa much of the economic profits were finally dissipated because of the common property nature of the resource. When the defense costs incurred by the potential quarry are added in, the total net impact of the slave trade was almost certainly negative even to the Africans who remained in Africa. Thus, the employers and purveyors of slaves gained from the trade only what they could have gained in the absence of the trade. The absence of the enforcement of private property rights in human beings probably made the society of the fishers of men net losers. The only group of clear gainers from the British trans-Atlantic slave trade, and even these gains were small, were the European consumers of sugar and tobacco and other plantation crops. They were given the chance to purchase dental decay and lung cancer at somewhat lower prices than would have been the case without the slave trade."[146]

God will not be mocked.

From Indentured Servitude to Racist Slavery

The issue of slavery casts a dark shadow over United States history. The Civil War (1861-65) was fought over the three questions: 1) will slavery be allowed to spread, 2) what to do with freed Negro slaves, and 3) should the Union be preserved?[147] After the war, Southern apologists focused on the third question, the preservation of the Union and the constitutionality of states' rights, as the legal justification of secession.[148] The idea that the war had been fought to defend slavery disappeared in the South as soon as Gen. Lee surrendered; many southerners, including Lee himself, professed relief that the war had destroyed slavery.[149]

---

146. Thomas and Bean, "Fishers of Men," *op. cit.*, p. 914.

147. This was the classroom assessment by the historian and remarkable Civil War bibliographer E. B. Long. I have never heard the causes of the war better summarized. Whether this was his own assessment or something he picked up from another historian, I do not remember.

148. See, for example, the two-volume book by the former Vice President of the Confederacy, Alexander H. Stephens, *A Constitutional View of the Late War Between the States*, (Philadelphia: National Pub. Co., 1867, 1870). On Stephens, see R. J. Rushdoony, *The Nature of the American System* (Fairfax, Virginia: Thoburn Press, [1965] 1978), ch. 3.

149. Richard E. Beringer, *et al.*, *Why the South Lost the Civil War* (Athens: University of Georgia Press, 1986), p. 361. In retrospect, the South's apologists offered other issues as the "true" reasons for the war: the defense of white supremacy, the Constitution (states' rights), and Southern honor: *ibid.*, ch. 16. Another reason, according to Southern apologists, was the high-tariff position of the industrial North: Robert L. Dabney, *Discussions*, 4 vols. (Vallecito, California: Ross House, [1892] 1980), IV, pp. 87-107. See the discussion of the 1861 Morrill tariff act in J. G. Randall and David Donald, *The Civil War and Reconstruction* (2nd ed.; Boston: D. C. Heath, 1961), pp. 286-87.

This was one of the most astounding cases of self-professed collective amnesia in human history.

The best estimate of the total number of slaves transported from Africa to the New World is 10 million people.[150] Fewer than 400,000 of these slaves were brought into British North America.[151] Compare this with over 1.6 million imported by the British Caribbean islands.[152] The slave system of the American South developed only in the late seventeenth or early eighteenth century. While the documentary evidence is somewhat elusive and incomplete,[153] it appears that prior to the 1640's, blacks and whites entered the region as temporary indentured servants. In 1640, however, the General Court of Virginia pronounced sentence on three escaped servants: a Dutchman, a Scot, and a black. The first two were ordered to serve their masters for an additional year; the black was returned to his master for life. Winthrop Jordan comments: "No white servant in any English colony, so far as is known, ever received a life sentence."[154] After 1640, surviving Virginia county court records began to mention black slavery for life.[155] Also, after 1640, records of prices paid for servants indicate a higher price for blacks, indicating a longer term of service. These higher prices may also indicate that blacks could be forced to do field work that whites refused to accept.[156] Beginning also in 1640 was a prohibition against blacks' bearing arms.[157] This was imitated in the North by Puritan Massachusetts in 1656, who excluded blacks from serving in the militia, and by Puritan Connecticut in 1660.[158]

Very few blacks were imported into the American colonies in the seventeenth century. In 1649, three decades after the arrival in Virginia of the first Africans, there were only 300 black laborers in

---

150. Philip D. Curtin, *The Atlantic Slave Trade: A Census* (Madison: University of Wisconsin Press, 1969), pp. 268-69.

151. *Ibid.*, p. 268.

152. *Idem.*

153. Historians who believe that the evidence is too incomplete to make any sure judgments regarding the terms of white and black indentures include Winthrop D. Jordan, "Modern Tensions and the Origins of American Slavery," *Journal of Southern History*, XXVIII (1962), p. 22; cf. Jordan, *White Over Black*, p. 75. See also Paul C. Palmer, "Servant Into Slave: The Evolution of the Legal Status of the Negro Laborer in Colonial Virginia," *South Atlantic Quarterly*, LXV (1966), p. 369.

154. Jordan, *White Over Black*, p. 75.

155. *Idem.*

156. *Ibid.*, pp. 76-77.

157. *Ibid.*, p. 78.

158. *Ibid.*, p. 71.

Virginia. About 80,000 Englishmen came to Virginia between 1630 and 1700, half in 1650-75. Only about 56 blacks per year were imported into Virginia, 1660-90.[159] Most of the laborers in Virginia were white until the end of the century.[160]

It was in the 1660's that the laws of various Southern colonies became openly racist, notably Virginia's and Maryland's.[161] From the mid-1660's, there was a declining pool of available white servants in the Chesapeake region.[162] Black slaves steadily replaced white indentured servants. A judicial transformation accompanied this economic shift to black slavery. Historian Kenneth M. Stampp describes this transformation: "During this decade various statutes provided that Negroes were to be slaves for life, that the child was to inherit the condition of the mother, and that Christian baptism did not change the slave's status. Even then it took many more years and many additional statutes to define clearly the nature of slaves as property, to confer upon the masters the required disciplinary power, to enact the codes by which the slaves' movements were subjected to public control, and to give them a peculiar position in courts of law."[163] Thus, what began in the Southern colonies as a biblically sanctioned system of indentured servitude was judicially transformed, probably beginning with the restoration in 1660 of the anti-Puritan Charles II as King of England, into an anti-biblical form of permanent slavery, one based exclusively on racial lines. This was the first stage of the American South's war against the Bible: the introduction of a Bible-prohibited permanent slave system.

A similar transformation had already taken place in the British West Indies under the reign of the Puritan saints, when sugar replaced tobacco as the primary export crop around 1640. Chattel slavery had been legalized in Barbados in 1636 during the reign of Charles I.[164] Charles was executed by the Puritans in 1649. Chattel slavery was

---

159. Wesley Frank Craven, *White, Red, and Black: The Seventeenth-Century Virginian* (Charlottesville: University of Virginia Press, 1971), p. 86.

160. Kenneth M. Stampp, *The Peculiar Institution: Slavery in the Ante-Bellum South* (New York: Vintage, 1956), p. 24.

161. Jordan, *White Over Black*, pp. 79-82.

162. See Russell R. Menard, "From Servants to Slaves: The Transformation of the Chesapeake Labor System," *Southern Studies*, XVI (1977), pp. 355-90.

163. Stampp, *Peculiar Institution*, pp. 22-23.

164. Richard N. Bean and Robert P. Thomas, "The Adoption of Slave Labor in British America," in Henry A. Gemery and Jan S. Hogendorn (eds.), *The Uncommon Market: Essays in the Economic History of the Atlantic Slave Trade* (New York: Academic Press, 1979), p. 388.

legalized in Virginia in 1670 under Charles II.[165] In between these reigns of these two kings, the Puritans ruled England. They did not attempt to abolish slavery.

Prior to 1660, at least on Barbados, the most profitable West Indies island in the mid-seventeenth century, the use of slave labor was not significantly cheaper than white labor, given the rising prices of slaves and their greater mortality in their early years of service. But the proportion of blacks nevertheless increased. Why? Perhaps because the slave traders of the Calvinist Netherlands continued to sell slaves to the Caribbean during the years of the English Civil War.[166] The Dutch also sold slaves on credit, a major incentive.[167] Another reason was the shift to sugar production; the field workers' living conditions deteriorated, and potential English emigrants were not easily induced to go to Barbados. Blacks had no choice.[168] By 1670, half of the population of the British West Indies was black; this proportion was not reached in the Chesapeake region of Virginia until 1750.[169]

Indentured servitude was basic to immigration to British North America from the Puritan migration of the 1630's until the American Revolution ended British rule. Something like one-half to two-thirds of all white immigrants came to the colonies as indentured servants.[170] In Virginia, the ratio was closer to three-quarters in the seventeenth century.[171] Indentured servitude began in Virginia as early as 1620.[172] It ended there seventy years later, replaced by black slavery.[173] But

---

165. *Ibid.*, p. 389.

166. Hilary McD. Beckles, "The Economic Origins of Black Slavery in the British West Indies, 1640-1680: A Tentative Analysis of the Barbados Model," *Journal of Caribbean History*, XVI (1982), pp. 36-56. I think this makes more sense than Bean and Thomas' argument that wages began rising in England from 1640 to 1645; hence, it became marginally less expensive to import slaves from Africa rather than indentured servants from England: *op. cit.*, pp. 393-94. I cannot imagine so rapid a shift from white indentured servitude to black slavery as a product of merely marginal price shifts.

167. *Ibid.*, p. 43n.

168. Richard S. Dunn, *Sugar and Slaves: The Rise of the Planter Class in the English West Indies, 1624-1713* (Chapel Hill: University of North Carolina Press, 1972), pp. 59-72, 110-16, 301-34.

169. Bean and Thomas, "The Adoption of Slavery in British America," *op. cit.*, p. 378.

170. Abbot Emerson Smith, *Colonists in Bondage, op. cit*, p. 336.

171. Craven, *White, Red, and Black*, p. 5.

172. David W. Galenson, "The Rise and Fall of Indentured Servitude in the Americas: An Economic Analysis," *Journal of Economic History*, XLIV (1984), p. 1.

173. Bean and Thomas, "The Adoption of Slave Labor in British America," *op. cit.*, p. 382.

indentured servitude did not end in the northern colonies; it persisted, though on a declining basis, through the first quarter of the nineteenth century.[174] On the other hand, the abolition of slavery in the British West Indies in 1833 revived the use of indentured servitude, with Asia furnishing the bulk of the immigrants.[175] This practice continued until 1917, when the British government made it illegal for people from India to indenture themselves in order to pay for their emigration from India.[176] Asians also came to Hawaii as indentured servants in the mid-nineteenth century.[177]

There is little doubt that voluntary indentured servitude was a rational economic response by both importing masters and immigrating servants, given the high costs of ocean transportation.[178] When these costs fell in the late nineteenth century because of the development of steamships, indentured servitude declined rapidly. The number of immigrants to the United States rose from 5 million in the entire antebellum period[179] to 10 million in the next 30 years, and 15 million in the 15 years thereafter.[180] "The change in countries of origin was equally dramatic: 87 percent of the immigrants were from northern and Western Europe in 1882, but twenty-five years later, 81 percent were from southern and eastern Europe."[181]

Southern Slavery

The eighteenth century saw the development of what became the antebellum slave system in the American South. By the eve of the American Revolution, half of Virginia's population was black, and two-thirds of South Carolina's.[182] By 1830, the Negro slave system had become permanent in the South. Southerners by then measured their rank in society, Stampp says, by counting their slaves.[183] At

---

174. Galenson, *op. cit.*, pp. 12-13. This is an excellent summary essay, and I have relied on it heavily. See also Galenson, *White Servitude in Colonial America: An Economic Analysis* (Cambridge, Massachusetts: Harvard University Press, 1981).

175. *Ibid.*, p. 14. See Galenson's footnote 38 for bibliography.

176. *Ibid.*, p. 26.

177. *Ibid.*, p. 15.

178. *Ibid.*, pp. 16-21.

179. The word "antebellum" refers to the pre-Civil War period in the United States.

180. Thomas Sowell, *Ethnic America: A History* (New York: Basic Books, 1981), p. 13.

181. *Idem.* For other possible economic explanations, see Galenson, *op. cit.*, pp. 21-24.

182. Stampp, *Peculiar Institution*, p. 24.

183. *Ibid.*, p. 27.

that point, the system stopped changing significantly. Its form was the same in 1860 as it had been in 1830.[184] Nevertheless, throughout the period, over half of the residents of the South were yeoman farmers, not plantation owners or "poor whites." "If there were such a thing as a 'typical' ante-bellum Southerner, he belonged to the class of landowning small farmers who tilled their own fields, usually without any help except from their wives and children. He might have devoted a few acres to one of the staples for a 'cash crop,' but he devoted most of his land and time to food crops for the subsistence of his own family."[185] Half of all slaves in the South in 1860 were owned by planters who owned 20 or more slaves.[186]

No doubt this section of the commentary will look quite dated in retrospect, perhaps within a few years. Historians continue to debate the issue of racism and modern slavery, but what seems to be the most accurate conclusion is that the system of short-term indentured servitude of the English-speaking colonies during the early seventeenth century was not a well-developed or politically entrenched permanent slave system, and that the deeply racist character of later slavery did not appear until the second half of the century, especially in North America.[187] In fact, it does not appear that there was extensive racial prejudice in the American South in the mid-seventeenth century,[188] although there are able historians who dispute this.[189] Slavery as a system came to North America in the early eighteenth century, and it was grounded in the racist prejudices that increased with every shipload of victimized blacks. Racism seems to have been the foundation of slavery rather than the reverse.[190]

---

184. *Ibid.*, p. 28.
185. *Ibid.*, p. 29.
186. *Ibid.*, p. 31.
187. The best current survey of the scholarly literature is William A. Green, "Race and Slavery: Considerations on the Williams Thesis," in Barbara L. Solow and Stanley L. Engerman (eds.), *British Capitalism and Caribbean Slavery: The Legacy of Eric Williams* (New York: Columbia University Press, 1987). I have relied on it heavily.
188. T. H. Breen and Stephen Innes, *"Myne Owne Ground": Race and Freedom on Virginia's Eastern Shore, 1640-1676* (New York: Oxford University Press, 1980), pp. 112-14.
189. Carl N. Degler, "Slavery and the Generation of American Race Prejudice," *Comparative Studies in Society and History*, XI (1959-60), pp. 48-66.
190. Jordan, *White Over Black*, pp. 93-98.

The Anti-Slavery Impulse: Very Recent

People forget how common slavery has been in human history. We also forget how recently it was that any group opposed slavery either religiously or philosophically. The Quakers (Society of Friends) were the first organized group in history to demand the abolition of slavery. They began their campaign within their own membership in the late 1750's, and took their criticisms public in the 1770's. The world ignored them at first. The idea was considered preposterous, yet it became triumphant in the Protestant West and the Russian East in less than a century. Professor Davis writes: "As late as the 1770s, when the Quaker initiative finally led to a rash of militant antislavery publications on both sides of the Atlantic, no realistic leader could seriously contemplate the abolition of New World slavery—except, on the analogy with European slavery and serfdom, over a span of centuries. Yet in 1807, only thirty-four years after a delegation of British Quakers had failed to persuade the Lord of Trade to allow Virginia to levy a prohibitive tax on further slave imports, Britain outlawed the African slave trade. Twenty-six years later, Britain emancipated some 780,000 colonial slaves, paying 20 million pounds compensation to their supposed owners. Only ninety years separated the first, cautious moves of the Philadelphia Quakers from the emancipation edicts of France and Denmark (1848), which left Brazil, Cuba, Surinam, and the southern United States as the only important slaveholding societies in the New World. It was barely a century after the founding of the London Society for Effecting the Abolition of the Slave Trade (1787), sixty-one years after the final abolition of slavery in New York State (1827), that Brazil freed the last black slaves in the New World. . . . From any historical perspective, this was a stupendous transformation. . . . From the distance of the late twentieth century, however, the progress of emancipation from the 1780s to the 1880s is one of the most extraordinary events in history."[191]

There is no New Testament biblical law or principle that abolishes the legitimacy of the Old Testament's system of fixed-term indentured servitude for debt repayment with a maximum term of seven years. The New Testament also does not abolish long-term or even lifetime slavery for criminals who are working off their obligations to their victims. (What the Bible does *not* sanction is long-term

---

191. Davis, *Slavery and Human Progress*, p. 108.

imprisonment by the State in place of restitution to the victims by the criminals.)[192]

The War Against the Bible

The American South had become morally content with slavery after 1820. The South was overwhelmingly Christian. Prior to the American Revolution, the North on the whole had been content with slavery. The North was also overwhelmingly Christian. New York passed a law in 1706 stating that "the baptizing of any Negro, Indian, or Mulatto slave shall not be any cause or reason for the setting them or any of them at liberty." The stated reason for this was that there were some slave-owners who wanted to baptize their slaves, but were afraid that this would require them to free them.[193] Similar laws had already been enacted in Maryland, Virginia, the Carolinas, and New Jersey.[194] Virginia enacted such a statute in 1668.[195] The next year, this was established as fundamental law by King Charles II's colonial charter establishing the Carolinas.[196]

Here is a special baptismal vow written by evangelist Francis LeJau in the early eigthteenth century. Before being baptized, the slave was required to make the following affirmation: "You declare in the presence of God and before this congregation that you do not ask for the holy baptism out of any design to free yourself from the Duty and Obedience you owe to your Master while you live, but merely for the good of Your soul and to partake of the Graces and Blessings promised to the Members of the Church of Jesus Christ."[197]

This sounds hypocritical to Christians today, but there is an Old Testament precedent for these laws. First, God required the Hebrews to circumcise every male child born into any household, including slave children (Gen. 17:12-13). Second, to gain access to the passover, a purchased adult foreign slave had to be circumcised (Ex. 12:44). This heritage of inter-generational slave circumcision had to persist unbroken for the full ten generations in order for the last generation to gain its freedom. Thus, the fact that slaves could be bap-

---

192. See Chapter 11: "Criminal Law and Restoration."

193. *Colonial Laws of New York*, Vol. I, pp. 597-98; in *Foundations of Colonial America: A Documentary History*, edited by W. Keith Kavenaugh, 3 vols. (New York: Chelsea House, 1973), II, p. 1198.

194. Jordan, *White Over Black*, p. 92.

195. *Foundations*, III, p. 2076.

196. *Ibid.*, III, p. 1773.

197. Cited in Scherer, *Slavery and the Churches in Early America*, p. 96.

tized but were not immediately freed is not hypocritical, given the assumption that Christians do not recognize that the abolition of the jubilee land tenure law also abolished permanent slavery.

Christianity and slavery were considered compatible until the 1770's. The geographical and ecclesiastical differences, North vs. South, did not lead to sharp differences of opinion regarding slavery until the early nineteenth century. Racist hostility to blacks in both the North and the South was common throughout the antebellum period.[198] These attitudes were inherently anti-biblical, but almost nobody recognized this prior to the late eighteenth century. This is why David Brion Davis calls this the problem of Western slavery.[199] It was, above all, a moral and theological problem.

The War Escalates

Let us not forget that the Bible-denying, Trinity-denying Unitarian abolitionists of the 1840's and 1850's in the United States had first decided to abolish the God of the Bible; only afterward did they turn their attention to the problem of abolishing Southern slavery.[200] Some of them had even decided to abolish the Union, calling the U.S. Constitution "a covenant with death."[201] William Lloyd Garrison concluded that the Bible must be subjected to the tests of reasonableness, historical confirmation, the facts of science, and man's intuition. "Truth is older than any parchment," he affirmed. His radical disciple, Henry Clarke Wright, proclaimed: "The Bible,

---

198. Leon F. Litwack, *North of Slavery: The Negro in the Free States, 1790-1860* (University of Chicago Press, 1961).

199. See the review of Davis' book by Moses I. Finley, "The Idea of Slavery," *New York Review of Books*, VIII (Jan. 26, 1967); reprinted in Allen Weinstein and Frank Otto Gatell (eds.), *American Negro Slavery: A Modern Reader* (New York: Oxford University Press, 1968), pp. 348-54.

200. Most of the Unitarian abolitionist leaders were or had been ministers. Otto Scott inserted the word "Rev." before the names of these men throughout the manuscript of his book, *The Secret Six: John Brown and the Abolitionist Movement* (New York: Times Books, 1979). When the page proofs came back from the printer, "Rev." had been removed. He marked the page proofs to indicate that the word should be reinserted. When the book was printed, these changes had not been made. The editor had known just how devastating these references to their ordination would appear, and he had kept them from appearing. I was told about this by Scott several years later.

201. Philip S. Paludan, *A Covenant With Death: The Constitution, Law, and Equality in the Civil War Era* (Urbana: University of Illinois Press, 1975). Cf. Staughton Lynd, "The Abolitionist Critique of the United States Constitution," in Martin Duberman (ed.), *The Antislavery Vanguard: New Essays on the Abolitionists* (Princeton, New Jersey: Princeton University Press, 1965), pp. 209-39.

If Opposed to Self-Evident Truth, is Self-Evident Falsehood." Charles Stearns said that the Old Testament is a tissue of lies, "no more the work of God than the Koran, or the Book of Mormon."[202] James B. Jordan is correct when he observes: "From the standpoint of abolitionism, Christianity is an immoral way of life."[203] He is equally correct when he observes that "insofar as Christian thinkers are subject to influence from anti-Christian philosophies, there is continuing need for a polemic designed to purge the Christian community of alien thought patterns."[204]

This has been a continuing problem for serious Christian thinkers. They tend to adopt too many of the assumptions of their enemies. Today, a major source of error is liberation theology, which, as Jordan remarks, "is laced with, when not actually grounded upon, radical egalitarian premises."[205] Two centuries ago, an important producer of error was Deism.[206] In the case of both liberation theology and Deism, Christians have given up too much philosophical territory. Professor Davis' insights into the effects of Deism on Christian faith in Britain in the eighteenth and nineteenth centuries are very important. He points out that the arguments of a handful of unpopular Deists in the early 1700's against the validity of the Old Testament called forth philosophical and theological defenses from orthodox Christians. But these defenses gave away too much to the haters of Christianity. Those Christians in our day who would disparage the laws of the Old Testament should take very seriously Davis' observations:

By the 1730s Christian apologists had learned that disputes over textual details could never drain the deepening pools of doubt. As a compromise, it was sufficient to insist on the centrality of the resurrection and the historical

---

202. David Brion Davis, *The Problem of Slavery in the Age of Revolution, 1770-1823* (Ithaca, New York: Cornell University Press, 1975), p. 523.

203. James B. Jordan, Slavery in Biblical Perspective, master's thesis, Westminster Theological Seminary, 1980, p. 3.

204. *Idem.*

205. *Idem.* Vladimir Bukovsky, the expelled Soviet dissident, writes: "The dream of absolute, universal equality is amazing, terrifying, and inhuman. And the moment it captures people's minds, the result is mountains of corpses and rivers of blood, accompanied by attempts to straighten the stooped and shorten the tall." Vladimir Bukovsky, *To Build a Castle: My Life as a Dissenter* (New York: Viking, 1978), pp. 106-7.

206. Henning Graf Reventlow, *The Authority of the Bible and the Rise of the Modern World* (London: SCM Press, [1980] 1984), Pt. III: "The Climax of Biblical Criticism in English Deism."

fulfillment of Old Testament prophecy. As [Leslie] Stephen sums up the pragmatic resolution, Englishmen could still believe everything in the Bible, "but nothing too vigourously"; if the book was not flawless, it was "true enough for practical purposes."

So far as slavery is concerned, the Deists pointed toward the future position of [Thomas] Paine and Garrison. Thus God, by definition, was good and just. Yet the God of the Bible had authorized slavery as a divine punishment, along with such barbarities as the stoning to death of stubborn children who refused to obey their parents. It followed that the Bible could not be God's word. [Matthew] Tindal specifically compared the Jewish enslavement of Canaanites to the Spanish conquest of Mexico. The claim of divine sanction should not lessen one's outrage over either crime.[207]

Ah, yes, those mean old Spaniards. They destroyed the Aztec and Inca cultures in which human sacrifice and ritual cannibalism were practiced regularly, where priests on top of pyramids would rip the hearts out of living sacrificial victims and eat them. In short, the Spaniards did to the Aztecs and Incas what the Hebrews did to the Canaanites, and for similar reasons: *to put an end to outrageous cultural sin.*

The Spanish used slavery to further empire; the Hebrews were not to establish an empire based on pagan slave labor, so God did not allow them to make slaves of the Canaanites. Instead, God told them to kill or expel from the land every Canaanite. In both cases, however — Spanish slavery and Hebrew slavery — "tender-hearted" (read: soft-headed) commentators many centuries later are appalled, not at the ritual murders that preceded the conquests, but at those who put a stop to ritual murder. For well over three centuries, the Spaniards have been seen as the cannibals, and the cannibals have been seen as the victims.[208]

Progress in Redemptive History

Nevertheless, this continuing bias of contemporary historiography does not relieve Christians of their difficulty: to explain how it was that Christianity did not pioneer the abolitionist movement, either in England or the United States, even though evangelical Christians later became ardent abolitionists in both nations.[209] Why did slavery

---

207. Davis, *The Problem of Slavery in the Age of Revolution*, p. 528.

208. For a corrective to the "Black Legend" story of Spanish atrocities in the New World, see Prof. Philip Wayne Powell's book, *Tree of Hate: Propaganda and Prejudices Affecting the United States Relations with the Hispanic World* (Vallecito, California: Ross House, 1985). Published originally in 1971 by Basic Books, New York City.

209. Bertram Wyatt-Brown, *Lewis Tappan and the Evangelical War Against Slavery* (Cleveland, Ohio: Case Western Reserve University, 1969).

flourish in the Christian West until the early nineteenth century? Why was there never an organized anti-slavery movement anywhere in the world until the Quakers of the mid-eighteenth century finally took steps to cleanse their ranks of this evil?[210] Christian evangelicals were the ones who successfully pushed laws through the British Parliament that abolished the slave trade (1808) and then slavery (1833),[211] but the Quakers had pioneered the abolition movement. Why the long delay?

William Westermann spent his academic career in pursuit of an answer. "One problem remains which presses insistently for an answer, however tentative it may be. It arises out of a conviction which has often been expressed both by students working in the field of the development of the early church and by several of the scholars who have interested themselves specifically in the slave system as it operated in the final centuries of the Roman Empire. This is the belief that the tenets of Christianity should have led to the overthrow of the slave institution, perhaps in the sixth century. If not then it must have occurred eventually at some unspecified period in which the conjunction of circumstances became favorable to that outcome."[212]

That final sentence is crucial. We need to ask his simple question: Why *must* abolition have occurred eventually at some unspecified period in which the conjunction of circumstances became favorable to that outcome? We can answer generally, "in the providence of God," but that is not the answer we need as historians. We need a far more specific answer. What was it *specifically* about Christianity that *had* to lead to the abolition of slavery? More to the point, what kinds of historical circumstances were so vital to the development of abolitionism that it took eighteen centuries after the death of the Founder of Christianity for the abolitionist movement to appear? And why were the Quakers the original proponents of abolition? Why not the Puritans, for example? Why so late in history—late in our view, that is?

---

210. Jordan, *White Over Black*, 194-95, 197-98, 271-76.

211. A very well written chapter on Wilberforce's career appears in Charles Colson's book, *Kingdoms in Conflict*, despite the book's self-conscious ethical dualism. The picture he presents on Wilberforce the Christian politician in Chapter 8 is in stark contrast to his favorable view of pluralism in Chapter 9. He cites these books on Wilberforce's career: Robin Furneaux, *William Wilberforce* (London: Hamilton, 1974); John Pollack, *Wilberforce* (New York: St. Martin's, 1978); Ernest Marshall House, *Saints in Politics: The Clapham Sect* (London, George Allen & Unwin, 1974); and Garth Lean, *God's Politician: William Wilberforce's Struggle* (Colorado Springs: Helmers & Howard, [1980] 1987).

212. Westermann, *Slave Systems*, p. 159.

Westermann keeps asking questions that he never really answers. "What were the elements inherent in Christian doctrine, whether original in Christianity or borrowed, and what were the factors in the later structure of Christian power which sanction the opinion that Christian teaching, the Christian way of life, and Christian organization must, in the final analysis, destroy slavery?"[213] The early church fathers were indifferent to the existence of the slave trade. Why?

Paul's answer, Westermann says, was that slavery is punishment for sin. It is indeed, and the Old Testament presents it as such, but how does this explain why the New Testament does not call for abolition? Isn't ours the new order of Christ? Why should Christians be placed in permanent bondage to pagans or to each other? Paul sent Onesimus back to Philemon. Why would he have done this if slavery is inherently wrong? Why condone it implicitly by not insisting that Philemon free Onesimus? Why encourage slavery by silence? John Murray, a twentieth-century Presbyterian theologian and ethicist, stated the ethical problem quite bluntly: "If the institution is the moral evil it is alleged to be by abolitionists, if it is essentially a violation of basic human right and liberty, if slave-holding is the monstrosity claimed, it is, to say the least, very strange that the apostles who were so directly concerned with these evils did not overtly condemn the institution and require slave-holders to practice emancipation. If slavery *per se* is immorality and, because of its prevalence, was a rampant vice in the first century, we would be compelled to conclude that the high ethic of the New Testament would have issued its proscription. But this is not what we find."[214]

Breaking With the Old Covenant

The biblical answer to Murray's question cannot be grasped without a redemptive-historical understanding of history. The definitive break with the Old Covenant was made with the death and resurrection of Christ. Then came His ascension and the coming of the Holy Spirit at Pentecost. Then came the New Testament, book by book. Finally, the fall of Jerusalem ended Israel's old order, leaving Christ's new order as the covenantal basis of redeemed society. All of

---

213. *Idem.*
214. John Murray, *Principles of Conduct* (Grand Rapids, Michigan: Eerdmans, 1957), p. 94.

this took at least 40 years. In other words, *it took time*, yet it was essentially *one event*, covenantally speaking: the coming of Christ's New World Order.

The legitimacy of lifetime heathen slavery and inherited slaves ended with Israel's final jubilee year in A.D. 70. In principle, that jubilee event came with Christ's announcement of the meaning of His ministry (Luke 4:16-21). But the development of this jubilee principle of release progressed for one generation until God destroyed Jerusalem, in order to destroy the liturgical and political foundations of the Jewish religious leaders who had refused to let their spiritual slaves go free. The leaders had rejected Christ's message of final jubilee release, and so had most of their spiritually enslaved followers; in response, God destroyed their civilization.

Jesus Christ was in principle an abolitionist, for He was the fulfillment of the jubilee year principle, the great year of release. His fulfillment of the jubilee year announced the advent of His New World Order. Nevertheless, *He did not verbally require an overnight (or seven-year) program of manumission or abolition.* As is the case with many of the implicit social and economic principles of the Bible, Jesus established the principle of abolition, and He was then content to wait for His people to acknowledge it and put it into action in history. He waited for seventeen centuries. (In the case of the biblical principle of judicially restrained debt, He is still waiting.)

The task of abolition was delayed until the advent of the modern world—specifically, until the Industrial Revolution made possible new sources of economic productivity that dwarfed anything that the old slave and serf systems could produce. This does not mean, however, that the Industrial Revolution as such led *inevitably* to the abolition of slavery. Historical causation is more complex than this. The issues and pressures behind abolitionism were far more complex than mere economic determinism or "mere" anything else.[215] Never-

---

215. Eric Williams argued that England's Caribbean slave colonies supplied much of the capital for England's Industrial Revolution, but then slavery became an economic drag on capitalism, leading to a shift of opinion toward anti-slavery among the new capitalist leaders of British society. Williams, *Capitalism and Slavery* (New York: Putnam, [1944] 1966). This thesis gained wide support among scholars for at least a generation, but both halves of this thesis have been seriously challenged in recent years. See especially Seymour Drescher, *Econocide: British Slavery in the Era of Abolition* (Pittsburgh, Pennsylvania: University of Pittsburgh Press, 1977). David Brion Davis now admits that he was incorrect in 1966 when he argued in *The Problem of Slavery in Western Culture* that "no country thought of abolishing the slave trade until its economic value had considerably declined." On the other hand, he says, no one has shown that the abolition of slavery retarded England's economic growth or was regarded by most English policy-makers as a threat to vital national interests. *Slavery and Human Progress*, p. 335, note 121. See also his bibliography in note 119.

theless, it was in non-slave cultures that the new industrialism flourished.[216] For the first time in history, long-term economic growth became a fixture in society, and a new era dawned. Men were ripe for radical changes as never before, especially changes in law and philosophy. They were ripe for abolitionism.

Christianity is a force for total transformation, even of the cosmos (Rom. 8:18-22). Nevertheless, it is not self-consciously revolutionary. It does not seek to overthrow civil governments by elitist-imposed force. Instead, it steadily overthrows all governments — personal, familistic, church, and civil — by the cumulative spread of the gospel and the process of *institutional replacement*. This is the New Testament kingdom principle of the leaven (Matt. 13:33).[217] In this God-ordained world, there is *a system of positive feedback* between new ideas and social change, but when the whole of a civilization refuses to consider a biblically valid new idea, God is content to allow members of that civilization to suffer the historical consequences.

When the Quakers at last began challenging the moral legitimacy of slavery in the late eighteenth century, God made possible the extension of this morally and judicially justified abolitionism into

---

216. I am implicitly dividing industrial England from its agricultural Caribbean colonies, and America's industrial North from its agrarian South. They rapidly became separate civilizations after 1780, as all sides agreed. This cultural division was maintained between North and South until air conditioning (1950's) made life in the South thinkable for outsiders, the civil rights movement (1960's) equalized the legal systems, and Southern university coaches' lust to recruit black athletes (1970's) equalized the regional win-loss records (especially in basketball). On the earlier post-Civil War division, see the testament of a dozen southern writers, *I'll Take My Stand: The South and the Agrarian Tradition* (New York: Harper Torchbooks, [1930] 1962); Alexander Karanikas, *Tillers of a Myth: Southern Agrarians as Social and Literary Critics* (Madison: University of Wisconsin Press, 1966).

217. The perversity of modern dispensational theology is seen in its combination of bad typology and anti-wine communion liturgy. *The New Scofield Reference Bible* insists (as did the original *Scofield*): "Leaven, as a fermenting process, is uniformly regarded in Scripture as typifying the presence of impurity or evil. . . . Leaven, as a symbolic or typical substance, is always mentioned in the O.T. in an evil sense (Gen. 19:3, marg.)." *The New Scofield Reference Bible* (New York: Oxford University Press, 1967), p. 1015n: Matthew 13:33. What is corrupt is not leaven but rather the exegesis of the Scofield note-writers, who systematically refuse to mention Leviticus 7:13 in this note, a verse which required the offering of a leaven sacrifice to God. Did God require a symbol of corruption on His altar? The note-writers say that He did: *ibid.*, p. 134n. For a refutation of this anti-kingdom, anti-wine (fermentation), anti-biblical nonsense, see my discussion in *Unconditional Surrender: God's Program for Victory* (3rd ed.; Tyler, Texas: Institute for Christian Economics, 1988), pp. 315-19, 325-26. What these fundamentalist legalists are really hostile to is wine in communion: *ibid.*, p. 223.

Western society at large.[218] *God's means of accelerating this specific histori-cal change was the advent of industrial capitalism, which opened the labor mar-kets to price competition and widespread social mobility.* In such a world, slavery appeared as a restraint on trade and production. Slavery be-came an economic anachronism in the opinion of the majority of those who believed in the rhetoric of the free market and republican institutions. Furthermore, capitalism urbanized the nation wherever it spread, and slavery could not exist in capitalist cities. Slavery re-quired a degree of social control over the slaves in leisure hours that urban capitalism simply did not permit. Slaves steadily disappeared from the South's cities throughout the nineteenth century.[219]

Diehards against abolitionism held out in the South, but they could not resist the floodgates of history. The diehards died hard, lit-erally, by the hundreds of thousands, but they did die. Both military and moral resistance to abolitionism ended in the United States at Appomattox in 1865.[220] Two decades later, it ended in Brazil, the last hold-out. (Three decades after that, slavery reappeared again in the Soviet Union, but this was a phenomenon of the State, not of private ownership.)

Does this mean that God works through history, bringing theo-logical anomalies to light, pressuring His people through historical forces to rethink their theological presuppositions? Quite clearly, He does exactly this. There is no better proof of this than the history of slavery.[221] Lifetime chattel slavery was wrong in principle from the

---

218. The Quaker founder of Pennsylvania, William Penn, was a slave owner. He once wrote to his steward regarding the benefits of black slaves over white inden-tured servants, "It were better if they were blacks, for then a man has them while they live." Cited by Scherer, *Slavery and the Churches in Early America*, p. 40.

219. In 1820, 37 percent of all town dwellers were blacks. Forty years later, the percentage was down to 17 percent. Urban slaves fell from 22 percent to 10 percent. Richard C. Wade, *Slavery in the Cities: the South, 1820-1860* (New York: Oxford Uni-versity Press, 1964), pp. 243-52.

220. When the Civil War was over, only Dabney remained as a public defender of the biblical legitimacy of "the peculiar institution" of chattel slavery. The greatest of the South's theologians vainly defended a slave system that Jesus had abolished in principle the day He publicly announced His ministry by reading Isaiah 61 in the synagogue. May God spare each of us such an ignominious end to an intellectually stellar career: one bit of theological leaven corrupted his theological reputation.

221. We could also discuss the invention of the printing press as a crucial techno-logical and economic factor in the coming of the Reformation. New doctrinal state-ments came like a flood from the pens of Protestant authors, because the printing press had created a market for the output of theologians' pens, as well as a valid eco-nomic incentive to widespread literacy. At last, the average person could afford a Bible and some strident theological pamphlets.

day that Jesus read in the synagogue (Luke 4), but it was not so great an evil that God felt compelled to reveal to the New Testament authors that they should stand against it publicly, making abolition a major dividing line between Christians and non-Christians. Slavery was not among the *adiaphora* — things of no importance — but it was not a major ethical issue, either. It was like representative constitutional government: implicit in the principles of biblical self-government, but not a top-priority theological issue in the first century. The church and the world could deal with other more pressing issues first.

When the economic means of abolition appeared — modern industrial capitalism — abolition could then become a top-priority issue in history, and did. The moral anomaly of slavery became too expensive an institutional anomaly for a Christian-influenced civilization to sustain. It was capitalism that made it too expensive. How? *By lowering the price of alternative social and economic relationships.* This economic process of social price competition combined with the newly popular philosophy of republican self-government (which was also an inevitable though delayed outgrowth of Christian social philosophy) to remove moral legitimacy from slavery.[222] The productivity of capitalism's mass-produced cotton gin on the plantation could not offset the moral and political effects of this erosion of slavery's moral legitimacy.[223] (This is also why Marxism is clearly doomed in history: the now-universally acknowledged reality of its economic failure has begun to reinforce the existing loss of faith in its moral legitimacy in every country where it is in control of the civil government.) Malcolm Muggeridge refers to England's Tory author, Samuel Johnson, who remarked in his *Taxation no Tyranny* that the loudest yelps for liberty in America were coming from the drivers of slaves.[224] The implicit schizophrenia of such a position could not indefinitely survive the stress placed on it by the republican political experiment.

That Paul did not write his epistle to Philemon in order to condemn chattel slavery should be no more surprising to modern readers than the fact that he did not write Romans 13 in order to promote

---

222. Cf. Edmund S. Morgan, *American Slavery — American Freedom: The Ordeal of Colonial Virginia* (New York: Norton, 1976).

223. In a very real sense, the economic effects of Eli Whitney's version of the cotton gin were defeated on the battlefield by Eli Whitney's vision (though perhaps not the actual production) of interchangeable parts for weapons. The South adopted the cotton gin, which reinforced slavery, while the North adopted mass-produced weaponry, which ended it.

224. Malcolm Muggeridge, *Chronicles of Wasted Time*, vol. 1, *The Green Stick* (New York: Morrow, 1973), p. 209.

parliamentary democracy. What should also not surprise us is that privately owned chattel slaves are today a thing of the past, as are kings. There are but five kings left in the world today, said deposed Egyptian "King" Farouk[225]: the king of England, and the kings of spades, hearts, clubs, and diamonds. This would not have been a believable possibility for most Europeans as recently as the beginning of the twentieth century. By the end of World War I in 1918, this was an inescapable reality. The kings departed or were dethroned. For the first time in three millennia, we no longer hear the cries of God's people: "We will have a king over us; that we also may be like all the nations" (I Sam. 8:19b-20a).

God still operates in history, making clear to His people what His principles are, and enabling them to conform their lives to His word. It takes time, but eventually we learn. He does not have to spell out everything in His inspired revealed word in order for us to work out His principles in our lives and in our societies over time. We have the Ten Commandments and the case laws; we do not need an edition of a heavenly version of the U.S. government's daily monstrosity, the *Federal Register*, with its 150 pages of new bureaucratic regulations.

The Permanence of Covenants

The economic thesis that underlies my whole discussion of slavery is that the fundamental issue of slavery is theological—the question of legitimate vs. illegitimate subordination—but its manifestation is primarily economic. Man is under God and over nature. There is no escape from hierarchy, the second point of the covenant. Individuals are always under the authority of other individuals; autonomy is impossible. The question then arises: How permanent is the subordination of anyone in any given relationship? The biblical answer must be: it depends on the covenant involved.

The model of the four covenants has been basic to Protestant social theory for centuries.[226] First, the *individual covenant*: an individual is always under God metaphysically, for God is the Creator, but he can switch gods covenantally. Man can rebel against one and

---

225. His father had been placed on an invented throne by the British after Britain replaced the Ottoman Empire in Egypt in World War I. Farouk was deposed in 1952 by an army revolt.

226. Richard Baxter used the four covenants as his structuring device for *A Christian Directory* (1673).

select another to rule over him. Once someone is adopted by God (John 1:12), he is a son forever (Rom. 8:28-35). Second, the *civil covenant*: men are always under a civil government, but they can move away from one by subordinating themselves to another. Third, the *marriage covenant*: legally, this is permanent until the death of one of the partners, including covenantal (legal) death.[227] Fourth, the *church covenant*. Men can leave local representatives of the church (congregations) but not the spiritual church. Once adopted by God, there is no escape from membership in the church. *Church membership is the only permanent covenant that carries into eternity.* Nevertheless, people have been granted the legal power to leave the local church, or cease attending any church, even though it is a great sin to do so. The ecclesiastical covenantal bond is still binding in God's court, but a positive compulsion to attend church is not the province of any civil court.[228]

Thus, a covenant is a *legal bond*, from which we derive the word *bondage*. In business, a long-term debt instrument is called a bond. This covenantal terminology reflects the biblical origins of modern capitalism. Biblically, there are only three public bonds because there are only three covenantal institutions: church, State, and family. All other legal bonds are in fact *contracts*, not covenants. When men endow any human relationship other than church, State, and family with the status of a covenant, they have violated God's law.[229] The only forms of lifetime servitude that are legal under biblical law are familistic: the permanent subordinate relationship of wives to husbands, and the voluntary subordination of servants to masters (Ex. 21:5-6).[230] People can escape covenantal bondage to either the institutional church or the State by revoking their vows and leaving. God does not allow the revocation of the family's covenantal bond

---

227. Ray R. Sutton, *Second Chance: Biblical Blueprints for Divorce and Remarriage* (Ft. Worth, Texas: Dominion Press, 1987).

228. It is biblically legitimate for a civil government to revoke the right to vote from those who have broken one or more institutional covenants. The State can lawfully establish positive criteria for a citizen's exercise of judicial authority (voting, jury duty), even though it is not authorized by God to impose economic or physical sanctions for not attending church.

229. North, *Sinai Strategy*, ch. 3: "Oaths, Covenants, and Contracts."

230. It could be argued that lifetime servitude by a criminal in order to make restitution is also an exception. This argument is incorrect. The period of a criminal's bondservice is limited by a specific sum of money owed to a victim, or owed to the buyer who has repaid the victim, not by a specific period of time owed to the buyer. The criminal bondservant can legally buy his way out of bondage, or another can buy his freedom for him.

except through the death, either physical or covenantal, of one of the partners.

This brings us back to the topic of slavery. The covenant is the key concept that distinguishes biblical slavery from indentured servitude. Heathen slavery in the Old Testament was a permanent (ten generations, minimum) relationship that was part of a covenant institution: church (tabernacle-temple), State, or family. As I mentioned earlier, the Gibeonites were servants of the *congregation*, meaning they were employed by the tabernacle (Josh. 9:27). All other forms of non-criminal personal subordination in Israel were limited by the terms of a contract, either stated or implied, and were restricted temporally. As we have seen, the one exception to this law of covenants — intergenerational heathen slavery — was abolished by Jesus Christ, through His fulfillment of the jubilee law. All economic relationships in New Testament times are therefore exclusively contractual; none is lawfully based on the invoking of a covenant, which is why contracts are less binding than covenants.[231] In economic affairs, there is a temporal limit on debt "bondage," precisely because *debt is not legally a covenantal bond.* That temporal limit is seven years (Deut. 15).[232]

Debt and Slavery: Limits on Capitalization

The contractual nature of New Testament economic relations means that it is illegal in the eyes of God for a person or an institution to capitalize another person's net future productivity beyond seven years. Individuals cannot legally promise to fulfill the terms of any contract beyond seven years. God's law points to a biblical principle: that no man can know the economic future accurately enough to allow him to make such legally enforceable promises. Thus, a man cannot legally capitalize his future beyond seven years. This is another way of saying that he cannot legally offer to sell for a lump sum his net future productivity beyond the seventh year. If he enters into such an agreement, no agency of civil or ecclesiastical government should enforce the terms of the contract.

We understand this with respect to chattel slavery. The seller of lifetime labor services is not supposed to make such an offer, except

---

231. North, *Sinai Strategy*, pp. 65-70.

232. The one exception is debt bondage that is imposed by the State against a criminal who must sell himself into long-term slavery in order to make restitution to his victims. This is a temporal manifestation of God's wrath against the criminal's breaking of the civil covenant. It is an involuntary relationship of subordination, once the criminal is convicted.

when he voluntarily becomes a second-class member of a family (Ex. 21:5-6). He should not sell himself into permanent bondage (I Cor. 7:21), although God allows this for weaker members of society. No one is ever to be enslaved against his will, except a convicted criminal, and this is not true lifetime enslavement, since he is allowed to buy his way out. If someone is sold into involuntary bondage, the civil government in a biblical society should prohibit the transaction.[233] The modern world understands that people are never to be allowed to sell themselves into lifetime chattel slavery. Even the term of en-listment in the armed forces should be limited to less than seven years, although people may lawfully re-enlist. Prior to 1780, the world did not understand that such covenantal capitalization of life-time *human* services is immoral and should be made judicially unen-forceable. Within a century, the world changed its collective mind.

A biblical society should abolish permanent lifetime slave con-tracts — *capitalized* streams of lifetime future service — as imitation covenants and therefore illegal. Jubilee bondservice of up to 49 years also disappeared judicially with Jesus' anullment of the jubilee land laws. Such contracts should not be enforceable in a civil court. In saying this, I am *not* saying that biblical society should refuse to en-force voluntary, interest-bearing debt contracts that are longer than seven years. The sabbitical-year limitation applied only to charitable loans, strictly defined as zero-interest, morally mandatory loans to destitute neighbors who offered as collateral the possibility of State-enforced servitude in case of their default. (See Chapter 23.) Long-term debt obligations that are collateralized by something other than personal service should be enforceable in a court of law.

This does not mean that a person is prohibited from becoming a lifetime servant as a gift of service, because the Bible makes provi-sion for this (Ex. 21:5-6). This is comparable to a marriage contract, meaning a marriage *covenant*. This decision does not involve a man's heirs, nor is any lump sum payment involved, which is also the case in marriage. Wives are not purchased for cash at an auction, at least

---

233. It should be pointed out that capitalizing a piece of long-"life" mechanical equipment is legal, which tends to subsidize the mechanization of industry. A machine may remain economically productive for decades, yet individuals are allowed to build or buy such equipment. Thus, by prohibiting lifetime slavery con-tracts, the civil government implicitly subsidizes mechanical substitutes for human labor. It is not accidental that the spread of the Industrial Revolution parallelled the abolition of slavery. On the one hand, the new technologies made possible the pro-duction of long-"lived" substitutes for human labor. On the other hand, the abolition of slavery subsidized the quest for and production of these mechanical substitutes.

not in this century. (The practice of husbands' auctioning off wives
who were no longer in favor, as an alternative to legal divorce, did go
on in England and Wales, but not in Scotland and Ireland, until the
late-nineteenth century, although the custom was not widely observed.)[234] Most important, *there is no capitalization process involved in
covenanting oneself to another man's household.* There is no cash payment
involved. In effect, an Old Testament servant became a second-
class, non-inheriting son by means of this contract, and it was in fact
a covenant, for it involved the shedding of blood ritually: a hole
bored in the ear.

A biblical society should permit the indentured servitude system
of Deuteronomy 15, for the New Testament did not abolish it, either
explicitly or implicitly. That a form of indentured servitude (apprenticeship) replaced permanent slavery in the British empire after 1833
until the abolition of apprenticeship contracts in 1917 should not be
surprising.[235] As mentioned earlier, it was an economically rational
response to a shortage of disciplined labor in the Caribbean islands,
a shortage of labor demand in Asia, and high transportation costs.
Nevertheless, indentured servitude is a second-best way of life, and
Paul recommends that Christians take their freedom if it is offered to
them (I Cor. 7:21). The same is true of debt. Debt contracts are still
legal, but the biblical ideal is zero debt (Rom. 13:8a). Freedom from
debt is a better way of life. People should take it if it is offered to
them.

When I was doing research in Jamaica on the history of the abolition movement, I came across a reprint of the original Abolition
Act of 1833. I discovered a most interesting provision of the Act: the
law adhered to the biblical sabbatical-year release principle. A tran-
sitional system of apprenticeship was established. Apprenticeship for
former slaves was to be compulsory from August 1, 1833 to August 1,
1840: a maximum of seven years. The apprentices by law could not
be compelled to work for plantation owners longer than 45 hours a

---

234. Samuel Pyeatt Menefee, *Wives for Sale: An Ethnographic Study of British Popular
Divorce* (London: Basil Blackwell, 1980).

235. Hugh Tinker, *A New System of Slavery: The Export of Indian Labour Overseas,
1830-1920* (London: Oxford University Press, 1974); William A. Green, *British Slave
Emancipation: The Sugar Colonies and the Great Experiment, 1830-1865* (Oxford, England:
Clarendon Press, 1976); Kay Saunders (ed.), *Indentured Servitude on the British Empire,
1834-1920* (London: Croom Helm, 1984). See also W. Kloosterboer, *Involuntary
Labour Since the Abolition of Slavery* (Leiden: E. J. Brill, 1960).

week.[236] It was illegal to dismiss a slave-apprentice if he was over age 49 or if he was mentally or physically infirm. If discharged from service prematurely for any of these reasons, his master then had to provide him with lifetime subsistence.[237] One class of apprentices, non-praedial apprentices, were under a less rigorous provision: full freedom in 1838.[238] As it turned out, all apprentices were released on August 1, 1838, and Jamaicans date the nation's liberation on this date. (I was in Jamaica on the 150th anniversary of liberation day. I had expected considerable public festivities. As it turned out, the government played down the event, substituting instead a national holiday celebrating liberation from British political rule in 1962.)

Government Debt and Servitude

The relationship between long-term government debt and servitude must be considered at this point. Unlike a voluntary private debt, a government debt does use the possibility of coercion and servitude—jail sentences for tax protesters—to collateralize its debt obligations. This places a government debt in a biblical judicial category different from a private debt. The government's debt is much closer to the emergency charitable debt of Deuteronomy 15: a morally (though not legally) mandatory extension of credit to a destitute neighbor who collateralizes his obligation by an agreement to go into debt servitude in case he defaults.

There are no legal or physical assets that collateralize any government debt. There is no way for creditors to repossess this collateral if the government should default. Taxpayers are then threatened by rising taxes. The State escapes the traditional political restraints of tax protests by means of perpetual debt. If the voters rebel against rising taxes, there is then a great temptation for a national government to sell its debt obligations to its national central bank, which uses these notes to collateralize an expansion of fiat money.[239] This leads to price inflation and the creation of the boom-bust business

---

236. Section V, *The Abolition Act of 1833* (reprint: Virgin Islands Public Library, 1984), [p. 16, Paragraph 3]. Other provisions included the slave's right of purchase out of bondage (Sect. VIII), a ban on the sale of slaves from off the island (Sect. IX), and a ban on separating former slave families (Sect. X).

237. *Ibid.*, Sect. VII.

238. *Ibid.*, Sect. VI.

239. Gary North, *Honest Money: The Biblical Blueprint for Money and Banking* (Ft. Worth, Texas: Dominion Press, 1986), ch. 8.

cycle.[240] Fiat money allows the government to lower the economic burden of its debts through monetary debasement. Economist Franz Pick always defined a government bond as a certificate of guaranteed confiscation.

To avoid repaying these debts, governments continue to roll them over by selling new debt obligations to pay off old ones. This is the philosophy of perpetual government debt for perpetual national (and now international) prosperity. This view of government debt has become basic to Western economic thought and practice ever since the creation of the privately owned Bank of England in 1694. This economic outlook has now spread to private debt markets, debt which is also collateralized by promises to pay rather than by actual physical assets. The world economy is now threatened by a combination of rising debt, lengthening debt maturities, fiat money, fractional reserve banking, uncollateralized private debt, and taxpayer collateralized government debt. The entire world is now caught in a demonic race against the inevitable: the extension of more debt, the threat of mass inflation, and the inevitable world depression that will hit when the debtors at last go into default.

Interestingly, it was only after the abolition of chattel slavery that the rapid spread of long-term indebtedness became a way of life in the West, first for the newly developed institutions known as limited liability corporations in the final third of the nineteenth century, and then for the modern State.[241] Only when creditors could no longer get the civil government to impose either a period of servitude (the biblical approach) or a jail sentence (the humanist solution prior to the late 1860's)[242] on those who defaulted did the modern institutions of debt capitalism and debt socialism become triumphant. Today this very institutional arrangement threatens to topple the world economy in a wave of defaults, either outright (unlikely) or inflationary (highly likely), taking with it the bloated remains of the culture of secular humanism.

Slavery is an inescapable concept theologically, as well as an inescapable concept economically, for as long as sin is in the world. The question is: Who will be enslaved, creditor or debtor? In the Old Testament, it

---

240. Mises, *Human Action*, ch. 20.

241. On the earlier period, see Carleton Hunt, *The Development of the Business Corporation in England, 1800-1867* (Cambridge, Massachusetts: Harvard University Press, 1936).

242. "Debt," in *The Encyclopaedia Britannica* (11th ed.; New York: Encyclopaedia Britannica, Inc., 1910), Vol. VII, p. 906.

was the defaulting debtor. The modern world has made a different decision: the creditor. There are more people who vote than people who lend — or more accurately, more indebted people who vote for inflation than people who perceive themselves as lenders. (Anyone who is owed a pension, or a bank deposit, or cash value life insurance is a creditor, but few people recognize this when making their political decisions.) The removal of major judicial penalties for defaulting on debt has subsidized the creation of debt on a scale undreamed of in history. The creditors do not recognize that the outlook of this age is hostile to them. They trust the promises of debtors, including the largest debtors of all: civil governments. Future economic productivity in the United States is now incapable of repaying principal and interest on this national and international debt, both private and public,[243] but creditors dare not admit to themselves what has happened. The banks continue to loan precious capital to the Third World socialist deadbeats and European former-Communist deadbeats in the desperate hope that they will themselves be paid off before the entire system goes bankrupt, even if other creditors will lose, and also in the hope that one more extension of funds will delay the day of financial judgment. The end result will be the destruction of capital (and people's dreams) on a scale never before imagined, through mass inflation, probably price and wage controls, and then economic depression.[244]

Then, perhaps, the Holy Spirit will persuade the world that Proverbs 22:7 is still in force in God's kingdom, if not in autonomous man's.

Modern Political Slavery

M. I. Finley writes concerning the slave societies of Greece and Rome that "three components of slavery — the slave's property status, the totality of the power over him, and his kinlessness — provided powerful advantages to the slaveowner as against other forms of involuntary labour. . . ."[245] In Israel, the indentured servant's property status was mitigated by law and by the seventh-year sab-

---

243. Alfred L. Malabre, Jr., *Beyond Our Means: How America's Long Years of Debt, Deficits and Reckless Borrowing Now Threaten to Overwhelm Us* (New York: Random House, 1987); Lawrence Malkin, *The National Debt* (New York: Henry Holt, 1987); Peter G. Peterson, "The Morning After," *The Atlantic* (Oct. 1987).

244. Gary North, *Government by Emergency* (Ft. Worth, Texas: American Bureau of Economic Research, 1983).

245. Finley, *Ancient Slavery*, p. 77.

batical year of release. The owner's power over him was neither total nor permanent, and he had kinship relations with people who were legally allowed to gain his freedom through purchase. Even in the case of the permanent heathen slave, the power over him was not legally unlimited. He could not be permanently injured physically and still be kept in slavery (Ex. 21:26-27).[246] The system of servitude established in the Bible was never intended to become the slavery of Greece or Rome. It was not true of Israel, as it was in classical antiquity, that "slaves were a logical class and a juridical class but not, in any usual sense of that term, a social class."[247] On the contrary, biblical slavery was governed by laws regarding the marriage of slaves, as we shall see in the next chapter, and where there is family law there is always an identifiable social class. The very requirement to circumcise all household members, including slaves, testifies to the inapplicability in Israel of Finley's assessment. Biblical servitude was a very different system from that which prevailed in the pagan classical world and which also prevails today in modern totalitarian societies, both of which fit Finley's *a priori* description far more closely.

When we come to the topic of slavery, the modern world is blind in one eye, just as the world was blind in the other eye prior to 1750. On the one hand, we reject the legitimacy of private property in human beings with the same intense moral outrage that everyone prior to 1750 would have directed against abolitionism. On the other hand, we are as blind to the moral evil of slavery to the State as our forebears were alert to the moral evil of political oppression.

For over seventeen centuries, the moral question of the legitimacy of slavery did not bother the vast majority of Christians (or Jews, for that matter).[248] Chattel slavery was an accepted institution, worldwide. Then, almost overnight, public opinion began to

---

246. See Chapter 13: "Freedom for an Eye."

247. *Idem.*

248. Roger Williams, ever the unheeded voice, especially after he fled to Rhode Island in 1636, protested in 1637 when Connecticut Puritans sold off defeated Indians into slavery after the Pequot War of 1636. Nevertheless, the first Negro slaves to arrive in Massachusetts were imported the next year, 1638, from Providence, Rhode Island, where blacks were already kept as perpetual servants: Winthrop Jordan, *White Over Black*, p. 67. There was also an attempt in 1688 by Dutch Quakers in Germantown, Pennsylvania, to circulate an anti-slavery petition, but nothing came of it. See J. Herbert Fretz, "The Germantown Anti-Slavery Petition," *Mennonite Quarterly Review*, XXXIII (Jan. 1959), pp. 42-59. It is reprinted in Samuel W. Pennypacker, "The Settlement of Germantown, and the Causes Which Led to It," *Pennsylvania Magazine of History and Biography*, IV (1880), pp. 28-30.

change in the late eighteenth century. A century later, slavery in the Bible had become an enormous embarrassment to Bible-believing people.

Finally — I should probably say "predictably" — within two generations after the abolition of chattel slavery, public opinion in the now-humanist West shifted once again. Slavery, if imposed "in the name of the People" — *Volk, Führer,* or Party — had again become acceptable. The slave societies of national socialism (Nazi Germany)[249] and international socialism (Communism) have dwarfed all previous slave societies. The spirit of Pharaoh has been reincarnated in modern totalitarianism — societies built on the model of the concentration camp.[250] Rushdoony is correct: "In virtually all the world today, the citizenry is moving into slavery to the state. The obligations of citizenship are being replaced by the obligations of slavery."[251]

What has become a retroactive embarrassment to Christians in the twentieth century is the profit-seeking, small-scale household indentured servitude that is authorized in the Bible. At the same time, slavery to the State has become a way of life (and death)[252] for millions. Pharaoh wants no competitors, either economically or, more important, in terms of sovereignty. We must understand this biblical truth from the beginning: *the right to own servants is an attribute of sovereignty.* God possesses this attribute, as we shall see, and He has delegated it to men under certain limited and specified conditions. Modern messianic States seek to replace God, and therefore seek also to abolish the biblical limitations on slave ownership. They wish to monopolize for themselves the right of slave ownership. They transform entire populations into slaves, and then select millions of

---

249. See Albert Speer, *Slave State: Heinrich Himmler's Masterplan for SS Supremacy* (London: Weidenfield & Nicholson, 1981). The Krupp arms manufacturing company hired slaves from Himmler's notorious SS, paying 3 to 4 marks per day in 1943. The firm hired about 5,000 slaves from concentration camps, 23,000 prisoners of war, and 70,000 foreign civilians. After the war, the head of the company was sentenced to 12 years in jail and forfeited all his property. Six years later he was paroled, and his property was returned to him. See Roger Sawyer, *Slavery in the Twentieth Century* (London: Routledge & Kegan Paul, 1986), pp. 37-44.

250. Hannah Arendt, *The Origins of Totalitarianism* (rev. ed.; New York: Harcourt Brace Jovanovich, 1966).

251. Rushdoony, *Politics of Guilt and Pity,* p. 27.

252. Gil Elliot, *Twentieth Century Book of the Dead* (New York: Scribner's, 1972). He estimated that at least 100 million people had died in this century by 1970, but this estimate assumed far fewer than 60 million deaths in Communist China.

them to serve in the concentration camps.[253] It was not simply for economic reasons that during Stalin's terror, the Soviet Union's dreaded NKVD (secret police) used churches and monasteries as torture and execution chambers.[254] The ability of dedicated covenant-breakers to image hell on earth in a church was too tempting. The Soviet authorities use churches and monasteries as prisons today.[255]

Men do not recognize tyranny on the part of their respective gods. For many decades, the liberal intelligentsia of the West denied that slave labor camps even existed inside the Soviet Union. Malcolm Muggeridge quotes Fabian founder Beatrice Webb, who announced at a small gathering of friends: " 'It's true,' she said suddenly, *a propos* of nothing, 'that in the USSR people *disappear.*' "[256] But as he reveals in his brilliant autobiography, such thoughts were not allowed to become public. He served as a Moscow correspondent for the liberal British newspaper, the *Manchester Guardian*, in the mid-1930's, and the Western correspondents there simply turned a blind eye such grim realities, faithfully reporting only what appeared in the Soviet press.[257] The Soviets controlled them by threatening them with the revocation of their visas, or by providing them with mistresses who would inform on them to the authorities.[258] But all of this made little difference to the newspapers back home. "Newspaper managements and broadcasting agencies have nonetheless been ready to pay out large sums of money to procure this tainted news just in order to be able to say that it came from Our Correspondent in Moscow. The image is, as always, preferred to reality."[259]

It was only with the publication of Solzhenitsyn's *Gulag Archipelago* in the mid-1970's that liberal intellectuals of the West at last grudgingly acknowledged the existence of the camps, I suspect primarily because Solzhenitsyn had won the Nobel Prize in literature in 1970. The intellectuals seemed to have reasoned that since the Nobel committee had concluded that he could write fiction with such power and

---

253. *U.S.S.R. Labor Camps*, Testimony of Avraham Shifrin, Hearings Before the Subcommittee to Investigate the Administration of the Internal Security Act and Other Internal Security Laws of the Committee of the Judiciary, United States Senate, 93rd Congress (Feb. 1, 1973).

254. Solzhenitsyn, *The Gulag Archipelago, 1918-1956*, p. 438.

255. *Ibid.*, pp. 479, 605.

256. Muggeridge, *The Green Stick*, p. 211.

257. *Ibid.*, p. 215.

258. *Ibid.*, p. 224.

259. *Ibid.*, p. 225.

grace, then perhaps he was telling the truth about Stalin. ("But Lenin? Must we believe such things about the Founder?") Solzhenitsyn broke the spell of the naive historical analysis articulated by Yugoslavian socialist Milovan Djilas, an analysis that had brought liberals comfort in the aftermath of the anti-Stalin "secret speech" by Khrushchev in 1956.[260] Djilas had set the tone for two decades of rhetoric: "Behind Lenin, who was all passion and thought, stands the dull, gray figure of Joseph Stalin, the symbol of the difficult, cruel, and unscrupulous ascent of the new class to its final power."[261] Solzhenitsyn showed that this was all mythical, that the Soviet system of terror and repression had been invented by Lenin, and merely perfected by Stalin.

Another example of this blindness to the tyranny of contemporary political gods is the obvious but universally ignored fact that in order to achieve the tax reform of 20 percent of income which the worst tyranny of the ancient world imposed on its people — Egypt (Gen. 47:26) — the nations of the West would have to *reduce* their total tax burden by at least 50 percent. Men are unwilling to admit that their god the State is a ruthless tyrant rather than a benevolent dictator who "makes occasional mistakes." They see the State as the sole representative of the people, and the people as god: *vox populi, vox dei.* This is the system of self-worship by self-proclaimed autonomous man.

Conclusion

Servitude exists because sin exists and because God's judgments in history and eternity also exist. This was Augustine's argument a millennium and a half ago, an argument which was old when he offered it: *slavery is one of God's penal sanctions against sin.*[262] Richard Baxter warned slave-owners in 1673: "If their sin have enslaved them to you, yet Nature made them your equals."[263]

---

260. Nikita Khrushchev, "Stalin and the Cult of the Individual" (Feb. 24-25, 1956), in Samuel Hendel (ed.), *The Soviet Crucible: The Soviet System in Theory and Practice* (2nd ed.; New York: Van Nostrand, 1963), pp. 383-415.

261. Milovan Djilas, *The New Class: An Analysis of the Communist System* (New York: Praeger, 1957), p. 52. Djilas did give evidence that Lenin was indirectly to blame, but the intellectuals chose to pass over these sections of the book.

262. Augustine, *City of God*, Book 19, Chap. 15. Cf. R. W. Carlyle and A. J. Carlyle, *A History of Mediaeval Political Theory in the West*, I, p. 113.

263. Baxter, *A Christian Directory*, Part II, *Christian Oeconomicks*, p. 71.

Covenant theology teaches that slavery is an inescapable concept. Slavery's positive model is the indentured servant who buys his way out of poverty, or who is released in the sabbatical year or jubilee year. He learns the skills and worldview of dominion. He becomes self-governed under God, a free man. Slavery becomes a means of liberation when coupled with biblical ethics. The fundamental issue, as always, is ethical rather than economic. His ability to buy his way out is indicative of a change in his ethical behavior.

Slavery's negative model is God's judgment of covenant-breakers throughout eternity. He consigns them first to hell and then, at the resurrection, to the lake of fire (Rev. 20:14-15). God places people on the whipping block, and then He flogs them forever. Of course, what they actually experience for eternity is far more horrifying than the comparatively minor inconvenience of an eternal whip. I am only speaking figuratively of whips; the reality of eternal torment is far, far worse than mere lashes. Thus, the legal right of some people to enslave others under the limits imposed by God's revealed law is based on the ultimate legal right of God to impose eternal torment on covenant-breakers. Biblical servitude is a warning to sinners as well as a means of liberation.

What I am arguing is simple: *it is not chattel slavery as such that appalls most covenant-breakers and their Christian ideological accomplices; rather, it is the doctrine of eternal punishment.* The denial of the New Testament doctrine of eternal punishment, above all other denials, is the touchstone of modern humanism. It is this doctrine, above all others, that humanists reject. They stand, clenched fists waving in the air, and shout their defiance to God, "You have no authority over us!" But He does. They proclaim, "There is no hell!" But there is. And the lake of fire will be even worse.

For all his protests, modern man nevertheless still accepts the legitimacy of slavery. Humanists understand implicitly that the right to enslave others is an attribute of God's sovereignty. They declare the State as the true God of humanity, and then they proclaim the right of the State to enslave men.[264] They have created the modern penal system, with its heavy reliance on imprisonment, yet have rejected the criminal's obligation to make restitution to the victim. They allow murderers to go free after a few years of imprisonment or

---

264. Libertarian anarchists are exceptions to this rule, since they do not acknowledge the legitimacy of the State.

incarceration in a mental institution, to murder again, for humanists are unwilling to allow the State to turn the murderer over to God as rapidly as possible, so that God can deal with them eternally. They regard man as the sovereign judge, not God; so they have invented the slave-master institution of the modern prison, while they have steadily rejected the legitimacy of capital punishment. Better to let murderers go free, humanists assert, than to acknowledge covenant-ally and symbolically that the State has a heavenly Judge above it, and that God requires human judges to turn murderers over to Him for His immediate judgment, once the earthly courts have declared them guilty as charged.

The nineteenth century's indiscriminate attack on all forms of privately owned servitude was ultimately an attack on God's law. This hostility to indentured servitude rested on a key assumption: that honoring God's revealed law is a criminal act. The humanist abolitionist tries to put God in the dock. He tries to put the State on the judgment throne of God. What he hates is the Bible, not slavery as such. The question is never slavery vs. no slavery. The question is: *Who will be the slave-master, and who will be the slave?* Autonomous man wants to put God and His law in bondage. On judgment day, this strategy will be exposed for the covenant-breaking revolution that it has always been. The abolitionists will then learn what full-time slavery is all about. It is a lesson that will be taught to them for eternity.

Pharaoh's spiritual heirs are with us still. Christians are in spiritual and cultural bondage to the theology of the power religion, and therefore to the State. They must prepare for another exodus, meaning they should be prepared to experience at least a share of the preliminary plagues, just as the Israelites of Moses' day went through the first three out of ten. It is nevertheless time to leave Egypt, leeks and onions notwithstanding. We must be prepared for numerous objections from Pharaoh's authorized and subsidized representatives inside the camp of the faithful. They owe their positions of influence to Pharaoh and his taskmasters, and they will not give up their authority without a confrontation. They will complain that their potential liberators are at fault for the increased burdens that Christians suffer (Ex. 5:20-21). They will continue to sing the praises of the welfare State. They will continue to sing the praises of tax-supported "neutral" education. They will tell the faithful that humanist slavery is freedom, and biblical freedom is barbaric. They will attract many followers within the camp, for there will always be camp followers close by any army. Choose this day whom you will serve.

Part II
COMMENTARY

5

SERVITUDE, PROTECTION,
AND MARRIAGE

If thou buy an Hebrew servant, six years he shall serve: and in the seventh he shall go out free for nothing. If he came in by himself, he shall go out by himself: if he were married, then his wife shall go out with him. If his master have [has] given him a wife, and she have born him sons or daughters; the wife and her children shall be her master's, and he shall go out by himself (Ex. 21:2-4).

It is a wise course to begin any discussion of the case laws of Exodus by pointing out that these laws are best understood theocentrically. God's relationship to man is the focus of many of these case laws, especially those involving slavery and marriage. The basic theme of this passage in Exodus is *protection through covenantal subordination.*[1] A subordinate theme, closely related to the first, is the *right of redemption* (buying back). These are fundamental themes in the Book of Exodus specifically and in the Bible generally. God delivers His bride from bondage in the household of a foreign master who has kept her in illegal slavery — slavery without the right of redemption.

The Pharaohs of the Mosaic period had attempted to do what the Pharaoh of Abram's day had attempted. Like Jacob, Abram had journeyed to Egypt in the midst of a famine (Gen. 12:10). As Abram had expected, Pharaoh captured Abram's bride, Sarai, and brought her to his house (12:15). God then sent plagues against Pharaoh's household (12:17). The Pharaoh of Moses' infancy instructed the Hebrew midwives to kill all the male infants but allow the females to live (Ex. 1:16). It is obvious what he intended: the capture of God's bride.

---

1. On the hierarchical nature of God's covenant, see Ray R. Sutton, *That You May Prosper: Dominion By Covenant* (Tyler, Texas: Institute for Christian Economics, 1987), ch. 2.

Exodus 21:2-4 presents the case law governing indentured servant marriages. God had just delivered a slave people out of bondage. He had removed them from the visible tyranny of Egypt, and He was preparing them for long-term service to Him in the promised land. It was not that servitude was being abolished; it was rather that a new Master had appeared on the historical scene. God had delivered them out of Pharaoh's household as intact families; God was now bringing them into His household as His servants. He was making Israel His bride.

The maximum legal period of the most rigorous form of noncriminal indentured servitude in Israel was a little over six years. This was the form of servitude in which the master had the right of corporal punishment, and the form in which the servant had to be provided with capital upon his release. During the seventh year, sometimes called the *sabbatical year* by Bible commentators, these servants went free in Israel, and simultaneously all zero-interest charitable debts were cancelled (Deut. 15). It is noteworthy that the year of release was also the year when the law was read to the assembled nation at the feast of the tabernacles (Deut. 31:10-13). God's law is to be understood as the means to freedom for those who obey it.[2]

---

2. I should mention here that the Jewish scholar Maimonides asserted in 1180 A.D. that a Hebrew can legitimately sell himself to another Hebrew for more than six years, but not beyond the jubilee year. Moses Maimonides, *The Book of Acquisition*, vol. 12 of *The Code of Maimonides*, 14 vols. (New Haven, Connecticut: Yale University Press, 1951), "Treatise V, Laws Concerning Slaves," Chapter Two, Section Three, p. 250. On the other hand, if the court sells him into servitude, which Maimonides says can only take place because the man is a thief who cannot afford to make restitution (Chapter One, Section One, p. 246), he can be required to work only six years (Chapter Two, Section Two, p. 249). I argue in this commentary that there were five different forms of Hebrew bondservice in Israel. See Chapter 4, pp. 123-36.

A major problem with the *Code* is its sparse or absent arguments and explanations for controversial assertions. In reading the *Code*, we must remember that Maimonides distinguished between a code and a commentary: "In a monolithic code, only the correct subject matter is recorded, without any questions, without answers, and without any proofs, in the way which Rabbi Judah adopted when he composed the Mishnah." A commentary records opinions, debates, and identifies sources and persons, he said: letter to Rabbi Phinehas ben Meshullam, judge in Alexandria: reproduced in Isadore Twersky, *Introduction to the Code of Maimonides (Mishneh Torah)* (New Haven, Connecticut: Yale University Press, 1980), p. 33. *The Code* was basic to Maimonides' thinking. Twersky writes: "The *Mishneh Torah* also becomes an Archimedean fulcrum in the sense that he regularly mentions it and refers correspondents and inquirers to it. The repeated references convey the impression that he wanted to establish it as a standard manual, a ready, steady, and uniform reference book for practically all issues" (p. 18).

In the national seventh year, these full-scale bondservants went free.[3] Why the statutory limitation? Probably because this sabbatical week of years pointed back to the symbolic work week that God imposed on man because of his sin. Adam had originally been given a one-six work week, with the first day as his day of rest. He sinned, seeking autonomy, and was then cursed by God with a six-one work week: six days of labor, with the promise of release and rest only at the end.[4] This new weekly structure was a curse on man, although a curse with the grace of sabbatical liberation promised at the end of the week's period of servitude. Thus, man's position as a *debtor to God* is manifested in the sabbatical-year system of debt and slavery. God offers covenant-breaking man a means of escaping his debt: faithful labor as a bondservant for a specified period.

Marriage and Servitude

Verse three is clear: a married man who goes into indentured servitude (probably because of debt)[5] takes his wife with him. She therefore departs with him when he goes out. Verse four is the difficult section for moralists: if he had been given a wife during his period of servitude, she and their children must remain behind with the master when the husband leaves.

The key question we need to ask ourselves is this: Where had the indentured servant received his wife if he originally brought her into the master's household? The answer is crucial to understanding this passage: *from her father.* He would have had to pay a *bride price* to her

---

3. This was not true of those who had indentured themselves to other Hebrews as permanent hired hands (Lev. 25:25-28), or those who had indentured themselves to resident aliens (Lev. 25:47-54).

4. Gary North, *The Dominion Covenant: Genesis* (2nd ed.; Tyler, Texas: Institute for Christian Economics, 1987), ch. 5: "God's Week and Man's Week."

5. Maimonides declared without argument or biblical citation that "One is not permitted to sell himself into servitude and lay the money away or buy merchandise or vessels with it or give it to a creditor. He can sell himself only if he needs the money for food and only after he has nothing left in the house, not even a garment." *Acquisition*, Chapter One, Section One, p. 246. The problem here is that it seems inconceivable that a man could be placed in servitude for over six years in order to raise enough money for his family's food. It seems far more plausible to believe that he was forced into servitude because of debts amassed over a lengthy period. Maimonides did say that the State may legitimately sell a man into bondage to someone who pays the man's unpaid taxes for him: *ibid.*, Chapter One, Section Eight, p. 248. Since he had already argued that the State can sell someone into slavery only for theft, he must have believed that the failure to pay a tax must be a form of theft.

father, thereby indicating his economic productivity, or at least his position as a man possessing inherited capital.[6] The bridegroom's payment of a required bride price is the key to understanding this case law.[7]

To Give a Wife

Jacob wanted to marry Rachel. He had no visible, transferable capital, for he was a fugitive, even though he had received Isaac's blessing. Without an assured inheritance, he had to pay Laban a bride price. That bride price was seven years of labor: "And Jacob served seven years for Rachel" (Gen. 29:20a). His words are significant: "Give me my wife, for my days are fulfilled" (Gen. 29:21a). *Give me my wife*, he insisted. The father had to *give* his daughter to the bridegroom, once he had met the terms of the bride price. Rachel now *belonged* to Jacob. He had paid the price.[8]

Exodus 21:4 reads: "If his master have *given* him a wife, and she have born him sons or daughters; the wife and her children shall be her master's, and he shall go out by himself." The language is the same as Jacob's to Laban: he has given her to him. This raises a second crucial question: Where did the master get a woman for his servant in order to be able to give her to him in marriage? Either she was a servant already owned by the master, or else she had been purchased by the master for the servant. Perhaps she had been some other family's servant. Perhaps she had been the daughter of a free man. The point is, the master now lawfully controls her as a lawful father. He can therefore give her to his servant.

---

6. The bride price would normally have been less than 50 shekels of silver. A man who seduced an unbetrothed virgin was required by law to pay 50 shekels to her father and then marry her, with no future right of divorce (Deut. 22:28-29). Additional evidence of this 50-shekel maximum: the bridegroom who falsely accused a new bride of not being a virgin at the time of their marriage, and who could not prove his accusation, had to pay a hundred shekels of silver to her father (Deut. 22:19). This was double restitution: two times fifty. On these points, see Chapter 21: "Seduction and Servitude."

7. See Chapter 6: "Wives and Concubines."

8. This is the covenantal basis of Jesus Christ's exclusive lifetime (eternal) ownership of His bride, the church (Eph. 5:22-24). The church is a true bride, not a concubine. A concubine in Israel was a wife who possessed no dowry. No bride price was paid for her, and no dowry was brought into the marriage by her. Legally, had Christ not died for the church, the church would be a concubine—a second-rate wife. This is why the church knows that she will never be divorced. This is why Paul could ask rhetorically: "Who shall separate us from the love of Christ?" (Rom. 8:35a). Christ paid the required bride price to the Father. The church is not a concubine, even though she brings neither virginity nor dowry into the marriage. The bride price was paid by Christ at Calvary.

If she had been the daughter of a free man, then the master would have had to pay a bride price to her father. This assured the father that the man who was taking *legal authority over his daughter* was competent financially. The father had been given economic evidence that the requested transfer of authority over his daughter to another man posed no threat to her economic future. The bride price served as evidence of her future husband's ability to support her; as a weaker vessel, she was legally entitled to such support.

If the master paid the bride price, and her father transferred to him the right to give her in marriage, then the master became her new father, *covenantally* speaking. He would remain legally responsible for her until she married a legally independent man. The master had the legal right to give her as a wife to a servant in his household, but only because she would remain in his household. He could not legally transfer to a servant the economic obligation to support her, for *the servant was not a covenantally free agent*, either economically or legally. Since the servant possessed no capital, the master remained her father covenantally until such time as the servant purchased her from him, that is, *until he paid the master the bride price owed to a father*.

This law provided additional assurance to the woman's natural father of the lifetime economic protection owed to his daughter. The master did not have the legal authority to transfer this economic responsibility to a former indentured servant until the latter had proven that he was able to pay the same bride price originally owed to the father. If this law had not been in existence, or if it was unenforced by civil law, then there would be no guarantee to the woman's natural father that the master would not later decide to escape his economic liabilities to the woman by transferring such responsibility to a former indentured servant who had not yet demonstrated his economic competence. The legal requirement that the released servant pay the master the bride price before his wife could leave the household of the master was the natural father's assurance of her continuing protection.

The modern world has pretended that it can somehow ignore the economic aspects of marriage. People assume that the ancient world was primitive,[9] and therefore the attention given by ancient law

---

9. Harry Emerson Fosdick, a liberal theologian and an immensely popular preacher for several decades, wrote: "We know now that every idea in the Bible started from primitive and childlike origins. . . ." *The Modern Use of the Bible* (New York: Macmillan, 1941), p. 11. See also Henry Schaeffer, *The Social Legislation of the Primitive Semites* (New Haven, Connecticut: Yale University Press, 1915). He begins with a consideration of Hebrew marriage. He argues that "the matriarchal clan was the dominant form of social organization prior to the settlement in Canaan" (p. 7). It is astounding the lengths to which people will go to escape the Bible's testimony concerning God and man.

codes to such matters as dowries and bride price payments is evidence of this primitivism.[10] But it is the modern world that is primitive, for it has abandoned a covenantal view of marriage, and has substituted easily broken mutual contracts, where fathers have no responsibilities to investigate the economic competence of prospective sons-in-law, and wives have little legal protection from the courts if husbands decide to break their marriage contracts.[11] Women have become the economic victims of divorce.[12]

The Family as the Primary Protection Agency

Marriage is not lawless. It is a covenantal institution.[13] It is the primary training ground for the next generation. It is the primary institution for welfare: care of the young, care of the aged, and education. It is the primary agency of economic inheritance. *The family is therefore the primary institutional arrangement for fulfilling the terms of the do-*

---

10. The Hammurabi Code devotes considerable space to these matters, paragraphs 128-84. *Ancient Near Eastern Texts Relating to the Old Testament*, edited by James B. Pritchard (3rd ed.; Princeton, New Jersey: Princeton University Press, 1969), pp. 171-74. Not equally detailed are the laws of Eshnunna, paragraphs 17-28: *ibid.*, p. 162; the Middle Assyrian laws, paragraphs 25-48: *ibid.*, pp. 182-84; and the Hittite laws, paragraphs 26-36: *ibid.*, p. 190.

11. In Victorian England, custody of the children automatically went to the divorced husband. This reduced the incentive for divorce on both sides. The husband feared the responsibility of taking care of the children, and the wife did not want to abandon them. As William Tucker comments: "The Victorian system favored neither men nor women: It favored families. . . . They loaded the system against the individual interests of men and women to keep both committed to the family." Only after 1910 did social workers and the courts shift the balance and begin to grant mothers automatic custody of the children. William Tucker, "Victorian Savvy," *New York Times* (June 26, 1983). The biblical approach is different: children go to the innocent victim of the sinning marriage partner.

12. Economic studies made in the 1980's indicate that in the United States, women who got divorced saw their standard of living drop by over 70 percent within a year, while divorced men saw an increase of over 40 percent in the same period. Lenore J. Weitzman, *The Divorce Revolution: The Unexpected Social and Economic Consequences for Women and Children in America* (New York: The Free Press, 1985), p. xii. As she writes, "the major economic result of the divorce law revolution is the systematic impoverishment of divorced women and their children. They have become the new poor." *Ibid.*, p. xiv; cited by George Grant, *The Dispossessed: Homelessness in America* (Ft. Worth, Texas: Dominion Press, 1986), p. 79. In 1940, one out of six marriages ended in divorce in the U.S.; in 1980, it was 50 percent. Grant comments: "With no-fault divorce laws in place, depriving women of alimony, child custody support, or appropriate property settlements, we can expect the feminization of poverty to continue to escalate exponentially" (p. 79).

13. Sutton, *That You May Prosper*, ch. 8. The code of Hammurabi specified that an aristocrat who acquired a wife without contracts for her did not have a wife: paragraph 128. *Ancient Near Eastern Texts*, p. 171.

minion covenant (Gen. 1:26-28). God honored this crucial dominion function of the family by placing restrictions on it. A servant is expected to defer marriage until he is an independent man. Later, as a husband in a position of authority, he can exercise dominion under God as the head of his family. The model here is Jacob (Gen. 29:20).

Both marriage and labor are normally to be part of the dominion covenant between man and God. Since the servant's dominion over his assigned portion of the earth is not independent of his master's authority, his authority over a wife taken during his term of service is also under his master's authority. There is a *human mediator* between God and the servant: *the master*. Therefore, it is the master, not the servant, who is directly responsible to God for the general care of the servant's wife. The servant takes orders from the master.[14]

The servant's protection comes from the master. The capital at his disposal comes from his master. He takes orders directly from his master or a representative of the master. If he is a foreman himself, he issues orders only as a representative of his master, since he is acting as an official under the master's general sovereignty. The master is responsible before God for any delegation of authority to a servant, so the mediatorial position of the master is not abrogated simply because he turns limited authority over to the servant.

This law made it clear to any woman who married a Hebrew indentured servant that *the ultimate human authority over her*, and therefore her legal protector, was not her husband but rather *her husband's master*. She was fulfilling the terms of the dominion covenant as a wife within a family unit, but the head of her family was her husband's master. Her husband was therefore only a *representative* of the head of her family. The covenant of marriage was in this instance four-way: 1) God, 2) the master of the house, 3) the indentured servant, and 4) the servant's wife. Since the protection of the wife and children was ultimately the legal responsibility of the master, the servant's wife and the children remained with the master when the husband, now released, departed.

The existence of such a law regarding servant families testifies to the importance of protection for a wife. Economic protection is one

---

14. A modern application of this biblical principle would be that a wife should remain a member of the Bible-believing church she is covenanted to even if her husband leaves the church and joins a more liberal church, let alone an apostate church. Her spiritual covering is provided by the church, mediated through her husband. Even though he has removed himself from the church's covering for the family, she is still entitled to it.

of the reasons why a woman marries. If the source of her financial protection is divided, then she faces dual loyalties. The problem of serving two masters arises. Which man possesses authority over her? If the master commands her husband, then her covenantal obligations to both men are unclear. This law forces the couple to recognize her ambiguous position as someone who owes loyalty to two men in the same household. This is a very difficult kind of in-law problem. The covenantal father-in-law actually owns the services of his covenantal son-in-law for a number of years, and literally owns his covenantal daughter until the servant becomes a free man and subsequently presents him with the bride price.

This law also forces both the servant and his prospective wife to consider carefully the costs, risks, and responsibilities of marriage. The husband's need for money to pay her bride price will remain a problem for them long after he regains his freedom. She may wind up with an occasional husband, should he decide to accept his independence and leave her behind. In this case, her master will become her day-to-day lord, unless her husband returns, either to buy her freedom or to become a permanent servant. Marriage to a man in bondage should not be entered into lightly. By asking her to marry him, the servant is asking her to subject herself to the covenantal authority of his master. A servant who married a woman was, in effect, acting as an agent of his master. The law testifies to her position of servitude as the wife of a servant. She may never be able escape this bondage. We can assume that the only woman ready to accept such bondage would be a household servant or the daughter of a poverty-stricken family (cf. Ex. 21:9).

Similarly, the servant has to consider the potential costs of marriage during his period of bondage. He may not be able to afford to redeem her and the children. In this case, he will face either a life of servitude or a life without his family. A future-oriented man probably would prefer to wait a few years, working out his term of service before bringing a woman into covenantal servitude under his master. By delaying marriage, he can then insure freedom for his future family. *Is freedom worth the delay?* This is the question facing a servant who is considering marriage. It is also the question facing his prospective bride.

Jacob's seven years of service for a wife had to be completed prior to his marriage. Similarly, a Hebrew bondservant, if he came into bondage as a single man, was expected to remain single throughout his term of service. He was under another man's administration, and he was therefore less able to fulfill the terms of the dominion covenant on his own initiative.

What about an indentured servant's children? The law did not permit law-abiding Hebrews to become involuntary lifetime servants to other Hebrews. A Hebrew could serve another Hebrew or a resident alien for up to 49 years, and he could become a member of the household through the pierced ear ritual, but nothing is said about the bondservant's children. Nothing needed to be said; the decision to become a servant, or even enforced servitude to repay a debt or make restitution, did not bind a man's children beyond the age of their maturity, for they were not permitted to be enslaved without their consent. Thus, it should be clear that the children of the released manservant, upon marriage for daughters or upon reaching the age of 20 for sons (Ex. 30:14), would have gone free. Presumably, an unmarried daughter who reached age 20 would have returned to her father's house or to her oldest brother's house, unless she, too, chose to become a lifetime servant in the master's house. Adult children no longer would have been in need of the legal protection of the master.

The wife, having married in terms of the servant status of her husband, in effect had already become *a voluntary lifetime servant to the master*, unless her husband came and redeemed her. Either she served her husband or her husband's former master, who remained her covenantal father until the bride price was paid.

The question arises, does the master own her future productivity, or does it belong to her husband? Maimonides wrote: "Though the master must support the wife and the children of his slave he is not entitled to the proceeds of their work. Rather do the proceeds of the wife's work and the things she finds belong to her husband."[15] Then what would be the economic incentive for a master to give the wife to the bondservant? He does not escape the legal and economic responsibilities of supporting her, yet he loses her productivity, which is transferred to the bondservant. Only if the master could escape the costs of supporting her would such a transaction have made sense. But the whole justification of this law regarding wives of bondservants is that it was the master's status as the provider of her protection that made it mandatory that she and the children remain with him upon her husband's departure. Because the responsibilities asso-

15. Maimonides, *Acquisition*, "Slave Laws," Chapter Three, Section Two, p. 254.

ciated with marriage would be a spur to the bondservant's productivity, marriage was also an incentive to liberty. Thus, contrary to Maimonides, it is difficult to imagine that the Bible would have created an economic disincentive for the master to provide his bondservant with a wife. He retained a portion of her productivity, and the productivity of any children born of the union, until the bondservant could afford to redeem her.

The Release Price

There were two ways of reuniting a broken Hebrew servant family. First, the servant could voluntarily become a lifetime servant. The sign of his bondage as an *adopted* household servant was a pierced ear (Ex. 21:6). This legal position as an adopted son would have been in effect until the jubilee year, when he would have returned as a free man to take possession of his family's inheritance in the land (unless he inherited land in his adoptive father's legacy).[16] Second, he could go out as a free man, returning intermittently for visitation rights with his wife, until such time as he earned funds to purchase his wife and children.

Understand, however, that no biblical text explicitly specifies this right of redemption by the husband if the wife was owned by a Hebrew master. Nevertheless, such a legal right is an inescapable conclusion of Exodus 21:7-8: "And if a man sell his daughter to be a maidservant, she shall not go out as the menservants do. If she please not her master, who hath betrothed her to himself, then shall he let her be redeemed: to sell her unto a strange nation he shall have no power, seeing he hath dealt deceitfully with her." The Hebrew daughter could be bought and sold as the Hebrew manservant could be. She could become a maidservant (Deut. 15:12). She could also be purchased by means of a *bride price*, that is, to become a wife. Her father could not legally abolish the God-given judicial, covenantal office of father; he could only transfer this office to another man who was promising to become her future husband or her future father-in-

---

16. Hebrew rabbis agreed that the word "forever" in Exodus 21:6 referred to the period remaining until the jubilee, said the medieval Jewish commentator, Rabbi Moshe ben Nachman (Ramban), *Commentary on the Torah: Exodus* (New York: Shilo, [1267?] 1973), pp. 348-49: Ex. 21:6. We do not know exactly when Nachmanides wrote this section; he did not complete his commentary on the Pentateuch until his arrival in Jerusalem in 1267. Charles B. Chavel, *RAMBAN: His Life and Teachings* (New York: Philipp Feldheim, 1960), p. 44. He died sometime around 1270, although the date of his death is not known: *ibid.*, p. 66. On "forever," see also Maimonides, *Acquisition*, "Slave Laws," Chapter Three, Section Seven, p. 255.

law. This transfer of office was legally possible only because *marriage is judicially a form of adoption.*[17]

We know this must have been the case because of the laws governing vows. A woman could take a vow, but the male head of household, father or husband, had to affirm it within 24 hours in order for it to be judicially binding before God (Num. 30:3-14). (This law appears, appropriately, in the Book of Numbers, the book corresponding to point four of the covenant: oath/sanctions.) Only a widow could make a judicially binding oath on her own (Num. 30:9). This indicates that a woman, unless a widow, was always legally under the hierarchical rule of a man. She was under a man's judicial authority: the office of household head. This office could not be transferred except through adoption or temporary maidservice. (A daughter could be used as collateral for a charity loan. A minor son could be, too, which is why the widow approached Elisha when the creditor threatened to make her sons into bondservants [II Ki. 4]. Elisha did not say that the creditor had broken the law. Instead, as her mediatory kinsman-redeemer [her pastor], he provided a miracle for this widow: oil that could be sold in order to redeem the debt.)

Daube's Hermeneutic: From Law to Theology

The prominent Old Testament scholar David Daube has gone so far as to argue that the original right of self-redemption by the Hebrew bondservant was strictly limited to cases of ownership of Hebrews by resident aliens.[18] Daube self-consciously prefers to argue from the legal to the theological,[19] but he then fails to deal with the actual judicial standards regarding redemption. This is why we need to argue theologically as well as judicially; otherwise, we will miss important aspects of both the theological and judicial character of God's revelation. Daube's hostility to theology is so great that he even argues that the priests and prophets who supposedly wrote the Pentateuch in the eighth century B.C. (or later) actually invented the idea of God's liberating His people from guilt.[20] Again, he is arguing from the judicial to the theological: a view based on the prior exclusively judicial concept of God as the liberator from physical bondage

---

17. See the section, "Marriage and Adoption," in Chapter 6, pp. 259-62.

18. David Daube, *Studies in Biblical Law* (Cambridge: At the University Press, 1947), p. 43.

19. *Ibid.*, pp. 1-3, 43.

20. See below, Appendix C: "The Hoax of Higher Criticism."

(the exodus), which in turn was based on the idea of His liberating
His people from debt servitude and economic oppression.[21] What he
refuses to acknowledge is that the liberation from debt, economic oppression, and slavery was first and foremost God's liberation of His
people from sin and idolatry. Again, we see a refusal to accept the
existence of the Bible-revealed relationship between covenant-breaking
and God's negative sanctions in history.

In contrast to Daube, I am arguing from the theological to the
legal. We need to explain the Bible's legal texts by analyzing them in
terms of the covenant. Covenant theology always governs Old Testament laws. The legal right of redemption from bondservitude
through offering a purchase price is implied throughout the Bible because of biblical religion's equating of personal freedom, economic
success, and ethical obedience to God. The biblical theme of national and personal liberation is always grounded in the general
commandment of liberation from the bondage of sin. The focus of
biblical law is primarily *ethical* rather than primarily legal, primarily
economic, or primarily political.

Covenant Sanctions

If a man is economically unskilled, his incompetence is expected
to lead him into poverty. This, in turn, tends to lead him into bondservice, where he can learn the biblical law of liberty—obedience to
God—through obedience to a covenantally self-disciplined person.
Why is it assumed in the Mosaic law that the owner of a bondservant
is covenantally faithful? Obviously, because he had sufficient wealth
to purchase the bondservant. Immoral and incompetent men do not
gain *and maintain* control over riches in a commonwealth governed
by biblical law (Deut. 28:15-68). This case law rests on the presupposition of a statistically relevant link between covenant-keeping and
long-term personal prosperity.

Because ethical behavior is best learned under a covenant-keeping
Hebrew master rather than under a covenant-breaking resident
alien, the preferred form of servitude is Hebrew over Hebrew. Thus,
contrary to Daube, the law regarding the redemption price would
have been applied in cases of Hebrew household bondservice, and

---

21. *Ibid.*, pp. 55-56. He writes: "The result that I wish to stress is that the idea of
God or Jesus redeeming mankind from sin and damnation, apparently a purely religious idea, derives from those ancient rules of insolvent debtors and victims of murder,
on the preservation of existing clans and the patrimony of clans." *Ibid.*, p. 59.

not just in cases of ownership by resident aliens. When the bondservant's incompetence is overcome, first by the master and then by himself, he is to be freed upon payment of the redemption price. He is expected to be able to earn the purchase price through faithful service. Here is the ethics-capital link in operation once again. The Bible recommends faithfulness, prosperity, and legal freedom. The Bible teaches that personal responsibility before God is enhanced by a person's legal status as a free man. This is why Paul tells Christian slaves to accept freedom if it is available to them (I Cor. 7:21).

Will Taxpayers Be Enslaved?

There are cases where righteous people fall into poverty or trials through no fault of their own. In order to give them a way back into profitable service as debt-free producers, God makes indentured servitude available to them. It is God's means of grace to them, a means of release from debt bondage. It is clear that the society at large is not supposed to become burdened with extra taxes in order to care for such people. Despite the fact that they may have come into hard times through no fault of their own, bondservice is still the Bible-sanctioned remedy for poverty. The society at large is presumed to be unable to sort out judicially on a case-by-case basis the righteous poor from the unrighteous poor. Thus, the same remedy for both is established by biblical law: indentured servitude. The poor man is expected to bear the unpleasant burden of becoming a bondservant as the means of his restoration economically. The taxpayers are not to become his servants. A welfare State cannot develop when the biblical laws of servitude are honored.

It should also be noted that in modern societies where these laws are not honored, the enslavement of taxpayers to the economically incompetent has become the political norm. Debt is seen as a blessing, bondservitude as a cursing, and theft by the ballot box as liberation. What the welfare State does is to put legally innocent, economically competent people into servitude to the economically incompetent. That Christian voters voluntarily resort to ballot-box coercion to care for their own parents (compulsory old age support programs), let alone the distant poor, testifies to the almost universal spread of antinomianism in our day. And when the welfare State goes bankrupt, there will be no one rich enough to pay its enormous debts. Its unproductive and economically dependent creditors will find themselves facing disaster. Bankruptcy cannot be avoided; it can only be deferred by transferring it to others. The bills are coming due.[22]

Prosperity Is Both the Standard and the Goal

The biblical economic standard for a righteous person, as with a nation or other covenantally bound groups, is prosperity. Thus, the man who has fallen into poverty needs guidance from one who is more skilled economically. There is presumably some flaw in the poor man's character or abilities that needs correction. (A physical or other catastrophe may also be the cause of the man's poverty, but the case law's provisions do not differentiate among the causes. The concern of biblical law is moral rehabilitation, which is then to lead to economic rehabilitation, or perhaps vice versa. The two forms of rehabilitation are assumed by the Bible to be connected.) Household servitude is a means of his release from this character flaw. It is the bankrupt person's first step to personal economic liberation. The case of a convicted thief who is sold into slavery to raise the funds to make restitution to his victims is an even more obvious example of being a slave to sin. Servitude is a means of progressive release for him. He is already in bondage to sin; bondservice in a righteous household is the first step in his redemption out of slavery.

The suggestion of any links in history between covenantal faithfulness under God and personal liberty, personal responsibility, and personal economic success is unacceptable to modern political liberals, including the vast majority of today's secular university-trained Christian social theorists. They implicitly understand that if such a covenantal relationship really exists, then biblical religion promotes the idea of the free market society, where individuals are to be held legally and economically responsible for their own mistakes. If the biblical covenant really does establish this connection, then any society that is faithful to the terms of God's covenant, meaning biblical law, will eventually become capitalist. There are few ideas more repugnant to the modern, liberal-minded, humanist-educated Christian social thinker. The Book of Deuteronomy, especially chapter 28, is the great offense, the great stumbling stone, for Christian

---

22. Alfred L. Malabre, Jr., *Beyond Our Means: How America's Long Years of Debt, Deficits and Reckless Borrowing Now Threaten to Overwhelm Us* (New York: Random House, 1987); Lawrence Malkin, *The National Debt* (New York: Henry Holt, 1987).

political liberals.[23] On the other hand, the dispensational fundamentalists' hostility to the idea of the continuing authority of Old Testament law makes it virtually impossible for them to present a specifically biblical-exegetical case for the free market economy, despite the fact that their instincts are generally conservative politically.

If this relationship between covenant-keeping and visible prosperity is denied, and poverty is not seen as statistically and covenantally correlated to ethical disobedience and a lack of self-discipline, then Old Testament servitude makes no ethical sense. Why should a man be put into legal bondage just because "random" events made him poor? If people's condition of poverty is in no statistically relevant way connected to their ethical condition, and if other people's condition of prosperity is in no statistically relevant way connected to their ethical condition, then indentured servitude, let alone intergenerational slavery, is ethically monstrous. This is exactly what modern liberal commentators say, *because above all they hate the idea of God's covenant sanctions in history.*

It is not random that the rise of Unitarianism (which tended to be deistic) and then Transcendentalism (which tended to be pantheistic) in New England were closely connected with the rise of abolitionism, 1820-1860.[24] What was common to both theological movements was a philosophy of *cosmic impersonalism.* Both theological systems were inherently anti-Christian and anti-covenantal. A representative statement of this anti-covenantal theology is provided by Unitarian Octavius Brooks Frothingham in his aptly titled book, *The Religion of Humanity* (1875): "The first sin was the first triumph of virtue. The fall was the first step forward. The advent of evil was the dawn of intelligence, discernment, enterprise, aspiration. Eden was the scene of humanity's birth. The tempter was Lucifer — the bringer

---

23. It was not an accident that William E. Diehl, a self-professed Keynesian, was so offended by my presentation of the biblical case for the free market economy. What really offended him was the Old Testament. He wrote: "That the author is strong on 'biblical law' is apparent. [What is also apparent is Diehl's hostility to biblical law: he placed the phrase in quotation marks, as if Old Testament law were not really biblical law — G.N.] The essay provides us with thirty-nine Old Testament citations, of which thirty-three are from the book of Deuteronomy. . . . [T]his essay might more properly be entitled, 'Poverty and Wealth according to Deuteronomy.'" Diehl, "A Guided-Market Response," in Robert G. Clouse (ed.), *Wealth and Poverty: Four Christian Views* (Downers Grove, Illinois: InterVarsity Press, 1984), p. 66.

24. C. Gregg Singer, *A Theological Interpretation of American History* (Nutley, New Jersey: Craig Press, 1964), ch. 2; R. J. Rushdoony, *The Nature of the American System* (Fairfax, Virginia: Thoburn Press, [1965] 1978), ch. 6.

of light. Thus even in him is something prophetic of salvation. The fault of Adam was disobedience to spoken law; but disobedience to arbitrary spoken decree, to unreasoning command, what is that but in essence obedience to the unspoken command of intelligence, and what is that but the soul of goodness?"[25] What God was not allowed to do in history in His name — bring covenant sanctions — the State was expected to do in the name of universal humanity.[26] The black slave became a tool in the statist plans of the North's Republican politicians. Congressman William D. ("Pig Iron") Kelley of Pennsylvania announced this messianic humanist vision: "Yes, sneer at or doubt it as you may, the negro is the 'coming man' for whom we have waited."[27] Frothingham recalled in 1875 the messianic viewpoint of his theological peers during the War: "The army of the North was to them the church militant; the leader of the army was the avenging Lord; and the reconstruction of a new order, on the basis of freedom for mankind, was the first installment of the Messianic Kingdom."[28] What should have been a biblical moral crusade against illegitimate lifetime chattel slavery became a humanist moral crusade against all forms of private, profit-seeking servitude. The result in the twentieth century has been the advancement of universal servitude to the State.

Protecting the Weak

The wife and children need lawful protection. They retained their lawful protection, either from the master or from an industrious, now future-oriented former bondservant, whether we are speaking of voluntary permanent servitude of the ex-bondservant husband or their purchase by him through the payment of a redemption price. But the husband would probably have retained little capital after having paid to buy freedom for his family. Nevertheless, it was his *time orientation and demonstrated industriousness* that were paramount for the subsequent protection of his family, not his remaining accumulated savings. This was also true, of course, with the bride price. A young man would probably give most of his capital to his father-in-law at the time of the marriage (although the father-in-law

---

25. Octavius Brooks Frothingham, *The Religion of Humanity* (New York: Putnam's, 1875), pp. 299-300; cited in Rushdoony, *Nature*, p. 89.

26. See especially the book by Unitarian Moncure D. Conway, *The Rejected Stone; or, Insurrection vs. Resurrection in America* (Boston: Walker, Wise, 1862).

27. *The Old Guard*, vol. I, no. IX (Sept. 1863), p. 240; cited in Rushdoony, *Nature*, p. 83.

28. Frothingham, *The Religion of Humanity*, p. 20; cited in Rushdoony, *idem.*

probably would have passed these assets to his daughter as her permanent dowry, in lieu of her inheritance of a portion of her family's land).[29]

Economically speaking, a master who wanted the lifetime services of a man had an incentive to find a man with a short-run time perspective to serve him, and then he might be able to persuade him to get married during his period of service. That way, the master would either have gained the woman as a lifetime servant, or both of them as lifetime servants, or the bride price. But in doing this, he risked having to take responsibility for servants with short-run outlooks, both husband and wife. He had no choice about accepting the servant as a lifetime servant; that decision was exclusively the servant's. As Mendelsohn points out, it was probably less expensive to hire workers part-time as needed than to buy someone's lifetime services.[30]

This law does not provide us with specific details of the redemption of a servant wife and children from a master. What would he have had to pay to free them? We might look at the prices associated with the redemption of temple vows. The official value of a woman dedicated to the temple by a vow was 30 shekels of silver (Lev. 27:4). The restitution payment for a male or female servant killed by a goring ox was also 30 shekels (Ex. 21:32).[31] On the other hand, the compulsory bride price owed to the father of a seduced virgin was 50 shekels of silver (Deut. 22:29). It seems more likely that the price would be the bride price paid by the master to the woman's father.

If the bride price was normally 50 shekels of silver, and the market price of a female servant fluctuated, the servant-master would

---

29. See the section, "Bride Price and Dowry," in Chapter 6, pp. 252-59.

30. Isaac Mendelsohn, *Slavery In the Ancient Near East* (New York: Oxford University Press, 1949), p. 119.

31. Children dedicated to the temple from five years old to age 20 were valued at 20 shekels for boys and 10 for girls. For young children, a month to five years old, it was five shekels and three shekels (Lev. 27:5-6). I presume, however, that no payment would have been required for children, since the master controlled them only as a covenantal grandfather, not as an owner. With the restoration of the covenantally independent family unit, the children would go out with their parents. If this was not the rule, and he had to buy his children, then with the birth of every child, the former servant would have been penalized. It is not likely that such a penalty would have been in force in a society designed by a God who favors population growth: Gary North, *Moses and Pharaoh: Dominion Religion vs. Power Religion* (Tyler, Texas: Institute for Christian Economics, 1985), ch. 1.

have been careful not to overpay. He would have preferred to buy a woman in the open market for less than 50 shekels. The servant might also have asked for a wife from the master's household servants, although the number of these servants was probably small in any household, as Mendelsohn's study indicates.[32] The servant probably would not have had many opportunities to meet girls outside this narrow household circle. He would have been dependent to a great extent on the servant-master's ability and willingness to locate a bride for him, unless he knew the prospective bride before he became a servant.

Why was the master entitled to payment from the former servant? *Because he was still covenantally the wife's father.* The man who gives a woman to another man to become his wife is covenantally her father. He is therefore entitled to a bride price — evidence that she will be protected in the new household.[33] The servant had taken the wife in advance, just as Jacob took Rachel after the switch had been made, and he owed the servant-master the required payment. In Jacob's case, the agreed-upon price was another seven years of service (Gen. 29:27-30).

How do we know that the husband would have been permitted to buy his family out of servitude? Because of the office of kinsman-redeemer. We know that the kinsman-redeemer was assigned the responsibility of buying his near-kinsman out of servitude to a stranger (Lev. 25:47-50). We know that the freed husband would have been his wife's kinsman-redeemer, as nearest of kin.

---

32. Mendelsohn, *Slavery In the Ancient Near East*, p. 121.

33. In the United States, fathers have historically paid for their daughters' weddings and post-wedding receptions. This is biblically foolish in a society in which the sons-in-law pay no bride price to the father. The prospective son-in-law should pay for everything. This is the father's evidence that the young man is thrifty, or at least a person who possesses inherited capital.

Like the dowry that once came from the father as a gift, but which was based on the size of the bride price, so today are the presents that come from the wedding guests. The larger the wedding expenditure, the more guests who will attend; the more guests, the larger the number of presents. But the size of the wedding, and therefore the size of the gifts (her dowry) should be determined by the husband's ability to pay for the wedding, not her father's ability. The gifts to the couple are really the bride's, for they constitute her dowry, her economic protection in case she is unlawfully divorced. Should the daughter bring assets of her own to the marriage, they should remain her property in case of a divorce. They are not "community property"; they are her protection. At her death, these assets would normally go to her children.

Normally, buying a wife out of servitude would have meant that the ex-servant had to earn these assets personally, unless his own kinsman-redeemer (or perhaps his wife's brother) voluntarily provided him with the funds. His ability to earn the redemption money testified to his capacity as an independent man under God. *Capital* was the *sign of independence and maturity* and therefore the means of securing his family's freedom.

Jesus Christ as Kinsman-Redeemer

God always allowed His people in bondage to be redeemed. This, of course, testified to the coming redemption of the nation of Israel by Jesus Christ. One way for a man to be reunited with his servant wife was for him to become adopted as a household servant, with the "circumcision of the ear" as the covenantal sign of household adoption. Only by adoption into God's family as a permanent bondservant can any person gain salvation (John 1:12). We become household servants in the family of faith.

Another important aspect of Christ's ministry is highlighted by the second avenue of escape from bondage, the bride-redemption system. Adam placed himself, his wife, and his heirs in spiritual bondage to sin. Eve suffered as a slave because of her husband's rebellious action. Ethically rebellious man still serves as a permanent slave to sin because he cannot pay the release price. But the *people of God* are referred to repeatedly in both testaments as being *God's bride.* "For thy Maker is thine husband" (Isa. 54:5a). Ezekiel 16 is built upon this analogy, as is Hosea 1-2. Christ referred to Himself as the bridegroom (Matt. 9:15). Paul wrote: "I have espoused you to one husband, that I may present you as a chaste virgin to Christ" (II Cor. 11:2b). Ephesians 5, which describes Christ's relationship to His church, is built on the analogy of marriage. The final consummation of this marriage comes with the resurrection and final judgment, when Christians shall indeed be spotless.[34] But in principle, *we are betrothed now.*

The Bridegroom, as kinsman-redeemer, has paid our release price.[35] He progressively delivers the bride ethically, though at a dis-

---

34. On the symbolic connections of circumcision to baptism, and the passover to communion, and all four sacraments to the marriage supper, see my essay, "The Marriage Supper of the Lamb," *Christianity and Civilization*, 4 (1985).

35. The Bridegroom is Jesus Christ. He also holds the office of kinsman-redeemer, the one who has the legal responsibility of buying his nearest of kin out of slavery, if the slave is in bondage to a foreigner (Lev. 25:47-49).

tance, helping her to mature in the spiritual independence from sin
that He has purchased. The church experiences *progressive liberation
from sin and bondage* in history—a progressive liberation based on the
Bridegroom's definitive redemption payment at Calvary. The Lord's
Supper covenantally represents this communion with the Bridegroom. The church now awaits His return at the final consummation.

We know that we are in principle set free from sin, but in history,
our sanctification is not yet complete. Our first husband, Adam,
died in slavery to sin, and we had been left behind, enslaved to
Adam's ethical master, Satan. Christ, like the brother who honors
the terms of the levirate marriage (Deut. 25:5-10), then married us,
thereby delivering us *legally* out of bondage to sin, but the consummation has not taken place. We wait for the return of our Bridegroom, who has redeemed us from the household of servitude. He
did not marry us as a servant marries. We will not remain in ethical
bondage. He completed His work on Calvary. The resurrection testifies to His condition as a free man. We are resurrected in Him in
principle—definitively set free *judicially and ethically* from sin as His
lawful bride (Gal. 4:7).[36] But in history, we still labor under the
bondage of sin (Heb. 2:8-18). Our sanctification in history is not yet
complete. We have not yet been presented as a chaste virgin before
Christ (II Cor. 11:2). One reason why there is no marriage after the
resurrection (Matt. 22:30) is that the church has but one husband,
Christ. There will be no divided family loyalties.

The marriage ceremony between Christ and His church did not
take place before Calvary. He was still laboring to complete His term
of service. He would not marry prematurely. It was the error of the
Jewish multitudes that they expected liberation—both marriage and
the consummation—in history, when they hailed Him as their earthly
king and placed palm branches before Him as He entered Jerusalem
in the final week of His pre-resurrection ministry (John 12:12-15).

The Fulfillment of the Jubilee Year

God's laws regarding Israel's land tenure system required that
every fiftieth year, each plot of ground in Israel be returned to the
heirs of the original family member who had it allocated to him after
the conquest of Canaan (Lev. 25:8-34). This land tenure system kept

---

36. Gary North, *Unconditional Surrender: God's Program for Victory* (3rd ed.; Tyler,
Texas: Institute for Christian Economics, 1988), pp. 66-71.

those outside a particular tribe from becoming permanent owners of rural land throughout Israel. This restricted the intermarriage of the tribes (Num. 36), and it also prohibited the consolidation of rural land by the Levites or the king. It kept the nation politically and economically decentralized. This system also kept strangers in the land — gentile alien residents — from ever becoming landowners rather than leaseholders, except through adoption into a Hebrew family.

We know that this land tenure system was both judicially fulfilled and historically annulled by Jesus, for He explicitly transferred the kingdom of God to the gentiles (Matt. 21:43). The "strangers to the land" inherited God's kingdom. This judicial transfer of ownership of the kingdom to the gentiles is the legal foundation of the inheritance of the earth by Christians.[37] The kingdom of God no longer is uniquely connected to the land of Palestine. The conquest of Canaan by Joshua is no longer judicially relevant to members of the kingdom. The jubilee's land-release system is therefore no longer judicially relevant in history, except as a type of Christ's redemptive work in history.

The historical transition from the Old Testament to the New Testament, which was completed with the fall of Jerusalem in 70 A.D.,[38] also abolished another law that governed the period of servitude for heathen slaves: the residency requirements for full citizenship in God's kingdom commonwealth. The law that delayed citizenship for the heirs of bastards for ten generations (Deut. 23:2-3) was annulled with the historic destruction of Moab and Ammon, and also with the inauguration of a New Testament definition of lawful citizenship in God's kingdom: faith in Christ and covenant membership in the church.[39] As the kingdom of God in history becomes progressively manifested in the affairs of men, mankind's legal institutions are supposed to reflect God's kingdom. Men's institutions are supposed to be conformed to the principles of God's law, just as men are supposed to be conformed to the image of God's Son, Jesus Christ (Rom. 8:29). To argue otherwise is to deny progressive sanctification in history, both for individuals and institutions.[40]

---

37. Gary North, *Inherit the Earth: Biblical Blueprints for Economics* (Ft. Worth, Texas: Dominion Press, 1987), ch. 5.

38. David Chilton, *The Days of Vengeance: An Exposition of the Book of Revelation* (Ft. Worth, Texas: Dominion Press, 1987).

39. This, of course, raises a whole host of problems for any theory of universal citizenship and therefore universal suffrage.

40. Gary North, *Dominion and Common Grace: The Biblical Basis of Progress* (Tyler, Texas: Institute for Christian Economics, 1987).

In New Testament times, any slave must be regarded legally as an indentured servant. Involuntary lifetime servitude was abolished when Jesus fulfilled the jubilee year; the only other form of servitude authorized by the Bible is indentured servitude. A slave in New Testament times is therefore entitled to be treated as a Hebrew servant was to have been treated in the Old Testament commonwealth, with his release delayed by no more than seven years, except in cases of criminal sanctions. His children must be freed upon reaching their maturity at age 20.

A Long History of Self-Serving Bible Interpretation

Purchasing lifetime slaves from pagan nations or resident aliens was biblically legitimate prior to Christ's fulfillment of the jubilee year, meaning prior to the abolition of its land tenure provisions. As we have seen, after Christ's death and resurrection, the Christian is to understand that slave-owning is for the purpose of liberating people from bondage, buying them out of demonic covenants. It is illegal to compel any male to remain in bondage beyond seven years, except in the case of criminals paying off debts to victims.

This abolition of permanent slavery was long ignored or unrecognized by Bible commentators. It took Christians and Jews over 1,800 years to come to the conclusion that lifetime slavery is illegitimate. The myth that the "curse of the children of Ham" refers exclusively to blacks was adopted by Jews, Christians, and Muslims in the Middle Ages.[41] (There had been a curse: Noah cursed Canaan, the son of Ham, but this curse was covenantal, not racial, and it was generally fulfilled by the conquest of the land of Canaan by the Israelites, and the subjection of the remnant as slaves.)[42] Winthrop

---

41. David Brion Davis, *Slavery and Human Progress* (New York: Oxford University Press, 1984), p. 87. (Davis is incorrect when he writes that the doctrine originated in the Middle Ages.) As late as 1867, Robert L. Dabney, the American South's greatest Calvinist theologian in the late nineteenth century, appealed to Genesis 9 and the curse of Canaan to justify the legitimacy of the idea of slavery in general: ". . . it gives us the origin of domestic slavery. And we find that it was appointed by God as the punishment of, and remedy for (nearly all God's providential chastisements are also remedial) the peculiar moral degradation of a part of the race." He did not argue that blacks are necessarily under this same curse, although he hardly denied it: "It may be that we should find little difficulty in tracing the lineage of the present Africans to Ham. But this inquiry is not essential to our argument." Dabney, *A Defence of Virginia* (New York: Negro University Press, [1867] 1969), pp. 103, 104.

42. Prof. Davis appeals to the liberal higher critic Von Rad to argue that "the original Yahwistic narrative had nothing to do with Shem, Ham, and Japheth, and the ecumenical scheme of nations which follows. It was rather an older story, limited to the Palestinian Shem, Japheth, and Canaan. . . ." Davis, "Slavery and Sin: The Cultural Background," in Martin Duberman (ed.), *The Antislavery Vanguard: New Essays on the Abolitionists* (Princeton, New Jersey: Princeton University Press, 1965), p. 5n.

Jordan has identified the source of the idea of Ham's curse as black skin: it first appeared in the Jewish Talmud and the Midrash.[43] Moses Maimonides ("Rambam"),[44] the influential Spanish-born Jewish Bible expositor and philosopher of twelfth century, who eventually wound up in Egypt as the court physician to the Muslim warrior Saladin, insisted that slaves should not be taught the Bible.[45]

The medieval church recognized that Christians were not to be enslaved by infidels (Jews, Muslims), although Christians could legally own Christian slaves and non-Christian slaves.[46] The seventeenth-century Puritans, as dedicated to Old Testament law as any Christian group in history, did not believe that the sabbatical year of release, or any other law of mandatory release, applied to Negro slavery, whether the slaves were Christians or not.[47] The price of slaves was kept high because slave-owners could capitalize the income stream of a lifetime of service, plus the lifetimes of the heirs of the slaves.

The classic example of "Christian" slavery is probably the case of the bequest by Christopher Codrington to London's Society for the Propagation of the Gospel (SPG) in 1710 of a plantation on Barbados with over 300 slaves. Did the SPG release them? Hardly. In 1732, a Codrington attorney suggested that the SPG cease branding the chests of newly purchased slaves with "SOCIETY." On the subject of slave marriage, the SPG was silent. The Society did not even enforce a sabbath day of rest; the slaves were worked for six days, and allowed to tend to their own plots and work on Sundays.[48]

Nevertheless, we must recognize that *these slaves had been rescued from the culture of demonism.* Those who were converted to Christ are unquestionably better off today than they would be if they had re-

---

43. Winthrop D. Jordan, *White Over Black: American Attitudes Toward the Negro, 1550-1812* (Chapel Hill: University of North Carolina Press, 1968), p. 18. He cites the *Babylonian Talmud* (Soncino Press edition), tractate *Sanhedrin*, vol. II, p. 745; *Midrash Rabbah* (Soncino Press edition), vol. I, p. 293. Reprinted by Bloch Pub. Co., New York.

44. Rabbi Moshe ben Maimon.

45. Maimonides wrote: "It is forbidden for a man to teach his slave the Scriptures. If he does teach him, however, the slave does not become free thereby." Maimonides, *Acquisition*, "Laws Concerning Slaves," Chapter Eight, Section Eighteen, p. 278.

46. David Brion Davis, *The Problem of Slavery in Western Culture* (Ithaca, New York: Cornell University Press, 1966), pp. 98-103.

47. *Ibid.*, pp. 203-7. Cf. Marcus W. Jernegan, "Slavery and Conversion in the American Colonies," *American Historical Review* (April 1916).

48. *Ibid.*, pp. 219-20.

mained slaves elsewhere, or even "free men," worshipping Satan under the fear of the local shaman. They did learn something of the Western, Protestant work ethic.

American Negro Slavery

The system of chattel slavery that existed in the antebellum (pre-Civil War) South had five extremely pernicious features:

> The denial of Christ's jubilee fulfillment
> No legal foundation for slave marriages
> No legal protection for the slaves
> No system of guaranteed redemption
> Gang labor was economically productive

The first four of the five great evils of the Southern slave system were primarily religious and judicial rather than economic. This is to be expected. Because biblical religion is ethical and judicial, the institutions that grow out of biblical law are to reflect this legal concern of God. Institutional rebellion will always reflect a denial of the ethical and judicial character of biblical religion. To focus on the economic aspects of life rather than the judicial is itself a manifestation of man's rebellion. That modern scholars, influenced by Marx's economic determinism, should redirect our interest away from the judicial and familial aspects of slavery, is simply another manifestation of the distorted presuppositions of modern humanism.

1. Denial of Christ's Jubilee Fulfillment

The South shared the view that had dominated Western civilization from the beginning: that Jesus has forever fulfilled Israel's jubilee land tenure system (Luke 4:16-21). Like the West in general, the South saw no connection between Jesus' fulfillment of the jubilee law regarding permanent chattel slavery (Lev. 25:44-46) and His abolition of the jubilee laws governing Israel's land tenure. Thus, Southerners imported foreign slaves from pagan nations and placed them and their children in permanent bondage.

As the nineteenth century progressed, people in the West began to recognize the evil of permanent chattel slavery. The Quakers pioneered the anti-slavery impulse, and it was adopted by evangelical revivalists and Unitarian abolitionists. Southerners continued to appeal to Leviticus 25 in defense of slavery. To do so, they had to ignore the jubilee-annulling aspects of Christ's ministry. Critics of slavery did not recognize the judicial implications of the abolition of the jubilee, thereby making it easier for Southern apologists to use the Old Testament as a way of defending the South for placing African Negroes in bondage for up to ten generations ("forever").

One abolitionist who did appeal to the jubilee year of release was Ralph Wardlaw, the British abolitionist. He appealed to the theme of the jubilee, but only as eschatological liberation: the judicial abolition of slavery by Parliament as the preparation for the earthly millennium. He saw the release of the slaves as the fulfillment of the jubilee year.[49] Thus, abolitionism was seen as the fulfillment of the jubilee.

This completely reversed the judicial terms of the jubilee. *What the jubilee year released was land, not slaves;* the jubilee law in fact was the *only* Old Testament law that authorized permanent slavery. Neither the opponents of slavery nor its defenders ever recognized this. Neither side argued that the jubilee had long-since been fulfilled by Christ, and therefore that the contemporary abolition of permanent chattel slavery should be seen as a covenantal affirmation of this previous judicial annulment. The modern abolition of slavery was not an announcement of the jubilee year of release, but rather a belated judicial acknowledgment of Christ's historical fulfillment of the jubilee and His *annulment* of its provisions. The jubilee law had authorized permanent slavery; its annulment therefore abolished permanent slavery, with the exception only of voluntary servitude, either by women who marry indentured servants or people who voluntarily choose it.

In the case of the South's slave system, every male should have been told that he could go free after having served for seven years, or upon reaching age 20, if he was the son of a slave. Every unmarried female should have been told the same thing. Civil and ecclesiastical law should have enforced this. Nobody argued along these lines in the nineteenth century. Until the late eighteenth century, no group had ever criticized the institution of chattel slavery.[50] It took a military defeat of the South to break the chains of slavery in the United

---

49. Davis, *Slavery and Human Progress*, pp. 120-21.

50. The law against slavery passed in 1652 in Rhode Island was never actually enforced. It was passed largely as a result of pressure from one man, Samuel Gorton. Charles M. Andrews, *The Colonial Period of American History*, 4 vols. (New Haven, Connecticut: Yale University Press, [1936] 1964), II, p. 30.

States. It then took a century of growing up by both races, plus more legislative pressure from the increasingly pagan North, to bring some degree of legal equality and social peace.

2. No Legal Foundation for Slave Marriages

The slave family had no legal existence, yet the very heart of the family as created by God is its position as a covenant institution, and the heart of the covenant is legal.[51] This absence of legal status for the family was equally true in the ancient pagan Near East.[52] In Egypt, it was rare for a male slave to be sold with his wife and children.[53] Without the possibility of attaining freedom for himself, his wife, or his children, the slave "husband" had far less incentive to work or to discipline himself or his family. The master reduced the likelihood of having any highly family-oriented male slave under his authority to bring personal dominion over members of the slave's household. Thus, the dominion training as head of a household that is so necessary for spiritual, economic, and ecclesiastical development (I Tim. 3) was not fully present in the slave society of the antebellum South.

There is no doubt that the most skilled Calvinist theologian of the South, Robert L. Dabney, was bothered slightly by this fact. In his post-bellum defense of slavery, he wrote: "The silence of our laws, then, concerning the marriage of slaves, means precisely this: that the whole subject is remitted to the master, the chief magistrate of the little integral commonwealth, the family." Thus, he asserted weakly, "the question whether our laws were defective . . . is only a question whether, in the distribution of ruling functions, those of the master were not made too large and responsible, herein."[54] Then he appealed to the patriarchs of Genesis. "What magistrate or legislature, other than Abraham, issued their marriage license? Who else enforced their marriage law or defined its rights?"[55] The fact that the

---

51. Sutton, *That You May Prosper*, ch. 2.

52. Mendelsohn, *Slavery In the Ancient Near East*, p. 40.

53. In some sixty documents, most of them from Egypt in late antiquity, that record sales of adult male slaves, not one wife or child accompanied the slave. M. I. Finley, *Ancient Slavery and Modern Ideology* (New York: Viking, 1980), p. 76. He cites K. R. Bradley, "The Age at Time of Sale of Female Slaves," *Arethusa*, II (1978), pp. 243-52.

54. Robert L. Dabney, *A Defence of Virginia [And Through Her, of the South]* (New York: Negro University Press, [1867] 1969), p. 229.

55. *Ibid.*, p. 230.

patriarchs were also civil rulers of a newly created covenant nation under God, and the fact that they could not sever a marriage whenever it was personally profitable to them to do so,[56] unlike the plantation owners who could sever a slave "marriage" at will,[57] he conveniently overlooked. If state laws in the South had been equally silent regarding the legal obligations of white partners, his argument would have been more plausible. It was, in fact, an example of the enormous self-deception of the best men in the South. Dabney was the South's greatest theologian, had served as Stonewall Jackson's aide and chaplain, wrote Jackson's biography, and later served as professor of political economy at the University of Texas. Yet he refused to face the ugly reality of southern slave non-marriages.

"The denial of legal marriage meant," writes Arnold Sio, "in conjunction with the rule that the child follow the condition of the mother, that the offspring of slaves had no legal father, whether the father was slave or free. The duration of the union between slaves depended on the interests of the master or those of the slaves. The union was subject at any time to being dissolved by the sale of one or both of the slaves. The children of these 'contubernial relationships,' as they were termed, had no legal protection against separation from their parents. In the law there was no such thing as fornication or adultery among slaves. A slave could not be charged with adultery, and a male slave had no legal recourse against another slave, free Negro, or white person for intercourse with his 'wife.' Nor could the slave present this abuse as evidence in his defense in a criminal charge of assault and battery, or murder."[58] Slaves could not own property, make wills, or inherit. In 1853, a North Carolina Supreme Court justice wrote that "our law requires no solemnity or form in regard to the marriage of slaves, and whether they 'take up' with each other by express permission of their owners, or from a mere impulse of nature, in obedience to the command 'multiply and replenish the earth,' cannot, in the contemplation of the law, make any sort of difference."[59]

---

56. "Polygamy and capricious divorce never were authorized by Old Testament law. . . ." *Ibid.*, p. 132.

57. *Ibid.*, p. 231.

58. Arnold A. Sio, "Interpretations of Slavery," *Comparative Studies in Society and History*, VII (April 1965); reprinted in Allen Weinstein and Frank Otto Gatall (eds.), *American Negro Slavery: A Modern Reader* (New York: Oxford University Press, 1968), p. 315.

59. Cited in Herbert G. Gutman, *The Black Family in Slavery and Freedom, 1750-1925* (New York: Pantheon, 1976), p. 52.

What is truly remarkable in retrospect is that actual practice throughout the South was very different from the civil law's lack of concern regarding slave marriages. The strong influence of the black churches before and after emancipation helped keep slave marriages intact.[60] White churches also sometimes pressured black slaves to remain married.[61] In a survey of blacks who were seeking to be legally married after emancipation in Mississippi in 1864-65, records indicate that perhaps one out of six reported that a prior marriage had been separated by forced sale, or 17 percent (therefore leaving 83 percent intact).[62] Obviously, this threat of separation was an important one in the owners' available sanctions against slaves, but it was one that had to be used sparingly if the black family structure was to remain intact. If breakups through forced sale had been common, then slave families would not have remained stable.

Planters also recognized that the maintenance of slave discipline required the formation of slave families. Gutman is correct: "Only those slaves who lived in affective familial groupings (and especially the greatly prized slave husband and father) could respond to indirect and direct incentives that exploited their familial bonds. Monetary rewards based on family labor (such as the slave garden plot) and incentive payments for 'extra' work balanced the threat of the sale of relatives and especially grown children. A husband and father might work harder to get extra rations for his children, to earn cash to purchase a luxury item for his wife, or to prevent his children from being sold."[63] Owners generally kept families together at least until the children reached adulthood.[64]

This story of the strong slave family structure was not recognized by most scholars of antebellum period until the pioneering studies by Herbert Gutman were published in the 1970's. The influential sociologist E. Franklin Frazier had painted a very different picture in the previous academic generation. Based on his accurate understanding of the South's civil laws regarding slave marriages, he drew conclusions that would have followed, had church law and actual custom not been radically different from the civil law. By removing the male as head of the slave household, he concluded, females tended to be-

---

60. *Ibid.*, pp. 70-75.
61. *Ibid.*, pp. 286-87.
62. *Ibid.*, pp. 146-47.
63. *Ibid.*, p. 79.
64. *Ibid.*, p. 149.

come dominant figures in the inevitably pseudo-families that were the product of sexual union. He writes: "Under slavery the Negro family was essentially an amorphous group gathered around the mother or some female on the plantation. The father was a visitor to the household without any legal or recognized status in family relations. He might disappear as the result of the sale of slaves or because of a whimsical change in his own feelings or affection. Among certain favored elements on the plantation, house slaves and skilled artisans, the family might achieve greater stability and the father and husband might develop a more permanent interest in his family. Whatever might be the circumstances of the Negro family under the slave regime, family and sex relations were constantly under the supervision of the whites. The removal of authority of masters as the result of the Civil War and Emancipation caused promiscuous sex relations to become widespread and permitted the constant change of spouses."[65]

After emancipation, he says, white missionaries from the North labored long and hard to persuade Negro males to formalize their sexual relationships with women. There was resistance by the now-emancipated males to establish a new form of "bondage." This undercut the development of the Negro family. "A large proportion of the Negro families among the freedmen continued after Emancipation to be dependent upon the Negro mother as they had been during slavery."[66] He admits that there were strong economic pressures on black males to marry. Freedmen absolutely refused to work as members of the gangs of laborers that had been basic to the antebellum plantation economy. Instead, they did their best to start farms as sharecroppers. The man or husband was required to sign a rent agreement. "The more stable elements among the freedmen who had been in a position to assimilate the sentiments and ideas of their former masters soon undertook to buy land. This gave the husband and father an interest in his wife and children that no preaching on the part of white missionaries or Negro preachers could give."[67] Leaders of the new post-emancipation black community also tended to be church members and church leaders.[68]

---

65. E. Franklin Frazier, *The Negro Church in America* (New York: Schocken, [1964] 1974), pp. 37-38.
66. *Ibid.*, p. 39.
67. *Idem.*
68. *Idem.*

What Frazier did not perceive is that slave-owners had early recognized the nature of economic incentives for black fathers, and had
responded appropriately. The fact is, the disintegration of the black
family is a very recent phenomenon. The primary institutional
causes of this disintegration were the rise of liberal theology in black
churches, which undermined the Protestant work ethic, and the
coming of the State-financed welfare system, which undermined
husbands' family responsibilities, but scholars do not want to tackle
the first topic or emphasize the second.[69] What we do know is that
the urban black family was generally stable prior to the 1940's.[70]
Gutman's studies of black families in Buffalo, New York, in 1855,
1875, 1905, and 1925 indicate a continuing pattern of black family
stability, with two-parent households dominant throughout the period: from 82 percent of the households to 92 percent. These were
mostly lower-class families.[71] He found the same pattern in New
York City households in 1905 and 1925.[72] Blacks had been moving
north for two generations in 1925. Where did this stable family pattern originate, asked Gutman, if not in slavery? He found that from
1864-65, the years of emancipation by northern armies, and in 1866
the year after the South surrendered, blacks all over the South rushed
to the civil authorities and churches to formalize their marriages.[73]
Over half of the couples in some districts of North Carolina claimed
to have been married for over a decade; around 9 percent for as long
as 30 years.[74]

Throughout the South, when a black slave became pregnant, her
owners and her peers expected her to marry and stay married. Most
of them did so.[75] This pro-family outlook was a major contributing
factor to the enormous fertility of the slaves. While only about 400,000

---

69. An exception is Charles Murray, *Losing Ground: American Social Policy,
1950-1980* (New York: Basic Books, 1984), ch. 9: "The Family." It is easy to blame
joblessness, but two questions must be asked: "Why did this problem arise after
1945? Was there greater racism after 1945 than in the previous three generations?"
Economic answers appear in Walter E. Williams, *The State Against Blacks* (New York:
New Press, McGraw-Hill, 1982); George Gilder, *Wealth and Poverty* (New York: Basic
Books, 1981), Pt. II.

70. Eleanor Holmes Norton, "Restoring the Traditional Black Family," *New York
Times Magazine* (June 2, 1985), p. 93.

71. Gutman, *Black Family*, p. xviii.

72. *Ibid.*, p. xix.

73. *Ibid.*, pp. 19-24.

74. *Ibid.*, p. 15.

75. *Ibid.*, pp. 62-75.

were imported from the beginning until the slave trade was made illegal in 1808, at least nine times this many slaves were freed in 1864-65. About 46 percent were imported from 1741 to 1780, and about 25 percent from 1781 and 1808.[76] Sowell has summarized this remarkable difference between American slavery and all other forms: "The United States held the largest number of slaves of any country in the Western Hemisphere — more than one-third of all the slaves in the hemisphere — in 1825. Yet other countries actually imported more slaves, and Brazil six times as many. The difference was that the United States was the only country in which the slave population reproduced itself and grew by natural increase. In the rest of the hemisphere, the death rate was so high and the birthrate so low that continuous replacements were imported from Africa."[77]

I have devoted considerable space to this aspect of Southern slavery because it is one that has been overlooked and misinterpreted for many years. The combined impact of church law, the white family's example, and economic incentives was far greater than scholars prior to Gutman had realized. We know little about marriage patterns in African tribes, but those traditions may also have played a role in stabilizing black marriages — a suggestion that is much more palatable to today's humanistic scholars. The fact is, however, that it was the decision of the slave-owner that was crucial with regard to the honoring of his slaves' biblical marriage patterns, and on the whole, the biblical standards were more honored than violated, except in civil law. It was the owner whose word was the slave's law in the South, for better or worse.

3. No Legal Protection for the Slave

The Bible's hierarchical appeals court system was denied to slaves, for the legal hierarchy, upward and downward, ended with the slave-owner. There was no government for the slave to appeal to. There was no civil or ecclesiastical government above the master that would be able to judge his behavior in terms of the biblical laws governing the treatment of slaves. This was a variation of the invariably perverse "divine rights" concept: a man who answers to no legal institutional authority above him with respect to his dealings with his slaves. Like the "divine right" of kings who were supposedly judged

---

76. *Ibid.*, p. 33; citing Philip D. Curtin, *The Atlantic Slave Trade: A Census* (Madison: University of Wisconsin Press, 1969).
77. Thomas Sowell, *Ethnic America: A History* (New York: Basic Books, 1981), p. 186.

only by God, the divine right of slave-owners was inherently tyrannical. The slave-owner was far more likely to be irresponsible with
regard to his slaves because he answered to no covenantal authority
above him, civil or ecclesiastical. Because of this, there was also a
less efficient servant below the typical slave-owner. This historical
development — less efficient slaves — was in conformity to the biblical
principle of dominion: a man must be governed *by* biblical law if he
is successfully to govern *by means of* biblical law. The economic blessings associated with the productivity fostered by adherence to biblical law were to that extent missing in southern slavery.

4. No System of Guaranteed Redemption

There was no way, guaranteed by civil law, for a slave to buy his
way out of slavery. This was not the case in the ancient Near East.[78]
Nor was any relative going to redeem him, as was possible in the ancient Near East. Because of the racial character of American Negro
slavery, there was also no likelihood of family adoption, another possible way of escape in the ancient Near East, although one infre-
quently used.[79] This left voluntary manumission and physical escape
as the only roads to freedom. The slave-owner's conscience, or his
understanding of human motivation (hard work in exchange for
guaranteed freedom in the future), was the slave's only earthly hope.
This offered most slaves very little earthly hope.

The self-discipline and future-orientation that would have been
stimulated within the slave society by a system of self-redemption
through thrift would have increased the sense of calling and economic responsibility among millions of slaves. God's original purpose for servitude — the increase of godly self-government — was
thwarted by the absence of a legally guaranteed system of economic
redemption. The work of Christ, as the kinsman-redeemer who buys
His people out of servitude, meaning the Bridegroom who buys the
bride out of servitude, had no visible institutional and judicial manifestation in the slave system of the American South in particular or
the world in general.

We do have one lonely example in the historical records of a
slave-owner who recognized the potential for a program of earned
manumission, John McDonogh. It offers evidence of what could

---

78. Mendelsohn, *Slavery In the Ancient Near East*, pp. 66-74.
79. *Ibid.*, pp. 79-83.

have been done throughout history with a system of indentured servitude combined with slavery. It would have increased slave output by giving at least partial obedience to the biblical standard, though not without the threat of lifetime, inherited slavery as the judicial "whip." John McDonogh was a Scottish Presbyterian slave-owner who lived in New Orleans in the first half of the nineteenth century. He was one of the richest men in the United States at the time of his death in 1850. He was famous in New Orleans because of his industrious slaves. They worked long hours for him, literally running to get their work done.

He did not tell his contemporaries his secret until late in his life. In 1825 he had conceived of a plan that would enable his slaves to buy their way to freedom. He hoped that they would go to Liberia, but only one did. As a strict sabbatarian, he would give them Saturday afternoons off for their own work if they promised not to work on Sundays. Other planters also gave their slaves Saturday afternoon off. But McDonogh made this offer: if they would work for him on Saturday afternoon, and two extra hours each day, he would pay them extra. He paid them 50 cents a day in winter and 62.5 cents in summer.

He established a set release price for males of $600 and $450 for females. This was somewhat less than the average market price for healthy field hands.[80] Once they had paid off one-sixth of this agreed-upon price, they would get one free day of their own. They could then use their earnings on this free day to speed up repayment. It took fifteen years for a slave to buy his way out of slavery.

The slaves ran his entire operation: rent collection from his white tenants, the agricultural operations, his urban real estate. A jury of six slaves handled all disciplinary matters, which he reviewed. He would overturn their punishments when they were too harsh. The slaves' jury tended to be overly rigorous in their judgments against fellow slaves.

He was a man of his word. He reported to them every six months concerning their progress. He later told his white contemporaries that slaves were in the best position to know a master's character, and the plan could work only if they trusted him to fulfill his promise.

---

80. In 1825, the average price of a male field hand in New Orleans was $800. This price was not to drop below $700 in McDonogh's lifetime. Prices rose steadily from $800 in 1830 to $900 in 1832 to $1,000 in 1834. In 1841 prices started dropping, reaching bottom ($700) in 1843-45, and then rose to $1,100 in 1850, the year of his death. Source: Alfred H. Conrad and John R. Meyer, "The Economics of Slavery in the Antebellum South," in Hugh G. J. Aitkin (ed.), *Did Slavery Pay?* (Boston: Houghton Mifflin, 1971), Table 17, p. 169.

He argued that merely by giving them their freedom, the owner could never get them to plan ahead. The owner might go back on his promise. But by *selling* a slave his freedom, this future-orientation would affect the slave's character positively. "Hope would be kept alive in his bosom; he would have a goal in view, continually urging him on to faithfulness, fidelity, trust, industry, economy, and every virtue of good work."[81] He did not honor the seventh-year automatic release, but he did understand that by allowing a slave to buy his way to freedom, the very effort would prepare him for independence. Meanwhile, the efforts of these independence-seeking slaves made him a rich man.

At his funeral, there were many weeping former slaves, but very few whites. He had broken covenant with his white contemporaries, getting rich by adhering to a biblical principle. He had begun to understand servitude as God had designed it: as a means of imparting self-discipline and eventual independence to the children of foreigners from demonic cultures. His peers had regarded slavery as the ancient Hebrews immediately had come to regard it: as a way to get rich through other men's permanent servitude. Judgment fell on the South, just as it had fallen on Israel. The Assyrians of the North invaded.[82]

It must be understood that McDonogh's system of slave management worked well only because of civil laws establishing the permanence of slavery. Only because the normal fate of a slave was to be born into slavery and die a slave, with his children inheriting his slave status, could the prospect of self-purchased manumission serve as a major incentive. Had the slave's release been automatic by law after a maximum of seven years of servitude, McDonogh's system would not have had comparable impact in the lives of his slaves. It was the ultimate negative earthly sanction of permanent servitude that enabled McDonogh to employ the positive sanction of liberty through purchase.

---

81. Cited by Carl N. Degler, *The Other South: Southern Dissenters in the Nineteenth Century* (New York: Harper & Row, 1974), pp. 43-44. Degler relies on two main sources: Lane Carter Kendell, "John McDonogh — Slave-Owner," *Louisiana Historical Quarterly*, XVI (1932), and William Talbot Childs, *John McDonogh: His Life and Work* (Baltimore, Maryland: Johns Hopkins University Press, 1939).

82. In the Old Testament, Assyria fell to Babylon. The international Babylon of our day is vastly more merciless than the Babylon of Jeremiah's day: Robert Conquest and Jon Manchip White, *What to Do When the Russians Come: A Survivor's Guide* (New York: Stein and Day, 1984).

Dual sanctions are an important aspect of biblical jurisprudence: there must always be a permanent negative sanction backing up economic sanctions such as purchasing one's freedom or paying restitution. The ultimate earthly sanction is capital punishment. The ultimate eternal sanction is perpetual agony in the lake of fire. These threats provide incentives for criminals and servants to suffer peacefully the "eye for eye" sanctions, and work to overcome them. God, however, has eliminated the legitimacy of the negative sanction of compulsory lifetime slavery in New Testament times. Even criminals who are sold into bondage in order to make restitution to their victims always have the legal right to buy their way out. The negative sanction is essentially economic rather than permanent. The criminal is legally an indentured servant, not a slave, even though the magnitude of his required restitution payment may in effect make him a lifetime servant unless someone else should pay his debt, or unless his victims at some point forgive him his debts. The liberty that Jesus Christ established must not be symbolically or judicially denied by the presence of permanent slavery in a Christian society.

5. *Gang Labor Was Economically Productive*

There was a fifth evil feature of Western slavery, and it was economic in nature: the economic efficiency of the slave gang system in harvesting key cash crops, especially sugar and cotton. This made large-scale private slave plantations profitable in a way not seen from the fall of the Roman Empire until the fourteenth or fifteenth century, in the case of sugar, and accelerating in the nineteenth century because of the invention of the cotton gin. As Prof. Davis says of the origin of Negro slavery in the fourteenth century, "It would have been better for the Christians' morals if they had remained content with honey. . . ."[83] Only the abolition of slavery by force of law and arms ended this evil. Within five years after the end of the Civil War, the South's plantation system was gone. Whites could no longer recruit blacks to serve as gang laborers.[84]

Thomas Sowell makes the point that "Crops requiring routine, mass-production labor that could be easily monitored by overseers were particularly suitable to slave labor."[85] He then draws some in-

---

83. Davis, *Slavery and Human Progress*, p. 59.
84. Roger L. Ransom and Richard Such, *One Kind of Freedom: The economic consequences of emancipation* (New York: Cambridge University Press, 1977), ch. 4.
85. Sowell, *Ethnic America*, p. 191.

teresting conclusions: "Relatively few slaves were ever used in the North, where the climate was unsuitable for plantation crops, and parts of the South likewise had little plantation slavery. One such southern area was the Piedmont, or foothill, region running through western Virginia, western North Carolina, eastern Kentucky, and eastern Tennessee. It is an erosion-prone region with 'lean soil,' unsuitable for plantation slave crops. Neither the slave plantation nor the racial ideology that justified it took as deep roots here as in the fertile Mississippi delta and the rich land of the 'black belt' stretching across Arkansas, Louisiana, Mississippi, Alabama, and Georgia. These Deep South states have historically been the most extreme and intransigent on racial issues — first slavery and later civil rights— — while the liberal elements in the South came largely from the Piedmont region."[86] The effects of geography on history and even applied theology should not be ignored.

Conclusion

The only form of non-criminal lifetime servitude authorized today by the Bible is for men who voluntarily become permanent household servants and for women who voluntarily marry these lifetime servants. A servant wife must go free upon her husband's payment of her bride price, but she is not automatically set free with her husband.

Her potential lifetime of institutional servitude to her husband's former master is an institutional manifestation of a married woman's lifetime of covenantal subordination — a subordination that is necessarily involved judicially in every marriage covenant. This idea appalls most modern Christian commentators. They simply refuse to take this law seriously. They have also begun to refuse to take biblical marriage seriously. (When was the last time you heard any Christian scholar call for the imposition by civil government of the death penalty for adultery, as specified by Leviticus 20:10?)[87] Christians have begun to think as humanists do. Twentieth-century humanism's view of Exodus 21:2-4 is matched by twentieth-century humanism's view of marriage.

God has imposed laws governing marriage, and therefore He has also imposed laws governing women who marry indentured ser-

---

86. *Idem.*

87. As to the question of whether the death penalty was automatic, as distinguished from the maximum penalty that the victim (the woman's husband) could demand, see below, pp. 300-7.

vants. Humanists reject these laws. This is the reason why wives are regarded today as not being legally entitled to the economic protection that biblical law mandates for wives. Husbands are allowed to break their marriage vows almost at will. They are increasingly permitted by church courts and civil courts to abandon most of their economic obligations to their former wives. Modern humanism's hostility to the God-imposed legal requirements of Exodus 21:2-4 is generally accompanied by an equal hostility to the idea of marriage as a God-required legal subordination of wives to husbands — that is, hostility to the biblical idea of marriage. Humanists take pride in defying God's law regarding servant wives, and then they take pride in ignoring God's laws regarding adultery. Innocent, non-adulterous wives are inevitably the victims.

Israel also defied God's laws regarding servitude. Prior to their captivity, Israel and Judah did not honor the terms of the sabbatical year, at least with respect to the resting of the land. Jeremiah says specifically that their removal from the land was required by God in order to give the land its accumulated sabbaths (Jer. 50:34; cf. II Chron. 36:21). Jeremiah's account also indicates that slaves had not been released, at least in his day (Jer. 34).

The institution of servitude is founded on the existing condition of all mankind as slaves to sin. Because of differences in ethical and moral capacities among men, some men find themselves unable to cope with their environment. Lacking an adequate degree of personal self-government, they need guidance in a disciplined but protected environment. The indentured servant system allows men to overcome their lack of self-discipline and lack of specialized knowledge of the requirements of dominion. For up to seven years, a regenerate person can be kept in servitude in order to pay off his debts. A criminal, however, can be kept beyond the seventh year in order to make restitution. Indentured servitude protects the victims, either creditors or victims of crime.

Wives of servants are entitled to protection. The husband of a wife married in servitude had not exercised personal self-discipline (or was overcome by his environment) prior to his marriage, and had been forced to become a bondservant. Subsequently, he did not exercise long-term deferred gratification in order to wait for his release before marrying. Thus, his lack of self-discipline and lack of future-orientation was institutionalized by the marriage. His wife was the property of her master until the day that her husband could buy her freedom as her closest relative, meaning her kinsman-redeemer. A relative could always redeem a servant, even one owned by a foreigner (Lev. 25:48-49). She received the protection of one man or another who was capable of dealing successfully with his environment, either her liberated husband or her original master.

The man who paid the bride price to a girl's father in order to provide a concubine[88] for his son or his servant thereby became her covenantal father. In this sense, the office of father was legally transferrable. *This transfer was based on a legal adoption.* Adoption is also the legal basis of marriage; the bride is adopted into the family of her husband.[89] Thus, the released male bondservant owed the slaveowner a bride price for the wife he had already been given, for the slave-owner had taken the office of covenantal father from her biological father. This is the reason why Jacob owed Laban seven additional years of service for Rachel: she had come to him in advance of any such payment. Until the bride price was paid to her owner, the servant wife would remain the master's *legally adopted daughter.* She would have to remain in his household. The payment of the bride price to her biological father by her master was the legal basis of her continuing position as bondservant in her master's house, but the payment of the release price by her released husband to her legal owner would be the legal basis of her emancipation. There was always the legal possibility of release from female indentured servitude by means of a payment of a release price or a bride price.

The goal of indentured servitude is to impart the economic and self-motivational skills of dominion to people who have in the past not demonstrated their ability to cope with a cursed, resistant environment. The goal is *ethical* self-government, but the starting point is *economic* self-government, which is the responsibility of all free men under God. A person who has been broken by some aspect of the external environment is given the tools of dominion—ethical, educational, motivational, and, after at most seven years of service, technological—by his close contact with, and subordination to, a competent master.

There was one major danger in this system. The master might decide to gain a lifetime pair of bondservants for himself by taking advantage of the present-orientation of the male bondservant. If he

---

88. A wife whose father had not provided her with a dowry.

89. Ray R. Sutton, *Second Chance: Biblical Blueprints for Divorce and Remarriage* (Ft. Worth, Texas: Dominion Press, 1987).

could persuade the man to accept a servant girl as his wife, he might be able to persuade the man later on to become a lifetime bond-servant by submitting to the ritual of the drilled ear (Ex. 21:5-6). There are always pitfalls for present-oriented men. But in ancient Israel, a man who wanted a wife or a concubine would have had to pay a bride price anyway. The difference was, a released man might be able to earn this by saving his money for several years after his release. By taking a bride before his release, he might find this too difficult, and so he might have been tempted to sell himself into life-time servitude. But this was the outgrowth of the moral flaw of the bondservant: his present-orientation.

6

WIVES AND CONCUBINES

And if a man sell his daughter to be a maidservant, she shall not go out as the menservants do. If she please not her master, who hath betrothed her to himself, then shall he let her be redeemed: to sell her unto a strange nation he shall have no power, seeing he hath dealt deceitfully with her. And if he have betrothed her unto his son, he shall deal with her after the manner of daughters. If he take him another wife; her food, her raiment, and her duty of marriage, shall he not diminish. And if he do not these three unto her, then shall she go out free without money (Ex. 21:7-11).

The servitude laws that govern female bondservants are tied directly to the laws governing marriage. The reason is simple, though not inherently obvious: *a Hebrew woman could not be permanently purchased; she could only be adopted.* She could not go out of her father's household "as the menservants do." The theocentric principle illustrated by this law is this: *adoption by God is the sole basis of man's deliverance.* God adopted cast-off Israel, who later became His bride (Ezek. 16). This symbolism was not to serve as a license for incest, which was (and still is) explicitly prohibited by biblical law (Lev. 18:6-7).[1] This symbolism was a defense of the biblical office of husband: he adopts a bride.

These laws governed female bondservants, and they also governed marriage. The marriage of a female bondservant was governed by laws different from those governing the marriage of a free woman. Why should this have been the case? How was marriage to a bondwoman different from marriage to a free woman? Why would God have established two different forms of marriage? Does such a distinction still apply to marriages in New Testament times?

We must begin our analysis with the biblical doctrine of the bride of God, a theme that appears throughout both Testaments. We must

---

1. This poses a difficult exegetical problem for those who deny the continuing authority of Old Testament law in the New Testament era: On what basis can one biblically and authoritatively deny the legality of incest?

begin with the covenantal marriage between God and Israel, for we recognize the theocentric nature of the Bible. God's covenantal relations with men should always be our starting point for any discussion of men's relationships with each other and with the environment. Therefore, before we examine the economics of this slave wife transaction, we must first understand the distinction between a wife and a concubine. *A wife came into an Old Covenant marriage with a dowry; the concubine did not.*

God Married Israel

God speaks of Israel as His bride in Ezekiel 16. The chapter begins with a description of Israel's illegitimacy. God told Ezekiel, "And say, Thus saith the Lord GOD unto Jerusalem; Thy birth and thy nativity is of the land of Canaan; thy father was an Amorite, and thy mother an Hittite" (Ezek. 16:3). The parents had ignored the child, not even cutting its navel or washing it (v. 4). The infant had been cast off by its parents, even as a bastard child is cast off, "to the loathing of thy person" (v. 5). Israel was therefore an orphan as well as a bastard.

God "passed by" Israel, and "saw thee polluted in thine own blood" (v. 6). He caused Israel to multiply, to come to maturity. God again "passed by" Israel, and looked with mercy on the nation. Then God married Israel: "Now when I passed by thee, and looked upon thee, behold, thy time was the time of love; and I spread my skirt over thee, and covered thy nakedness: yea, I sware unto thee, and entered into a covenant with thee, saith the Lord GOD, and thou becamest mine" (v. 8). The imagery is very similar to the imagery in Ruth 3, where rich Boaz spread his own cloak over poverty-stricken Moabitess Ruth (v. 10), as a testimony of his covenantal promise to marry her (v. 13).

Concubine or Bride?

The question is: Was Israel a concubine or a true bride? Ezekiel 16 assures us that Israel was a true bride. Ezekiel describes God's provision for His bride:

Then washed I thee with water; yea, I throughly washed away thy blood from thee, and I anointed thee with oil. I clothed thee also with broidered work, and shod thee with badgers' skin, and I girded thee about with fine linen, and I covered thee with silk. I decked thee also with ornaments, and I put bracelets upon thy hands, and a chain on thy neck (vv. 9-11).

The description continues: God gave Israel a jewel for her fore-
head, earrings, a crown, fine linen, and the best food (vv. 11-13).
"And thy renown went forth among the heathen for thy beauty: for it
was perfect through my comeliness, which I had put upon thee, saith
the Lord GOD" (v. 14). But then Israel played the whore, trusting in
her own beauty (vv. 15-31). "But as a wife that committeth adultery,
which taketh strangers instead of her husband! They give gifts to all
whores: but thou givest thy gifts to all thy lovers, and hirest them, that
they may come unto thee on every side for thy whoredom" (vv. 32-33).

Israel was God's bride, not His concubine. What was the difference between a bride and a concubine? It was the presence of a
dowry in the original marriage covenant. The concubine possessed
no dowry. Israel had possessed nothing of her own to bring into the
marriage. God had discovered Israel as a man discovers a cast-off infant at the side of the road. Upon her maturity, God graciously
washed her and "covered her nakedness" with his own garment (v.
8a), a symbolic reference to marriage: "yea, I sware unto thee, and
entered into a covenant with thee" (v. 8b). There is no question:
Israel was God's bride. Her adultery was therefore much worse than
if she had been a mere concubine. She had been decked in ornaments, the proof of her status as a wife, yet she had traded them for
the pleasures provided by male whores, meaning the gods and
rituals of the surrounding nations. Worse than a whore who was in it
for the money, Israel was a wife who was in it for the sheer pleasure
of covenant-breaking. It was the difference between the low-passion,
income-seeking sin of the professional prostitute and the high-
passion, self-conscious rebellion of the adulterer. Prostitution was
not a capital crime in Israel; had it been a capital crime, there would
have been no need for a law prohibiting the high priest from marrying
a prostitute (Lev. 21:14). Adultery was a capital crime (Lev. 20:10).
This was the heart of Israel's self-conscious perversion: "And the contrary is in thee from other women in thy whoredoms, whereas none
followeth thee to commit whoredoms: and in that thou givest a reward, and no reward is given unto thee, therefore thou art contrary"
(v. 34). It was Israel's position as a bride with her own assets, enabling her to pay for her consorts, that marked her as uniquely evil.

Grace and Marriage

God's marriage to Israel was an act of grace. God recognized that
Israel was a bastard nation, an orphan. Ultimately, this is the spiritual and legal condition of all humanity, for humanity is fallen, dis-

inherited by God because of Adam's rebellion. Nevertheless, God singled out Israel as uniquely fallen, uniquely in need of God's grace. Without God's grace, there could be no life, marriage, or future. Thus, God displays His common grace to all people by giving them life, marriage, and a future. But He displays His special grace to His people by entering into a covenant with them, one so intimate that only the marriage analogy suffices to explain it (Eph. 5:22-33).

If God had not stopped to give life to Israel, the people would have perished. Moses' generation was to learn this lesson again and again in four decades of wandering. If God had not married Israel, the Hebrews would have had neither protection nor hope for the future. God granted them both life and protection. He granted them legitimate hope.

For Israel to become a fully protected bride, she had to receive a dowry. The dowry served the bride as her token of security in case her husband divorced her or in other ways abused her. The dowry was her token of independence. A free woman was a wife who could survive economically even if her husband broke his covenant with her. God provided a huge dowry to Israel in Ezekiel 16 as a visible manifestation of His grace and protection. What husband would endow a wife with such wealth if He intended to divorce her? Thus, the very magnitude of His visible grace testified to her permanently protected legal status under God.

Israel then squandered her dowry in repeated acts of covenantal rebellion. She impoverished herself through idolatry and whoredom. Step by step, she placed herself in the economic position of a concubine: an unendowed wife. But she was far worse than a concubine, who would have possessed no dowry of her own to squander; she was an adulteress who had squandered God's marriage gifts. She was clearly deserving of death (Lev. 20:10). It was only God's grace to Israel in not bringing her before the bar of justice that enabled her to maintain her status as even God's concubine.[2]

What this testifies to is that *even the concubine's status is a position that depends on grace.* God recognizes that societies and individuals fall into sin, and from sin into poverty (Deut. 28:18). Thus, His law made it

---

2. At the end, national Israel pronounced judgment against Jesus Christ and joined with her false lover, Rome, in a fatal affair. Both perished, but national Israel perished first, when she twice proved false to Rome in rebellion, in A.D. 69-70, and in A.D. 132-34 under Bar Kochba. The Jews were scattered throughout the empire by the Romans in 135. See Heinrich Graetz, *History of the Jews*, 6 vols. (Philadelphia: Jewish Publication Society of America, [1893] 1945), II, chaps. 15, 16.

possible for a daughter of a poor Israelite to marry into a family that could afford to pay a bride price. In effect, *this option of concubinage was a poor girl's way out of poverty.* Her father had no way to protect her economically. If every marriage had required a dowry, she might never have been able to marry. Her future as a mother would have been cut off. So God graciously established a way out: concubinage.

What this points to is something that the Bible never says explicitly, but which Ezekiel 16 points to: the biblical requirement of the bride price. *A wife must be purchased.* Without the payment of a bride price, there can be no marriage and no future for the prospective bride. The dowry was optional in the Old Testament economy; the bride price was mandatory.

Bride Price and Dowry

God gave Israel jewels and bracelets. This is reminiscent of the gifts to Rebekah from Abraham's servant: "And the servant brought forth jewels of silver, and jewels of gold, and raiment, and gave them to Rebekah: he gave also to her brother and to her mother precious things" (Gen. 24:53). Abraham, as Isaac's father, used his capital to pay the girl and her relatives. The property would ultimately have become Isaac's, however, for it was part of his inheritance. Abraham acted as a *representative* of his son. He supplied the bride price, and his own agent acted in Isaac's best interests. The gifts from Abraham served as her dowry, and the gifts to the relatives served as a bride price. This indicates that the bride price could be separated from the dowry, meaning that *the family could keep part of the total payment without passing the total bride price to the daughter as her dowry.* This could become a means of increasing the capital base of the family of the bride. This would clearly have made the daughter an economic asset for her family.

There was a covenantal reason for this economic obligation on the part of a bridegroom. The father of the prospective bride represented God to his daughter. This covenantal authority before God — this position as *God's representative* to his daughter — had to be lawfully transferred from the father to the bridegroom. By paying the bride price to her father, *the bridegroom ritually swore to a lifetime of faithfulness to his wife as God's representative over her,* faithfulness comparable to what her father's faithfulness to her had been. This is precisely what Jesus swore to God the Father in His role as the cosmic Bridegroom. He paid the price at Calvary. God then transferred all authority over heaven and earth to Christ as His lawful representative (Matt. 28:18-20).

Cancelling the Daughter's Obligation

The dowry functioned in Israel as an alternative to inheritance by daughters. Sons inherited the family land in the Old Testament, not daughters. Sons had the responsibility of caring for aged parents, not daughters and sons-in-law.[3] To whom much is given, much is expected (Luke 12:47-48). Since the daughter could not inherit, she was not obligated to share in her parents' support. But because she would not share in her parents' support, she was not supposed to receive her dowry from her father's capital, for this would deplete the portion remaining to her brothers. The system was consistent.

Normally, the bride price was used to repay the family for the expense of the dowry. Such a system guaranteed that being a daughter would not be regarded by her family as being an economic liability. The bride price kept daughters from draining the inheritance that normally went to sons. A daughter did not normally remain economically responsible for her parents; she became responsible for her husband's parents. Why? Because legally she was *adopted* into the family of her husband. Thus, inheritances in Israel went to sons, who later cared for aged parents, and dowries went to daughters, who extended their original family's ethical standards over time, though not the family's name.

To enable a girl to leave her father's household as a free woman — a wife with a dowry — the bridegroom paid the bride price. Most of the bride price or perhaps all of it would have passed to his wife as her dowry. By paying her father the equivalent of the girl's dowry, *he was relieving both her and himself from the legal obligation to support her parents in their old age.* The girl's father would officially provide the dowry. The daughter would therefore be in a position to take a portion of the family's inheritance now, indicating her future obligation. Then the bridegroom would replace the dowry with the payment of the bride price, thereby relieving her and himself of the future responsibilities associated with supporting her parents. Her brothers lost nothing, she gained a dowry, and he escaped the future obligation of supporting her parents.

Whether she brought a dowry into the marriage or not, the bridegroom had to pay the bride price to her father or to her brothers. This indicated that *in principle*, he owed the family of the bride some form of service if he was going to be permitted to marry

---

3. R. J. Rushdoony, *The Institutes of Biblical Law* (Nutley, New Jersey: Craig Press, 1973), p. 180.

the daughter. He was allowed to substitute a bride price for actual service. In Jacob's case, for example, he actually had to serve Laban for fourteen years in payment for Rachel and Leah, for he had no capital to pay the bride price because he had fled from his father's house without bringing his inheritance (Gen. 29). Why did Jacob owe such service? Because in each marriage, he wanted a wife with a dowry, but if their father had unilaterally paid the dowry each time as their brothers' representative, then in effect the brothers were paying the sisters to leave the family and join themselves to another family. This would have been the economic equivalent of the daughters' taking present family assets, yet also avoiding future family responsibilities.

Without the existence of the bride price requirement, a girl's brothers would have been tempted to regard her as a liability, a potential drain on the family's capital, meaning their own inheritance.[4] They would have had an incentive to refuse to allow any man to marry her, for her services in the existing household would have been valuable. Why give her up to serve another, and also allow her to take with her present family capital? Who could be sure that she and her husband would support the aged parents in the future? How could her brothers enforce such a requirement? In contrast, with a bride price system operating, there was even a possibility for family gain as well as loss, as the case of Rebekah's family indicates. Old Testament law nowhere specified that all of the bride price would become the girl's dowry. The bride price might sometimes actually exceed the dowry.

The final allocation of the bride price would have been established by competitive bargaining of her father and the potential bridegroom or by their representatives.[5] Shechem's father Hamor

---

4. In India, a Hindu with many daughters is ruined. If he also has sons, they will inherit little. The cost of the dowries will wipe out his capital. This makes daughters a liability. A similar rule prevailed in early modern Europe, where fathers had to supply the dowry to the grooms. "Girls became, in such a system, a liability." Rushdoony, *Institutes*, p. 177. He cites Iris Origo, *The World of San Bernardino* (New York: Harcourt, Brace & World, 1962), pp. 52-53.

5. This same competitive outlook regarding arranged marriages prevailed in seventeenth-century New England; so did the system of family representation. Edmund Morgan describes the process of marriage bargaining: ". . . in many cases the wooing of a lady consisted largely in financial bargaining. In the case of widows and widowers the haggling took place directly between the parties concerned, but in most first marriages the parents fought out the sordid pecuniary details while the children were left to the business of knitting their affections to each other. The latter process, however, was usually supposed to follow rather than precede the financial agreement." Edmund S. Morgan, *The Puritan Family: Religion and Domestic Relations in Seventeenth-Century New England* (rev. ed.; New York: Harper Torchbooks, 1966), pp. 56-57.

dealt with Jacob and Dinah's brothers in the matter of his son's seduction of Dinah, although the text indicates that Shechem was also present (Gen. 34:6-11). In general, bargaining being what it is, the two payments would have been similar in magnitude, except in the case of a seduction. In this unique case, the bride price was far more likely to exceed the normal dowry. Because Shechem was a seducer, he was in no position to bargain: "Ask me never so much dowry and gift, and I will give according as ye shall say unto me: but give me the damsel to wife" (Gen. 34:12).

Why couldn't the father have agreed with the bridegroom on allowing a marriage with neither dowry nor bride price? The girl would not deplete her brothers' inheritance by taking a dowry with her, and the bridegroom would not be required to come up with the bride price. After all, if the size of the bride price was even close to the dowry, the marriage could presumably take place without either of the ritual asset transfers: bridegroom to father, father to daughter. What would have been wrong with this? There are three reasons: 1) the bride price served as a screening device; 2) it served as a ritual sign of subordination; and 3) the dowry served as the woman's protection against the short-sightedness of her husband and perhaps also her father and brothers.

1. Screening Device

By the payment of the bride price, the groom was also acknowledging that he was capable of being as good a supporter of the girl as her father had been. He needed to assure her family of her future economic protection, thereby releasing her father and brothers from this legal responsibility. His ability to follow through on this covenantal guarantee was revealed by his ability to pay the bride price. The bride price was therefore an economic screening device for the family of the girl. The bridegroom's ability to pay a bride price was evidence of his outward faithfulness to the terms of God's covenant.[6] The parents were transferring legal responsibility to a new covenantal head. They were participating in the establishment of a new family. Thus, the in-laws had to serve as God's agents. Rushdoony

---

6. Those who deny that there has ever been any relationship between individual productivity and personal faithfulness to the external requirements of the covenant (Deut. 28:1-14) will reject this explanation of the usefulness of the bride price. Those who think it makes sense as a screening device will be led to conclude that there must have been a predictable relationship between economic performance and faithfulness to the covenant's external requirements.

writes that "the Hebrew word for bridegroom means 'the circumcised,' the Hebrew word for father-in-law means *he who performed the operation of circumcision*, and the Hebrew word for mother-in-law is similar. This obviously had no reference to the actual physical rite, since Hebrew males were circumcised on the eighth day. What it meant was that the father-in-law ensured the fact of *spiritual circumcision*, as did the mother-in-law, by making sure of the covenantal status of the groom. It was their duty to prevent a mixed marriage. A man could marry their daughter, and become a bridegroom, only when clearly a man under God."[7]

The bride price was also a sign of the bridegroom's future-orientation and self-discipline. Because Jacob came without capital into Laban's household, he first had to work for Laban as a servant for seven years in order to prove his capacity to lead his own household. To lead covenantally, you must first follow. To rule, you must also have served. Dominion is by covenant, and covenants are always hierarchical.[8] This hierarchical structure of the biblical covenant is, above all, the message of the Book of Exodus.[9] Israel was to be visibly under God's administration, not Pharaoh's.

Finally, the bride price was proof of the bridegroom's lawful subordination to his own father, under whom he had probably worked in an agricultural society, or from whom he had received the bride price as part of his inheritance.[10]

2. Symbol of Subordination

The bride price was an extension of the bridegroom's productivity to the girl's household. The bride price was therefore symbolic of the son-in-law's devotion and subordination to her father, *as if he were a family member*, although this was not an actual contract to become a son who would inherit. The bride price testified to the covenantal requirements that sons-in-law owe to fathers-in-law. It testified that the bridegroom had previously served someone else (probably his father) productively, and he had amassed capital equivalent to what could be accumulated during a period of subordination to the father-

---

7. Rushdoony, *Institutes*, p. 344.

8. Ray R. Sutton, *That You May Prosper: Dominion By Covenant* (Tyler, Texas: Institute for Christian Economics, 1987), ch. 2.

9. Gary North, *The Dominion Covenant: Genesis* (2nd ed.; Tyler, Texas: Institute for Christian Economics, 1987), pp. x-xi.

10. Christ's faithful service to His Father during His earthly ministry was the basis of His ability to provide a bride price for the church.

in-law. He then transferred this capital to his father-in-law as a *ritual sign of his subordination.*

The bride price compensated the father for the expense of the daughter's dowry. From a purely economic standpoint, the dowry could have been delivered directly from the bridegroom to the daughter. Why did God require this seemingly unnecessary intermediate step, the payment of the bride price to the father? *Because the formal transfer of the bride price to her father pointed to the bridegroom's requirement of covenantal subordination to her father.* We see this clearly in the case of Saul's insistence on payment from David, despite the fact that Saul did not ask David to supply Michal's dowry. Saul could require the payment of a bride price. In fact, the killing of Goliath was in effect the bride price. He promised his daughter to the one who defeated Goliath (I Sam. 17:25b). Saul was demanding the payment of an additional bride price, the hundred foreskins of Philistines. Neither the death of Goliath nor the foreskins of the Philistines would have served as an economic dowry for his daughter.

David knew that he could not afford the bride price appropriate to a king's daughter, for he was a poor man (I Sam. 18:23b). Only if Saul fulfilled his promise and supplied David with great riches (I Sam. 17:25b) could David afford the bride price. The king, by implicitly agreeing to supply her with her dowry, was in effect backing away from his original promise to give Goliath's victor great riches. What he insisted on instead was the payment of a second bride price that he believed was in his own interest, though not his economic interest. "Thus shall ye say to David, The king desireth not any dowry, but an hundred foreskins of the Philistines" (I Sam. 18:25a). He hoped to see David killed in an attempt to pay it (I Sam. 18:25b). David delivered the hundred foreskins to Saul in place of the normal bride price, much to Saul's surprise and consternation (I Sam. 18:29). *The issue was not economics; it was covenantal subordination.* David was obedient to Saul continually.

The passage in Ezekiel 16 does not mention the payment of a bride price by God to Israel's parents. This is because Israel was a bastard. The parents — Amorites and Hittites — had cast out the nation of Israel. Israel was covenantally not only a bastard but also an orphan. So, God intervened and paid Israel's dowry directly to the bride by dressing her. He owed nothing to the Amorites or Hittites. He was in no way obligated to any pagan culture.

3. Protection for the Wife

The dowry was an extension of the father's reputation and his family's reputation to his daughter and her children. It was a sign of future-orientation on his part. The dowry testified to the father's covenantal obligation to future generations born through his daughters, even though they would not inherit his name or his land. It also acknowledged that daughters were not covenantally inferior to sons.

The dowry assured the daughter a degree of economic independence if her future husband proved incompetent or died without leaving her much immediately useful capital, or if he divorced her. The dowry served as a kind of "incompetence insurance." What if her husband divorced her, and her father and brothers should lose their wealth at the same time? The wife could not easily return empty-handed to her father's household under such conditions. With a dowry she would be protected from this sort of dual calamity.

God in his grace protects women. Brides need protection. The Old Testament required payment to the bride's family. This insured at least some degree of competence on the part of bridegrooms or their families. But God also acknowledges the legitimacy of marriage despite a girl's poverty. She was not absolutely required to bring a dowry into the marriage, the way the bridegroom was required to bring a bride price. Her father's improvidence was not to make her marriage impossible; his improvidence was not supposed to trap her in his household if there was a way for her to improve her economic position.

The evidence of a slave marriage's forced status was the fact that her father kept the bride price. By keeping it, he was acknowledging that he had been improvident, and that he either cared little for his daughter's future protection against an unjust husband, or that he simply could not afford to give her the dowry she needed. In either case, his failure to provide her a dowry lowered her future legal status to that of concubine (slave wife). On the other hand, there were economic benefits to compensate her for her lowered legal status.

If a girl's father was so defenseless economically that he decided to sell her, she obviously had very little, if any, choice in the matter. Nevertheless, it was better for her to be provided for in a new household than to live hand to mouth in her father's household. But to improve her economic position by moving out of her impoverished family's household, she had to sacrifice her legal status as a free woman. This would be a marriage of necessity, a slave marriage.

This was the legal meaning of concubinage. She was going to be put into the position of a slave. She could not veto this slave marriage (concubinage), any more than a male Hebrew slave could veto a decision by his master to sell him to a new master.[11]

This is indirect evidence that daughters in Israel did have the right to veto *conventional* arranged marriages. That was part of what it meant to be a free woman: neither completely dependent on an improvident father nor on an improvident or unjust future bridegroom. The dowry system provided this protection, thereby making her a free woman. *Wealth revealed her legal status.*

Marriage and Adoption

The text reads: "And if a man sell his daughter to be a maidservant, she shall not go out as the menservants do. If she please not her master, who hath betrothed her to himself, then shall he let her be redeemed: to sell her unto a strange nation he shall have no power, seeing he hath dealt deceitfully with her" (Ex. 21:7-8). What does it mean, "she shall not go out as the menservants do"? This refers to the girl's special position of covenantal subordination. She could not be bought and sold by resident aliens in the same way that sons could be.[12]

The text says that "to sell her unto a strange nation he shall have no power, seeing he hath dealt deceitfully with her." Does this mean that female servants who had not been deceived could be sold into a foreign nation, meaning outside the land? It could not possibly mean this, because no Hebrew could be sold lawfully to anyone outside the land. The Hebrews were sojourners with God *in the land* (Lev. 25:23). The term "strange nation" must be interpreted here as "strange people." These were resident aliens in Israel. A Hebrew

---

11. Maimonides supported half of my contention. On the one hand, he denied that a Hebrew male servant could be sold to any other family. Moses Maimonides, *The Book of Acquisition*, vol. 12 of *The Code of Maimonides*, 14 vols. (New Haven, Connecticut: Yale University Press, 1951), "Treatise V: Laws Concerning Slaves," Chapter Four, Section Ten, p. 262. On the other hand, he did affirm that the young bondwoman could reject the proposed marriage: *ibid.*, Chapter Four, Section Eight, p. 262.

12. Maimonides concluded that the phrase, "she shall not go out as the menservants do," meant that if her master knocked out her tooth or blinded her in one eye, she would not become a free woman, although a male bondservant injured this way did go out free. This, in spite of the plain reading of the text: "And if a man smite the eye of his servant, *or the eye of his maid*, that it perish; he shall let him go free for his eye's sake" (Ex. 21:26). *Ibid.*, Chapter Four, Section Six, p. 261.

male servant could be sold to any Hebrew inside the land. (If the
Hebrew buyer adopted her, so could a Hebrew girl.)[13] Normally, the
resident alien was not under the limitations of the sabbatical year; he
was only under the terms of the jubilee year. Since the resident alien
could capitalize up to 49 years of service from a Hebrew male bondservant (Lev. 25:47-52), he was in a position to offer a higher purchase price. This would have created a major source of profit: buying
sabbatical-year bondservants and selling them to pagans. Therefore,
we have to conclude that if a sabbatical-year bondservant was sold to
a resident alien, the stranger would have had to abide in this unique
instance by the terms of the sabbatical year. *It is illegal to sell what you
do not own*; a Hebrew who purchased a sabbatical-year Hebrew servant did not own any claim on his services beyond the sabbatical
year.[14]

What this passage establishes, at the very least, is that a Hebrew
girl could not be sold to a stranger.[15] There was a covenantal reason
for this restriction: *hierarchy*. A woman was always covenantally subordinate to a man, except for a widow (Num. 30:9). She was inherently in a position of covenantal subordination. It was therefore illegal to sell her into a pagan household ruled under pagan household
deities. This cultural influence was too dangerous for her, compared
to the risks for a man. A father could not sell a daughter into a foreign household, for he was her lawful representative before God. His
son could lawfully be sold into servitude to a resident alien.[16]

Adoption

The daughter referred to in the text is someone who has been
bought from her father to become a wife, either for the master or for
his son. Thus, she was bought by means of *a permanent transfer of authority*. The master, as either a future husband or future father-in-

---

13. Maimonides denied this: "The Hebrew slave may neither be sold by her master or given away to another man, regardless of whether he is a stranger or a kinsman." Maimonides, *Acquisition*, Chapter Four, Section Ten, p. 262. He went so far
as to say, "Neither may one sell or give away to another a Hebrew male slave." *Idem.*
14. A Hebrew convicted of a crime and sold into bondservice was therefore legal
to sell again to a resident alien on the same terms: service for full restitution.
15. Rabbi Moses ben Nachman [Ramban], *Commentary on the Torah: Exodus* (New
York: Shilo, [1267?] 1973), pp. 352-53.
16. This has nothing to do with Christ's serving as a substitute. Christ served as a
substitute for His brothers, not for His Father, just as Judah offered to serve as a
substitute for Benjamin (Gen. 44:18-34).

law, was making a permanent purchase. If he bought her to give to his son, then *he was covenantally becoming her father.* He would thereby take full responsibility *as her covenant father* for giving her to his own son, who would guarantee her a lifetime of support. He was in effect *adopting* her into his household. It was not a seven-year or less guarantee, but rather a lifetime guarantee.[17]

Look at Ezekiel 16. At first, Israel is described as a discarded infant. God "passes by" her, picks her up, and raises her until she becomes an adult (vv. 6-7). This was clearly an act of adoption. Then the same phrase occurs again, God "passes by" her (v. 8). This time, however, God married her. Thus, with respect to God's salvation of Israel, *covenantal adoption took place before covenantal marriage.* This is why Exodus 21:8 says, "If she please not her master, who hath betrothed her to himself, then shall he let her be redeemed." The master was not allowed to keep her if he did not marry her and if some relative would buy her. He was able to buy her only as a bridegroom purchases a wife for himself, or as a father purchases a wife for his son.

The text says, "And if he hath betrothed her unto his son, he shall deal with her after the manner of daughters" (v. 9). He was required to treat her as if he were her father, for covenantally speaking, *he had in fact become her father.* When Abraham sent his servant to find a wife for Isaac, he was in effect adopting Rebekah into his household. He was taking parental responsibility for her. He was promising to watch over her as conscientiously as her own father or brothers would.

Similarly, when a bridegroom took a wife, he was becoming her covenantal brother.[18] This is why Abraham was not lying to Abimelech when he called Sarah his sister (Gen. 26:7). This is why the betrothed man in the Song of Solomon exclaimed, "Thou hast ravished my heart, my sister, my spouse. . . . How fair is thy love, my sister, my spouse!" (Song 4:9a, 10a). The bridegroom promised to care for the woman as if he were her brother. Covenantally, she

---

17. Maimonides viewed her tenure as an espoused bride as ending when she reached puberty, after age 12. Fathers could not sell daughters, he argued, once they reached puberty: *Acquisition*, "Slave Laws," Chapter Four, Section One, p. 259. She had to consent to the marriage, Chapter Four, Section Eight, p. 262. If the master refuses to marry her, either to himself or his son, "she shall go out free for nothing" at puberty: Section Nine, p. 262. He was silent about the explicit biblical text, "let her be redeemed" (v. 8). If the master fails to marry her, her father or kinsman-redeemer can redeem her. The text says nothing about going out for free, or her puberty, or any restriction against the sale of daughters beyond puberty.

18. Sutton, *That You May Prosper*, pp. 149-51.

was adopted into the family of her husband. The Western practice of giving the bride the last name of her husband indicates her adoption into the bridegroom's family. This is also why both sets of parental in-laws are usually referred to as Mom or Dad by the children. It is a verbal acknowledgment of the covenantal relationship of adoption.

The Concubine

Rachel and Leah complained that their father Laban had squandered the inheritance that they and their children were entitled to (Gen. 31:14-16), treating them as if they had been sold into slavery. They had in mind the accumulated earnings of fourteen years of Jacob's labors to pay their bride prices. Jacob had earned this wealth back from Laban, as they recognized (v. 16), but this meant that it once again belonged to Jacob; they still had no dowries. They were being relegated by their father to the status of concubines, not wives.

In ancient Israel, keeping the bride price was the economic equivalent of selling a daughter into slavery. When a father in this way sold his daughter to a husband, he was legally making her a concubine. He did not pass on to her any portion of the money he had received from the bridegroom or her future father-in-law. He kept it all. This is why the transaction was a purchase. His daughter was becoming a bondservant inside another man's household. This bondservice would not be governed by the sabbatical principle of the year of release. Also, her father did not retain the right of redeeming her as her kinsman-redeemer, unless the man who bought her decided before the marriage to return her, and her father could and would repay him his bride price. Thus, a concubine was a permanent bondservant who worked at the discretion of her husband.

Does this mean that her betrothed husband could have sold her to another Hebrew at will? To answer this question, we must first look at the covenantal nature of her position. The text speaks of "her master, who hath betrothed her." The betrothal constituted a marriage promise, but because she was not a free woman, meaning a woman with a dowry, this was not a totally binding vow on his part. It was not the same legally as a promise to marry a free woman for whom a bride price had been paid, and who brought a dowry into the marriage. We know that it was not the same, because it was not considered adultery for another man to have sexual relations with her. The two would be scourged but not executed, "because she was not free" (Lev. 19:20). If a woman possessed a dowry, then a betrothal was the same covenantally as a marriage vow. Sexual relations with such a woman was a capital crime (Deut. 22:23-24). Thus, there were two kinds of betrothals; they were covenantally and legally different. The covenantal sign that distinguished between them was the dowry. The difference was covenantal — free vs. unfree — but the visible manifestation of this difference was economic.

The question then arises: Which was the determining factor in determining her status, the legal or the economic? *The Bible always places the foundational status of all human relationships in the legal sphere, not the physical, intellectual, emotional, or economic sphere.* It is this legal relationship that governs all of God's relationships with mankind, either saved or lost. What was the covenantal basis of her legal status as a wife? Her position as an *adopted daughter.* Her father allowed her to be adopted by another family. He relinquished his position as her covenantal representative before God.

What about her status as a concubine? Her father determined the economic terms of her adoption. He chose to keep the bride price for himself. In so doing, he placed her in a second-best legal status. His motivation was no doubt deeply tied to his personal or familistic economic goals, but the basis of her status as a concubine was the result of a *legal transfer of covenantal authority over her,* not economics as such. Her primary status was that of wife, meaning an adopted sister (Song 4:9-10). Her secondary legal status as a concubine stemmed from the nature of the one-step transfer of wealth from the bridegroom to her father. Biblical law recognized her vulnerability and took steps to protect her. Her father determined her legal status; economics was his motivating factor in making this legal determination.

Consummation and Legal Protection

Once their sexual union had taken place, the marriage was covenantally complete. It then became a capital crime for another man to take her sexually. Thus, she became a true wife. We now return to the original question: Could her husband then sell her to anyone who would pay him what he had paid to her father? The text does not indicate any such right on his part. He could sell her to another Hebrew during the betrothal period, with her family's consent. He could thereby transfer her covenantal position as an *adopted woman,* though not to a resident alien, who did not have the legal right of adopting Hebrews into his household. But once covenantally bonded sexually before God, she became his wife. He could not divorce her, except insofar as any wife could be divorced. The Bible is silent about any special divorce proceedings available to him under concubinage.

On the other hand, the concubine could divorce him under certain specified circumstances. She had the three rights of any wife: food, clothing, and sexual relations. This meant that she had the right to be given an opportunity to bear children. The text says, "If he take him another wife; her food, her raiment, and her duty of marriage, shall he not diminish. And if he do not these three unto her, then shall she go out free without money" (vv. 10-11). Why list food and clothing here? Any bondservant had the right to food and clothing. Masters could legally not starve their servants, nor force them to go naked. Thus, what the right to food and clothing must have meant in this case was food and clothing *comparable to that received by the new wife.*

If her husband did not treat the concubine equally, then she could leave his household free of charge. She could not be legally compelled to remain in her husband's household if she could prove to the authorities that she was being treated as a second-class wife. In other words, her legal status as a free woman had been lost when her father sold her, but once married, she became a wife who could not be overtly discriminated against. Her second-class legal status disappeared upon sexual consummation; only her second-class economic status remained. She could take no economic assets out of the marriage, other than her children, but other than this, she possessed equal status with her husband's other wives. Of course, she was tied to him economically to the extent that her lifestyle outside her husband's care might have looked even worse to her, and she possessed no dowry. Nevertheless, she retained the formal legal right to leave his household. Her father kept the original purchase price, and she went free.

Would she have been able to bring her children with her? It could be argued that the concubine would have had to leave her children behind, for children of a bondservant wife stayed with the master when the servant left (Ex. 21:4), and the master in this case was her husband. But this would miss the point. The children did go with the concubine when her former slave husband redeemed her. The ex-slave husband's payment of the redemption price (bride price) to his former master made her his wife rather than a concubine, for her children served as her dowry. Hagar took Ishmael when she was forced out of Abraham's household (Gen. 21:9-14). She was not divorcing Abraham because he had refused her anything; rather, he was divorcing her. Sarah's decision to remove Ishmael from Abraham's household and from any inheritance necessarily involved Abraham's divorce of Hagar; otherwise, Abraham possessed no legal authority to send Ishmael out of his household. Abraham disinherited Ishmael. How? *By revoking the adopted status of Ishmael's mother.* Ishmael then became a member of his mother's household, not Abraham's.

Does this mean that children should today go with their lawfully divorced mother? No. The Old Testament allowed husbands to divorce wives for reasons other than the wives' commission of capital crimes (Deut. 24:1). Jesus said that such a law had been given by Moses because of the hardness of their hearts (Matt. 19:8). The new Testament requirement is far more rigorous: only the capital crimes of the Old Testament serve as lawful grounds of divorce—in effect, divorce by *covenantal death*.[19] Covenantally dead people should not be allowed to take their children with them. The children should remain with the innocent injured party.

Upon what legal principle could the mistreated concubine have taken her children with her? By an appeal to her own legal status. The legal basis of the marriage had been her adoption into the master's family. By the husband's treating her in such a way that she had legally regained her freedom, she was no longer an adopted member of his family. As the innocent victim, she had reclaimed her former legal status. Biblical law always defends the innocent party. She would therefore keep the children when she left her husband's household. She would then be in the position of a widow who was the head of her own household (Num. 30:9). The legal issues in biblical covenant arrangements are based on ethics, not blood or biology. Her husband had not treated her righteously. If she remained single and outside any man's household authority, she became both father and mother to her children, just as a widow became.[20] If she remarried, the new husband adopted her and her children into his family. If she returned to her father's house, he became the true father of her chil-

---

19. Rushdoony, *Institutes*, pp. 401-15; Ray R. Sutton, *Second Chance: Biblical Blueprints for Divorce and Remarriage* (Ft. Worth, Texas: Dominion Press, 1987).

20. If the Numbers 30:9 principle governed her, meaning that she refused to return to her father's house, she became both father and mother. She became a daughter of God, which is why a widow was allowed to take a vow before God without getting approval from anyone. Her legal subordination to God no longer required a visible male head of household as her representative. Biblically, Jesus Christ became her intermediary.

dren. Fatherhood in all cases was by adoption, not biology. This legal principle reflects our own covenantal status before God: we are either disinherited children because of Adam's sin, or else we are adopted children in God's household because of Christ's death and resurrection (John 1:12).

Then in what visible way was a former concubine different from a former wife? Only in terms of her capital. She took no dowry with her when she left, for she had brought no dowry to the marriage when she came. A bride price transaction without a dowry for the daughter in fact was *a servant purchase price*. A concubine had no personally held economic protection. If treated unequally compared to another wife, she could return to her father's household, and she could marry again. She could also remain single and alone, although that was rare in any agricultural society, except for a few urban occupations such as tavern-keeping and prostitution, and the court would probably remove her children from her if she became a prostitute. Nevertheless, an honest, moral woman was legally able to leave her husband's house with her children: her new dowry.

She could return to her father's household without a sense of becoming a needless burden, because her father had been paid. He had kept all of the bride price, which made it more strictly an economic transaction. She had borne the risk of winding up with a husband who mistreated her, so her father could have no legitimate complaints about her returning home.

New Testament Applications

Jesus Christ paid the bride price to God through His death at Calvary. This is the basis of His marriage to the bride, the church. It is also the basis of all marriages through God's common grace.[21] Christ paid the bride price for all of humanity, for each individual, for Old Covenant Israel, and for New Covenant Israel. It was the highest price that has ever been paid. Old Covenant Israel looked forward to this payment, while New Covenant Israel now looks backward.[22]

---

21. If we do not maintain that Christ's payment of the bride price is the foundation of all marriages through common grace, then we must conclude that there is still a valid form of concubinage among non-Christians. We would have to argue that only Christian brides are exempt from the requirements of the bride price/dowry system.

22. Genetic Old Covenant Israelites (the Jews of today), described in Romans 11 as the branches that were cut off (v. 17-19), still look forward to this payment, but God requires them to join themselves to the church and begin to look backward. There is only one bride, the church of Jesus Christ. God is not a polygamist. The old bride, national Israel, was executed for her whoredoms in A.D. 70. See David Chilton, *The Days of Vengeance: An Exposition of the Book of Revelation* (Ft. Worth, Texas: Dominion Press, 1987).

This is the proper New Testament starting point for any discussion of the bride price.

One conclusion is inescapable: *there are no more concubines in the New Testament economy.* That institution was done away with by Calvary. If concubinage still were lawfully in force, it would point away from Christ's definitive overcoming of mankind's slavery to sin, the ultimate form of bondage. Permanent servitude, except as a criminal penalty (restitution), is no longer biblically sanctioned as a valid institutional arrangement.

The concubine's second-class legal status always ended with the consummation of the marriage. It applied only to the betrothal period. The whole imagery of the marriage supper of the lamb[23] points to the status of the church as a free woman, a full bride in legal possession of a vast dowry, the whole earth.[24] There are no slave wives any more; all lawfully married women are regarded by God as having entered marriage as free women. They gained their status as free women by means of Christ's payment of the bride price at Calvary. This payment serves as the legal basis of *God's adoption of His people into His eternal family.* The covenantal distinctions between the betrothed slave wife and the betrothed free wife have disappeared. "For as many of you as have been baptized into Christ have put on Christ. There is neither Jew nor Greek, there is neither bond nor free, there is neither male nor female: for ye are all one in Christ Jesus" (Gal. 3:27-28). Galatians 4 is the chapter above all others in the Bible that deals with spiritual adoption — "the adoption of sons" (v. 5) — and our deliverance out of the family of the bondwoman into the family of the free woman, the "Jerusalem which is above" which is free, "the mother of us all" (v. 26). The church rather than the family is the agency of covenantal adoption in New Testament times. It is the agency that publicly represents the new birth.[25]

---

23. Gary North, "The Marriage Supper of the Lamb," *Christianity and Civilization*, 4 (1985).

24. Gary North, *Inherit the Earth: Biblical Blueprints for Economics* (Ft. Worth, Texas: Dominion Press, 1987).

25. In churches that fully honor this principle, infants are baptized. Parents hand over the infant to the pastor, who then baptizes it, and hands it back. This is the public symbol of the inability of parents in their own strength to give eternal life to their children. The church *adopts* children publicly, and then hands them back to parents as the designated agents of the church — the covenanted, international, trans-historical institution known as the bride of Christ. This does not guarantee the continuing covenantal faithfulness of the children, but it does honor the legal principle that without adoption into the family of God, each person stands condemned before God.

The justification of divorce for the concubine was that her husband treated another wife with greater favor. The New Testament's standard is monogamy, for only through membership in Christ's bride, the church, can people find salvation. God is not a bigamist; Israel as a bride has been lawfully divorced because of her rebellion. He has not taken an additional new wife; the church is the replacement for the lawfully divorced wife. Israel must become part of the church if she is ever to regain her status as bride (Rom. 11). Therefore, men are not supposed to be bigamists. Monogamy was the legal standard for Hebrew kings (Deut. 17:17), and this "one wife" standard is explicitly stated as a requirement for church elders (I Tim. 3:2).

Brides can no longer legally be offered for sale by fathers. Fathers are no longer allowed to demand a bride price as a condition of a daughter's marriage. Institutionally, there is no longer any necessity for the bride price, except in cases of criminal penalties imposed by the church or State on offending males in cases of the seduction of a virgin.[26] Church symbols and church discipline have replaced the original functions of the bride price/dowry system. First, baptism and church membership have become the screening devices. Second, baptism and church membership also have become the evidence of covenantal subordination to the family of God. Third, various economic contracts and legal provisions for the protection of the innocent victim of a divorce become the proper protective devices. Finally, husbands are not allowed to take extra wives, so there is clearly no purpose in establishing special divorce laws to protect a concubine who is not being treated equally to the new wife.[27]

From Circumcision to Baptism

Because daughters receive the covenantal sign of baptism, the New Testament's position is that in all but biological respects, *adult women are now covenantally equal with adult men*. The only exception is that women are not allowed to speak in church worship services (I Cor.

---

26. See Chapter 18: "Seduction and Servitude."

27. There is this exception to the rule against divorce laws for concubines. If a polygamous culture converts to Christ, the missionaries would be foolish to impose monogamy retroactively on existing polygamous households. The husbands would then throw wives out of their homes, whether they wanted to stay or not. Who would protect them or remarry these divorced wives? They would be tempted to become prostitutes. In such mission situations, biblical law would protect concubines who were subsequently treated as second-class wives. They could lawfully leave their husbands if they chose to.

14:34). Circumcision as a required rite is no longer binding in the New Testament era. It is significant that Paul inserts his famous statement on the irrelevance of circumcision in the middle of his chapter on marriage: "Circumcision is nothing, and uncircumcision is nothing" (I Cor. 7:19a).

The locus of authority for approving a marriage has shifted from the family to the church. This is manifested symbolically by the fact that baptism has replaced circumcision as the covenantal sign of family membership. The bride's father therefore no longer serves as the "circumciser" of the bridegroom, for the rite of circumcision no longer has any role to play covenantally. The church is the ultimate covenantal screening agent today. The church sanctions the spiritual condition of the bridegroom, through its control over membership standards. The churches have failed in this role by not policing their members in terms of strict moral and confessional requirements, and also by not placing under severe discipline members who wilfully marry nonbelievers. But this failure has been matched by Christian fathers who have failed to enroll their daughters in Christian schools, kindergarten through college, thereby increasing drastically the likelihood that they will marry pagans. There has been a general breakdown in the willingness of covenantal authorities to supervise and restructure in terms of the Bible the marital customs of the West.

A father who prohibits his daughter from marrying can be overruled by the church or churches to which the communicant prospective partners belong. The idea that a non-Christian father can lawfully and legitimately prohibit his Christian daughter from marrying a Christian man is outrageous theologically. The assertion that the couple is legally defenseless, and that they must confine their efforts to praying that her father will change his mind, is an indirect attack on the legitimate authority of the church.[28] Similarly, a father may authorize the marriage of his Christian daughter to a pagan young man, but the church can lawfully before God veto the proposed marriage and place the daughter under discipline if she follows her father's advice. She cannot biblically claim her father's authorization of the marriage as somehow validating it.

---

28. In effect, such an argument makes a father the equivalent of the Pope. It is odd that Protestants sometimes use such arguments, for such a view of paternal authority transforms the New Testament family into a pagan, patriarchal, humanistic institution, one whose standards are autonomous, governed by neither church nor State.

The abolition of concubinage did not abolish the covenantal principle of hierarchy. Someone must represent the bride. Who represents the girl in the name of Jesus Christ in today's marriage arrangements? Obviously, the girl's father does, unless the church has intervened to sanction the marriage if her father has immorally denied permission. But the father represents his daughter as the *agent of the church* rather than as the agent of the bloodline family. The church, as the true covenantal family of the God-adopted believer, retains its sanctioning authority. It is this *fundamental transfer of authority from the family to the church*, as symbolized ritually by the abolition of circumcision and the substitution of baptism, that has made the bride price and dowry legally optional. Christ has paid the bride price for His church, and His church now has become the locus of primary covenantal authority for conducting marriages, enforcing the terms of the marriage covenant, and screening the prospective partners. The bridegroom submits himself to the jurisdiction of the church.

We have seen that the bride price-dowry system was part of a program of inheritance. The daughter received a dowry in lieu of receiving her share of her father's inheritance. Her husband relieved her of the requirement to support her aged parents. I am arguing that Christ's establishment of His church has made optional this transfer of funds. The church has become the new screening agent. This raises fundamental questions concerning family inheritance. Does this mean that the church becomes the primary agent for the care of older people, replacing the children? No. The church does become the agent of last resort if families fail in their responsibilities. Older widows (age 60 and older) whose families fail to support them are to be supported by the church (I Tim. 5:9-10). Family members of such widows thereby identify themselves covenantally as infidels (v. 8), and would be excommunicated. The church then becomes the covenantal kinsman-redeemer of the widows.

Today, sons and daughters inherit. They both receive expensive educations. Daughters also share in the various responsibilities of caring for aged parents, to the extent that daughters possess independent capital. Their husbands know that they may be called upon to assist aged in-laws. There is no clear line of authority for establishing institutional responsibility for aged parents, nor is there a clear structure of inheritance. It was far easier to establish such responsibility when blood lines and gender determined inheritance. Inheritance in the New Testament is expressly covenantal rather than familistic. This blurs the formal, legal lines of economic responsibility.

Membership in the church is of far greater consequence than membership in the family. Jesus was at war with any view of the human family that elevated it to equality with the church. "For I am come to set a man at variance against his father, and the daughter against her mother, and the daughter in law against her mother in law. And a man's foes shall be they of his own household" (Matt. 10:35-36). The biblical economic goal is to increase the dominion of Christians, not families as such; the institutional focus is on the kingdom rather than the family. Thus, parents should not leave great wealth to apostate children. Parents should normally leave their wealth to believing children, *assuming* that the children are economically competent and faithful to the external requirements of the covenant. If they are not, then parents should consider setting up trusts governed by competent church members. The only exception to these guidelines is where the apostate children give evidence that they are lawful, parent-honoring, responsibility-affirming people who are far more competent economically than the family's creed-affirming children, and who appear to be willing and able to support the aged parents. As a matter of self-defense, parents would transfer sufficient wealth to these children to compensate them for the expected future burden of caring for them in old age. Unbelieving children who abide by the external terms of the covenant are to this extent sanctified — set apart — by believing parents.

Parents must use their wealth to endow those who will carry their religious vision into the future, though not necessarily their names. Covenantally faithful daughters should inherit. Christian charities should also inherit. The Christian vision is far broader than family or tribe. The transfer of the kingdom to the "nation" of the church (Matt. 21:43)[29] testified to this shift in sovereignty away from tribal, regional, and even familial groups.

Inheritance or Dowry?

Because of their change in covenantal status in the New Testament, there is no reason to believe that daughters should not inherit, even if they have brothers. Sisters without brothers were allowed to inherit in the Old Testament: the case of the daughters of Zelophehad. Because of the operation of the jubilee land tenure law, daughters who inherited were required to marry only inside the tribe of their

---

29. Gary North, *Healer of the Nations: Biblical Blueprints for International Relations* (Ft. Worth, Texas: Dominion Press, 1987), Introduction.

fathers (Num. 36:8). With Jesus' fulfillment of the jubilee law (Luke 4),[30] and with the destruction of Israel in A.D. 70, these restrictions on inheritance disappeared. Nevertheless, family responsibilities did not disappear just because tribal responsibility did. If daughters can lawfully inherit, then *daughters who inherit and their husbands necessarily become legally responsible for the care of her aged parents*. Thus, the husband of a daughter who prefers to inherit rather than accept a dowry should legally agree in advance to become equally liable for the care of her parents as any of her brothers. Because the West ignores such responsibilities, it has ignored these sorts of legitimate family legal contracts. As a result, families have not been careful to take care of aged parents. This furthered the expansion of the welfare State, for its proponents have successfully appealed to guilt-ridden voters in the name of indigent aged parents. The welfare State has steadily made itself the primary heir.[31]

The dowry is legitimate, though not required, as an alternative to inheritance. If a father decides to pay for the education of his daughter, he should tell her in advance the terms of the arrangement. If this is not her dowry, but is instead an advance payment of her lawful inheritance, then he need not seek to collect a bride price from her future husband, but she and her husband will be expected to bear their share of the costs of supporting the parents in their old age. If her education or a very expensive wedding is her dowry, this constitutes a formal admission on her part and on the part of her husband of their obligation to repay him in the form of a bride price — highly unlikely in our day — either before the marriage or in the years following the marriage.

Since the bride price is seldom paid today, daughters and bridegrooms implicitly do become responsible for the support of her parents. Such implicit support is no longer regarded as enforceable by civil law, however. Thus, the State has steadily encroached on the family as the primary agency for the support of aged parents. Taxes have replaced both the bride price and financial support by children. There has been no escape from these biblical economic and legal responsibilities; there is only a shift in institutional authority for collecting and distributing the funds.

---

30. Gary North, "The Fulfilment of the Jubilee Year," *Biblical Economics Today*, VI (April/May 1983).

31. Gary North, *The Sinai Strategy: Economics and the Ten Commandments* (Tyler, Texas: Institute for Christian Economics, 1986), ch. 5.

Alternatives to the Dowry

The economic consequences of divorce are the big economic problem that has arisen from the disappearance of the bride price and/or dowry system. When the husband walks out of the marriage, all he generally is required by law to pay is child support. Alimony payments to wives have become far less common in the United States since the mid-1970's. Divorced wives receive very little, except in cases where there is a major distribution of property. Few families possess that much debt-free property to divide. There is a slogan that says that "the husband gets the mortgage, and the wife gets the house." Then the husband stops paying on the mortgage, and the lending institution gets the house. At the youngest child's eighteenth birthday, the father's responsibility ends. The wife and her parents are cut off.

If there were not so much debt in society, then community property laws would protect wives far better. By requiring the husband to forfeit half of their property to the divorced wife, the State does act as an intermediary. What should be required, however, is the honoring of the biblical principle of covenantal death. The offending party should take nothing; the injured party should keep everything, including all the children. The offending party should not even be given visitation rights. If biblical law were enforced, the offending party would often be publicly executed. Only because the State has been negligent in its duty to enforce the biblically required standards and sanctions have divorce settlements become a problem. Community property laws — the automatic division of family assets — were the precursor of no-fault divorce, which in a debt-ridden society is another way of guaranteeing the impoverishment of divorced wives.

One way to protect the daughter and her parents would be for the church (which becomes ultimately liable economically for indigent members) to require the prospective bridegroom to agree in writing to give his wife sufficient funds for her to take out a paid-up life insurance policy on his life. The policy would be owned by his wife or owned by a diaconate-managed trust in the name of the wife. He would do the same for her parents, with the premium money being given by the bridegroom to both wife and parents in advance of the wedding. He would sign the policy immediately after the wedding ceremony: no signature, no consummation. A refusal to sign would annul the marriage. He would not own the policy; therefore, he could not name new beneficiaries, or cancel the policies, should he walk out of the marriage. He would subsequently pay additional annual premiums each year, so that the paid-up policies would be extended over time, or new policies be purchased. If we had a Christian society, life insurance companies would allow the wife and her parents to collect built-up assets in the paid-up policies upon the civil government's announcement of the divorce, if the husband was declared the guilty party. On the other hand, if the State should determine that the wife was guilty, then the assets in both policies would be transferred to the husband. Covenantal death would be regarded as the legal equivalent of actual death, not to the extent of requiring the immediate payment of the face value of the policies (which are sold on the basis of physical death statistics rather than the much less stable divorce statistics), but at least to the extent of paying out the built-up assets in the policies.

Another way to reduce the likelihood of his walking out is to require him to agree in advance to create irrevocable trusts for his wife each time the couple buys any major investment, with her father or the diaconate as the trustee. Everything they buy that costs over, say, five ounces of gold during the first decade of their marriage is placed into this trust. The father-in-law should require the son-in-law to agree in writing to put at least ten percent of his salary into an automatic savings account inside the wife's trust. The husband would be legally allowed only to suggest where this money should be invested. Her brother (or someone covenantally responsible) would be named in the trust as the successor trustee, in case of the father-in-law's death.

All of this today would be regarded as "crass" and "mercenary." So was the bride price and dowry system of the Old Testament. The system offered economic protection to the economically vulnerable.

Freedom and Risks

All women in New Testament times have been freed from the Old Testament's requirement of bringing dowries into their marriages in order to avoid the second-class status of concubinage. This testifies to their status as wives whose bride price has been paid. The economic reality of this transformation was not visible in history for many centuries, but only because Western capitalism had not made it economically feasible for most young women and young men to leave home and marry, with or without parental financial support. The growth of highly urbanized capitalism has changed this picture in the twentieth century. This recent development has placed heavy new economic and moral responsibilities on the shoulders of single adult women. With greater authority inevitably comes greater responsibility. They can set the terms of their own marriages. What we have seen is that they have proven to be tragically incompetent bargainers. No one represents them any more. With the rise of no-fault divorce, not even the civil government protects their interests any longer. In the United States, one year after a divorce, the woman's standard of living has fallen by over 70 percent, while her former husband's has risen by over 40 percent.[32]

To ignore these economic realities in the name of formal biblical law would be foolish. The dowry is not legally required in order to avoid concubinage, since concubinage is no longer a biblical office, but this does not solve the economic problem of the economic vulnerability of wives, especially in an increasingly humanistic civilization in which divorce is regarded as some sort of opportunity to escape responsibility — an economic subsidy to lawless, irresponsible males if there ever was one. When husbands walk out of a marriage, leaving the care of children to the wives, as well as the wives' support of themselves, the division of labor is restricted. Wives must become self-supporting, even when husbands pay child support, and in millions of cases, they refuse. With this contraction of the division of labor, wives' personal productivity necessarily falls, and therefore their net income falls. The husbands find younger wives to marry, but divorced wives over age 35 with children seldom find husbands. The majority of divorced husbands win; the majority of divorced wives lose. Thus, wives without dowries are still unprotected economically, just as they were in the Old Testament. The difference is, concubines had biblical laws to protect them in the Old Testament. So did their aged parents. Today, these economic problems must be dealt with early by voluntary contract rather than by civil law. They seldom are, except in second marriages[33] or in cohabitation.[34] In the

---

32. Lenore J. Weitzman, *The Divorce Revolution: The Unexpected Social and Economic Consequences for Women and Children in America* (New York: The Free Press, 1985), p. xii; cited by George Grant, *The Dispossessed: Homelessness in America* (Ft. Worth, Texas: Dominion Press, 1986), p. 79. I referred to these statistics in the previous chapter. Remember, this is a commentary; many readers will read only one chapter or section at a time.

33. Georgia Dullea, "Prenuptial Agreements the 2nd Time Around," *New York Times* (June 7, 1982).

34. So widespread in the United States is cohabitation without marriage that lawyers now draw up cohabitation agreements that deal with such issues as individual and joint bank accounts, real estate contracts, equal obligations (expenses), and em-

latter cases, women recognize more clearly how vulnerable they are legally and economically.

Conclusion

The Old Testament authorized two forms of marriage contracts: free marriage and concubinage. The free wife brought a dowry into the marriage; the concubine did not. Both forms of marriage were lawful, but concubinage was less desirable. It left wives far more vulnerable to divorce or neglect by husbands.

The bride price was a requirement for marriage. If the father used the money to endow his daughter, she entered the marriage as a free woman. If he kept the bride price for himself, she entered as a concubine. The system allowed poor girls to escape from a life of poverty in their fathers' households.

The basis of Old Testament marriage was adoption. In effect, it was a symbol of the new birth, which is also a covenantal adoption (John 1:12). The bridegroom adopted the girl into his family. He had to gain the cooperation of her father in this transfer of family membership from her family to his. Fathers used the bride price system to screen out bridegrooms who were more likely to be economically irresponsible. When fathers transferred to bridegrooms their covenantal office as God's representative for their daughters, they wanted some visible sign that the recipient would be responsible. The payment of the bride price was a manifestation of the bridegroom's competence and also a symbol of his subordination to the girl's family.

The New Testament annulled the bride price system by transferring the marital adoption process to the church. There are no lawful concubines today. Christ's payment of the bride price to God the Father at Calvary marked Him as the Bridegroom to the true bride, the church. The church is today the appropriate agency of the covenantal adoption process of marriage. Like God, who found abandoned Israel as an infant and raised her, and later married her (Ezek. 16), so the church baptizes children and then later sanctions

---

ployment obligations. See Barbara B. Hirsch, *Living Together* (Boston: Houghton Mifflin, 1976). Something like 3 million couples are presently unmarried in the U.S. reports Gary S. Meyers, "'Unmarriage contract' can help protect cohabitants' rights," *Dallas Times Herald* (Feb. 15, 1987). In 1978, the figure was about 1.1 million out of 48 million husband-wife households: Robert Reinhold, "Census Finds Unmarried Couples Have Doubled From 1970 to 1978," *New York Times* (June 27, 1979). The growth in cohabitation is accelerating rapidly.

the human marriage bond that reflects Christ's love of His church (Eph. 5:22-33). Christian fathers still screen prospective bridegrooms, but as delegated agents of the church rather than as agents of the extended bloodline family.

The church is the ultimate protector of unlawfully divorced wives. The preaching of the gospel is to lead to the rewriting of the divorce laws. The legal structure should protect the innocent partner and impose heavy sanctions on the offending partner, up to and including the death penalty for capital crimes identified by the Bible. The State should recognize in its statutes that biblical divorce is always and only by death, and this includes covenantal death.

When marriage partners are not Christians, the State should become the judicial sanctioning agency, for its laws also govern marriage and divorce. It becomes the primary agency by default. The State alone possesses the lawful monopoly of violence. It can punish those who disobey certain of God's standards, including certain aspects of marriage. The family no longer possesses any legal authority to marry or divorce couples. Fathers can lawfully prevent marriages under some circumstances, but they cannot perform lawful marriages simply and solely because they hold the office of father.

7

VICTIM'S RIGHTS VS.
THE MESSIANIC STATE

And he that smiteth his father, or his mother, shall be surely put to death (Ex. 21:15).

And he that curseth his father, or his mother, shall surely be put to death (Ex. 21:17).

The theocentric principle here is obvious: God the Father must not be attacked by His children. Parents are God's covenantal agents in the family, which is a hierarchical, oath-bound covenantal institution. They are God's covenantal *representatives* in the family. To strike an earthly parent is the covenantal equivalent of striking at God. It is an act of moral rebellion so great that the death penalty is invoked.

The doctrine of hierarchy, which includes the doctrine of representation,[1] is point two of the biblical covenant model. The Book of Exodus, the second book in the Pentateuch, is primarily concerned with point two of the covenant, for the Pentateuch is itself structured in terms of the biblical covenant's five-point structure.[2] It is appropriate that questions relating to representation should be the focus of several of the case laws of Exodus.

The covenant's representation principle is built into the creation. We know that the visible creation testifies to the existence of the invisible God. "For the invisible things of him from the creation of the world are clearly seen, being understood by the things that are made, even his eternal power and Godhead; so that they are without excuse" (Rom. 1:20). Men, as creatures, cannot strike at God directly.

---

1. Ray R. Sutton, *That You May Prosper: Dominion By Covenant* (Tyler, Texas: Institute for Christian Economics, 1987), pp. 46-47.

2. Gary North, *The Dominion Covenant: Genesis* (2nd ed.; Tyler, Texas: Institute for Christian Economics, 1987), pp. x-xiv.

They must act through intermediaries. Men strike some aspect of God's creation in their attempt to strike at God. A crime is committed in history against God-created men and the God-created environment, but always in the creation's capacity as reflecting God. Men are creatures, so they must use the creation as the only available means of any attempted attack on God. As Cornelius Van Til once wrote, the child must sit on the father's lap in order to slap his face.

Biblically and covenantally speaking, the earthly victim of a crime is always the secondary victim; *God is always the primary victim.* Ours is a theocentric universe, not anthropocentric. This means, additionally, that the criminal acts in his own interests secondarily; when committing a biblically prohibited act, he acts primarily as Satan's representative, just as Adam did. This judicial principle — the doctrine of covenantal representation — is not intuitively apparent to those who are not trained to think theocentrically and covenantally. We must learn to think theocentrically and representatively (covenantally) when we think about crime and punishment.

Christians and Jews should therefore begin any consideration of the principles of biblical jurisprudence with this fundamental legal principle: *God is always the primary victim of every sin and every crime.* This leads to a crucial conclusion: *the victims of any crime or unlawful attack become the legal representatives of God.* The victim of a crime is authorized by God, the Author of history, to initiate a covenant lawsuit against the suspected criminal. He and he alone is so authorized. While it is legitimate to speak of primary and secondary earthly victims of crime, we must always bear in mind that the primary cosmic victim is always God.

Because of the somewhat intricate nature of my arguments in this chapter, I think it is best if I state my conclusion in advance, so that the reader will be better able to assess the cogency of my argumentation. The conclusion that I have come to after having studied in detail this and other biblical case laws is that the following judicial principle is dominant in the Bible: *if the victim of a crime fails to initiate this covenant lawsuit, then the other covenantal agents of God must honor this decision* — the civil magistrate, the church officer, and the head of a household. They are not authorized in this instance to step in and prosecute in God's name as God-ordained covenantal judges. They are unquestionably judges.[3] But they are allowed by God to bring

---

3. Gary North, *When Justice Is Aborted: Biblical Standards for Non-Violent Resistance* (Ft. Worth, Texas: Dominion Press, 1989), ch. 2.

charges against the suspected criminal only if they can persuade the court that they have become victims by the original victim's failure to prosecute.

What we must understand is that in biblical jurisprudence, *it is the victim whose rights must always be upheld*, not simply because he was harmed by the criminal, but also because *he served as God's surrogate when he became the victim*. God is the primary victim, and His rights must be upheld first and foremost. His specified judicial sanctions must be enforced by His designated covenantal representatives. His case laws provide mankind with the proper guidelines of how His honor is to be upheld in various cases.

There is another Bible-sanctioned office to consider, the office of *witness*. The witness is authorized to bring relevant information to one of these covenantal judges, so that the judge can initiate the covenant lawsuit against the suspected violator.[4] The witness plays a very important role in the prosecution of God's covenant lawsuits. Without at least two witnesses, it is illegal to execute anyone (Deut. 17:6). Also, the affirming witnesses in a capital lawsuit must be the first people to cast stones (Deut. 17:7).

The Biblical Hierarchical Structure

Adam was allowed to do anything he wanted in the garden, except eat from the forbidden tree. There was a specific sanction attached to that crime, a capital sanction. This reveals a fundamental biblical judicial principle: *anything is permitted unless it is explicitly prohibited by law, or prohibited by an extension of a case law's principle.* This principle places the individual under public law, but it also relies on self-government as the primary policing device. It creates the bottom-up appeals court character of biblical society. Men are judicially free to act however they please unless society, through its various covenantal courts, has been authorized by God's Bible-revealed law to restrict certain specified kinds of behavior.

The bottom-up appeals court structure of the biblical hierarchy is in opposition to the principle of top-down bureaucratic control. Under the latter hierarchical system, in theory nothing is permitted

---

4. The hostility of siblings against "tattle tales" in a family is easily explainable: youthful law-breakers resent judgment. They resent witnesses whose action brings the dreaded sanctions. But what about parents? Parents who side with the critics of "tattle tales" are thereby attempting to escape their God-given role as judges. They are saying, in principle, "We don't want to know about it. We don't want to serves as judges, despite our position as God's designated representative agents in this family."

except what has been commanded. The decision-making private individual is tightly restricted; the centralized State is expanded. This is the governing principle of all socialist economic planning. It assumes the omniscience and omnicompetence of distant central planners.[5]

What a free society needs is predictable law.[6] The maximum sanction for any crime must be specified in written law or at least in traditional legal precedent. The criminal must know the maximum negative consequences of conviction. He is under law, but so are his judges. The State as well as the criminal are restrained under biblical law. The State is placed under tight judicial restraints, and first and foremost of these restraints is the requirement that crimes and their respective sanctions be announced in advance. There must be no *ex post facto* statutes or sanctions. This reduces the arbitrary authority of judges to apply sanctions or increase sanctions beyond what is specified in the law code. They sometimes possess the authority to reduce the specified sanctions, as this chapter argues, but never to increase them. This restriction drastically reduces the growth of arbitrary civil power. (By adhering to this biblical principle of responsible freedom under specified law, the West made possible the development of modern capitalism and its accompanying high per capita wealth.)

The limits on the biblical State's ability to impose arbitrary sanctions are derived from three case-law principles. First, the God-given authority of the victim to refuse to prosecute, and also his authority to reduce the applicable sanctions upon conviction of the criminal, restricts the power of the civil magistrate. Second, the maximum sanction allowed by existing law keeps the State under restraint. Third, the *pleonasm of execution*—"dying, he shall die"—inhibits the authority of the judges to subsidize outrageous crimes by imposing reduced sanctions in specific cases: where the State has lawfully initiated the covenant lawsuit because there is no earthly victim who could initiate it. To deny any of these principles is to promote the advent of the messianic State.

To describe the working of these three case-law principles, we need to begin with the maximum civil sanction: execution. Because public execution is the maximum civil sanction allowed by God's law, it has the most critics.

---

5. Gary North, *Marx's Religion of Revolution: Regeneration Through Chaos* (Tyler, Texas: Institute for Christian Economics, [1968] 1989), Appendix A: "Socialist Economic Calculation."

6. F. A. Hayek, *The Constitution of Liberty* (University of Chicago Press, 1960).

Capital Punishment: Yesterday and Today

One of the complaints against the continuing legitimacy of biblical law is that the death penalty is too rigorous to be applied as a sanction against most of the capital crimes specified by the Old Testament. Therefore, conclude the Mosaic law's critics, execution is no longer a valid civil sanction today, except in the case of murder.[7] This line of argumentation leads to the peculiar conclusion that in the Old Covenant era, covenantally faithful people were expected by God to be a lot more rigorous about prosecuting criminals, and were therefore expected to be more willing to see God's civil sanctions enforced. This rigorous "Old Testament attitude" toward criminals is no longer valid, it is said, because of the coming of the New Covenant. But if Christians are to be less rigorous regarding crime and its appropriate civil sanctions, then God also must have adopted a more lenient attitude, which is supposedly reflected in His New Covenant law. A major problem with this line of reasoning is the fact that God's New Covenant standards seem to be more rigorous, e.g., the prohibition of easy divorce (Matt. 19:7-9).[8] With greater maturity and greater revelation, Christians are supposed to be less lenient about sin. After all, more is expected from him to whom more has been given (Luke 12:47-48). The New Testament gives Christians greater revelation and assigns us far more responsibility than was the case in the Old Covenant era. Christ's resurrection is behind us. The Holy Spirit has come.

It could be argued, of course, that because greater mercy has been shown to us, we should extend greater mercy. With respect to the judicial principle of victim's rights, I quite agree. The victim should be more merciful, so long as his mercy does not subsidize further evil. He must judge the character of the criminal. But this does not answer the question of designated capital crimes. Is it the State's responsibility to adopt the principle of reduced New Covenant sanctions, despite the explicit revelation of the Old Covenant case laws? Should the State adopt a judicial principle different from that which prevailed in the Old Covenant? I answer no. Furthermore, I also answer that civil judges in Old Covenant Israel had the God-given authority to reduce the severity of the specified sanctions under certain circumstances. I develop the evidence for this conclusion in this chapter.

---

7. For example, see John Murray, *Principles of Conduct* (Grand Rapids, Michigan: Eerdmans, 1957), p. 118.

8. See below: "Divorce by Covenantal Death," pp. 289-90.

Critics of capital punishment also argue that righteous and sensitive jury members today are unwilling to hand down "guilty" verdicts against offenders in many cases, since the death penalty is much too harsh. If the death penalty is kept on the statute books, critics argue, serious criminal behavior is therefore indirectly subsidized by victims' unwillingness to prosecute and juries' unwillingness to convict. Thus, conclude the critics, we should ignore the Old Testament's capital sanction in all but the case of premeditated murder. Some Christian critics would even abandon capital punishment in this instance, following the lead of secular humanist criminologists and jurists.

It is my belief that in the twentieth century, there are three affirmations the denial of which best indicates the presence of Christian heresy. Heresy is easy to conceal in a world of endless qualifications and maneuvering. But three affirmations go right to the heart of the neo-evangelical and neo-orthodox rejection of biblical revelation. The first is the inerrancy of the Bible, as delivered in the original manuscripts. The second is the doctrine of eternal punishment. The third is the doctrine of capital punishment, as specified in the Old Testament case laws (unless modified by a specific New Testament revelation). I think the third is related to the second: God's merciless torturing of His covenant-breaking enemies, and the State's merciless delivery of capital crime-committing offenders into the court of the eternally torturing Judge. Therefore, the affirmation of the legitimacy of case-law specified capital punishment is an initial step back on the road to Christian orthodoxy.

The Rebellious Son

One of the Christian antinomians' most effective arguments today against the revealed law of God is the law which requires the execution of the rebellious son. This brings us to the passages under consideration in this chapter: the execution of a son who strikes his father (Ex. 21:15) or assaults his parents verbally (Ex. 21:17). Both of these passages contain the phrase, "he shall surely be put to death." Literally, the Hebrew phrase reads: "dying, he shall die"—a pleonasm. There is no question that biblical law specifies execution as the appropriate penalty for *adult* rebellious sons.[9] Biblical law's critics see this as a grave defect in the case law system, almost as if God made a horrendous mistake in the Old Testament, which He

---

9. The sons are drunkards (Deut. 21:20).

somehow rectified in the New Testament. If capital punishment is automatic upon conviction, say the critics of capital punishment, then the parents will probably refuse to take him before the judges. They will swallow their injured pride and tolerate evil in their midst. So runs the argument against a specific capital punishment specified in the Mosaic law. It is a representative argument that is subsequently used against virtually all of the biblical case laws to which the capital sanction is attached.

The obvious preliminary response to this line of reasoning is this: Were parents in the Old Covenant significantly different from parents today? Were they more willing to see their sons executed? There is something inherently unconvincing about the critics' line of argumentation. It assumes too great a discontinuity between the emotional make-up of righteous people in the Old Testament and righteous people today. Furthermore, if the biblically required sanction of execution is too harsh today, was God too harsh in ancient Israel? What has changed? God's character? Men's character? Men's emotions? Social circumstances? The critics become conveniently vague at this point. They prefer not to speculate about the reason or reasons for the supposed change. But the questions do not go away.

Until we have surveyed the evidence that undergirds the biblical concept of victim's rights, we must defer considering the judicial problem of executing the rebellious son who strikes his parent. This sanction can be understood properly only in terms of the Bible's concept of victim's rights. We will return to it later in this chapter. But as we consider the question of victim's rights, we need to keep in mind this question: *Is execution really what these texts require in every instance of the stated infractions, striking and cursing parents?*

I am devoting much of this chapter to a detailed consideration of the key phrase, "shall surely be put to death." It requires a lengthy excursion in order to deal with some things not intuitively obvious from the text. The conclusion that I reach will prove useful in interpreting the next verse in Exodus, one which specifies capital punishment for kidnappers. The same problem of interpretation occurs throughout Exodus, Leviticus, and Numbers, though not Deuteronomy, since the phrase "he shall surely die" does not occur in Deuteronomy.

I begin my discussion by considering the theological basis of all prosecutions by any court, the covenant lawsuit.

The Covenant Lawsuit

Adam and Eve had to serve as witnesses and judges in the garden. There was no escape from these two offices. The serpent had forced their hand. They had heard Satan's temptation, namely, that they could be as God if they disobeyed God (Gen. 3:5). They had become witnesses. They could not escape from their knowledge of the serpent's words. He had spoken in their presence.[10] They could stand with God and God's law by obeying God's word concerning Himself, the forbidden fruit, and the promised sentence of execution, or they could stand with Satan and his word concerning God, the forbidden fruit, and the promised execution. But when called upon by God to testify in His court, they would be required to testify, either against themselves if they stood with Satan or against Satan if they stood with God.[11] They both sought to escape self-incrimination. Adam blamed Eve, and Eve blamed the serpent. Still, there was no available judicial escape. Their fig leaves testified against them. They knew they were guilty, and their wardrobes testified to their sense of guilt.

They also had to serve as judges. They could issue a condemnation of God by eating the forbidden fruit, or they could issue a condemnation of Satan, either by eating of the tree of life, or by eating from any tree except the forbidden one, or by not eating anything at all. But they could not avoid serving as judges. They had to *decide*. They had to *act*. They had to *render judgment*.[12]

The two offices, witness and judge, were inherent in their position as God's authorized representatives on earth (Gen. 1:26-28). Because of Satan's rebellion and his temptation of them, they were forced to decide: *Against whom would they bring the required covenant lawsuit:*

---

10. This assumes that Adam was at Eve's side when the serpent spoke. If he was not, then only Eve heard him speak. She should then have gone to Adam for confirmation, and he would have had to ask the serpent to repeat his claim. As I argue in my study of the incident, in order for Satan to gain the biblically specified pair of witnesses against God, they both had to act against God's law. I think that Adam was next to Eve when the serpent spoke. Adam let her act in his name. He allowed her to test the serpent's claim.

11. This is the theological foundation of the idea of the subpoena. The State has a legitimate right to compel the appearance of an individual in court, as well as compel his truthful testimony. This right is denied by some libertarians. Cf. Murray N. Rothbard, *For a New Liberty: The Libertarian Manifesto* (rev. ed.; New York: Collier, 1978), p. 87.

12. North, *Dominion Covenant: Genesis*, Appendix E: "Witnesses and Judges."

God or Satan? They brought it against God. They served as Satan's agents. They implicitly claimed to be the victims of God's discriminatory restrictions against them, for God had denied them access to the forbidden fruit, and He had obviously lied to them concerning His power to enforce His will. They must have regarded His promised sanctions as a lie. Why else would anyone commit automatic suicide for a bite of forbidden fruit? They brought their covenant lawsuit against God *in absentia* by partaking of the forbidden fruit in the presence of Satan, thereby indulging in a satanic sacrament, an unholy communion service. They ate a ritual meal in the presence of the prince of demons. This is what Paul warns against: eating at the table of demons (I Cor. 10:21).

From the day that the serpent tempted Adam and Eve by testifying falsely concerning God's revealed word, there has been a designated victim of all criminal behavior: God. Satan needed to recruit human accomplices in his war against God. He needed two witnesses, the required number to prosecute anyone successfully for a capital crime (Deut. 17:6). But the moment that Adam and Eve brought their false testimony into God's court, they became subject to the penalty for perjury: suffering the same punishment to which the falsely accused victim was subject (Deut. 19:16-19). If their testimony had been true, then God must have lied about who is truly sovereign over the universe. He would have given false testimony against the true god, man. God would have been guilty of calling man to worship a false god, which is a capital offense (Deut. 13:6-9). He would also have been guilty of false prophesying, another capital offense (Deut. 13:1-5). Adam and Eve had sought to indict God for a capital offense; they were subsequently executed by God. So are all their heirs who persist in refusing to renounce the judicial accusations of their parents, who represented them in God's court.

In His grace, God offered them a judicial covering, a temporary stay of execution, which was symbolized by the animal skins (Gen. 3:21). This symbolic covering required the slaying of an animal. God offered them time on earth to repent. He offered them a way to make restitution to Him: the blood sacrifice of specified animals. He did this because He looked forward in time to the death of His Son on the cross, the only possible restitution payment large enough to cover the sin of Adam and his heirs.

His Son's representative death is the basis of all of God's gifts to mankind in history. *Grace is an unearned gift*, meaning a gift earned by

Christ at Calvary and given by God to all men in history. Christ's restitution payment serves as the basis of *common grace* to covenant-breakers in history and *special grace* to covenant-keepers in history and eternity.[13] The words of Christ on the cross are the basis of common grace in history: "Then said Jesus, Father, forgive them; for they know not what they do" (Luke 23:34). Ignorance of the law is no excuse, but Jesus Christ grants grace to the ignorant anyway. He paid God's price; He suffered God's sanctions; so He has the right to grant temporal (common) forgiveness on no terms at all, and eternal (special) forgiveness on His own terms.

Criminal and Victim as Covenantal Representatives

Adam and Eve served as Satan's representatives when they had communion with him, thereby bringing a covenant lawsuit against God. Had they refused to take Satan's advice, they would have served as God's representatives against Satan. The point is, *representation is an inescapable concept.* The issue is never this one: "To serve or not to serve as the covenantal representative of a supernatural being." The question is rather: "Which supernatural being shall I represent covenantally?" There is no escape from this decision and its consequences.

What does the word *covenant* mean biblically? God has created a legal relationship to man, one which is based on a legal *bond.* There is no personal relationship between God and man apart from this legal bond. The covenant structure has five parts:

1. Transcendence yet presence of God
2. Hierarchy (representative authority)
3. Ethics (law)
4. Oath (judgment and sanctions)
5. Succession (inheritance and continuity)

By combining the first letters, we get an acronym: THEOS, the Greek word for God. God's three covenantal institutions are governed in terms of this five-point structure. These institutions of God-authorized government are: church, State, and family. The covenant structure is an inescapable concept.[14]

---

13. Gary North, *Dominion and Common Grace: The Biblical Basis of Progress* (Tyler, Texas: Institute for Christian Economics, 1987).
14. Sutton, *That You May Prosper, op. cit.*

When a man sins, he thereby brings a covenantal lawsuit against
God. His action violates all five points of the covenant. First, he
denies that God is who He says He is: the Law-giver and eternal
Judge. Second, he declares himself no longer under God's hierarchical authority. Third, he says that God's ethical standards do not
apply to him. Fourth, he denies that God can or will apply His sanctions, either in history or eternity. Fifth, he asserts that covenant-
breakers shall inherit the earth.

Let us consider in greater detail point two: hierarchy. By rebelling against God, he thereby places himself under the hierarchical
authority of Satan. *He becomes Satan's representative.* This is why Christ
spoke to Peter so harshly when Peter denied that Christ would soon
go to His death: "Get thee behind me, Satan" (Matt. 16:23a). Men's
actions are always representative. This is why God judges between
the saved and lost, between sheep and goats, on judgment day
(Matt. 25:32). The eternal life-and-death question on that great and
terrible day will be: *Which sovereign did you represent and serve on earth,
God or Satan?*

It is clear that Adam and Eve sinned directly against God. More
specifically, they sinned against the God who walked in the garden
(Gen. 3:8). This is the character of all sin: a denial of God's word,
His authority, His ethical character, His sanctions, and His ability to
disinherit covenant-breakers. *Sin is a representative denial of God's covenant*: His transcendence, His authority, His law, His judgment, and
His inheritance. Man sins against God covenantally. He would steal
the very throne of God if he could. "For thou hast said in thine heart,
I will ascend into heaven, I will exalt my throne above the stars of
God: I will sit also upon the mount of the congregation, in the sides
of the north: I will ascend above the heights of the clouds; I will be
like the most High" (Isa. 14:13-14). What will be the result of this attempted theft of God's glory? "Yet thou shalt be brought down to
hell, to the sides of the pit" (Isa. 14:15).

The Trial of Jesus

Jesus Christ was the judicial victim of a corrupt Jewish court,
false witnesses, and a corrupt civil government. The Jewish leaders,
in their capacity as the God-ordained representatives of the Jewish
people, had brought a false covenant lawsuit against Jesus.[15] They

---

15. Gary North, *The Sinai Strategy: Economics and the Ten Commandments* (Tyler,
Texas: Institute for Christian Economics, 1986), pp. xxiii-xxiv.

had convicted Him of a capital crime: claiming to be God. There were two ways that He could be exonerated: if there were no witnesses who could prove that He had made the claim, or if proof were presented that His claim was true. They had hired false witnesses and had not proved that His claim was false.

The Roman State acted as the sanction-imposing agent of the Jewish people. The people had chosen Barabbas as the recipient of their mercy rather than Christ (Matt. 27:21). The Jewish leaders had been faithful representatives of the people's will. Jesus would die on the cross.

Ultimately, there is no escape from a decision either for or against Jesus Christ, Israel's only true messiah and mankind's only true savior. The old truth of Christian evangelism is correct: "No decision is still a decision." Either men vote against Jesus Christ with the Jews and the Romans as their covenantal representatives, or else they vote with Jesus Christ against the Jews and Romans as their covenantal representative. Either the decision of the Jews and Pontius Pilate represents their views, both intellectually and judicially, or else God's affirmation of His son represents them. Men bring a covenant lawsuit either against Jesus, as the Jews did, or against those who crucified Him, as Peter did (Acts 3). There is no escape. *Men must bring a covenant lawsuit in this life.* They must designate both the criminal and the victim at the drama on Calvary. Their designation will reflect their covenant status as either covenant-keepers or covenant-breakers.

Divorce by Covenantal Death

I have argued that *sin is always a representative act*. It is the act of bringing a covenantal lawsuit against God. A crime is a special kind of sin: a publicly verifiable act against God's civil law. It is an act of defiance against God's civil covenant with either an individual or some aspect of the environment as God's representative agent.

We can see the principle of victim's rights more clearly by focusing on marital divorce as a covenant lawsuit. Jesus sets forth this law regarding divorce: "It hath been said, Whosoever shall put away his wife, let him give her a writing of divorcement: But I say unto you, That whosoever shall put away his wife, saving for the cause of fornication, causeth her to commit adultery: and whosoever shall marry her that is divorced committeth adultery" (Matt. 5:31-32).

In this chapter, I do not want to cover all the theological ground that Ray Sutton covers in his book, *Second Chance: Biblical Blueprints for Divorce and Remarriage.*[16] I agree with his argument that divorce is above all a covenantal act, and that any crime listed in the Old Testament as a capital offense constitutes legal grounds for divorce today. Jesus did not abrogate the Old Testament case laws that governed divorce and remarriage, except to make them more rigorous. The principle of New Testament divorce is the same as it was in the Old Testament: *divorce by covenantal execution.* There may also be physical execution involved, but in both Old and New Testament law, *covenantal execution is primary*; eternal execution in God's heavenly court is of greater consequence than physical execution by the civil government's court. Biblically speaking, physical execution is simply the God-ordained legal consequence of specific forms of covenantal execution. This has also been argued by R. J. Rushdoony[17] and Greg Bahnsen[18] with respect to divorce. I do not try to prove this argument in this chapter; I begin with the assumption that it is biblically correct. Those who disagree should consult these other sources.

This line of reasoning from the Old Testament's case laws raises an important practical and legal issue. When a spouse commits an act that produces covenantal death—judicial death in the eyes of God—and when this is proven in one or more of God's authorized earthly courts, ecclesiastical and civil, either by the injured spouse or by other witnesses, the covenantally dead person becomes subject to covenantal sanctions. In a systematically biblical civil government, the maximum penalty attached to many of these crimes would be death. This would lead to divorce by physical execution because there has *already been* divorce by covenantal execution.

John 8

The standard response from those who reject such a "harsh" (i.e., God-established) penalty is an appeal to John 8, the case of the woman who was taken in adultery. I believe that this passage was in the original Bible text. Biblical "higher critics" and many orthodox Christians deny this, since most of the older Greek manuscripts do

---

16. Ft. Worth, Texas: Dominion Press, 1987.

17. R. J. Rushdoony, *The Institutes of Biblical Law* (Nutley, New Jersey: Craig Press, 1973), pp. 401-15.

18. Greg L. Bahnsen, *Theonomy in Christian Ethics* (2nd ed.; Phillipsburg, New Jersey: Presbyterian & Reformed, 1984), pp. 105-16.

not include John 7:53-8:11.[19] Most modern translations of the Bible provide a marginal note to this effect. But if this passage is not in the Bible, then surely the Old Testament's capital sanction against adultery has not been altered. If John 8 is not in the biblical canon, then there is no other passage that supports the case for an alteration of the capital sanction against adulterers except Joseph's forgiving Mary, which we will examine in detail later.[20]

John 8 deals with a woman who was discovered in the very act of adultery (v. 4). Her accusers (witnesses) brought her before Jesus, challenging Him to render judgment. This was clearly an attempted trap on their part, for Jesus was neither a civil nor an ecclesiastical official. The woman's accusers were also judicially corrupt. They were law-breaking deceivers, for they were being highly selective: her partner was not brought before Jesus. (Might he have been one of their ecclesiastical or professional associates?)

Jesus challenged them: "He that is without sin among you, let him first cast a stone at her" (v. 7b). Then He stooped down and wrote something in the dirt (v. 8) — the only instance recorded in the New Testament of His writing anything. (Might He have written the names of women who were well known — biblically speaking — by the woman's accusers?) We do not know what He wrote. We do know that her accusers immediately decided to leave. Discretion was the better part of valor, in their view. They did not continue to press charges against her. Thus, *without the presence of two witnesses, she could not be legally convicted of a capital crime, according to Old Covenant law* (Deut. 17:6). The witnesses had to cast the first stones (Deut. 17:7), but they all had departed. So, Jesus asked her an obviously rhetorical question: "Woman, where are those thine accusers? Hath no man condemned thee? She said, No man, Lord. And Jesus said unto her, Neither do I condemn thee: go, and sin no more" (vv. 10b-11).

Jesus knew she was guilty as initially accused. He told her to go and sin no more, making clear to her that He knew she was guilty. But adultery is a civil matter. *Without witnesses, she could not be lawfully convicted.* She acknowledged Him as Lord in her own words; He warned her not to do this thing again.

---

19. See Appendix C: "The Hoax of Higher Criticism."

20. The loss of this supposed defense of a New Testament alteration in the adultery sanction would be a bitter pill to swallow for neo-evangelicals, far too many of whom are prone to accept the hoax of higher criticism, and virtually all of whom spend their intellectual careers seeking exegetical ways around the Old Testament case laws and their sanctions.

There are millions of short-sighted, instinctively law-breaking and covenant-denying Christians who argue that this incident proves that adultery is no longer a capital crime. They invariably point to Jesus' words, "He that is without sin among you, let him first cast a stone at her." They challenge those who affirm the law: "You see, we [meaning *you*] are not to judge anyone unless we [meaning *you*] have no sin." This interpretation of Christ's words is utter lunacy. Its implications are preposterous. If pressed, these "he who is without sin" interpreters will admit that the New Testament does allow the State to enforce penalties against criminals (Rom. 13:1-7). But then their whole argument collapses. He who is sinful *must* cast the first stone, for all people have sinned and come short of the glory of God (Rom. 3:23). If their argument is taken seriously, then John 8 prohibits all capital punishment, and probably all punishment by anyone, any time. If true, this principle of interpretation would make all covenantal sanctions impossible to enforce: family, church, and State. It would mean the end of all human government. It cannot possibly mean this.

In the Old Testament, God established the death penalty for various crimes. Were Old Covenant judges and witnesses without sin? Obviously not. So, what did Jesus really mean?

This Particular Sin

The most obvious explanation is that He meant "He that is without *this particular* sin, let him cast the first stone." Then He started writing something in the dirt. The witnesses immediately departed. The biblical judicial principle is this: those who have committed a particular crime, but who have not been tried and convicted by a lawful court, or who have not privately offered to make restitution, and who have therefore not been forgiven by the victim, are not fit to serve as witnesses or judges of those who are accused of having committed the same crime. This is a reasonable interpretation, and a reasonable view of justice. It does not necessitate the scrapping of all civil law, all capital sanctions, and the sanction of death for men who commit adultery with other men's wives.

When Jesus told her to go and sin no more, did He really expect her to be able to avoid all sin for the rest of her life? Of course not. But what He did expect her to be able to do was to avoid the sin of adultery. He did not have *sin in general* in mind in this passage when He used the word *sin*, but rather the *particular sin of adultery*. Thus, it is totally misleading for people to use this passage as a proof text that Jesus established a new civil penalty, or even no penalty at all, for the civil crime of adultery. He did not abandon the Mosaic law in John 8. On the contrary, He followed the Mosaic law's procedural requirements to the letter. *She was publicly innocent in terms of the procedural requirements of the Mosaic law.* Thus, He did not execute His historical wrath upon her in His capacity as perfect humanity. Only the witnesses were allowed to do that, and they had departed. He would deal with her later as God, the perfect Witness, on judgment day in His court; until then, she was granted time to repent and reform her ways. So are all the rest of us.

Obvious, isn't it? Yet for several generations, pietists and antinomians (those who reject biblical law) have persuaded Christians that John 8 represents some remarkable break with the Old Testament. Christians who hate God's law also hate the New Testament, so they do whatever they can to distort it and misinterpret it, even when their misinterpretations lead to obviously preposterous conclusions. They do not worry about preposterous conclusions; they worry instead about a sovereign God who threatens individuals and society with judgments in history for sin. They are in principle adulterers themselves, and they are looking for an escape from God's authorized civil sanctions against adultery, should they someday fall into this sin. They are looking for loopholes — civil, ecclesiastical, and psychological.

Witnesses as Unauthorized Prosecutors
There is another aspect of this incident that must be considered. Jesus dealt directly with the sins of the witnesses. He did not focus on questions of legal procedure. He did not point out that they should have gone immediately to a civil court. He did not ask them rhetorically, "Who made me a judge over you?" He did not remind them that the other guilty party was missing. It is clear that His main concern was not with the procedural details of the incident; He preferred instead to deal positively with the sinful condition of the accused woman. She was the focus of His concern, not her accusers. He acted to remove them from His presence, so that He might restore her to moral and judicial wholeness. This was His tactic in all of His public confrontations with His accusers. He did this with Israel in 70 A.D. He removed Israel from His presence, so that He might restore the gentiles to moral and judicial wholeness. (When He has accomplished this, He will then redeem Israel: Romans 11.)

He could also have asked these two questions: "Where is the victim? Why is the victim not here to press charges?" More to the point, He could have asked: "By what authority have you, the witnesses, substituted your judgment for the victim's? Who made you the authorized prosecutors of this covenant lawsuit? On whose behalf are you acting?" He did not ask these questions, not because they were irrelevant to the situation, but because they were secondary to His main concern: dealing positively with the sin of the woman.

Did the Mosaic law give to witnesses an independent authority to prosecute the covenant lawsuit as agents solely of the State? If so, then the State has the right to prosecute despite the decision of the victim not to prosecute. This would clearly compromise the judicial principle of victim's rights. I am arguing in this chapter that *the State possesses no independent authority to prosecute if the victim voluntarily decides not to prosecute*, an argument based heavily on Joseph's decision as a just man to put Mary away privately. (See below: "The Victim's Decision.") The victim's decision is final until God intervenes directly — sickness, calamity, death, or at His Second Coming — to bring His own covenant lawsuit. Thus, the witnesses in John 8 were violating yet another principle of the Mosaic law. The whole incident was one of utter lawlessness and rebellion, which is the characteristic feature of every challenge to the God-given authority of Jesus Christ.

Extending Mercy

As the cosmic lawgiver, God has the right to set the penalties for crimes. Biblical law provides society with God's specified penalties. What is crucial to understand is that the biblical principle of *God as the victim who names the penalty* leads to a derivative principle: the earthly victim of the prohibited act is also allowed to name the penalty to be imposed on the criminal, so long as it does not exceed the limits specified by the Bible.

There is one exception to this rule, argue some biblical scholars: if the specified penalty is death, and if a particular phrase appears in the text, then the State must enforce whenever it unilaterally prosecutes and convicts the criminal. The phrase is: "surely he shall die" or "dying, he shall die." This phrase, which biblical scholars call a *pleonasm*, initially appears to be an identifying mark of infractions of God's law that inescapably require the death penalty. I argue that this is an incorrect interpretation of the use of the pleonasm, but I could be wrong. This is why we need to explore the usage of this pleonasm in the section below, "Dying, He Shall Die." First, however, we must consider the principle of victim's rights.

We know that sanctions against non-capital crimes are to be imposed by the civil government at the discretion of the victim. He can refuse to accept any restitution payment or a reduced restitution payment. He can lawfully cancel the debt owed to him (Matt. 18:23-35). I argue that this principle of forgiveness also applies to capital crimes in which there is an identifiable human victim who is capable of bringing a covenant civil lawsuit against the criminal. We see this judicial principle in action at the crucifixion. Jesus requested that the Father not immediately destroy His executioners. "Then said Jesus, Father, forgive them; for they know not what they do" (Luke 23:34a). He extended additional time to them. This was His unmerited favor or gift to them, just as God had extended life to Adam, Eve, and Cain. As both the primary victim (God) and the secondary victim (perfect man), Jesus Christ possessed the right to extend temporal mercy to His enemies, even for this capital crime. His divinity authorized this extension of mercy. So did His perfect humanity, for He was the victim of a rigged trial. I argue that as the victim, He could lawfully extend mercy only before He physically died.

The question is: Are victims allowed to extend mercy in cases where the State appears to be required by the presence of the pleonasm, "surely he shall die," to execute the convicted criminal? We know that in his capacity as a lawful prosecutor of God's covenant lawsuit, the earthly victim does possess the right—the legal authorization from God—to extend mercy to a convicted criminal for any crime other than a capital crime. He can lawfully forgive the restitution payment owed to him. Why not also in the case of a capital crime?

The State as God's Prosecutor

In order to answer this question, we need to understand that the victim is not the only one who can lawfully initiate a covenant lawsuit against a suspected criminal. God has more than one covenantal agent in society. Witnesses can bring incriminating information to an authorized agent of covenantal government, and this agent can lawfully institute covenant lawsuit proceedings against any criminal, *but only if there is no earthly victim of the crime who is capable of bringing charges.*[21] If there is an identifiable earthly victim, then he

---

21. For a list of capital crimes and an identification of those cases in which the State is authorized to initiate the covenant lawsuit, see the subhead at the end of this chapter: "Addendum: Cases to Which the Pleonasm Is Attached."

alone becomes the exclusive agent who is authorized to initiate a covenant lawsuit against the suspected criminal. This restriction on State's authority to initiate a covenant lawsuit is an implication of the doctrine of victim's rights. The victim possesses the right to forgive. The State is not authorized to ignore or supersede this right.

The interests of the community are upheld by identifying the criminal or member of the criminal class. Remember, God is the primary victim of crime; He has authorized *representatives* to defend the integrity of His name. If a community refuses to do this—if church, State, and family governments break down—God threatens to bring His negative sanctions through other agencies: war, pestilence, and famine (Deut. 28:15-68). This is why an unsolved murder in a field required a public blood sacrifice by the nearest city's civil magistrates, not the priests (Deut. 21:1-9).[22]

A Legal Claim

Who acts as God's authorized agent in the bringing of a covenantal civil lawsuit? The victim, the witnesses, or those who are authorized agents of the civil government. If the initiator of the lawsuit is the victim, he is not acting primarily on his own behalf, but as an agent of God because of his position as the victimized intermediary between the criminal and God, the ultimate victim. He is acting secondarily in his own behalf, for any restitution payment will go to him. Similarly, witnesses who bring evidence to the State for use in prosecuting the covenant lawsuit are acting as representative agents of God through the civil government. They do not act on their own behalf, for they have *no legal claim* on the resources of the person who is being charged with the crime, should he be convicted. Witnesses are not victims. They are acting in the name of God as authorized and oath-bound agents of the State when they testify in a civil court. *Where there is no direct legal claim, there is no direct covenantal relationship.* Thus, witnesses are acting as indirect agents of God as participants in the civil commonwealth.

Because crimes are always crimes against God, the State has a law-enforcement role to play, for the State possesses God's authorized monopoly of the sword: the imposition of physical sanctions. The State in turn implicitly delegates the office of witness to those who view a crime or who have information relevant to the State's

---

22. Clearly, the Book of Hebrews has annulled this practice today.

prosecution of a covenant lawsuit. (This is the judicial basis of what in English common law is known as "citizen's arrest," although it is seldom invoked today.) This is why the State can lawfully compel honest testimony from a witness: the witness is under the authority of the State. It is in fact unlawful to withhold evidence of a crime when subpoenaed. While the State may offer a reward for the capture and conviction of a criminal (a positive sanction: blessing), this is at the discretion of the State. The witness who seeks an announced reward has a claim on the State, not on the criminal.

The most important example in history of a reward-seeking witness is Judas Iscariot, who collected 30 pieces of silver from the Jewish court to witness against Jesus Christ. He later returned the money, not because it is inherently wrong to accept money as an honest witness, but because he knew he had been a false witness in a rigged, dishonest trial. The Jewish leaders self-righteously replied, "What is that to us?" (Matt. 27:4b). They felt no sense of guilt, so why should he? They also recognized the tainted nature of the money, which was the price of blood, and as true Pharisees, they refused to accept his repayment (Matt. 27:6). Committing murder by rigging a court was irrelevant in their view, a means to a legitimate end; getting paid for false witness-bearing, however, was seen by them as a sin. This is the essence of Pharisaism, the classic historical example of Pharisaism in action. They were happy to serve as the most corrupt court in man's history, but they judiciously refused to accept money for their efforts. (What is not recognized by most Christian commentators is that the testimony of a witness in a Hebrew court was invalidated, at least by the law of the Pharisees, if he had received payment for testifying.)[23]

What is my conclusion? Only that witnesses have no legal claim on the criminal. The authorized agents of God in the prosecution of a covenant lawsuit are officers of one of the three courts — church, State, and family — and the victim of the crime.

The Right of Refusal

If the authorized biblical penalty is economic restitution, then the victim whose covenant lawsuit is successfully prosecuted by the civil government has the right to refuse payment, or the right to take less than what biblical law authorizes. Like the creditor who has the

---

23. *Bekhoroth* 4:6, in *The Mishnah*, edited by Herbert Danby (New York: Oxford University Press, [1933] 1987), p. 534.

right to take less in repayment, or to extend the debtor more time to repay, or even to forgive the debt, so is the victim of a criminal who has been convicted in a court of law. The nineteenth-century Jewish commentator S. R. Hirsch remarked that the victim of a theft "can renounce altogether his right to repayment by the sale of the male-factor, and content himself with a signed promise to pay as soon as the circumstances of the thief improve."[24]

What if the victim refuses to prosecute? I see no warrant in most cases for the State then to prosecute. The court can lawfully serve as the agent of the victim in certain exceptional cases. Two examples would be victims who are orphaned minors or mental incompetents. Nevertheless, under normal circumstances, a decision not to prose-cute by a victim who is legally competent to initiate a covenant lawsuit is a binding decision. He thereby loses his legal claim on any future restitution payments by the convicted criminal. If he is willing to suffer this loss, then the State must honor his or her decision. The individual, not the State, is the victim; the principle of victim's rights is binding on the State. Only if the criminal act in some way also in-jured the State or society could the State then prosecute, but only on its own behalf.[25]

The case of Judah and Tamar is representative. Judah refused to prosecute Tamar for whoredom when she brought tangible evidence that he was the guilty party and that she had merely been claiming her legal right to the levirate marriage (Gen. 38:26). On the other hand, the victim also escapes the threat of a counter-lawsuit from the accused if the latter should be declared innocent by the court. Again, the case of Judah and Tamar is representative. Judah did not want to be convicted of false witness-bearing, for he had committed the crime with her, and he was therefore not authorized to bring accusa-tions against her in his own name. As the head of both his family and the local civil government, he dropped all charges.

Civil Sanctions

Old Testament law specifies that criminals are subject to several types of civil sanctions: corporal punishment—lashings, but with no

---

24. Samson Raphael Hirsch, *The Pentateuch Translated and Explained*, translated by Isaac Levy, 5 vols., *Exodus* (3rd ed.; London: Honig & Sons, 1967), p. 295: at Exodus 21:6.

25. Treason that also involves theft would be an example. The victim of the theft might not prosecute, but the State could, for treason is an act of attempted murder against the society.

more than forty lashes (Deut. 25:3) and the slicing of a woman's hand in one instance (Deut. 25:12)[26] — economic restitution, banishment, and the death penalty.

The punishment of lashing is curious. No crime in the Bible is specifically said to require lashing. The language of the King James Version indicates an exception to this rule: the required scourging of a bondmaid who is betrothed to one man and who then commits fornication with another man (Lev. 19:20). However, the Hebrew word translated as "scourge" does not necessarily mean physical scourging; it is better translated as "punishment," or even "inquiry." Nevertheless, the lack of any reference to specific crimes with which this physical sanction is associated does not mean that no public crime is subject to lashing, or else there would be no prohibition against imposing more than forty lashes. This is a sanction to be imposed at the discretion of the judges in cases where there is *no identifiable victim who has suffered either economic loss or physical or verbal abuse.* Presumably, this sanction is appropriate for such acts as public nudity by adults, prostitution, public drunkenness, repeated disturbances of the peace, and public acts prohibited by God, but for which no identifiable victim can be found. The victim of such "victimless crimes" — God — is entitled to restitution: lashes. *Eternal punishment is the model: God is repaid through the suffering of the criminal.*

In the Old Testament era, if the restitution payment to the victim was larger than the criminal or his kinsman-redeemer could afford to pay, the criminal was sold into slavery. The purchase price went to the victim. This was the only way that a Hebrew could become an involuntary lifetime slave in Israel, and even in this instance, it was lifetime slavery only if he could not earn enough to meet the restitution payment or if his kinsman-redeemer refused to pay. Non-criminal Hebrew debt slaves were to be released in the seventh, "sabbatical" year (Deut. 15); voluntary jubilee year slaves were to be released in the year of jubilee (Lev. 25:39-41).[27] The criminal became a slave to another person because he had been a slave to sin — specifically, he had committed a criminal act that had seriously damaged someone else's property or body.

---

26. The language of the King James makes it appear that the woman's hand is to be cut off. This is incorrect: it is permanently injured, but not cut off: James B. Jordan, *The Law of the Covenant: An Exposition of Exodus 21-23* (Tyler, Texas: Institute for Christian Economics, 1984), pp. 118-19.

27. See Chapter 4, above, pp. 125-31.

The Death Penalty

Some crimes are so great that God authorizes the death penalty. This means the criminal's immediate deliverance into God's court. This in turn leads to his subsequent delivery into permanent slavery in hell and the lake of fire unless he repents prior to his physical execution by the civil government. This removal of temporal life is restitution to God for a criminal's major transgression of God's covenant laws. *The death penalty points clearly to God's position as the primary victim.* It also points to His status as eternal Judge.

In cases of murder, the State becomes the delegated representative of God. The deceased obviously cannot initiate the covenant lawsuit. The State therefore initiates it on behalf of both the deceased and God. No restitution payment is possible to the deceased; thus, God must judge the criminal directly in His court. The State is required to deliver the criminal's soul immediately into the hands of God, who is the primary victim and also the legal representative of the deceased victim. The State must not allow a murderer to escape immediate entry into God's court—physical execution—by the payment of a fine: "Moreover ye shall take no satisfaction for the life of a murderer, which is guilty of death: but he shall be surely put to death" (Num. 35:31).

Christ's resurrection is the basis of man's escape from God's immediate and direct imposition of the death penalty, both the first death (physical death) and the eternal second death (Rev. 20:14). Because Jesus Christ rose from the dead, His previous grant of temporary forgiveness to Rome and Israel received God's sanction. It was also on the basis of this resurrection that God granted a stay of execution to Adam and Eve. But judgment eventually comes in history: Adam and Eve died, and Israel and Rome fell. The question then arises: Does the resurrection of Jesus Christ also serve as the basis of a man's legitimate escape from the death penalty from a civil court? If so, in which cases and on what judicial basis?

"Dying, He Must Die"

We need to deal with a problem of interpretation that confronts us over and over in Old Testament case laws. It is a phrase that occurs in many passages.[28] A person convicted of a specified crime "shall

---

28. These verses are displayed under the subhead at the end of this chapter: "Addendum: Cases to Which the Pleonasm Is Attached."

surely be put to death." As mentioned earlier, the Hebrew phrase is what scholars call a pleonasm: "dying, he shall surely die." It is emphatic language. We find it in Exodus 21:12: "He that smiteth a man, so that he die, shall surely be put to death." James Jordan commented in 1984: "The emphasis means that the death penalty cannot be set aside by any payment of money."[29] But because of a series of problems in interpretation, he subsequently changed his mind about the meaning of this pleonasm.[30]

What Is the Problem?

Why should the interpretation of this pleonasm of execution be such a problem? Because the same phrase appears in the case of crimes that we normally would not think would involve automatic capital punishment. These include crimes that have no immediate human victims: sabbath-breaking (Ex. 31:14-15) and bestiality (Ex. 22:19; Lev. 20:15-16). These also include crimes in which no one dies: assaulting parents physically (Ex. 21:15) or verbally (Ex. 21:17), adultery that involves another man's wife (Lev. 20:10), blasphemy against God (Lev. 24:16), and wizardry and witchcraft (Lev. 20:27). One crime to which this pleonasm is attached is often regarded by modern societies as a capital crime: kidnapping (Ex. 21:16).[31]

To survey the nature of the exegetical problem, let us consider in greater detail the case of adultery that involves a man with another man's wife: "And the man that committeth adultery with another man's wife, even he that committeth adultery with his neighbour's wife, the adulterer and the adulteress shall surely be put to death" (Lev. 20:10). The pleonasm of execution appears here: "shall surely be put to death." Capital punishment for both of the adulterers can legitimately be imposed at the insistence of the victim, the woman's husband. Why? *Because the government of the covenantal family was broken by adultery.* The injured party, meaning the head of the household, is the lawful covenantal representative of God. He is authorized to bring charges against the adulterers as the injured party and also as the head of the family unit. Because the Bible specifies adultery as a civil crime, he also brings this lawsuit in civil court.

The victimized husband can lawfully file the covenant lawsuit in up to three covenantal courts: family, church, and State. A covenant

---

29. Jordan, *Law of the Covenant*, p. 96n.
30. They are not the same objections that I raise in this chapter.
31. See Chapter 8: "Kidnapping."

lawsuit is first presented by the victimized husband to the suspected partner, and then (at the discretion of the victimized husband) it is presented in the appropriate court or courts. The institutional church has a legitimate role to play if either of the marriage partners is a member. It pronounces the sentence of covenantal death against the offending party. Thus, adultery can sometimes affect all three covenantal institutions. The victim declares that the covenantal bond of marriage has been broken, and that the adulterers have now come under God's wrath. If the suspected adulterous male partner is married, his wife can also file appropriate lawsuits against her husband. Biblical law makes it clear, however, that *the husband of the adulterous wife has primary authority to specify the penalty*. It is his covenantal household office as the head of the family that has been attacked by the adulterers. If he decides on the death penalty for his wife, as we shall see, the criminal consort cannot escape her fate. As the officer of his family's government, the victimized husband specifies the penalty; the wife of the adulterer cannot stay the hand of the civil magistrate.

Two questions arise. Can the husband legally grant mercy to the wife if she is convicted, that is, can he specify a lesser punishment? Furthermore, if he can, and if he does this, must he show equal mercy to the convicted man?

No Respect for Persons

The example of Jesus on the cross indicates that the victim can lawfully spare the criminal. He asked His Father to forgive them, meaning Jews and Romans (Luke 23:34). He spared both of the "adulterers," Israel and her consort, Rome. Israel again and again in Old Testament history committed spiritual adultery with foreign gods and nations, yet God always spared the nation until A.D. 70.[32] The Book of Hosea centers on this theme of the husband's forgiveness of an adulterous wife. Romans 11 indicates that genetic Israel will someday be re-grafted into the church through mass conversion,[33] so God has still withheld the death penalty from Israel as a covenantal people (though not necessarily as the modern political unit that we call the state of Israel).

---

32. David Chilton, *The Days of Vengeance: An Exposition of the Book of Revelation* (Ft. Worth: Dominion Press, 1987).

33. This postmillennial position has been defended by such Calvinist commentators on Romans 11 as Charles Hodge, Robert Haldane, and John Murray. The Larger Catechism of the Westminster Confession of Faith also teaches it: Answer 191.

What is the problem here? The pleonasm appears in Leviticus 20:10, "dying, they shall die." If the language of inescapable death is accepted at face value, then the husband of the adulteress cannot lawfully request a reduced penalty, such as the forfeiture of her dowry to him, rather than insist on her execution. But is he so restricted? God spared Israel time after time. It would seem reasonable that the injured husband might prefer a lesser penalty, just as God did with Israel. Maybe he still loves her. Maybe this is her first transgression. He feels deeply injured, but not enough to have her executed. Perhaps she is a good mother. Perhaps he wants to keep her as his wife. Perhaps not. What if he wants a divorce? This would be granted by the State. He could also require her to transfer her dowry to him.

By showing mercy to his wife, he must also show mercy to her consort. In the case of adultery involving another man's wife, the two adulterers must receive the same negative sanction. The judges are not permitted to show partiality to persons in rendering official judgment. The victimized husband who decides to prosecute is acting as a judge, for if the adulterers are convicted, he specifies the penalty. If he wants total vengeance against the man, he must also demand the same penalty for his wife. If he shows leniency to her, he must show the same leniency to him. Why? Because in our capacity as God-ordained judges, men are not to show partiality, or as the Bible says, "respect of persons" (Deut. 1:17; 16:19; II Sam. 14:14; Acts 10:34). When Joseph decided as a just man to put Mary away privately, he necessarily also decided not to seek civil justice against any suspected consort.

The Bible does not directly discuss the question of leniency by the victim. The pleonasm "dying, they shall die" is attached to this crime of adultery (Lev. 20:10). Nevertheless, I am arguing that the victim can specify a lesser penalty for the adulterers. If I am correct, then in such cases, the criminals do not "surely die" at the hands of the court. But if they are not automatically executed upon conviction, then what does the presence of the pleonasm mean? Why is it found in some biblical texts specifying capital punishment, but not in all of them? The pleonasm is there for emphasis, the lexicographers say.[34] Then what exactly does it emphasize? Not the ab-

---

34. *Genesius' Hebrew Grammar* (Oxford, [1910] 1974), sect. 113n, p. 342; cited by Jordan, *The Death Penalty in the Mosaic Law* (Tyler, Texas: Biblical Horizons, 1988), p. 9.

solute necessity of the death penalty in every case in which it appears, if I am correct in my reasoning. It does not apply in cases where the victim shows leniency. The victim decides.

The Victimized Wife

The Old Testament specifies the death penalty for wives who commit adultery. It does not specify the death penalty for a husband who commits adultery. Is this an oversight? Or does this indicate that God does respect persons, leaving victimized wives more vulnerable than victimized husbands? Does the Mosaic law in fact show respect for persons, discriminating against victimized wives?

The answer is found in the nature of the lawsuit. The victimized husband brings the lawsuit in his capacity as head of his household. The family is one of God's three covenantal governments. It is marked by a covenantal oath. Thus, the death penalty as the maximum for an adulterous wife places the decision in the hands of a covenant head. It is not that the Bible discriminates against victimized wives. It simply places the primary authority for prosecuting the covenant lawsuit in the hands of the covenantal head of the household.

If the adulterous wife could be executed at the discretion of the wife of her adulterous consort, then the primary authority to impose the penalty would be removed from the head of the household and transferred to the subordinate member of another household. The victimized husband who had decided to keep his wife would lose her if the wife of her consort prosecuted, saw her husband convicted, and asked for the death penalty. Since the court is not allowed to discriminate, it would also have to execute the adulterous wife. Thus, the adulterous wife's husband would lose control over the sanction.

The victimized wife can lawfully sue for divorce. The judges are authorized to grant this. Even if the husband of the adulterous wife does not insist on a divorce, the victimized wife is allowed to gain legal separation. Why, if there must be equality of negative sanctions placed on both adulterers? *Because the judges' announcement of the divorce is not the imposition of a negative sanction; it is simply a legal announcement of a broken marriage.* The marriage was covenantally broken by her husband's act of adultery; the wife is simply declaring her formal acceptance of her new legal status as an unmarried woman. She asks the court to make this declaration public. Biblical law always protects the innocent party. She is not compelled to re-adopt her husband back into the marriage. But she cannot lawfully insist on physical execution of her adulterous husband. The wife of an adulterous husband has only secondary rights as a victim because in this two-party sin, she is the secondary earthly victim. She is not the head of her household. She cannot lawfully seek the execution of the victimized husband's wife by insisting on the execution of her husband.

The Bible is silent regarding the execution of an adulterous husband who commits adultery with an unmarried woman. It is clear, however, that his wife is the primary earthly victim. It seems to me that the wife, as the primary earthly victim, then gains the legal authority to prosecute the two adulterers to the limit of the law. She can require the execution of both partners if they are convicted of adultery by a civil court.

If I am correct about this, then we now know why there is no civil sanction against prostitution specified in the Old Testament, except for the required execution of the daughter of a priest who becomes a prostitute. "And the daughter of any priest, if she profane herself by playing the whore, she profaneth her father: she shall be burnt with fire" (Lev. 21:9). If the victimized wife can have her convicted husband executed for having committed adultery with a prostitute, then the prostitute is required to share his fate. Thus, there is no need for an explicit civil sanction against prostitution. The victimized wife decides. If this view is correct, then the threat of the capital sanction would tend to confine prostitution to unmarried persons. It would therefore reduce prostitution's assault on marriage.

The Victim's Decision

What would it take to get a victim to accept a reduced penalty? The criminal would make a public confession of guilt and repentance, and then offer to pay restitution to the victim. This might work. Then again, it might not. *The key to the criminal's escape from death is the decision of the victim.* The victim cannot lawfully demand a penalty greater than the one specified in the case law, but he can accept something less.

In a later essay, James Jordan took another look at the pleonasm, "surely he shall die."[35] He cites Numbers 35:30-31: "Whoso killeth any person, the murderer shall be put to death by the mouth of witnesses: but one witness shall not testify against any person to cause him to die. Moreover ye shall take no satisfaction for the life of a

---

35. Jordan, *Death Penalty*, p. 9.

murderer, which is guilty of death: but he shall be surely put to death." The law specifically says that there can be no substitute payment. The question then arises: Which is more authoritative, the pleonasm's language or the automatic penalty attached to murder? Is murder unique? Is it only in murder cases that the State must invariably impose the death penalty? Or is the death penalty the inescapable consequence of the pleonasm? Does the presence of the pleonasm indicate the idea of "accept no substitutes" wherever it occurs, or is it merely emphasis? If merely emphasis, what exactly does it emphasize?

If adultery always requires the death penalty (Lev. 20:10), Jordan asks, then why did Joseph decide to put Mary away quietly rather than prosecuting her (Matt. 1:19)? My answer: *victim's rights*. The primary earthly victim always has the legal right not to prosecute. This was Joseph's decision. The civil government was not to intervene, nor was the priestly government. Similarly, the decision to forgive was also Christ's decision at the cross, although He had earlier warned the Jewish leaders that He would eventually bring judgment on them (Luke 21), which He did in A.D. 70.

Joseph forgave Mary. This was clearly a decision made under the terms of Old Covenant law. The New Covenant had not yet been established. Thus, when the text identifies Joseph as a just man, its frame of reference is the Old Covenant law. *Joseph was not violating any principle of the Mosaic law when he showed mercy to Mary and refused to prosecute.* He chose to put her away quietly in order to avoid having to bring a civil covenant lawsuit against her. In his capacity as the betrothed husband, Joseph decided to break off the betrothal. Only if Mary's family had protested — unlikely, given the apparent circumstances of her pregnancy and the capital sanction involved (Deut. 22:20-21) — would he have been required to pursue his accusation in a civil or ecclesiastical court in order to defend his decision to break the betrothal.

The first question then is this: If the victim does decide to prosecute, and the person is convicted, can the victim then specify a lesser penalty? I think the answer is yes. I offer this explanation: the principle of victim's rights still applies, but in the case of murder, the victim cannot volunteer to accept a reduced penalty; thus, the State must impose the maximum penalty. This leads me to a general principle: *When the State becomes the prosecuting agent of case laws where this pleonasm occurs, it must enforce the death penalty on conviction.* There are no exceptions.

The second question is this: If the victim decides not to prose-cute, can any other court intervene and prosecute in God's name? The case of Joseph and Mary indicates that Joseph's decision would have been authoritative and final. Her pregnancy would have been visible to all, yet if he had chosen not to prosecute, she could remain free of concern about any other court bringing charges against her. Had she actually been an adulteress, and had her consort been mar-ried, then the victimized wife could bring charges against them, but she could gain only a divorce: the court's declaration of a broken marriage. She could not require civil penalties against Mary, and therefore also not against her husband. Joseph, not the victimized wife, was the primary earthly victim and therefore the one who pos-sessed the option of freeing his betrothed wife from any civil penalties.

What Does the Pleonasm Emphasize?

I think the pleonasm identifies *crimes that are the highest on God's list of abominations.* The normal penalty for these crimes is death; any-thing less than this which the victim specifies is a manifestation of great mercy. By upholding the principle of victim's rights, biblical law also creates incentives for criminals to deal less harshly with vic-tims during the actual crime. If the victim is not brutalized, he may decide to show leniency if the criminal is later convicted. This pro-tects the victim. Biblical law is designed to protect the victim.

Must civil judges impose the *maximum penalty* allowed by biblical law when the State is the victim, or when by law the State is God's designated agent to protect the community by upholding God's rights and enforcing His sanctions? Not always. The principle of vic-tim's rights governs the imposition of civil sanctions. Judges have the God-given authority to impose a reduced penalty according to cir-cumstances. The only exceptions to this rule are those cases in which the pleonasm occurs; the judges cannot reduce the sanctions in such cases. This is the meaning of the pleonasm: *the elimination of judicial discretion in imposing sanctions when the State initiates the lawsuit.*

Consider two alternative lines of reasoning. First, if we argue that the judges must impose the *maximum* penalty in *all* cases that specify the death penalty, irrespective of the presence of the pleonasm, then the emphasis aspect of the pleonasm disappears judi-cially. If all capital crimes require the death penalty, of what purpose is the pleonasm? This would indicate that the pleonasm has some function other than judicial emphasis. I cannot imagine what this other function might be. The presence of the pleonasm must indicate *the legitimacy of judicial discretion in cases where the pleonasm is missing.* By requiring judges to impose the maximum penalty in all cases, judicial discretion disappears. The judicial principle of victim's rights would therefore disappear.

Second, if we argue that the judges can in *all* cases legitimately impose a *lesser* penalty, then the emphasis aspect of the pleonasm also disappears judicially. Cases that are governed by the pleonasm would then become indistinguishable from those that are not. The pleonasm would lose its force.

My conclusion is this: if the pleonasm of execution is understood to have any judicial effect in distinguishing capital cases, and if the principle of victim's rights is also to be honored in all cases, then the pleonasm should be interpreted as *eliminating judicial discretion in applying sanctions in all cases in which prosecution has been lawfully initiated by the civil government.* The judges must not reduce the sanction of execution in any case in which 1) the State lawfully initiates the lawsuit, and 2) the sanction is marked by the pleonasm.

Thus, the pleonasm applies *only* to a unique set of capital crimes: where there is no identifiable human or institutional victim who could specify a reduced sanction. The victim is God alone. The State therefore is authorized to initiate the covenant lawsuit. *There is no earthly victim who has the authority to reduce the sanction.* The community through the civil government is called upon to execute the convicted criminal. In short, in the so-called "victimless crimes" in which the pleonasm of execution applies, civil judges have no choice in deciding on the appropriate sanction. The sanction is always execution. *"Dying, he shall die" binds the judges in capital crimes where the State acts as the covenant lawsuit's prosecutor without the presence of an intermediary or representative human victim.*

The pleonasm is not a denial of the principle of victim's rights because God, as the primary cosmic victim, has specified the appropriate sanction. This sanction must be imposed by the State in the absence of any secondary victim—a victim who is always authorized to speak in God's name. In the absence of such a representative, the pleonasm takes effect. The pleonasm must therefore *not* be understood as a limitation on the judicial principle of victim's rights. It limits the discretion of civil judges in those cases where there is no identifiable earthly victim, but it does not limit the discretion of the victim. Biblical law allows the victim, as God's representative, to reduce the penalty.

Rabbinic Law

Rabbinic law also recognizes the legitimacy of the victim's option of reducing or forgiving a criminal, as S. R. Hirsch's previous comments indicate, but not in capital crimes. While he did not refer to the pleonasm, Hirsch summarized the principle of Jewish law with respect to capital crimes. "The whole idea of the right to grant clemency or mercy was entirely absent in the Jewish Code of Law. Justice and judgment is [sic] the perogative [sic] of God not Man. When the very precisely defined Law of God, — giving Man no scope for his own judgment or arbitrary discretion — ordains death for a criminal, the carrying out of this sentence is not an act of harshness to be commuted for any consideration whatsoever, it is itself the most considerate atonement, atonement for the community, atonement for the land, atonement for the criminal. . . ."[36]

The Christian cannot legitimately speak of atonement through a criminal's execution in this post-Calvary era, but he can and should speak of delivering the criminal directly into God's court, thereby placing him under God's sanctions rather than placing the community under God's sanctions for its unwillingness to obey God's law. The community that allows a criminal convicted of a capital crime to live is like a community that offers sanctuary to someone who is supposed to be tried in God's court. The community is required by God to extradite him. It cannot legitimately offer the evil-doer sanctuary. The text of Exodus 21:14 is clear: ". . . thou shalt take him from mine altar, that he may die." If a criminal is not to be granted sanctuary from a human civil court at the very altar of God, then surely a human civil court cannot legitimately grant him sanctuary by refusing to extradite him to God's heavenly court by executing him.

---

36. Hirsch, *Exodus*, p. 306: at Exodus 21:14. Hirsch immediately abandons this rigorous judicial principle in his discussion of kidnapping. The Talmud sets up so many extra stipulations regarding the definition of kidnapping that it is virtually impossible to execute a kidnapper under Jewish law. Hirsch says that the kidnapper is to be executed only "if he has made the man feel that he is being treated as an object, a thing" (p. 306). This sounds more like Immanuel Kant than the God of the Bible. Jewish lawyer and Talmudic scholar George Horowitz comments on the Talmudic view of kidnapping: "That the Rabbis considered the death penalty too severe for this wrong to society and the individual, seems quite plain from the foregoing rules. But they were bound by the express command of Scripture; hence they devised such requirements as made conviction virtually impossible. There is no record, moreover, that a regular court ever convicted a person of Manstealing." Horowitz, *The Spirit of Jewish Law* (New York: Central Book Co., [1953] 1963), pp. 197-98.

Taking a Rebellious Son to Court

At the beginning of this chapter, I raised the question of the parents' willingness to take a rebellious son to court. Would they do this if the death penalty were inescapable upon his conviction? Probably not. The key question then is this: Is the death penalty absolutely required by the pleonasm of execution? The point I have tried to make in this exposition is that *this pleonasm applies only in cases where the State is authorized to initiate the prosecution*, i.e., in cases where there is no earthly victim who can bring charges. This is not the situation in cases involving a rebellious son. Parents can and must bring their son before the civil authorities and complain about his conduct. God requires them to bring him to the civil court. The judges would then enforce a penalty specified by the parents, although they might first recommend an appropriate penalty. The son would obey his parents far more readily in the future, since he would know that the parents could take him back and insist on escalating penalties up to the death penalty if he committed similar infractions again. This fear would reinforce the parents' authority in the home.

What if they refuse to bring a formal charge against their rebellious son? Then they have implicitly subsidized evil behavior. They have implicitly *sanctioned* it. They know that they are risking the possibility that he will become an incorrigible adult. If he does, they will lose him anyway. Better to bring him before the civil court early. Better to obey God. Better to avoid God's sanctions against the family for the parents' refusal to obey. The son may learn fear of the civil court even though he has no fear of the family court.

If they bring him several times, the court will undoubtedly recommend increased sanctions. He has been identified as an incorrigible youth. The day that he commits a crime against someone outside his family, the court will be able to demonstrate to the victim that leniency is no solution, that this man is a habitual criminal. Thus, by allowing parents to insist on the death penalty, but by also allowing them to be lenient, God encourages parents to identify rebellious sons before the latter become incorrigible criminals. The court can take steps to enforce parentally recommended sanctions before it is too late.

This law, Rushdoony perceptively argues, is a law against the development of a professional criminal class. "But the godly exercise of capital punishment cleanses the land of evil and protects the righteous. In calling for the death of incorrigible juvenile delinquents, which means, therefore, in terms of case law, the death of incorrigible adult delinquents; the law declares, 'so shalt thou put evil away from among you; and all Israel shall hear and fear' (Deut. 21:21)."[37]

What is true of this case law is true of all the other capital cases in which this pleonasm occurs and in which the victim is the specified agent who brings the covenant lawsuit. The victim has the option of specifying the penalty. If the case is one in which the State lawfully prosecutes in God's name, then the pleonasm is binding. Execution is mandatory.

Noah's Covenant and Execution

Dispensational authors H. Wayne House and Thomas D. Ice present a weak case for their speculations regarding the pre-New Covenant legal order as it applied to the nations. They insist that "Nowhere in the nations is capital punishment obligatorily extended beyond the penalty for taking human life. . . ."[38] They assert, though do not prove, that none of the Mosaic law's sanctions ever applied directly or even was intended in principle to apply to the nations, except the capital sanction for murder. This unique sanction is binding on all men always, they argue, so its authority came from Noah to Moses; it in no way went from Moses to the nations.

This is a clever attempt to escape the suggestion that in the New Covenant era, Christians have a responsibility to pressure civil governments to impose specific sanctions against specific crimes on the basis of biblical revelation. Such a view of "Noahic biblical law," if correct, would allow Christians to avoid personal responsibility in civil affairs, since they could not speak authoritatively in the name of the Lord when it comes to specifying civil crimes or penalties. The price of such a theological position regarding biblical law is, predictably, the cultural, political, and judicial irrelevance of Christianity. This is why dispensationalism is in principle culturally retreatist and culturally irrelevant, and why no dispensationalist in over a century and a half has published a book on Christian social ethics during the so-called "Church Age."

---

37. Rushdoony, *Institutes of Biblical Law*, pp. 77-78; cf. p. 188. See below, pp. 410-11.

38. H. Wayne House and Thomas D. Ice, *Dominion Theology: Blessing or Curse?* (Portland, Oregon: Multnomah Press, 1988), p. 90.

House and Ice go on to say that "in Israel this penalty [execution] was exacted for various crimes. . . ."[39] If they mean merely that in Israel, the maximum sanction of execution could be required by the victim in several capital crimes, then they are correct. If they mean that in those cases where the State lawfully prosecuted in God's name as His designated representative, and where the pleonasm "dying, he shall surely die" was attached to the biblical sanction, then they are also correct. If this is all they mean, however, then they have not said anything very significant. They have not shown that God restricted these judicial principles to Old Covenant Israel.

The judicial principle of a *maximum allowable sanction for any given crime* was also in principle God's requirement for the nations. Without this God-imposed judicial restriction, the State can lawfully become all-powerful, messianic, and therefore demonic. There will always be sanctions imposed by civil government. The only question is: Whose law establishes the specified judicial limits of State-imposed sanctions, God's or self-proclaimed autonomous man's?

To answer, as House and Ice do, that it depends upon when and where you live in God's world, is to abandon the concept of universal biblical ethics and therefore also to abandon the principle of universally restricted civil governments. Any attempted distinction between the Old Covenant nations and Mosaic Israel which is based on a theory of differing judicial sanctions for the same civil crimes is misguided. Civil sanctions are always specified by God because *God always wants limits on the State and always wants to see victims protected.* In other words, He always wants judicial limits on the pretensions of autonomous man. God killed nations under the Old Covenant, just as He kills New Covenant nations, because they failed to apply His civil sanctions in history. If this was not the message which Jonah brought to Nineveh, what was?

The principle of victim-imposed sanctions is also God's requirement for all nations in this New Covenant era, now that the death, resurrection, and ascension of Jesus Christ, plus the sending of the Holy Spirit and the creation of the church, have extended *God's now-resurrected law-order* to the nations. The New Covenant is truly new; its Bible-specified laws and sanctions have been *universalized definitively in history* by the earthly ministry of Jesus Christ. The resurrection is behind us. Surely the sanctions of God's law for the nations are no less binding today than before Christ arose from the dead and

---

39. *Idem.*

incorporated His church! Yet House and Ice insist that the Mosaic sanctions are even less binding, for the Mosaic law does not even bind national Israel any longer, and so the law has no visible geographical example and testimony, as it had in the Old Covenant era (Deut 4:5-8).

House and Ice do their dispensational best to create a false dichotomy between the God-required social laws of nations and the Mosaic social laws of Israel. They also try to create a dichotomy between New Covenant social laws and the Mosaic social laws. They want to place all Christians under the penal sanctions of the Noahic covenant (as the Calvinist ethicist John Murray sought to do before them),[40] both in the Old Covenant era and in the New Covenant era.[41]

Noah's Covenant: Low Content

Why this preference by modern conservative theologians for Noah's covenant? Because in Noah's covenant *only one civil infraction*

---

40. Murray wrote: "It is conceivable that the progress of revelation would remove the necessity for the penal sanction [in the case of murder]. This is the case with the death penalty for adultery. And the same holds true for many other penal sanctions of the Mosaic economy. Does the same principle apply to the death penalty for murder?" John Murray, *Principles of Conduct*, p. 118. He goes on to argue that the sanction of execution is still valid because "murder is the capital sin." *Idem.* I find it interesting that dispensationalist antinomians House and Ice should have come to the same judicial conclusion that Calvinist Murray reached. Whether this ought to embarrass House and Ice more than it ought to embarrass Professor Murray's Calvinist disciples is a question I like to ask myself, but do not have the time or energy to answer.

I think Ray Sutton's assessment of Murray's theological motivation is plausible. Murray did not share Scottish Presbyterianism's rigorous view of the sabbath: for example, making illegal all public transportation services on Sunday. In the U.S., however, he was regarded as a rigorous sabbatarian. He did not give examinations on Mondays, since students would be tempted to study on Sunday. The pleonasm is attached to the sabbath laws (Ex. 31:14, 15), which indicates that the Scottish view of the sabbath is an embarrassingly watered-down version of the Old Testament's sabbatarianism. Thus, in order to avoid having to adopt a view of the sabbath like the one I offer in *The Sinai Strategy* — that the locus of sovereignty of sabbath enforcement has been shifted in the New Covenant era, and therefore all of its civil and ecclesiastical sanctions have been removed — Murray preferred to defend the abolition of all capital sanctions in New Testament times, except the one for murder. Thus, he could retain a watered-down version of sabbatarianism, yet not be forced to admit that the O.T. sabbath's sanctions had been uniquely singled out by God for a drastic modification in the New Covenant era. The cost of this theological strategy was very high: his adoption of an essentially dispensational view of biblical law — the House-Ice view of Noah's one-law, one-sanction covenant as God's covenant for the nations.

41. "The Noahic covenant is perpetual. It serves as a basis of God's relationship and the standards imposed upon the nations." House and Ice, *op. cit.*, p. 127.

is specified: murder; and *only one penal sanction*: execution (Gen. 9:5). This absence of judicial specifics allows the civil government to specify as criminal whatever behavior it disapproves of, and also allows it to impose whatever sanctions it wants to, without any mandatory reference to any other biblical law or sanction. This political perspective is basically an application of pre-Darwinian humanism's social contract or social compact theory of the State, pioneered by Thomas Hobbes in *Leviathan* (1651) and developed by John Locke (1690) and Rousseau (1762). This older viewpoint was originally a secularized version of, and reaction against, the Puritans' biblical covenant theory of civil government.[42] It imputes primary sovereignty to the people rather than to God and His revealed law.[43]

What is judiciously not discussed by the defenders of the "Noahic covenant theory of the State" is that *the older social contract theory relied completely on the concept of natural law, and in Locke's case, natural rights.* This epistemologically naive view of civil law has been refuted from two sides: by Darwinism's view of the evolving universe and by Van Til's presuppositional apologetic. Without the doctrine of natural law or some version of natural rights theory to govern their theory of the State, *defenders of the "Noahic covenant" theory have implicitly granted judicially unlimited power to the modern State*, no matter how much they protest against such a development. They may be political conservatives personally; it makes no difference. Their personal political preferences become just that: personal preferences. Their personal political preferences are self-consciously and explicitly unconnected with any biblical-theological system of social ethics and political theory.[44]

Such a view of Noah's low-content covenant grants enormous authority to self-proclaimed autonomous man and his representative, the messianic State. The power-seeking covenant-breaker is as pleased with such a view of the State as the responsibility-freeing Christian pietist is. This is why there is now and always has been *an implicit judicial alliance between antinomian Christians and humanist statists.* Here is an ideal way to silence Christians in all judicial matters ex-

---

42. A. D. Lindsey, *The Modern Democratic State* (New York: Oxford University Press, [1943] 1959), ch. 5.

43. Rousseau's version of the sovereignty of the General Will might best be described as the Cole Porter theory of the State: "Anything Goes."

44. I studied systematic theology under John Murray. In private, he was an anti-New Deal conservative. In public, he was politically mute. Both Wayne House and Tommy Ice are political conservatives. In terms of a developed social and political theory, however, they are equally mute.

cept murder: insist that "The Bible doesn't offer a blueprint for civil law!" With this judicial affirmation, antinomian, responsibility-fleeing Christians sound the retreat, and secular humanists and other covenant-breaking power-seekers sound the attack. The victim is in principle victimized even further by this view of Noah's drastically restricted covenant, and the messianic State is unchained by it. *All this is accomplished in the name of a "higher" view of theistic ethics than the Mosaic law supposedly offered to the Israelites.*

This supposed dichotomy between Noah's covenantal sanctions and Moses' covenantal sanctions, and also between Moses' covenantal sanctions and Jesus' covenantal sanctions, cannot survive a careful examination of the biblical principle of victim's rights, which is also the principle of the judicially limited State. The biblical judicial principle is this: victims of criminal acts possess the God-granted legal right to specify no penalty or any penalty up to the maximum limit allowed by God's Bible-revealed law. Neither the State nor the humanistic sociologist is entitled by God to increase or reduce this victim-specified penalty. But in order to keep the principle of victim's rights from becoming tyrannical, God's law specifies maximum penalties. Men must be restrained by law, including victims. To argue that there ever was, ever is, or ever will be a time when men are not under God's specified judicial sanctions is to argue that they are under sanctions imposed by autonomous man, meaning the self-proclaimed autonomous State. In short, to argue this is inescapably to argue also that God has in history authorized either the tyranny of the unchained State or else the implicit subsidizing of criminal behavior through the State's unwillingness to impose God's specified sanctions. In either case, victims lose. This is what antinomians of all varieties refuse even to discuss, let alone answer biblically.

There will always be sanctions. The relevant questions are: Which sanctions? What laws? Who judges? There will always be *judicial chains*, either attached to Satan (Rev. 20:1-2), his demonic host (II Pet. 2:4; Jude 6), and his covenantal earthly representatives, or else attached to the righteous victims of Satan's covenantal representatives (Acts 12:7; 21:33). The modern antinomian Christian and the modern power-seeking statist want to break God's judicial chain, His revealed law. The result is the victimization of the judicially innocent and the expansion of the messianic State.

Conclusion

All sins are against God and God's law. All sinners are criminals in the hand of a temporarily merciful Victim. God sits on His throne as final Judge and even temporal Judge (e.g., He slew Ananias and Sapphira: Acts 5:5, 10). But to sin against God, men usually must sin against something in the creation.[45] The Bible provides case laws that define those sins against any aspect of the creation which constitute civil, familial, or ecclesiastical infractions. Where a sin does constitute an infraction, *the victim must represent God by becoming a plaintiff against the sinner.* He upholds the integrity of the injured party and also seeks restitution. In some cases, restitution is made only to the victim; in other cases, it must also be made to God through a payment to His church (Lev. 6:1-7).

The Bible provides five remedies for criminal behavior: 1) flogging (up to 40 lashes), 2) the slashing of a woman's hand; 3) economic restitution, which can be large enough to require 4) up to a lifetime of bondage, and 5) execution. The goals of these penalties include: 1) upholding God's interests by enforcing His law (civil worship)[46]; 2) penalizing criminal behavior, sometimes by removing the criminal from this world (vengeance); 3) warning all people of the eternal judgment to come (evangelism); 4) protecting civil order (deterrence); and 5) protecting the interests of victims (justice). Ultimately, all of these goals can be summarized in one phrase: *upholding God's covenant.*

Notice that there is no mention of imprisonment. Hirsch wrote a century and a half ago: "Punishments of imprisonment, with all the attendant despair and moral degradation that dwell behind prison bars, with all the worry and distress that it entails for wife and child, are unknown in Torah jurisprudence. Where its power holds sway, prison for criminals does not exist. It only knows of remand custody, and even this, according to the whole prescribed legal procedure, and especially through the absolute rejection of all circumstantial evidence, can only be of the shortest duration."[47]

The law upholds the victim's interests. The criminal is to make restitution to his victim. The victim has the right to extend mercy,

---

45. An exception could be mental sins, yet in a sense even these are sins against the creation: a misuse of man's gift of reason.

46. If civil magistrates are ministers, as Paul says they are (Rom. 13:4), then there is an element of worship in their enforcement of God's law. Sanctions are imposed in God's name.

47. Hirsch, *Exodus*, p. 294: at Exodus 21:6.

but that is his decision, not the judge's. Judges are to serve as agents of the victim, who is God's primary earthly representative in criminal affairs. The primary goal of criminal justice theory should be to discover and enforce civil penalties that uphold victim's rights within the guidelines established by Scripture.

When the victim refuses to prosecute, the other covenantal courts are required by God to honor this decision. The criminal is not to be prosecuted by any covenantal court without the co-operation of the victim. When the State is the victim, or when a victim cannot be identified (e.g., a speeding violation), the judges are allowed to impose penalties up to the limit of God's Bible-revealed civil law, or when a penalty is not specified by the Bible, up to the limit of the written statute.[48] They can also impose reduced penalties, except where the pleonasm occurs. Where the pleonasm occurs, and where the State is not itself the victim, the judges must act as God's agents and impose the penalty that the pleonasm requires. This is the judicial function of the pleonasm of execution: *a restriction on leniency by civil judges when punishing "victimless crimes."* The judges must execute the convicted criminal without mercy. God requires him to be delivered speedily into His court.

Those who reject my thesis regarding the pleonasm must solve some very difficult problems. First, on what legal basis other than victim's rights did Joseph, said by the text to be a just man, fail to prosecute Mary either in a priestly court or a civil court? Had the law's sanction been changed by God before the birth of Jesus Christ? What is the evidence for such a view of the law's sanctions? Second, on what legal basis other than victim's rights did Jesus announce the temporal forgiveness of those who had crucified Him? Third, on what legal basis other than victim's rights had God refused to execute Israel for her adulteries? Put differently, what was the judicial basis of the Book of Hosea? Fourth, on what legal basis other than victim's rights did God divorce Israel when He transferred His kingdom to the church (Matt. 21:43), yet also allow her to survive another generation after the crucifixion of Jesus Christ and the

---

48. The Bible does not specify the amount of a proper fine for a speeding violation. It lays down the general principle of protecting potential victims. The civil authorities must then decide what the fine should be by balancing the risks to people as pedestrians vs. the benefits to people as drivers. Fines should vary according to speed and also according to geographical safety considerations such as school zones. See Chapter 11: "Criminal Law and Restoration," under the subhead, "Fines Should Compensate Victims," pp. 395-96.

incorporation of the church by the Holy Spirit? Not until critics provide consistent, well-developed, Bible-supported answers to these and related judicial questions should they abandon the principle of victim's rights.

Addendum: Cases to Which the Pleonasm Is Attached

I have put in bold face those case laws in which the State in Old Testament Israel was required to initiate the prosecution, and therefore those cases in which the convicted criminal had to be put to death.

He that smiteth a man, so that he die, shall be surely put to death (Ex. 21:12).

And he that smiteth his father, or his mother, shall be surely put to death (Ex. 21:15).

And he that stealeth a man, and selleth him, or if he be found in his hand, he shall surely be put to death (Ex. 21:16).

And he that curseth his father, or his mother, shall surely be put to death (Ex. 21:17).

Whosoever lieth with a beast shall surely be put to death (Ex. 22:19).

Ye shall keep the sabbath therefore; for it is holy unto you: every one that defileth it shall surely be put to death: for whosoever doeth any work therein, that soul shall be cut off from among his people (Ex. 31:14).

Six days may work be done; but in the seventh is the sabbath of rest, holy to the Lord: whosoever doeth any work in the sabbath day, he shall surely be put to death (Ex. 31:15).

Again, thou shalt say to the children of Israel, Whosoever he be of the children of Israel, or of the strangers that sojourn in Israel, that giveth any of his seed unto Molech; he shall surely be put to death: the people of the land shall stone him with stones (Lev. 20:2).

For every one that curseth his father or his mother shall be surely put to death: he hath cursed his father or his mother; his blood shall be upon him (Lev. 20:9).

And the man that committeth adultery with another man's wife, even he that committeth adultery with his neighbour's wife, the adulterer and the adulteress shall surely be put to death (Lev. 20:10).

And the man that lieth with his father's wife hath uncovered his father's nakedness: both of them shall surely be put to death; their blood shall be upon them (Lev. 20:11).

And if a man lie with his daughter in law, both of them shall surely be put to death: they have wrought confusion; their blood shall be upon them (Lev. 20:12).

If a man also lie with mankind, as he lieth with a woman, both of them have committed an abomination: they shall surely be put to death; their blood shall be upon them (Lev. 20:13).

And if a man lie with a beast, he shall surely be put to death: and ye shall slay the beast (Lev. 20:15).

And if a woman approach unto any beast, and lie down thereto, thou shalt kill the woman, and the beast: they shall surely be put to death; their blood shall be upon them (Lev. 20:16).

A man also or woman that hath a familiar spirit, or that is a wizard, shall surely be put to death: they shall stone them with stones: their blood shall be upon them (Lev. 20:27).

And he that blasphemeth the name of the LORD, he shall surely be put to death, and all the congregation shall certainly stone him: as well the stranger, as he that is born in the land, when he blasphemeth the name of the LORD, shall be put to death (Lev. 24:16).

And he that killeth any man shall surely be put to death (Lev. 24:17).

I the LORD have said, I will surely do it unto all this evil congregation, that are gathered together against me: in this wilderness they shall be consumed, and there they shall die (Num. 14:35).

For the LORD had said of them, They shall surely die in the wilderness. And there was not left a man of them, save Caleb the son of Jephunneh, and Joshua the son of Nun (Num. 26:65).

And if he smite him with an instrument of iron, so that he die, he is a murderer: the murderer shall surely be put to death. And if he smite him with throwing a stone, wherewith he may die, and he die, he is a murderer: the murderer shall surely be put to death. Or if he smite him with an hand weapon of wood, wherewith he may die, and he die, he is a murderer: the murderer shall surely be put to death (Num. 35:16-18).

But if he thrust him of hatred, or hurl at him by laying of wait, that he die; Or in enmity smite him with his hand, that he die: he that smote him shall surely be put to death; for he is a murderer: the revenger of blood shall slay the murderer, when he meeteth him (Num. 35:20-21).

Moreover ye shall take no satisfaction for the life of a murderer, which is guilty of death: but he shall be surely put to death (Num. 35:31).

No instances of the pleonasm appear in the Book of Deuteronomy. I do not think that this has any biblical-theological significance. The biblical hermeneutical principle of the continuity of a God-revealed law is that unless a law or its sanction is repealed by a subsequent biblical revelation, it is still judicially binding. The pleonasms did not have to be repeated in Deuteronomy in order for them to be binding in the land. God's laws in Exodus, Leviticus, and Numbers were not exclusively "wilderness laws," with the laws of Deuteronomy alone to serve as the law of Israel in the land. In any case, the severity of God's sanctions tends to increase over time as men's maturity increases. This is a basic principle of biblical jurisprudence: *men's knowledge of God increases over time, and so does their personal and corporate responsibility.* "The lord of that servant will come in a day when he looketh not for him, and at an hour when he is not aware, and will cut him in sunder, and will appoint him his portion with the unbelievers. And that servant, which knew his lord's will, and prepared not himself, neither did according to his will, shall be beaten with many stripes. But he that knew not, and did commit things worthy of stripes, shall be beaten with few stripes. For unto whomsoever much is given, of him shall be much required: and to whom men have committed much, of him they will ask the more" (Luke 12:46-48). Because they were required by God to exercise greater responsibility in the Promised Land, as testified to by the ending of the miraculous agricultural subsidy of the manna (Josh. 5:12), the law's civil sanctions did not decrease in rigor; if anything, they increased. The pleonasm was still judicially binding in Canaan. The equivalent phrase in Deuteronomy is, "so shalt thou put [purge] evil away from among you" (Deut. 17:7; 19:19; 21:21; 22:21; 24; 24:7).

8

KIDNAPPING

And he that stealeth a man, and selleth him, or if he be found in his hand, he shall surely be put to death (Ex. 21:16).

In Chapter 7, I set forth my thesis that the pleonasm, "he shall surely be put to death," is binding on the civil authorities when the State initiates the prosecution of the covenant lawsuit, but it does not bind the victim when he initiates the prosecution. We must examine the implications of this principle in the case of kidnapping, a crime that is bound by the terms of the pleonasm.

Before getting to this problem, however, we must search for the theocentric principle that governs the crime of kidnapping. James Jordan quite properly lists kidnapping under the general heading of *violence*. The nature of violence biblically is that it represents an attempted assault on God, an attempt to murder God by murdering His image.[1] He lists other aspects of violence: the desire of sinful men to play god, the desire to achieve autonomous vengeance, and sado-masochism.[2] Violence should be understood as a sinner's rebellious attempt to achieve dominion by power.[3] It is a form of *revolution*. The preaching of the gospel is intended to reduce violence.

Ultimately, this crime and its civil penalty should be understood in terms of the assumption of a *theocentric* universe. Jordan's assessment is valid: "The death penalty is appropriate because kidnapping is an assault on the very person of the image of God, and as such is a radical manifestation of man's desire to murder God. Like rape, it is a deep violation of personhood and manifests a deep-rooted contempt for God and his image."[4]

---

1. James B. Jordan, *The Law of the Covenant: An Exposition of Exodus 21-23* (Tyler, Texas: Institute for Christian Economics, 1984), p. 93.
2. *Ibid.*, pp. 93-96.
3. *Ibid.*, p. 95.
4. *Ibid.*, p. 104.

Nevertheless, the crime of kidnapping goes beyond the question of the image of God in man. Kidnapping is more than an assault against God's image in man. It is not simply man's blood that is inviolate (Gen. 9:6); it is also his life's *calling*. It is not simply his image that commands respect from other men; it is also his *God-ordained assignment in life*. Perhaps it would be better to argue that man's imaging also includes the calling. God is revealed in Genesis 1 as a God who works and who judges. Man images this God. Kidnapping is therefore an assault on both of these aspects of man's imaging.

Who is the true owner of the kidnapper's victim? God is. God owns the whole world (Ps. 50:10). Nevertheless, stealing a privately owned animal is not a capital crime (Ex. 22:1). Why the special case of a man? The answer is found in man's special position: subordinate under God and possessing authority over the creation. Man is made in God's image (Gen. 1:27; 9:6). By interfering with a man's God-given calling before God, the kidnapper disrupts God's revealed administrative structure for subduing the earth. Each man must work out his salvation—or, presumably, work out his damnation—with fear and trembling (Phil. 2:12). The kidnapper asserts his presumed autonomy and illegitimate authority over the victim, as if he were God, as if he possessed a lawful right to determine what another man's responsibilities on earth ought to be.

The Death Penalty

The Bible recognizes that there are two potential criminals involved in kidnapping: the actual kidnapper and the person to whom he sells the victim. The international slave trade did exist. (White slavery—kidnapping of white girls who are then sold into the Middle East or other foreign areas—still appears to exist.) The passage deals with both types of criminal: "And he that stealeth a man, and selleth him, or if he be found in his hand, he shall surely be put to death." Both the kidnapper and the recipient of the stolen victim are subject to the death penalty.[5]

The obvious problem with a universally mandatory death penalty is that a crime whose effects are less permanent than murder bears the same permanent penalty that murder does. Consider the case of kidnapping. The kidnapper has a strong incentive to kill the victim if he thinks that the authorities are closing in on him. The victim may

---

5. Dale Patrick, *Old Testament Law* (Atlanta, Georgia: John Knox Press, 1985), p. 74.

later identify him as the kidnapper; better to kill the source of the incriminating evidence. After all, the penalty for murder is the same as
the penalty for kidnapping. A person can only be killed once by the
civil government. Jordan recognizes this problem.[6] So do humanist
legal theorists.

Then why does the Bible specify the death penalty for kidnapping? Isn't this dangerous for the victim? Other ancient Near Eastern law codes — if we can accurately call them codes[7] — did not impose such a harsh penalty. The code of Hammurabi specified the
death penalty for kidnapping only when an aristocrat kidnapped the
young son of another aristocrat.[8] What lies behind the rigorous biblical penalty?

The Bible does not limit the death penalty to cases involving
physical harm to the victim. The person who is kidnapped in order
to be sold as a slave is not said to have been harmed. If anything, the
kidnapper who intends to sell the victim into servitude has an economic incentive not to harm the victim, since an injury would
presumably reduce the market value of "the property." Yet the kidnapper potentially faces the most fearful penalty that society can inflict. Why such a concern for this crime?

Sacrilege

To steal from God involves sacrilege. Rushdoony has made an
interesting study on the meaning and implications of sacrilege, and
his general comments apply in the case of kidnapping. "*Theft* is basic
to the word, and sacrilege is theft directed against God. It is apparent from this that the idea of sacrilege is present throughout Scripture. . . . The concept of sacrilege rests on God's sovereignty and
the fact that He has an absolute ownership over all things: men and
the universe are God's property. The covenant people are *doubly*

---

6. James B. Jordan, *The Death Penalty in the Mosaic Law* (Tyler, Texas: Biblical
Horizons, 1988), p. 17.

7. Shalom Paul cites the 1963 warning of his teacher, E. A. Speiser, regarding the
famous Code of Hammurabi: "The handful of jurists . . . seem agreed that what we
have before us is not properly a code or a digest but 'a series of amendments to the
common law of Babylon' (Driver and Miles, *Babylonian Laws* I, p. 41)." Shalom Paul,
Studies in the Book of the Covenant in the Light of Cuneiform and Biblical Law (Leiden: E. J.
Brill, 1970), p. 3n. But Yehezkel Kaufman insists that Deuteronomy "is unquestionably intended to be a law code in the ancient Near Eastern sense." *The Religion of
Israel* (University of Chicago Press, 1960), p. 46.

8. Hammurabi Code, paragraph 14: *Ancient Near Eastern Texts Relating to the Old
Testament*, edited by James B. Pritchard (3rd ed.; Princeton, New Jersey: Princeton
University Press, 1969), p. 166.

God's property: *first*, by virtue of His creation, and, *second*, by virtue of His redemption. For this reason, sin is more than personal and more than man-centered. It is a theological offense."[9] So serious is the crime of sacrilege that it is compared by Paul to adultery and idolatry (Rom. 2:22), both of which were capital crimes in the Old Testament.[10] (The code of Hammurabi specified the death penalty for those who stole the property of either church or State, and also for those who received the stolen goods.)[11]

Because sacrilege is theft, it requires restitution.[12] Since sacrilege is theft against God, it requires restitution to God. In this case, the crime is so great that the maximum restitution is the death of the criminal. No lower payment can suffice if the State prosecutes and convicts in God's name. The implied assertion of autonomy by the criminal, who seeks to play God, represents a form of idolatry, worshipping another God. The kidnapper steals God's property — a person made in His image — and seeks to profit from the asset. This is the essence of the crime of Adam, to be as God (Gen. 3:5).

Future Deterrence

The death penalty is final. Its beneficial effects for society are twofold: it restrains the judgment of God on society, and it provides a deterrence effect — deterring the criminal from future crime (he dies), deterring other criminals from committing similar crimes (fear of death), and deterring God from bringing His covenant judgments on the community for its failure to uphold covenant law (fear of God's wrath). Capital punishment is God's way of telling criminals, whether convicted criminals or potential criminals, that they have gone too far by committing certain crimes. It also warns the community that God's law is to be respected. Obviously, there is no element of rehabilitation for the convicted criminal in the imposition of the death penalty. The State speeds the convicted criminal's march toward final judgment. The State delivers the sinner into the presence

---

9. R. J. Rushdoony, *Law and Society*, vol. II of *Institutes of Biblical Law* (Vallecito, California: Ross House Books, 1982), p. 28.

10. *Ibid.*, p. 31.

11. CH, paragraph 6; *Ancient Near Eastern Texts*, p. 166. There was an exception: if the person stole an ox or a sheep from church or State, he paid thirty-fold restitution; it was ten-fold restitution if the animal had belonged to a private citizen: CH, paragraph 8, *idem*.

12. Rushdoony, *Law and Society*, p. 33.

of the final and perfect Judge.[13]

If we interpret the presence of the pleonasm as making the death penalty mandatory, irrespective of the wishes of the victim, then we create a problem for the victim. *A mandatory death penalty may actually increase the risk to the victim, once the criminal act has taken place.* First, the victim may have seen the criminal. His positive identification of the kidnapper and his testimony against him can convict him. Second, should the criminal begin to suspect that he is about to be caught by the authorities, he may choose to kill the victim and dispose of the body. By disposing of the evidence of the crime, the victim loses his life, while the criminal reduces his risk of being detected. This is a good reason to suppose that the death penalty for kidnapping is a maximum allowable penalty, one which a victim can impose but need not impose on a convicted kidnapper.

What if the kidnapper has stolen more than one adult person? What if one adult victim asks the court to impose the death penalty, but the other victim asks for leniency? Or, if the kidnapper has stolen more than one minor, what if the parent or legal guardian of one asks for the death penalty, but the parent or legal guardian of the other recommends leniency? The victim who demands execution is sovereign. The extension of mercy is not mandatory. The pleonasm of execution is attached to this law. The presence of the pleonasm indicates that capital punishment is the normal sanction. Anything less than execution is abnormal: a unique sign of leniency by the victim. The victim who specifies execution is adhering to God's written law. He is upholding the sanctity of the sanction against sacrilege. His decision is final.

Can the State prosecute if the victim declines? Only if the State is itself a victim. It seems reasonable to allow the State to recover the costs of searching for the victim. The kidnapper has stolen from the State by his criminal act. If the State successfully prosecutes a kidnapper, judges can impose a double restitution penalty payment for the costs incurred. But the judges cannot lawfully impose the capital sanction. They must uphold the principle of victim's rights.

---

13. One reason why the torture of a convicted criminal prior to his execution is immoral is that it symbolically arrogates to the State what God reserves exclusively for Himself: the legal authority to torture people for eternity. It is not that torture is inherently wrong; rather, it is a right that God exercises exclusively. By torturing a person prior to his execution, the State asserts that its punishments are on a par with God's, that the State's penalties are to be feared as much or more than God's judgment is. Humanist theology lies at the base of such punishments.

Confession Before Conviction

There is the possibility that in other circumstances, the threat of the death penalty may reduce the risk to the victim. A criminal in the Bible is allowed to go to the authorities before he has been caught and make a 20 percent restitution payment, plus the capital value of the stolen property or unpaid vow (Lev. 6:1-7). The kidnap victim in the Old Testament presumably would have been sold as a servant. The market price of this sort of servant could have been calculated in the Old Testament.[14] The judges could also have used the Bible's fixed price system for a servant killed by a goring ox: 30 shekels of silver (Ex. 21:32). Or perhaps the prices listed for human vows to the temple could have been used by the judges (Lev. 27:3-7). The Bible always offers opportunities for repentance. By allowing the kidnapper to escape the threat of the death penalty by surrendering to the authorities, biblical law reduces the threat to the kidnap victims in those cases where a kidnapper repents before he is arrested.

Ransom

But what about the modern form of kidnapping, where the kidnapper demands a ransom? The same principle operates: the repenting but as yet unarrested kidnapper offers to the victim the value of the ransom demanded, plus one-fifth. In most cases, this would mean a lifetime of servitude to repay the debt. Servitude for the kidnapper is better for the victim and society than what the modern criminal justice system imposes. The modern criminal justice system would probably impose a life sentence in jail for the criminal, at the expense of taxpayers, with parole possible (likely) in a few years. The kidnap victim gets nothing.

---

14. Writes the early nineteenth-century Jewish commentator S. R. Hirsch: "The value of any human life can not be expressed in pounds, shillings and pence. But atonement-money has to be paid in certain cases. This 'atonement-money' the token value of his own life, in the case of a free man, is estimated at the amount he would fetch if sold in the market as a slave. There is no other way of fixing the amount of human life in terms of hard cash." Samson Raphael Hirsch, *The Pentateuch Translated and Explained*, translated by Isaac Levy, 5 vols., *Exodus* (3rd ed.; London: Honig & Sons, 1967), p. 323; at Exodus 21:32. This ignores another valid means of estimating a kidnapped man's hard-cash value: the ransom payment demanded by the kidnapper (what economists call "reservation value"). Another problem with Hirsch's restricted means of estimating a person's value is that today there is no lawful slave market operating. He must have known that this would complicate things for the judges.

There was a motion picture in 1956 called *Ransom*. The hero of the film is a rich businessman. His son is kidnapped, and the kidnappers demand a huge ransom. The police tell him that kidnap victims wind up dead about half the time, whether a ransom is paid or not. The father decides not to pay. He goes to his bank and gets the money demanded by the kidnappers. He then calls in the local television station, which broadcasts his announcement. In front of him on a desk is the money, in cash. He says to all those listening that if his son is murdered, he intends to pay every cent of the money to anyone who will tell him the name of the person who kidnapped his son. He offers to pay the accomplices to the crime. He reminds the kidnapper of the risk of relying on the reliability of his accomplices. He then points to the money and declares to the kidnapper, "This is as close to this money as you'll ever get." When he returns home, his neighbors are outraged. They throw rocks through his window. He had not shown filial piety. He deserves to be an outcast. But at the end of the movie, his son is returned to him. The kidnapper was fearful of being turned in for the reward.

What the movie's hero did was to place a greater priority on *bringing the criminal to justice* than he placed on public acceptance of his act. (The statistical risk to his son, he had been told, was the same, whether he paid the ransom or not.) By using the ransom money in a unique way—as a reward that would increase the likelihood of someone's becoming an informant—the father increased the odds in favor of his son's survival. (The majority of crimes are probably solved as a result of informants.)[15] He relied on the threat of punishment more than he did on the good will of the criminal in honoring the terms of the transaction, his son's life for a cash payment. He turned to the law for protection, not to the criminal's sense of honor.

In 1973, the grandson of J. Paul Getty, one of the world's richest men, was kidnapped in Italy. The kidnapping received worldwide attention. The kidnappers demanded over a million dollars as the ransom.[16] Getty publicly refused to pay. He said that if he did, this would place his fourteen other grandchildren in jeopardy. By not paying, he said, he was telling all other potential kidnappers that it was useless to kidnap any of his relatives. The kidnappers cut off the youth's ear and sent it to his mother. Still the grandfather refused.

---

15. Edward Powell, "The Coming Crisis in Criminal Investigation," *Journal of Christian Reconstruction*, II (Winter 1975-76), pp. 81-83.

16. The price of gold was then about $100 an ounce.

Privately, he lent $850,000 to the boy's father to pay the ransom — at 4 percent, of course. Getty never missed an opportunity for profit.[17] The gamble paid off: the kidnappers released him.[18] No other Getty relatives became victims.[19]

Equal Penalties or Equal Results?

The Bible does not forbid the victim's family to pay a ransom, but the threat of the death penalty makes the risk of conviction so great that few potential kidnappers would take the risk, except for a very high return. The average citizen therefore receives additional but indirect protection because of this biblical law. The penalty to the convicted kidnapper is so high that the money which the middle-class victim's relatives could raise to pay the ransom probably would not compensate most potential kidnappers for the tremendous risk involved. Presumably, kidnappers will avoid kidnapping poorer people.

In effect, *the threat of the death penalty increases the likelihood that members of very rich families or senior employees of very rich corporations will be the primary victims of kidnappers.* Also, in cases of politically motivated kidnappings, the famous or politically powerful could become the victims. They seem to be discriminated against economically by biblical law: high penalties make it more profitable for kidnappers to single their families out for attack. On the other hand, these people possess greater economic resources, making it more likely that they can more easily afford to protect themselves and their relatives.

From the point of view of economic analysis, the stiff penalty for kidnapping protects society at large, though not always the actual victim of the crime, and it protects the average citizen more than it protects the rich. The law applies to all kidnappers equally; it has varying effects on different people and groups within the society. Be-

---

17. Fellow billionaire industrialist Armand Hammer refers to him as "that tight old weasel." Armand Hammer (with Neil Lyndon), *Hammer* (New York: Putnam's, 1987), p. 386. Hammer did respect him as an entrepreneur, however.

18. The grandson later suffered a stroke as a result of alcohol and drug abuse, and is paralyzed and blind. *Time* (March 17, 1986), p. 80.

19. I have instructed my wife never to pay a ransom for me under any conditions. I have also told her that I will not pay a ransom for her or any of our children. The goal is to reduce the risk of kidnapping before it takes place, not to increase the likelihood of the victim's survival. The evil of kidnapping should not be rewarded. It should be made devastatingly unprofitable. The same should be true for terrorist kidnappings. The policy of the state of Israel regarding terrorist kidnappings is correct: a kidnapper-for-victims exchange before any victim is harmed, but no compromise thereafter.

cause the Bible requires *equality before the law,* it produces *different results.* To equalize the results — equal risk for rich families and poor families — the Bible would have to impose the death penalty only for kidnappers of rich people. (This, as we have seen, is what Hammurabi's Code did: it imposed the death penalty only on those who kidnapped the sons of aristocrats.) The economic payoff would have to be made lower in the case of a kidnapper who steals a poor person. Therefore, in order to put poor families at risk as high as that borne by rich families, the law would have to discriminate between kidnappers of the poor and kidnappers of the rich. But *the kidnapper sins primarily against God,* so the death penalty can be specified by the victim in both cases. God is not a respecter of persons, meaning those convicted of a capital crime. The question is not the economic status of the victims, but the nature of the crime (sacrilege) and the sanctions specified by the victims (victim's rights). Thus, a consistent application of this law in every case of kidnapping increases the risk of being kidnapped for the rich.

Equality

This brings up a very important question relating to the word "equality." When men demand equality, what do they really want? If they demand *equality before the law* — "Equal penalties for identical crimes, irrespective of persons!" — then they are simultaneously demanding *unequal economic results.* This is not true only in the case of the variation of risk for different economic groups when a society demands the death penalty for all kidnappers. This is true of the economy in general. When men demand *equal economic results,* they are simultaneously demanding *inequality before the law.* Hayek's analysis is correct: "From the fact that people are very different it follows that, if we treat them equally, the result must be inequality in their actual position, and that the only way to place them in an equal position would be to treat them differently. Equality before the law and material equality are therefore not only different but are in conflict with each other; and we can achieve either the one or the other, but not both at the same time. The equality before the law which freedom requires leads to material inequality. Our argument will be that, though where the state must use coercion for other reasons, it should treat all people alike, the desire of making people more alike in their condition cannot be accepted in a free society as a justification for further and discriminatory coercion."[20]

---

20. F. A. Hayek, *The Constitution of Liberty* (University of Chicago Press, 1960), p. 87.

Biblical law is clear: *equality before the civil law is the God-sanctioned concept of equality.* Equality of results does not apply to the sanctions that God imposes after a person dies, either positive sanctions or negative sanctions. The principle of *positive sanctions* is specified in I Corinthians 3:11-15: "For other foundation can no man lay than that is laid, which is Jesus Christ. Now if any man build upon this foundation gold, silver, precious stones, wood, hay, stubble; Every man's work shall be made manifest: for the day shall declare it, because it shall be revealed by fire; and the fire shall try every man's work of what sort it is. If any man's work abide which he hath built thereupon, he shall receive a reward. If any man's work shall be burned, he shall suffer loss: but he himself shall be saved; yet so as by fire." The principle of *negative sanctions* is specified in Luke 12:47-48: "And that servant, which knew his lord's will, and prepared not himself, neither did according to his will, shall be beaten with many stripes. But he that knew not, and did commit things worthy of stripes, shall be beaten with few stripes. For unto whomsoever much is given, of him shall be much required: and to whom men have committed much, of him they will ask the more."

Time Perspective

The establishment of the death penalty is necessary to increase risk to the potential kidnapper — risk that is proportional to the magnitude of his proposed crime. By calculating in advance the permanent nature of the penalty (death), the criminal is forced to come to grips with the future. The criminal presumably is present-oriented.[21] Certainly, he ignores the eternal consequences of his acts. He generally lives for the moment. His long-term fate is total destruction on the day of judgment. He discounts this, refusing to act in terms of this knowledge. That day seems too far away chronologically, and God is not visible. "Perhaps God is not going to enforce the promised penalty. Maybe God doesn't even exist," the criminal thinks to himself. Therefore, God sets the civil government's penalty so high that even a present-oriented criminal will feel the restraining pressure of extreme risk, even if his psychological rate of discount is very high.

---

21. Edward C. Banfield, "Present-Orientedness and Crime"; Gerald P. O'Driscoll, "Professor Banfield on Time Horizon: What Has He Taught Us About Crime?" in Randy E. Barnett and John Hegel III (eds.), *Assessing the Criminal: Restitution, Retribution, and the Legal Process* (Cambridge, Massachusetts: Ballinger, 1977).

The severity of the earthly punishment testifies to the severity of the eternal punishment. It serves as an "earnest" or down payment on eternity.

The Bible teaches us that history is linear. History has a beginning and an end. The Bible also teaches us that our thoughts, as well as our deeds, have consequences in history and also in eternity beyond the grave (Matt. 5:28). It tells men to redeem (buy back) their time (Eph. 5:16), to work while there is still light (John 9:4). If God-fearing people must be educated and motivated for them to believe such doctrines, then we have to come to grips with the reality of a world in which members of a criminal class reject all these doctrines. More than this: members of a professional criminal class self-consciously live in terms of *a rival set of attitudes* toward time, personal responsibility, and the consequences of human action.

The possibility of the death penalty for kidnapping forces the potential kidnapper to count the cost of his transgression. Remember, *a person's perception of total cost (including risk) is affected directly by his perception of time.* If men discount the future greatly, as Esau did with respect to his birthright, then they will accept low cash bids for future income.[22] Present-oriented men discount future benefits and future curses alike; the distant future is of very little concern to them. As Harvard political scientist Edward Banfield comments: "At the present-oriented end of the scale, the lower-class individual lives from moment to moment. If he has any awareness of a future, it is of something fixed, fated, beyond his control: things happen *to* him, he does not *make* them happen. Impulse governs his behavior, either because he cannot discipline himself to sacrifice a present for a future satisfaction or because he has no sense of the future. He is therefore radically improvident: whatever he cannot use immediately he considers valueless. His bodily needs (especially for sex) and his taste for 'action' take precedence over everything else — and certainly over any work routine."[23]

A law-order must recognize present-oriented people for what they are. The kidnapper may be somewhat more future-oriented than the lower-class man. He makes plans, counts costs, and takes risks. But he discounts the long-term consequences of his acts. He does not care about the effects on the victim, his family, or the com-

---

22. North, *Dominion Covenant: Genesis*, pp. 126-28, 182-83.
23. Edward Banfield, *The Heavenly City Revisited* (Boston: Little, Brown, 1973), p. 61.

munity. It is this *radical lack of concern for the lives and callings of other men* that makes him a menace to society. To catch his attention, to convince him of the seriousness of his crime, the Bible stipulates the death penalty. Richard Posner, an economist and also a judge for the U.S. Court of Appeals, acknowledges the validity of relationship between a criminal's time perspective and the need for capital punishment, but only in a footnote: "Notice that if criminals' discount rates are very high, capital punishment may be an inescapable method of punishing very serious crimes."[24]

The total discontinuity involved in the execution of the kidnapper favors *continuity in the lives of the innocent*. It is the innocent people of society who deserve continuity, not the kidnappers. The decision to prosecute, or to specify a penalty other than death, is in the hands of the victim or his survivors. The victim is allowed by biblical law to bargain with the kidnapper in order to obtain his freedom. (The kidnapper would have no way to get even with a victim who subsequently changed his mind and called for the death penalty.)

Kidnapping and the Slave Trade

The abolition of slavery has made kidnapping less profitable financially. Before slavery was abolished by law, the slave market offered a profit to kidnappers because *they could capitalize the entire working lifetime of the victim*. There were numerous buyers who were willing to bid against each other for the lifetime output of kidnap victims. Today, only families, major corporations, and civil governments are willing and able to buy back a victim, and very often not primarily because of the victim's earning power.

The slave trade existed for many centuries because of the ready market for its victims. The purchase of slaves by slave-buyers created the market price of the slaves, from ancient Greece until the not-so-ancient 1960's. As recently as 1960, in the words of Britain's Lord Shackleton, African Muslims on pilgrimages sold slaves on arrival, "using them as living traveller's cheques."[25] Slavery was officially outlawed in Saudi Arabia in 1962 and by Oman in 1970.[26] Nevertheless, though African slavery declined sharply in the 1960's, "slave-trading continued to flourish in Mauritania, Mali, Niger, and Chad, along the drought-stricken southern fringe of the Sahara."[27]

---

24. Richard Posner, *Economic Analysis of Law* (Boston: Little, Brown, 1986), p. 212n.
25. Cited by David Brion Davis, *Slavery and Human Progress* (New York: Oxford University Press, 1984), p. 317.
26. *Ibid.*, p. 319.
27. *Idem.*

As recently as 1981, the United Nations Human Rights Commission reported that there were 100,000 slaves in Mauritania. Other estimates place the total number of slaves at 250,000 among the nomadic tribes of the drought-ridden Sahel in North Africa.[28] The slave-owners are Moors (Islamic), while the slaves are blacks from Senegal. There are no open slave markets because the trade is officially illegal. The biggest part of the trade is in children. They belong to the owners of the mothers.[29]

A steady economic demand for slaves created the demand for new victims. The *slave traders*, so hated and despised in the eighteenth and nineteenth centuries by "respectable" English-speaking society, including most slave owners, and equally despised by slave-owning writers in the ancient world,[30] were, from a strictly economic point of view, nothing less than *the paid agents of the buyers*. They were performing specialized work as purchasing agents for slave-buyers. The Arab and native African kidnappers were, to that extent, merely the specialized collection agents of the slave-buyers. They were economic middlemen, entrepreneurs. The entrepreneur necessarily serves the wants of consumers.

In every free market transaction, the potential consumers of any economic good or service are competing with other consumers for control over all scarce economic resources. They compete directly and indirectly for the final output of the economy. The outcome of this competition establishes prices, quality standards, and costs related directly to the production of all economic goods. The middlemen (entrepreneurs) simply serve those consumers whose competing bids are expected to produce the highest profits. *Consumers ultimately determine prices and therefore also costs.*[31] This economic process was no less true of the slave trade. It is one of the peculiar aspects of "the peculiar institution" of American Negro slavery that the "final consumers" refused to recognize their own personal responsibility, as economic actors and political voters, for the operations of the entire slave-delivery system.

---

28. Roger Sawyer, *Slavery in the Twentieth Century* (London: Routledge & Kegan Paul, 1986), p. 14.

29. Bernard D. Nossiter, "U.N. Group Gets Report on Slaves in Mauritania," *New York Times* (Aug. 21, 1981).

30. Thomas Wiedemann, *Greek and Roman Slavery* (Baltimore, Maryland: Johns Hopkins University Press, 1981), pp. 6, 106-7.

31. Murray N. Rothbard, *Man, Economy, and State* (New York: New York University Press, [1962] 1979), pp. 301-8.

What we should recognize here is the relationship between the abolition of compulsory slavery and the reduction of involuntary servitude for citizens in general. By making illegal the *market* for imported slaves, Western nations reduced the demand for imported slaves in the early 1800's. This in turn reduced the risk of being kidnapped for the average African.[32] A policy of State-enforced coercion against slave-buying reduced the profit-seeking private coercive activity of kidnapping Africans thousands of miles away.

This policy worked only because 1) the British navy enforced its regulations against the slave traders, 2) a majority of citizens in the recipient nations were steadily educated to reject the idea of the legitimacy of involuntary servitude, and 3) slavery's defenders were defeated on the battlefield, in the case of the American South in the 1860's. The economic lesson: disregarding the needs and preferences of slave-holders (the final users) by outlawing slavery led to the reduction of the entire slave trade. The profitability of the international slave trade was reduced. We learn that there are cases where State coercion is valid, when that coercion is directed against private coercers. The anti-slave trade legislation recognized the complicity of slave-owners (final users) in the coercive international slave trade. The market for slaves was not a free market, for the supply side of the equation was based on coercion.

Monopoly Returns and Reduced Crime

There is a curious myth that laws against evil acts do not reduce the total number of these acts that criminals commit. Some critics even go so far as to argue that the very presence of the law subsidizes evil, as in the case of laws against the sale of illegal drugs or laws against prostitution. Somehow, passing a law makes the prohibited market more profitable, and therefore the law leads to greater output of the prohibited substances or services. This is a very odd argument when it comes from people who defend the efficiency and productivity of laissez-faire economics.

---

32. This falling demand for imported slaves was offset by an increase in demand for legal, domestically produced slaves. This transformed some plantations into slave-breeding centers, especially in the Virginia tidewater region, where soil-eroding agricultural techniques had reduced the land's output, and therefore had reduced the regional market value of the human tools who produced the output. This region began to export slaves to buyers who cultivated the fresher soils of Louisiana and Mississippi. See Alfred H. Conrad and John R. Meyer, "The Economics of Slavery in the Ante-Bellum South," *Journal of Political Economy*, LXVI (April 1958); reprinted in Robert W. Fogel and Stanley L. Engerman (eds.), *The Reinterpretation of American Economic History* (New York: Harper & Row, 1971), ch. 25.

A fundamental principle of economics is this: the division of labor is limited by the extent of the market. This was articulated by Adam Smith in Chapter 3 of *Wealth of Nations* (1776). Another basic principle is this one: the greater the division of labor, the greater the output per unit of resource input — in short, the greater the efficiency of the market. When the market increases in size, it makes possible an increase in cost-effective production. Advertising and mass-production techniques lower the cost of production and therefore increase the total quantity of goods and services demanded. This is well understood by all economists.

Nevertheless, there are some people who still believe that laws against so-called "victimless crimes" — sins that they do not regard as major transgressions, I suspect — actually increase the profitability of crime. On the contrary, such laws increase the risk of the prohibited activities, both to sellers and consumers. Prices rise; the market shrinks; per unit costs rise; efficiency drops. What such laws do is create monopoly returns for a few criminals. But the critics of such laws conveniently forget that *monopoly returns are always the product of reduced output*. This, in fact, is the conventional definition of a monopoly. Thus, civil laws do reduce the extent of the specified criminal behavior.[33] They confine such behavior to certain criminal subclasses within the society. Biblically speaking, such laws place *boundaries* around such behavior.

There is no doubt that nineteenth-century laws against the slave trade drastically reduced the profitability of the international slave trade. These laws increased the risks for slavers, reduced their profits, and narrowed their markets. The result was a drop in output (slavery) per unit of resource input.

Household Evangelism

Apart from the one exception provided by the jubilee law, the Old Testament recognized the legitimacy of involuntary slavery of foreigners only when the slaves were female captives taken after a battle (Deut. 20:10-11, 14). To fight a war for the *purpose* of taking slaves would have been illegitimate, for this was (and is) the foreign policy of empires. It is true that the jubilee law did allow both the importation of pagan slaves and the purchase of children from resi-

---

33. Cf. James M. Buchanan, "A Defense of Organized Crime?" in Ralph Andreano and John J. Siegfried (eds.), *The Economics of Crime* (New York: Wiley, 1980), pp. 395-409.

dent aliens, but the purpose of this practice was primarily covenantal: bringing slaves of demon-possessed cultures into servitude
under Hebrew families that were in turn under God.

Once the New Testament gospel became an international phenomenon that spread outward from local churches rather than from
a central sanctuary in Jerusalem, there was no longer any need to
bring potential converts into the land through purchase. Jesus completely fulfilled the terms of the jubilee law, including the kingdom-
oriented goals of the imported slave law. He transferred the kingdom
from the land of Israel to the church international: "Therefore say I
unto you, The kingdom of God shall be taken from you, and given
to a nation bringing forth the fruits thereof" (Matt. 21:43).[34] He
abolished the jubilee's land tenure laws, as well as the slave-holding
laws associated with the land of Israel as the exclusive place of temple sacrifice and worship.

Adoption

Nevertheless, in principle there remains a modern Christian practice that resembles the Old Testament jubilee slave law. It is the practice of adoption. Christians pay lawyers to arrange for the adoption of
infants whose pagan parents do not want them. This is true household
adoption rather than permanent slavery, but biblical law requires
children to support parents in their old age, so the arrangement is not
purely altruistic. The practice of adoption is governed by civil law in
order to reduce the creation of a market for profit,[35] therefore discouraging the kidnapping of infants, but the economics of modern adoption are similar to the Old Testament practice of buying children from
resident aliens. Adoption is a very good practice. Children are bought
out of slavery inside covenant-breaking households.

Rushdoony refers to kidnapping as "stealing freedom."[36] He

---

34. Gary North, *Healer of the Nations: Biblical Blueprints for International Relations* (Ft.
Worth, Texas: Dominion Press, 1987), Introduction.

35. Actually, the adoption laws have created a profitable market for babies, but
only state-licensed lawyers and adoption agencies are legally allowed to reap these
profits. This is a legitimate licensing arrangement, similar in intent and economic
effect as the licensing of physicians: to control a potentially coercive market phenomenon. Physicians control access to addictive drugs, and lawyers and adoption agencies
control access to babies offered for adoption. This reduces the threat of kidnapped
babies. By centralizing access to the flow of babies offered for adoption, the civil
government can more successfully impose restrictions on the market for babies by
guaranteeing that parents make the decision to supply this market, not kidnappers.

36. Rushdoony, *The Institutes of Biblical Law* (Nutley, New Jersey: Craig Press,
1973), p. 484.

comments: "The purpose of man's existence is that man should exercise dominion over the earth in terms of God's calling. This duty involves the restoration of a broken order by means of restitution. To kidnap a man and enslave him is to rob him of his freedom. A believer is not to be a slave (I Cor. 7:23; Gal. 5:1). Some men are slaves by nature; slavery was voluntary, and a dissatisfied slave could leave, and he could not be compelled to return, and other men were forbidden to deliver him to his master (Deut. 23:15, 16). . . . The purpose of freedom is that man exercise dominion and subdue the earth under God. A man who abuses this freedom to steal[37] can be sold into slavery in order to work out his restitution (Ex. 22:3); if he cannot use his freedom for its true purpose, godly dominion, reconstruction, and restoration, he must then work towards restitution in his bondage."[38]

Conclusion

Kidnapping is a crime against God, man, and the social order. It steals men's freedom. It asserts the autonomy of the kidnapper over the victim. It substitutes the kidnapper's profit for the calling God gives to each man. It attacks God through His image, man. The kidnapper is therefore subject to the death penalty, at the discretion of his victim.

The potential imposition of the death penalty produces unequal risks for different economic classes. The rich are more likely to be victims in a non-slave society, where the quest for a ransom payment is the primary motivation for the kidnapper. *Equality before the law* is the fundamental principle of biblical law enforcement; *inequality of economic results* is therefore inescapable. By imposing a single penalty, death, the law increases the percentage of rich kidnap victims.

The legislated abolition of slavery reduces the market demand for stolen men, thereby reducing the profit accruing to kidnappers, and increasing the safety from kidnapping for the average citizen. To be effective, however, the majority of potential slave-owners must agree with the abolition, or else be fearful of violating the law. A profit-seeking black market in slaves would thwart the economic effects of this law, namely, reduced demand for slaves. The high

---

37. Rushdoony obviously does not mean "freedom to steal"; he means a person who "abuses his freedom by stealing," or "in order to steal." The use of the infinitive, "to steal," could lead to confusion.

38. *Ibid.*, p. 485.

penalty imposed on both kidnapper and buyer, if coupled with the moral education of potential buyers of slaves (the final users), reduces the size and therefore the efficiency of the slave market. (Remember Adam Smith's observation: the division of labor is limited by the extent of the market.)[39]

Finally, the death penalty overcomes the short-run, present-oriented time perspective of the potential kidnappers. The magnitude of the punishment calls attention to the magnitude of the crime. A death penalty forces the criminal to contemplate the possible results of his actions.

As with all other crimes except murder, the victim has the final authority to specify the appropriate penalty, up to the biblically specified limit of the law. Rushdoony does not consider the concept of victim's rights in his *Institutes*. He writes that "the death penalty is mandatory for kidnapping. No discretion is allowed the court. To rob a man of his freedom requires death."[40] I would agree with this statement if it were qualified as follows: "The death penalty is mandatory for kidnapping. No discretion is allowed the court, once the victim has specified the death of the kidnapper as his preferred penalty." To deny the victim the legal right to specify the appropriate sanction is to deny the concept of victim's rights.

39. Smith, *The Wealth of Nations* (1776), ch. 3.
40. Rushdoony, *Institutes*, p. 486.

9

THE COSTS OF PRIVATE CONFLICT

And if men strive together, and one smite another with a stone, or with his fist, and he die not, but keepeth his bed: If he rise again, and walk abroad upon his staff, then shall he that smote him be quit: only he shall pay for the loss of his time, and shall cause him to be thoroughly healed (Ex. 21:18-19).

The theocentric principle here is that man is God's image, and that for anyone to strike another person unlawfully or autonomously is an attempt to commit violence against God. It is man as God's representative that places him under the covenantal protection of civil government. The State is required by God to protect men from the physical violence of other men.

One of the primary earthly goals of any godly society is the elimination of conflict among its citizens. The establishment of a reign of peace is one of the most prominent promises in the Old Testament's prophetic messages. Peace is therefore a sign of God's blessing and also a means of attaining other blessings, such as economic growth. Men who strive together in private battle testify to their own lack of self-discipline, and a godly legal order must provide sanctions against such disturbances of public order.

The Bible reminds men that they are responsible before God and society for their private actions. Specific costs are imposed by biblical law on the victor in any physical conflict. The eventual loser is to be protected and so is his family, whose rights he cannot waive simply by stepping into the arena. The loser is to be compensated for his loss of time while in bed and also for his medical expenses. In short, the victor must make *restitution* to the loser. The mere possession of superior strength or combat skills is not to be an advantage in the resolution of personal disputes.

We see a similar perspective in the Hittite laws: "If anyone batters a man so that he falls ill, he shall take care of him. He shall give a man in his stead who can look after his house until he recovers. When he recovers, he shall give him 6 shekels of silver, and he shall also pay the physician's fee. If anyone breaks a free man's hand or foot, he shall give him 20 shekels of silver and pledge his estate as security. If anyone breaks the hand or foot of a male or a female slave, he shall give 10 shekels of silver and pledge his estate as security."[1] Men must pay the costs of restoring the injured party to physical wholeness.

Winners and Losers

These economic restraints on victors remind men of the costs of injuring others. There are economic costs borne by the physical confrontation's loser. There are also costs borne by society at large. A man in a sickbed can no longer exercise his calling before God. He cannot labor efficiently, and the products of his labor are not brought to the marketplace. If he is employed by another person, the employer's operation is disrupted. By forcing the physical victor to pay for both the medical costs and the alternative costs (forfeited productivity on the part of the loser), biblical law helps to reduce conflict. The physical victor becomes an economic loser. The law also insures society against having to bear the medical costs involved. The immediate family, charitable institutions, or publicly financed medical facilities do not bear the costs.

The Mishnah, which was the legal code for Judaism until the late nineteenth century, establishes five different types of compensation. First, compensation for the injury itself, meaning damages for permanent injury that results from the occurrence. Second, compensation for the injured person's pain and suffering. Third, compensation for the injured person's medical expenses. Fourth, compensation for the injured person's loss of earnings (time). Fifth, compensation for the embarrassment or indignity suffered by the victim.[2] Not all five will be found in each case, of course.[3]

---

1. "The Hittite Laws," paragraphs 10-12, in *Ancient Near Eastern Texts Relating to the Old Testament*, edited by James B. Pritchard (3rd ed.; Princeton, New Jersey: Princeton University Press, 1969), p. 189. Paragraphs 13-16 continue the restitution theme: monetary penalties for biting off noses and ears of free men or slaves.

2. *Baba Kamma* 8:1, *The Mishnah*, edited by Herbert Danby (New York: Oxford University Press, [1933] 1987), p. 342.

3. Emanuel B. Quint, *Jewish Jurisprudence: Its Sources and Modern Applications*, 2 vols. (New York: Harwood Academic Publishers, 1980), I, p. 126. Maimonides wrote: "If one wounds another, he must pay compensation to him for five effects of the injury, namely, damages, pain, medical treatment, enforced idleness, and hu-

The judicially significant point is that the person who wins the conflict physically becomes the loser economically. The one who is still walking around after the fight must finance the physical recovery of the one who is in bed. The focus of judicial concern is on the victim who suffers the greatest physical injury. Biblical law and Jewish law impose economic penalties on the injury-inflicting victors of such private conflicts. As Maimonides put it, "The Sages have penalized strong-armed fools by ruling that the injured person should be held trustworthy. . . ."[4]

Games of Bloodshed

The murderous "games" of ancient Rome, where gladiators slew each other in front of cheering crowds, violated biblical law. The same is true of "sports" like boxing, where the inflicting of injuries is basic to victory. The lure of bloody games is decidedly pagan. Augustine, in his *Confessions*, speaks of a former student of his, Alypius. The young man had been deeply fond of the Circensian games of Carthage. Augustine had persuaded him of their evil, and the young man stopped attending. Later on, however, in Rome, Alypius met some fellow students who dragged him in a friendly way to the Roman amphitheater on the day of the bloody games. He swore to himself that he would not even look, but he did, briefly, and was trapped. "As he saw that blood, he drank in savageness at the same time. He did not turn away, but fixed his sight on it, and drank in madness without knowing it. He took delight in that evil struggle, and he became drunk on blood and pleasure. He was no longer the man who entered there, but only one of the crowd that he had joined, and a true comrade of those who brought him there. What more shall I say? He looked, he shouted, he took fire, he bore away with himself a madness that should arouse him to return, not only with those who had drawn him there, but even before them, and dragging others along as well."[5] Only later was his faith in Christ able to break his addiction to the games.

---

miliation. These five effects are all payable from the injurer's best property, as is the law for all who do wrongful damage." Moses Maimonides, *The Book of Torts*, vol. 11 of *The Code of Maimonides*, 14 vols. (New Haven, Connecticut: Yale University Press, 1954), "Laws Concerning Wounding and Damaging," Chapter One, Section One, p. 160. Maimonides made one strange exception: if a person deliberately frightens someone, but does not touch him, he bears no legal liability, only moral liability. Even if he shouts in a person's ear and deafens him, there is no legal liability. Only if he touches the person is there legal liability: *ibid.*, Chapter Two, Section Seven, pp. 165-66.

4. *Torts*, Chapter Five, Section Four, p. 177.

5. *The Confessions of St. Augustine*, trans. by John K. Ryan (Garden City, New York: Image Books, 1960), Book 6, ch. 8.

In the city of Trier (Treves) in what is today Germany, alien hordes burned the town in the early fifth century, murdering people and leaving their bodies in piles. Salvian (the Presbyter) records what took place immediately thereafter: "A few nobles who survived destruction demanded circuses from the emperors as the greatest relief for the destroyed city."[6] They wanted the immediate reconstruction of the arena, not the town's walls, so powerful was the hold of the bloody games on the minds of Roman citizens.

Chaos Festivals

Roger Caillois, in his book, *Man and the Sacred* (1959), argues that the chaos festivals of the ancient and primitive worlds served as outlets for hostilities. These festivals are unfamiliar to most modern citizens, or in the case of the familiar ones, such as Mardi Gras in New Orleans, carnival in the Caribbean, or New Year's Eve parties in many nations, they are not recognized for what they are. He writes: "It is a time of excess. Reserves accumulated over the course of several years are squandered. The holiest laws are violated, those that seem at the very basis of social life. Yesterday's crime is now prescribed, and in place of customary rules, new taboos and disciplines are established, the purpose of which is not to avoid or soothe intense emotions, but rather to excite and bring them to climax. Movement increases, and the participants become intoxicated. Civil or administrative authorities see their powers temporarily diminish or disappear. This is not so much to the advantage of the regular sacerdotal caste as to the gain of secret confraternities or representatives of the other world, masked actors personifying the Gods or the dead. This fervor is also the time for sacrifices, even the time for the sacred, a time outside of time that recreates, purifies, and rejuvenates society. . . . All excesses are permitted, for society expects to be regenerated as a result of excesses, waste, orgies, and violence."[7]

It was these festivals, he argues, that in some way drained off the violent emotions inherent in men. (On the contrary, such festivals

---

6. Salvian, *The Governance of God*, in *The Writings of Salvian, the Presbyter*, Jeremiah F. O'Sullivan, trans. (New York: Cima Publishing Co., 1947), Bk. VI, Sect. 15, p. 178. Salvian was a contemporary of St. Augustine, in the fifth century. This was probably written around A.D. 440.

7. Roger Caillois, *Man and the Sacred* (Glencoe, Illinois: The Free Press, 1959), p. 164.

stimulated violent emotions.)[8] The festivals, he argues, were therefore basic to the preservation of social peace. Without these ritual celebrations of lawlessness, he argues, there will be an increase of actual wars. In other words, men innately require the tension and release of violence. Prohibit the socially circumscribed ritual chaos of Mardi Gras, carnival, and New Year, and we therefore supposedly risk the outbreak of war. Because modern man has suppressed such ritual chaos, he concludes, we have seen the increase of wars and their intensity and devastation.[9]

In contrast to Caillois' analysis stands the Bible. Leaders in a godly social order should strive to eliminate such chaos festivals and "circumscribed violence." The laws requiring restitution for anyone injured in a brawl are related to the general prohibition against individual violence. Lawlessness is to be suppressed. Man is not told to give vent to his feelings of violence; he is told to overcome them through self-discipline under God. Wars and violence come from the lusts of men (Jas. 4:1). These bloody lusts are to be overcome, not ritually sanctioned. The celebration of communion is God's sanctioned bloody ritual which gives men symbolic blood, but the Bible forbids the drinking of actual blood (Lev. 3:17; Deut. 12:16, 23; Acts 15:20).

Biblical Law Confronts the "Honorable Duel"

The Bible informs us that the civil government is to protect human life. Each man is made in God's image, and men, acting as private citizens, do not have the right to attempt to attack God indirectly by attacking His image in other men. Men are not sovereign over their own lives or over the lives of others; God is (Rev. 1:18). God delegates the right of execution to the civil government, not to individual men acting outside a lawful institution in the pursuit of lawful objectives.

The private duel is just such a threat to human life and safety. Fighting is a threat to social peace. It is disorderly, willful, vengeful, and hypothetically autonomous. It poses a threat to innocent by-

---

8. It is interesting to note that modern political liberals criticize graphic violence on television because it may produce violent behavior, especially in children. In contrast, they argue that graphic sex in magazines, books, and moving pictures is harmless, and in no way can be shown to produce deviant sexual behavior. In other words, liberals are opposed to violence and favor open sex. Conservatives have a tendency to reverse these two preferences and argue the opposite positions.

9. *Ibid.*, ch. 4.

standers (Ex. 21:22-25). It can destroy property. When a death or serious injury is involved, a duel can lead in some societies — especially those that place family status above civil law — to an escalation of inter-family feuding and blood vengeance.

The premise of the duel or the brawl is the assertion of the existence of *zones of judicial irresponsibility.* Men set aside for themselves a kind of arena in which the laws of civil society should not prevail. There may or may not be rules governing the private battlefield, but these rules are supposedly special, removing men from the jurisdiction of civil law. The protection of life and limb which is basic to the civil law is supposedly suspended by mutual consent. "Common" laws supposedly have no force over "uncommon" men during the period of the duel. Somehow, the law of God does not apply to private warriors who defend their own honor and seek to impose a mutually agreed-upon form of punishment on their rivals.

But the laws of God *do* apply. "The Bible does not permit the use of force to resolve disputes, except where force is lawfully exercised by God's ordained officer, the civil magistrate. To put it another way, the Bible requires men to submit to arbitration, and categorically prohibits them from taking their own personal vengeance (Rom. 12:17-13:7)."[10]

An obvious implication of the biblical law against dueling is the prohibition of gladiatorial contests, which would include boxing. A boxer who kills another man in the ring should be executed. Another implication is the necessity of rejecting the notion of a "fair fight." There is no such thing as a fair fight. Flight is almost always preferable to private fighting, but where fighting is unavoidable, it should be an all-out confrontation. Should a person "fight fair" when his wife is attacked? Should women under attack from a man "fight fairly"? The answer ought to be clear.[11] Thus, the code of the duel is doubly perverse: first, it imputes cowardice to a man who would seek to keep the peace by walking away from a challenge to his honor; second, it restricts a man's lawful self-defense to a set of agreed-upon "rules of the game." Fighting is not a game; it is either an evil assertion of personal autonomy or else a necessary defense of life, limb, and perhaps property.

---

10. James B. Jordan, *The Law of the Covenant: An Exposition of Exodus 21-23* (Tyler, Texas: Institute for Christian Economics, 1984), p. 110.

11. *Ibid.*, p. 112.

Duel to the Death: Murder

One implication of Exodus 21:18-19 is that a death resulting from a duel or a brawl is to be regarded as murder.[12] This is a concept of personal responsibility that is foreign to societies that allow private violence. In such societies, the quest for personal power and prestige overrides the quest for public peace. The autonomy of man is affirmed by the ritual practices of the duel and brawl. Wyatt-Brown writes of the antebellum (pre-1861) American South: "Ordinarily, honor under the dueling test called for public recognition of a man's claim to power, whatever social level he or his immediate circle of friends might belong to. A street fight could and often did accomplish the same thing for the victor. Murder, or at least manslaughter, inspired the same public approval in some instances. Just as lesser folk spoke ungrammatically, so too they fought ungrammatically, but their actions were expressions of the same desire for prestige."[13]

Under biblical law, injured bystanders are protected from deliberate violence on the part of other people on an "eye for eye" basis.[14]

---

12. Robert L. Dabney, *Lectures in Systematic Theology* (Grand Rapids, Michigan: Zondervan, [1878] 1972), pp. 404-6. Dabney was by far the most insightful Presbyterian theologian in the nineteenth-century South. He had served for several months, before becoming too ill to continue, as Gen. Thomas "Stonewall" Jackson's chaplain, as well as his Chief of Staff. He later wrote a biography of Jackson, so he cannot be considered a man hostile to military virtues. Cf. Thomas Cary Johnson, *The Life and Letters of Robert Lewis Dabney* (Richmond, Virginia: Presbyterian Committee of Publication, 1903), ch. 13.

13. Bertram Wyatt-Brown, *Southern Honor: Ethics and Behavior in the Old South* (New York: Oxford University Press, 1982), p. 353.

14. A somewhat different problem is raised if a person defends himself from another person who has initiated violence. What if, in defending himself, a person injures a bystander? Clearly, it was not the bystander's fault. The person responsible for inflicting the injury should pay damages. Should it be the person who initiated the violence or the defender who inadvertently harmed the bystander? For example, what if a man attacks another man, and the second person pulls out a gun and fires at the attacker, hitting a bystander by mistake? A humanistic theory of strict liability would produce a judgment against the defender, for his defense was misguided, or excessive, or ineffective. But what if the attacker had grabbed the defender's "shooting hand," causing him to fire wildly? The injury to the bystander would seem to be the fault of the attacker. On the other hand, if the original attacker was using only his fists, and the defender had pulled out a gun and started shooting—a seemingly excessive response—would this make the original attacker a defender when he attempted to grab the weapon? Judgment is complicated, for life is complicated.

The Bible places restraints on violence. The goal of the God-fearing man should be to reduce private physical violence. Thus, if the attacker uses fists, and the defender has a weapon, the attacker should be warned to stop. The victim does have the right to identify the attacker and press charges. The civil government should inflict the penalty. But if the attacker still challenges the person with the weapon, then the person has the right to stop the attacker from inflicting violence on him.

An injured loser who walks again is entitled to full compensation. But in the case where the loser dies, the judges are required to impose a capital sentence on a surviving fighter. When the loser cannot "walk abroad," the victor must not be "quit." At best, he would have to pay an enormous fine to the family of the dead man, but even this would seem to be too lenient, since the only instance of a substitution of payment for the death sentence involves criminal negligence — the failure to contain a dangerous beast which subsequently kills a man — but not willful violence (Ex. 21:29-30). The autonomous shedding of man's blood, even to "defend one's good name," is still murder. There is the perverse lure of such "conflicts of honor."

It is clear that if a biblically honorable man refuses to fight because the civil law supports his position by threatening him with death should he successfully kill his opponent, he can avoid the fight in the name of personal self-confidence. He says, in effect, "I know I can probably kill you; therefore, I choose not to enter this fight because I will surely be executed after I kill you." Thus, he can avoid being regarded as a coward. This breaks the central social hold that the *code duello* has always possessed: the honorable man's fear of being labeled a coward. But in order to deflect this powerful hold, the State must be willing to enforce the death penalty on victors.

The Duel in American History

The enforcement of legal prohibitions against private duels is basic to the culture of the industrial and post-industrial (i.e., service-oriented) West. The duel is based upon essentially pre-industrial concepts of personal honor and personal pride.[15] In the years from the American Revolution until 1800, the duel was a familiar though illegal activity in both North (outside of Puritan New England)[16] and South. Two important facts are not generally recognized by

---

15. Marc Bloch writes of late medieval society: "A theory at that time very widely current represented the human community as being divided into three 'orders': those who prayed, those who fought, and those who worked. It was unanimously agreed that the second should be placed much higher than the third. But the evidence of the epic goes farther still, showing that the soldier had little hesitation in rating his mission even higher than that of the specialist in prayer. Pride is one of the essential ingredients of all class-consciousness. That of the 'nobles' of the feudal era was, above all, the pride of the warrior." Bloch, *Feudal Society* (University of Chicago Press, [1961] 1965), pp. 291-92.

16. Richard Buel, Jr., *Securing the Revolution: Ideology in American Politics, 1789-1815* (Ithaca, New York: Cornell University Press, 1972), pp. 80-81.

those who are not specialized historians. First, the South had civil sanctions against duelling in the late eighteenth century, including North Carolina's threat to impose the death penalty without benefit of clergy on the survivor of a duel in which a man was killed.[17] (In Tennessee, it was discovered that about 90 percent of the duels were fought by lawyers, so a prospective lawyer was required to swear that he would never be a participant in a duel in order to gain admission to the bar.)[18] Second, the duel was relatively common in the North. Thus, in both North and South, civil laws against duelling were ineffectual prior to 1800. After 1800, social opinion changed in the North, and duels disappeared. Not so in the South. Social opinion was therefore the dominant force regarding the practice of duelling in both regions, not civil law.

Hamilton and Burr, 1804

In the North prior to 1800, it was considered a loss of honor to avoid a "legitimate challenge" from a man of upper class standing, a fact revealed by Alexander Hamilton's unwillingness in 1804 to refuse the challenge from his old political rival Aaron Burr, for fear of eroding his political influence.[19] Both were legal residents of New York State. Burr was at the time the Vice President of the U.S. because, under the old rules of presidential elections, he had tied with Jefferson in the Electoral College vote in 1800, and Hamilton's influence in the House of Representatives, which legally had to settle the tie, had elected Hamilton's political rival Jefferson, whom Hamilton hated less than he hated Burr.[20] Burr had actually campaigned for Governor of New York in 1804, a race which he lost a few months before the famous duel, in part because of Hamilton's efforts against him.

Hamilton had repeatedly insulted Burr in private conversation: "He had insulted Burr's family, impugned his honesty, and accused him of almost every imaginable crime from taking bribes to cowardice in the army."[21] Hamilton had used the word "despicable" in a private conversation regarding Burr, and this had become public

---

17. Dickson D. Bruce, Jr., *Violence and Culture in the Antebellum South* (Austin: University of Texas Press, 1979), p. 27.

18. *Idem.*

19. *Ibid.*, p. 42.

20. His opposition to Burr had also cost the latter a seat in the U.S. Senate and the governorship of New York State: Robert Hendrickson, *Hamilton II (1789-1804)* (New York: Mason/Charter, 1976), p. 629.

21. *Ibid.*, p. 626.

knowledge. He felt he could not retract the statement without calling the man who repeated it in public a liar, which was the only way he could avoid the duel. Hamilton believed that to avoid the challenge from Burr would ruin his influence within the Federalist Party.[22]

Hamilton had come close to other duels in his life. His brother-in-law Robert Church had been involved in several duels, including one with Burr.[23] His eldest son Philip had died in a duel with a Burr supporter in 1801. All this in one prominent family. Thus, the duel in late-eighteenth-century America was not uncommon within the upper classes, North and South. Hamilton and Burr fought their duel across the Hudson River from New York City in Weehawken, New Jersey. This was a common practice of duelers: fighting the duel in a neighboring state.[24] Hamilton's son Philip had been killed on this very spot; it was a popular place for New York City residents to conduct their duels.[25] New York's laws against dueling were strict, though not so strict as Exodus 21:18. Conviction for the mere issuing of a challenge could result in a prohibition on his holding State office for 20 years.[26] Burr shot Hamilton on July 11, 1804, and the latter died the next day. Hamilton had expressed his intention of not shooting Burr, a practice which remained common but risky in subsequent duels in the South.[27] The legend that Hamilton fired into the air while Burr fired into Hamilton is a myth; Burr fired first, and Hamilton's pistol went off as he fell.[28]

Hamilton knew full well that the duel was illegal and immoral, which he stated in his diary. He insisted that his "religious and moral principles strongly opposed the practice of duelling." It would give him pain, he wrote, "to shed the blood of a fellow in a private combate forbidden by the laws."[29] Nevertheless, the pressure he felt regarding his honor left him no choice: "To those, who with abhorring the practice of duelling, may think that I ought on no account to have added on the number of bad examples, I answer that it is my *relative* situation, as well in public as private appeals, enforcing all

22. *Ibid.*, p. 627.

23. *Idem.*

24. Bruce, *Violence and Culture*, p, 27.

25. John C. Miller, *Alexander Hamilton and the Growth of the New Nation* (New York: Harper Torchbooks, 1959), p. 573.

26. *Idem.*

27. Bruce, *Violence and Culture*, p. 36.

28. Hendrickson, *Hamilton II*, pp. 638-39.

29. *Ibid.*, p. 634.

the considerations which constitute what men of the world denominate honour, impressed on me (as I thought) a peculiar necessity not to decline the call."[30]

Grand juries in both New York and New Jersey indicted Burr: New York's for violating the anti-dueling laws, even though the duel had taken place in New Jersey, and New Jersey's for murder.[31] He did not return to New York for several years. (Neither indictment was ever tried in court; both were allowed to lapse.) Burr's political career was permanently destroyed as a result of the duel. He served out his term as Vice President and headed west in 1805, involving himself in actions that led to his 1807 trial to commit conspiracy against the U.S., at the end of which he was declared not guilty.

Northern sensibilities, Burr learned to his regret, had shifted from the region's former views. These views, argues Bruce, had been essentially those of the classical Enlightenment: that man's nature is inherently violent; therefore, institutions and customs must be designed to channel this violence for socially acceptable purposes. The duel was one of these accepted channeling devices. This emphasis on the classic dualism between virtue and violence faded in northern political and social philosophy after 1800, but not in the South. "After 1800, however, the ideas which gave duelling its meaning were increasingly confined to the South, and, as Southerners became aware of this, they saw in the duel an expression of their distinctive character and of the views which, they felt, made them distinct. Southern civilization and Southern distinctiveness were, that is, symbolized in the practice of duelling, and this would account for its growing acceptance after 1800."[32]

The Southern Duel

The duel had numerous community functions: the relief of boredom,[33] the preservation of a chivalrous concept of honor, and an attempted reinforcement of traditional status distinctions between

---

30. *Ibid.*, p. 635.

31. Milton Lomask, *Aaron Burr: The Conspiracy and Years of Exile, 1805-1836* (New York: Farrar Straus Giroux, 1982), p. 24.

32. Bruce, *Violence and Culture*, p. 42.

33. Wyatt-Brown, *Southern Honor*, p. 328. Boredom is one possible explanation for the rise of the medieval tournament in France. Prior to the twelfth century, there were enough real wars to keep the knights occupied. Sidney Painter, *French Chivalry: Chivalric Ideas and Practices in Medieval France* (Ithaca, New York: Great Seal Books, a division of Cornell University Press, [1940] 1961), p. 46.

gentlemen and commoners. The duel was considered a cut above the street brawl, even though the duel's use of handguns could easily result in the death of one or both rivals. It also offered the possibility of placing restrictions around the conflicting individuals, so that the potentially lethal conflict did not result in a lengthy feud between extended families. Wyatt-Brown writes:

Feuds were generally much deplored, particularly among the gentry, because quite obviously they disrupted community life grievously, and incited conflicts of loyalty among related family members and their friends. Duels, in contrast, provided structure and ritual. Referees assured the fairness of the fight and witnesses reported back to the public on the impartiality of the proceedings. Moreover, the rites of challenge and response afforded time and means for adjustment of differences through third parties. . . . In addition, the duel set the boundaries of the upper circle of honor. They excluded the allegedly unworthy and therefore made ordinary brawling appear ungentlemanly, vulgar, and immoral. In a hierarchical society, all these factors were socially significant. They made violence a part of the social order even in the upper ranks, but at least duels helped to restrict the bloodletting, which otherwise would have been much more chaotic and endlessly vindictive.

It would be a mistake, however, to argue that duels were as much deplored as Southern hand-wringing would lead an observer to believe. Hardly more than a handful genuinely considered duels socially beneficial, although some apologists claimed that the prospect of dueling forced gentlemen to be careful of their language and cautious in their actions. The criticism of outsiders, the clear opposition of the church, the recognition that valuable members of the community sometimes fell for reasons that retrospectively seemed petty—these attitudes placed duelists on the defensive. As a result, most of them explained their general opposition to the *code duello* in almost ritual words, but in the next breath gave reason for its continuation.[34]

He offers evidence that the duel became a familiar aspect of the coming to maturity of young gentlemen in the South. Teenage duels were not uncommon in New Orleans and South Carolina.[35] At the center of the duel was the pride of man:

In 1855 Alfred Huger of Charleston, for instance, rejoiced in the news that the son of a friend had killed his rival in a contest. The boy had showed

---

34. *Ibid.*, pp. 352-53.
35. *Ibid.*, p. 167. The rituals associated with dueling were well known only in Charleston and New Orleans: *ibid.*, p. 355.

commendable willingness to be "cut to pieces rather than give an inch or abate a tittle" of his honor, Huger declared. When James Legaré's son was killed in a similar affair, Huger commiserated with the father, but pointed out, "Would you call him back today, with his noble spirit tamed or with his brave & manly bearing humbled! to see him 'live' without the sensibility to perceive what was due his Honour?". . . It could be claimed that these sentiments, as well as the duels themselves, were merely fancies peculiar to romantic personalities. Such was not the case. From sons' early childhood, fathers prepared their boys to observe the rules by which honor was upheld, as a mark of status and a claim to leadership. [36]

The practice of dueling had been introduced to the United States during the American Revolution by British and French aristocrats. [37] The concepts underlying the formal duel are essentially feudal and military in origin. The hierarchical privileges of rank are to be respected in such a code. Military codes of justice still reflect this: officers are not permitted to strike enlisted officers (sergeants)[38] or enlisted men. Such loss of self-control is considered beneath an officer; it is a breach of social status. A man who cannot exercise such self-control with those beneath him in status is considered incompetent to lead. When Gen. George Patton in a rage struck an enlisted man in 1943, he was forced by Gen. Dwight Eisenhower to offer a public apology in front of numerous units under Patton's command. Patton could have been court-martialled and removed from command.

When extended to civilian society, such a military code necessarily thwarts the civilian goal of social peace. This is why the original code restricted it to a military caste. There was another good military reason for this. After the middle of the twelfth century, as society became more differentiated and less subject to invasion and war, the common man was no longer permitted to carry professional instruments of war (or poaching), such as bows and arrows or a sword. [39] The medieval story of the fight between Robin Hood and Little John reflects this: they fought with walking sticks that could be used as bludgeons against commoners, or to unseat a knight on horseback.

---

36. *Ibid.*, p. 167.

37. *Ibid.*, p. 354.

38. The term "sergeant" comes from the medieval word for a peasant in service to a warrior's household. They were men of a servile social status, yet they steadily gained rights of inheritance to their office for their sons. Marc Bloch, *Feudal Society*, pp. 337-44.

39. *Ibid.*, pp. 289-90.

But as the weapons of conflict were steadily democratized by mass production, the code itself was partially democratized. Aristocratic private citizens were allowed by social custom to adopt the *code duello*. This democratization culminated in the ritualized gun fights of the American West, 1865-90, which were not battles between gentlemen.

This aristocratic function of the duel was not successfully confined to its original social status in the South. A democratic imitation spread into the community at large. Community standards governed behavior, and these standards were heavily influenced by the code of honor, even though that code originally was expected to be the monopoly of a minority social elite. "It was democracy perhaps, but a kind of democracy that placed primary stress on white, manly virtue. Those who failed to set the appropriate standard were soon unseated. Duels were a method for ascertaining who should exercise the power that the community of men was willing to accord the winners."[40] Thus, the steady erosion of authority of civil law by the democratization of the late medieval code of military honor was a feature of the pre-industrial American South. Among the "plain folk" of the South, fist fights were common and socially acceptable. "The violent planter was a deviant; the violent yeoman was not."[41]

The South saw the duel as a means of controlling verbal passions, slurs against another man's character.[42] But in confining its legitimacy to the aristocratic class of gentlemen, the South was saying, in effect, that only upper class aristocrats have character worth defending with one's life. This anti-democratic and anti-Christian attitude was destroyed when the South lost the Civil War to "upstart and uncultured yankees," with their mass democracy and mass production of weapons. The ideal of the Southern gentlemen as an aristocratic warrior changed radically overnight. He became a soft-spoken gentleman who would achieve his revenge in more subtle ways.

Courts and Vigilantes

Legal predictability is crucial to the preservation of an orderly society. The breakdown of predictable justice in any era can lead to a revival of blood vengeance. Those who are convinced that the court system is unable to dispense justice and defend the innocent are

---

40. Wyatt-Brown, *Southern Honor*, p. 357.
41. Bruce, *Violence and Culture*, p. 91.
42. *Ibid.*, pp. 38-39.

tempted to "take the law into their own hands." The rise of vigilante groups that take over the administration of physical sanctions always comes at the expense of legal predictability. This is a sign of the breakdown in the legal order, and it is accompanied by a loss of legitimacy by "establishment" institutions.[43] Eventually, vigilante movements are either stamped out by the existing social order or else they become the foundation of a new social order: the warlord society.

The various vigilante movements of the United States in the nineteenth century arose when the civil authorities would not or could not enforce the law.[44] Vigilantes were common in the American West after the Civil War prior to the establishment of local and regional judicial order. The most famous vigilante group in U.S. history is the Ku Klux Klan. The original Ku Klux Klan of the American South, 1865-71, was a defensive movement.[45] The organization was self-consciously occult in its regalia. Members wore white sheets with holes cut out for eyes, so that they would resemble the folklore version of ghosts, thereby adding to the terror of superstitious former slaves. The Klan was highly liturgical, its rituals filled with diabolic symbols, hidden signs, and other elements of secret societies, and it

43. This appears to be beginning in large cities in the United States. Citizen's patrols became common in certain Jewish districts in the New York City area in the late 1960's. A parallel group of inner-city youths sprang up in the late 1970's, the Guardian Angels, initially composed mostly of Puerto Ricans. This group has spread across the United States. By 1988, its leaders claimed 60 chapters and 6,000 members. Citizen's patrols have now spread to black neighborhoods and middle class neighborhoods, especially in response to the advent of "crack" houses: the modern equivalent of the opium dens of the nineteenth century. In some cases, local police departments do cooperate with these citizen's patrols, and to this extent they are not pure vigilante organizations. See "Neighbors Join to Rout the Criminals in the Streets," *Insight* (Nov. 28, 1988), pp. 8-21.

44. Richard Maxwell Brown, "The History of Vigilantism in America," in H. Jon Rosenbaum and Peter C. Sederberg (eds.), *Vigilante Politics* (Philadelphia: University of Pennsylvania Press, 1976); see also Brown, *Strain of Violence: Historical Studies of American Violence and Vigilantism* (New York: Oxford University Press, 1975).

45. The early-twentieth-century trilogy of novels by Thomas Dixon eulogized this early Klan. *Birth of a Nation*, the epic D. W. Griffith silent film of 1915, was based on Dixon's second novel in this trilogy, *The Clansman* (1905). This moving picture was the first modern "spectacular," and was shown to large audiences across the United States. It had the support of President Woodrow Wilson (an old college classmate of Dixon's) and the Chief Justice of the U.S. Supreme Court, a former Klansman. See David M. Chalmers, *Hooded Americanism: The First Century of the Ku Klux Klan, 1865-1965* (Garden City, New York: Doubleday, 1965), pp. 26-27. The film, unfortunately, led to a revival of the Klan: *ibid.*, ch. 4. (The 17-year-old star of Griffith's movie, Lillian Gish, also starred in *The Whales of August* in 1987, making hers the longest film career in history.)

predictably degenerated into violence and lawlessness within a few years. It was officially disbanded in 1869, and when local "dens" persisted, it was stamped out by the U.S. military. An imitation of the old Klan rose again to national political prominence in the 1920's,[46] only to fade nationally in the 1930's and in the South in the 1940's. Today, numerous local Klan-type groups exist, but they have little influence.[47] But the Klan's former power testifies to the fact that when civil courts fail to dispense justice and therefore lose their legitimacy in the eyes of large numbers of citizens, societies will eventually see the rise of private dispensers of "people's justice."

Without a sense of legitimacy, the authority of public courts is threatened. The courts need legitimacy in order to gain the long-term voluntary cooperation of the public, meaning self-government under law, without which law enforcement becomes both sporadic and tyrannical. No legal system can afford the economic resources that would be necessary to gain full compliance to an alien law-order in a society whose members are unwilling to govern themselves voluntarily in terms of that law-order.[48] If the courts do not receive assent from the public as legitimate institutions, they can maintain the peace only by imposing sentences whose severity goes beyond people's sense of justice, which again calls into doubt both legitimacy and legal predictability.

Judicial Pluralism and Social Disintegration

A civil government that refuses to defend a law-order that is seen as legitimate by the public is inviting the revival of the duel, the feud, and blood vengeance. If the public cannot agree on standards of decency, then the courts will be tempted to become autonomous. Widespread and deep differences concerning religion lead to equally

---

46. It was the victory of an anti-Klan candidate for governor in the Republican Party's primary in the state of Oregon which led the Klan to jump to the Democratic Party. They elected the Democratic candidate, plus enough members of the legislature to pass a law mandating that all children between the ages of eight and sixteen attend a government-operated school. Chalmers, *Hooded Americanism*, p. 3. This law was overturned by the U.S. Supreme Court in 1925 in a landmark case, *Pierce v. Society of Sisters*, which has remained the key Court decision in the fight for Christian schools.

47. As one southerner described the Klan: "It is made up mainly of gasoline station attendants and FBI informers. The members can easily spot the informers: they are the only ones who pay their monthly dues."

48. Gary North, *Moses and Pharaoh: Dominion Religion vs. Power Religion* (Tyler, Texas: Institute for Christian Economics, 1985), pp. 291-94.

strong disagreements over morality and law. Religious pluralism leads to moral and judicial pluralism, meaning unpredictable courts. Religious pluralism is an outgrowth of polytheism. Polytheism inescapably leads to what we might call "polylegalism." Too many law courts decide in terms of conflicting moralities. Only the strong hand of centralized and bureaucratic civil government can enforce a single standard of law on a religiously divided public, which is why religious and judicial pluralism ultimately leads to tyranny: the grab for power. Long-term judicial pluralism is a myth: one group or another ultimately must decide what is right and what is wrong, what should be prohibited by civil law and what shouldn't.[49]

The myth of judicial pluralism has hidden from the people (including Christians) the reality of the inescapable *intolerance* of all civil government. There can no more be religious neutrality on earth than in heaven, and as time moves toward that final court decision, the impossibility of pluralism is becoming more obvious. Either God or Satan will execute final judgment; either God's law or man's law will be imposed on eternity. The covenant representatives of each kingdom will, on earth and in history, progressively present their respective supernatural sovereign's case to the world. There is no way to reconcile these competing claims. Marxism cannot be reconciled with Christianity, and neither system can be reconciled with Islam. The liberal humanist's hope in treaties, arms control, and endless tax-supported economic deals with Communist nations is as doomed to failure as the conservative humanist's faith in the peace-promoting reign of neutral natural law.[50] Elijah's challenge is inescapable: "How long halt ye between two opinions? If the LORD be God, follow him: but if Baal, then follow him." Then as now, the people delay making a decision: "And the people answered him not a word" (I Ki. 18:21).

They did not remain silent forever. The fire came from heaven and consumed the sacrifice on God's altar. The people saw, understood, and acted: they brought the 850 priests of Baal to Elijah, who killed them (I Ki. 18:40). The nation for the moment sided with God's prophet. The "priests of Baal" of any era can delay judgment for a while, but eventually *judgment comes in history*. Nevertheless,

---

49. Gary North, *Political Polytheism: The Myth of Pluralism* (Tyler, Texas: Institute for Christian Economics, 1989).

50. Gary North, *Healer of the Nations: Biblical Blueprints for International Relations* (Ft. Worth, Texas: Dominion Press, 1987), ch. 3.

without a change in heart, the people eventually return to their old ways. The Revolution consumes its own children. The prophet is again put on the run (I Ki. 19).

The humanist courts of our day appeal to religious pluralism, yet they are creating judicial tyranny.[51] The anti-feud, anti-clan,[52] anti-duel ethic of once-Christian Western bourgeois cultures — societies in which social peace has fostered economic growth — is being undermined by judges who are creating lawlessness in the name of a purified humanist legal system. Judicial pluralism must be replaced, but not from the top down, and not from the vigilante's noose outward. The satanic myth of legal pluralism must be replaced by the power of the Holy Spirit in the hearts of men. The Holy Spirit is the enforcer in New Testament times.

Conclusion

Social order requires a degree of social peace. When biblical law began to influence the civil governments of the West, an increase of social peace and social order took place. This, in turn, led to greater economic growth and technological development.[53]

Christian culture is orderly. The Christian West steadily abolished or redirected the chaos festivals of the pagan world, until the growth of humanism-paganism began to reverse this process.[54] Legal systems became predictable, as the "eye for eye" principle spread alongside the gospel of salvation. The unpredictable violence of State power was thereby reduced. In private relationships, men were not allowed to vent their wrath on each other in acts of vio-

---

51. Carrol D. Kilgore, *Judicial Tyranny* (Nashville, Tennessee: Nelson, 1977).

52. Weber wrote: "When Christianity became the religion of these peoples who had been so profoundly shaken in all their traditions, it finally destroyed whatever religious significance these clan ties retained; perhaps, indeed, it was precisely the weakness or absence of such magical and taboo barriers which made the conversion possible. The often very significant role played by the parish community in the administrative organization of medieval cities is only one of the many symptoms pointing to this quality of the Christian religion which, in dissolving clan ties, importantly shaped the medieval city." He contrasts this anti-clan perspective with that of Islam. Max Weber, *Economy and Society: An Outline of Interpretive Sociology*, edited by Guenther Roth and Claus Wittich (New York: Bedminster Press, [1924] 1968), p. 1244.

53. Gary North, *The Sinai Strategy: Economics and the Ten Commandments* (Tyler, Texas: Institute for Christian Economics, 1986), pp. 223-26.

54. Peter Gay aptly titled the first volume of his study of the Enlightenment, *The Rise of Modern Paganism* (New York: Knopf, 1966). The two-volume study is titled, *The Enlightenment: An Interpretation* (New York: Knopf, 1966, 1969).

lence. Those who violated this law became economically liable for their actions.

The duel or brawl is by nature a direct challenge to the authority and legitimacy of the civil government. It transfers to individuals operating outside the State — the God-ordained monopoly of violence — a degree of legal immunity from civil judgment. It transfers sovereignty in the administration of violence from the State to the individual. It is not surprising, therefore, that one program of legal reform recommended by some contemporary libertarian anarchists is the legalization of dueling. The duel is seen as a private act between consenting adults and therefore sacrosanct. (Sacrosanct: from *sacro* = sacred rite, and *sanctum* = holy and inviolable. Also related to *sanction* = legal and sovereign authority, or a judgment by a legal and sovereign authority.)

The abolition of the private duel in the late nineteenth century is a case in point. While this development came during an era of increasing secularism, it was consistent with a Christian view of civil law. Personal self-control within a social framework of predictable biblical law is to replace physical violence. The failure of Christian culture in the antebellum South to eliminate the imported feudal tradition of duelling in the name of gentlemanly honor eventually was rectified. The Southern duel disappeared with Gen. Lee's surrender to Gen. Grant at the Appomattox courthouse in 1865.

Yet even in the South, there were strict limits placed on this *code duello*. It had been a highly ritualized procedure, as the duelling handbook of the era indicated, a book written by a Governor of South Carolina, John Lyde Wilson's *Code of Honor* (1838). It is significant that custom recognized the immunity of serious Christians to the formal ritual of the honorable duel. Wyatt-Brown comments: "Of course, among Christians and older men who were not expected to show youthful passions excessive violence was considered inappropriate. As Henry Foote noted, devout churchmen could forgo duels or, in fact, any other form of physical redress without incurring public censure. For other men a different standard prevailed."[55] Bruce, also citing Foote's statement, concurs: "Only a known Christian, appealing to religious scruples, could refuse to challenge another gentlemen with public approval. . . ."[56] It was only the de-

55. Wyatt-Brown, *Southern Honor*, p. 354.
56. Bruce, *Violence and Culture*, p. 28.

feat of the South on the battlefield that finally transformed the model of a Southern gentlemen from a man ready to defend his honor with personal violence into a self-disciplined, soft-spoken person who gains his revenge for an insult to his honor in non-violent ways. (A similar transformation of Japanese aristocratic ideals, also closely tied to feudal and military concepts of honor, took place after Japan lost World War II.) A military defeat is an expensive way for a society to learn to conform its social standards to the requirements of biblical law.

10

THE HUMAN COMMODITY

And if a man smite his servant, or his maid, with a rod, and he die under his hand; he shall be surely punished. Notwithstanding, if he continue a day or two, he shall not be punished: for he is his money (Ex. 21:20-21).

Exodus 21:20-21 clearly teaches that an owner may legitimately beat permanent heathen slaves and indentured Hebrew bondservants. The theocentric principle here is that *the slave-owner is God's representative agent to the slave.* God deals with all men hierarchically. This is very clear in the case of master and slave. The slave is in an inferior position institutionally, though not necessarily morally. His servitude may be the result of some flaw in his character or his skills, or it may be because of uncontrollable external circumstances. The case laws do not distinguish between the servant who is a moral failure and the servant who has suffered a temporary but uncontrollable setback. The bondservice laws apply to all bondservants and all masters equally. The bondservant's legal status is judicially binding on the civil magistrates; they are not to make arbitrary exceptions to God's authorized sanctions in terms of their evaluation of the servant's moral condition. In this way, *the State is placed under limits,* which is even more important than placing masters and slaves under limits.[1] Jesus fulfilled the jubilee laws and thereby abolished the legal

---

1. Critics of competitive free market capitalism sometimes argue that personal wealth can result from "luck" as well as from hard work, from the "accident of birth" as well as from successful entrepreneurship. They want the civil government's bureaucrats to determine whether other men's wealth is morally deserved, and then redistribute wealth by compulsion in terms of the "deserving character" of the recipients. But because civil law must be general in scope, the proponents of compulsory wealth redistribution must then generalize their criticisms of the more economically successful. One legislative result is the graduated ("progressive") income tax, which assumes that all high-income earners have been rewarded disproportionately to their productivity, and all low-income people therefore deserve a share in the high-income people's gains. The economically successful must subsidize the unsuccessful. Thus, there can be no neutrality with respect to the Bible in tax policy. We should

foundation of permanent chattel slavery; He did not abolish the State. The State is a far more important institution historically and judicially than private chattel slavery ever has been.

Sanctions and Moral Reform

The master is supposed to be an agent of moral reform; his training, support, and example are supposed to serve as the bondservant's pathway back to self-government and productivity. The master therefore exercises lawful discipline in God's name, including physical discipline. He brings *covenantal sanctions*. Because the servant is made in God's image, there are limits placed on the master's authority. This authority to impose sanctions is not unlimited; it is restrained by civil law and, as we shall see, by economic self-interest.

So severe is a Bible-sanctioned beating that a servant may even die a few days later. This is regarded as a case of *accidental death*, and the owner is not to be held responsible. It is acknowledged by God that servants can be rebellious to the point that they may be severely beaten. This is the passage that so disturbs Christian family counsellor James Dobson: "Do you agree that if a man beats his slave to death, he is to be considered guilty only if the individual dies instantly? If the slave lives a few days, the owner is considered not guilty (Exodus 21:20-21)[?] Do you believe that we should stone to death rebellious children (Deuteronomy 21:18-21)? Do you really believe we can draw subtle meaning about complex issues from Mosaic law, when even the obvious interpretation makes no sense to us today? We can hardly select what we will and will not apply now. If we accept the verses you cited, we are obligated to deal with every last jot and tittle."[2] He is correct; we are required to take seriously every last jot and tittle.

---

affirm the biblical standard, namely, that civil law must not distinguish between the morally deserving or undeserving nature of income recipients, so long as they did not use force or fraud in gaining their wealth. The alternative is to conclude that civil law must assume that either the successful deserve special treatment at the expense of the less successful, or vice versa. The law must "take sides." It must discriminate. This makes the State arbitrary and dangerous.

If the case laws of Exodus do not distinguish between slaves and masters in terms of their comparative moral stature or their prior outward circumstances, then there is no way biblically to justify the creation of welfare State wealth-redistribution schemes based on people's comparative moral stature or their prior outward circumstances.

2. James Dobson, "Dialogue on Abortion," in Dobson and Gary Bergel, *The Decision of Life* (Arcadia, California: Focus on the Family, 1986), p. 14.

All human authority is limited by God's law. Man is not autonomous (*autos* = self; *nomos* = law). There are therefore God-imposed judicial limits on the master's lawful authority to impose physical sanctions. What are these limits? The first limit is mechanical. The bondservant must be punished with a rod, not with a lethal weapon. If the master used a lethal weapon to administer the punishment, such as a rock, and the slave died a few days later, the protection normally afforded to him by this law would become the basis of his conviction for murder.[3]

The second limit is the threat of the execution of the master if a servant dies on the day of the beating. "And he that killeth any man shall surely be put to death" (Lev. 24:17). The owner is not exempted from this law. He is in a position of authority, and he must not abuse this position of authority. He who exercises dominion is always under lawful authority. Men are not autonomous. It should be noted at this point that this law was unique in the legal collections of the ancient Near East. No other collection even deals with a master who kills a slave.[4]

Obviously, it would be difficult to prove that a master deliberately killed his servant if the servant survived the beating for several days.[5] Biblical civil justice is concerned with criminal intent, but only to the extent that such intent can be deduced from the external events. The State is not allowed to seek to get inside a person's mind. (This is why lie detector exams must never be made mandatory, nor regarded as anything more than circumstantial evidence. Hypnotism, being demonic in origin and frequently leading to more overt signs of demonic possession,[6] should itself be regarded as a crime, let alone adopted as a tool of crime detection or courtroom evidence.)

The third limit is the loss suffered by the servant. If the owner breaks a servant's tooth or puts out an eye—representative injuries indicating any major permanent disfigurement—the servant goes free (Ex. 21:26-27). Also, if the servant dies a few days later, the owner has just lost a major capital investment. His self-interest in-

---

3. Walter C. Kaiser, Jr., *Toward Old Testament Ethics* (Grand Rapids, Michigan: Zondervan Academie, 1983), p. 102.

4. Shalom Paul, *Studies in the Book of the Covenant in the Light of Cuneiform and Biblical Law* (Leiden: E. J. Brill, 1970), p. 69.

5. *Idem.*

6. Gary North, *Unholy Spirits: Occultism and New Age Humanism* (Ft. Worth, Texas: Dominion Press, 1986), pp. 106-7.

structs him to restrain his wrath.[7] The Bible recognizes this economic self-interest on the part of the owner, when it refers to the servant as "his money" (Ex. 21:21). A rational, calculating owner is not
going to destroy his own asset needlessly. *It is the very fact of the "servant
as commodity" that protects him from excessive abuse.* It is his commodity
status that enables the civil government to leave him in the hands of
his owner. Self-government by the owner is encouraged by economic
self-interest.[8]

If the economic self-interest of bondservant-owners is biblically
legitimate, and even a factor in the self-restraint of owners, as the
Bible says is the case, then this implies that *men can legitimately be regarded by others in terms of the economic value that their services offer those other
people.* Bondservants command a price in a market. Thus, they are
regarded by purchasers as economic commodities. Workers also
command a contract price. Thus, they too are regarded by purchasers
as economic commodities. The question then is: To what extent?

Marx on Workers as Commodities: A Myth

A familiar criticism of capitalism is that it treats people as if they
were commodities rather than human beings. The capitalist order
supposedly dehumanizes man by defining him as a thing, a part of
the production process, a cog in a great machine. The solution, we
are told, is to permit men to organize collectively in labor unions (even
Christian labor unions),[9] or to overturn the capitalist order, or to get
Christians in labor and management to have prayer meetings together.

---

7. Kaiser, *Toward Old Testament Ethics*, p. 102.

8. None of this provides any insight into the rule of Maimonides regarding the
deliberate injuring of other men's slaves: "One's slave is regarded as his own person,
but his animal is regarded as his inanimate property. Thus, if one places a burning
coal on the breast of another's slave so that he dies, or if one pushes a slave into the
sea or into a fire from which he can escape but he does not escape and dies, the injurer is exempt from paying compensation. If, however, one does the same to
another's animal, it is regarded as if he had placed a burning coal on another's clothing and burned it, in which case he is liable for payment. The same rule applies in
all similar cases." Moses Maimonides, *The Book of Torts*, vol. 11 of *The Code of Maimonides*, 14 vols. (New Haven, Connecticut: Yale University Press, 1954), "Laws Concerning Wounding and Damaging," Chapter Three, Section Twenty-two, p. 176.
The reader is left on his own; this one is beyond me. I cannot fathom what general
principle of jurisprudence Maimonides' case law represents.

9. See the essay by Gerald Vandezande, "On Strikes and Strife: A Critique of the
Status Quo," in John H. Redekop (ed.), *Labor Problems in a Christian Perspective*
(Grand Rapids, Michigan: Eerdmans, 1972).

You might imagine that such a moralistic argument against capitalism is a variation of Marxism. Such is not the case. Marx's few references to workers as commodities appear only in his youthful and unpublished *Economic and Philosophic Manuscripts of 1844*, which were not translated into English until the mid-1960's, and which had zero influence on traditional Marxist thought.[10] Marx was quite matter-of-fact in his published writings concerning human labor as a commodity. In his major theoretical work, *Capital* (1867), Marx argued that the "free laborer," meaning the wage-earner in a capitalist economy, sells his own commodity, labor power, to the capitalist. He "must constantly look upon his labour-power as his own property, his own commodity, and this he can only do by placing it at the disposal of the buyer temporarily, for a definite period of time."[11] Original Marxist theory presumes that if the legally free laborer can legitimately look at his own labor power as a commodity, then so can the capitalist buyer. Marx argued that the terms of sale involve exploitation by the capitalist, but he did not argue that the item sold, human labor, is somehow not a commodity.

Years earlier, Marx had distinguished between slave labor, in which the worker is a commodity, and free labor under capitalism, in which he isn't. He discussed labor power, not the worker as a commodity. "Labour power was not always a *commodity*. Labour was not always wage labour, that is, *free labour*. The *slave* did not sell his labour power to the slave-owner, any more than the ox sells its services to the peasant. The slave, together with his labour power, is sold once and for all to his owner. He is a commodity which can pass from the hand of one owner to that of another. He is *himself* a commodity, but the labour power is not *his* commodity."[12] Popular Marxism may occasionally use the idea of "proletarian man, the commodity" to gain converts, but traditional Marxism has always focused on Marx's exploitation theory, his surplus value theory, and other more arcane topics. Thus, to criticize capitalism because of its alleged result — workers as commodities — is a most un-Marxist line of rea-

10. These statements appear in the essay, "Antithesis of Capital and Labor. Landed Property and Capital." Two brief references to workers as commodities from this essay are the only ones listed in *Karl Marx Dictionary*, edited by Morris Stockhammer (New York: Philosophical Library, 1965), p. 268.

11. Karl Marx, *Capital* (New York: Modern Library, [1867] 1906), ch. 6, pp. 186-87. The Modern Library version is a reprint of the Charles H. Kerr edition.

12. Marx, *Wage Labour and Capital* (1849), in Karl Marx and Frederick Engels, *Selected Works*, 3 vols. (Moscow: Progress Publishers, 1969), I, p. 153.

soning. Marx believed that it was feudalism and especially capitalism that destroyed slavery, the system in which workers supposedly did become commodities.

Reductionism and Impersonalism: Costly Errors

What we need to ask ourselves is this question: Is everything that commands a price nothing more than a commodity? The phrase "nothing more than" is crucial. Whenever we encounter it, either explicitly or implicitly, we are encountering a form of economic reductionism.

In any sort of scientific analysis, there lurks the threat of reductionism. This is especially true in the case of social science. Man and man's personal relationships can be reduced to "merely" economics, or "merely" induced responses to stimuli, or "merely" chemical responses, or even nothing more than a figment of his imagination (solipsism). By reducing our explanation of man and his actions to one seemingly all-encompassing model, we become "monocausational" (single cause) thinkers. Monocausational theories invariably become tautological — a repetition of the same concept using different words — and wind up explaining little, throwing little light on most of man's actions. An otherwise useful explanation of some *aspect* of man or society becomes a misleading concept when we attempt to explain *everything* in terms of it.

Economic analysis can easily be misused. Man's labor is sometimes discussed as *nothing more than* an impersonal commodity on an impersonal market. The producers of human labor then are formally reduced to *nothing more than* suppliers of a useful commodity. Man is treated as if he were *nothing more than* a commodity. But what we find in free market societies is that such attitudes on the part of employers (renters of human labor services) lead to reduced profits. Workers resent being treated as machines or as beasts of burden. They respond to such treatment by reducing their output, sometimes in subtle ways that cannot be easily monitored by their supervisors. Thus, on a free market, economic reductionism is self-penalizing for employers. Those who treat workers better, acknowledging the cosmic personalism of all existence, are more likely to bring forth positive, productive efforts from those who are employed by them. The false assumption of impersonalism therefore pays a price. Those who indulge themselves in the fantasy of economic reductionism and im personalism pay for the privilege.[13] Reductionism is not a zero-price intellectual resource.

The Commodity Factor

At the same time, those who categorically assail the idea that the laborer is *in part* a commodity, or that man's labor power is *in part* a commodity, have abandoned both the Bible and economic analysis. Obviously, if a man can exchange his labor services for scarce economic resources, then the person who purchases his labor services must regard these labor services as scarce economic resources. In short, *the buyer regards labor services as commodities.* Why else would the buyer (employer) give up scarce economic resources (wages) in order to obtain labor services?

Let us take the next step. Why would someone purchase an indentured servant? Why would he forfeit the ownership of present scarce economic resources in order to buy the future services of a person? The answer is obvious: he expects to gain from the transaction. Buyer and seller agree on a present price that they both believe is approximately equal to the *discounted* (by the relevant interest rate) value of that expected future stream of income, in the form of labor services.[14] The buyer buys the future services of the man by using the same process of economic estimation that he uses when buying the services of any tool of production. To get those future economic services from a machine, he must take delivery of the machine that supplies him with the services. Because indentured servitude is rare today, buyers normally rent the services of laborers for a day, a week, or a month at a time.[15] But under a system of indentured ser-

---

13. A good book on the positive effects of managers treating workers as human beings is R. C. Sproul's *Stronger than Steel: The Wayne Alderson Story* (New York: Harper & Row, 1980). Alderson took a faltering steel fabrication company that was 24 hours away from bankruptcy and made it one of the top ten in terms of efficiency, in less than two years, and without an infusion of new financial capital, simply by setting up daily prayer meetings open to all employees, and by requiring managers and foremen to show at least some minimal concern about the lives of the workers. He called forth the latent reserves of productivity from previously disgruntled, resentful workers.

14. Technically speaking, the exchange takes place because the *present value of the expected future stream of labor services* from the servant (minus the costs of maintaining the servant) is more valuable, in the eyes of the purchaser, than the expected future income stream of the asset he gives up in the exchange. The buyer and the seller *capitalize the expected future value of the servant.*

15. One of the few exceptions to this rule in the United States is the purchase of a professional athlete's future services. The best amateur athletes usually receive large

vitude, these *labor services* are legally capitalized at the time of purchase, and the buyer takes delivery of the *person* who is to supply them.

Slaves and indentured servants command a sale price. Why? Because their expected labor services are valuable. These services can be capitalized. The purchaser calculates the present market value of this expected stream of income in *exactly the same way* that he capitalizes the expected future income stream of any commodity. The same rate of interest establishes the discount of the future services of man, land, and machine, and to the same degree. The buyer estimates the proper purchase price of all forms of capital by means of the same statistical techniques.[16] To this extent, the transaction appears to be impersonal, "treating men like machines." But if we look closer, we find that all such transactions are ultimately personal. The wise (profit-seeking) slave-buyer calculates the expected future services of the slave in terms of how well he will treat the slave. He does the same when he estimates the value of a piece of farmland. He even makes such calculations regarding machinery. We speak of "babying" a tool when we really mean treating it with care by lubricating it, servicing it, and recognizing its limits in service. The rate of interest is itself an impersonal number that is the product of all the highly personal time-preferences (discounts for future goods and services) of the many economic decision-makers in the society. Ultimately, there can be no impersonalism in a universe created and providentially sustained by God.[17]

The very fact that bondservants command a price, and owners make rational economic decisions about how much to pay for bondservants, testifies to the reality of the commodity aspect of human labor. The existence of a market for bondservants indicates that men's labor services can be treated as commodities. In short, expected future labor services can be *capitalized*—converted into capital

---

bonuses in advance when they sign their professional contracts, as well as receiving a guaranteed wage for a specified period of time. They can legally quit the team and forfeit the agreed-upon wage income, but they are legally prohibited from offering their services to a rival team within the same sports league. The bonus capitalizes a portion of their future productivity.

16. If the tax laws recognized indentured servitude, bondservants would probably be depreciated the way a machine or any other depreciating asset would be. The United States tax code allows animals and fruit-bearing trees to be depreciated in this fashion.

17. Gary North, *The Dominion Covenant: Genesis* (2nd ed.; Tyler, Texas: Institute for Christian Economics, 1987), ch. 1.

goods that can be bought and sold in the present. This is the definition of every economic commodity: a producer of expected future income that can be priced — bought and sold — today. Present goods (the price) are exchanged for expected future services (income).

If a buyer expects a plot of land to produce a net income of one ounce of gold per year indefinitely, and he also expects a married pair of slaves to produce a net income of one ounce of gold per year, including the value of their children over an indefinite period, then he will pay the same price for the plot of land that he will pay for the slaves, other things being equal. The same estimating process governs both transactions, as does the same rate of interest. Both the land and the slaves are capitalized. Their expected future net incomes, when discounted by the prevailing rate of interest, produce the same sales price.

The Image of God

The Bible sets forth laws that regulate indentured servitude. This is another example of God's recognition of the image of God in man. It is immoral to treat men as if they were *nothing more than* beasts or burden. He allowed the Israelites to suffer under the crushing burden of slavery in Egypt in order to demonstrate to them the way in which rebellious men who worship other gods — demonic spirits — view their servants: as beasts to be sacrificed, as *nothing more than* commodities. The Egyptian Pharaohs who enslaved them were *reductionists*. They viewed the Israelite males only as beasts of burden or as potential future military enemies (Ex. 1:10). The Pharaoh was willing to kill all of Israel's male infants (Ex. 1:16), just as he might have slaughtered animals. He refused to acknowledge that there are God-ordained limits placed on bondservant-owners. God warns men not to make such an assumption. Men are more than beasts or machines. The commodity factor in human labor is only one aspect of man. A slave is more than the commodity that Aristotle described as "property with a soul."[18]

Nevertheless, the commodity factor is unquestionably one factor. Because the expected income stream produced by human labor can be capitalized according to the rules governing all other expected in-

---

18. I am using M. I. Finley's translation of *Politics* 1253b: Finley, *Ancient Slavery and Modern Ideology* (New York: Viking, 1980), p. 73. Sir Ernest Barker's translation is less graphic: "an animate article of property." *The Politics of Aristotle* (New York: Oxford University Press, [1946] 1960), pp. 9-10.

come streams, there is a potential market for permanent slaves and indentured servants. The Old Testament legitimized a system of private ownership of the *human* means of production. It has been only during the last two centuries that this outlook has become unacceptable.[19]

The Command to Labor

The second principle of the biblical covenant is "hierarchy."[20] The dominion covenant reflects this general covenantal principle: 1) God is over man, 2) man is over his wife, 3) parents are over children, and 4) mankind is over nature. To exercise effective, long-term *dominion over nature*, men must become *subordinate under God*.[21]

Modern democratic theory has steadily begun to reject all four points of this hierarchical worldview. First, God is seen as mythical, or at best a distant, powerless uncle. He does not intervene in human history. He does not "take sides" in mankind's disputes (at least not since World War II). Second, marriage is not seen as hierarchical; divorce has been legitimized legislatively for "unreconcilable differences," and the women's liberation movement has asserted radical equality between the marriage partners. Third, parents are understood as unreliable supervisors generally; a State-operated school system is to be substituted for parental authority. There is also a growing "children's rights" movement which promotes a program that includes such provisions as self-determination for children, the right to leave home, the right to all information available to adults, the right of self-education, the right of freedom from physical punishment, the right to sexual freedom, and the right to vote and hold political office.[22] We should recall Isaiah's words:

---

19. See Chapter 4's subsection, "The Anti-Slavery Impulse: Very Recent," pp. 181-82.

20. Ray Sutton, *That You May Prosper: Dominion By Covenant* (Tyler, Texas: Institute for Christian Economics, 1987), ch. 2.

21. North, *Dominion Covenant: Genesis*, chaps. 7, 8. Humanist theologian John C. Raines has written of Calvin: "Calvin understood the Christian life not as 'a vessel filled with God' but as an active 'tool and instrument' of the Divine initiative. But this is precisely our point. Active toward the world, the Christian knows himself as utterly passive and obedient toward God, whose Will it is his sole task to discover and obey." Raines, "From Passive to Active Man: Reflections on the Revolution in Consciousness in Modern Man," in Raines and Thomas Dean (eds.), *Marxism and Radical Religion: Essays Toward a Revolutionary Humanism* (Philadelphia: Temple University Press, 1970), p. 114.

22. Richard Farson, *Birthrights* (New York: Macmillan, 1974); cited by John Whitehead, *Parents' Rights* (Westchester, Illinois: Crossway, 1985), pp. 24-25. This movement began to be noticed in the mid-1970's: "Drive for Rights of Children," *U.S. News and World Report* (Aug. 15, 1974).

"And I will give children to be their princes, and babes shall rule over them" (Isa. 3:4). Finally, the more radical of the ecology movement's advocates have denied that men are over nature.[23] They have even argued that the idea of man over nature is a terrible legacy of Christianity, and that it has led to mass pollution.[24]

Unfaithful Servants and Indentured Servitude

Some people are unfaithful servants. They seek to escape the moral and institutional obligations of God's dominion covenant. One of the ways historically that God has put men visibly under the terms of His dominion covenant is through indentured servitude. Some ethical rebels can be made more effective laborers in God's kingdom through indentured servitude. Indentured servitude is an earthly manifestation of the authority-hierarchy relationship. The New Testament reconfirms the Old Testament view of marriage as a covenantal yoke,[25] and it reminds men that this yoke is analogous to the relationship of Christ to His church (Eph. 5:21-28). We must become servants of God in order to avoid remaining slaves to Satan.

Human slavery testifies to the reality of sin, as well as to the need of some rebels and some weak people for institutional subordination. Private property in slaves therefore testified to the need for men to learn submission to God, who is the personal Sovereign who owns the universe.[26] This thought is repulsive to the modern democratic faith. Modern democratic theory rejects the idea that private prop-

---

23. This view of the "autonomous" environment became part of the U.S. Park Service's policies regarding forest fires. Unless a fire was started by a camper or an arsonist, it was left alone to burn itself out "naturally." In the drought-ridden summer of 1988, a series of lightning-induced fires began in Yellowstone National Park. They spread, as the saying goes, like wildfire. By the time winter snows began to fall, these fires had burned about a million acres of land in three states. The President of the U.S. later admitted that he had not known about this "let it burn" policy. For an analysis critical of the United States Park Service, see Alston Chase, *Playing God in Yellowstone: The Destruction of America's First National Park* (New York: Atlantic Monthly Press, 1986).

24. See, for example, Lynn White, Jr., "The Historical Roots of Our Ecological Crisis," *Science* (10 March 1967); reprinted in Garrett de Bell (ed.), *The Environmental Handbook* (New York: Ballentine, 1970). For a critique of White's thesis, see R. V. Young, Jr., "Christianity and Ecology," *National Review* (Dec. 20, 1974); North, *Dominion Covenant: Genesis*, pp. 33-35.

25. Gary North, *The Sinai Strategy: Economics and the Ten Commandments* (Tyler, Texas: Institute for Christian Economics, 1986), ch. 7: "The Yoke of Co-operative Service."

26. On God's ownership of the creation, see Gary DeMar, *Ruler of the Nations: Biblical Blueprints for Government* (Ft. Worth, Texas: Dominion Press, 1987).

erty in the form of indentured servants can deal effectively with such issues as depravity, rebellion, laziness, and crime. Democratic theorists refuse to acknowledge the legitimacy of indentured servitude as a God-ordained private hierarchy that promotes the fulfillment of the dominion covenant. They attack private slavery as the greatest of all evils in history. Then they pass laws that make people slaves to the State. They do not reject the hierarchical structure of slavery; they merely substitute the State for the private slave-owner, and then they rename this relationship with a term more acceptable politically, such as "public welfare" which is to be paid for by "progressive taxation." They raise taxes above 40 percent of a family's income, and they call this "paying your fair share." Ancient Egypt, which under Joseph suffered from a 20 percent income tax rate, is called "oriental despotism."[27] Contemporary taxation at twice or three times this level is called progressive democratic fiscal policy.

Two Kinds of Ancient Slavery

Democratic theorists make no ethical distinction between the Hebrews' slave status in ancient Egypt and the enslavement of heathens in ancient Israel. All private chattel slavery is dismissed as evil. "Slavery is an example of an institutionalized evil," writes theologian Ronald Sider.[28] The Bible, however, does distinguish sharply between permanent slavery that was regulated by God's law and slavery that was antinomian — unregulated by God's law. This is why Paul was quite ready to have the escaped slave Onesimus return to the Christian household of Philemon (Phm. 10-12).

Men must serve one of two masters (Matt. 6:24). Each supernatural master has used slavery as part of his particular program of kingdom development. We are either under God's yoke or Satan's (Matt. 11:29-30). Christ's yoke is freedom; Satan's is bondage (Gal. 5:1). The ethical question of slavery — which form is righteous and which form is evil — must be answered by an appeal to biblical law. *A retroactive condemnation of all ancient slavery is biblically illegitimate; it reflects the critics' ethical submission to Satan.* When the Bible affirms the legitimacy of any institution, even if only for a millennium or two, then it is sin to call that institution universally evil, without qualifi-

---

27. Karl Wittfogel, *Oriental Despotism: A Comparative Study of Total Power* (New Haven, Connecticut: Yale University Press, 1957).

28. Ronald J. Sider, "Words and Deeds," *Journal of Theology for Southern Africa* (Dec. 1979), p. 38.

cation or respect to time. Such an accusation is analogous to calling God evil. Theologians and social philosophers who call God evil are dancing at the edge of permanent slavery in the lake of fire.

Why would God authorize indentured servitude? Because rebels sometimes seek to escape the requirements of the dominion covenant. They may work in ways prohibited by God. God therefore has placed some men under indentured servitude as a *means of evangelism*, and also as a means of extracting from them the *service due to Him*. Men who would otherwise perish are also placed under the care of a godly household. The most famous example in the Bible of this is the case of the Gibeonites, who tricked Joshua into taking them as permanent slaves — hewers of wood and drawers of water (Josh. 9:27) — rather than perish at his hand or be forced out of the land of Canaan.

American Negro Slavery

The slave system of the American South was neither exclusively "Pharaonic" nor "Mosaic." It was a mixed system, although it leaned more heavily toward the Pharaonic because it made no provision for the slaves to earn their freedom, nor did it allow slaves to go free in the seventh year. The system did not survive, among other things, the onslaughts of the West's evangelical preaching,[29] New England's Unitarian abolitionist moralizing, South Carolina's self-immolating secessionist hot-heads,[30] the Confederacy's self-destructive mass inflation,[31] mass-produced Yankee weaponry, and the North's superior numbers of soldiers.[32]

The debate over the biblical legitimacy of slavery in the South escalated in the mid-nineteenth century.[33] But this shift toward abo-

---

29. Bertram Wyatt-Brown, *Lewis Tappan and the Evangelical War Against Slavery* (Cleveland, Ohio: Case Western Reserve University Press, 1969).

30. Rushdoony is correct: the responsible leaders of the South, including Jefferson Davis, had been opposed to secession. R. J. Rushdoony, *The Nature of the American System* (Fairfax, Virginia: Thoburn Press, [1965] 1978), p. 78n. "In 1828-32, many Southern conservatives had refused to support South Carolina and [John C.] Calhoun in the nullification controversy because of the liberal theological orientation of its leaders. Thomas Cooper, president of the University of South Carolina, a major champion of nullification, was a noted Deist and Unitarian." *Ibid.*, p. 49.

31. Richard Cecil Todd, *Confederate Finance* (Athens, Georgia: University of Georgia Press, 1954), ch. 3.

32. Richard N. Current, "God and the Strongest Battalions," in David Donald (ed.), *Why the North Won the Civil War* (New York: Collier, 1960).

33. See, for example, Thornton Stringfellow, "A Brief Examination of Scripture Testimony of the Institution of Slavery" (1841); reprinted in Drew Gilpin Faust (ed.),

litionism in the thinking of Christians in the North was not originally the result of changes in orthodox trinitarian theology. As discussed in Chapter 4, the first group to change its views was the Society of Friends (Quakers),[34] who certainly did not emphasize the Trinity. It would be much easier to defend the argument that the advent of the Industrial Revolution in the late eighteenth century was a far greater factor in the rise of abolitionism than the pioneering efforts of the great theologians of the world, who never pioneered abolitionism anyway. Cheap mechanical labor no doubt made it less expensive for men whose societies benefitted from these technological developments to consider at long last the possibility of freeing other men's human slaves without suffering substantial decreases in economic production and national wealth.[35]

A team of four historians demonstrated in *Why the South Lost the Civil War* (1986) that the South's morale began to falter after the military defeats of July, 1863 (Vicksburg and Gettysburg), and then accelerated in the fall of 1864. Preachers began to call into question the original righteousness of the Confederate cause. When, in early 1865, the Confederate government voted to allow slaves to be brought into the army, with the understanding that the slaves would have to be promised their freedom if they served faithfully, the case for any supposed "innate slave mentality of the Negro" collapsed. Nobody wants to be defended militarily by innate slaves. Even before the war ended, the war to defend slavery had been reinterpreted by its supporters as a campaign to defend states rights or white supremacy or Southern honor. Nobody in the South called for the reimposition of slavery after the war ended.[36] Military defeat by the anti-slavery North, not slavery's alleged economic inefficiency, doomed the South's slave system.[37]

The Ideology of Slavery: Proslavery Thought in the Antebellum South, 1830-1860 (Baton Rouge: Louisiana State University Press, 1981), ch. III. See also Eric L. McKitrick (ed.), *Slavery Defended: The Views of the Old South* (1963) and John L. Thomas (ed.), *Slavery Attacked: The Abolitionist Crusade* (1965), both published by Prentice-Hall, Englewood Cliffs, New Jersey.

34. See above, p. 181.

35. Again, as I said in Chapter 4, let me stress the fact that I am not arguing that the Industrial Revolution made abolitionism inevitable.

36. Richard E. Beringer, et al., *Why the South Lost the Civil War* (Athens, Georgia: University of Georgia Press, 1986), chaps. 13-16.

37. On the continuing profitability of legalized slavery, so long as the soil of the land owned by the final purchasers of slaves had not become depleted, see the classic essay by Alfred H. Conrad and John R. Meyer, "The Economics of Slavery in the Ante-Bellum South," *Journal of Political Economy*, LXVI (April 1958); reprinted many times, e.g., Robert W. Fogel and Stanley L. Engerman (eds.), *The Reinterpretation of American Economic History* (New York: Harper & Row, 1971), ch. 25.

While it lasted, though, slavery had positive educating effects for the slaves. The critics of Western slavery are seldom aware of the overwhelming impact of demonism on persons and cultures.[38] The close relationship between sub-Sahara Africa's animism and its perpetual poverty is not discussed in university classrooms. This is one reason why humanist scholars have such difficulty in explaining why State-to-State foreign aid programs do not produce long-term economic growth in backward nations. An understanding of the demonism-poverty relationship is fundamental to any valid economic, political, and social analysis of primitive cultures. This relationship is denied by most modern scholars, on those rare occasions when it is even considered. Scholars ignore the obvious: The slaves imported from Africa were former savages.[39] They were the victims of kidnapping by other savages, who then sold them to Arabs or directly to Western slave traders.

The high bids of English-speaking slave-owners can be said to have rescued some of these savages from Arab slavery, or from rival tribal slavery. It also can be said, however, that the high bids increased the demand for slaves, which in turn led to more slaves being hunted and taken. In any case, the slave-buyers should have known what they were doing: they were buying slaves from kidnappers. They simply preferred not to think through the economics of consumer sovereignty: consumers, not sellers, determine prices. Final demand creates intermediate demand. They were buyers of stolen goods. They were the accomplices of kidnappers. As such, they became subject to the death penalty (Ex. 21:16). God imposed this penalty on the South during the war, over half a century after slave imports from abroad had ceased. The South's slave-owners had ceased being the accomplices of kidnappers, but had instead become slave farmers: raising people as if they were cash crops, which they were, economically speaking.[40] Like the enslavement of the Hebrews by the Egyptians, it took two centuries for this judgment to be imposed on the South, but eventually God's patience ran out.

---

38. North, *Unholy Spirits*, ch. 8.

39. Resistance to any discussion of black Africans or Amerindians as savages, except possibly in the eighteenth-century context of "noble savages," is common in modern humanist circles. Theological savages come in many forms; tens of thousands of them hold Ph.D's in the social sciences and humanities.

40. The fact that slaves may only have been sold occasionally by any particular slave-holding family does not alter the accuracy of this economic analysis. Even if the slaves were not regarded as primary cash crops, they were surely regarded as legally transferrable capital assets. They were like seed corn held in reserve.

Academic Hostility to the Protestant Ethic

African blacks were savages who were being delivered by Southern slavery from earthly bondage to demons. They were being given the opportunity to improve their religious commitment, improve their skills, and ultimately achieve spiritual freedom. Scholars do not recognize that *covenantally faithful people who achieve spiritual freedom by the grace of God in history cannot forever be enslaved.* They lose their status as slaves to sin. This new judicial and ethical status eventually is manifested in history. This is a major theme of the Book of Exodus. *Spiritual freedom under Jesus Christ eventually produces political and economic liberty, though seldom in a single generation.* Conversely, spiritual bondage under Satan eventually produces political and economic bondage, though seldom in a single generation. *History is not covenantally neutral.* There is ethical cause and effect in mankind's institutional history, a covenantal fact denied vehemently by humanists and pietists alike. It is this denial which is the foundation of the operating alliance between humanists and pietists,[41] the defenders of the power religion and the defenders of the escape religion.[42]

There are five steps in the securing of this institutional liberty. They match the five points in the biblical covenant model. The first step is spiritual: faith in Jesus Christ as the sovereign Lord and Savior, the redeemer of men and institutions in history. The second step is the recognition of God's hierarchical covenants: the requirement of faithful labor under guidance from those who possess authority. The third step is covenantal faithfulness to the ethical terms of God's covenant. The fourth step is self-government (self-judgment) with the hope of God's blessings, both in heaven and in history. The fifth step is confidence concerning the long-run earthly effects of one's efforts. This confidence leads to a more efficient management of time and capital. In short, for any people to become liberated, they must change their perception of God, man, law, judgment, and time. They must then discipline their lives in terms of this covenantal worldview. In short, the way to liberty is by means of the Protestant ethic.

Technically oriented economic historians often not only ignore the capacity for self-transformation that the Protestant work ethic

---

41. Gary North, *Political Polytheism: The Myth of Pluralism* (Tyler, Texas: Institute for Christian Economics, 1989), Part 2.

42. Gary North, *Moses and Pharaoh: Dominion Religion vs. Power Religion* (Tyler, Texas: Institute for Christian Economics, 1985), pp. 3-5.

possesses, they openly deny it. One historian of ideas does not ignore it, Daniel Rodgers.[43] He writes of the fusion of the work ethic and economic growth in preindustrial America: "By the middle of the nineteenth century, the process had created in the American North an expansive, though still largely pre-industrial, economy and an unequaled commitment to the moral primacy of work."[44] But economic historians are usually more skillful technicians than "mere" intellectual historians, so they are more readily cursed with the tendency to believe the myth of value-free economic science.

Two skeptics regarding the moral and economic benefits of slaves' exposure to the Protestant work ethic are economic historians Roger Ransom and Richard Sutch. They reproduce a statement in 1900 by Hollis Burke Frissell, a prominent Southern educator. It is a statement that could hardly be quarrelled with, yet they quarrel with it. The first sentence is, admittedly, preposterous: "It is only fair to call attention to the part which the South performed in the education of the barbarous people forced upon her," but the authors ignore it. Why preposterous? Because the slaves were not educated by "the South," meaning the vast majority of southerners who were not slave-owners. It is misleading to equate "the South" with the slave system. To some extent these free citizens had the slave system forced on them, or at least "sold" to them by the aristocrats who had always dominated the South. Furthermore, those who did the educating of slaves, prior to 1865, did not have the slaves forced on them; they paid for them, and paid a lot. But the authors do not criticize these words. Instead, they criticize what follows: "The Southern plantation was really a great trade school where thousands received instruction in mechanic arts, in agriculture, in cooking, sewing, and other domestic occupations. . . . The training which the black had under

---

43. Daniel T. Rodgers was a student of a powerful triumvirate of American historians, Yale University's David Brion Davis, C. Vann Woodward, and Edmund S. Morgan. Rodgers writes in his Introduction to his book, *The Work Ethic in Industrial America, 1850-1920* (University of Chicago Press, 1978): "This is at bottom a study not of work but of ideas about work. In particular it is a study of those threads of ideas that came together to affirm work as the core of the moral life. By now reiteration of that claim has dulled its audacity. But in the long run of ideas it was a revolutionary notion. In and of itself work involves only an element of burden and, for most people, the goad of necessity. Few cultures have presumed to call it anything more than a poor bargain in an imperfect world. It was the office of ideas to turn the inescapable into an act of virtue, the burdensome into the vital center of living. That presumption — the work ethic — begins in a momentous act of transvaluation" (p. xi).

44. *Ibid.*, p. xii.

slavery was far more valuable as a preparation for civilized life, than the freedom from training and service enjoyed by the Indian on the Western reservations. For while slavery taught the colored man to work, the reservation pauperized the Indian with free rations; while slavery brought the black into the closest relations with the white race and its way of life, the reservation shut the Indian away from his white brothers and gave him little knowledge of their civilization, language or religion."[45]

The critics' comments reveal a great deal about the attitude of modern scholars towards the Protestant work ethic: "Frissell's suggestion that slavery imbued the slave with a work ethic indispensable to success as a free laborer has recently reappeared in the work of Robert Fogel and Stanley Engerman. These authors insist that the American slave internalized the 'Protestant work ethic.' Slaves were 'diligent,' 'responsible,' and 'hardworking,' 'virtues' they presumably carried with them into freedom. Upon closer examination, however, Fogel and Engerman's argument has been shown to amount to nothing more than a curious interpretation of the well-known fact that slaves were worked hard."[46] We are once again face to face with reductionism: *nothing more than*.

Even if this were true — nothing more than the fact that "slaves were worked hard" — it would be enough. Learning the rigors of disciplined labor is no minor achievement.[47] Being in a culture that expected people to work six days a week, with few vacations and little idleness, provided a competitive model that had its effects on the post-Civil War black freedmen. It is economic reductionism which leads otherwise sensible and painstaking scholars to write that "freedmen worked hard, not because they had actually been imbued with the Protestant work ethic as slaves, but because of the powerful

---

45. Cited by Roger L. Ransom and Richard Sutch, *One Kind of Freedom: The economic consequences of emancipation* (New York: Cambridge University Press, 1977), p. 20.

46. *Idem.* The authors refer in a footnote to another essay co-authored by Sutch, an essay whose very title tells all: "Sambo Makes Good, or Were Slaves Imbued with the Protestant Work Ethic?" in Paul A. David, *et al.*, *Reckoning with Slavery: A Critical Study in the Quantitative History of American Negro Slavery* (New York: Oxford University Press, 1976).

47. The restructuring of the outlook and personal habits of self-discipline of factory workers was necessary to the coming of the Industrial Revolution in Britain. It took a generation for managers and churchmen to accomplish even a rudimentary shift in the habits of the laboring classes. Sidney Pollard, *The Genesis of Modern Management: A Study of the Industrial Revolution in Great Britain* (Cambridge, Massachusetts: Harvard University Press, 1965), ch. 5: "The Adaptation of the Labour Force."

influence of self-interest. . . . The freedmen were the beneficiaries of emancipation, not of slavery."[48]

They forget that emancipation from demonism is the first step toward long-term economic success. The slaves went through two stages of social emancipation: first, when the original Africans were transported by force to the insufficiently Christian South; and second, when their heirs were emancipated from their insufficiently ethical masters. Although the original acts of kidnapping were immoral, their long-term results were to the benefit of those victimized Africans who survived the Atlantic passage and the early years of their enslavement.[49] The critics also forget that what men regard as economic self-interest varies widely across the globe, culture to culture. Men respond to incentives and opportunities (problems) in different ways. To imagine that the freedmen of 1865-80 responded to their economic environment in approximately the same way that their savage, demon-worshipping, shaman-manipulated forebears would have responded is not only naive, it is positively denigrating to the economic and spiritual wisdom of the freedmen.[50] More to the point, it is all too favorable to their ancestors, not to mention the pagan gods that they worshipped.

What we must recognize is that bondage to sin produces bondage in other areas of life, both personal and cultural. Neither judicial emancipation nor slavery is in itself a solution to the bondage of sin. Slavery in tribal Africa would not have solved the black African's spiritual poverty, but slavery in a spiritually compromised Christian culture eventually led to his hoped-for emancipation. Hard work as slaves within the cultural framework of a generally free and generally Christian society was a better training ground for a slave's eventual emancipation than hard work as a slave within some shaman-governed tribe.

Freedom begins with internal regeneration, and then steadily works its effects outward. If spiritual freedom is not allowed by civil

---

48. Ransom and Sutch, *One Kind of Freedom.*, p. 22.

49. It would be preposterous to deny the benefits to Israel of Solomon's wisdom just because he was the product of a marital union originally based on adultery and murder. The undeniable evil of the latter does not negate the equally undeniable benefits of the former.

50. I have no doubt that the proportional representation of saints in heaven is much higher for nineteenth-century American slaves than it is for twentieth-century economists. The bulk of the economists will be spending eternity with the shamans who stayed behind in Africa.

rulers to work its way toward political and economic freedom, then God at last breaks the chains of bondage that restrain the covenantal blessings of freedom. This is the message of the Book of Exodus. Antinomian Christians do not believe this, and humanistic scholars do not admit this, but God says that this is the way He runs His world.

Economic Self-Interest

A slave is not usually an efficient worker. At times, he must be forced to work. Like draftees, or even volunteers in military service, fear motivates slaves. Yet it is also true that a military unit that is run exclusively by fear is not likely to fight as well as units that also combine honor, loyalty, comradeship, a taste for victory, a sense of purpose, and the possibility of personal advancement up through the ranks, not to mention the prospect of an honorable discharge. An army of perpetual recruits, of perpetual boot camps, is not going to win many battles. We are back to reductionism: the idea that people respond to *nothing more than* fear. Societies that are based on the assumption of any kind of reductionism do not survive. Man and society are more than any single characteristic.

Fogel and Engerman, whose evaluation is so despised by Ransom and Sutch, have concluded the obvious, something any sensible observer might have known before the two began their detailed study of slavery—a study which received a firestorm of criticism from the academic and literary world. They write: "While whipping was an integral part of the system of punishment and rewards, it was not the totality of the system. What planters wanted was not sullen and discontented slaves who did just enough to keep from getting whipped. They wanted devoted, hard-working, responsible slaves who identified their fortunes with the fortunes of their masters. Planters sought to imbue slaves with a 'Protestant' work ethic and to transform that ethic from a state of mind into a high level of production."[51]

Slavery was the boot camp that God provided for half a million African "draftees"; emancipation gave their heirs a discharge out of "the service." It was the great historic evil of the slave-masters that slaves had been expected to spend their lives as recruits forever— and productive, loyal, hard-working recruits at that. When slaves became Protestants, in faith as well as ethic, the obvious hypocrisy of their masters must have been even more oppressive. Their masters

---

51. Robert William Fogel and Stanley L. Engerman, *Time on the Cross: The Economics of American Negro Slavery* (Boston: Little, Brown, 1974), p. 147.

simply did not take seriously biblical law and the Protestant doctrine of the priesthood of all believers. The military defeat of the South, like the defeat of Israel and Judah, should have served as a lesson in Protestant theology, how God uses the "rod" of an invading army — even an army drafted into service by pagan Boston abolitionists[52] — to bring His people to repentance.

The abolition of chattel slavery in the South did not end either racism or the South.[53] It launched a new phase in southern history, one which culminated a century later in the civil rights protests of the early 1960's.[54] That Karl Marx believed that the end of slavery would not only destroy the South but also destroy the United States is just one more piece of evidence that Marx was a third-rate prophet, a level of performance that matched the quality of his economic analysis. In 1847, he wrote:

Direct slavery is just as much the pivot of bourgeois industry as machinery, credits, etc. Without slavery you have no cotton; without cotton you have no modern industry. It is slavery that gave the colonies their value; it is the colonies that created world trade, and it is world trade that is the pre-condition of large-scale industry. Thus slavery is an economic category of the greatest importance.

Without slavery North America, the most progressive of countries, would be transformed into a patriarchal country. Wipe North America off the map of the world, and you will have anarchy — the complete decay of modern commerce and civilization. Cause slavery to disappear and you will have wiped America off the map of nations.[55]

Conclusion

Men can legitimately be evaluated as commodities, meaning as scarce economic resources that are still in demand at a price above zero. A man whose services are not in demand at zero price — a man

---

52. On the conspiratorial aspects of the Civil War, see Otto Scott, *The Secret Six: John Brown and the Abolitionist Movement* (New York: Times Books, 1979).

53. C. Vann Woodward, *The Strange Career of Jim Crow* (New York: Oxford University Press, 1957); Woodward, *Origins of the New South, 1877-1913* (Baton Rouge: Louisiana State University Press, 1951).

54. David J. Garrow, *Bearing the Cross: Martin Luther King, Jr., and the Southern Christian Leadership Conference* (New York: William Morrow, 1986); Taylor Branch, *Parting the Waters: America in the King Years, 1954-63* (New York: Simon & Schuster, 1988).

55. Karl Marx, *The Poverty of Philosophy* (Moscow: Foreign Languages Publishing House, [1847]), p. 107. In 1885, Engels added an unconvincing footnote: "This was perfectly correct for the year 1847." But what are we then to make of Marx's next statement? "Thus slavery, because it is an economic category, has always existed among the institutions of the peoples." *Ibid.*, pp. 107-8.

who is not a producer of the commodity of labor—is in sorry shape unless he has a great deal of income-producing capital.

The Bible's slave laws confirm this obvious economic truth. So valuable is "man, the commodity," that specific rules which limit the exploitation of this commodity by other men have been established by God. The key limitation is the seven-year maximum period of indentured servitude (Deut. 15:12). This limitation keeps down the price of the human commodity by *restricting the period of time in which his services can be lawfully capitalized by an owner.* Even in the case of life-time slavery, Old Testament law restricted slave-owners in their dealings with slaves. It is not true, as M. I. Finley asserts, that "The failure of any individual slaveowner to exercise all his rights over his slave-property was always a unilateral act on his part, never binding, always revocable."[56] In Greece and Rome, perhaps; not in ancient Israel. God, then as now, always warned those under the terms of His covenant that those in authority over men are also under the authority of other men, and that all men are under God and His law.

The Bible uses the economic self-interest of the owner to supplement the self-government and therefore the self-restraint that owners are expected to demonstrate to those under their authority. The bondservant is a valuable commodity. God tells bondservant-owners, "Handle with care, for these people are made in My image!" If they refuse to listen to God, then perhaps they will listen to the market. If they refuse to listen either to God or to the market, then the civil government must step in and enforce the law of God regarding indentured servitude. If the civil government refuses to obey God in this way, then God imposes other forms of negative sanctions: war, pestilence, or famine. There is no better example of this inescapable covenantal process in New Covenant history than the history of slavery in the American South.

Modern democratic theory has denied the legitimacy of biblical indentured servitude, but it has substituted a new form of slavery, which is in fact a very ancient form of slavery: *slavery to the State.* The State is a slave-owner which wants no private competition. It wants people placed in permanent bondage to the State. It establishes what sociologist Max Weber described as the bureaucratic cage.[57] It calls this system democratic freedom.

---

56. Finley, *Ancient Slavery*, p. 74.

57. Gary North, "Max Weber: Rationalism, Irrationalism, and the Bureaucratic Cage," in North (ed.), *Foundations of Christian Scholarship: Essays in the Van Til Perspective* (Vallecito, California: Ross House Books, 1976).

11

CRIMINAL LAW AND RESTORATION

If men strive, and hurt a woman with child, so that her fruit depart from her, and yet no mischief follow: he shall be surely punished, according as the woman's husband will lay upon him; and he shall pay as the judges determine. And if any mischief follow, then thou shalt give life for life, eye for eye, tooth for tooth, hand for hand, foot for foot, burning for burning, wound for wound, stripe for stripe (Ex. 21:22-25).

The theocentric principle here is that man is made in God's image and therefore must be protected by civil law. The husband of the victimized woman represents God the Judge to the convicted criminal. The State is required to impose sanctions specified by the husband. The violent person who has imposed on the woman and the child the risk of injury or death must compensate the family. The judges do retain some degree of authority in specifying the appropriate sanction. The criminal must pay "as the judges determine." In the absence of actual physical harm, there is no rigorous or direct way to assess the value of this risk of injury or death, so the State does not allow the husband to be unreasonable in imposing sanctions.

Where physical damage can be determined objectively, the criminal must pay on an "eye for eye" basis. This is the judicial principle known as the *lex talionis*. The punishment must fit the magnitude of the violation; the violation is assessed in terms of the damages inflicted.

Controversy Over Abortion

Exodus 21:22-25 has recently become one of the most controversial passages in the Old Testament. Prior to the 1960's, when the abortion issue again began to be debated publicly in the United States after half a century of relative silence,[1] only the second half of

---

1. Marvin Olasky, *The Press and Abortion, 1838-1988* (Hillsdale, New Jersey: Lawrence Erlbaum Associates, 1988), ch. 6. This book shows that in the late nineteenth century, the battle over abortion, as revealed in the press, was widespread.

this passage was controversial in Christian circles: the judicial requirement of "an eye for an eye." The abortion aspect of the argument was not controversial, for the practice of abortion was illegal and publicly invisible. A physician who performed an abortion could be sent to jail.[2] It was clearly understood by Christians that anyone who caused a premature birth in which the baby died or was injured had committed a criminal act, despite the fact that the person did not plan to cause the infant's injury or death. The abortion described in the text is the result of a man's battle with another man, an illegitimate form of private vengeance for which each man is made fully responsible should injury ensue, either to each other (Ex. 21:18-19) or to innocent bystanders. If this sort of "accidental" abortion is treated as a criminal act, how much more a deliberate abortion by a physician or other murderer! Only when pagan intellectuals in the general culture came out in favor of abortion on demand did pro-abortionists within the church begin to deny the relevancy of the introductory section of the passage.

This anti-abortion attitude among Christians began to change with the escalation of the humanists' pro-abortion rhetoric in the early 1960's. Christian intellectuals have always taken their ideological cues from the humanist intellectuals who have established the prevailing "climate of opinion," from the early church's acceptance of the categories of pagan Greek philosophy to the modern church's acceptance of tax-funded, "religiously neutral" education. As the humanists' opinions regarding the legitimacy of abortion began to change in the early 1960's,[3] so did the opinions of the Christian intellectual community. Speaking for the dispensationalist world of social thought, dispensationalist author Tommy Ice forthrightly admitted

---

2. Julius Hammer, the millionaire physician father of (later) billionaire Armand Hammer, in 1920 was sent to Sing-Sing prison in Ossining, New York, for performing an abortion in 1919. The woman had died from the operation. Hammer was convicted of manslaughter. (If all women died after an abortion, there would be fewer abortions performed.) Predictably, several physicians protested the law, but to no avail. Armand Hammer, *Hammer* (New York: Putnam's, 1987), pp. 74-82. Contrary to Hammer's glowing tribute to his father, the press was hostile to Julius Hammer. See Joseph Finder, *Red Carpet* (New York: Holt, Rinehart & Winston, 1983), p. 18. (This book was reprinted in paperback by the American Bureau of Economic Research, Ft. Worth, Texas, in 1987). Julius Hammer had been a member of the Socialist Labor Party, a precursor of the American Communist Party. He became a millionaire by trading in pharmaceuticals with the USSR. He actually served as commercial attaché for the USSR in the United States. *Ibid.*, pp. 12-16.

3. Olasky, *The Press and Abortion*, chaps. 10, 11.

in a 1988 debate: "Premillennialists have always been involved in the present world. And basically, they have picked up on the ethical positions of their contemporaries."[4] (He defended this practice, it should be noted.) The shift in Christian opinion regarding the illegitimacy of abortion took place throughout the 1960's and early 1970's.

The moral schizophrenia of contemporary pietism can be seen when anti-abortion picketers confront killer physicians at their offices with some variation of "Smile! God loves you" or "God hates abortion but loves abortionists." On the contrary, God hates abortionists, and He demands that the civil government execute them. Where are Christian protesters who pray the imprecatory psalms, such as Psalm 83? Where are they calling publicly on God to bring judgment against abortionists and their political allies?[5] Only when Christian anti-abortionists freely and enthusiastically admit that the Bible demands public execution for all convicted abortionists, and also for the women who pay for them, will they at last be proclaiming the Bible's judicial requirements.

The fact that they draw back from proclaiming this testifies to the appalling lack of biblical thinking that prevails in contemporary Christianity. *The vast majority of Christians hate God's revealed law far more than they hate either abortion or abortionists.* They would far rather live in a political world that is controlled by humanists who have legalized abortion than in a society governed by Christians in terms of biblical law. So, God has answered the desire of their hearts. He has done to modern Christians what He did to the Israelites in the wilderness: "And he gave them their request; but sent leanness into their soul" (Ps. 106:15).

The Legalized Slaughter of the Innocents

I do not intend to deal in detail with the question of abortion in this context.[6] There is no doubt that these verses apply to abor-

---

4. Cited in Gary DeMar, *The Debate Over Christian Reconstruction* (Ft. Worth, Texas: Dominion Press, 1988), p. 185. The debate was Dave Hunt and Tommy Ice vs. Gary North and Gary DeMar. A pair of audio cassette tapes or a videotape of this April 14, 1988 debate are available from the Institute for Christian Economics.

5. Gary North, *When Justice Is Aborted: Biblical Standards for Non-Violent Resistance* (Ft. Worth, Texas: Dominion Press, 1989), pp. 88-94.

6. J. J. Finkelstein points out that some variation of this law — the jostled woman who aborts her infant — is found in many of the ancient law sources. Finkelstein, *The Ox That Gored* (Philadelphia: American Philosophical Society, 1981), p. 19n. It is treated at length in Hammurabi's laws (209-14), Hittite laws (17-18), and Middle

tion.[7] The legal issue is clear: *victim's rights*. In all cases of public evil that the Bible prohibits, there must be judicial representatives of God: the victims are the primary representatives, and the various covenant officials are secondary representatives. When the victims cannot defend their interests, then the covenantal officers become the legal representatives of the victims.[8] The potential victims in this case are the unborn infants whose lives are sacrificed on the altar of convenience. Because they are incapable of speaking on their own behalf, God empowers their fathers to speak for them, or in cases where a father remains silent, God empowers the civil government to speak for them: first to prohibit abortion, and second to impose the death penalty on all those who are involved with abortion, either as murderers (mothers) or as their paid accomplices (physicians, nurses, office receptionists, and so forth).

False Prophets

All this is conveniently ignored by Christian abortionists and their academically respectable false prophets.[9] Examples of pro-abortionists, especially physicians, in evangelical churches can be found in a book put out in 1969 by the Christian Medical Society, *Birth Control and the Christian: A Protestant Symposium on the Control of Human Reproduction*, edited by Walter O. Spitzer and Carlyle L. Saylor.[10] Bruce K. Waltke, then a Dallas Theological Seminary professor, and presently a professor at Westminster Theological Seminary in Philadelphia, explicitly stated in that book that Exodus 21:22 teaches that "the fetus is not reckoned as a soul."[11] (He subsequently reversed his pro-abortion stance.) Dr. M. O. Vincent, psychiatrist, reported that the symposium moved him to conclude that "the foetus has great and developing value, but is less than a human being. It

---

Assyrian laws (21): *Ancient Near Eastern Texts Relating to the Old Testament*, edited by James B. Pritchard (3rd ed.; Princeton, New Jersey: Princeton University Press, 1969), Part II, Legal Texts. Finkelstein argues that the text is probably a literary device rather than legal, since the likelihood of an abortion occurring in this way is minimal. What he does not consider is that as a case law, it was intended to be a minimal application example: if, in this biologically unlikely situation, the one causing harm is fully liable, how much more the liability of an actual abortionist.

7. R. J. Rushdoony, *The Myth of Over-Population* (Fairfax, Virginia: Thoburn Press, [1969] 1975), Appendix 3.

8. North, *When Justice Is Aborted*, ch. 2.

9. *Ibid.*, Appendix A.

10. Wheaton, Illinois: Tyndale House, 1969.

11. *Ibid.*, p. 11.

will be sacrificed only for weighty reasons."[12] Predictably, he refused to spell out in detail what these weighty reasons are. Dr. William B. Kiesewetter, before leading the reader to his conclusion that a Christian physician friend was doing the right thing when he "terminated the pregnancy" (never seen as terminating the baby) of a missionary's wife, warns us against "Rigid, authoritarian evangelicals [who] so often extract from the Word of God precepts which they then congeal into a legalism by which everyone is admonished to live."[13] (His main problem is not with rigid, authoritarian evangelicals. His main problem is with the rigid, authoritarian God who commanded Moses to write Exodus 21:22-25. This is the main problem faced by all false prophets who blithely deny the continuing judicial authority of God's Bible-revealed law, and who then proceed to recommend the violation of God's law whenever convenient.)

In short, it is not necessarily immoral to take money for performing an abortion, provided that you are licensed by the medical profession to do so. These self-deluded physicians would bring a non-physician to court for practicing an abortion — an infringement on their state-licensed monopoly — but not a licensed colleague. Such is the state of twentieth-century medical ethics, including the ethics of self-professed Christians.

A book by D. Gareth Jones, Professor of Anatomy at the University of New Zealand, *Brave New People: Ethical Issues at the Commencement of Life* (1984), created a national Christian protest in the United States against its neo-evangelical, "liberal whenever remotely possible" publisher, Inter-Varsity Press. The book promotes a view of the "foetus" that would allow abortion in uncertain, undefined cases. Franky Schaeffer, the son of Francis Schaeffer (*Whatever Happened to the Human Race?*), mounted a protest in 1984 which led to the resignation of the editor of IVP and the scrapping of the book. Eerdmans republished it the next year. It is still published by IVP in Britain.[14]

A Question of "Barbaric" Sanctions

Christian scholars generally choose to ignore Exodus 21:22-25, and then they spend their time defending mass murder in the name of biblical ethics and "compassion" — compassion for murderous

---

12. *Ibid.*, p. 213.

13. *Ibid.*, p. 561.

14. For a critique of this book, see Gary North, *Moses and Pharaoh: Dominion Religion vs. Power Religion* (Tyler, Texas: Institute for Christian Economics, 1985), pp. 350-58.

women and their well-paid, state-licensed accomplices. Meanwhile, these critics of biblical law are busy challenging any defenders of the law with criticisms along these lines: "You would reimpose the barbaric principle of poking out a man's eye or cutting off his hand. This is nothing but vengeance, a return to savagery. What possible good would it do the victim to see the assailant suffer physical damage identical to his own? Why not impose some sort of economic restitution to the victim? To inflict permanent injury on the assailant is to reduce his productivity and therefore the wealth of the community. By returning to Old Testament law, you are returning to the tribal laws of a primitive people."[15] (This line of criticism incorrectly assumes that the *lex talionis* principle was not in fact designed by God to encourage economic restitution to the victim from the criminal. Chapter 12 will demonstrate that *lex talionis* promotes economic restitution.)

Nevertheless, the question remains: *Which is truly "barbaric," mass murder through legalized abortion or the required judicial sanctions revealed in biblical law?* The Christian antinomians of our day—that is to say, virtually all Christians—have voted for the barbaric character of biblical law. They are faced with a choice: Minimal sanctions against abortion or the civil enforcement of biblical law? Their answer is automatic. They shout to their elected civil magistrates, "Give us Barabbas!" Better to suffer politically the silent screams of murdered babies, they conclude, than to suffer the theocratic embarrassment of calling for the public execution of convicted abortionists.[16] The babies who are targeted for destruction have only a confused, inconsistent, waffling, squabbling, rag-tag army of Christians to

---

15. Henry Schaeffer wrote a book called *The Social Legislation of the Primitive Semites* (New Haven, Connecticut: Yale University Press, 1915). The title is revealing. He did not comment on the "eye for eye" passages.

16. We must not miss the point: the inevitable issue here is *theocracy*. When a Christian calls for the execution of the convicted abortionist, he is necessarily calling for the enforcement of God's revealed law by the civil magistrate. This fear of being labeled a theocrat is why James Dobson chooses to weaken his response to a pro-abortion physician by not dealing forthrightly with Exodus 21:22-25: "Do you agree that if a man beats his slave to death, he is to be considered guilty only if the individual dies instantly? If the slave lives a few days, the owner is considered not guilty (Exodus 21:20-21)[?] Do you believe that we should stone to death rebellious children (Deuteronomy 21:18-21)? Do you really believe we can draw subtle meaning about complex issues from Mosaic law, when even the obvious interpretation makes no sense to us today? We can hardly select what we will and will not apply now. If we accept the verses you cited, we are obligated to deal with every last jot and tittle." Dobson, "Dialogue on Abortion," in James Dobson and Gary Bergel, *The Decision of Life* (Arcadia, California: Focus on the Family, 1986), p. 14.

speak for them authoritatively in God's name inside the corridors of political and judicial power. Their defenders are agreed: "Abortion is the lesser of two evils, if the alternative is theocracy."[17]

In stark contrast is the tiny handful of Christians[18] who confidently believe in the whole Bible, including Exodus 21:22-25, and who have therefore confidently voted against abortion as the true barbarism and for biblical law as the sole long-term foundation of Christian civilization. But most Christians have self-consciously suppressed any temptation to think about this dilemma, one way or the other. The thin picket lines in front of abortion clinics testify to the thoughtlessness of Christians in our day. (So do the thin shelves of the Christian bookstores.)[19]

Restitution and Vengeance

The "eye for an eye" principle is known by the Latin phrase, *lex talionis*, or "law of retaliation." The English word, "retaliate," is derived from the same Roman root as "talionis." Today, "retaliate" means to inflict injury, but earlier English usage conveyed a broader meaning: *to pay back or return in kind*, including good will.[20] According to one source, the *lex talionis* was a Roman law that specified that anyone who brought an accusation against another citizen but could not prove his case in the courts would suffer the same penalty that he had sought to inflict on the defendant.[21] (This was a perverted version of the biblical principle of the law governing deliberate perjury, found in Deuteronomy 19:16-21, which concludes with a restatement

---

17. Christian anti-abortionists will attempt to find a third choice. It may be natural law. It may be emotion. It may be the will of the people. It may be to some less familiar version of common-ground philosophy, meaning baptized humanism. What it will not be is an appeal to the whole Bible as the sole authoritative will of God.

18. Christian Reconstructionists or theonomists.

19. James Jordan's book, *The Law of the Covenant: An Exposition of Exodus 21-23* (Tyler, Texas: Institute for Christian Economics, 1984), was removed from the shelves of a local Christian bookstore in Tyler when the store's owner discovered that Jordan had called for the execution of the aborting physician and the mother. The owner dared not take the heat for selling a book which announced: "Until the anti-abortion movement in America is willing to return to God's law and advocate the death penalty for abortion, God will not bless the movement. God does not bless those who despise His law, just because pictures of salted infants make them sick" (p. 115).

20. See the *Oxford English Dictionary*: "retaliate."

21. *Cyclopaedia of Biblical, Theological, and Ecclesiastical Literature*, edited by John McClintock and James Strong (New York: Harper & Bros., 1894), Vol. X, p. 165: "Talionis, Lex."

of the "eye for eye" requirement in verse 21. The law reads: "Then shall ye do unto him [the false witness], as he had thought to have done unto his brother: so shalt thou put the evil away from among you" [v. 19].[22] Only if the innocent person could prove perjury on the part of his accuser could he demand that the civil government impose on the latter the penalty that would have been imposed on him.[23])

Not every Bible commentator has seen the "eye for eye" sanction as primitive. Shalom Paul writes: "Rather than being a primitive residuum, it restricts retaliation to the person of the offender, while at the same time limiting it to the exact measure of the injury— thereby according equal justice to all."[24] W. F. Albright, the archeologist who specialized in Hebrew and Palestinian studies, wrote: "This principle may seem and is often said to be extraordinarily primitive. But it is actually not in the least primitive. Whereas the beginnings of *lex talionis* are found before Israel, the principle was now extended by analogy until it dominated all punishment of injuries or homicides. In ordinary Ancient Oriental jurisprudence, men who belonged to the higher social categories or who were wealthy simply paid fines, otherwise escaping punishment. . . . So the *lex talionis* (is) . . . the principle of equal justice for all!"[25] Albright understood some of the implications of the passage for the principle of equal justice for all, meaning equality before the law. Nevertheless, the myth of "primitive" legislation still clings in people's minds.[26] It seems to some Christians to be a needlessly bloody law. In a reaction against the rigor of this judicial principle, liberal scholar Hans Jochen Boecker goes so far as to argue that Old

---

22. The same rule applied in Hammurabi's Code: "If a seignior came forward with false testimony in a case, and has not proved the word which he spoke, if that case was a case involving life, that seignior shall be put to death. If he came forward with (false) testimony concerning grain or money, he shall bear the penalty of that case." CH, paragraphs 3-4: *Ancient Near Eastern Texts*, p. 166.

23. A moral judicial system would impose on the accuser or his insurance company all court costs, plus the costs incurred by the defendant in defending himself.

24. Shalom Paul, *Studies in the Book of the Covenant in the Light of Cuneiform and Biblical Law* (Leiden: E. J. Brill, 1970), p. 40.

25. W. F. Albright, *History, Archaeology, and Christian Humanism* (New York, 1964), p. 74; cited in *ibid.*, p. 77.

26. Hammurabi's "code" has similar rules: "If a seignior has destroyed the eye of a member of the aristocracy, they shall destroy his eye. If he has broken a(nother) seignior's bone, they shall break his bone." CH, paragraphs 196-97. If an aristocrat has destroyed the eye of a commoner, however, the *lex talionis* did not apply: he paid one mina of silver (CH 198). *Ancient Near Eastern Texts*, p. 175.

Testament law was not actually governed by *lex talionis*,[27] that it only appears in three instances, and that it is a holdover of early nomadic law.[28]

"Vengeance Is Mine"

Vengeance in the Bible is God's original responsibility. "To me belongeth vengeance, and recompence; their foot shall slide in due time: for the day of their calamity is at hand, and the things that shall come upon them make haste" (Deut. 32:35). "If I whet my glittering sword, and mine hand take hold on judgment; I will render vengeance to mine enemies, and will reward them that hate me. I will make mine arrows drunk with blood, and my sword shall devour flesh . . ." (Deut. 32:41-42a). All nations are required to rejoice because of God's willingness and ability to avenge His people: "Rejoice, O ye nations, with his people: for he will avenge the blood of his servants, and will render vengeance to his adversaries, and will be merciful unto his land, and to his people" (Deut. 32:43). These passages, and many others in the Old Testament, are the foundation of Paul's summary statement: "Vengeance is mine; I will repay, saith the Lord" (Rom. 12:19b). "For we know him that hath said, Vengeance belongeth unto me, I will recompense, saith the Lord. And again, The Lord shall judge his people" (Heb. 10:30).

God makes it clear that He sometimes intervenes personally in history and brings bloody vengeance on His enemies. The State, under limited and Bible-defined circumstances, possesses an analogous authority. It is therefore highly inaccurate to say that the authority to impose vengeance in history is exclusively God's prerogative. God has delegated to the civil government its limited and derived sovereignty to impose physical vengeance. The State is allowed, by the testimony of witnesses, to impose the death penalty and other physical punishments. *Perfect justice must wait until the day of judgment; so must perfect vengeance.*[29] But men do not have to wait until the end of time in order to see preliminary justice done, and therefore preliminary vengeance imposed.

Vengeance is a form of *restitution*. "Vengeance is mine; I will *repay*." This repayment is in the form of punishment and even perma-

---

27. Hans Jochen Boecker, *Law and the Administration of Justice in the Old Testament and Ancient East*, translated by Jeremy Moiser (Minneapolis, Minnesota: Augsburg, [1976] 1980), pp. 171-72.

28. *Ibid.*, pp. 174-75.

29. North, *Moses and Pharaoh*, ch. 19: "Imperfect Justice."

nent judgment. God *pays back* what is owed to the sinner. It is *repay-ment in kind,* an original meaning of "retaliate." Capital crimes require the public execution of the guilty person. In the case of crimes less repugnant to God than capital crimes, economic restitution is often paid by the criminal to the victim. But restitution is ultimately owed to God.[30] The victim, as God's image bearer, deserves his restitution, just as God deserves His. When repayment in kind is not made, a sense of injustice prevails. The victim, or the family members who survive the victim, understand that a convicted criminal who is not forced to make restitution has evaded justice. Such an escape is seen as being unfair.

Fair Warning

God reminds His people that His ultimate justice cannot be evaded. This testimony of a final judgment is provided by the sanctions imposed by the authorities. Historical sanctions are designed by God to fit the crime in order to persuade men that *the universe is ultimately fair, for both time and eternity are governed by the decree of God.* God's people should not despair because some men escape the earnest (down payment) of the final justice that is coming. The 73rd Psalm is a reminder of the seeming injustice of life, and how the wicked are finally rewarded according to their deeds. "For I was envious at the foolish, when I saw the prosperity of the wicked" (Ps. 73:3). David was beaten down by events (v. 2), yet he saw all the good things that come to the wicked in life (vv. 4-5, 12). He flayed himself with such thoughts, "Until I went into the sanctuary of God; then understood I their end. Surely thou didst set them in slippery places: thou castedst them down into destruction. How are they brought into desolation, as in a moment! They are utterly consumed with terrors" (vv. 17-19). David finally admits: "So foolish was I, and ignorant: I was as a beast before thee" (v. 22).

The relationship between covenantal faithfulness and external prosperity is clearly taught in the Bible (Deut. 28:1-14). So is the relationship between covenant-breaking and calamity (Deut. 28:15-68). This system of sanctions applies to the whole world, not just in Old Testament Israel. Deny this, and you have also denied the possibility of an explicitly and exclusively Christian social theory. Christians who deny the continuing relevance of Deuteronomy 28's sanctions in

---

30. R. J. Rushdoony, *The Institutes of Biblical Law* (Nutley, New Jersey: Craig Press, 1973), pp. 525-30.

post-Calvary, pre-Second Coming history should be warned by David's admission that he had been foolish to doubt these relationships. The concept of *slippery places* is not often discussed, but it is very important. God sets people high *in order to make them slide*, visibly, before the world. God said to Pharaoh: "For now I will stretch out my hand, that I may smite thee and thy people with pestilence; and thou shalt be cut off from the earth. And in very deed for this cause have I raised thee up, for to show in thee my power; and that my name may be declared throughout all the earth" (Ex. 9:15-16). The temporary prosperity of the wicked must not be viewed as evidence that would call into question the long-term relationship between covenant-breaking and destruction.

Vengeance is legitimate, but not as a private act. It is always to be covenantal, governed by God's institutional monopoly, civil government. James Fitzjames Stephen said it best: "The criminal law stands to the passion of revenge in much the same relation as marriage to the sexual appetite."[31] The private vendetta is always illegitimate; public vengeance is sometimes legitimate. There are many examples of private vengeance not sanctioned by God: gangster wars, clan feuds, the murder of those who testify against a criminal or syndicate, and murders for breaking the code of silence of a secret society. It is a crime against God Himself to take any oath that testifies to the right of any private organization or voluntary society to inflict physical violence, especially death, for breaking the oath or any other violation of the "code," even if this oath's invoked penalties are supposedly only "symbolic" rather than literal. I refer here to Masonic oaths,[32] but also to any other similar oath. For example,

---

31. James Fitzjames Stephen, *A History of the Criminal Law in England* (London: Macmillan, 1863), II, p. 80. Cited by Ernest van den Haag, *Punishing Criminals: Concerning a Very Old and Painful Question* (New York: Basic Books, 1975), p. 12.

32. That the Freemasons adopt a covenantal view of the self-maledictory oath is admitted in *The Encyclopedia of Freemasonry*, a standard Masonic publication. The author of the section on "Oath" discusses the objections raised in the nineteenth century by the Roman Catholic Church and the Scottish seceders to Masonic oaths. He refers to the "sacred sanction" of an oath, and insists on the legitimacy of "the invocation of the Deity to witness" the oath. He cites Dr. Harris' *Masonic Discourses*: "What the ignorant call 'the oath,' is simply an obligation, covenant, and promise, exacted previously to the divulging of the specialties of the Order, and our means of recognizing each other; . . ." Explaining away the accusation that these secret oaths are taken in religious ceremonies, the author says: "Oaths, in all countries and at all times, have been accompanied by peculiar rites, intended to increase the solemnity and reverence of the act. . . . In all solemn covenants the oath was accompanied by a sacrifice; . . ." He admits that a Masonic oath may have sanctions attached, even

the oath of an Entered Apprentice of the Masonic order ends with
these words: ". . . binding myself under no less penalty than that of
having my throat cut from ear to ear, my tongue torn out by its roots
and buried in the rough sands of the sea at low-water mark where
the tide ebbs and flows twice in twenty-four hours, should I ever
knowingly or willingly violate this my solemn oath and obligation as
an Entered Apprentice Mason."[33] Such an oath affirms the legitimacy of private institutional vengeance — vengeance applied by institutions that have not been assigned the State's limited sovereignty
to serve as God's agency of vengeance.[34] This sort of physical vengeance is prohibited by biblical law, but the Bible does not condemn
all earthly vengeance. The State is an agency of God's vengeance. So
is the church, but the church may not lawfully impose physical vengeance, while the State can. Therefore, no church can legitimately
invoke oaths or oath signs similar in form to secret society blood
oaths. A church that does this has marked itself as a cult.

Limiting the State

The authority to impose vengeance is limited. This authority is
too easily abused for God not to place Bible-revealed restraints on it.
The officers of the civil government readily overstep their authority. The
State has often been seen as divine because it possesses the ability to
impose the death penalty and other punishments. What the Bible
presents as a limited, derived sovereignty, men have defined as an
ultimate, original sovereignty. To combat this false interpretation,
biblical law restrains the officers of the State by imposing strict limitations on their enforcement of law. It is God's law that must be enforced, and this law establishes criteria of evidence and a standard of
justice. This standard is "an eye for an eye." A popular slogan in the
modern world promotes a parallel juridical principle: "The punishment should fit the crime."

---

a capital penalty. All oaths do, he insists. This is "an attestation of God to the truth
of a declaration, as a witness and avenger; and hence every oath includes in itself,
and as its very essence, the covenant of God's wrath, the heaviest of all penalties, as
the necessary consequence of its violation." Albert G. Mackey, *The Encyclopedia of
Freemasonry and Its Kindred Sciences*, 2 vols. (rev. ed.; New York: Masonic History Co.,
1925), II, pp. 522-23.

33. *King Solomon and His Followers* (New York: Allen Pub. Co., 1943); cited in E.
M. Storms, *Should a Christian Be a Mason?* (Fletcher, North Carolina: New Puritan
Library, 1980), p. 63.

34. Gary North, *The Sinai Strategy: Economics and the Ten Commandments* (Tyler,
Texas: Institute for Christian Economics, 1986), pp. 55-58.

The Punishment Should Fit the Crime

Why should the punishment fit the crime? What ethical principle leads Western people to believe that the Islamic judicial practice of cutting off a pickpocket's hand is too severe a punishment? After all, this will make future pickpocketing by the man far less likely. Why not cut off his other hand if he is caught and convicted again? People who have grown up in the West are repelled by the realization that such punishments have been imposed in the past, and are still imposed in Muslim societies.[35] Why this repulsion? Because they are convinced that the punishment exceeds the severity of the loss imposed on the victim by the thief.

The Bible teaches that the victim must have his goods restored two-fold (Ex. 22:4, 7), four-fold (for stealing a sheep), or five-fold (for stealing an ox) (Ex. 22:1).[36] The passage on restitution in Leviticus 6 indicates that if the thief turns himself in before the authorities identify him as the thief, he must restore the principal (6:4), and must also add a 20 percent payment — a double tithe — presumably because of the false oath (6:5). The restitution is equal to the value of

---

35. This is Islam's *Shari'a* law. It is officially the civil law in Mauritania, where such amputations are still imposed: Roger Sawyer, *Slavery in the Twentieth Century* (London: Routledge and Kegan Paul, 1986), p. 15. *Shari'a* was reimposed in Sudan in 1988. Complains M. Ismail of Arlington, Virginia in a letter to the editor: "As a Sudanese, I feel that the previous legal code, which was an adoption of the British secular code, was a colonial yoke that disfigured our national independence." *Washington Times* (Oct. 3, 1988). Better to disfigure pickpockets than Sudan's national independence, Mr. Ismail is saying.

36. The seven-fold restitution of Proverbs 6:31 appears to be a *symbolic statement* regarding the comprehensive nature of restitution. The hungry thief who is destitute and who steals food must repay "all the substance of his house," meaning that what little he owns is forfeited when the normal two-fold restitution payment is imposed. A rich man who steals bread would not be made destitute by a two-fold payment. The poor thief has to pay to the limits of his wealth, despite his "extenuating circumstances," while the rich thief who steals for the love of evil-doing is barely touched financially. In short, the law plays no favorites. It does not respect persons. The perverse rich thief is not required to pay any greater percentage than the impoverished thief.

The seven-fold vengeance of God against anyone who might persecute Cain is another example of the language of fullness (Gen. 4:15). It means full judgment. Christ's words in Matthew 18 also indicate fullness: "Then came Peter to him, and said, Lord, how oft shall my brother sin against me, and I forgive him? Till seven times? Jesus saith unto him, I say not unto thee, Until seven times: but, Until seventy times seven" (vv. 21-22). "Seventy times seven" is hyperbolic language; seventy times "fullness" means totality. Such forgiveness is not to be forgiveness apart from biblical restitution, however; the principle of forgiveness is not to be used to subsidize evil: Rushdoony, *Institutes*, p. 463.

the item stolen, and the penalty is one-fifth of this.[37]

The Bible does not teach that a convicted man's future productivity should be utterly destroyed by the judges, except in the case of capital crimes. The dominion covenant imposes a moral obligation on all men to labor to subdue the earth to the glory of God. A man whose body has been deliberately mutilated probably will become a less productive worker. He may find it difficult to earn enough wealth to repay his debt to the victim. By cutting off the pickpocket's hand, the State is saying that there is no effective regeneration in life, that God cannot restore to wholeness a sinner's soul and his calling. Because he is a convicted pickpocket, he must be assumed to be a perpetual thief by nature; therefore, the State must make his future labor in his illegal calling less efficient. His hand is not being cut off because his victim lost a hand; it is being cut off simply as *an assertion of State power*, and as a deterrent against crime.

Boecker correctly observes that "The intention of the talion was not, therefore, to *inflict* injury — as it might sound to us today — but to *limit* injury."[38] But then he gets everything confused once again. He says that this law restrained the institution of blood revenge.[39] He never bothers to apply this principle of restraint to the modern State. The Bible teaches that excessive penalties imposed by the State violate a fundamental principle of biblical obedience, both personal and civil: "Ye shall observe to do therefore as the LORD your God hath commanded you: ye shall not turn aside to the right hand or to the left" (Deut. 5:32). Conclusion: neither is the State to *cut off* the pickpocket's right hand or his left.[40]

The Punishment Should Benefit the Victim

Societies that are not governed by biblical law do not place the proper emphasis on the principle of economic restitution. The con-

---

37. The King James translation reads: "he shall even restore it in the principal, and shall add the fifth part more thereto" (6:5). The New English Bible is clearer: "He shall make full restitution, adding one fifth to it." The New American Standard reads: "[H]e shall make restitution for it in full, and add to it one-fifth more." The restitution payment would appear to be the penalty payment equal to the item stolen.

38. Boecker, *Law and the Administration of Justice*, p. 174.

39. *Ibid.*, pp. 174-75.

40. The Hammurabi Code specified death for any thief who had taken an oath that he had not stolen: CH, paragraphs 9-10. There was a 30-fold restitution for stealing animals belonging to the State: paragraph 8. *Ancient Near Eastern Texts*, p. 166.

cern of the judicial system becomes *punishment of the criminal* rather than *restitution to the victim*. W. Cleon Skousen, a lawyer and former law enforcement official, has described the prevailing situation: "Under modern law, fines are almost invariably paid to the city, county or federal government. If the victim wants any remedy he must sue for damages in a civil court. However, as everyone knows, by the time a criminal has paid his fines to the court, he is usually depleted of funds or consigned to prison where he is earning nothing and therefore could not pay damages even if his victim went to the expense of filing a suit and getting a judgment. As a result, modern justice penalizes the offender, but does virtually nothing for the victim."[41] In later stages of the development of humanism, State officials begin to substitute the shibboleth of "rehabilitation" for punishment, although the form this "rehabilitation" takes makes the State's officers even more arbitrary than before.

Biblical law restrains the arbitrariness of the State's officers. If the punishment must fit the crime, then the judges do not have the authority to impose lighter judgments or heavier judgments on the criminal. The victim decides the penalty, not the judges.[42] The criminal is to be given sufficient freedom to repay the victim, even if he must be sold into indentured servitude for a specific period of time in order to raise sufficient funds to pay off the victim. As a servant, he learns the discipline of work, and perhaps sufficient skills to give him a new calling and a new life when his debt is paid. But the debt is always to a private party: to the victim originally, and the slave-owner secondarily. Where a specific victim is involved and can be identified, the debt is not owed as a fine to the State. It is owed to the victim. The man who causes a premature birth in which the baby is not harmed nevertheless pays a fine to the family because of the risk to which he subjected the pregnant woman and her child.

Fines Should Compensate Victims

This should not be understood as an argument against fines to the civil government for so-called "victimless crimes." For example, a person is prohibited from driving a car at 70 miles an hour through a

---

41. W. Cleon Skousen, *The Third Thousand Years* (Salt Lake City, Utah: Bookcraft, 1964), p. 354. Skousen served in the Federal Bureau of Investigation (FBI) for 16 years and also served as Chief of Police in Salt Lake City in 1956. He became Editorial Director of *Law and Order* in 1960, the leading professional law enforcement journal in the United States.

42. See above, Chapter 7: "Victim's Rights vs. the Messianic State."

residential district or school zone. There are potential victims who deserve legal protection. The speeding driver is subjecting them to added risk of injury or death. Clearly, it is more dangerous statistically for children to attend a school located near an unfenced street on which drivers are travelling at 70 miles an hour rather than 25. The imposition of a fine helps to reduce the number of speeding drivers. Because they increase risks to families, drivers who exceed the speed limit can legitimately be fined, since the victims of this increased statistical risk cannot be specified. These fines should be imposed locally: to be used to indemnify future local victims of crimes that go unpunished.

The State is not to use fines to increase its operating budget or increase its control over the lives of innocent citizens. The State is to be supported by tax levies, so that no conflict of interest should occur between honest judgment and the desire to increase the State's budget. The proper use of fines is the establishment of a *restitution fund for victims of crimes whose perpetrators cannot be located or convicted*, analogous to the Old Testament sacrifice of the heifer when a murderer could not be found (Deut. 21:1-9). Such a fund is a valid use of the civil law. Even if law enforcement authorities are unable to locate and convict a criminal, the victim still deserves restitution, just as God deserved restitution for an unsolved murder in Israel in the form of a sacrificed heifer. A reasonable way of funding such a restitution program is to collect money from those who have been successfully convicted by law enforcement authorities.

Hayek's Three Principles

Lex talionis binds the State. This so-called "primitive" principle keeps the State from becoming arbitrary in its imposition of penalties. *Citizens can better predict in advance what the penalty will be for a specific crime.* This is extremely important for maintaining a free society. The three legal foundations for a free society, Hayek argues, are known general rules, certainty of enforcement, and equality before the law. I argue that the principle of "eye for eye" preserves all three.

1. General Rules

First, with respect to general rules, Hayek writes that these rules must distinguish private spheres of action from public spheres, which is crucial in maintaining freedom: "What distinguishes a free from an unfree society is that in the former each individual has a recognized private sphere clearly distinct from the public sphere, and the private individual cannot be ordered about but is expected to obey only the rules which are equally applicable to all. It used to be the boast of free men that, so long as they kept within the bounds of the known law, there was no need to ask anybody's permission or to obey anybody's orders. It is doubtful whether any of us can make this claim today."[43] If men must ask permission before they act, society then becomes a *top-down bureaucratic order*, which is an appropriate structure only for the military and the police force (the "sword").[44] The Bible specifies that the proper hierarchical structure in a biblical covenant is a bottom-up appeals court structure (Ex. 18).[45]

Adam was allowed to do anything he wanted to do in the garden, with only one exception. He had to avoid touching or eating the forbidden fruit. He did not have to ask permission to do anything else. He was free to choose.[46] This biblical principle of legal freedom is to govern all our decisions.[47] This is stated clearly in Jesus' parable of the laborers who all received the same wage. Those who had worked all day complained to the owner of the field. The owner responded: "Friend, I do thee no wrong: didst not thou agree with me for a penny? Take that thine is, and go thy way: I will give unto this last, even as unto thee. Is it not lawful for me to do what I will with mine own? Is thine eye evil, because I am good?" (Matt. 20:13-15). Neither the owner nor the workers had to get permission in advance from some government agency. God leaves both sides free to choose the terms of labor and payment.

Because God alone is omniscient, He controls the world perfectly. Men, not being omniscient, must accept judicial restrictions on their own legitimate spheres of action. In doing so, they acknowledge their position as creatures under God. They must face the reality of their own limitations as creatures. They must not pretend that they can foresee the complex outcome of every activity of every per-

---

43. F. A. Hayek, *The Constitution of Liberty* (University of Chicago Press, 1960), pp. 207-8.

44. Ludwig von Mises, *Bureaucracy* (Cedar Falls, Iowa: Center for Futures Education, [1944] 1983), ch. 2. Distributed by Libertarian Press, Spring Mills, Pennsylvania.

45. Ray R. Sutton, *That You May Prosper: Dominion By Covenant* (Tyler, Texas: Institute for Christian Economics, 1987), ch. 2.

46. Milton and Rose Friedman, *Free to Choose: A Personal Statement* (New York: Harcourt Brace Jovanovich, 1980).

47. Grace Hopper, who developed the computer language Cobol, and who served as an officer in the U.S. Navy until she was well into her seventies, offered this theory of leadership: "It's easier to say you're sorry than it is to ask permission."

son in society. The complexity of life is too great. Men can only make guesses about the consequences of human action. *To bring the greatest quantity of accurate knowledge to bear on society at any point in time, men must be allowed great latitude in their personal decision-making.* This division of intellectual labor is what provides society with the best available knowledge at a price people are willing to pay.[48] If men pretend that a committee of experts can plan for an entire economy, they have denied God's exclusive omnipotence and omniscience. Hayek is correct: ". . . the demand for conscious control is therefore equivalent to the demand for control by a single mind."[49] He goes on to argue: "Indeed, any social processes which deserve to be called 'social' in distinction from the action of individuals are almost *ex definitione* not conscious. Insofar as such processes are capable of producing a useful order which could not have been produced by conscious direction, any attempt to make them subject to such direction would necessarily mean that we restrict what social activity can achieve to the inferior capacity of the individual mind."[50] Worse; in a socialist society, we restrict what social activity can achieve to what a responsibility-avoiding, government-protected committee can achieve.

By decentralizing decision-making within a system of known rules, and by allowing a competitive system of market-imposed rewards and punishments, society preserves individual freedom, individual and corporate productivity, and personal responsibility. This decentralized decision-making process is what is established by the profit management system.[51]

The principle of "eye for eye" is easily understood. It allows people to evaluate in advance their potential liabilities for actions that inflict physical harm on others. This encourages personal responsibility. It also encourages people to make accurate assessments of potential costs and benefits of their actions. This is the biblical principle of *counting the cost* (Luke 14:28-30). It is basic to biblical liberty that individuals count the costs of their behavior.

---

48. Hayek, *Individualism and Economic Order* (University of Chicago Press, 1948), ch. 4: "The Use of Knowledge in Society."

49. Hayek, *The Counter-Revolution in Science: Studies on the Abuse of Reason* (Indianapolis, Indiana: Liberty Press, [1952] 1979), p. 153.

50. *Ibid.*, p. 154

51. Mises, *Bureaucracy*, ch. 1.

2. *Legal Predictability*

Second, there is the crucial issue of legal predictability. "There is probably no single factor which has contributed more to the prosperity of the West than the relative certainty of the law which has prevailed here."[52] He makes a very important point in this regard. The certainty of law is important, not just in cases that come before the courts, but also in those cases that do not lead to formal litigation because the outcome is so certain. "It is the cases that never come before the courts, not those that do, that are the measure of the certainty of the law."[53] In the United States, there is seemingly endless litigation, precisely because of the unpredictability of the courts.[54] Men go into the courts seeking justice because they do not know what to expect from the courts. If they knew what to expect, fewer people would bother to litigate. They would settle out of court or perhaps even avoid the original infraction.

The law of God establishes the "eye for eye" principle. Men can assess, in advance, what their punishment is likely to be if they transgress the law. They can count the potential cost of violence. This is a restraining factor on all sin. A person can imagine the costs to his potential victim of losing an eye or a tooth. If convicted, the criminal will bear a comparable cost.

Rulers must be aware that the *lex talionis* principle is not simply limited to crimes by private citizens. Judgments fall on nations, both blessings and cursings (Judges, Jonah, Lamentations). The list of promised *national* cursings in Deuteronomy 28:15-68 is a detailed extension of the list of promised blessings in verses 1-14. When nations defy God in specific ways, they will be judged in specific ways — mirror images of the promised blessings to covenantally faithful nations. Instead of going out in war (a national endeavor, not private) and scattering their enemies, they will go out to war and be scattered by their enemies. Instead of lending to their enemies, they will become debtors to their enemies. The principle of "eye for eye" is essential to all of life. From him to whom much has been given, much is expected (Luke 12:47-48).

---

52. Hayek, *Constitution of Liberty*, p. 208.
53. *Idem.*
54. Macklin Fleming, *The Price of Perfect Justice* (New York: Basic Books, 1974).

3. Equality Before the Law

"The third requirement of true law is equality."[55] Equality before the law, as Albright has said, is reinforced by the "eye for eye" principle.[56] The rich man, as well as the poor man, wants to avoid the loss of an eye or a tooth. Therefore, the rich man, like the poor man, must avoid inflicting such injuries on other people. There must be equality before the law (Lev. 19:15). The judges must not impose a tooth's worth of punishment for an eye's worth of damage just because the convicted person is rich or famous. People can then trust the law and the courts, for they know that the law is being enforced because God is sovereign over the affairs of men. The law does not become a weapon of oppression to be used by one class over another. The law, to use Marx's terminology, is not to become a superstructure which is built on the foundation of an economic substructure. The law of God is the substructure in terms of which the economy, the political order, and the pattern of society develop.

Thus, the general legal principle of "eye for eye" in the imposition of civil punishments is a crucial foundation of human freedom, for it binds the civil government in advance. Hayek's discussion is very useful for understanding the State-binding purposes of the *lex talionis*. There are three legal principles that undergird a free society, he argues: general legal rules that 1) distinguish private from public spheres of action; 2) provide legal predictability; and 3) provide equality before the law. The judicial principle of *lex talionis* supports all three.

Restoration, Repentance, and Restitution

Men have failed to understand the fundamental goal of biblical law: *restoration* — restoration of the covenantal relation between God and a formerly rebellious man, and restitution between the criminal and his victim. Rushdoony writes: "Emphatically, in Biblical law the goal is *not punishment but restoration*, not the infliction of certain penalties on criminals but the restoration of godly order."[57] The criminal is to make restitution to the victim. This restores the victim's position

---

55. Hayek, *Constitution of Liberty*, p. 209.

56. "So the *lex talionis* (is) . . . the principle of equal justice for all!" W. F. Albright, *History, Archaeology, and Christian Humanism*, p. 74, as cited in Shalom Paul, *Studies in the Book of the Covenant, op. cit.*, p. 77.

57. Rushdoony, *Institutes*, p. 515.

prior to the crime, plus it increases his holdings to compensate him for the trouble the crime caused him. He is as fully repaid as the court system can lawfully determine. The innocent members of society can feel more confident about their lives and property because the State is obeying God and punishing criminals in a way that preserves the dominion covenant. They can work hard, knowing that the State is working to reduce crime and help them keep the fruits of their labor. At the same time, the criminal now knows that his debt is paid, and that *the burden of guilt is removed*. He can then return to a lawful calling and begin to exercise dominion as a free man. This is what Rushdoony means when he speaks of restoration, of maintaining godly order.

The Bible teaches restitution, repentance, and restoration. The criminal must make outward restitution to the victim, no matter what his feelings are. The State lawfully enforces this. Second, he is morally required by God to repent, and to declare himself at the mercy of God. No human government can lawfully enforce this. Finally, in response to both external restitution and internal repentance, God restores the sinner to wholeness.

The State cannot legitimately require the internal act of repentance; officers cannot know the criminal's heart. The State cannot legitimately require a public statement of theological faith from all residents in a society. The "stranger within the gates" may believe what he wants about God, man, and law.[58] The State can legitimately claim only the right to compel outward conformity to the law, including the law of economic restitution. *Outward conformity to the law* is sufficient to create the conditions of *external social order*. This is the function of civil government: *the preservation of external social order through the administration of justice*. At the same time, we must recognize that apart from widespread inward repentance, no social order can be preserved in the long run, for men will chafe at the requirements of God's law, including the law of restitution. Men will not

---

58. This does not mean that the State cannot legitimately require a statement of faith from those who seek citizenship, and therefore the right potentially to serve as judges "within the gates." In the United States, citizens are required to uphold and defend the Constitution; resident aliens make no such profession of faith. They are required to obey the terms of laws that are based on the Constitution, but they are not required by law to swear that they will uphold and defend it. This is one reason why foreign citizens should be exempt from military conscription: soldiers, as covenanted officials of the national government, are required to uphold and defend the Constitution. They wear the marks of their civil office (uniforms) and carry "swords": weapons.

honor God's law indefinitely, apart from widespread conversions. *Regeneration ultimately undergirds long-term social order.*[59] Nevertheless, it is not the State's function to seek to enforce inward regeneration. The State is not the Holy Spirit.

Concern for the Victim

Concern for the victim rather than with rehabilitation of the criminal often marked so-called "primitive" societies. English common law has also tended to focus on retribution, not the rehabilitation of the criminal. It seeks to punish men in specific ways for specific evil acts. In contrast, modern humanistic theories of jurisprudence, in the name of humanitarianism, to a great extent have promoted a messianic view of the State. Prof. Lon Fuller has summarized the contrasting views, and the heart of the controversy is the assertion of the ability of the State to *recreate* man: "The familiar penal or retributive theory looks to the act and seeks to make the miscreant pay for his misdeed; the rehabilitative theory on the other hand, sees the purpose of the law as recreating the person, or improving the criminal himself so that any impulses toward misconduct will be eliminated or brought under internal control. Despite the humane appeal of the rehabilitative theory, the actual processes of criminal trials remain under the domination of the view that we must try the act, not the man; any departure from this conception, it is feared, would sacrifice justice to a policy of paternalistic intervention in the life of the individual."[60] This fear is well-deserved: continual interventions into the lives of men by a self-professed omniscient paternalistic State is exactly where a legal theory of "trying the man rather than his acts" does lead. A jury can make the criminal "pay for his crime" by paying the victim because members of the jury can make reasonable estimates of the economic effects of the convicted criminal's acts. On the other hand, jurors cannot read the convicted criminal's mind. When men try to read other men's minds, the result is tyranny.

Restitution by the criminal to the victim is one way of restoring wholeness to the victim. It also reduces the likelihood of private at-

---

59. Appendix A: "Common Grace, Eschatology, and Biblical Law."

60. Lon Fuller (1969), cited by Richard E. Laster, "Criminal Restitution: A Survey of Its Past History and an Analysis of Its Present Usefulness," *University of Richmond Law Review*, V (1970), p. 97. Laster's study concludes that the role of the victim in criminal law has steadily diminished (p. 97).

tempts at vengeance.[61] It is a way of dealing with guilt. In this sense, it is a means of restoring wholeness to the criminal, too.

Israel's history can legitimately be classified in terms of a series of incidents by which this three-fold relationship — repentance, restitution, and restoration — was illustrated in a covenantal, communal, and national way. Israel's deliverance from Babylon is a good example of this restorative process. It is also illustrated in the instance of David's adultery and his murder of Uriah the Hittite. David repented (II Sam. 12:13); the child died (12:18), and so did three of his adult sons — Amnon, Absalom, and Adonijah — thereby making four-fold restitution on a "four lives for one" basis.[62] Four-fold restitution was the required payment for the slaughter of a lamb (Ex. 22:1). Nathan the prophet had used the analogy of the slaughtered ewe lamb in his confrontation with David (II Sam. 12:4). David recognized that the culprit was worthy of death (v. 5). David therefore could not escape making the four-fold restitution payment to God's sense of justice (adultery and murder are both capital crimes in the Bible). Subsequently, David and Bathsheba were covenantally restored in their marriage, which God testified to publicly by the birth of Solomon (12:24), who became the lawful heir of David's throne.

We must understand capital punishment as God's required restitution payment. The death penalty is not a means of revenge alone or deterrence alone. It was imposed on Adam and his heirs, and also on the second Adam, Jesus Christ. For any civil crime too great to be compensated for by a monetary restitution payment to the victim, God requires the civil magistrate to impose the death penalty, God's restitution payment. Homicide, for example, could not be paid for in Israel by anything less rigorous than life for life (Num. 35:31), a law which is without parallel in the laws of the ancient Near East.[63] It was only later rabbinic Judaism that abandoned the principle that all murderers are subject to the death penalty, in order to reduce the penalty for Jews who kill resident aliens or gentiles. Maimonides was quite open about this: "If an Israelite kills a resident alien, he does not suffer capital punishment at the hands of the court, because Scripture says, *And if a man come presumptuously upon his neighbor* (Exod.

---

61. Laster, *ibid.*, p. 75.

62. Herbert Chanan Brichto, "Kin, Cult, Land and Afterlife — A Biblical Complex," *Hebrew Union College Annual*, XLIV (1973), p. 42.

63. Shalom Paul, *Book of the Covenant*, p. 61.

21:12). Needless to say, one is not put to death if he kills a heathen."[64]

Restitution, repentance, and restoration are equally fundamental concepts in Christian theology. Without Christ's restitution payment to God for the sins of mankind, there could have been no history from the day Adam fell. Without repentance, the individual cannot claim to be free from the requirement to make the restitution payment to God. Eternal judgment is God's lawful vengeance on all those who have not made restitution, meaning all those who have not placed themselves at the mercy of God by claiming to be under Christ's general repayment. The absolute righteousness of God is demonstrated by His eternal punishment of those who have not made full restitution to Him. The punishment fits the crime of ethical rebellion against a sovereign, holy God.

Restitution in Practice

Various forms of restitution have been adopted by civil governments for centuries.[65] Experiments by state and local governments in the United States since the mid-1970's also indicated that such a system can provide significant benefits to victims. The state of Minnesota began its experiment in October of 1973. Based on one year's data, researchers made a study of opinions and results. Restitution was a condition of probation of the criminals in one-fourth of all probation cases. "Restitution was used in a straightforward manner by most courts. Full cash restitution was ordered to be paid by the offender to the victim in more than nine out of ten cases. Adjustments in the amount of restitution because of limited ability of the offender were rare. In-kind, or service, restitution to the victim or community was ordered in only a few cases. . . ."[66]

The program was limited primarily to non-violent criminal offenders who were considered able to pay, which generally meant white middle-class criminal offenders.[67] This limits the empirical reliability of the conclusions concerning the overall effectiveness of

---

64. Moses Maimonides, *The Book of Torts*, vol. 11, *The Code of Mainonides*, 14 vols (New Haven, Connecticut: Yale University Press, [1180] 1954), Chapter Two, Section Eleven, p. 201.

65. J. A. Gylys and F. Reidy, "The Case for Compensating Victims of Crime," *Atlanta Economic Review*, XXV (May/June 1975).

66. *Summary Report: The Assessment of Restitution in the Minnesota Probation Services*, prepared for the Governor's Commission on Crime Prevention and Control (Jan. 31, 1976), p. 1.

67. *Idem.*

the program. Also, the amount of restitution was limited to the amount of the economic loss by the victims, not two-fold restitution, as required by the Bible. The original state-level trial program was dropped in 1976, but the principle has been instituted at the local level. Judges in every jurisdiction now impose restitution as a penal sanction.

The *Summary Report* states that "Most judges and probation officers favored the use of restitution. Similarly most judges and probation officers expressed the belief that restitution had a rehabilitative effect." Furthermore, "most victims believed that restitution by the offender to the victim is the proper method of victim compensation. Victims who were dissatisfied tended to be those who felt that they had not been involved in the process of ordering or aiding in the completion of restitution." And perhaps most revealing of all, "Most offenders thought that restitution as ordered was fair."[68] Only ten of the offenders (14.4 percent) would have preferred a fine or a jail sentence.[69] It is understandable why we have seen a renewed interest in restitution as a form of punishment.[70]

Prisons

The prison as a correctional and rehabilitative institution was the invention of the early nineteenth-century reform movement in the United States. Visitors from all over Europe came to see these correctional "wonders." The most famous of these visitors was Alexis de Tocqueville, who came from France in 1831 to see our prisons, and who then wrote the most insightful study of American institutions in the nineteenth century, which also became the earliest major work in the discipline of sociology, *Democracy in America* (1835, 1840). He and his colleague Gustave de Beaumont produced a report on their observations, *On the Penitentiary System in the United States* (1833).[71]

---

68. *Idem.*

69. *Ibid.*, p. 26.

70. Joe Hudson and Burt Galloway (eds.), *Considering the Victim: Readings in Restitution and Victim Compensation* (Springfield, Illinois: Charles C. Thomas, 1975); O. Hobart Mowrer, "Loss and Recovery of Community," in George M. Gazda (ed.), *Innovations to Group Psychotherapy* (Springfield, Illinois: Charles C. Thomas, 1975). Such interest has never been entirely absent: see Irving E. Cohen, "The Integration of Restitution in the Probation Services," *Journal of Criminal Law, Criminology and Police Science*, XXXIV (1944), pp. 315-26.

71. *Tocqueville and Beaumont on Social Reform*, edited by Seymour Drescher (Santa Fe, New Mexico: Gannon, 1968).

Parallel tax-supported institutions were developed during this same era: the insane asylum, the orphanage, the reformatory for youthful delinquents, and the large-scale public almshouse.[72] It was also the era of the first "religiously neutral" (humanistic) tax-supported day schools in the United States.[73]

In Israel, there was no prison system. Egypt had prisons; Israel did not.[74] Why not? Because prisons do not offer adequate opportunities for criminals to repay their victims. *A prison restricts the criminal's ability to make restitution, and restitution is the very essence of biblical punishment.* Prisons restrict men's ability to repay; they also make it difficult for men to exercise dominion over nature.

In a sense, the prison is analogous to the final judgment. There is no restitution to victims by those in hell or in the lake of fire. There is permanent restitution to God, but not to man. In this sense, hell is outside history and the process of restitution and restoration. Hell is described as a debtors prison in Jesus' parable of the unjust debtor. The debtor is cast into prison until every last payment is made (Matt. 18:23-35). The debtor could get out only if someone else paid his obligations. Clearly, this is a picture of Christ's payment of His people's ethical debts to God, as their kinsman-redeemer. This substitute payment is available to mankind only in history. Thus, the prison is illegitimate because it represents a denial of history and the opportunities of history. That Egypt should have prisons is understandable; Egyptians had a static view of time. Israel did not. Old Testament law did not allow imprisonment.[75]

---

72. David Rothman writes: "Americans in the colonial period had followed very different procedures. They relieved the poor at home or with relatives or neighbors; they did not remove them to almshouses. They fined or whipped criminals or put them in stocks or, if the crime was serious enough, hung them; they did not conceive of imprisoning them for specific periods of time. The colonists left the insane in the care of their families, supporting them, in case of need, as one of the poor. They did not erect special buildings for incarcerating the mentally ill. Similarly, homeless children lived with neighbors, not in orphan asylums. . . . The few institutions that existed in the eighteenth century were clearly places of last resort. Americans in the Jacksonian period reversed these practices. Institutions became places of first resort, the preferred solution to the problems of poverty, crime, delinquency, and insanity." David J. Rothman, *The Discovery of the Asylum: Social Order and Disorder in the New Republic* (Boston: Little, Brown, 1971), p. xiii.

73. The two leaders in this self-consciously anti-Christian public school movement were Horace Mann and James G. Carter: R. J. Rushdoony, *The Messianic Character of American Education: Studies in the History of the Philosophy of Education* (Nutley, New Jersey: Craig Press, 1963), chaps. 3, 4.

74. Rushdoony, *Institutes*, pp. 514-16.

75. Samson Raphael Hirsch, *The Pentateuch Translated and Explained*, translated by Isaac Levy, 5 vols., *Exodus* (3rd ed.; London: Honig & Sons, 1967), p. 294: at Exodus 21:6.

Western Europe abandoned debtors prison during the decade 1867-77.[76] Legislators at last recognized that it did victims no good to see a debtor cast into prison until he paid, since he could not earn his way out. It is not coincidental that Europe passed such legislation in the same era that the United States and Russia abolished slavery, another system that also did not provide a way for people to buy their way out.

The ultimate earthly prison is the concentration camp. While the modern Soviet camp has economic functions, the cruelty of long sentences is obvious. Under Stalin, these sentences were incredibly grotesque. As many as 30 million people were sent into the camps, never to return.[77] The magnitude of the crime against humanity seems irrationally cruel.[78] They were irrational, according to Solzhenitsyn. The first thought of the arrested person was always, "Me? What for?"[79] From 1934 on, a soldier captured in wartime was automatically given a ten-year sentence upon being freed from the enemy.[80] Encircled military units got ten-year sentences after 1941.[81] Failure to denounce specified evil acts carried an indeterminate sentence.[82] Quotas for arrests made the diversity of the camps fantastic, he says; there was no logic to them.[83] A chance meeting with a condemned man could get you ten years.[84] Owning a radio tube was worth ten years.[85] In 1948, the average sentence increased to 25 years; juveniles received ten.[86]

The classic story he tells was of a district Party conference in Moscow Province. At the end of the conference, someone called for a tribute to Stalin. A wave of applause began, and continued. Everyone was afraid to be the first person to stop clapping, for fear of

---

76. France abolished debtors prison in 1867; England abolished it by the Debtors Act of 1869. Ireland followed in 1872, Scotland in 1880. Switzerland and Norway abolished it in 1874, Italy in 1877. "Debt," *Encyclopaedia Britannica* (11th ed.; New York: Encyclopaedia Britannica, Inc., 1910), VII, p. 906.

77. Robert Conquest, *The Great Terror: Stalin's Purges of the Thirties* (rev. ed.; New York: Collier, 1973), p. 710.

78. Van den Haag, *Punishing Criminals*, p. 43.

79. Aleksandr Solzhenitsyn, *The Gulag Archipelago, 1918-1956: An Experiment in Literary Investigation, I-II* (New York: Harper & Row, 1974), p. 4.

80. *Ibid.*, p. 61.

81. *Ibid.*, p. 79.

82. *Ibid.*, pp. 67, 363.

83. *Ibid.*, p. 71.

84. *Ibid.*, p. 75.

85. *Ibid.*, p. 78.

86. *Ibid.*, p. 91.

being arrested. It went on for eleven minutes. Finally, one man, a factory director, stopped clapping and sat down, then the whole group immediately stopped and sat down. That night the man was arrested, and he then received a ten-year sentence.[87]

There is only one way to explain this: *the desire of the State to become God and to impose hell on earth.* It became a goal of State policy to destroy men's lives, to leave them without earthly hope in the future. It was easy to go to jail without a trial. The Special Boards attached to the secret police, the OSO's,[88] handed down "administrative penalties," not sentences. "The OSO enjoyed another important advantage in that its penalty could not be appealed. There was nowhere to appeal to. There was no appeals jurisdiction above it, and no jurisdiction beneath it. It was subordinate only to the Minister of Internal Affairs, to Stalin, and to Satan."[89] It is not surprising that the camps became the closest thing in recorded history to hell on earth.

The prison is a bureaucracy, not a market-oriented institution. It is run by the State through taxes; it is a bureaucratic management system, not a profit management system.[90] Men are trained to follow orders, not to innovate, take risks, and meet market demand. There are many arguments against prisons, as revealed by an enormous bibliography on alternatives to prisons,[91] but the most important one is that they thwart the biblical principle of restitution.

The prison also creates other horrors, such as homosexuality and training in criminal behavior for the younger inmates by the "skilled" older inmates. It puts too much power in the hands of prisoners, who can commit rape and even murder with their AIDS infections.[92] It

---

87. *Ibid.*, pp. 69-70.

88. *Ibid.*, p. 275.

89. *Ibid.*, p. 285.

90. See Gary North, "Statist Bureaucracy in the Modern Economy," in North, *An Introduction to Christian Economics* (Nutley, New Jersey: Craig Press, 1973), ch. 20. See also Ludwig von Mises, *Bureaucracy.*

91. James R. Brantley and Marjorie Kravitz (eds.), *Alternatives to Institutionalization: A Definitive Bibliography,* published by the National Criminal Justice Reference Service of the National Institute of Law Enforcement and Criminal Justice, a division of the Law Enforcement Assistance Administration, U.S. Department of Justice (May 1979), 240 pages.

92. National columnist Mike Royko has actually recommended prison sentences for computer file break-ins rather than fines because intelligent middle-class prisoners will be raped in jail. "If the computer vandals are as bright as they think they are, they'll decide that they don't want to be forcibly betrothed to some hulk of a cellmate with a shaved head and 10 tatoos." Mike Royko, "No software in his heart for hackers," *Washington Times* (Nov. 11, 1988). This is a politically conservative newspaper.

puts too much power in the hands of guards, who can then indulge their tastes in brutality. It puts too much power in the hands of parole boards, who can shorten a man's sentence irrespective of the crime, thereby making the punishment fit the board's assessment of the criminal, not the judge's assessment of the effects of the crime — or more to the point, making the punishment fit the latest humanistic theory of criminal behavior and social responsibility, not the crime.[93]

Left-wing humanists have begun to see the threat to justice posed by the indeterminate sentence.[94] Mitford has described the indeterminate sentence as "a potent psychological instrument for inmate manipulation and control, the 'uncertainty' ever nagging at the prisoner's mind a far more effective weapon than the cruder ones then [in the 1870's] in vogue: the club, the starvation regime, the iron shackle."[95] Because of doubts regarding the prison as a means of correcting evil behavior, we have seen an increasing resistance by juries and judges to send first offenders or minor offenders to prison. But because restitution has not yet become a common means of punishing criminals, these "minor" criminals receive no punishment, other than having to report occasionally to an overburdened probation or parole officer.[96]

These same humanists look at the "eye for eye" principle, and react in horror. They do not react with equal consternation when

---

93. C. S. Lewis, "The Humanitarian Theory of Punishment," in Lewis, *God in the Dock: Essays on Theology and Ethics*, edited by Walter Hooper (Grand Rapids, Michigan: Eerdmans, 1972), pp. 287-300.

94. Jessica Mitford, *Kind and Usual Punishment: The Prison Business* (New York: Knopf, 1973), ch. 6. Those who have opposed capital punishment have denounced it as cruel and unusual. Mitford's attack implies that imprisonment is, too. What, then, is legitimate punishment? The Bible gives us guidelines; few humanists do.

95. *Ibid.*, p. 82.

96. Charles Manson, who led the "family" (gang) of murderers who killed actress Sharon Tate and several others in 1969, was on parole from prison at the time. Others in his "family" were also on probation. As the prosecuting attorney later wrote: "Manson associated with ex-cons, known narcotics users, and minor girls. He failed to report his whereabouts, made few attempts to obtain employment, repeatedly lied regarding his activities. During the first six months of 1969 alone, he had been charged, among other things, with grand theft auto, narcotics possession, rape, contributing to the delinquency of a minor. There was more than ample reason for parole revocation." Vincent Bugliosi, *Helter Skelter: The True Story of the Manson Murders* (New York: Norton, 1974), p. 420. Manson's parole officer stated in court that he could not remember whether Manson had been on probation or parole; the man was responsible for overseeing 150 persons (p. 419). Manson had actually begged to be allowed to remain in jail when they released him in 1967; at that time, he was 32 years old, and had spent 17 years in penal and reform institutions (p. 146).

they confront the problem of the late twentieth century's increase in violent crime. Statistics on crime for the United States are readily available and comprehensive, and I am including a brief survey of this material in order to present an overview of the crisis facing Western, humanist culture.[97] At the end of an age, we expect to see an increase in criminal behavior, as lawlessness becomes a way of life for a dedicated, pathological minority, while religious and cultural relativism and self-doubt render citizens and their elected authorities helpless to stem this tide of consistent lawlessness. Gilbert Murray, the great student of Greek civilization, characterized the last days of Greek religion as "the failure of nerve."[98] This seems to fit late-twentieth-century Western humanism quite well.

Emptying Prisons and Stoning Sons

Prisons need to be emptied. The biblical way to accomplish this is to revive the biblical practices of execution for habitual criminals (Deut. 21:18-21), corporal punishment (Deut. 25:1-3), and restitution. It is interesting that the justification for executing habitual criminals rests on that bugaboo of all pietism, the execution of the rebellious son. It is a case of "if *this*, then how much more *that*." If it is mandatory that a man bring his incorrigible adult son before the elders for gluttony, drunkenness,[99] and verbal rebellion, how much more ready will a society be to execute repeatedly violent individuals or members of a professional criminal class! Remove from the law books the law regarding the civic execution of the rebellious son, and you thereby remove the one *and only* biblical sanction for executing professional criminals. The "three-time loser" penalty of American jurisprudence[100] has disappeared; in its place has come a criminal class of far more than three felony convictions — and most of these professionals are paroled early.

Incorrigible sons and incorrigible criminals are to be removed from society: ". . . so shalt thou put evil away from among you; and all Israel shall hear, and fear" (Deut. 21:21b). Rushdoony has identified the importance of this law for society: "Such persons were thus

---

97. Appendix F: "Violent Crime in the United States, 1980."

98. Gilbert Murray, *Five Stages of Greek Religion* (1925 edition), reprinted by AMS Press and Greenwood Press.

99. Seven-year-olds are not drunkards; this verse deals with adult rebels.

100. A man convicted of a felony for the third time used to receive life imprisonment without possibility of parole.

blotted out of the commonwealth. When and if this law is observed, ungodly families who are given to lawlessness are denied a place in the nation. The law thus clearly works to eliminate all but the godly families."[101] The point here is that if incorrigible sons are to be executed, how much more the members of the professional criminal class. The case law is based on the idea that this maximum sanction, if applied to a seemingly minimal infraction, is surely to be applied in an analogous major infraction. The infraction is repeated lawlessness as a lifestyle: *incorrigibility.*

The prison is a second-best device. It does keep some habitual criminals locked up for part of their lives. It is sometimes argued that by keeping them out of circulation, the overall crime rate drops. There is only spotty evidence to prove this. The problem is, when one criminal is locked up, others move into the "vacuum" of crime.[102] It may take time for the new entrants to become equally skilled, however.

Still, prison is a threat. If a society refuses to execute professional criminals, then it must impose some kind of sanctions if evil is not to be indirectly subsidized. In short, biblical law is a package deal. It will not suffice to empty the prisons until the whole of biblical criminal law is on the law books and enforced, especially the death penalty against rebellious sons. Those who are appalled by this law are not sufficiently appalled by professional criminal behavior.

Conclusion

The biblical principle of an eye for an eye protects society from a lawless State which recognizes no limitations on its power. This law establishes the fundamental judicial principle that the punishment should fit the crime. This principle, sometimes called *lex talionis*, requires that the criminal *pay back* to the victim whatever was stolen, and in some cases an additional penalty payment is required.

There is no doubt that this law is based on vengeance, but vengeance is a basic principle of biblical law. God extracts a vengeance payment from evil-doers: perfect vengeance at the day of judgment, and imperfect vengeance through the civil government. Vengeance is a form of restitution to God.

The fundamental goal of biblical law is *restoration*. Evil people are to be restored by God to righteousness. The State cannot save man-

---

101. Rushdoony, *Institutes*, p. 380.
102. Van den Haag, *Punishing Criminals*, pp. 53-60.

kind, except in the sense of healing through enforcing justice, but it can impose external punishments that make social and economic restoration possible. Restitution by the criminal to the victim is an effective way of restoring wholeness to both parties. It upholds a basic principle of civil law: the punishment should benefit the victim.

Prisons are a second-best system of punishment. They keep hardened criminals off the street, but they do very little for the past victims. While they should eventually be emptied, except for holding suspects for trial at the local level, this would be too risky before all three biblical sanctions are restored to civil law: the death penalty, corporal punishment, and economic restitution.

But the question still must be faced: How could a society literally enforce the "eye for eye" principle without becoming barbaric? We have seen the theory of what *lex talionis* is supposed to accomplish for a biblical social order. How could a literal application work in practice? This is the subject of the next chapter.

12

THE AUCTION FOR SUBSTITUTE SANCTIONS

If men strive, and hurt a woman with child, so that her fruit depart from her, and yet no mischief follow: he shall be surely punished, according as the woman's husband will lay upon him; and he shall pay as the judges determine. And if any mischief follow, then thou shalt give life for life, eye for eye, tooth for tooth, hand for hand, foot for foot, burning for burning, wound for wound, stripe for stripe (Ex. 21:22-25).

In the previous chapter, I discussed the biblical rationale for the principle of *lex talionis*: upholding the principle of victim's rights while limiting the State. It provides a means of restoration: to the victim, to the criminal, and to society. In this chapter, we need to consider how this principle could be applied in the modern world.

As the reader considers how this system might work in practice, he must keep in the back of his mind an outline of how the modern criminal justice system works, for it is surely more criminal than just. We are not here comparing a pair of theoretical ideals, biblical vs. humanistic. We are attempting to compare rival systems in action, although because there has been such hostility to the *lex talionis* principle, we have not seen the biblical system in operation historically. This is why this chapter is in part hypothetical — how things could work — yet also a self-conscious attempt on my part to deal with the real world.

The reason why we have no real-world examples of how the *lex talionis* system has worked is because Christians and Jews have never seriously attempted to enforce it in civil law, or if they have, they have left few records of these attempts.[1] They have instead adopted

---

1. Again, this could be the product either of an historical blackout on the part of professional historians or the ignorance of the historians regarding biblical law. We need generations of trained historians who will comb the records of Western legal history and examine the documents from the point of view of biblical law.

as their operational models the judicial systems of contemporary covenant-breaking societies. They have "baptized" or "circumcised" prevailing judicial practices. But these judicial standards have usually been opposed to the Bible's *lex talionis* standard. There is little doubt that the covenant-breaker is hostile to the judicial principle of "an eye for an eye." First, it reminds him of the existence of a sovereign God who will judge him perfectly, so he prefers to affirm a more "merciful" judicial standard. He understands the biblical principle proclaimed by Jesus Christ: "For with what judgment ye judge, ye shall be judged: and with what measure ye mete, it shall be measured to you again" (Matt 7:2.) Second, he also wants to worship autonomous man through worshipping the State, so he wants the State to be more rigorous than God in imposing historical sanctions, as a testimony to autonomous man's might. These goals are clearly contradictory. By pursuing both, autonomous man produces judicial schizophrenia.

In some societies, covenant-breakers have regarded *lex talionis* as too lax. This is surely the case in totalitarian societies today. The Gulag Archipelago of the Soviet Union is clearly not the product of biblical law. Yet in other societies, *lex talionis* is regarded as inhumane. Western humanists today regard biblical law as primitive and brutal. We must ask: Is the concern of humanists for the "brutality" shown by the Bible's "eye for eye" principle misguided? Shouldn't their concern be focused instead on the brutality of the criminal against the innocent victim? Isn't the *lex talionis* principle a deterrent to crime, especially repeated crimes by a criminal class? Shouldn't our concern be with the victims of violent crime rather than with the criminals who commit them?

What we find today in the United States is a perverse mixture of judicial laxness and tyranny, both of which are inevitable in any society that rejects biblical law as its civil standard. Members of the voting public occasionally perceive this judicial schizophrenia, but they have no understanding of its cause or its biblical solution. They have denied the authority of biblical law so systematically that they no longer have any awareness of how God's judicial standard would provide justice for modern civilization. This judicial blindness is as true of seminary theologians and pastors as it is of the average covenant-breaker. There has been a deliberate Christian blackout regarding the legitimacy of biblical law for over three centuries.[2]

---

2. By the 1680's, the Puritan pastors of New England had ceased preaching sermons on the need for specific pieces of civil legislation in the name of the Bible. Gary North, *Puritan Economic Experiments* (Tyler, Texas: Institute for Christian Economics, 1988), pp. 35-39, 57-59.

Dear Abby

Nevertheless, from time to time, Americans briefly recognize the injustice that the court system produces on a daily basis. In "Dear Abby," the nationally syndicated question-and-answer newspaper column of "Abigail Van Buren" (a pen name for a very smart Jewish lady, whose equally smart sister writes a similar column under the pen name of "Ann Landers"), "Abby" reproduced the following letter from a concerned reader:

> I am enclosing two items clipped today from the *Atlanta Constitution*. They appeared one directly above the other. The first reports that a Mineola, New York, driver was racing down the street at 100 miles per hour. His car crashed into a limousine carrying a wedding party. Instantly killed were the groom, age 27, and his brother, who was the best man, age 29. The bride (age 24) died 18 days later without learning of her husband's death.
>
> The driver of the car that killed them was sentenced to 28 months to seven years in prison.
>
> The other item was about a man in Lubbock, Texas, who was sentenced to 10 years in prison for biting off part of a police officer's ear! The jury deliberated only 10 minutes before arriving at the sentence.
>
> Am I mistaken? Or is this a case of misplaced priorities?[3]

"Abby" answered correctly, as far as she went: the first sentence was too lenient, while the second was too harsh. But how could she be sure? She did not say what would have been proper sentencing. Furthermore, why did her correspondent sense that something was wrong with these judicial decisions? Answer: because both the correspondent and the columnist have been strongly influenced by the biblical ideal of the *lex talionis*. Even the headline for the column (probably selected by a local newspaper staff member) points to the influence of the *lex talionis* principle: "Punishment fails to fit these crimes." The influence of the biblical judicial standard is still occasionally visible, but only as an unenforced ideal. The *lex talionis* principle is ignored in practice. It is like a sinner's conscience which he systematically ignores when making his decisions. The intellectuals, the legislators, the judges, and the juries refuse to honor the "eye for eye" principle. So do the theologians and pastors. If they were to take this biblical judicial principle seriously, they would also have to

---

3. *Dallas Times Herald* (Nov. 17, 1988).

begin to take seriously all the specifics of the biblical case laws. This, above all, they do not want to do. They would much prefer to suffer injustice, but all in the name of avoiding the supposedly greatest injustice of all, Old Testament law.

Were Christians to begin to identify the injustice of this era as the product of humanism and the self-proclaimed autonomy of man and his civil law, they would then be confronted with the awesome task of reclaiming civil law for Jesus Christ. They would have to rethink the whole of Western civilization. They would have to study the whole Bible carefully. They would face the exegetical task that so disturbs James Dobson: "Do you agree that if a man beats his slave to death, he is to be considered guilty only if the individual dies instantly? If the slave lives a few days, the owner is considered not guilty (Exodus 21:20-21)[?] Do you believe that we should stone to death rebellious children (Deuteronomy 21:18-21)? Do you really believe we can draw subtle meaning about complex issues from Mosaic law, when even the obvious interpretation makes no sense to us today? We can hardly select what we will and will not apply now. If we accept the verses you cited, we are obligated to deal with every last jot and tittle."[4]

My response? It is time for us to start dealing!

Thumb for Thumb, Toe for Toe

We read of Adoni-bezek in the first chapter of Judges. Adoni-bezek (Lord of Bezek) was a Canaanitic king. The Israelites fought him and defeated him. "But Adoni-bezek fled; and they pursued after him, and caught him, and cut off his thumbs and his great toes. And Adoni-bezek said, Threescore and ten kings, having their thumbs and their great toes cut off, gathered their meat under my table: as I have done, so God hath requited me. And they brought him to Jerusalem, and there he died" (Jud. 1:6-7). This Canaanitic king's confession reveals that he recognized the justice of the punishment imposed on him by his conquerors.[5] He had cut off the toes and thumbs of kings; now he had suffered the same punishment. He had removed their anatomical "tools of dominion"; now he had his

---

4. James Dobson, "Dialogue on Abortion," in Dobson and Gary Bergel, *The Decision of Life* (Arcadia, California: Focus on the Family, 1986), p. 14.

5. The Hammurabi Code specifies mutilations on an "eye for eye" basis, paragraphs 196-201. *Ancient Near Eastern Texts Relating to the Old Testament*, edited by James B. Pritchard (3rd ed.; Princeton, New Jersey: Princeton University Press, 1969), p. 175.

removed.[6]

This incident raises some difficult exegetical questions. Was the "eye for eye" principle literally applied in ancient Israel after the defeat of Canaan? Did Israel's courts really poke out people's teeth and eyes? If not, why not? Or is it merely that there are no clear-cut biblical records of such physical penalties being imposed by Israelite judges on Israelite citizens?

The incident also raises some difficult historical questions. In the Christian West, judges have consistently refused to impose "eye for eye" physical penalties. In non-Christian societies, permanent physical vengeance is quite common, e.g., Islam's *Shari'a* law. Why not in the West? What is it about inflicting permanent physical mutilation — in contrast to whippings or other relatively impermanent forms of physical violence — that so repels Westerners?

The West's Future-Orientation

The West's impulse toward dominion in history is one possible answer. The West has been future-oriented, as a direct result of its Christian eschatological heritage: *a faith in linear history*, with a God-created beginning, a God-sustaining providence, and a God-governed final judgment.[7] This vision of linear time made possible the development of modern science.[8] The future-orientation of the West, especially from the seventeenth century onward, and especially in Protestant societies, led to faith in long-term progress, including long-term economic growth.[9] Western people have understood the importance to the community of full production from all members. There is (or was) the psychological and social phenomenon called "the Protestant Ethic."[10] Begging, for example, has not

---

6. Without a thumb, a person cannot grasp a tool or weapon. Without a big toe, he cannot balance himself easily. See James B. Jordan, *Judges: God's War Against Humanism* (Tyler, Texas: Geneva Ministries, 1985), pp. 4-5.

7. Karl Löwith, *Meaning in History* (University of Chicago Press, 1949), ch. 11: "The Biblical View of History."

8. Stanley Jaki, *The Road of Science and the Ways to God* (University of Chicago Press, 1978), chaps. 1, 2; *Science and Creation: From eternal cycles to an oscillating universe* (Edinburgh and London: Scottish Academic Press, [1974] 1980); "The History of Science and the Idea of an Oscillating Universe," in Wolfgang Yourgrau and Allen D. Beck (eds.), *Cosmology, History, and Theology* (New York: Plenum Press, 1977).

9. Gary North, "Medieval Economics in Puritan New England, 1630-1660," *Journal of Christian Reconstruction*, V (Winter 1978-79), pp. 157-60.

10. Max Weber, *The Protestant Ethic and the Spirit of Capitalism* (New York: Scribner's, [1904-5] 1958). See also Gary North, "The 'Protestant Ethic' Hypothesis," *Journal of Christian Reconstruction*, III (Summer 1976); Daniel T. Rodgers, *The Work Ethic in Industrial America, 1850-1920* (University of Chicago Press, 1978).

been favored in Protestant nations. Idleness has been frowned upon. Therefore, the realization that physical punishment can permanently reduce the productivity of any citizen repels the Westerner. The Western judge asks: What happens to the criminal after he has "paid his debt"? Why should the criminal, his family, his future employers, and consumers be deprived of his full future productivity? Why should any man be hampered in working out his own salvation with fear and trembling (Phil. 2:12)? Wouldn't permanent physical mutilation tend to impair his future employment, thereby luring him back into a life of crime? What if he should experience a moral transformation in the future? Western justice seems to recognize such problems, and so it has rejected physical mutilation as a legal sanction.

Figuratively Speaking?

Are we to interpret the "eye for eye" passage figuratively? Jesus said in the Sermon on the Mount, "If thy right eye offend thee, pluck it out, and cast it from thee. . . . And if thy right hand offend thee, cut it off, and cast it from thee" (Matt. 5:29a, 30a). We recognize that He spoke figuratively. He meant that the lusts of the flesh are so dangerous spiritually that even the loss of eye or hand is to be preferred. Therefore, avoid moral contamination; avoid lust (5:28). But the issue in Exodus 21:24-25 is that there has been physical injury inflicted on another person. The eye which the victim has lost is a literal eye. To interpret the "eye for eye" passage figuratively because Jesus interpreted "eye" figuratively in a very different context is not legitimate.

There is no doubt that the "thumb for thumb" penalty was literally applied to Adoni-bezek. He recognized the justice of the penalty. Permanent physical mutilation is legitimate when applied to one who has committed a crime that has produced the same mutilation in another person. Yet the resistance of Western judges to impose this physical penalty on their own nation's citizens indicates that they have sought other ways to deal with criminals and victims in crimes involving permanent physical mutilation. Question: In cases other than manslaughter — the death of an innocent third party as a result of unwarranted violence — as in the abortion of Exodus 21:22-23, *may some other penalty legitimately be imposed*, one which meets God's standards of justice, as well as men's sense of justice?

Option: Economic Restitution

Say that an ox has been known to gore people in the past. It gets loose again and kills someone. The owner in this instance is held legally liable; in fact, he is to be put to death (Ex. 21:29). However,

Exodus 21:30 provides an exception to the requirement that a crime that results in a person's death be punished by the execution of the person responsible. "If there be laid on him a sum of money, then he shall give for the ransom of his life whatsoever is laid upon him." The death penalty is set aside at the discretion of the judges and the victim's heirs. *The man pays a ransom for his life.* The text does not specifically say that the ransom is paid to the victim's next of kin, but this is the familiar pattern in the Old Testament. The payment would become part of the dead person's estate, as if he were still alive and had been merely injured by the beast. The ransom is a restitution payment. There is no evidence that the ransom would go anywhere else except to the victim's heirs.

The question can be raised: If the death of the owner of the ox does not benefit the victim's heirs, while the ransom does benefit them, does the *lex talionis* allow a comparable solution to the problem of the physically mutilated person? Instead of physically mutilating the criminal, may the judges legitimately impose a restitution payment?

Jewish Commentaries

Traditional Jewish explanations of the *lex talionis* principle point to a payment in lieu of physical mutilation. Nachmanides wrote in the thirteenth century concerning "eye 'tachath' (for) eye":

It is known in the tradition of our rabbis that this means monetary compensation. Such a usage [of the term *tachath* to indicate] monetary compensation is found in the verse: *And he that smiteth a beast mortally shall pay for it; life 'tacheth' life* [Lev. 24:18], [in which case *tacheth* surely indicates monetary compensation]. Rabbi Abraham ibn Ezra commented that Scripture uses such a term to indicate that he really is deserving of such a punishment, [that his eye be taken from him], if he does not give his ransom. For Scripture has forbidden us to take *ransom for the life of a murderer, that is guilty of death* [Num. 35:31], but we may take ransom from a wicked person who cut off any of the limbs of another person. Therefore we are never to cut off that limb from him, but rather he is to pay monetary compensation, and if he has no money to pay, it lies as a debt on him until he acquires the means to pay, and then he is redeemed.[11]

Nachmanides' citation of Abraham ibn Ezra indicates that he was disturbed by the literal wording of the "eye for eye" stipulation. By

---

11. Rabbi Moses ben Nachman [Ramban], *Commentary on the Torah: Exodus* (New York: Shiloh, [1267?] 1973), p. 368.

refusing to call for a literal application of the verse in the case of a poor criminal, and also by their refusal to call for indentured servitude as a way to repay the debt, these two Jewish medieval commentators softened the threat of the punishment.

There are difficulties with this interpretation. It is ingenious, but it has no explicit biblical precedent, and it may therefore be incorrect, even though it appears to conform to the implicit meaning of "eye for eye." It involves speculation that relies heavily on the precedent of economic restitution in the case of the ox that gores someone to death (Ex. 21:30) — a separate case law that may not apply to the *lex talionis* law of Exodus 21:24-25. But this view became common in the interpretation of Jewish law. Rabbi Samson Raphael Hirsch commented on Exodus 21:25 in the early nineteenth century: ". . . the taking of this legal canon literally, in the sense of an eye for an eye, would be morally impossible for any idea of equity; . . ." Further, "the whole spirit of the text is what the traditional Halacha [Jewish law] teaches, viz., that here it is only speaking of monetary compensation for the injury inflicted. . . ."[12]

Restitution and Equity

In principle, the interpretation of the *lex talionis* as allowing economic restitution in place of physical mutilation raises some fundamental questions. First, is the requirement of vengeance compromised by the imposition of a restitution payment? Is there some fundamental aspect of justice, or men's sense of justice, that should allow a man to "buy his way out" of an injury that he has inflicted on another person? If so, what is this long-neglected aspect of justice?[13]

Second, does this law so interpreted lead to class antagonism? What if the criminal is poor? He cannot pay what a rich man can afford to pay. Is it fair to allow a rich man to forfeit only money, when the poor man must forfeit his eye or tooth or else become an indentured servant to pay off the debt? Will violent rich people become more careless than violent poor people with regard to injuring others? Are the rich being taught to care less for the law of God than the poor do? If the rich can buy their way out, is society thereby allowing the development of resentment among the poor, who feel

---

12. Samson Raphael Hirsch, *The Pentateuch Translated and Explained*, translated by Isaac Levy, 5 vols., *Exodus* (3rd ed.; London: Honig & Sons, 1967), p. 315.

13. I argue that three principles of justice lead us to such a view of *lex talionis*: victim's rights, the criminal's right to seek mercy through making a substitute payment, and the limitation of the judges' authority.

that the law is working against them? Is society implicitly subsidizing rich criminals?

The most important questions are these: Has the "eye for eye" principle been abandoned when economic restitution is substituted for physical punishment? Will God honor a society that abandons this literal principle?

But what if the economic interpretation of *lex talionis* is denied? Would the requirement that all criminals pay the full physical price rather than economic restitution really be beneficial to their victims? The victim may need additional capital to compensate for his loss of productivity as a result of the injury. What benefit is it to him that the criminal becomes equally hampered physically?

Furthermore, there are important social consequences of denying the economic interpretation. What benefit is it to society that two people now will suffer from some physical impairment rather than only one? Is the dominion covenant better fulfilled when two men lose an eye or an arm rather than only one man? After he makes economic restitution to the victim, the criminal can work hard and perhaps regain his lost wealth, but he can never regain a lost eye. Society may benefit more in the long run because of the productivity that the convicted man retains. If he repents and becomes a law-abiding member of the community, his greater productivity increases the wealth of all those consumers whom he will serve as a producer.

These questions deserve biblical answers. We can begin to discover answers by examining in detail how the substitution of economic restitution for physical mutilation might work.

Establishing a Fair Payment

Let us begin with the case of a victim who has lost his eye. A partially blinded person could insist on a particular restitution payment from the convicted criminal. He could say to the judges, "Tell that man that he can keep his eye, but only if he pays me 100 ounces of gold." The judges would then present this option to the criminal: *your gold or your eye.*

If the criminal values his body more highly than he values the economic restitution demanded by the victim, he can pay the money. This is the principle of *victim's rights* in action. On the other hand, if he values the payment higher, or if he simply cannot afford to pay, then he can forfeit his eye. This is the principle of *maximum specified sanctions* in action. The criminal could also make payment by selling himself into indentured servitude, with the buyer paying the victim. But perhaps the convicted man would prefer to lose the use of part of his body rather than becoming a bondservant. He could reject the demand of the victim for economic restitution and insist instead on his legal right under biblical law: to suffer the same physical mutilation that he had imposed on the victim.

The Right to Punishment

Each of the parties in this judicial dispute has biblically specified legal rights. The victim has the right to insist on the biblically specified maximum physical sanction: eye for eye. He also has the right to offer the criminal an alternative, one which appears to be less severe than the biblically specified physical sanction. If the alternative offered to the criminal is not regarded by him as less severe, then he has the legal right to insist on the imposition of the biblically specified maximum sanction. He therefore possesses the *right to be punished by the specified biblical sanction*. His punishment is limited by the extent of the injury which he imposed on his victim. The punishment fits the crime.

It is basic to the preservation of liberty that the State not be allowed to deny to either the victim or the criminal his right of punishment. While this principle of the right to punishment is at least vaguely understood by most people with respect to the victim, it is not well understood with respect to the criminal. The right to be punished is a crucial legal right, one which Paul insisted on at his trial: "For if I be an offender, or have committed any thing worthy of death, I refuse not to die: but if there be none of these things whereof these accuse me, no man may deliver me unto them. I appeal unto Caesar" (Acts 25:11).

If the State can autonomously substitute other criteria for deserved punishment, such as personal or social rehabilitation, then society loses its right to be governed by predictable laws with predictable judicial sanctions. The messianic State then replaces the judicially limited State. Neither the victim nor the criminal can be assured of receiving justice, for justice is defined by the State rather than by God in the Bible. If punishment is not seen as *deserved* by the criminal, and therefore his *fundamental right*, then he is delivered into the "merciful" hands of elitist captors who are not bound by written law or social custom. No one has described this threat more eloquently than C. S. Lewis: "To be taken without consent from my home and friends; to lose my liberty; to undergo all those assaults on my personality which modern psychotherapy knows how to deliver; to be re-made after some pattern of 'normality' hatched in a Viennese laboratory to which I never professed allegiance; to know that this process will never end until either my captors have succeeded or I grown wise enough to cheat them with apparent success — who cares whether this is called Punishment or not? That it includes most of the elements for which any punishment is feared — shame, exile, bondage, and years eaten by the locust — is obvious. Only enormous ill-desert could justify it; but ill-desert is the very conception which the Humanitarian theory has thrown overboard."[14]

The State represents God in history in His capacity as cosmic Judge (Rom. 13:1-7). When a civil government's leaders say that the State represents any other agent or principle, the State has begun its march toward either tyranny or impotence. Either it will bring judgment on men and other states in the name of its deity, its official source of law,[15] or else some other State will bring judgment on it and those governed by it in the name of a foreign deity. Only a rare nation like Switzerland can defend its borders for centuries, and then only by renouncing all thought of conquest in the name of defense and international neutrality.[16]

The mark of this transformation of the State is when the State insists on imposing the punishment in terms of the supposed "needs of society," meaning ultimately the needs of the State's officers. When the State collects fines for use by the State rather than to pay victims, when it imposes prison sentences paid for by the taxes of law-abiding citizens, and when it insists that every convicted criminal "pay his debt to society," then the messianic State has arrived. God has specified that the victim is His representative in criminal cases, not the State, unless the victim is legally unable to represent himself, in which case the State acts as his trustee. Only if the State is the victim can it lawfully demand restitution. When the State presents itself as

---

14. C. S. Lewis, "The Humanitarian Theory of Punishment," in Lewis, *God in the Dock: Essays on Theology and Ethics,* edited by Walter Hooper (Grand Rapids, Michigan: Eerdmans, 1972), pp. 290-91.

15. R. J. Rushdoony, *The Institutes of Biblical Law* (Nutley, New Jersey: Craig Press, 1973), p. 4.

16. It had better have high mountains, civil defense, an armed population, and services such as private banking and a geographical "King's X" facilities for overthrown rulers. See John McPhee, *La Place de la Concorde Suisse* (New York: Farrar, Strauss, Giroux, 1984).

the universal victim of all crime to which is owed universal restitution by criminals and taxpayers alike, it has asserted its own divinity.

Benefits of Alternative Sanctions

The proposed economic solution to the dilemma of the *lex talionis* offers at least three very real benefits. The first benefit is judicial: *the victim has the right to specify the appropriate punishment.* This punishment is limited only by the maximum penalty specified by biblical law, *eye for eye.* The biblical principle of victim's rights is upheld by the judges. If the victim believes that the criminal's act was malicious, and if he wishes to inflict the same damage on the criminal which he himself suffered, this is his legal option.

To take this retributive approach, however, he necessarily forfeits all the economic advantages he might have received from a restitution payment from the criminal. He can exercise his legitimate desire for vengeance — his desire to reduce the criminal to a physical condition comparable to his own — but this desire for vengeance has a price attached to it. He is made no better off financially because of his enemy's suffering. In fact, he could be made slightly worse off: he, as a member of the economic community, loses his portion of the other man's lost future productivity, assuming the man cannot overcome the effects of his lost eye or limb. *Vengeance in the Bible's judicial system has a price tag attached to it.* This inevitably reduces the quantity of physical vengeance insisted on by victims, for biblical civil justice recognizes the judicial legitimacy of a fundamental economic law: "The higher the price of any economic good, the less the quantity demanded."

The second benefit of this interpretation of *lex talionis* is also judicial: *the criminal who is about to lose his eye or tooth is permitted to make a counter-offer.* He has the right to be punished to the limit of the written law, but he also can suggest a less onerous punishment — less onerous for him, but possibly more beneficial to his victim. He can legally offer money or services in exchange for the continued preservation of his unmutilated body. The system puts him in the position of being able to pay in order to retain his limbs. *He places a price tag on his body.*

This price tag makes it costly for the victim to pursue an emotion which, had there been no crime, would be called envious: the desire to tear another person down, irrespective of the direct benefits to the person who is envious.[17] But because there has been a crime, envy is legitimate in this case. It must be understood that "getting even" with a convicted criminal is a legitimate goal for the victim of a crime. God eventually "gets even" with Satan and his followers who have sinned against Him; He pulls them down from their positions of power and influence. This process of pulling Satan down began with Jesus' ministry, an event which was manifested by the power of His disciples. "And the seventy returned again with joy, saying, Lord, even the devils are subject unto us through thy name. And he said unto them, I beheld Satan as lightning fall from heaven. Behold, I give unto you power to tread on serpents and scorpions, and over all the power of the enemy: and nothing shall by any means hurt you" (Luke 10:17-19). The victims of violent crime are in an analogous position with God: innocent people who deserve to be avenged. But grace still abounds in history, so the criminal is allowed to make a counter-offer to his victim, just as the sinner can make a counter-offer to God.[18]

The third benefit of this interpretation is social: *the integrity of the legal system is upheld in the eyes of all the nation.* Members of society at large cannot complain that the judges are playing favorites. The judges are not "respecting persons." If a rich man loses money, while the victim has lost the use of his body, this result has been the decision of the victim, not the judges. What is essentially a private dispute, victim vs. criminal, rather than a conflict between classes, has been settled by the disputants. The victim has made his choice. Outsiders therefore have no valid moral complaint against the judicial system. This keeps the ideology of class conflict from spreading to the general population. This is a very important feature of the justice system in an era of class conflict, meaning an era of rhetoric by competing elites in the name of various classes.

---

17. Of course, the desire to gain compensation would be regarded as jealousy, in the absence of a crime: the desire to gain at another person's expense. The crime, naturally, does make a difference: the right of the State to avenge the victim is crucial; pseudo-envy or pseudo-jealousy are just that: pseudo. These are legitimate emotions when a crime has been committed that has cost the victim the use of part of his body.

18. When sick or injured people learn that they are about to die, one common reaction is to make a deal with God: specific service for an extension of the gift of life. Contrary to secular humanists and theological liberals, this makes good sense. The dying individual is thereby admitting that God is in control of life and death. This is another reason why dying people deserve to be told that they are dying.

Insurance for Criminals?

Should the victim be denied the option of specifying the form of vengeance? Does it thwart justice to set up a judicial system where a rich criminal can offer to "buy his way out"?[19] Worse, what if his rich insurance company can offer to buy his way out?

If criminals could escape the likelihood of physical violence by means of monetary restitution, they might start buying insurance contracts that would enable them to escape the economic penalty of inflicting physical violence. This could be regarded as licensing criminal behavior. No one is going to co-insure another man's eye with his own eye, but the public has already set up co-insurance for monetary claims. Thus, by allowing economic restitution for crimes of violence, criminal behavior might be made less costly to the criminals.

One answer to this objection is that insurance companies are unlikely to insure a person from claims made by victims if the man is a repeat violator. The risk of writing such contracts is too high. Private insurance contracts are designed to be sold to the general public, and to keep premiums sufficiently price competitive, sellers exclude people known to be high risks. Low-risk buyers do not want to pay for high-risk buyers. Furthermore, insurance policies often specify that the coverage is for civil damages rather than criminal acts. This is true of most automobile insurance policies. Policies specify exactly what is to be covered—the famous insurance industry principle of "the large print giveth, but the fine print taketh away."

Policies actually designed by criminals to co-insure would be extremely unlikely. Violent criminals seldom think ahead. They do not work well with others. They are essentially anti-social people. A system of insurance company-subsidized crime could not last very long without government financial aid.

The Auction for Human Flesh

By allowing the substitution of an economic payment for actual physical disfigurement, the judges unquestionably do authorize an auction for human flesh. If a convicted criminal is allowed to pay the victim in order to avoid physical mutilation, he is participating in an auction. Such an implicit auction may sound crass, but so does pok-

---

19. If the criminal could "buy his way out" by bribing the judges, then justice would be thwarted. But judges in a biblical system represent the victims, not the State. If they represent a victim who wishes to be "bought off," where is the injustice?

ing out an innocent person's eye. So does all criminal behavior. Covenant-breaking men may not like to think of criminal behavior in such terms, but this is what the Bible teaches. Sin is the evil, not economic restitution.

We begin our economic analysis of this auction process with a consideration of the victim. Let us assume that he has lost his eye. He tells the judges that he wants to see the other man's eye poked out, just as his was. He offers the criminal no choice between mutilation and restitution. Because the victim initially offers no alternative sanction, the criminal is then allowed to make a single counter-offer, if he wants to. Assume that he makes this counter-offer: 100 ounces of gold instead of losing his eye.[20] Perhaps he is a skilled craftsman who needs both eyes. Perhaps he fears disfigurement. In any case, he places a high premium on his eye. He bids 100 ounces of gold to retain it.

Once the victim receives an offer from the criminal, he may change his mind about his commitment to seeing the criminal disfigured. Perhaps he did not suspect that he could get this much money from the criminal. Perhaps his wife has seen the wisdom of taking the money. He may conclude that he would much prefer 100 ounces of gold to the joy he would receive in seeing (with his remaining eye) his enemy brought low. After all, seeing his enemy part with 100 ounces of gold is also seeing him brought low, and the event brings other benefits, such as all the pleasures or security the 100 ounces of gold can buy. So he accepts the counter-offer. The criminal keeps his eye.

In this case, the criminal is the high-money bidder. The victim values the gold more than he values the criminal's eye. The criminal places more value on his eye than the gold. Each man gets what he most prefers. The criminal has bought the right to determine what happens to his own body. He has bought the right to avoid mutilation.

Consider the victim's other possible choice. He is still outraged at what has befallen him. He wants the criminal to share the same physical limitation. He is unwilling to accept the financial counter-

---

20. As we shall see, this counter-offer is allowed because the victim did not offer the criminal a choice between mutilation and economic restitution. If the victim specifies a choice between mutilation and a money payment, he is not entitled to accept less money, since this would indicate that he had not been honest when he specified the initial conditions. On the other hand, if the criminal should propose a non-monetary payment, the victim would be entitled to consider it, since this would constitute a different kind of offer from that specified by the victim. See subsection below, "Limiting One's Original Demands," pp. 430-31.

offer. Now, economically speaking, the criminal had just placed 100 ounces of gold into the victim's lap. He had been willing to pay. The victim is not impressed, or not sufficiently impressed. He figuratively hands the 100 ounces of gold back to the criminal. "Keep your filthy money, you butcher! Keep your only remaining eye on your money." The victim has now matched the money bid of the criminal. He has forfeited the 100 ounces of gold that he might have received. He places a higher value on his legal ability to blind the other man's eye than he does on 100 ounces of gold. So the victim gets what he values most, the joy of seeing the other man lose his eye. But he pays 100 ounces of gold for this pleasure. The pleasure is biblically legitimate, but it is expensive.

The criminal's 100 ounces of gold did not constitute a high enough bid. The victim might have agreed for more than the 100 ounces, but the criminal had not been willing to pay this much. The criminal keeps what he wants: the 100 + ounces of gold that the victim might have accepted in payment, but which the criminal refused to offer. The criminal would rather have this larger quantity of gold than keep his eye. There is what the economists call "reservation demand" for this money; the criminal pays with his eye for his continued possession of the money.

None of this suggests that the criminal can buy justice. Justice is what the court provides when it tries the case and imposes the victim's preferred sanction, up to the limit of the law. The criminal is buying a specific sanction that he prefers by offering the victim an alternative which the criminal hopes the victim will prefer. It is an auction for flesh, not an auction for justice.

The Private Slave Market

To give the criminal access to capital sufficient to make the offer, the State must allow another auction for flesh: a slave market. Deny this, and the criminal is thwarted in gaining what he wants, and so is his victim. The most valuable asset a criminal may possess is his own ability to work. If he is denied the legal right to capitalize this asset, he may not be able to offer a sufficiently high bid to the victim to avoid mutilation.

The modern democratic theorist professes horror at such a thought. Why? *Because the modern State's disciples want the State to have a monopoly on the slave market.* The State imposes prison as the alternative to both restitution and slavery — an alternative which benefits neither the victim nor the potentially productive criminal.

At this point, we return once again to the basic theme of the Book of Exodus: *the choice between slavery to man and service to God.* It is therefore the question of *representation*: Who is represented by the State, God or autonomous man? When autonomous man is represented by the State, then tyranny or impotence is the result. Autonomous man seeks to enslave others, for he seeks to imitate God, just as Satan imitates God. The State becomes the primary agency of this enslavement process. It should not be surprising to learn that the call for the abolition of chattel slavery in the United States began in the 1820's in the Northeast, where the new state prison systems were also being implemented.[21]

Slavery may seem brutal. The *lex talionis* also may seem brutal. Judicially unregulated violence is more brutal. Injustice in the face of crime is more brutal yet. The high penalty imposed on the convicted criminal is intended to impress the criminal, potential criminals, and all ethical rebels of *the majesty of God's law,* and the high price God will impose eternally on those who break it. This no doubt repels the sense of justice of covenant-breakers, but God is not concerned about the ethical sensibilities of covenant-breakers. He is concerned primarily about His own majesty, which is reflected in His law, including the penalties imposed on those who transgress its provisions.

Technological Progress and Restitution

With the advent of modern technology, it might be possible for the victim to secure a replacement eye. He might demand an operation, with the criminal's eye being transplanted as a replacement. Or an exchange might be set up: the criminal's eye goes to an eye bank in exchange for an eye that might be more compatible biologically with the victim's system. Alternatively, the judges could allow the criminal to pay for an operation for the victim, and give the victim an additional payment equal to the value of the operation. The criminal would lose the money, but the victim would see again.

This sort of economic resolution to the problem of "eye for eye" standard is ideal: the victim gains what he had lost, and the criminal

---

21. David J. Rothman, *The Discovery of the Asylum: Social Order and Disorder in the New Republic* (Boston: Little, Brown, 1971). This same era saw Horace Mann's call for the establishment of a "theologically neutral" tax-financed day school movement, meaning a call for social morality without Christian supernaturalism. When American society began to abandon the God of the Bible, it also began to abandon the institutional foundations of freedom.

pays for it, plus restitution for the victim's pain, fear, and trouble. The technological advances brought by Western — and initially Christian[22] — civilization make possible the best solution for both parties, namely, the restoration of the injured man's sight, but at the expense of the criminal. The technological progress that would be brought by a thoroughly Christian civilization would make possible a better set of options for both victim and criminal. The more faithful society's commitment to enforcing God's law, the more rapid the technological progress is going to be.

Limiting One's Original Demands

The threat of actual physical mutilation for the convicted violent criminal will always be present in a biblical legal order. The victim has lost his eye or tooth; the criminal deserves to lose his. But few criminals would sacrifice an eye if they could make restitution in some other way. They might sacrifice a tooth, but not an eye. The victim can legitimately demand the removal of the other man's eye, but there is not much doubt that he would prefer a large cash settlement to help him recover his lost productivity and forfeited economic opportunities. He might even be able to get a new eye through surgery. The rich man is allowed to "buy his way out," but only at the discretion (and direct economic benefit) of the victim. On the other hand, the victim can demand his "pound of flesh," but only by forfeiting the money that he might have been paid.

What if the victim is really vindictive? What if he demands 1,000 ounces of gold for the other person's tooth? In all likelihood, the criminal would prefer to forfeit the tooth. *Under this kind of judicial system, the victim must estimate carefully in advance just what the convicted person might be willing and able to pay.* There must be no "fall-back position" after the victim submits his pair of demands to the judges: physical mutilation or a specified financial restitution payment.

Under a biblical system of economic substitution, the victim would be required by the court to specify the minimum amount of money he would be willing to accept in exchange for not having mutilation imposed on the criminal. The victim would not be allowed to present a false estimate about how much restitution he would be willing to accept. This would be false witness, or perjury. He could not come back a second time, after the criminal has refused to

---

22. See footnote #8, above.

pay the 1,000 ounces of gold, and say, "All right, I'll accept 500 ounces of gold instead of his tooth." By lowering his new demand, he would be admitting that his initial offer had been higher than his minimal demand. In short, the injured victim must know in advance that by making an excessive initial financial demand, he might "price himself out of the market"; he therefore has to be reasonable if he is really after money. He might wind up with nothing except the pain and disfigurement of the criminal as his reward. He must ask for less money in order to increase his likelihood of collecting anything.

The judges would present the victim's specified choices to the criminal, and the criminal would have the option of refusing to pay the 1,000 ounces. The judges would then have the physical penalty imposed.

The man condemned by the victim to permanent physical mutilation would have the option of making a counter-proposal if the victim had offered no option to mutilation. The victim could then consider it. Again, the criminal would be allowed only one offer; if the victim still says no, and the criminal then makes a higher offer, he can be presumed to have given false witness when he made the first offer. By limiting the victim to presenting the criminal with only one set of options, and by giving the criminal the opportunity to make a single counter-offer only when no alternative option has been offered by the victim, the judges can obtain honest offers from the beginning.

The court would allow only one form of second-chance bids. If the criminal is unwilling to pay the victim the money payment demanded, but he is willing to pay in some other way than money, he would have the opportunity to present the alternative or group of alternatives for the victim to choose from. But if the victim turns this counter-offer down, the criminal will then have to undergo mutilation. He is governed by the equivalent rule that governs the victim: honest bidding. He offers his highest price or best bid. If it is rejected, he must suffer the physical consequences.

The Authority of the Judges

The integrity of society's covenantal civil judges is fundamental to the preservation of social order. The Bible warns rulers and judges to render honest judgment. They are forbidden to take bribes (although it is *not* forbidden for righteous people to offer bribes to corrupt judges).[23] Judges are to render honest judgment because the

---

23. See Chapter 26, section on "The Righteous Bribe," pp. 793-800. Cf. Gary North, "In Defense of Biblical Bribery," in Rushdoony, *Institutes of Biblical Law*, Appendix 5.

Bible requires it and because God requires it, not because it is made personally profitable for them to do so. When citizens distrust the judicial system, a fundamental weakness exists in the society. Bribes are a sign of such weakness and distrust.

The judges establish the initial penalty payment in the case of a notorious ox that has killed a person (Ex. 21:30). What about in the case of the crime of mutilation? Shouldn't the judges set the penalty? In the case of a non-injurious, accidental, premature birth caused by another man's violent behavior, the husband establishes the penalty, and the judges then impose it. "If men strive, and hurt a woman with child, so that her fruit depart from her, and yet no mischief follow: he shall be surely punished, according as the woman's husband will lay upon him; and he shall pay as the judges determine" (Ex. 21:22). This implies that the judges can overrule the husband if the penalty is thought by them to be excessive. The authority of the judges is supreme in this case.

If it is true that the Bible requires that in the case of bodily mutilation, the judges must assess the penalty, as they do in the case of criminal manslaughter (the owner of the notorious ox), then they must make the decision: economic restitution or physical restitution. Both are legitimate forms of vengeance; both are true forms of restitution. If the judges are solely responsible for making this determination, then sovereignty is transferred to them and away from the victim and the criminal, who might prefer to come to a different, more mutually beneficial transaction. This raises the question of righteous judgment. Why should the victim and the criminal be excluded from the process of the setting of the penalty? After all, in the case of the non-injurious premature birth, the husband has the opportunity of setting a preliminary penalty. Why not in the case of mutilation?

One solution to this dilemma would be to allow the judges to assess the original penalty, estimating what the defense of an eye is worth in the open market, and then make a preliminary announcement of the size of the payment. Then either of the two contending parties could make a counter-offer, which the judges would accept if both parties agree. In this way, the authority of the law would have a visible manifestation — rule by the judges — but the type of restitution could be modified at the discretion of the affected parties. It would be analogous to parents making an arranged marriage: either of the two children can legitimately protest and refuse the other, but initiating the marriage would be the right of the parents.

It is important that collusion between the judges and either the victim or the convicted criminal be prevented. To help prevent such collusion, dual rights are established: the right of the victim to demand different restitution from that set by the judges, and the right of the criminal to make a counter-offer to the victim when he receives notice of the judges' initial proposal.

There is another factor to consider. Economic value is both objective and subjective.[24] The judges are required by God to attempt to assess the cost to the victim, as well as the cost to the criminal, but they may make a mistake. There is no scientifically or theoretically valid way for judges to assess the comparative costs of injuries, since these costs are based on other people's subjective utilities. For example, if either the victim or the criminal is a right-handed skilled craftsman whose hand is his calling, and he has lost (or is faced with the threat of loss of) his right hand, the penalty is not easily fitted to the crime. Say that the victim has lost his right hand, and he is the craftsman. The criminal is a left-handed lawyer whose right hand is seemingly less crucial to him than the right hand of the victim. Is the loss of the criminal's right hand really a case of "hand for hand"? How can the judges determine what is a really comparable penalty? Hasn't the victim suffered far greater loss? Of course, the reverse could be true: a left-handed lawyer loses his right hand, and the criminal is a right-handed craftsman. Is the *physically* identical penalty really comparable in terms of the costs to each person?

The System in Operation

Consider a hypothetical case. A criminal is convicted for having mutilated another man's hand. Let us consider three possible outcomes. *First,* the judges determine that the criminal should lose his hand. Why would they impose this penalty? Perhaps the criminal is a known brawler. He used a weapon to bash a victim's hand, making it permanently useless. The judges decide that the best thing for society would be for the criminal to have his hand bashed into uselessness or amputated, so that he could not easily repeat the offense.

The victim at this point might prefer economic restitution. The brawler also might be willing to pay to keep his hand. In such a case, the judges would be placing their perception of the public's need for future social peace above the economic needs of the victim.

---

24. Gary North, *The Dominion Covenant: Genesis* (2nd ed.; Tyler, Texas: Institute for Christian Economics, 1987), ch. 4.

The victim would have the option of asking for a different kind of punishment. The victim may want money, so he appeals the decision, and demands monetary compensation. The judges then go to the criminal. Is he willing to pay the victim the proposed monetary restitution? The criminal has three choices: pay the money, accept the judges' original penalty, or offer a third proposal to the victim. If the criminal turns down the request of the victim to be paid, and if the victim rejects the criminal's counter-offer, then the judges' original sentence would be carried out. He would lose the use of his hand.

Second, the judges impose a monetary penalty that is too low in the opinion of the victim. He demands more money. The criminal has a new set of choices: pay the higher penalty, make a counter-offer of something other than money, or lose his hand. He no longer has the option of paying the original penalty established by the judges. The victim has overruled the judges on the question of the appropriate monetary penalty.

Third, the judges impose a monetary penalty. The victim is outraged. He believes that the criminal should lose his hand, just as he lost his. The judges then go to the criminal. You must lose your hand, the victim says. Do you wish to offer the victim more money than we determined originally, or offer something other than money? The criminal makes his decision. If he decides to offer more money or another non-monetary option, he has only one opportunity to persuade the victim. If the victim refuses to accept the counter-offer, the criminal loses his hand.

By allowing the victim to demand different compensation — money or service rather than physical mutilation, or more money than the judges have imposed, or physical mutilation rather than money — the proposed restitution process allows subjective value to assert itself. The *victim* determines whether or not the judges have really offered him what his loss is worth to him personally. If he thinks he is being cheated, he can demand that his enemy pay more or suffer the same physical loss. The *criminal* also has the right to substitute the loss of an appendage, if the judges determine that he should lose the appendage, rather than pay what he believes is an excessive economic demand by the victim, if the demand is higher than the judges originally set.

The Bible does not anywhere indicate that the criminal has any legal, formal ability to overturn the final decision of the highest civil court of appeal. If the judges impose a particular penalty — mutilation, for example—and the victim is satisfied, then the criminal has no formal right of appeal. He cannot override the decision of the judges. But in fact he really does have the indirect ability to appeal— an appeal through the victim. He or his representatives can approach the victim with a counter-proposal. "Look, I would be willing to pay 100 ounces of gold if you would appeal the decision of the judges to have me mutilated." If this is satisfactory to the victim, he then appeals the decision, and the criminal agrees to the new terms of restitution. The judges are not allowed to overturn this mutually agreed-upon form of restitution.

If the court sets an economic penalty, and the victim agrees, the criminal still has a legal, formal ability to substitute his own mutilation for the economic restitution. He can demand the explicit physical sanction of the law: *lex talionis*. This means that the law upholds his right to demand the punishment specified by God. Bargaining is legitimate, but both the victim and the criminal can insist on the specified penalty. If the victim insists on physical mutilation, the criminal has no choice. If the criminal insists on physical mutilation, the victim has no choice. Bargaining, however, is likely.

By establishing the three-way system of establishing penalties— judges, victim, and convicted criminal—the judicial system receives a means of making *objective* approximations of the inescapably *subjective* "eye for eye" standard—subjective to both victim and criminal. By permitting subjective estimations of loss by both the victim and the criminal, the judges find a way to offer compensation to the victim that he believes is comparable to the crime. The criminal, however, is allowed to counter-offer a different, economic form of restitution penalty if he believes that the cost of a physical penalty is too high.

Conclusion

My discussion of the possible outworkings of the "eye for eye" passage should not be understood as the last word on the subject. It is, however, a "first word." I want readers to understand that the biblical justice system is just, workable, and effective. The *lex talionis* should not be dismissed as some sort of peculiar juridical testament of a long-defunct primitive agricultural society. What the Bible spells out as judicially binding is vastly superior to anything offered by modern humanism in the name of civic justice.

The problems in dealing with the actual imposition of the *lex talionis* principle are great. The history of the people of God testifies

to these difficulties. We have few if any examples of Christian societies that have attempted to impose the "eye for eye" principle literally. The basic principle is clear: *the punishment should fit the crime.* By
allowing the victim to demand restitution in the form pleasing to
him, and by allowing the criminal to counter-offer something more
pleasing to him, the penalty comes close to matching the effects of
the crime, as assessed by the victim.

Each party gets to make one offer. If the victim offers a choice between penalties, the criminal chooses which one he prefers, or can
offer something completely different. If the victim specifies one and
only one penalty, mutilation, the criminal is entitled to counter-offer.
If the victim specifies only a money payment, but the criminal
prefers mutilation on an "eye for eye" basis, then he has the right to
choose mutilation.

The judges can establish the original restitution payment, whether
physical or economic, but the two affected parties should have the
final determination. This places limits on the State. The economic
assets involved in this auction process are transferred (or retained)
by the person who is more concerned with economic capital than
with physical mutilation. In this way, biblical justice is furthered.

The modern Western world has not imposed deliberate, permanent physical mutilation on violent criminals. These criminals,
when convicted, have been imprisoned. They have been compelled
to pay fines to the State. In very few cases have they been compelled
to make monetary restitution to the victims. The result has been
escalating violence against private citizens, as well as the escalating
power of the State.

Biblical law imposes penalties on violent criminals that tend to
reduce the amount of violent crime. Biblical penalties encourage
criminals to count the cost in advance. In the case of "crimes of passion," the convicted passionate criminals would be reminded of the
benefits of self-control. That stump at the end of an arm is a better
reminder than a string tied around a finger. So is the loss of several
years' worth of savings, or several years as an indentured servant.
What men sow, that shall they also reap (Gal. 6:7-8). A godly society's
criminal justice system, organized around the *lex talionis* principle,
provides criminals with a glimpse of (or preliminary down payment
to) this cosmic principle of justice.

FREEDOM FOR AN EYE

And if a man smite the eye of his servant, or the eye of his maid, that it perish; he shall let him go free for his eye's sake. And if he smite out his manservant's tooth, or his maidservant's tooth; he shall let him go free for his tooth's sake (Ex. 21:26-27).

The law concerning the striking of a bondservant[1] seems to be in conflict with the immediately preceding verses. The "eye for eye" principle of verse 24 does not seem to be upheld in this passage. The master who has blinded his slave is not to be blinded by the judges. This in turn seems to be a violation of the principle of equality before the law: "One law shall be to him that is homeborn, and unto the stranger that sojourneth among you" (Ex. 12:49). If the master may strike a Hebrew bondservant, putting out his eye, why shouldn't he suffer the same physical consequences? Why is he allowed to retain his sight? Is the law unfair?

Whenever we find a variation in the application of some general biblical law, we should search the context to discover which special circumstances of the case have made mandatory the variation. We must bear in mind that *in principle,* the general law is still in force. God does not change His mind concerning ethics. The ethical terms of His covenant do not change. Nevertheless, in order for the law to apply fairly to those under the terms of the covenant, *differences in circumstances must be respected.* Some people deserve more protection than others because of their place in society. Young children are one example. Widows and orphans are another. So is the bondservant.

---

1. Reminder: I use the word "bondservant" rather than slave, except when referring to permanent ownership of non-Hebrew slaves.

The Bondservant's Special Position

The Bible recognizes the legitimacy of the institution of indentured servitude. It places this institution under specific laws, and the law governing the injuring of a bondservant is one such law. On the one hand, as we shall see, the master needs special legal protection from the false claims of a disobedient bondservant. On the other hand, the dependent bondservant needs special legal protection against excessive discipline by the master. This law governing physical punishment protects both master and bondservant.

We need to examine the biblical principles that undergird this law. First, it must be understood that the master has legitimate authority over the bondservant. The bondservant is a form of property. The master is allowed to assign tasks to the bondservant that produce profit for the master. In this sense, the bondservant is his property, for the fruits of the bondservant's productivity belong to the master, as if he were a beast or a tool. The master may not mistreat the bondservant, however, as this law indicates. The bondservant is not without legal protection, but he is not a free man. The "eye for eye" principle is applied differently in the case of a bondservant because the legal relationships are different from those governing free men.

Second, ownership is an inescapable social function. We say that ownership necessarily involves *stewardship*. The ownership of an asset imposes certain inescapable costs on the owner. He must make decisions about how to use an asset, or whether or not to divest himself of ownership. If he uses the asset in one way, he cannot use it in another. By earning income (or attempting to) by using an asset in one productive process, he necessarily forfeits whatever income he might otherwise have produced with the asset.[2] He must choose what to do with whatever assets he legally controls. This is called *allocation*.

Market Pricing

The bondservant's owner has a capital asset at his disposal. The bondservant can produce income for him. An economically rational purchaser of a bondservant looks at the expected future stream of income — net income, after caring for the bondservant's physical needs — and he then discounts this by the prevailing rate of interest. He will pay no more for a bondservant than he will pay for any other

---

2. Gary North, *An Introduction to Christian Economics* (Nutley, New Jersey: Craig Press, 1973), ch. 28: "Ownership: Free but Not Cheap."

capital asset that is expected to produce the same net output, nor will the seller sell the bondservant for less.[3] If he pays more, he will lose money on the investment. On the other hand, he cannot buy the bondservant for less, since the competitive bids of other potential buyers keep the bondservant's price high. The bondservant's market price will be the same as the market price of a piece of land that is leased for the period of his bondage, or a bond, mortgage, or any other productive asset that produces the same net economic return over the same period of time.

It may bother some people to learn that the market price of the human bondservant is governed by the same economic forces that govern all other economic assets that are expected to produce the same rate of return. This seems to equate people with things. But we also know that buyers and sellers make their economic decisions in terms of economic costs and benefits. Unless the buyers are sadists who love to mistreat people (and who are therefore willing to pay more than the market price of leased land or a bond in order to assure their ownership of a bondservant),[4] the market price of the bondservant will equal the market price of any economic asset that is expected to produce the same rate of return. As we shall see, this equation of market prices for all equally productive assets is one of the aspects of a market economy that protects the bondservant from abuse.

So, from the point of view of economic return on the investment, the bondservant is not in a special position. But the Bible teaches that he is a human being, not a beast of burden or a machine. He is therefore singled out for special protection by civil law.

Self-Interest and Self-Restraint

The bondservant-owner's quest for profit places limits on his relationship with his bondservant. The bondservant is expected to be a producer of net income. The owner risks losing this income, or part of the income, if he permanently mutilates the bondservant. First, there will be the loss in productivity associated directly with the bond-

---

3. There is this exception: to the degree that owning a slave is a prestige factor, the buyer will pay more, and the seller will demand more. The value of the slave in this case reflects his position as both a capital good and a consumer good.

4. This really does not invalidate the general rule. The sadist is receiving nonmonetary returns psychologically through the suffering he imposes on the slave. Thus, he will pay more to buy the human asset.

servant's physical loss. Second, there could also be loss as a result of the mistreated bondservant's resentment. He will not perform as expected. *The market's forces of profit and loss restrain the bondservant-owner.* The civil authorities can presume that the bondservant-owner is not going to mistreat his bondservant physically to the extent that the bondservant's performance will be seriously impaired. *Because of the competitive market for the bondservant's economic output, civil authorities can more safely delegate authority to the bondservant-owner.* This decentralizes power in the society. The competitive market, through the self-interest of the bondservant-owner, serves as an institution that restrains the illegitimate use of power. The economic costs of lawless behavior are borne by the bondservant-owner. This is true of all capital resource ownership. This is why the bondservant's economic position as a capital asset protects him.

Bondservants are understood to be potentially rebellious. This is clearly true in the case of criminals who are sold to masters in order to raise money for the restitution payment to the victims. But rebellion is not limited to criminals. Men are by nature rebellious. They resist authority, both lawful and unlawful. Adam rebelled against God; bondservants rebel against masters. Without a means of enforcing lawful authority, no form of external government could exist. The bondservant system is an aspect of family government in the Bible. Thus, the bondservant-owner possesses the legitimate authority to inflict limited physical punishment. What the Bible restrains is punishment that inflicts *permanent physical damage.*

There are several reasons that we can presume for this prohibition. *First,* men are made in God's image, and therefore they deserve protection. *Second,* interpersonal relationships between people are threatened when one person has seemingly unlimited power to impose his will on another. Punishment is supposed to increase respect for the law, the master, and God on the part of the bondservant, not foster an urge to revenge because of the outrageous nature of some type of punishment. Evil calls forth evil. *Third,* permanent injuries generally restrict people's ability to exercise dominion. Punishment is not to thwart the dominion covenant. *Fourth,* a man's spirit can be broken by continual, ruthless beatings. Without the protection of law, the victim may see himself as exploited and without hope. This also conflicts with the psychology of dominion. The law provides him with an area of safety. He is to increase his dominion by his subservience to God's law. This, in fact, is one of the functions of inden-

tured servitude: to bring men under God's law. *If there is no protection,
then there is no law. Without law, there can be no dominion.* Indentured servitude is supposed to teach this biblical principle of life.

Judicially Unrestrained Violence:
The Lure of Autonomy

There is a fifth reason why it was illegal for bondservant-owners
to inflict permanent physical damage on their slaves. This reason is
more narrowly theological in nature. It is one which contemporary
Christians do not want to think about: *eternal punishment.*

Slavery and bondservice point to man's subordinate relationship
to God. This relationship, being covenantal, is governed by the inescapable aspect of all covenants, judgment. There are two forms of
covenantal judgment: blessing and cursing.[5] The blessing side of
slavery is the *judicially guaranteed prospect of release.* A slave who
matures and learns to be self-disciplined and productive is to be released, and civil law is to enforce his right to freedom by establishing
specific performance standards for slaves. This hope of eventual
release must not be destroyed.[6] Thus, slavery points to covenantal
blessing. It points to God's final release of covenant-keepers from
bondage to sin and death.

On the other hand, slavery also points to the other side of God's
final judgment, the eternal curse: the lake of fire (Rev. 20:14). It
points to God's position as cosmic Slavemaster. In the lake of fire, the
"whipping" never ceases. The physical sanctions are eternal. These
physical sanctions have no redeeming value, meaning no redemptive
purpose. God whips rebels forever in order to satisfy His own sense
of justice. But the inflicting of permanent cursing is exclusively
God's decision and activity. Men are never to imitate God in this
respect. *Men in history are never to be given the power to impose non-
redemptive sanctions, either physical or spiritual.* Even capital punishment
is legally only a change in venue: convicted criminals are transferred
to God's court for final trial and sentencing. This is why the Bible
provides no authorization for torturing those who have been legally
condemned to execution.

---

5. Ray R. Sutton, *That You May Prosper: Dominion By Covenant* (Tyler, Texas: Institute for Christian Economics, 1987), ch. 4.

6. Even in the case of permanent heathen slaves, there was a temporal limit: ten
generations. See Chapter 4's subsection: "Ten Generations to Freedom," pp. 147-52.

The American South: No Civil Protection

Slavemasters who symbolically violate this principle by inflicting permanent damage on a slave are therefore supposed to be removed from legal authority over the slave. Slavery in the American South violated this principle. Unlimited authority to inflict punishment was given to slave masters by Southern custom. Just as there was no judicially enforced hope of release for the slave, so was there no judicially enforced limit on physical punishment of the slave. The slave system of the South rested on violence. Every slave system does. In fact, both State and family rest on the threat of violence, but not unlimited violence. Violence is always supposed to be judicially restrained. This was not the case with Southern slavery.

In plantation management handbook after handbook, owners were told that the slave had to submit unconditionally. John Stuart Skinner's 1840 essay in the *American Farmer* is representative of the mentality of the Southern slave-owner: "Absolute, unqualified authority is asserted and exercised on the part of the master."[7] His focus was on the absoluteness of the relationship. "Whenever the authority of the master becomes qualified — whenever his dominion is relaxed, and the submission of the slave ceases to be absolute, the relation between the two loses its homogenious [sic] distinctness. The one is no longer master, the other no longer slave, in the sense and degree of absoluteness which produces uniformity of action and feeling between them."[8]

There is no absolute human authority present in man's institutions. Men are not God. Only God establishes absolute relations with others. Only He possesses absolute authority. Thus, the judicial mark of the inherent perversity of Southern slavery was this assertion of absolute judicial authority of master over slave. The Southern slave-owner was allowed to impose any sanctions he chose for whatever reason he deemed significant. Whatever civil laws may have been on the statute books regarding limits on a master's punishment of slaves, they were seldom enforced, just as the dueling laws in the South were seldom enforced. Social custom sometimes differed from judicial forms, and social custom was the operational law of the region.

---

7. John S. Skinner, "Mortality among Slaves in Mississippi," *American Farmer*, 3rd ser. (1840), p. 170; cited in Dickson D. Bruce, Jr., *Violence and Culture in the Antebellum South* (Austin: University of Texas Press, 1979), p. 116.

8. *Ibid.*, p. 117.

The Whip

Deuteronomy 25:3 specifies 40 lashes ("stripes") as the maximum allowed. To beat a person with more than 40 lashes would make the person seem "vile," in the language of the King James. The New American Standard translates the word as "degraded." In other words, it would make him seem less than human, meaning someone not protected by law in spite of his imaging of God.

The Massachusetts Body of Liberties (1641) recognized the degrading aspect of whipping, and specifically protected gentlemen from this form of punishment. "No man shall be beaten with above forty stripes, nor shall any true gentleman nor any man equal to a gentleman be punished with whipping, unless his crime be very shameful and his course of life vicious and profligate."[9] This fastidiousness about whipping gentlemen violated the second listed liberty: equality before the law (the rule of Exodus 12:49). "Every person within this jurisdiction, whether inhabitant or foreigner, shall enjoy the same justice that is general for the plantation, which we constitute and execute toward another without partiality or delay. . . ."[10] Ex-slave Henry Bibb expressed his position well: "I was brought up in the Counties of Shelby, Henry, Oldham, and Trimble. Or, more correctly speaking, I was *flogged up*; for where I should have been receiving moral, mental, and religious instruction, I received stripes without number, the object of which was to degrade and keep me in subordination."[11] Bibb's eloquence seems to have been influenced at this point by the very terminology of Deuteronomy 25:3: "stripes without number," "to degrade me."

It was considered a mark of personal weakness for a Southern slave-owner to rely too heavily on the whip. Certainly, he was warned by social custom and written manuals to be fixed, predictable, and self-restrained in his exercise of plantation discipline. A gentleman was expected to be in self-control at all times. Bruce summarizes the social standard: "The plantation was supposed to be a system in which places were known and rules observed. Regularity and order were to be its main features. The slave's behavior was to be highly

---

9. The Body of Liberties (1641), reprinted in David Hawke (ed.), *U.S. Colonial History: Readings and Documents* (Indianapolis: Bobbs-Merrill, 1966), p. 126.

10. *Ibid.*, p. 125.

11. Henry Bibb, *Narrative of the Life and Adventures of an American Slave, Written by Himself* (1849), p. 13; cited in *ibid.*, p. 147. Bibb's *Narrative* has been reprinted by several publishers, including the Negro University Press and Greenwood.

predictable and the master, in turn, was to be predictable in his own actions."[12] This was the ideal. In fact, it was the continual complaint of ex-slaves that their masters had not been predictable in imposing sanctions.[13]

Other sanctions were available besides the whip: the demotion of household slaves to the status of field slaves; the denial of passes to leave the plantation temporarily; confiscation of crops in the slaves' personal gardens; time in the stocks; or even solitary confinement in a plantation jail (some plantations were large enough to have a jail).[14] But in the last analysis, the whip was the key to slave discipline. It was the emblem of the master's authority.[15] It could be used in an orderly manner: more lashes for more serious infractions. Also, there were several kinds of whips, some more painful than others (e.g., rawhide). But the goal of the plantation ethic was to reduce whipping to a minimum.[16]

Limiting Passion

There is no doubt that one of the great concerns of Southern social thought before the Civil War was to place limits on passion. Bruce's book makes this clear. Southerners feared disorder. They wanted limits — judicial, customary, and institutional — placed on men's outward acts of violence. This was one reason why the gentleman class placed such great stress on personal manners. They feared the "natural man," a man of passion and violence. They identified him by his tendency to violence. But when it came to slavery, they defied the fundamental biblical principle of social order: *self-government under God's revealed law.* They refused to establish a judicial hierarchy, an appeals court that would bring every person under the rule of law, including slave and master. They made the tight little "family" of the plantation into a sovereign judicial entity. The "children" — slaves — were to remain in the status of perpetual children. Their "father" — the master — would retain perpetual and judicially unlimited authority over them. This was a denial of the very foundation of liberty under God, a fact recognized by Jefferson, Madison, and many other Southern spokesmen, but they could not bring them-

---

12. Bruce, *Violence and Culture*, p. 118.
13. *Ibid.*, pp. 138-40.
14. Kenneth M. Stampp, *The Peculiar Institution: Slavery in the Ante-Bellum South* (New York: Vintage, 1956), pp. 172-73.
15. *Ibid.*, p. 174.
16. *Ibid.*, pp. 177-79.

selves to abandon the institution that denied their first principle of government: self-government under law.[17]

The defenders of Southern slavery could always insist that brutality on the part of masters was not the norm but rather an exception. This was Presbyterian theologian Robert L. Dabney's argument. "Now, while we freely admit that there were in the South, instances of criminal barbarity in corporal punishments, they were very infrequent, and were sternly reprobated by publick opinion."[18] Dabney was using rhetoric to make his point. There were no acts of criminal barbarity by slave-masters in the South because there were no criminal sanctions against such acts in the South's judicial code. Such acts could not be criminal acts, except in terms of a higher civil law than the South's. Dabney was using the word "criminal" in a general moral sense, i.e., criminal in the eyes of God and men, meaning "socially unacceptable." In any case, how he could know how frequent such acts of "criminal barbarity" were? Intuition? There were no published records for Yankees and other "outside agitators" to appeal to. The system's defenders expected slavery's critics simply to accept their word on the matter. How sternly or frequently public opinion "reprobated" floggers was another question that could not easily be settled by an appeal to reliable public records. What is not open to question is the nature of the sanctions of the South's judicial system against the physical mistreatment of slaves: there were none.

Formal Sanctions and Deviance

The same kind of defense could be made regarding the splitting up of slave families: an occasional event. Dabney made it, too. Again, he appealed to the integrity of the court of public opinion: ". . . when the separation was not justified by the crimes of the parties, it met the steady and increasing reprobation of publick opinion."[19] The weakness of this defense is that it fails to acknowledge the heart of the matter, namely, that such supposed deviations on the part of slave-owners were legal. There were no judicially enforceable sanc-

---

17. Winthrop D. Jordan, *White Over Black: American Attitudes Toward the Negro, 1550-1812* (Chapel Hill: University of North Carolina Press, 1968), ch. 12: "Thomas Jefferson: Self and Society."

18. Robert L. Dabney, *A Defence of Virginia [And Through Her, of the South]* (New York: Negro University Press, [1867] 1969), p. 221.

19. *Ibid.*, p. 231.

tions against such supposedly deviant behavior.[20] Thus, the behavior was not in fact deviant by Southern standards but at most merely exceptional. *Without judicial sanctions, a society has no formal way of identifying deviant behavior.* There is always a court of public opinion, and its acceptable jurisdiction is more broad than that of civil courts, but if this court is not supported by judicial sanctions, then it is an informal court. The slaves would have found it difficult to make accurate predictions about the degree of safety such informal sanctions could provide. Without a formal court of appeal, the degree of safety would be far more indeterminate.

Deviant behavior requires sanctions to identify it. Sociologist Kai Erikson, in his study of law enforcement in Puritan Massachusetts, offers this useful definition of deviance: the term "refers to conduct which the people of a group consider so dangerous or embarrassing or irritating that they bring special sanctions to bear against the persons who exhibit it."[21] "The deviant is a person whose activities have moved outside the margins of the group, and when the community calls him to account for that vagrancy it is making a statement about how much variability and diversity can be tolerated within the group before it loses its distinctive shape, its unique identity."[22] Those who defended slavery could and did appeal to the supposedly deviant character of its evils and the common character of its benefits. *But the key element in defining deviance is establishing the nature of the sanctions against it.* It is not the task of biblical civil government to make men perform moral tasks; its job is to restrict them from performing biblically immoral acts. The benefits of slavery should not be the civil government's legitimate concern; reducing the public evils associated with it is its legitimate concern.

Massachusetts legislation during the first full year of the colony's existence (1630) repeated the biblical standard, although with two modifications: "If any man smite out the eye or tooth of his manservant or maid-servant, or otherwise maim or much disfigure them, unless it be by mere casualty, he shall let them go free from his ser-

---

20. Legislation in the American South imposed no penalties on slave owners who physically injured their slaves: Arnold A. Sio, "Interpretations of Slavery," *Comparative Studies in Society and History*, VII (April 1965); reprinted in Allen Weinstein and Frank Otto Gatell (eds.), *American Negro Slavery: A Modern Reader* (New York: Oxford University Press, 1968), pp. 316-17.

21. Kai T. Erikson, *Wayward Puritans: A Study in the Sociology of Deviance* (New York: Wiley, 1966), p. 6.

22. *Ibid.*, p. 11.

vice and shall allow such further recompense as the court shall adjudge him."[23] If the injury was clearly an accident, the servant stayed; this provided an escape clause for the owner that the Bible does not mention. On the other hand, if it was deliberate, the servant not only went free but might also receive additional compensation. This went beyond the biblical penalty. The Massachusetts Puritans, at least with respect to their public law code, were concerned about violating the spirit of the law of slave injuries. They understood this law as prohibiting deliberate injuries by the master, so they relaxed the automatic release provision of the law, yet they also tried to honor another important principle of biblical law, economic restitution. They unquestionably placed servant-owners under the threat of civil sanctions.

It was the absence of judicial sanctions against these evils that made the character of Southern slavery judicially perverse. The South did not impose formal, public sanctions against those slave-owners who clearly mistreated their slaves. The Bible is clear about the proper response of society to such deviant behavior: for the slave so mistreated, the court's granting him his freedom is the appropriate sanction against the owner.

Because the South's courts refused to impose this biblical sanction on deviant slave-owners within their jurisdiction, God then imposed his sanctions on the courts. The slaves were freed by the courts of the South's conquerors. When self-government fails to produce proper results, external sanctions are appropriate. God brought the South under a kind of temporary servitude that lasted a little over a decade militarily,[24] over half a century politically,[25] and just over a century economically, socially, and culturally. (When Martin Luther King, Jr., ended his unforgettable "I Have a Dream" speech at the 1963 "March on Washington" with the words, taken

---

23. *Foundations of Colonial America: A Documentary History*, edited by W. Keith Kavenaugh, 3 vols. (New York: Chelsea House, 1973), I, p. 405. Also reprinted in Hawke (ed.), *U.S. Colonial History*, p. 127.

24. William A. Dunning, *Reconstruction: Political and Economic, 1865-1877* (New York: Harper Torchbooks, [1907] 1962); Kenneth M. Stampp, *The Era of Reconstruction, 1865-1877* (New York: Knopf, 1965); John Hope Franklin, *Reconstruction: After the Civil War* (University of Chicago Press, 1961); Harold M. Hyman (ed.), *New Frontiers of the American Reconstruction* (Urbana: University of Illinois Press, 1966); C. Van Woodward, *Reunion and Reaction: The Compromise of 1877 and the End of Reconstruction* (New York: Doubleday Anchor, [1951] 1956).

25. C. Vann Woodward, *Origins of the New South, 1877-1913* (Baton Rouge: Louisiana State University Press, 1951).

from an old hymn, "Free at last! Free at last! Thank God Almighty, we are free at last!"[26] he spoke prophetically for the American South, which during the next five years abandoned that distinctive degree of racism, intellectual and judicial, that had kept it separated from the rest of the nation for two centuries. Well could he announce in 1968 in Memphis, Tennessee, in his last public speech before his assassination: "And He's allowed me to go up to the promised land. I may not get there with you. But I want you to know tonight, that we, as a people will get to the promised land."[27] Judicially, blacks in the South were already as close to his vision of a racial promised land as the North was.)

Freedom: The Best Compensation

Biblical law makes the presumption that *a master who is not self-restrained is incapable of exercising responsible dominion over the bondservant.* Dominion is always to be in terms of God's law. The master is in a weak position to teach the bondservant the basics of the dominion covenant if he is himself not self-restrained. Self-government is the fundamental level of government in human affairs. God's law promotes self-government.

The bondservant's owner may misuse his authority by inflicting excessive punishment. The bondservant loses the use of his eye or tooth. How is he to be compensated? By a *non-literal* application of the "eye for eye" principle. The Bible recognizes the ultimate earthly desire of a God-fearing bondservant who is in bondage to a master who does not exercise self-restraint: *freedom.* The civil authorities do not put out the master's eye or knock out a tooth. If his master were to lose an eye to match his eye, then the bondservant would be no better off, and the brooding master might attempt to murder the bondservant in order to gain revenge.

The injured bondservant is rewarded with his freedom. This reminds the bondservant of the essential righteousness of God's law. It also reminds the undisciplined former owner of the same thing, as well as the necessity of his exercising self-restraint in the future. *The bondservant is taken out of the jurisdiction of a lawless man.*

The victim receives compensation for the loss he has sustained. While his physical ability to exercise dominion may be permanently

---

26. David J. Garrow, *Bearing the Cross: Martin Luther King, Jr., and the Southern Christian Leadership Conference* (New York: William Morrow, 1986), p. 284.

27. *Ibid.*, p. 621.

impaired by a physical injury, the increase of the scope of his authority compensates him. The former bondservant's freedom also benefits society, if the bondservant becomes successful in some free market activity. The lure of self-interest which the market provides may off-set the loss of productivity which results from the physical injury. Thus, the terms of the dominion covenant are more closely fulfilled. Output increases because of the incentives provided through freedom. The bondservant will now receive the fruits of his labor, not the former master. This increased productivity benefits both the bondservant and consumers.

The bondservant is not compensated in any other way. The law does not require the master to provide him with tools or other capital assets. This indicates that the value of personal freedom is very high — so high, in fact, that the loss of a tooth barely compares with it. Freedom is such an advantage that it can barely be compared with the losses associated with physical impairment. Freedom is the reward for both the loss of a tooth or an eye. It is so valuable in comparison with physical impairment that no additional compensation is granted to the bondservant who has lost an eye, even though an eye is more valuable than a tooth. So precious is freedom that the eye-less bondservant cannot legitimately protest to God or the authorities that he has received the compensation "only" of the tooth-less man.[28] He does not receive "freedom plus." Freedom is sufficient.

Biblical law substitutes the bondservant's freedom for a retaliatory loss of the master's tooth or eye. This substitution may or may not be to the liking of the master. The economic loss of the bondservant may be greater in the opinion of the master than the loss of his own tooth, but he has no choice in the matter. He must allow the bondservant to go free.

This substitution is evidence of the legitimacy of substitution in other non-capital "eye for eye" crimes. In cases involving free men, the victims can demand compensation other than the literal inflicting of physical mutilation of the criminals. *The goal is dominion.* Free men are allowed to "get even" with those who have mistreated them, not necessarily by pulling their enemies down to their physically damaged level (although this is the victim's option), but rather by in-

---

28. I had never noticed a curiosity of the English language before I wrote this sentence. "Eyeless" is a term for a totally blind man, not "eyesless." The same is true of "toothless" rather than "teethless." We have no convenient terms for "one eye less" and "one tooth less."

creasing their own wealth and productivity. This is also how the mis-treated bondservant is supposed to "get even." The guilty party does lose, just as the victim has lost, but *the loss is a form of economic compen-sation to the victim* — a grant of capital (freedom) to the victim that may enable him to perform the tasks of dominion more effectively. The criminal is "pulled down," but the victim is also "raised up."[29] The motivation of the bondservant is not to be envy — pulling down the master without any compensating move upward on the part of the bondservant.[30]

Protecting the Bondservant-Owners

The "freedom for an eye" law also protects the bondservant-owning class. This may not be immediately apparent. Consider an alternative rule: strict eye-for-eye vengeance. Let us say that a bond-servant-owner faces an unruly bondservant. He knows that he must maintain order in his household — defined in the broadest sense — and without his ability to inflict physical punishment, this particular bondservant is unlikely to respond to his commands. Inflicting phys-ical damage on him is always risky. The bondservant might be per-manently damaged. The owner might lose the production that the bondservant would otherwise have provided. Additionally, the owner might be convicted by a court of illegitimate brutality, and have his own body mutilated. Nevertheless, the bondservant would not go free.

What if the bondservant finds the owner alone in a field and attacks him? How is the owner to defend himself? If he puts out the eye of his attacker, but *there are no witnesses* who can testify that his ac-tion was in self-defense, the bondservant has him at a disadvantage. The bondservant can claim in a court that he had been thoughtlessly or maliciously mutilated by the owner. This will not gain him his freedom, but the master will lose his eye if the bondservant loses his.

---

29. We have seen in Chapter 11 that "pulling down" the criminal is lawful in the case of the "eye for eye" law between free men (Ex. 21:22-25). The victim can de-mand physical punishment of the criminal. This prerogative is unlikely to be exer-cised often. Men generally want capital more than physical revenge. The option of demanding physical vengeance is more important as a device for pressuring the criminal to pay what he really regards as a fair price to the victim — a payment to avoid the same injury. It creates incentive for the criminal to pay the appropriate economic compensation to the victim.

30. On the distinction between envy and jealousy (meaning covetousness), see the classic book by sociologist Helmut Schoeck, *Envy: A Theory of Social Behavior* (New York: Harcourt Brace Jovanovich, [1966] 1970).

An envious bondservant might accept this loss, to "bring down" a person who possesses authority over him. After all, if the bond-servant cannot gain his freedom as a result of his loss, and the master will be punished physically, then an envious bondservant might think to himself: "If I attack this man, I get even. If he defends him-self and really hurts me, I can still get even. The power to inflict pain at will is transferred to me, if I'm willing to accept the risk of physical loss. The master may even be afraid to fight back, for fear of injuring himself by injuring me. I have him at a disadvantage. All I need to do is to be willing to risk the loss of my tooth or eye. I will be worse off, but so will he. He has more to lose than I do. I'm only a bond-servant. I'm used to hardship. He isn't. He will be more afraid of me than I am of him. I have the upper hand, for I have the willingness to suffer more physical damage than he does."

The bondservant-owners need to maintain their authority. The way that we exercise dominion is to submit ourselves to God's law. *Self-restraint leads to dominion.* It is no different for bondservant-owners. The master must be able to impose his will on the bondser-vant in external ways. To make more certain that the bondservant is restrained, there must be incentives for the bondservant to comply. *The bondservant, no less than the master, needs self-government.* The bond-servant, no less than the master, needs to count the costs of rebellion. A bondservant who is granted the ability by law to inflict permanent damage on his master merely for the price of suffering the same in-jury, is a dangerous bondservant. If he is willing to accept the pain, and the master isn't, then the bondservant is given the upper hand. The social order of society is threatened. Power is transferred from those who will not accept pain to those who will. But power in a godly society should be based on *moral authority*, not the comparative ability to withstand pain. Power should be based on *ethical standing before God*, not tolerance for pain.

A bondservant-owner in a society whose civil law recognizes the principle of "freedom for an eye" who is attacked without witnesses present knows that he can defend himself to the utmost. If he cannot prove self-defense in the court, then the worst he will suffer is the loss of the bondservant. But at the moment a man is attacked, the thought of the removal of the bondservant from his presence is not really that repugnant to him. The bondservant-owner will not hesi-tate to defend himself under such circumstances. The bondservant knows this.

The freedom-seeking bondservant might think to himself: "If I attack the man in private, and he mutilates me, I can go free. I will do it. I want my freedom more than I want my tooth. On the other hand, he might punch out my eye. There are risks here. I can go free in a few years anyway. This is not a permanent position of servitude. Is it worth the possible loss of my eye to gain my freedom a few years early? I may not be able to hurt him very much, and he will not hesitate to beat me to a pulp. Is an attack worth the risk?" The bondservant counts the cost. In a Christian society governed by biblical civil law, in which servitude is not permanent, but can extend at most for seven years, will he risk forfeiting his eye for the rest of his life? He must pay a high price for rebellion-based freedom. The court may decide against him anyway and convict him of assault on the owner. Attacking the bondservant-owner in secret is a very risky act. The bondservant is restrained by the threat of physical punishment by the owner, and the court may not impose any penalty on the owner. The master is restrained, at most, by the threat of losing the bondservant. The master has the edge in this case.

The Foreign Slave

The foreign slave, like the committed criminal sold into permanent bondage, was in a different situation. He was not guaranteed release after a fixed period of time (Lev. 25:44-46). He therefore might have been willing to attack the slave-owner in secret, not fearing physical retribution, for the reward would be freedom. Provoking a Hebrew master to excessive punishment might have been to the advantage of a foreign slave. The price of freedom was mutilation — a price that some slaves might have been willing to pay.

This would have been an incentive for masters to avoid being alone with foreign slaves. In the absence of witnesses, the slave could do two evil things. First, he might attack the owner in order to cause the owner to mutilate him in self-defense. Then he could claim to be the victim. Second, he might self-mutilate himself and then claim that the owner had struck him. In the absence of witnesses, the court might decide in his favor, especially if the slave-owner had a reputation for violence. These possibilities increase the risks to an owner of being alone with a foreign slave.

By separating foreign slaves from Hebrew masters, the law also tended to separate the religious rites of foreign slaves from their masters. In the Old Testament commonwealth, there would have been fewer opportunities for Hebrew masters to learn the secret rites of demon-worshipping foreign slaves. An owner would have been more likely to have witnesses present in his dealings with foreign slaves, and therefore capital punishment for his worship of false gods would always have been far more likely. Intimate contacts between foreign slaves and Hebrew masters would have been less likely. In private, the master would have been at a disadvantage to the slave, compared to the advantage he possessed in public. The slave would have had more to gain from such contacts than the master: 1) an opportunity to attack him and provoke a freedom-producing response; 2) an opportunity to fake an attack through self-mutilation; and 3) an opportunity to convert him to the worship of the slave's hidden gods of darkness.

There are other intimacies between master and slave that would have borne great risks to the Hebrew master. Secret encounters with foreign slaves for sexual contact would have been made less likely because of the law that offered freedom to mutilated slaves. The slave might argue in court that the master had attempted to violate her (or him, in the case of sexual deviation), and when she resisted, he attacked her physically. This might actually be true; resistance by the slave might provoke a lawless master to violence. Or it could be a lie—perhaps the lie most easily believed by a court. In either case, secret associations with a foreign slave would be reduced if the "freedom for an eye" law were enforced. Only the most trustworthy foreign slave would have had access to a master in total privacy.

The Jubilee Year

With respect to the jubilee law, which alone authorized Hebrews to own permanent foreign slaves, this "freedom for an eye" law served to separate Hebrew masters from their foreign slaves. This was probably more of a protection for Hebrew masters than foreign slaves. Hebrews under the Old Covenant were highly vulnerable to the lure of foreign gods. The Old Testament laws concerning ritual pollution, which included the dietary laws, pointed to the defensive position of the Hebrews spiritually: death contaminated them ritually because theologies of death lured them repeatedly. It was only after Christ's ministry cleansed the ground, making possible the annulment of the laws concerning ritual pollution,[31] that God's people

---

31. James Jordan writes: "In the Old Covenant, the land was perpetually defiled, and only provisionally cleansed by a variety of cleansing actions, the most promi-

could at last be self-confident in their offensive campaign against evil. It was only then that the conquest of the nations became ritually easy.

At that point in covenantal history, however, the jubilee laws were abolished. All of Leviticus 25 became a dead letter. This included the law allowing permanent household slavery. No longer were slaves allowed to be imported from the lands around God's people, for God's people were now enabled to extend the kingdom of God far more easily than before Christ's death and resurrection cleansed the earth ritually. There were to be no more "heathen that are round about you" nationally (Lev. 25:44); heathen would henceforth be immediately round about God's people, because God's people were to enter heathen lands, bringing the gospel and discipling the nations (Matt. 28:19). God's people were to be in close contact with racially and culturally foreign household slaves, even in private, sometimes as brothers in the faith. At that point, the law of permanent household slavery had to go, to protect the slave-owner as much or more than to protect the slave.

Conclusion

The goal of servitude in the Bible is liberation through self-discipline, dominion through service. This is true for both the master and the bondservant. Each must show self-restraint or else suffer penalties. A lawless, undisciplined, violent master therefore loses legal control over his bondservant. This law reminds us that the exercise of power must be governed by law; he who holds power is supposed to hold it by means of his moral authority as well as by the sword. To the extent that the master is handed the sword by the civil government, as an agent of the civil government, he is under restrictions imposed by God's law through the civil government.

---

nent being the annual cleansing on the Day of Atonement (Lev. 16). Apart from this, the holy land of Canaan would revert to a defiled status. Within this annual provisional cleansing, there was the possibility of local, occasional defilements. . . . In the New Covenant, the land is perpetually cleansed. It is only the occasional defilement which must be dealt with. The ceremony of dealing with it is not the sacrifice of slaying an animal, or the death of a Church leader, but the ceremony of the Church's declaring a man forgiven and permitting him to partake of the Holy Eucharist, which applies the finished sacrifice to him. Such a ceremony would be an important part of a Christian society." James B. Jordan, *The Law of the Covenant: An Exposition of Exodus 21-23* (Tyler, Texas: Institute for Christian Economics, 1984), pp. 101-2. This is why any attempt to revive the ritual slaying of animals, even as a "memorial," is a return to the heresy of the Judaizers. Baptism and Holy Communion, not the slaying of animals, are the only remaining memorials of rituals of cleansing.

This law protects slaves from lawless tyrants. It also protects masters from cost-calculating, envious, violent slaves. The penalty of losing the slave raises the price of lawlessness to the master. Simultaneously, the inability of the court to impose physical retribution on the owner restrains the envious bondservant in any attempt to "get even" with the master by provoking a physical attack on himself. By limiting the duration of debt servitude to seven years, the incentive to revolt is minimized among bondservants. An act of physical rebellion against a master which might cost the bondservant an eye is less advantageous in a society with a time limit on slavery. If bondservants wait a few years, they will keep their eyes and also gain freedom. Better to bear the rule of the master patiently.

God defines deviant behavior in His law. Individuals and societies that transgress these standards of deviance are eventually placed under God's formal judicial sanctions, in history (Deut. 8:19-20) and beyond history (Matt. 25:31-46). The South was not deviant in terms of ancient historical precedent regarding permanent slavery; the North was. The fact is, the South was deviant in terms of God's written standards, for its legislators and judges honored neither Old Testament laws governing servitude nor Jesus' abolition of permanent slavery in His abolition of Israel's jubilee land tenure laws. It took a long time, but God eventually imposed His sanctions by means of Northern aggression, for the North had more closely approached the biblical norms regarding permanent slavery.

14

THE RANSOM FOR A LIFE

If an ox gore a man or a woman, that they die: then the ox shall be surely stoned, and his flesh shall not be eaten; but the owner of the ox shall be quit. But if the ox were wont to push [gore] with his horn in time past, and it hath been testified to his owner, and he hath not kept him in, but that he hath killed a man or a woman; the ox shall be stoned, and his owner also shall be put to death. If there be laid on him a sum of money, then he shall give for the ransom of his life whatsoever is laid upon him. Whether he have gored a son, or have gored a daughter, according to this judgment shall it be done unto him (Ex. 21:28-31).

The Bible tells us that we live in a universe which was created by God at the beginning of time and history, and that this world is sustained by Him, moment by moment. The doctrines of creation and providence are therefore linked. The universe which God created, He presently sustains. We live in a world of cosmic personalism.[1] God's answer to Job, beginning in chapter 38 and continuing through chapter 40, presents a summary of the total control of all events by God.

In such a world, men cannot escape full responsibility for their actions. God holds them responsible for everything they think, say, and do. "But I say unto you, That every idle word that men shall speak, they shall give account thereof in the day of judgment" (Matt. 12:36). "But I say unto you, That whosoever looketh on a woman to lust after her hath committed adultery with her already in his heart" (Matt. 5:28). Everything people do is done within a personally sustained, God-ordained universe (Rom. 9). They succeed or fail in terms of God's decree. They run to God ethically, or they run away

---

1. Gary North, *The Dominion Covenant: Genesis* (2nd ed.; Tyler, Texas: Institute for Christian Economics, 1987), ch. 1.

from God unethically; they cannot run away from Him metaphysically. God is everywhere; there is no escape: "Whither shall I go from thy spirit? Or whither shall I flee from thy presence? If I ascend up into heaven, thou art there: if I make my bed in hell, behold, thou art there" (Ps. 139:7-8). "Am I a God at hand, saith the LORD, and not a God afar off? Can any hide himself in secret places that I shall not see him? saith the LORD. Do not I fill heaven and earth? saith the LORD" (Jer. 23:23-24).

Human action is always personal, never impersonal. First, it is personal primarily with respect to God. God is the ultimate, inescapable fact of man's environment, not sticks and stones. Second, human action is secondarily personal with respect to oneself: one's goals, choices, and assets. Third, human action is personal with respect to other human actors, both as individuals and as covenantal groups. Fourth, human action is personal with respect to the environment, which God has created and presently sustains, and over which He has placed mankind. Man's responsibility extends *upward* to God, *inward* to himself, *outward* toward other men, and *downward* toward the environment. It is comprehensive responsibility. When we speak of "responsible men," we should have this four-part, comprehensive responsibility in mind, not just one or two aspects. A person may appear to be responsible in one or two areas of his life, but whether he likes it or not, or whether he is adequately instructed or not, he is covenantally responsible before God in all four ways, and he will be held totally accountable for his thoughts and actions on the day of judgment.

Liability for Damages

Although God holds each person fully responsible, no agency of human government has the power to do so. This is why we must affirm as Christians that with respect to the decisions of human governments regarding men's personal responsibility, there must always be *limited liability*. No agency of human government is omniscient; none possesses the ability of God to read the human heart or to assess damages perfectly. We must wait for perfect justice until the day of final judgment. To insist on perfect justice from human government is to divinize that agency. It will also lead to its bankruptcy and the destruction of justice.[2]

---

2. Gary North, *Moses and Pharaoh: Dominion Religion vs. Power Religion* (Tyler, Texas: Institute for Christian Economics, 1985), ch. 19: "Imperfect Justice."

The case laws of Exodus function as the groupings under which many different kinds of disputes over liability for damages can be classified. This has been recognized by Jewish scholars for at least two millennia. Later Jewish law created various categories of offenses subject to private lawsuits ("torts") that were based on the case laws of Exodus. Jewish legal scholar Shalom Albeck writes:

> Four principal cases are considered: (1) where someone opens a pit into which an animal falls and dies (Ex. 21:33-4); (2) where cattle trespass into the fields of others and do damage (Ex. 22:4 [English version, 22:5]); (3) where someone lights a fire which spreads to neighboring fields (Ex. 22:5 [Eng., 22:6]); (4) where an ox gores man or beast (Ex. 21:28-32, 35-6). To those has to be added the case where a man injures his fellow or damages his property (Ex. 21:18-19, 22-5; Lev. 24:18-20). The Talmud calls the cases contained in the Torah primary categories of damage (*Avot Nezikin*) and these serve as archetypes for similar groups of torts. The principal categories of animal torts are: *shen* (tooth) — where the animal causes damage by consuming; *regel* (foot) — where the animal causes damage by walking in its normal manner; and *keren* (horn) — where the animal causes damage by goring with the intention of doing harm or does any other kind of unusual damage. The other principal categories of damage are: *bor* (pit) — any nuisance which ipso facto causes damage; *esh* (fire) — anything which causes damage when spread by the wind; and direct damage by man to another's person or property. These principal categories and their derivative rules were expanded to form a complete and homogeneous legal system embracing many other factual situations. As a result they were capable of dealing with any case of tortious liability which might arise.[3]

The key issue, then, is personal responsibility. Who is responsible for damages sustained, and what are the appropriate penalties? The case laws provide us with the governing standards for assigning legal responsibility for damages and the appropriate penalties.

Responsibility: Upward and Downward

Man's responsibility outward and downward is seen in this section of Exodus. A man owes protection to his fellow man, which includes women, as the passage at the beginning of the chapter clearly

---

3. "TORTS. The Principal Categories of Torts," in *The Principles of Jewish Law*, edited by Menachem Elon (Jerusalem: Keter, 1975?), col. 319. This compilation of articles taken from the *Encyclopedia Judaica* was published as Publication No. 6 of the Institute for Research in Jewish Law of the Hebrew University of Jerusalem.

points out. This passage also teaches that "dumb animals" under a man's personal administration are responsible, through him, for their actions. They are responsible upward to mankind through their master, as well as outward to other beasts through their master (v. 35). Human society enforces sanctions against lawless behavior, whether in the animals or their owners. Domesticated animals are responsible to mankind through their owners, and therefore society holds the owners responsible for those animals under their control. Animals that are not domesticated — neither trained nor tamed — are to be under physical restraint, at the owner's expense.

Domesticated Beasts

The shedding of man's blood is illegal, either by man or beast. "But flesh with the life thereof, which is the blood thereof, shall ye not eat. And surely your blood of your lives will I require; at the hand of every beast will I require it, and at the hand of man; at the hand of every man's brother will I require the life of man. Whoso sheddeth man's blood, by man shall his blood be shed: for in the image of God made he man" (Gen. 9:4-6). The ox that gores a man to death cannot escape the sanctions of biblical law. Neither can other man-killing animals.

In the case of the ox, the animal is presumed to be domesticated, for if it were dangerous, the owner would be required to restrain it. The owner becomes legally liable because what was, in fact, a dangerous animal had been publicly treated by him as if it had been safe. *The owner deliberately or inadvertently misinformed the public about the risks.* He did not place restraints on it. The victim died because of the neglect of the owner. The owner should have placed restraints on the beast, or else he should have placed warnings for bystanders.

Why shouldn't bystanders recognize that the animal is dangerous? Why are they considered judicially innocent? Don't people know that bulls charge people and gore them? They do know, which is why the Hebrew usage, as in English, indicates that "ox" in this case must refer to a castrated male bovine. The castrated beast is not normally aggressive. It is easier to bring under dominion through training. In this sense, a castrated male bovine is unnaturally subordinate.

As an aside, the question of unnatural subordination (lack of male dominion) can also be raised with respect to the prohibition against eunuchs worshipping in the congregation (Deut. 23:1). Presumably, this was because eunuchs could not produce a family, and to that extent they were cut off from the future. Rushdoony writes (unfortunately using the present tense): "Because eunuchs are without posterity, they have no interest in the future, and hence no citizenship."[4] This was true enough in ancient Israel, where land tenure, bloodlines, political participation (elders in the gates), and the national covenant were intermixed. The New Testament forever abolished this biological-geographical intermixture. Spiritual adoption[5] became forthrightly the foundation of heavenly citizenship (Phil. 3:20), and therefore the only basis of church membership. The baptism of the Ethiopian eunuch by Philip the deacon (Acts 8)[6] indicates that the Old Testament rule lost all meaning, once Jesus, the promised seed, had come and completed His work.

The goring ox is also judicially guilty. He is therefore treated as a responsible moral agent—not to the extent that a man is, of course, but responsible nonetheless. We train our domestic animals. We beat them and reward them. Modern scientists call this training "behavior modification." In other words, we deal with them on the assumption that they can learn, remember, and discipline themselves. Anyone who has ever seen a dog that looks guilty, which slinks around as if it has done something it knows is wrong, can safely guess that the dog *has* done something wrong. It may take time to find out what, but the search must begin. The dog *knows*.

An Ethically Unclean Beast

The goring ox is to be treated as if it were an unclean beast. It has become an ethically unclean beast. Because of its ethical uncleanness, it is still subject to this punishment in New Testament times, despite the New Testament's abandonment of the category of physical and ritual uncleanness. James Jordan comments on the biblical meaning of unclean animals:

All unclean animals *resemble the serpent* in three ways. They eat "dirt" (rotting carrion, manure, garbage). They move in contact with "dirt" (crawling on their bellies, fleshy pads of their feet in touch with the ground, no scales to keep their skin from contact with their watery environment). They revolt

---

4. R. J. Rushdoony, *The Institutes of Biblical Law* (Nutley, New Jersey: Craig Press, 1973), p. 100.

5. John 1:12; Romans 8:15; Galatians 4:5; Ephesians 1:5.

6. That a deacon performed this baptism, as well as many others in Samaria, creates a presently unsolved theological problem for all denominations that specify elders as the only ordained church officers with a lawful call to baptize.

against human dominion, killing men or other beasts. Under the symbolism of the Old Covenant, such Satanic beasts represent the Satanic nations (Lev. 20:22-26), for animals are "images" of men. To eat Satanic animals, under the Old Covenant, was to "eat" the Satanic lifestyle, to "eat" death and rebellion.

The ox is a clean animal. The heifer and the pre-pubescent bullock have sweet temperaments, and can be sacrificed for human sin, for their gentle, non-violent dispositions reflect the character of Jesus Christ. When the bullock enters puberty, however, his temperament changes for the worse. He becomes ornery, testy, and sometimes downright vicious. Many a man has lost his life to a goring bull. *The change from bullock to bull can be seen as analogous to the fall of man*, at least potentially. If the ox rises up and gores a man, he becomes unclean, fallen. . . .

The *unnaturalness* of an animal's killing a man is only highlighted in the case of a clean, domesticated beast like the ox. Such an ox, by its actions, becomes unclean, so that its flesh may not be eaten. . . .

The fact that the animal is stoned indicates that the purpose of the law is not simply to rid the earth of a dangerous beast. Stoning in the Bible is the normal means of capital punishment for men. Its application to the animal here shows that animals are to be held accountable to some degree for their actions. It is also a visual sign of what happens when a clean covenant man rebels against authority and kills men. Stoning is usually understood to represent the judgment of God, since the Christ is "the rock" and the "stone" which threatens to fall upon men and destroy them (Matt. 21:44). In line with this, the community of believers is often likened to stones, used for building God's Spiritual Temple, and so forth. In stoning, each member of the community hurls a rock representing himself and his affirmation of God's judgment. The principle of stoning, then, affirms that the judgment is God's; the application of stoning affirms the community's assent and participation in that judgment.[7]

Covenantal Hierarchy and Guilty Animals

"But if the ox were wont to push [gore] with his horn in time past, and it hath been testified to his owner, and he hath not kept him in, but that he hath killed a man or a woman; the ox shall be stoned, and his owner also shall be put to death." The owner had been warned that the beast was dangerous. (We shall consider in the next section what constitutes valid evidence of habitual goring.) He had withheld this information from the victim. How? By refusing to place ade-

---

7. James B. Jordan, *The Law of the Covenant: An Exposition of Exodus 21-23* (Tyler, Texas: Institute for Christian Economics, 1984), pp. 122-24.

quate restraints on the beast. The victim had every reason to believe that the ox was fully domesticated, meaning that it was *self-disciplined* under the general authority of its owner. Again, it is *self-government under God's law* which is the crucial form of government.

The Bible is unique in establishing the judicial requirement of self-government to beasts in general. At the very least, any beast is to be held accountable if it kills a human being. (Maimonides made one exception regarding a domesticated beast: it is not responsible if it kills a heathen, meaning a gentile.)[8] Since the days of Noah, they have had the fear of man placed in them by God (Gen. 9:2). A beast must somehow suppress this fear—an internal warning from God—in order to kill a man. Beasts are responsible creatures; they are to be hunted down and killed for this form of rebellion. Some domesticated beasts are responsible outward to other beasts, upward to man, and, through their masters, upward to God.[9]

The Bible deals with the liability problem by making owners personally responsible for the actions of their animals. If their animals cause no problems, there will be no penalties. The more dangerous the animals, the more risky the ownership. Clearly, Exodus 21:30 is a case-law application of a general principle regarding the responsibilities of ownership. The principle can be extended to ownership of other animals besides oxen, and also to related instances of personal financial liability for damages in cases not involving animals.

The law makes it clear that the owner may not profit in any way from the evil act of the beast. He is not permitted to salvage anything of value. The beast is stoned—the same death penalty that a guilty human would receive—and the owner does not receive the carcass. Its flesh may not be eaten (v. 28). The beast is treated as if it were a human being. Its evil act brings death—not the normal killing of oxen, which allows owners to eat the flesh or sell it to those who will, but the death of the guilty. The guilty beast is no longer part of the dominion covenant. It can no longer serve the economic

---

8. "If an ox kills a person anywhere, whether an adult or a minor, a slave or a freeman, it incurs death by stoning whether it is innocuous or forewarned. However, if it kills a heathen, it is exempt in accordance with heathen law." Moses Maimonides, *The Book of Torts*, vol. 11 of *The Code of Maimonides*, 14 vols. (New Haven, Connecticut: Yale University Press, 1954), "Laws Concerning Damage by Chattels," Chapter Ten, Section One, p. 36.

9. The incomparable biblical example of upward responsibility of an animal toward man is Balaam's ass. "And the ass said unto Balaam, Am not I thine ass, upon which thou hast ridden ever since I was thine unto this day? Was I ever wont to do so unto thee? And he said, Nay" (Num. 22:30).

purposes of men, except as an example. It has to be cut off in the midst of time, just as a murderer is to be cut off in the midst of time.

Why Stoning?

J. J. Finkelstein discusses at considerable length the question of the stoning of the ox. While similar laws regarding the goring ox are found in many ancient Near Eastern law codes, the Hebrew law is unique: it specifically requires stoning of the ox that kills any human being, even a slave. Finkelstein concludes that this requirement testified to the ox's crime as being of a different order than the crime of its negligent owner. It points to *treason*, a rebellion against the cosmic order, a crime comparable to a Hebrew's enticing of a family member to worship foreign gods, which was also to be punished by stoning (Deut. 13:6-11). It is an offense against the whole community, and the whole community is therefore involved in the execution. "The real crime of the ox is that by killing a human being—whether out of viciousness or by an involuntary motion—it has objectively committed a *de facto* insurrection against the hierarchic order established by Creation: Man was designated by God 'to rule over the fish of the sea, the fowl of the skies, the cattle, the earth, and all creatures that roam over the earth' (Gen. 1:26, 28). Simply by its behavior—and it is vital here to stress that intention is immaterial; the guilt is objective—the ox has, albeit involuntarily, performed an act whose effect amounts to 'treason.' It has acted against man, its superior in the hierarchy of Creation, as man acts against God when violating the Sabbath or when practicing idolatry. It is precisely for this reason that the flesh of the ox may not be consumed."[10]

Finkelstein traces this biblical law forward into the Middle Ages. In medieval Europe, trials for animals were actually held by the civil government. Defense lawyers in secular courts were hired at public expense to defend accused beasts. Witnesses were called. Guilty animals were destroyed as a civic act. In some cases, they were publicly hanged.[11] Few people know about this side of European history, although specialized historians have known all along. Some of the great minds of Western philosophy, including Aquinas and Leibniz,

---

10. J. J. Finkelstein, *The Ox That Gored* (Philadelphia: American Philosophical Society, 1981), p. 28.

11. A painting of the hanging of a pig in Normandy in 1386 appears on the cover of the 1987 reprint of E. P. Evans' 1906 book, *The Criminal Prosecution and Capital Punishment of Animals* (London: Faber & Faber). The painting shows the pig dressed in a jacket.

attempted to explain this practice rationally.[12] Yet the specialized historians have generally remained silent, and few professional historians have ever heard of such goings-on, nor are they aware that in ancient Athens, the courts tried inanimate objects, such as statues that had fallen and killed someone. If convicted, the object was banished from the city.[13] Why the silence? Why don't these stories get into the textbooks? As Humphrey asks: "Why were we never told? Why were we taught so many dreary facts of history at school, *and not taught these?*"[14]

He answers his own question: modern historians can make little sense out of these facts. There seems to be no logical explanation for the way our ancestors treated guilty animals. What is a guilty animal, anyway—a legally convicted guilty animal? How can such events be explained? Finkelstein cites the theory of legal scholar Hans Kelsen that such a practice points to the "animism" of early medieval Europe, since to try an animal in court obviously points to a theory of the animal's possession of a soul.[15] Kelsen says that this reflects early Europe's older primitivism. Finkelstein then attacks Kelsen's naive approach to an understanding of this practice. In contrast to primitive societies, it is only in the West that such legal sanctions against offending animals have been enforced. "*Only* in Western society, or in societies based on the hierarchic classification of the phenomena of the universe that is biblical in its origins, do we see the curious practice of trying and executing animals as if they were human criminals."[16] Then he makes a profound observation: "What Kelsen has misunderstood here—and in this he is typical of most Western commentators—is the sense, widespread in primitive societies (as, indeed in civilized societies of non-Western derivation), that the extra-human universe is *autonomous* and that this autonomy or integrity is a quality inherent in every species of thing."[17] Because Western society long denied such autonomy to the creation, it has in the past adhered to the biblical requirement of destroying killer animals; in Europe, they were even given a formal trial.

---

12. Nicholas Humphrey, Foreword, *ibid.*, p. xviii.

13. W. W. Hyde, "The prosecution of animals and lifeless things in the middle ages and modern times," *University of Pennsylvania Law Review* (1916). Finkelstein is somewhat suspicious of these accounts.

14. Humphrey, Foreword, p. xv.

15. Finkelstein, *Ox That Gored*, p. 48. He cites Kelsen, *General Theory of Law and State* (1961), pp. 3-4.

16. Finkelstein, *op. cit.*, p. 48.

17. *Ibid.*, p. 51.

Expiation

What none of the scholars discusses is the need for expiation, a need which is both psychological and covenantal. The animal's owner and the community at large, through its representatives, must publicly disassociate themselves from the killer beast. They must demonstrate publicly that they in no way sanction the beast's murderous act. There is an Old Testament precedent for the need for this sort of formal expiation: the requirement in ancient Israel that civic officials sacrifice a heifer when they could not solve a murder that had taken place in a nearby field (Deut. 21:1-9). "So shalt thou put away the guilt of innocent blood from among you, when thou shalt do that which is right in the sight of the LORD" (v. 9). In New Testament times we no longer need to sacrifice animals (Heb. 9, 10), but the need for formal procedures for the expiation of the crime of man-killing is still basic. To ignore this need is to unleash the furies of the human heart.

The medieval world understood this to some degree, however imperfectly; the modern humanistic West does not understand it at all, and seeks to deny it by abolishing any trace of such ritual practices. We cannot make sense of the so-called "primitive folk practices" of medieval and early modern Western history that dealt with this fundamental civic and personal need, and so we refuse even to discuss them in our history books. We execute murderers in private when we execute them at all. (In the State of Massachusetts in the early 1970's, the median jail term served by a murderer was under two and a half years.)[18] Humanist intellectuals in the non-Communist West seek to persuade the public that society is itself ritually guilty for maintaining the "barbarous" practice of capital punishment. Meanwhile, in the year of our Lord 1988, in the streets of southern California, motorists were shooting each other during traffic jams, and teenage gang members were executing at least one victim per day.[19] God is not mocked at zero cost to the mockers.

Personal Liability and Self-Discipline

The convicted owner of the habitually goring ox in Exodus 21:28 implicitly misinformed the ox's victim. He had known that the ox had been violent in the past, yet he did not take steps to restrain it.

---

18. James Q. Wilson, *Thinking About Crime* (New York: Basic Books, 1974), p. 186.
19. An estimated 80,000 gang members were in the county of Los Angeles.

The beast was roaming around as if it had no prior record of violence. The victim did not recognize the danger involved in being near the beast.

The Bible does not reveal in these passages regarding goring oxen the evidence that constitutes judicially binding prior knowledge. What kind of information did the owner have to possess in order for the court to declare him guilty? The rabbinical specialists in Jewish law said that the animal had to have gored someone or other animals on three occasions before the owner became personally liable.[20] Maimonides spelled it out in even greater detail: any domesticated animal must first kill three heathen (gentiles), plus one Israelite; or kill three fatally ill Israelites, plus one in good health; or kill three people at one time, or kill three animals at one time.[21]

This is an excessive number of prior infractions in order to activate capital sanctions. Subsequent victims need more protection than these Talmudic rules would provide. It is far more reasonable to conclude that a single prior conviction should suffice to identify the beast as dangerous. What should be obvious in any study of traditional Rabbinic laws regarding killer oxen is the extent to which the rabbis would go in order to exempt the owners. Maimonides' example is remarkable, found in Chapter Ten of the first treatise on torts, "Laws Concerning Damage by Chattels":

11. No owner need pay ransom unless his animal kills outside his premises. But if it kills on his premises, then although it is liable for stoning, the owner is exempt from paying ransom. Thus if one enters a privately owned courtyard without the owner's permission—even if he enters to collect wages or a debt from the owner—and the householder's ox gores him and he dies, the ox must be stoned, but the owner is exempt from paying ransom since the victim had no right to enter another's premises without the owner's consent.

12. If one stands at the entrance and calls to the householder, and the householder answers, "Yes," and he then enters and is gored by the householder's ox and dies, the owner is exempt, for "Yes" means no more than "Stay where you are until I speak to you."[22]

He even exempted the owner of a notorious ox that has gored a pregnant woman whose child is born prematurely. "For Scripture im-

---

20. Albeck, *Jewish Law*, col. 322.
21. Maimonides, *Torts*, "Laws Concerning Damage by Chattels," Chapter Ten, Section Three, p. 36.
22. *Ibid.*, p. 38.

poses liability to pay the value of such infants on humans only."[23] Because the ox did it, and is not a human, its owner is exempt; the transfer of liability upward to the owner is cut short, because the ox cannot be held responsible. He did admit that if the ox gores a pregnant bondwoman, and the same thing happens, the owner is financially liable in this case, "for this is as if the ox gored a she-ass about to foal."[24] Oxen are responsible for damaging other animals, so this responsibility is transferred upward to owners, unlike the previous case.

On the other hand, Maimonides was very hard on the animal associates of a condemned criminal ox. "If its trial has been concluded and it then becomes mixed with other oxen—even with a thousand others—all must be stoned and buried and are forbidden for use, as is the rule concerning any animal condemned to be stoned."[25] Owners of friendly oxen were forewarned by Maimonides: don't let your law-abiding beasts fall in with bad company![26] (After reading Maimonides' *Code* in detail, this gentile begins to suspect that premodern Rabbinic reasoning regarding the case laws is very different from his own.)

We know that an ox that had gored another ox had to be sold by its owner to a third party (Ex. 21:35). Thus, to be the owner of an ox that had been convicted of goring, he would have had to go out and repurchase the offending ox, or else he is the person who bought the offending ox. In either case, he had taken active steps to buy a known offender. To have done this, and then to have refused to take active measures to restrain it, should make him legally vulnerable to the charge of negligence.

Would other evidence rather than a prior conviction be a sufficient warning? What if neighbors had reported the beast to the authorities? If the authorities had issued a formal warning to the owner, would this serve as evidence of its status as a habitual

---

23. *Ibid.*, Chapter Eleven, Section Three, p. 40.

24. *Idem.*, Section Four.

25. *Ibid.*, Chapter Eleven, Section Ten, p. 41.

26. What Maimonides and the rabbis failed to understand is this: the guilt of a murderous animal is covenantal, not metaphysical. The evil that the animal has committed is not passed to other animals by mere physical contact or proximity. The evil act of the animal was rebellion against the fear of man that God places in every animal's heart (Gen. 9:2). It had trespassed the moral boundaries that God placed in its heart. Maimonides was more concerned about the boundary between the convicted animal and other animals than with the boundary inside the animal between it and mankind, and the physical boundary between the animal and his last three human victims.

offender? If we answer yes, then this raises the issue of "innocent until proven guilty." There had been no proven evidence against the beast. Perhaps neighbors were hostile to the ox's owner, and reported false information. On the other hand, perhaps they were telling the truth, and the owner was negligent in not taking steps to restrain the ox.

The easiest way to resolve the issue is to rely on the biblical principle of the double witness (Deut. 17:6). If two different witnesses each reports a different infraction — neither of the infractions had a double witness — then the authorities must issue a warning to the owner. This formal warning can then serve as evidence in a future trial.

David Daube's Judicial Subjectivism

David Daube, dazzled by the legerdemain of biblical higher criticism, argues that this law was written much earlier than the law in Exodus 21:35-36. He argues that there was a strict rule of evidence in this instance: a formal warning given to the owner of the ox. "This means that the judge need not examine whether or not you were really clear on the point — which might be difficult for him to discover. He need only examine whether or not the necessary announcement was made to you — a very easy thing to find out. If the announcement was made, you are responsible for everything that has happened since; and it would be no excuse to say that you personally had not believed that the ox was so savage. If no announcement was made, you are not responsible even if you yourself had seen all the time how dangerous the ox was."[27] The decision of the judge is to be made "on a strict, archaic, 'objective' kind of proof," Daube says. Notice his characterization of objective proof as archaic. He contrasts this supposedly archaic legal rule with a supposedly more advanced rule of law that governed the supposedly later law of Exodus 21:35-36.

The judge does not raise the freer, more advanced, "subjective" question: Did you or did you not know about the nature of the ox? Now in the other, later paragraph, on the case where your ox kills an ox, we do get this "subjective" element. No mention is here made of the necessity of a formal announcement: the responsibility is yours from the moment you are aware, or should be aware, that your ox is not to be trusted. At this more advanced

---

27. David Daube, *Studies in Biblical Law* (Cambridge: At the University Press, 1947), p. 87.

stage of the law, the judge must investigate the affair much more closely; he must, above all, search men's hearts. If he reaches the conclusion that you knew the beast was dangerous, he will find you guilty even though no announcement was ever made to you in the matter.[28]

Daube does not discuss the differing criteria of evidence in terms of the differing impact of the crime and differences in the resulting liability: the death of a human being vs. the death of someone else's ox. He fails to recognize that the formal criteria that govern evidence of liability in the case of an ox that kills another ox are less rigorous because the crime is less damaging. In a case of an ox that slays another ox, biblical law does not require that a formal warning be given by the authorities to the owner; prior general knowledge is sufficient to convict: "Or if it be known that the ox hath used to push [gore] in time past, and his owner hath not kept him in; he shall surely pay ox for ox; and the dead shall be his own" (Ex. 21:36). *Public knowledge rather than a formal complaint to the civil authorities is sufficient to convict the owner in this instance.* It can be safely assumed by the judge that if the public knew about the beast's habits, then the owner must have known. In contrast, the potential liability of the owner is far greater when an ox kills a human being. It is too dangerous to allow the judge to make his ruling in terms of the assumption of general knowledge. By requiring more rigorous standards of evidence, biblical law restrains the discretionary authority of the State's representative in the more serious cases of negligence. This restrains the State.

Daube ignores this explanation in order to argue that the later rule was chronologically later in Israel rather than merely later in the biblical text. He also argues that the later rule was governed by a more mature concept of legality, a legal development that allows the judge to search the hearts of the disputants. He is a faithful representative of contemporary humanism: a man who weakens men's confidence in the integrity of God's revealed word and the reliability of His law, and thereby strengthens the arbitrary power of the State.

Daube's view of the State is the modern humanist's view: the State as an agency that possesses the judicial authority and obligation to search men's hearts, and to render formal judgment in terms of its findings. This view of State power asserts that the State possesses an ability that only God possesses: the ability to know man's heart. The prophet Jeremiah asked rhetorically: "The heart is deceit-

---

28. *Idem.*

ful above all things, and desperately wicked: who can know it?" (Jer.
17:9). His answer was clear: "I the LORD search the heart, I try the
reins, even to give every man according to his ways, and according
to the fruit of his doings" (Jer. 17:10). The human judge can make
causal connections based on public evidence, but he cannot search
the defendant's heart. Any assertion to the contrary necessarily involves an attempt to divinize man, and in all likelihood, divinize
man's major judicial representative, the State.

The Economics of Negligence

We know from the text that the ox's owner had been warned
about the dangerous ox, yet he did nothing visibly to restrain it.
Why would an owner neglect a warning from someone else regarding the threat of his ox to others? There are several possible reasons.
First, he may not trust the judgment of the person bringing the
warning. The beast may behave quite well in the owner's presence.
Is he to trust the judgment of a stranger, and not trust his own personal experience? But once the warning is delivered, he is in jeopardy.
If the beast injures someone, and the informant announces publicly
that he had warned the owner, the owner becomes legally liable for
the victim's suffering.[29]

Second, the owner may be a procrastinator. He fully intended to
place restraints on the ox, but he just never got around to it. This
does not absolve him from full personal liability, but it does explain
why he failed to take effective action.

Another reason for not restraining the ox is economics. It takes
extra care and cost to keep an unruly beast under control. For example, over and over in colonial America, the town records reveal that
owners of pigs, sheep, and cattle had disobeyed previous legislation
requiring them to pen the beasts in or put rings in their noses.
Apparently, the authorities were unable to gain compliance, for this
complaint was continual and widespread throughout the seventeenth century.[30] The costs of supervising the animals or maintaining fences in good repair were just too high in the opinion of count-
less owners. Even putting a ring in the beasts' noses, making it easier

29. Because a serious penalty could be imposed on the liable owner, the informant would have to have proof that he had, in fact, actually warned the owner of the
beast's prior misconduct. Otherwise, the perjured testimony of one man could ruin
the owner of a previously safe beast which then injured someone.

30. Carl Bridenbaugh, *Cities in the Wilderness: The First Century of Urban Life in
America, 1625-1742* (New York: Capricorn, [1938] 1964), pp. 19, 167, 323.

for others to put a rope through the ring and pull a beast home or to some other location, was simply too much trouble.[31] Boston imposed stiff fines on the owners of wandering animals, which helped to reduce the problem.[32]

In one case, the unwillingness or inability of a woman to control her wandering pig literally changed the political history of the United States. Litigation over the ownership of a wandering pig between Goodwoman ("Goodie") Sherman and the well-to-do Boston merchant, Robert Keayne, led in 1644 to a deadlock in the General Court (legislature) of Massachusetts between the deputies or direct representatives of the people (who favored Sherman) and magistrates (who favored Keayne). The result was the division of the two groups into separate legislative houses — the origin of bicameralism in America.[33] As Bridenbaugh notes, "The frequency with which the hog appears in town records is mute proof that despite many 'good and sufficient' measures the problem was never solved, and the bicameral legislature of Massachusetts remains a monument to its persistence."[34] Passing laws is not sufficient. Sanctions must be imposed that alter human behavior.

Limited Liability

The Bible imposes liability on owners of animals known to be dangerous. Penalties are imposed that vary according to the nature of the infraction and the degree of prior knowledge by the owner. These penalties are intended to reduce uncertainty about potentially violent beasts. By extending the principle of legal liability, we can derive principles of liability for owners of inanimate objects.

Man is a limited creature. His knowledge is therefore limited. Because his knowledge is limited, God limits man's legal liability.

---

31. In my research on my doctoral dissertation on colonial American Puritanism, I came across no case where an owner was executed for the act of his beast, nor do I recall locating an example where heavy restitution was paid to a victim.

32. Bridenbaugh, *Cities in the Wilderness*, p. 168.

33. On the "sow" incident, see Charles M. Andrews, *The Colonial Period of American History*, 4 vols., *The Settlements* (New Haven, Connecticut: Yale University Press, [1934] 1964), I, pp. 450-51. Cf. Gov. John Winthrop, *Winthrop's Journal: "History of New England," 1630-1649*, edited by James Kendall Hosmer, 2 vols. (New York: Barnes & Noble, [1908] 1966), II, pp. 64-66, 120-21.

34. Bridenbaugh, *Cities in the Wilderness*, p. 19. I put a question mark in the margin of my book upon first reading it. I had not yet heard of the Keayne-Sherman conflict, and Bridenbaugh never explained what he meant. Scholars can sometimes be too cryptic.

Man is not to be judged by standards that could apply justly only to an omniscient being. If a State seeks to impose perfectionist standards of liability, the legal system will cease to function. It will begin to produce unjust decisions, and there will be an increase of uncertainty and also an increase of arbitrary decisions — precisely what biblical law is designed to prevent. Such judicial uncertainty would make economic decision-making prohibitively expensive. The economy would be threatened.

Consider the case of a potentially dangerous beast which broke its rope or knocked down a restraining fence in Old Testament Israel. The owner would be in the same position as a man who was using an axe which he thought was safe. The axe head flew off and killed someone. This was a case of accidental manslaughter. Immediately, the man would have fled to a city of refuge, in order to escape the dead man's avenger of blood. At that point, the avenger of blood would have demanded a trial, and the elders of the city would have held it. If judged guilty of premeditated murder, the guilty man would have been delivered up to the avenger. If judged innocent, he would have had to remain in the city until the death of the high priest (Num. 35:22-28).

A Broken Rope

Consider the dangerous beast in our day which breaks his restraining rope and kills someone. The victim's heirs sue the owner. They argue that the owner should have used a more sturdy rope. If convicted, the owner then has to prove that the rope's manufacturer was the true culprit. The court then investigates the rope manufacturer. Should he be held liable? To defend himself, he charges the hemp growers with selling a substandard product. Each stage in the case gets more technical and more expensive. The quest for perfect justice is suicidal. It increases the costs of litigation to such an extent that real victims cannot ever afford to attain restitution, for the case never ends. The courts become clogged with expensive cases that can never be resolved by anyone other than God. Only the lawyers profit. God's law does not exist in order to create employment for lawyers.

The State that attempts to impose standards of personal responsibility that imply omniscience and omnipotence will eventually make life impossible. Sometime before civilization grinds to a strangled halt, however, the bureaucrats will back down or else there will be a revolution which removes these messianic standards of personal and corporate responsibility from the law books. The price of perfect liability laws, like the price of perfect justice, or the price of a risk-free society, is death.[35] Such justice will be available only at the end of history. At that point, it will not only be available, it will be inescapable.

This passage therefore has implications for the concept so popular in modern economies, that of *limited liability.* The modern corporation is protected by limited liability laws. In case of its bankruptcy, creditors cannot collect anything from the owners of the corporation's shares of ownership. The corporation is liable only to the extent of its separate, corporate assets.

Legitimate Limitations

Certain kinds of economic transactions that limit the liability of either party, should one of them go bankrupt, are valid. For example, a bank that makes a loan to a church to construct a building cannot collect payment from individual members, should the church be unable to meet its financial obligations. It can repossess the building, of course, something that few banks relish doing. It is bad publicity, and a church building is a kind of white elephant in the real estate world: only churches buy them, and almost all of them are short of funds. This is why bankers prefer to avoid making loans to churches, other things being even remotely equal.[36]

---

35. It should be understood that the selection of "socially appropriate risk" is like any other selection process: it involves subjective valuation and "aggregation" through politics and market forces of the "socially appropriate" mixture of risk and productivity. See Mary Douglas and Aaron Wildavsky, *Risk and Culture: An Essay on the Selection of Technological and Environmental Dangers* (Berkeley: University of California Press, 1982).

36. A wise banker would recommend to the church's officers that church members refinance their homes or assume debt using other forms of collateral, and then *donate* the borrowed money to the church. This ties the loans to personal collateral that a banker can repossess without appearing to be heartless. It makes church members personally responsible for repayment. (Co-signed notes are also acceptable from the banker's point of view, but questionable biblically: e.g., prohibitions against "surety.") Members cannot escape their former financial promises by walking away from the church. It also keeps the church out of debt as an institution, which is godly testimony concerning the evil of debt (Rom. 13:8a). Since a loan is not taxable to the recipient as income (in U.S. tax laws), and since repayments on interest for home loans are tax-deductible, and since donations to a church are tax-deductible, the borrowers receive tax advantages through this arrangement. The interest payments would not constitute a tax advantage if the church borrowed the money, since income to churches is not normally taxable. This approach is illegal in the state of Texas, however; it is illegal to refinance your home in Texas, except to make home improvements — a very stupid law that is left over from the older "populist" mentality.

The same sorts of limited liability arrangements ought to be legally valid for other kinds of associations, including profit-seeking corporations,[37] limited partnerships, or other private citizens who can get other economic actors to agree voluntarily to some sort of limited liability arrangement. For example, a "daredevil" who accepts a very dangerous job, such as putting out an oil well fire, is probably willing to release his employer from all legal damages in case he gets killed. He is paid more than a normal wage for his services in order to compensate him for the risk. A normally dangerous job, such as uranium mining or handling radioactive substances, may carry with it an economic obligation to release the employer from any responsibility for injury or death. The very existence of the danger keeps other workers from applying, thereby lowering the competition and keeping economic wages higher than would have been the case, had the job been safe. The laborer is compensated fairly. He gets more money for being willing to bear greater risk. Without the limited liability provision, the employer might not be willing to employ anyone. The dominion assignment might not be completed in this field until some new technological development reduces risk. Some tasks in life cannot be actuarially insured at a profit, but this does not mean that they should not be performed by people who are aware of the risks and who agree to "self-insure" themselves.[38]

---

37. Robert Hessen, *In Defense of the Corporation* (Stanford, California: Hoover Institution, 1979). I disagree with R. J. Rushdoony's condemnation of limited liability. See Rushdoony, *Politics of Guilt and Pity* (Fairfax, Virginia: Thoburn Press, [1970] 1978), Part III, ch. 8: "Limited Liability and Unlimited Money." What persuaded me that he is incorrect here was a careful consideration of the legal implications of the imposition of unlimited personal liability of church members for the decisions of pastors and church officers. Could the church function if every member were made potentially liable to the limits of his capital for the illegal activity of the church's officers?

38. After the fatal explosion of the launch vehicle of the Challenger space shuttle in January of 1986, it was revealed that the seven government-employed "astronauts" had been required by the government to forego all but minimal life insurance benefits as a condition of participating in the launch. The one civilian, a school teacher, had been given anonymously a one-trip life insurance policy for a million dollars, insured by Lloyd's of London. Months later, the heirs of four of the astronauts received payments totalling $7.7 million, or about $1.9 million per family. (Gold: $350/oz.) The federal government paid 40% of this, and the firm that constructed the rocket paid 60%. This was a political decision; the actual figures paid were kept secret by the government, and only became public fifteen months later when legal action was taken by seven news organizations. *New York Times* (March 8, 1988). It is not yet public knowledge what was paid to the heirs of the other three astronauts.

Other Cases

On the other hand, consider the case of citizens who once lived near an atomic bomb test site. They were assured by government officials (who were presumed to be knowledgeable and therefore were legally responsible) that there were no excessive risks involved in remaining where they were, when there is evidence that these officials knew or should have known about the risks. The citizens who sustain long-term radiation-related injuries as a result of the explosion have every reason to sue and collect from the federal government, even if those officials cannot be located today, or are dead. It is the policy of deliberate misinformation ("disinformation") concerning risks which is the issue. The civil government cannot escape these responsibilities. "I was just following orders," is no excuse for some bureaucrat's deliberately misinforming the civilian victims.

There are other cases that are more difficult to assess. A chemical firm buries toxic wastes. It uses means that are at the time of burial believed to be safe by private health experts or government health officials — people whose tasks are part of the quarantine function of the civil government (cp. Lev. 13, 14). The firm's managers have not deliberately misinformed anyone. Neither have public health officials. They acted with good intentions to the best of their ability, according to the best technical knowledge generally available at the time of the decision. They are like a man who ties up a dangerous beast with a rope generally believed to meet standards of strength, but which snaps unexpectedly, allowing the beast to escape and injure or kill someone.[39] Men are limited creatures; they cannot be held to be liable for every unforeseen act. This was also the conclusion of the rabbinical experts of Jewish law.[40]

"Ransom" Insurance

The Bible provides only one explicit example of a capital crime that can be punished either by execution or a fine: this one. Murder has to be punished by the death penalty (Num. 35:31). In this case, the ox is executed, so the general principle of "life for life" is maintained. Genesis 9:4-6 is not violated by Exodus 21:28-30. The owner, because he is not directly guilty of committing a capital crime,

---

39. See Chapter 16: "Knowledge, Responsibility, and the Presumption of Guilt."

40. Writes Shalom Albeck: "The foreseeability test as the basis of liability for damage led the rabbis to conclude that even where negligent the tortfeasor would only be liable for damage that he could foresee." *Principles of Jewish Law*, col. 322.

although fully responsible before the law for the actions of his beast, can escape execution. It is not stated that the judges make this decision: death or restitution. The victim's family probably makes this decision. Perhaps both judges and family do.[41] Restitution is owed to the relatives, as heirs of his estate; legally, the payment is made to the dead victim. The economic incentive of the family is clear: money is more useful than the death of the victim.

The restitution payment normally would be high. A man has to pay. There is no escape. If he cannot pay what is demanded, either through liability insurance, personal capital, or selling himself into slavery, then he dies. Restitution is mandatory.

The development of personal liability insurance is one way that Western society has dealt with the problem of the catastrophic judgment. The question then arises: Should *criminal negligence* be covered? The civil government must face the questions raised by economic analysis. If the criminal is criminally negligent, yet covered by liability insurance, can the insurance firm be forced by law to pay, even if its contract with the convicted person says that it must? Is a third-party payment to the victim in the name of the criminal an immoral contract and therefore illegal? Does it reduce the economic threat of personal bankruptcy to such an extent that criminal negligence is thereby subsidized? Is criminal negligence a legitimate event to insure against? Should such contracts be made illegal — not just unenforceable in a court of law, but illegal?

There is another problem. If the "deeper pocket" of the insurance company is available for the victim's family to reach into, will they demand "all the traffic will bear," irrespective of justice? If the owner were not insured, would the victim's family ever demand such a high restitution payment? In the absence of insurance, the victim's heirs would probably have to limit their demands. Question: Should judgments be based on the merits of the case or the "depth of the pocket" of the insurance company?

Limiting the Insurer's Liability

To sell personal liability policies, insurance companies have to limit their liability. They do so by placing maximum monetary limits on all pay-outs. They also limit their liability by insuring people who have reputations for being reliable. High-risk buyers raise the prem-

---

41. Finkelstein, *Ox That Gored*, p. 29.

iums that low-risk buyers are forced to pay. There is an economic incentive for companies to seek out lower-risk buyers for any given type of policy. They can insure a special class of higher-risk people, but only by charging all members high premiums. Eventually, they run out of volume sales when they seek out more and more high-risk buyers. They eventually stop selling policies to the highest-risk people.

Personal liability insurance, to be profitable, must be sold to a *particular class* of insurable people. The very concept of "insurable class" refers to a group of people to whom the actuarial laws of probability apply. Groups to which these laws do not apply cannot be safely and profitably insured by private firms selling voluntary policies. Thus, insurance companies attempt to sell to people who are members of a large, insurable class.[42] Insurance firms limit their risk by enlarging the number of policy buyers within a particular large class. They do not want to be bankrupted by one or two large settlements; to avoid bankruptcy, they must sell large numbers of policies. The larger the number of policy holders, the closer the "fit" between the actuarial laws — "laws of large numbers" — and the actual number of cases in which the company must pay victims of negligence.

Liability insurance therefore will cover occasional cases of criminal negligence, for any given policy holder may occasionally be criminally negligent. For example, personal liability coverage on automobile drivers covers those rare cases in which a driver may be criminally negligent.[43] But the firms will not insure people who have received numerous traffic tickets for speeding, and especially for drunk driving. It is true that high-risk drivers can purchase automobile and liability insurance, but only because state governments require the auto insurance industry to set up high-risk pools for otherwise uninsurable drivers do the companies sell policies to these people. *Today's civil governments are requiring private firms to insure people who are more likely to be regarded by the courts as criminally negligent.* These laws reduce political pressures from those classified as criminally negligent; they continue to be allowed to drive. The states also avoid having to set up taxpayer-financed insurance programs for the high-risk drivers — programs that might bring complaints from low-risk drivers who also vote. The legislators require all drivers to carry per-

---

42. Ludwig von Mises, *Human Action: A Treatise on Economics* (3rd ed.; Chicago: Regnery, 1966), p. 109.

43. Some policies may exclude such coverage. It is in the self-interest of policy-buyers to read the fine print of their insurance contracts before they buy.

sonal liability policies — "ransoms for lives" — but they also require insurance companies to sell high-risk drivers this coverage.

If the law did not compel the purchase of auto insurance, or
strongly encourage it by requiring visible evidence of a driver's ability to self-insure himself, the insurance firms would be trapped.
They could not easily pass on to low-risk drivers the added costs of
insuring high-risk people. Low-risk drivers are forced by the state to
pay higher premiums for their policies than would have been the
case had the high-risk drivers been refused coverage and thereby
forced off the roads. Without this compulsion, they would not purchase the policies. The companies would then suffer losses because
of the reduced sales. In fact, they do suffer some losses; some buyers
drop coverage and drive illegally. The sellers cannot pass on all the
additional costs to buyers.[44]

Thus, the concern about criminals' being able to escape justice
because of private insurance contracts is misplaced. The greater
problem is the civil government's demand that people who are more
likely to be convicted of criminal negligence be covered by insurance, whether or not they are insurable by private firms on a voluntary basis. It is not that the State *allows* insurance companies to pay
"ransoms for the lives" of criminally negligent people; it is rather that
the State *compels* private firms to sell such coverage to people or firms
that are more likely to be convicted of criminal negligence.

The State as Insurer

The State even enters as the "insurer of last resort" when no private firms will insure extremely high-risk people or industries. One
example in the United States — which is common in Western industrial nations, though not in Japan[45] — is the government-guaranteed
coverage for accidents connected with the generation of electricity
through nuclear power. Power companies are government-licensed

---

44. Part of these costs are passed on to uninsured or under-insured drivers who
would have liked the coverage but who cannot afford the higher premiums. Also, the
company's shareholders bear some of these costs. They suffer capital losses because
the companies cannot sell policies to all those who would be willing to buy policies if
the costs were lower. It is erroneous to argue that higher costs can be passed on to
customers indiscriminately or at zero cost to companies. See Murray N. Rothbard,
Power and Market: Government and the Market Economy (Menlo Park, California: Institute for Humane Studies, 1970), pp. 66-68.

45. H. Peter Metzger, *The Atomic Power Establishment* (New York: Simon &
Schuster, 1972), p. 218.

public utilities that possess regional monopolies. The "Price-Anderson" legislation of the 1950's sets relatively low ceilings for financial liability by such firms — $560 million per accident[46] — and then the federal government collects the premium money. By limiting its liability, the federal government forces residents who live near nuclear power sites to co-insure against a disaster, since there is a maximum pay-out per accident. The larger the local population that could be affected, the more each resident co-insures, for the lower the per capita payments would be. Taxpayers also co-insure: in case of an accident, the tiny federal nuclear accident insurance fund could not pay off more than 2 percent of a single $560 million damage suit. Money taken from the federal government's general fund would have to make up the difference. Because of this federal legislation, public utilities have been able to expand the use of nuclear power generation. In this sense, today's nuclear power industry has not been the product of a free market economy; it has been the product of special-interest legislation in the form of liability maximums and compulsory State insurance coverage.[47]

The Free Market's Response

Liability insurance is another example of a free market, scientific development that protects the victims without bankrupting those who are personally responsible. The victims receive more money

---

46. *Idem.*

47. Anti-nuclear power advocates tend to be anti-free market, and usually blame the free market for the nuclear power industry. Nuclear power proponents usually are pro-free market, so they seldom talk about the statist nature of the subsidy. But when the chips are down, the pro-nuclear power people accept federal subsidies to *their* program as being economically and ideologically valid. Writes nuclear power advocate Petr Beckman: "Yes, the American taxpayer has paid $1 billion to research nuclear safety, and I consider that a good investment. . . ." Beckman, *The Health Hazards of NOT Going Nuclear* (Boulder, Colorado: Golem Press, 1976), p. 154. He also argues that the Price-Anderson insurance program makes money for the federal government because power companies pay premiums to Washington, along with money sent to private insurance pools. "You call that a subsidy?" he asks rhetorically (p. 156). Of course it is a subsidy. The premium rates are far below market rates, even assuming private firms would insure against a nuclear power plant disaster, which is doubtful. The maximum liability is fixed by law far below what would be demanded in a court if some major nuclear accident took place in a populated area. This is why the Price-Anderson legislation was enacted in the first place: to subsidize the power industry by reducing its legal liability and its insurance rates. Furthermore, taxpayers are co-insuring: the fund which is to cover all power companies nationally was $8 million, as of 1976; the liability was $560 million per accident. Taxpayers would have to make up the difference.

than the private, uninsured citizen or firm would otherwise have been able to pay. The lifetime income loss suffered by the family of the victim is compensated by the insurance company. The negligent person still could be executed, should the plaintiffs desire it, but it is far more likely that they would prefer to accept money from the insurance firm. The "ransom for a life" is higher; thus, the guilty person is more likely to survive. This extends the dominion covenant; the victim's family carries on, but the guilty man suffers no loss of capital, except possibly his ability to buy insurance subsequently.

Does the State have a biblically sanctioned right to compel people to buy liability insurance or else proof of sufficient capital to make restitution? In the case of drivers' liability insurance, where death and serious injury to innocent parties are common, and the drivers are using the State's highway system, the answer is yes. The State can establish rules and regulations for drivers who wish to qualify to use its highways. One of these regulations is liability insurance. Another requirement might be an annual auto safety inspection.[48] The automobile is like a large beast; if it becomes dangerous through neglect by its owner, innocent people can be killed. Insurance companies can be used as screening agents. They may be able write cheaper policies for those who drive inspected automobiles.

Other forms of liability insurance should not be mandatory, unless the situation is comparable to the "dangerous beast in a State-owned place" analogy, but civil government should recognize the legitimacy of the victim's heirs to call for the execution of the criminally negligent party. This would encourage people to buy sufficiently large personal liability insurance policies so that the victim's heirs would have a strong financial incentive to allow the guilty man to live.

The Goring of a Slave or a Child

"If the ox shall push [gore] a manservant or a maidservant; he shall give unto their master thirty shekels of silver, and the ox shall be stoned" (Ex. 21:32). Normally, the death penalty could be imposed on the owner of the ox. In this case, however, the penalty was fixed by law: 30 shekels of silver.

---

48. This assumes that there is statistically valid evidence that state-mandated auto inspections do in fact reduce accidents and injuries. This evidence is frequently unclear. What *is* clear is that such legislation provides an initial increase in the net worth of those who are granted the licenses to perform these inspections, and that a continuation of such laws brings a stream of rents to those who possess these licenses.

The wording here is peculiar. To "push" means, in this instance, to kill. In verse 29, "push" did not mean to kill. "But if the ox were wont to push with his horn in time past, and it hath been testified to his owner, and he hath not kept him in. . . ." Had "to push" meant "to kill," the ox would have been executed upon conviction. An ox that killed someone was stoned to death (v. 28). Thus, "push" in verse 29 had to mean something other than killing. But with respect to servants, the word "push" or "gore" is used in the sense of "gore to death." This is why the ox is executed: a human being has died.

Why the comparatively small penalty?[49] Why is the death of a servant dealt with less severely? Because the servant's owner has not suffered a loss comparable to the loss suffered by the heirs of a free man or woman. He has lost part of an investment in human capital— one which he would have had to part with after a set term of years. He has not suffered the loss of a relative. The primary issue is covenantal. The owner has not suffered a covenantal loss; he has suffered only an economic loss. He is not entitled to place penalties on the owner of the goring ox larger than the economic penalty specified by law.

If a male bondservant had brought a wife and children into the household of the owner, they would now go free, which serves them as a form of compensation. The master would have recouped his investment from the owner of the ox, thereby freeing the slave's heirs from further service.

What if the deceased bondservant had married after becoming a bondservant? In this instance, the heirs probably would have had the option of either remaining as servants in the owner's household or going free. Whether they would go free or not would depend on the size of the penalty payment to the bondservant-owner, compared to what he had paid for the bondservant. If the death occurred shortly before the bondservant was to have gone free, then the penalty payment would have constituted an overpayment, and the extra money probably would have functioned as a release price for the wife and children of the bondservant. But if the penalty payment was approximately what the owner had spent to pay off the bondservant's debt —the original cause of his going into slavery—then the bondservant's family would have remained with the owner, as specified in Exodus 21:4.

---

49. Thirty pieces of silver were a lot of money in terms of what they could buy, but not compared to what the victim's heirs could normally impose.

An interesting connection can be seen between the death of
Christ on the cross and the death of the gored servant. James B. Jordan
has commented on this connection: "As we have seen, our Lord
Jesus Christ was born into the world as a homeborn slave-son, for
His incarnation was His ear's circumcision. On the cross, he was
made sin for us, and thus came under condemnation of death. He
became an abject slave, that we might be elevated into the status of
adopted slave-sons. He was killed by the wild beasts, the lions of paganism, and the apostate unclean goring bulls of Israel: 'Many bulls
have surrounded Me; strong ones from Bashan have encircled me.
They open wide their mouth at me, as a ravening and a roaring lion.
. . . Save Me from the lion's mouth; and from the horns of the wild
oxen Thou dost answer Me' (Ps. 22:12, 13, 21). Thus, the price given
for Christ's death was the price of the gored slave, thirty pieces of silver (Matt. 26:15). At His resurrection, however, our Lord overcame
the bulls and trampled on the silver for which He was sold: 'Rebuke
the beasts of the reeds, the herd of bulls with the calves of the peoples, trampling under foot the pieces of silver; He has scattered the
people who delight in war' (Ps. 68:30). Thus, Judas found no joy in
his silver, and it was used to buy a burying field for dead strangers,
pagans destroyed by the wrath of God (Matt. 27:2-10)."[50]

The Goring of a Child

"Whether he have gored a son, or have gored a daughter, according to this judgment shall it be done unto him" (Ex. 21:31). This is an
important biblical principle: the imposition of a fine rather than the
execution of the ox's owner or his child (a pagan practice of the ancient Near East). The Bible places this example under the general
rule that allows the substitution of a fine for the death of the owner.
This means that the evil practice of the ancient Near East, killing a
man's child if he kills another man's child, is prohibited.[51] The
Hammurabi Code specified: "If a builder constructed a house for a
seignior, but did not make his work strong, with the result that the
house which he built collapsed and so has caused the death of the
owner of the house, that builder shall be put to death. If it has
caused the death of a son of the owner of the house, they shall put the

---

50. Jordan, *Law of the Covenant*, pp. 127-28.
51. Dale Patrick, *Old Testament Law* (Atlanta, Georgia: John Knox Press, 1985),
p. 78.

son of that builder to death."[52]

This sharp difference from Babylonian law would appear to be an application of the principle of Deuteronomy 24:16: "The fathers shall not be put to death for the children, neither shall the children be put to death for the fathers: every man shall be put to death for his own sin."

Conclusion

The Bible establishes the principle of cosmic personalism as the foundation of the universe.[53] There is no way that men can escape their responsibilities before God. Because biblical law recognizes this principle, it establishes the judicial principle of restitution to victims by the negligent. The general rule is: an eye for an eye, a life for a life.

The Bible affirms the principle of limited liability before men. The State is not God. It cannot know every aspect of historical causation. Neither can men. The State therefore cannot lawfully impose unlimited liability on those convicted of negligence, irrespective of their knowledge, decisions, and contractual arrangements.

In this unique instance, the case of a dangerous ox that kills a person, the guilty owner can legitimately escape death, though his beast cannot, because the victim's heirs are allowed to impose an economic restitution payment on the negligent individual. This law of criminal negligence is much broader than simply oxen and owners; it applies to all cases of death to innocent parties that are the result of negligence on the part of owners of notorious beasts or notorious machinery — capital that is known to be risky to innocent bystanders. Automobiles, trucks, certain kinds of occupations, nuclear power plants, coal mines, and similar examples of dangerous tools are covered by this general principle of personal liability.

This law should not be understood as applying to workers who voluntarily work in dangerous callings and who have been warned in advance of the risks by their employers, nor should it be used as a justification for the creation of a messianic State that attempts to discover criminal negligence in every case of third-party injury, despite the lack of knowledge of risks by the owners or experts in the field.

---

52. Code Hammurabi, paragraphs 229-30. *Ancient Near Eastern Texts Relating to the Old Testament*, edited by James B. Pritchard (3rd ed.; Princeton, New Jersey: Princeton University Press, 1969), p. 176.

53. North, *The Dominion Covenant: Genesis*, ch. 1.

Personal liability insurance is a development of the West that allows criminally negligent people a greater opportunity to escape the death penalty by means of high payments to the heirs of their victims. Purchasing such insurance is not to become mandatory, except in cases related to the use of State-financed capital (e.g., highways). Nevertheless, the risk is so high — execution — and the cost of premiums so low in comparison to the risk, that personal liability coverage is available to most people. Only the very poor, who would not normally own "oxen" (expensive capital equipment), or people convicted repeatedly of criminal negligence or actions that would lead to convictions for criminal negligence (e.g., drunk driving), or people who manage or own businesses that create high risks for innocent bystanders, would normally be excluded from the purchase of such insurance coverage. They would have to learn to handle their "oxen" with care.

15

THE UNCOVERED PIT

And if a man shall open a pit, or if a man shall dig a pit, and not cover it, and an ox or an ass fall therein; the owner of the pit shall make it good, and give money unto the owner of them; and the dead beast shall be his (Ex. 21:33-34).

Here is another variation of the restitution principle. A man digs a pit for some reason, and fails to cover it. This is negligent behavior. He knows that unsuspecting people or animals could fall into the pit and be harmed. His failure to go to the expense of covering the pit is an example of what economists call "externalities." He imposes the risk of an injured beast on the owner of the beast. *By saving time and money in not covering the pit, he thereby transfers the economic burden of risk to someone else.* This is a form of theft. Someone who cannot benefit from the use of the pit is expected to pay a portion of its costs of operation, namely, the risk of injury to any animal that might fall into it. This is the meaning of economic "externalities": those who cannot benefit from an economic decision are forced to pay for part of the costs of operation.

Biblical civil law settles the question of property rights and the responsibilities of ownership. Because the Bible affirms the rights of private ownership — meaning *legal immunities* from interference by either the State or other private citizens in the use of one's property — it therefore imposes *responsibilities* on owners. The law regulating uncovered pits is not an infringement on private property rights. On the contrary, it is an *affirmation* of such rights. By linking personal economic responsibility to personal, private ownership, biblical civil law identifies the legal owner of the pit, namely, the person who is required to pay damages should another person's animal be killed by a fall into the unsafe pit. He receives some sort of advantage from the pit, and therefore he must bear the expense of making it safe for other people's animals.

"Pit" in Rabbinical Literature

"Pit" is a classification used for centuries by the rabbis to assess responsibility and damages. The Mishnah specified that any pit ten handbreadths deep qualifies as deep enough to cause death, and therefore is actionable in cases of death. If less than this depth, the pit is actionable in case of injury to a beast, but not if the beast died.[1] Writes Jewish legal scholar Shalom Albeck: "This is the name given to another leading category of tort and covers cases where an obstacle is created by a person's negligence and left as a hazard by means of which another is injured. The prime example is that of a person who digs a pit, leaves it uncovered, and another person or an animal falls into it. Other major examples would be leaving stones or water unfenced and thus potentially hazardous. The common factor is the commission or omission of something which brings about a dangerous situation and the foreseeability of damage resulting. A person who fails to take adequate precautions to render harmless a hazard under his control is considered negligent, since he is presumed able to foresee that damage may result, and he is therefore liable for any such subsequent damage."[2]

Samson Raphael Hirsch, the brilliant mid-nineteenth-century Jewish Torah commentator, analyzed the economics of negligence under the general heading of property, and property under the more general classification of guardianship. "Man, in taking possession of the unreasoning world, becomes guardian of unreasoning property and is responsible for the forces inherent in it, just as he is responsible for the forces of his own body; for property is nothing but the artificially extended body, and body and property together are the realm and sphere of action of the soul — *i.e.*, of the human personality, which rules them and becomes effective through them and in them. Thus is the person responsible for all the material things under his dominion and in his use; and even without the verdict of a court of law, even if no claim is put forward by another person, he must pay compensation for any harm done to another's property or body

---

1. *Baba Kamma* 5:5, *The Mishnah*, edited by Herbert Danby (New York: Oxford University Press, [1933] 1987), p. 338.
2. "Avot Nezikin: (2) Pit," *The Principles of Jewish Law*, edited by Menachem Elon (Jerusalem: Keter, 1975?), col. 326. This compilation of articles taken from the *Encyclopedia Judaica* was published as Publication No. 6 of the Institute for Research in Jewish Law of the Hebrew University of Jerusalem.

for which he is responsible."[3] The guardian is always responsible before God for the administration of everything under his legal authority.

Hirsch goes so far as to say that our willingness to indemnify a victim is not enough, morally speaking; we must take care not to allow damage in the first place. "Once you have done harm the only thing you are able to do is to pay compensation; you can never undo the harm and wipe out all its consequences."[4] A righteous person should become a blessing for those around him. "You, with all your belongings, should become a blessing; be on your guard that you and your belongings do not become a curse! Watch over all your belongings so that they do no harm to your neighbour! And also what you throw away or pour away — see to it that it do no harm; you ought to bring good, so do not bring evil!"[5] Thus, our economic responsibility is an *active* responsibility. We must actively seek to avoid harming others. It is within this moral framework that the Bible discusses the uncovered pit.

Animals and Children

This case law deals specifically with animals. It does not mention people. Why not? Because the pit is almost certainly located on the land of the person who digs it. An animal that wanders onto the man's property has no understanding of private property rights. Presumably, no fence has restrained it from coming onto the property. If a fence is present, then the animal would have to knock it down to get onto the property. The damage to the fencing would then be the responsibility of the owner of the animal. He should have restrained his animal. *The fence in such an instance serves as the legal equivalent of a cover.* But unrestrained access to the area of the uncovered pit places the responsibility on the land-owner. An animal is not expected to honor the law against trespassing.

What holds true for an animal is also true for a young child. If the child is not restrained by a fence or a cover over the pit, then the owner is liable. Like an ox with a reputation for violence, so is the uncovered pit. The owner is responsible. The parents of a child who is killed by a fall into an uncovered pit are entitled to the same restitution as the heirs of a victim of an ox that was known to be dangerous.

---

3. Samson Raphael Hirsch, *Horeb: A Philosophy of Jewish Laws and Observances,* trans. I. Grunfeld (New York: Soncino, [1837] 1962), pp. 243-44, paragraph 360.

4. *Ibid.,* p. 247, paragraph 367.

5. *Ibid.,* p. 248, paragraph 367.

A responsible adult who comes onto another person's property and falls into a pit has to have a legitimate reason for being there. If the uncovered pit is located on a path over which a visitor might normally pass, and the pit is not easily visible, then the owner becomes legally responsible. The visitor, in this instance, is like a dumb animal: he is not aware of special prohibitions against walking in the vicinity of the uncovered pit. But if the visitor has climbed over a fence and is wandering over the property in the dead of night, where he has no reason to be, then the owner is innocent. If the intruder ignores "No Trespassing" signs, he is also unprotected by the "covered pit" law. He is not to be treated in a literate culture as if he were a dumb animal. Albeck comments: "If the *bor* [pit] (i.e., the hazard) is adequately guarded or left in a place where persons or animals do not normally pass, such as one's private property, no negligence or presumed foreseeability can be ascribed and no liability would arise."[6]

The pit-digger is required to reimburse the owner of the dead beast. The latter can then buy a replacement for the dead animal. The pit-digger becomes the owner of the dead animal. In Israel, he could have sold it or eaten it, since it died of a known cause; it did not die "of itself," which would have made it forbidden meat for Israelites (Deut. 14:21). The pit-digger does not suffer a total loss.

In modern times, people build swimming pools on their property. These are certainly uncovered most of the swimming season. They are holes in the ground. Are these the modern equivalent of a pit? No. A pit is a hole in the ground which is not expected. It is not readily visible. A swimming pool has a cement deck around it. It may have a diving board. It is plainly visible in the back yard. It is anything but inconspicuous. Besides, if an animal falls into it, it will swim out. If a small child falls into it, liability could be imposed on the owner only under the "railed roof" statute (Deut. 22:8), not under the "uncovered pit" statute. The pool is a place of entertainment and recreation, just as flat-roof housetops were in the ancient world. It is not a pit which men stumble into unexpectedly. The so-called "attractive nuisance" problem—a dangerous object to which small children are attracted—falls under the railing statute.

Public "Pits"

There are areas of life that are almost always the responsibility of the civil government. Highways are one example. If people are to

---

6. Albeck, "Pit," *Principles of Jewish Law*, col. 326.

use the highways, they need protection, both as drivers and pedestrians. The civil government erects stop signs and stop lights; it places other road signs along the highways, so that drivers can drive more safely and make better high-speed decisions. Similarly, residential areas and school zones are restricted to slower traffic. This protects pedestrians and home owners who would otherwise face the continual threat of high-speed vehicles that are difficult to control in tight quarters.

The posting of a speed limit is essentially the same as a private citizen who posts a "no trespassing" sign, or a "beware of dog" sign on his property. The sign serves as a substitute for the "cover for the pit"; the sign, like the cover, is a device for *protecting the innocent.* Where children in cities are forced to cross busy streets, local governments hire crossing guards to control traffic and help younger children across the street. Sometimes, older students in a grammar school serve as unpaid crossing guards in a safety patrol. In some communities, fenced, overhead ramps are built across busy highways. The fence serves as a means of protection for 1) pedestrians who might fall off the overpass and 2) motorists who face risks from vandals who would drop heavy rocks onto the passing cars beneath. But fences are expensive, and they cannot be built in every residential area. Thus, the civil government establishes speed limits, and it posts signs that warn drivers of these limits.

A philosophy of nearly risk-free existence would impose speed limits of no more than a few miles per hour on all drivers, except perhaps on specially designed highways. But voters, who are both pedestrians and drivers, would not long tolerate such utopian restrictions. In most places in the United States, voters drive far more hours during the day than they walk. So they will not allow defenders of the rhetoric of risk-free living to have their way. They make judgments as individuals that legislators must respect in the aggregate: *speed limits that meet the needs of voters,* both as drivers and pedestrians, or the parents of pedestrians. Once the speed limit is posted, people make personal adjustments, both as drivers (by slowing down to approach the legal limit, but letting pedestrians look out more for themselves) and as pedestrians (by reducing their watchfulness about cars, so long as cars are moving at or near the posted limit). Voters compromise: slower speeds close to schools, but faster speeds on highways.

Drivers who violate these limits are increasing the statistical risks of walking in a neighborhood. Residents believe that they have been granted a degree of safety by the authorities—not perfect safety, since automobiles are still permitted in the area, but *calculable safety*. They use the streets and sidewalks in terms of this greater degree of safety. But pedestrians and other (slower) drivers are threatened by those who refuse to honor the posted speed limit. They have made decisions in terms of a given environment ("25 m.p.h."), and a law-breaker unilaterally alters this environment. He has, in effect, torn down the protective fencing. He has "uncovered the pit."

Fines and Restitution

What is the proper remedy? Most communities impose fines for excessive speeding, with the fines proportional to the violations: a higher fine for a higher speed. Can a fine be justified biblically? Yes. *The fine is imposed because a specific victim cannot be identified.* No one was injured by the speeding vehicle. Therefore, the civil government collects a *restitution payment* in the name of all the victims who had their lives and property *threatened* by the speeder's act.

A statistically measurable risk of injury was transferred by the speeder to those in the area of his speeding vehicle. This is another case of "externalities": people are being forced by the speeder to bear risks involuntarily. The fines should be used to establish *a trust fund for future victims of "hit and run" auto accidents*, where the guilty party cannot be located and/or convicted. The perpetrator of this "victimless crime" becomes a source of restitution payments for the subsequent victims of this same criminal act by an unconvicted agent. *Fines are therefore an acknowledgement by the authorities of the limits placed on their knowledge.* If law enforcement authorities were omniscient, all restitution payments in a biblical society would go from the known criminal to the known victim.

Fines should be imposed by local authorities for a specific purpose: to make restitution payments to victims who reside in the same general neighborhood. The civil government acts as a *trustee* for future victims in cases where the authorities cannot locate or convict the violator. *Fines are not to be regarded as a normal source of revenue for the civil government.* The civil government must enforce biblical law without prejudice. The bureaucrats' fond hope of collecting municipal operating revenues from fines creates prejudice. In a biblical commonwealth, taxes are supposed to finance civil government—*predictable* taxes that are collected from every responsible adult in a community. Citizens must know what law enforcement is really costing them. Setting up "speed traps" along the highway so that non-residents can be forced to finance the local government is a gross perversion of the function of the fine. This subsidizes local bureaucrats rather than assisting future victims.

Drunk Drivers

An individual who deliberately distorts his own perceptions is implicitly attacking God and his God-created environment.[7] He is saying by his actions that God has not been fair to him in placing him in such an environment. He then makes decisions under the influence of alcohol or drugs that can physically damage others because of his self-induced distorted perceptions. Drunk drivers are therefore to be prosecuted as criminally negligent, should their acts cause damage. They have "torn off the pit cover" with impunity. Their injury-inflicting acts are not to be considered as accidents, meaning low-probability events that cannot reasonably be predicted in advance in the life of any specific individual. Their injury-inflicting actions are rather the product of an act of moral rebellion: the implicit denial of their own personal responsibility for their actions.

Drunk drivers impose increased statistical risks on their potential victims. The victim or the heirs must be given the legal option of imposing a heavy restitution payment, under the guidance of the judges (see Chapter 6). Where there is no victim, the drunk driver must pay the fine.

Repeated convictions for drunk driving indicate moral rebellion. Here is a person who has the equivalent of a notorious ox: the lawless "beast" is inside him. Worse: he is responsible in a way that a beast is not. He has moral insights concerning the consequences of his acts that a beast does not possess. The authorities can legitimately "tie him up" by revoking his right to operate a vehicle until he has demonstrated his continued sobriety for a fixed period of time. Like a notorious ox that must be fenced until it becomes self-disciplined, so is the drunk driver, or the repeat speeder, or the driver who drives under the influence of drugs. There may not be identifiable victims, but there are certainly *statistical victims* whose interests need protection.

---

7. Obviously an exception is the person who has accepted an anesthetic in order to reduce his pain. Thrashing around in agony during a medical operation clearly reduces the likelihood of a successful operation. But such people are always placed under medical observation and supervision. They are not legally responsible agents during their period of distorted perceptions.

The same principles of economic analysis that apply to speeding and drunk driving can be applied to other areas of life in which the State is the primary protector of life and limb. Fines to the civil government should be imposed on convicted violators only in cases where the civil government is acting as a trustee for future unknown victims.

Political Hypocrisy

The problem today is that society refuses to accept the morally and legally binding nature of Old Testament legal principles of criminal negligence. First, legislators do not consistently make "pit owners" legally liable for damages, as the Bible requires. The most flagrant example is the failure of state and local governments to impose stiff fines on all drunk drivers, and capital punishment on drunk drivers whose unsafe driving leads to someone else's death. Furthermore, politicians do not impose fines on themselves or city employees for failing to repair public streets with potholes which cause damages to people's cars or which cause accidents.

Second, politicians pass safety laws (or allow the bureaucracy to define and then enforce earlier laws) whose costs to the general public are not immediately perceptible. They may require automobile companies to install seat belts that buyers do not want to pay for, and which occupants subsequently refuse to use, but politicians are not about to pass a law that would impose fines on families for refusing to install smoke detectors in their own homes. The first piece of legislation would not gain the reprisal of voters; the second probably would. In short, they pass pieces of legislation with minimal political and statistical impact (for good or evil) in terms of the utopian principle of "better to spend millions of dollars than to suffer one dead victim," but fail to honor it in statistically relevant cases because of the equally relevant (to them) political backlash they would receive from voters. The proclamation of the "better millions of dollars than. . . ." principle has been, is, and will continue to be the product of economic ignorance and political hypocrisy.

This is not to say that it is always wrong to require owners to pay more in order to save lives, but the Bible provides us with the proper guidelines, not some hypothetically universal utopian principle that would necessitate the creation of a messianic State. The general principle is simple: *those who own a known dangerous object are legally responsible for making it safer for those who are either immature or otherwise unwarned about the very real danger.*

Conclusion

Ownership is a social function. There is a link between the costs and benefits of lawful ownership. He who *benefits* from the use of private property must also bear the *costs* of ownership. He cannot legitimately pass on the costs to other people who have not voluntarily agreed to accept these costs. He is also responsible for the risks of physical damage that he imposes on them without their prior knowledge and consent.

The pit-digger must cover the pit or be responsible for the consequences. The owner of an unpenned notorious ox is equally responsible. Beasts are not expected to understand property rights; the owner must fence his property, or cover his pit, or pay restitution to the dead beast's owner. He cannot legitimately pass on the risks associated with uncovered pits to his neighbors.

The civil government has an analogous responsibility to protect those who use the property which belongs to, or is administered by, the State. Thus, speed limits, crossing guards, and school safety patrols are created. Patrol cars monitor traffic in neighborhoods. Fines are collected from speeders and other traffic violators. Why fines? Because there are limits on the knowledge of law enforcement authorities; thus, fines are used as a way to collect restitution payments from known violators, and to make payments to victims of unknown violators.

Responsibility is personal, and it involves every area of authority exercised by any individual. The civil government has the obligation of setting forth principles of judicial interpretation that will prevail in any civil court. The court will look at the circumstances surrounding the injured party, and determine who was responsible. If the property owner was attempting to pass on involuntarily to innocent third parties the risks of ownership, the court will find the owner guilty. All property owners know this in advance, and they can take steps to reduce their legal risks by reducing involuntary risks borne by innocent third parties.

The Bible does not warrant the establishment of a huge bureaucracy to define every area of possible risk, promulgate minute definitions of what constitutes unlawful uses of property, and describe in detail every penalty associated with a violation. The Bible certainly does not indicate that the civil government is warranted to step in and proclaim a potentially injurious action illegal, except in cases where the violator could not conceivably make restitution to all the potential victims (e.g., fire codes) or in cases of repeated violations (the "notorious ox" principle). The Bible simply reminds property owners of the consequences of creating hazards to life and limb for third parties who were not consulted in advance concerning their willingness to bear the risks. The property owner is assumed to be competent to make judgments for himself concerning the consequences of his actions, and then take the steps necessary to reduce his risks.

16

KNOWLEDGE, RESPONSIBILITY,
AND THE PRESUMPTION OF GUILT

And if one man's ox hurt another's, that he die; then they shall sell the live ox, and divide the money of it; and the dead ox also they shall divide. Or if it be known that the ox hath used to push [gore] in time past, and his owner hath not kept him in; he shall surely pay ox for ox; and the dead shall be his own (Ex. 21:35-36).

The crucial fact in these verses is that two different sorts of offending oxen are dealt with: a previously peaceful ox and a notorious ox. Because of these differences, the penalties differ. The question is: Why?

An ox is a domesticated work animal. It is under the dominion of its owner. The owner therefore incurs certain responsibilities for the behavior of his animal. The animal is to refrain from attacking man or other animals of its own species. The owner must take steps to train the animal to respect the life and limbs of others, or else he is to restrain its ability to inflict such injuries.

The concept of a domesticated animal points to the ability of men to train and discipline lower species. Animals are responsible to man, and by implication, to God. The owner of a dangerous beast must see to it that others in the vicinity do not become involuntary risk-bearers as a result of the animal's lack of self-discipline. To create judicial incentives for owners of oxen to train or restrain their beasts, the Bible sets forth principles of economic responsibility.

Say that a man's previously passive ox gores another ox to death. Because the ox has gored another animal, and not a human, it is not to be killed by the original owner. It is to be sold to a third party. The third party who subsequently buys it may kill it if he wishes; if he does, he reduces his risks of ownership. The ox has become a notorious ox. There are risks associated with the ownership of such a beast. There are costs of fencing it or restraining it in some fashion. The new owner may decide not to keep it alive.

There is also no biblical law that restricts the original owner from making an offer to buy back (redeem) the ox from the third party, but the law requires that the beast be sold initially.

The case of the notorious ox is different. The owner is fully responsible, exactly as the owner of the uncovered pit is responsible. This case law presumes that for the owner to be liable, the notorious beast not be penned in or otherwise restrained, just as in the case of the notorious ox that gores a human (Ex. 21:29). The owner has to pay the full value of the dead beast to the beast's owner. Again, he is allowed to keep the dead animal. He is also allowed to keep the offending animal.

Why isn't the offending animal stoned to death for killing another beast, as would be required in the case of an unpenned notorious ox that gores a man or woman to death? The reason should be clear to anyone who understands the implications of the dominion covenant. An ox is *responsible upward*, toward man. It suffers the death penalty for killing a man. The *innate fear of man* which is in all animals (Gen. 9:2) serves as its *restraining factor*, a kind of "fence" which it knows it must not break through. By killing a man, the ox has demonstrated that it actively transgressed this God-imposed restraint. It is therefore rebellious and deserving of death. It is acting like the serpent of Genesis 3, and therefore it suffers the same penalty. But it is not held responsible "to the death" for killing another animal. It is not "responsible outward," toward other beasts. Its owner is responsible for its behavior "outward," not the ox.

Who Pays?

Who pays for damages? The owner of the surviving ox pays. Under normal circumstances, the individual who is legally and financially responsible is the owner of the offending ox that initiated the attack. But there is a problem here. Whose beast took the initiative? Can this be determined in a court of law? Were there witnesses? Can we understand the motivation of oxen? These questions are almost self-explanatory. The assessment of which animal "started it" is most problematical. The ox cannot be placed under oath and cross-examined.

The Bible's solution is to divide the proceeds from the sale of the surviving animal, and to divide the carcass of the dead one. Each owner has an incentive to maximize the proceeds from the sale of the survivor, since both of them gain an equal share of the sale price. The owner of the dead beast cannot come before the judges and claim that his beast was worth ten times as much as it really was worth. The judges do not have to call in specialists in assessing retroactively the value of dead cattle. They can leave it to both owners to settle their differences. Each man has an incentive to get the transaction over with. Neither can trick the other (or the judges) as to the former value of the dead beast. The market then reveals the live beast's value.

The dead beast is also worth something. The Old Testament rules prohibiting the sale of unclean dead beasts (Deut. 14:21; Lev. 17:15) do not apply in the New Covenant era. Even under the Old Covenant, the beast could be sold to a resident alien gentile (Deut. 14:21b). Today, the beast can lawfully be sold to Jew or gentile if the carcass meets public health standards. Each owner receives an equal share of the returns.

What if a run-of-the-mill bull kills a champion? The owner of the champion suffers the greater loss. But since it cannot easily be determined which bull initiated the violence, the court is not required by God to examine the detailed question of what is owed to the owner of the dead beast. This law implicitly recognizes the limitations on courts in assessing responsibility in the case of the behavior of animals. Owners of prize animals are forewarned to take care of their property.

Jewish Law: Whose Ox Is Gored?

The Mishnah makes some very peculiar exemptions to this law. "If an ox of an Israelite gored an ox that belonged to the Temple, or an ox that belonged to the Temple gored the ox of an Israelite, the owner is not culpable, for it is written, *The ox of his neighbour* [Ex. 21:35] — not an ox that belongs to the Temple."[1] This is most peculiar. One would think that if any ox was to be protected by the threat of damages imposed on the owner of the killer ox, it would be an ox belonging to the temple. Why the word "neighbor" excluded the temple is not explained.

The Mishnah continued: "If an ox of an Israelite gored the ox of a gentile, the owner is not culpable. But if the ox of a gentile gored the ox of an Israelite, whether it was accounted harmless or an at-

---

1. *Baba Kamma* 4:3, *The Mishnah*, edited by Herbert Danby (New York: Oxford University Press, [1933] 1987), p. 337.

tested danger, the owner must pay full damages."[2] Almost a millennium later, Maimonides agreed: he exempted the Israelite owner from being required to pay damages, whether or not he was forewarned about his beast, if his ox gores an ox belonging to a heathen. He adds reasons for the Mishnah's discriminatory law. The "heathen do not hold one responsible for damage caused by one's animals, and their own law is applied to them." (This is truly preposterous, and he offers no evidence.) On the other hand, the heathen is fully liable, whether or not he was forewarned, if his ox gores the ox of an Israelite. Why? Because "should they not be held liable for damage caused by their animals, they would not take care of them and thus would inflict loss on other people's property."[3] This is a classic example of different laws for different residents, in open violation of Exodus 12:49.

Maimonides argued that if the ox was unowned at the time of the goring, and is subsequently appropriated by someone else, before the plaintiff can seize it, the new owner is not liable for previous damages.[4] This would leave the victim without recourse, and it would leave the animal immune from judgment, for it would not serve as payment—ox for ox—for the damages it caused. (Rabbi Judah had early argued that "A wild ox, or an ox belonging to the Temple, or an ox belonging to a proselyte who died are exempt from death, since they have no owner.")[5]

Even more incredibly, Maimonides argued that if the existing owner renounces ownership after the goring takes place, but before the trial, "he is exempt, for there is no liability unless the ox has an owner both at the time it causes the damage and at the time the case is tried in court."[6] This would destroy personal legal liability in the most serious cases. The owner would be allowed to separate himself retroactively from the social responsibilities of ownership, as if ownership of a physical object were all that is involved in ownership, and not also the legal immunities and legal responsibilities that are inescapably bound up with possession of the object. Maimonides did

---

2. *Idem.*

3. Moses Maimonides, *The Book of Torts*, vol. 11 of *The Code of Maimonides*, 14 vols. (New Haven, Connecticut: Yale University Press, 1954), "Laws Concerning Damage by Chattels," Chapter Eight, Section Five, p. 29.

4. *Idem.*

5. *Baba Kamma* 4:7, *Mishnah*, p. 337. The Talmud also specifies that the ox had to have gored on three previous occasions for the owner to become personally liable: Shalom Albeck, "TORTS. The Principal Categories of Torts," in *The Principles of Jewish Law*, edited by Menachem Elon (Jerusalem: Keter, 1975?), col. 322.

6. Maimonides, *Torts, loc. cit.*

not say that the victim could not demand that the beast be destroyed or sold in order to compensate him. He did say that if the owner sells the animal, the victim can collect compensation from the animal, and the buyer must reclaim damages from the defendant.[7]

Maimonides also added that the testimony of certain witnesses is invalid: slaves, shepherds, children, and women. "One must not think that because only slaves, shepherds, or similar persons are generally found in horse stables, cattle stalls, or sheep pens, these should be heard if they testify that one animal has caused damage to another, or that children or women should be relied on if they testify that one person has wounded another or if they testify about other types of damage."[8]

The Christian commentator finds little that he can appeal to in confidence in Jewish laws regarding the goring ox. It is no better in the case of the notorious ox. How many occurrences establish a pattern of habitual action? How many gorings need to take place before the beast is identified as a notorious beast? It was the opinion of Rabbi Meir that the court should identify as an "attested danger" any ox against which three separate proven accusations of damage have been brought in the past.[9] Maimonides did not indicate how many accusations were required, unlike the Mishnah and Talmud, but he indicated that it must be more than one. "An animal is called *mu'ad,* 'forewarned,' with respect to actions which it does normally and habitually, and *tam,* 'innocuous,' with respect to actions which it does only exceptionally and which are not normally done by members of its species — as, for example, if an ox gores or bites. If an animal, having acted abnormally once, makes it a habit to repeat the abnormal action on numerous occasions, it becomes 'forewarned' with respect to the particular action which it has made a habit. For Scripture says, *Or if it be known that the ox was wont to gore* (Exod. 21:36)."[10]

We need better guidelines than this.

The Notorious Ox

Responsibility is more easily assessed by a court in the case of an ox that was known in the past to be a violent animal. The owner had

7. *Ibid.*, "Laws Concerning Damage by Chattels," Chapter Eight, Section Six, p. 29.

8. *Ibid.*, "Laws Concerning Damage by Chattels," Chapter Eight, Section Thirteen, p. 31.

9. *Baba Kamma* 1:4, *Mishnah,* p. 333.

10. Maimonides, *Torts,* "Laws Concerning Damage by Chattels," Chapter One, Section Four, pp. 4-5.

been given a previous warning concerning the behavior of the beast under his jurisdiction. Perhaps the court had convicted this beast of a prior violation; perhaps witnesses had independently complained to the civil authorities, and they had issued the owner a formal warning. There is no indication that three warnings are required; one warning should be sufficient to persuade the owner to take additional steps to restrain his beast. From the time of the warning, it becomes the owner's responsibility to keep the beast penned in or in some way restrained from inflicting damage on others.

This case law applies to an owner who chose to keep possession of the beast. Thus, he simultaneously chose to bear the additional risks associated with the behavior of that particular beast. The owner also chose not to take the time and trouble necessary to restrain the beast. This is his lawful decision. No one is sent by the civil government to inspect the quality of the fence or the strength of the rope around its neck. But its owner is prohibited by biblical law from passing on these now-known risks of ownership to innocent third parties. *Self-government under law*—written laws with specified, predictable sanctions—is the biblical standard, not a legal order based on a top-down bureaucratic enforcement system.

The judicial problem with this rule regarding the notorious ox is its vagueness: How much information is enough? The Bible says that if the ox was known to gore in the past, it becomes for legal purposes a notorious beast. Known by whom? By the owner, certainly. But how can this knowledge be proven in court to have been in the possession of the owner? Only through previous publicly provable complaints registered by neighbors, either to the owner or the public authorities, or by a single prior conviction of the beast. If the owner has publicly provable evidence that the ox gored someone in the past, he becomes legally liable.

Obviously, if the beast has gored on several occasions, it is a known offender. But society needs to defend the property of those victims of the beast in the meantime. This passage of Scripture establishes that the issue of legal liability in the case of the damage-producing actions of a dangerous domestic animal is to be established in terms of *the judges' ability to assess comparative knowledge between the plaintiff and the defendant*. The owner is presumed to have better information concerning his beast's behavior than an outsider possesses. Thus, a single proven case of previous bad behavior on the part of an ox places its owner at risk judicially.

Ox for Ox

"Or if it be known that the ox hath used to push [gore] in time past, and his owner hath not kept him in; he shall surely pay ox for ox" (Ex. 21:36). What is the meaning of "ox for ox"? In the previous case of a beast whose dangerous behavior had not been a matter of public knowledge, the owner of the dead beast does not receive a replacement ox. He only receives half of the proceeds of the sale of the live ox and the dead ox's carcass. But this case is different. The goring beast is known to have gored in the past. The owner of the dead ox is to be fully reimbursed, "ox for ox."

Does this mean that the owner of the dead beast is simply to be given the surviving ox? This would be a very unlikely interpretation. First, the surviving ox is now a known renegade. It is a menace, as the owner of the dead ox knows only too well. The owner of the survivor therefore would be transferring ownership of a high-risk beast to the owner of the victim. But a high-risk property always commands a lower sale price than a low-risk property, for obvious reasons. The buyer has to be compensated for the added expense he is accepting by purchasing the high-risk property.

Second, the market value of the dead beast may be far higher than the transgressing survivor, irrespective of the risk factor. Perhaps the dead beast was a prize-winning beast. The victim now can sue for damages. He is to be reimbursed, "ox for ox." In other words, he is to be reimbursed like for like, value for value. On the one hand, as the owner of a champion bull, he has a financial incentive to keep his high-value beast away from any potentially dangerous beast that has not been identified as dangerous. On the other hand, it is the responsibility of the owner of a known renegade beast to keep it away from other bulls, especially champion bulls. The economic burden now shifts to the owner of the killer beast.

What is the difference between the two cases? In both cases, one man loses his beast, and another man's beast survives. The difference has to do with differences in *knowledge*: by the court, by the dead beast's owner, and by the surviving beast's owner. Greater knowledge establishes greater responsibility (Luke 12:41-48).

This principle of comparative knowledge leads to the conclusion that certain animals that are by nature dangerous, and only marginally and sporadically responsive to human training, are automatically considered notorious. Maimonides defined such animals as those that kill by goring, biting, clawing, or similar action. Following the Mishnah,[11] he listed the wolf, lion, bear, panther, and leopard. He also added snakes, but strangely enough, only those that have bitten in the past.[12] These species would today be classified as "exotic animals." Most communities in the United States place legal restrictions on the private, non-institutional ownership of such animals, and in many cases such ownership is banned by law. To these species should probably be added species of dogs that have been bred to be fighters. The very possession of such breeds places the owners at risk. The individual animal may not be known to be dangerous, but it can be presumed in advance by the owner to be dangerous, and therefore also by the court retroactively.

Limited Knowledge

The court's knowledge is limited, yet it has to have evidence to make a judgment. The only evidence sufficiently reliable to allow the court to presume guilt on the part of a beast is the beast's previous public record. Why must the court presume guilt? Because there is no way for the court to determine guilt with the same degree of accuracy that must prevail in deciding human transgressions of the law, where the innocence of the accused is presumed.[13]

First, let us consider the case of the goring of a prize-winning beast by a previously peaceful ox. The prize-winning beast's owner has to bear the increased risks associated with ownership of a champion beast. He has to assess the risks of putting it in close contact with other beasts. Neither he nor the owner of the previously tame beast had special knowledge of the future behavior of either beast. Neither owner possessed a uniquely inexpensive way to gain such knowledge. Therefore, neither owner is to be assessed by the court with special burdens of responsibility, since the knowledge of each is presumed to be the same. It might have been the champion beast that was the potential killer.

Second, in the case of the owner of a known renegade beast, the court can presume that he had access to better knowledge concerning the behavior of his beast than the dead beast's owner had with respect to either beast. Because the owner of the renegade had greater

---

11. *Baba Kamma* 1:4, *Mishnah*, p. 332.

12. *Torts*, "Laws Concerning Damage by Chattels," Chapter One, Section Six, p. 5.

13. I am speaking here of common law societies. Napoleonic Code societies do presume that the accused is guilty unless proven innocent.

knowledge concerning his beast's behavior—knowledge which was *less expensive* for him to obtain than for the owner of the dead beast to have obtained—the law finds him guilty of negligence. He had the responsibility to keep his beast away from other beasts, especially championship beasts. The *burden of economic responsibility* is different because the *costs of obtaining better knowledge* are different.

This is why "ox for ox" refers to a *replacement of equal value*. The owner of the dead beast is entitled to full-value compensation. Nevertheless, it must be borne in mind that championship beasts can become renegades, too. It would not be fair for the owner of a newly vicious beast that is worth, say, 100 ounces of gold, to be forced to sell his beast and split the proceeds with the victim's owner, just because his beast killed a beast worth, say, one ounce of gold. He is required to pay the owner what it will cost him to buy a replacement beast, but no more. Were it otherwise, it would pay owners of average beasts to place their beasts in close proximity to the champion but possibly violent beast, in the hope that a fight would take place in which the less valuable beast is killed. The Bible does not recommend laws that promote profit-seeking violence.

The owner of the survivor gets to keep the carcass of the dead beast. "If the ox hath used to push [gore] in time past, and his owner hath not kept him in; he shall surely pay ox for ox; and the dead shall be his own." He has paid the owner of the dead beast, ox for ox. But the owner of the dead beast is not entitled to everything. The man who is required to pay at least gets something.

Guilt Is Presumed

Again, this recognizes the limitations of judges to make perfect assessments concerning which beast was responsible. The victim does not lose anything, economically speaking, but he is not given a bonus payment, either. Why doesn't the owner of the survivor owe a penalty payment to the victim? Because the courts cannot ascertain that the renegade was completely responsible. Guilt is *presumed* by the court; it need not be established beyond reasonable doubt, unlike a case involving human behavior. In a legal dispute involving human beings, the present guilt of a previously convicted criminal is not to be presumed by the court; it must be proven. But a decision must be rendered by the court in order to honor God's law and to preserve the juridical foundation of social peace. So the court is required to presume one beast's guilt, and therefore its owner's responsibility.

The Bible is silent with respect to fights between two known renegade beasts, but by an extension of this argument, it can safely be concluded that the first example becomes the standard. The surviving beast is sold and the proceeds are divided. The court cannot presume to know which beast started the fight.

Conclusion

Biblical law favors neither the rich nor the poor. It places a greater burden of responsibility on the owner who has access to better or cheaper information concerning the probable behavior of a domesticated beast under his command. Biblical law implicitly recognizes that *knowledge is not a zero-cost economic resource*, and therefore neither courts nor owners should be treated as if they were omniscient.

Where two beasts with clean records fight, and one is killed, the owners split the proceeds. Where the surviving beast was known to be a greater risk, its owner must fully compensate the victim for his economic loss, on the basis of equal value restored. The court is not required to presume which beast was responsible in the first example, but it is required by God's law to make this presumption automatically in cases involving a known renegade. The important thing, however, is that judgment be rendered by the court. Without judgment, social peace cannot long be maintained.

17

PROPORTIONAL RESTITUTION

If a man shall steal an ox, or a sheep, and kill it, or sell it; he shall restore five oxen for an ox, and four sheep for a sheep. . . . If the theft be certainly found in his hand alive, whether it be ox, or ass, or sheep; he shall restore double (Ex. 22:1, 4).

In any attempted explanation of a Bible passage, we must have as our principle of interpretation the Bible's revelation of the theocentric nature of all existence. God created and now sustains all life. Thus, a sin against a person is first and foremost a sin against God. Restitution must always be made to God. God demands the death of the sinner as the only sufficient lawful restitution payment. But God allows a substitute payment, symbolized in the Old Testament economy by the sacrifice of animals. These symbols pointed forward in time to the death of Jesus Christ, which alone serves as the foundation of all of life (Heb. 8). Jesus Christ made a temporary restitution payment to God in the name of mankind in general (temporal life goes on) and a permanent one for His people (eternal life will come).[1] Adam deserved death on the day he rebelled; God gave him extended life on earth because of the atonement of Christ. The same is true for Adam's biological heirs. We live because of Christ's atonement, and only because of it.

Crimes can also be against men. This means that restitution must be made to the victim, and not just to God. There is no forgiveness apart from restitution: Christ's primarily, and the criminal's secondarily. As images of God, victims are entitled to restitution pay-

---

1. Gary North, *Dominion and Common Grace: The Biblical Basis of Progress* (Tyler, Texas: Institute for Christian Economics, 1987), chaps. 3, 6. The Bible passage that indicates these two aspects of salvation is I Timothy 4:10: "For therefore we both labour and suffer reproach, because we trust in the living God, who is the Saviour of all men, specially of those that believe."

505

ments from criminals. Since crimes differ in terms of their impact on victims, penalties also vary. The biblical principle is a familiar one in Western jurisprudence: the punishment must fit the crime. Since economic restitution is the form that punishment must take in the case of theft, *economic restitution must therefore "fit the crime."* It must fit the crime in at least three ways: first, by restoring to the victim as closely as possible the value of what had been stolen; second, by compensating the victim for his suffering in losing the item or items; third, by compensating the victim for the costs of detecting the thief.

Costs of Retraining: The Traditional Explanation

R. J. Rushdoony's discussion of multiple penalties, which he calls multiple restitution, is important for the light it sheds on the first aspect of restitution, the payment necessary to compensate the victim for the loss he suffered as a result of the theft. Unfortunately, Rushdoony follows rabbinical tradition and introduces an extraneous issue which confuses the discussion, namely, the *use-value of the animals.* He writes: "Multiple restitution rests on the principle of justice. Sheep are capable of a high rate of reproduction and have use, not only as meat, but also by means of their wool, for clothing, as well as other uses. To steal a sheep is to steal the present and future value of a man's property. The ox requires a higher rate of restitution, five-fold, because the ox was trained to pull carts, and to plow, and was used for a variety of farm tasks. The ox therefore had not only the value of its meat and its usefulness, but also the value of its training, in that training an ox for work was a task requiring time and skill. It thus commanded a higher rate of restitution. Clearly, a principle of restitution is in evidence here. Restitution must calculate not only the present and future value of a thing stolen, but also the specialized skills involved in its replacement."[2] Walter Kaiser agrees.[3] The Jewish scholar, Cassuto, argues along similar lines: *"He shall pay five oxen for an ox, and four sheep for a sheep*—less for a sheep than for an ox, possibly because the rearing of a sheep does not require so much, or so prolonged, effort as the rearing of herds."[4] In

---

2. R. J. Rushdoony, *The Institutes of Biblical Law* (Nutley, New Jersey: Craig Press, 1973), pp. 459-60.

3. Walter C. Kaiser, Jr., *Toward Old Testament Ethics* (Grand Rapids, Michigan: Zondervan Academie, 1983), p. 105.

4. U. Cassuto, *A Commentary on the Book of Exodus,* translated by Israel Abrahams (Jerusalem: The Magnes Press, The Hebrew University, [1951] 1974), p. 282.

fact, this interpretation is quite traditional among Jewish scholars.[5]

This interpretation seems to get support from the laws of at least one nation contemporary with ancient Israel. The Hittites also imposed varying penalties according to which animal had been stolen. Anyone who stole a bull and changed its brand, if discovered, had to repay the owner with seven head of cattle: two three-year-olds, three yearlings, and two weanlings.[6] A cow received a five-fold restitution payment.[7] The same penalty was imposed on thieves of stallions and rams.[8] A plow-ox required a 10-fold restitution (previously 15).[9] The same was true of a draft horse.[10] Thus, it appears that trained work animals were evaluated as being worth more to replace than the others. Anyone who recovered a stolen horse, mule, or donkey was to receive an additional animal: double restitution.[11] The original animal that had received training was returned; thus, the thief did not have to pay multiple restitution.

It seems reasonable to conclude that the Bible's higher payment for a sheep or ox is based on the costs of retraining an equivalent animal. But what seems reasonable at first glace turns out to be mistaken.

Discounted Future Value and Capitalization

We need to consider carefully the argument that the higher restitution penalty is related to the increased difficulty of training domestic animals. No doubt it is true that the owner must go to considerable effort to retrain a work animal. But is a sheep a work animal? Does it need training? Obviously not. This should warn us against adopting such an argument regarding any restitution payment that is greater than two-fold.

It is quite true that the future value of any stolen asset must be paid to the victim by the thief. What is not generally understood by non-economists is that *the present market price of an asset already includes its expected future value.* Modern price theory teaches that the present

---

5. See the citations by Nehama Leibowitz, *Studies in Shemot*, Part 2 (Jerusalem: World Zionist Organization, 1976), p. 364.

6. "Hittite Laws," paragraph 60. *Ancient Near Eastern Texts Relating to the Old Testament*, edited by James B. Pritchard (3rd ed.; Princeton, New Jersey: Princeton University Press, 1969), p. 192.

7. *Idem.*, paragraph 67.

8. *Idem.*, paragraphs 61, 62.

9. *Idem.*, paragraph 63.

10. *Idem.*, paragraph 64.

11. *Idem.*, paragraph 70.

price of any scarce economic resource reflects the estimated future value of the asset's net output (net stream of income, or net rents), discounted by the market rate of interest for the time period that corresponds to the expected productive life of the asset.[12] For example, if I expect a piece of land to produce a net economic return (rent) equivalent to one ounce of gold per year for a thousand years, I would be foolish to pay a thousand ounces of gold for it today. The present value to me of my thousandth ounce of gold is vastly higher than the present value to me of a thousandth ounce of gold a thousand and one years in the future. When offering to buy the land, I therefore discount that expected income stream of gold by the longest-term interest rate on the market. So do all my potential competitors (other buyers). The cash payment for the land will therefore be substantially less than the expected rental payments of one thousand ounces of gold.

This discounting process is called *capitalization*. When we capitalize something, we pay a cash price — an actual transaction or an imputed estimation — for a future stream of income. Capitalization stems from the fact, as Rothbard argues, that "Rents from any durable good accrue at different points in time, at different dates in the future. The capital value of any good then becomes the sum of its expected future rents, discounted by the rate of time preference for present over future goods, which is the rate of interest. In short, the capital value of a good is the 'capitalization' of its future rents in accordance with the rate of time preference or interest."[13] This is not a difficult concept to grasp; unfortunately for human freedom and productivity, very few people have ever heard about it.

What is most important to understand is that this discounting process applies to *all* capital goods (including durable consumer goods) in the market; it is not simply the product of a money economy. Monetary exchanges are as bound by the process of discounting expected future income (rents), as are all other transactions. Put a different way, *the phenomenon of interest is basic to human action everywhere and throughout history; it is not a unique product of a money economy.*

If economists could persuade people of this fact, there would be less freedom-restricting legislation such as usury laws. Govern-

---

12. Murray N. Rothbard, *Man, Economy, and State* (New York: New York University Press, [1962] 1979), ch. 7.

13. Murray N. Rothbard, Introduction; Frank A. Fetter, *Capital, Interest, and Rent: Essays in the Theory of Distribution* (Kansas City, Kansas: Sheed Andrews and McMeel, 1977), p. 13.

ments sometimes pass usury laws that establish a price ceiling on interest rates. These laws are almost always applied only on monetary transactions. As with any price control, a usury law will reduce the number of transactions at the coercively fixed price. It will reduce the supply of loanable funds, since lenders do not wish to loan money at an artificially undervalued rate of return.[14] Usury laws are the destroyers of civilization, for they impede the free flow of capital. Indeed, if they could be fully enforced, usury laws that prohibit all interest payments would make impossible the creation of capital goods, for capital goods are the product of 1) human labor (including intellectual insight and entrepreneurship) combined with 2) raw materials 3) over time.[15] All three must be paid for: labor (wages), raw materials (rent), and time (interest). Usury laws deny the legitimate return of the third component of a capital good.[16]

This process of capitalization means that the higher the prevailing interest rate, the smaller the cash payment that a buyer will offer for a piece of land today: the buyer applies a *higher discount* to its ex-

---

14. A low official rate of interest makes it appear as though people are discounting future income at a lower rate than is actually the case. Thus, a legislated (or fiat-money-induced) lower rate of interest will make it appear as though buyers are willing to offer higher prices for land bought by means of long-term debt contracts (mortgages). But this is an illusion created by the government's usury law. In the case of property sold by a seller who is willing to finance the sale by accepting a long-term debt contract from the buyer, he will have to accept a lower price if the market's true rate of interest exceeds the official interest rate ceiling; otherwise the buyer will not buy. A usury law, like any price control, is analogous to placing a limit on a thermometer's scale. A cap on a thermometer does not reduce the fever of the sick person; it simply keeps people from assessing the true conditions. A usury law creates an illusion of a lower rate of discount than market transactors voluntarily agree upon.

15. Rothbard, *Man, Economy, and State*, ch. 6.

16. There is no surer way to identify a crackpot theory of economics than to examine what the economist's theory of interest is. If he denies the legitimacy of interest in morally legitimate profit-seeking transactions, he is not an economist; he is a monetary crank. If he denies interest as a theoretically inescapable tool of economic analysis, he is a true crackpot, as nutty as a man who promotes the idea of the possibility of a perpetual motion machine. But he is far more dangerous: legislators do not listen to "scientists" who would propose making illegal all machines except perpetual motion machines. Legislators have on occasion passed usury laws that are based on the idea that interest is illegitimate. The most precise discussion of interest is still Eugen von Böhm-Bawerk's classic study, *History and Critique of Interest Theories* (1884), which is volume 1 of *Capital and Interest*, 3 vols. (South Holland, Illinois: Libertarian Press, 1959). This publishing firm is now located in Spring Mills, Pennsylvania.

pected stream of income.[17] Always bear in mind, however, that no one knows for certain what the future value of an asset's output will be, nor does anyone know precisely how much the interest rate will fluctuate over the expected productive life of the asset. Obviously, no one is sure just what the productive life of any asset will be. Market forecasting involves a great deal of uncertainty.

Uncertainty is the origin of what some economists call entrepreneurial or "pure" profit.[18] When the estimates of the various competing entrepreneurs — market forecasters-investors[19] — are brought to bear in the capital goods markets, the outcome is a price for any capital asset.[20] Today's demand is a composite of demand for present use (shear, kill, and eat a sheep today) and future use (shear a sheep repeatedly over several years and then kill and eat it). Today's price is the product of the competitive interaction between *today's demand* — which includes an estimation of future demand and an estimation of future supply — and *today's supply.*

----

17. If we expect a lower rate of interest in the future than presently prevails, we will be willing to pay the prevailing cash price, since the annual rate of return will be discounted subsequently by a smaller number. Thus, we buy today at a nice, fat "discount for cash," and we will be able to sell the property later on for a smaller discount for cash when the rate of discount (interest) drops. If we expect rates to rise, we will only buy at less than the prevailing cash market price, which means, of course, that we will not be able to buy it, since the owner can sell it for more to someone else. The new buyer will then suffer economic losses, if our expectation is correct. He will get a smaller "discount for cash" when he buys today, and if he wants to sell later on, he will have to accept a larger discount, since the rate of interest will have risen. The market value of his land will drop.

18. Frank H. Knight, *Risk, Uncertainty, and Profit* (New York: Harper Torchbooks, [1921] 1965). See also Gary North, *The Dominion Covenant: Genesis* (2nd ed.; Tyler, Texas: Institute for Christian Economics, 1987), ch. 23.

19. Some economists distinguish between the capitalist owner-investor and the future-predicting entrepreneur. I have not found this distinction particularly helpful. A forecaster who does not invest capital is not a participant in the market. If someone invests in terms of what the capital-deficient forecaster has said, then the investor becomes the significant participant. Like the race track tout who refuses to invest his own money, and who therefore has no effect on the odds at the ticket window unless he gets someone to bet in terms of his forecasts, so is the entrepreneur who is not a capitalist. Both are economically irrelevant in practice. I prefer to avoid distinctions that are irrelevant in practice. For examples of this distinction, see Israel Kirzner, *Competition and Entrepreneurship* (University of Chicago Press, 1973), pp. 47-52; Henry Manne, *Insider Trading and the Stock Market* (New York: Free Press, 1966), pp. 117-19.

20. Yes, there can be various prices, depending on market information concerning other buyers and sellers, including substitute producer goods, as well as transportation costs, insurance rates, and so forth. But the tendency of competition is to produce a single market price for a given piece of equipment in a particular geographical region.

In short, the present price of any scarce economic resource already includes its expected future price, discounted by the applicable period's market rate of interest.[21]

I. The Economics of Restitution

Having said this, we now consider the economics of restitution. The task of the judges in estimating a morally legitimate restitution payment is easier than it seems. Judges can safely ignore the question of just how much the future value of a stolen asset might be. The best experts in forecasting economic value — entrepreneurs — have already provided this information to the judges, all nicely discounted by the market rate of interest. The judges need only use *existing market prices* in order to compute restitution payments.

A restitution payment is normally twice the prevailing market price of the asset. When the stolen ox is returned by the authorities to the owner (the thief neither slaughtered it nor sold it), the thief pays double restitution. "If the theft be certainly found in his hand alive, whether it be ox, or ass, or sheep; he shall restore double" (Ex. 22:4). Rushdoony follows the traditional rabbinical interpretation when he argues that this 100 percent penalty above the market price is the minimum amount by which the thief expected to profit from his action.[22] The thief must return the original beast, plus his expected minimum "profit" from the transaction, namely, the market value of the stolen beast. He forfeits that which he had expected to gain. Maimonides wrote of the requirement that the thief pay double: "He thus loses an amount equal to that of which he wished to deprive another."[23] Akedat Yizhak concurs: "The thief is treated differently from the one who causes damage. The latter who caused damage through his ox or pit did not intend to deprive his fellow of anything. He is therefore only required to make half or total restitution. The thief who deliberately sets out to inflict loss on his fellow deserves to have a taste of his own medicine — to lose the same amount that he deprived his fellow of. This can only be achieved

---

21. The prevailing rate of interest for loans of any given duration, like the prevailing price of any asset, is the product of the best guesses of entrepreneurs (speculators) concerning the future of interest rates of that duration.

22. Rushdoony, *Institutes*, p. 460.

23. Moses Maimonides, *The Book of Torts*, vol. 11 of *The Code of Maimonides*, 14 vols. (New Haven, Connecticut: Yale University Press, [1180] 1954), "Laws Concerning Theft," Chapter One, Section Four, p. 60.

through double restitution."[24] This is analogous to the perjurer who is subject to the judicial penalty which his lie, had it been believed by the judges, would have imposed on the innocent person (Deut. 19:16-21).[25]

Victim's Rights

"If a man shall steal an ox, or a sheep, and kill it, or sell it; he shall restore five oxen for an ox, and four sheep for a sheep" (Ex. 22:1). What if a stolen sheep or ox had been sold by the thief? The thief may know where the animal is. If the authorities convict him of the crime, would he be given an opportunity to buy back the stolen animal and return it to the owner, plus the 100 percent penalty, and thereby avoid the four-fold or five-fold restitution penalty? This would seem to violate the third goal of proportional restitution (see below): increasing the risk for thieves who steal sheep or oxen, and who then dispose of the evidence by destroying them or selling them, thereby making it more difficult to convict them in court. The thief would still have to pay the four-fold or five-fold penalty, *unless the victim decides otherwise*. The fundamental judicial principle here is *victim's rights*. The victim decides the penalty, up to the limits of the law.

The victimized original owner should always have the authority to offer the convicted criminal an alternative which is more to the victim's liking. Perhaps he is emotionally attached to the missing ox, especially if he personally trained it. He may even be attached emotionally to the stolen sheep — less likely, I suspect, than attachment to an ox that he had personally trained. What if he offers to accept double restitution if 1) the criminal will tell him where the sold beast is, and 2) the beast is returned to him alive? What if the thief then tells the victim and the civil authorities where the missing beast is? The authorities would then compel the new owner — who, legally speaking, is not truly an owner, as we shall see — to return the animal to the original owner.

The buyer of the stolen beast now has neither beast nor the forfeited purchase price. He has become the thief's victim. The thief therefore owes him some sort of restitution payment. The question is: How much? This is a difficult question to answer. It would be either a 20 percent penalty or a 100 percent penalty. I believe that it is a 20 percent penalty.

---

24. Cited by Leibowitz, *Studies in Shemot*, p. 362.

25. This section of Deuteronomy is explicitly a case-law application of the "eye for eye" principle.

Timely Confession Receives Its Appropriate Reward

Here is my reasoning. Say that the convicted thief confesses his crime of having either sold or slaughtered the stolen beast. The court is not sure which he did, but the penalty is the same in either case: four-fold (sheep) or five-fold (ox) restitution. In an attempt to persuade the original owner to accept the return of his animal plus a 100 percent penalty, he now confesses that he sold it. Say that the owner agrees to accept two-fold restitution if the thief can get the animal back (the victim need not consent to this). The thief must now return the stolen beast. He goes to the buyer and tells him that the animal was stolen and must be returned to the original owner. He now also owes the victimized buyer the purchase price of the beast, plus a penalty payment of 20 percent (Lev. 6:2-5).

If the initial buyer has already sold the beast, then it is the responsibility of the thief, not the buyer, to trace down its present location. The person who has final possession when the State intervenes and requires him to return it to its original owner is the defrauded buyer to whom the thief owes the restitution payment. Because the "bundle of rights" associated with legal ownership could not be transferred by the thief to the various buyers, the final buyer has no legal claim on the animal. He is in receipt of stolen goods.

By cooperating with the original victim, the thief may be able to reduce his overall liability. Instead of paying the original owner five-fold restitution for an ox, he now pays less. How much less is determined by the victim. Let us assume that the victim agrees to two-fold restitution. First, the thief agrees to return the stolen beast to the true owner: basic restitution. Second, the thief then must pay that person the equivalent value of the beast. Third, he also owes the defrauded purchaser the return of his purchase price plus a penalty of 20 percent. Thus, in this example, he pays 3.2-fold restitution, plus the cost of locating and transporting the beast, rather than five-fold or four-fold restitution. Obviously, the thief is better off if he cooperates with the true owner, and tells him who bought the stolen ox or sheep from him.

Why assume that the thief only owes the victimized buyer 20 percent? Because biblical law recognizes that thieves have *better information* about what they did than other people do. It is best for the law to offer thieves a reduced penalty for confession in order to elicit better information from them before the costs of the trial must be borne. To encourage the criminal to tell the truth, there has to be a threat hanging over him: the possibility that someone with the missing information will come to the judges and present it. Thus, if the thief remains silent about the person who bought the sheep or ox, he bears greater risk.

The Silent Thief

A silent thief faces an additional threat. Assume that the original owner demands four-fold (sheep) or five-fold (ox) restitution. Still, the thief says nothing because he knows that if he admits that he sold the beast, he will also have to pay the victimized buyer 120 percent, yet the original owner may nevertheless refuse to deal with him, and may demand (as is his legal right) either four-fold or five-fold restitution. Once the thief has sold a stolen a sheep or ox, the victim can legally demand the higher penalty payment. The victim is owed the four-fold or five-fold restitution whether or not the thief locates the stolen beast, buys it back, and returns it to its original owner. *The very act of selling a stolen ox or sheep invokes the law's full penalty.* It is very much like the crime of kidnapping; the family of the kidnapped victim or the judge or the jury can legally insist on the death penalty even if the kidnapper offers to identify the person to whom the victim had been sold into bondage.

Why would the thief remain silent about the whereabouts of the stolen animal? One reason might be his fear of revenge from an accomplice in the crime. Laying this motivation aside, let us consider other possible motivations for the thief's remaining silent. First and foremost, the thief may believe that he will not be convicted of the crime. After all, the beast is missing. It is not in the thief's possession. Second, he may believe that the victim is hard-hearted and will insist on the maximum restitution payment even if the thief can get the beast back by identifying the defrauded buyer and paying him the purchase price plus a penalty payment of 20 percent.

He remains silent. He may be convicted anyway. If so, he now faces a new problem: he not only owes four-fold or five-fold restitution to the victim, he could also wind up owing the victimized buyer whatever the buyer paid him for the stolen animal. Why? Because the victimized buyer may later discover that he has purchased a stolen beast. If he then remains silent, he breaks the law. He is a recipient of stolen goods. He has become an accomplice of the thief. His silence condemns him. Additionally, he may feel guilty because he is not its legal owner.

How can the defrauded buyer escape these burdens? He can go to the original owner who has already received full restitution from the thief (or from the person who has purchased the thief as a slave), and offer to sell the animal back to him. Once the victimized buyer identifies himself, the thief now owes restitution to the defrauded buyer: double restitution, minus the purchase price that the defrauded buyer receives from the original owner. The thief has stolen from the buyer through fraud. As is the case with any other victim of unconfessed theft, the defrauded buyer is entitled to double restitution from the thief. Therefore, as soon as the thief gets through paying his debt to the original owner, he then must pay the victimized buyer the penalty payment.

If the original owner declines to buy the beast, the buyer becomes its legal owner. The original owner does not want it back. He has also been paid: restitution from the thief. But the defrauded buyer remains a victim. He keeps the beast, but he is also entitled to restitution from the thief equal to the original purchase price charged by the thief.

If the thief confesses before the trial, he can avoid the risk of the extra payment to the defrauded buyer. Even if the victim demands four-fold or five-fold restitution, by paying it, the thief thereby becomes the owner of the beast. *The criminal's act of timely confession, plus his agreement to pay full restitution to the victim, atones judicially for the theft.*[26]

But what about the defrauding of the buyer? I think the confessed thief would owe the buyer a restitution payment of 20 percent of the purchase price because he had involved the buyer in an illegal transaction. Having repaid both owner and buyer, he has legitimized the new ownership arrangement. The buyer has gained full legal title to the animal plus restitution, so he is no longer a defrauded buyer. He now has no additional complaint against the thief. He cannot demand any additional restitution payments.

Without confession and restitution, the thief would owe the buyer at least 100 percent restitution if discovered, which is an important economic incentive in getting the buyer to identify himself. Thus, the thief's silence at the trial regarding the existence of a defrauded buyer hangs over him continually.[27]

---

26. Obviously, I am speaking here only of the earthly court. Atonement means "covering."

27. If the victimized buyer waits for several years before identifying the stolen beast, the court might decide that the stolen beast has aged too much, and that it constitutes half of the payment owed. Still, the thief would have to make the 100% penalty payment to him.

Let us assume that he is convicted. He pays his maximum restitution to the victim. He still has an economic incentive to confess.
He tells the judges that he had sold the animal. He tells them who
the defrauded buyer is. He now owes the defrauded buyer the 20
percent restitution payment. This is better than paying the defrauded buyer 100 percent (or two-fold restitution minus any repurchase price from the original owner), should the buyer learn that
the beast was stolen property and decide to confess to the original
owner or the judges.

Biblical law puts a premium on timely confession. The criminal
who confesses receives a lighter penalty than the criminal who refuses to confess, and who is then subsequently convicted.[28] There is
an economic incentive for him to confess. There is also an economic
threat if he refuses to confess: the possibility of two-fold restitution
provides an incentive for a defrauded buyer to reveal the existence of
the stolen animal to the original owner. The Bible's penalty structure
for theft provides economic incentives for all parties to present accurate information to the civil authorities. Once again, biblical law
recognizes that accurate information is not a zero-price resource.

Considering an Alternative Arrangement

If there were no risk to the thief attached to his remaining silent,
what would be his economic incentive to tell the owner that he knows
where the stolen beast is? I can see none. Assume that the thief owes
no mandatory penalty payment to the defrauded buyer once he has
paid restitution to the victim. He pays full restitution to the owner,
and the defrauded buyer then hears about this, realizes that he has
purchased stolen property, and comes to the owner. He offers to sell
back the missing beast to the owner at the market price the beast was
worth to the owner when the beast was stolen (presumably, the price
he paid to the thief). If the thief owes nothing to the defrauded
buyer, he is still out only four-fold or five-fold restitution by having
concealed evidence. He is under no additional financial obligation.

What is wrong with this interpretation of the restitution statutes?
Answer: the thief has entangled the buyer in an illegal transaction

---

28. In modern U.S. jurisprudence, plea bargaining is used by defense attorneys
to reduce their clients' sentences by persuading criminals to confess to milder crimes
than they actually committed. In biblical law, the criminal also is given an opportunity to escape a heavier sentence by confessing before the trial; the confessed
crime, however, remains the same.

that was inherently filled with uncertainty for the buyer. The latter might have been convicted of being a "fence"—a professional receiver of stolen goods. He has therefore been defrauded by the thief. He deserves restitution.

What if the original owner says that he does not want to buy the beast from the defrauded buyer? The buyer has now in effect purchased the beast from its rightful owner. He now owns the "bundle of rights" associated with true ownership. But the thief has nevertheless exposed him to the discomfort of being involved in an illegal transaction. Shouldn't the thief still owe the seller a 100 percent restitution payment? My assessment of the principle of victim's rights leads me to conclude that biblical law does in principle allow the defrauded buyer to come to the judges and have them compel the thief to pay him 100 percent of the price he had paid the thief. This has nothing to do with whether he has sold the beast to the original owner or whether the owner has allowed him to retain legal possession of it.

Transferring Lawful Title

Why must we regard the sale of the animal as fraudulent? Why can the authorities legitimately demand that the purchaser return the animal to the original owner? Because the thief implicitly and possibly explicitly pretended to be transferring an asset that he did not possess: *lawful title*. The thief did not possess lawful title to the property. This illuminates a fundamental principle of biblical ownership: *whatever someone does not legally own, he cannot legally sell*. Ownership is not simply possession of a thing; it is possession of certain *legal immunities* associated with the thing. It involves above all the *right to exclude*. Writes economist-legal theorist Richard Posner: "A property right, in both law and economics, is a right to exclude everyone else from the use of some scarce resource."[29] This right to exclude was never owned by the thief; therefore, he cannot transfer this bundle of legal immunities to the purchaser. The purchaser can legally demand compensation from the thief, but he does not lawfully own the stolen item. The civil authorities can legitimately compel the buyer to transfer the property back to the thief, who then returns it to the original owner, or else compel him to return it directly to the original owner.

The explicit language of the kidnapping statute provides us with the legal foundation of this conclusion regarding the transfer of own-

---

29. Richard A. Posner, *The Economics of Justice* (Cambridge, Massachusetts: Harvard University Press, 1983), p. 70.

ership. "And he that stealeth a man, and selleth him, or if he be found in his hand, he shall surely be put to death" (Ex. 21:16). Even to have a stolen man in your possession was a capital crime, unless you could prove that you did not know that he or she was stolen. Just because a kidnapper sold you a stolen person as a slave did not mean that this person would remain in your possession as a slave. The same was true of other property. It still is true.

English common law does not recognize this biblical standard. Receiving stolen goods was not made a crime until the nineteenth century. Common law had recognized no such crime; it took statute law to make it a crime.[30] While it is no doubt true that it is expensive to research every title before making a purchase, especially in a premodern society, the responsibility to do so is biblically inescapable if the buyer wishes to reduce his risk of purchasing stolen goods — goods that must be returned to the original owner. Not only is the childhood chant of "finders, keepers; losers, weepers" not biblical, neither is common law's "buyers, keepers; victims, weepers." A far better rule is the traditional *caveat emptor*: let the buyer beware.

What if the thief has already spent the purchase money, and is therefore unable to repay the defrauded buyer? Say that the thief confesses, and the original victim agrees to accept two-fold restitution if the original beast is returned to him unharmed. The thief owes the restitution payment (the animal) to the original owner, plus the 100 percent penalty; he also owes the purchase price plus 20 percent restitution to the defrauded buyer. It may take him years to repay. Who has first claim on the thief's money? The original owner does. He is the primary earthly victim. He made the offer or at least accepted a reduced payment from the thief. Without his willingness to accept less, he would have been entitled to four-fold (sheep) or five-fold (ox) restitution. For him to grant legal relief to the thief in exchange for the return of the stolen animal, he will presumably want at least double restitution.

The defrauded buyer has had to forfeit both the purchase price and the stolen animal, which must be returned to the true owner. The initial claim to restitution belongs to the owner of the beast, which has now been returned to him, leaving the purchaser with neither money nor beast. The defrauded buyer has now become the primary

---

30. Wayne LaFave and Austin Scott, Jr., *Handbook on Criminal Law* (Minneapolis, Minnesota: West, 1972), pp. 681-91: "Receiving Stolen Property." My thanks to Prof. Gary Amos for this reference.

economic victim of the thief. This position as *secondary legal victim* but primary economic victim imposes added risks on buyers: they must take special care to see to it that the goods they purchase are accompanied by valid titles. If the original owner is willing to bargain with the convicted thief, the purchaser then becomes the major loser. Legal initiative lies with the initial victim of the theft. Under biblical law, it pays buyers of goods or valuable information to be sure they are buying legal title as well.

II. Protecting the Victims

We think of the criminal's victims as being people who have lost their animals or money. But there are other victims: the animals themselves. This is analogous to the crime of kidnapping. The restitution system that the Bible establishes for oxen and sheep reflects this special concern by God for helpless animals. What makes sheep and oxen special is their status in the Old Testament as symbolically helpless animals. So, biblical law protects both the animals and their owners. Let us consider each in turn.

A. Symbolically Helpless Animals

Why the requirement of five-fold restitution for a slaughtered or sold ox? Oxen require training, meaning a capital investment by the owner, in order to make them effective servants of man in the tasks of dominion, but so do other animals, such as horses and donkeys, yet only two-fold restitution is required for them. Also, a thief who is found with a living ox in his possession pays only double restitution. What makes a slaughtered or sold ox different? Answer: *the ox is symbolic of the employed servant*. It is my contention that this symbolism has more to do with its five-fold restitution penalty than the value of its training does.

The law forbids the muzzling of oxen when they are working in the field (Deut. 25:4). Paul cited this verse on two occasions: first, to make the point that God cares for His people, and that our spiritual labors will not be in vain (I Cor. 9:9); second, to point out that the laborer is worthy of his reward, and that elders in the church are worthy of double honor (I Tim. 5:17-18). It pays to train an ox, just as it pays to train human workers in their jobs. Unquestionably, a trained ox is worth more to the owner than an untrained steer, just as a trained worker is worth more than an unskilled worker, and just as an elder is deserving of double honor (payment). Furthermore, the ox is a dominion beast, but the steer is only a source of food and leather. The ox is productive until the day it is killed by man or beast; the steer is simply fattened for the slaughter.

Sheep are undoubtedly quite different from oxen. They are stupid animals. Shepherds care for them, sheep dogs monitor their movements, but wise men do not invest a lot of time and energy in trying to train them for service. They are not active work animals like oxen, which pull plows; they are far more passive. A sheep is in fact the *classic passive animal* — an animal whose main purpose in life is to get *sheared*. They are helpless. For this reason, they are symbolic in the Bible of the poor.[31]

How do we make sense of the four-fold restitution payment for a stolen sheep which is subsequently killed or sold by the thief? Why is this loss (as indicated by the size of the restitution payment) so great to the owner, compared to the double restitution payment he receives if the stolen sheep is restored to him by the thief? Economic analysis of a sheep's output does not throw much light on this problem, except in a negative sense: there is no strictly economic reason. A beast of burden such as a donkey has to be trained, and was unquestionably a valuable asset in the Old Testament economy. So was a horse. Yet neither slaughtered horses nor slaughtered donkeys are singled out in the law as entitling their owners to four-fold or five-fold restitution. What is so special about a sheep? Is its wool production that much more valuable than the economic output of a horse or donkey? Clearly, the answer is in the negative. We are forced to conclude that the distinguishing characteristic between a slaughtered stolen donkey and a slaughtered stolen sheep has nothing to do with the comparative economic value of each beast's output. Instead, it has a great deal to do with the sheep's *symbolic subordinate relationship to the owner.*

Of Sheep and Men

In the Bible, animals *image* man.[32] Sheep are specifically compared to men throughout the Bible, with God as the Shepherd and

---

31. James B. Jordan, *The Law of the Covenant: An Exposition of Exodus 21-23* (Tyler, Texas: Institute for Christian Economics, 1984), pp. 267-69.

32. Animals in men's image: *ibid.*, p. 122. He cites Prov. 6:6; 26:11; 30:15, 19, 24-31; Dan. 5:21; Ex. 13:2, 13. When I use the noun "image" as a verb, I am reminded of one cynic's remark: "There is no noun in the English language that cannot be verbed."

men as helpless dependents. The twenty-third psalm makes use of the imagery of the shepherd and sheep. David, a shepherd, compares himself to a sheep, for God is described as his shepherd (Ps. 23:1). Christ called Himself the "good shepherd" who gives His life for His sheep (John 10:11). He said to His disciples on the night of His capture by the authorities, citing Zechariah 13:7, "All ye shall be offended because of me this night: for it is written, I will smite the shepherd, and the sheep of the flock shall be scattered abroad" (Matt. 26:31). He referred to the Jews as "the lost sheep of the house of Israel" (Matt. 10:6), echoing Jeremiah, "Israel is a scattered sheep" (Jer. 50:17a) and Ezekiel, "And they were scattered, because there is no shepherd: and they became meat to all the beasts of the field, when they were scattered" (Ezk. 34:5). Christ spoke of children as sheep, and offered the analogy of the man who loses one sheep out of a hundred. The man searches diligently to locate that one lost sheep and rejoices if he finds it. "Even so it is not the will of your Father which is in heaven, that one of these little ones should perish" (Matt. 18:14).

It is thus the *helplessness* of sheep rather than their value as beasts of burden or dominion that makes four-fold restitution mandatory.[33] Shepherds regard sheep as their special responsibility. The position of sheep is therefore unique. *Sheep are representative of the utter helplessness of men.* An attack on the sheep under a man's control strikes at his position as a covenantally responsible steward. David risked his life to save a lamb (or perhaps lambs) captured by a bear and a lion, and he slew them both (I Sam. 17:34-36), taking the lamb, apparently unharmed, out of the mouth of the lion: "I caught him by his beard" (v. 35). As God had delivered him out of the paw of both lion and bear, David told Saul, so would He deliver him out of the hand of Goliath (v. 37). Again, David was comparing himself (and Israel) with the lamb, and comparing God with the shepherd. Thus, the recovery of a specific lost or stolen sheep is important to a faithful shepherd or owner, not just a replacement animal.

Perhaps the best example of sheep as a symbol for defenseless humans is found in Nathan's confrontation with King David con-

---

33. Maimonides ignored all this when he insisted that if a thief "butchers or sells on the owner's premises (an animal stolen there), he need not pay fourfold or fivefold. But if he lifts the object up, he is liable for theft even before he removes it from the owner's premises. Thus, if one steals a lamb from a fold and it dies on the owner's premises while he is pulling it away, he is exempt. But if he picks it up, or takes it off the owner's premises and it then dies, he is liable." Maimonides, *Torts*, "Laws Concerning Theft," Chapter Two, Section Sixteen, p. 67.

cerning his adultery with Bathsheba, wife of Uriah the Hittite. Nathan proposed a legal case for David to judge. A rich man steals a female lamb from a poor neighbor, and then kills it. "And David's anger was greatly kindled against the man; and he said to Nathan, As the LORD liveth, the man that hath done this thing shall surely die: And he shall restore the lamb fourfold, because he did this thing, and because he had no pity" (II Sam. 12:5-6). Then Nathan replied to him, "Thou art the man." Uriah had been the neighbor; Bathsheba is the ewe lamb who, biblically speaking, has been killed, the death penalty being applicable in cases of adultery (Lev. 20:10).

David recognized that the four-fold restitution was applicable in the case of stolen and slaughtered sheep. But in fact, Nathan was not talking about a lamb; he was talking about a human being. He used the symbol of the slaughtered sheep for the foolish woman who consented to the capital crime of adultery. The woman had been entitled to protection, especially by the king. Instead, she had been placed in jeopardy of her life by the king. The king had proven himself to be an evil shepherd.

What was the penalty extracted by God? First, the infant born of the illicit union would die, Nathan promised (II Sam. 12:14). On the seventh day, the day before its circumcision, the child died (v. 18). The next section of Second Samuel records the rape of Tamar by David's son Amnon. Absalom, her brother, commanded his servants to kill Amnon, which they did (II Sam. 13:29). Absalom revolted against David and was later slain by Joab (II Sam. 18:14). Finally, Adonijah attempted to steal the throne, but Solomon was anointed (I Ki. 1), and Adonijah tried again to secure the throne by asking Solomon to allow him to marry David's bed-warmer. Solomon recognized this attempt to gain the throne through marriage, and had him executed (I Ki. 2:24-25). Thus, four of David's sons died, fulfilling the required four-for-one punishment for his adultery and his murder of Uriah.[34]

---

34. The Jewish scholar Brichto recognizes the connection between Exodus 22:1 and the death of four of David's sons. His comment on the fourth of the four-fold penalty that God imposed on David is pertinent: "The execution of Adonijah, occurring after David's death has, in this context, escaped general notice: even of scholars, who have been conditioned not to count as significant (for biblical man) what happens to a man's son(s) after his demise." Herbert Chanan Brichto, "Kin, Cult, Land and Afterlife — A Biblical Complex," *Hebrew Union College Annual*, XLIV (1973), p. 42.

Shepherds and Sheep

By striking at a man's lawful position of personal stewardship, the sheep-stealer takes an extra risk. It is far less risky to steal gold or silver and then sell it than to steal and sell a sheep; he will pay only two-fold restitution if he is captured for stealing and then selling gold. The sheep-stealer strikes at the very heart of a man's dominion assignment, in which a man has invested love and care on helpless, dependent beasts. *The shepherd's calling (vocation) is the archetypal calling: it points analogically to the cosmic personalism and providential goodness of God.* It is therefore specially defended by biblical law.

We see the archetypal nature of the shepherd's calling in the office of church elder. We call ministers of the gospel "pastors," a word derived from the same root as "pastoral." They are shepherds. Christ three times told Peter that his task would be to feed Christ's sheep (John 21:15-17). Peter later instructed elders of the church to "Feed the flock of God which is among you, taking the oversight thereof" (I Pet. 5:2a). The shepherd's role as caretaker and protector is analogous to God's care and protection of the world and Christ's care and protection of His church (John 10).

It is significant that the Israelites had been shepherds of cattle and sheep when they came into Egypt. The Egyptians despised shepherds. Because of this, Joseph instructed his brothers to ask Pharaoh for a separate land, Goshen, where the Hebrews would not come into contact with the Egyptians (Gen. 46:33-34). God's law, delivered so soon after their escape from a land in which their calling was despised, dealt with that calling and its risks and responsibilities.

The Egyptians had despised shepherds, whose task is to care for flocks. These same Egyptians had placed the Israelites in bondage. The Egyptians were repulsed by an occupation that is based on a covenantal model of God's responsibility for the care and protection of His people. They were also repulsed by the concept of a society based on the idea of a ruler's covenantal responsibility for the care and protection of men. This hostility is understandable: Egypt was a bureaucratic, tyrannical State.[35] The Hebrews' experience in Egypt was designed by God to teach them that men are not allowed to do to cattle and sheep something that they are unquestionably not to do to other men: treat them unmercifully and carelessly or steal them and

---

35. Gary North, *Moses and Pharaoh: Dominion Religion vs. Power Religion* (Tyler, Texas: Institute for Christian Economics, 1985), ch. 2: "Imperial Bureaucracy."

illegally slaughter them. Thus, God imposed His four-fold restitution on the Egyptians: He destroyed them.

Sheep, being stupid, are inescapably dependent. They have to trust their master if they are to survive. The shepherd is not to betray this personal trust until it is time to kill the sheep for food or, in Old Testament times, for sacrifice. Christ pointed to the intimate relationship between the shepherd and his sheep: "And when he putteth forth his own sheep, he goeth before them, and the sheep follow him: for they know his voice. And a stranger will they not follow, but will flee from him: for they know not the voice of strangers" (John 10:4-5). When removed from the care of their shepherd, forcibly or otherwise, the sheep become lost.

Symbolism or Training?

At this point, I must resort to a somewhat speculative hypothesis in order to make sense out of the four-fold restitution payment for a missing or dead sheep and the five-fold restitution payment for a missing or dead ox. I am arguing that the high penalties are imposed because of the symbolic nature of sheep and oxen, although I cannot absolutely prove it.[36] But to make sense of Exodus 22:1, we have to go beyond considerations of strictly financial profit and loss. Economics as such does not provide a clear-cut answer to a fundamental question: *Why doesn't God's law impose five-fold or four-fold restitution payments for the slaughter or sale of stolen horses or donkeys or other beasts of burden (dominion)?* They require the capital investment of training, just as an ox does. The value of this training is forfeited when the thief cannot return the actual stolen beast to the owner. We might presume that the principle of the four-fold and five-fold restitution payment does, by implication, apply to these other beasts, if they have received training or other capital investments that set them apart from untrained beasts of the same species. Nevertheless, the Bible never says this explicitly. It specifically singles out sheep and oxen. Why?

I see two possible reasons. First, unlike horses, donkeys, and other domesticated animals that might be trainable, sheep and oxen were commonly *slaughtered and eaten*, as they are today. Thus, they

---

36. Jordan, *Law of the Covenant*, Appendix G. I discussed my thesis in the present chapter with Jordan prior to the publication of his book, and he expanded on the idea.

need special protection from thieves. A thief who slaughters an ox or sheep is subject to more stringent penalties. The higher penalty tends to restrain him in his blood-letting. This is a more strictly economic argument, one based on the economic effects of the law. Second, both sheep and oxen are *symbolic in the Bible of mankind*: oxen for men of power or office, and sheep for dependent, spiritually helpless people. Oxen are normally peaceful, dominion beasts that are used for plowing the fields, never for war. Sheep are passive creatures that require special care on the part of shepherds. Thus, as archetypes of man in his relationship to God—*creatures in need of care*—oxen and sheep receive special consideration by the law.

Why a five-fold restitution payment for oxen? Why not four-fold? Probably because oxen are beasts of burden and therefore living tools of dominion. They are dependent,[37] though not so dependent as sheep, but they are also symbolic of God's dominion covenant. The number five is associated with the covenant in the Bible. Also, Israel marched in military formations based on the number five.[38] The number five is associated with dominion. By killing a stolen ox, the thief is symbolically sacrificing another person's economic future for the sake of his own present enjoyment. This is what Satan attempted to do to Adam, and only the grace of God in Christ prevented Satan's successful slaughtering of humanity.

This law of restitution singles out oxen and sheep as being special creatures. Other passages in the Bible do the same. What the stringent restitution penalties of Exodus 22:1 point to is a general principle: *how you treat oxen and sheep is indicative of how you treat other men.* The ox is worthy of his hire; how much more a man! The sheep is helpless, and is deserving of protection; how much more a man! A society whose legal order protects oxen and sheep from thieves who would slaughter them is a society whose legal order is likely also to protect men from oppression, kidnapping, and murder. A biblical social order offers special protection to oxen, sheep, and men.[39]

---

37. I believe that the male ox in this case law is castrated and not a bull. Castration reduces its threat to men, yet the animal's strength can still be harnessed for man's purposes. It is more dependent on man than a bull would be.

38. James B. Jordan, *The Sociology of the Church* (Tyler, Texas: Geneva Ministries, 1986), pp. 215-16.

39. David Daube's comments on the four-fold and five-fold restitution requirements acknowledge none of this. Instead, he returns to his favorite theme, like a dog returns to its vomit: the "later addition" thesis. He contrasts the two-fold restitution requirement with the four-fold and five-fold requirements. The higher penalties are

B. Owners

The penalty paid to the victim by the criminal *compensates him for his trouble*, while it simultaneously serves as a *deterrent to future criminal behavior*. Biblical restitution achieves both goals — compensation of the victim and deterrence of criminal behavior — by means of a single judicial penalty: restitution. In contrast, modern humanistic jurisprudence has until quite recently ignored the needs of the victim by ignoring restitution.[40] Edward Levi, who served as President Gerald

---

evidence of an earlier law. ". . . the older rule makes a rather primitive distinction between theft of an ox and theft of a sheep: for one ox you have to give five, but for one sheep only four. No such distinction occurs in the later rule. Whatever kind of animal you steal, you have to restore two for one." Daube, *Studies in Biblical Law* (Cambridge: At the University Press, 1947), pp. 94-95. He uses a similar line of argumentation to distinguish Exodus 21:28-31 from 21:35-36: *ibid.*, pp. 86-87.

40. This two-fold purpose of criminal law was ignored by modern American jurisprudence until the 1960's, when the subject of restitution to victims at last became a topic of discussion among legislators and law enforcement authorities. Cf. Burt Galaway and Joe Hudson (eds.), *Offender Restitution in Theory and Action* (Lexington, Massachusetts: Lexington Books, 1977); Randy E. Barnett and John Hegel III (eds.), *Assessing the Criminal: Restitution, Retribution, and the Legal Process* (Cambridge, Massachusetts: Ballinger, 1977). See the special feature, "Crime and the Victim," in *Trial* (May/June 1972), the national legal news magazine of the American Trial Lawyers Association.

The Department of Corrections of Minneapolis, Minnesota began a "restitution and release" experimental program in 1974, the Minnesota Restitution Center, in which criminals involved in crimes against other people's property compensate the victims. Only 28 men were admitted to the experiment during its first year. Violent criminals were not accepted: *Los Angeles Times* (April 21, 1974). By 1978, 24 of the 50 states in the United States had adopted some form of compensation to victims of violent crimes.

This policy had begun in the mid-1960's in Great Britain. In the United States, the first state to introduce such a program was California, in 1965. Such costs as legal fees, money lost as a result of the injured person's absence from work, and medical expenses are covered in some states. In cases of death or permanent disability, maximum payments were anywhere from $10,000 to $50,000. Average payments in 1978 were $3,000 to $4,000 (with the price of gold in the $175-240 per ounce range). Nonviolent crimes were not covered, nor were property losses in violent crimes. Only a small percentage of citizens are aware of these laws; only a small percentage (1% to 3%) of victims received such payments. Also, the states compensated victims from state treasuries; the criminals did not make the payments: *U.S. News and World Report* (July 24, 1978). Predictably, state officials want the federal government to fund most of these payments. A bill to pay 90% of such costs through the Law Enforcement Assistance Administration (L.E.A.A.), the Victims of Crime Act, passed the U.S. Senate in 1973, but did not pass the House and was not signed into law. Hearings were held in 1972 and 1973. It was a sufficiently important topic to be included in Major Issues System of the Congressional Research Service of the Library of Congress beginning in 1974: *Crime: Compensation for Victims and Survivors*, Issue Brief 74014.

Ford's Attorney General (1974-76), pinpointed the origin of the penitentiary: the ideal of the savior State. "While the existence of jails dates back to medieval times, the idea of penitentiaries is modern — indeed, it is American. Largely it is the product of the Quaker notion that if a wrongdoer were separated from his companions, given a great length of time to think about his misdeeds, and with the help of prayer, he would mend his ways. This late-18th-century concept was the beginning of what has come to be known as the rehabilitative ideal."[41] Here is the great irony: it was Quaker theology that led both to the freeing of the slaves and the imprisoning of criminals whose productivity should be put into service of their victims. Prior to the rise of Quaker jurisprudence, Roger Campbell reports, "Massachusetts law in 1736 provided that a thief should be whipped or fined for his first offense. The second time he was apprehended and proven guilty of that crime he would be required to pay three times the value of the property stolen to the victim and was forced to sit on the gallows for one hour with a rope around his neck. On the third offence, the trip to the gallows was for real."[42]

Restitution and Deterrence

We are required by God always to begin our analysis of any problem with the operating presupposition of the theocentric nature of all existence. Modern jurisprudence refuses to begin with God. It begins with man and man's needs, and generally progresses to the State and the State's needs. This is why modern jurisprudence is in near-chaos. It is also why the court system is in near-chaos.[43]

Deterring God's Wrath in History

Whenever we speak of deterring crime, we must speak first of the deterrence of God's wrath against the community because of the courts' unwillingness to impose God's justice within the community. The civil government is required by God to seek to deter crimes be-

---

41. Edward H. Levi, speech at the dedication ceremony for the Federal Bureau of Prisons Detention Center, Chicago, Illinois, October 15, 1975; cited in Roger F. Campbell, *Justice Through Restitution: Making Criminals Pay* (Milford, Michigan: Mott Media, 1977), p. 63. By far, the best historical account of this transition from town punishments to the state penitentiary system is David J. Rothman's prize-winning study, *The Discovery of the Asylum: Social Order and Disorder in the New Republic* (Boston: Little, Brown, 1971).

42. *Ibid.*, p. 64.

43. Macklin Fleming, *The Price of Perfect Justice* (New York: Basic Books, 1974).

cause all crimes are above all *crimes against God*. An unwillingness on the part of civil magistrates to enforce God's specified sanctions against certain specified public acts calls forth God's specified covenantal cursings against the community. This threat of God's sanctions is the fourth section of God's covenant; without this covenant, either explicit or implicit, no community can exist.[44] Only when we clearly recognize the theocentric nature of deterrence — and when we are ready to seek to have it recognized publicly *in our civil and ecclesiastical statute books* — can we legitimately begin to speak about deterring criminal behavior for the protection of the community.

The Bible does not distinguish between civil law and criminal law. All sins are crimes against God, for they break His law. All public sins must be restrained by one or more of God's covenantal agencies of government: family, church, and State. Certain public transgressions of God's law are specified as acts to be punished by the civil magistrate. In the modern world, we call these acts crimes. (The King James Version uses the word "crime" only twice, and "crimes" only twice.) The civil government enforces biblical laws against such acts. The general guideline for designating a particular public act as a crime is this: if by failing to impose sanctions against certain specified public acts, the whole community could be subsequently threatened by God's non-civil sanctions — war, plague, and famine — then the civil government becomes God's designated agency of enforcement. *The civil government's primary function is to protect the community against the wrath of God* by enforcing His laws against public acts that threaten the survival of the community.

The perverse practice of modern jurisprudence of allowing a person who has been declared legally innocent of a crime to be subsequently sued for damages in civil court by alleged victims cannot be found in the Bible. There is no distinction in the Bible between criminal law and civil law; if the *civil* magistrates are entitled to enforce a rule or law, then this rule or law should be classified in the modern world under a *criminal* statute. Because the State is not omniscient, God allows self-proclaimed victims of lawless behavior to sue other individuals in the presence of a civil magistrate, which we call civil procedure or torts, but if the State is the lawful agency of enforcement, then we are always talking about criminal acts. Con-

44. Ray R. Sutton, *That You May Prosper: Dominion By Covenant* (Tyler, Texas: Institute for Christian Economics, 1987), ch. 4.

tinued injustice, *if* it can be biblically defined and publicly identified in advance through statute or judicial precedent, because it goes unpunished by the civil government, calls forth the wrath of God on the community. So, there is ultimately no Bible-based distinction between civil law and criminal law.

The Bible encourages the *legitimate division of labor* in identifying all types of criminal behavior, including such acts of injustice as breaking contracts or polluting the environment. The Bible recognizes that the State is not God. It is not omniscient. The initiation of public sanctions against all criminal acts therefore must not become a monopoly of civil officers. Citizen's arrest and torts—where one person sues another in order to collect damages—are modern examples of the outworking of this biblical principle of the decentralization of law enforcement. All government begins with self-government. The bottom-up, appeals court structure of covenant society (Ex. 18) is protected by not requiring that agents of the civil government initiate all of the civil government's sanctions against criminal behavior. Nevertheless, all disputes into which the State can legitimately intervene and settle by judicial decision must be regarded in a biblical commonwealth as criminal behavior. There is no biblical distinction between criminal law and civil law.

It is therefore preposterous to argue, as liberal scholar Anthony Phillips argues concerning the Mosaic law, that "A crime is a breach of an obligation imposed by the law which is felt to endanger the community, and which results in the punishment of the offender in the name of the community, but which is not the personal concern of the individual who may have suffered injury, and who has no power to stop the prosecution, nor derives any gain from it."[45] It is preposterous because every transgression of the civil law that goes unpunished by the authorities raises the threat of God's judgment on the community, which is why unsolved murders required expiation in the Old Testament: 1) the sacrifice of a heifer (Deut. 21:1-7); and 2) the elders were required to pray, "Be merciful, O LORD, unto thy people Israel, whom thou hast redeemed, and lay not innocent blood unto thy people of Israel's charge. And the blood shall be forgiven them" (Deut. 21:8). The State must regard as crimes against God all public transgressions for which the Bible specifies restitution payments to victims. Such acts are criminal acts against the community.

---

45. Anthony Phillips, *Ancient Israel's Criminal Law: A New Approach to the Decalogue* (New York: Schocken, 1970), p. 10.

Why? Because if they go unpunished, God threatens to curse the community. Thus, criminal law in the Bible was not enforced "in the name of the community," but *in the name of God*, so as to protect the community from God's wrath.

Restitution to God

Phillips is consistent in his errors, at least; he also argues that Hebrew covenant law was *exclusively* criminal law, meaning that its goal was solely the enforcement of public morals, rather than civil law (torts), in which restitution to the victim was primary.[46] This definition, if correct, would remove from covenant law all biblical statutes that require restitution to victims. What he is trying to do is separate the case laws of Exodus from the Ten Commandments. If believed, this argument would make it far easier for antinomians to reject the continuing validity of the case laws in New Testament times, for the case laws of Exodus and other books rest heavily on the imposition of restitution payments to victims. The antinomians could publicly claim allegiance to the Ten Commandments, but then they could distance themselves from the specific applications of these commandments through the case laws, for they have concluded that the case laws are unconnected to the Decalogue because these are "civil" laws rather than "criminal" laws.[47] Phillips writes: "But it is the contention of this study that Israel herself understood the Decalogue as her criminal law code, and that the law contained in it, and developed from it, was sharply distinguished from her civil law."[48]

If true, then all you need to do to escape from the covenantal, State-enforced requirements of the Decalogue is to make the Ten Commandments appear ridiculous. This he attempts in Chapter 2. "Initially only free adult males were subject to Israel's criminal law, for only they could have entered into the covenant relationship with Yahweh. . . . But women did not enter into the covenant relationship, and were therefore outside the scope of the criminal law. They had no legal status, being the personal property first of their fathers

---

46. *Ibid.*, pp. 10-11.

47. Phillips says that the "Book of the Covenant," meaning Exodus 21-23, was a product of David's reign, with some of it quite possibly written by David himself. *Ibid.*, ch. 14.

48. *Ibid.*, p. 11.

and then of their husbands."[49] The Decalogue is clearly preposterous, he implies. Presto: modern man is freed from *any* covenantal relationship to God. Man is on his own in the cosmos. He is autonomous. He shall be as God.

His case rests, first and foremost, on his distinguishing of criminal law from civil law in terms of the presence of restitution requirements in civil law. Next, he excludes women from the covenant. Then he turns them into chattel slaves. His tactic is obvious: to make God's law appear ridiculous. But it is Phillips who is ridiculous, not the Bible. Like all humanists, he does not begin with the presupposition of a theocentric universe. He therefore does not begin his discussion of crimes and restitution with the understanding that all crimes are ultimately crimes against God, and all restitution payments belong ultimately to God as the ultimate injured party. It does not occur to him that *all of God's curses are His imposition of restitution payments to Himself as the ultimate Victim.* Because covenant-breakers do not voluntarily repay to God what they owe Him as the innocent victim — the ultimate object of their moral rebellion — He therefore repays them with inescapable final judgment. "Vengeance is mine; I will repay, saith the Lord" (Rom. 12:19b).

All sins are crimes against God. All sins are therefore judged by God: "For the wages of sin is death" (Rom. 6:23a). Each person is a sinner in God's eyes, and therefore a criminal. The key question that must be answered during each person's life on earth — acknowledged by him or not — is this one: Will I allow Jesus Christ's payment of the God-imposed eternal penalty to serve as my substitutionary restitution payment to God, or will I instead choose to ignore the magnitude of this looming restitution payment and cross death's threshold autonomously? Anyone who makes the second choice will spend eternity in God's non-rehabilitative torture chambers.

"Victimless Crimes" and Civil Judgment

In the ultimate covenantal sense, it is improper to speak of victimless crimes. Every person who entices another to sin is bringing that person under the threat of God's negative sanctions, in time and

---

49. *Ibid.*, pp. 14, 15. He does say that Deuteronomy later made women full members of the covenant. *Ibid.*, p. 25. This is the standard liberal dismemberment of the Pentateuch into the hypothetical documents of the play-pretend scribes, J, E, D, P, and their as-yet unidentified accomplices. It should be a great comfort for Christians to realize that God will dismember these scholarly covenant-dismemberers throughout eternity.

in eternity. God therefore threatens the whole community for its failure to impose civil sanctions against such crimes. If there were no threat of God's sanctions against the community for the failure of the magistrates to enforce all statutes assigned by the Bible to the civil magistrates for enforcement, then there would be no biblical justification for sanctions against such "victimless crimes" as prostitution, pornography, and drug dealing. Because he rejects the idea of such a covenant, classical liberal economist and legal theorist F. A. Hayek rejects laws against "victimless crimes," saying that they are illegitimate interventions of the civil government, "At least where it is not believed that the whole group may be punished by a supernatural power for the sins of individuals. . . ."[50] But that is the whole point: such a community-threatening God *does* exist.

Many actions that are specified in the Bible as sins are not to be tried and judged by the civil magistrate, but this is not evidence of neglect by God; it is instead *a restraint on the growth of messianic civil government*. The absence of civil penalties against such designated sinful behavior indicates only a postponement of judgment until the sinner's final and eternal restitution payment to God. Through their public enforcement of God's law, civil magistrates warn people of the necessity of obeying God, the cosmic Enforcer: "By the fear of the LORD men depart from evil" (Prov. 16:6b). This legitimate fear is to be both personal and national, for God's punishments in history are imposed on individuals and nations: "If thou wilt not observe to do all the words of this law that are written in this book, that thou mayest fear this glorious and fearful name, THE LORD THY GOD; then the LORD will make thy plagues wonderful, and the plagues of thy seed, even great plagues, and of long continuance, and sore sicknesses, and of long continuance" (Deut. 28:58-59).

The necessity of making restitution reminds the covenanted nation to fear the God who exacts a perfect restitution payment to Himself on judgment day, and who brings His wrath in history as a warning of the final judgment to come. He brings His wrath either through lawfully constituted civil government or, if civil government refuses to honor the terms of His covenant, through such visible judgments as wars, plagues, and famines. This is why the nation was warned to fear God, immediately after the presentation of the Ten Commandments: ". . . God is come to prove you, and that his fear may be before your faces, that ye sin not" (Ex. 20:20b).

---

50. F. A. Hayek, *Law, Legislation and Liberty*, 3 vols. (University of Chicago Press, 1973), I, p. 101.

Jesus was not departing from the biblical view of judicial sanctions when He warned: "Fear him which is able to destroy both soul and body in hell" (Matt. 10:28b). It is eternal punishment which is to serve as the covenantal foundation of all judicial sanctions. Civil government is supposed to reflect God's government. Public punishments deter evil. They remind men: better temporal punishment that leads to repentance (personal and national) than eternal punishment that does not lead to repentance (personal). Repentance is possible only in history.

Capital Punishment

Phillips is consistently incorrect when he writes: "Modern theories of punishment are therefore totally inapplicable when considering reasons why ancient Israel executed her criminals, for the punishment was not looked at from the criminal's point of view. This extreme penalty was not designed to deter potential criminals, nor as an act of retribution, but as a means of preventing divine action by appeasing Yahweh's wrath."[51] If criminal law was "not looked at from the criminal's point of view," then why does the Bible repeatedly refer to the fear of external punishment by the civil authorities as a means of leading men to fear God and to obey His law? "And all Israel shall hear, and fear, and shall do no more any such wickedness as this is among you" (Deut. 13:11). Deterring future crimes is certainly one of the functions of capital punishment in a biblical law-order. Capital punishment is also an act of retribution and restitution. And, yes, it is also "a means of preventing divine action by appeasing Yahweh's wrath." It is erroneous to argue exclusively in terms of "either-or" when considering the potential social motivations for capital punishment or any other required civil sanction in the Bible.[52]

---

51. Phillips, *Ancient Israel's Criminal Law*, p. 12.

52. I do not want to give the reader an inflated opinion of Phillips' importance. He is just another obscure liberal theologian toiling fruitlessly in the barren wilderness of higher criticism. I have included this brief survey of some of his ideas as an example of just how intellectually sloppy liberal theology can be, not because he is an important thinker. He is simply a convenient foil. He is all too typical of a small army of liberal theologians whose works would be immediately forgotten if they had ever been read in the first place. These scholars will eventually make full restitution to God for their efforts to deceive their readers concerning the Bible.

Liberal scholars are always looking for a new angle to justify the publication of yet another heavily footnoted, utterly boring, totally useless book, especially books like Phillips', which is a rewritten doctoral dissertation — the most footnoted, boring, and useless academic exercise of all. Doctoral dissertations should be interred quietly, preferably in private, with only the author and close family in attendance. If such interment must be public, then it should be as a summary published in a scholarly journal, where the remains' entombment will seldom be disturbed again. Ashes to ashes, dust to dust.

Capital punishment points to the final judgment as no other civil penalty does. It reminds sinners of the ultimate restitution penalty that God will impose on all those who refuse to accept His Son's payment on their behalf. The civil government acknowledges that its most fearful form of punishment is to speed convicted criminals along into the courtroom of the cosmic Judge. The magistrate announces that there is no way to restore the convicted criminal to fellowship in earthly society. He visibly becomes what he already is in principle: a sinner in the hands of an angry God.

Final Judgment

We see the ultimate example of this two-fold aspect of restitution in the final judgment. Satan and his host, both human and angelic, pay for their rebellion with their lives. Their leavening power of corruption in history is reduced to zero. Their assets are transferred to God's people, who inherit the earth. From a biblical standpoint, this transfer of legal title to the world was accomplished by Christ at Calvary.[53] Then the rebels are thrown into the lake of fire (Rev. 20:14-15).

This eternal, continual restitution payment honors God, while it simultaneously acts as the perfect deterrent to crime — a covenantal warning that remains before God's servants, both human and angelic, throughout eternity. Resurrected people will never sin again, whether they are covenant-breakers or covenant-keepers. Righteous people will not choose to sin, and resurrected sinners will not be able to. In the lake of fire there is only impotence. The ability to adhere to any of the terms of the dominion covenant cease when grace ceases, and there is no grace in the lake of fire.

Then why speak of the deterrence effect of eternal damnation? Because God's judgment is covenantal: blessings and cursings (point four of the Biblical covenant).[54] There are always conditional aspects to God's covenant promises, as well as unconditional aspects. The promises of God are part of the structure of the covenant. There will be promises and blessings in the post-resurrection new heaven and new earth. Cursing and blessing are eternal, which reminds everyone of the covenant's conditions. Thus, the lake of fire can be spoken of covenantally as a perfect deterrent, for it deters all God-defying

---

53. Gary North, *Inherit the Earth: Biblical Blueprints for Economics* (Ft. Worth, Texas: Dominion Press, 1987), ch. 5.

54. Sutton, *That You May Prosper*, ch. 4.

behavior forever. It also complements and reinforces the perfect obedience of covenant-keepers who know perfectly well about the perfect
torment of covenant-breakers, with their perfect bodies that possess
the terrifying ability, like the burning bush that Moses saw, of not
being destroyed by a perfect fire. God's perfection is manifested in
His perfect wrath.

It is not God's grace that keeps alive covenant-breakers, with
their perfect bodies that are so sensitive to every subtle aspect of their
endless torment; it is instead His uncompromising *wrath* that keeps
them alive.[55] Covenant promises, conditions, and sanctions are eternally perfect.[56] The soul and body of every covenant-breaker are reunited perfectly at the resurrection, so that each can experience the
eternal torments of covenant judgment as unified and fully human.
There is no dualism of body and soul in the lake of fire.[57]

---

55. On this point, I disagree with John Calvin's reference to God's grace in keeping souls alive: "And although the soul, after it has departed from the prison of the
body, remains alive, yet its doing so does not arise from any inherent power of its
own. Were God to withdraw his grace, the soul would be nothing more than a puff
or blast, even as the body is dust; and thus there would doubtless be found in the
whole man nothing but mere vanity." Calvin, *Commentary on the Book of Psalms* (Grand
Rapids, Michigan: Barker Book House, 1979), Baker's volume VI, p. 138: Ps.
103:15. There is no grace shown by God to the souls of covenant-breakers in hell or
the lake of fire. Grace is shown only to the souls of covenant-keepers. Calvin's loose
language here is misused by Edward William Fudge in his book-long attempt to
deny the biblical doctrine of eternal torment: *The Fire That Consumes: A Biblical and
Historical Study of Final Punishment* (Houston, Texas: Providential Press, 1982), p. 74.

56. Fudge attempts to trace Protestantism's doctrine of the immortality of the soul
to Calvin, and Calvin's doctrine of the immortality of the soul to Plato. This argument
is nonsense, though representative of similar arguments used by heretical theologians
to reject Bible doctrines in the name of rejecting Greek speculation, when in fact they
have adopted some variation of humanist speculation. The Bible's doctrine of the immortality of the soul and also its doctrine of eternal torment of the wicked are both
grounded in the doctrine of the covenant. It is not surprising that Fudge finds in the
Calvinist tradition the most tenacious die-hard defense of the doctrine of eternal punishment. Fudge, *ibid.*, pp. 26n, 466. There is a reason for this tenacity. Calvinism,
more than any other Christian tradition, is grounded in the doctrine of the covenant.

57. Fudge and several of the drifting theologians whom he cites continually refer
to the orthodox doctrine of souls in hell as implicitly dualistic. The doctrine of hell is
no more dualistic than the traditional doctrine of heaven. The issue is not heaven or
hell, for both are temporary way stations for souls until God's final judgment; the
issue is the post-resurrection world, where souls and bodies are reunited. Fudge
fudges this issue, as he does so many others. He covers his flanks with a whole series
of peripheral issues — theological and historical rabbit trails for non-covenant theologians to pursue until exhaustion. The fundamental issue is the covenant: God's
eternal dead-end judgment for covenant-breakers. This is the issue Fudge never discusses in chapter 20, "Focusing on the Issue," with its subsection, "Traditional
Arguments Summarized." It is not man who is central to discussions of final judgment, but God and His eternal covenant.

Perfect justice brings with it a resurrection life permanently devoid of sin. Furthermore, the punishment perfectly fits the ethical crime of rebellion against God. It is a punishment whose magnitude God made quite plain from the beginning: "But of the tree of the knowledge of good and evil, thou shalt not eat of it: for in the day that thou eatest thereof thou shalt surely die" (Gen. 2:17). Absolutely proportional restitution at the final judgment creates the conditions necessary to establish a perfect society beyond the final resurrection.

Lex Talionis

Throughout the section of Exodus that immediately follows the Ten Commandments, we are given case-law applications of these commandments. In these case laws we discover an operating principle: "an eye for an eye," the *lex talionis*. This principle is the theological foundation of all punishment, and therefore serves as the basis of restitution. This is why God required a living sacrifice, life for life, to atone for mankind's sin. A perfect man had to die in order to atone for the sin of another formerly perfect man, Adam. This is why the author of the Epistle to the Hebrews could write concerning the life and work of Jesus Christ: "For it is not possible that the blood of bulls and of goats should take away sins. Wherefore when he cometh into the world, he saith, Sacrifice and offering thou wouldest not, but a body hast thou prepared me: In burnt offerings and sacrifices for sin thou hast had no pleasure" (Heb. 10:4-6). Again, "Neither by the blood of goats and calves, but by his own blood he entered in once into the holy place, having obtained eternal redemption for us" (Heb. 9:12). This should have come as no surprise to anyone who had read and believed Exodus 21-22. Atonement for sins against God requires more than the slaughter of animals. Slaughtering an animal does not compensate God for man's sin. *The principle of proportional restitution testified from the beginning against the autonomous adequacy of the Mosaic sacrificial system. It pointed to a greater sacrifice to come.* A perfect man would have to die, and more than a perfect man: God's Son.

As history's pre-resurrection society begins to approach, though never attain, the perfect justice of proportional restitution, it will thereby approach, though never attain, institutional perfection.[58] In

---

58. Perfection is an ethical requirement, for each individual and for all covenant institutions. It is a mandatory goal: "Be ye therefore perfect, even as your Father which is in heaven is perfect" (Matt. 5:48). Christ was simply citing an Old Testament principle regarding sanctification, or holiness (Lev. 11:44). Perfection cannot be attained prior to the day of resurrection, however: "If we say that we have no sin, we deceive ourselves, and the truth is not in us. If we confess our sins, he is faithful and just to forgive us our sins, and to cleanse us from all unrighteousness. If we say that we have not sinned, we make him a liar, and his word is not in us" (I John 1:8-10).

God's pre-resurrection cultural "earnest" to His people—His down payment or pledge (Rom. 8:19; Eph. 1:14)—which is the earthly beginning of the new heavens and new earth (Isa. 65:17), people will still die, proving that it will be an era prior to the final judgment, but they will normally live extraordinarily long lives (Isa. 65:20). It will be a period of reduced immorality (Isa. 1:25; 4:2-4), more equitable judgment (Isa. 1:26-27), and greater productivity as a result of universal peace (Isa. 65:22-23). There is an earthly relationship between righteous living (progressive sanctification), godly civil justice, and economic growth.[59]

III. Offsetting Reduced Risks of Detection

The thief who steals a specially protected beast must suffer greater risks for stealing it when compared to any other kind of property. The sheep or ox can easily be slaughtered and eaten. This makes it far more difficult for the civil authorities to discover who the thief is and then prove it in court. Thus, the thief who steals an ox or sheep seems to have a greater likelihood of getting away with the crime. The law therefore imposes far higher penalties in cases of ox-stealing or sheep-stealing. This offsets part of the self-subsidy—the reduction of the risk of detection—that the thief receives when he slaughters the animal, thereby destroying the evidence.

But what about selling the animals? This is the equivalent of kidnapping, for these particular animals represent man. Thus, there is a higher penalty attached to their theft. This higher penalty relates to the *symbolic aspect* of the forbidden act of man-stealing. Selling a useful beast that can be taken into a different part of the country makes it easier for the thief to escape detection. The thief does not wear a stolen jewel or use a stolen tool, which would make it easier to detect his crime locally. The animal, which was under the personal protection of its owner, is separated from the owner permanently. Biblical law therefore stipulates that the thief who does sell the beast is placed under greater risk; should he be proven to be the thief, he will be required to pay four-fold or five-fold restitution to the victim.

This explanation may seem strained, but it is necessary if we are to make sense of Exodus 22:9, which regulates property placed in trust with a neighbor. If the neighbor loses the goods, they both must

---

59. Gary North, *Unconditional Surrender: God's Program for Victory* (3rd ed.; Tyler, Texas: Institute for Christian Economics, 1988), pp. 101-15.

go before the civil magistrates. If the neighbor is found guilty, he pays double restitution. "For all manner of trespass, whether it be for ox, for ass, for sheep, for raiment, or for any manner of lost thing, which another challengeth to be his, the cause of both parties shall come before the judges; and whom the judges shall condemn, he shall pay double unto his neighbour."

Why should the neighbor be required to pay only double restitution for a sheep or ox in this case? What about five-fold and four-fold restitution? My answer: because the neighbor cannot conceal the crime the way that the outsider can when he slaughters or sells the animal. In short, *it is easier for the victimized owner to prove his legal case against a neighbor than it is for him to prove his case against an unknown thief who disposes of the evidence.* Thus, the penalty imposed on the neighbor is double restitution, which is the standard requirement for the theft of all other goods except slaughtered or sold oxen and sheep. Since the owner faces reduced difficulties in recovering his property, and the thief therefore faces increased risk, the penalty payment is reduced.

Conclusion

What will be the marks of civil justice during an era of biblical justice? Victims will see the restoration of their stolen assets, while criminals will see their ill-gotten capital melt away because of the financial burden of making restitution payments. The dual sanctions of *curse and blessing* — part four of the biblical covenant model[60] — are invoked and imposed wherever the principle of restitution is honored in the courts, both civil and ecclesiastical. Restitution brings both *judgment and restoration*, which affect individual lives and social institutions.

There are limits to biblical restitution. First, the full value of whatever was stolen is returned by the thief to the original owner. Second, the thief makes an additional penalty payment equal to the value of the item stolen. To encourage criminals to admit their guilt and seek restoration before their crimes are discovered, the Bible imposes a reduced penalty of 20 percent on those who admit their guilt voluntarily (Lev. 6:2-5).

There are two exceptions to double restitution. The law singles out oxen and sheep as deserving special protection in the form of five-fold and four-fold restitution in cases where the stolen animals are killed or sold. Because oxen and sheep are symbolic of mankind, the law thereby points to the need of protecting men from oppression

---

60. Sutton, *That You May Prosper,* ch. 4.

and slavery. He is given responsibility over oxen and sheep, implying that he is also given responsibility over other men in various circumstances. To thwart a man in the exercise of his lawful calling is a crime against dominion man, and is punishable by God.

Proportional restitution is imposed by the civil government as God's lawful representative on earth. The three economic goals of proportional restitution are these: 1) restoring full value to the victim; 2) protecting future potential victims by means of the deterrence effect of the penalty payment (Deut. 13:11): a) animals, especially those symbolic of man's helplessness (sheep and oxen), and b) property owners; and 3) offsetting the lower economic risks of detection associated with certain kinds of theft — the slaughter or sale of specially protected edible animals.

Biblical restitution also has at least three civil goals in addition to the three economic goals. The first civil goal of restitution is to make life easier for the law-abiding citizen by fostering external social conditions in which he can live in peace and safety. Peace and safety are the fully legitimate goals of all biblical justice, which God has promised to bring to pass in world history through His church during a future period of earthly millennial peace. The nations will come to God's church ("the mountain of the house of the LORD") in search of true justice (Mic. 4:1-5).

A second civil goal of biblical restitution is to make possible the full *judicial* restoration of the criminal to society after he has paid the victim what he owes him.[61] The State is not to concern itself with the psychological restoration of the criminal, the victim, or society in general. The State's jurisdiction is strictly limited to the realm of the judicial: *restitution*. The psychological state of the criminal is between himself and God, as is the psychological state of the victim. Nevertheless, as in the case of the salvation of any individual by God's grace, judicial restoration is the first step toward psychological restoration.

The third civil goal of biblical restitution is not intuitively obvious, but it may be the most important goal for the modern world. A system of biblical restitution is required in order to reduce the likeli-

---

61. The modern U.S. practice of never again allowing convicted felons to vote is clearly immoral. Under biblical law, a convicted criminal becomes a *former* convicted criminal when he has made full restitution to his victims. In this sense, he is "resurrected" judicially. After he has paid his debt to his victims, he must be restored to full political participation. To segregate the former convicted criminal from any area of civic authority or participation is to deny judicially that full civil restoration is made possible by means of God's civil law.

hood that citizens will come to view the civil government as an agency that lawfully initiates programs leading to personal or social transformation. The State's task is to assess the economic damage that was inflicted on the victim and then impose judgment on the convicted criminal that will reimburse the victim for his loss, plus a penalty payment. Normally, this means double restitution. The State is not an agency of creative transformation. It is not a savior State. Men should not seek to make the State an agency of social salvation. It is supposed to enforce biblical civil law — no more, no less. The State is not supposed to seek to make men righteous; its God-assigned task is to restrain certain specified acts of public evil. Theft is one of these acts.

Civil government is an agency of visible judgment in history. Justice demands judgment. The judgments handed down by civil government acknowledge the historic judgments of God, as well as point to the final judgment of God. The goal of civil justice is always restoration; restoration through restitution or restoration through execution. This two-fold system of civil judgment also characterizes God's judgments, which are equally judicial.

When God deals with His people in a harsh way in history, it is a means of restoration: *judgment unto restoration*, not judgment unto destruction. The atoning work of Jesus Christ at Calvary points the way to a better world in history; restitution has been made to God by the only possible ethically acceptable representative of man, the Son of God. The Christian's expectation of better earthly times is therefore valid. Christ's restitution payment has been made, on earth and in history.

One thing which is needed to translate His atonement into social reality is the progressive transformation of the criminal justice system in terms of biblical law, something which cannot take place until the humanistic theology which undergirds the existing system of justice is replaced by biblical orthodoxy. Anyone who denies that such a progressive transformation of the criminal justice system is possible in history is thereby also denying that the atoning work of Christ can be manifested progressively in history. Anyone who denies that such a progressive transformation of the criminal justice system will actually take place in history is thereby also denying that the atoning work of Christ will be actually manifested progressively in history. People should therefore consider carefully the economic, social, political, and ethical implications of their eschatological views. When they make eschatological pronouncements, they are inescapably also making implicit economic, social, political, and ethical pronouncements. Eschatology and ethics cannot be successfully separated.

18

POLLUTION, OWNERSHIP, AND RESPONSIBILITY

If a man shall cause a field or vineyard to be eaten, and shall put in his beast, and shall feed in another man's field; of the best of his own field, and of the best of his own vineyard, shall he make restitution. If fire break out, and catch in thorns, so that the stacks of corn, or the standing corn, or the field, be consumed therewith; he that kindled the fire shall surely make restitution (Ex. 22:5-6).

The theocentric issue raised by this passage rests on the recognition of each person's legal obligations as a responsible steward over private property in a world in which God is the absolute owner of the world. As part of His providential administration over the world, God establishes boundaries in life. These boundaries are ultimately ethical: the boundaries between covenant-keepers and covenant-breakers. The existence of these ethical boundaries is reflected in every area of life. Man cannot think or act apart from boundaries of various kinds. These ethical boundaries are reinforced by legal boundaries that separate the use of property. Boundaries are therefore inescapably tied to the legal issue of personal responsibility before God and man.

God parcels out property to his subordinates. The very phrase, *parcels out*, reflects the noun, a parcel. God places specified units of land under the administration of specific individuals, families, and institutions. This division of authority is an aspect of God's overall system of the division of labor. Responsibility for the administration of specific property units can therefore be specified by law. The allocation of legal responsibility matches the allocation of property. God holds specific people responsible for their stewardship over specific pieces of property. This enables owners to evaluate their own performance as stewards, and it also allows the free market and God-ordained governmental authorities to evaluate owners' specific performance. The ultimate economic issue is each person's stewardship over property in history and God's judicial response, in history and at the final judgment. The temporal institutional issues of ownership-stewardship are covenantally related to this ultimate issue.

These verses make plain at least three facts. First, the Bible affirms the moral and legal legitimacy of the private ownership of the means of production. Fields and cattle and crops are owned by private individuals. Second, private property rights (legal immunities from action by others) are to be defended by the civil government. The State can and must require those people whose activities injure their neighbor or their neighbor's property to make restitution payments to those injured. Third, owners are therefore responsible for their own actions and for the actions of their subordinates, including wandering beasts.[1]

This combination of 1) privately owned property, 2) personal liability, and 3) predictable court enforcement of private property rights is the foundation of capitalism. It surely was a major aspect of the West's long-term economic growth.[2] But as this chapter argues, this property ownership arrangement is also important for the reduction and allocation of pollution.

We begin with the case of the wandering animal. It wanders from its property and invades another man's corn field. It eats some of this corn. The owner of the beast owes the victimized neighbor the equivalent of whatever has been destroyed.[3] The owner of the beast must not short-change the victim; he pays from the best of his field. The legal principle is that the injured party is entitled to the replace-

---

1. Hammurabi's Code penalized a man who neglected to repair a dike on his property, which in turn broke and allowed his neighbor's property to be flooded: CH, paragraph 53. If he allowed water to flow through his canal and onto his neighbor's property, he was liable: CH, paragraph 55. *Ancient Near Eastern Texts Relating to the Old Testament*, edited by James B. Pritchard (3rd ed.; Princeton, New Jersey: Princeton University Press, 1969), p. 168.

2. Nathan Rosenberg and L. E. Birdsell, Jr., *How the West Grew Rich: The Economic Transformation of the Industrial World* (New York: Basic Books, 1986), ch. 4: "The Evolution of Institutions Favorable to Commerce."

3. Maimonides made this peculiar exception: "If an animal eats foodstuffs harmful to it, such as wheat, the owner is exempt because it has not benefited." Moses Maimonides, *The Book of Torts*, vol. 11 of *The Code of Maimonides*, 14 vols (New Haven, Connecticut: Yale University Press, [1180] 1954), Chapter Three, Section Three, p. 12. That the victim must suffer an economic loss just because his neighbor's animal did not profit biologically from its invasion of the former's property is a principle of justice that needs a great deal of explaining. Maimonides provided no further discussion; he just laid down this principle of Jewish law, and went on.

ment of his damaged goods by the best of the responsible party's possessions. What is the theocentric principle that this legal principle reflects? It is this: *God, in imposing an appropriate restitution payment from rebellious mankind, is entitled to the best that man has to offer.* This is why man was not allowed under the Old Covenant to bring to God's sacrificial altar any injured or blemished animal (Lev. 1:10). "But cursed be the deceiver, which hath in his flock a male, and voweth, and sacrificeth unto the Lord a corrupt thing" (Mal. 1:14a). When Ananias and Sapphira brought only part of their pledged money to the church, but claimed that they were bringing in all of it, God killed them (Acts 5:1-10). They had violated a fundamental biblical principle. They became publicly cursed deceivers. "And great fear came upon all the church, and upon as many as heard these things" (Acts 5:11).

This theocentric principle governing restitution to God points to the ultimate principle governing the atonement: *only a perfect offering for sin can placate the God of perfect wrath.* Anyone who attempts to bring a blemished sacrifice to the altar of God will be destroyed. This, of course, is the underlying soteriological requirement that made necessary the incarnation, death, resurrection, and ascension of Jesus Christ. Only a perfect man, God's own Son, can serve as an acceptable sacrifice for sinful mankind (Heb. 2:14-18; 9:12-14). A sinful man will perish eternally if he attempts to short-change God by offering anything on judgment day in place of exclusive faith in the true mediator and high priest, Jesus Christ.

Initially, Exodus 22:5-6 may seem self-explanatory. Nevertheless, when we consider the passage in the light of the many intellectual and institutional problems related to the whole question of pollution and ecology, its application in society becomes an enormously complex judicial task. Without the legal guidelines established by the passage, we could not deal effectively with the pollution problem.

Pollution: Socialist and Free Market

Contrary to many of the twentieth-century critiques of both capitalism and pollution, socialist commonwealths have not produced reasonable, cost-effective, workable solutions to the pollution problem.[4] Think of Poland's Katowice region, in which the sulphuric and nitric acids released into the atmosphere by coal and steel plants

---

4. Fred Singleton (ed.), *Environmental Misuse in the Soviet Union* (New York: Praeger, 1976).

have so corroded the railway tracks that the trains are not allowed to
go over 25 miles per hour.[5] Think of the workers in Cracow's steel
plant, where in 1980, 80 percent of those leaving the plant received
disability payments, and 7.5 percent died while still employed.[6] The
problem is inherent in the State's ownership of the means of production; the means of production necessarily must include the workers.
The State owns their labor. Ultimately, the radical socialist and
Communist States assert actual ownership of the workers, disposing
of them however the bureaucrats see fit. It is "common ownership" —
bureaucratic ownership — which creates most of the economic incentives to pollute and exploit the environment, because leaders within
the civil government's hierarchy become the unnoticed beneficiaries
of the increased output of lower-cost industrial processes that produce the pollution. The plant managers meet their State-assigned
output quotas less expensively (for their local plants) by transferring
some of the costs of production to the public: smoke, noise, chemical
wastes, etc. Politically acceptable solutions to widespread pollution
have never been successfully implemented in socialist societies because
it is the private ownership of the means of production that serves as a
key element in any successful program of pollution control.[7]

At the same time, free market economists have not been able to
produce theoretically acceptable solutions to the problem of pollution
that do not rest heavily on the idea of the necessity of government intervention into market operations. The problem then becomes: How
much intervention is appropriate in any given case? There is no theoretically acceptable answer to this problem. In fact, because of the
very nature of modern economic theory, there never will be a theoretically acceptable solution that is consistent with contemporary
economics. I have added   Appendix D to prove this assertion. It
deals with the crucial, neglected, and somewhat technical problem:
determining social cost. I have added it in order to demonstrate that
conventional humanist economic theory is incapable of dealing with
the problem of pollution — or any problem of applied economics, for
that matter — because there is no self-consistent way for the economist to go from modern economics' methodological individualism to
collective decision-making in terms of the presuppositions of modern

---

5. Lloyd Timberlake, "Poland — the most polluted country in the world?" *New
Statesman* (22 October 1981), p. 248.

6. *Ibid.*, p. 249.

7. See Appendix E: "Pollution in the Soviet Union."

economic theory. The economists almost never discuss this embarrassing fact, although the more sophisticated members of the economics profession have been aware of it since at least 1938, but it is nonetheless a fact.

Thus, both collectivism and free enterprise face a growing problem, the problem of minimizing the negative effects of pollution without simultaneously destroying the benefits of economic growth. Neither variety of secular economic theory has a scientific answer to this problem. This is why Christian economics is needed. This is why we must begin our economic analysis with Exodus 22:5-6.

Capturing Economics for Christ

The theoretical and practical problems associated with the pollution question are numerous. The problems are ethical, technical, theoretical, and ultimately philosophical. Economists do not like to admit that all problems in applied economic theory have inherent and inescapable ethical and philosophical aspects, so they tend to ignore or even suppress these aspects of applied economics when discussing them in their scholarly journals. This is why modern economics to a great extent is fraudulent — a mental contrivance to conceal fundamental ethical issues, a series of rarified mental exercises devised for agnostics by agnostics. But the agnostics maintain monopoly control over the professional journals because they control the funds, the academic institutions, and the certification of younger scholars. This epistemological agnosticism must change if economics as a discipline is to be saved, but only self-consciously Christian scholars can redeem it.

How should Christians go about redeeming any academic discipline? By beginning with the whole Bible as academically and professionally authoritative. Christians must begin to tackle those intellectual problems for which the humanists have no consistent answers. In the case of economics, Christians must follow the lead set by Cornelius Van Til in philosophy. Van Til did not ask: "Is Christian philosophy valid?" He started with the premise that there is no valid philosophy except Christian philosophy. That is what I have asserted with regard to Christian economics. The humanists have run out of internally consistent answers. In fact, they never had accurate answers that were not implicitly based on biblical presuppositions, and the farther away the economists get from the Bible, the fewer accurate answers they can provide.

We can see this drift away from theoretically consistent answers by a study of a specific problem of applied economics, pollution. This chapter can serve as an introduction to the kinds of theoretical and practical problems that face professional economists, and that also face Christians who are intent upon redeeming economics for Christ. It is a scaled-down study, not overly technical (except for Appendix D, on social costs). It is only an introduction. Nevertheless, the topic's complexity may scare off Christian laymen. Because of this complexity, I need to list in advance some of the basic themes in this lengthy chapter. The reader should be prepared to think through some fundamental ethical issues. This is the price of the first phase of Christian reconstruction.

How to assess true costs and benefits
Overusing "free" resources
Private property vs. disputes
Fire as pollution
Damage and restitution
Restitution in advance (discounts)
Allowing prior pollution to continue
Voluntary contracts that allow pollution
Pollution and the varying costs of knowledge
Risks that can be insured against
Undiscovered risk and legal liability
Retroactive penalties vs. innovation
Externalities: forcing you to pay me
How to allocate pollution regionally
A pollution auction
Wastes and stewardship: Who pays?
Pollution as trespassing
The problem of moving fluids: liability
Automobile emissions: noise and exhaust
Fire codes: Are they biblical?
Organizing injured victims
Exchanging risks voluntarily
Increased wealth and pollution complaints
Localism and pollution control
Subsidizing the politically skilled
The anti-dominion impulse
Claims of future generations
Incentives and sanctions
Pollution and responsibility
State officers as surrogates
Information and pollution: Who knew?
Incentives and sanctions to stop
Zero pollution: a messianic quest

The "Tragedy of the Commons"

A fundamental economic problem in any system of common ownership is the problem of assessing true costs and benefits. Historically, one of the most familiar of these systems of common ownership has been commonly held land. From the Middle Ages through at least the late seventeenth century, these property units were known as "the commons," and the term still persists in some regions of the United States, referring usually to city parks.

Where the community allows citizens to place their grazing animals on the commons, a whole series of difficulties emerges. The economic benefits accrue directly to the man who places his animal on the "free" land, but the costs are borne by everyone in the community who would like to use the property for any other purpose. In Puritan New England in the seventeenth century, roaming animals uprooted plants and overgrazed pastures. Townspeople cut down trees in the night for firewood or fencing.[8] Similar problems have plagued the commons in every culture. This is the direct result of a system of ownership in which *economic gains go to individual users* and *costs are borne by non-users*.

Such a system inevitably produces economic waste and personal disputes over the proper use of the common property. Those who benefit directly from their personal use of the commons have few direct economic incentives to conserve the commons' scarce economic resources, for these resources are obtained at nearly zero cost to the private users. The cost of running one additional animal on the commons is minutely felt by any single taxpayer-owner, but he receives the full benefits immediately. There is an economic incentive to overgraze the commons, for economic restraints are minimal (e.g., taking your animals to the pasture), while the benefits are direct. This creates a system of "positive economic feedback" rather than "negative feedback." It leads to a situation described by some scholars as "the tragedy of the commons."[9] It involves such phenom-

---

8. Gary North, "The Puritan Experiment in Common Ownership," *The Freeman* (April 1974); reprinted in *Puritan Economic Experiments* (Tyler, Texas: Institute for Christian Economics, 1988), ch. 1.

9. Garrett Hardin, "The Tragedy of the Commons," *Science* (13 Dec. 1968); reprinted in Garrett de Bell (ed.), *The Environmental Handbook* (New York: Ballentine, 1970). Hardin calls for greater government intervention rather than an expansion of private property rights. A solid refutation of Hardin is C. R. Batten's "The Tragedy of the Commons," *The Freeman* (Oct. 1970). See also Robert J. Smith, "Resolving the Tragedy of the Commons by Creating Private Property Rights in Wildlife," *Cato Journal*, I (Fall 1981), pp. 439-68, and "Comment" by Walter N. Thurman, pp. 469-71.

ena as overgrazing, soil exhaustion, and pollution. J. H. Dales correctly observes: "The economic effect of making common property available for use on a no-rule basis, so that it may be freely used by anyone for any purpose at any time, is crystal clear. Common property will be over-used relative to both private property and to public property that *is* subject to charges for its use or to rules about its use; and if the unrestricted common property resource is depletable, over-use will in time lead to its depletion and therefore to the destruction of the property."[10]

Private Ownership

The private ownership of property drastically reduces these problems. Private costs are more readily, accurately, and inexpensively assessed than public or social costs, precisely because *private owners directly face the effects of their own economic decisions.* The cost of adding another animal to the land is borne directly by the man who expects to profit from the decision, if the owner of the animal is also the owner of the land.[11] When the private costs of adding one more animal to the land exceed expected future benefits, owners will stop adding new animals. *Private costs and private benefits tend to balance over the long run.* The better the knowledge that owners have about costs and benefits, the more rapidly these costs and benefits will be balanced. Scarce economic resources are thereby better conserved in a legal system that affirms and enforces private ownership of the means of production, i.e., the free market system.

Nevertheless, men are continually tempted to pass on their costs of operation to their neighbors, while retaining personally all the benefits of production. In private affairs, this quite properly is called *theft.* One man may sneak his animals into another man's field. The other man is harmed economically — robbed of a portion of his land's productivity. The injured party has an immediate economic incen-

---

10. J. H. Dales, *Pollution, Property, and Prices: An Essay in Policy-Making and Economics* (Toronto: University of Toronto Press, 1968), p. 63.

11. In the case of land which is rented or leased, the renter may attempt to pass some of these costs to the owner. He may allow his animals to overgraze, or he may allow the soil to be depleted or damaged in other ways. Profit-seeking owners need to consider these costs when they draw up the terms of the lease. The original lease contract may impose penalties on renters who damage the property, or it may include incentives so that he will care for it. These economic-legal problems plagued Irish tenant farming during the centuries of absentee English ownership: Richard A. Posner, *Economic Analysis of Law* (Boston: Little, Brown, 1986), pp. 63-65.

tive to put a stop to his neighbor's practice of transferring production costs to him. His incentive as an injured private owner to stop the practice is far greater than it would be in a system of common ownership, where the injury is spread over the entire population of so-called owners. (Do we really own common property? If a man cannot *disown* a piece of property, it is difficult to see how he can be said to own it.[12] At best, the costs of "disownership" are high; they involve political mobilization, not simply a private offer to sell.)

The desire to reduce costs is strongly felt on both sides of the fence that separates privately owned properties. In fact, *the very existence of the fence testifies to a man's desire to keep outsiders from transferring their costs to him.* Of course, a fence also testifies to people's desire to avoid having their "benefits" wander off, especially if they might cause damage to another person's property, assuming restitution is the law of the land. As the American poet Robert Frost put it in his poem "Mending Wall," good fences make good neighbors. What we need is a system of law that encourages people to mend their own fences. We need to do better than Talmudic Judaism, which simply forbade Jews to breed cattle, sheep, and goats anywhere near towns or settlements. These animals could be legally bred only in desert areas.[13]

Fences Reduce Conflicts

The Bible affirms that those who violate fences or property lines must make full restitution to the economically injured neighbor. The assessment of harm is easier to make than under common ownership. "*His* cows ate *this* row of corn in *my* cornfield." The owner of the damage-producing animals is responsible. Responsibility and ownership are directly linked under a system of private property rights. Under a system of private ownership, *property lines* are in effect *cost-cutting devices*, for they serve as *cost-assessing devices*. Without clearly defined property rights for men, and therefore clearly defined responsibilities, the rights of "property" — God's living creatures and a created environment under man's dominion (Gen. 9:1-17)[14] — will be sacrificed.

---

12. "The corollary of the right of ownership is the right of disownership. So if I cannot sell a thing, it is evident that I do not really own it." F. A. Harper, *Liberty: A Path to Its Recovery* (Irvington-on-Hudson, New York: Foundation for Economic Education, 1949), p. 106.

13. Aaron Levine, *Free Enterprise and Jewish Law: Aspects of Jewish Business Ethics* (New York: Ktav Publishing House, Yeshiva University, 1980), p. 68. He cites the Talmudic book, *Baba Kamma*, 79b, 80a. He also cites numerous rabbinic sources: Maimonides, Karo, etc. (p. 194, note 42).

14. See "The Ecological Covenant," in Gary North, *The Dominion Covenant: Genesis* (2nd ed.; Tyler, Texas: Institute for Christian Economics, 1987), ch. 14. (Cited hereafter as *Genesis*.)

Carefully defined property rights also help to reduce social conflicts. Dales writes: "Unrestricted common property rights are bound to lead to all sorts of social, political, and economic friction, especially as population pressure increases, because, in the nature of the case, individuals have no legal rights with respect to the property when its government owner follows a policy of 'anything goes.' Notice, too, that such a policy, though apparently neutral as between conflicting interests, in fact always favours one party against the other. Technologically, swimmers cannot harm the polluters, but the polluters can harm the swimmers; when property rights are undefined those who wish to use the property in ways that deteriorate it will inevitably triumph every time over those who wish to use it in ways that do not deteriorate it."[15] Common ownership of large bodies of water, when coupled with an opportunity to pass on private costs of polluted production, increases the extent of water pollution. It is a bad system for the swimmers of this world.

In questions of pollution and environmental quality, there can be no neutrality. There are always winners and losers, although net winners may suffer some losses (air polluters breathe, too), and net losers may gain some benefits (asthmatics may earn high incomes by working for firms that sell raw materials to local polluting factories). It is the task of biblical exegesis to establish the ethical and legal foundations that enable civil judges to do the following: 1) identify the winners and the losers; 2) adjudicate cases properly in the sight of God; and 3) determine what is fair compensation to the losers from any unauthorized winners. One thing is certain: we cannot hope to attain a zero-pollution environment. All life is a form of pollution.

Fire and Pollution

Each owner is also responsible for whatever actions that his animate or inanimate objects do that injure others. A fire that a man kindles on his land must be kept restrained to his property. If the fire spreads to his neighbor's field, he is fully accountable for all the damages. Men therefore have an incentive to take greater care when using potentially dangerous tools or techniques.

The problem of pollution should be subsumed under the general principle of responsibility for fire. A fire is a physical cause of physical damage. From the case-law example in Exodus 22:5, it is clear

---

15. Dales, *Pollution*, p. 67.

that the fire which a man starts is his responsibility. *He cannot legally transfer risks to his neighbor without his neighbor's consent.*

The Bible is not talking here about some shared project in which both men expect to profit, such as burning fields to get rid of weeds or unwanted grass. In such a mutually shared project, the case-law example of the man who rents his work animal to a neighbor, but who stays with the animal the whole time, is applicable. The neighbor is not required to pay anything beyond the hiring fee to the owner (Ex. 22:14-15). If the animal is hurt or killed, the neighbor owes nothing. (If the two men start a fire that spreads to a third party's property and damages it, English common law holds both of them responsible, though not necessarily in equal economic portions, since the victim can collect more money from one than another[16] — what we might call "deeper pockets jurisprudence." Such a legal tradition makes joint activities between rich men and poor men less likely; the rich person, if he is aware of the law, knows that he will be required by the court to pay the lion's share of any joint restitution, simply because he can pay it more easily.)

There is no doubt that the fire-starter is responsible for all subsequent fires that his original fire starts. Sparks from a fire can spread anywhere. A fire beginning on one man's farm can spread to thousands of acres. Fire is therefore essentially unpredictable. Its effects on specific people living nearby cannot be known with precision. I adopt the principle of *uncertainty*, meaning the unpredictability of the specific, individual consequences of any fire, as the governing principle of my discussion of restitution for damage-producing fires, as well as laws relating to the regulation of fire hazards.

What about pollution? Specifically, what about the uncertainty aspect of pollution? A Christian economist should argue that a man must not pollute his neighbor's property without making restitution to him for any *new* damaging effects. If existing pollution is discovered to be more harmful medically or ecologically than had been understood before, the polluter should be required to reimburse those who are *subsequently* affected adversely by the pollutant after the information concerning the danger is made public by the State or becomes known within the polluting industry. (I will consider the legal and economic problems associated with retroactive responsibility in a subsection of this chapter, "Undiscovered Risk.")

---

16. Posner, *Economic Analysis of Law*, pp. 171-73.

Land Discounts: Restitution in Advance

But what if the complaining neighbor had purchased his land knowing all about *present nuisance effects* (as distinguished from subsequently discovered nuisance effects) of the pollution process that was going on next door to his property? Does he now have the legal right to sue his neighbor, who is doing exactly what he was doing before the contiguous property was sold? After all, the buyer bought the property at a *discount* as a result of the depressing effect on local land prices produced by the pollution. There is no doubt that there is an inverse relationship between the damage caused by pollution and land rents (and therefore the market price of land): the greater the pollution, the lower the rents.[17] The purchase price of land — the capitalization of expected net returns over time — reveals this inverse relationship.

Economic analysis informs us about the costs and benefits of biblical morality, and biblical law tells us who should bear these costs and receive these benefits. As potential buyers, we look at the discount in the purchase price of the land next door to a polluting production process, and we can conclude that this discount serves as *an advance payment of restitution to the buyer.* It is an advance payment for *specified, known kinds of expected future "spillovers."* The nuisance effects of these spillovers from the property next door are implicitly agreed to by the buyer when he receives his discount from the seller. Any subsequent attempt by the buyer to demand financial compensation from the polluter under such circumstances is simply a demand for a statist, compulsory redistribution of private property. So is any legislation that would force the polluter to reduce pollution, unless new information regarding the dangers of the pollution is discovered. It would be a demand for restitution in addition to the discount already received by the buyer when he bought the property.

Economist Murray Rothbard has used the concept of the "homesteading principle" to defend the legal right of a polluter to continue to pollute. By developing a previously unused piece of land, the polluter has created an *easement right* to whatever polluting processes he adopts, so long as these processes do no physical harm to those people who owned nearby property when he bought or discovered his land. He "owns the right" to emit noise or other forms of pollu-

---

17. T. D. Crocker, "Externalities, Property Rights, and Transaction Costs: An Empirical Study," *Journal of Law and Economics*, XIV (Oct. 1971), p. 452.

tion, assuming his original neighbors were unaffected. In the case of pollution, he calls this a *pollution easement*.[18]

The Christian economist could also argue that a protesting "pro-environmentalist" who demands that the civil government put a stop to his neighbor's pollution is seeking to achieve a less polluted lifestyle at his neighbor's expense, despite the fact that he bought the property at a discount because of the pollution. Would the protester be willing to pass on to the polluter any increase in the value of his property that results from the reduction of pollution, to help defray the costs of reducing the pollution? Or would he be willing to return an amount of money equal to the increased property value to the original seller, who had to take a discount in order to sell the property? If not, why not? Economically speaking, he is demanding double compensation: initially from the seller, who took a discount, and then from the polluter. Is this fair, even in the name of ecology?

Sewers and Property Value

Perhaps we can better understand the economic issues that are involved here by examining the economics involved in the installation of water or sewer lines in a region of town which had previously been dependent on wells and septic tanks. The municipal government could make an offer to local residents who are about to see their property values rise as a result of the new municipal service. The city says: "If you want to hook up to the new lines, you must pay a high hook-up fee to the municipal water company — a fee closer to the full value of the resulting increase in your property's value." In short, the resident who receives the increase in the value of his land must pay for this appreciated value. This is the way that new sewer projects should be financed, not by assessing all taxpayers in the community. Those who benefit directly and immediately should bear the full costs of the project, or at the minimum, should be required to pay the equivalent of the immediate increase in the value of the property, perhaps in the form of higher assessments per month for a fixed period of time. If sewers were financed this way, there would probably be less political resistance from local taxpayers to local growth.[19]

---

18. Murray N. Rothbard, "Law, Property Rights, and Air Pollution," *Cato Journal*, II (Spring 1982), p. 77.

19. Gary North, "Public Goods and Fear of Foreigners," *The Freeman* (March 1974).

What is the economic principle involved? Simple: *one person should not be compelled by the State to finance the exclusive increase in value of another person's property.* The taxpayer whose property is unaffected by the increased benefits associated with a new water or sewer line should not suffer economic losses (higher property taxes or water bills) because he has to pay for another resident's economic windfall (waterfall?). The beneficiary should pay for the benefit.

So it is with pollution. The beneficiary of the improved environment — a benefit extracted through compulsion by the civil government — should pay for this improvement. He should compensate the neighbor for the costs borne by the neighbor in reducing the existing level of pollution.

Private Contracts

This raises a very interesting point. Why should the civil government get involved in the dispute at all? Why shouldn't the benefit-seeker approach the polluter directly and offer him direct compensation? The beneficiary knows approximately what it would be worth to him to escape from the pollutant. The polluter knows approximately what the value of being able to pollute means to him. If the benefit-seeker's price is high enough, he can persuade the polluter to sign a contract guaranteeing to reduce or eliminate the polluting activity. In effect, the benefit-seeker pays to the polluter part or all of the discount he initially received from the seller.

The polluter may reject the offer. Under the assumptions of this hypothetical example, this is his legal privilege. But it costs him to reject it. He forfeits the economic benefit offered by the pollution-avoider. His cost of continuing to pollute has just risen appreciably. He can no longer pollute at zero cost. He has an economic incentive to stop polluting the environment.

Bear in mind that we are speaking here of *pollution that was known in advance,* and for which the buyer of the adjacent property received a discount. We are not speaking of new pollution or an older pollution process which, through improved scientific knowledge, is now understood to be more of a physical hazard than had been understood before.

Summary

By assigning to individuals the economic and legal responsibilities of ownership, God imposes on individuals the burden of assessing the costs and benefits of their actions. There is no escape from this economic responsibility. "No decision" is still a decision. If an asset is squandered, the owner loses.

The chief failure of what is commonly referred to as collective ownership is that no individual can be sure that his assessment of the costs and benefits of a particular use of any asset is the same assessment that those whom he represents would make. The tendency is for individuals who are legally empowered to make these representative decisions to decide in terms of what is best for them as individuals. There is also a tendency for the decision-maker to make mistakes, since he cannot know the minds and desires of the community as a whole.

The common property tends to be wasted unless restraints on its use are imposed by the civil government. The "positive feedback" signals of high profits for the users are not offset by equally constraining "negative feedback" signals. Users of a scarce economic resource benefit highly as immediate users, yet they bear few costs as diluted-responsibility collective owners. Thus, in order to "save the property from exploitation," the civil government steps in and regulates users. This leads to political conflicts.

The biblical solution to this problem is to establish clear ownership rights (legal immunities) for property. The individual assesses costs and benefits in terms of his scale of values. He represents the consumer as an *economic agent* only because he has exclusive use of the property as *legal agent*. He produces profits or losses with these assets in terms of his abilities as an economic steward. The market tells him whether he is an effective agent of the competing consumers.

The legal system simultaneously assigns responsibility for the administration of these privately owned assets to the legal owners. It becomes the owners' legal responsibility to avoid damaging their neighbors through the use of their privately held property. The specific biblical classification of fire damage governs pollution in general.

There is no doubt that living close to a source of pollution increases the risk of suffering economic losses. The market reveals this by forcing sellers of polluted or nearly polluted land to offer discounts to buyers. This leads us to conclude that if a person has bought a piece of property at a discount because of its proximity to a known source of pollution, the buyer has no legal claim against the polluter unless the latter adds to the level of pollution or else new dangers regarding the pollution itself are subsequently discovered.

The civil government should not tax one group in order to reward exclusively some other group. Thus, individuals should pay to gain access to a cleaner environment if they are the only (or primary) beneficiaries of the cleaner environment. Each person should assess the costs and benefits of living in a cleaner environment. Nevertheless, when someone begins to damage his neighbor's physical environment, the victim should be able by law to put a stop to the polluter's activity or else be compensated by the polluter.

Pollution and the Costs of Knowledge

If pollution is really equivalent to fire's damaging effects, and because we see that the Bible makes all fire-starters legally liable for damages, then is this economic analysis of pollution and damages — the concept of the purchase price discount as a form of restitution payment — ethically biblical? Shouldn't all damage-inflicting pollution be banned, whether or not the buyer next door knew in advance about it? After all, he may also have known that the man next door started fires regularly, but he would also know in a biblical commonwealth that the fire-starter is personally liable for all future damages that his fire might cause. Why should the polluter be allowed to go on with his polluting without paying damages, yet the fire-starter be required to pay for all damages, irrespective of the neighbor's discount? Are the two cases ethically the same or different?

The Economics of Uncertainty

They are the same cases in principle, but they are different in application. To understand the differences in application, we must return to the issue of uncertainty. The specific effects of noise and smoke are known by the general public. They are nuisance effects. They are effects that buyers can estimate, at least to the extent that discounts are offered by sellers to buyers for agreeing to live next door to smoke and noise pollution. In contrast to the known effects of a familiar form of pollution, *the specific effects of any given fire are uncertain.* They can be negligible or catastrophic. A fire may affect people far distant from the point of origin. Thus, the fire-starter is warned: be extremely careful. Biblical law warns all fire-starters: "You are legally responsible for all damages caused by your actions. We all know how dangerous fires are; do not attempt to transfer the side-effects to a neighbor." Under biblical law, society is partially protected from essentially unpredictable catastrophes, because those who light the fires are restrained by the threat of full financial responsibility for damages that the fires inflict.

The difference between "traditional" polluters — smoke, noise, smells — and fire-starters is primarily *a difference in men's knowledge of each action's future effects*. The specific local effects of a familiar form of pollution are approximately known in advance to those who choose to live near pollution. The specific effects of specific fires caused by local fire-starters are not well known to nearby residents. Whether specific sparks from a specific fire will be harmless or will ignite this or that field, or this or that neighborhood, cannot be known in advance. We must focus our exegetical attention on these specific effects.

Insurable Risk

The existence of fire insurance does not invalidate this analysis of "the economics of specific effects." While it is often possible for a person to buy fire insurance, the reason why fire insurance is available at all is because companies insure many different regions, thereby taking advantage of "the law of large numbers." They can insure specific properties economically only because fires have known effects in the aggregate. If there were no known statistical pattern to fires in general, insurers would not insure specific properties against fire damage.

This is not to say that the following arrangement should be prohibited by law. A person who wishes to begin a business which is known to be dangerous approaches others who could be affected. "I'll make you a deal," he says. "I will pay for all increases in your insurance coverage if you let me begin this business in the neighborhood." If they agree, and if the insurance companies agree to write the policies, then he has met his obligations. He has made himself economically responsible for subsequent damages. Instead of paying for damages after the fact, he has paid in advance by providing the added insurance premiums necessary to buy the insurance.

What if some resident says "no"? The prospective producer of danger can then offer to buy him out by buying his property. If the offer is accepted, the prospective danger-producer can then either keep the property or sell it to someone who is willing to live with the risk, if the discount on the land's selling price is sufficiently large. But if the original owner refuses to sell, and if he also refuses to accept the offer regarding insurance premiums, then the first man should not be allowed to force out the original owner. If he begins the

dangerous production process, the existing property owner can legitimately sue for damages. The court may require a money payment
from the danger-producer to the potential victim. If it does, then
many other people may sue for damages. This threat will inhibit the
dangerous production. The court need not necessarily prohibit the
activity altogether.

Judges must do the best they can in estimating the costs and benefits to the community, *including the perceived value to citizens everywhere*
of the preservation of private property rights by the State. They cannot estimate perfectly, for they cannot know the psychic costs and benefits
involved in the minds of the conflicting parties. But they can make
general, "unscientific" estimations, given the image of God in all
men, and given the created environment in which all men live. This
is an important application of biblical revelation to economics: if
there is no universal humanity (no universal human nature) and no
Creator who serves as the basis for man's image, and no creation
governed by the Creator in terms of His value and His laws, then it
is impossible for the judges legitimately to have confidence in their
estimation of social costs, social benefits, private costs, and private
benefits. Without our knowledge of objective economic value provided by God's plan and His image in man, objective economic
value becomes epistemologically impossible.[20] Judges would then be
blind in a sea of exclusively subjective economic values in which it is
philosophically impossible for men to make interpersonal comparisons of subjective utility.[21]

Undiscovered Risk

If the case of the polluter and the fire-starter is essentially the
same case ethically, then we have another legitimate question to deal
with. Should the polluter be held fully responsible for any *yet-to-be-*
discovered effects of his pollution? Should judges require polluters to
make *retroactive* penalty payments to victims if dangerous effects of
the pollution are discovered? After all, a man who starts a fire cannot escape responsibility for the damage his fire inflicts on others.
Why should the polluter escape? Again, the ethical principle is the
same, but the application is different. Again, the difference in application relates to the question of knowledge.

---

20. North, *Genesis*, ch. 4: "Economic Value: Objective and Subjective."
21. See Appendix D: "The Epistemological Problem of Social Cost."

Men know about fire's *general* potential for creating damage. It is a dangerous tool. In contrast, a particular form of pollution may *not* be known to be *dangerous generally*, although it *is* known to be a *nuisance specifically*. The nuisance factor is what provides the victim with his discount when he buys the neighboring property — a discount appropriate to the *known* side-effects of the polluting process. The limited but known effects of the polluting activity can be dealt with by the victims. They receive compensation in advance in the form of discounted land purchase prices for *relatively predictable damages*.

The problem of uncertainty concerning pollution has increased since the end of World War II. The development of the petrochemical industry has created new problems associated with toxic wastes. The physiological effects of today's forms of pollution may not be well known. Uncertainty increases, making some forms of pollution more like the example of uncontrolled sparks than like smoke, whose effects are not lethal. The modern legal system has struggled with the implications of the new technology:

However, modern chemicals are suspected of causing physical injuries, such as cancer, and certain emotional dysfunctions having etiologies that are little understood by science or medicine. One of the most significant characteristics of the development of these types of diseases is their latency, the time between exposure and expression of the disease. For example, a few types of cancer have a latency period of 20 to 30 years while some mutagenic diseases may take a generation or more to become evident. Moreover, chemicals suspected of causing such diseases often function at low concentrations, e.g., parts per billion, or perhaps a single molecule. In addition, pollution injuries, unlike common traumatic injuries, may be inflicted on many persons located far from the pollution source.

Particularly baffling is their unpredictability. If a heavy beam falls upon a worker, the injury will be much the same regardless of who is struck. Exposure to identical concentrations of a given pollutant, however, may produce reactions varying from no observable ailment to a life-threatening emergency.

These characteristics create unprecedented uncertainty, thereby challenging the ability of the judicial system to perform its traditional role of balancing the availability of compensation for individual injury against the social benefits of the injury-causing agent.[22]

---

22. Robert K. Best and James I. Collins, "Legal Issues in Pollution-Engendered Torts," *Cato Journal*, II (Spring 1982), pp. 104-5. See also Peter Huber, *Liability: The Legal Revolution and Its Consequences* (New York: Basic Books, 1988), pp. 67-70, 112-14.

Retroactive Payments vs. Innovation

The question of a retroactive payment in the future for late-appearing medical or ecological harm that was produced by the pollutant before the pollutant was regarded as dangerous is a controversial topic. Polluting when the specific effects are not presently regarded as dangerous seems to be a case of *accidental harm without personal liability.* Men are not omniscient. They should not be held personally liable for harm that results from seemingly harmless activities or activities that were known to be nuisance-producing, but for which the victims had received compensation, either directly (e.g., restitution) or indirectly (e.g., a discount on land purchase price).

This is an aspect of the judicial problem of negligence. Traditional Jewish law recognized that where no foreseeability was possible, individuals should not be held legally liable for damages that result from their actions. "Cases where the defendant is entirely exempt from liability because he was in no way negligent are of two kinds: (1) the plaintiff himself was negligent because he should have foreseen the possibility of damage, i.e., where the defendant acted in the usual way and the plaintiff acted in an unusual way and the damage was therefore unforeseeable; (2) neither party could have foreseen the possibility of damage and therefore neither was negligent."[23] These conditions are theoretical; seldom are real-life situations able to be defined this clearly. In the older common law tradition, if the courts determine that both parties are negligent, the victim must pay for his own losses — the doctrine of contributory negligence.[24] The point is clear, however: a legal system must not be constructed that rests on the operating presupposition that people can be expected to possess perfect foreknowledge.

If civil law does hold innovators financially responsible for possessing knowledge before even specialists have it, then innovation will be inhibited. Developers of potentially dangerous production methods will be afraid to produce anything new. The more rigorously the law links long-run damage to a particular new technology, the more that any given innovation will be regarded by producers as

---

23. Shalom Albeck, "TORTS. The Principle Categories of Torts," *The Principles of Jewish Law,* edited by Menachem Elon (Jerusalem: Keter, 1975?), col. 321.

24. In recent years, a new doctrine has emerged: comparative negligence. It examines "relative fault" in accidents. It is a means of forcing some people or businesses to provide insurance for negligent accident victims. Posner, *Economic Analysis of Law,* pp. 156-57. See also Huber, *Liability,* pp. 78-79.

potentially dangerous. The costs of testing all possible effects could conceivably wipe out most innovation. (By requiring perfect testing, and by enforcing this requirement perfectly, the civil government could wipe out all innovation perfectly.) At the very least, newer, more innovative but undercapitalized firms would be forced out of the market, which is one reason why large, bureaucratic, lawyer-filled, conventional, and heavily capitalized firms tend to favor government rules and regulations that make the introduction of a new technology expensive. If such legislation is passed, existing firms can then buy up innovative processes at prices lower than those that would otherwise have prevailed.

The costs (forfeited opportunities) borne by many members of society as a result of the innovation that is not introduced could easily be far greater than the damage inflicted by a mistake in the early stages of a production process. A classic example of just this sort of retarded technology is the American pharmaceutical industry, which is hemmed in by extremely expensive testing requirements — requirements that are designed more to protect the careers of the federal bureaucrats who are empowered by law to regulate the industry than designed to protect the public.[25]

Common law recognizes a category of activities called *ultrahazardous*. Strict liability applies to them. Those who are involved with them are held fully responsible, no matter what. Such things as blasting with explosives are included, as well as the ownership of wild animals. But "ultrahazardous activity" is a vague concept. There is a tendency to affix the label to new activities. Posner argues that because we do not know much about their effects, the best way to prevent damage may be to take greater care. This means imposing the law of strict liability until society gains more knowledge about them. This is a means of accident control.[26] The proper biblical response to this State-enforced limitation of innovation is to allow contracting parties to waive their right to sue in case damage results. The case of a terminally ill patient who is willing to try an experimental drug is an obvious example. Needless to say, this is rarely allowed by the bureaucrats.

---

25. Sam Peltzman, *Regulation of Pharmaceutical Innovation* (Washington, D.C.: American Enterprise Institute, 1974); Peltzman, "The Benefits and Costs of New Drug Regulation," in R. Landau (ed.), *Regulating New Drugs* (University of Chicago Center for Public Policy Study, 1973); Robert B. Helms (ed.), *Drug Development and Marketing* (Washington, D.C.: American Enterprise Institute, 1975).

26. Posner, *Economic Analysis of Law*, pp. 163-64.

We must begin with the premise that men are not omniscient; knowledge is not a free good. *A society generally should not make an increase of knowledge a retroactive liability on those who make a discovery and implement it.* Retroactive compensation statutes would put too great a liability on polluters who discover a dangerous effect from the effluent that their company produces. The firm's officers would have too great an incentive to hide the results of their findings. It is better to encourage them to admit the existence of the problem and then remove the offending product or manufacturing process, or remove it geographically, in order to avoid any future judgments against them. Penalties could legitimately be imposed in cases where prudent research — "prudent" ultimately being defined retroactively by a *jury* — into the dangerous effects of a production process or a product was deliberately avoided by the producer. But from the standpoint of passing legislation in the United States, Article I, Section 9 of the U.S. Constitution prohibits *ex post facto* laws that declare some action illegal, and then retroactively impose damages on those who broke the law before it became a law — a wise, State-restraining provision of the Constitution.

Summary

Men are not omniscient; therefore, information must be paid for. Accurate information is even more expensive. Any approach to economics that does not honor this principle from start to finish will be filled with errors. [27]

Individual sparks from a fire are unpredictable in their effects. We can make guesses about the overall effects of a fire, but an area of uncertainty is inescapable. Thus, when we analyze pollution damage in terms of the damage produced by a fire, we must be careful. There are differences of available knowledge in the two types of cases, and therefore different solutions to the respective threats.

Living next door to a fire-starter may be tolerable. Farmers start fires to burn grasses or timber, for example. We do not call for a complete banning of all open fires. We do make people responsible for damage produced by fires that they start. The greater the danger of fire, the more concerned nearby residents must be. Sometimes, the public bans fires altogether.

The same is true of pollution. Sometimes polluters are allowed to continue to pollute the environment, especially if they have been

---

27. Thomas Sowell, *Knowledge and Decisions* (New York: Basic Books, 1980).

polluting it for a long time, and those nearby have purchased land at a discount. But with respect to newly discovered dangers, the polluter is warned: continue polluting, and you will be required to make restitution to victims. This is analogous to the warning to fire-starters if the wind shifts or increases. What was acceptable before may be unacceptable now.

Because no one can know everything, it is impossible to preserve life by eliminating every possible danger before taking any action. It would make human action impossible. We are not God; society must not expect people to perform as if they were God. Thus, there must always be limited legal liability in life. Nevertheless, for those actions that are known to be dangerous, people must be made legally responsible for their actions. This does not justify holding people fully responsible for actions made in terms of earlier knowledge. With greater knowledge comes greater responsibility (Luke 12:47-48). If society tries to impose damages retroactively on actions that were taken yesterday based on yesterday's information, it would destroy the legal foundation of progress.

There can be no life without pollution. There can be no life without risk and uncertainty. We must not strive to build a zero-pollution, zero-risk world. What we must do is to restrain those who would impose added known risks in the lives of neighbors without the latter's permission. We find the legal rule that provides this restraint in Exodus 22:5-6.

Externalities

A man should not be prosecuted for polluting his own land, so long as the form of pollution does not have measurable, physical, and undesired effects on anyone else's life, health, or property. Because it is his own land, *he has internalized the costs of pollution.* (By "internalize," I do not mean simply a mental calculation; I mean that *his property alone* suffers from his actions.) He risks starting a fire on his own property, or he runs a herd of cattle on his own property. The man making the estimate of benefits is the same person who makes the estimate of costs; it is the same man who will reap what he sows.

Once he sells a section of his land, he no longer internalizes costs and benefits on the section that was sold. Another person is now involved: his neighbor. The first man must not be allowed to pass on to his neighbor the risks of living next door to a person who sets fire on his property. The fire-starter cannot legally transfer to his neighbor the *generally known* but highly unpredictable *specific, individual* production costs of fire. *Economic analysis must begin with the Bible's assessment of personal responsibility for a man's actions.* It must begin with the presupposition of the rights (legal immunities) of private property. These rights must be protected by civil law and custom.

The act of polluting someone else's environment is a crime in those cases where either production costs or consumption costs[28] (including risks) that are known to a polluter but unknown to the victim are deliberately imposed on the victim. It is also a crime when someone begins a new and previously unpredicted polluting process without getting permission from future victims. In both cases, it is an attempt on the part of a beneficiary to "externalize" his costs of production or consumption by passing them along to others who do not profit directly from the production process or consumption activity. He lowers his costs by transferring a portion of these costs to innocent victims.

We can grasp the economics of pollution quite easily in the case of a manufacturer. Polluting allows him to retain a greater net income when he sells the goods, and it eventually allows him to increase output until his *personally borne* marginal costs equal his *personally received* marginal revenues, i.e., until he arrives at that level of output at which he loses money by producing one more item. But the total costs of production are higher than his personally borne marginal costs. These additional costs — costs above his personally borne costs — are involuntarily borne by the victims of his pollution. So he continues to expand production above the level of output that he would have produced had he borne the full costs of his production process. If he is not required by law to share these marginal benefits with victims (restitution), and if he is also allowed to continue to pass on some of his production costs to them, then the law has created an incentive to overproduce this particular product.

It must be understood that there are many beneficiaries of this overproduction — overproduction that is *subsidized by the victims* of the pollution. Obviously, the owner of the firm benefits. Another group of beneficiaries is his *customers*, who can buy more goods at the same price, or the same number of goods at a lower price, than before the pollution process began. Third, there are *employees* of his company.

---

28. An example of a consumption cost which produces net losses for a neighbor would be the keeping of pets that bark or bite or otherwise disturb the neighbor.

These groups of beneficiaries can become allies of the polluter in any political dispute concerning the continuation of the polluting practices. Edwin Dolan's comment is applicable: "If he has to clean up he may pass part of the cost along to his customers in the form of a price increase, so his customers may testify on his behalf before the city council. If less of the product can be sold at the higher price, he may have to lay off some of his workers, and thus his employees may join the propollution faction. The addition of these allies does not alter the normative analysis of the situation, for if the act of pollution itself is a crime then these allies are nothing but partners in crime. The customers of the firm are in a position analytically identical to the recipient of stolen goods. The producer kept his price low only by forcing the residents adjacent to his establishment involuntarily to subsidize the cost of production, by permitting their lungs and noses to be used as industrial waste disposal units, substituting for the mechanical units which should have been installed at the plant. The customers no more deserve to benefit from this tactic than the owner himself."[29]

Notice that Dolan explicitly uses *normative* economic analysis. He does not ignore ethics. To ignore ethics as a matter of methodological objectivity, as most humanistic free market economists *claim* that they must,[30] is to subsidize immorality. They are importing immorality into their "neutral" economic analysis, all in the name of scientific objectivity. There are always unrecognized and uncompensated victims of "neutral" economic analysis, at least in those cases when policymakers take seriously an economist's suggestion (sometimes called "a conclusion of scientific economics").

Allocating Pollution

Dolan's analogies are both clever and graphic: consumers as "recipients of stolen goods," and nearby residents as "unpaid organic pollution-absorption devices." We need to pursue the analogy of the consumer as a receiver of stolen goods. If a buyer of a domestically produced consumer good is enabled to make the purchase at a lower

---

29. Edwin G. Dolan, *TANSTAAFL: The Economic Strategy for Environmental Crisis* (New York: Holt, Rinehart & Winston, 1971), pp. 42-43. TANSTAAFL, the book's cover tells us, stands for: "there ain't no such thing as a free lunch."

30. In fact, they sneak in their ethical views through the back door of applied economics — evaluating economic policies — and also through aggregation. See Appendix D: "The Epistemological Problem of Social Cost."

price than would have been possible, had the producer not been a
polluter, then he has benefitted at the expense of the residents who
have "absorbed" the pollution. The consumer is a participant in the
pollution process, even if he is unaware of the reason why he has
been offered an opportunity to buy a product at a low price. The
consumer has transformed private costs into social costs, for he in
effect "hires" the polluter as his production agent when he makes the
purchase. He provides the seller with money, which in turn encourages the producer to continue producing the product.

Should the consumer be held legally responsible and economically responsible? No. The consumer must assume that the producer
is violating no laws in anyone's community. He cannot investigate
every instance of lower-than-normal prices. He must act in terms of
what is presented before him — product and price — and not become
a full-time, one-man investigative agency. He assumes that the local
civil government in the producer's region is serving as the agent of
any injured local victims of pollution. The State should not attempt
to impose on consumers all the producers' costs of knowledge in
every economic transaction.

If the civil government in the producer's community steps in and
requires the producer to install pollution-control equipment, and if
the producer then discovers that he is in a position to pass these costs
along to the buyer, at least temporarily, the buyer may begin to shop
for a cheaper substitute. In this sense, the pollution-control equipment is essentially a *tax*. Contrary to popular opinion, *taxes cannot be
shifted forward to consumers*, at least not without risk, precisely because
consumers may begin shopping around for cheaper, untaxed goods.[31]
Now, what if some "foreign" producer — in a foreign nation, or a "for-

---

31. Murray Rothbard is the one economist who has stressed this point. "It is generally considered that any tax on production or sales increases the cost of production
and therefore is passed on as an increase in price to the consumer. Prices, however,
are never determined by costs of production, but rather the reverse is true. The
price of a good is determined by its total stock in existence and the demand schedule
for it on the market. But the demand schedule is not affected at all by the tax. The
selling price is set by any firm at the maximum net revenue point, and any higher
price, given the demand schedule, will simply decrease net revenue. A tax, therefore, *cannot* be passed on to the consumer. It is true that a tax *can* be shifted forward,
in a sense, if the tax causes the supply of the good to decrease, and therefore the
price to rise on the market. This can hardly be called shifting *per se*, however, for
shifting implies that the tax is passed on with little or no trouble to the producer."
Rothbard, *Power and Market: Government and the Economy* (Menlo Park, California: Institute for Humane Studies, 1970), p. 67.

eign" state or province across the nation, or in a "foreign" city across the state — is in a position to get the authorities in his region to allow the production of a comparable product at a more competitive price, by using the same polluting methods that the authorities in the first community banned? The foreign producer is allowed to pollute — to externalize production costs without getting permission from the victims.

Voting for Pollution

What if a majority of the "victims" — local townspeople — want jobs more than they want clean air or water? What if they agree, implicitly, with the decision of their civil authorities to allow the pollution? In other words, what if most residents in a different community are willing to receive income in the form of wages rather than in the form of a clean environment? The polluting process will then be transferred to the new region where this form of pollution is not so great a concern. *The free market allocates pollution through competition.*[32] The manufacturer in the first region, where voters prefer a cleaner environment to higher monetary income for local firms and higher income for those servicing those firms, will lose his share of the market to the producer in the second region.

Is the buyer of *legalized* higher pollution goods still "a receiver of stolen goods," economically speaking? (At no time is the consumer morally or legally guilty of receiving "stolen" goods. It is only a question of formal economic analysis — the economist's attempt to show

---

32. There is a problem here with majority rule. What if one person in the community objects to the polluting factory? If social policy by civil governments always had to attain unanimous consent in order to be implemented, there could be no civil government. The economic goals of a few people sometimes must be sacrificed for the sake of the majority. There are obligations and benefits for both the "one" (the society) and the "many" (individuals). The problem for humanistic economists is that if unanimous consent is not achieved within the electorate, then there is no way for economists to know whether a particular intervention by the State has maximized social welfare: John Burton, Epilogue, in Steven N. S. Cheung, *The Myth of Social Cost* (San Francisco: Cato Institute, [1978] 1980), pp. 62-63.

The Bible gives us guidelines for establishing the necessary balance between the two. In the case of the anti-pollutionists in a community, they can sell their property to others who want to take advantage of a better "environment for jobs." Higher pay scales will tend to offset declines in property values that result from pollution. If a property owner believes that his losses are too great, he can sue the polluting company. Local legislation should not make such law suits impossible; it should only reflect a community's consent concerning the *approximate* level of pollution which a particular facility is permitted to emit. If one man's property is damaged excessively (wind patterns, etc.), then he should be allowed by law to take his claim before a jury of his peers.

who wins, who loses, and why, in terms of economic theory.) No, he is not guilty. Why not? Because a majority of voters in the manufacturer's community really are not deeply worried about the particular form of pollution involved in the specific manufacturing process, possibly because local air currents or water flows disperse the pollution effectively. The voters have announced, in principle, "go ahead and buy our local manufacturer's lower-priced goods, for we are willing to accept the costs that his manufacturing process imposes on us as 'pollution absorbers.'"

The consumer cannot be held accountable, economically speaking, since he cannot know the local opinions of the townspeople. He has to assume that the goods are being produced lawfully. If residents are willing to put up with the pollution for the sake of the local economy, then in effect they are being compensated by the polluter. The *higher wages or other economic benefits* accruing to local residents as a result of the employment opportunities offered by the polluting company are, economically speaking, *the equivalent of restitution*. Victims are being compensated for their suffering. Therefore, *the goods are no longer "stolen."*

The Pollution Auction

Most people in the economically developed nations live in urban areas. These urban centers are noted for their smog-filled air, the noise of trucks rumbling down highways, traffic jams, noisy power lawn mowers, and other "spillover" effects. Yet people in the United States refused to move back to small towns until the 1970's, and even then, the move out of the major cities amounted to little more than a trickle. Few people in Western nations are moving to the small town or farming community. For that matter, few people in any nation are moving to small towns; the phenomenon of urbanization is international. A nation's major economic opportunities are generally concentrated in cities. Yet there is little doubt that industrial pollution is nonexistent in most of these rural areas.

What is a legitimate conclusion regarding this fact of urbanized life? Simple: most people do prefer clean air and quiet streets, but they want them at *very low prices*. The demonstrated preference of the vast majority of Western citizens is for the city, with all its pollution. The polluted environment of the city is preferable to the *differently polluted* environment of the rural countryside. It may have something to do with rural insects, dust, or pollen; it may have more to do with loneliness or the hard work of subduing a rural environment. It almost certainly has a lot to do with comparative opportunities for monetary income. But it is a fact that most people have chosen to live in the industrially or mechanically polluted environments that a vocal minority decries publicly. Most people prefer an urban type of pollution to a rural type, *given today's array of prices.* Change the array of prices, and people may well move out of the city.[33]

In effect, people in various regions are involved in a giant auction — a *pollution auction.* Some people bid high. They announce, in effect, "We'll put up with a lot of smog for the sake of high incomes to match our sunny climate" (Southern California). Or they say, "We'll put up with noxious fumes from wood pulp mills in order to live in the green outdoors" (Oregon). People in particular regions are more concerned about one form of pollution than another. This preference may be strictly aesthetic, or it may be due to special problems posed by the fluid in question. For example, a region's stagnant air but free-flowing, aerated streams may make liquid effluents more acceptable than smoke effluents. In another region, the reverse may be the case. What we find, then, is that *voters in regions "buy" the quantity and kind of pollution they most prefer.*

There will always be some pollution where there is life. Francis Schaeffer wrote a book called *Pollution and the Death of Man.* I much prefer the title, *Pollution and the Life of Man.* Pollution is inescapable. We are all polluters. We are all exhalers and excreters. What we need are legal and institutional arrangements that allow us as individuals to make our own decisions concerning what kind of pollution we are willing to put up with, and at what price.

This is the legal and institutional framework that is produced by biblical law and free market economics. Each region selects a particular form of pollution in the quantity it can tolerate at prices it is willing to pay. Each community is forced to give up particular forms of a clean environment in exchange for other benefits. *There are no free lunches in life; there are also no pollution-free environments.* Scarcity is inescapable (Gen. 3:17-19). *At zero price,* there is always more demand for clean air and pure water than there is available supply.

---

33. If people presently dwelling in American cities should become convinced that the Soviet Union plans to attack all American cities with nuclear missiles next year, the array of prices will shift. The same would also be true if people became convinced that some deadly plague is specifically urban and expected to become an epidemic.

The Mobility of Capital

The free market's *mobility of capital* allows communities to make the choice among various mixtures of pollution and economic benefits, but local regulations also force polluters to participate in this choice. Production can shift, industry by industry, to those regions of the globe where the particular form of pollution involved is most acceptable. The *free movement of capital* combines with *competitive markets for consumer goods* to make it possible for regions to make effective "bids" for the "pollution-income package" they prefer. At the same time, local legislation that restricts certain kinds of locally less desirable pollutants forces plant managers to come to grips with the true costs of production in that region. They can then decide if it would pay to shut down the factory and relocate elsewhere. And even if they simply shut down the factory and go out of business, another firm using the same production methods can always go to a community where the firm's polluting is acceptable *at some price*. So consumers, by responding or failing to respond to offers by sellers, force a *redistribution of pollution* from one region to another. But to do this, consumers in effect work with local civil governments.

Anthony Y. C. Koo has remarked that two countries with identical economic resources and technologies could engage profitably in trade if the two populations had different environmental preferences. He also warns against the danger of globally enforced, uniform environmental standards. People in underdeveloped nations will be suspicious about the imposition of Western standards. "The movement could be construed as an attempt to impose pollution controls that will prevent them from taking full advantage of comparative cost. . . ."[34]

Summary

Pollution is a side effect of production (including life). What is a side effect? It is an effect that the affected people do not like. Effects are effects; the "side" aspect of an effect is an assessment made by observers.

In any production process, there are costs to be borne and benefits to be reaped. The goal of a biblical legal order is to create an institutional order that will allocate costs and benefits fairly. What is fair? The Bible is clear: a man reaps what he sows. Those who seek

---

34. Cited in James C. Hite, *et al.*, *The Economics of Environmental Quality* (Washington, D. C.: American Enterprise Institute for Public Policy Research, 1972), p. 35.

the benefits must bear the costs. But men are advantage-seekers. If they can pass on costs of operations to others, their net return on their property increases. Thus, the legal order must see to it that costs are paid by those who can legally claim the benefits of any action. In short, costs ("side effects") must be allocated, just as benefits ("effects") must be.

What we must recognize is that there are costs involved in achieving the benefits of reduced pollution. Production involves costs; therefore, the production of a cleaner environment produces costs. We speak of externalities, but there are two kinds of externalities in any production process: cursings (costs) and blessings (benefits). A person who is not an owner of a firm may suffer from its pollution, but he may also make a living by selling goods or services to people employed by the polluting firm. Thus, for him to see the reduction of the costs (pollution), he may also find the reduction of the benefits (income). Non-owners who are affected will differ in their personal cost-benefit analysis of the effects of the local production process. Some of them will seek economic restitution or political allies in stopping the pollution; others will bear the costs and even organize politically to defeat those who have organized a zero economic growth–clean air lobbying group.

The allocation of pollution is in part political and in part economic. The free market requires a legal order to protect it (benefit); one of the costs of obtaining this legal order is the risk that the owners of any particular production process will lose wealth when the production process is hampered by regulations or legally shut down by those who have become "pollution absorbers" in the community.

The civil government is one institutional means through which the competing individual assessments of costs ("side effects") and benefits ("effects") are weighed and acted upon. The decision may be made in terms of "one man–one vote," or it may be made representatively by a council or a judge; it may be made representatively by a jury. Civil governments also compete against each other, bidding for or against polluting industries. The other institutional means of assessing costs and benefits is the free market itself: "high bid wins." Consumers vote with their money (productivity). It is the interaction of these competing assessments that results in the allocation of pollution. The owner of the production facility then responds to the highest bid: market plus civil government. He may close the factory, or install pollution-control devices, or pay the fines, but it is the owner who is ultimately responsible. This is why ownership is ultimately a social function, an aspect of representative government. The owner is inescapably a steward.

Identifying the Polluter

We cannot live in a pollution-free world. We pollute the environment simply by being alive. Even when we die, we "pollute" as we rot; but one species' pollution is another species' life-support system. The question is: How can we see to it that pollution is distributed according to the needs of individuals, social units, and the non-human environment? How can we best adhere to our responsibilities under the ecological covenant?[35]

Some forms of pollution may be totally illegitimate. Permanent or near-permanent toxic wastes, including radioactive waste and waste from burning coal, may place such a burden on future generations and future environments that toxic waste-producing processes should be abandoned until cost-effective disposal methods are developed. The problem is, the public has been misled about the risks. Waste from radioactive materials is a legitimate problem. It should be understood, however, that the major creator of radioactive wastes is the federal government, which is involved in the production of nuclear weaponry. Both the production and (of course) the ultimate use of these weapons are sources of such waste. Second, the risks of peacetime radiation are not overwhelmingly great, *compared to coal wastes*. The waste-disposal problem is a real one; there are real economic costs involved in solving this problem. Nevertheless, scientific evidence points to the ability of radioactive waste-producers to reduce risks to a minimum, especially cancer risks. Even in the much-feared and highly improbable case of a core meltdown of a nuclear reactor, the risks are not that great, especially compared to the very real risks of dying from pollution from coal-fired plants.[36]

The public is not aware of the huge waste-storage problems associated with coal-fired electricity. Coal ash is being disposed of in landfills. A 1,000 megawatt plant must dispose of 36,500 truckloads a year. "The tens of millions of tons of ash generated by U.S. coal-fired plants every year are dumped in landfills. . . . There are no

---

35. North, *Genesis*, ch. 14.

36. For a carefully argued presentation of the evidence in this regard, see Bernard L. Cohen, "Radiation Pollution and Cancer: Comparative Risks and Proof," *Cato Journal*, II (Spring 1982).

provisions to prevent the poisons in coal ash being leeched out by rainwater (they are dumped close to the surface) and creeping into aquifers. . . . The radioactivity of the radium and thorium isotopes in coal ash exposes the public to [up to 50] times[37] the dose received from nuclear plants of equal capacity and would violate NRC [Nuclear Regulatory Commission] standards if the NRC were responsible for coal-fired plants, but it isn't. The radionuclides contained in coal ash are chemically active and soluble in water; yet the stuff is dumped close to the surface without strict control and without even any monitoring."[38]

The best way to achieve increased safety from toxic waste is for the State to establish safety criteria for dumping sites and then *to require producers to bear the full costs of waste disposal.*[39] This includes the cost of dismantling nuclear power plants after their economic life is over.[40] The State has increasingly begun to require this, but two problems have appeared. First, organized crime has moved into the "midnight waste disposal business." Highly toxic wastes are being dumped at below-market prices by criminals who pick up the liquid wastes in tank trucks and deposit these effluents in public sewers or on private property.[41] The civil government is almost helpless in the

---

37. In the 1976 book, the author used the figure "at least 180 times," but he has revised this downward as of 1988: letter to author.

38. Petr Beckmann, *The Health Hazards of NOT Going Nuclear* (Boulder, Colorado: The Golem Press, 1976), p. 107. Beckman is a professor of electrical engineering at the University of Colorado.

39. Cohen writes: "One important aspect of the high-level waste disposal question is the quantities involved: The waste generated by one large nuclear power plant in one year is about six cubic yards. This waste is 2 million times smaller by weight and billions of times smaller by volume than wastes from a coal-burning plant. The electricity generated by a nuclear plant in a year sells for more than $200 million, so if only one percent of the sales price were diverted to waste disposal, $2 million might be spent to bury this waste. Obviously, some very elaborate protective measures can be afforded." Cohen, *op. cit.*, p. 266.

40. The important economic and political argument against the commercial use of nuclear power is that the State, because of the military applications of nuclear power, and because of its declared monopoly over the supply of nuclear materials, has an implicit monopoly over electricity generated by nuclear power. This centralizes the production of electricity. The free market solution should be a *decentralized* distribution system. Free market power generation should be as localized and independent of the State as economically feasible, such as power produced by cost-effective solar energy, with rooftop solar panels. The sooner consumers can "unplug" from municipal power companies — or at least can sell back excess power their panels produce during the day — the better it will be for the cause of freedom.

41. Michael Brown, "Toxic Waste: Organized Crime Moves In," *Reader's Digest* (July 1984). The problem of toxic wastes from commercial manufacturing processes appeared only after the Second World War, with the development of the petrochemical industry.

face of this activity. It is an evasion of the problem to blame the government for imposing compulsory waste-disposal costs on private firms, as one libertarian economist does.[42] If the government has imposed too many regulations, then economists need to show what an appropriate program would be. But anarchist economists reject this responsibility. They simply announce: "There is no government solution to pollution or to the common-pool problem because government is the problem."[43]

The second problem arises when the State and its licensed agencies are the prime polluters. This is especially true in the case of water pollution. Municipalities have saved money by reducing expenditures on sewage treatment facilities. How can the State compel itself to be responsible to God, men, and the non-human environment? Jerome Milliman, a specialist in the field of the economics of water distribution and environmentalism, has commented on this problem:

In 1972 Congress established the Federal Water Pollution Control Act in which the Environmental Protection Agency was given responsibility to "restore and maintain the chemical, physical, and biological integrity of the nation's waters." Two national goals of "swimmable and fishable" in 1983 and "zero-discharge" in 1985 were set forth. . . .

As of 1980, EPA reported that the industrial dischargers had a compliance rate of 80 percent. By contrast, municipal dischargers have been slow to comply despite being eligible for construction grants, with a compliance rate of 40 percent with the 1977 requirements. In February 1980, EPA estimated that 63 percent of major municipal treatment facilities were not yet in compliance with the original July 1977 deadline. By the end of 1979, EPA had obligated $24.4 billion in construction grant appropriations (75 percent of construction costs) to municipalities for sewage treatment plants. Construction had begun on 6,623 projects but only 1,552 were in operation. EPA inspections of operating municipal sewage plants reveal that less than one half perform satisfactorily because of operation and maintenance problems. Apparently, EPA is in a poor bargaining position with reluctant municipalities to require compliance because of lack of effective sanctions.[44]

Milliman also points to another problem — a problem that no one so far has been able to deal with successfully, either theoretically or

___

42. "Already existing regulations and laws make it too costly for honest firms to dispose legally of these wastes." Gerald P. O'Driscoll, Jr., "Pollution, Libertarianism, and the Law," *Cato Journal*, II (Spring 1982), p. 51.

43. *Ibid.*, p. 50.

44. Jerome W. Milliman, "Can Water Pollution Policy Be Efficient?" *ibid.*, pp. 165-66.

institutionally: *non-point sources of water pollution*. All our energy and effort has been lavished on the question of how to reduce *point sources*, such as manufacturing plants, municipal sewage treatment centers, and other "piped" effluents. But what about agriculture? What about topsoil runoff and livestock urea runoff? In the cities, what about storm water runoff? Over half of all pollutants coming from non-point sources were uncontrolled, as of the early 1980's, and over half of all pollutants entering surface waters come from non-point sources.[45] As he says, "In contrast to the limited progress that has been made in cleaning up point discharges, progress with nonpoint sources is almost negligible."[46]

What Christians must proclaim is that *this world is God's, and we are His stewards*. When certain forms of pollution are beyond our ability as creatures to deal with effectively, we should abandon the production processes that leave the uncontrollable wastes. But this also means that *we have a responsibility to develop economically and institutionally workable allocation systems to dispose of the wastes that we can control.* A combination of private ownership, private responsibility, public sanctions, and the free flow of capital makes possible an efficient spreading of pollution into those communities that can deal with them most effectively. There is a division of labor in the world. There are different environments in different regions of the earth. *We need a cost-effective allocation of pollutants in order to protect the earth's entire environment.* More specifically, we need a program of market incentives and State sanctions to distribute pollution in such a manner that concentrated and dangerous pollutants are rendered harmless, either by safety packaging or by dilution through geographical dispersion. Without the free market, it is unlikely that the earth's total pollution will be allocated efficiently. Civil government alone cannot do it.

Private Property Rights

Dolan links the crime of pollution with the crime of *trespassing*.[47] Pollution is therefore an invasion of the rights of private ownership. This explains why it is legitimate to bring in the civil government to reduce "pollution invasions" in a neighborhood. By placing pollution

---

45. *Ibid.*, pp. 166, 190.
46. *Ibid.*, p. 190.
47. Dolan, *TANSTAAFL*, p. 69.

within a moral framework, his study avoids a sense of unreality, something that too many other economists have not avoided.

What do we mean by "private property"? Writes legal theorist and economist Richard Posner: "A property right, in both law and economics, is a right to exclude everyone else from the use of some scarce resource."[48] Professor Steven Cheung agrees, but adds two important qualifying aspects of this legal right to exclude: a property right is the *right to exclude* others from using an asset, the *right to benefit* from an asset's productivity, and the *right to transfer* either or both of these two rights to others.[49] This is an ideal definition, as he admits. In practice, exclusivity and transferability are matters of degree.

It should be clear why questions of pollution arise more readily in cases where private property rights have not been (or cannot be) established. The great area of pollution is the area of *moving fluids*, namely, air and water. Who owns the air? Who owns the oceans? Who owns the river? Everyone? No one? Economically, it makes little difference which we conclude, everyone or no one. There is a tendency for men to waste resources under either assumption. As Dales says, "There is an old saying that 'everyone's property is no one's property,' the inference being that no one looks after it, that everyone over-uses it, and that the property therefore deteriorates. History bears out the truth of this saying in many sad ways. Property that is freely available to all is unowned except in a purely formal, constitutional sense, and lack of effective ownership is almost always the source of much mischief."[50] There is an economic incentive to convert private costs (smoke, heat, effluents, noise) into social costs — costs borne by others in society.

Automobile Emissions

The problem is especially acute when there are multiple and basically unidentifiable polluters. Very often those who pollute the

---

48. Richard A. Posner, *The Economics of Justice* (Cambridge, Massachusetts: Harvard University Press, 1983), p. 70.

49. "A good or an asset is defined to be private property if, and only if, three distinct sets of rights are associated with its ownership. First, the exclusive right to *use* (or to decide how to use) the good may be viewed as the right to exclude other individuals from its use. Second is the exclusive right to receive *income* generated by the use of the good. Third, the full right to *transfer*, or freely 'alienate,' its ownership includes the right to enter into contracts and to choose their form." Steven N. S. Cheung, *The Myth of Social Cost*, p. 34.

50. Dales, *Pollution*, pp. 63-64.

environment also suffer from the pollution. For example, a man starts an automobile engine. He becomes a polluter of the air (exhaust emissions, noise). His car's contribution to the overall level of exhaust emissions pollution is infinitesimal — probably unmeasurable from five feet away, unless the car is old and smoking. Yet three million cars in a valley like California's Los Angeles and Orange counties create pollution that is all too measurable. If total air pollution in a particular region is to be reduced, then all the permanent polluters in that region — e.g., people whose automobiles are licensed locally, but not visitors from outside the region — must be restrained by law.

Economically speaking, the emissions-control device on a car is no different from the exhaust muffler, although the latter is more readily understood. Both devices raise the price of the car, reduce its engine's efficiency, and increase gasoline consumption. Both protect innocent bystanders: less noise, less bad air. Both protect the owner of the car: less noise, less bad air. The protection of the innocent bystander is the focus of the law, however. If the owner were the only person affected, the law would not be legitimate. He should be allowed to do what he wants with his own eardrums and lungs.

It must be understood that neither of these emissions-control devices will be paid for entirely by the automobile manufacturers, for manufacturers are not the only ones involved in the pollution process. Pollution-control or noise-control devices are, economically speaking, a kind of sales tax that is paid by consumers, despite the fact that the "collection" of the sales tax is made by the auto companies when they sell the cars. Drivers are the local polluters; auto manufacturers are their accomplices. Drivers usually prefer to convert private costs (lower performance, the cost of the device) into social costs (noise and air pollution), especially if they believe that other drivers are allowed to do the same thing. Car buyers are therefore required by law to pay for the control devices when they purchase the cars. But in most cases, pollution control devices are not required for older model cars; the laws only apply to current production models and future models.

The automobile companies also lose, as the new car drivers' "accomplices," for they cannot automatically "pass along" the added costs of production to buyers. Some buyers may decide to keep driving older, "hotter" performance cars, especially if new car prices rise. This raises the question of who pays. If the public insists on buying new cars, and if all new cars must be fitted with the equipment, then the companies will more readily attempt to "pass on" the extra costs to the buyers. But this is always risky. If buyers have acceptable substitutes — mass transit, for example, or keeping older model cars — then the car manufacturers may not be able to pass on costs without losing buyers. Substitutes or not, total sales of cars could drop as a result of higher prices, and total revenues might fall. The auto manufacturers cannot be certain in advance. They tend to resist any new legislation that would raise their costs of production because of this uncertainty.

Managers do not want to risk the threat of the wrath of the legal owners of the automobile companies. Who are the legal owners of these firms? Those people who own shares of ownership. How can they retaliate against the senior managers? By selling their shares, thereby depressing the price of the shares and reducing the value of the capital owned by the senior managers. We know that a very important form of compensation to the senior managers of a firm is the appreciation of their shares of stock in the firm.[51] They do not want to risk seeing the price of the shares drop. Why would the share owners start selling? Because of the very real possibility that the company's total net revenues will drop in response to reduced sales of the now higher priced cars. Therefore, the costs of pollution-control devices cannot be passed on by the company to the customers at zero price (zero risk) *to* the company — its managers, workers, and share owners.

Mandatory pollution-control devices, biblically, are like spark-retarding devices: they protect other people's property. Where there are multiple polluters, only the civil government can effectively restrain a significant number of polluters, for all are bound equally under civil law.

Summary

There are always problems in identifying polluters, since all of life is a pollution process. The media have focused on nuclear power plants, but they have generally ignored waste materials produced by coal-fired plants. The politicians studiously ignore the pollution produced by their own production facilities. Also, there are non-point

---

51. Henry Manne, *Insider Trading and the Stock Market* (New York: Free Press, 1966), ch. 8.

sources of pollution that cannot be regulated effectively by law. There are limits to bureaucratic regulation, in other words. If self-government fails, then civil government will fail, too.

The world is under a curse. This curse cannot be escaped, only modified. The land brings forth thorns (Gen. 3:18) — "side effects," in other words, meaning unwanted effects. Pollution can be reduced through self-discipline, better scientific knowledge, market incentives, and the threat of punishment. It cannot be eliminated, however, because man's knowledge is limited, and so is his power over the many known effects of human action. The best that we can hope to accomplish is to identify major sources of known dangerous pollution, to study the effects of legislation in reducing the production of such pollution, and then persuade voters to impose workable sanctions against polluters. When criminals are convicted for illegally dumping known toxic wastes into public sewers, and then sold into lifetime servitude to pay the fines, we will see less toxic waste dumped into sewers. There will always be some, however.

All government begins with self-government. Self-government must become more important in regulating pollution, for it is not possible to identify all polluters, and it is also not possible to eliminate every known form of pollution. When polluters know that they will suffer economic sanctions and public ostracism when convicted, they will modify their behavior. They will not modify economically profitable behavior until the public is willing to impose civil sanctions, however. We can see this in the case of abortion. If physicians are willing to get rich by aborting babies, we should not be surprised to find that ordinary businessmen are willing to dump effluents into rivers, even dangerous effluents. If the voting public and its judges cannot distinguish between the effects of abortion (legal) and the effects of the agricultural use of DDT (illegal), then we should not expect to see the spread of self-restraint by industrial polluters. When members of a state-licensed guild are allowed to get rich by killing babies, few people will take seriously warnings against pollution. Acid rain is hardly the threat to life and limb that uterine saline solutions are.

Legitimate State Coercion

In the case of a single violator or a few potential violators, there are two reasons justifying the coercive intervention of the civil government. *First*, to use the biblical example of fire, a man who permits a fire to get out of control may see an entire town burned to the ground. There is no way, economically, that he can make full restitution. In fact, it would be almost impossibly expensive to estimate the value of the destroyed physical property, let alone the loss of life, or the psychological anguish of the victims. Therefore, in high-risk situations, the civil government can legitimately establish minimum fire prevention standards. (Analogously, the civil government can also legitimately establish medical quarantines to protect public health: cp. Lev. 13, 14.)

Carl Bridenbaugh, in his study of urban life in seventeenth- and early eighteenth-century colonial America, discusses this problem in detail. "The specter of fire has ever haunted the town-dweller. This necessary servant may, amidst crowded town conditions, buildings of inflammable construction and the combustible materials of daily housekeeping and commerce, become his deadly enemy. Even in Europe the means of fighting fire were very crude in the seventeenth century, and only towards its close did the great cities, driven by a series of disasters, begin to evolve a system for combatting it."[52] Such measures infringed on personal freedom, and they increased costs on citizens, but they were necessary to help protect people from each other's mistakes — mistakes that the person responsible could not have paid for. In fact, it could easily be argued that the very inability of anyone to pay for them is in itself an incentive for people to take such risks. As Posner says, "An injurer may not have the resources to pay a very large damages judgment; and if not, his incentive to comply with the law will be reduced. . . ."[53]

Marginal Damages and Profit Centers

A *second* reason for allowing State coercion, though far less relevant, is that there may be cases of identifiable polluters who injure many neighbors in a minor, though measurable, way. The costs of assembling all the injured parties — search costs, lawyer fees, delays in court hearings, injury assessments — into one or more legitimate complaining units may be too high for each member of the group to bear. Another way to gain restitution is the establishment of fines for polluters, including graduated fines as the levels of pollution increase. Least desirable, probably, is the outright abolition of the

---

52. Carl Bridenbaugh, *Cities in the Wilderness: The First Century of Urban Life in America, 1625-1742* (New York: Capricorn, [1938] 1964), p. 55.
53. Posner, *Economic Analysis of Law*, p. 344.

pollution-producing activity, although the costs of pollution abatement may in effect serve as outright prohibitions for marginally profitable firms.

The buyers of a particular product may save a few cents or many dollars because the costs of producing it are passed along, involuntarily, to residents living close to the plant, but this does not justify polluting, nor do considerations of the comparative wealth of buyers and injured parties. Coercion in the form of unforeseen and injurious pollution can legitimately be met by coercion from the civil government.

On the other hand, as we have seen earlier in this chapter, such pollution is not necessarily evil, if those who are injured have voluntarily assented to the injury. For example, consider the "company town," a town whose houses and public facilities have been built by a profit-seeking company that employs most of the town's residents. The firm's employees are given access to low-cost housing as part of their pay. They breathe the fumes of the factory, but they also gain the benefits of employment. A required anti-pollution program might make production costs skyrocket and force the closing of the factory. The benefits of employment at that location would then disappear. Workers may very well prefer noxious fumes to unemployment. Even in a normal community, where employees and non-employees live side by side and breathe the same foul air, a majority of voters may prefer the fumes to the economic effects of unemployment. This is especially true if the factory, or industry in general, is a primary employer in a particular region. Bad air may be preferable to most local residents, compared to the firm's bankruptcy. The poorer a community—the fewer economic and employment alternatives available to people—the more likely it is that people will choose bad air to unemployment.

If specific physiological dangers exist because of the fumes that are dumped into the atmosphere or some water-carried effluent that is dumped into the public water supply system, then those affected must be warned. The problem of toxic wastes is a real one. When the victims do not have the technical expertise to discern a measurable, statistically relevant danger to people's health, the civil government can legitimately require the polluter to warn them. But smoke is a familiar fact of life. So is smog. So is noise. If people choose to put up with these nuisances for the sake of employment or for a stronger local economy, then they should be allowed to do so.

Permitting Voluntary Exchange

Suppose, for example, that there is a very desirable piece of land overlooking a lake which is in the path of a proposed runway for jet planes. The land sells at a discount because of the expected noise. Potential buyers are warned in writing of the proposed airport. The buyer takes a risk. He buys his land less expensively, assuming that he will get used to the noise (which most people do). Perhaps the runway will never be built. Then he may find himself the owner of a far more valuable piece of property. Or perhaps the airport will be built, and the land appreciates anyway. (Empirical research indicates that almost without exception, land adjacent to proposed airports rises in value after the construction of the airport.)[54]

Question: Should the civil government forbid such a transaction if the seller has warned the buyer in writing concerning the risk? Why should the civil government be given such power? Perhaps a potential buyer cannot afford to buy a piece of land near a lake in any area not subject to a negative factor like noise. Wouldn't an outright prohibition on land sales be harmful to potential buyers and potential sellers? Wouldn't such legislation be discriminatory against poorer members of the community? Why should men be forbidden to trade off money against noise? On the other hand, should the airport be shut down by law because people who bought the land at a discount later decide that they want a noise-free environment, and then decide that a lawsuit is the way to get it? Is this not another case of theft, a coercive redistribution of wealth from the airport and airlines to the buyers of discounted land?

This example should not be construed to validate the case of a person who buys land at a high price and then is informed that the city council has voted to build the runway. Here is a case of a violation of his property rights. The Bible says that he must be compensated for any resulting loss. The beneficiaries of the council's action, the airlines that use the airport facility, should pay the victims either directly or indirectly, through taxes collected by the city and passed on to the victims. What should the compensation be? A payment equivalent to any drop in the market value of the property caused by the airport, plus moving costs, if owners decide to leave.

Something else should be considered. One reason why Western industrial nations have become so concerned with pollution is that

54. Cheung, *Myth of Social Cost*, p. 20.

they are wealthy.[55] As men's per capita income rises, they tend to worry less about where the next meal is coming from and more about their "quality of life," meaning their physical environment. The West does pollute the environment, but as men get richer, they tend to buy more services than goods. As national wealth increases, capital shifts to the service sector, and to high-technology, low-pollution production. Yet as the level of pollution may be dropping — or shifting from, say, horses to autos, from manure-filled streets and flies to smog and stinging eyes[56] — people's *concern about pollution* may be rising. As they become financially capable of reducing pollution levels, they demand action, even in the face of less dangerous forms of pollution than before. The smoke-filled skies of the great steel towns of the late-nineteenth century are sometimes smog-filled today. Are we so confident that we suffer from more pollution today? Women can safely hang clothes out to dry on a clothes line in Pittsburgh today; in the 1930's, the clothes — and even curtains in their homes — would often be covered with soot in a few hours.[57] (Of course, most women use clothes driers today, which were not available to consumers in the 1930's.) The main reason why Pittsburgh's air is cleaner today is that so many steel mills have shut down due to foreign competition.

Regional Standards

When it comes to the problem of reducing the costs (increasing the efficiency) of assessing the effect of injuries, *local* civil governments are best equipped to enforce pollution (cleanliness) standards. The larger the administrative or geographical unit, the more difficult it is to assess costs and benefits. Only when conflicts across political or jurisdictional boundaries are involved — county vs. county, state vs. state — should higher levels of civil government be called in to re-

---

55. Lester Lave, "Health, Safety, and Environmental Regulations," in Joseph A. Pechman (ed.), *Setting National Priorities: Agenda for the 1980s* (Washington, D.C.: Brookings Institution, 1980), pp. 134-35.

56. Milwaukee, Wisconsin, in 1907 had a population of 350,000 people, and a horse population of 12,500. The city had to dispose of 133 tons of horse manure daily. In 1908, when New York City's population was 4,777,000, it had 120,000 horses. Chicago in 1900 had 83,300 horses. This was in the early era of the streetcar and automobile. There were still three and a half million horses in American cities and seventeen million in the countryside. Joel A. Tarr, "Urban Pollution — Many Long Years Ago," *American Heritage*, XXII (October 1971).

57. Ted O. Thackery, "Pittsburgh: How One City Did It," in Marshall I. Goldman (ed.), *Ecology and Economics: Controlling Pollution in the 70s* (Englewood Cliffs, New Jersey: Prentice-Hall, 1972), pp. 199-202.

dress grievances. Local conditions, local standards of cleanliness, silence, or whatever, involve local conflicts: these are best settled by local governmental units.

For example, if a national civil government imposes general pollution-control standards for clean air, local communities could be damaged economically. A community may have a polluting factory as its primary employment base. The factory is bankrupted by the newly applied national standards. Its owners, or rival producers of similar goods, may choose to move capital into a foreign nation whose political leaders are more anxious to create jobs than to avoid pollution. The pollution is simply shifted "off shore." This may be a good thing, overall; perhaps this particular sort of pollution will be less of a problem in some other geographical environment that is blessed with pollution-reducing wind patterns. Or a foreign nation may have a less dense population. The first question is: *Who knows best?* Is some political body or bureaucratic agency thousands of miles away from the affected areas sufficiently informed about local effects of such decisions?

A second relevant question is: *Who pays?* Rich voters in some regions of a country may be making political decisions that adversely affect poorer voters in different regions whenever national environmental standards are imposed. Are such national standards really that crucial to the survival of the environment? Can local geographical regions really destroy the ecology of the entire nation? What kind of proof can the defenders of national pollution-control standards present to defend their conclusion that such standards are exclusively a matter of national self-interest?

Subsidies to the Politically Skilled

One reason why we get national ecology or pollution-control standards is because of the *costs of political mobilization.* It is less expensive for special-interest groups to lobby a few hundred politicians in the nation's capital or to gain control over a Washington bureaucracy than it is to conduct a lobbying campaign in every regional legislature and local town council. The national civil government then preempts the regional units of civil government. This *centralizes political power*, which leads increasingly to a reduction of everyone's political freedom.

Why should residents of Los Angeles, California, or Denver, Colorado, who live in peculiar geographical environments (stagnant air currents, breeze-reducing surrounding mountains) impose their environmental standards on drivers in wide-open Texas or Wyoming? Why should they lobby for national auto pollution emission standards that will necessarily reduce the performance and increase the purchase price of all cars produced in the United States? *They are demanding a subsidy:* lower costs per unit for required pollution-control equipment (as a result of higher production of regulated cars), but increased costs for most other drivers whose communities are not in need of such devices. In this case, *national pollution-control legislation is a politically acceptable wealth-redistribution scheme.* If people in Southern California want mandatory pollution-control devices for cars registered in their region, they can vote accordingly. Indeed, given the vast number of cars in this region, they *must* vote for emission standards if they are to improve the quality of the air they breathe. But they should not insist on a subsidy from car buyers and operators in other regions of the country.[58]

Why should those who worry about pollution be allowed to extract a subsidy from those who do not worry so much? Those who hate pollution are allowed to move to a less polluted region of the country. But they prefer to achieve their goal of living in a cleaner environment at the expense of local factory workers, whose jobs are "up in the air." How many factory workers are enthusiastic and dedicated supporters of the ecology movement, or were in its early days in the late 1960's? Aren't the movement's white-collar supporters better paid, more highly educated (at taxpayers' expense), and more mobile than the blue-collar working people whose jobs are at stake? The leather goods–selling "street people" with university degrees in sociology were more likely to be at the forefront of the ecology movement in 1968 than the average employee with General Motors. As one book points out, "Preliminary studies indicate in fact the opposite result from that expected by critics; that is, wealthy people tend to be lovers of [ecological] purity while the very poor are more interested in other problems."[59]

Some readers may think I am exaggerating. Not so. The Sierra Club is perhaps the most active lobbying organization for ecology in the world, along with Friends of the Earth. The group took out an advertisement in *Advertising Age* magazine, to attract advertisers for

---

58. To some extent, this principle is honored. Emissions-control standards have in the past been far more stringent for California than for other states in the U.S.
59. James C. Hite, *et al.*, *Economics of Environmental Quality*, p. 34.

their magazine, *Sierra*. Why advertise in *Sierra*? Money! "Sierra readers have very good taste. Each month 81 percent serve domestic or
imported wines, 27 percent serve bottled mineral water and 42 percent offer their guests imported beer."[60] In other words, they say of
their readers, here are the educational and financial *elite*. Kevin
Phillips, the conservative political commentator, has referred to environmentalists as "the wine and cheese belt."[61] The same theme is
pursued brilliantly by William Tucker, in his 1982 book, *Progress and
Privilege: America in an Age of Environmentalism.*[62] We should ask ourselves: To what extent is the concern about pollution a concern of the
highly educated, higher-income intellectuals who have more skills in
media manipulation and political manipulation than those who are
not equally skilled, or who do not trust in salvation by political action?

Economist Thomas Sowell, who grew up in rural North Carolina
and the Harlem "ghetto" of New York City in the depression and war
years,[63] has put his eloquent finger on the problem: the majority
poor have too much money in the aggregate for the minority rich to
compete against successfully. The poor are foreclosing on the rich
because the poor have more money. "There are infinitely more of
them, and real estate dealers and developers would rather get $10
million from 10,000 people than get $1 million from one millionaire."[64]
You will not see economic analysis like this in *Sierra* magazine:

> In the natural course of economic events, the non-rich would end up
> taking more and more land and shore away from the rich. Spectacular
> homes with spectacular views would be replaced by mundane apartment
> buildings with only moderately pleasant vistas. A doctor or movie mogul
> who can now walk the beach in front of his house in splendid isolation
> would be replaced by whole families of ordinary grubby mortals seeking a
> respite from the asphalt and an occasional view of the sunset.
>
> The climax of the story is when the affluent heroes are rescued by the
> government. In the old days, this used to be the cavalry, but nowadays it is
> more likely to be the zoning board or the coastal commission. They decree
> that the land cannot be used in ways that would make it accessible to the

---

60. "Briefing," *New York Times* (Nov. 8, 1982).

61. *Idem.*

62. Garden City, New York: Anchor Press/Doubleday.

63. Thomas Sowell, *Black Education: Myths and Tragedies* (New York: David
McKay, 1972).

64. Thomas Sowell, *Pink and Brown People and Other Controversial Essays* (Stanford,
California: Hoover Institution Press, 1981), p. 104. This essay appeared originally in
the *Los Angeles Herald Examiner* (March 23, 1979): "Those Phony Environmentalists."

many, but only in ways accessible to the few. Legal phrasing is of course more elaborate and indirect than this, but that is what it all boils down to. This is called "preserving the environment" (applause) from those who would "misuse" it (boos).[65]

The Anti-Dominion Impulse

James Jordan is correct: biblical law is essentially anti-aristocratic in the field of economics. The main anti-aristocratic feature of biblical economics is the familistic aspect of capital. The reason for the anti-aristocratic provisions is *dominion*.

If language is the first stage and prerequisite of dominion, property is the second. Adam was given the garden to beautify and protect (Gen. 2:15). He was to name it, get power over it, and creatively remold it. The eighth commandment protects private property, as do other provisions in the law of God (cf. esp. Lev. 25:13; and see I Ki. 21). Every man is to have his own garden. His marriage and his garden (work) are the major axes around which the ellipse of the temporal life is drawn. In pagan aristocratic societies, few men have gardens, and many men are slaves. Moreover, such aristocrats often exercise only minimal dominion, preferring to war or entertain themselves.

Under the influence of Christian concepts of familistic property, the free market has acted to break up such large aristocratic holdings. The industrious poor eventually buy out the lazy rich, and anyone with thrift can eventually obtain his own garden. Dominion is multiplied.[66]

Public concern, meaning media headlines, for both the "population explosion" and the "ecology crisis" hit overnight, around 1967. As Marshall Goldman commented in 1967, "Today's news media devote almost as much attention to air and water pollution as to the problems of poverty. Virtually overnight pollution seems to have become one of America's major issues."[67] The rapid rise and fall of both issues as "media events" indicate that a deeply felt concern over these issues in the minds of large numbers of voters was never present. Can we be sure that much of the motivation behind the once loudly proclaimed "concern for the environment" was not really a hatred of

---

65. *Idem.*

66. James B. Jordan, *The Law of the Covenant: An Exposition of Exodus 21-23* (Tyler, Texas: Institute for Christian Economics, 1984), p. 133.

67. Marshall I. Goldman, "Pollution: The Mess Around Us," in Goldman (ed.), *Ecology and Economics, op. cit.*, p. 3. This book was first published in 1967 under the title, *Controlling Pollution: The Economics of a Cleaner America.*

free enterprise, a hatred of economic growth as such?[68] Is a major underlying (and unstated) intellectual impulse behind the ecology movement
an anti-dominion, anti-progress, anti-Christian Eastern mysticism,
or a "back to nature" ideology that hates modern industrialism?[69]

It is difficult to take seriously anyone who writes, as the leading
anti-growth economist, E. J. Mishan, has written in a purportedly
scholarly work: "The private automobile is, surely, one of the greatest, if not *the* greatest, disasters that ever befell the human race. For
sheer irresistible destructive power, no other creation of man — save,
perhaps the airliner — can compete with it. . . . One could go on, for
the extent of its destructive powers is awesome to contemplate.
Criminal success, especially of robbery and violence, has come to
depend heavily on the fast get-away car."[70] (The get-away car? He
must have been watching too many late-night gangster movies on
television. Besides, the police have cars, too.) He should write a
book called *The Sinister Ambulance*. Mishan's radical elitism is clear
enough in his discussion of the terrible effects of jet planes. They
have allowed hordes of middle-class people to travel to the former
pleasure spots of the rich: ". . . the airliner has conspired with the
automobile to create a tourist explosion that, within a few years, has irrevocably destroyed the once-famed beauty spots of the Mediterranean
coastline."[71] In the name of "the good life" and "the quality of life,"
the supposedly democratic and equalitarian academic scribblers are
proclaiming the wonders of a world in which the middle class and
the poor will not have the economic opportunity to "dirty up the environments" of the rich. "No growth" means less competition from
the "unwashed masses" for those who have already arrived at the top.

Are there objective scientific standards of pollution? Yes. Are the
physiological, ecological and economic effects of these pollutants
universally agreed upon by scientists and other professionals?
Seldom. Can economists assess the costs and benefits of pollution —
or anything else — scientifically? No. As Dales says, "The important

---

68. See, for example, two books by Prof. Ezra J. Mishan, *The Costs of Economic
Growth* (New York: Praeger, 1967) and *The Economic Growth Debate: An Assessment*
(London: George Allen & Unwin, 1977).

69. Ayn Rand argued that the ecology movement is intensely anti-progress: "The
Anti-Industrial Revolution," in her book, *The New Left: The Anti-Industrial Revolution*
(New York: Signet, 1971), ch. 8. A similar thesis is presented by John Maddox, the
editor of the British scientific journal, *Nature*, in his book *The Doomsday Syndrome*
(New York: McGraw-Hill, 1972).

70. Mishan, *The Economic Growth Debate*, pp. 122-23.

71. *Ibid.*, p. 123.

question is *how much* 'better quality environment' we would be willing to buy at different 'prices' in terms of higher taxes and higher costs of goods, and most of us are not sure about this. As was suggested in the last chapter, the only way to answer the question may be to have the politicians start charging us for better quality air and water and then keep 'upping the ante' until we say 'Enough! No more!' The trouble is that when we call a halt about half of us will think that we are already spending too much to improve the environment, and about half of us will want to spend more; therefore very few of us will be very happy with the outcome."[72] A perfect environment will not come from political pressure.

Few people are aware that the whole debate over carcinogens (cancer-producing substances) in the environment has been conducted with virtually no evidence. In her study of 15,000 scientific papers and books, Edith Efron discovered that the scientific community has identified very few clear threats to human health in the modern environment. The public discussions of carcinogens in the environment have been conducted primarily by special-interest groups, political propagandists, social scientists, and a handful of scientists, often those employed by government regulatory agencies whose survival is dependent on continuing public funding. As she says, "the government has systematically fed the public the views of one faction in the academic world while the views of others have been largely withheld."[73] She correctly pinpoints the underlying problem: a commitment to a particular view of man and nature by modern scientists. Rachel Carson, whose apocalyptic book on the environment, *Silent Spring* (1962), launched the modern political ecology movement, operated in terms of a view that man is an invader in nature. Efron is correct: ". . . the apocalyptic approach to cancer rests, fundamentally, on the 'axiom' of a largely benevolent nature — on a vision of a largely noncarcinogenic Garden of Eden now defiled by the sins of pride and greed."[74] This deeply religious perspective has produced faith in a political solution: ". . . the 'axiom' of nature's minimal role in cancer causation led to a political conception of the disease of cancer and to a political solution. . . . The underlying 'axiom' of nature's virtual noncarcinogenicity was tacitly accepted, and the

---

72. Dales, *Pollution*, pp. 71-72.
73. Edith Efron, *The Apocalyptics: Cancer and the Big Lie* (New York: Simon & Schuster, 1984), p. 12.
74. *Ibid.*, p. 127.

little packet of ideas that followed from that 'axiom' soon became the conventional wisdom: 'Man,' not nature, was responsible for the evil . . .'man' meant the men who made and used chemicals . . .'man' meant industry . . . cancer was fundamentally a political disease."[75] The scientific facts prove otherwise: man's natural environment is itself carcinogenic.[76]

What is the biblical perspective? The Bible teaches that man is cursed, and so is nature. Neither man nor nature is normative, ethically or biologically. Man sickens and dies because he is under a curse, but no one environmental source is the primary cause of man's condition. To assume that nature is not carcinogenic is an exercise in fantasy.

Summary

There are certain kinds of damage that can become so widespread that those who produce them endanger too many people. In the case of some form of pollution that is known to be so damaging that the producer could not possibly make restitution to those injured, the State possesses the lawful authority to prohibit or isolate the activity. The example of fire codes is representative. Similar codes for polluting processes can and should be worked out by experts who are hired by the government, with the politicians invoking the required regulations. The legal justification for outright prohibition must be the known inability of damage-producers to pay their victims, should a crisis take place. The more widespread the production process is, and the more widespread its spillover effects, the less likely that any one producer could afford to make restitution. Thus, the civil government restricts the process.

The civil government is the necessary agent for settling disputes that cannot be worked out voluntarily and peaceably. It is an agent of last resort, for it uses coercion, a very dangerous monopoly to be invoked by anyone. The public should be willing to permit people to settle disputes over pollution on a mutually profit-seeking basis. The most obvious example is to allow people to accept known environmental defects in order to gain discounts on land purchases.

The assessment of risks (costs) and rewards is a cultural phenomenon.[77] Cultural preferences are expressed locally. They are more

---

75. *Ibid.*, p. 128.
76. *Ibid.*, pp. 125-75.
77. Mary Douglas and Aaron Wildavsky, *Risk and Culture: An Essay on the Selection of Technical and Environmental Dangers* (Berkeley: University of California Press, 1982).

identifiable and distinct. Thus, the regulation of pollution should be limited judicially. The judicial authority to which voters assign the tasks of regulation should be closely restricted to the geographical region in which that type of pollution is being produced. There will therefore be less distorting of the pollution allocation preferences of the people who are involuntarily affected by the particular pollutants.

A major reason why regional pollution preferences are ignored is that those who are politically skilled in imposing their views on politicians prefer to concentrate their efforts and resources at the national level. A region-by-region political fight is expensive and essentially open-ended; the results will not be clear cut, for many regional politicians will resist the arguments of the anti-pollution forces. It is cheaper for the anti-pollution lobby to risk losing nationally on any particular vote and then try again than it is to try to win each region separately.

Dominion involves costs and risks. Those who want anything like a perfectly safe environment are calling for the extinction of the human species—a very high-risk program. It is ultimately a religious program. This anti-dominion religion is not Christianity. The biblical goal is the progressive sanctification of the environment as an effect of the progressive sanctification of a growing number of individuals through God's grace. The environment must be progressively healed as a result of God's judgment of blessing on covenant-keeping men, for it was first polluted as a result of God's judgment against covenant-breaking mankind (Gen. 3:18).

Brokers Between Generations

All government is representative. Each individual represents God, for better or worse. Each person is responsible before God. We are all stewards. There is no escape. The final judgment is sure.

The question then arises: Why should the civil government be a better long-run steward of resources than individual or corporate owners? The fact is, if ownership becomes political, then the only true ownership is the ability of the politician to maintain himself in political office. If ownership is bureaucratic, then it is based on considerations of tenure and bureaucratic advancement. If it is private, familial, or corporate, then ownership is governed by competitive market considerations. The public is always represented by owners, just as God is; the question is: Which form of representation is appropriate? Which form is most responsive to God and to the public in any given instance?

R. H. Coase quite properly called attention to the problem of State enterprise and responsibility for damages. He remarked that "it is likely that an extension of Government economic activity will often lead to this protection against action for nuisance being pushed further than is desirable. For one thing, the Government is likely to look with a benevolent eye on enterprises which it is itself promoting. For another, it is possible to describe the committing of a nuisance by public enterprise in a much more pleasant way than when the same thing is done by private enterprise. . . . There can be little doubt that the Welfare State is likely to bring an extension of that immunity from liability for damage, which economists have been in the habit of condemning. . . ."[78]

A proper analysis of ownership, pollution, and responsibility quite properly begins with F. A. Harper's observation that if I do not have the right to *disown* an asset, I do not really own it. Murray Rothbard extends Harper's comment and applies it to the question of who really owns "public" property. Very important, Rothbard concludes, is the *short-run perspective of government owners.*

While rulers of government own "public" property, their ownership is not secure in the long run, since they may always be defeated in an election or deposed. Hence government officials will tend to regard themselves as only transitory owners of "public" resources. While a private owner, secure in his property and its capital value, may plan the use of his resource over a long period of time in the future, the government official must exploit "his" property as quickly as he can, since he has no security of tenure. And even the most securely entrenched civil servant must concentrate on present use, because government officials cannot usually sell the capitalized value of their property, as private owners can. In short, except in the case of the "private property" of a hereditary monarch, government officials own the current *use* of resources, but not their capital value. But if a resource itself cannot be owned, but only its current use, there will rapidly ensue an uneconomic ex-

---

78. R. H. Coase, "The Problem of Social Cost," *Journal of Law and Economics*, III (Oct. 1960), pp. 26-27. A classic example of this unwillingness of the federal government to police its own agencies is the case of the radioactive waste disposal sites that are believed to be leaking wastes into local environments. Seventeen of these nuclear weapon production facilities in 12 states are owned by the U.S. Department of Energy. Congressman Albert Bustamante of Texas admitted: "Anytime we get into a problem like now, nobody on the committee knows what is what. We just delegate things to the Department of Energy." Fox Butterworth, "Trouble at Atomic Bomb Plants: How Lawmakers Missed the Signs," *New York Times* (Nov. 28, 1988).

haustion of the resource, since it will be to no one's benefit to conserve it over a period of time, and yet to each owner's advantage to use it up quickly. It is particularly curious, then, that almost all writers parrot the notion that private owners, possessing time preference, must take the "short view" in using their resources, while only government officials are properly equipped to exercise the "long view." The truth is precisely the reverse. The private individual, secure in his capital ownership, can afford to take the long view because of his interest in maintaining the capital value of his resource. It is the government official who must take and run, who must exploit the property quickly while he is still in command.[79]

Harold Demsetz has argued that the private owner serves as a *broker between generations*. "In effect, an owner of a private right to use land acts as a broker whose wealth depends on how well he takes into account the competing claims of the present and the future. But with communal rights there is no broker, and the claims of the present generation will be given an uneconomically large weight in determining the intensity with which the land is worked. Future generations might desire to pay present generations enough to change the present intensity of land usage. But they have no living agent to place their claims on the market. Under a communal property system, should a living person pay others to reduce the rate at which they work the land, he would not gain anything of value for his efforts. Communal property means that future generations must speak for themselves."[80]

Because private owners can personally capitalize their efforts to conserve resources ("land"), and pass this asset on to children, or sell it to other private parties who will want to pass the capitalized assets on to future generations, the property's future value can be estimated by a private owner—the demand by future consumers for the output of the resource in question, discounted by the prevailing rate of interest. The lower the rate of interest,[81] of course, the higher the present value of the capitalized asset. Why? Because the rate of in-

---

79. Murray N. Rothbard, *Man, Economy, and State* (New York: New York University Press, [1962] 1979), pp. 828-29.

80. Harold Demsetz, "Toward a Theory of Property Rights," *American Economic Review*, LVII (May 1967); reprinted in Furubotn and Pejovich (eds.), *Economics of Property Rights*, pp. 38-39.

81. Lower interest stems from: 1) a lower risk premium (to compensate for debtors' defaulting), 2) a lower price inflation premium (to compensate lenders for the loss of purchasing power of the monetary unit), and 3) a lower social rate of time preference (the more citizens are future-oriented).

terest discounts the present market value of the expected future stream of income (including personal use value) of a capital asset. The higher the discount, the less the asset is worth in the present. A future-oriented society has a lower rate of interest than a present-oriented society. A lower rate of interest therefore allows future generations to "shout their bids" more effectively to this generation's "brokers" or "auctioneers." It generally takes private, profit-seeking "auctioneers" to hear those bids clearly and act in terms of them. In short, *the more a society conforms itself to a biblical concept of private ownership and a biblical concept of time, the higher the capitalized value of privately owned assets, as a result of the greater attention that profit-seeking owners will pay to the perceived demand of future owners and users.*

Summary

The question of resource conservation is intimately tied to the question of time perspective. When we ask ourselves questions concerning resource conservation, we are asking questions regarding conservation *for future consumption.*

The debate over ecology has been dominated by people who believe (or say they believe) that the civil government has the most responsible view of the future. They do not raise the obvious question: What motivates the individuals who control the various agencies of civil government? What is their motivation regarding pollution and resource conservation compared to the motivation of private owners?

Free market economists stress the long-range motivations of those who own property. When a person sells an asset, he is capitalizing in the present the expected future net productivity of that asset. The individual who can sell an asset owns it. The government bureaucrat cannot legally sell it and pocket the money, so he does not own it. Thus, his motivation is to use the asset in such a way that his income or prestige is increased. He is not paid to represent future generations of users; the private owner is paid to represent those living in the future, for an asset's present price depends heavily on the expected stream of net income it will generate over time.[82]

What we find is what economics predicts concerning the motivation of managers under socialist ownership of the means of production. Managers in socialist nations tend to pollute the environment, use State-owned resources, and ignore the complaints of the politi-

---

82. The other major considerations are selling costs and the prevailing rate of interest.

cally impotent public. This is especially true of the Soviet Union.[83] Managers use the State's resources to benefit their own careers, which means meeting State-assigned production quotas. The subtle pressures and rewards of private ownership are missing; socialist plans are crude and focus on aggregate output. Little else matters to the manager, except possibly laying up hidden reserves to barter with or steal and then sell into the black market. He must make his factory's quota (plus a few percentage points more, to earn his bonus). The environment suffers as a direct result.

Pollution is controlled by a combination of widespread private ownership, and local and regional civil government enforcement of Exodus 22:5-6. Socialist ownership is guaranteed to produce pollution because it places at the top of the list the goals of non-owning factory managers.

Solutions to Pollution

The first step is to recognize that *men are responsible for their actions*. The man who pollutes the environment in such a way that it infringes on the way of life of his neighbors must be made to pay restitution. He is responsible; he must pay.

There are always problems in applying this rule. Here are some basic ones. *First*, it may be impossible to identify a single polluter as the major source of pollution. An entire region may be filled with polluting industries. In this case, the local civil government or governments will have to begin to formulate general policies that encourage all polluters to reduce their polluting activities, even though each polluter cannot be matched precisely with all those who are harmed by the pollution.

This raises some very hard legal questions. The main one is that of *strict liability*.[84] If a plaintiff cannot prove that a specific polluter

---

83. See Appendix E: "Pollution in the Soviet Union."

84. Richard Epstein, an articulate defender of strict liability, contrasts his position with what he calls a *negligence* theory of law. "The development of the common law of tort has been marked by the opposition between two major theories. The first holds that a plaintiff should be entitled, prima facie, to recover from a defendant who has caused him harm only if the defendant intended to harm the plaintiff or failed to take reasonable steps to avoid inflicting the harm. The alternative theory, that of strict liability, holds the defendant prima facie liable for the harm caused whether or not either of the two further conditions relating to negligence and intent is satisfied." Epstein, *A Theory of Strict Liability: Toward a Reformulation of Tort Law* (San Francisco: Cato Institute, 1980), p. 5. He distinguishes four cases governing private tort (law

hurt his property in a specific physical way, and that he thereby suffered a specific economic loss, then how can he legitimately receive restitution from a supposed polluter? Is a defendant presumed innocent until proven guilty or not? Paul Downing writes: "Currently, a party who has been damaged by air pollution must prove in court that emitter A damaged him. He must establish that he was damaged and emitter A did it, and not emitter B. This is almost always an impossible task."[85] Comments Murray Rothbard, a proponent of a zero-civil government society: "If true, then we must assent uncomplainingly. . . . Are defendants now to be guilty until they can prove themselves innocent?"[86] Rothbard prefers to live with pollution rather than live with a civil government that does not honor the principle of strict liability in courts of law.

The proper biblical response is that the officers of the State must act as surrogates for injured citizens in this instance. The State must of course prove its case, namely, that the physical effects of the polluting substances are harming specific people in a specific region, or, in the case of noisy automobiles, that the pollutant — "noise" — in almost all known cases involves an infringement on the property rights of citizens who will never be able to locate and prosecute all violators of their rights (legal immunities). Civil law should not ignore the effects on *existing* property rights that are produced by such social changes as new technology, the crowding of residential areas, the high costs of proving specific damages in a multi-polluter environment, and the desire of people to reduce the assault on their bodies and their property.

No perfect system of pollution control (or allocation) can be devised, either by the free market or the State. But to leave the polluters

---

suit) action: *A* hits *B*; *A* frightens *B*; *A* coerces *B* to hit *C*; and *A* creates dangerous conditions. He advocates the adoption of a rigorous concept of *causation*. Because he relies so heavily on the nearly absolute nature of private property rights, Epstein's position has become the foundation of the legal theory most popular with anarcho-capitalists of the "Austrian" School of economics. It should be noted that he admits that in actual cases, the same outcome is reached by judges who adopt either of the two approaches. "Hence the choice between these two systems comes down to the few, but still important, cases where the outcome will rest upon choice of theory." *Ibid.*, p. 135.

85. Paul B. Downing, "An Introduction to the Problem of Air Quality," in Downing (ed.), *Air Pollution and the Social Sciences* (New York: Praeger, 1971), p. 13; cited by Murray N. Rothbard, "Law, Property Rights, and Air Pollution," *Cato Journal*, II (Spring 1982), p. 88.

86. *Idem.*

free to pollute just because there are a lot of them to prosecute will only lead to a growth in their numbers and the amount of pollution. Civil law should not subsidize pollution's involuntary transfers of wealth by adhering to man-made legal principles that were not designed to deal with every conceivable technological problem — legal rules that have never been applied perfectly anyway.

Nevertheless, there is a definite legal problem here, and Christians should not ignore it. The State can become over-zealous in its prosecution of every known form of pollution. The messianic State is a greater menace to civilization than pollution has ever proven to be. People can at least move away from polluters. Also, the polluters generally live in the local environment, so they have an incentive to restrict the polluting processes. The messianic State is not equally self-limiting or limited by the direct response of the public, especially a public that has lost faith in the God of the Bible and His law.

The main restraint on the advent of a messianic State in a Christian commonwealth will be the inability of the State financially to expand its influence, since the taxing powers of the combined levels of civil government, local to federal, will be limited to less than 10 percent of national income (I Sam. 8), and it will not have the legal ability to debase the currency, either through debasing precious metals (Isa. 1:22) or by fractional reserve banking (Ex. 22:26).[87] This general restraint on the growth of State power limits the State specifically in the area of pollution control (and in all other areas).

A *second* problem of enforcing responsibility for pollution is that there may be no way for victims to organize cost-effectively in order to gain restitution. The costs of organizing and proving damages in a court of law may exceed the actual, or at least demonstrable, injuries from the pollution.[88] Crocker calls these "informational, contractual, and policing costs." *Third*, the complexity of the situation may make it difficult for a court to determine just what is fair with respect to compensation. Which firm's smoke hurt what home owner in exactly what proportion of the total pollutants in a valley? And

---

87. Gary North, *Honest Money* (Ft. Worth, Texas: Dominion Press, 1986). Cf. North, *An Introduction to Christian Economics* (Nutley, New Jersey: Craig Press, 1973), ch. 1: "The Biblical Critique of Inflation." For an even more detailed analysis, see North, "Isaiah's Critique of Inflation," *Journal of Christian Reconstruction*, VII (Summer 1980).

88. For an instance of just such a situation, see T. D. Crocker, "Externalities, Property Rights, and Transaction Costs: An Empirical Study," *Journal of Law and Economics*, XIV (Oct. 1971), pp. 461-62.

how much was he hurt? Contrary to the rarified discussions found
in professional economics journals, there is no known scientific way
to come up with an answer to the question of damages.[89] There is a
lot of guesswork or intuition involved. (Economists should not object
too strenuously, since intuition is the bedrock foundation of all humanistic economics anyway.)[90] Nobody can use the complex mathematical and logical formulas found in the scholarly journals to solve
the "externalities" problem.[91]

There are other issues to consider. *First*, did the property owner
know in advance about the pollution, and did he buy the property at
a discount? In short, has he already been compensated economically
for his suffering? *Second*, has new information on the danger of a particular form of pollution recently become available? If so, did the
victim pay too much for the property, even with the discount, and is
he entitled to more compensation? *Third*, is the danger so great to
the whole community that the pollution should be stopped entirely?
Fourth, if regulations need to be passed to control regional pollution,
will the enforcement mechanism be too powerful and arbitrary to
preserve freedom, or will it be too weak to achieve its goals? Who decides? What kinds of self-compliance incentives can be built into the
law to encourage the polluters to discipline themselves?

Incentives and Sanctions

The economists debate about incentives and sanctions. There
are several recommended approaches. *First*, an outright ban on
polluting. This is seldom wise. The costs are too high: costs of lost
freedom and capital to producers, costs of lost jobs for employees,
costs of forfeited tax revenues to the civil government, and lost economic growth when new factories fail to move in for fear of arbitrary,
retroactive decisions by regional authorities. Also, it transfers too
much power to enforcing agencies.

---

89. See Appendix D: "The Epistemological Problem of Social Cost."

90. Gary North, "Economics: From Reason to Intuition," in North (ed.), *Foundations of Christian Scholarship: Essays in the Van Til Perspective* (Vallecito, California: Ross
House Books, 1976).

91. For an example of such unrealistic and utterly useless mathematical models,
see S. A. Y. Lin and D. K. Whitcomb, "Externality Taxes and Subsidies," in Lin
(ed.), *Theory and Measurement of Externalities* (New York: Academic Press, 1976). The
authors' model assumes that: 1) private firms and the civil government have perfect
and costless information; and 2) the costs of policing are zero. See John Burton's
comments, Epilogue, to Steven N. S. Cheung, *The Myth of Social Cost*, p. 60.

Second, tax credits (deductible against taxes owed to the community or civil government agency that is imposing the law) for installing pollution-control equipment. This gives the polluters an incentive to install the pollution-control devices. It also puts pressure on civil governments to reduce their expenditures to compensate for falling revenues — almost always a desirable political effect. If the civil government raises taxes from other sources, it risks a tax revolt. If it succeeds, however, taxpayers are then forced to pay for cleaner air or water. But if they had bought land under the older conditions — at a discount because of the pollution — they are going to be compensated by rising property values and a more pleasant way of life. This makes higher taxes more bearable.

The problem with the tax credit approach, on the face of it, is that polluters are not penalized. The Bible's rule that the victims should be compensated by the trespassers is seemingly not being honored. The best answer is that the rising concern for ecological purity is placing new environmental standards on producers — standards that did not prevail when they moved into the region to start business. The local residents got the benefits — more jobs, lower-priced land, perhaps a lower property tax rate — and are not entitled to direct restitution, except by the better environment they will receive. Thus, if residents want less pollution, they have to pay for it. One way to pay for this is to allow profitable manufacturers the right to pay fewer taxes.

Third, progressive fines for polluters: the more pollution, the higher the fines. In effect, this allows polluters to "buy" the right of polluting. They must assess the value to them of continuing to pollute. They get no more "free lunches" in the form of an open sky or stream. The fines can be experimented with by the local civil government to reduce the worst kinds of pollution without bankrupting local businesses. If the money is used to reimburse victims directly or indirectly by lowering tax rates, this follows the biblical injunction.

If the fines are used by the bureaucrats and politicians to expand the civil government, then this is not what the Bible requires. There is always a great temptation by the civil government to use the fines to expand their power. The tax credit approach seems to be a better way to restrict the expansion of civil government. Higher taxes unquestionably act as an incentive to make changes as the output of pollutants increases. If the goal is to "put a lid" on pollution, a graduated fine system is effective. But there are problems with defining legitimate fines or charges for any given level of pollution. There is no science of appropriate fines.[92]

Fourth, in the case of a localized polluter that is affecting only land close by, the civil government can establish specific pollution standards, such as parts per million. The company can then be given a choice: meet the standards, or buy the lands that are being affected. This was done in Polk County, Florida, in the late 1950's when phosphate producing plants were reducing the value of adjacent cattle land and citrus properties. The companies could then decide which to do: pay for more pollution-control equipment or pay for the land. Increasingly, they bought the land, as the marginal cost of each additional increase in pollution control climbed much higher. In the mid-1950's, the companies had owned 50 percent of the affected land; by 1964, they owned 80 percent.[93]

There are other possible solutions, but any workable long-term solution will have to be at bottom voluntaristic. We need greater decentralization of our population. It is the concentrated population of the modern city that is the great burden to the environment. The advent of decentralized power-generation systems, such as inexpensive solar power, should enable people to move to less expensive land in presently less populated regions. The strain on the environment will be reduced. If a low-cost system of international telecommunications becomes available, with two-way wireless communications, then another barrier to small town and rural living is gone. If we can power our modern lifestyles without wires and centralized power plants, if we can educate and entertain ourselves without hooking up to wires, then "wireless" living could begin to approach low-pollution living. If technologically advanced societies continue to sell information rather than manufactured goods, substituting high-technology, low-pollution manufacturing for older steel mills and automobile plants, then we can escape both big government and pollution. Something approaching the kind of decentralized utopia outlined by Toffler may not be that far away, technologically speaking.[94]

What must be understood is that all talk in scholarly economic journals about the ability of science to discover socially "optimal"

---

92. Peter Lewin, "Pollution Externalities: Social Cost and Strict Liability," *Cato Journal*, II (Spring 1982), pp. 214-15; Jerome Millimen, "Can Water Pollution Policy be Efficient?", *ibid.*

93. Crocker, "Externalities," pp. 456-59.

94. Alvin Toffler, *The Third Wave* (New York: Random House, 1980).

levels of pollution is as far-fetched as science's ability to come up with socially optimal anything (especially an optimal investment of scarce economic resources in scientific reports). Because humanistic economists cannot scientifically make interpersonal comparisons of subjective utility, it is illegitimate to assert the ability of any economist or other scientist to offer advice or data on how to achieve socially optimal anything. All the equations in the world will not add one iota of knowledge that will prove useful to any economist who relies exclusively on subjective economic theory in his search for socially optimal levels of pollution. (If the equations are sufficiently elegant to be utterly irrelevant, they could, on the other hand, win the developer a Nobel Prize in economics.)

The modern State is becoming messianic. Its supporters believe that salvation is essentially political. Thus, they promote State action in their efforts to heal the environment. Instead, we should begin with the issue of legal responsibility. Individuals are to be held accountable for their actions — by God, by the civil government, and by the free market.

When many polluters are harming many people, the State must intervene and impose sanctions against all producers of the particular type of generally unwanted pollution. But in doing so, the officials must count the costs to society of the intervention's effects of people's faith in private ownership. The intervention must be made in terms of a defense of private property rights, not its abolition. The rise of the messianic State is a greater threat to liberty than pollution is. Pollution is a recognized evil; the messianic State is the agent of a rival religion.

A whole system of incentives and sanctions is available: fines, tax credits, pollution control standards, and even outright prohibition. What must be recognized is that the quest for zero pollution is messianic. It is a program that covers the real intent of its promoters: salvation by legislation. If men do not restrain themselves voluntarily as both polluters and pollution-fighters, the social order will be torn apart by the messianic quest for the perfect environment. Such an environment is available only after the final judgment, when the curse is removed (Rom. 8:19-22).

The Messianic Quest for Zero Pollution

The question of pollution, ultimately, is a question of *stewardship*, meaning personal responsibility. The Bible affirms that each man is responsible for his actions. No man is to pass along the costs of his activities to his neighbor, apart from the latter's consent. Where there is ownership (legitimate sovereignty), there must also be responsibility.

Perfect justice in this regard is impossible, and any attempt to create a completely pollution-free environment is doomed to failure. After all, men exhale — a form of pollution that unquestionably has some environmental consequences. Furthermore, it is not possible to assess the full costs of pollution, since estimating costs necessarily requires men to make interpersonal comparisons of subjective utility, and such comparisons can be made only imperfectly.[95] Arbitrary estimates must be made by judges, arbitration committees, or administrative bureaucracies in charge of pollution-control programs. These will not be "scientific" estimates, for such measurable estimates cannot be made in economics. As Dales admits, "the economist is quite unable to draw up a neat table showing all benefits and all costs of all anti-pollution policies that are proposed (or that might be proposed); he is therefore quite unable to say that one policy is demonstrably superior to all others. . . . At the moment, the subject is humility."[96] Perfection here cannot be achieved at any cost.

The example of the phosphate companies of Polk County, Florida, is representative. Achieving 95 percent efficiency in controlling emissions was economically possible. The last 5 percent would have bankrupted the companies. "Once an efficiency level of 95 per cent has been attained, it is clear that further increases in efficiency become relatively unresponsive to additional capital outlays. For plants at least ten years old in 1965, it is unlikely that the 97 per cent efficiency level can even be reached. The plant less than ten years old required an outlay of almost one-half million dollars to move from a 98 to a 99 per cent level of efficiency. Two two-year old plants needed a quarter million dollars to increase their control efficiency from 99.1 to 99.2 per cent."[97] In 1968, the Pennsylvania Power Company of Newcastle, Pennsylvania spent $2 million on a facility to reduce fly ash and suspended particulates discharged by the plant. To attain 99 percent removal, the firm had to spend an additional $4 million.[98]

Citizens must use self-discipline in their quest for a better world. If every citizen is forever suing his neighbor for each perceived infringement

---

95. North, *Genesis*, ch. 4.
96. Dales, *Pollution*, pp. 39, 40.
97. Crocker, "Externalities," p. 458.
98. Hite, *Economics of Environmental Quality*, p. 25.

on his environmental lifestyle, society will perish. This is the great danger of class-action suits by one person in the name of an unspecified number of others in a supposed "class" of victims. Each person can sue a company, which may be operating within the law, thereby imposing endless legal fees on the firm. This could tie up a firm's legitimate operations. Such suits could be brought by anyone for almost any perceived infraction: automobile safety, national defense, and on and on.[99] Those who bring class-action suits that are determined by a jury to constitute unwarranted harassment of a business must be put "at risk" for their actions. Everyone must become responsible for his actions, not just producers.[100]

Ours is not a perfect world, and any attempt to impose perfect standards on it, without acknowledging the limits imposed by scarcity, and therefore the costs involved, is demonic. The whole community will be harmed. "As costs rise for persons who must treat more and more of their wastes so that other persons can enjoy more and more purity, it will become apparent that the party who wants pure water is hurting the environment for the party who wants food, clothing, and shelter."[101]

Any civil government that attempts to reduce pollution to anywhere near zero is messianic. The results of a quest for zero pollution will be similar to the results of a quest for perfect justice: bankruptcy of the treasury, bankruptcy of producers, judicial arbitrariness, and an increasing number of economic disruptions.[102]

The following piece of legislation, Senate Bill 2770, passed by the U.S. Senate by a vote of 86 to 0 in 1971, is indicative of this sort of messianic role for the State: "This section establishes a policy that the discharge of pollutants should be eliminated by 1985, that the natural chemical, physical, and biological integrity of the Nation's waters be restored, and that an interim goal of a water quality allowing fish propagation and suitable for swimming should be reached by 1981. The states are declared to have the primary responsibility and right to implement such a goal."[103] At least the Senate was wise

---

99. *Ibid.*, p. 91.

100. On the legal problems associated with class-action suits, see the critical comments by Murray N. Rothbard, "Law, Property Rights, and Air Pollution," *Cato Journal*, II (Spring 1982), pp. 93-97. Cf. Huber, *Liability*, ch. 5.

101. Hite, *Economics of Environmental Quality*, p. 91.

102. Macklin Fleming, *The Price of Perfect Justice* (New York: Basic Books, 1974).

103. Cited in Hite, *op. cit.*, p. 92.

enough to pass along "primary responsibility" to achieve these unattainable goals to the state governments. Since these goals were not
attained, should someone ever remind the politicians about this bill,
the Senate can blame someone else for its failure. Should the national government decide to impose sanctions in a futile attempt to
achieve zero water pollution, it will mean the end of personal freedom for United States' citizens.

Summary

The Bible tells us to count the costs of our actions (Luke
14:28-30). We cannot avoid the inescapable reality of scarcity in our
cursed world. We are creatures who labor under a curse, and our environment is also under a curse. *It is therefore as messianic to expect to be
able to achieve a zero-pollution world in history as it is to expect to be able to
achieve a sin-free world in history.* The pollution that we experience is
simply a "side effect" of man's sin — the thorns and weeds with which
God has cursed us (Gen. 3:18).

We are told to be perfect, even as our Father in heaven is perfect
(Matt. 5:48). Perfection is the standard by which we are judged by
God in both time and eternity. We are to strive toward this goal, but
never in the hope of being able to achieve it in history, and never by
means of political power alone. The same standard of perfection exists for our environment. Mankind is supposed to dwell in a
pollution-free environment that matches his sin-free environment.
When God's curse is removed from the creation after the final judgment, sin will no longer be a problem for mankind. Neither will
pollution. But that perfect environment will be trans-historical.

To devote scarce resources to reduce sin is legitimate judicially
and morally mandatory. To devote resources to reduce pollution is
equally legitimate judicially and morally mandatory. Nevertheless,
the task of reducing sin is not God's monopoly assignment to the
State; neither is the reduction of pollution. We must avoid perfec-
tionism and its institutional concomitant, the messianic State.

Conclusion

The Bible provides us with moral and legal guidelines that will
permit those who abide by biblical law to serve as stewards of God's
resources. As in any stewardship activity, sin reduces our ability to
achieve perfection. The earth is cursed. We cannot legitimately expect to achieve perfect results. Nevertheless, we can expect God's

blessings on our activities if we faithfully apply ourselves to the terms of the dominion covenant.

The free market allows us to estimate individual costs and benefits. A combination of political authority and free market allocation is needed to allocate the disposal of waste products. It is sometimes impossible to allocate private property rights, including waste disposal responsibilities, and the civil government has a role to play in this allocation process. The local civil government, governed by the value preferences of local residents, should have the primary responsibility in this regard. Larger units of civil government are to enter into the allocation process only because there are disputes between local units of government. The goal is to assign responsibility for cleaning up waste products to private beneficiaries of waste production (lower-cost producers and their clients), or when this proves too costly for them to remain in business, then to allow community standards of the majority to allocate the production and distribution of pollution in order to retain the local economic benefits that these polluters also produce.

Without market pricing of resources, underpriced resources tend to be overused by profit-seeking (cost-reducing) users. This has led to the so-called tragedy of the commons. Commonly owned property is treated as a cost-free resource. The individual users overgraze, overpollute, or generally abuse it because they receive the immediate benefits (lower costs of production) and share in the liabilities only as members of a large, diffused group — the "owners."

We must treat the pollution issue as a "spillover" effect. The Bible's case law regarding fire is applicable to pollution in general. One man's actions impose costs on other people, and this should not be allowed without their express or implicit permission. He who imposes damage must make restitution to the victims. But we must recognize that buying property at a discount because of existing pollution constitutes "restitution in advance." It is often legitimate under such circumstances to allow polluters to continue polluting.

Pollution is not always harmful (e.g., a bakery's scent). Sometimes some form of pollution is harmful, but people may not recognize this. To hold men accountable retroactively for the recently recognized harmful effects of prior pollution is to treat people as if they were omniscient. If such penalties were automatically imposed as a matter of law, innovation would be stifled.

The civil government enters as an indirect allocator of pollution when markets fail to allocate pollution efficiently. This is necessary in most instances because property rights cannot be assigned to moving fluids. The State protects victims of unauthorized pollution. But this task is generally a local responsibility, for people in different communities may be willing to tolerate more pollution than others, if the economic payoff is high enough. The market then allocates pollution, given the State-enforced liability system. The State creates a kind of auction for pollution where the "high bid" (high tolerance) wins.

Pollution should be seen as a form of trespassing. It is an invasion of private property. The State has a responsibility to enforce property rights against trespassers; similarly, it has a responsibility of enforcing laws against polluters. This would include legislating fire codes (pre-pollution restrictions) and automobile emissions and noise-reduction devices.

We must recognize, however, that many of the most vocal opponents of pollution are in fact wealthy people who are attempting to keep less wealthy people from invading "their" common property. The ecology movement is dominated by upper-middle class people and the rich. They are articulate. They are threatened by the combined economic bidding of poorer people. They have mobilized people to pressure the politicians to pass laws that favor a narrow special-interest group. By passing such all-encompassing legislation, especially at the national level, politicians are subsidizing the politically skilled minority whose interests frequently are at odds with the less skilled majority. The language of environmental ethics can be easily misused. In our day, the ecology movement has reflected a general attitude that is hostile to dominion. It has proclaimed the sovereignty of nature over covenant man.

Biblical Intuition vs. Humanist Science

Nevertheless, it is not possible to make a valid biblical case against all pollution legislation. Some defenders of the autonomous free market deny that the civil government has any responsibility in the area of pollution control. This clearly is a policy recommendation. When these intellectual defenders of the free market are challenged to answer one crucial question—the question of how economists can scientifically formulate social policy if they cannot make interpersonal comparisons of subjective utility—they are forced by the logic of their position to affirm a sort of intellectual agnosticism. As scientists, they must remain silent about social policy. They cannot possibly tell us as citizens or tell society's judges just *how much* pollution is "socially optimal," or *how much* restitution is "efficient" in the reduction of pollution. They do not accept the idea that God-directed and biblical law-affirming civil judges have the ability to make these intuitive judgments, but if economists are intellectually honest, they must also admit that *all* such judgments are necessarily intuitive, not "scientific."[104] There can be no "scientific" economic judgments regarding social policy in a world in which it is impossible to make interpersonal comparisons of subjective utility. I keep stressing this point throughout *The Dominion Covenant* because it is the Achilles heel of modern subjectivist economics. Nowhere is this epistemological problem more crucial or less solvable than in the field of pollution control.

The Christian knows that God can and does make such interpersonal comparisons. God knows how much pollution is optimal in any society at any point in time. His law-order is designed to enable God-fearing and biblical law-honoring societies to approach this optimum level of pollution, though not attain it perfectly. Christians who understand and believe Deuteronomy 28:1-14 also know that God has promised great blessings to those who seek to conform themselves to His law. These blessings presumably include reduced pollution, both as a benefit to man and the environment, but also because man is responsible for this environment. Such blessings are the product of a property rights system that honors the Bible's guidelines. The Bible gives us moral and legal guidelines, and biblical economics alerts us to the costs and benefits involved in the resolution of disputes concerning the proper level of pollution.

Our long-run goal is perfection, of course — ethical perfection. But we know that we are cursed sinners living in a cursed world. We aim at perfection as an ethical ideal, but we do not wring our hands in despair because we cannot attain perfection, in time and on earth. We know the costs associated with State-enforced programs that promise perfection and establish sanctions against those who do not achieve it. Those costs are too high.

---

104. Gary North, "Economics: From Reason to Intuition," in North (ed.), *Foundations of Christian Scholarship*.

19

SAFEKEEPING, LIABILITY,
AND CRIME PREVENTION

If a man shall deliver unto his neighbour money or stuff to keep, and it be stolen out of the man's house; if the thief be found, let him pay double. If the thief be not found, then the master of the house shall be brought unto the judges, to see whether he have put his hand unto his neighbour's goods. For all manner of trespass, whether it be for ox, for ass, for sheep, for raiment, or for any manner of lost thing, which another challengeth to be his, the cause of both parties shall come before the judges; and whom the judges shall condemn, he shall pay double unto his neighbour (Ex. 22:7-9).

Part of ancient Israel's concept of neighborly hospitality[1] involved taking care of the neighbor's property from time to time. Exodus 22:7-9 deals with inanimate property as well as animals. Exodus 22:10-13 deals exclusively with animals entrusted to another's care.[2] The existence of case laws governing safekeeping testifies to the fact that it was considered socially acceptable for an Israelite to ask his neighbor to safeguard his goods temporarily. This should also be true for modern Christians. Neighborly safekeeping is clearly a benefit to a man who is taking his family on a journey. He needs someone to watch over his possessions.

The neighbor is expected by both God and man voluntarily to accept this caretaking responsibility. Why? Because God accepted this same responsibility in ancient Israel. God promised to serve the Israelites as the safekeeper of their goods when they journeyed to Jerusalem to celebrate the feasts. "For I will cast out the nations before thee, and enlarge thy borders: neither shall any man desire thy land, when thou shalt go up to appear before the LORD thy God

---

1. James B. Jordan, "God's Hospitality and Holistic Evangelism," (1981), in Jordan, *The Sociology of the Church: Essays in Reconstruction* (Tyler, Texas: Geneva Ministries, 1986), pp. 207-20.
2. See Chapter 20: "Caretaking and Negligence."

608

thrice in the year" (Ex. 34:24). Men are therefore to imitate God by guarding their neighbors' property when the latter go on journeys. God the cosmic Safekeeper and Caretaker is the theocentric frame of reference for these verses. Covenant-keeping man must be like God.

Adam was entrusted with the task of guarding God's property in the garden. God told Adam that the tree of the knowledge of good and evil was off-limits to him. Then God departed from Adam's presence, as if going on a journey — the theme of the New Testament's parable of the talents (Matt. 25:15).[3] God tested Adam's faithfulness in a particular way: to see if Adam would protect God's property from an invader during His absence. Instead of defending God's property from this invader, the serpent, Adam and Eve listened to the invader and did what he suggested: join in a covenantal alliance with him by sharing a covenant meal in his presence at the forbidden tree. God also tested Adam to see whether he would "put his hand unto his neighbour's goods." God was Adam's neighbor, a special privilege for Adam. But to maintain good relations with this cosmic Neighbor, Adam and Eve had to pass the test of hospitality. They failed the test. Thus, they owed God double restitution: death in history and death in eternity.

Representative Laws

Because God tested Adam's covenantal faithfulness by testing Adam's commitment to be an honest safekeeper, we should conclude that the Exodus case laws governing safekeeping have broad implications for the life of man. The caretaking laws are therefore representative laws. Samson Raphael Hirsch, the nineteenth-century Jewish commentator, wrote that verses 7-15 (6-14 in the Hebrew Torah) deal with "responsibilities which are incurred in the case of duties which are voluntarily undertaken." He divided the cases in terms of four participants: the unpaid custodian, the paid custodian, the borrower, and the hirer. "In working out the different responsibilities incurred, and in the laws laid down regarding them, many general basic laws of civil law and justice are incidentally laid down, laws which have far-reaching application."[4]

---

3. Elijah taunted the priests of Baal with this suggestion: "And it came to pass at noon, that Elijah mocked them, and said, Cry aloud: for he is a god; either he is talking, or he is pursuing, *or he is in a journey*, or peradventure he sleepeth, and must be awaked" (I Ki. 18:27).

4. Samson Raphael Hirsch, *The Pentateuch Translated and Explained*, translated by Isaac Levy, 5 vols., *Exodus* (3rd ed.; London: Honig & Sons, 1967), p. 348.

It should be noted in advance that this passage covers criminal behavior: *theft*. It specifically refers to a *trespass*. In contrast, Exodus 22:10-13 deals with the caretaker's *negligence*. The requirement here that double restitution be imposed by the judges indicates that this law deals with a criminal trespass. Not so in the case of Exodus 22:12: "And if it be stolen from him, he shall make restitution unto the owner thereof." Double restitution is the penalty for criminal theft; value-for-value restitution is the penalty for negligence.

This passage does not indicate that the neighbor who receives the goods is given any kind of payment for his trouble. The rabbis so interpreted it.[5] Hirsch said that this passage deals with "a custodian who is not responsible if the object left in his charge is stolen from him," whereas the custodian in verses 10-13 is "one who has to pay compensation in such a case . . . and who is only free from responsibility if the property is lost in a manner which could not possibly have been prevented." Citing the Talmud,[6] he added: "A non-paid custodian in accepting custody, implicitly undertakes to give the entrusted goods the same care that he normally gives to his own property e.g., that at night time he places them in a securely closed place. But a paid custodian (unless of course, special conditions are agreed) implicitly accepts the duties of a watchman, so that even if he leaves it out of his personal surveillance he would be responsible even if it were stolen by thieves breaking in to properly closed premises."[7] I am not persuaded that Hirsch was correct about the legal distinction here being based on paid vs. unpaid custodianship, since I believe that the dividing issue is theft vs. negligence, but his comments indicate that he and the rabbis had given considerable thought to the meaning and application of these verses. He devoted ten pages to expositing just Exodus 22:7-9, more than he devoted to almost any other passage in the case law section of Exodus.

Preserving Godly Social Order

It is not specified in the text just why the owner would transfer his assets to a neighbor, although an obvious reason would have been an upcoming journey. The fear of thieves would have moti-

---

5. Rabbi Moses ben Nachman [Ramban], *Commentary on the Torah: Exodus* (New York: Shilo, [1267?] 1973), pp. 378-79.

6. *Baba Kamma* 57a; *Baba Metzia* 93b.

7. Hirsch, *Exodus*, p. 348.

vated a man to entrust his capital to a neighbor. The nature of the liabilities imposed by this and the related safekeeping passage (Ex. 22:10-13) indicates that the primary intent of the laws governing safekeeping was to reduce crime. Members of the covenant community are expected voluntarily to take on certain limited responsibilities in order to place the criminal at a disadvantage. It is the maintenance of godly social order that is the goal of these laws.

A thief, then as now, would have looked for telltale signs of an abandoned house. When houses are empty, they are vulnerable to attack. The motif of the "empty house" is found throughout Scripture, most notably in the threat of God to abandon the House of Israel, symbolized by His departure from the temple, should Israel rebel against Him (Ezek. 8-11). Covenantal emptiness is a spiritual condition which is to be avoided. It cannot be maintained; something will always fill a covenantally empty place, whether an individual soul or a social order. In Jesus' parable of the swept house, He compared a house to man's heart, and then to the spiritual condition of the Jewish culture of His day. When a man "sweeps" out an evil spirit, but then leaves his "house" empty, the spirit returns with seven other spirits, all worse than the first, and reoccupies the house (Matt. 12:43-45). In short, from a spiritual standpoint, "you can't beat something with nothing." The covenantal "house" is not to be left empty. There can be no ethical or spiritual vacuums in life.

Stewardship and Dominion

The case laws governing safekeeping point to this important covenantal truth. Valuable property must be under someone's administration if it is to be protected. It must be cared for. The thief who finds an empty house is more likely to be able to commit his crime undetected. *Guarding private property is therefore an important aspect of the dominion covenant.* Since all property belongs to God, the steward is required to be faithful in caring for whatever property has been assigned to him by God to guard, just as Adam was to care for God's garden. The steward must seek to preserve it intact. In cases when a person needs to go on a journey, and cannot carry all of his property with him, or fears to carry it because of highway robbers, he must locate a local guardian. Keeping thieves from breaking in and taking property is very important.

Because ownership is inescapably covenantal, and because neighbors are involved in a civil covenant with each other, the owner transfers limited and temporary control over his property to his neighbor. Neighbors have an incentive to reduce crime in the neighborhood. This was especially true in agricultural ancient Israel. Rural neighbors are more dependent on each other than urban neighbors are. There is less commerce with those outside the local community than there is in a city, which is a trade center. In other words, there is a reduced division of labor in a rural area. Rural residents are therefore more dependent on each other's productivity than residents of a city are. This was especially true before the revolutionary development of mail-order catalogue marketing.[8] Rural residents have a unique economic incentive to preserve the wealth of their neighbors, for it is always better to have a prosperous neighbor nearby, since a wealthy neighbor has more goods to exchange with his neighbors, and more assets to help them in a crisis.

Additionally, wealthier neighbors are a social asset. This is why the influx of richer neighbors into the neighborhood has a tendency to increase the market value of local real estate.[9] Envy and jealousy against those with greater wealth are evil impulses that threaten the covenantal integrity of a neighborhood, for they make the wealthier residents secretive and distrustful of their neighbors.[10] These twin evils therefore reduce voluntary local cooperation and planning.

When neighbors can be trusted to care for each other's goods, a society probably has a strong covenantal bond. Residents see the thief's threat to the neighborhood, and they cooperate in order to make the thief's task more difficult. A similar bond is seen in the urban "neighborhood watch" societies, in which residents of a neighborhood join together in a voluntary agreement to keep an eye on each other's homes, and to report anything suspicious to the police.

---

8. Peter Drucker, *Management: Tasks, Responsibilities, Practices* (New York: Harper & Row, 1974), ch. 5: "Managing a Business: The Sears Story."

9. The best example of such a process in the United States in recent years is the movement of upper-middle-class whites into crime-ridden urban ghetto areas, especially in Washington, D.C. Crime drops, housing is improved by the new owners, and then unimproved local property values rise. This does lead to the displacement of former residents, however. But "movement in" usually involves "movement out" in real estate transactions.

10. The sociologist Helmut Schoeck argues that envy—the desire to tear down someone simply because he is better off—is always a phenomenon of social proximity. Helmut Schoeck, *Envy: A Theory of Social Behaviour* (New York: Harcourt, Brace & World, [1966] 1970), pp. 20, 40, 62, 121, 189, 220, 237, 273, 349, 355. Social proximity is commonly very closely related to geographical proximity, at least in modern urban societies.

The social atomization of the typical modern urban neighborhood, in which people do not know the names of their next-door neighbors, or the neighbors two houses down the street, favors the thieves.[11]

Accepting Responsibility

So common was the entrusting of goods to neighbors in Israel that the case laws established rules governing the practice. The case law's provisions still govern similar relationships today. When a man accepts the task of guarding his neighbor's property, he thereby accepts a considerable degree of personal liability. Control is inescapably tied to ownership.[12] Yet, in this case, the controller is not the legal owner. This places certain disadvantages on him.

We must distinguish here between legal responsibility and economic responsibility, lest there be any confusion about the nature of the responsibility of the safekeeper. Ownership is inescapably connected to economic responsibility. Ownership is a social function; it is a stewardship function.[13] Owners must decide, moment by moment, what to do with the assets they own. Moment by moment, others are bidding in the market for the services, animate and inanimate, that each person owns. The moment this bidding process ceases, the price of the asset in question falls to zero, and therefore it ceases to be a scarce economic resource. The existence of a price testifies to the existence of the competing bids for ownership. There is

---

11. A profitable tactic for thieves in urban America is to buy, hire, or steal a large moving van, paint counterfeit company symbols on its sides, drive up to a house while the family is away, load the van with the family's household goods, and drive away. So impersonal are most American neighborhoods that the neighbors seldom report this activity to the police as it is taking place. They simply assume that the family is moving away. They do not regard it as remarkable that the departing family never said goodbye to anyone. American families seldom say hello to anyone living next door or across the street, year after year.

12. This is why the fascist states of the 1930's were really socialist economies. Ownership of industry was officially retained by private individuals, but control over industrial assets was placed in the hands of State bureaucrats. Cf. Guenter Reimann, *The Vampire Economy: Doing Business Under Fascism* (New York: Vanguard, 1939). It is remarkable that after half a century of books, monographs, and doctoral dissertations, there is still not a single book by a well-known economist or economic historian that surveys the actual operations of the German economy of the 1930's, despite the fascination of all things Nazi by the book-buying public. (There is also no full-length book by a professional historian on the occult theology and occult practices of the Nazi Party, 1920-45.)

13. Gary North, *An Introduction to Christian Economics* (Nutley, New Jersey: Craig Press, 1973), ch. 28: "Ownership: Free But Not Cheap."

no escape for a property owner from these God-imposed economic functions and responsibilities. Arrangements can be made to distribute these ownership functions among those who are willing to bear certain kinds of risk, such as through insurance contracts, but with the ownership of legal titles to property inevitably comes a "bundle of rights" (legal immunities from specified kinds of physical interference) and therefore a "bundle of responsibilities" (economic obligations to the market).[14]

Exodus 22:7-15 is not speaking about inescapable, God-imposed economic responsibilities of ownership. It speaks instead about certain *legal* responsibilities that pass to the safekeeper even though he is not the owner of the property. Biblical law spells out these legal responsibilities. A neighbor can be held accountable in a court of law for his actions. In the case of missing goods, the man to whom the property has been entrusted must give an account for the missing property. "For all manner of trespass, whether it be for ox, for ass, for sheep, for raiment, or for any manner of lost thing, which another challengeth to be his, the cause of both parties shall come before the judges; and whom the judges shall condemn, he shall pay double unto his neighbour" (Ex. 22:9). This is the case of suspected *trespass*. It involves a suspicion of criminal behavior. Double restitution is therefore the penalty upon conviction (Ex. 22:4).

Why Only Double Restitution?

Notice that the passage specifies double restitution for a stolen sheep. Clearly, the convicted caretaker has either eaten the sheep or has sold it; otherwise, there would be no court case: the animal would be in the caretaker's herd. The suspected neighbor would simply return the animal to its owner. Then why only double restitution in this instance? Four-fold restitution is imposed on the thief who kills or sells a sheep (Ex. 22:1). The answer is that one of the reasons

---

14. These economic responsibilities stem directly from the legal immunities of others in the marketplace. Consumers in a free society possess a legal right to bid for ownership of certain forms of property. This is sometimes called *consumers' sovereignty.* (An early use of this term is found in W. H. Hutt, "The Nature of Aggressive Selling," *Economica,* 12 (1935); reprinted in *Individual Freedom: Selected Works of William H. Hutt,* edited by Svetozar Pejovich and David Klingaman [Westport, Connecticut: Greenwood, 1975], p. 185. Hutt died in 1988.) The present owner is also a consumer: he holds the property for himself. The interaction of the bidders determines the price of the good. Responding to these offers is the inescapable economic responsibility of the present legal owner: no response is in fact a response of "no."

why there is a higher penalty imposed for stealing and destroying a sheep or ox (specially protected because of their symbolizing mankind) is that it is difficult to locate and convict the unknown thief.[15] In the case of a neighbor, there is greater ease (i.e., less expense) of conviction; the owner knows who had possession of it last. Since there is lower risk of detection for a stranger who commits the theft, there are increased criminal penalties to offset this lower risk.

There are risks for both of the disputants when they go to court to settle the conflict. The neighbor who brings a false accusation, as distinguished from a mistaken accusation, risks being condemned by the judges. He would then be required to pay double restitution to the falsely accused victim, the same penalty that the latter would have suffered (Deut. 19:18-19). Bringing a false accusation is a form of perjury, and the law of perjury applies: forfeiting to the victim what the victim would have been required to forfeit as a result of the false testimony (Deut. 19:19). Understand, however, that the victim would have to prove that the accuser had knowingly accused him falsely.

Implied Trust and Presumed Innocence

Because of the implied trust that the first man had in the character of the second person, it becomes difficult for the judges to convict the second man for theft, a criminal act. The owner's original decision to trust the neighbor indicates that he believed the person to be honest. The judges must therefore operate with the presumption of the innocence of the accused, just as the owner had himself originally operated. This difficulty of gaining a conviction adds to the risk borne by the accuser if he decides to charge his neighbor with criminal trespass (Ex. 22:7-9) rather than mere negligence (Ex. 22:10-13).

If the property owner is unwilling to bear the full legal responsibilities and costs of ownership (i.e., by paying someone to perform this service), and he therefore decides to transfer some of this legal responsibility to a neighbor, then he himself must bear an added degree of risk. His neighbor may turn out to be a criminal or negligent, but the former will be difficult to prove. If his neighbor is willing to lie to the judges, then it will be very difficult to prove criminal action. "If a man deliver unto his neighbor an ass, or an ox, or a sheep, or any beast, to keep; and it die, or be hurt, or driven away, no man seeing it: Then shall an oath of the LORD be between them

---

15. See Section III of Chapter 17, pp. 537-38.

both, that he hath not put his hand unto his neighbour's goods; and
the owner of it shall accept thereof, and he shall not make it good"
(Ex. 22:10-11). Thus, there is *shared risk*: the owner imputes trustworthiness to the neighbor, and the neighbor takes on added legal responsibility. The requirement of the oath reduces risk to the property
owner, however, if the safekeeper believes in God. (The modern loss
of faith in God has unquestionably increased the level of risk in society, as well as having increased the difficulty of gaining judicial convictions.) The compulsory oath is an important biblical device for
promoting civil justice.[16]

Judicial Oaths

Why should the Bible authorize the civil government to require
covenant oaths from witnesses? Why should the accused be required
to testify under oath, and therefore be under the threat of both civil
and ecclesiastical sanctions? *Because the State is not allowed by God to attempt to read the mind of a witness.* Far from being a means of enhancing
State power, the compulsory oath is a device that is intended to restrain State power. By making it possible for the State to impose
sanctions against convicted perjurers, biblical law removes from the
judges any presumed authority to read the mind of a witness. The
witness' own public testimony can condemn him, but not his hidden
thoughts. He is not allowed to hide his thoughts because *the State is
not allowed to imitate God by claiming to be able to search the hearts of men.*
For instance, testimony based on "lie detector" tests or on such
satanic skills as mind-reading, hypnotism, and information revealed
in dreams or trances is biblically invalid.

The witness is required to tell the truth, the whole truth, and
nothing but the truth. He is not to place his accuser under the risk of
loss by offering false testimony. The court is God's agency of justice
and temporal judgment. The civil judges represent God in history. A
witness is no more allowed to testify falsely to a lawful civil court
than he is allowed to testify falsely to God.[17] He is therefore required

---

16. Is the State authorized by God to compel testimony from the oath-taker if he
is the accused? Yes, except in cases when the accused is being charged with the sin of
blasphemy against God or treason against the State, as Jesus was. He refused to answer Herod (Luke 23:9) and Pilate (Matt. 27:14). His silence was the fulfillment of
Isaiah's messianic prophecy (Isa. 53:7). This was not a case involving alleged
damages suffered by another oath-taking individual, as in Exodus 22:11.

17. False testimony is legitimate when the court is illegal, or is demanding information that it is not entitled to. For example, Pharaoh's "court" was not entitled to

to reveal everything he knows about the facts of the case when asked specific questions under cross-examination. The court needs accurate information in order to render honest judgment. The court is legally *entitled* to accurate information from all witnesses who are called by law to testify. The compulsory oath is God's authorized means of lowering the court's cost of attaining such knowledge.

The witness is required to swear an oath before God, and not just before the earthly judges. He invokes God's name and therefore invokes God's sanctions. The civil court-imposed oath is therefore a true covenantal oath, for all covenantal oaths are self-maledictory under God.[18] By invoking God's sanctions by taking a judicially valid oath, the witness faces negative sanctions, not just from the court in case his perjury is detected, but from God who knows all hearts. The witness is reminded by the oath that *God will condemn him if he gives false testimony, for God knows the thoughts of men.* This is why offering false testimony under oath places a man under God's sanctions, and why the sinner owes a trespass offering to the church, God's agency of excommunication, rather than to the State, God's agency of the sword: "And he shall bring his trespass offering unto the LORD, a ram without blemish out of the flock, with thy estimation, for a trespass offering, unto the priest" (Lev. 6:6).

Hammurabi's Code

The oath was also used in Hammurabi's Babylon. Speaking of the seignior, or aristocrat, the law states: "If a seignior deposited grain in a(nother) seignior's house for storage and a loss has then occurred at the granary or the owner of the house opened the storage-room and took grain or he has denied completely (the receipt of) the grain which was stored in his house, the owner of the grain shall set forth the particulars regarding his grain in the presence of god and the owner of the house shall give to the owner of the grain double the grain that he took."[19] The one who was said to have stored the grain

---

accurate information from the midwives regarding the birth of male Hebrew children. They could legitimately lie to Pharaoh because they were under covenant to a different God who was in the process of bringing Pharaoh and his society under judgment. Cf. Gary North, *Moses and Pharaoh: Dominion Religion vs. Power Religion* (Tyler, Texas: Institute for Christian Economics, 1985), ch. 4: "Illegitimate State Power."

18. Gary North, *The Sinai Strategy: Economics and the Ten Commandments* (Tyler, Texas: Institute for Christian Economics, 1986), ch. 3.

19. Hammurabi Code, paragraph 120. *Ancient Near Eastern Texts Relating to the Old Testament*, edited by James B. Pritchard (3rd ed.; Princeton, New Jersey: Princeton University Press, 1969), p. 171.

was assumed to be guilty, once the accuser had made an oath in the presence of a god. Whether theft was involved or simply negligence, the granary owner paid double. But this was not a case of voluntary safekeeping. This was a commercial transaction. The law imposed a fixed price for storing grain.[20]

The Code of Hammurabi did not rely exclusively on an oath before a god in every case. It also relied on written contracts and witnesses. (There is no reason to believe that this was not also true in ancient Israel. But in an illiterate culture, not everyone can afford such written documents. The Code of Hammurabi was almost entirely concerned with laws governing the oligarchy. This was not the case with biblical law. Thus, Old Testament rules of evidence were based on verbal promises and oaths, since it set down general laws that governed all people in Israel.) Anyone who wished to have someone else store silver, gold, or anything else for safekeeping had to show witnesses what was being entrusted to another. Contracts were drawn up.[21] "If he gave (it) for safekeeping without witnesses and contracts and they have denied (its receipt) to him at the place where he made the deposit, that case is not subject to claim."[22] On the other hand, if there were witnesses, the person who accepted the property for safekeeping paid the depositor double.[23] There is no reason to doubt that the same sorts of evidence could be used in a Hebrew law court, but the case law does not mention types of formal evidence.

If the safekeeper's house was broken into, and both his property and the depositor's stored property were missing, he was presumed by law to be careless. The law declares: he "shall make (it) good and make restitution to the owner of the goods, while the owner of the house shall make a thorough search for his lost property and take (it) from its thief."[24] First, the language indicates that the safekeeper did not pay double, but only restored what was lost, making good the loss. This corresponds to the provision of Exodus 22:12: "And if it be surely stolen from him, he shall make restitution unto the owner thereof." Second, this law indicates that any property subsequently returned by the thief to the safekeeper who had paid restitution to his neighbor would be kept by him as compensation for his loss.

---

20. *Idem.*, paragraph 121.
21. *Idem.*, paragraph 122.
22. *Idem.*, paragraph 123.
23. *Idem.*, paragraph 124.
24. *Idem.*, paragraph 125.

The most interesting section of the Code refers to a man who claimed that his property was lost, when it was not lost. The law says that he has deceived the city council. The council set forth the facts of the case "in the presence of god," and he then paid double restitution to the city council, not to the person who was falsely accused.[25] This is in stark contrast to biblical law, which makes the false accuser liable for damages he sought to impose on a private party. It is much closer to modern concepts of jurisprudence, where fines are paid to the State.

The other major difference between Hammurabi's Code and the Bible is that these laws applied only to aristocrats. Nothing is said about the legal relations between aristocrats and commoners. The law protected aristocrats in their relations with each other, but no legal protection was guaranteed for other classes.

Escaping an Erroneous Accusation

Once the accuser has made his accusation, the accused has a lawful way of escape: the oath.[26] "Then shall an oath of the LORD be between them both, that he hath not put his hand unto his neighbour's goods; and the owner of it shall accept thereof, and he shall not make it good" (Ex. 22:11). There can be no escape from this oath. There is no "fifth amendment" in this dispute, as there is in the U.S. Constitution — no right to remain silent in a court concerning one's guilt.[27]

---

25. *Idem.*, paragraph 126.

26. Boecker makes the observation that oaths were taken only by the accused in Israel's courts. There is no case in the Bible that an oath was taken by a witness, he says. Hans Jochen Boecker, *Law and the Administration of Justice in the Old Testament and Ancient East*, translated by Jeremy Moiser (Minneapolis, Minnesota: Augsburg, [1976] 1980), p. 35. This seems to be true with respect to formal oath-taking, but Boecker's observation is also irrelevant. The witness who gave his testimony in a Hebrew court was implicitly under an oath, for he was under the threat of civil covenant sanctions. Perjury on the part of the witness, when discovered and proven, subjected the lying witness to the punishment that would have been imposed on the victim (Deut. 19:15-21). Where there are covenant sanctions, there is inevitably a covenant oath, either implicit or explicit.

27. The Fifth Amendment of the United States Constitution prohibits the federal government from forcing an individual to testify in court against himself. This provision is clearly opposed to the requirement of biblical law that a person swear before God that he is innocent: he may not remain silent. Until the ratification of the Fourteenth Amendment in 1868, the first eight amendments did not apply to the states. Chief Justice John Marshall articulated this position in his famous decision, *Barron v. Baltimore* (1833). See *The Constitution of the United States of America: Analysis and Interpretation*, Congressional Research Service, Library of Congress (Washington, D.C.: Government Printing Office, 1973), pp. 899-90. The Committee of Eleven, to

As we shall see, added economic penalties were imposed by the civil magistrates and also by ecclesiastical officers on a man who offered false testimony under oath.

Hirsch argued that the double restitution penalty is to be imposed only after the thief has sworn falsely.[28] I disagree. Once the trial has begun, the convicted thief owes double restitution, with or without the oath. Only if he confesses before the trial can he escape double restitution, in which case he pays to the victim full value restitution plus 20 percent.[29] It is not simply that theft is to be penalized; false oaths must also be penalized. The Book of Leviticus specifies that a trespass offering to God must be made by anyone who makes a false oath. The Old Testament trespass offerings for swearing falsely (Lev. 5:4) involved ritual animals: lambs, turtledoves, or pigeons (Lev. 5:6-7). The priest made atonement for the guilty person (Lev. 5:6).

In New Testament times, such ritual atonement offerings have not been applicable (Heb. 9). This does not mean that there are no valid penalties against false oaths. A payment must go to the church as a means of support (Lev. 6:6). This also reminds the civil court that it is not the only valid court in society. The church, as God's representative court over the individual's moral conscience, is entitled to a payment, although the civil judges are to specify the size of this payment. "And he shall bring his trespass offering unto the LORD, a ram without blemish out of the flock, *with thy estimation*, for a trespass offering, unto the priest" (Lev. 6:6).

Confession and Restitution

I argue in this commentary that once a person commits a theft, he automatically owes the victim at least a 20 percent payment in addition to the return of his principal. The case does not have to come to trial for this penalty payment to be owed by the thief. I derive this conclusion from the case law's texts regarding theft, but also from the example of the archetypal theft: Adam and Eve's stealing of

---

whom the Bill of Rights (first ten amendments) had been referred by Congress in 1789, rejected any suggestion that these amendments be applied to state governments as well as to the federal government: Raoul Berger, *Government by Judiciary: The Transformation of the Fourteenth Amendment* (Cambridge, Massachusetts: Harvard University Press, 1977), p. 134n.

28. Hirsch, *Exodus*, p. 349.
29. See Chapter 17: "Proportional Restitution," pp. 513-17.

God's forbidden fruit. The moment they touched it, they were guilty. They owed God at least a ritual apology. In the Old Testament, anyone who touched a forbidden (unclean) thing was himself unclean until evening (Lev. 11:24-25). I think this is because God had originally returned in judgment to the garden in the cool of the day (Gen. 3:8), meaning at evening. It may not have hurt God's net asset value for them to have merely touched the fruit, but it was a violation of His law, His ethical boundary.

They went beyond mere touching; they stole the fruit and ate it. This was theft. It was corrupt caretaking. It was also the equivalent of eating a forbidden sacrifice, for it was a ritual meal eaten in the presence of the serpent. The penalty for this in ancient Israel was separation from God's people: "But the soul that eateth of the flesh of the sacrifice of peace offerings, that pertain unto the LORD, having his uncleanness upon him, even that soul shall be cut off from his people. Moreover the soul that shall touch any unclean thing, as the uncleanness of man, or any unclean beast, or any abominable unclean thing, and eat of the flesh of the sacrifice of peace offerings, which pertain unto the LORD, even that soul shall be cut off from his people" (Lev. 7:20-21). This penalty pointed back to the garden, where God separated Adam and Eve from Himself by casting them out of the garden.

God, however, is merciful to sinners. Why else would He have created the sacrificial system? Thus, had Adam and Eve come to God as He entered the garden, admitting their sin and pleading for mercy, He would have spared mankind the ultimate penalty of eternal separation from Him. In fact, had they prayed a prayer of confession rather than spending their time sewing fig leaves for themselves, they would have escaped the death penalty — full restitution payment to God. This very act would have constituted a pre-trial confession of guilt. It would have been an act of symbolic communion with God — a judicial, sanctions-governed act of repentance. But instead they tried to cover their own guilt through their own efforts: sewing fig leaves. God therefore announced His sentence of death against them: dust to dust. Those who wait until the end of the trial must make full (multiple) restitution.

My conclusion is that a pre-trial confession of guilt by the criminal is punished less rigorously than a crime in which the criminal is

convicted on the basis of the judges' inquiry. A person is always encouraged by God to confess his sins. If these sins are public sins,
then his confession must also be public, if not to a court, then at least
to the victim. For example, if a worker steals cash from his employer,
but later replaces it before the theft is discovered, he still must confess his crime to the owner. The fact that no human being detected
the crime does not affect the question of guilt and sanctions in God's
eyes. The thief did impose the *risk* of permanent loss on the victim,
even though the victim suffered no known loss; the victim therefore
deserves compensation. This upholds the biblical principle of
victim's rights. The victim, like God, should strive to be merciful,
but biblical law teaches that he is entitled to be informed that mercy
is now in order.

Leviticus 6

The Bible actually subsidizes public confession. If a man confesses, he can escape the multiple restitution requirement: he is required only to repay the stolen principal, plus 20 percent.

If a soul sin, and commit a trespass against the LORD, and lie unto his
neighbour in that which was delivered him to keep, or in fellowship, or in a
thing taken away by violence, or hath deceived his neighbour; or have
found that which was lost, and lieth concerning it, and sweareth falsely; in
any of all these that a man doeth, sinning therein: Then it shall be, because
he hath sinned, and is guilty, that he shall restore that which he took violently away, or the thing which he hath deceitfully gotten, or that which was
delivered him to keep, or the lost thing which he found, or all that about
which he hath sworn falsely; he shall even restore it in the principal, and
shall add the fifth part more thereto, and give it unto him to whom it appertaineth, in the day of his trespass offering (Lev. 6:2-5).

There appears to be an inconsistency here. The penalty for theft
is here stated to be 20 percent, yet in other verses, restitution for
theft in general is two-fold, and sometimes four-fold or five-fold.
Why the apparent discrepancy? We know that Leviticus 6 is dealing
with cases in which the guilty person has sworn falsely to the authorities. Later, however, he voluntarily confesses the crime and his false
oath. I conclude that the multiple restitution penalty is therefore imposed only in cases where a formal trial has begun. The provision in
Leviticus 6 of a reduced penalty is an economic incentive for a guilty

person to confess his crime before the trial has begun, or at least before the court hands down its decision.

The thief has testified falsely to the authorities, either before the trial or during it. This is why he owes a trespass offering to the priest (Lev. 5:1-13; 6:6). I argue here that he can lawfully escape the obligation to pay double restitution if he confesses after his initial denial, but before the trial begins. He cannot lawfully escape paying double restitution and making the trespass offering if he swears falsely during the trial. He has to confess before the oath is imposed and the trial begins. At the very least, he must confess before it ends.[30]

As always, we should search for a theocentric principle lying behind the law. There is one in this case: the correlation between this *reduced criminal penalty* for voluntary, public confession of sin, when accompanied by economic restitution, and God's offer of a *reduced (eliminated) eternal penalty* for people who make public Christian confession of sin prior to their physical death, if this confession is also accompanied by economic or other kinds of restitution.[31] If we wait for God's formal trial at the throne of judgment, we are assured of being forced to pay a far higher restitution penalty.

Why do I believe that Leviticus 6 refers to a pre-trial voluntary confession? Because of the context of Leviticus 6. Leviticus 5 deals with sins against God that must be voluntarily confessed: "And it shall be, when he shall be guilty in one of these things, that he shall confess that he hath sinned in that thing" (Lev. 5:5). The sinner in

---

30. Achan confessed to his theft of the forbidden items after the trial had begun, and he was then executed (Josh. 7:20). However, this case may not be a relevant example; he confessed only after Israel had suffered a military defeat, with the loss of 36 men (Josh. 7:5). His trespass required life for life at that point, confession or no confession. Thus, I do not appeal to this test case to defend my thesis. Still, I could be wrong about this. It may be that even after the trial begins and the oath is imposed, but prior to the decision of the jury or the judges, he has an opportunity to repent. But once the court hands down its decision, he is trapped.

31. I am not arguing that salvation is by works. It is by grace (Eph. 2:8-9). But let us not forget Ephesians 2:10: "For we are his workmanship, created in Christ Jesus unto good works, which God hath before ordained that we should walk in them." I am arguing that without obedience, our faith is dead. James 2:18 says: "Yea, a man may say, Thou hast faith, and I have works: shew me thy faith without thy works, and I will shew thee my faith by my works." And in James 2:20, we read: "But wilt thou know, O vain man, that faith without works is dead?" The outward obedience of the criminal is supposed to be demonstrated by his willingness to make restitution to his victim.

Israel then brought a trespass offering to the priest (Lev. 5:8). This made atonement for the trespass: "And he shall offer the second for a burnt offering, according to the manner: and the priest shall make an atonement for him for his sin which he hath sinned, and it shall be forgiven him" (Lev. 5:10). Why would he make such a public confession? Because of his fear of the ultimate penalty that God will impose on those who offer false testimony in His courts.

We then note that Leviticus 6 also deals with trespasses against God. It is specifically stated in Leviticus 6:2 that the 20 percent penalty payment applies to "a trespass against the LORD" in which the sinning individual has lied to his neighbor about anything that was delivered to him by the neighbor for safekeeping. The context indicates that the sinner has voluntarily confessed his crime against God and his neighbor, just as he voluntarily confessed his trespass against God in Leviticus 5.

The question is inevitable: Are there two penalties of 20 percent implied in Leviticus 6, or only one? In other words, is there a 20 percent penalty only for making a false oath, with the payment going to the victim, and with a trespass offering also going to the church court, or is there also a 20 percent penalty to the victim in cases of pre-trial confession? Here is the text in Leviticus:

And the LORD spake unto Moses, saying, If a soul sin, and commit a trespass against the LORD, and lie unto his neighbour in that which was delivered him to keep, or in fellowship, or in a thing taken away by violence, or hath deceived his neighbour; Or have found that which was lost, and lieth concerning it, and sweareth falsely; in any of all these that a man doeth, sinning therein: Then it shall be, because he hath sinned, and is guilty, that he shall restore that which he took violently away, or the thing which he hath deceitfully gotten, or that which was delivered him to keep, or the lost thing which he found, Or all that about which he hath sworn falsely; he shall even restore it in the principal, and shall add the fifth part more thereto, and give it unto him to whom it appertaineth, in the day of his trespass offering (Lev. 6:1-5).

Restitution Plus a Trespass Offering

Here is the problem the commentator faces. The text in Exodus 22 states that the court is to require double restitution from the neighbor who has "put his hands to" his neighbor's goods. He is therefore to be treated as a common thief. But if double restitution is the required penalty, then what is the 20 percent penalty of Leviticus 6:5 all about?

It has been argued by some Jewish commentators that the 20 percent penalty in Leviticus 6:5 is to be imposed only in cases where there has been a public oath before a rabbinical court. They argue that the penalty payment does not apply to cases of voluntarily confessed theft as such, meaning secret or even undetected thefts, but only to cases of forcible robbery in which the thief is identified, arrested, and brought before an *ecclesiastical* (i.e. synagogue) court, where he gives a false oath of denial, and later admits this lie. Writes Jacob Milgrom: "Since the point of this law is to list only those cases that culminate in the possessor's false oath, it would therefore be pointless to include the term 'theft' which assumes that the possessor-thief is unknown."[32] He goes so far as to argue that the Leviticus passage deals only with religious law, not civil law. "All that matters to the priestly legislator is to enumerate those situations whereby the defrauding of man leads, by a false oath, to the 'defrauding' of God. The general category of theft in which the thief remains unidentifiable is therefore irrelevant to his purpose."[33] Eight centuries earlier, Maimonides wrote that the thief who confesses of his own accord owes only the value of the asset he stole, not double restitution. He did not mention the 20 percent penalty.[34]

If Milgrom's view were correct, this would mean that there would be no court-imposed restitution penalty payment from criminals to victims in (oathless) cases of pre-trial, self-confessed theft. Why wouldn't there be such compensation? Because the one-fifth penalty is assumed by Milgrom to be applicable only in cases where there has been a false oath. This interpretation therefore eliminates the 20 percent penalty payment for pre-trial, self-confessed crimes.

While this judicial implication follows the premise, it is not in accord with the biblical principle of victim's rights. The victim has been deprived of his property, and he has suffered a sense of loss, assuming that he had actually discovered that the stolen item was missing, yet the Bible supposedly makes no provision to compensate him for these obvious burdens. On the face of it, this conclusion seems highly unlikely, yet it follows inevitably from the initial claim

---

32. Jacob Milgrom, *Cult and Conscience: The "Asham" and the Priestly Doctrine of Repentance* (Leiden: E. J. Brill, 1976), p. 100.

33. *Ibid.*, pp. 100-1.

34. Moses Maimonides, *The Book of Torts*, vol. 11 of *The Code of Maimonides*, 14 vols. (New Haven, Connecticut: Yale University Press, [1180] 1954), "Laws Concerning Theft," Chapter One, Section Five, pp. 60-61.

that the 20 percent penalty only applies to cases where there has been a false oath to a court.

Why do I believe that this interpretation is unlikely? Because the Bible is emphatic that *victims are to be protected*, and that *criminals are to suffer losses in proportion to their crimes*. The thief who confesses before a trial is not on a par judicially with a neighbor who has, through negligence, lost or inadvertently ruined an item placed in his safekeeping. The negligent neighbor pays only for what he lost; the self-confessed thief has to pay more. The principle of *lex talionis* applies here as elsewhere: the penalty must fit the crime.[35] To argue that the penalty is the same for theft and negligence — merely the return of the stolen item or its equivalent value — is to deny *lex talionis*.

If thieves were granted the legal option of returning stolen goods whenever it appeared to them that they might be discovered, but before they are put under oath, then it would be far less risky to steal. If there is a 20 percent penalty only after a false oath is given, but before a trial, then a theft that is confessed before the oath is administered would become virtually risk-free for the thief. He could escape any penalty simply by confessing his crime and by returning the stolen property. The option of self-confession would remain as an escape device whenever the authorities began to close in. If God's law did not impose penalties on theft, it would implicitly be subsidizing criminal behavior. God does not subsidize rebellion.

The express language of the passage militates against Milgrom's interpretation of Leviticus 6. After listing all sorts of theft and deception, the text says, "he shall even restore it in the principal, and shall add the fifth part more thereto" (v. 5). To whom must this penalty payment be paid? To the victim: "Or all that about which he hath *sworn falsely*; he shall even restore it in the principal, and shall add the fifth part more thereto, and *give it unto him to whom it appertaineth*, in the day of his trespass offering" (Lev. 6:5b). While the passage does mention a false oath, this does not render null and void a penalty for each of the crimes that preceded verse 5.

The sense of the passage is not that a false oath must accompany each of the list of transgressions in order for the penalty to be invoked; on the contrary, *each of the victims of these crimes is to be compensated by a 20 percent penalty payment*. The crimes are separate acts; thus, translators used the English word "or" in listing them, indicating that

---

35. Chapter 11: "Criminal Law and Restoration."

any one of these criminal infractions automatically invokes the 20 percent penalty, not merely the taking of a false oath. The false oath invokes its own independent penalty payment: the trespass offering, a ram without blemish (Lev. 6:6). So, the criminal must pay the victim 20 percent, with or without a false oath. The false oath makes the trespass offering to the priest an additional requirement.

Leviticus 6 is not in opposition to Exodus 22:9. Exodus 22:9 requires double restitution either from the false accuser who perjured himself (Deut. 19:16-19) or from the criminal neighbor (thief). Assume that the criminal neighbor swears falsely before the judges in order to avoid having to pay double restitution to his victim; if successful in his deception, he then collects double restitution from him. He now owes him four-fold restitution. What if he then repents of his false oath before it is discovered? He still owes the original double restitution, plus the return of the falsely collected double penalty, plus a 20 percent penalty payment on everything (Lev. 6:1-6). Thus, if the stolen object was worth one ounce of gold, the restitution payment owed to the victim by a now-confessed perjured thief would be 4.8 ounces of gold: 2 ounces (the original double restitution payment), plus 2 ounces (the falsely extracted penalty) plus .2 times 4 ounces, meaning .8 ounces = 4.8 ounces.

What about the perjured thief who refuses to admit his guilt and who is later convicted of this perjury? Because he had been paid double restitution by his victim (Ex. 22:9), he now owes him *six-fold restitution*: double whatever he had stolen (2 × 1) plus double whatever he had unlawfully collected (2 × 2). This threat of six-fold restitution serves as an economic incentive for the perjured thief to confess to the court that he had offered false testimony earlier. We see once again that *biblical law rewards timely confession*.

Exodus 22:9 establishes double restitution for stolen sheep and oxen, not four-fold or five-fold. This is because neighbors are involved. What if the court does not have proof that the accuser testified falsely against his neighbor, yet also does not have sufficient proof to convict the neighbor? The thieving neighbor escapes paying two-fold restitution. What if he then repents and confesses? He owes his neighbor a 2.4 restitution penalty (2 × 1, plus 2 × .2). What if his crime is discovered later? He owes four-fold restitution for perjury: double what he would have owed if he had been convicted originally.

What would he have owed to the temple in the case of unconfessed perjury? If the trespass offering was one animal if he had confessed after making a false oath or oaths, presumably the penalty was double this.[36] This follows from my thesis that *there is an escalation of penalties.* At each step of the legal proceedings, he can confess and bear a reduced penalty. For each level of deception, there are increased sanctions.

God is honored by the very act of self-confession, when such confession has a penalty attached to it. Oath or no oath, the two primary goals of laws governing theft are the *protection of property* and the *compensation of the victim.* Earthly civil courts are therefore to safeguard the property rights of the victims, making sure that the appropriate penalty is extracted from the criminal and transferred to the victim. There is no requirement of an additional money penalty payment to the civil court because of a false oath regarding theft. A trespass or guilt offering must be paid to the church.[37]

The false oath before God invokes the threat of the ultimate penalty: the eternal wrath of God, preceded by the physical death of the criminal. Unless a person confesses his false oath in this life, makes appropriate restitution to his victim and brings a transgression offering, God will collect His own restitution payment, and it is far greater than 20 percent. Ananias and Sapphira lied to church authorities concerning the percentage of their economic gains that they had voluntarily donated to the church. When asked individually by Peter if what they had told the authorities was true, they lied, and God struck each of them dead on the spot, one by one (Acts 5:1-10). This served as a very effective warning to the church in general (v. 11). Presumably, they could have confessed their crime at that point, paying all the money from the sale into the church's treasury, since God was the intended victim of their lies (Acts 5:4). They chose instead to lie. So, God imposed His more rigorous penalty.

After the Accusation, but Before the Trial

What if the thief stole an animal, especially a sheep or an ox, and then sold it? If the civil authorities have brought the thief to trial, but the trial has not been held, would he be given the opportunity to

---

36. It could be argued that the penalty was death: a high-handed false oath that was not confessed.

37. The question arises: Which church? To the church that the convicted thief belongs to, since it suffers the public humiliation. If he belongs to no church, then it should probably go to the victim's church, or if he also does not belong to a church, to a local church selected randomly or in predictable sequence by the civil judges.

confess to the victim, and then go to the buyer, confess his crime, buy it back at the purchase price plus 20 percent, and return it to the true owner, plus 20 percent? This would seem to be a reasonable conclusion. His confession would reduce the cost of prosecuting him and convicting him. Understand, however, that the thief has committed two crimes: the original theft and the defrauding of the buyer. The buyer was led to believe that the thief possessed the legal right of ownership, which was being passed to the new buyer.[38] Thus, the defrauded buyer is also entitled to a 20 percent penalty payment, as well as the return of his purchase price. This would make the total penalty 40 percent, since he had defrauded two people: the first by means of the theft and the second by means of his lie.

The thief's confession reduces the possibility that a guilty man will go free and an innocent victim will be defrauded. Apart from this admission, the judges might make a mistake, especially if the thief commits perjury during the trial. His confession eliminates this judicial problem.

The modern judicial system has adopted an analogous solution: plea bargaining. A criminal confesses to having committed a lesser crime, and the judge accepts this admission and hands down a reduced penalty. This is the way that prosecuting attorneys unclog the court system. The Bible rejects this approach. Plea bargaining leaves the main crime officially unsolved, and it allows the guilty person to appear less of a threat to society than his behavior indicates that he is. The Bible does recognize the institutional problem, however: the risks and costs of gaining a conviction. Instead of having the criminal plead guilty to a lesser crime, it encourages him to plead guilty to the actual crime before the trial, and thereby receive a reduced penalty.

Who Pays What?

The judges must determine the nature of the negligence, and therefore the size of the restitution payment. A thief pays double (v. 7). If the neighbor himself is the thief, he pays double (v. 9). But verse 12 speaks of "restitution," not a double payment: "And if it shall be stolen from him, he shall make restitution unto the owner thereof." In this case, "restitution" means "making good the loss." We can see

---

38. See Chapter 17, "Proportional Restitution," under the subsection, "The Economics of Restitution," pp. 511-19.

this in verse 13, where it says that when he can produce the torn remains of the animal, "he shall not make it good." "Making it good" and "restitution" are identical words in Hebrew, and should be regarded as equivalents here.

Restitution in the context of the obligation of the negligent safekeeper is *a payment equal to the value of what had been lost.* The responsible neighbor did not intend to profit from the theft. Indeed, he voluntarily took on added responsibilities by agreeing to serve as a protector. Negligence on the part of the safekeeper is not the same as criminal intent on the part of the thief; therefore, the penalties are different. The thief pays the victim an extra penalty equal to his hoped-for profit: double restitution. There is no additional penalty payment imposed on the safekeeper, for he had not hoped to profit by the transaction. To make safekeepers responsible for large restitution payments associated with criminal action would be to break down the covenantal bonds of the community, since too high a risk factor would be transferred to safekeepers. Men would no longer be so willing voluntarily to accept the liabilities of safekeeping. This reduction in voluntary safekeeping activities would tend to subsidize the criminal class, which is certainly not the intent of biblical law.

The "hospitality of safekeeping" is designed to make theft more difficult for professional thieves. Clearly, it makes theft easier for previously honest neighbors. Nevertheless, the law has been given by God. So, the focus of judicial concern has to be on the professional thief. A man delivers his inanimate goods to a neighbor, above all, to keep them from being stolen. The recipient therefore must take care to see to it that the property is not stolen. He cannot guard against every conceivable loss, but he is required to make life more difficult for thieves. The law makes this responsibility inescapably clear: "And if it be stolen from him, he shall make restitution unto the owner thereof" (v. 12). The safekeeper has to repay the depositor. This motivates the safekeeper to seek to capture the thief.

If subsequently apprehended and convicted, the thief must pay the victimized safekeeper double. The safekeeper has already had to repay the depositor. It should be obvious that if the safekeeping neighbor has been assessed a compensating restitution payment, he has "bought" the missing beast from the original owner. Therefore, half of what the thief has returned to him serves as compensation for the loss he incurred by repaying the depositor. The other half of the double restitution payment is his compensation for having been put into a bind by the thief's actions.

The principle of ownership does not change in the case of the stolen ox or sheep. If the thief had stolen and killed or sold a sheep or an ox, and therefore must make a five-fold or four-fold restitution payment, the safekeeper receives the total restitution payment. He has become the victim, not the original owner, who has been compensated by the safekeeper; therefore, the safekeeper should receive the four-fold or five-fold restitution payment.

Conclusion

Accepting the responsibilities associated with safekeeping is a voluntary act which affirms the existence of covenantal bonds. There are judicial bonds with the neighbor, with the community, and with God. By acting as a steward of another man's property, the safekeeper becomes an agent of the neighbor, the community, and God. He must do his best to keep thieves at bay. He is not responsible for every possible loss that might befall these entrusted goods, but he is responsible to see that thieves do not break in and take them. He is responsible up to the value of the stolen goods, beast for beast, good for good.

The neighbor who is a thief jeopardizes covenantal social order. He is to be brought before the judges by the victim. This passage refers exclusively to criminal behavior. This is why double restitution is imposed in each case. Double restitution is biblical law's sanction against criminal intent: an additional restitution payment is imposed that is equal to the gross return that the thief hoped to gain from the transgression. If the case comes to trial, the accused must take an oath before God and the court that he is innocent. The thief takes great risks in giving a false oath. A false oath involves him in a second theft: the attempt to avoid paying the victim his lawful restitution. If he later admits his false oath, he will have to make an additional payment of 20 percent of the required double restitution to the victim, plus a trespass offering to the church. If he never admits it, and his false oath is subsequently proven in court, he will have to make quadruple restitution to the victim, or six-fold restitution, plus at least a double trespass offering to the church.

The judicial principle here is that *there are progressively greater sanctions as criminal behavior escalates.* Confession before each stage of rebellion brings with it reduced penalties.

20

CARETAKING AND NEGLIGENCE

If a man deliver unto his neighbor an ass, or an ox, or a sheep, or any beast, to keep; and it die, or be hurt, or driven away, no man seeing it: Then shall an oath of the LORD be between them both, that he hath not put his hand unto his neighbor's goods; and the owner of it shall accept thereof, and he shall not make it good. And if it be stolen from him, he shall make restitution unto the owner thereof. If it be torn in pieces, then let him bring it for witness, and he shall not make good that which was torn (Ex. 22:10-13).

The previous case law (Ex. 22:7-9) dealt with property that has been put in safekeeping with a neighbor, and the property is then stolen from the safekeeper, or is said by the safekeeper to have been stolen. The present passage is an extension of the previous one. It begins with the same phrase as verse 8 does: "If a man deliver unto his neighbour. . . ." If verse 8 refers to a non-commercial transaction, as it seems to,[1] then so does this passage.[2] There is no indication that the neighbor is a professional who is hired for a fee. The relationship is neighborly, not commercial. If this were a commercial transaction, it would necessarily involve the transfer of much greater responsibility for taking care of the animals to the person receiving payment. The owner is paying the professional to become his *delegated surrogate*, someone who is therefore to protect the animals from danger.[3] The

---

1. Rabbi Moses ben Nachman [Ramban], *Commentary on the Torah: Exodus* (New York: Shilo, [1267?] 1973), pp. 378-79; Samson Raphael Hirsch, *The Pentateuch Translated and Explained*, translated by Isaac Levy, 5 vols., *Exodus* (3rd ed.; London: Honig & Sons, 1967), p. 348.

2. Hirsch said that this section does involve a commercial transaction, but he offered no evidence from the biblical text: *Exodus*, p. 348.

3. The Hammurabi Code specified that if a hired shepherd lost a sheep or ox, he had to restore the equivalent animal to the owner: CH, paragraphs 263-64. If he sold an animal or switched its brand, and the owner proved it, he had to restore tenfold: 265. *Ancient Near Eastern Texts Relating to the Old Testament*, edited by James B. Pritchard (3rd ed.; Princeton, New Jersey: Princeton University Press, 1969), p. 177.

person renting the skills of a shepherd or cattle drover expects this hired professional to do his job responsibly.

If the thief cannot be located, the neighbor immediately may fall under suspicion and can be brought before the judges (Ex. 22:9). (The Hebrew word here translated as "judges" is transliterated as *elohim*, one of the names of God [Gen. 1:1]. Some commentators translate the word in Exodus 22:9 as "God," arguing that suspects were actually brought before God in expectation of a divine judgment. But the verb used here with *elohim* is plural, indicating men who serve as God's authorized judicial representatives rather than God Himself as the immediate Judge. The meaning is comparable to the meaning of *elohim* in Psalm 82:6: "I have said, Ye are gods. . . .")[4] The judges must determine which of the contending parties is lying and therefore who owes restitution to whom. The principle of "eye for eye" also applies to cases of false witness (Deut. 19:17-21).

Animals

This case law focuses exclusively on animals. An inanimate object remains where it was placed until someone or something moves it. An animal is mobile. The problems of taking care of an animal are greater, generally, than the problems of guarding inanimate objects. The animal has to be cared for as well as protected from thieves and wild animals. There is greater expense involved in taking care of an animal, and greater risk of its getting in trouble.

The punishments vary for the deliberate theft of an animal. Twofold restitution is required in the case of most stolen animals and all stolen inanimate property. Five-fold restitution is required for a stolen ox, while four-fold restitution is sufficient in the case of a stolen sheep. These high penalties were imposed only when the animal had already been killed or sold by the time of the thief's capture (Ex. 22:1). Double payment was required from the man who still had the living animal in his possession when caught by the authorities (Ex. 22:4). Contrary to commentators who argue that the differences

---

4. DeMar and Leithart point out that virtually all Protestant commentators interpret "gods" of Psalm 82:6 as "judges." They cite Charles H. Spurgeon, H. C. Leupold, Thomas Scott, F. S. Delitzsch, J. J. Stewart Perone, David Dickson, Joseph Addison Alexander, William S. Plummer, John Calvin, Matthew Henry, Matthew Poole, and Woodrow Michael Kroll. Gary DeMar and Peter J. Leithart, *The Reduction of Christianity: A Biblical Response to Dave Hunt* (Ft. Worth, Texas: Dominion Press, 1988), pp. 78-81.

in the size of the fines were based on the difference in cost of training certain animals, the differing penalties were probably imposed because of the *special symbolism of sheep and oxen* — symbols that represent mankind — and also because of differing levels of difficulty in apprehending and convicting the thief.[5]

Cases of known theft (Ex. 22:1-4), as well as cases of carelessness concerning fire or pollution (Ex. 22:5-6) — the coercive transfer of operating costs to one's neighbor — are easier for the authorities to adjudicate than those cases in which the responsibility for someone's loss is hidden. Verses 7-15 deal with several of these more difficult cases involving loss: 1) the safekeeping or storage of inanimate objects; 2) caretaking of animals; 3) borrowing goods; and 4) renting goods.

These passages indicate that it was a common practice among the Hebrews to ask their neighbors to act as temporary guardians for their property, thereby transferring to their neighbors the risks of supervision. This was one of the costs of "neighborliness," and the law established legal limits of responsibility, risk, and restitution. One of the advantages of this safekeeping system was the *greater physical mobility* it permitted to Hebrew families.

Passover

When would such mobility have been most important? At Passover and at the other celebrations in Jerusalem. There is no way that families could have left their flocks and herds at home without supervision. At the same time, it is inconceivable that they could have brought the animals with them to Jerusalem. Thus, neighbors would have taken turns in caring for the animals of their neighbors.

Wasn't Passover absolutely required for all Hebrews every year? Not necessarily. It was required for all adult males who were numbered (Num. 1:1-4). It was not required of all women. For instance, Jesus and His disciples met together for Passover; there is no indication that women or children were present (John 13-17). Furthermore, men on very distant journeys probably were not required to attend. Getting back on time from North America or other far-away lands might not have been possible.[6] A second Passover celebration was established a month after the first one for those who legitimately

---

5. See my exegesis of Exodus 22:1 in Chapter 17: "Proportional Restitution."

6. On evidence that Middle Eastern and European traders were operating in North America long before Roman times, see Barry Fell, *Bronze Age America* (Boston: Little, Brown, 1982).

missed the first one, either for having been in contact with a dead body or for having been on a journey, presumably one in the Mediterranean area (Num. 9:10-11). While caretaking for a neighbor's animals was not listed as one of the reasons for missing the Passover legitimately, it must have been one of them.

If we argue that Passover was required for every Hebrew at one time, then the only explanation of who kept the animals would seem to be permanent foreign slaves, meaning that Passover was a major economic incentive for every Hebrew family to become owners of permanent foreign slaves, and to place all the mobile property of the land into their hands at least once a year. This seems to be an unlikely ritual incentive in biblical law.

Restitution, Risk, and Knowledge

The case of a dead or lost animal is different from the case of a stolen animal. The caretaker has to swear before God that he did not steal it, destroy it for his own use, or sell it. If he is willing to swear this, he is not required to restore the missing animal. The owner has to accept this oath as binding (Ex. 22:10-11). The sacred nature of the oath has to be recognized; the original owner thereby acknowledges his faith in God's final judgment and His perfect restitution. Vengeance belongs to God, and He will impose judgment. Social peace is therefore far easier (cheaper) to attain in a community of men who believe in a living God who serves as perfect Judge. The judges will have fewer cases to adjudicate, for self-discipline increases in such a society. The likelihood of blood vengeance and clan feuds is also reduced. Socially disrupting suspicions and accusations can be put to rest.

The caretaker cannot escape his responsibility for the stolen animal. He only escapes the additional penalty for criminal activity (Ex. 22:11b). If the animal has been stolen from him, he has to make a restitution payment to the original owner (Ex. 22:12). This payment is equal to the value of the goods stolen or lost.[7] (Exodus 22:12 indicates that if the thief is found, he must make proportional restitution to the caretaker, who is now the economic victim, since the caretaker had made the restitution payment to the owner.)

---

7. See my exegesis of Exodus 22:7 in Chapter 19: "Safekeeping, Liability, and Crime Prevention."

The Wild Beast

One kind of negligence is not penalized: a loss imposed by a wild beast. Verse 13 provides the details: "If it be torn to pieces, then let him bring it for witness, and he shall not make good that which was torn." If a bear, wolf, lion, or a pack of dangerous animals rips apart a beast that has been entrusted to a neighbor, he is not liable. He is not required to risk his life trying to save the animal from wild beasts.

Why should he escape this requirement in the case of an animal carried away by a beast? Why should he be less liable? After all, the animal is gone. The loss to the owner is just as great as it would be if the animal had been stolen. If the loss is as great, why shouldn't the restitution be equal? One answer relates to comparative risks to the life of the caretaker. He is under no pressure judicially to challenge a bear or other dangerous beast in order to protect his neighbor's property, any more than he has a legal obligation to challenge a dangerous beast in order to defend his own property.[8] There are limits on his responsibilities as a neighbor. Second, men in general cannot be expected to know the habits of another man's animal. Perhaps it can lift a latch with its nose, or maybe it runs away as soon as it gets outside its pen. If it exposes itself to danger in this way, it has to bear responsibility for its actions. If it removes itself from the protection of the caretaker, it is not the caretaker's fault.

An animal can kill itself or injure itself in many ways. A man cannot be expected to provide free caretaking services for every contingency. He is dealing with an unfamiliar animal, and the animal is in unfamiliar surroundings. The predictability of its behavior is reduced, compared to its predictability under the dominion of its owner. The owner may recognize certain patterns of behavior that point to injury or sickness that a neighbor would probably ignore. The neighbor does not have equally accurate background information on the animal.

The Witness

Why is the safekeeper responsible when something inanimate is stolen, but not in the case of animals that are torn apart? Verses 10 and 11 provide the solution: "If a man deliver unto his neighbor an ass, or an ox, or a sheep, or any beast, to keep; and it die, or be hurt,

---

8. Challenging a criminal, or at least doing what is necessary to bring him to justice, is a different situation. The law-abiding citizen is to take risks to restrict evil people. They are a greater threat to social order than wild beasts are.

or driven away, *no man seeing it*, then shall an oath of the LORD be between them both, that he hath not put his hand unto his neighbour's goods; and the owner of it shall accept thereof, and he shall not make it good."[9] Verse 10 deals with the death, injury, or driving away of an animal. If no one has seen what happened to the missing animal, then there is no way to prove that some wild animal did not do it, or that the protected beast did not hurt itself. Wild animals might drive away or carry away a sheep; they might drive away an ox or donkey. The presumption is that a wild animal dragged away the animal that was being guarded.

The dead carcass of the animal serves as a witness to the honesty of the safekeeper, so in this case there is no need to go before the judges and swear an oath. There is a *witness* in this case: the carcass itself. The carcass is evidence that a wild beast destroyed it. The safekeeper did not profit from its death, nor did any thief. There is no human being to be held accountable for the loss. This allows the safekeeper to escape legal liability for the return of the animal or its equivalent value.

When it comes to defending against thieves, however, men are expected to possess approximately the same information. Men understand the ways of other men. Locking or blocking a door at night to restrict access to the home is a universal practice. So is listening to animals, since they tend to cry out, bark, or stamp around when strangers approach. What the absent neighbor wants is to reduce the likelihood of theft by placing his animal under someone else's protection, so as to avoid the "empty house" problem. The neighbor's house is a safer place for his animals. He expects his neighbor to provide him with safety from thieves.

How could the complaining neighbor prove that the other man should be held economically responsible? He would have to prove that the safekeeper sought to profit from the loss of the animal, or failed to do his duty in stopping a thief. To prove the latter case, he would have to have a witness. The key phrase is, "no man seeing it" (v. 10). Some witness would have to come forward and testify that he

---

9. Maimonides argued that in cases where there are witnesses, the oath is not to be imposed. Moses Maimonides, *The Book of Civil Laws*, vol. 13 of *The Code of Maimonides*, 14 vols. (New Haven, Connecticut: Yale University Press, [1180] 1949), "Hiring," Chapter Three, Section One, p. 12. This would seem to eliminate the use of the oath between the disputing parties in any courtroom where there are witnesses available to testify. God is called upon through the oath only when there are no "normal" sources of resolving the dispute.

saw someone snooping around the home of the safekeeper during the night of the theft, and that he had warned the safekeeper (indicating that he, the witness, was not an accomplice or a guilty, silent on-looker), or that he saw the beast penned in the night before it disappeared (indicating that a thief had released it). The safekeeping neighbor has to spend time and capital in making sure that his neighbor's property is protected. This is his voluntary contribution to his neighbor, the neighborhood, and God. He acts as a steward to keep the property protected from the criminal class.

Inanimate Goods

Inanimate goods are a less difficult case. They are not "driven off." They are stolen by a criminal or lost by the safekeeper. The man who accepts his neighbor's goods in trust must be willing to see to it that precautions are taken to protect these goods from theft. If he cannot honestly swear that the goods had been lost, or if a witness can point to signs that the man was criminally negligent — negligent in failing to protect the property against criminal action — then he has to pay. This gives him added incentive to take some risks in stopping a thief who breaks into his home. He will bear the penalty if the thief gets away with the crime. Thus, in the case of a thief who breaks in, he has both the legal right and the economic incentive to stop the thief, even to the point (at night) of killing him (Ex. 22:2). Again, the focus of concern of these case laws is the *reduction of criminal activity in the local community*, namely, the prevention of theft. A thief must be specially guarded against.

Borrowed Property

In the case of borrowed property, any loss or damage is not the responsibility of the borrower if the owner accompanies his property when it is being used: "And if a man borrow ought of his neighbour, and it be hurt, or die, the owner thereof being not with it, he shall surely make it good. But if the owner thereof be with it, he shall not make it good: if it be an hired thing, it came for his hire" (Ex. 22:14-15). The owner retains his oversight over it, and therefore bears the full responsibility for its proper use. He can see how the borrower is using the property when the accident occurred.[10]

_____

10. Maimonides cites the Jewish oral tradition as saying that the lender needed to be present with the borrower only when the property was transferred, but not after-

On the other hand, if he does not accompany his property, then the borrower has to pay simple "like for like" compensation, not double or quadruple restitution, for criminal activity is not involved in the loss, only carelessness. James Jordan writes: "Since this is the kind of thing that happens every day, a few comments are in order. Let us assume that you borrowed your neighbor's punchbowl and broke it. How should you make compensation? First, don't tell her in advance that you broke the punchbowl, unless you have to. That only gives her an opportunity to say she doesn't need a replacement. People say things like, 'Oh, well, forget it. It's not important,' but in fact they don't forget. Second, don't just give her the money. She is likely to refuse to take it. Also, why should she have to go to the trouble of purchasing a new bowl, when you are the one who broke it? Third, don't buy a more expensive punchbowl. It may not match her set. Let her use the receipt and exchange it if she wants to. Fourth, don't neglect the opportunity to witness for Christ. You are not doing this because it seems nice and neighborly. You are doing it because Christ your Lord tells you to. Let her know that." What if you are the person who has had an item broken? What if the person who broke it wants to reimburse you? "If someone wants to make compensation to you, don't despise him by refusing to accept it. Accept it graciously as from the Lord."[11]

Finally, in the case of rented property, the borrower is not legally responsible for loss, for the property "came for his hire." The risk premium or insurance premium is included in the rental fee. *The owner-renter is self-insuring his own property.* (The translation of the Hebrew in the second half of Exodus 22:15 is disputed, however; it may refer to a hired servant who accompanies his master's property as the owner's representative, in which case, no restitution is owed.)

What is in focus in these laws is the particular "bundle of rights" that is transferred along with the physical property. With rights of ownership come certain responsibilities for preserving the quality of

---

wards, in order for the lender to escape liability. Even more peculiar, "if the lender was not with him at the time of the borrowing, though he was present at the time of the death or capture, the borrower is liable." Maimonides, *Civil Laws*, "Treatise I, Laws Concerning Hiring," Chapter One, Section Three, p. 5. This makes the law difficult to interpret from an economic standpoint. The focus of the passage is on the risk borne by the owner-lender because, being present with his property, he has the legal authority to call a halt to some high-risk use of it.

11. James B. Jordan, *The Law of the Covenant: An Exposition of Exodus 21-23* (Tyler, Texas: Institute for Christian Economics, 1984), p. 143.

the goods loaned out. All property is God's; He delegates certain rights and responsibilities to specific people. The goal of this delegation of this stewardship system is to extend God's dominion on earth. Thus, ownership has inescapable legal implications, that is, *covenantal* implications. There cannot be ownership without legal responsibility. These laws set forth the limits of the "bundle of rights" in three types of lending transactions: 1) when the owner or his agent accompanies his property, 2) when he does not accompany his property, and 3) when he rents his property for a fee. In the first case, the rights and therefore responsibilities of ownership remain with the owner. In the second, they shift to the borrower. In the third, they remain with the owner.

There is a system of strict liability operating here. The borrower assumes risks when he borrows a work animal. He is asking another person to give him something free of charge. He is asking for *grace*. The borrower becomes responsible for the proper administration of the other person's property. If the animal dies of natural causes, the borrower has to repay the owner. Who can be sure what killed it? Was it overworked or not? When the borrower asks for grace from his neighbor, he must not expect unlimited grace. Biblical law establishes the limits of his responsibility.[12]

Conclusion

This section of the case laws refers to the voluntary, charitable care of a neighbor's animals. Rules are established regarding the extent of personal responsibility for the caretaking of animals. There is no penalty imposed on the caretaker if an animal is carried off when no one sees it, if he swears before the judges that he has not stolen the animal. He is responsible for restoring, like for like, any animal

---

12. Maimonides argued that if the animal died of natural causes during normal work activities, the borrower is exempt: *Civil Laws*, "Treatise II, Laws Concerning Borrowing and Depositing," Chapter One, Section One, p. 52. Incredibly, he argued that if a man asks another man for a drink of water and also to borrow his work animal, no matter what happens to the animal, he owes the lender nothing. Why? Because this is a case of "the owner thereof be with it" (Ex. 22:13). "Whether the commodatary borrowed the services of the owner or hired them, whether he borrowed the services for the same work, or for other work, or for anything in the world . . . it is a case of borrowing with the owner and the commodatary is quit. If, however, he borrowed the animal first, and then the owner gave him water to drink, it is not a case of borrowing with the owner. And so it is in all similar cases." *Ibid.*, Chapter Two, Section One, p. 55. This sort of reasoning places barriers of extreme legalism in between neighbors. Legal technicalities can overwhelm personal relationships.

that is stolen from him. If the beast's torn carcass is located, the caretaker is not held responsible.

Charity is basic to social order. Property needs protection when owners are away from their homes. Men's geographical mobility would be heavily restricted if they could not occasionally trust their neighbors to look after their property. But there are legitimate limits to people's willingness to bear risks. By establishing rules in advance that govern the judges' assessment of responsibility in the case of theft or loss, the Bible allows neighbors to estimate more precisely the extent of the risk they are being asked to bear in these instances. This assists them in making an estimate concerning the amount of charity they are willing to extend, for that is what caretaking involves: extra work and extra responsibility.

The costs of litigation are lowered by the fear of God and the fear of the restitution payment owed to God because of false oaths. The fear of having to make equal restitution increases the costs of carelessness. As we have seen in Chapter 17, the fear of double restitution increases the costs of theft when the animals are not immediately sold or killed, or when the stolen property is inanimate. *Restitution and the fear of God are basic to social order.*

21

SEDUCTION AND SERVITUDE

And if a man entice a maid that is not betrothed, and lie with her, he shall surely endow her to be his wife. If her father utterly refuse to give her unto him, he shall pay money according to the dowry of virgins (Ex. 22:16-17).

The theocentric principle that governs this case law seems to be the defense of God the Father's covenantal authority over the family of man. This case law governs a man's seduction of an unmarried and unbetrothed (unengaged) virgin. It is not a capital crime. Adultery, in contrast, is a capital crime (Deut. 22:22). Why is there a difference in the punishments? Because the seduction of a virgin does not involve the breaking of a covenant vow. In fact, it involves *taking* a covenant vow. It involves the physical bonding associated with the consummation of a binding marriage vow. In biblical law, physical consummation is itself the mutual vow of betrothal.

Adultery was involved in the sins in the garden of Eden. Eve's spiritual seduction by Satan was an adulterous attack on her existing covenantal bond with her husband Adam. She had been given by God to Adam. It had been an arranged marriage, one to which both partners had freely consented. She was therefore "spoken for" covenantally at the time of her temptation, either as a betrothed woman or as a consummated bride. She was Adam's wife. Satan intervened and lured her into disobeying God, her husband's master. This was a capital crime, even though she, unlike Adam, was deceived into sinning (I Tim. 2:14). She could not claim ignorance of God's law as justification of her crime. Because Adam consented to this act of adultery, and participated in it, he also came under God's condemnation of death. He became, in effect, a covenantal pimp for his own wife.

642

The Age of Lawful Independence

Fornication by unmarried and unbetrothed partners was a crime in the Old Testament, if the daughter was still living in the household of her father. The question arises: At what age did the father's authority legally cease or become drastically reduced? The Bible is silent on this point. Sons in the Old Testament became subject to a military draft at age 20 (Ex. 30:14). This "age of independence" may also have applied to a daughter who lived outside her father's home, although the Bible does not say so explicitly. The dividing line of authority seems to have been her presence in her father's house: "These are the statutes, which the LORD commanded Moses, between a man and his wife, between the father and his daughter, being yet in her youth in her father's house" (Num. 30:16). If she was outside his house, unmarried, yet economically self-sufficient—highly unlikely, given the ancient world's agricultural economy and Israel's jubilee land tenure system (Lev. 25)—she would have been beyond his legal responsibility over her. She would have been free to conduct her life as she saw fit, for good or evil, without calling his judgment into question, although he could have disinherited her by refusing to provide any dowry for her.[1]

In the New Covenant era, seduction remains an attack on the covenantal authority of the girl's family. There is no indication that the legal terms have changed. Fornication is behavior that covenantally faithful families should seek to impair, and the civil government is required to back up the family with the threat of sanctions against the seducer. The father becomes the lawful prosecutor of the seducer, and the State supports him in his decision. In this sense, the father becomes a lawful agent of the State, the State's representative. This is why the seduction is a crime.

The State enforces all sorts of contracts, but this case is different. The magnitude of the potential penalty is so great, as we shall see, that in order to impose it, the State must number the transgressor among felony criminals, such as major thieves. In the case of a seduction, biblical law transfers to the girl's father a monopoly position in set-

---

1. We cannot take seriously the comment by Nachmanides, who said that the father's authority over her decision to marry lasted only from age twelve and one day to twelve and a half, and that after this she had passed her maidenhood and was considered lawfully able to decide for herself whom she would marry, with or without fornication's having preceded the marriage. Nachmanides, *Commentary on the Torah: Exodus* (New York: Shilo, [1267?], 1973), p. 388.

ting the terms of the bride price.[2] The magnitude of the sanctions against seduction is such that only the State could enforce them without risking a clan war or other violence. The act of seduction therefore came under the jurisdiction of Israel's criminal statutes.

Consenting to a girl's marriage is normally a family responsibility, not primarily a civil government or church responsibility, except in those rare cases when the couple appeals the negative decision of the father to the church or churches to which they belong.[3] The father does not have a final say, for no single human agent ever possesses an absolutely final say in any legal decision, including the State,[4] but he has the primary responsibility to sanction the marriage of his daughter. His decision can lawfully be appealed to the church, but in general his decision stands. In the case of dealing with the seduction of a virgin, however, the father's authority is supplemented by civil authority, according to biblical law.

Consummating the Vow

A lawful marriage normally requires three things in the following order: a mutual vow of the proposed marriage partners, a public transfer of covenantal authority from the girl's father to the bridegroom, and sexual consummation. A verbal vow (betrothal) is to precede the formal ritual of public, covenantal marriage; physical consummation follows. But when private physical consummation itself becomes the form the vow takes, then a public act must follow: either the seducer's payment to her father (or brother)[5] of an unspec-

---

2. As we shall see, there is a judicial distinction between the bride price, which is paid by the bridegroom to the girl's family, and the dowry, which is paid to the girl by her family.

3. The case of a pagan father who refuses to sanction the marriage of his Christian daughter to a Christian man would be a case that the couple could lawfully appeal to the church or churches that possess covenantal sovereignty over them. To deny this right of appeal would be to absolutize the father's word, and to designate him as the sole authorized agent under God over the daughter. This would elevate the father's word to a sovereign position comparable to the Roman Church's post-1870 view of the Pope.

4. The father can appeal this decision to the civil magistrate. The decision of the civil magistrate would then confirm either the father's decision or the church's. The State serves only as a settler of disputes between lawful authorities, not as the initiator of laws regarding marriage, except when public health considerations are involved, e.g., compulsory testing of both parties for disease. The State's word is not autonomously final; it simply confirms the decision of one of the disputants in the case.

5. Abraham's servant dealt with Rebekah's brother Laban and her mother (Gen. 24:29, 53, 55) even though her father Bethuel was alive (v. 50). The sons of Jacob set the terms of Shechem's dowry, even though Jacob was present with them (Gen. 34:13).

ified bride price plus a marriage ceremony, or his payment of "the dowry of virgins" without a marriage ceremony. *The physical consummation constitutes covenantal betrothal.* It is a binding oath. It is a *bond.* Her father then determines whether a marriage will consummate the vow, or whether the payment of the formal bride price, the "dowry of virgins," will alone consummate it.[6] But payment of some sort is necessary to consummate the vow.

The consent of the girl to her seduction is the equivalent of her private betrothal. She takes a binding covenant vow with the seducer by means of her body. The seducer does the same with his body. She implicitly agrees to marry the seducer, and he implicitly agrees to marry her. Neither of them has the option of breaking the vow. Only her father does. An unmarried girl has no independent authority to take a vow if her father refuses to accept it (Num. 30:3-5). Numbers 30:3 refers to a binding vow as "a vow unto the LORD." Thus, this passage in Exodus informs us that her father, as God's covenantal agent over her until her marriage, has the authority to deny the consummation of his daughter's vow through marriage.

The girl must immediately inform her father of the act-vow. If she refuses, she has identified herself before God as a promiscuous woman, a prostitute. She has accepted the legitimacy of sexual union outside of marriage, the essence of prostitution. She has thereby become an idolater. If she marries later on, and neither she nor her father formally informs her suitor prior to the betrothal, her discovered lack of virginity could lead to her public execution (Deut. 22:20-21). Also, should she become pregnant, she would soon be publicly identified as a prostitute. If she was the daughter of a priest in Israel, she would be stoned to death, with her body burned after (Lev. 21:9; see Josh. 7:25), but only after the birth of her child. This, of course, drastically increased the risks of fornicating with the promiscuous daughter of a priest. If she knew she was pregnant from an earlier act, she might immediately seduce some other young man — as Eve seduced Adam by means of the forbidden fruit — and then announce the act to her father, as if the night before had been her first time, in order to get herself a husband or a bride price, and thereby avoid the death penalty.

---

6. In the United States, it has long been a crime to seduce a woman by promising to marry her later, and then refusing to marry her. The crime is called "breach of promise." It clearly parallels this biblical case law. It is seldom enforced today.

The Father's Status

Why does the seducer owe money to the father, rather than to the girl? Because the father is legally liable for the girl and for his family's reputation. But this liability is limited by the extent of his knowledge. He cannot know everything she does. He always needs better information. Biblical law creates incentives for the transfer of appropriate knowledge to those who are God's legally responsible representatives.

The daughter's original consent to the act of seduction does not itself constitute whoredom. Her failure to tell her father immediately of the seduction is what constitutes her whoredom, for whoredom (as distinguished from adultery) is defined biblically as sexual bonding apart from a marriage vow.[7] If she accepts the legitimacy of her sexual union apart from a marriage vow, then she has become a whore. She had taken the vow implicitly by her consent to the act, but her unwillingness to tell her father of the act that constituted her vow thereby establishes her covenantally as a whore.

She remains "in her father's house" (Num. 30:16), and under his covenantal jurisdiction, yet she is no longer a virgin. The presence of this unannounced non-virgin daughter brings disgrace on her house and on Israel when she is discovered. Because she has willfully broken her covenantal bond with her father, but has refused to acknowledge her implicit vow with her seducer, biblical law considers her a whore. The capital penalty can subsequently be imposed if she marries another man who has been asked to pay a bride price to her father, if the new husband immediately decides to prosecute her (Deut. 22:13-19).

If the father had known of her act, yet took no steps to receive payment from the seducer, he thereby consented to the theology of sexual bonding without covenantal bonding. He has also become an implicit idolater. He has no legal excuse. He has identified himself as

---

7. This indicates that Jesus' announcement that divorce is legitimate only because of fornication (*porneia*) must have been based on a far broader definition of *porneia* than mere sexual bonding. The King James translators too narrowly defined the word as fornication. Under Old Testament law, once a marriage had taken place, fornication was always defined as adultery, a capital offense. Obviously, divorce through execution was possible, and Jesus would not have had to raise the issue. He would have used the term for adultery rather than fornication. Rushdoony, *The Institutes of Biblical Law* (Nutley, New Jersey: Craig Press, 1973), pp. 406-14; Greg L. Bahnsen, *Theonomy in Christian Ethics* (2nd ed.; Phillipsburg, New Jersey: Presbyterian & Reformed, 1984), pp. 105-9.

a pimp for his own daughter. To avoid this humiliation, there must be a consummation of the marriage vow by the seducer, either through marriage plus payment of the bride price or payment without marriage. Thus, the father's insistence on receiving the bride price is a legal announcement of his rejection of whoredom in his household and in Israel. His daughter is declared not to be a whore, for he has received the bride price. *Without payment of the bride price by the seducer, the father's house and his family's name are polluted.*

Once the bride price has been paid, the father cannot legitimately collect it from another man. Thus, if someone else lies with his daughter, he is protected from a forced marriage. He has identified himself as a whoremonger, but not as a bridegroom. She identifies herself as a prostitute as soon as she identifies the second seducer. She has no legal claim on any man who does not voluntarily agree to marry a non-virgin, nor does her father have any economic claim on him, even if he decides to marry her. A daughter is entitled only to one dowry per marriage, and her father is entitled to one bride price per marriage. (Negotiations between a father and a prospective bridegroom are legitimate, though not mandatory, for a widow who wishes to remarry, for she is taking on another set of responsibilities, and is in need of economic protection from potentially bad decisions of the next husband. The reason why negotiations are not mandatory is that she no longer is required to have her vows authorized by her father [Num. 30:9].)

The Formal Bride Price

We have seen earlier that the payment of a bride price by the bridegroom is a sign of his subordination and obligation to the bride's family.[8] This text discusses "the dowry of virgins." The text does not specify how much this was. The reason for this omission is that *this payment was negotiable between families* within each economic class. The Bible could not specify a particular price without either placing it out of reach for most Israelites or else trivializing it for the rich. The price was not set so high that the poor would be forced to adopt concubinage—marriage without a dowry—or so low that the rich could dismiss it as nothing more than a mere ritual. Also, if a poor man wanted to marry a rich girl, her father could set a bride price lower than his intended dowry for her in order to test the will-

---

8. See Chapter 6: "Wives and Concubines," pp. 253, 256-57.

ingness of the prospective bridegroom to work hard to earn what for him would be a large sum, but which would nevertheless be a pittance for the father. This was the problem David faced (I Sam. 18:23). The bride price was, first, a ritual sign of subordination; second, it was a screening device for the girl's parents; and third, it was a means of compensating the girl's family for the expense of the dowry. The first two aspects were more important than the third. Thus, a fixed bride price was not set by biblical law. The existence of its requirement was far more important than the actual money involved, with only two judicial exceptions: the case of seduction (Ex. 22:16-17) and the case of accused harlotry (Deut. 22:13-19).

Seduction

Let us consider the case of seduction. There is no doubt that the father, under the jurisdiction of the judges, was allowed to establish a bride price requirement for the seducer, and even prohibit the marriage after having collected it. Obviously, only the State could have lawfully enforced such a penalty.

When the State enters the picture to enforce a private decision, there must be upper limits on the punishment if liberty under predictable law is to be preserved. At the same time, the penalty must be high enough to deter the immoral behavior. Thus, the maximum bride price that could be imposed by the father with the consent of the judges could and would be different from normally negotiated bride prices. We know what that upper limit was: 50 shekels of silver. I call this compulsory maximum the *formal* bride price, in contrast to the normal or negotiated bride price, in which the State was not involved. It is specified in Deuteronomy 22:28-29:

> If a man find a damsel that is a virgin, which is not betrothed, and lay hold on her, and lie with her, and they be found; then the man that lay with her shall give unto the damsel's father fifty shekels of silver, and she shall be his wife; because he hath humbled her, he may not put her away all his days.

The formal bride price of 50 shekels of silver specified here was far higher than the common dowry in Israel. This was a great deal of money. It was not required of every suitor. The Old Testament did not establish a fixed price so high that only a few women could have become wives, with most of them being forced by a government-imposed price floor to settle for status as concubines (wives without dowries) instead. What the law did was to establish *a penalty price so high that it discouraged seduction*. It also discouraged false accusations of whoredom.

The threat of the imposition of the formal bride price was designed to restrain the present-orientation of the couple—in this case, the lure of instant sexual gratification. The bride price jumped automatically to 50 shekels of silver in such instances. This economic threat forced marriage arrangements into specific patterns as family-authorized covenants, with the parents and older brothers of the girl as the agents with primary authority to inaugurate or veto her decision. This threat also forced irresponsible, short-sighted young men to save for the future, to develop good character traits. The normal bride price was a covenantal screening instrument; the formal bride price was a covenantal disciplining instrument.

The seducer placed himself outside the normal competitive position of a suitor. He was in no legal position to bargain effectively with the girl's father. Shechem pleaded: "Ask me never so much dowry and gift, and I will give according as ye shall say unto me: but give me the damsel to wife" (Gen 34:12). The father of a seduced girl was in a position to demand up to 50 shekels of silver from the young man, which probably would have involved many years of servitude on his part, unless his family was rich. The seducer could even be required to pay her father the 50 shekels of silver, and then not be allowed to marry the girl.

Establishing the Formal Bride Price

The Jewish commentators agree that it was 50 shekels of silver, although they do not always precisely explain their line of reasoning. Those who say that it was 50 shekels frequently connect this passage to Deuteronomy 22:19.[9] This passage provides rules for penalizing a bridegroom who falsely accuses his new bride of not being a virgin. A new husband in ancient Israel who falsely accused his wife of not being a virgin at the time of marriage was obviously after two things: 1) permanent separation from the girl; and 2) the return of his bride price. He may also have been after an additional penalty payment of 50 shekels from her father. I am assuming here that a bride price had been paid before the marriage; if not, then by his accusation, he was

---

9. Nachmanides, *Exodus*, p. 256; Haim H. Cohn, "Sexual Offenses," *The Principles of Jewish Law*, edited by Menachem Elon (Jerusalem: Keter, [1975?]), col. 485.

trying to avoid paying it. I believe, however, the bride price was normally paid before the marriage, which is why Jacob worked seven years for Laban before Laban was required to give him Rachel (Gen. 29:18-20).

Why 100 Shekels?

The required penalty owed to the father of a falsely accused girl was 100 shekels of silver (Deut. 22:19). The question then is: Does this provide us with evidence that confirms my suggestion concerning the size of the original bride price? We know that the Old Testament's authorized penalty payments were double damages, quadruple damages (a slaughtered sheep),[10] and quintuple damages (a slaughtered ox). In this case, double damages were required. Half of a hundred is 50. Why 50 shekels? Because this was the maximum bride price that could be imposed by law. We must think through the issue with 50 shekels as the starting point.

Notice that the girl was executed if she was convicted, but her bridegroom was not executed if she was exonerated. This seems to be opposed to the principle of Deuteronomy 19:15-21, which states that the false witness must suffer the penalty that the falsely accused person would have suffered if convicted. Instead, the bridegroom paid a heavy penalty to her father. All he owed his bride was a lifetime guarantee of no divorce. What he owed her father, however, was a lifetime of servitude, unless he was very rich. He became a slave to her father twice over, for the formal price of the lifetime slave for purposes of making a sanctuary vow was 50 shekels of silver (Lev. 27:3).

This is the only instance in the Bible of a false witness who is not subject to an equal penalty, as required by Deuteronomy 19:16. The falsely accused bride was to receive lifetime economic support from him rather than making her a divorcée by means of his execution. This exception to Deuteronomy 19:16 may be because of the difficulty in proving for certain either that she had or had not lost her physical evidence of virginity by some means other than copulation. The circumstantial nature of the required evidence — "tokens of virginity" — reduced the penalty for the false accuser, but it also made it

---

10. David insisted on the four-fold restitution payment when he heard Nathan's story, but in this case, the "ewe" was another man's wife (II Sam. 12:6). His "slaughter" of Bathsheba was the result of their adultery, not his seduction of a virgin as an unmarried man.

possible for the wife to escape the death penalty if she had not broken her hymen during a previous sexual liaison. The threat of the death penalty was great; a bride who suspected that the "tokens" would not appear would have warned the bridegroom in advance, and this could have led to his offering her father a reduced bride price, since he could not be sure of her explanation affirming her virginity. This reduced bride price would then have served as a substitute for her lack of the "tokens."

But if he owed his father-in-law 100 shekels, then in some way the father-in-law would have owed him 50 shekels if the accusation had been confirmed by the court. The text does not say this, but it is implied by the double restitution provisions of the case laws. We need to search for an implied theft of 50 shekels from the bridegroom on the part of the father-in-law, had the girl been guilty as charged.

Defrauding the Bridegroom

Let us assume that the bridegroom's accusation was accurate: she had not been a virgin at the time of marriage. The father-in-law was entitled only to one bride price per vow and marriage; whether collected by him or voluntarily forfeited, it could not be collected a second time, unless the girl was a widow, and the bridegroom agreed to pay it. (Because a widow would bring her original dowry into the subsequent marriage, she was not legally a concubine.) This payment was the formal bride price. The second man had owed her father nothing. By collecting a normal bride price from him, her father had cheated him. It was not his legal responsibility to pay.

Her father could have collected up to 50 shekels from the original seducer, but he failed to do so, either through ignorance of her condition, or through misplaced pity for the seducer, or through fear of the seducer's family, or because he knew that his daughter was promiscuous and not truly entitled to the first *discovered* seducer's bride price. In the last case, he had willfully allowed whoredom in his house, or, if he really had not known about it, then the daughter had to pay the maximum penalty for her deliberate concealment. In any case, the bridegroom would have been entitled to the return of his bride price. The text is silent about this, but it is implied; if this were not the case, then the father-in-law would have profited from his daughter's whoredom at the expense of the injured party, the bridegroom. Biblical law does not subsidize evil. It protects the innocent.

If the bridegroom had been informed of the girl's loss of virginity, then he would not have paid her father a bride price. The bride price would have already been paid by the seducer, even though her father had not consented to their marriage. I am arguing that *the bride price owed to the father by the seducer was 50 shekels, the settlement price of a lifetime male slave in formal judicial disputes* (Lev. 27:3).[11] This compulsory bride price should have been passed on to the daughter as her dowry, but passed on in a specific formal way, as I discuss below: first to the bridegroom, then back to her father, and then to the girl. If her father had not collected the money from the seducer, assuming that he knew of the seduction, he nevertheless owed a dowry to the daughter; otherwise, she would become a concubine. Without a dowry from her father, she was a concubine, yet only her father could pay for it this time; no subsequent bridegroom could be asked to pay a second bride price for a non-virgin non-widow.

The bridegroom had been forced to pay a bride price to the girl's father. Her father had either kept the 50 shekels that had been paid to him by the seducer, thereby making his daughter a concubine, or, if he had not collected the 50 shekels, he then owed the 50-shekel dowry out of his own assets. Again, the bridegroom had believed he was marrying a free woman who was bringing a dowry to the marriage, not a concubine. He was not legally required to pay the bride price because of her status as a non-virgin, so the father must have been required to pay it. Her father had not paid it. The bridegroom had been forced to pay. This constituted fraud. Although the actual fraud involved whatever his negotiated bride price payment had been, for judicial settlement purposes, the fraud was assumed to be the maximum required formal bride price, and therefore the required dowry, of 50 shekels.

How Much Had He Actually Paid?

I am assuming for the sake of argument that the bridegroom was in fact the victim of a conspiracy between the girl and her family, or else at least the victim of the girl, who had kept her status a secret from her father. After the marriage, the bridegroom then decided to get rid of the wife on the official grounds that she was not a virgin. He had not been informed of her status. How could he prove this? Because he had paid the bride price, which would not have been required of him in the case of a non-virgin; her seducer should have

---

11. An exception: the owner of a slave killed by a goring ox always was reimbursed by payment of 30 shekels of silver (Ex. 21:32).

provided the bride price. Her father had not delivered the required 50 shekels to her as her dowry; he had delivered only the bride price unjustly collected from the bridegroom. If the bridegroom could prove that he had been defrauded by the girl, or by her and her father, he could get back his bride price that had been unjustly extracted from him.

He had paid something for the girl, but probably not 50 shekels of silver. Why would the court not have returned whatever bride price he had paid? What has precisely 50 shekels got to do with it? The bridegroom was saying in effect that 50 shekels should have been given to him by her father as a ritual sign of her family's dependence on his merciful willingness to marry a non-virgin. There was *mutual subordination* involved, so her father should have provided this bride price to the bridegroom, and then the bridegroom would have ritually returned it to her father. Just as the bride price was a ritual sign of his subordination to the father-in-law, so was the father-in-law's provision of a bride price to the bridegroom a ritual sign of his dependence on the bridegroom. It was a sign that her father was in no position to bargain under such circumstances because of his daughter's defiled status. But her father had been unwilling to pay him the 50 shekels that would have served as his bride price payment, so that he could in turn pay the 50 to the father, who would then endow the daughter. The symbolism of the bridegroom's dependence was basic to the bride price-dowry transaction. Even without the formal double transaction, the father's payment of the daughter's dowry was implicitly a form of his dependence on the bridegroom. But I believe that the double formal transaction would have been carried out, as a public manifestation of the daughter's lack of virginity. Such a formal public transaction would have secured her from future prosecution by her husband.

The bridegroom was saying that he had never been informed of the girl's status. Her father had treated him unjustly, defrauding the bridegroom of whatever bride price he had been asked to pay. Thus, from a strictly economic standpoint, her father owed him at least the return of the original bride price that he had paid. Her father may also have owed the 50 shekels that should have been given to him by the seducer. The text does not say this, and I may be reading too much into it. It may be that the death of the daughter was regarded by the court as a sufficient penalty on her family. The death of the daughter may have replaced the implicit 50-shekel payment owed by the father. The father lost his daughter forever, and the bridegroom regained his original bride price payment.

What is clear is that in these formal judicial proceedings, the court was implicitly using 50 shekels as the formal penalty that would have been implicitly or actually owed to the bridegroom if the wife had been convicted. Why? Because the payment owed to the father by the original seducer was 50 shekels, the judicial price of an adult male slave.

Restitution: Double or Triple?

If the bridegroom lost the case, he was required to pay to the father-in-law the formal restitution penalty of the 50 shekels he had sought to collect through divorce by execution, plus another 50 shekels as a penalty. The court recognized the bridegroom as someone involved in intent to defraud the girl's father, whose reputation (and possibly 50 shekels) was at stake.

Thus, we conclude that *the penalty payment from the false accuser was directly related to the compulsory formal bride price of the seducer.* The new husband had accused his father-in-law of having cheated him out of the bride price. He never legally owed it, he insisted, yet his father-in-law had taken it. The court denied his accusation, so he was then forced to pay 100 shekels to his father-in-law.

The bridegroom had paid a negotiated bride price to the girl's father. Her father had transferred all or a part of this to her as her dowry. She was now formally accused by her husband of being a whore. If she was convicted, her father would probably have been forced to pay the bridegroom the formal (50-shekel) bride price; the bridegroom would also have kept her dowry, as her lawful heir after her execution. If she was declared innocent, the bridegroom owed double restitution to the father-in-law: twice the amount of the formal bride price that the father-in-law would have owed to him upon her conviction. The wife of course kept her dowry.

To repeat: since the court's decision in this example went against the bridegroom, he had to pay the father a hundred shekels of silver, meaning that he returned the maximum bride price of 50 shekels, plus an additional 50—double restitution. Furthermore, he could never divorce her in the future (Deut. 22:19), except by public execution for a capital crime. This indicates that the maximum formal bride price was 50 shekels of silver. It also indicates that any husband bringing such an accusation against his bride believed that he had a good case. His wife and father-in-law did not possess the required tokens of virginity, and he imagined that the court would uphold him.[12]

This indicates that for purposes of establishing *public restitution payments*, a very high initial bride price would have been established by law. Once the dispute became a matter of public decision by the court, the formal penalties became very high. In this case, a price of 50 shekels was assumed as binding.

Slavery: Male or Female?

We know that in the formal sanctuary vow, the adult female slave was valued at 30 shekels (Lev. 27:4). We also know that the false accuser was required to pay double restitution. Why wasn't his required penalty 60 shekels? Because he was not paying double restitution for the "purchase price" of a "female slave," meaning his bride. It was the adult male slave whose vow price was 50 shekels. Thus, the penalty was not related to the supposed formal slave price of the girl, but to the formal slave price of the seducer or the false accuser. It was the male seducer, not the daughter, who was judicially marked as the slave.

Now we begin to understand the magnitude of the penalty for seduction. The seducer could be required to pay the girl's father 50 shekels of silver. This would have constituted a judicial sentence of lifetime bondservice against him. It was the sort of sentence handed down to major thieves with a lifetime of restitution payments to make to victims.

When the false accuser made his charges, he also faced lifetime servitude. He became a "double slave": 100 shekels worth of servitude. He had to pay 100 shekels of silver as double restitution to his father-in-law, the equivalent of two lifetimes of service, or the equivalent of two male slaves. Few young men could afford this. Thus, either the father-in-law took him in as a lifetime bondservant, or else the man had to sell himself into lifetime servitude. There was very little likelihood that the young man would ever escape this double

---

12. If corrupt, the father-in-law might have faked the blood stains on the cloth. To prevent this, the bridegroom would normally have insisted on a formal presentation in the presence of some authority. In case of his suspicion regarding his new wife, the young man would have had to complain immediately to the authorities. He would have had to keep his wife under close surveillance, to keep her from faking the tokens and presenting them to the authorities. On the other hand, a corrupt husband might have tried to destroy the evidence that defended her. Thus, it would have become a formal public matter the day after the wedding, under public supervision.

servitude. He had accused his father-in-law's household of being in slavery to sin; now he would experience a lifetime of slavery. His wife went with him into servitude. She had subordinated herself covenantally to a man who had poor judgment, and she could not escape the consequences of her decision. Once he made the accusation against her, she would either have been executed or would have become a lifetime bondservant's wife. She was the loser in these proceedings. God's law made it plain: girls should carefully examine the moral character of prospective bridegrooms.

Purchasing Power

What was the value of 50 shekels of silver? We cannot know for sure, since at different times in the ancient world, silver's value would have fluctuated, just as it fluctuates today. We know that the atonement money paid by Israelite adult males when they were numbered for military service was half a shekel (Ex. 30:15).[13] If this was half a shekel of silver, then the maximum bride payment was a hundred times this large. An ox that killed another person's bondservant brought a payment of 30 shekels of silver to the owner of the servant (Ex. 21:32). An adult male slave was valued at 50 shekels of silver for the purpose of making a vow payment to the sanctuary (Lev. 27:3). This was a form of servitude to God.[14] We know that the ownership of slaves was sufficiently expensive so that very few families could afford them in the ancient world.[15]

The price of twenty shekels of silver for a male slave under age twenty (Lev. 27:5) corresponds with the twenty shekels paid to Joseph's brothers by the caravan that bought Joseph (Gen. 37:28). This indicates a remarkably stable monetary system throughout the Middle East, from Joseph's day at least until the giving of the Mosaic law over two centuries later.[16] Mendelsohn provides slave

---

13. Chapter 32: "Blood Money, Not Head Tax." Cf. James B. Jordan, *The Law of the Covenant: An Exposition of Exodus 21-23* (Tyler, Texas: Institute for Christian Economics, 1984), Appendix D.

14. Wenham writes: "The legal fiction underlying these payments is that a man could vow himself or a member of his family to the service of God (I Sam 1:11). He made himself God's slave as it were (II Sam 15:8, cf. Ps 116:14-18)." G. J. Wenham, "Leviticus 27:2-8 and the Price of Slaves," *Zeitschrift für die Alttestamentliche Wissenschaft*, XC (1978), p. 264.

15. Isaac Mendelsohn, *Slavery In the Ancient Near East* (New York: Oxford University Press, 1949), pp. 119-21.

16. Gary North, *Moses and Pharaoh: Dominion Religion vs. Power Religion* (Tyler, Texas: Institute for Christian Economics, 1985), Appendix A: "The Reconstruction of Egypt's Chronology."

prices in the surrounding cultures, and these are reasonably commensurate with the prices listed in Leviticus 27.[17] The purchase of a slave gained the buyer the net return from a lifetime of service from a slave. We are not talking about merely a Hebrew's seven-year term of service, for the caravan bought Joseph for resale into permanent servitude. Thirty shekels of silver must have been a lot of money; 50 shekels was that much more.[18]

Lifetime Servitude

Would the seducer have come under the provisions of the debt-release provisions of the sabbatical year (Deut. 15)? Probably not. If these sabbatical year provisions had applied to this crime, they would have subsidized seductions in the years immediately preceding a year of release by lowering their financial risk. To avoid this implicit subsidy of sin, the young man would probably have been regarded by the court as the equivalent of a thief who had to make full restitution to his victims, even if it meant lifetime servitude. He could not escape the payment of the bride price.

In effect, the young man would have come under his father-in-law's jurisdiction for many years. This would have been an appropriate form of judgment for his having lured the girl into making a covenant vow autonomously. They would both be brought under the jurisdiction of the girl's father as a punishment, but also as a way to bring them greater respect for his authority in the future.[19]

All or most of the bride price eventually came to the daughter, and from her to her children. It was her protection against an incom-

---

17. Mendelsohn, *Slavery In the Ancient Near East*, pp. 117-18.

18. There is a hidden danger in one account of a purchase in the Old Testament, David's apparent purchase, for fifty shekels of silver, of the threshing floor that later became the site of the temple (II Sam. 24:24). This was a very desirable location on a mountain top in the midst of the capital city of the nation. How could he have purchased this for the price of a slave? The answer is that he actually paid 600 shekels of gold (I Chron. 21:25). The fifty shekels probably bought only the oxen used in the sacrifice.

19. United States Senator Daniel Moynihan (New York) has proposed a sweeping reform of the national welfare system. One of these reforms would make mandatory that unmarried parents under the age of 18 years old be required to live with their own parents, or in a foster home or a maternity home, if they receive welfare payments. The system presently encourages a teenage mother to move away from her home by paying her more money if she moves out. Suzanne Fields, "Welfare Reincarnate: Seeking new life for a gasping system," *Washington Times* (July 28, 1987), Sect. D, p. 1.

petent husband. It was administered on her behalf by her father. It was held in trust by him in her name, unless he delivered it to her at the time of her marriage as her dowry. In this case, her father would have collected the bride price, year by year, in the form of wages from the son-in-law, unless the son-in-law sold himself into bondage to another buyer, with the money going to his father-in-law. If he sold himself to his father-in-law, this would have built up his heirs' capital indirectly. He would learn future-orientation (deferred gratification) the hard way.

Thus, the risk of seducing a virgin was very great, even if the father accepted the seducer as a son-in-law. Seduction had tremendously negative consequences. There were heavy economic sanctions against seduction. The worst sanction, however, was a father's refusal to allow her to marry him. He would still have to pay the bride price. The girl's father could extract the full penalty, up to 50 shekels of silver. If the father was vindictive, or if he believed that the young man was morally corrupt or an economic incompetent, he could choose to get him away from his daughter by selling him into lifetime slavery. Then the young man could marry only at the discretion of his new master. If kept by the girl's father, he faced the prospect of a life without a wife, if the man was vindictive and refused to provide a wife for him.

All this risk for a few moments of unauthorized ecstasy. Unauthorized ecstasy carried a high price under the Old Covenant.

The Seducer's Legal Right to Pay

The fundamental principles of this case law are still in force. Consider this law's implications. The seducer was not entitled to the girl, but he was entitled (and required) to pay her father. Being "entitled to pay" the equivalent of a large fine may seem a peculiar way to describe his legal position, but the right of payment was important to the judicial standing of the seducer. If he was to be regarded by God and the community as one who stands behind his vows, he had to be allowed to pay the formal bride price. Otherwise, it would seem to the community that he was a man who willingly visited prostitutes (promiscuous women). Such evil men prefer paying token fees for sexual favors rather than paying a large bride price once.

The implicit vow of the seducer was not rendered null and void just because the girl's father denied her permission to marry him. He was required by God to consummate his vow, not in marriage, but through the payment of the formal bride price to the father. The adult male, as the initiator of the vow, had to fulfill its terms. In this case, any male old enough to seduce a woman was considered an adult whose vow was binding.

If he had not been required to pay her father, it would then have appeared as though her father had no legal ground to collect the formal bride price, meaning that he recognized that his daughter was a whore, and also that he had been implicitly or explicitly consenting to the fact. A whore is not simply a woman who charges money for sexual favors. A whore is anyone who experiences sex outside of marriage, except the first time through an implicit vow which is then consummated either in marriage or the payment of the formal bride price. If her father knew that she was no longer a virgin, and still consented to her repeated contacts, he was thereby identifying his own household as a house of prostitution.

How would a young man who fornicates with a non-virgin, believing her to be a virgin, subsequently defend himself against compulsory marriage to a promiscuous woman if she then goes to her father and claims that this young man is her first seducer? He is very nearly defenseless judicially. To escape marrying her, he must either prove in court that she is promiscuous or else pay the 50 shekels to her father and hope that he refuses to allow the marriage. How can he prove that she is a promiscuous woman? Only by identifying a previous seducer. This would probably be very difficult without the earlier consort's willingness to identify himself voluntarily. What would be another man's incentive to admit this? Only to satisfy his sense of righteousness—a moral sense that previous fornicators might not possess in abundance. While her father could no longer compel any man to marry her, since she would be publicly identified as promiscuous, the confessed seducer would lose his reputation. Furthermore, had he been a married man at the time of the seduction, his wife could legally insist on his execution. Thus, seducing a presumed virgin was a highly risky activity in Old Covenant Israel: a man could wind up in debt servitude, married to a whore.

Could the average young man have afforded a bride price of 50 shekels of silver? Only by selling himself into lifetime service to someone. This is the amount of money appropriate to the purchase of a criminal who was being sold into lifetime servitude in order to raise enough money to repay his victims. Obviously, it was not the intention of God to force each bridegroom into slavery in order to marry. Thus, the 50-shekel payment indicates an extreme.

Why would this penalty be imposed? Because the young man unilaterally arrogated to himself the right to lure her into making a vow that only her father could rightfully sanction. He acted as her advisor, as if he possessed the authority of her father. Thus, he becomes responsible for paying the bride price that will serve as her future dowry for marriage to another man. He acted in place of her father; he now pays her dowry in place of her father.

The Bridegroom's Covenant Lawsuit

The girl now is no longer a virgin. In a God-honoring society, any future suitor would have to be informed of this fact before a betrothal. If the marriage takes place, she will be discovered by the bridegroom not to be a virgin. If he has not been informed of her status, he can break the marriage through divorce, including *divorce by execution*, "because she hath wrought folly in Israel, to play the whore in her father's house" (Deut. 22:21). He does not have to have her executed, for Joseph decided to put Mary away quietly for her perceived unfaithfulness (Matt. 1:19), but in a biblical commonwealth, the bridegroom would have the legal option of requiring her death. He would not know if the violation had taken place after the betrothal unless he had been informed of her condition before the betrothal.

Notice that the law in Deuteronomy does not say that she has sinned against the bridegroom, although he surely had been deceived. He had paid the bride price to her father, yet she had implicitly taken a vow to another. The Bible says that she has sinned against her *father* and against *Israel*, the priestly nation. Why then does the bridegroom bring formal charges against her? Because the bridegroom has become *the lawful covenantal agent of Israel and her father*.

The bridegroom is the only one who can legally discover her lack of biological evidence attesting to her own virginity.[20] If he does not present the biological tokens of her virginity to her father or an agent of civil or church government, then her father cannot subsequently

---

20. Today, a gynecologist could also legally discover this. This raises the legal question of the authority of the physician to remain silent. Biblically, the daughter who is still living at home is not an independent legal agent. An unmarried daughter living at home is under her father's covenantal administration. The physician's contractual obligation to provide information is with her father, not with her. Thus, biblically speaking, the physician has an obligation to inform her father of the lack of evidence of her virginity, including her pregnancy. This principle also governs the covenantal obligation of anyone dispensing contraceptives to an unmarried male or female minor to receive written permission from the head of household first.

prove that his daughter had not played the whore under his household administration.[21] Her father is therefore legally powerless to defend her life. In fact, only by remaining silent can he demonstrate publicly that his household is free from the bridegroom's accusation of whoredom, and that he is not a pimp. The bridegroom is the covenantal agent of the holy community and also the covenantal agent of a righteous father's household. His public accusation allows her father to preserve his family's good name by implicitly supporting his charge by not coming to her defense. He has replaced her father as the covenantal head over her. He brings a covenant lawsuit against her as a whore in the name of her father and the priestly nation.

Jesus Christ, the Bridegroom

Biblically speaking, Jesus Christ brought a covenantal lawsuit when He charged Israel with spiritual whoredom. He was Israel's divine Bridegroom, sanctioned by Israel's Father, yet He caught Israel worshipping false gods. He publicly called the rulers of Israel "sons of your father, the devil" (John 8:44).

Whoredom had been Israel's problem from the beginning, which the entire Book of Hosea was written to illustrate, and which Ezekiel 16 was devoted to explaining. In God's eyes, as Israel's Father, His daughter was deserving of death as a whore. But Jesus Christ came to pay the bride price for all mankind, including Israel. He paid it to God the Father, as required. This restored God's reputation among His enemies as the cosmic Judge.[22] Without this payment, God's authority as cosmic Judge would have been compromised, for He would be viewed as a God who cannot bring His word to pass in history. He would be viewed as a Father who cannot control the actions of his promiscuous or adulterous daughter. His only other option would have been to bring His daughter to the authorities for burning, as the fornicating daughter of a priest (Lev. 21:9). This is what God did with national Israel in A.D. 70.

---

21. If her lack of physical evidence for her virginity was the result of something other than previous sexual intercourse, then she would have to inform her father, who would in turn warn the prospective bridegroom before the betrothal, and get from him a signed statement or other suitable courtroom evidence of his acceptance of this explanation in lieu of the physical tokens.

22. The family name of God is always *the* key motivation in God's decision to bring judgment. Moses appealed to God to spare the Hebrews by appealing to God's reputation among His enemies (Ex. 32:11-14). Nathan reminded David that his adultery and murder had given the enemies of God a cause to blaspheme (II Sam. 12:14).

Israel needed the payment of this bride price by the Bridegroom in order to be married. Without His acceptance of her, He could have had her executed. The period from Christ's resurrection to the fall of Jerusalem in 70 A.D. was the period in which Israel could accept this bride price, and covenant with Jesus. But to do this, Israel had to align herself with the gentile church, the new bride of Christ. This implication is what the Jews and the Judaizers in the church resisted.

It was clear what it meant if the church really is God's new bride. If Jesus was the true Bridegroom, and if Israel was truly promiscuous and in need of acceptance by the Bridegroom, then Old Covenant Israel was about to be publicly burned by God. Jesus had identified Israel as a whore, a spiritual adulteress. Israel was doomed to certain death. The daughter of a priest was under special restraints.

It is quite likely that the Judaizers who kept infiltrating the early church understood what was coming. If Israel was truly required to covenant with Christ, becoming His bride through church membership, then it meant that the old bride, Old Covenant Israel, would be cut off by divorce, making the consummation of Christ with His new bride legitimate. God would consummate His marriage with the church, the new wife, through *divorce by execution*. Thus, the Judaizers worked hard to bring the gentiles under the covenantal signs of the older covenant. The gentiles had to be made members of the Jewish bride. Not to do so would have been to admit that covenantal judgment was coming to the nation of Israel.

Israel's destruction can be viewed symbolically in several ways: first, as God the Father's burning of her as the promiscuous daughter of a priest; second, as Jesus Christ's successful prosecution of her as the Bridegroom of a non-virgin bride; third, as God's adulterous bride (Hosea). The Father would have burned her, but He offered her one last possibility: marriage to the Bridegroom who knew of her fornication, but who was willing to pay the bride price, as if she were righteous. When Israel rejected this offer of marriage, God the Father had His Son serve as the instrument of His wrath. Israel was publicly burned. Fire from heaven is what was poured forth symbolically on Israel in 70 A.D., the comprehensive judgment of God.[23]

The Bridegroom, in His mercy, still has left alive a remnant of the old bride: genetic Israel. He offers full covenantal restoration to

23. David Chilton, *The Days of Vengeance: An Exposition of the Book of Revelation* (Ft. Worth: Dominion Press, 1987).

fallen Israel, and He promises to bring her into union with Him when the fullness of the gentiles has come (Rom. 11). But Israel will come in only as part of the church, not as a separate body. *God publicly divorced Israel by execution in 70 A.D.* Once a covenantally valid divorce has taken place, and one partner has remarried, there can never be a remarriage between the lawfully divorced partners (Deut. 24:4). Genetic-covenantal Israel as genetic-covenantal Israel can never again become God's bride. Only by joining new covenant Israel can genetic-covenantal Israel be reunited in marriage to God.[24]

New Testament Applications

We have already seen how the principle of the bride price and dowry could apply in New Testament times.[25] What about the possible applications of the laws regarding seduction? Are they still mandatory in New Testament times? If so, have they been modified in any way?

Dowries

What would be the equivalent of the mandatory bride price for seducers? It would be at least the economic equivalent of a girl's dowry from her father. Most Western nations have abandoned formal dowries, but the principle of endowing a daughter is still recognized. Instead of jewelry or land, a daughter receives an expensive formal education and a wedding paid for by her parents. Friends bring presents to the wedding, but parents pay for it.

The Old Testament principle was far better: the bridegroom paid the father, who then either paid the daughter in capital goods (not presents), or else he held the assets for her and the grandchildren. The collections of laws from the ancient Near East devoted considerable space to discussing dowries and obligations. Hammurabi's Code from paragraph 128 through 184 deals with dowries, the longest section in the Code.[26] These rules were generally well thought-out and sensible. Examples: "If, when a seignior acquired a wife, she

---

24. This line of argumentation based on Deuteronomy 24:4 rejects the teaching of dispensationalism that the ritual signs and symbols of the Old Covenant will be the basis of membership in the New Covenant during a future millennium. This is the underlying theology of the Judaizers.

25. Chapter 6: "Wives and Concubines."

26. *Ancient Near Eastern Texts Relating to the New Testament*, edited by James B. Pritchard (3rd ed.; Princeton, New Jersey: Princeton University Press, 1969), pp. 171-74.

bore him children and that woman has then gone to (her) fate, her father may not lay claim to her dowry, since her dowry belongs to her children" (paragraph 162). All right, what if she died, leaving no children? Should the son-in-law inherit the dowry? That depends on who keeps the bride price. "If a seignior acquired a wife and that woman has gone to (her) fate without providing him with children, if his father-in-law has then returned to him the marriage-price which that seignior brought to the house of his father-in-law, her husband may not lay claim to the dowry of that woman, since her dowry belongs to her father's house. If his father-in-law has not returned the marriage-price to him, he shall deduct the full amount of her marriage-price from her dowry and return (the rest of) her dowry to her father's house" (paragraphs 163-64). It was all spelled out in advance. Each party knew where he stood.

The Absence of Monetary Specifics

In the Old Testament era, 50 shekels of silver was a great deal of money, the vow price of an adult male slave (Lev. 27:3). Today, because of the vast increase in mining, 50 one-ounce silver coins are not worth much. A one-ounce silver coin would not buy a dinner at an average restaurant. It would buy one ticket to a two-hour motion picture. Thus, the imposition of a 50-shekel bride payment would not be meaningful in an advanced society.

What is the basis for arguing that in principle, the obligation of the bride price is still in force, yet the specific penalty is no longer in force? Can the spirit of the law be maintained while violating the Old Testament letter of the law? If so, on what basis?

With the death in 70 A.D. of national Israel, the harlot daughter and harlot wife, God removed the specific monetary penalties attached to the land. Christ's payment fulfilled the specific terms of the law, as did the death of the law-breaker, national Israel. Penalties that involve physical pain (whipping, for example), or the loss of life (capital punishment), or percentages forfeited (proportional restitution) retain their permanent character as punishments to be avoided irrespective of time or place. This is comparable to the principle of the tithe: the required percentage remains constant, but the currency unit is not specified by biblical law.

On the other hand, punishments that were tied to Israel's land and the nation's historical role are no longer binding, such as specific money prices for a slave gored by an ox, or the bride price, or the

military atonement price (the erroneously named "head tax"),[27] or
the sacrifices of specific animals for specific transgressions, or specific
ritual washings. The common latrine in a military camp is now the
technical substitute for going outside the camp and using a personal
spade to dig an individual hole (Deut. 23:13).

The Old Testament, unlike the law collections of contemporary
nations, did not impose many specific monetary fines. There were
also no price controls in Israel, unlike the laws of Eshnunna, which
is basically a listing of fixed prices for goods, services, and fines,[28] or
Hammurabi's Babylon,[29] or the Hittites.[30] Thus, with very few exceptions, Old Covenant law avoided detailed monetary penalties. It
did not presume to interfere with competitive bargaining. Only in a
handful of instances were specific prices mentioned, and these were
in the context of ritual payments to the temple and restitution payments to victims. Percentages, not specific amounts of metal, were
the rule for imposing punishments. This makes it more difficult to
understand in retrospect the magnitude of a handful of specified
monetary penalties, but it also made it possible for biblical law to
stand without revision until 70 A.D.

Modern Equivalents

Let us consider what the ideal situation would be, when enforced
by family, church, and civil authorities. A man seduces an unmarried woman. They immediately go to her father and admit their
physical bond. He then decides whether to allow the marriage. If he
is willing to listen to the man, he demands a bride price, probably
high. The man has no choice in the matter. He may have to sell
everything he has, or even accept bondservice to the father for a period of time. The civil government would enforce the father's decision. The father retains the option of denying them the right to
marry. If he is supported in this decision by church and State—
which would be normal—he can impose on the man the equivalent
of her dowry.

27. See Chapter 32: "Blood Money, Not Head Tax."
28. *Ancient Near Eastern Texts*, pp. 161-63.
29. *Ibid.*, pp. 167-77: paragraphs 17, 24, 51, 88, 90, 111, 114, 116, 121, 156, 203-4,
207-9, 211-17, 220-24, 228, 234, 239, 241-43, 251-52, 257-61, 268-77. End of text: 282.
30. *Ibid.*, 189-97: paragraphs 4-18, 20, 22-25, 26(B), 42, 77-78, 81-89, 91-97,
101-5, 107-9, 119-48, 150-62, 164-65, 167-68, 170, 172, 177-86 (extremely detailed
price controls), 200. End of text: 200.

What is the modern dowry? A monetary payment equivalent of a college education or other formal training, plus the cost of a wedding. This would probably involve the equivalent of many years of net income, after minimal support for himself. If the girl had received no advanced education, he would pay for it. If she had been sent to private high school and college by her father, the father would be reimbursed for the expenses, plus interest from the time of the seduction until final payment. The seducer would pay for her dowry.

The next potential bridegroom could not be asked to pay something. She has become a liability. In a God-honoring society, her lack of virginity would be an initial liability, depending on the circumstances of her rebellion. A righteous young man would fear a flaw in her moral character. But if she brings skills and money into the marriage, plus several years of righteous behavior, he may be willing to consider her.

In our day, all this sounds very old fashioned, even archaic. These days, so does chastity. This marks the moral decline of the West, not its moral maturity. With Christ's payment behind us, all sins can be covered in each person's experience, but this does not obliterate the need for visible evidence of progressive sanctification. The words of moral warning of the father to his son in the first nine chapters of Proverbs are still valid.

Conclusion

This case law indirectly brings up the threat of slavery. This is the integrating theme of the case laws of Exodus 21-23. The penalties of public sinning are always of such magnitude that flagrant public sinning could and probably would involve a return to slavery for most publicly condemned sinners. This, of course, is the whole message of the Book of Exodus: God delivers His covenant people from slavery, but He threatens them with a return to slavery if they should continue to break His covenant. Ultimately, He threatens them with public execution.

The bride price paid to the father by the seducer is a classic example of this return to slavery. The short-run perspective of the seducer is essentially the time perspective of Satan and his followers: a few moments of ecstasy in defying God, and eternity in bondage to repay Him. These forbidden moments of ecstasy began in the garden and will end at the final judgment.

In the Old Covenant era, the seducer might be allowed to become a righteous husband, but only at the discretion of the seduced girl's father. He became a righteous husband—with or without a bride—through the public payment of a very high bride price. The maximum of 50 shekels of silver points to a lifetime of bondservice to repay. If the father allowed the marriage, the heirs of the sinner would inherit, but he himself paid the price. Wealth was transferred from the older generation to the younger.

This was Israel's lesson in the wilderness. The fathers were still mental and moral slaves. They rejected God when they tried to stone Joshua and Caleb (Num. 14:10). They were forced to wander in the wilderness until their children could inherit the land. Even Joshua and Caleb suffered, just as Jacob had suffered at the hand of Laban, for the unrighteousness and cowardice of their covenantal peers. They had to wait for an extra generation before they could enter the land. God extracted the bride price from that seducing and adulterous generation, so that their heirs might inherit it. God gave them sufficient capital to raise the next generation, and then they died in the wilderness. Delivered by God's grace from Egyptian slavery, they nevertheless remained in lifetime bondservice to God in the wilderness.

The New Testament standard is analogous, not identical. The land of Israel has lost its covenantal relevance. The price of silver has changed. But the judicial principle has remained the same: the seducer must pay for the bride's dowry, whether her father allows the couple to marry or not. The civil government is supposed to enforce this penalty. Seduction is not to be indirectly subsidized by the removal of economic sanctions.

22

OPPRESSION, OMNISCIENCE, AND JUDGMENT

Thou shalt neither vex a stranger, nor oppress him: for ye were strangers in the land of Egypt. Ye shall not afflict any widow, or fatherless child. If thou afflict them in anywise [any way], and they cry at all unto me, I will surely hear their cry; and my wrath shall wax hot, and I will kill you with the sword; and your wives shall be widows, and your children fatherless (Ex. 22:21-24).

The theocentric principle here is the office of God as the kinsman-redeemer, and therefore the blood avenger (the same office). "Speak unto the children of Israel, When a man or woman shall commit any sin that men commit, to do a trespass against the LORD, and that person be guilty; Then they shall confess their sin which they have done: and he shall recompense his trespass with the principal thereof, and add unto it the fifth part thereof, and give it unto him against whom he hath trespassed. But if the man have no kinsman to recompense the trespass unto, let the trespass be recompensed unto the LORD, even to the priest; beside the ram of the atonement, whereby an atonement shall be made for him" (Num. 5:6-8). In lieu of a family kinsman-redeemer, God serves in this office.

God protects the vulnerable members of His covenant family when they have no one to act in their behalf. So should we. Men's treatment of the helpless reflects their willingness or unwillingness to serve as representatives of God in His capacity as the defender of the oppressed. How men treat other people indicates their attitude toward God, for man is made in God's image. How they treat others tells God how He would be treated by them if they got the opportunity. Speaking of the final day of Judgment, Jesus said:

Then shall the King say unto them on his right hand, Come, ye blessed of my Father, inherit the kingdom prepared for you from the foundation of the world: For I was an hungred, and ye gave me meat: I was thirsty, and ye gave me drink: I was a stranger, and ye took me in: Naked, and ye clothed me: I was sick, and ye visited me: I was in prison, and ye came unto me. Then shall the righteous answer him, saying, Lord, when saw we thee an hungred, and fed thee? or thirsty, and gave thee drink? When saw we thee a stranger, and took thee in? or naked, and clothed thee? Or when saw we thee sick, or in prison, and came unto thee? And the King shall answer and say unto them, Verily I say unto you, Inasmuch as ye have done it unto one of the least of these my brethren, ye have done it unto me (Matt. 25:34-40).

If one's protection of the weak testifies to one's willingness to honor God, then God in turn will protect those who offer protection. Men are weak in the sight of God. They need His protection. How they treat the weak in history will determine how God treats them in history. "And he said unto them, Take heed what ye hear: with what measure ye mete, it shall be measured to you: and unto you that hear shall more be given" (Mark 4:24).

Restraint and Protection

Strangers, widows, and orphans: these three examples, along with the poor, are seen in the Bible as being especially vulnerable to oppression.[1] "Also thou shalt not oppress a stranger: for ye know the heart of a stranger, seeing ye were strangers in the land of Egypt" (Ex. 23:9). They deserve protection. If the Hebrews remained faithful to God in this matter of dealing with strangers, God promised, they would retain their own civil liberties. If the judges of the land remained so committed to the ethical terms of God's covenant that they would restrain the oppression of strangers, widows, and orphans by fellow Hebrews, then all righteous Hebrews could safely retain confidence in their judges. On the other hand, if a system of bribes or special favors corrupted the judges, and they began to show favor to the interests of Hebrews in their legal disputes with resident aliens, widows, and orphans, then this would be a preliminary manifestation of looming tyranny, domestic and then foreign. "Your wives shall be widows, and your children fatherless" (v. 24).

Why does God single out the widow, the orphan, and the resident alien? They must be representative of a general class of people. If we search for the distinguishing characteristic of all three — their

---

1. Charles F. Fensham, "Widow, Orphan and the Poor in Ancient Near Eastern Legal and Wisdom Literature," *Journal of Near Eastern Studies*, XXI (1962), pp. 129-39.

representative feature — we find that there is only one: *their lack of covenantal representation*. It is appropriate that this should be the focus of the law in the Book of Exodus, the premier book in the Bible and in the Pentateuch on hierarchical representation. The widow has no husband; the orphan has no parents; the resident alien has no tribe and no legal status in the assembly. The first two have no family head above them; the third has no ecclesiastical or judicial place in the hierarchy. No earthly agent *speaks* for the resident alien in the assembly. No one *listens* to the widow and orphan. No one has a major cultural incentive to protect them.

Nevertheless, they are not covenantally defenseless. Their lack of a covenantal intermediary between them and God does not leave them without judicial recourse. Prayer can bring them before the judgment seat of the King. Their prayers indicate that they honor God in their hearts by subordinating themselves to Him. Prayer testifies to a person's faith in the hierarchical nature of the universe. God will therefore listen to them. "If thou afflict them in anywise [any way], and they cry at all unto me, I will surely hear their cry." God will protect them. They have honored His sovereignty and His hierarchy through their prayers. In contrast, their oppressors have ignored His revealed law. He will therefore uphold His law. He will intervene, acting on their behalf: "And my wrath shall wax hot, and I will kill you with the sword; and your wives shall be widows, and your children fatherless." He will bring judgment in history, on the basis of *lex talionis*: an eye for an eye, a dead husband for the victim's dead husband, dead parents for the victim's dead parents. The invisible God of the Bible will intervene in history as their representative agent. He becomes their kinsman-redeemer, and in doing so, He becomes the wicked oppressor's blood avenger. He cuts off the oppressor's inheritance. In short, God defends all five parts of His covenant.

God's Negative Sanctions in History

God says that Biblical law is to be honored by individuals and their courts above all considerations of race, family, or other personal relationships. Judges are required to uphold its terms without respect to persons. "Ye shall not respect persons in judgment; but ye shall hear the small as well as the great; ye shall not be afraid of the face of man; for the judgment is God's: and the cause that is too hard for you, bring it unto me, and I will hear it" (Deut. 1:17). If for any reason the civil courts should fail to uphold the law, God warned the Israelites, then the nation as a whole would be held responsible for having broken the terms of His covenant. God would bring His negative sanctions against the whole nation.

But if ye will not hearken unto me, and will not do all these commandments; And if ye shall despise my statutes, or if your soul abhor my judgments, so that ye will not do all my commandments, but that ye break my covenant: I also will do this unto you; I will even appoint over you terror, consumption, and the burning ague, that shall consume the eyes, and cause sorrow of heart: and ye shall sow your seed in vain, for your enemies shall eat it. And I will set my face against you, and ye shall be slain before your enemies: they that hate you shall reign over you; and ye shall flee when none pursueth you. And if ye will not yet for all this hearken unto me, then I will punish you seven times more for your sins. And I will break the pride of your power; and I will make your heaven as iron, and your earth as brass: And your strength shall be spent in vain: for your land shall not yield her increase, neither shall the trees of the land yield their fruits. And if ye walk contrary unto me, and will not hearken unto me; I will bring seven times more plagues upon you according to your sins. I will also send wild beasts among you, which shall rob you of your children, and destroy your cattle, and make you few in number; and your high ways shall be desolate. And if ye will not be reformed by me by these things, but will walk contrary unto me; Then will I also walk contrary unto you, and will punish you yet seven times for your sins. And I will bring a sword upon you, that shall avenge the quarrel of my covenant: and when ye are gathered together within your cities, I will send the pestilence among you; and ye shall be delivered into the hand of the enemy (Lev. 26:14-25).

The decision to ignore God's law by the civil and priestly representatives of a nation is inescapably a covenantal decision, God has always insisted. Citizens under the judges' authority in ancient Israel were be held responsible for the injustice of the judges, for they possessed the power to replace the judges for unrighteousness (Ex. 18:21). Furthermore, their long-term public consent to the faithless decisions of Israel's civil magistrates meant that God would hold them responsible as a nation. There could be no lawful appeal to God by any private citizen that "I was only following orders." There could be no successful appeal by the citizens as a covenantal unit that "our leaders did these things against our will." The existence of a covenantal cause-and-effect relationship between the moral character of a nation's rulers and the moral character of a majority of its cit-

izens is why we know that evil, incompetent, and cowardly leaders are a curse brought by God to self-consciously evil citizens.
Those who prefer to be ruled by the laws of men rather than the laws
of God shall be given their heart's desire: tyranny and high taxes
(I Sam. 8).

Protection

If the people of Israel oppressed strangers, they could do this
only by ignoring God's law. God's Bible-revealed law was designed
by God to be the judicial means of civic righteousness throughout
history. It was designed to *protect* men. But in ancient Israel, men
soon learned that if they were compelled by the civil government to
obey God's law, they could not effectively oppress the stranger, the
widow, and the orphan. Yet exploiting these victims proved so profitable in the short run that short-run thinkers decided to abandon
God's law. Short-run thinkers always do.[2] They think that God will
not see what they do.

> They break in pieces thy people, O LORD, and afflict thine heritage.
> They slay the widow and the stranger, and murder the fatherless. Yet they
> say, The LORD shall not see, neither shall the God of Jacob regard it.
> Understand, ye brutish among the people: and ye fools, when will ye be
> wise? He that planted the ear, shall he not hear? He that formed the eye,
> shall he not see? He that chastiseth the heathen, shall not he correct? He
> that teacheth man knowledge, shall not he know? (Ps. 94:5-10).

The false prophets of every era, who come before God's people
and tell them not to pay any attention to the specifics of God's revealed law, are sure that God will not impose His negative sanctions
in history. "Then said I, Ah, Lord GOD! behold, the prophets say unto
them, Ye shall not see the sword, neither shall ye have famine; but I
will give you assured peace in this place" (Jer. 14:13). They lie. They
are the apologists for oppression, the watchmen who are asleep.

---

2. Today, however, a strange transformation has taken place. Humanists and
pietists agree: God's revealed law is tyrannical, inherently a source of oppression.
They have abandoned God's revealed law in the name of universal principles of
"right reason" and "religiously neutral civil justice." Because they view God's revealed law as the source of oppression rather than its cure, they call for the extension
of humanist civil law. They cannot seem to understand why oppression has multiplied in the twentieth century, but they know what is needed to cure it: more of
the same.

Evangelism Through Law

The treatment that Hebrew judges displayed officially to the resident alien was the primary civil symbol of the nation's honoring of the terms of God's covenant. The uncircumcised stranger was outside the ecclesiastical covenant, but he was not outside both the restraint and the protection of the civil law. Everyone inside the geographical boundaries of the nation of Israel was bound to the judicial terms of the civil covenant. Each resident was therefore compelled to affirm his subordination to God, not necessarily as a member of God's ritual household, but as one who was nevertheless under God's visible authority.

To achieve the comprehensive external blessings of the covenant, aliens were required by God to place themselves inside Israel's geographical and covenantal boundaries. Isaiah predicted that one sign of Israel's covenantal faithfulness would be that the nations would pour into the land to worship at Mt. Zion (Isa. 2:2-3). When this happens, Isaiah said, the Lord will judge the nations and turn swords into ploughshares (Isa. 2:4). This did not mean that every person on earth was to take up permanent residence in tiny Israel. It meant that the borders of Israel were to be extended *covenantally* to cover the whole earth. The sign of this geographical expansion would be the willingness of the nations to covenant with the God of Israel. They would accept His law and His sacrifices as their own. They would replace their false gods with the God of the Bible. To say that they were not to do this is to say that God's salvation was in principle offered only to the Israelites. It would mean that there was supposed to be no evangelism prior to the ministry of Jesus Christ, no preaching of God's word and the need for repentance outside the geographical boundaries of Palestinian Israel. Does any Christian want to maintain such a view of 1,400 years of biblical religion in Old Testament Israel? (Officially, no; practically, yes.)

How could the gentile nations learn of the wonders of God's judgment and His blessings (Deut. 4:6-8)? One way would be through the information sent back from fellow countrymen living in Israel. Placing resident aliens under the protection of God's civil law was therefore to be a preliminary stage of international evangelism.

Greek Mythology: Justice for All

This was an evangelism program unique to ancient Israel. It was common in the ancient world to regard resident aliens as outside the protection of civil law. This was true even of "enlightened" Greece and Rome.[3] To be a citizen meant that you had to participate in the religious rites of the city. Only those born into or adopted by families that had been "present at the creation" of the city-state had lawful access to these civil sacrifices; only they were citizens.[4] This is why exile was so devastating to an ancient citizen; he was permanently cut off from his family's religious rites as well as his city's rites, yet he could not participate in the rites of his new residence. Fustel wrote:

> We can easily understand that, for the ancients, God was not everywhere. If they had some vague idea of a God of the universe, this was not the one whom they considered as their providence, and whom they invoked. Every man's gods were those who inhabited his house, his canton, his city. The exile, on leaving his country behind him, also left his gods. He no longer found a religion that could console and protect him; he no longer felt that providence was watching over him; the happiness of praying was taken away. All that could satisfy the needs of his soul was far away.
>
> Now, religion was the source whence flowed civil and political rights. The exile, therefore, lost all this in losing his religion and country. Excluded from the city worship, he saw at the same time his domestic worship taken from him, and was forced to extinguish his hearth-fire. He could no longer hold property; his goods, as if he was dead, passed to his children, unless they were confiscated to the profit of the gods or of the state. Having no longer a worship, he had no longer a family; he ceased to be a husband and a father. His sons were no longer in his power; his wife was no longer his wife, and might immediately take another husband. . . . It is not surprising that the ancient republics almost all permitted a convict to escape death by flight. Exile did not seem to be a milder punishment than death. The Roman jurists called it capital punishment.[5]

Israel Was Different

The unbreakable link between the family's religious rites and the possession of civil rights did not prevail in Israel's holy commonwealth. Adoption was required for access to the nation's religious rites, but *this adoption was open to all people*, irrespective of the decision

---

3. Numa Denis Fustel de Coulanges, *The Ancient City: A Study on the Religion, Laws, and Institutions of Greece and Rome* (Garden City, New York: Doubleday Anchor, [1864] 1955), Bk. III, ch. XI, pp. 192-93.

4. *Ibid.*, Bk. III, ch. III. Occasionally, citizenship was granted to an individual who had served a city faithfully or to skilled immigrants in times of acute labor shortages, but this was rare until late Roman times.

5. *Ibid.*, Bk. III, ch. XIII, pp. 200-1.

of a particular Hebrew family to adopt an alien son or daughter. God adopted individuals into His family, just as He had adopted Israel as a nation. The sign of God's adoption was circumcision. First, a person could gain access to civil and ecclesiastical rites through circumcision (Ex. 12:48). Access to membership in the biblical covenant in Old Testament Israel was not achieved through incorporation into one of the nation's founding families. Circumcised foreigners and their families were outside the jubilee land redistribution law (Lev. 25), but they were nonetheless full citizens, although they would have had to live in the cities, where this law did not apply, or else live as renters or long-term leaseholders in rural areas. Second, resident aliens who chose not to be circumcised were under the civil law of Israel (Ex. 12:49), for the God of Israel is a universal God.

It was His assertion of universality that made the claims of the God of the Hebrews unique in the ancient world. For example, the theology of ancient Israel taught, in contrast to the theologies of rival pagan civilizations, that the defeat of His people militarily did not mean that the gods of Israel's military conquerors had triumphed over the God of Israel (Isa. 9-11). The Israelites could be scattered geographically, yet still remain under the terms of God's covenant law (Deut. 28:64-68). Why? Because God is a universal God who judges all men wherever they are in terms of His law or the work of the law written in their hearts (Rom. 2:14-15). All of the ancient world was therefore under the ethical requirements of God's revealed law. The ancients were supposed to conform themselves to the Ten Commandments and the case laws that applied these commandments in daily living. Foreign nations were supposed to see the application of the legal principles outlined in the Ten Commandments in the actual daily operations of Israelite society, and they were supposed to imitate Israel. The resident alien was able to acknowledge this fact in a more visible way than those living outside the land of Israel.

Resident Aliens Deserve Legal Protection

Any attempt on the part of the judges of Israel to place the resident alien outside the protection of God's law would have represented an attempt to pervert God's universal standards of justice. By not honoring God's law in every dispute between a Hebrew and a resident alien, the judge was in effect announcing: "God's law is binding only in terms of circumcision. Those outside this blood covenant are therefore not under the law's protection. This means that they are outside any general covenant that God has established with mankind. This in turn means that mankind is not required by God to honor the judicial terms of His covenant. God imposes no final claims on those outside the covenant, which is marked exclusively by physical circumcision of male heads of households. He is, therefore, a God of Palestine rather than the cosmic Creator. There is no universal covenant."

Obviously, such a view of God is foreign to everything God teaches regarding His absolute sovereignty as the Creator. To respect persons in rendering judgment, the judges would be denying God's holiness, His general covenant with mankind, the universality of His civil laws, and the absolute claims He places on all mankind. Thus, the stranger was entitled to full protection under the law, even though he could not become a citizen, meaning that he could not become a judge or own land permanently inside the nation (Lev. 25:11-17).[6]

Furthermore, if the judges refused to succumb to pressures by Hebrews to favor their cause just because of their racial characteristics, as marked by their circumcised flesh and their families' permanent ownership of land inside Israel, then they would probably not succumb to other pressures to withhold justice. The law of God made it clear that a Hebrew's treatment of bondservants, strangers, widows, orphans, the poor, and animals represented his treatment of all mankind. These weaker people and creatures were frequently under his authority, just as he was always under God's authority. As he treated those under him, so would God treat him. This is a very common theme in both Testaments, but especially in the case laws of Exodus, which is why so much space is devoted to setting forth the legal principles governing bondservants, maidservants, widows, the poor, and animals. God reminds them again and again that they had been strangers in Egypt. They needed the protection provided by righteous judgment, and so did the strangers in the land.

This is why their years as slaves in Egypt were so important covenantally. They had suffered at the hands of lawless judges who refused to honor God's law. Such is tyranny throughout history: civil courts that deny the specific terms of God's revealed covenantal law. To avoid tyranny, God told them, render righteous judgment regardless of race, color, or creed. Place all people dwelling inside the *geographical boundaries* of Israel under the *ethical boundaries* of God's

---

6. Gary North, *Moses and Pharaoh: Dominion Religion vs. Power Religion* (Tyler, Texas: Institute for Christian Economics, 1985), ch. 14: "The Rule of Law."

civil covenant. This was to remind residents of Israel that all men are born under the ethical terms of God's covenant, and they will all be held accountable in time and eternity for their disobedience. Thus, any refusal by the judges of Israel to honor God's law would inescapably damage God's testimony to the *sanctity* of His law, which necessarily meant His *sanctions*: blessing and cursing.[7]

If a Hebrew judge cursed a publicly righteous stranger in order to bless a publicly law-breaking Hebrew, then that judge was implicitly testifying to the partiality of God regarding the enforcement of His law, a false god who respects persons more than he respects the integrity of his law. This is false testimony to a false and unjust god who had been invented by the corrupt judge, and Jehovah God promises to bring judgment against any nation that continues to promote such false testimony through civil injustice.

Christian Antinomians Deny This

Those today who deny that the Old Testament case laws also applied judicially to the ancient world as far as God was concerned must therefore take the position that: 1) the Ten Commandments were never intended by God to be more than a local, temporary, tribal legal code; or 2) the Old Testament's case laws were not connected judicially to the Ten Commandments; or 3) both of the above. I have several questions for those who maintain such a position. Didn't God want pagans to worship Him? Didn't He want them to avoid worshipping idols, avoid using His name in vain, and avoid breaking the sabbath? Didn't He want them to honor father and mother, avoid murder, avoid adultery, avoid stealing, avoid bearing false witness, and avoid covetousness? Which of the Ten Commandments didn't apply to the ancient pagan world? And I would also ask this: Which of the case laws has nothing to do judicially with one or more of the Ten Commandments? (Yes, I know. I'm a "legalist.")

Christians really do not want to maintain such a position publicly, yet their endlessly repeated statements against the legitimacy of biblical law forces them to take this position. "Should the Nations Be Under the Mosaic Law?" ask two dispensationalists, theologian H. Wayne House and pastor Thomas D. Ice.[8] They answer their ques-

---

7. Ray R. Sutton, *That You May Prosper: Dominion By Covenant* (Tyler, Texas: Institute for Christian Economics, 1987), ch. 4.

8. H. Wayne House and Thomas D. Ice, *Dominion Theology: Blessing or Curse?* (Portland, Oregon: Multnomah Press, 1988), ch. 7.

tion clearly: *no.* "The nations surrounding Israel were never called to adopt the law of Moses; rather Israel's obedience to the law would attract nations. Deuteronomy 4:6-8 says that the surrounding nations would be attracted to Israel and consider it wise."[9] This is the theological equivalent of saying: "The people surrounding the church are never called to adopt the religion of Christianity; rather Christians' obedience to the Christ should attract people. Matthew 28:18-20 says that the surrounding nations will be attracted to the church and consider it wise." That the authors' logic is internally schizophrenic should be clear to anyone who can follow an argument. To put it bluntly, this line of reasoning is utter nonsense. It is the argument that the specifics of God's revealed law are wise but they are not now nor were they ever in any way judicially binding on those outside of tiny Israel.

What can it possibly mean to argue that the law of God is wise but not morally or judicially binding? It means only this: those who argue this way prefer not to obey God's revealed law, except when they can prove to themselves and others that any particular biblical law is "wise." Their implicit (but always undefined) universal standard for wisdom is therefore something other than God's revelation of Himself in His law. But then the nagging question arises: *On what other basis than God's revealed law are men and nations condemned by God, in history and at the final judgment?* By what other standard will the sheep be separated from the goats? "And before him shall be gathered all nations: and he shall separate them one from another, as a shepherd divideth his sheep from the goats: And he shall set the sheep on his right hand, but the goats on the left" (Matt. 25:32-33). To put it in terms that even a dispensationalist can understand: *Is it wise to want to avoid eternal damnation?* If so, then isn't is also wise to have faith in Jesus Christ? Isn't it wise to obey Jesus? "If ye love me, keep my commandments" (John 14:15). "And hereby we do know that we know him, if we keep his commandments. He that saith, I know him, and keepeth not his commandments, is a liar, and the truth is not in him" (I John 2:3-4). Faith requires obedience to validate its reality. "Even so faith, if it hath not works, is dead, being alone. Yea, a man may say, Thou hast faith, and I have works: shew me thy faith without thy works, and I will shew thee my faith by my works. Thou believest that there is one God; thou doest well: the devils also

---

9. *Ibid*, p. 128.

believe, and tremble. But wilt thou know, O vain man, that faith without works is dead?" (James 2:17-20).

One of these faithful works is to avoid oppressing the weak.

Economic Oppression

The question then arises: Is economic oppression a matter of civil action? Is it a criminal offense to oppress a stranger, widow, or orphan? In my comments on Exodus 22:1, 4, I wrote, "The general guideline for designating a particular public act as a crime is this: if by failing to impose sanctions against certain specified public acts, the whole community could be subsequently threatened by God's non-civil sanctions—war, plague, and famine—then the civil government becomes God's designated agency of enforcement. *The civil government's primary function is to protect the community against the wrath of God* by enforcing His laws against public acts that threaten the survival of the community."[10] The language of Exodus 22:24 surely indicates that God will avenge the oppressed by bringing curses on the community. "My wrath shall wax hot, and I will kill you with the sword."

Should the State pass specific legislation against economic oppression? Should the courts enforce legal precedents against economic oppression? The answers depend on whether the laws and penalties can be *formulated clearly and interpreted predictably* on the basis of biblical revelation. I also wrote this regarding the legitimate jurisdiction of civil government: "Continued injustice, *if* it can be biblically defined and publicly identified in advance through statute or judicial precedent, because it goes unpunished by the civil government, calls forth the wrath of God on the community, so there is ultimately no Bible-based distinction between civil law and criminal law."[11] Can a specific law against oppression be "biblically defined and publicly identified in advance through statute or judicial precedent"? This is the key judicial problem facing the civil magistrate. It is also the key judicial problem facing a free society: the problem of the *messianic State*, whose mark of oppression is its *judicial arbitrariness*.[12]

Economic theory provides no definition of the concept of "economic oppression" in the case of voluntary transactions. Only where coercion is involved—the threat of physical violence—can the econo-

---

10. See above, p. 528.
11. See above, pp. 528-29.
12. F. A. Hayek, *The Constitution of Liberty* (University of Chicago Press, 1960).

mist be confident that oppression is involved. This does not mean
that a definition of oppression is impossible, but it does mean that no
appeal to modern humanistic economic theory can provide a clear-
cut definition. The use of the coercive power of the civil government
to extract resources from other people can be regarded as oppression
in most instances, but there are no clearly defined criteria of oppressive voluntary transactions made in a free market. The mere
presence of competitive bargaining between unequally rich or unequally skillful bargainers does not constitute economic oppression,
as the bargain between Jacob and Esau indicates (Gen. 25:29-34).[13]
Nevertheless, there *are* acts of economic oppression, even if conventional economic theory cannot state the criteria scientifically (neutrally).

Oppression and affliction are related concepts. The translators of
the King James Version translated the Hebrew word for "oppression"
(*lah-'gahtz*) as "affliction" in I Kings 22:27: "bread of affliction" and
"water of affliction." The word is translated as "crush" in Numbers
22:25: "and crushed Balaam's foot." The Hebrew word for "affliction"
(*guh-nah*) is also translated as "humble" in several instances.[14] Oppression can be judicial oppression (Ex. 23:7-9). Examples of this
would be rendering false judgment or testifying falsely. It sometimes
carries the meaning of sexual abuse of a defenseless woman.[15]

Protecting Women

One of the complaints of the so-called "women's movement" of
the 1970's and 1980's has been that women in the work force are frequently told by their supervisors or employers that they must compromise themselves sexually in order to retain their jobs or to advance
their careers. This practice of "sexual harassment" is unquestionably
an instance of affliction, as defined by the Bible. Women have called
for legal penalties on men who resort to such tactics.[16]

It might be argued by defenders of pure laissez-faire capitalism
that such a request by an employer may (or may not) be immoral,
but that there should be no law against it. "After all, the woman does
not have to submit. If she chooses not to prostitute herself, it could

---

13. See Gary North, *The Dominion Covenant: Genesis* (2nd ed.; Tyler, Texas: Institute for Christian Economics, 1987), ch. 18: "Competitive Bargaining."

14. Ex. 10:3; Jud. 19:24, Ps. 35:13, etc.

15. Deut. 21:14, 22:24, 29; II Sam. 13:22; Lam. 5:11; Ezek. 22:10-11.

16. Men who find themselves employed by women who make the same demand
would be equally entitled to protection by civil law.

cost her dearly in terms of her career, but this is the free market's way: if you are not willing to pay the price demanded by the seller — in this case, the seller of the job — you have no valid complaint. After all, any attractive woman who decides not to become a prostitute thereby gives up the economic income that she might have earned. The only strictly economic difference between this woman and the woman who has been solicited by her employer is that she may not have been asked to become a prostitute by some man. But the economics of the two examples are the same: forfeited income for lack of consent. Each woman pays to retain her moral integrity. But the civil government should have nothing to say in either case." So might run the arguments of an "anarcho-capitalist."

The Bible prohibits prostitution. "Do not prostitute thy daughter, to cause her to be a whore; lest the land fall to whoredom, and the land become full of wickedness" (Lev. 19:29). To profane or pollute the land morally was a sin in the Old Testament. Today, it is a direct sin against Christ, who now spews out evil (Rev. 3:16), as the land was said to do in the Old Testament (Lev. 18:25). To pressure a woman to become a prostitute is itself an act of defilement. If either the woman or the employer is married, then the demand that she submit is also a call to commit the capital crime of adultery, for which both parties could be executed if discovered and convicted in a civil court, if the woman's husband so insists (Lev. 20:10). While there is no civil penalty attached to the command not to afflict the weak, it is clear that the judges have the authority in this instance — sexual harassment — to penalize the offender. Oppression as such is not penalized, but this specific form of oppression is, since biblical civil law deals with it.

Without the civil government's authority to inflict a penalty, this crime of demanding the performance of a capital crime could not easily be exposed to the civil authorities by the victim. The employer would suffer no civil penalty, and the woman would probably lose her job for having complained publicly. Thus, the enforceability of the law of God would be compromised. Sin would encounter less restraint. The *enticement* to commit a sin to which a civil penalty is attached is therefore itself a civil crime, punishable by civil law, analogous to the case of someone who secretly enticed a family member to worship a god other than the God of the Bible, a crime punished by the authorities (Deut. 13:6-11). The judges might use public flogging as a first-time penalty, and execution for the second infraction.

The question at hand, therefore, is this: To what extent is the practice of oppression or affliction a matter of civil jurisdiction? What is the responsibility of the civil government in suppressing economic oppression by means of its legal monopoly of violence? Furthermore, is an ecclesiastical court responsible in some way to step in and call a halt to economic oppression? Will the criteria used by ecclesiastical courts be different from those used by civil courts? Such questions have baffled Christian commentators for centuries.

Criteria of Oppression

What, precisely, are criteria of economic oppression? The medieval scholastic theologians struggled long and hard with questions relating to the "just price," and "usurious loans." What is a "fair profit"? Without exception, the analytical attempts of the scholars failed to survive the test of applying the criteria. The late-medieval scholastic theologians actually defined the "just price" as the *competitive market price*, so long as the market price was not the result of price fixing by public or monopolistic concerns.[17]

The same problem disrupted the attempts of the early New England Puritans to establish formal standards of economic justice. A famous instance was the trial of Capt. Robert Keayne, a Boston merchant, who was convicted in 1639 of having taken unjust profits on the sale of foreign commodities (specifically, above 50 percent in some instances, and above 100 percent in others).[18] The fine was set by the deputies (the "lower" court, or lower chamber of the legislature-court of the Massachusetts Bay Colony) at £200; the magistrates ("upper" court) reduced it to £100.

He was punished, Gov. Winthrop argued, because the colony's leaders were determined to take action. "For the cry of the country was so great against oppression, and some of the elders and magis-

---

17. Marjorie Grice-Hutchinson, *The School of Salamanca: Readings in Spanish Monetary Theory, 1544-1605* (Oxford: The Clarendon Press, 1952); Joseph Schumpeter, *History of Economic Analysis* (New York: Oxford University Press, 1954), pp. 98-99; Raymond de Roover, "The Concept of the Just Price: Theory and Economic Policy," *Journal of Economic History*, XVIII (1958), pp. 418-34; Murray N. Rothbard, "Late Medieval Origins of Free Market Economic Thought," *Journal of Christian Reconstruction*, II (Summer 1975); Alejandro A. Chafuen, *Christians for Freedom: Late-Scholastic Economics* (San Francisco: Ignatius, 1986), ch. 7.

18. The account of his conviction is found in the diary of Gov. John Winthrop: *Winthrop's Journal: "History of New England," 1630-1649*, edited by J. Franklin Jamison, 2 vols. (New York: Barnes & Noble, [1908] 1966), I, pp. 315-16.

trates had declared such detestation of the corrupt practice of this man (which was the more observable, because he was wealthy and sold dearer than most other tradesmen, and for that he was of ill report for the like covetous practice in England, that incensed the deputies very much against him)." The politics of envy seems to have been in full force against Capt. Keayne. Gov. Winthrop's five-point explanation of why the magistrates showed leniency to him is revealing, especially the fifth: 1) because there was no law on the statute books prohibiting his rate of profit; 2) because merchants all over the world raised prices when market conditions allowed them to do so; 3) because he was not alone in this fault; 4) because all men throughout the colony were guilty of "like excess in prices" in the sale of cattle, corn, and labor; and 5) "Because a certain rule could not be found out for an equal rate between buyer and seller, though much labor had been bestowed in it, and divers laws had been made, which, upon experience, were repealed, as being neither safe nor equal."[19]

The Colony had passed and repealed just price and maximum wage laws on numerous occasions during its first decade (1630-39), without being able to solve the theological and economic problem of defining economic injustice.[20] After 1676, the legislators capitulated: there was virtually no "just price" legislation in Massachusetts for a century, until the American Revolution's wartime controls.[21]

The decision to specify a maximum price or rate of profit as universally evil is clearly arbitrary. Legislators, judges, and defendants all can point to "special circumstances" that supposedly justify or invalidate the charge of economic oppression in any specific instance. By what specific, authoritative, predictable, and generally agreed-upon standard can the civil or ecclesiastical authorities render judgment? This is the problem of *formal law*: the establishment of a written standard relating to ethics which does not rest on some appeal to external circumstances (as interpreted by the judges) or human conscience.

In the case of voluntary economic transactions, the Bible gives no specific guidelines as to what constitutes economic oppression, apart from oppression in the form of commands to perform a civil crime

19. *Ibid.*, I, p. 316.

20. See Gary North, "Medieval Economics in Puritan New England, 1630-1660," *Journal of Christian Reconstruction*, V (Winter 1978-79), pp. 171-77.

21. Gary North, "From Medieval Economics to Indecisive Pietism: Second-Generation Preaching in New England, 1661-1690," *ibid.*, VI (Summer 1979), pp. 165-70. See also North, *Puritan Economic Experiments* (Tyler, Texas: Institute for Christian Economics, 1988), pp. 35-39.

(e.g., adultery, prostitution). There are laws that prohibit false weights and measures or other crimes involving fraud, but these are general rules for the whole population. They are not laws designed specifically to protect widows, the fatherless, and strangers. Apart from the law regarding weights and measures, *the Bible does not authorize legislation or court decisions against perceived cases of economic oppression.*[22] There are no biblical (or economic) guidelines that define "price gouging" or "rent-racking," or similar unpopular practices. The attempt of governors and judges, whether civil or ecclesiastical, to go beyond the enforcement of specific laws against fraud is necessarily an expansion of arbitrary rule. Legal predictability suffers, and therefore human freedom also suffers. The power-seeking State expands at the expense of individual freedom.

This is not to argue that such evil economic practices do not exist. No doubt they do exist. The question is: What, if anything, is the civil government or a church court supposed to do in any formal case of alleged oppression? The problem that freedom-seeking Christian societies must deal with is the preservation of the judicial conditions necessary for maintaining personal liberty. How can a society avoid oppression by unjust civil magistrates if the legal system offers great latitude for civil judges to define arbitrarily and retroactively what constitutes an economic crime? Civil government is a God-ordained monopoly of violence. Allow arbitrary and unpredictable power here, and the entire society can be placed under the bondage of oppressors — oppressors who legally wield instruments of physical punishment. In contrast, economic oppression is an individual act by a specific person against a handful of people locally. It is a temporary phenomenon, limited at the very least by the continuing wealth of the oppressor, the continuing poverty of the victims, and the lifespans of both the oppressor and the oppressed. There are no comparably effective restraints on oppression by those who control the administration of civil justice. Society-wide, monopolistic, State-enforced sin is generally a far greater threat to potential victims of oppression than localized, privately financed sin.

Despite this limitation on the sanctions that can be legitimately imposed by the civil government, individuals are warned against oppressing the weak. Men are told in this passage that God will make

---

22. The laws requiring gleaning and prohibiting interest-bearing charitable loans to fellow Hebrews had no civil penalty attached to them.

widows of their wives if they are themselves oppressors. The *lex talionis* principle of "eye for eye" undergirds the principle of doing unto others what you would have others do unto you and your family. God, not the civil government, knows men's hearts. God is the Enforcer.

Judges possess lawful authority to impose sanctions against lawbreakers. Civil magistrates possess a legal monopoly of violence. Ecclesiastical authorities possess the lawful authority to keep covenant-breaking people from lawfully partaking of the sacraments. Because they possess these monopoly grants of power—monopolies granted by God (Rom. 13:1-7)—judges must be restrained by law from acting arbitrarily, in order to avoid widespread, monopolistic oppression (Isa. 1). In short, "oppression" is not a monopoly of private individuals; it is also a temptation open to men who hold the office of judge. Indeed, the ability to oppress the defenseless is far easier for a judge, for he possesses a God-ordained monopoly of power, or at least an "oligopoly" of power (since men can usually appeal to other judges). Nevertheless, each participant in a voluntary transaction must take care not to exercise his civil or institutional freedom to the detriment of the defenseless, and ultimately to the detriment of himself and his own family.

Defending the Institutionally Defenseless

The Bible singles out three representative groups as being uniquely defenseless: widows, the fatherless, and strangers. Strangers in the Hebrew commonwealth were politically at the mercy of the rulers and those citizens who were upheld judicially by the rulers. Widows and the fatherless were economically disadvantaged, having lost a reliable source of family income. The division of labor which prevails in a covenantal family unit had been broken by the death of the husband. The per capita productivity of the other members of the family normally drops under such circumstances. Thus, the biblical concept of oppression encompasses both forms of weakness, political and economic. The weak are not to be afflicted. They are not like Esau, who was in a position of presumed defenselessness only because of a flaw in his character.[23]

All three disadvantaged groups were entitled in Old Testament times to their portion of the feast of weeks and the feast of taber-

---

23. North, *Dominion Covenant: Genesis*, ch. 18: "Competitive Bargaining."

nacles (so were the landless Levites: Deut. 16:11, 14), as well as to the third-year tithe (Deut. 14:28-29). These injunctions would have been enforced by the priests.

Positive Injunctions

To protect these groups, biblical law imposes morally mandatory forms of charitable giving on the part of neighbors. But there is no civil sanction attached to this moral obligation. Biblical civil law does not compel people to do good things for others; it imposes sanctions on those who do evil things to others. Biblical civil law is therefore a barrier to the creation of a State-funded, State-mandated welfare system.

Interest payments (usury) are prohibited in the case of a morally obligatory loan to a poor brother in the faith.[24] Thus, since usury — defined very strictly in the Bible as a *charitable* loan with an interest payment attached — is prohibited, the oppressed victim can sue a lender in a civil court and recover double damages upon the lender's conviction, meaning twice the judicially prohibited interest payment. Such a lawsuit is legitimate because there are civil sanctions against specified activities. What the State cannot lawfully do is compel lenders to make charitable loans. God is the enforcer in this instance. He brings *positive sanctions* to those who obey His *positive injunction.* "Beware that there be not a thought in thy wicked heart, saying, The seventh year, the year of release, is at hand; and thine eye be evil against thy poor brother, and thou givest him nought; and he cry unto the LORD against thee, and it be sin unto thee. Thou shalt surely give him, and thine heart shall not be grieved when thou givest unto him: because that for this thing the LORD thy God shall bless thee in all thy works, and in all that thou puttest thine hand unto" (Deut. 15:9-10). The State is not authorized by God to bring positive sanctions.

It is not lawful to ask for the cloak of a widow as collateral (Deut. 24:17), but it is legal to ask for a cloak as collateral from a poverty-stricken Hebrew man (Ex. 22:26). The Bible recognizes degrees of vulnerability and degrees of responsibility. Farmers are told to permit strangers, widows, and the fatherless to glean the fallen fruit and unharvested corners of their fields (Lev. 19:9-10; Deut. 24:19-21), but being a positive injunction, it is not a judicially enforceable law in

---

24. On the other hand, usury is permitted in loans to religious strangers (Deut. 23:20).

civil court. Because this is a moral injunction, religious leaders can advise people to obey God. A church court cannot lawfully impose physical sanctions, but it can teach people to obey God's positive injunctions. Can it also legitimately impose the sanction of excommunication against those who are morally stiffnecked? Biblical law places great restrictions on those who bear the sword, but what about church discipline? The same rule seems to bind an ecclesiastical court: no arbitrary law enforcement. There have to be written rules, or at least known rules that are predictable. Men need to govern their actions in terms of their expectations regarding the decisions of courts, including church courts.

If the mark of the messianic State is arbitrary law, what of the church? The threat is far less. First, the State controls everyone within a geographical territory. The church does not. Second, there are competing churches locally; there are not competing civil governments, at least not in the same sense. Third, the State taxes people by force; the church does not. Fourth, the State inflicts physical punishment; the church does not. Thus, moral persuasion is far safer in the hands of a church court than a civil court. But the problem still remains: What is to restrain the judges in a church court? What is to make their decisions predictable? I can see only one answer: predictable written law, including case law precedents, announced in advance. Without this, the rule of moral persuasion must serve as the church's tool of discipline. The church is not to enforce God's positive injunctions apart from the specifics of Bible-revealed law.

The reason given to the Israelites for these morally (but not judicially) *mandatory* forms of *individual* charity — the State, it must be stressed, is not God's authorized agency of charitable wealth redistribution — was straightforward: God had delivered the Hebrews from bondage and oppression, and their acts of charity were to serve as reminders and symbols of their *total dependence on God* for their wealth and freedom (Deut. 16:11-12; 24:22). To oppress the weak, therefore, is equivalent to throwing off the covenant, reproaching God, and returning to the bondage of sin: "He that oppresseth the poor reproacheth his Maker: but he that honoreth him hath mercy on the poor" (Prov. 14:31). Isaiah charged the rulers of the land with just this crime: refusing to render lawful judgment to the widows and the fatherless (Isa. 1:23). Judah's rulers had become oppressors.

The decline of charitable giving is one sign of an increase in economic oppression within a society. The law of gleaning and the law of the tithe are to be upheld by ecclesiastical law. There is no New Testament evidence that either tithing or gleaning has been abolished as a moral and ecclesiastical requirement. Gifts to the poor, we are told, are made to God, and He promises to repay them (Prov. 19:17). He brings positive sanctions to those who obey His positive injunctions. He leaves to the priests the task of imposing moral sanctions for His positive injunctions. For example, the church enforces the tithe, and it grants a positive sanction to those who pay: the right of voting membership. The church also supports poor widows when relatives cannot or refuse to do so (I Tim. 5:3-10). It excommunicates relatives who can support widows but refuse, for they are worse than infidels (I Tim. 5:8).

Limited Knowledge

A voluntary exchange can be oppressive to a weaker party, biblically speaking, even though economic analysis does not provide the civil or ecclesiastical authorities the guideline, and therefore the ability, to render lawful judgment in specific cases. Why is the institutional government limited? Because there are *limits on the knowledge available* to observers of any economic transaction. Each party entered the transaction hoping to benefit. Sometimes men may cry "oppression" when they are secretly pleased with the bargain: "It is naught, it is naught, saith the buyer: but when he is gone his way, then he boasteth" (Prov. 20:14). No man can measure another man's subjective benefits; no man or committee of men can compare the gains of each party in a voluntary exchange.[25] But God can make such estimations, as Jesus demonstrated when He assessed the extent of the economic sacrifice of the widow who gave away her two "mites," or small coins (Mark 12:42-44). The fact that the authorities are not omniscient does not relieve sharp bargainers from their obligation of being alert to the weak position of the defenseless, and to make adjustments in favor of the weak in their exchanges with them.

By not seeking maximum profits in such transactions, strong bargainers thereby grant a *non-humiliating form of charity*. A good bargainer always seeks to guess what the other man is willing and able to *pay*. If he is confident in his ability to make this exceedingly difficult estimation, then he should have comparable confidence in his ability to make an estimation of how much the other, weaker bargainer may *need*.

---

25. North, *Dominion Covenant: Genesis*, ch. 4: "Economic Value: Objective and Subjective."

Biblical Law or Revolution

The quest for a zero-oppression society in history is demonic. It implicitly denies that mankind is burdened by sin and the effects of sin throughout history. When we ask questions regarding the proper means of bringing healing to social relations and institutions, we need to be clear about the fundamental question of sovereignty. Who is to heal man in history, God or the State? This raises the question of the Messiah. Who is this Messiah, Jesus Christ or the State? Who are the Messiah's chosen representatives? What are the Messiah's designated means of achieving this reduction of oppression: Biblical law or violent revolution? What is the goal of this social quest: The kingdom of God or the kingdom of man? Is this goal of perfection to be approached as a limit in a historically sin-filled world, or to be achieved in history by a scientific program of remaking man? As Rushdoony warns: "There is thus a dimension of victory in history, Jesus Christ. The alternative plan of victory is social science, and history as a social science. This means the totalitarian socialist state, the world of *1984*. For the Christian this is rather the dimension of hell, not of victory; . . ."[26]

Those who proclaim the legitimacy of such a quest apart from the preaching of the gospel and the extension of biblical law into every area of life want to lodge absolute sovereignty in the centralized "scientific" State. They begin their quest with the presupposition that there is no God who applies visible sanctions in history, either blessings or cursings. If there is a God, they assume, He reveals Himself only at the final judgment, and few of them assume that there will be even a final judgment. He is a God outside of history, they believe. This was exactly what the Pharaoh of the oppression assumed, as did the Pharaoh of the exodus. "Who is the LORD, that I should obey his voice to let Israel go?" he asked rhetorically (Ex. 5:2). Similarly, Nebuchadnezzar rhetorically asked the three Hebrew youths: "Who is that God that shall deliver you out of my hands?" (Dan. 3:15b). Pride goeth before destruction (Prov. 16:18), and pride before God is the ultimate form of pride. These kings in their rebellion had become opponents of covenant theology, which teaches that God imposes visible sanctions in history.[27]

---

26. R. J. Rushdoony, *The Biblical Philosophy of History* (Phillipsburg, New Jersey: Presbyterian & Reformed, [1969] 1979), p. 27.

27. Sutton, *That You May Prosper*, ch. 4.

Christians vs. the Covenant

One reason for the growth of 1) private oppression, 2) messianic movements against private oppression, and 3) statist tyranny in the name of relieving oppression is that Christians in the twentieth century have for the most part accepted implicitly the anti-covenantal view of God that is proclaimed by the humanistic defenders of the messianic State. Christians today believe that historical affairs will get progressively worse and worse for righteous people until Jesus comes again, either to establish a bureaucratically enforced millennium in which He will rule from the top in person (premillennialism), or to impose the final judgment (amillennialism). Such a view of God in pre-Second Coming history agrees with the pessimistic conclusions of humanists and liberation theologians who say that God does not reveal Himself in history.

Christian eschatological pessimists do admit one minor exception to the absence of God's covenant sanctions in history: representative acts of voluntary private charity by Christians that do assist a handful of people to survive a little longer or in a little more comfort. Would-be liberationists also admit an exception: representative acts of revolutionary violence against the innately oppressive social institutions of capitalist society. Nevertheless, both groups are agreed: God will not redeem society through His church's preaching of the gospel and the extension of Bible-revealed law across the face of the earth. They are agreed that God will not impose in history His dual sanctions of external blessings for covenant-keepers and external cursings for covenant-breakers. They are agreed that the Old Testament civil covenant of God is irrelevant in New Testament times, and therefore God's sanctions in history are today either nonexistent or confined exclusively to the hearts and minds of men. They insist that the visible authority of God's law and His church is steadily removed from history, and His kingdom is steadily shoved into the historically impotent realm of undefinable spirit.[28]

---

28. God will be victorious in history, premillennialists claim, only when He returns physically in awesome power to judge the nations in history for a thousand years. But this is the direct imposition of judgment; it is not based on representative judgment in history by God's elect people in His name, while He is in heaven and His people are on earth. This rulership only takes place after the church—meaning you and I—are physically dead and gone. Premillennialists and amillennialists are agreed: the church is impotent in history to change history through the preaching of the gospel and through covenantal faithfulness to God's law. As dispensationalists House and Ice insist: "Because the Bible speaks of things progressing from 'bad to

Such a view of God is implicitly or explicitly a denial of both the creation and the resurrection. Rushdoony has pointed to these implications of anti-covenant theology:

> The purpose of Biblical history is to trace the victory of Jesus Christ. *That victory is not merely spiritual; it is also historical.* Creation, man, and man's body, all move in terms of a glorious destiny for which the whole creation groans and travails as it awaits the fulness of that glorious liberty of the sons of God (Rom. 8:18-23). The victory is historical and eschatological, and it is not the rejection of creation but its fulfilment.
>
> This victory was set forth in the resurrection of Jesus Christ, Who destroyed the power of sin and death and emerged victorious from the grave. As St. Paul emphasized in I Corinthians 15, this victory is the victory of all believers. Christ is the firstfruit, the beginning, the alpha and omega of the life of the saints. Had Christ merely arisen as a spirit from the grave, it would have signified His lordship over the world of spirit but His surrender of matter and history. But by His physical resurrection, by His rising again in the same body with which He was crucified, He set forth His lordship over creation and over history. The world of history will see Christ's triumph and the triumph of His saints, His church, and His kingdom. History will not end in tribulation and disaster: it will see the triumph of the people of God and the manifestation of Christian order from pole to pole before Christ comes again. The doctrine of the resurrection is thus a cornerstone of the Biblical dimension of victory.
>
> The doctrine of the resurrection, however, does not last long in any church or philosophy which surrenders or compromises the doctrine of creation. Creationism asserts that the world is the creative act of the triune God, Who made it wholly good. Sin is a perversion of man and a deformation of creation. The goal of the Messianic purpose of history is the "restitution of all things" (Acts 3:21), their fulfilment in Jesus Christ, first in time and then in eternity.[29]

Because modern Christians have abandoned the Biblical doctrine of the six-day creation, they have failed to understand the Biblical doctrine of God's providential control over history in terms of His covenant. Because the vast majority of the handful of scientists who teach the six-day creation have been either premillennialists or

worse,' of men 'deceiving and being deceived' (2 Timothy 3:13), we look out at our world and see how bad things really are. . . . Common grace is on the decline, especially God's restraint of evil. This accounts for the rising apostasy and the decline of Christianity. North is wrong and Van Til [an amillennialist] is right on this issue." House and Ice, *Dominion Theology*, p. 183.

29. Rushdoony, *Biblical Philosophy of History*, pp. 25-26.

amillennialists, their defense of creationism has been based on humanistic science's theory of entropy (the second law of thermodynamics), which rests on the inescapability of God's curse of the cosmos in Genesis 3:17-19, rather than the doctrine of Christ's definitive restoration of all things by His resurrection, and the progressive (though imperfect) restoration of the pre-Fall world through the power of the Holy Spirit and the extension of biblical law. Thus, modern Bible-affirming Christians have found it difficult to refute by an appeal to the Bible the modern messianic quest for socialistic perfection.[30] They cannot successfully defend the idea of the free market economy as an institutional manifestation of the fourth point of the biblical covenant, the principle of judgment-sanctions: blessing and cursing, profit and loss.[31]

The Free Market's Auction Process

The pricing principle enunciated by the villain in Frank Norris' turn-of-the-century novel, *The Octopus*, is a morally valid principle for commercial transactions: "All the traffic will bear." At an auction, the highest-bidding buyer gets the sought-for asset. This principle reigns at every auction: *the high bid wins*. Yet, there is hardly any principle of capitalism that is more hated, and more criticized, than this one. The only one that receives greater criticism is the capitalist principle of economic inequality, especially inequality of inheritance at birth. But the right (legal immunity) of unequal inheritance is the legal manifestation of point five of the biblical covenant, inheritance-disinheritance.[32] In short, capitalism is hated because visible institutional manifestations of God's covenant are hated.

The free market economic system is essentially a giant auction. If potential buyers at an auction were repeatedly frustrated when low-bidding competitors were favored by the auctioneer, it would eventually destroy the auction. Similarly, if sellers of goods and services in a free market economy were unwilling to honor this principle of "high bid wins" *most of the time* (though not necessarily in every case), they would destroy the market as an institution for producing and allocating scarce economic resources. By refusing to honor the "high

---

30. Gary North, *Is the World Running Down? Crisis in the Christian Worldview* (Tyler, Texas: Institute for Christian Economics, 1988).

31. Gary North, *Inherit the Earth: Biblical Blueprints for Economics* (Ft. Worth, Texas: Dominion Press, 1987), ch. 9.

32. Sutton, *That You May Prosper*, ch. 5.

bid wins" principle, *sellers of goods* ("auctioneers") would thereby force potential *sellers of money* (buyers or "bidders") to search out another, less preferable system of allocating scarce economic resources. Alternatively, new sellers of goods and services would appear who would honor the auction principle of "high bid wins," and thereby recapture the buyers. In coercive societies, such alternatives are called black markets.

"All the traffic will bear" is simply another way of saying "the high bid wins." This arrangement benefits those consumers who at any point in time are willing and able to pay the highest price offered by all known buyers. It also benefits all other consumers — the "excluded buyers" — who learn the rules of the free market, and who can plan their own economic futures accordingly. They can enter other markets next time where they will be the highest bidders. The fact that some consumers are excluded from ownership on any given day is the fact of scarcity: at zero price, there is greater demand for scarce economic resources than there is supply of those resources. Every economic system must face the fact of scarcity, not just capitalism.

"All the traffic will bear" is a rational response of sellers to competitive bids by all known buyers. It honors the principle of *consumer sovereignty*. When we affirm that sellers of goods and services have the right (legal immunity) to request "all the traffic will bear" from competing buyers (sellers of money), we are simultaneously saying that buyers have the right to make "the lowest bid possible."[33] If the final bid for an item is one ounce of gold, the State should not insist that the buyer pay the seller two ounces of gold "because the seller deserves it," or because "stable markets for sellers is a benefit to the economy," which is precisely what civil governments do when they legislate tariffs, import quotas, and other monopoly-producing restraints on voluntary trade. "All the traffic will bear," "high bid wins," and "final bid wins" are three ways of expressing a single principle of market competition: the right (legal immunity) of free people to agree upon a familiar standard for conducting voluntary exchange.

Civil and ecclesiastical governments should respect the lawful authority of men to operate in terms of this auction principle when

---

33. It must also be understood that "sellers" are also buyers in every transaction. Each party gives up something in order to get something. But we normally do not speak of "sellers of goods and services" as "buyers of money." As "buyers of money," we all try to offer the lowest price (in goods and services) that we can get away with. Thus, we all make the lowest bid possible, and still get what we want: sometimes we make the lowest bid possible in money (when we are "buyers"), and sometimes we make the lowest bid possible in goods and services (when we are "sellers").

making their voluntary exchanges. There is no way for judges to distinguish "oppressive" transactions from "just barely oppressive" transactions and "not quite oppressive" transactions by means of an appeal to percentages, such as 8 percent profit per sale or 15 percent profit on invested capital (both of which are at least 50 percent above the normal rate of before-tax profits in the United States).[34] To make lawful judicial decisions, judges need *moral constants*; but economic percentages change over time. The question, "How much of anything should be universally illegal?", has baffled moral philosophers for millennia. Only in rare instances, such as the tithe of 10 percent, does the Bible give a specific answer to a question regarding a legal minimum percentage.[35]

The Lawful Domain of Conscience

Conscience is a valid, though not exclusive, guide to individual action. It is *self-government* which regulates the overwhelming majority of all human actions. Men must not be burdened with unnecessary guilt, nor should they become libertines, sinning against themselves because some other agency of government is not authorized by God to step in and call a halt to their activities. The question is: What are the proper standards for men to use in determining whether or not a specific transaction is oppressive, biblically speaking?

The Bible mentions strangers, widows, the poor, and the fatherless as the representative examples of people who are easily exploited. In dealing with these people, what questions should the sharp bargainer ask himself? What kinds of offers would be innately immoral?

---

34. What is not understood by most Americans, as a poll taken annually by the Opinion Research Corporation reveals year after year, is that the average rate of net after-tax profit on sales in the United States is about 5 percent or less. See, for example, "Public Attitudes Toward Corporate Profits," *ORC Report to Management* (Aug. 1981). The average rate of before-tax profits on invested capital (excluding banks and savings & loan associations) is around 10 percent. In 1964, the profit rate was about 16 percent. This figure declined steadily in the United States, 1964-80, corresponding to the coming of inflation and the vast expansion of the welfare State. After taxes, of course, it is substantially less. See Dale N. Allman, "The Decline in Business Profitability: A Disaggregated Analysis," *Economic Review*, Federal Reserve Bank of Kansas City (Jan. 1983). Employee compensation varies between 85 percent and 90 percent of after-tax business income, year after year.

35. Then the experts debate over the question, "10 percent of *what*?" They also debate: "Does the Bible require a third-year additional tithe?"

1. An Immoral or Illegal Act

The request that the economically weaker party perform an immoral or illegal act is a form of oppression. The civil government can enforce sanctions against anyone who entices another person into illegal acts, but enticement is both difficult and expensive to prove in a court of law. Nevertheless, no such enticement is legitimate, for the charge will be easy to prove in God's court of law on judgment day.

2. Forestalling

Forestalling is the act of holding goods off the market in order to drive up the price. "He that withholdeth corn, the people shall curse him: but blessing shall be upon the head of him that selleth it" (Prov. 11:26). It should be noted that the people will curse the forestaller, but the State is not authorized in the Bible to be a price-setting agency or a confiscating agent "in the name of the people." Also, it is God, not the State, who is the rewarder of those who sell.

The man who is criticized here for holding the corn off the market in expectation of a higher price is obviously holding back *sufficient quantities of food to make a difference in price in the market*. There is no implication in this passage that someone who buys food for his own use, who has a refrigerator full of food or a freezer full of beef, is in some way an exploiter. (This is not a hypothetical argument on my part. Ronald J. Sider has criticized Christians who eat beef because it takes twice as much grain to produce the same quantity of protein in a steer as in a chicken. Christians should eat more chicken, he says. This is a moral imperative, he says.[36] His vegetarian socialist peers no doubt would regard this as a woefully weak argument, smacking — perhaps even lip-smacking — of capitalist exploitation.) The exploiter is a person who is holding back the sale of a great deal of food — so much, in fact, that the market price would be affected if he brought it to market. Not many farmers or sellers have this much food at their disposal, given the huge size of the international grain markets. This is one of the strongest arguments in favor of free markets and against tariffs and import quotas of any kind: *economic freedom reduces the possibility of successful local or regional forestalling*.

In a godly society, no honest man curses the entrepreneur (risk-taking forecaster) who "buys low" during the bounty of the harvest

---

36. Ronald J. Sider, *Rich Christians in an Age of Hunger: A Biblical Study* (Downers Grove, Illinois: Inter-Varsity Press, 1977), p. 43.

and plans to "sell high" in the winter. Rational people understand, for example, that fruits and vegetables in the off-season are more expensive: supplies are limited, and they must be imported. Distant sellers must be lured into the local market through the hope of receiving higher prices for their produce than they can receive locally. In short, *someone* has to store the food, harvest season through off-season; few users have the storage facilities. The economic function of allocating food across the seasons and across regions has to be performed by someone.

Profit-seeking (uncertainty-bearing) entrepreneurs are the most responsible, least bureaucratic people for this task.[37] Why? Because if they guess wrong, they lose. If they charge too little, they run out of food before they run out of buyers. They lose sales that they could have made, and therefore they lose money. On the other hand, if they charge too much, they lure in competitors who take away potential buyers and leave them sitting on a lot of unsold food. They lose sales that they could have made, and therefore they lose money. Conclusion: they have an economic incentive not to overcharge or undercharge the consumers.

3. A Government-Enforced Monopoly

Any offer that lacks a competitive alternative offer because of *interference by the civil government in the market* is potentially immoral, unless the civil authorities are regulating the market as a "public utility." (Even if they are regulating the market in the name of the consumer, such a monopoly may still be exploitative, for collusion between the regulators and the regulated is not only possible, it is predictable.)[38]

---

37. North, *Dominion Covenant: Genesis*, ch. 23: "The Entrepreneurial Function."

38. This is understood by representatives of the far left wing of American politics: e.g., Gabriel Kolko, *The Triumph of Conservatism: A Reinterpretation of American History, 1900-1916* (New York: The Free Press of Glencoe, 1963); Robert C. Fellmeth, *The Interstate Commerce Commission: The Public Interest and the ICC*, The Ralph Nader Study Group Report on the ICC (New York: Grossman Publishers, 1970). It is also recognized by free market economists: e.g., Milton Friedman, *Capitalism and Freedom* (University of Chicago Press, 1962), ch. 9: "Occupational Licensure"; Friedman, *Free to Choose* (New York: Harcourt Brace Jovanovich, 1980), ch. 7: "Who Protects the Consumer?"; Mary Bennett Peterson, *The Regulated Consumer* (Ottowa, Illinois: Green Hill Publishers, 1971); Thomas Gale Moore, *Trucking Regulation: Lessons from Europe* (Washington, D.C.: American Enterprise Institute-Hoover Institution, 1976); Yale Brozen, *Is Government the Source of Monopoly? and Other Essays* (San Francisco: Cato Institute, 1980); Harold Flemming, *Ten Thousand Commandments: A Story of the Antitrust Laws* (New York: Prentice-Hall, 1951).

If the seller of a good or service is protected by the judges from other competitors who might otherwise enter the market and make the buyer a better (lower price) offer, then the seller is oppressing the buyer. He may not have approved of this legislation or judicial interpretation, but he is now the beneficiary. If such restrictive legislation is in force, then the seller must do his best to sell his product or service to the buyer at a price that would prevail if there were open competition.

The problem, of course, is that *in the absence of a free market, no one can really be sure just what such a free market price might be.*[39] Without the information made available through market competition, buyers and sellers are left without reliable indicators of the true conditions of supply and demand.[40] Moral decisions concerning "fair" pricing are therefore made more difficult — more expensive to solve — by the State's interference with the flow of economic information. The prevailing price in a government-regulated market raises moral questions concerning fairness precisely because it is not a competitive market price. Moral dilemmas for honest sellers are created by the State's interference because this interference creates opportunities for sellers to extract monopoly profits from buyers. The "non-monopoly" price can only be guessed at by judges, buyers, and sellers.

4. Better Information

The economically stronger party in a transaction may have better information at his disposal. How much of this is he morally required to give to the economically weaker seller? If he asks a lower price, then he is, economically speaking, transferring the value of his information to the other party in the exchange.

The civil government should not compel the transfer of such information. If such a law were passed, it would inhibit the quest for better information on the part of all participants, which would eventually harm all people in the society.[41] Besides, judges would face that age-old problem, defining exactly *how much* of his information the economically stronger seller (or buyer) is required to give up to the other person before a voluntary exchange is legal. For that mat-

---

39. Ludwig von Mises, "Economic Calculation in the Socialist Commonwealth" (1920), in F. A. Hayek (ed.), *Collectivist Economic Planning* (London: Routledge & Kegan Paul, [1935] 1963); T. J. B. Hoff, *Economic Calculation in the Socialist Society* (London: Hodge, 1949), reprinted by Liberty Press, Indianapolis, Indiana, 1981; Hayek, *Individualism and Economic Order* (University of Chicago Press, 1948), chaps. 7-9.

40. Thomas Sowell, *Knowledge and Decisions* (New York: Basic Books, 1980), ch. 8.

41. Gary North, "Exploitation and Knowledge," *The Freeman* (Jan. 1982).

ter, how can the economically stronger party be precisely determined? The question, "How much stronger?" is closely related to the
other question, "How much information?"[42]

What governing principle does the Bible offer to the individual
conscience? If the economically weaker party would be able to locate
someone who would make a better offer if it were not for the particular circumstance — pressures on a widow or orphan, legal discrimination against a stranger, etc. — then the economically stronger party
should offer a price comparable to what the person might reasonably
expect to receive. A person who finds "a pearl of great price" on
another person's property has a moral right to sell what he has and
offer to buy that property in order to get ownership of the pearl
(Matt. 13:44).

But what if the seller is blind, and would never have had an opportunity to find that pearl? There is no explicit biblical law here,
but the discoverer should remember that God is not blind. The
buyer of the field might choose to give, say, half of the net profits in
the transaction to the economically weaker party, in order to avoid
inflicting economic oppression. (Again, there are no fixed rules
available to us, but a 50-50 split is a good operating principle.)
Nevertheless, the Bible is silent with respect to any State prohibition
against such a transaction, either retroactively or in advance. To
write a legal code that would attempt to cover every similar transaction would become a nightmare of confusion and uncontrolled State
power in a short period of time. The behavior of monopolistic bureaucrats is not noticeably superior to profit-seeking buyers of hidden pearls. At least such oppression by private entrepreneurs is not
subsidized by the taxpayers.

There are those who deny the legitimacy of a "pearl of great
price" type of transaction under any circumstances. They do not
understand (or choose to deny) the inescapable fact of *man's lack of
omniscience*. They assume, consciously or unconsciously, that accurate knowledge is (or ought to be) a zero-price resource — a resource that really ought to be available free of charge to all, either
naturally or through the intervention of the State.

---

42. There are other questions, of course: "How much capital does each participant have in reserve?" "What are the living expenses that each participant incurs
while he is waiting to complete the transaction?" "How much time does each participant have to complete the transaction?" "What are the transaction (exchange) costs
incurred by each participant?"

The Pearl of Great Price

This kingdom parable is important for a proper understanding of entrepreneurship—*forecasting* the economic future and *efficient (low waste) planning* in terms of the forecast. Jesus said: "Again, the kingdom of heaven is like unto treasure hid in a field; the which when a man hath found, he hideth, and for joy thereof goeth and selleth all that he hath, and buyeth that field" (Matt. 13:44).

Consider what the buyer in this parable is doing. He stumbles across an important piece of information: there is a valuable treasure hidden in a field. He is not sure just who it was who hid it there, but now he knows where it is. He presumes that the person who hid it was not the present owner of the field.[43] He hides the treasure, and then goes out and sells everything he owns in order to buy the field. Notice that he does not steal the treasure. He is not a thief. He is simply the possessor of information.

He may have done some preliminary investigating, just to see if the present owner of the field is willing to sell it. Still, the present owner may change his mind before the sale is completed. Perhaps the owner may sell it at what he knows is a higher-than-normal market price, since he knows that the treasure has been left there by a vicious criminal who stole it. Perhaps the stolen treasure will be confiscated by the police and turned over to the victim, or the victim's insurance company, as soon as it appears on the market. It is even possible that the treasure is a fake: the owner may have placed a phony treasure on his land just to lure in some ecstatic discoverer.[44] The discoverer cannot be sure. But he takes a chance, meaning that he decides to bear some uncertainty in hope of economic profit. He sells what he owns and buys the field.

Now he owns the treasure. Assume that the police do not confiscate it, and some criminal does not return to collect it. The new owner did take advantage of a special situation: his knowledge of this treasure in his newly purchased field. He took a risk and sold every-

---

43. If the owner of the field hid the treasure, then before he sells it, he will go and search for it. When he does not find it, he can report it lost to the authorities. At that point, the discoverer is required by biblical law to return it to the owner (Ex. 23:4). The Bible does not teach "finders-keepers, losers-weepers."

44. In the gold rush days of the American West, mine owners would sometimes place grains of gold in a shotgun and fire at one of the mine's walls. This was called "salting a mine," and buyers could be lured into paying a high price for the mine, in order to profit from the perceived ignorance of the seller.

thing. Now he has his reward. He has benefitted himself, and he has given the original owner of the field all that he asked for. If the treasure is worth selling, then someone who buys it will gain access to his heart's desire. Who loses?

Clearly, the original owner might have stumbled across that treasure. On the other hand, he might never have found it. Is it a moral obligation on the discoverer to run to the owner of the field and tell him? Jesus did not indicate that it was. The discoverer has a potentially valuable asset: information. He lacks ownership of the field. The owner of the field also has a potentially valuable asset: title to the treasure. But he lacks knowledge of its presence on his property. Each man possesses something of potential value, but neither man can make personal use of his potential asset: the owner of the field has no knowledge of the pearl, and the man who knows where the pearl is has no economic incentive to make this knowledge public unless he owns the field. Society gets no use of it until the potential asset is translated through market exchange into a known asset. The *opportunity for profit* is what translates that potential asset into a marketable asset. The discoverer buys the field. In this way, potential assets become market assets.

The modern socialist is outraged at this parable. The entrepreneur (uncertainty-bearing forecaster) who discovered the treasure is seen by the socialist as immoral. First, the land he was on should have been owned by "the people" through the State. Second, he had no business being on the land, since he had no official papers entitling him to be on the State's property. Third, he should never have hidden the treasure again. It belonged to the State. Fourth, if the land was not yet the property of the State, then he should have notified the present owner of the field about the existence of this newly discovered treasure. Fifth, failing to do this much, he was immoral in making an offer to buy the field. He was really stealing from the owner of the field. Sixth, should he attempt to sell the treasure, the State ought to tax his profits at a minimum rate of 50 percent, and probably more. Seventh, if he refuses to sell, the State should impose a capital tax or property tax in order to force him to sell.

Socialists Resent Limitations

What the socialist-redistributionist objects to, in the final analysis, is *mankind's lack of omniscience*. The socialist believes, implicitly or explicitly, that the economy should operate as smoothly, as efficiently, and as profit-free as a hypothetical economy in which each participant has equally good knowledge — perfect knowledge — as all other participants. Knowledge, in a "decent" social order, should be a zero-price resource, equally available to all, and equally acted upon by all. Socialist arguments implicitly assume that it is only the *temporary* existence of such factors as private property, personal greed, and people's willingness to exploit the poor, that has created a world of scarcity, profits, and losses. Knowledge concerning the future should be regarded as a free good, they implicitly assume. Profits are therefore evil, not to mention unnecessary, in a sound economy. This has been the underlying line of reasoning for centuries of all those who equate economic profits with exploitation.

Men are not omniscient. This angers the socialists. They strike out in wrath against the free market institutional order that encourages men to seek out better information, day by day, so that they might profit individually from its application in economic affairs. The socialists prefer to create legislative barriers that interfere with the operation of the market's "auction for information."

It should be clear why so little innovation takes place in socialist economies. The development — or rather, the lack of development — of commercial technology in the Soviet Union is a representative historical example.[45] Innovation is not a service that people normally offer free of charge to others. It involves creativity, capital, and the willingness to take risks. In a socialist commonwealth, the entrepreneur who is willing to bear uncertainty cannot legally receive payment for the full economic value to society — as determined by market forces — of his innovation. For entrepreneurs to receive full value for services rendered, the socialist commonwealth would have to abandon the collective ownership of the means of production-distribution.[46]

Those who discover treasures in "collectively owned" fields, meaning State-controlled and bureaucracy-administered fields, have

---

45. Antony Sutton's three-volume study of Soviet technology, 1917-1965, indicates that almost none of the Soviet Union's industrial technology (as distinguished from its military technology) originated in the U.S.S.R. Out of 75 different major technologies surveyed, the percentage of Soviet technology was zero, 1917-30, 10 percent, 1930-45, and 11 percent, 1945-65. "It should be emphasized that this is the most favorable interpretation possible of the empirical findings." Sutton, *Western Technology and Soviet Economic Development, 1945 to 1965* (Stanford, California: Hoover Institution Press, 1973), p. 370.

46. Svetozar Pejovich, "Liberman's Reforms and Property Rights in The Soviet Union," *Journal of Law and Economics*, XII (April 1969).

these choices: 1) provide information, free of charge, of the treasure's whereabouts to bureaucratic officials of the State; 2) say nothing and save themselves a lot of trouble; 3) work out an illegal deal with some official; or 4) steal the treasure. In the Soviet Union, predictably, the final three possibilities are the ones people choose; the first choice is simply not taken seriously as a sensible alternative.[47]

Conclusion

The Bible forbids economic oppression, but only vaguely defines it. Economic theory provides even fewer guidelines than the Bible. About all that economic theory can say is that when the threat of violence is imposed on someone, there is oppression. But violence must not be defined as a market participant's threat of refusing to trade with someone else, unless the violation of an existing contract is involved, or unless someone is being asked to commit a crime or immoral act. Sharp bargaining is not automatically considered oppressive, either in the Bible or economic theory.

Without specified infractions, it is very difficult to develop a system of civil law. The law must specify the action that is being prohibited. It must be sufficiently clear that juries can make judgments, and that their judgments can be predicted with better than 50-50 accuracy by most people, especially potential criminals. If the decisions of juries are random, then the law will not protect innocent people on a predictable basis. This means that civil law no longer serves its God-given purpose of providing social order.

Defining oppression clearly is very difficult. Oppression must be defined in such a way that the courts do not easily become tyrannical or arbitrary in their decisions. But as I have said, a definition of economic oppression that is both equitable and tyranny-resistant when it is applied to a large number of cases over time has not yet been discovered. This is why economic oppression rarely can be legislated against without creating more harm than benefits for the potential victims of oppression. The legislation itself becomes a major source of oppression.[48] The medieval notion of the "just price" is one of the best examples of this problem in history, especially when interpreted centuries later by civil magistrates who were not familiar with the late-medieval Scholastic theologians' distrust of government price-fixing.

---

47. Konstantin Simis, *USSR: The Corrupt Society* (New York: Simon & Schuster, 1982).
48. See Chapter 24: "Impartial Justice and Legal Predictability."

This points to the fact that human conscience must rule over all pricing decisions in voluntary exchanges, not because the individual conscience is in any way autonomous, but because *only God is legitimately sovereign over the minds of men.* He alone, not human authorities, can make accurate comparisons of interpersonal subjective utility. He alone knows precisely how much one person has benefitted from a transaction, and to what extent the magnitude of his gain was based on the defenselessness of the other participant in the exchange. Therefore, penalties against those who are suspected of acting oppressively in economic transactions — apart from those cases specified in Scripture — are not to be imposed by human institutional governments, precisely because omniscience is God's monopoly. This is why men can rest assured that God's penalties against cases of economic oppression are utterly certain and will be applied precisely by God, according to the magnitude of each oppressive act. *The self-governed individual under God,* not institutional governments, is the proper agent of earthly enforcement. If this human agent fails to render God-honoring judgment, then God will bring him under judgment.

The Bible does mandate certain forms of charity to relieve oppression, including morally mandatory interest-free loans to the deserving, covenanted poor, gleaning, and the prohibition against asking a widow for her cloak as collateral. But there are no specified penalties for violating these laws, and the civil government is not specified as the enforcing institution. In the case of hoarding goods in order to increase the market price of the particular good, the Bible says that the penalty is public censure: "He that withholdeth corn, the people shall curse him: but blessing shall be upon the head of him that selleth it" (Prov. 11:26). The people can lawfully curse him, but no physical violence or fines are to be imposed on the culprit.

God is the Enforcer. He brings *judgment in history.* Because modern man refuses to acknowledge this, he seeks to become his own God by making the State an enforcer. He does not believe that God enters into the historical affairs of men to bring judgment. Because many Christians today have adopted this same "God is beyond history" theology — God as Judge only on the day of final judgment, or only during the supposed millennial reign of Christ in person — they have fallen into the same State-expanding worldview. They want an enforcer. More than this: they want a *near-omniscient* enforcer. But in calling for such an enforcer, they are denying the very basis of civil freedom: civil law that is biblically specific as to what constitutes illegal behavior, and biblically specific as to what constitutes appropriate punishment.

When such an enforcer is constructed by antinomian man, economic oppression will become universal.

Those who argue today that God's law does not and should not apply to all men have in mind the restraining aspects of civil law. Christians today insist, alongside the humanists, that God has not entrusted Christians with the responsibility of "telling other people how to live." Christians do not understand that biblical civil law never was intended to tell men how to live; it tells them how *not* to act in public. What modern antinomian Christians systematically ignore is this: if God's law does not restrain the stranger as well as the believer, it therefore does not protect either the stranger or the believer. Christians forget all about the protective benefits of God's civil law. They have implicitly accepted humanism's lie: that biblical law is inherently tyrannical, and that "true" humanist law is beneficent. (Problem: no one ever seems to be able to discover what this beneficent "true" humanist law is.)

Christians today hate the law of God as surely as the humanists do. They hate the idea of God's judgments in history. But God's judgments are always both positive and negative, blessings and cursings. Christians today much prefer to live under the negative civil sanctions of humanism and thereby forfeit the positive sanctions of God's law rather than suffer the embarrassment and personal responsibility of enforcing biblical law. The result is that Christians have become strangers in their own land.[49] And the astounding fact is this: they prefer it this way. It provides them with the psychologically necessary self-justification for their own cultural impotence.

---

49. Martin E. Marty, *Pilgrims in Their Own Land: 500 Years of Religion in America* (Boston: Little, Brown, 1984).

23

THE PROHIBITION AGAINST USURY

If thou lend money to any of my people that is poor by thee, thou shalt not be to him as an usurer, neither shalt thou lay upon him usury. If thou at all take thy neighbour's raiment to pledge, thou shalt deliver it unto him by that the sun goeth down: For that is his covering only, it is his raiment for his skin: wherein shall he sleep? And it shall come to pass, when he crieth unto me, that I will hear; for I am gracious (Ex. 22:25-27).

The context of these verses indicates that they are an extension of the immediately preceding verses: "Ye shall not afflict any widow, or fatherless child. If thou afflict them in any wise, and they cry at all unto me, I will surely hear their cry; And my wrath shall wax hot, and I will kill you with the sword; and your wives shall be widows, and your children fatherless" (Ex. 22:21-24). The general category of all these verses is affliction or oppression. In the first case, the law singles out a particular judicial category of victims: people without covenantal representation. In this case, the law singles out another class of potential victims: poor people. They, too, are vulnerable. They, too, deserve sympathy and protection — in this case, economic protection.

What is the category that links all of these people? Not their legal status, for the poor brother in Israel had full legal status, unlike the stranger in Exodus 22:21. There must be some other link. There is: their status as economically vulnerable. The presumption is that they share one thing in common with the previous three: *they are economically vulnerable through no fault of their own.* They are the "victims of circumstances" rather than the victims of their own evil behavior. The poor man here is presumed by God to be a sober, righteous person, not a drunk who drinks up his family's substance, and not a previous oppressor of the vulnerable who has now come under God's promised sanctions. The Bible is clear: *we are not to subsidize evil.*

Charity which deliberately subsidizes visible moral evil or failure that is the product of moral failure is itself morally corrupt.

In Exodus 22:21-24, the theocentric principle is that God is the kinsman-redeemer. How we treat the judicially most vulnerable people in the commonwealth reflects our covenantal response to God. It identifies those who will and who will not act voluntarily as kinsmen-redeemers for the helpless. The issue in Exodus 22:21-24 is the legal status of the oppressed as covenantally unrepresented. Because the legal status of the poor Hebrew in Exodus 22:25-27 is different from the legal status of the widow, orphan, or resident alien, we need to search for some theocentric principle other than God as protector and judge, kinsman-redeemer and blood avenger.

God Is the Owner

Because this case law is tied directly to economics, the theocentric category must also be economic. The foundational biblical economic principle is always this one: *God is the owner of all the earth.* "The earth is the LORD's, and the fulness thereof; the world, and they that dwell therein" (Ps. 24:1). "For every beast of the forest is mine, and the cattle upon a thousand hills" (Ps. 50:10).

God delegates ownership to mankind in terms of a leasehold contract. Men owe Him a tithe as His legitimate return. They are required to pay God representatively by paying their tithes to His church. But men do not want to pay God this rental fee. They want autonomous ownership without any obligation to pay rent. They despise the very thought of paying rent to God (or anyone else) because it testifies that they are not the ultimate owners. Paying a tithe to God is a public admission that they are not the sovereign owners, not the autonomous creators. Paying rent or sharing the crop means that they are *subordinate.* They are therefore under a hierarchy, not over it. They deeply resent their position as subordinate stewards. They would rather become murderers than remain rent-payers. Since they cannot kill the true Owner, they seek to kill His lawful representative. Instead of collecting their rent in the Owner's name, his highest representative will collect their vengeance. This is the message of Jesus' parable of the vineyard:

Hear another parable: There was a certain householder, which planted a vineyard, and hedged it round about, and digged a winepress in it, and built a tower, and let it out to husbandmen, and went into a far country:

And when the time of the fruit drew near, he sent his servants to the husbandmen, that they might receive the fruits of it. And the husbandmen took his servants, and beat one, and killed another, and stoned another. Again, he sent other servants more than the first: and they did unto them likewise. But last of all he sent unto them his son, saying, They will reverence my son. But when the husbandmen saw the son, they said among themselves, This is the heir; come, let us kill him, and let us seize on his inheritance (Matt. 21:34-38).

God judges a person's attitude toward Him by judging his attitude toward His servants. Sometimes these servants are in positions of authority, as in the parable of the vineyard. Sometimes they are in positions of weakness (Matt. 25:34-40). A good steward must be obedient to those over him and merciful to those under him. God judges our performance as stewards in terms of this upward and downward covenantal responsibility.

This brings us to the topic at hand: the prohibition of interest payments from the poor fellow believer. God establishes a rule with respect to loans to poor fellow believers: *no interest payment may be imposed on charity loans*. The lender who violates this law is violating the terms of God's leasehold arrangement.

God-Mandated Charity

By prohibiting an interest return on charitable loans, the Bible requires a form of charitable giving on the part of lenders, namely, the *forfeited use* of their present goods over the life of the loan. It is one of the very few examples in the Bible of God-required wealth redistribution.

What are the predictable results of such a moral (though not civil) law? When it is obeyed, there will be fewer loans available for other kinds of investments, *other things remaining equal*. But God promises that things will not remain equal in such a society; things will get better. "For the LORD thy God blesseth thee, as he promised thee: and thou shalt lend unto many nations, but thou shalt not borrow; and thou shalt reign over many nations, but they shall not reign over thee" (Deut. 15:6). So, there will be more wealth, and faithful commonwealths will have money to lend to foreigners — and at a profit. This distinguishes the biblical view of progressive history from the cyclical classical Greek view. There is a covenantal relationship between obedience to God's revealed law and economic growth, something that the Greeks ignored or even denied.[1]

---

1. As do premillennialists H. Wayne House and Thomas D. Ice: *Dominion Theology: Blessing or Curse?* (Portland, Oregon: Multnomah Press, 1988), ch. 8; cf. p. 183.

People may choose not to obey God's directive, of course. Potential lenders can simply refuse to make loans to brothers in distress, and there is nothing in biblical law that allows the authorities to take any kind of legal action against them. Poor people can only appeal to a lender's conscience. For another, lenders can get around the prohibition in many ways, such as by unofficially requiring the borrower to perform some sort of service, or requiring the borrower to buy goods or services that the lender sells. (This latter restriction is a familiar requirement of certain kinds of U.S. government loans and economic aid to foreign nations: they are required to buy goods from U.S. companies.) Nevertheless, God's law is clear: all such subterfuges are immoral, and the victims will cry out to God, who will hear their complaints (Ex. 22:27).

Another product of this prohibition against usury would be political pressures from lenders in a money economy to reduce prices by reducing the money supply. If the money supply is stabilized, or even lowered, this will tend to reduce prices. Thus, a return of the same amount of gold, silver, or paper money will in effect grant lenders increased wealth. They can buy a greater quantity of goods and services when the loan is repaid. Should this political pressure fail to achieve its goal, and should monetary inflation continue, then lenders will prefer to loan goods rather than money, with repayment denominated in goods of equal quality. They will at least regain an equal quantity of goods that have appreciated in value (as denominated in the depreciating monetary unit).

The prohibition on usury clearly and absolutely prohibits interest payments on all charitable loans to other Christians. This includes loans to churches and other non-profit institutions that come to Christians in the name of Christ. The church is not a business. The Christian who loans the church anything, at any time, for which he requires an extra amount in repayment, is violating the law against usury. Any leader in a church or non-profit Christian organization who encourages Christians to make interest-bearing loans to it is involving its supporters in the sin of usury. This restriction on "church bonds" is almost universally ignored by denominational leaders today. They ignore the prohibition against usury. The Bible is clear on this point: usury is a terrible crime (Jer. 15:10). The prophet Ezekiel announced that it is actually a capital crime in the eyes of God, and will not go unpunished (Ezek. 18:8-9, 13). Yet church and Christian school leaders in almost every denomination can be found offering

"Christian stewardship" (usury) contracts to their people.[2]

A church may request a loan from a bank or other thrift institution. This is unwise, given the fact that the borrower is servant to the lender (Prov. 22:7). Nevertheless, the bank is not wrong in taking an interest return from a church. The bank is not a Christian. It is not a member of a church. It does not face damnation or salvation. The church does not approach it in the name of Jesus, or with the promise of future rewards in heaven. The bank is strictly a commercial lending institution. The bank is the agent of depositors of all religious faiths.

But is the zero-interest loan exclusively a charitable loan? Some expositors deny this.[3] We need to examine the biblical texts to learn the truth.

Charitable Loans

The text is clear: "If thou lend money to any of my people that is poor by thee, thou shalt not be to him as an usurer, neither shalt thou lay upon him usury" (v. 25). This verse does not compel a person to make a loan to the poor person, but if the lender decides to make such a loan, he may not ask the recipient to pay interest. The text in Leviticus 25, the chapter on the jubilee year, is equally clear: "And if thy brother be waxen poor, and fallen in decay with thee; then thou shalt relieve him: yea, though he be a stranger [*geyr*], or a sojourner [*to-shawb*]; that he may live with thee. Take thou no usury of him, or increase: but fear thy God; that thy brother may live with thee. Thou shalt not give him thy money upon usury, nor lend him thy victuals for increase" (Lev. 25:35-37). It begins with the determining clause: "If thy brother be waxen poor."

The interpretation of the Leviticus 25 passage initially seems difficult because of the King James translation of Deuteronomy 23:20: "Unto a stranger [*nok-ree*] thou mayest lend upon usury; but unto thy brother thou shalt not lend upon usury: that the LORD thy God may bless thee in all that thou settest thine hand to in the land whither thou goest to possess it." We must begin with the presupposi-

---

2. Gary North, "Stewardship, Investment, and Usury: Financing the Kingdom of God," in R. J. Rushdoony, *The Institutes of Biblical Law* (Nutley, New Jersey: Craig Press, 1973), Appendix 3; reprinted also in Gary North, *An Introduction to Christian Economics* (Nutley, New Jersey: Craig Press, 1973), ch. 31.

3. For example, S. C. Mooney, *Usury: Destroyer of Nations* (Warsaw, Ohio: Theopolis, 1988).

tion that God's revealed law is not inconsistent. But here we have what appears to be two rules regarding the stranger: you may not lawfully charge the stranger interest, yet you may lawfully charge him interest. How can we reconcile these two statements?

The answer is that the Hebrew word used in Leviticus 25:35, transliterated *geyr* [gare], is not the same as the Hebrew word in Deuteronomy 23:20. Similarly, "Sojourner" [*to-shawb*] is related to *yaw-shab*,[4] meaning "sit," and implying "remain," "settle," "dwell," or even "marry."[5] *To-shawb* therefore means *resident alien*. The stranger [*nok-ree*] referred to in Deuteronomy 23:20 was simply a foreigner.[6] Two different kinds of "stranger" are referred to in the two verses. Thus, if the resident alien was poor, and if he was willing to live in Israel under the terms of the civil covenant, then he was entitled to a special degree of civil legal protection. What was this legal protection? If he fell into poverty, he was not to be asked to pay interest on any loan that a richer man extended to him. With respect to usury, he was to be treated as a poverty-stricken Hebrew. Not so the foreigner.

What must be understood is that the economic setting is clearly *the relief of the poor*. The recipient was any poor person who had fallen into poverty through no ethical fault of his own, and who was willing to remain under God's civil hierarchy.

There is a parallel passage in Deuteronomy 15. Deuteronomy 15 lists the economic laws governing Israel's national sabbatical year. In this national year of release, the text literally says, all debts *to neighbors* are to be forgiven: "At the end of every seven years thou shalt make a release. And this is the manner of the release: Every creditor that lendeth ought unto his neighbour shall release it; he shall not exact it of his neighbour, or of his brother; because it is called the LORD's release" (Deut. 15:1-2). The text is clear: the neighborly loan is the focus of the law.

At least one kind of loan was explicitly exempted by the text: loans to non-resident foreigners: "Of a foreigner [*nok-ree*] thou mayest exact it again: but that which is thine with thy brother thine hand shall release" (Deut. 15:3). This could have been a traveller or

---

4. James Strong, "Hebrew and Chaldee Dictionary," in *The Exhaustive Concordance of the Bible* (New York: Abington, [1890] 1961), p. 123.

5. *Ibid.*, p. 52.

6. This is the translation given in the Revised Standard Version, the New American Standard Bible, and the New International Version. The alien and the sojourner were equivalents judicially in Old Covenant law. The NIV translates Leviticus 25:35 as "an alien or a temporary resident."

foreigner who owned a business locally. It could have been a business contact in another country. It was not a poverty-stricken resident alien, who was treated by biblical civil law as a neighbor.

Who Is My Neighbor?

Because all debts to a neighbor are to be forgiven, the legal question legitimately arises: "Who is my neighbor?" This was the question that the lawyer asked Jesus (Luke 10:29). Jesus answered this question with His parable of the good Samaritan. The Samaritan finds a beaten man on the highway. The man had been robbed. He looked as though he was dead. He was in deep trouble *through no fault of his own*. He was on the same road that the Samaritan was traveling. The Samaritan takes him to an inn, pays to have him helped, and goes on his journey. He agrees to cover expenses. He is the neighbor. He showed mercy to the man. The lawyer admitted this (Luke 10:37).

So, the context of the parable is not simply geographical proximity in a neighborhood. It is *proximity of life*. Samaritans did not live in Israel. They had very little to do with the Israelites. But this Samaritan was walking along the same road as the beaten man, and he was in a position to help. He saw that the man was a true victim. The latter was in trouble through no visible fault of his own. He therefore deserved help—morally, though not by statute law—but the priest and the Levite had refused to offer him any help. The Samaritan was being faithful to the law.

This parable was a reproach to the Jews. They knew what Jesus was saying: they were too concerned with the details of the ceremonial law to honor the most important law of all, which the lawyer had cited: "Thou shalt love the Lord thy God with all thy heart, and with all thy soul, and with all thy strength, and with all thy mind; and thy neighbour as thyself" (Luke 10:27). What they also fully understood was that Jesus was predicting that the gentiles (Samaritans) who did obey this law of the neighbor would eventually rule over the Jews, for this is what Deuteronomy 15 explicitly says. *He who shows mercy to his neighbor will participate in his nation's rule over other nations.* "Only if thou carefully hearken unto the voice of the LORD thy God, to observe to do all these commandments which I command thee this day. For the LORD thy God blesseth thee, as he promised thee: and thou shalt lend unto many nations, but thou shalt not borrow; and thou shalt reign over many nations, but they shall not reign over thee" (Deut. 15:5-6). Notice also that the means of exercising this rule is through extending them credit.

This is a very significant covenantal cause-and-effect relationship. If a nation is characterized by the willingness of its citizens to loan money, interest-free, to their poverty-stricken neighbors, including resident aliens, the nation will eventually extend its control over others by placing them under the obligation of debt. "The rich ruleth over the poor, and the borrower is servant to the lender" (Prov. 22:7). This is why it was legal to take interest from the foreigner who was living outside the land. It was a means of subduing him, his family, and his God-defying civilization. It was (and is) a means of dominion.

Moral Compulsion

Because these charitable loans were supposed to be cancelled in the seventh year, the national sabbatical year, there was an obvious temptation to refuse to make such loans as the sabbatical year approached. God recognized this temptation, and He warned against it.

> If there be among you a poor man of one of thy brethren within any of thy gates in thy land which the LORD thy God giveth thee, thou shalt not harden thine heart, nor shut thine hand from thy poor brother: But thou shalt open thine hand wide unto him, and shalt surely lend him sufficient for his need, in that which he wanteth. Beware that there be not a thought in thy wicked heart, saying, The seventh year, the year of release, is at hand; and thine eye be evil against thy poor brother, and thou givest him nought; and he cry unto the LORD against thee, and it be sin unto thee. Thou shalt surely give him, and thine heart shall not be grieved when thou givest unto him: because that for this thing the LORD thy God shall bless thee in all thy works, and in all that thou puttest thine hand unto (Deut. 15:7-10).

This indicates that God placed a moral obligation on the heart of the more successful man. He was supposed to lend to his neighbor. But this was not statute law enforceable in a civil court. God would be the avenger, not the State.

The context of the obligatory loan of Deuteronomy 15, like the zero-interest loan of Exodus 22:25-27, is poverty. There will be poor people in the promised land, Moses warned. Because of this, these special loans are morally mandatory. There must be a year or release, "Save when there shall be no poor among you; for the LORD shall greatly bless thee in the land which the LORD thy God giveth thee for an inheritance to possess it" (Deut. 15:4). Does this mean that these loan provisions would eventually be annulled? No. "For the poor shall never cease out of the land: therefore I command thee, saying, Thou shalt open thine hand wide unto thy brother, to thy poor, and to thy needy, in thy land" (Deut. 15:11). Everything in Deuteronomy 15 speaks of poverty and biblical law's means of overcoming it. *Deuteronomy 15 is not dealing with business loans; it is dealing with charity loans.*

But let the reader be forewarned: biblical law is a broader category than biblical civil law. There was no statute law that imposed sanctions on anyone who refused to make an interest-free loan.

Defining Poverty by Statute

Why was this not a statute law? Because biblical civil law presents only negative injunctions. It prohibits publicly evil acts. Biblical civil law does not authorize the State to make men good. It does not authorize the State to force men to do good things. It does not authorize the creation of a messianic, salvationist State. The State cannot search the hearts of men. God does this, as the Creator and Judge, so the State must not claim such an ability. The State is only authorized by God to impose negative sanctions against publicly evil acts. It is not authorized to seek to force men to do good acts. In short, the Bible is opposed to the modern welfare state.

There is no way for biblical statute law to define what poverty is apart from the opinions of those affected by the law, either as taxpayers, charitable lenders, or recipients of public welfare or private charity. "Poverty" is too subjective a category to be defined by statute law. The State needs to be able to assign legal definitions to crimes, in order that its arbitrary power not be expanded. Yet economic definitions of wealth and poverty that are not arbitrary are simply not available to the civil magistrates for the creation of positive legal injunctions. Thus, God's civil law does not compel a man to make a loan to a poor person.

Nevertheless, the civil law does prohibit taking interest from poor people. How can it do this without creating the conditions of judicial tyranny through arbitrariness? If the magistrates cannot define exactly what poverty is for the purpose of writing positive civil injunctions, how can they define what a charitable loan is? How can the State legitimately prohibit interest from a charity loan if the legislators and judges cannot define poverty with a sufficient degree of accuracy to identify cases where a charity loan is legally obligatory for the potential lender?[7]

The lender decides who is deserving of his loan and who is not. This is his moral choice. God will judge him, not the State. However, once the lender grants this *unique, morally enjoined charity loan*, he may not extract an interest payment. This is a negative injunction — not doing something which is forbidden by law — and therefore it is legitimately enforceable by civil law, as surely as the civil magistrates in ancient Israel were supposed to enforce the release of debt slaves[8] in the seventh (sabbatical) year (Deut. 15:12-15). The requirement to lend to the brother in need under the terms specified in biblical law, being a positive injunction, therefore comes under the self-government provisions of the conscience and the negative sanctions of God. This positive injunction is not under the jurisdiction of the civil courts. On the other hand, the prohibition against interest on these unique loans, being a negative injunction, does come under the enforcement of both civil courts and church courts.

The key to understanding the Bible's civil definition of poverty is the loan's contract. There must be a mutually agreed-upon contract, explicit or implicit, in order to establish a legally enforceable loan. If the borrower comes to the lender and calls upon him to honor Deuteronomy 15:7-8, then the borrower admits that his is a special case, a charity loan, and it is governed by the civil law's terms of the sabbatical year and the prohibition against interest. The borrower makes his request a matter of conscience.

In so doing, he necessarily and inescapably places himself under the terms of biblical civil law. *If he cannot repay his debt on time, he can be legally sold into bondservice.* This is not a collateralized commercial loan. The borrower is so poor that he has no collateral except his land. He chooses not to use his land as collateral. He therefore chooses not to become a landless man, meaning landless until the next jubilee year. Yet he is still in dire need. All he can offer as collateral is his promise, his cloak, and his bodily service until the next sabbatical year should he default. Thus, the borrower admits that he in principle has already become a bondservant. He admits through

---

7. This is the question that S. C. Mooney raises in his attempt to remove any distinction between charity loans and business loans. Mooney, *Usury*, pp. 123-27.

8. A debt slave was a person who had asked his neighbor for a morally mandatory, zero-interest charity loan, and who had then defaulted. He was then placed in bondage until the sabbatical year, or until his debt was paid.

the loan's contractual arrangement that the borrower is servant to the lender. If he cannot repay, he will go into bondservice until the next sabbatical year, or until his debt is repaid, whichever comes first.

How would the civil magistrate in Israel know which kind of loan was in force, commercial or charitable, and therefore whether interest was valid or illegal? By examining the nature of the loan's collateral. If a loan went to an individual who, if he should default on the loan, would be placed in debt slavery, then this was a charitable loan governed by the provisions of Deuteronomy 15. This is why the year of release applied to both kinds of servitude: debt servitude and bodily servitude that arose because of a man's default on a charity loan.

Furthermore, if it was a loan with the individual's cloak as security, then it was also a zero-interest loan. The collateral described in Exodus 22:25-27 insured little more than that the individual was a local resident—he had to come to the lender to get it back each evening—and that the loan was temporary. (It also made multiple indebtedness more difficult.)[9] It would have been a very small loan. This is clearly not a business loan. A business loan would have a different kind of collateral: property that was not crucial to personal survival on a cold night. If the borrower defaulted on a commercial loan, he would forfeit the property specified in the loan contract. He would not forfeit his freedom or his children's freedom. In short, the Old Testament biblical texts governing lending specify that certain kinds of loans would have certain kinds of collateral, and wherever these forms of collateral appeared, the lender could not legally demand an interest payment.

Biblical civil law is exclusively negative law—prohibiting evil public deeds—not positive law, which enjoins the performance of righteous public deeds. An example of this distinction is the enforcement of the tithe: church courts can legitimately require voting members to tithe as a condition of maintaining their voting church membership; the State cannot legitimately require residents to tithe to a church or other organization on threat of civil punishment.

Once the contract is made, the lender is placed under the limits of the civil law. He may not extract interest from the borrower, even a resident alien. But the borrower also is placed under limits: if he defaults, he can be sold into bondservice. Each party is under limits. Each has decided that this is a true poor loan situation. Each

---

9. See below: "Multiple Indebtedness," pp. 738-40.

agrees to a unique set of contractual obligations by entering into this arrangement.

Thus, once the contract was made, either implicitly or explicitly, the State had a legal definition of poverty. If the borrower was legally subject to the possibility of being sold into bondservice for defaulting on the loan, then the lender could not lawfully extract interest from him. On the other hand, if the borrower was unwilling to place his own freedom in jeopardy, then he was unwilling to define himself as a poor man for the sake of the civil law's definition. Thus, he had to pay interest on the loan, *and his obligation to repay the loan extended beyond the sabbatical year.* If he was not under the threat of bondservice, he was not under the protection of the sabbatical year or the zero-interest provisions against usury.

Revising Past Mistakes

No one likes to admit publicly that he was wrong in the past, but honesty requires it. For two decades, I followed R. J. Rushdoony's lead on the question of the sabbatical year of debt release. I taught that no debt should be contracted by the debtor that is longer than seven years (Rushdoony says six years).[10] I adhered to this in my own finances. It has cost me a great deal of money. I sold a rapidly appreciating investment property I wanted to keep because my seven years had run out, and I did not want to pay $45,000 cash to pay off the loan. I have paid off other real estate investment loans in the seventh year. I stayed out of other real estate investments I really should have made. I did my best to honor in practice what I had taught in theory. God holds us responsible for obeying our own interpretations of His law, even when we have misinterpreted the law. This is how we learn to obey. This is also how we show Him that we are serious about being covenantally faithful. But now I realize that I was wrong in my interpretation. I no longer wish to mislead people.

I was forced to rethink my position by S. C. Mooney. Mr. Mooney has written a truly misguided book on usury. He says that interest on all loans is immoral and should be illegal in a Christian society. He also correctly concludes that this law against all forms of interest would have to apply to all rents, something previous critics of interest have been unwilling to say in print. Thus, he concludes,

---

10. R. J. Rushdoony, *The Institutes of Biblical Law* (Nutley, New Jersey: Craig Press, 1973), p. 510.

no Christian can lawfully collect either interest or rent on his investment capital. This is economically preposterous, as well as biblically unwarranted. This was also the official position of the Roman Catholic Church until the sixteenth century, and it collapsed of its own weight.[11] It collapsed because it was not biblical.

Mr. Mooney's book offered a challenge to me. He observed, correctly, that I had previously argued that the interest-free loans of the Bible were (and are) charitable loans. I have always argued that business loans were (and are) loans of a completely different ethical and judicial character, and therefore lenders can legitimately ask for an interest payment. But I had also said that no loan beyond seven years is valid. He quite properly called me to account. If Rushdoony and I appeal to Deuteronomy 15 in order to defend the seven-year (or six-year) maximum on *all* loans, yet Deuteronomy 15 is also the basis of our arguing that morally compulsory *charity* loans — zero-interest loans — are unique, then we are mixing our judicial categories. He asked: "Why do they not hold that only the debts of 'poor' brethren are to be cancelled, and [thus] infer from this that it is lawful for one to continue to exact the debts of the 'rich'? The present writer agrees with their views concerning the remission of debts, particularly as cited above."[12]

When I read that, I instantly changed my views. In the twinkling of an eye, I abandoned my old argument that there must be a seventh-year debt cancellation by civil law.[13] Mooney is correct: either Christians must accept the fact that there is no biblically valid judicial distinction between charity loans and profit-seeking loans, and therefore no biblically legitimate economic distinction, or else we must interpret Deuteronomy 15 exclusively in terms of charity loans. Either all loans are to be zero-interest loans, or else charity loans alone are under the temporal restrictions of the sabbatical year principle. Thus, from this point on, I will argue, to cite Mr. Mooney, that "it is lawful for one to continue to exact the debts of the rich."

---

11. For a very clear summary of the transition in the Church away from the medieval position, see John T. Noonan, "The Amendment of Papal Teaching by Theologians," in Charles E. Curran (ed.), *Contraception: Authority and Dissent* (New York: Herder & Herder, 1969), pp. 41-75.

12. Mooney, *Usury*, p. 131.

13. This was not a paradigm shift, but it surely was a sub-paradigm shift. They can take place very rapidly.

Who Are the Rich?

Who are the "rich," judicially speaking? Those who are not judicially poor. We have seen what constitutes poverty judicially: those who go to the potential lender and 1) remind him of his moral obligation to lend to the deserving poor 2) at zero interest, and 3) offer to go into bondage for as much as seven years to pay off the note if they should default on the loan.

This formula therefore tells us who the rich are, judicially speaking: all those people who are willing to sign a strictly voluntary, interest-bearing debt contract that is collateralized by something other than the threat of placing them in bondservice if they should default on their obligation. If the lender extends them credit on the basis of their signatures, or because they have offered him other collateral, including their real estate, then they are not considered poor people judicially. They come to him on the basis of a business opportunity, not on the basis of his moral obligation to lend them an interest-free loan.

What about the jubilee year? The jubilee law has been completely fulfilled in history by Jesus. This means, as I argue in Chapter 4, that the Old Testament's ten-generation slave system for foreigners has been legally abolished. It also means that the land tenure laws of ancient Israel are legally abolished. There is no longer any legal obligation to return a piece of rural property to the original owner or his heirs. *Thus, a debtor can legitimately collateralize a loan with his property.* If he defaults on the loan, he loses his property unless he buys it back later on. (While this revision of my views will not please Mr. Mooney, I hope it will satisfy Greg Bahnsen, who once wrote that he did not agree with "Gary North's view of home mortgages."[14])

This is not to say that the debtor should do this. It is a great embarrassment to a man if he loses ownership of his family's property — his home — even in an urban society. If he is evicted from his home, he loses face. It is best if a man can own his home debt-free. He then does not face the threat of eviction and the embarrassment associated with eviction. But it is his legal right biblically to sign a debt contract to buy or refinance a home.[15]

---

14. Greg L. Bahnsen, *Theonomy in Christian Ethics* (2nd ed.; Phillipsburg, New Jersey: Presbyterian & Reformed, 1984), p. xix.

15. This does not mean that the State should subsidize this practice, as the U.S. government does, by offering deductions from total income, for income tax reporting purposes, for interest paid on mortgages. It also does not mean that the govern-

A Millennium of Misinterpretation

Medieval Roman Catholics and early modern Protestants misinterpreted these verses. They interpreted them as if they were prohibitions against all forms of interest, rather than prohibitions against interest earned from charitable loans to fellow believers, as the Exodus 22 text explicitly says: "If thou lend money to any of *my people that is [are] poor.* . . ." The church's hostile view of interest had its origin in the teaching of Aristotle. Aristotle's economic analysis, rather than the explicit teaching of the biblical texts, always was the unstated intellectual foundation of the church's prohibition on interest-bearing business loans.

Aristotle taught that money is sterile — that it cannot increase by moving from person to person over time — and therefore undeserving of any return beyond the principal. Economist Joseph Schumpeter writes of Aristotle: "He condemned interest — which he equated to 'usury' in all cases — on the ground that there was no justification for money, a mere medium of exchange, to increase in going from hand to hand (which of course it does not do). But he never asked the question why interest was being paid all the same. This question was first asked by the scholastic doctors. It is to them that the credit belongs of having been the first both to collect facts about interest and to develop the outlines of a theory of it. Aristotle himself had no theory of interest."[16] Neither did the early church.

From the beginning, the West's view of interest was clouded by the association of interest rates and physical production. They are not linked in economic theory. It was also clouded by the association of interest with money. Furthermore, the Greeks were hostile to the

---

ment should create (or promise) deposit insurance for those who put their money in savings institutions, with the legal right of immediate withdrawal, when the institutions then use this money to lend on 30-year mortgages. The length of the loan must be the same for both lender and debtor. The institutions must not be allowed by civil law to "borrow short" and "lend long." President-elect George Bush in January of 1989 faced the bankruptcy of some 500 savings and loan companies and also the bankruptcy of the Federal Savings & Loan Insurance Corporation (FSLIC), a non-government or quasi-government insurance scheme, established in 1934, which had failed. It was expected that the government would have to bail out the FSLIC by granting it cash or credits of between $50 billion to $100 billion. By August, the bill had soared to $166 billion. The crisis is still not over. Bad economics eventually produces bad results.

16. Joseph A. Schumpeter, *History of Economic Analysis* (New York: Oxford University Press, 1954), p. 65.

idea of long-term progress.[17] They believed that time does not bring economic growth to society as a whole. This view was basic to all Greek thought. This pessimism about the economy dominated Western social thought until the Protestant Reformation. In this sense, the Greeks were not future-oriented, and Aristotle's analysis of money was clouded by this view of time. Only with the Reformation, and especially the Calvinist branches, did men begin to abandon this pessimistic view of the earthly future, and also begin to abandon medieval interest theory.

We need to recognize that early medieval theologians were unaware of Aristotle's specific arguments; copies of his manuscripts were not available until the eleventh century.[18] Later, Aquinas did follow Aristotle in condemning interest.[19] On the other hand, some of the late-medieval scholastic theologians broke with Aristotle on this point.[20] With or without Aristotle, however, the Roman Church remained officially hostile to usury throughout the medieval period. We still find a few isolated Roman Catholic theologians who try to defend the view of those medieval Scholastic theologians who opposed all interest as usury.[21] Sadly, we occasionally find Protestant non-theologians and non-economists who say the same thing.[22]

Not Interest as Such

There has been a great deal of confusion over the years regarding the "true meaning" of the English word *usury*, and how usury relates

---

17. On this point, I have always been in opposition to the opinion to the contrary of my teacher Robert Nisbet. See Nisbet, *Social Change and History: Aspects of the Western Theory of Development* (New York: Oxford University Press, 1969), ch. 1; *History of the Idea of Progress* (New York: Basic Books, 1980), ch. 1. I wrote "The Metaphor of Growth" for him in 1967 or thereabouts as a rebuttal to his position: Gary North, *Moses and Pharaoh: Dominion Religion vs. Power Religion* (Tyler, Texas: Institute for Christian Economics, 1985), ch. 17.

18. John T. Noonan, *The Scholastic Analysis of Usury* (Cambridge, Massachusetts: Harvard University Press, 1957), p. 12.

19. Mr. Mooney recommends both Aristotle and Aquinas in this regard: Mooney, *Usury*, pp. 43-45.

20. Alejandro A. Chafuen, *Christians for Freedom: Late-Scholastic Economics* (San Francisco: Ignatius, 1986), ch. 7.

21. Patrick Cleary, *The Church and Usury: An Essay on Some Historical and Theological Aspects of Money Lending* (Hawthorne, California: Christian Book Club of America, [1914] 1972). This publishing house is closely related to Omni Books, a Social Credit-oriented publishing house. They are the primary publishers in the United States of "greenback" or "populist" tracts.

22. Mooney is a good example. See Appendix F: "Lots of Free Time: The Existentialist Utopia of S. C. Mooney."

to *interest*, and how both words relate to the Bible. It is common for those without training in either economic theory or biblical studies to go rummaging around in 200-year-old English dictionaries in search of the "true meaning" of usury and interest. They have the illusion that what "Webster says" — any Webster — is somehow authoritative in economics or biblical studies. They may even pick up a Bible dictionary or two. Anyone who has looked up a word in the *Oxford English Dictionary* knows that there may be dozens of uses of the word. For example, look up "fix" or "set." The same is true of any other dictionary, including a Hebrew or Greek dictionary. Usage varies.

The Bible expositor must look at the uses of words in the actual texts, sorting out how the words and the meanings they convey can be conformed to each other. It is long, hard work. This commentary is a good example of what the expositor must do. It is surely not accomplished in a short paragraph in a Bible dictionary. Why, then, do otherwise literate people think that a Bible dictionary — perhaps one written a century ago — is the last word on the meaning of a hotly disputed word? I think it is because they never took a graduate school course in anything. When the college student gets beyond the textbook level of learning, he finds out how difficult words and meanings are in texts as recent as half a century ago — or in specialized disciplines with extensive jargons, the day before yesterday.

Where do the writers of textbooks and dictionaries go in search of meanings? To fat, academic studies such as this one. They have no time to research the meaning of every word. They rely on specialists. It is strange, then, to find that critics of a book like this will offer as supposedly serious evidence against it the fact that several dictionaries do not agree with the specialist's findings.

A common error historically has been the idea that usury in the Bible means high (undefined) interest, but not interest as such. Such an interpretation first appeared in the Christian era, and is not supported by any Hebrew text.[23] This definition of biblical usury obviously cannot be reconciled with Deuteronomy 23:19, which prohibits any interest return whatsoever: "Thou shalt not lend upon usury to thy brother; usury of money, usury of victuals [food, or "vittles"], usury of any thing that is lent upon usury." The question of the rate of interest is irrelevant; any charge above zero is prohibited.

---

23. Walter C. Kaiser, Jr., *Toward Old Testament Ethics* (Grand Rapids, Michigan: Zondervan Academie, 1983), p. 215.

The question then must be raised: Does this prohibition apply to every type of loan? The biblical answer is no. The Bible does indeed prohibit any increase from *charitable* loans to the *impoverished* neighbor or brother, if he is willing to live in terms of the *biblical civil covenant*, and if he is not in poverty because of laziness or rebellion. It is not the moral obligation of the Christian to subsidize laziness or evil. The impoverished person must be part of the *deserving poor.* All four of these qualifications must be present in order to qualify someone as a candidate for a morally mandatory, interest-free loan. Deuteronomy 23:19-20 does not mention poverty. The other texts do, including Ezekiel 18, which warns against a son who "Hath oppressed the poor and needy, hath spoiled by violence, hath not restored the pledge, and hath lifted up his eyes to the idols, hath committed abomination, Hath given forth upon usury, and hath taken increase: shall he then live? he shall not live: he hath done all these abominations; he shall surely die; his blood shall be upon him" (Ezek. 18:12-13). The specific texts that detail the limiting conditions should be used to interpret Deuteronomy 23:19-20.[24]

The Bible allows other types of interest payments. First, it does not prohibit interest payments on business loans, as Jesus' parable of the talents indicates (Matt. 25:27). Second, the Old Testament specifically exempted the foreigner from the protection of the prohibition against interest. It was legal to charge him interest (Deut. 23:20). Thus, any attempt to argue that the Bible always prohibits interest payments is untenable.

Positive Injunctions

Any attempt to argue that the very nature of interest payments is illegitimate because they involve demanding "something for nothing," and therefore necessarily involve cheating, is inescapably an attempt to deny the universalism of the ethics of the Bible. The Bible specifies that certain kinds of *positive charity* are appropriate for believers in certain circumstances, but are not required in our dealings with unbelievers in the same circumstances. On the other hand,

---

24. Those who would place a universal ban on all interest-bearing loans interpret all Old Testament verses regarding usury in terms of the general, unqualified prohibition of Deuteronomy 23:19-20. They also are forced to deny the plain teaching of Jesus' parable of the talents in Luke 19:23: "Wherefore then gavest not thou my money into the bank, that at my coming I might have required mine own with usury?" See below: "Interest-Seeking Loans," pp. 744-46.

the Bible never allows the *judicial oppression* of anyone; all people under the jurisdiction of a God-covenanted civil society are entitled to equal protection of the law. "One law shall be to him that is home-born, and unto the stranger that sojourneth among you" (Ex. 12:49).[25]

Thus, if interest payments truly involved collecting something for no service received in return, then interest payments for every kind of loan would fall under the general biblical prohibitions against fraud and theft. Why would interest be allowed from loans to foreigners if interest involves taking something for nothing? Why would people be so foolish as to pay something for nothing, millennium after millennium? Interest does not involve collecting something for nothing, as we shall soon see.

Interest: Time, Risk, and Price Inflation

The prohibition against interest payments for charitable loans was not limited to money loans; "usury of anything that was lent" was prohibited (Deut. 23:19b). By refusing to make any distinction between money loans and loans "in kind" (goods or services), the Bible avoids a very serious analytical error. The Bible announces clearly that *the phenomenon of interest is not confined to money loans*. Had the church fathers understood the implications of this from the beginning, perhaps the church would have avoided over a millennium of error, 300 to 1550.

Confusion over the two forms of loans — money loans and loans in kind — for centuries kept incipient economists and other intelligent observers from coming to grips with the phenomenon of *interest as a universal aspect of human action*. Only with the writings of Eugen von Böhm-Bawerk in the late nineteenth century, and the writings of Ludwig von Mises and Frank Fetter in the early twentieth century, did modern economists at last unravel this aspect of interest. These economists classified interest payments under the general economic phenomenon of *time-preference*.[26] Time-preference is an inherent

---

25. North, *Moses and Pharaoh*, ch. 14: "The Rule of Law."

26. Eugen von Böhm-Bawerk, *History and Critique of Interest Theories*, vol. 1 of *Capital and Interest*, 3 vols. (South Holland, Illinois: Libertarian Press, [1921 ed.] 1959); available from Libertarian Press, Spring Mills, Pennsylvania; Frank A. Fetter, *Capital, Interest, and Rent: Essays in the Theory of Distribution*, edited by Murray N. Rothbard (Kansas City, Kansas: Sheed Andrews and McMeel, 1977); Ludwig von Mises, *The Theory of Money and Credit* (Indianapolis, Indiana: Liberty Classics, [1912] 1981); Mises, *Human Action: A Treatise on Economics* (3rd ed.; Chicago: Regnery, 1966), ch. 19; Murray N. Rothbard, *Man, Economy, and State* (New York: New York University Press, [1962] 1979), chaps. 5-7.

aspect of human action; it is therefore inescapable. This explanation denies the Aristotelian idea that the phenomenon of interest is solely a function of money.

The prevailing market rate of interest is a component of three factors, modern economics informs us: 1) time-preference, or the originary rate of interest (as Mises calls it); 2) a risk premium; and 3) the inflation premium. Few economic textbooks ever explain this, and no proponents of zero-interest free market loans ever discuss it.

1. Time-Preference

The originary interest rate, or time-preference factor, is the least understood and yet the most fundamental aspect of the phenomenon of the market rate of interest.[27] Other things remaining equal, a given quantity and quality of *future* goods is worth less in the free market (and in people's minds) than the same basket of goods today. This is not because, in the words of an old proverb, "a bird in hand is worth two in the bush." I am *not* speaking here about *comparative risks* of obtaining ownership, "in hand" vs. "in the bush," meaning present vs. future. I will discuss the risk factor later on. I am speaking here about interest as *a fundamental category of human action*.

We live in a universe that is structured by the category of *time*. We necessarily live and act in the present. We cannot escape the constraints of time. We prefer satisfaction now. A brand-new automobile (or anything else) is more valuable to me right now than the delivery of an identical car a year from now (other things — public tastes, market value, gasoline prices, etc. — being equal). I act in the present. I choose to do in a *sequence of events* those things that I am capable of doing with whatever assets I possess. I plan for the future, but I am not immediately responsible for the future, for I have no control over it. I am responsible only in the present. Thus, what happens in the present is more relevant for me than what I expect in the earthly future, since I must live in the present in order to get to the future. I am responsible in the here and now, not in the there and then.

Let us consider all this in more general terms. Biblically speaking, an individual is responsible to God in the present. He cannot escape this covenantal responsibility. As a person created in God's image, he must place higher value on action in the present than action in the future. He is not yet responsible for what he will do in the

---

27. Mises, *Human Action*, ch. 19.

future. Thus, an individual does those things first that he rates as most important in a calculated sequence of events. He places higher value on present goods and services than on future goods and services because he has a proposed plan of action: first, second, third, etc. in a plan of sequential events. He does not control future goods; he controls only present goods. He must act in the present. Thus, *the goods that he owns in the present are worth more to him than those same physical goods in the expected future.* There is a premium for present goods over identical future goods in the world of human action because of the time-constrained nature of covenantal responsibility before God. "Take therefore no thought for the morrow: for the morrow shall take thought for the things of itself. Sufficient unto the day is the evil thereof" (Matt. 6:34). Also sufficient unto the day are the pleasures thereof.

A lender will require an interest return on a loan in order to compensate him for the loss of his use of his present goods. The borrower should not expect to get something for nothing. Critics of interest claim that the lender gets something for nothing. On the contrary, if there is no interest return on the loan, *the borrower gets something for nothing.*[28] The borrower is offering the lender nothing for something when he asks the lender to transfer to him something worth more (a presently owned good, e.g., money) in exchange for something worth less (that same or a comparable good in the future). The rate of interest expresses the difference in present market value between *present goods* and physically identical *future goods.* It does not matter whether a loan is made in the form of money or any other commodity; the same discount on the market price of future goods exists for all commodities.

The more *future-oriented* the lender is — the more he values the future in relation to the present — the lower the rate of interest he will require in order to persuade him to make the loan. This is why future-oriented cultures experience greater economic growth per capita than present-oriented cultures. It is easier to obtain capital loans in such societies, meaning that at any given rate of interest, more loans are available. This is another aspect of consumer sover-

---

28. Obviously, I am assuming here that market competition has eliminated differences in the retail price of the goods. Some sellers will offer goods or services on the basis that the buyer does not have to pay any interest on the loan for a month, three months, or whatever. The economically literate buyer knows better. There is a concealed interest rate in the selling price.

eignty. If consumers in one society value future wealth more highly
than consumers in another society do, both groups "buy" the future
they prefer. How? The former save more (defer consumption) at any
given rate of interest than the latter do.

Consider the case of two societies, each possessing capital equipment and land of equal value. If consumers in Civilization A place
higher value on future goods (low time-preference) than the people
of Civilization B place on future goods (high time-preference), it
therefore means that Civilization A places lower value on present
goods than Civilization B does. If people in both societies plan production equally accurately — if their respective entrepreneurs and laborers are equally skilled — then the consumers in Civilization A who
prefer future goods will get what they want: higher future income.
They must pay for that higher future income by foregoing present
income. They save more. They allocate more present goods for increased future consumption than citizens of Civilization B do.
Citizens of Civilization B also get what they want: higher present income than the future-oriented citizens Civilization A enjoy, but
lower future income. They save less. The free market interest rate is
the economic indicator that reflects and guides the respective concerns of consumers, present goods vs. future goods.

If there were no market rate of interest, it would be impossible
for anyone to make rational economic plans. It would be irrational
to expect anyone to be able to plan rationally if all prices were compelled by law to be the same. It would be equally irrational to expect
anyone to be able to plan rationally if the price of future goods were
compelled by law to be the same as the price of present goods.
Future goods are less valuable than present goods. Passing a law
does not make them of equal value.[29]

What is really being said by those who pass "usury laws" is that
capital is free of charge. ("Capital" = land + labor over time.) Thus,
when capital's rental price is lowered below the market rate — or
worse, to zero — the supply of this supposedly free good dries up.

What must be understood clearly at this point is that *interest is not
the "product" of capital*. Interest does not originate with the productivity
of capital. Economic *rent* is the stream of income which is produced
by a capital asset. The interest rate (people's time-preference) is ap-

---

29. The only reason the Bible's law against interest can be expected to function is
to admit that such loans are charitable loans. Such a moral (though not civil) law requires the lender to give the borrower something for nothing.

plied to the future value of this expected stream of income. A better way to put this is to say that the prevailing rate of interest *discounts* the future expected value of this expected stream of income.[30]

Similarly, *interest is not the "product" of a loan.* It is simply the discount applied to the future stream of income called repayment. Interest arises from the present-orientation of human beings as creatures of the present; it is applied to the future as a discount. Economist Murray Rothbard writes: *"The time market is therefore not restricted to the loan market. It permeates the entire production structure of the complex economy."*[31] It is such a simple concept, yet it took so long for anyone to figure it out. Not many people understand it even today.

2. Risk Premium

The market rate of interest also contains a risk premium. The risk that a particular borrower will not repay his loan must be shared among all borrowers within any particular class of borrowers — class in this case referring to a statistical grouping of borrowers according to lending risks. General Motors will pay a lower rate of interest to borrow money than a buyer of a used General Motors car will have to pay. A nation of people who believe that the wicked borrow and do not repay (Ps. 37:21), and who believe that God judges the wicked, will experience lower rates of interest than a nation of "devil-may-care, but God doesn't" borrowers.

If the national government is trusted by the public, then its debt will be able to be sold at the lowest rate of interest. Major corporations will enjoy the privilege of paying rates slightly higher than the national government. At the bottom of the pile are those who are least credit-worthy. They will be able to get only small loans from pawn shops that demand collateral (highly discounted, in case the lender defaults), or, worst of all, from "loan sharks" who charge very high rates, and who are willing to accept this risk of default only because they are also willing to impose physical violence on those who refuse to pay on time. They do not "re-schedule" loans without re-arranging faces.[32]

---

30. Fetter, *Capital, Interest, and Rent*, pp. 192-221: "The Relations between Rent and Interest."

31. Rothbard, *Man, Economy, and State*, p. 322.

32. There are many New York bankers in three-piece, blue pin-striped suits who wish they could impose similar penalties on Third World nations that demand to have their loans rescheduled.

3. Price Inflation Premium

The inflation premium becomes an increasingly important factor in the market rate of interest in a society which permits or encourages monetary debasement, including fractional reserve banking. Loans will contain an inflation premium component — interest rates higher than the mere originary rate, or "present goods vs. future goods" component. The lender of money will lose if money of less purchasing power is returned to him. Inflation raises long-term interest rates.[33]

One way around price inflation is to make loans in kind. The lender loans gold coins, for example, and demands repayment of both principal and interest in gold coins. Or perhaps the loan is made in a comparatively stable foreign currency. The loan's price inflation premium then disappears.

Summary

The reason why interest rates never fall to zero is that a lender does not need to transfer an asset to anyone else merely to have that same asset returned to him in the future. He can hold onto the asset and achieve the same economic return in the future. Meanwhile, he has the asset ready for immediate use, should a profitable opportunity arise. Therefore, should someone voluntarily lend any asset at a zero rate of interest, it is because the person is making a *charitable loan*, or else he is buying safer storage for the asset. In the latter case, he is then paying an *implicit fee for storage*: the interest that he is forfeiting that the borrower will receive by re-lending the asset, or the immediate access to the asset that he is forfeiting. A negative interest rate, should it ever appear on a voluntary market, is clearly evidence of a storage fee.

People do not voluntarily give up something for nothing unless they are confused about the details of the transaction.[34] Thus, all talk about a zero rate of interest in a time-bound, risk-bound, free market world is nonsense.[35] In an attempt to achieve such a world, the civil government would have to prohibit all profit-seeking lend-

---

33. Monetary inflation can temporarily lower short-term interest rates: Mises, *Human Action*, ch. 20.

34. In the case of making a zero-interest charitable loan, the lender is honoring God. He is thereby building up treasures in heaven (Matt. 6:20), to be received in the future (I Cor. 3:12-14).

35. Rothbard, *Man, Economy, and State*, p. 326.

ing and borrowing, including mortgages; but that would not be a world of voluntary exchange. It would also be a world of barbarism: the destruction of all capital by consumption.[36]

Inescapable Interest

The phenomenon of interest is inescapable in any economy. It is not something "extracted" from borrowers by lenders. It is inherent in the very way we all think about the future, whether as borrowers or lenders. We are creatures. We are always *time-constrained*. We live in the present. Those items which we presently possess are of greater use to us — and therefore of greater economic value to us — right now than the prospect of using those same physical items in the future. We are covenantally responsible *now* for the use of whatever we presently own or control. We therefore *discount future value* as against present value. It is this present market discount of future value, above all, which is the reason why there is an interest phenomenon in economics.

Any attempt to legislate away the inescapable effects of the rate of interest (discount for time-preference) should be seen as a doomed attempt to escape both time and creaturehood. To put it as bluntly as possible, anyone who argues that an economy can operate apart from the effects of the time-preference factor has adopted the *economic equivalent of the perpetual motion machine*. Both arguments — perpetual motion physics and zero interest economics — rely on men's obtaining "something for nothing."

In fact, anyone who would recommend civil legislation against all interest payments is far more dangerous than a person who would argue for legislation prohibiting all machines except perpetual motion machines. The second person is instantly recognized as a crackpot whose proposed legislation would destroy civilization, assuming that the civil government would seriously attempt to enforce it. The anti-usurer isn't as readily recognized as a dangerous crackpot, even though his recommendation, if seriously enforced by civil law, would be equally a threat to the survival of civilization. Both forms of legislation, if enforced, would decapitalize society. The crackpot amateur physicist, however, cannot do what the crackpot amateur economist can do and has done in the past: present himself as a defender of "love" in social theory, a protector of society's "bank-oppressed" little people, and a person who has found a long-neglected way to elimi-

---

36. *Ibid.*, pp. 341-42, 385-86.

nate from this world a group of corrupt money middlemen and their
extortionate ways, thereby making everyone else a little bit richer.
Even worse, the anti-interest destroyer of nations who would ruin
society by making illegal all interest payments can easily present his
case in the name of the Bible. The nut (or outright occultist) who
would prohibit by civil law all non-perpetual motion machines cannot easily appeal to any body of literature in the history of moral
thought. Nevertheless, both types of self-professed reformers—the
perpetual motion "physicist" and the zero-interest "economist"—are
ultimately appealing to the occult or to magic, but the anti-usurer's
appeal is not recognized as such, even by many Christians. Usury
laws are the destroyer of nations.

Let's Make a Deal

To make my point clear—that interest is inescapable—let us
assume that you are a potential buyer of my piece of property, a gold
mine. I persuade you that you can earn one ounce of gold per year
net profit from this land, after all expenses are paid, simply by paying
someone to dig the gold ore and selling it to a refiner. Furthermore,
we both agree (and all other potential buyers agree) that the mine
will probably be able to produce this profit for a thousand years,
with the first ounce coming in one year. Then I ask you to pay me
one thousand ounces of gold, cash, for the mine.

You, of course, protest. It is not worth a thousand ounces, cash. I
counter by showing you that you have already agreed that the land
will produce a thousand ounces of gold, so why shouldn't I be entitled to a thousand ounces? We all agree: equal for equal, right?
Where is my argument incorrect?

The error has to do with the value to you *today* of those *future*
ounces of gold. I am asking you to give me gold, ounce for ounce, in
advance. But what is the gold mine's thousandth ounce, delivered a
thousand and one years from now, really worth to you? Will you
give up your thousandth ounce of gold today (and all that it will buy)
for that thousandth ounce in the distant future for some unnamed
heir of yours? I doubt it. Why won't you? *Because you apply a cash discount to that future stream of income.* An ounce of gold a thousand and
one years down the road isn't worth as much to you today as your
thousandth ounce is worth to you today. You will not be here to enjoy that future thousandth ounce; you can enjoy whatever your presently owned thousandth ounce will buy today.

Now, think about this process of discounting for cash. We call this process *capitalization*. Let us assume that you own an ounce of gold today. An ounce of gold fifty years from now, or twenty years from now, is not worth your ounce of gold today. A future ounce of gold, whether scheduled to be received a year from now or a thousand and one years from now, is discounted in your mind. We have therefore discovered a law of human action (which applies in economics): *the present cash market value of expected future goods is always discounted compared with the present cash market value of the identical physical goods.*

What is this discount called? It is called the *rate of interest*. You discount the future value to you of any good compared to what that same good is worth to you immediately, whether it is that automobile or an ounce of gold from that piece of property. For me to get you to hand over the present good today (money), I have to promise to return it to you in the future, plus extra money or other benefit. In other words, I have to pay you *interest*.

Let us consider another example. You win a brand new Rolls-Royce automobile. These cars do not change in styling very often. They actually look more like a 1953 Packard than like a new car. But they are status symbols. Assume that all taxes are paid by the prize-granter. You are now offered a choice: delivery of the car today or in a year. The style probably will not change (low risk factor). Tastes of the very rich public for Rolls-Royces probably will not change. The car will be taken care of, you are assured. Make your choice: the car now or the car in a year. The choice is obvious. Why is it obvious? Because of interest, meaning time-preference. "Better now than later!"

Why do some people seriously believe that your preference here is pathological, the product of your morally diseased mind? Because they are utopians.

Utopianism: A World Without Scarcity

It would be nice if I did not have to mention any of the following crackpot theories of economics. The reason why this task is unavoidable is that these ideas have spread far and wide in Christian circles. Christian economics has been an ignored topic for centuries. What has passed for Christian economics in the past has either been baptized moralism or baptized humanism. Numerous crackpot schemes have been promoted in the name of Christian economics, and still are being promoted. The closer we get to the question of monetary policy and interest, the more likely we are to discover pamphlets claiming to be Christian.[37]

Anyone who seriously discusses the possibility of judicially compulsory zero-interest loans in a "free" or "wise" economy is a monetary crank, a person with no formal training in economics or social theory, and a person dangerously devoid of understanding regarding the human condition. You know for sure that you are listening to an economic amateur when you hear someone seriously propose the possibility of an economy without any legal debt, meaning an economy without legally enforceable contracts to deliver goods or services in the present in exchange for a greater quantity of goods or services in the future. This would be an economy run exclusively in terms of zero-interest business loans.

There has never been such a phenomenon as a zero-interest business loan. There never will be. Why not? Because *time is not a zero-price resource*.

There have been a lot of these "anti-usury" amateur economists on the fringes of the American conservative movement ever since the days of the "greenback" movement and the politically radical Populist movement of the late nineteenth century. These views on debt were associated with calls for inflation and the free coinage of silver.[38] Radical conservatives and radical leftists have cooperated for over a century in these Populist-type movements.[39] The Technocracy movement and the Social Credit movement are contemporary examples.[40] Both groups gained their prominence during the economic confusion of the 1930's.[41] Defenders of such views on interest-free debt

---

37. See Appendix F: "Lots of Free Time: The Existentialist Utopia of S. C. Mooney."

38. Allen Weinstein, *Prelude to Populism: Origins of the Silver Issue, 1867-1878* (New Haven, Connecticut: Yale University Press, 1970); Willis A. Carto (ed.), *Profiles in Populism* (Old Greenwich, Connecticut: Flag Press, 1982). See the three-volume reprint of *"Money": A Monthly Magazine* (New York: Money Pub. Co., 1897-1900).

39. The most obvious example of a liberal promoter of such views is Jerry Voorhis, the California Democrat who lost his seat in Congress in 1946 to a young Richard Nixon. He later became associated with the co-operative movement. See his books, *Out of Debt — Out of Danger* (New York: Devin-Adair, 1943), published by a conservative publisher, and *Beyond Victory* (New York: Farrar & Rinehart, 1944).

40. The Social Credit movement of Canada (especially in the province of British Columbia) no longer takes seriously the monetary theories of the founder of Social Credit, Major Douglas. The Party may sell Major Douglas' books or pamphlets based on them, such as Maurice Colbourne's *The Meaning of Social Credit* (Edmondton, Alberta: Social Credit Board, 1933). But once in office, Social Credit politicians never mention Social Credit monetary theory.

41. Frank Arkright, *The ABC of Technocracy* (New York: Harper & Bros., 1933); E. S. Holter, *The ABC of Social Credit* (New York: Coward-McCann, 1934).

are also to be found in certain Christian circles.[42] Very traditional Roman Catholics have promoted such ideas, most notably the notorious anti-Semitic radio priest of the 1930's, Rev. Charles Coughlin.[43] Today, the "British Israel" or "Identity" movement is filled with tract-writers who offer such monetary theories, all claiming that their views are Bible-based.[44] Two of the monetary crank paperback books in my library are written by dentists and physicians.[45] Another was written by a Nobel Prize-winning chemist, Frederick Soddy.[46] Few, if any, of these books have been written by a trained economist.[47] All of them display bad typography, and many of them reprint 1930's-style (or earlier) political cartoons. (Occasionally, they are printed from computer print-outs.)[48] There is a peculiar combined scent of forgotten used books and fresh mimeograph ink that emanates from the American and Australian Social Credit movement.[49]

---

42. Cf. George F. MacLeod, *Money: A Christian View* (Glasgow: William Mac-lellan, 1963). In Australia, the Social Credit movement is heavily dependent on support by Christians. Cf. Eric D. Butler, *Social Credit and Christian Philosophy* (Melbourne: New Times Limited, 1956). The Australian movement, never having achieved any political influence, still takes Major Douglas seriously.

43. Rev. Charles E. Coughlin, *The New Deal in Money* (Royal Oak, Michigan: Radio League of the Little Flower, 1933); *Money! Questions and Answers* (Royal Oak, Michigan: National Union for Social Justice, 1936). On his national influence, see Sheldon Marcus, *Father Coughlin: The Tumultuous Life of the Priest of the Little Flower* (Boston: Little, Brown, 1973). Another Catholic priest whose books have promoted these monetary theories is Rev. Denis Fahey. Cf. Fahey, *Money Manipulation and Social Order* (Dublin: Browne and Nolan, 1944).

44. J. Taylor Peddie, *The Economic Mechanism of Scripture: The Cure for the World Crises* (London: Williams & Norgate, 1934); C. F. Parker, *Moses the Economist* (London: Covenant Pub. Co., 1947); C. O. Stadsklev, *New Money for the New Age* (Hopkins, Minnesota: Gospel Temple, 1968).

45. Cf. Edward Popp, D.D.S., *Money — Bona Fide or Non-Bona Fide* (Port Washington, Wisconsin: Wisconsin Educational Fund, 1970); Charles Norburn, M.D., *Honest Money* (Asheville, North Carolina: New Puritan Library, 1983).

46. Frederick Soddy, *Wealth, Virtual Wealth and Debt: The Solution of the Economic Paradox* (3rd ed.; Hawthorne, California: Omni, 1961).

47. A pamphlet by Georges-Henri Levesque, O.P., *Social Credit and Catholicism* (Hawthorne, California: Omni, [1936]), seems to be an exception. He taught economics at Laval and Montreal Universities, the pamphlet says. He was a graduate of the School of Social and Political Sciences, Lille, France. To say that he was not a well-known figure is putting it mildly.

48. Richard Kelly Hoskins, *War Cycles — Peace Cycles* (Lynchburg, Virginia: Virginia Group, 1985).

49. For a critique of these doctrines, see Gary North, *An Introduction to Christian Economics* (Nutley, New Jersey: Craig Press, 1973), ch. 11: "Gertrude Coogan and the Myth of Social Credit."

The Crackpot Economics of J. M. Keynes

I have said that no trained economist has taught such doctrines. There is one glaring exception, which may not be an exception after all: John Maynard Keynes. Mr. Keynes actually earned only a bachelor's degree in mathematics. He never took a graduate degree in economics or any other subject. His father, Cambridge University economist John Neville Keynes, got him a job teaching economics at Cambridge. From that privileged pulpit, he began to make his international reputation.

Mr. Keynes taught that "Interest to-day rewards no genuine sacrifice, any more than does the rent of land. The owner of capital can obtain interest because capital is scarce, just as the owner of land can obtain rent because land is scarce. But whilst there may be intrinsic reasons for the scarcity of land, there are no intrinsic reasons for the scarcity of capital."[50] His liberal followers do not want to admit that he believed such nonsense, and the right-wing monetary cranks who do believe it do not want to be associated with him or his ideas. Nevertheless, he is one of theirs, meaning both ideological groups.

Keynes promoted the theories of Silvio Gesell, a true monetary crank and socialist, whom he referred to as "the strange, unduly neglected prophet."[51] He spent several pages of the *General Theory* praising Gesell. Referring to the preface of Gesell's *Natural Economic Order* (1916), Keynes said that "The answer to Marxism is, I think, to be found along the lines of this preface."[52] He went on: "He argues that the growth of real capital is held back by the money-rate of interest, and that if this brake were removed the growth of real capital would be, in the modern world, so rapid that a zero money-rate of interest would probably be justified, not indeed forthwith, but within a comparatively short period of time."[53] But can the money rate of interest be reduced to zero? Of course, Keynes said.

Keynes praised Gesell's plan[54] for the government to issue paper money with a date stamped on it; to keep the money legal, the users would have to get their money re-stamped each month. There would be a stamping tax on the money. Keynes highly recommended this

---

50. John Maynard Keynes, *The General Theory of Employment, Interest, and Money* (New York: Macmillan, 1936), p. 376.

51. *Ibid.*, p. 353.

52. *Ibid.*, p. 355.

53. *Ibid.*, p. 357.

54. And also Irving Fisher's, another prominent academic proponent of government-produced fiat money.

scheme. "According to my theory it [the stamping tax] should be roughly equal to the excess of the money-rate of interest (apart from the stamps) over the marginal efficiency of capital corresponding to a rate of new investment compatible with full employment."[55] But Keynes also taught that the marginal efficiency of capital could fall to zero "within a single generation. . . ."[56] In fact, he said that it would be "comparatively easy to make capital-goods so abundant that the marginal efficiency of capital is zero. . . ."[57] Thus, when the marginal efficiency of capital falls to zero, then there will be no economic reason for the rate of interest not to do the same. Just tax interest and rents out of existence! In short, under his system of economics, "the rentier would disappear. . . ."[58]

This is so clearly an example of crackpot economic utopianism that his respectable academic disciples have spent two generations either ignoring it or explaining it away as really meaning something else. But he meant what he said. One reason why the *General Theory* is so incoherent, in sharp contrast to his earlier economic writings, is that it is an attempted defense of a program to produce the impossible: a world without scarcity, a world where capital is free for the asking, a world without interest.

It is not surprising, therefore, to find that Keynes was also a promoter of the basic monetary theory and policy of Social Credit. Social Credit economics teaches that the government should create fiat money to match the aggregate economic growth of the nation. This, we are told, will keep effective demand high enough to promote full employment. This is what Keynes taught, too: "There will be a determinate amount of increase in the quantity of effective demand which, after taking everything into account, will correspond to, and be in equilibrium with, the increase in the quantity of money."[59] Keynes was unquestionably a monetary crank.

I agree with Sir Eric Roll, at least on this one point: the growth of such utopian ideas represented a reaction to the Great Depression of the 1930's, and it also represented a decline in the influence of rational economic reasoning. "In particular, the social and political roots of the monetary doctrines of Major Douglas, of the mystical

---

55. *Idem.*
56. *Ibid.*, p. 220.
57. *Ibid.*, p. 221.
58. *Idem.*
59. *Ibid.*, p. 299.

views on wealth and debt of Professor Soddy, of the 'free land' and 'free money' agitation of Silvio Gesell, would form an interesting subject of analysis. What needs, however, to be pointed out is that the keen discussion which those views evoked and the many adherents which they could claim, particularly in the years immediately after the Great Depression, were both a symptom and an aggravating cause of the decline of relevance and of authority of economic theory."[60] I regret only that Professor Roll did not have the academic courage to list Keynes in this menagerie of cranks.

Capitalization: Human vs. Non-Human

I fully acknowledge that men, in their quest for autonomy from God, are willing to become slaves of sin, and therefore in principle to become slaves of other men. I recognize the accuracy of the New Testament principle that it is best to owe no man anything (Rom. 13:8a). I also recognize that modern economics has promoted the ideal of perpetual debt for perpetual prosperity, and that a world so constructed will eventually collapse if, as happens when governments control the issue of money, political pressures from debtors create steady monetary inflation. Long-term debt tends to lure debtors into the illusion that monetary inflation benefits them more than it harms society. In the short run, they may be correct; not in the long run.

Nevertheless, the long-term capitalization of inanimate equipment, agricultural land, and work animals is biblically legitimate. (So, in the Old Testament economy, was the capitalization of foreign heathen slaves, although not for resale to foreign nations.) The borrower owns an economically valuable asset. The lender may be willing to lend money if this asset serves as collateral for the loan. The borrower owes the lender something, but it is something that he already owns. He can "buy his way out" of the loan contract by turning over to the lender the agreed-upon collateral. He does not place himself in bondage with this type of loan. He can pay off the loan at any time, either by turning over cash or the collateral to the lender. Thus, the capitalization of long-term rents is legitimate today.

In a biblical society, governments would not be allowed to issue money.[61] Neither would fractional reserve banks.[62] This would elim-

---

60. Eric Roll, *A History of Economic Thought* (3rd ed.; Englewood Cliffs, New Jersey: Prentice-Hall, 1956), p. 457.

61. Gary North, *Honest Money: The Biblical Blueprint for Money and Banking* (Ft. Worth, Texas: Dominion Press, 1986), ch. 10.

62. *Ibid.*, ch. 11.

inate the primary biblical objection against collateralized debt: the subsidy that monetary inflation offers to debtors. They could not pay off their debts with depreciated money.

What about unsecured debt? That has to be the decision of the lender. Are the risks worth it? He decides. He should have the legal right to extend credit. The creditor believes that debt is to his advantage. The Bible says that such personal debt is best avoided (Rom. 13:8), but it does not forbid debt. In some cases, debt may actually be to the benefit of the debtor. Debt to finance a higher education is one example. But the debtor must always understand that by taking an unsecured debt, he is risking disgrace. He has in principle become a bondservant (Prov. 22:7).

In a biblical social order, a defaulting debtor would be required to sell everything he owns to pay his creditors. "The wicked borroweth, and payeth not again: but the righteous sheweth mercy, and giveth" (Ps. 37:21). There must be sanctions against such public wickedness as defaulting on a loan. When a person declares bankruptcy, he is publicly announcing that the total value of his possessions is insufficient to repay his creditor or creditors. He violates the terms of the loan's contract if he retains any personal assets after declaring bankruptcy. He must turn over everything he owes to his creditor up to the amount specified in the contract. (Some societies may allow him to retain some of his possessions, but this exception was known to lenders beforehand, and the added risk to the creditor was already built into the loan's risk premium.) He cannot legitimately be sold into indentured servitude unless this was specified in the loan contract, and if it was, then the loan had to be a zero-interest charity loan, as I have argued above ("Defining Poverty by Statute"). (There should be little doubt that the abolition of debtors prison in the West during the late-nineteenth century was an act in conformity with biblical law's standards of debt and repayment.)

If such laws were on the statute books, there would be a lot less consumer debt.

Collateral

The lender is permitted to take a poor man's cloak as collateral, but the cloak must be returned at night. This is a strange form of collateral, since the lender cannot use it when it is most needed. Its purpose is two-fold. *First*, to restrict loans of charity to *local regions* whenever possible. Lenders are supposed to be in close contact with borrowers. They should know their character. Lenders are very likely employers. They can distinguish a true emergency from a disguised

consumer loan. *Second*, to reduce *multiple indebtedness*. While the
lender cannot use the cloak during the night, the debtor cannot use it
during the day. He cannot use the same cloak as collateral for several
loans at the same time.[63] He is limited in his ability to indebt himself
and his future.

Character: A lender is not required to take any form of collateral.
This indicates that a major form of collateral for a loan is the lender's
perception of the borrower's character and his ability to repay the
loan. Character, in fact, is a better form of collateral, since the
lender does not have to go to the trouble of returning the cloak each
evening. This reduces transaction costs. The less trustworthy the
borrower's character, the more likely that a lender would require the
cloak, fearing multiple indebtedness.

Multiple Indebtedness

There is a very important application of the law of collateral, one
that is seldom discussed. Consider the case of a poor man who comes
in search of an emergency loan from his neighbor. The neighbor
assesses the man's character, and concludes that the man is likely to
repay the loan. The lender has made a mistake. The man may visit
several people to ask for an emergency loan. If he collects from all of
them, he may waste the money. Even if he repays these loans, he has
dealt fraudulently with lenders by accepting numerous interest-
bearing loans. They have unknowingly borne added risk.

But what if the lender suspects that the borrower is somewhat
unreliable. The lender wants to honor God, so he intends to make
the loan. But he wants collateral. He wants to give the borrower an
economic incentive to repay the loan as soon as possible. The man is
poor. He has no collateral of value. But the lender can still demand the
man's cloak. He is not allowed to take the widow's cloak (Deut. 24:17).

What good is this cloak to the lender? He must return it in the
evening, when the man needs it. It cannot be sold. It cannot be used
by anyone in the lender's household. It is a nuisance, for it must be
returned each evening. But it has two important economic functions. First, the borrower has to come back every evening to get it
back. This is an inconvenience. He will have an added incentive to

---

63. This was the opinion of the twelfth-century Jewish scholar, Ibn Ezra, citing
Saadia Gaon. Nehama Leibowitz, *Studies in Shemot*, Part 2 (Jerusalem: World Zionist Organization, 1976), p. 418.

repay the loan early. Second, since the garment is in the possession of the lender during the day, it cannot be used as collateral with another lender. One piece of collateral can be used for only one loan at a time, if the lender demands collateral. If the borrower kept it, and simply signed a note saying that it stands as collateral for the loan, he may sign several such notes for several lenders. If he defaults, they cannot all collect their collateral. Therefore, by permitting the lender to demand half a day's collateral, biblical law reduces the temptation on the part of borrowers to commit fraud.

Fractional Reserve Banking

Modern banking is based on the flagrant flouting of the prohibition against multiple indebtedness. For every asset a bank owns, there are many claims—legal claims—against that asset. The bank keeps fewer reserves on hand to meet demands of lenders to the bank—depositors— than the bank has promised to deliver on demand. This is called *fractional reserve banking*. It is the universal form of banking and has been since the early modern period. It was an invention of the Renaissance.

Depositors believe that their money is available on demand. The banks have promised them that it is available on demand. But it isn't. If every depositor came to the bank one day and began to withdraw his money, the bank would go bankrupt. The bank loaned out the depositors' money in order to earn interest on the loans. Part of this return is paid to depositors as interest on their accounts. The depositors know this, but they all assume (as do the bank's managers) that not all depositors will try to get their money out on the same day. They assume that withdrawals will tend to equal deposits on any given day. Usually, this assumption is correct. The day men lose faith in the solvency of the bank—in the bank's ability to repay those few depositors who demand their money—a bank run ensues. Everyone wants his money at once. The bank defaults. It has run out of "raiment."

Without the protection of state and federal government agencies, fractional reserve banking would face the prospect of bank runs, as lenders (depositors) would lose faith in overextended (multipally indebted) banks. The most important form of collateral a bank should have is its reputation for honesty and conservative (minimal fractional reserves) investing policies. In a truly biblical society, banks would be required to have 100 percent reserves.[64] In the twentieth

---

64. North, *Honest Money*, ch. 7.

century, however, a commercial bank's most important from of collateral in the United States is the legal backing of the federal government, which stands ready to bail out bankrupt banks—a guarantee
which is ultimately backed up by the printing press money of the
Federal Reserve System, the nation's central bank.[65] We have guaranteed inflation by ignoring the warning against multiple indebtedness.

Fractional reserve banking is inflationary, for it creates credit
money—money which is backed only by faith. When a person
deposits his money on the condition that he can write a check and
spend it, the inflation is about to begin. The banker loans, say, 90
percent of this money to a borrower. The borrower then spends the
money. Whoever gets the borrower's money then either spends it or
deposits it in *his* bank, and the process continues. As a theoretical
limit (though not in practice), for every dollar deposited in a banking
system with 10 percent reserves, nine additional dollars will eventually come into circulation.[66] Thus, fractional reserve banking is inherently inflationary.[67] It also creates inflationary booms and their
inevitable consequences, depressions.[68]

Warehouse Receipts

Say that a person brings in ten ounces of gold to a warehouse for
safekeeping, and the warehouse issues a receipt for ten ounces of
gold. The owner pays a fee for storing the money, but he presumably
increases the safety of his holdings. The warehouse specializes in
protecting money metals from burglars. The depositor pays for this
specialized service. It is somewhat like a safety deposit box in a
bank, except that the warehouse issues a receipt.

The receipt may begin to function as money. If people trust the
warehouse, they will accept a receipt for all or part of this gold in
payment for goods and services. A piece of paper authorizing the
bearer to collect a specified amount of gold is just about the same as
the actual ounce of gold. Besides, the gold is safer in storage, and
paper is a lot more convenient than pieces of metal.

But a problem threatens the system. What if the warehouse
owner recognizes that people in the community trust him? They

---

65. On the operations of the Federal Reserve System, see North, *ibid.*, ch. 9.
66. The process is described, step by step, in a free book which is published by
the Federal Reserve Bank of Chicago, *Modern Money Mechanics.*
67. North, *Honest Money*, ch. 8.
68. Mises, *Human Action*, ch. 20.

know that he has a lot of guards watching everything, and that he has always been scrupulously honest. He then betrays this trust. He issues warehouse receipts for gold for which there is no gold in reserve. He then loans these receipts to borrowers. The receipts serve as money. People accept them in exchange for goods and services. These warehouse receipts are considered "as good as gold." Why? Because they are always exchangeable for gold upon demand. Just take the piece of paper to the warehouse, and get your gold. No problem!

But now there *is* a problem. There are more receipts for gold than there is gold in reserve to pay all the potential bearers on demand. These "demand deposits" are now vulnerable to that most feared of financial events, a *bank run*. Depositors who have receipts come down and demand repayment. There is not enough gold in reserve to meet the total demand.

The warehouse has placed itself in a position similar to that of the poor man who immorally secures loans from a dozen lenders on the basis of one piece of collateral. The warehouse owner has become a banker. He makes loans, for which borrowers agree to pay him interest in the future, along with a return of the principal. But the money, once loaned out, is gone until the day that repayment comes. The warehouse is vulnerable to a run on the deposits. The warehouse owes gold to the depositors. It is indebted to them. The deposits are legal liabilities to the bank. The bank has become multipally indebted.

The Creation of Money

The warehouse receipt circulates as if it were gold. Now, if gold serves as money in that society, the pieces of paper will also serve as money.

When these pieces of paper are pure money-metal substitutes, nothing changes. Physical gold is taken out of circulation and put into a warehouse. A piece of paper (a warehouse receipt) substitutes for the physical gold. No new money has come into circulation. No money has been taken out of circulation. Nothing fundamental changes, except for convenience. But if the warehouse owner writes up a warehouse receipt for gold when there is no new gold on deposit, then he has increased the money supply in the community. No one has come to the warehouse and deposited gold (taken it out of the day-to-day economy). So the warehouse receipt is inescapably *inflationary*. It is an addition of money into the economy. (I am defin-

ing "inflation" as "an increase in the money supply," the way dictionaries and economists defined it before 1940. The result is either:
1] rising prices, or 2] prices will not fall as far as they would otherwise have fallen.)

Here is what normally would happen. The warehouse receipt
circulates as if it were gold. If the warehouse owner is very cautious,
and issues only a few extra receipts, probably nobody will find out.
He will collect a little interest from borrowers, and everyone will be
happy. Prices of goods (as denominated in gold) may rise only a little, or perhaps not at all. But other warehouse owners hear about
their competitor. So he is lending out money, is he? Well, two can
play at that game. So can five or six. They all begin to issue their
warehouse receipts to borrowers. They too get in on the banking
game. The money supply now starts to increase.

Prices start to rise, as denominated in paper money. But gold
bullion's currency-denominated price does not rise, for all the unbacked receipts to gold are "as good as gold," and therefore supposedly identical to gold. The increase in circulation of these receipts
does not initially push up gold's paper money-denominated price. So,
those who hold gold get hurt initially. They see the paper money-
denominated prices of other goods rising, but the market price of
stodgy old gold is unchanged. It looks as though lots of newly mined
gold is coming onto the market. But statistics are available to show
that this is not true. So, the increase must be coming from the issuers
of warehouse receipts. So, receipt-holders do the rational thing: they
start buying goods and services before the price of these goods gets
any higher. This puts upward pressure on prices, *as denominated in
gold receipts*. That is to say, the market value of these receipts falls.
Holders of these warehouse receipts try to pass them to other people.
The decline in their market value continues.

Then what happens? Store owners continue to take a lot of paper
receipts. They steadily deposit them with their local banks. Unlike
the general public, bankers understand how the fractional reserve
system works; at least, they understand the risks associated with
issuing more receipts for gold than there is gold to redeem the receipts. *Bankers become increasingly suspicious of each other's gold receipts.*
Too many receipts are being deposited by their customers. Many of
the bankers know that there is not this much new gold coming into
circulation. What if the public figures this out, too? They think to

themselves, "Maybe it would be smart to cash in these receipts and demand delivery of gold, just in case some receipt-issuing competitor is hit with a bank run." They start demanding gold for the receipts issued by suspected banks. This places added downward pressure on the gold-related price of some banks' receipts, and possibly on many banks' receipts. Thus, the bankers have an incentive individually to pull the plug on their own fractional reserve scheme. So do market speculators. Specialist traders suspect that the price of gold will zoom when the deception is discovered, once the general public starts cashing in their warehouse receipts for their hoped-for gold. Thus, bankers and speculators begin the run on the banks' gold hoards—a run that the bankers fear the public will initiate if the bankers don't get in line first. They dearly want to get in line first. They want their gold before their fractionally reserved competitors run out.

This is why bankers and other sophisticated holders of gold receipts eventually go to the warehouses and start demanding their gold. They understand that at least some of the banks are technically insolvent. They are not sure which ones are weakest, so all the banks risk getting hit. Receipt-holders want their gold now, while they can still get it on demand. The run on the warehouses begins. Warehouse receipts for gold continue to fall in value compared to gold. Other people then rush down to get their gold (which is now rising in value compared to the warehouse receipts people are holding). The insolvent banks collapse, or else they are forced to delay repayment to receipt-owners.

This declaration of insolvency (insufficient reserves) is similar to the action of the wicked cloak-owner who has multipally indebted himself, and then leaves his creditors standing out in the cold. Thus, fractional reserve banking violates two biblical principles: 1) honest weights and measures, and 2) no multiple indebtedness. Fractional reserve banking is inflationary while people accept the checks, and deflationary when confidence in the banks finally collapses.

Understand, however, that the evil of fractional reserve banking is not created by the phenomenon of interest (time preference) as such. It is not money-lending as such that is condemned by the Bible; rather, it is *borrowing with collateral that you do not have* and *lending what you do not have* (i.e., issuing receipts for commodities not held in reserve).

Interest-Seeking Loans

The prohibition against usury only appears in the context of charitable loans. The Bible does not prohibit loans that draw interest in business dealings, as Jesus' parable of the talents indicates (Matt. 25:27).[69]

Consider the problem faced by the person who argues, as medieval theologians argued, that all interest is immoral. What if the banker comes to the potential depositor and made this offer? "Sir, you have money that you do not need for immediate consumption. I have several prospects for earning money on invested capital. Let us make a bargain. You loan me the money for a year. I, in turn, will see to it that your money gets into the hands of low-risk borrowers who have some excellent business opportunities, if they can only locate some capital at reasonable rates of interest. I will retain a percentage of the money they pay me for having located your money. This is my service fee. But you will do much better on this loan than you could if you loaned the money to people you know. I will save you the time, expense, and trouble of seeking out reputable borrowers. They come to me. That is my job.

"I must make this stipulation, however. For the agreed-upon period of the loan, you won't be able to get your money. The money will be used by the borrowers in their business operations. After all, we can't spend the same money at the same time! So you forfeit the use of your money for a year; the borrower gets the use of your money for a year; he pays you for the privilege of using your money, and I will take a small percentage for my services. Everyone wins, including consumers who will benefit from the increased production."

This sounds good. But the lender wants security. "Mr. Banker, I will agree to this on the following condition. I want security for my investment. I will buy an insurance policy from you. If the businessman you loan the money to should go bankrupt and be unable to repay me, then you will pay me the agreed-upon rate of interest anyway. I have to pay for this protection, of course, but you know so many businessmen, and can spread the investments of all depositors over so many different investments, that we all can gain greater security if you act as an insurance agent for our loans."

Reasonable? Certainly. It is so reasonable that the medieval prohibition against all interest payments, including business loans, was

---

69. North, *Honest Money*, ch. 7.

destroyed by just this kind of insurance contract. Medieval business-men agreed to finance various maritime enterprises, but only if the shipper guaranteed repayment. Instead of taking a percentage of the profits from a particular ship's voyage, the less risk-oriented investors agreed to a fixed percentage (interest rate), leaving more profits (or more losses) to the adventurer.

Then third parties entered into the transaction, probably beginning in the fourteenth century. They agreed to act as insurers for ship owners who did not want to offer such a guarantee to investors, or who could not because they owned only one ship, and if its voyage failed, there was no way to repay the loans. This third-party loan was called the *contractus trinus*, and it eventually sank the usury prohibition to the bottom of the historical sea.[70] For what was the "insurer" offering, if not a guaranteed, fixed-interest return on loans? It may have been called shipping insurance, but it was identical to the medieval definition of usury. Yet it took over a century for even one scholastic commentator to spot the problem, and no one paid any attention to him.[71]

When the insurance feature of non-shipping business contracts was first introduced, it was initially rejected by the theologians. In partnerships, where there was shared risk of failure, interest payments had always been acceptable, but not in contracts where there was a guaranteed rate of return, irrespective of the outcome of the particular business or business venture. But step by step, the resistance of the church to interest payments in business loans was weakened. By Luther's day, the old prohibitions were almost gone. Incredibly, by the late fifteenth century, the Roman Church had actually approved charitable loans (called "contracts") that paid 5 percent to 6 percent per annum, the *montes pietatis*.[72] The church by the late medieval period had reversed the original meaning of the biblical prohibition, which forbids interest from charitable loans, but which places no restraints on interest from business loans. The church prohibited interest from business loans and itself collected interest from charitable loans.

The prohibition against interest could not be sustained. The future is always discounted. So when we read in the Bible about loans without interest, we are talking about charitable loans, not

---

70. Noonan, *The Scholastic Analysis of Usury*, pp. 202-3.
71. *Ibid.*, p. 203. His name was John Consobrinus.
72. *Ibid.*, p. 295.

business or consumer loans. We are talking about destitute borrowers, not high-flying upwardly mobile lawyers, accountants, professionals, and entrepreneurs.

The Moral Legitimacy of 100 Percent Reserve Banking

While I normally do not insert lengthy expositions of the New Testament in my Old Testament commentaries, it is necessary that I devote considerable space to Jesus' parable of the talents. Christians who have been influenced by the "economists of love" and their zero-interest fantasies need to know that the New Testament teaches clearly that what I have said regarding interest is valid, that there is no biblical rule against interest-bearing loans. The following passage verifies this point:

> For the kingdom of heaven is as a man travelling into a far country, who called his own servants, and delivered unto them his goods. And unto one he gave five talents, to another two, and to another one; to every man according to his several ability; and straightway took his journey. Then he that had received the five talents went and traded with the same, and made them other five talents. And likewise he that had received two, he also gained other two (Matt. 25:14-17).

This parable is a kingdom parable. It follows the five-point covenant model that was first discovered by Ray Sutton.[73] First, the master calls his servants before him (sovereignty). Second, he delegates authority to them as his economic representatives by transferring money to them (hierarchy/representation). Third, while it is not stated explicitly, he commands them to make a profit (law/dominion). We know this because all three immediately take steps to obey his implicit economic command. Fourth, he returns and imposes positive sanctions: blessings to the profitable servants. Fifth, the blessings that he gives them involve rulership (succession/continuity). He then imposes negative sanctions against the unprofitable servant, casting him into outer darkness (disinheritance).

This parable contains several theological messages, but the three main ones are these: first, God owns all things; second, He delegates temporary control over these things to men; third, men are required to increase the value of whatever God has entrusted to them.

---

73. Ray R. Sutton, *That You May Prosper: Dominion By Covenant* (Tyler, Texas: Institute for Christian Economics, 1987).

There are also secondary implications. First, it should be noted that the servants were required to act on their own initiative for a long period. The master was not present to tell them precisely what to do. He imposed *a profit management system of control, a bottom-up hierarchy.* It was not the management alternative, a non-market, top-down bureaucracy.[74] He wisely decentralized his investment portfolio before he departed. He allowed his subordinates to make their own decisions regarding the proper use of his capital. He subsequently held them legally responsible for the results.

Marxism as Covenant-Breaking

What about the person who takes no risks, buries his talent, and returns to the master only what he had been given initially? This man has produced losses. He is an evil, unprofitable servant. He has not performed according to minimum standards.

Like so many other incompetent, slothful people in history, the servant of the parable tries to justify his poor performance by blaming the master. He accuses the master of being a thief, or at least an unscrupulous exploiter. "Then he which had received one talent came and said, Lord, I knew thee that thou art an hard man, reaping where thou hast not sown, and gathering where thou hast not strawed. And I was afraid, and went and hid thy talent in the earth: lo, there thou hast that is thine" (vv. 24-25).

What was the slothful servant's accusation of the master? Clearly, he was accusing him of being a *capitalist*. The master is rich, yet he does not go into the fields to labor. He expects a positive return on his money, even though he goes away on a journey. In short, *the servant is an incipient Marxist.* He believes, as Marx did, in the labor theory of value. He also believes in Marx's exploitation theory of profits. Anyone who gets money without working for a living is nothing but an exploiter, living on the labor of the poor. The servant calls him "a hard man." (Theologically speaking, this is the covenant-breaker's accusation against God: God is an unfair exploiter.)

The master accepts the ideological challenge. He reminds the servant that he is indeed a hard man, meaning someone who has the lawful authority to establish standards of profitable performance, as well as the authority to hand out rewards and punishments. He admits freely to the servant that as a successful capitalist, he does not

---

74. Ludwig von Mises, *Bureaucracy* (Spring Mills, Pennsylvania: Libertarian Press, [1944] 1983).

personally go into the fields to plant and reap, yet he reaps a profit. "His lord answered and said unto him, Thou wicked and slothful servant, thou knewest that I reap where I sowed not, and gather where I have not strawed" (v. 26). Then he tells the servant the minimum that he is entitled to, an interest return: "Thou oughtest therefore to have put my money to the exchangers, and then at my coming I should have received mine own with usury" (v. 27). Luke 19:23 reads: "Wherefore then gavest not thou my money into the bank, that at my coming I might have required mine own with usury?"

The Legitimacy of Interest

The King James translators used the English word *usury* to translate a Greek word that is more accurately translated as *interest*. This discussion of interest here is very revealing, for two reasons. First, this parable of God's kingdom acknowledges that *interest-taking is legitimate*. God eventually comes to every person and demands a positive return on whatever had been entrusted to him by God. The master had done without the use of his funds during his absence. He is therefore entitled to a minimum return: interest.

Second, *the parable clearly distinguishes between profits and interest.* The other two stewards each produced a profit of 100 percent. They received the greater praise and greater visible rewards. The minimum required performance was an interest payment. The slothful servant had been unwilling to take even the minimal risk of handing the money over to specialists in money-lending, who would seek out entrepreneurs to lend the money to, entrepreneurs who would then pay a competitive return to the money-lenders on this passively managed investment.

In other words, the master's capital was supposed to become productive. Each steward had to become an entrepreneur, or else had to seek out an entrepreneur who would put the money to economically productive uses. The talent was not to sit in the earth; it was to perform a socially useful function.

The Entrepreneur and the Banker

The economic agent who is on the cutting edge of both prediction and production is the entrepreneur. The first two men in the parable were entrepreneurs. They went out and found ways of investing the master's money that produced a positive rate of return. As the parable presents it, this rate of return was higher than what could have been earned by depositing the money with money-lenders. Thus, the entrepreneur is understood to be someone who bears much greater risk than someone who deposits money in a bank. The economist calls this form of risk *uncertainty*. It cannot be estimated in advance.[75] It involves guesswork, unlike the depositor who is promised a specific rate of interest when he deposits his money.

The only way that the banker can afford to pay out a promised return is because he successfully seeks out final borrowers (entrepreneurs) who produce an even higher rate of return. The banker makes his living on the difference between the interest payment which the final borrower pays to him and what he in turn pays to the depositors. He makes it "on the spread."

The future is uncertain to men. We do not know it perfectly. We barely know it at all. We see the future as though we were peering through a darkened glass. Nevertheless, all of life involves forecasting. There is no escape. We must all bear some degree of uncertainty. But some people are willing to bear more of it than others, and of these, some are more successful in dealing with it. In economic terminology, some produce greater profits than others. Profit is a *residual* that remains, if at all, only after all costs of the business have been paid, including interest.

Banking: Reducing Uncertainty

The banker is able to offer a special service to investors. He can diversify depositors' uncertainty by lending to many people — people who, like the servants in the parable, have performed successfully in the past. They have "a track record," to use the language of racing. By lending out money to many borrowers, the banker therefore converts a portion of the depositors' uncertainty into risk, meaning from the statistically incalculable to the statistically calculable. The banker is like an insurer. In fact, in the Middle Ages, the bank was an insurance company, since both church and State had made it illegal for Christians to ask or pay interest.[76] The modern profession of banking grew out of the marine insurance guild, which was legal in the Middle Ages.[77]

---

75. Frank H. Knight, *Risk, Uncertainty and Profit* (New York: Harper Torchbooks, [1921] 1965).

76. Jews could legally lend to Christians, which is why Jews from the middle ages onward have been found in banking. It was a near-monopoly granted to them by Christian legislators.

77. Noonan, *The Scholastic Analysis of Usury*, ch. 10.

What does an insurance company do? Its statisticians (actuarians) calculate the likelihood of certain kinds of undesirable events in large populations. These unpleasant events cannot be statistically calculated individually, but they can be calculated collectively if the population involved is large enough. The seller of insurance then persuades members of these large populations to pay periodic premiums so as to "pool" their risks. When one member of the pool suffers the event that has been insured against, he is reimbursed from the pool of assets. Hence, some of life's inescapable and individually incalculable uncertainties are converted to calculable risk by means of diversification: "the law of large numbers."

The same is true of banking. Borrowers will seldom all go bankrupt at once. Most borrowers will repay their debts as specified in their loan agreements. Bad loans are more than offset by the good ones. Thus, the banker can offer a fixed rate of return to depositors. In almost all cases, depositors will be repaid as promised because most of the borrowers repay their loans as promised. (The exception is in a depression, when banks fail. Depressions are the result of prior monetary inflation, which in our day means fractional reserve banking.[78])

What we must understand is that *the master in this parable protects his funds in much the same way.* He seeks out a group of potential entrepreneurs. He gives each of them an amount of money to invest. He makes predictions regarding their future performance based on their past performance, and then he allocates the distribution of his assets in terms of this estimation. He protects his portfolio by diversification.

He is not an interest-seeking banker, however. The money he invests is his own. He is not acting as the legal agent of other depositors. He legally claims all of the profits. He does not contract with borrowers who agree in advance to pay him a fixed rate of interest. The entrepreneurs are strictly his legal subordinates, unlike the relationship between banker and borrower.

Yet in the Old Testament era, there was a relationship of *economic subordination* between lender and borrower: the borrower was servant to the lender (Prov. 22:7). This economic subordination was based on the legal authority of the lender to place the borrower in indentured servitude for up to six years (Deut. 15). Because the borrower today can lose his collateral or his reputation, there is still a mild

---

78. Mises, *Human Action*, ch. 20.

form of economic subordination in every debt contract. Debt is still a threat, even though it can also be very productive. It is like fire: a useful tool, but a danger if it gets out of control.

The Forfeited Productivity of Inaction

The master in the parable is outraged by the coin-burying servant. The parable is intended to show the subordinate (indebted) position of all men before God. The servant was cast into outer darkness because he was an unprofitable servant (v. 30). The parable stands as a warning to all men because the Bible teaches that all people are unprofitable servants (Luke 17:10).[79] This is why we need a profitable servant as our intermediary before God, our perfect sin-bearer. But to understand our relationship of indebtedness to God, the parable's language must be taken seriously. We cannot make accurate theological conclusions about the broader meaning of the parable if the symbolic reference points of the parable are themselves inaccurate.

There is no question that the master not only approves of taking interest, he sends the servant to the nether regions for not taking it. This is strong imagery! *The interest payment belongs to the master.* By having refused to deposit the master's money with the money-lenders, the servant has in effect stolen the master's rightful increase. The servant was legally obligated to protect the master's interests, and interest on his money was the minimum requirement. He failed. The master's judgment of the servant's past performance had been accurate; he was entitled to only one talent initially, for he had not demonstrated competence previously. Had he been given more, he would have wasted more.

The idea that the interest return was the master's minimum expectation leads us to the question of *the origin of interest*. Why did the master deserve an interest return? Because he had possession of an asset that could have been put to productive use, but was not. He had forfeited an economic return that could have been his. This concept of the *forfeited return* appeared in medieval economic literature as the doctrine of *lucrum cessans*. The owner of money who could have made a profit by investing it elsewhere, but who loaned the money to someone, was said by some theologians to be entitled to an interest payment from the borrower because of the income he had forfeited. Interest compensated the lender for the opportunity he had missed.

---

79. Gary North, "Unprofitable Servants," *Biblical Economics Today* (Feb./March 1983).

This raises the whole question of *cost*. What is the cost of any action or any purchase? It is the value of whatever has to be forfeited, i.e., the value of *the most valuable foregone use*. If I do one thing with my money, I cannot do something else with it. The value of whatever I would actually have done but did not do is what it costs me to do whatever I do.

The lender who transfers to another person the use of an asset, monetary or nonmonetary, has given up whatever other opportunities might have been available to him. There are always other opportunities available. There is therefore always a cost to the lender of lending money.

The master in the parable was being gracious to the servant. He recognized from the beginning that the man was not very competent. The master did not tell the servant that he had failed because he had not made 100 percent on the money entrusted to him. He told him only that he had failed because he had not earned an interest payment. This is the least that the master could have expected.

The master probably could have doubled his money by entrusting it to either of the first two servants. But he had sought greater economic safety instead. He had adopted the principle of *risk reduction through portfolio diversification*. You get a lower rate of return but a more sure return. But the master had been cheated. He could have deposited his money directly with the money-lenders instead of giving it to the servant. That would have been safer — greater diversification through the bank — and it almost certainly would have produced a positive rate of return, however low. Instead, he received only his original capital in return.

He had forfeited his legitimate interest payment because he had transferred the asset to the slothful, risk-aversive servant. This servant is a model of wickedness, not because he was actively evil, but that he was *passively unproductive*. He did nothing with that which had been entrusted to him. Doing nothing is sufficient to get you cast into hell, when doing the minimum would at least quench the master's wrath. (Warning: only one man in history has ever performed this minimum: Jesus Christ.)

Interest and Capitalization

Is interest-taking morally legitimate? This debate has been going on since at least the days of Aristotle, who called money sterile and interest illegitimate. But if money is sterile, why have men throughout history paid to gain access to its use for a period? How are so many people fooled into paying for the use of a sterile asset? Besides, interest is a phenomenon of every loan, not just loans of money. Modern economics teaches this; so does the Bible.

It is obvious that the phenomenon of interest is not confined to money. Aristotle was incorrect. *The phenomenon of interest applies to every scarce economic resource.* We always discount future value. Whatever we own in the present is worth more to us than the promise of owning that same item in the future. Promises to repay can be broken (the risk factor), but more to the point, *the present commands a price premium over the future.*[80]

We live in the present. We make all of our decisions in the present. We enjoy the use of our assets in the present. While wise people plan for the future by purchasing streams of future income by buying assets that they expect to produce net income over time, they purchase these hoped-for streams of income at a discount. The *rate of discount* that we apply to any stream of expected future income is called the *rate of interest*. Mises called it *time-preference*.

Thus, the rate of interest is not exclusively a monetary phenomenon. *Interest is a universal discount that we apply to every economic service that we expect to receive in the future.* We buy a hoped-for stream of rents; we can buy them for cash; but we expect a discount for cash. This purchase at a discount for cash is called *capitalization*. It is the heart of capitalism. It is the heart of every society more advanced than the utterly primitive.

The person who lends money at zero interest is clearly forfeiting a potential stream of income. He will seldom do this voluntarily, except for charitable reasons. The ownership of the asset offers him an expected stream of income: psychological, physical, or monetary. If it did not offer such a stream of income, it would be a free good. It would not be demanded. It would therefore not command a price. The owner expects to receive a stream of income. He chooses the degree of risk that he is willing to accept, and he then refuses to lend the asset for less than the interest rate appropriate to this degree of risk.

The borrower compensates the owner for the use of the asset, or its exchange value, for a specified period of time. He borrows it only because he values its stream of services more highly than he values

---

80. Mises, *Human Action*, ch. 19.

its rental fee (interest). He expects to make a profit of some kind on the temporary exchange of control over it.

Summary

Non-fractional reserve banking and the taking of interest are both biblically legitimate. The parable of the talents should be sufficient proof for anyone who is not trying to make an overnight theological reputation for himself based on the promotion of the utterly fantastic. We should take the Bible seriously in preference to Aristotle, and also in preference to the economics of love.[81] The capitalization of long-term assets, including human services is biblically legitimate.

Again, I acknowledge that men, in their quest for autonomy from God, are willing to become slaves of sin, and therefore in principle slaves of other men. I recognize the New Testament principle that it is best to owe no man anything (Rom. 13:8a). I also recognize that modern economics has promoted the ideal of perpetual debt for perpetual prosperity, and that a world so constructed will eventually collapse. But to place temporal limits on the judicial enforceability of the discounting of future long-term human services, because the Bible requires that we restrain man's overconfidence about his long-term future, is not the same as denying that there is an inescapable discounting (capitalization) process between the present value of present goods and the present value of expected future goods.

With respect to capitalized debt, if both the lender and the borrower agree that a piece of collateral is acceptable in exchange for the defaulted loan, then the debtor is not in debt, net. He has an offsetting asset. He wants the money in cash; the lender would rather have the money over time. The existence of the collateral reduces the likelihood that the debtor will default. The debtor is therefore not a servant of the lender in this case. Nevertheless, if the loan involves the potential loss of a man's home, meaning his status and his own self-evaluation, then he is in a form of bondage. But if he owns investment assets (a house, for example) with a mortgage on it, and he risks losing the house if he defaults, then this voluntary transaction is merely a shifting of risk to the liking of both transactors. The lender feels better about the future with a stream of income guaranteed by the value of

---

81. See Appendix F: "Lots of Free Time: The Existentialist Utopia of S. C. Mooney."

the collateral. The borrower feels better about owning the collateral and paying the money. Neither is a servant; neither is a master.[82]

Conclusion

The confusion throughout the Middle Ages and early modern period concerning the evil or illegitimacy of interest came as a result of not paying attention to the biblical texts, and then mixing in the fallacious economic opinions of Aristotle. The Bible is clear: there is to be no interest return from money loaned to the poverty-stricken neighbor. This applies to money loans or loans of goods. But the definition of poverty must be the willingness of the borrower to serve as a bondservant of the lender should he be unable to repay the loan. The larger the loan, the longer the term of service that will be required to repay it. Ordinarily, though, charity loans would be small, and the time to repay would probably not be seven years, unless it was for something like the payment of physicians' bills or lawyers' fees.

There is no prohibition on interest returns from loans to distant pagans or from business loans. The term translated as "usury" in the King James Bible is narrow and precise in its application: *interest derived from morally mandatory charity loans, either from poverty-stricken righteous brothers in the faith or from resident aliens who live alongside believers in nations that are formally covenanted under the God of the Bible.* The word does not mean "exorbitant" interest. That usage was the product of the early modern period, and is not the product of biblical analysis. Any interest taken from a loan to the poor brother in the faith is usurious; no maximum rate of interest from other loans is ever mentioned in the Bible.

Interest is inescapable. It is not a uniquely monetary phenomenon. It is the discount we apply to future goods as against present goods. This process goes on continually, whether or not there is a money market, whether or not published loan rates are available. We are mortal. We die. We live in an uncertain world. We cannot know the future. Thus, we discount the value of future goods, and we also confront the phenomenon of risk whenever we defer present consumption. If nothing else, we may not live long enough to enjoy the future.

Fractional reserve banking is prohibited in the Bible, for two reasons: 1) it violates the prohibition against false weights and mea-

---

82. Warning: do not take a loan if it is not 100 percent collateralized by an asset you are willing to lose.

sures because it creates money, and 2) it violates the principle against multiple indebtedness. But interest-producing loans on a truly deferred basis — no check-writing on money already loaned out — are biblically valid.

24

IMPARTIAL JUSTICE AND
LEGAL PREDICTABILITY

Thou shalt not raise a false report: put not thine hand with the wicked to be an unrighteous witness. Thou shalt not follow a multitude to do evil; neither shalt thou speak in a cause to decline [bend] after many to wrest judgment: Neither shalt thou countenance a poor man in his cause (Ex. 23:1-3).

Thou shalt not wrest the judgment of thy poor in his cause. Keep thee far from a false matter; and the innocent and righteous slay thou not: for I will not justify the wicked (Ex. 23:6-7).

God is the cosmic Judge. "And the heavens shall declare his righteousness: for God is judge himself. Selah" (Ps. 50:6). "A father of the fatherless, and a judge of the widows, is God in his holy habitation" (Ps. 68:5). "But God is the judge: he putteth down one, and setteth up another" (Ps. 75:7). "Arise, O God, judge the earth: for thou shalt inherit all nations" (Ps. 82:8).

Few doctrines alienate modern man as much as this one does. I believe that the doctrine of final judgment, above all others, is the biblical doctrine that most repels the unbeliever. The rise of modern evolutionary science can be traced back to the idea that infinite space and nearly infinite time have shoved God out of the universe.[1] Man wants some other judge besides God: either the heat death of the universe or cosmic crushing, in eternal cycles of creation and contraction.[2] By default, the modern State becomes the judge for man, substituting its temporal judgments for God's.[3]

---

1. Gary North, *The Dominion Covenant: Genesis* (2nd ed.; Tyler, Texas: Institute for Christian Economics, 1987), pp. 249-50, 279, 379. (Cited hereafter as *Genesis*.)

2. Gary North, *Is the World Running Down? Crisis in the Christian Worldview* (Tyler, Texas: Institute for Christian Economics, 1988), ch. 2.

3. Gary North, *Heaven or Hell on Earth: The Sociology of Final Judgment* (forthcoming).

When He judges men, God does not respect persons. He respects His covenant law, not the social or economic position of the person being judged, whether rich or poor. This concept of highly personal but even-handed justice is basic New Testament doctrine. "For there is no respect of persons with God" (Rom. 2:11). "And if ye call on the Father, who without respect of persons judgeth according to every man's work, pass the time of your sojourning here in fear (I Pet. 1:17). It is also Old Testament doctrine, reflected in the requirement that human judges are to honor God by imitating Him in His capacity as Judge. "Ye shall not respect persons in judgment; but ye shall hear the small as well as the great; ye shall not be afraid of the face of man; for the judgment is God's: and the cause that is too hard for you, bring it unto me, and I will hear it" (Deut. 1:17). "Thou shalt not wrest judgment; thou shalt not respect persons, neither take a gift: for a gift doth blind the eyes of the wise, and pervert the words of the righteous" (Deut. 16:19). "These things also belong to the wise. It is not good to have respect of persons in judgment" (Prov. 24:23).

There was a time when this doctrine of even-handed justice in terms of biblical law alienated the rulers of the world because they served as agents of the rich, who would not countenance the thought of honest judgment for the poor. James warned against this very temptation within the church:

My brethren, have not the faith of our Lord Jesus Christ, the Lord of glory, with respect of persons. For if there come unto your assembly a man with a gold ring, in goodly apparel, and there come in also a poor man in vile raiment; And ye have respect to him that weareth the gay clothing, and say unto him, Sit thou here in a good place; and say to the poor, Stand thou there, or sit here under my footstool: Are ye not then partial in yourselves, and are become judges of evil thoughts? Hearken, my beloved brethren, Hath not God chosen the poor of this world rich in faith, and heirs of the kingdom which he hath promised to them that love him? But ye have despised the poor. Do not rich men oppress you, and draw you before the judgment seats? Do not they blaspheme that worthy name by the which ye are called? If ye fulfil the royal law according to the scripture, Thou shalt love thy neighbour as thyself, ye do well: But if ye have respect to persons, ye commit sin, and are convinced of the law as transgressors (James 2:1-9)

Today, on the other hand, there are many rulers and would-be rulers who refuse to tolerate this biblical doctrine because it sounds as though God is on the side of the rich simply because He will not bend judgment in the name of the poor. Their court theologians and would-be court theologians dutifully reinterpret the biblical texts to fit the rulers' socialist goals: "The God of the Bible is on the side of the poor just because he is *not* biased, for he is a God of impartial justice."[4] The fact is, however, it is the idea that *rulers are under God and under the obligation to enforce God's revealed law* that most antagonizes rulers, not to mention their court theologians. Whether they represent the poor, the rich, or the "middling sort," rulers refuse to represent God's court of justice. To do so would point to God as final Judge, and this doctrine is too repulsive for autonomous man.

Judicial Stability

God's justice is the goal for the entire commonwealth, and all members of society are personally responsible before God to meet all of the demands of His law. The 23rd chapter of Exodus provides us with some specific details of what constitutes biblical justice. False reports are prohibited (23:1, 7). Evil acts by men in crowds are banned (23:2). Favoritism of the rich or poor is banned (23:3, 6). Animals that belong to a hated neighbor must be assisted and returned to him (23:4-5). The acceptance of bribes by leaders is banned (23:8). Oppression of strangers is prohibited (23:9). God's law is to rule over the affairs of men, irrespective of anyone's personal emotions concerning the "worthiness" of a man or his cause. All men are worthy to receive God's justice, just as all men are worthy of the wrath to come.

God's justice is *constant*.[5] It is constant because it is *theocentric*.[6] It reflects the unchanging character of God. God's justice on judgment day will be reliable. Therefore, human judges are required by God to strive to become analogously reliable. They are to render decisions in terms of the fixed principles of biblical law.

This does not mean that the application of the law's principles is essentially a near-mechanical operation. While the principles of biblical justice do not change, the *applications* of God's general principles in specific instances can change over time, for history has meaning.[7] Christ's replacement of the Mosaic ritual ordinances with new ones, baptism and communion, is indicative of the nature of the relation-

---

4. Ronald J. Sider, *Rich Christians in an Age of Hunger: A Biblical Study* (Downers Grove, Illinois: Inter-Varsity Press, 1977), p. 84.

5. James B. Jordan, *The Law of the Covenant: An Exposition of Exodus 21-23* (Tyler, Texas: Institute for Christian Economics, 1984), pp. 11-17.

6. *Ibid.*, pp. 1-3.

7. *Ibid.*, pp. 12-17.

ship between God's law and history.[8] With the coming of Christ, the last and greatest high priest — a member of the tribe of Judah (Matt. 1:2), not Levi — God changed some of the specifics of outward and inward obedience to the permanent principles He set forth.[9] He annulled through perfect fulfillment the jubilee laws governing land and slaves in Israel (Lev. 25; Luke 4:18-21).[10] He transferred His kingdom to a new nation (Matt. 21:43). History is not static. Neither Jews nor Christians worry today about eating from the tree of the knowledge of good and evil; that transgression is behind us. Jews and Christians do not worry about the absence of animal sacrifices in the temple. The principle of obedience nevertheless is with us still, and will be throughout eternity, in heaven and hell, in the resurrected new heavens and new earth, and also in the lake of fire.

Men discover new areas of dominion, for good and evil, that were not previously covered by judicial interpretations in courts of law. But this does not invalidate the unchanging judicial principles of biblical law. Men are responsible for the correct matching of the Bible's case laws to specific circumstances, either before they take action as individuals (self-government), or as judges who hear cases after others have taken action and are in court because of it.

Personalism and Intuition

The dispensing of justice is not an impersonal activity, meaning a computerized, mathematical operation, since it is men who serve as both judges and judged, and men are not machines. The affairs of men are not purely mechanical or numerical; neither are their formal legal conflicts.[11] Fitting case laws to circumstances necessarily

---

8. Cf. Greg L. Bahnsen, *Theonomy in Christian Ethics* (2nd ed.; Nutley, New Jersey: Presbyterian & Reformed, [1977] 1984), ch. 9.

9. Jews no longer sacrifice bulls and lambs to God, indicating that they, too, recognize this relationship between unchanging law and changing history.

10. See Chapter 4, pp. 144-45.

11. One naive attempt to find an impersonal program for dispensing justice by computer has already begun. General Robotics Corp., a private firm, set up an experiment in 1983 to offer people an "electronic jury." People send in information concerning pending cases (federal criminal law) and have a computer analyze these cases. The president of the company, an engineer, stated that federal cases are the easiest to quantify. A spokesman for the firm announced: "We are attempting to replace the warm, living, human juries with a cold, dead, robot jury so that citizens may have a plain and speedy adjudication or arbitration of their disputes. Our slogan is 'Equal Justice Under the Law,' which will be a welcome relief to anyone who has ever had a trial by jury." *Infoworld* (Feb. 28, 1983), p. 1. The experiment failed the test of the marketplace: profit and loss. It had to. Men think analogically; elec-

involves reasoning by analogy, frequently an intuitive process — a process beyond the scope of mathematics.[12] Hayek writes: "That the judge can, or ought to, arrive at his decisions exclusively by a process of logical inference from explicit premises always has been and must be a fiction. For in fact the judge never proceeds in this way. As has been truly said [by Harvard's Dean Roscoe Pound], 'the trained intuition of the judge continuously leads him to right results for which he is puzzled to give unimpeachable legal reasons.'"[13] Or as Nicholas Georgescu-Roegen, perhaps the most brilliant epistemologist that the economics profession has ever seen, has described the problem: "And it is because society and its organization are in constant flux that genuine justice cannot mean rigid interpretation of the words in the written laws."[14]

Human reasoning cannot function without intuition. Reason can be *progressively disciplined* by either covenant-keeping intuition or covenant-breaking intuition, but in either case, reasoning is not a mechanical-numerical process. "Between the plasticity of the brain and the mechanistic structure of a computer there is an unbridgeable gap. . . ."[15] Intuition is the inescapable element of the incalculable in all human thought and decision-making. Intuition connects the "steps" in the human reasoning process, a process which in fact cannot be shown to consist of a series of discrete, identifiable steps. The process of reasoning is a continuum, and it is applied to change over time, which is also a continuum.[16] Georgescu-Roegen writes, "The

---

tronic computers do not think at all; computer programs are structured numerically (digitally). As computer programmer A. L. Samuel said so well, computers "are giant morons, not giant brains." Samuel, "Artificial Intelligence: A Frontier of Automation," *Annals of the American Academy of Political and Social Science*, CCCXL (March 1962), p. 13.

12. Higher mathematics, as with all human speculation, also involves the use of intuition. The popular understanding of mathematics ignores this. Fitting the aesthetic purity of mathematics to the external world also involves such things as faith, genius, and insight. It is not a predictable, automatic process, and therefore not "mathematical."

13. F. A. Hayek, *Law, Legislation and Liberty*, vol. I of *Rules and Order*, 3 vols. (University of Chicago Press, 1973), pp. 116-17. Hayek goes on to say that "The other view is a characteristic product of the constructivist [top-down planning] rationalism which regards all rules as deliberately made and therefore capable of exhaustive statement" (p. 117).

14. Nicholas Georgescu-Roegen, *The Entropy Law and the Economic Process* (Cambridge, Massachusetts: Harvard University Press, [1971] 1981), p. 82.

15. *Ibid.*, p. 90.

16. *Ibid.*, pp. 60-72.

intuitive continuum belongs to that special category of concepts about which we can discourse with each other without being able to define them."[17] This statement does not go far enough: *all* logical concepts possess this same quality of not being able to be defined precisely. The human mind is not omniscient; absolutely precise definitions are always elusive to man's mind. The mathematician-philosopher Alfred North Whitehead said, "As soon as you leave the beaten track of vague clarity, and trust to exactness, you will meet difficulties."[18] You will meet more than difficulties: you will meet failure. As Georgescu-Roegen notes, "any vocabulary is a finite set of symbols."[19] The structure of vocabulary "does not have the power of the continuum."[20] In short, there is an inescapable element of *uncertainty* in exercising judgment. "A measure for all uncertainty situations, even though a number, has absolutely no scientific value, for it can be obtained only by an intentionally mutilated representation of reality. We hear people almost every day speaking of 'calculated risk,' but no one yet can tell us how he calculated it so that we could check his calculations."[21]

Men are not omniscient. They cannot know another man's heart (Jer. 17:9). Only God knows men's hearts (Jer. 17:10). "But the LORD said unto Samuel, Look not on his countenance, or on the height of his stature; because I have refused him: for the LORD seeth not as man seeth; for man looketh on the outward appearance, but the LORD looketh on the heart" (I Sam. 16:7). But we do not need to render perfect justice in order to render adequate justice. We render preliminary justice, and leave the rest to God. This is why capital punishment is required by God: it turns over the person immediately to the highest court of all, the throne of God. God does not wait for a judicially convicted person's "biological time clock" to deliver him into His presence for God's preliminary judgment.[22]

---

17. *Ibid.*, p. 66.

18. Whitehead, *Science and Philosophy* (New York: Littlefield, 1948), p. 136; cited in *ibid.*, p. 90.

19. *Ibid.*, p. 73.

20. *Idem.*

21. *Ibid.*, p. 83.

22. This judgment by God is preliminary because God confines a soul either to heaven or hell, both of which are temporary places of residence. Final judgment comes at the resurrection, when body and soul are reunited perfectly, and people are sent either into the eternal lake of fire (Rev. 20:14-15) or into the final manifestation of the new heaven and new earth (Rev. 21).

Inescapable Casuistry

Despite the impossibility of man's ability to declare and impose perfect, comprehensive judgment, judges must not be consciously partial in the inescapable process of fitting biblical law to public facts regarding historical circumstances. Judges must not give men legitimate reasons to complain that biblical law is not a trustworthy guide for rendering judgments in history. God's law *alone* is trustworthy for rendering judgments in history, for at least three reasons. First, it reflects certain aspects of God's nature, both ethical and ontological (being). His law is permanent. Second, it is constructed to meet the needs of men, who in turn are made in the image of God. The law is suited to men and their circumstances. Third, biblical law fits the creation and therefore serves as man's tool of dominion. *Biblical law links God, man, and the creation in a hierarchical chain of command.*[23]

The doctrine of creation provides us with a concept of *transcendent law*. The source of all law is external to the universe. It can therefore be permanent in the face of changes within the universe. This view of law stands in radical contrast to the Darwinian view of law as totally immanent to — immersed in — the creation. Darwin and his intellectual heirs have explained all life in terms of random changes: random mutations and adaptations within a framework of random, or nearly random, impersonal environmental change.[24] (Post-Heisenberg science has increasingly abandoned the Newtonian view of a deterministic, predictable environment.)[25] All human laws in a

---

23. Gary North, *Unconditional Surrender: God's Program for Victory* (3rd ed.; Tyler, Texas: Institute for Christian Economics, 1988), pp. 94-115. See also Ray Sutton, *That You May Prosper: Dominion By Covenant* (Tyler, Texas: Institute for Christian Economics, 1987), ch. 2.

24. North, *Genesis*, pp. 259-62, 267, 395-97.

25. German physicist Werner Heisenberg in 1927 announced an important finding of modern physics, the *uncertainty principle*. An undergraduate college textbook describes it in language reasonably close to English: "This principle, which is derivable from wave mechanics, says that, irrespective of technical errors of measurement, it is *fundamentally impossible* to describe the motion of a particle with unlimited precision. We may specify the position of a particle with increasing precision, but in so doing we introduce uncertainty into its motion, in particular into its momentum. Conversely, we may observe the momentum with increasing precision, but then we introduce uncertainties into its position." G. S. Christiansen and Paul H. Garrett, *Structure and Change: An Introduction to the Science of Matter* (San Francisco: Freeman, 1960), p. 558.

This observation about the limits of observation in the world of subatomic physics led to another disconcerting discovery: the light wave which enables the scientist to observe phenomena itself upsets the observation (or makes observation

Darwinian world must be relative. Law is part of the overall evolutionary process. Any correspondence between the *one* (general law) and the *many* (specific circumstances) may last for no longer than an instant. Darwinism produces *process philosophy*: the assertion of a world devoid of permanent standards.[26] A sea of randomness engulfs Darwin's universe, threatening to overcome islands of permanence. Randomness also engulfs the mind of self-professed autonomous man.[27]

Legal Predictability

Justice is simultaneously personal and impartial. God does not respect persons, a doctrine that is repeated again and again in Scripture, as we have seen.[28] *Cosmic personalism*, meaning God's comprehensive judgment of every fact in the universe, requires *judicial impartiality* for human law courts. Men are to think God's thoughts after Him, within the limits of their creaturehood. Truth is placed before friendship or hatred, class or status. Biblical law is not class law, contrary to Marxists. It is not the product of class conflict. It is accurate to say that the *arena* of biblical law's application is the historical product of ethical conflict between man and God. Conflicts between men are a result of this ethical conflict between man and God (James 4:1), but these conflicts are not the origin of biblical law. Bib-

---

impossible) at the level of subatomic physics. The positions between electrons are far smaller than the smallest light wave, so the light serves as a kind of blanket which covers up what is going on. If smaller gamma rays could ever be employed in a "microscope," these would strike the electrons and "kick" them, thereby changing their momentum. In short, *the observer interferes with the observed.* "A quantitative analysis of this argument shows that beyond any instrumental errors there is, as stated by the uncertainty principle, a residual uncertainty in these observations." *Ibid.*, p. 559. As a result, the optimism of scientists regarding Newtonian mechanics as a perfect description of the physical universe has disappeared.

But this textbook summary for undergraduates avoids the real problem of modern quantum mechanics. The uncertainty of the universe is now said to be fundamental, and not just our uncertainty of measurement. The unobserved "real world" is said to be statistical rather than physical at the subatomic level. See North, *Is the World Running Down?*, ch. 2.

26. North, *Genesis*, pp. 273, 287, 323-24, 333-35, 339, 351, 355, 419-20.

27. Cornelius Van Til, *The Defense of the Faith* (2nd ed.; Philadelphia: Presbyterian & Reformed, 1963), pp. 124-28. For a detailed defense of this thesis from a humanistic viewpoint, see William Barrett, *Irrational Man: A Study in Existential Philosophy* (New York: Doubleday Anchor, [1958] 1962).

28. Deut. 10:17; II Chr. 19:7; Job 34:19; Acts 10:34; Rom. 2:11; Gal. 2:6; Eph. 6:9; Col. 3:25; I Pet. 1:17.

lical law, to use Marx's terminology, is not the "superstructure" which has been produced by the "substructure" of class conflict. The legitimacy and eternally binding character of God's law have nothing to do with the success or failure of an economic class. Neither rich nor poor can legitimately claim special privileges under biblical law. Therefore, neither rich nor poor can legitimately claim the right to favorable arbitrary treatment by the judges. Judicial arbitrariness is to be reduced to a minimum.

The characteristic feature of biblical justice is therefore its *predictability*. Residents in a biblical commonwealth have access to the law. They can understand it. They can exercise self-government in their relationships, for they know what it means to transgress the law. They know what God expects from them positively, and they know the sanctions He will bring against them negatively. This same confidence in and understanding of biblical law can be transferred to society's law-enforcement system. Men know that the judges are restrained by the same law that restrains them. They know what to expect from their earthly judges because they know what to expect from their heavenly Judge. He has revealed Himself to them in His law.

The Jury System

To insure that the decisions of the courts do not become dependent on professional lawyers and judges, a free society establishes juries. The priesthood of all believers is the theological foundation of juries: every redeemed person is a Levite. The Levites studied the law and gave advice to the courts. In civil society, every citizen is a judge. Citizens can make arrests, and citizens sit on juries, declaring other people's guilt or innocence. In order to insure that common people retain in their possession the authority to interpret and apply civil law (including criminal law), the doctrine of double jeopardy comes into play. Once a person has been declared innocent, he may not be retried. The historic roots of this judicial procedural principle can be found in the Bible.[29] The modern practice in U.S. courts of allowing civil suits against people declared innocent of criminal charges is perverse.

Any weakening of the right of trial by a jury of one's peers — including "scientific screening" of jurors by attorneys — is an assault on

---

29. Greg L. Bahnsen, "Double Jeopardy: A Case Study in the Influence of Christian Legislation," *Journal of Christian Reconstruction*, II (Winter, 1975), pp. 40-54.

the integrity of the predictability of the law. It is an attempt to make law the plaything of full-time legal technicians rather than the jury's application to trial court evidence of general laws that can be understood by the vast majority of those who are covenantally under its provisions. This is why judges are to be selected in terms of their reputation for honesty (Ex. 18:21). Ethics, not mental gymnastics by highly trained legal specialists, is God's screening system for judges. This is also why God required that His law be read publicly to all residents of Israel during the year of release, once every seven years (Deut. 31:9-13). He wants people to know in advance what He requires of them ethically.

Judges and Justice

Law enforcement is ideally to be immune to a judge's personal connections to the accused, whether pro or con. Enemies deserve justice. So do close relatives. All men deserve justice, meaning the impartial (but never impersonal) application of biblical law to every aspect of their lives—judgments imposed not just by the State, or even primarily by the State, but by all forms of government, including self-government. The emotions of the judge are not the issue; *external justice* is the issue. An emotion-filled judge is commanded by God to provide the same impartial judgment which would be rendered by a disinterested judge. The issue is not emotion; the issue is self-government under biblical law. God is emotional. He *hates* covenant-breakers as passionately as He loves covenant-keepers. How else could He create the eternal lake of fire for His enemies? Out of His love for them? Hardly. Why else would He recommend that we do good deeds to our enemies, so that we might heap coals of fire on their heads (Rom. 12:20)? David could say, "Do not I hate them, O LORD, that hate thee? And am I not grieved with those who rise up against thee? I hate them with perfect hatred: I count them mine enemies" (Ps. 139:21-22). Nevertheless, to render anything less than impartial justice is to impugn the character of both the law and the Law-giver.

The doctrine of the atonement affirms this principle of impartiality despite emotion. The demands of the law must be met. God the Father spared not His own Son, despite His emotional involvement with His Son. Emotions may be present in certain judicial cases, but they are not to influence the application of God's standards to these cases.

We must distinguish *feeling* in judicial administration — feeling in the sense of intuition — from *emotions* regarding the people who are being judged. Feeling is inescapable in the judicial process, meaning the informed yet intuitive "feel" for the connections between permanent law and specific cases which a judge develops after years of studying and hearing cases. This sort of feeling is inherent in the judicial process. Emotion may or may not be present in the mind of a judge during a particular trial, but its influence is to be suppressed by the individual judge. Should his emotions deflect the imposition of the law's requirements, and therefore affect the outcome of the case, the appeals court can overrule him.

Oppression and Envy

The law of God protects private property. An enemy's lost animals must be returned by the finder, and the animals must be aided by the one who finds them in trouble (Ex. 23:4-5). Animals are not to run wild, for they are under the dominion of man. Domesticated animals are tools used by man in his dominion assignment. In other words, both man and beast are under law. Neighbors are required by God to forfeit time and effort, suppressing any emotions of vengeance, in order to see to it that the tools of dominion are returned to the lawful owner. Finders are not to become keepers unless they become buyers. In one sense this is a requirement of charity; in another sense it is simply respect for the order of creation and its law-based hierarchy of command and responsibility.

No group within the commonwealth may legitimately be singled out for oppression. The context here places "oppression" within the category of legal judgment, not private economic oppression. There must not be false or partial justice. (By "partial," I mean both "deliberately incomplete" and "not impartial.") The productivity of those who would otherwise be likely victims of judicial discrimination can flourish when they know that they will be permitted to keep the fruits of their labor. The division of labor increases as a direct result, because men are more willing to cooperate with each other in production. Output per capita increases, and therefore so does wealth per capita. Legal predictability, the product of impartial justice and permanent legal standards, produces greater wealth than any other system of justice.

With Justice for All

The court is to be a place of justice for all men, without respect to their economic position. Bearing false witness is described in Exodus 23 as being an aspect of oppression. The innocent are to be protected (v. 7), bribes are to be rejected by judges (v. 8), and the stranger is not to be oppressed (v. 9). When men can have reasonable faith in the content of the law and the reliability of the judges, they can cooperate with each other less expensively. The division of labor increases, along with voluntary exchange. Productivity increases throughout the society. The "miracle of the market," with its benefits to all individuals who serve their neighbors by responding efficiently to consumer demand, becomes so familiar to the beneficiaries that they may forget the source of their blessings: God and His law-order.

A society that is filled with envy-driven false witnesses who "uphold the cause of the poor" by means of courtroom lies, university indoctrination, guilt-manipulation from the pulpit, and orchestration of the public by the mass media, is a doomed society if it continues in its rebellion. The self-righteousness of the envious will not alter the reality of the economic effects of envy. All the rhetoric about "healing unjust social structures" and "providing justice for the oppressed" will not delay the judgment of God if the content of the promised utopian reformation is founded on the politics of envy.[30]

By perverting judgment, men tear down the foundation of their liberties and the foundation of their wealth, especially their freedom to profit from their own ingenuity, labor, and thrift. They find that others are increasingly hesitant to display visible signs of their prosperity. Economic prosperity cannot survive when productive members of a society withdraw from entrepreneurial activities — the uncertainty-bearing, future-oriented, consumer-satisfying quest for profit — and instead become content to consume their wealth (and hide it) rather than face the slander of false witnesses who rise up against them in the name of the poor.[31]

Justice and Productivity

As capital, including human capital, is steadily withdrawn from

---

30. Gonzalo Fernández de la Mora, *Egalitarian Envy: The Political Foundations of Justice* (New York: Paragon House, [1984] 1987).

31. Helmut Schoeck, *Envy: A Theory of Social Behavior* (New York: Harcourt, Brace, [1966] 1970), pp. 46-47, 88, 290-91.

the marketplace and consumed, almost everyone loses.[32] Like the kulaks (successful independent small farmers) of the Soviet Union in the early months of 1930 who killed their livestock and ate them rather than put them into the newly collectivized farms,[33] so envy-besieged entrepreneurs are buying Rolls-Royce automobiles and "state of the art" stereo systems. At least they are able to enjoy their depreciating capital base while it lasts. This form of capital consumption is taking place all over the democratic and socialist West,[34] although not in the capitalist Far East. The cost to society? All the forfeited opportunities — employment, innovation, and general productivity — that this capital base, if invested wisely, would have produced.

Through their continual false witness against biblically legitimate forms of wealth, the envious promote the destruction of society's capital base. So do all those who tolerate envy and do not fight it, or who fail to recognize it for what it is. And most incongruous of all are the wealthy victims of envy who indulge their masochism (or their desperate quest for acceptance) by continuing to attend and support envy-preaching churches, and who send money to envy-promoting evangelical associations, colleges, and politicians — all in the name of Jesus![35]

Without legal predictability, capitalism as a social system cannot flourish. Max Weber listed calculable law as one of the five major features of the capitalist economic system.[36] The bulk of Hayek's legal and economic studies, from *The Road to Serfdom* (1944) to the trilogy, *Rules and Order* (1973-80), has been devoted to a demonstration of the links between formal, general, predictable law on the one hand, and economic freedom and the market economy on the other.

---

32. Short-run winners: competitors who no longer feel the heat of competition from the oppressed, productive capitalists who withdraw; government bureaucrats and corrupt judges, who gain access to bribes; and those who are better able to prosper in the black market, which is where the hidden transactions will take place as the civil government becomes debauched.

33. On the forced collectivization of Soviet agriculture, see Lazar Volin, *A Century of Russian Agriculture: From Alexander II to Khrushchev* (Cambridge, Massachusetts: Harvard University Press, 1970), pp. 224-34.

34. George Gilder, *Wealth and Poverty* (New York: Basic Books, 1981), ch. 15.

35. See my discussion of this suicidal phenomenon in Appendix 4 in David Chilton's book, *Productive Christians in an Age of Guilt-Manipulators: A Biblical Response to Ronald J. Sider* (4th ed.; Tyler, Texas: Institute for Christian Economics, 1986). For evidence of the theological drift toward liberalism of the major evangelical colleges, see James Davison Hunter, *Evangelicalism: The Coming Generation* (University of Chicago Press, 1987), pp. 165-80.

36. Max Weber, *General Economic History*, translated by Frank H. Knight (New York: Collier, [1920] 1961), p. 208.

Too many economic resources are wasted under social systems characterized by judicial arbitrariness — scarce resources that might
otherwise be used to reduce uncertainty in forecasting uncertain
future consumer demand rather than uncertain future judicial decisions. By reducing judicial uncertainty, biblical justice frees up resources that can then be used to increase output per unit of resource
input. Nevertheless, biblical law should not be interpreted as the
product of capitalistic institutions; on the contrary, capitalism is the
historic product of a world-and-life view favorable to the kind of
legal predictability which is produced by respect for biblical law.[37]

False Witness and Organized Envy

Individuals are commanded not to raise a false report. This is a
specific application of the law against bearing false witness (Ex.
20:16). Raising a false report is the equivalent of slander; God cuts
off the slanderer (Ps. 101:5). By raising a false report, men endanger
their victimized neighbor, as well as the peace of the community. By
misleading the judges, and by luring them into making improper decisions, the man who bears false witness endangers the trust which
other men place in the judges and the biblical system of justice. This
is why a stiff penalty is imposed on perjurers: the penalty that would
have been imposed on the victim of the falsehood (Deut. 19:16-19).

The focus of concern in this passage is with false witnesses, corrupt judges, and the oppressed rich. The "oppressed rich"? Yes. The
law warns against upholding the poor man in his cause or lawsuit.
But if we are not to uphold the poor as such, then the poor man or
men must be bringing a case against someone or some group that is
not equally poor. This classification of "non-poor" included successful strangers (v. 9), who were willing to remain as resident aliens in
urban areas. Economic success, or the hope of success, motivated
the stranger to remain. Once successful, he would be less likely to
return to his people and the society governed by the religion of his
people.[38] The phenomenon of the successful outsider is a familiar

---

37. Gary North, *The Sinai Strategy: Economics and the Ten Commandments* (Tyler,
Texas: Institute for Christian Economics, 1986), especially the Conclusion.

38. It is worth considering the possibility that one reason for the economic and
academic success of Jews in the twentieth century is the combination of modern secularism and remnants of historic discrimination. Secularism assumes that religious
differences that are based on dogma or theology are irrelevant, or should be. This
has opened up universities, businesses, professions, and most other institutions to

one: Chinese in Southeast Asia and the United States, Indians in Africa, West Indies blacks in New York, and Jews everywhere.[39]

This raises an interesting question. What if the false witnesses accuse successful people *in general* of wrongdoing? What if they argue that the rich are inescapably economic oppressors unless they give their wealth, or a major portion of their wealth, to the poor? False witness need not be directed against an individual in order to have evil consequences. It can be directed against any group: religious, racial, national, or class. In this case, false witness against "rich men in general" falls under God's condemnation.

A philosophy or ideology that condemns the rich in general is equally as perverse as a philosophy that condemns the poor in general. If men are rich because they or their entire society have conformed themselves to biblical law (Deut. 28:1-14), they are not to be condemned. *To condemn them is to condemn God and His law-order.* Conversely, if men are poor because they or their entire society are in rebellion against God and God's law (Deut. 28:15-68), they are not to be upheld. *To uphold them is to uphold Satan and his law-order.*[40]

The twentieth century has seen the temporary triumph of many philosophies that advocate State-enforced policies of compulsory wealth redistribution. Generally, these philosophies are promoted in the name of democracy. In effect, advocates of these philosophies propose a revision of the eighth commandment: "Thou shalt not steal, except by majority vote." Other versions of collectivism are promoted as elitist programs that need to be imposed on the "rich" in the name of the poor, even when a majority of voters are opposed to

---

hard-working Jews. At the same time, the lingering sense of being set apart from the society at large has given Jews a sense of covenantal mission: to outperform the gentile majority. If the acids of modernism do their predictable work, economic and social success will tend to produce Jews who no longer have the "outsider's" mentality, and the humanistic quest for unity will undermine the sense of covenantal or family mission. We are seeing this in the United States today, where Jews commonly marry non-Jews, since they come into social contact with each other in the secular universities. As Schumpeter said of capitalism, Jewish performance is likely to fail in the long run because of its success. The very secular institutions that allow Jews to compete without religious, social, or racial restrictions will undermine their sense of "Jewishness."

40. R. J. Rushdoony, "The Society of Satan," *Christian Economics* (July 7 and Aug. 4, 1964); reprinted in *Biblical Economics Today*, II (Oct./Nov. 1979).

39. Thomas Sowell, *The Economics and Politics of Race: An International Perspective* (New York: William Morrow, 1983), Pt. I.

the programs. These philosophies universally bear false witness against the rich in general, charging that the rich have exploited the poor throughout history. Marxism is only the most successful and most consistent of these philosophies of organized envy. There are many others: fabian socialism, national socialism (Nazism), the corporate State (fascism), social democracy, populism, liberation theology, Christian socialism, the New World Order, the New International World Order, New Age communalism, and hundreds of variants. These philosophies have produced political movements that have pressured politicians to pass legislation that oppresses the productive: the present rich (though seldom the "super rich")[41] and the future rich, meaning all those who would like the opportunity to become rich, i.e., the middle class entrepreneur, the independent businessman, and the potentially productive but presently poor person, whose avenues for advancement are cut off.[42]

Conclusion

Because all men are under God and responsible to God, justice is to be impartial and predictable. It is not to be arbitrary, for God is not arbitrary. Law is both constant and theocentric, although applications of God's fixed laws can and have changed, as a result of new historical circumstances. The Bible gives us our standards of application, just as it gives us God's law.

Men are to judge in terms of God's law. This process of rendering judgment is not mechanical. It is personal and covenantal. It involves the use of intuition, either Bible-based or humanistic. There is no escape from the "humanness" of human judgment. What is needed to restrain men from arbitrariness in rendering judgment is a system of biblical law which restrains the flights of judicial fancy of intuition-guided judges. But we can never totally eliminate uncertainty from the judicial process. The price of perfectly certain justice is astronomical; it would destroy justice.

Legal predictability is one of the fundamental historical foundations for the development of capitalism in the West. The rise of envy-based political and economic systems is now threatening the productivity

---

41. Ferdinand Lundberg, *The Rich and the Super Rich* (Secaucus, New Jersey: Lyle Stuart, 1968).

42. See, for example, Walter Williams, *The State Against Blacks* (New York: New Press, McGraw-Hill, 1982).

and very survival of the West. Judges are rendering decisions in terms of who people are — the "generally oppressed" or the "general oppressors." This means that law is beginning to "respect persons" *as members of economic or political classes.* Men are rendering *false witness* against the institutions and laws that grew out of Christianity, and which gave us modern prosperity.

25

FINDERS SHOULD NOT BE KEEPERS

If thou meet thine enemy's ox or his ass going astray, thou shalt surely bring it back to him again. If thou see the ass of him that hateth thee lying under his burden, and wouldest forbear to help him, thou shalt surely help with him (Ex. 23:4-5).

This case law, since it deals with property, is governed by the theocentric principle of God as the cosmic Owner. He has delegated temporary ownership of selected portions of His property to individuals and organizations, so that they might work out their salvation or damnation with fear and trembling (Phil. 2:12). Because God has delegated responsibility for the care and use of His property to specific individuals or organizations, who are held responsible for its management, others are required to honor this distribution of ownership and its associated responsibilities.

Exodus 23:4-5 requires the person who finds a stray domesticated beast to return it to its owner, an enemy. Why specify an enemy? Because if a person is obedient to this narrowly defined law, he will also be obedient to the wider implications of the law. It is not that one may lawfully ignore a friend's lost animal, but return an enemy's. The Lawgiver assumes that anyone who will do a favor for an enemy will also do a favor for a friend.

There are several beneficial results of such a moral injunction whenever it is widely obeyed. First, it upholds the sanctity of the legal rights of property owners. Second, it reasserts man's legitimate control over the animal creation. Third, it reduces hostilities between enemies. Fourth, the passage of time makes it easier to identify thieves. Fifth, it provides an incentive to develop marks of private ownership. It must be stressed from the beginning, however, that this law is not a civil law, for there is no way to develop a system of compulsory charity or compulsory righteousness through the civil

774

government. Exodus 23:4-5 is rather a moral law to be enforced through self-government.

Owner's Rights

There is a rhyme that English-speaking children chant, "Finders, keepers; losers, weepers." When one child finds a toy or possession of another, he torments the owner with this chant. Yet his very chanting testifies to the fact that the tormenter really does not believe in his ethical position. If he really wanted to keep the object, he would not admit to the victim that he had found it. He would forego the joys of tormenting the victim for the pleasure of keeping the object. The tormenter can always appeal to his own parents, who will then go to the parents of the tormenter. In Western society, most parents know that the discovered object is owned by the loser.

From time to time, someone discovers a very valuable lost object, such as a sack of money that had dropped out of an armored car. When he returns it to the owner, the newspapers record the story. Invariably, the doer of the good deed receives a series of telephone calls and letters from anonymous people who inform him that he was a fool, that he should have kept the money. Again, this is evidence of the West's dominant ethical position: the critics prefer to remain anonymous.

Rights of Disposal

From a legal standpoint, the reason why the law requires the finder to return the lost item to the owner is that the owner owns the rights of use and disposal of the property. What is owned is the *right to exclude* other people from using the property. This "bundle of rights" is the essence of ownership. The capitalist system is not based on "property rights"; it is based on the legal rights to control the use and disposal of property. Nothing inheres in the property that gives these rights.

There is another familiar phrase, "possession is nine-tenths of the law." This is incorrectly stated, if by "possession" we mean physical control over some object. The possession which is nine-tenths of the law is the possession of the *legal right to exclude*, not possession of the physical object itself. The object does not carry this legal right with it when it wanders off or is lost by the owner.

We can see this easily when we consider the case of a lost child. The fact that someone discovers a lost child obviously transfers no legal right to keep the child. The child is to be returned to the parents or to the civil authorities who act as legal agents of the parents. Possession is clearly not nine-tenths of the law. If anything, possession of a long-lost child subjects a person to the threat of being charged with kidnapping. Because God is the ultimate owner of mankind, He has delegated the legal right to control children to parents, except in cases of physical abuse by parents which threatens the life of the child. In short, parental sovereignty is nine-tenths of the law, not merely possession of physical control over a particular child.

When someone who discovers another person's property is required by God to return it to its owner, there can be no doubt concerning the Bible's commitment to the private ownership of the means of production. Biblical moral law undergirds a capitalist economic order. Socialism is anti-biblical. Where biblical moral law is self-enforced and biblical civil law is publicly enforced, capitalism *must* develop. The reason why most modern Christian academics in the social sciences are so vocal in their opposition to biblical law is that they are deeply influenced by socialist economic thought. They recognize clearly that their socialist conclusions are incompatible with biblical law, so they have abandoned biblical law.[1]

Dominion Through Judgment

This case law extends man's dominion over nature: domesticated animals are not to "run wild." They are under man's care and protection. This reasserts man's place under God but above the animals: point two of the biblical covenant model, hierarchy[2] — appropriate for the Book of Exodus, as the second book of the Pentateuch.

A law requiring a man to help an animal that has fallen because of too heavy a burden is similar in intent to the law regarding wandering animals. The owner is present with the animal, however: "thou shalt surely help with him." He has overburdened his animal, and it has fallen. The typical response of an enemy would be, "Well, that good-for-nothing has now gone too far. He has broken the back of his own animal. Let him find out just how much trouble it is to set

---

1. A good example of such antinomian socialist reasoning is John Gladwin, "Centralist Economics," in Robert Clouse (ed.), *Wealth and Poverty: Four Christian Views of Economics* (Downers Grove, Illinois: InterVarsity Press, 1984), ch. 4. See also my response, *ibid.*, pp. 198-203.

2. Ray R. Sutton, *That You May Prosper: Dominion By Covenant* (Tyler, Texas: Institute for Christian Economics, 1987), ch. 2.

things straight. Let him untie all the packages, lift up the beast, and repack." The problem with this approach is that the beast is suffering for the errors of its owner. The owner is having trouble, but so is the innocent beast. Should the beast suffer needlessly? The law directs a passerby to go over and help lift the beast back to its feet. This is a two-person job: one to help up the beast, and the other to help lift its burden. Man is to be a protector of those under his authority, including animals.

A lost animal can damage other people's property (Ex. 22:5). It can wander into a pit and get hurt or killed (Ex. 21:33-34). It can injure men or other animals (Ex. 21:35-36). To have a domesticated lost animal wandering without any form of supervision testifies against the dominion covenant. It is a sign that God's required moral and hierarchical order has broken down. It is an aspect of God's curse when beasts inherit the land (Ex. 23:29). In short, domesticated animals require supervision by man.

No man's knowledge is perfect. Men can lose control over their domestic work animals. When they do, it becomes a moral responsibility for other men to intervene and restore order. This is done for the sake of biblical social order: 1) for the individual who has lost control over his animal and who is legally responsible for any damage that it might perform, and 2) for the sake of the animal itself.

A domesticated animal is a capital asset, a tool of production. It is mankind's development of tools of production that is the basis of economic growth. The loss of a trained work animal reduces its owner's ability to subdue his portion of the earth. This sets back the fulfillment of God's dominion covenant with mankind. This loss of production reduces the per capita economic growth of the whole community, even though the loss may not be large enough to be perceived. The person who finds a lost animal is required to restore it to the owner, even though this involves economic sacrifice on his part. In the long run, this implicit sanctioning of privately owned capital will produce increased wealth for all.

The biblical imagery of the lost sheep of Israel is indicative of the central concern of the Bible: the restoration of moral and legal order, the overcoming of sin and its effects. The lost sheep in history need a shepherd. They are wandering toward destruction. God intervenes and brings them home. The New Testament imagery of Jesus as the great shepherd points to the theme of restoration.

Righteous Judgment

There is a principle of justice visible here. These verses appear in between verses dealing with civil justice. The first three verses of Exodus 23 deal with impartial justice. Verses four and five deal with the lost or fallen animal. Then verses six and seven return to the original theme of justice: "Thou shalt not wrest the judgment of thy poor in his cause. Keep thee far from a false matter; and the innocent and the righteous slay thou not: for I will not justify the wicked." The idea that links these verses is this: *if you treat an animal well, you will probably treat other people well*. If you will care for your enemy's helpless beast, you will probably not pervert justice when dealing with a helpless person.

This law is also a way of bringing God's eternal judgment on one's enemy. "If thine enemy be hungry, give him bread to eat; and if he be thirsty, give him water to drink: For thou shalt heap coals of fire upon his head, and the LORD shall reward thee" (Prov. 25:21-22). One destroys a covenant-breaking enemy forever by treating him lawfully. Every good deed done to a covenant-breaking enemy, if he remains a covenant-breaker, adds to his eternal agony. This is a basic New Testament doctrine: "Therefore if thine enemy hunger, feed him; if he thirst, give him drink: for in so doing thou shalt heap coals of fire on his head. Be not overcome of evil, but overcome evil with good" (Rom. 12:20-21).

The Reduction of Personal Hostilities

When your enemy goes out of his way to restore a lost asset to you, it becomes more difficult to hate him. He has demonstrated his commitment to God's law. This identifies him as someone who respects the terms of God's covenant. This covenant is personal, not impersonal. All those who affirm the covenant are personally bonded to God, and therefore to each other. Thus, whatever the dispute may be between them, it becomes more difficult to ascribe comprehensive evil motives to anyone who honors this moral injunction. He has gone to some expense to restore a lost animal to its owner. This is a visible affirmation that the law of God is more important than the personal disputes of life.

Obviously, it would be close to impossible to gain a court's conviction against anyone who ignores this law. There would have to be witnesses. The accused person could claim that he had never seen the animal or other lost object. It is also difficult to imagine what civil penalties might be attached to this law. We therefore should conclude that the enforcement of this law is based on *self-government under God's law.* The person who returns a lost object to its owner is demonstrating that he acted out of concern for the law, not out of concern for the civil magistrate. He is a person who exercises self-government under law. Again, it becomes more difficult to entertain suspicions about his overall ulterior motives.

Maimonides' Rule and Social Conflict

Clearly, Moses Maimonides' rule would drastically increase hostilities between Jews and gentiles: "The lost property of a heathen may be kept, for Scripture says, *Lost thing of thy brother's* (Deut. 22:3). Furthermore, if one returns it, he commits a transgression, for he is supporting the wicked of the world."[3] In other words, returning lost property to a gentile is primarily a form of economic subsidy, not primarily an honoring of the principle of owner's rights. It is revealing that he cited Deuteronomy 22:3, which refers to the lost property of one's brother, and made no mention of Exodus 23:4-5, which explicitly deals with the lost property of enemies.

He did add this qualification: "But if one returns it in order to sanctify God's name, thereby causing persons to praise the Israelites and realize that they are honest, he is deemed praiseworthy. In cases involving a profanation of God's name, it is forbidden to keep a heathen's lost property, and it must be returned."[4] In other words, in order to maintain the appearance of honesty, the property should be returned. The problem was, of course, that eventually these rules would become known to the gentile community, and they would learn the truth about those Jews who follow Maimonides' precepts: they are governed by a very different concept of honesty from what the Bible itself establishes. At that point, the rule of expediency would be recognized for what it is, and would therefore backfire, bringing reproach on the Jewish community. This is not the way to increase social peace between hostile religious groups in a community.

If the town is equally inhabited by Jews and gentiles, he said, the Jew has to advertise that he has found lost property.[5] But if the town

---

3. Moses Maimonides, *The Book of Torts*, vol. 11 of *The Code of Maimonides*, 14 vols. (New Haven, Connecticut: Yale University Press, [1180] 1954), "Laws Concerning Robbery and Lost Property," Chapter Eleven, Section Three, p. 128.

4. *Idem.*

5. *Ibid.*, Section Six, p. 129.

is less than half populated by Jews, and the lost property is found where heathen generally congregate, or in a highway, the Jew is blameless in keeping it, since "whatever he finds belongs to him, even if an Israelite comes along and identifies it."[6] Maimonides warned his fellow Jews that if the owner is a Jew, and he claims the property, the Jew who wishes to follow "the good and upright path and do more than the strict letter of the law requires" should return it to him.[7] Nevertheless, he is not required by law to do this.

The following rule is literally a corker. "If one finds a cask of wine in a town containing a majority of heathen, any benefit from the wine is forbidden, but the cask may be retained as lost property." Leave the cork in the cask. Presumably, Maimonides was worried about some sort of ritual pollution problem associated with gentile food. That fear is solved as soon as a Jew asserts ownership of the lost cask: ". . . if an Israelite comes and identifies it, the finder may drink the wine."[8] What a system! As soon as a Jew identifies himself as the legal owner, he loses legal ownership. This is not the best way to reduce personal hostilities within the Jewish community.

Maimonides does provide one rule that makes sense, toward the end of Chapter Eleven: "If one follows the good and upright path and does more than the strict letter of the law requires, he will return lost property in all cases, even if it is not in keeping with his dignity."[9] But this *is* the strict letter of the law: Exodus 23:4-5. Any form of dignity that is not in keeping with it is a form of pride, and should be eliminated, or at least suppressed through self-discipline. Obeying the law regarding lost property is a good place to begin the process.

Identifying Thieves

The person who steals and is immediately arrested could offer this excuse: "I found this animal wandering in the area, and I was simply returning it to its owner. I did not know who owned it, so I was taking it home until I could make further inquiries." This might work once or twice. The man could appeal to the case law in Deuteronomy:

---

6. *Ibid.*, Section Seven, p. 129.
7. *Idem.*
8. *Ibid.*, Section Eight, p. 129.
9. *Ibid.*, Section Seventeen, p. 131.

Thou shalt not see thy brother's ox or his sheep go astray, and hide thyself from them: thou shalt in any case bring them again unto thy brother. And if thy brother be not nigh unto thee, or if thou know him not, then thou shalt bring it unto thine own house, and it shall be with thee until thy brother seek after it, and thou shalt restore it to him again. In like manner shalt thou do with his ass; and so shalt thou do with his raiment; and with all lost thing of thy brother's, which he hath lost, and thou hast found, shalt thou do likewise: thou mayest not hide thyself (Deut. 22:1-3).

This would not be a suitable excuse three or four times. If a person lives in a society that has developed an information reporting system, he has a legal requirement to report the whereabouts of lost articles to the civil authorities if he does not know who the owner is. Thus, as time passes, the "excuse of the wandering animal" fades. The owner who discovers his animal in another's possession has a far stronger legal case than if this case law were not in God's law-order. A lost animal is not supposed to remain indefinitely in another person's possession, especially after the person who lost it broadcasts its loss publicly. "Thou shalt bring it unto thine own house, and it shall be with thee until thy brother seek after it."

Marks of Ownership and Reduced Search Costs

This case law makes it far more likely that a lost animal will be immediately returned to the owner. Thus, the law increases the economic return from marking property. This is an incentive to promote the spread of owner's rights that can be legally protected. A person's property is brought under his own administration through a mark of ownership.

By marking property, the owner reduces future search costs: his search for the animal and the finder's search for the owner. It reduces search costs for a neighbor whose crops have been eaten or ruined by a wandering beast. He can then gain restitution from the owner (Ex. 22:5). This is an incentive for someone who wants to protect his property (the beast) from thieves or to protect his neighbor's property (crops) from loss by building a fence or by restraining the animal in some way.

Branding also reduces search costs for the civil authorities if the animal should be stolen. By burning an identifying mark into an animal's flesh, or by attaching a tag to its ear or other flesh, the owner increases risks to the thief. It also increases risks to those who would buy from the thief. The identifying mark makes it possible for buyers to avoid the possibility that they will be charged with having received stolen property. As I mentioned in Chapter 17, English common law recognizes no such crime; it took statute law in the nineteenth century to make it a crime. [10] Biblical law does make it a crime to receive stolen property knowingly, and even when the buyer does not know that the property is stolen, the owner has the right to have it returned to him. The thief never possessed the "bundle of rights" necessary for biblical ownership. God delegates ownership; he does not delegate it to thieves.

God's use of circumcision in the Old Testament era is an obvious parallel to the brand. So was the hole punched in the ear of a slave (Ex. 21:6). These were both marks of ownership. The New Testament practice of baptism leaves no visible mark, but it leaves a legal description in the records of a continuing third party institution, the church. It is also a mark of God's primary ownership. The same is true of property registration generally. Titles, deeds, and other marks of legal ownership have developed over the centuries, thereby extending the dominion of mankind through the development of the institution of private property. By identifying legal owners, society increases the level of personal responsibility. This, too, is a basic biblical goal.

Not a Case of State-Enforced Charity

The discoverer must sacrifice time and effort to see to it that the beast is returned to its owner. This might be seen as a form of judicially mandated charity, one of the few examples of compulsory charity in the Bible. Compulsory charity, however, is a contradiction. Charity must always be voluntary. It is governed by the legal principle that the recipient has no judicially enforceable entitlement to the gift. This is why the modern welfare State is careful to label its compulsory wealth-redistribution programs as *entitlements*. The creators of these programs want to get away from any suggestion of voluntarism, which implies that the donor has the right to refuse to make the gift. Thus, this case law is not related to charity. The owner has a legal claim on the property. He has an entitlement. The person who finds the lost animal is expected to honor this legal claim, even though it costs him money or time to do so.

---

10. Wayne LaFave and Austin Scott, Jr., *Handbook on Criminal Law* (Minneapolis, Minnesota: West, 1972), pp. 681-91: "Receiving Stolen Property."

This law requires a form of wealth-redistribution. The one who discovers the lost animal owes it to the owner to return it. This is a positive injunction. So is the law to assist an enemy whose animal has fallen down. Yet biblical civil law, I have argued, does not issue positive injunctions. It does not compel anyone to do good; it merely prohibits people from doing public evil. Thus, I conclude that this law is not a civil law, but is rather a moral injunction. There is no civil sanction attached to it, nor is there any general judicial principle of restitution that would enable the judges to determine a proper sanction. The civil government therefore has no role to play in the enforcement of this law.

The civil government can become involved if the person who owns the beast discovers it in someone else's possession. The suspicion of theft immediately arises. This threat is an incentive for the discoverer to return it to its owner, in order to avoid future criminal prosecution for theft. But this is a separate issue. The case law in question should be seen as a moral responsibility placed on the individual directly by God, and not as a civil statute.

Conclusion

The righteous person is not to use circumstances to gain revenge on his enemy at the expense of the innocent and helpless. He must do what he can to restore order — economic and moral — in his dealings with his enemies. This means that God's purposes for society are more important than men's short-term personal feuds. This is not to say that society is always more important than the individual is; it *is* to say that *God's purposes* are more important than man's purposes, either for society or for individuals.

God's requirement of returning a lost animal or lifting up a fallen domestic animal is imposed in order to restore harmonious relations among enemies, and to help fulfill the dominion covenant. While a short-run burden is placed on the man who comes across a lost or fallen animal, he knows that in the long run his own interests as a property owner are improved when people honor this law. If he refuses to honor it, then others may also refuse. Thus, honoring the terms of the law improves the safety and security of all members of society.

This case law is an example of a biblical injunction that is narrowly circumscribed, but which in fact has wide application. The finder is to return the lost animal to the owner, an enemy. Does this

mean that he need not return a lost animal to his friend? No; the
focus of the law is on the case where the temptation is greater to keep
the animal: the enemy's beast. The law assumes that if you are required to obey it in the difficult case, you surely are required to obey
it in the easier case.

26

BRIBERY AND JUDGMENT

And thou shalt take no gift: for the gift blindeth the wise, and per-
verteth the words of the righteous (Ex. 23:8).

God is a righteous Judge. His judgment cannot be purchased by anyone. He honors His law, not gifts from men. "Wherefore now let the fear of the LORD be upon you; take heed and do it: for there is no iniquity with the LORD our God, nor respect of persons, nor taking of gifts" (II Chron. 19:7). He sets the standard for rendering judgment; human judges are to follow it. "Thou shalt not wrest judgment; thou shalt not respect persons, neither take a gift: for a gift doth blind the eyes of the wise, and pervert the words of the righteous" (Deut. 16:19).

The context of this law is official judgment rendered by a court. Judges are not to render false judgment in favor of a poor man (Ex. 23:3) or against him (Ex. 23:6). People are not to offer false witness in a court against a righteous person (Ex. 23:7). They are not to oppress a stranger (Ex. 23:9). Such corrupt judicial acts constitute oppression, which points to the most common source of oppression in society: a misuse of God's authorized monopoly of justice, the courts.[1] *Oppression is therefore primarily judicial*: either the court renders false judgment or else it refuses to prosecute a righteous person's cause. "They afflict the just, they take a bribe, and they turn aside the poor in the gate" (Amos 5:12). The court indulges in official sins of commission or omission. It is supposed to uphold God's *mission* by rendering righteous judgment as a means of national and international evangelism.

Behold, I have taught you statutes and judgments, even as the LORD my God commanded me, that ye should do so in the land whither ye go to possess

---

1. See Chapter 22: "Oppression, Omniscience, and Judgment."

it. Keep therefore and do them; for this is your wisdom and your understanding in the sight of the nations, which shall hear all these statutes, and
say, Surely this great nation is a wise and understanding people. For what
nation is there so great, who hath God so nigh unto them, as the LORD our
God is in all things that we call upon him for? And what nation is there so
great, that hath statutes and judgments so righteous as all this law, which I
set before you this day? (Deut. 4:5-8).

Misusing a Legitimate Monopoly

In the analysis of oppression that is offered by modern socialists,
the free market is the source. Competition is seen as ruthless, immoral, and man-destroying. Capitalism in this view is not a system
governed by the principle of consumer's sovereignty,[2] but rather a
system of consumer exploitation by unscrupulous businessmen
whose goal is to hold down wages and raise prices. (In fact, free market firms raise wages through their mutual competition for scarce
labor services,[3] and also by investing in capital that increases the
productivity of the workers.[4] They reduce prices in their endless
quest for new consumers.[5] They are forced to do this through the
competitive market process, since they are economic agents of the
consumers.[6]) Karl Marx concluded volume 1 of *Das Kapital* (the only
volume published in his lifetime) with these words: ". . . the capitalist mode of production and accumulation, and therefore capitalist
private property, have for their fundamental condition the annihilation of self-earned private property; in other words, the expropriation
of the labourer."[7] A few pages earlier, he had prophesied the inevitable communist revolution in these envious and apocalyptic terms:
"The knell of capitalist private property sounds. The expropriators
are expropriated."[8]

---

2. W. H. Hutt, "The Nature of Aggressive Selling," *Economica*, 12 (1935);
reprinted in *Individual Freedom: Selected Works of William H. Hutt*, edited by Svetozar
Pejovich and David Klingaman (Westport, Connecticut: Greenwood, 1975).

3. Gary North, "Exploitation and Knowledge," *The Freeman* (Jan. 1982).

4. Percy L. Greaves, Jr., "How Wages Are Determined," *The Freeman* (July
1970); reprinted in Bettina B. Greaves (ed.), *Free Market Economics: A Basic Reader*
(Irvington, New York: Foundation for Economic Education, 1975).

5. Gary North, "Price Competition and Expanding Alternatives," *The Freeman*
(Aug. 1974); cf. North, *An Introduction to Christian Economics* (Nutley, New Jersey:
Craig Press, 1973), ch. 9: "Downward Price Flexibility and Economic Growth."

6. Gary North, "Who's the Boss?" *The Freeman* (Feb. 1979); Greaves, *op. cit.*

7. Karl Marx, *Capital* (New York: Modern Library, [1867] 1906 ed.), p. 848.

8. *Ibid.*, p. 837.

Such rhetoric has been highly influential in academic circles, including Christian academic circles. Liberation theology is the most consistent and most visible theological by-product of such a view of the free market, but liberation theology's rejection of capitalism is quite common in neo-evangelical colleges and seminaries that do not openly teach liberation theology. Evidence of this bias is provided by George Grant, who in 1987 and 1988 visited 116 evangelical Protestant colleges, relief and development agencies, missionary groups, and charities in the U.S. He asked for copies of their recommended reading lists; at the colleges, he got the required reading texts. After many months of this, he compiled a list of over three dozen of the most common titles. Without exception, they all share an essentially anticapitalist outlook. There was not a single openly pro-free market book on the list. Five of these titles were published by Orbis Books, the publishing outlet of the Roman Catholic Maryknoll Order, and the primary liberation theology publishing house in the U.S.[9]

By focusing on what is no more than a secondary source of economic oppression, the free market, critics of capitalism have misled people. The free market is not the source of the problem, although the visible manifestations of oppression frequently are found in economic transactions. The source of the problem is the misuse of a biblically legitimate monopoly, the civil court system. Political oppressors in the West from the medieval period until the late seventeenth century were generally the allies of unscrupulous, power-seeking and rent-seeking[10] agricultural aristocrats, and from the eighteenth century until the Great Depression were allies of unscrupulous, power-seeking and rent-seeking businessmen. Since the early 1930's, they have more likely also been the allies of unscrupulous, power-seeking

---

9. *Good News to the Poor* by Julio de Santa Ana, *God So Loved the Third World* by Tom Hanks, *Christ Outside the Gates* by Orlando Costas, *The Bible of the Oppressed* by Elsa Tamez, *The Militant Gospel* by Alfredo Fierro.

10. I use the term "rent" as the so-called "public choice" school of economics does: *a stream of income.* These streams of income are not limited to real estate investments. Income from government-created economic monopolies is surely a form of rent. The most prominent figure of the public choice school is Nobel laureate James Buchanan. Gordon Tullock, a law professor-turned-economist, was for many years Buchanan's intellectual partner, and should have been awarded the Nobel Prize in economics with Buchanan in 1986. He told me in 1988 that he had received two votes in the committee. I suspect the fact that he had never taken an economics course proved too embarrassing to the committee. A good introduction to public-choice economics is the textbook by James D. Gwartney and Richard Stroup, *Economics: Private and Public Choice* (New York: Academic Press, 1979).

and rent-seeking socialists, Communists, fascists, Keyenesian inter-
ventionists, and lifetime bureaucrats whose main goal in life is to
expand their ability to tell other people what to do.[11] Long-term economic monopolies, ancient and modern, have almost always been
the creation of civil governments.[12]

Bribes

Why do judges become allies of economic oppressors, thereby
making possible continuing oppression? This verse tells us why.
Citizens take a portion of their capital and "invest" it. They bribe a
court officer to render unrighteous judgment or to look the other way
and refuse to prosecute unrighteous public behavior. This verse
focuses on direct bribes, but the principle of bribery goes beyond a
direct payoff to a personally corrupt official. Bribes can come in
many forms, including promises for financial or other support during the next election.[13] Roman Catholic moralist and legal scholar
John Noonan's massive and brilliant book, *Bribes*, lists two pages of
bribe prices in history: gold, cash, percentages, etc.[14] Even the definitions of what constitutes a bribe vary widely. Noonan lists four
sources of the possible definitions of bribery, "that of the more advanced moralists; that of the law as written; that of the law as in any
degree enforced; that of common practice. If one is to say that an act
of bribery has been committed, one should know which standard one
is using."[15] But whatever the definition, in whatever society, bribes
are officially disapproved.[16]

This disapproval causes problems for explaining a nation's history. We forget or ignore the fact that some of our greatest heroes
have been bribees or bribers. Societies prefer to avoid accusing some

---

11. This is not to say that big business has not also remained the beneficiary of the
politicians. Big business has itself become the subsidized ally of socialists, Commu-
nists, fascists, and Keynesians. On this point, see Gabriel Kolko, *The Triumph of
Conservatism* (New York: Free Press of Glencoe, 1963); Carroll Quigley, *Tragedy and
Hope: A History of the World in Our Time* (New York: Macmillan, 1966), especially
Chapter 17.

12. D. T. Armentano, *Antitrust and Monopoly: Anatomy of a Policy Failure* (New York:
Wiley, 1982); Walter Adams and Horace M. Gray, *Monopoly in America: The Govern-
ment as Promoter* (New York: Macmillan, 1955); Mary Bennet Peterson, *The Regulated
Consumer* (Ottawa, Illinois: Green Hill, 1971).

13. John T. Noonan, *Bribes* (New York: Macmillan, 1984), pp. xxi-xii.

14. *Ibid.*, Appendix.

15. *Ibid.*, p. xii.

16. *Ibid.*, p. xx.

great national historical figure with the valid accusation of having been involved in this kind of scandal. Noonan comments: "Francis Bacon, Samuel Pepys, Warren Hastings are not merely respectable; they are heroes — respectively the founders, in the view of their admirers, of British science, the British navy, and British India. Bacon was a bribee by the law as actually enforced; Pepys a bribee by his own measure; Hastings a bribee by the law that was being made. Apologists by the score have hesitated to give their bribetaking its proper name. As for bribers, judgment has always been even more charitable, the underlying assumption being that they are the victims of extortion. When the persons involved have been preeminently just, judgment has often been entirely suspended. Who thinks of Thomas Becket or John Quincy Adams as giving bribes?"[17]

The Power of the Bribe

The power of the bribe is very great. This verse tells us that wise men are blinded, and righteous men become perverse through bribes. The Bible repeats its warning against bribe-taking judges in Deuteronomy 16:19, Isaiah 1:23, Amos 5:12, Psalms 26:10, and I Samuel 12:3. It was this sin that Samuel's two evil sons practiced (I Sam. 8:3), and it led to the people of Israel calling for a king (I Sam. 8:5), which Samuel warned against (I Sam. 8:11-18). The judges' sin of bribery led step by step to the call for a stronger, more centralized civil government. It was difficult for Samuel to take a stand against the inauguration of the kingship when the judicial failure of his sons was the occasion of the people's demand.

Records from the ancient Near East do not indicate any actual prosecutions for bribe-taking. There are no Mesopotamian examples yet translated of any official's being punished for this crime — this, out of a total 100,000 cuneiform tablets in museums.[18] Nothing in the records of Egypt indicates that any official was prosecuted for this crime.[19] Nowhere in the ancient Near East was there a specific civil law against bribery, with punishment specified. This is even true of the ancient Israel. "Reliance is not on human enforcement but on divine assistance."[20] But Noonan understands that this is true

---

17. *Ibid.*, p. xiii.
18. *Ibid.*, p. 11. It should be recognized that only a small proportion of these tablets has been translated. Translators seldom translate as much as 15 percent of existing Near Eastern tablets.
19. *Ibid.*, p. 12.
20. *Idem.*

of biblical history generally: "The enforcement of any law by actually applied human sanctions is not a prominent feature of biblical history. Vengeance is normally divine."[21] Noonan overstates his case with respect to biblical law, however. Deuteronomy 19 specifies that a false witness must suffer the same punishment that he had sought to inflict on his victim (Deut. 19:19). There is no reason to believe that a judge and the one who bribed him would be any less subject to this penalty.[22] Case laws frequently specify the less obvious infraction in order to affirm the more obvious, e.g., requiring a person to return his enemy's stray animal to him (Ex. 23:4), therefore indicating that this should surely be done with a friend's stray animal. If a false witness is to receive punishment on the *lex talionis* basis, surely a corrupt judge should suffer like-for-like retribution!

The combination of civil monopolistic power and the wealth transmitted by a bribe is too great for even good men to handle, so God prohibits bribe-taking. We never receive something for nothing, except by God's grace. When a bribe is offered, it is not offered free of charge. *A bribe is not a friendly gift; it is payment for services received or hoped for.* But these services are usually corrupt.[23] When bribery becomes extensive, it is either because the rulers are corrupt already, or because the bribers intend to corrupt them. Bribes are therefore a sign of widespread corruption.

This widespread acceptance of bribery as a way of life threatens the social order. When men believe that they can buy the civil judgment they prefer, they lose sight of the true character of God and the looming threat of His judgments, both temporal and eternal. People will eventually lose faith in a bribe-ridden social order, for a social order is sustained by men's faith in the character of God (real or imagined) and the trustworthiness of His sanctions. In a society marked by bribery, the guardians of social order no longer guard in the name of God and by means of His law. They make it appear as though they can sell God's judgment to the highest bidder. In response, God visits His judgment on them and their society. The *lex talionis* of the civil covenant cannot be annulled by civil legislation. It is basic to God's creation order. Societies will reap what they sow.

---

21. *Ibid.*, p. 23.

22. Why Noonan contrasts the Deuteronomic law regarding false witness with the absence of a law regarding bribe-taking is a mystery to me: *ibid.*, p. 24.

23. Not in every case, however; see below: "The Righteous Bribe," pp. 793-800.

Beyond Civil Corruption

The corruption of the bribe goes beyond the civil order. It will affect family government, too. Noonan's insight is perceptive: *bribery is linked culturally and theologically to adultery*. "Metaphors drawn from the vocabulary of sexual sin are used to describe the bribetaker. Since the time of the Roman Republic, 'to corrupt' has meant both to seduce a woman and to pay off an officeholder. One 'betrays' a lover or an office. One is 'faithless' to a spouse or a public trust. The same religions, the same kind of commandments and examples, the same kind of sanctions have addressed acts of bribery and acts of unlawful intercourse. Taken at a certain level of generality, the same substantive goods are protected and promoted by both ethics. Each sets enormous store by fidelity. Each lays down the lines that separate a gift, understood as an identification of one person with another person, from the manipulative or exploitative use of one person by another person. As the sexual ethic disintegrates, or appears to disintegrate, before our eyes, we can ask whether the ethic governing bribes will follow suit."[24]

Bribery is also similar to witchcraft, he argues. Both bribery and sorcery are ways of influencing the outcome of an event by illegal means. Both are believed to be widely practiced, though no one admits being involved personally. The formal accusations of both offenses increase during times of moral ambiguity and institutional disruption.[25] That adultery in the Bible is also connected to witchcraft and idolatry should come as no surprise. However, the fact that bribery, witchcraft, and adultery are linked in terms of ethics, language, and social function in the history of the West is not intuitively obvious.

Bribes and Higher Courts

It should be obvious that local church courts are uniquely vulnerable to being swayed by considerations of money. The local church, unlike the civil government, faces the problem of its dependence on essentially voluntary contributions. Even if the tithe is mandatory in a local congregation,[26] a person's continuing membership would not be judicially enforceable by civil law in a biblical society. Civil courts do not face this problem of voluntarism. Civil govern-

---

24. *Ibid.*, p. xvii.
25. *Ibid.*, p. xviii.
26. This is virtually unheard of in twentieth-century churches.

ments can compel the payment of taxes by threat of violence, such as confiscation of property. Few people ever voluntarily offer lots of extra money to the tax collector, just to be nice. But people who consistently bring tithes and offerings to the local church, and especially rich people who bring extensive additional offerings on a regular basis, automatically become important figures in that congregation. The more debt the church carries, the more influential such people become. (The borrower is not only servant to the lender, he is servant also to his employer; the deeper in debt he is, the more dependent he is on his employer.)

In a dispute between a tithing rich person and a tithing poor person, or especially a non-tithing poor person, a local church court may be tempted not to render an adverse verdict against a demonstrably guilty but very rich man. *This is one reason why higher church courts are so necessary: to allow a poor man to appeal to a more distant court that is less dependent financially on one rich man's contributions.* While a bribe may not have been offered to the church's highest officer, the pastor, the economic equivalent of a bribe may have been offered to him: continued local employment. If the rich man in his dispute in any way threatens to cease giving his tithe, or threatens to stop giving the extra offerings, or threatens to leave the church altogether, then his previous offerings have in fact become *retroactive bribes*. This is a practical reason why it is imperative for all voting members[27] of a congregation to be required by church law to tithe to the local church. The church's source of income must be wide and deep, in order to reduce the influence of any particular member.

The direct bribe is more likely to be offered to a civil magistrate than to a church officer. Why? First, because it is illegal to offer a bribe to a civil servant. Second, because the civil magistrate receives a guaranteed salary that is relatively independent of competitive pressures. Unlike a pastor whose church could be thrown into a crisis if a disgruntled rich person leaves, the civil judge has considerable coercive power over those who are tried by his court. Those standing before him cannot autonomously walk out and transfer

---

27. I am not saying that all communicant members should be forced to tithe as a condition of membership; only the voting members should be. Those members who refuse to pay their God-required share of the ministry should not be given judicial status in the government of the church. If they refuse to place themselves under the ecclesiastical requirements of God's law, then they should not exercise authority over others in terms of the God's law. They should not hold any ecclesiastical office. Voting is an aspect of exercising citizenship, an office of judge.

membership to another jurisdiction before the trial begins.[28] The people in his court are paying their taxes to a third party, the tax collecting agency. The judge will probably not lose his job if he renders an adverse judgment against one of them, unless one of them is a political power broker or a celebrity who is popular with the public. If he is a lifetime judge, nothing but threats of coercion or promises of secret rewards may sway him. Thus, if he is to be influenced by a bribe, it is because he is *personally* after the money or other economic asset, such as inside information of economic value.[29] In short, the bribe to a specific civil officer is far more likely to be obvious to the recipient; the bribe to the church court is more likely to be indirect.

Again, one of the reasons why a civil court of appeal is necessary is to insure honest judgment for those without money or local influence. The more distant higher court is less likely to be swayed by questions of a person's local influence. Also, the person who offers a bribe locally will find it more expensive and more risky to continue to offer bribes to higher courts' officers. Thus, the potential payoff of bribing a local judge is also reduced; on appeal, the favorable local decision may be overthrown. The more visibly corrupt the paid-for local verdict is, the more likely it will be overturned on the basis of law.

The Righteous Bribe[30]

Exodus 23:8 forbids the judge's acceptance of a bribe. A bribe perverts the wise and righteous person. Thus, the judge who is righteous is characterized in part by his refusal to accept a bribe. The law of God is to be applied to each case before the court, irrespective of the personal advantage of a judge. The court has been granted a monopoly by God. It represents God in a covenantal hierarchy.[31] A judge is not to seek personal gain through altering justice, either to render a corrupt judgment or a righteous one.

But what of the unrighteous judge who rules in a corrupt society? What can righteous people do about him? If a righteous person is

---

28. A "change of venue" plea can be offered, of course. The accused can request a trial in a different court. But such pleas can be turned down by the local court.

29. Henry Manne [MANee], *Insider Trading and the Stock Market* (New York: Free Press, 1966).

30. The original version of this section appeared as Appendix 5 in R. J. Rushdoony, *The Institutes of Biblical Law* (Nutley, New Jersey: Craig Press, 1973). I have yet to receive a single criticism of the thesis.

31. Ray R. Sutton, *That You May Prosper: Dominion By Covenant* (Tyler, Texas: Institute for Christian Economics, 1987), chaps. 2, 12.

brought before an unrighteous judge or an unrighteous court, how does he gain righteous judgment? What if he is a stranger in some society that expects bribes from those seeking justice? An analogous example is the salesman who seeks to sell military equipment or other goods to nations governed by corrupt State officials. What if that nation's customs regarding State purchases recognize the legitimacy, or at least the necessity, of kickbacks and payoffs to public officials? In other words, what if some nation's traditions would rather have foreign capitalists pay part of the salaries of public officials, even though this means using tax money to buy possibly substandard foreign products? Obviously, to make such payments is to subsidize evil — corrupt officials — to some degree. On the other hand, to allow corrupt officials to continue to make personally profitable but socially bad decisions is also to subsidize evil to some degree. Wouldn't it be better to have a bribe-seeking public official profit from a good decision rather than from a bad decision? The question then arises: Are righteous people allowed to pay bribes, even though officials are forbidden by the Bible to receive them?

Contrary to most people's expectations, the Bible says yes. The Bible recognizes that in order to gain legitimate goals in life, righteous people are allowed to pay bribes to corrupt officials. In the same way that a bribe to a righteous judge is designed to twist righteous justice, a bribe to an unrighteous judge is designed to straighten out unrighteous judgments.

Solomon's Recommended Strategy

Solomon the wise understood this biblical principle of productive bribery:

A gift is as a precious stone in the eyes of him that hath it: whithersoever it turneth, it prospereth (Prov. 17:8).

A gift in secret pacifieth anger: and a reward in the bosom strong wrath (Prov. 21:14).

Notice the phrase, "a reward in the bosom." It produces a mental image of a secret gift, one tucked away in one's cloak. Nevertheless, someone might argue that Solomon did not have civil government in mind when he wrote these two proverbs. Perhaps Solomon had in mind only personal friendship rather than civil justice. But to argue in this fashion makes it very difficult to interpret Solomon's use of the parallel phrase "a gift out of the bosom" in reference to paying bribes to civil magistrates:

A wicked man taketh a gift out of the bosom [under his cloak] to pervert the ways of judgment (Prov. 17:23).

He had in mind a judge, someone who has the power "to pervert the ways of judgment." Solomon was not talking about gifts of friendship; he was talking about gifts to produce favorable judgments.

It might also be argued that Solomon was simply commenting on the reality of the success of bribery, but not promoting the offering of bribes. If so, then why would he say of a bribe that "whithersoever it turneth, it prospereth"? Does evil always prosper? Not in the long run, certainly. So, he seems to have had in mind the *righteous bribe* — a gift to an unrighteous judge from a righteous person in order to gain righteous judgment.

Other Biblical Examples

There are several examples of such bribery in the Bible. When Jacob passed through the land controlled by his brother Esau, he had his servants present Esau with a series of presents, each nicer than the previous gift. He self-consciously decided to buy off his brother's wrath by a systematic program of bribery (Gen. 32:13-21).[32] Why was this necessary? Because his brother was a corrupt and present-oriented person. It was better, Jacob decided, to pay bribes to Esau in advance than to risk a military confrontation with him. The bribe, unlike tribute, was offered voluntarily in advance of Esau's rendering of judgment against Jacob. Esau did not impose a military defeat on Jacob and then ask for tribute from him. Instead, Jacob acted in advance of what he wisely expected to be a losing military effort when he passed through his brother's jurisdiction.

We also have examples of *negative bribes*: the imposition of unpleasantness on judges, with an implicit offer to stop, once judgment is rendered. Jesus told a parable of an unjust judge and a righteous widow. The judge, first of all, "feared not God, neither regarded man" (Luke 18:2). The widow comes to him to be avenged of her adversary. He refuses to render a decision. So she comes again. And again. She refuses to let him alone. Finally, he can stand it no

---

32. Gary North, *The Dominion Covenant: Genesis* (2nd ed.; Tyler, Texas: Institute for Christian Economics, 1987), ch. 20: "Contingency Planning."

longer. He announces, in desperation: "Though I fear not God, nor regard man; yet because this widow troubleth me, I will avenge her, lest by her continual coming she weary me" (vv. 4b-5). Let us not miss the economics of all this: the widow had offered the judge a bribe. "Render judgment," she was saying, "and I will give you peace. I will stop demanding judgment. I will *pay* you by going away and leaving you in peace." She was entitled to judgment, and she insisted on getting it. It was a reverse bribe: "I will pay you after the judgment is rendered." She did not ask for unrighteous judgment; she merely asked for prompt judgment. She asked for what God says that she was entitled to.

I realize that Bible commentators are not used to thinking in terms of subtle economic concepts such as reverse bribery. Yet we use a similar approach all the time when dealing with our children. We offer "carrots" for good behavior, and we offer "sticks" for bad behavior. We keep telling them to obey, with the harshest, most fearsome tone of voice we can muster; we make them feel uncomfortable. We implicitly promise to leave them alone if they obey. They dearly want to be left alone. When they do what we tell them, we once again speak pleasantly to them. They want to avoid our harsh words, so we devise a system of negative rewards that uses this desire to our advantage. We also use positive rewards. We offer them payment if they obey. The goal of each kind of reward is the same: *gaining their cooperation*. The same is true of negative bribes and positive bribes: we seek to gain corrupt officials' cooperation.

The Sermon on the Mount

Consider also Jesus' recommendations in His famous Sermon on the Mount. He set forth suggestions for daily conduct in a world controlled by unrighteous people.

Agree with thine adversary quickly, whiles thou art in the way with him; lest at any time the adversary deliver thee to the judge, and the judge deliver thee to the officer, and thou be cast into prison (Matt. 5:25).

And if any man will sue thee at the law, and take away thy coat, let him have thy cloak also. And whosoever shall compel thee to go a mile, go with him twain (Matt. 5:40-41).

Jesus informed His followers that they should give to those in power over them—i.e., if anyone can *compel* our cooperation—an extra measure of cooperation. Give him your cloak also, He said. If such a gift were truly voluntary, we would call the extra gift a tip for good service or charity to the needy. What, then, should we call such cooperation under conditions involving the threat of external compulsion? *Obviously, this is bribery.* A bribe is a gift to a public official over and above what is legally required or officially asked for. Such a bribe enables a Christian to escape the full force of the wrath that, in principle, a consistent pagan ruler would impose on Christians if he realized how utterly at war Christ and His kingdom are against Satan and his kingdom. In other words, a bribe pacifies the receiver, just as Solomon said.

The ethic of the Sermon on the Mount is grounded on the principle that a godly bribe (of goods or services, cloak or walk) is sometimes the best way for Christians to buy temporary peace and freedom for themselves and the church, assuming that the enemies of God have overwhelming temporal power. Jesus was giving suggestions for a captive people who labored under the domination of the Roman Empire. This is also the context of His famous recommendation to turn the other cheek (Matt. 5:39). His advice should not lead us to believe that the proper Christian attitude under all circumstances should be to agree with our enemies. Perpetual forgiveness and endless toleration of evil should not be our attitude when we are given lawful authority over evil-doers. When we are given the lawful authority to prosecute, convict, and punish evil people in the civil courts, we should do so.

Jesus warned His listeners to "resist not evil" (Matt. 5:39). Is this a universal rule applicable in all circumstances? Not at all. James tells us, "Submit yourselves therefore to God. Resist the devil, and he will flee from you" (James 4:7). Why the difference in the recommended strategies? Because Jesus' words were directed toward a captive people who were under the heel of frequently evil local rulers who were the agents of Rome. He had in mind civil conduct by a captive nation. His advice? "Do not become violent revolutionaries. Don't provoke a head-on armed conflict with military power that exceeds yours." In contrast, James set forth a principle of moral conduct: resist the devil. Sometimes the best way to resist the devil is to cooperate temporarily with his subordinates, the way that Obadiah cooperated with King Ahab in order to save the lives of a hundred prophets (I Ki. 18:13). We cooperate with evil-doers for the purposes of subversion. In effect, we become spies for God's kingdom in a strategy of conquest. We do what Moses did as a young man in

Pharaoh's court, Rahab did in Jericho, Ehud did with Eglon when he brought the king a "present," and Jael did with Sisera before he slept. We "play ball" long enough to get an opportunity to crush their skulls with the bat.

Does an evil civil ruler deserve obedience? No; he deserves eternal punishment. Is it wise for Christians to render an evil civil ruler obedience? Yes, but only if his judgments cannot be successfully overturned in court by superior magistrates or if he cannot be successfully overthrown by lower magistrates.[33]

To the extent that a Christian's position in some period of history resembles the plight of the Christians under Roman rule, he should take heed of the Sermon on the Mount. He should remain outwardly cooperative with civil magistrates. Under the rule of a Hitler or a Stalin, the Christian's proper response is outward subservience. He should bribe the dictator's lieutenants, join a Christian underground, and continue preaching the gospel, both openly (where legal) and clandestinely (where illegal). Bribes and outward cooperation gain people time and influence. The Christian can then continue his work of reshaping people's religious views, thereby undermining the power base of the tyrant. He should be as wise (and deadly) as a serpent by appearing as harmless as a dove.

This raises the practical question of how to deal with the Christian who insists in advance that he will inform on other Christians who break any civil law, or at the very least will tell the truth to any civil magistrate who asks him a question about someone else's law-breaking. First and foremost, such a compulsive truth-teller has not understood the Bible, especially the case of Rahab the God-honoring liar.[34] Second, in a major crisis where the State threatens the church or obedience to biblical principles, it then becomes the moral responsibility of other Christians to lie to, confuse, and generally misinform any "blabbermouth for Jesus" in their midst. A real-world example of the threat of this sort of self-righteousness would be the case of Christians in Europe who hid Jews in their homes. Immediately after a successful invasion of a country, the Nazis insisted that all

---

33. John Calvin, *Institutes of the Christian Religion* (1559), Book 4, Chapter 20. See also Michael Gilstrap, "John Calvin's Theology of Resistance," *Christianity and Civilization*, 3 (1983), pp. 180-217.

34. Gary North, "In Defense of Biblical Bribery," in R. J. Rushdoony, *Institutes of Biblical Law*, pp. 838-42. Jim West, "Rahab's Justifiable Lie," *Christianity and Civilization*, 2 (1983).

Jews report to local police headquarters. It was clear that the Jews were being shipped to concentration camps. Many Christians in the Netherlands, for example, hid Jews on their farms or in other hiding places. It was imperative that informers, Christian and non-Christian alike, not be given evidence of such activities. Lying to Christian informants was as ethical as lying to the State officials who were being served by collaborating Christians as their agents.

The Failure of Neutrality

If a bribe offered by a righteous man to an unrighteous court is legitimate in God's eyes, yet an offer of a bribe to a righteous judge is illegitimate, then a problem arises: How to discover a common definition of criminal behavior that encompasses the visible, prosecutable activity of paying off a judge? Can a proper definition be found that allows prosecution without relying on an investigation into the question of demonstrable intent of the briber? Can a biblically sanctioned legal definition of criminal action be imposed that does not raise the question of the legitimacy of the judgment sought by the briber? Can both the briber and the bribee be legitimately convicted, irrespective of the intent of the briber?

The Bible's answer is clearly no. No common-ground definition of bribery is possible. There are biblically legitimate bribes as well as biblically condemned bribes. Judges must never accept bribes, the Bible teaches, but bribers are sometimes acting legitimately. Thus, *no common-ground, natural-law principle can be invoked to define specific visible acts that invariably constitute criminal bribery.* Noonan, as a Roman Catholic defender of natural law principles, searches in vain to provide a single definition of bribery that can be imposed on any society, irrespective of that society's theological roots. It is interesting that Thomas Aquinas did not invoke natural law theory in his discussion of bribery, and in this, Noonan says, "Thomas is representative of the medieval theologians working in the natural law tradition."[35]

Here is what I wrote in the early 1970's. I have not changed my opinion: "There can be no neutral, universal application of a word like 'bribery,' for, to make such a universal definition, we would have to assume the existence of some universal, neutral, and completely accepted legal code. That is the basic presupposition of humanism, but Christianity denies such neutrality. Neutrality does not exist.

---

35. Noonan, *Bribes*, p. 212.

Everything must be interpreted in terms of what God has revealed. The humanistic goal of neutral language (and therefore neutral law) was overturned at the Tower of Babel. Our *definitions* must be in terms of *biblical revelation*. Resistance to unjust laws is not anarchy; resistance to just laws is anarchy. Rahab was right, though her apostate state would have regarded her as treasonous; Judas Iscariot was wrong, though an apostate state regarded his actions as exemplary, and rewarded him handsomely. There is no universal definition of a concept like treason. God's law and His specific guidance determine what is or is not treasonous or anarchistic. Rahab was the saint and Judas was the traitor."[36] I linked treason and bribery together because they are obvious examples, biblically, of the impossibility of finding a universal definition of crime without any appeal to biblical ethics. What I did not recognize until I read Noonan's book is that treason and bribery are the two crimes mentioned by name in the U.S. Constitution.[37]

The legitimacy of certain forms of bribery points directly to the moral necessity of theocracy: the rule (*kratos*) of God (*theos*). If God's revealed law in the Bible is not acknowledged by the civil courts as the ultimate standard of civil law, then the State will of necessity convict people who are biblically innocent of any crime, or else fail to convict others who are guilty as charged. Once we recognize this fact with respect to crimes as important as treason and bribery, we also ought to recognize it with respect to the whole of civil law. To fail to recognize this is to continue to deny the moral and civil legitimacy of biblical law itself. Natural law theory is a myth. It is time for Christians to abandon it.

Highest Bid Wins: Illegitimate for Governments

We hear of bribes offered to public officials. We seldom hear of bribes offered to businessmen. We expect to hear of businessmen offering bribes, but we do not expect to hear of businessmen being offered bribes. Why not? Because the concept of bribery is linked almost exclusively to the misuse of a God-sanctioned monopoly, a judicial office. A bribe is a payment to an official. When one capitalist makes a cash payment to another in order to gain his cooperation,

---

36. North, "In Defense of Biblical Bribery," in Rushdoony, *Institutes of Biblical Law*, p. 843.
37. Noonan, *Bribes*, p. xvi.

this is called market competition, not bribery.[38]

This illustrates a very important economic principle: *different systems of financing govern different sovereign spheres of society.* The principle of "highest money bid wins" governs the competitive free market. If this principle were not honored, then the auctions (competitive open markets) of the world could not function, as we shall examine in detail below. Men always have expectations of how resources are to be distributed in any social order. If the principle of private ownership is maintained by the civil authorities, then people know that they have the *right to exclude others* from access to their property. The civil government is expected to uphold ownership *boundaries.*[39] Only by offering higher and higher bids can other people hope to gain access to my assets and the key legal right (immunity) associated with ownership, namely, the right to exclude. The principle of *highest bid wins* is inherent in any society that upholds the private property system. The rules of economic order are known in advance, and people can make economic plans for the future in terms of these judicial assumptions.

The difference between the operation of the free market and the operation of the court system is that God has granted a legal monopoly of enforcement to church government and civil government. Courts must serve as the final voice of civil authority.[40] They are to be neither open nor competitive.[41] This means that they are not to

---

38. An exception: a salesman who pays a bribe to a purchasing agent who is in a position to place a large order using his firm's money. They in effect "split the commission." This is a violation of company policy on the part of the purchasing agent, who is misusing company funds in order to get a personal reward. It is a criminal offense. This must be recognized for what it is: a violation of company policy. It is not inherently a "capitalist act." It is a thief's act.

39. This is point three of the biblical covenant model: Gary North, *The Sinai Strategy: Economics and the Ten Commandments* (Tyler, Texas: Institute for Christian Economics, 1986), ch. 8.

40. If a national (or international) supreme court possesses, as a side-effect of rendering judgments in court cases, the constitutional authority to declare an act of the legislature illegal or unconstitutional—a power possessed by the U.S. Supreme Court (though not by many other nations' courts)—this power should be tempered by the right of the legislature and the executive to combine (if they are divided) in a decision to overturn the supreme court's decision, if the vote of the legislature is large enough (say, three-quarters of both houses of the legislature). Without this right of appeal beyond the supreme judicial court, a single agency of civil government gains the exclusive voice of authority, a power trustworthy only in the hands of God. On the accelerating power of the U.S. judiciary, see Carrol D. Kilgore, *Judicial Tyranny* (Nashville, Tennessee: Nelson, 1977).

41. The legitimacy of a system of exclusively private, competitive, profit-seeking, free market civil courts is promoted by Bruno Leoni, *Freedom and the Law* (Princeton, New Jersey: Van Nostrand, 1961); cf. Murray N. Rothbard, "On Freedom and the

be governed by the capitalist principle of "highest bid wins." No man is supposed to be able to pay a court to gain his preferred decision, nor should people be able to "shop around" in search of a court more likely to be favorable to them.

A church government has been granted a unique monopolistic authority over those who have voluntarily covenanted with it (or whose parents have). A civil government has been granted a unique geographical monopoly over those who have covenanted with it (or whose parents have). The State represents God to those within its geographical boundaries, and it possesses an authority defined by constitutional law or custom. Thus, a court is not governed by the principle of "highest money bid wins." To imagine that such a principle governs the courts is to imagine that God honors the same principle in His rendering of judgment. It would mean that rich people could buy a decision from God. But they cannot do this, even if they owned the whole world. "For what shall it profit a man, if he shall gain the whole world, and lose his own soul?" (Mark 8:36). God honors Himself alone by honoring His law. All men are judged by His law. He does not respect persons, including those who could offer him a higher bid. The basis of rewards in eternity is righteousness.

Highest Ethical Bid?

Now, it might be argued that the principle of "highest bid wins" still operates in God's courtroom of final judgment, in the sense that righteousness should be the true "coin of the realm," and therefore those who pay the most, ethically speaking, will receive the highest rewards (I Cor. 3:13-15). But there is a fundamental difference in the operating principles of the competitive market for goods and the closed monopoly of God's final judgment. The free market for goods operates in terms of *objective prices*, irrespective of one's relative capacity to pay. In contrast, God's monopoly of final judgment operates in terms of one's objective performance *relative to one's gifts*. The story of the widow's two mites informs us of this latter principle. Those rich people who gave much into the treasury did not give nearly so much as the poor widow who cast in two small coins, for this was all she possessed. Jesus said, "For all they did cast in of their abundance; but she of her want did cast in all that she had, even all

Law," *New Individualist Review*, I (Winter 1962), pp. 37-40; reprinted in one volume by Liberty Fund, Indianapolis, Indiana, 1981, pp. 163-66; Rothbard, *For a New Liberty: The Libertarian Manifesto* (rev. ed.; New York: Collier, 1978), pp. 227-34.

her living" (Mark 12:44). God, unlike man, can search each heart. He knows what we possess and what it has cost us to give up something.

The principles that govern God's final judgment are predictable. They are revealed to everyone in the Bible. The principle of "highest ethical bid wins" *does* govern God's court: the perfect life of Jesus Christ, and His full payment on the cross. God's wrath is placated alone by this voluntary act of covenantal mercy on the part of Jesus Christ. Those who place themselves under Christ's jurisdiction thereby escape the perfect wrath of God. They then receive rewards in terms of their ethical performance, but only because they have first built on the foundation that Jesus Christ laid at Calvary (I Cor. 3:9-11). These rewards are granted on the basis of 1) gifts originally given to him by God and 2) the individual's lifetime ethical performance in terms of these gifts. The high bids are relative, not absolute. They are bids in terms of ethical performance, not financial performance.

A human court cannot search the heart in this way. The judges do not know what is in people's hearts; at best they can estimate. Human courts must render judgment in terms of public evidence regarding people's *objective external acts*; judges and juries can only indirectly search for a person's motives, for they must rely on objective, corroborated public testimony in the collection of facts. They cannot know what "ethical assets" any person possesses. Thus, a human court must judge human guilt or innocence in terms of people's objective conformity to God's revealed law. Whatever subjective motivations may have existed in the mind of someone who has committed a trespass, these motivations must be ascertainable through public evidence.

Financing Human Courts

This leads us to definite conclusions concerning the financing of human courts. The principle of the "widow's mite" cannot be invoked to justify any particular financing system for a court. The "widow's mite" principle of sacrificial giving can be legitimately invoked only by God in rendering His judgments, in time and eternity, for He alone can search men's hearts. The Bible informs us of the principle of financing for the local church: the tithe. Samuel informed the Hebrews that the future king would also invoke the requirement of the tithe (I Sam. 8:15, 17). It was the level of civil taxation that Samuel warned against—a level equal to God's tithe—rather than the principle of equal proportional taxation.

Human courts should not be financed by requiring all people to pay the same fixed money price, for this would allow rich people to escape their obligations too lightly.[42] It would also either destroy the finances of the poor or strangle the courts. *The principle of the tithe must govern the two monopolistic human courts, church and State*: each person under the jurisdiction of the monopolistic government pays the same percentage of the net increase of his income. This way, the poor person knows that the system is fair. He will receive justice because he has paid as much — a known percentage of his net income — as the rich man. He is therefore entitled to the same impartial justice.

On the other hand, the graduated income tax — making rich people pay a larger percentage of their income than other pay — is as corrupt as the so-called "head tax" system. Coupled with democratic voting privileges, the graduated income tax transfers legal control over one group's wealth into the hands of another. Karl Marx believed that when a graduated income tax is imposed on a nation, in principle it has taken one of the ten steps toward communism.[43] The almost universal acceptance in the twentieth century of the legitimacy of the "progressive" income tax is indicative of just how far the modern world has drifted (or run) from the Bible. Even economists who defend the free market have frequently accepted its legitimacy.[44] That Christian social thinkers should promote the graduated income tax in the name of Jesus is almost beyond belief; that one of them should call for a "graduated tithe" — a graduated ten percent? — indicates the extent of the moral and intellectual corruption of our day.[45]

Civil courts should be financed through tax revenues raised by equal proportional giving by the rich, the middle class, and the poor, either by sales tax or income tax. The principle of proportionality must govern civil governments, for they are closed monopolies, not

---

42. The so-called "head tax" of Exodus 30:11-16 was not a civil tax at all, contrary to Rushdoony. It was an atonement payment that was required before the Hebrews marched to war. See Chapter 32: "Blood Money, Not Head Tax." See also James B. Jordan, *The Law of the Covenant: An Exposition of Exodus 21-23* (Tyler, Texas: Institute for Christian Economics, 1984), Appendix D. Rushdoony's comments are found in *Institutes of Biblical Law*, pp. 281-82, 492, 510, 719.

43. Karl Marx and Frederick Engels, *Manifesto of the Communist Party* (1848) in Marx and Engels, *Selected Works*, 3 vols. (Moscow: Progress Publishers, [1969] 1977), III, p. 126.

44. Walter J. Blum and Harry Kalven, Jr., *The Uneasy Case for Progressive Taxation* (University of Chicago Press, 1953).

45. Ronald J. Sider, *Rich Christians in an Age of Hunger: A Biblical Study* (Downers Grove, Illinois: Inter-Varsity Press, 1977), pp. 175-78.

open competitive markets. The predictability of the courts' enforcement
of God's law is the foundation of justice, both civil and ecclesiastical.
It is also the foundation of social peace. Taking a bribe corrupts a
Bible-based judicial system, for it introduces uncertainty and judicial self-interest into the court. The poor person never knows if he
can trust the court, since a rich man may pay a small percentage of
his assets to a judge—an absolute amount that is far beyond the
capability of the poor person to match. A judge should no more take
a bribe to pervert biblical justice than God would.

Highest Bid Wins: Mandatory for Markets

What I am arguing should be clear to everyone: *different forms of
sovereignty require different forms of financing.* For example, to propose a
financing system that is appropriate for the church or State as the
proper way to run a competitive market system is to propose the destruction of the free market, as surely as the free market's financing
principle would destroy the integrity of the church or State.

To examine how an institution can be destroyed by an inappropriate principle of financing, let us examine the operations of a competitive free market. Those potential buyers who bid the highest
amount of money are thereby able to gain, through *voluntary transfer,*
legal access to the sought-after goods, unless a seller for some reason
prefers to forfeit money that is available to him in order to deliver the
goods to someone making a lower bid. Such a below-market wealth
transfer is a form of charity, not a profit-seeking business. While
such decisions on the part of sellers are legal, they are not common.
The highest bid usually wins. In any case, the highest bid inescapably forces the seller to consider the personal cost of not honoring the highest bid, i.e., forfeited income.

In a free market, auctions (the market process) are conducted in
terms of public bids that are legally unconnected to considerations of
the size of the bids in relation to the potential buyers' income level
(the tithe principle) or net asset level (the "widow's mite" principle).
They must be separated, if increasing economic output and the competitive performance of producers are to be furthered.

Net-Worth Bidding

Consider the alternative. What if a society by civil law required
all economic transactions to be conducted in terms of this principle:
"the highest percentage of presently owned assets offered in ex-

change wins the auction"—an economy based on the "widow's mite" principle? Bidders would not know who won the auction until a detailed study of each bidder's present net worth was conducted. Producers would be forced by law to sell expensive items and services to people who own almost nothing but who are willing to pay a very high percentage of their assets in order to buy something. Obviously, production would grind to a halt. People would begin to produce only for their own personal use—outside of the open market. They would be afraid to bring their goods and services to sell to "highest percentage" bidders. The division of labor would collapse. So would per capita productivity and income.

An example may help to illustrate this. An automobile salesman would be required by law to sell a car to the person who offered the highest percentage of his present assets. Instead of a price sticker on the car's window that says so much money, it would list a percentage number. "This week only: 35 percent of your net worth!" What would be the quickest way to buy the car? *Lower your net worth.* Instead of competition in terms of the production of assets, we would see competition in terms of destruction of assets. *The spendthrifts would inherit the earth.*

A poor man who really wanted a car to drive (or park it with an empty gasoline tank in front of his home) might be willing to give up almost everything he owns to buy it. He would therefore willingly come close to making the automobile into an idol. But he would not be pressured by the market to increase his personal productivity in order to buy it. In such a social order, no strictly objective performance is required: exactly so much money in exchange for the car. Instead, the test would be the percentage of his bid in relation to his present assets. This would virtually destroy the predictability of market pricing. A person with greater net worth who wanted to buy the car, either for personal use or business use, would be outbid by the person willing to make the car into a near-idol. Unless the second man was also willing to make the car into his own near-idol, sacrificing nearly everything he owns to buy it, he would not be able to buy the car.

Future-Orientation

The competitive free market encourages people to plan for the future, to become productive. It pressures them to use their skills and capital to create value—value registered in terms of competitive bids by potential consumers. To become a consumer, you must first become a producer, unless you are being supported by your inheritance, or by charity, or by the privately wielded sword (criminals), or by the civil government's sword (welfare recipients). The market steadily pressures participants to become productive because it is governed by the principle of "highest bid wins"—bids usually registered by money, but at least in goods or services (barter). The market also pressures people to become future-oriented. They have to earn money through personal productivity in order to make future purchases.

If the principle of "highest money bid wins" is abandoned, then the economic system becomes intensely present-oriented. People would look only to their present assets as the basis of their ability to buy what they want. They would be able to buy things by becoming poorer. If they can reduce their net worth sufficiently, and can squeeze their living standards down to the near-starvation level, they can buy their one dream item for practically no money, just as long as the purchase price absorbs a very high percentage of their assets. They sacrifice nearly everything they own, once, in order to make that one dream purchase. Attaining their dream impoverishes them. If this is not a form of implicit idol-worship, what is? The principle of the "widow's mite," which is appropriate for sacrificial *giving*, becomes a means of personal and cultural idolatry when it becomes sacrificial *buying*.

Another very efficient and pleasant way to reduce your net worth is to go deeply into debt for consumer goods and services that depreciate faster than the obligation is reduced. This, too, is counterproductive. It is a decision based on a deeply entrenched present-orientation.

The Sellers' Dilemma

We have been speaking of buyers. What about sellers? Consider the car salesman. He sells cars, but he also buys cars. How would he be able to order a replacement car for every car sold? Only by offering the highest percentage of his dealership's assets. Small, struggling, very high-risk dealerships that order a very small number of cars could get delivery precisely because they have so *few* cars in inventory—i.e., so little net worth. Obviously, the number of automobile orders would drop as small, struggling dealers became the legally competitive bidders. Fewer orders would lower the factories' efficiency by increasing the cost-per-unit-produced, thereby reducing output. Reducing output is not the way to national prosperity.

Meanwhile, in the international competition for scarce resources, everyone outside the nation would be operating in terms of highest money bid wins. If you were a resource owner in another nation, to whom would you sell your assets? To residents of a nation governed by highest *money* bid wins or residents of a nation governed by highest *percentage of assets* bid wins? Probably you would sell it to whichever bidder brought in the highest price. So, any nation operating in terms of "highest percentage of assets presently owned" would remove itself from the world's market. Thus cut off, it would grow steadily poorer. It would be a nation characterized by falling production and the consumption of present assets. It would be a capital-consuming society.

Privacy

There is another factor to consider. Every transaction would require the seller to examine the assets of every potential buyer. The buyer (seller of money) would have to bring with him a government-authorized statement of exactly what he owned at that moment. It would be like paying your income tax every time you went to the market. It would be worse; it would be like going through an audit by the civil tax collector or ecclesiastical tithe collector every time you went to the market. No shred of financial privacy would remain in the society. It would also lead to the creation of counterfeit asset evaluations, for these would serve as the new currency of the realm. You can see where the principle of "highest percentage of owned assets offered in exchange" would lead to: reduced national competitiveness, reduced savings, falling income, petty tyranny, and massive cheating. In short, it would lead to bankruptcy and national extinction.

What I have described is a topsy-turvy economic world. It makes no sense. It sounds like a scene out of *Alice in Wonderland*. So why dwell on the obvious? Because not all people acknowledge the obvious. They seek to operate one sphere of human existence in terms of financing principles appropriate for another sphere. Today we have far too many self-professed Christian social theorists who recommend taxing and financing policies that would drastically hamper or even destroy the free market. It is necessary to demonstrate clearly that the free market operates under a different set of financing principles from those governing a God-ordained monopoly government.

The *voluntarily accepted* principle of "highest money bid wins" governs the free market. The principle of the *God-required* tithe governs the church. The principle of the *coercive* fixed percentage of net income (income tax) should govern the civil government, or else a fixed percentage of market purchase price (sales tax or use tax).[46] In short, a monopolistic court is not an open competitive market. Both church and State are monopolistic courts.

Conclusion

Noonan's book on bribery is built around a single theme: that a bribe is a form of *reciprocity*. Why is it, his book asks, that reciprocity is basic to human life, yet in the case of bribery, it is condemned? His book provides no real answer. The biblical answer is primarily theocentric: *God's dual character as Judge and also as Creator-Redeemer.* Secondarily, it rests on the difference between a monopolistic court and an open market. The court does not operate in terms of economic reciprocity; the market does. The court enforces the law of the God who declares that which is criminal and who specifies appropriate penalties. The reciprocity associated with a court is found in its imposition of a restitution program. The criminal repays his victim. The principle of reciprocity is enforced by the court on those who stand before it, righting wrongs and restoring order. There is no reciprocal economic relationship between the court and those being judged.

Men are wicked if they take bribes to pervert righteous judgment. God's laws are supposed to be every judge's standard. He is not to respect persons. He is not to favor one or the other. The court is to imitate God as the cosmic Judge: "Wherefore now let the fear of the LORD be upon you; take heed and do it: for there is no iniquity with the LORD our God, nor respect of persons, nor taking of gifts" (II Chron. 19:7). Yet we are told that God *does* take gifts: "And many brought gifts unto the LORD to Jerusalem" (II Chron. 32:23a). God never takes a gift or bribe in His capacity as Judge: "For the LORD your God is God of gods, and LORD of lords, a great God, a mighty, and a terrible, which regardeth not persons, nor taketh reward" (Deut. 10:17).

John Noonan writes, "As a believer in religion, I have asked how

---

46. The best tax is the gasoline tax, if the revenues are used exclusively to build and repair roads in the region where the tax is collected. If you do not drive, you do not pay the tax.

prayer and sacrifice to God are different from bribes."[47] What is the difference? It is the difference between worship and judgment. We do not lawfully ask God to pervert judgment when we pray or bring sacrifices to him. We honor Him as Creator and Redeemer, not as Judge. Civil judges are not to receive gifts because they are neither to be worshipped nor asked to pervert judgment; they serve as representatives of God's justice, not God's character as Creator and Redeemer.

The evil of taking gifts is the evil of threatening unrighteous judgment through respect of persons. Taking a bribe is synonymous with perverting judgment; it is prohibited in the affairs of civil or ecclesiastical judgment. It is not wrong for pastors to receive gifts to the church in the name of God, but to the extent that these gifts are received in order to pervert justice, they are regarded by God as bribes. Thus, church rulers have a more difficult task in identifying bribery than civil judges do. The civil magistrate does not represent God in His capacity as Creator and Redeemer, but only in His capacity as Judge. He is unlikely ever to be given a gift, except in his capacity as judge. This is not true of the church officer, who receives gifts in the name of the church.

The Bible does not teach that bribe-offering is always wrong. If given by a righteous person who seeks righteous judgment from an unrighteous judge, it is valid. If given by someone to pervert God's law, it is evil. The quest for a neutral definition of bribery which equates both practices is a biblically illegitimate quest.

---

47. Noonan, *Bribes*, p. xvi.

27

SABBATICAL LIBERTY

Also thou shalt not oppress a stranger: for ye know the heart of a stranger, seeing ye were strangers in the land of Egypt. And six years thou shalt sow thy land, and shalt gather in the fruits thereof: But the seventh year thou shalt let it rest and lie still; that the poor of thy people may eat: and what they leave the beasts of the field shall eat. In like manner thou shalt deal with thy vineyard, and with thy oliveyard. Six days thou shalt do thy work, and on the seventh day thou shalt rest: that thine ox and thine ass may rest, and the son of thy handmaid, and the stranger, may be refreshed (Ex. 23:9-12).

It is not immediately clear how these verses of the Bible should be linked together, because they appear to be separate units. The reference to the stranger in verse 9 seems to be linked to the reference to the stranger in verse 12. In between are laws relating to the sabbath: the sabbath year rest of the land, and the sabbath day rest of domestic animals, servants, and strangers. The question needs to be raised: Why should the section on sabbath rest begin and end with references to the stranger?

To answer this, we need to discover the theocentric principle of the passage: *God as Deliverer or Liberator.* James Jordan has argued that the theme of the Book of Exodus is God's deliverance of His people from bondage to sabbath rest. "The instructions for the design of the Tabernacle culminate in sabbath rules (31:12-17), and the procedure for building the Tabernacle commences with sabbath rules (35:1-3). The book closes with the definitive establishment of Old Covenant worship on the very first day of the new year. Thus, the book moves from the rigors of bondage to the sinful world order, to the glorious privilege of rest in the very throne room of God."[1] I

---

1. James B. Jordan, *The Law of the Covenant: An Exposition of Exodus 21-23* (Tyler, Texas: Institute for Christian Economics, 1984), p. 75.

argue that the placement of the Book of Exodus as the second book
of the Pentateuch indicates that its central theme is that of the second
point of the biblical covenant, hierarchy. What we find is that these
two themes are inseparably linked: the deliverance of God's covenant people from the rigors of Egyptian slavery, and their subsequent ratification of the covenant with God at Mt. Sinai.

Sabbath Rest

The theme of sabbath rest is one that should have been easily
understood by the Hebrews. The rigors of endless toil under Pharaoh's
taskmasters had caused them to cry out to God, the true Monarch,
and He heard their cries (Ex. 3:7-9). He responded by sending
Moses and Aaron with a request to Pharaoh: to allow His people to
go three days' journey, to sacrifice to God, and then return—a seven-
day round trip, a sabbath week of service to God rather than to
Pharaoh (Ex. 5:3), although a week with the day of sacrifice taking
place midweek. This was unacceptable to Pharaoh, who piled extra
work on them as a punishment by forcing them to produce bricks
without straw (Ex. 5:6-19). Thus, they saw the contrast: labor with
sabbath rest periods under God versus endless toil under Pharaoh.
They could have a feast with God on a day of rest (Ex. 5:1), or else
they could remain in a strange land as slaves.

Initially, they chose slavery in a strange land, for their hierarchical
representatives, the officers of Israel, complained against Moses and
Aaron for having stirred up trouble (Ex. 5:19-21). They did not want
to bear the responsibility of challenging a State that had attempted to
slay their children and that had brought them into slavery to a self-
proclaimed divine monarch. They preferred the familiar trials of slavery to what seemed to them to be a high-risk encounter with Pharaoh,
not to mention the Red Sea, the wilderness, and the Canaanites.

Nevertheless, the prospect of rest from their labors had to be a
tempting one. God offered them a sabbatical week of respite from
their lives of unrelieved toil. *This sabbatical week was in fact symbolic of
their deliverance.* Pharaoh fully understood this, which is why he refused
to permit it. To grant them a week outside of his jurisdiction meant
that in principle he would be acknowledging the sovereignty over
him of the God of the Hebrews. This is what he dared not allow,
given the theology of theocratic Egypt.[2] Granting sabbath rest to the

---

2. Gary North, *Moses and Pharaoh: Dominion Religion vs. Power Religion* (Tyler,
Texas: Institute for Christian Economics, 1985), ch. 10: "Total Sacrifice, Total
Sovereignty."

Hebrews would have involved acknowledging symbolically his own covenantal subordination to God. The issue of sabbath rest is in fact an issue regarding God's sovereignty, meaning covenantal subordination.[3]

The Heart of a Stranger

The Hebrews are told not to oppress a stranger because they "know the heart of a stranger." How can they know this? Because they, too, had been strangers in the land of Egypt. This raises a crucially important issue in philosophy, the issue of epistemology: "What can men know, and how can they know it?"

The question here is the question of empathy. It tells us that because we can look within ourselves, we can make judgments regarding the feelings of others. What they feel is sufficiently close to what we feel to enable us to make ethical judgments. This ability undergirds the so-called golden rule: "Do unto others as you would have others do unto you." This phrase is one of those famous phrases attributed to Jesus that He never quite said. What He said was, "Therefore all things whatsoever ye would that men should do to you, do ye even so to them: for this is the law and the prophets" (Matt. 7:12). It is closely related to Paul's words: "For all the law is fulfilled in one word, even in this; Thou shalt love thy neighbour as thyself" (Gal. 5:14). This is the requirement of Leviticus 19:18, which Jesus cited in Matthew 22:39-40: love your neighbor as yourself.

The humanist has a problem with this moral injunction. The problem was best stated in George Bernard Shaw's play, *Man and Superman* (1903): "Do not do unto others as you would they should do unto you. Their tastes may not be the same." There is an implicit lawlessness in this, as he says forthrightly in the same play: "The golden rule is that there are no golden rules." If each man is autonomous, and therefore utterly unconnected with other men by feelings

---

3. I have elsewhere argued that the New Testament places the locus of enforcement regarding the sabbath with the individual conscience (Rom. 14:5-6; Col. 2:16). Gary North, *The Sinai Strategy: Economics and the Ten Commandments* (Tyler, Texas: Institute for Christian Economics, 1986), ch. 4, Appendix A. To head off arguments that I am now denying my former arguments by making sabbath observance an issue of covenantal subordination, I need to point out that there are four biblical covenants: personal, familial, civil, and ecclesiastical. The New Testament's covenantal subordination is directly personal under God, meaning that sabbath enforcement is no longer a judicial responsibility of family (when dealing with legal adults), church, or State. A person should not be disinherited, excommunicated, or executed because of his or her failure to observe the sabbath.

and interpretations, then life is anarchy. But on the basis of the logic of autonomous man, there is no sure reason to believe that there are such connections. It may be convenient to believe that there are, if only to make sense of reality, but there is no way to prove that empathy serves as a means of unifying mankind.

But there *is* a link, the Bible tells us: the image of God in man. Man is made in God's image, and he is therefore responsible to God covenantally (Gen. 1:26-27). There are common emotional and ethical bonds in all men. These bonds can be actively suppressed, in the same way that the knowledge of God is actively suppressed by sinful men (Rom. 1:18-22). Nevertheless, these bonds serve as the basis of social cooperation, which in turn requires people to make ethical judgments.

The Israelites were reminded that they had been strangers in Egypt. They should therefore not imitate their tyrannical captors by imposing unrighteous judgments on those who are under their God-given authority. If they should do so, then God will remove this authority from them and punish them in the same way. To escape God's temporal covenantal judgments, men must obey God's law. *They must subordinate themselves to this law in order lawfully to execute righteous judgment on those beneath them.* As they do unto others, so will God do to them.

Then what about differing tastes? What about using our feelings as guides for dealing with others? If tastes are ethically random, or even ethically neutral, how can we rely on introspection as a guide to external behavior? The biblical response is clear: tastes are neither random nor ethically neutral. Tastes are inherent in men as God's creatures, although this testimony can be suppressed and twisted to covenant-breaking purposes. Because of sin, tastes must be governed by the standards of God's law. The Hebrews were supposed to remind themselves of what it meant to be an oppressed slave in a foreign land. They were required to eat bitter herbs each year at passover (Ex. 12:8). Tastes are not random; bitter herbs for one person will taste bitter for others. The memory of the bitterness of slavery would be preserved by the bitter taste in people's mouths each year at the Passover feast.

The memory of their ancestors' years in Egypt was important for the life of the nation. This memory was to stay with them through the history taught to them as children at the Passover feast (Ex. 12:26-27), in the readings from the Torah, and from their instruction in the law. *Covenant ethics and covenant history could not lawfully be sepa-*

rated in Israel. Because they shared a common covenant history, they were under covenant law. God had told them centuries before when *they* were slaves in Egypt not to forget to remind their heirs of this experience.

How could later generations remember? In what way had they been slaves in Egypt? How could God expect later generations to remember what had never in history happened to them personally? Because *life is covenantal.* In the same sense that all men have rebelled in Eden's garden, so were the Hebrews to regard themselves as having served a term as slaves. That sense is covenantal — personal, hierarchical, ethical, judgmental, and historical. God reminded the generation of the exodus that they had been slaves, and that they, meaning their heirs, would return to slavery in a foreign land again if they disobeyed Him (Deut. 28:64-65). Their heirs were required to remember this, too, long after that first generation had died in the wilderness.

The stranger in the land wants rest from his labors. He needs hope that at the end of his work, there will be rest. This is the equivalent of saying that at the end of his period of bondage, there will be liberty. This is the message of the Book of Exodus: *liberty comes through God's covenant blessings to those who serve God and other men faithfully through dedicated labor.* It was the denial of hope in future rest or future liberty that marked Pharaoh's Egypt. It marks every bureaucratic civilization.

Sabbath and Providence

The sabbath is an aspect of God's grace to man and the creation. It is the promise of rest and eventual liberty from bondage, primarily the bondage of sin. The Bible is clear: what man hopes to be his external reward from God he must therefore offer to all those under his authority. This includes not just people, but also animals and the land itself. The discipline of ethics goes from the lesser case to the greater. If man is to give even the land rest, then he is surely to give rest to the animals of the land. If he is to give animals rest, then he must surely be required to give strangers rest. If he is to give strangers rest, then surely he must give his servants rest. And if he is to give his servants rest, then he must surely give himself rest.

But how can he afford to give himself rest? Who is to guard the garden while he is resting? Who is to care for the needs of his family, his servants, strangers in the land, animals, and the land itself? Without man as the guardian and administrator, how will civilized life go on? The answer, of course, is theocentric: the sovereignty of God. *It is God who gives man rest, for it is God who providentially sustains man's environment and man himself.* If God refuses to give man rest, then rest becomes too expensive for man, too dangerous. Accepting rest from God requires a visible commitment to the covenant, faith that things will work out for the best for those who are obedient to God (Rom. 8:28). Only this faith in God and His covenant blessings can relieve man of the worry that without his own efforts, all will be lost.

The sabbatical week is designed to persuade covenant man that he can trust God for one day per week. It breaks man of his spirit of self-centeredness. By resting from his labors on the sabbath, man learns to rest his mind and soul as well. He sees, week by week, that life goes on, that the system holds, even though he has not worked for one day in seven. This self-discipline is designed to increase his faith in the sustaining providence of God.

From Miracles to Weekly Thrift

For that first generation, the miracle of the daily manna was supposed to persuade them of God's providence. So was the fact that any manna collected beyond a day's use would rot (Ex. 16:20). They were taught to rely on God before they were taught to save for the future. The suspension of the law of rotting manna for the double portion they collected on the morning before the sabbath served as a double witness to God's providence: they had to gather a double portion to sustain them on the sabbath, when the manna would cease (Ex. 16:5). This taught them short-term thrift. But it was thrift within the context of daily miracles. On the day that the miracle of new manna ceased, the miracle of non-rotting manna replaced it.

Once they crossed over the Jordan River, the miracle of the daily manna ceased (Josh. 5:12). They had to transfer their faith in the miracle of the manna to the less visibly miraculous six-one weekly pattern. They would have to get their work done in six days, just as they had been required to collect a double portion of manna on the sixth day. Now, however, they could structure their workweek more rationally. There would be no equivalent of the rotting second portion of manna. They could accumulate the excess production of each day in order to survive the seventh day of rest without a crisis. They learned the principle of thrift by accumulating goods for the future through abstaining from maximum present consumption. They worked a little harder in the present in order to enjoy a period of rest in the future. This future-orientation would have been limited to six days at a time, had it not been for the law of the sabbatical year.

Long-term thrift was forced on them whenever they obeyed this law governing agriculture (Ex. 23:9-12). What they had learned in the wilderness through the miracle of the manna, they were to apply to their daily labors in the land. What they learned in their weekly efforts to save for the future, they were to apply to the God-imposed sabbatical year cycle. One year in seven they were to allow the land to rest.

If the land was entitled to rest, then how much more the animals. If the animals were entitled to rest, how much more strangers within the land, and so on, right up the hierarchical chain of command to the master of the household himself. Everyone could look forward to rest, if each did his labor diligently, and if each saved a portion of his output for that future day.

The Psychology of Growth

Each person is supposed to be self-disciplined. As he matures in his Christian faith, he is supposed to operate faithfully under God without prodding from a superior. The sluggard is supposed to abandon his slothful ways:

Go to the ant, thou sluggard; consider her ways, and be wise: Which having no guide, overseer, or ruler, Provideth her meat in the summer, and gathereth her food in the harvest. How long wilt thou sleep, O sluggard? When wilt thou arise out of thy sleep? Yet a little sleep, a little slumber, a little folding of the hands to sleep: So shall thy poverty come as one that travaileth, and thy want as an armed man (Prov. 6:6-11).

The Hebrews were warned a generation before they entered the land what would be required of them. They would have to rest one day in seven, and rest the land one year in seven. They would have to save enough goods daily to get them through the day of rest, and they would have to save enough goods yearly to get them through the year of rest. The required self-discipline of future-orientation and thrift, coupled with the legal requirement to honor the sabbath, helped to create a particular attitude that leads to increased per capita output and lower interest rates.[4]

---

4. Because the rate of interest is a reflection, in part, of individuals' time-preference or future-orientation, with high interest rates stemming from intense present-orientation, the requirement of the sabbatical year fostered greater future-orientation and therefore lower rates of interest.

Reduced interest rates lead to greater output, for people are more willing to forego present consumption in favor of increased future consumption. This greater output could then be used to lend money or goods to non-Israelites, thereby gaining authority over them. This ability to lend is a sign of God's blessings:

> The LORD shall open unto thee his good treasure, the heaven to give the rain unto thy land in his season, and to bless all the work of thine hand: and thou shalt lend unto many nations, and thou shalt not borrow. And the LORD shall make thee the head, and not the tail; and thou shalt be above only, and thou shalt not be beneath; if that thou hearken unto the commandments of the LORD thy God, which I command thee this day, to observe and to do them (Deut. 28:12-13).

If a nation filled with future-oriented people who are willing to lend money at 5 percent per annum encounters a more present-oriented society filled with people who are willing to pay 10 percent to finance their consumption or production, the people living in the first society can easily become the lenders to people living in the second. It is necessary for the lenders to monitor the ability and willingness of the borrowers to pay back the loans, of course. For a safe commercial transaction to take place, the differential between the respective interest rates must not be the product of a high risk premium — fear of outright default — or the product of a price inflation premium — fear of disguised default through loss of purchasing power.

The extension of dominion by lending at interest is legitimate for both lender and borrower. There are always risks associated with dominion, however. Lending to present-oriented consumers may later become a curse for the lender: he trusts in his riches but forgets that he is becoming dependent on present-oriented debtors. But it may also be that the foreign debtors are not consumers, but merely intelligent producers in the other country. In this case, the lender helps future-oriented foreign producers to become more productive by supplying them with capital more cheaply than they can borrow it at home. Dominion is by covenant. Lending to the foreigner at interest brings him indirectly under the sanctions of God, but these sanctions can be either blessing or cursing.[5] So, it is always a question of intent

---

5. The possibility of blessing eludes utopian author S. C. Mooney, who refuses even to comment on Deuteronomy 28:12-13, since it clearly says that it is legitimate to make loans at interest. He insists that "Usury enslaves. The brethren are not to be enslaved." S. C. Mooney, *Usury: Destroyer of Nations* (Warsaw, Ohio: Theopolis,

on the part of both lender and borrower. What is the goal of the lender, passive escapism or active expansion of his capital? To what purposes will the borrowed money be put, productive or unproductive? The raw numbers do not tell us these things.

Gleaning and Liberation

"But the seventh year thou shalt let it rest and lie still; that the poor of thy people may eat: and what they leave the beasts of the field shall eat." This verse makes it clear that the poor are allowed to enter the field and glean whatever grain has come up of its own accord. The same rule applied to the vineyards. This is an extension of the rule prohibiting the owner of the land to reap every nook and cranny of his fields. He had to allow poor people to enter his fields and glean the corners — the areas more difficult to harvest (Lev. 19:9-10). The Bible specifically identifies the poor who were to be invited in: the stranger, the orphan, and the widow (Deut. 24:21). Why is the landowner told to do this? Predictably, it is because of Israel's years in Egypt: "And thou shalt remember that thou wast a bondman in the land of Egypt: therefore I command thee to do this thing" (Deut. 24:22).[6]

Is this a form of government-required public welfare? No. There are no negative sanctions mentioned, and it is difficult to imagine how anyone who felt abused could sue for damages. Where there are no civil sanctions, there can be no crime. None is listed, and it is difficult to imagine the basis by which appropriate sanctions could be devised by the civil judges. *Lex talionis*? Would he be kept from gleaning for a year? By double restitution? Double what? How much could the potential gleaner have gleaned from the field? How many local potential gleaners could sue? All of them? Does each of them have a lawful claim against the landowner, no matter how small his fields?

1988), p. 98. On the contrary, usury does not always enslave. Becoming a debtor for productive reasons — to go to college, for example — or to start a business, can be liberating. It depends on what the borrower intends to do with the money. Like fire, debt is risky. The older you get, the less you should rely on it. But young men and citizens in pagan nations that are trying to advance themselves economically can legitimately go into debt for productive purposes. Debt is no more of a curse than personal apprenticeship with a master is — a form of personal and professional discipline that Mr. Mooney would have been wise to consider before he wrote his book.

6. That this law applies to the New Testament Christian gentile stems from the fact that we are covenantally Israelites through the new birth. "But he is a Jew, which is one inwardly; and circumcision is that of the heart, in the spirit, and not in the letter; whose praise is not of men, but of God" (Rom. 2:29).

God instructs owners to allow poor people to glean. The land is His (Lev. 25:23); the whole earth is His (Ex. 19:5;[7] Ps. 24:1). As the permanent owner, God can tell his stewards how to administer His property. But God is the disciplining agent. He acts as Kinsman-Redeemer or as Blood Avenger, depending on the obedience or disobedience of the landowner. The law is in the form of a positive injunction, and biblical civil law is negative in scope: forbidding public evil.

There is no doubt that this form of morally compulsory charity on the owner's part involved hard work on the part of the recipients. They are be allowed to glean the corners and difficult places only after the "easy pickings" have been gleaned by the hired harvesters. They are invited into the open fields only in the sabbatical year in which there has been no previous season's planting. They have to earn every bit of the produce they collect. It is not a chosen profession for sluggards. But for those who are willing to work, they will not perish at the hands of men who systematically used their competitive advantage to create a permanent class of the poor.

There is another great advantage to this form of morally enforced charity: it brings hard-working, efficient poor people to the attention of potential employers. There is always a market for hard-working, efficient, diligent workers. Such abilities are the product of a righteous worldview and a healthy body, both of which are gifts of God. It always pays employers to locate such people and hire them. In effect, the employers can "glean" future workers. Gleaning appears initially to be a high-risk system of recruiting, for it requires landowners to forfeit the corners of their fields and one year's productivity in seven. Nevertheless, God promises to bless those who obey Him. It really is not a high-risk system. Israel's gleaning system made the charity local, work-oriented, and a source of profitable information regarding potential employees. Thus, the system offered (and offers) hope to those trapped in poverty. They can escape this burden through demonstrated productivity. This is how Ruth, a stranger in the land, began her escape: she caught the attention of Boaz (Ruth 2:5).

---

7. Horror of horrors! I have just discovered an economic verse in Exodus 19 — the chapter that I skipped in *Moses and Pharaoh*. If you think I intend to add a whole chapter to that book, pay for new typesetting, and re-index it, then you have not judged the cost-benefit ratio from the same subjective value framework as I have.

We Are All Gleaners

Because each person is in bondage to sin, God has made gleaners of everyone. He cursed the ground, making it to bring forth thorns and thistles. This in effect put us all in the position of people who are not entitled to the best of the field. God removed the "easy pickings" from mankind as a result of mankind's rebellion. But at least he did not destroy the field (the world). He promises not to interfere directly with it until the final judgment (Matt. 13:29-30, 49). We must work harder than before the curse, but God graciously grants us access to the field. Those who are content with second-best are given an opportunity to escape their economic bondage through faith in the great Gleaner, Jesus Christ, who served God faithfully unto death, buying our way out of spiritual bondage. God observes us, to see who is efficient and who is a sluggard. He uses history as a giant gleaning operation for recruiting servants for eternity. Those who do not demonstrate faithfulness under adversity are not given access to the fields of the post-judgment world, but instead are cast out into the fire.

In a very real sense, biblical evangelism prior to the great millennial outpouring of the Holy Spirit is a form of gleaning. We seem to reap small harvests. We get the spiritual leftovers, after the local tyrants, the humanist school system, the Marxists, the cults, and the drug dealers have passed through the field and have picked off "the best and the brightest." Successes on the missions field are minor, the biological reproduction of God's enemies is now becoming exponential, and we have few reliable models to imitate. Evangelism seems futile. But to be a gleaner always tempts us to accept second-best as a way of life. The gleaner may not recognize or appreciate his God-given opportunity. He may not see that he is being called into the Master's field in order to demonstrate his competence in the face of adversity. He may view his plight as something undeserved, not recognizing that after Adam, all that any man deserves is death and eternal wrath. He does not recognize the stripped field as a garden of opportunity. He imagines that all he can hope for is a sack of leftover grain. His time horizon is too short. His future-orientation suffers from a lack of vision, and also a lack of faith in God's grace. He forgets how few and far between faithful workers are, and how the opportunity to glean the leftover harvest is a God-given way to demonstrate his character as a man with a future precisely because he has confidence in the future.

Eschatologies of the Stripped Field

Because the church has seen so few examples of successful evangelism, and because even the successful examples seem to fall back into paganism within a few centuries, Christians have come to adopt eschatologies that deny liberation for gleaners. They see themselves and their spiritual colleagues as people who are locked in a vicious "cycle of poverty," to borrow the language of paganism's modern welfare economics. They see no hope beyond the stripped field. Life only offers minimal opportunities for harvesting souls, they believe. "What we have today as gleaners is all that we or our heirs can expect in history." They lose faith in the jubilee year, when the land of their fathers reverts to them. They lose faith in the ability of the heavenly Observer to identify and hire good workers and to place them in new positions of responsibility. So, Christians have invented eschatologies that conform to their rejection of any vision of temporal liberation — *eschatologies of the stripped field*. Men with battered spirits preach that nothing Christians can do as spiritual gleaners will ever fill the sacks to overflowing. They see no covenantal cause-and-effect relationship between gleaning and liberation. They preach a new gospel of the kingdom — *the kingdom of perpetual leftovers*. They do not recognize that there is a valid historical function of gleaning: the public identification of those bondservants who actively seek liberation and who pursue every legitimate avenue of escape.

New Testament Applications

In Israel, the sabbatical year of release was national and simultaneous. It was a negative injunction, and therefore a civil law, for it forbade something that was a positive evil: working the land without a break. We know what an appropriate penalty might have been: double restitution of that year's harvest, with the produce going to the priests as a payment to God. To pay that, the owner would probably have had to sell himself into slavery: a symbol of the transition from grace to wrath, a symbolic return to Egypt.

Today, there is no common year of release, nationally or internationally. The reason for this lack of a common year of release is because the enforcement of the New Testament sabbath has been decentralized. God now assigns to individuals the responsibility of deciding how to observe the sabbath. This decentralization of the locus of enforcement has led to the abolition of a common sabbatical year in which all fields are required to lie fallow in the same year, and charitable debts are cancelled in that same year (Deut. 15:1-6).[8]

How can the requirement of the sabbatical year be observed today? Farmers can honor it by refusing to plant their fields one year in seven, and inviting in gleaners. The land rests, the nematodes (earthworms) multiply, and the soil is rejuvenated. The land is given an opportunity to recover from the mistakes the farmer might have made, including the latest chemical fad. Or farmers may choose to rest one-seventh of their tillable land each year. The point is, farmers honor the principle by visibly conforming to the law of the sabbatical year.

This is not to become a matter of civil law. It is no longer the State's responsibility to enforce sabbath requirements. Owners can do what they please, but God watches closely. Those who own land that is leased to others can certainly require the lease-holders to abide by a fallow-rotation system, so that the land's productivity can be preserved.

Similarly with the injunction that all zero-interest charitable debts be cancelled every seventh year. The State is not to enforce such a requirement. Instead, the State should simply refuse to enforce any charitable debt contract beyond the seventh year. If creditors can collect what is owed to them by poor debtors without resorting to violence, that is their business, but the coercive authority of the State will not be used to enforce a contract that clearly violates the terms of the covenant. The State should no more enforce a morally mandatory charitable debt obligation beyond the seventh year than it should enforce any other kind of inherently immoral contract. There are limits to the legitimacy of voluntary contracts.

We should understand that the gleaning requirement from the beginning applied only to agricultural operations. It was not extended to the cities in the Old Testament, and it should not be extended beyond agriculture today. To the extent that the modern world has become urban, the year of release applies far more to society's debt structure than to its agriculture. Debt slavery is far more common today than agricultural slavery. Today, it is the farmer who has sold himself into bondage in his lust for more land and more comfortable tractors. He has collateralized the present value of his

---

8. North, *Sinai Strategy*, pp. 243-48, 253-55.

land, and he has prayed for the future value of his land's produce.[9]
The process of urbanization continues.

Conclusion

The stranger in the land was to be the beneficiary of the civil laws
of Israel. This was to serve as a testimony to the nations. It was not
only those who were born in the land who could experience the external blessings of God.

The land was to be given its rest every seventh year. The gleaners and the animals were not restricted from the unsown fields.
Whatever output of value that the land produced in these years became the lawful possession of the propertyless poor who worked to
claim it. Landowners rested, while the poor labored.

The sabbath was instituted in order to teach men about the necessity of relying on God to sustain them. Honoring the sabbath revealed to men that God sustains those who obey Him, no matter
how improbable that might seem. It also taught people habits of
thrift, future-orientation, and diligence. People had to get their work
done in six days, not seven; they had to store up necessities out of the
excess output of the days of lawful labor. This enforced system of
sabbath discipline was intended to reshape the slave mentality of
covenant-breakers.

What God taught them first with the miracle of the manna, He
later taught their heirs with the weekly sabbath, then the sabbatical
year, and finally with the year of Jubilee (Lev. 25). Because the people of Judah did not honor the law of the sabbatical year, God threatened to drive them into captivity for seventy years, that the land
might obtain its lawful rest (Jer. 50:34). They did not repent; Judah

---

9. This entrepreneurial hope faded in the early 1980's in the English-speaking,
grain-exporting nations of Canada, the United States, and Australia as the world at
long last learned to feed itself. The heart of this profound worldwide change was not
the innovative technology of the "green revolution"; it was rather the revolution of
freedom that free market agriculture promoted. The green revolution may now be
reaching its limits. The new rice strains that were introduced in Asia in the 1960's
have begun to reach inescapable limits of growth in output per acre. The law of
diminishing returns still holds. Rice production in Indonesia in the late 1980's began
to press against limits of land, labor, and affordable fertilizers, yet population continues to grow rapidly. *Wall Street Journal* (April 1, 1988), p. 1. Nevertheless, this long-
prophesied Asian crisis will not necessarily lead Asians to learn at last to enjoy a diet
based on the West's wheat. As one biologist notes, "Rice-eating people would often
rather starve than eat wheat or barley, which are unknown to them." Richard H.
Wagner, *Environment and Man* (3rd ed.; New York: Norton, 1978), p. 523.

then fell to Babylon. "To fulfil the word of the LORD by the mouth of Jeremiah, until the land had enjoyed her sabbaths: for as long as she lay desolate she kept sabbath, to fulfil threescore and ten years" (II Chron. 36:21).

God enforced His law when men refused to.

28

FEASTS AND CITIZENSHIP

Three times thou shalt keep a feast unto me in the year. Thou shalt keep the feast of unleavened bread: (thou shalt eat unleavened bread seven days, as I commanded thee, in the time appointed of the month Abib; for in it thou camest out from Egypt: and none shall appear before me empty:) And the feast of harvest, the firstfruits of thy labours, which thou hast sown in the field: and the feast of ingathering, which is in the end of the year, when thou hast gathered in thy labours out of the field. Three times in the year all thy males shall appear before the Lord GOD. Thou shalt not offer the blood of my sacrifice with leavened bread; neither shall the fat of my sacrifice remain until the morning. The first of the firstfruits of thy land thou shalt bring into the house of the LORD thy God. Thou shalt not seethe a kid in his mother's milk (Ex. 23:14-19).

God is the King who owns the land and who invites His people to join in corporate celebrations with Him. Those who harvest His crops are His judicial subordinates, and they publicly testify to this by their participation in His required feasts. They are to provide God with the firstfruits of the land. Those who refuse to attend the required feasts of God are in open rebellion against Him, for they are declaring publicly that they are not under His jurisdiction and that they owe him no firstfruits.

God's Sharecroppers

The sharecropping farmer does not own his own land. He may not even own his own tools. The owner provides these capital assets to the worker, who then agrees to share a fixed percentage of the crop with the owner.

The owner gains several advantages through this legal arrangement. He does not have to supervise the worker on a day-to-day basis. This had been the problem with the southern slave system prior to its abolition in 1865.[1] The owner can therefore concentrate his attention on more economically profitable tasks, such as marketing the crop. Second, the owner teaches his subordinate independence, which should increase the latter's total productivity. Third, the owner provides incentives for the worker to maximize his output. The lower the percentage demanded by the owner, the greater the economic incentive of the worker to maximize his output, since the latter keeps the lion's share of the product.

God requires a tithe. He also required the feasts of the Old Covenant era. This brought his workers before him on a regular basis. They had to sacrifice time, energy, and money to journey to Jerusalem and eat the required feasts. They had to bring the token firstfruits as a ritual testimony to their faith in God as the true owner of their land: "The first of the firstfruits of thy land thou shalt bring into the house of the LORD thy God" (Ex. 23:19a).

The Festivals and Civic Judgment

The feasts reminded them three times a year that the King of heaven requested their presence before Him. It reminded them who owned the land. Yet it was also an honor to attend. It also reminded them that the Creator and Sustainer of the universe protected them. He promised to protect the wives, children, and land during their absence. "Thrice in the year shall all your menchildren appear before the Lord GOD, the God of Israel. For I will cast out the nations before thee, and enlarge thy borders: neither shall any man desire thy land, when thou shalt go up to appear before the LORD thy God thrice in the year" (Ex. 34:23-24).

This passage appears at the end of a longer passage dealing with oppression. Men are warned not to raise a false report or render false judgment (Ex. 23:1-3). They are warned to return a lost animal to its owner, as well as help an enemy's fallen beast of burden (Ex. 23:4-5). Men are again reminded not to render false judgment or testify falsely (Ex. 23:6-7). They must not take bribes (Ex. 23:8). They must not oppress a stranger (Ex. 23:9). They must honor the sabbatical year and rest the land: no harvesting in the seventh year (Ex. 23:10-11). They must honor the weekly sabbath: no working

---

1. On the economic rationality of sharecropping in the post-Civil War American South, see Roger L. Ransom and Richard Sutch, *One Kind of Freedom: The economic consequences of emancipation* (New York: Cambridge University Press, 1977).

(Ex. 23:12). They must not mention any other God (Ex. 23:13). Then they are given the requirement of attending the three annual feasts.

Why bring up the requirements associated with the feasts in a section of the law that deals with civil judgment and economic oppression? Does participation in the feasts have some connection to the rendering of civil judgment? It does. *A circumcised male in Israel who failed to attend the required sacramental feasts lost his inheritance in the land and therefore also lost his citizenship.* He lost his eligibility to become a civil magistrate in Israel. This chain of judicial events is not immediately apparent from the text in Exodus 23, which is why this chapter is a detailed exposition of implications based on other texts, especially New Testament texts regarding Israel's loss of the kingdom through covenantal rebellion.

An Open Invitation to Israel's Closed Feasts

There were three required annual feasts in ancient Israel. This law applied to the circumcised members of the congregation. The feasts were open to all those in Israel who were circumcised, including converts from foreign nations and household slaves. The model feast was the Passover:

> And the LORD said unto Moses and Aaron, This is the ordinance of the passover: There shall no stranger eat thereof: But every man's servant that is bought for money, when thou hast circumcised him, then shall he eat thereof. A foreigner and an hired servant shall not eat thereof. In one house shall it be eaten; thou shalt not carry forth ought of the flesh abroad out of the house; neither shall ye break a bone thereof. All the congregation of Israel shall keep it. And when a stranger shall sojourn with thee, and will keep the passover to the LORD, let all his males be circumcised, and then let him come near and keep it; and he shall be as one that is born in the land: for no uncircumcised person shall eat thereof. One law shall be to him that is homeborn, and unto the stranger that sojourneth among you (Ex. 12:43-49).

The Passover was originally a household feast that was actually celebrated in the home. This is why hired servants were not allowed to participate. They would have to return to their own households in order to celebrate the feast. They were hired by money, and therefore not under the protection of the hiring family's covenant. The covenant was established by physical birth and circumcision, not by an economic contract. A stranger who was circumcised could participate in Passover, but only if all those under his household jurisdiction were also circumcised. The *mark of covenantal subordination* had to be on the flesh of every male participant, and it had to be on all those males under his family jurisdiction. (Moses' failure to circumcise his son is what brought God against Moses just before he re-entered Egypt [Ex. 4:24-26].)[2]

Sacrificial Offerings

After the Israelites arrived in the promised land, God made certain changes in the Passover ritual. Families were henceforth required to journey to a central location to celebrate the Passover: "Thou shalt therefore sacrifice the passover unto the LORD thy God, of the flock and the herd, in the place which the LORD shall choose to place his name there" (Deut. 16:2). The text makes it plain that the celebration was corporate, and it was not to be in a man's home town: "Thou mayest not sacrifice the passover within any of thy gates, which the LORD thy God giveth thee: But at the place which the LORD thy God shall choose to place his name in, there thou shalt sacrifice the passover at even, at the going down of the sun, at the season that thou camest forth out of Egypt" (Deut. 16:5-6). While the passage in Exodus 23 indicates that only the circumcised males were required to come to the various feasts, in fact the whole family was required to come to the place where the tabernacle was, and later on, where the temple was. The Exodus passage speaks representatively, but the parallel passage in Deuteronomy 16 is more specific:

Thou shalt observe the feast of tabernacles seven days, after that thou hast gathered in thy corn and thy wine: And thou shalt rejoice in thy feast, thou, and thy son, and thy daughter, and thy manservant, and thy maidservant, and the Levite, the stranger, and the fatherless, and the widow, that are within thy gates. Seven days shalt thou keep a solemn feast unto the LORD thy God in the place which the LORD shall choose: because the LORD thy God shall bless thee in all thine increase, and in all the works of thine hands, therefore thou shalt surely rejoice. Three times in a year shall all thy males appear before the LORD thy God in the place which he shall choose; in the feast of unleavened bread, and in the feast of weeks, and in the feast of tabernacles: and they shall not appear before the LORD empty: Every man shall give as he is able, according to the blessing of the LORD thy God which he hath given thee (Deut. 16:13-17).

---

2. Gary North, "The Marriage Supper of the Lamb," *Christianity and Civilization 4* (1985), pp. 209-26.

The men were to appear together at a corporate ritual at some point during each of these three feasts. They were to appear in their official covenantal capacity as judges of their households. Wives and children came to the city, but there must have been a separate ritual "before the Lord" at which only men were in attendance. It was there that the priests or Levites offered the families' sacrifices, which were required offerings: "they shall not appear before the LORD empty." In their capacity as *household priests*, the men were required to bring a sacrificial offering before God. Fathers no longer killed the sacrificial animals and ate them with their families in their own homes, as they had at the first Passover. The priests or priestly aides killed the animals for them representatively. Presumably each father took his portion of the sacrifice and returned to his family to eat it before the night was over: "neither shall the fat of my sacrifice remain until the morning."

It was during the feast of tabernacles that a week-long total of 70 bulls was sacrificed for the 70 nations, plus one for Israel: $13 + 12 + 11 + 10 + 9 + 8 + 7(+ 1) = 71$ (Num. 29:13-36). Israel sacrificed bulls representatively for the nations.[3] Because these sacrifices were priestly and therefore mediatorial, only circumcised males could lawfully participate in the actual ritual. God is only represented by males in the sacrifices, which is the reason why women cannot lawfully be ordained to church offices (I Cor. 14:34-35).

Every Man a Priest

The Protestant doctrine of "every man a priest" was equally in force in Old Covenant Israel: "Now therefore, if ye will obey my voice indeed, and keep my covenant, then ye shall be a peculiar treasure unto me above all people: for all the earth is mine: And ye shall be unto me a kingdom of priests, and an holy nation. These are the words which thou shalt speak unto the children of Israel" (Ex. 19:5-6). *God's covenant, ownership, kingdom, and priesthood*: all are linked together here. The hierarchical subordination of each man under God — a subordination marked physically by circumcision — entitled any man to serve as the priest of his own household. This was why the stranger who wanted to participate in Passover had to have all the males in his household circumcised. "And when a stranger shall

---

3. James B. Jordan, *The Sociology of the Church: Essays in Reconstruction* (Tyler, Texas: Geneva Ministries, 1986), pp. 101-2. This was what I would call a "common grace" sacrifice. It accomplished ritually what Jesus' death on the cross fulfilled: a covering for the nations of the earth that allowed them to survive temporally.

sojourn with thee, and will keep the passover to the LORD, let all his males be circumcised, and then let him come near and keep it; and he shall be as one that is born in the land: for no uncircumcised person shall eat thereof" (Ex. 12:48). He had to be marked as a priestly representative of God within his own home. He had to be a member of a judicially marked covenantal hierarchy.

Israel as a Sanctuary

This *family priestly office*, hierarchical in structure, opened the door to another office, that of *civil magistrate*. To be a citizen in Israel, a man first had to be under the jurisdiction of a family covenant,[4] either by physical birth into his own family or by adoption (including a woman's marriage)[5] into a Hebrew family.[6] This family-based order of governmental authority and office helps to explain an otherwise difficult exegetical problem. Immediately following the passage in Deuteronomy that deals with the feast of the tabernacles we read: "Judges and officers shalt thou make thee in all thy gates, which the LORD thy God giveth thee, throughout thy tribes: and they shall judge the people with just judgment. Thou shalt not wrest judgment; thou shalt not respect persons, neither take a gift: for a gift doth blind the eyes of the wise, and pervert the words of the righteous. That which is altogether just shalt thou follow, that thou mayest live, and inherit the land which the LORD thy God giveth thee" (Deut. 16:18-20).

Here we find once again that *the laws of the festivals are closely associated with the laws of civil justice*. The civil judge is warned not to accept a bribe. He shall not render false or perverted judgments. The context is a court of law. The promise is that those who render righteous judgments will live and inherit the land. All three are tied together: required attendance at the festivals, rendering honest civic judgment, and inheriting family-owned land.

---

4. Just as a church officer must first serve as the head of his household (I Tim. 3:2, 4).

5. For example, Rahab and Ruth.

6. Adoptions into Hebrew households took place on a widespread basis during the first century of Israel's stay in Egypt, which is why their population was growing so rapidly by Moses' day. See Gary North, *Moses and Pharaoh: Dominion Religion vs. Power Religion* (Tyler, Texas: Institute for Christian Economics, 1985), ch. 1: "Population Growth: Tool of Dominion."

Sanctuary: Equality Before the Law

Any man who was willing to subordinate himself to God by living in the land of Israel as a stranger was entitled to the benefits of God's revealed civil law, including its protection. He had access to civil justice by his very presence in God's geographical sanctuary, the land of Israel.

This sanctuary was man's sanctuary. *The land of Israel was every resident's boundary of judicial protection from the civil laws of false gods.* The promise of equality before the civil law was the judicial sanctuary offered by God to all those who would voluntarily remain within the geographical boundaries of those nations that formally covenanted with Him. This sanctuary status of a biblically covenanted nation was therefore geographical rather than ritual.

Biblical law is quite clear: there is to be one civil law-order governing all people because everyone is under the jurisdiction of God, who rules by covenant. God holds men and nations accountable for their obedience to His laws. Even though not all men are willing ritually to admit their subordination to God as creatures, all are to be governed by the requirements of the same civil law-order that God established as His representative model in Israel (Deut. 4:4-5).[7] This is God's wisdom for all mankind. Wisdom cannot legitimately be observed by autonomous man on a "take it or leave it basis"; covenantal religion is not smorgasbord religion, picking and choosing in terms of what sounds good to unregenerate minds. Wisdom must be *obeyed.* Wisdom is part of God's national covenant: "Keep therefore and do them; for this is your wisdom and your understanding in the sight of the nations, which shall hear all these statutes, and say, Surely this great nation is a wise and understanding people" (Deut. 4:6).[8]

---

7. Some may deny that this was true in the era of the Old Covenant, although they must contend with Greg L. Bahnsen in this regard: Greg L. Bahnsen, *By This Standard: The Authority of God's Law Today* (Tyler, Texas: Institute for Christian Economics, 1985), ch. 24. But Christians cannot escape the judicial and civil implications of Matthew 21:43: "Therefore say I unto you, The kingdom of God shall be taken from you, and given to a nation bringing forth the fruits thereof." When God transferred His kingdom to the church, an international covenantal institution, he brought all nations under the covenantal obligations of his law, including civil law. Gary North, *Healer of the Nations: Biblical Blueprints for International Relations* (Ft. Worth, Texas: Dominion Press, 1987), ch. 2.

8. In their path-breaking and ground-surrendering study of biblical law, neo-dispensationalists H. Wayne House and Thomas D. Ice argue that the Mosaic Law is not binding today and was never binding on the ancient pagan world, yet the Mosaic Law offers wisdom. "Wisdom differs from law in that law provides the legal

Because pagan nations in the Old Covenant era did not acknowledge their judicial obligations in this regard, God created a geographical sanctuary in Israel for men to flee to when they decided to place themselves under the civil covenant of God.

Judicial Distinctions

The question then arises: What was the judicial distinction between an uncircumcised resident and a circumcised resident? One distinction was inheritance: rural land reverted back to the original owner's family in the 50th year (Lev. 25:13). But this law did not govern property within walled cities or towns (Lev. 25:31). Does this mean that in walled cities, there was no judicial distinction between Jew and gentile? There must have been some sort of distinction, or else the gentiles could have captured the cities of Israel, *including Jerusalem*, simply by moving into them, buying up the property, and taking over each city's civil government. The strangers within the gates could thereby have inherited the land.

---

stipulations which regulate the covenantal agreement and can be enforced by civil penalties. . . . On the other hand, wisdom is advice with no legal penalties." House and Ice, *Dominion Theology: Curse or Blessing?* (Portland, Oregon: Multnomah, 1988), p. 186. They argue for wisdom apart from any covenant law or covenant sanctions. Therefore, one has to conclude, outside the narrow geographical confines of ancient Israel, God's Ten Commandments become the Ten Suggestions. The wisdom of Proverbs becomes a lot of wise sayings. But Solomon was a king whose fame spread because of his ability to impose *wise sanctions*. After the incident of the two prostitutes and the baby, we read: "And all Israel heard of the judgment which the king had judged; and they feared the king: for they saw that the wisdom of God was in him, to do judgment" (I Ki. 3:28). They are saying that because of the resurrection of Jesus Christ, who suffered the ultimate sanctions, there are no further biblically required covenant sanctions in history (except execution for murder, a Noahic covenant sanction: p. 130) until His Second Coming. Autonomous man therefore gets to make up his own civil laws as he goes along. If you suspect that this view of civil law without specific biblical sanctions can easily become a license to sin, personally and nationally, and also a license to commit statist tyranny, you have correctly grasped their argument: *no biblical sanctions — no biblical crimes.*

They write: "There is a big difference between law and wisdom, though often the net effect will be the same since the regenerate believer will want to apply the wisdom of God's law" (p. 187). This is *theobabble* (theological doubletalk that evades confronting difficult problems). They are trying desperately to avoid appearing as the social antinomians that they are, one last attempt to save the decaying remains of dispensational ethics from the acids of antinomianism and ethical dualism — an attempt that clearly comes a century too late. On the morally and theologically devastating antinomianism of modern dispensationalism, see the book by dispensationalist theologian and pastor John MacArthur, *The Gospel According to Jesus* (Grand Rapids, Michigan: Zondervan Academie, 1988).

It was in fact legally possible for strangers in the gates to buy up houses and buildings inside the gates, but this did not make them citizens. Nor would the post-exilic revised terms of land ownership that God instructed Ezekiel to announce to Israel make citizens of strangers in the land: "And it shall come to pass, that ye shall divide it by lot for an inheritance unto you, and to the strangers that sojourn among you, which shall beget children among you: and they shall be unto you as born in the country among the children of Israel; they shall have inheritance with you among the tribes of Israel. And it shall come to pass, that in what tribe the stranger sojourneth, there shall ye give him his inheritance, saith the Lord GOD" (Ezek. 47:22-23). Citizenship in the biblical commonwealth of Israel was not by property ownership as such. Citizenship was by covenant. Citizenship was by *circumcision and feast*, by covenant mark and covenant renewal.

There was a judicial distinction between circumcised and uncircumcised residents. This distinction was explicitly not a difference in the God-required application of the civil law to different people (Ex. 12:49). This distinction must therefore be found elsewhere than in some supposed inequality before the law. There is to be no inequality before God's civil law.[9] Thus, the difference had to have been in the very definition of citizenship, meaning *the exercise of civil rulership*. Citizenship was closely tied to one's participation in the three required annual feasts in Jerusalem. As was the case in the ancient world generally, *if a man could not legally participate in the religious rites of the city, he could not become a citizen.*[10] What made Israel different was the widespread use of adoption, which mirrored God's gracious adoption of Israel (Ezek. 16:3-7). Paul connected God's adoption and God's covenant with Israel when he spoke of his kinsmen according to the flesh, "Who are Israelites; to whom pertaineth the adoption, and the glory, and the covenants, and the giving of the law, and the service of God, and the promises" (Rom. 9:4). Thus, unless he was a bastard, a Moabite, an Ammonite, an Edomite, or an Egyptian (Deut. 23:2-8), he had to be granted immediate access to the feasts: "And if a stranger shall sojourn among you, and will keep the passover unto

---

9. North, *Moses and Pharaoh*, ch. 14: "The Rule of Law."
10. Numa Denis Fustel de Coulanges, *The Ancient City: A Study on the Religion, Laws, and Institutions of Greece and Rome* (Garden City, New York: Doubleday Anchor, [1864] 1955), Bk. III.

the LORD; according to the ordinance of the passover, and according to the manner thereof, so shall he do: ye shall have one ordinance, both for the stranger, and for him that was born in the land" (Num. 9:14).

Feasts and Sanctions

The uncircumcised resident male and his household did not gain access to God's sanctuary, the temple. To gain this priestly access, he was required first to accept a visible mark in his flesh, as were all the males under his family jurisdiction. He had to accept God's "brand" on him, God's sign of adoption. *God owns all men, and circumcision was a man's acknowledgment of God's lawful claim on him.* A man carried this servile mark in his flesh, and he was reminded daily of his judicial condition as a servant to God. For as long as he lived, he bore this mark of judicial subordination.

A circumcised man declared ritually and physically that he was under God's judicial authority; only then was he given access to the three annual feasts. These feasts were held in a central location. Attendance was mandatory for all circumcised men who were residents of the land.[11] A resident male who refused to attend the feasts of the King of heaven came under the king's condemnation. One did not lawfully turn down the King's invitation. This was the message of Jesus' parable of the king's feast.

The kingdom of heaven is like unto a certain king, which made a marriage for his son, And sent forth his servants to call them that were bidden to the wedding: and they would not come. Again, he sent forth other servants, saying, Tell them which are bidden, Behold, I have prepared my dinner: my oxen and my fatlings are killed, and all things are ready: come unto the marriage. But they made light of it, and went their ways, one to his farm, another to his merchandise: And the remnant took his servants, and entreated them spitefully, and slew them. But when the king heard thereof, he was wroth: and he sent forth his armies, and destroyed those murderers, and burned up their city. Then saith he to his servants, The wedding is ready, but they which were bidden were not worthy. Go ye therefore into the highways, and as many as ye shall find, bid to the marriage. So those servants went out into the highways, and gathered together all as many as they found, both bad and good: and the wedding was furnished with guests. And when the king came in to see the guests, he saw

---

11. Men could go on journeys and escape this obligation. Passover could be celebrated late by those who had been on long journeys (Num. 9:10-11).

there a man which had not on a wedding garment: And he saith unto him,
Friend, how camest thou in hither not having a wedding garment? And he was
speechless. Then said the king to the servants, Bind him hand and foot, and
take him away, and cast him into outer darkness; there shall be weeping and
gnashing of teeth. For many are called, but few are chosen (Matt 22:2-14).

There is no doubt that Jesus was referring here to Israel. The
Pharisees understood His accusation. "Then went the Pharisees, and
took counsel how they might entangle him in his talk" (Matt. 22:15).

There were two crimes associated with the festivals of the kingdom: 1) refusing to come when invited and 2) refusing to bear the appropriate mark of subordination: in Israel, circumcision; in the parable, a wedding garment.[12] It is an honor to be invited and a curse to
refuse to come. It is an honor to attend, but only those who have
subordinated themselves publicly to the heavenly King should dare
to enter His presence.

The annual festivals of Israel were mandatory for those males
who were under God's ecclesiastical jurisdiction. These were members of the congregation. The question then arises: If it was required
that every circumcised male attend the feasts, what were the sanctions for non-attendance? Who imposed them?

What Kind of Negative Sanctions?

I have argued throughout this volume that biblical civil law does
not set forth positive injunctions to do good. It only enforces laws
against publicly evil acts, as defined by God's revealed law. This law
of the compulsory feasts initially appears to be an exception to this
rule. It is not an exception. Because no negative sanction is mentioned in the various texts dealing with the required festivals, we
should initially conclude that this was not a civil law. Only if we can
derive appropriate civil sanctions by examining the nature of the
crime should we conclude that this was a civil law. I can see no appropriate sanctions. There was no earthly victim of a crime who
could bring charges. There seems to be no appropriate fine to be distributed to some future victim of an unknown criminal. Whipping
seems inappropriate, since the crime is not a positive assault on public morality.

It seems a likely inference that the appropriate negative sanction was
excommunication from the priestly congregation. By failing to attend the re-

---

12. This is clearly symbolic of baptism.

quired feasts, the man had placed himself in the camp of the uncir-cumcised strangers. He would have been kept from attending future ritual feasts. He would have been barred from attendance at local worship conducted by the priests. If he was an Israelite with an in-heritance in the land, he would also have forfeited this inheritance, for he had renounced his family's ownership rights in Israel when he renounced God's ownership rights over Him and His family. Only if his sons or distant heirs later denied their father's rebellion and affirmed the family covenant under God when they became adults could they reclaim the forfeited inheritance. However, this re-covenanting pro-cedure did give them the ability to reclaim what had been legally removed. This was God's promise to the future dispossessed sons of Israel whenever they were removed from the land:

And ye shall perish among the heathen, and the land of your enemies shall eat you up. And they that are left of you shall pine away in their iniquity in your enemies' lands; and also in the iniquities of their fathers shall they pine away with them. If they shall confess their iniquity, and the iniquity of their fathers, with their trespass which they trespassed against me, and that also they have walked contrary unto me; And that I also have walked con-trary unto them, and have brought them into the land of their enemies; if then their uncircumcised hearts be humbled, and they then accept of the punishment of their iniquity: Then will I remember my covenant with Jacob, and also my covenant with Isaac, and also my covenant with Abra-ham will I remember; and I will remember the land (Lev. 26:38-42).

If a man had no inheritance in the land, he had no legal access to judicial office. This was another aspect of God's threat of imposing the physical sanction of removing them from their geographical sanctuary in the land. They would become slaves and strangers in a foreign land. Only through extraordinary faithfulness did certain Israelites become leaders in foreign lands, as Joseph had become in Egypt, as Daniel later became in Babylon and Medo-Persia, and as Esther became in Medo-Persia. Israelites would suffer by becoming subordinates to foreign gods whose spokesmen did not respect the principle of equality before the law. They would not again serve as judges in the land, declaring God's civil law, unless they repented.

To be an uncircumcised stranger in Israel was to be someone outside the congregation. Circumcision was a judicial act. It was a physical mark of covenantal subordination, not a magical mark of initiation. A man could make his circumcision null and void by rejecting the terms of the covenant. Refusing to attend the feasts was such a rejection.

Family Sanctions

Inheritance was familistic in Old Covenant Israel.[13] The civil government was supposed to enforce the laws of inheritance, but the seat of family covenantal authority was in the father as the family priest. When a man died, his sons inherited. If he had no sons, his daughters inherited. If he had no daughters, his brothers inherited (Num. 27:8-10). "And if his father have no brethren, then ye shall give his inheritance unto his kinsman that is next to him of his family, and he shall possess it: and it shall be unto the children of Israel a statute of judgment, as the LORD commanded Moses" (Num. 27:11). The kinsman redeemer (ga'al), meaning the blood avenger (Deut. 19:6), inherited the property as his closest next of kin.

What about a man who had voluntarily abandoned the feasts? He had thereby publicly abandoned the covenant. This was a form of *covenantal death*.[14] Covenantally, it was as if the original owner had died. His heirs inherited. But because he had cut off all those who were under his immediate covenantal authority in his family, his brothers immediately inherited, unless his sons broke covenant with him. If he had no brothers, then his next of kin inherited. His brothers or his closest relatives could then go to the civil magistrate and compel the transfer of title to the land, which would presumably go into effect at the time of his physical death or the jubilee year, whichever came first.[15] This confiscation of the man's property was not the sovereign act of the civil government. It was not a negative civil sanction. It was a family sanction that was lawfully enforced by the civil government. The terms of land ownership had been set by God before they conquered Canaan. As the ultimate Owner, God had the legal right to specify in advance the judicial terms of the leaseholds.

Similarly, the removal of the man's status as someone eligible to serve as a civil magistrate was not a negative civil sanction. It was

---

13. Gary North, *The Sinai Strategy: Economics and the Ten Commandments* (Tyler, Texas: Institute for Christian Economics, 1986), ch. 5: "Familistic Capital."

14. On covenantal death, see Ray R. Sutton, *Second Chance: Biblical Blueprints for Marriage and Divorce* (Ft. Worth, Texas: Dominion Press, 1987), chaps 2, 4.

15. He would have been given time to repent. Also, while civil law in Israel had to abide by the terms of ownership, the original terms did not specify that immediately upon the covenantal death of a man he would be eligible to be thrown off his land. The sanction had to do with lawful inheritance. Inheritance was governed by the inheritance laws of Numbers 27 and the jubilee laws of Leviticus 25.

simply a *public acknowledgment* by the civil government of the individual's change in legal status when he withdrew from the congregation by ceasing to attend the feasts. It was the removal of a covenant privilege open only to members of the congregation. The State merely confirmed what the former congregation member had publicly announced: he was no longer a citizen or judge in Israel.

Jesus and the Disinheritance of Israel

The kinsman-redeemer inherited because of the covenantal death of the covenant-breaker. This was the legal basis for Jesus Christ, the kinsman-redeemer and also the blood avenger of Israel, to inherit the kingdom and to pass this inheritance to those under His covenantal administration. Thus, Jesus prophesied to the Jews of His day: "Therefore say I unto you, The kingdom of God shall be taken from you, and given to a nation bringing forth the fruits thereof" (Matt. 21:43).

Israel had renounced the ethical terms of God's covenant, despite the fact that all the men bore the mark of covenantal subordination in their flesh. "Woe unto you, scribes and Pharisees, hypocrites! For ye pay tithe of mint and anise and cummin, and have omitted the weightier matters of the law, judgment, mercy, and faith: these ought ye to have done, and not to leave the other undone" (Matt. 23:23-24). The Jews crucified their kinsman-redeemer, Jesus Christ, who exercised the office of blood avenger after His resurrection. Jesus destroyed Jerusalem and the temple in 70 A.D., so that never again could they honor the feasts. The great tribulation came in 70 A.D.[16] The days of vengeance came in 70 A.D.[17]

Never again would the temple sacrifices in Jerusalem serve as a legal covering for the nations. This meant that the Hebrews would never again serve as judges in God's Holy Commonwealth. Once they had lost title to the land, they could be expelled. Once removed from the land of promise, they no longer lawfully imposed biblical law's civil sanctions, either on themselves or on the gentiles.

Talmudic law recognized their new legal status. As I wrote in Chapter 1, when the Romans captured Jerusalem and burned the temple in A.D. 70, the ancient official Sanhedrin court came to an end. The rabbis, under the leadership of Rabbi Johanan ben Zakkai,

---

16. David Chilton, *The Great Tribulation* (Ft. Worth, Texas: Dominion Press, 1987).
17. David Chilton, *The Days of Vengeance: An Exposition of the Book of Revelation* (Ft. Worth: Dominion Press, 1987).

then took over many of the judicial functions of the Sanhedrin.[18] They established as a principle that every Jewish court must have at least one judge who had been ordained by the laying on of hands (*semikah*), and who could in principle trace his ordination back to Moses. This laying on of hands could take place only in the Holy Land. Legal scholar George Horowitz comments: "A court not thus qualified had no jurisdiction to impose the punishments prescribed in the Torah."[19] After the Bar Kochba revolt, the Jews were scattered across the Roman Empire in the diaspora. "The Rabbis were compelled, therefore, in order to preserve the Torah and to maintain law and order, to enlarge the authority of Rabbinical tribunals. This they accomplished by emphasizing the distinction between Biblical penalties and Rabbinical penalties. Rabbinical courts after the second century had no authority to impose Biblical punishments since they lacked *semikah;* but as regards penalties created by Rabbinical legislation, the Rabbis had of necessity, accordingly, a whole series of sanctions and penalties: excommunications, fines, physical punishment, use of the 'secular arm' in imitation of the Church, etc."[20] Thus, by the time of the writing of the Mishnah, which was Rabbi Judah the Prince's authoritative late-second-century compilation of rabbinical laws, Jewish courts had already abandoned any attempt to enforce the Old Testament sanctions.

Covenantal Restoration

But there is always a qualification to God's historical judgments, the same one open to the Hebrews who had been scattered before in Babylon (Lev. 26:38-42): the Jews can repent, affirm the terms of the covenant, be adopted by God into His church, and serve as judges again. In fact, they will surely repent, Paul promised in Romans 11. They will be restored to faith.

I say then, Have they stumbled that they should fall? God forbid: but rather through their fall salvation is come unto the Gentiles, for to provoke them to jealousy. Now if the fall of them be the riches of the world, and the diminishing of them the riches of the Gentiles; how much more their fulness? For I speak to you Gentiles, inasmuch as I am the apostle of the Gen-

---

18. George Horowitz, *The Spirit of Jewish Law* (New York: Central Book Co., [1953] 1963), pp. 92-93.

19. *Ibid.*, p. 93.

20. *Idem.*

tiles, I magnify mine office: If by any means I may provoke to emulation them which are my flesh, and might save some of them. For if the casting away of them be the reconciling of the world, what shall the receiving of them be, but life from the dead? For if the firstfruit be holy, the lump is also holy: and if the root be holy, so are the branches. And if some of the branches be broken off, and thou, being a wild olive tree, wert graffed in among them, and with them partakest of the root and fatness of the olive tree; Boast not against the branches. But if thou boast, thou bearest not the root, but the root thee. Thou wilt say then, The branches were broken off, that I might be graffed in. Well; because of unbelief they were broken off, and thou standest by faith. Be not highminded, but fear: For if God spared not the natural branches, take heed lest he also spare not thee. Behold therefore the goodness and severity of God: on them which fell, severity; but toward thee, goodness, if thou continue in his goodness: otherwise thou also shalt be cut off. And they also, if they abide not still in unbelief, shall be graffed in: for God is able to graff them in again. For if thou wert cut out of the olive tree which is wild by nature, and wert graffed contrary to nature into a good olive tree: how much more shall these, which be the natural branches, be graffed into their own olive tree? For I would not, brethren, that ye should be ignorant of this mystery, lest ye should be wise in your own conceits; that blindness in part is happened to Israel, until the fulness of the Gentiles be come in. And so all Israel shall be saved: as it is written, There shall come out of Sion the Deliverer, and shall turn away ungodliness from Jacob: For this is my covenant unto them, when I shall take away their sins (Rom. 11:11-27).

Next time, however, they will not have to settle for restoration of their ownership of tiny Israel. As members of the church, they will inherit the earth. "His soul shall dwell at ease; and his seed shall inherit the earth" (Ps. 25:13).

Citizenship by Birth Within the Covenant

On the eighth day, the Hebrew male child was to be circumcised (Lev. 12:3). This gave him the mark of citizenship. Birth gave him access to circumcision, and circumcision gave him citizen's rights. He could lose his citizenship by violating the terms of the covenant in specific ways, most notably by refusing to attend the required festivals. The feasts were ritual acts of covenant renewal,[21] and these acts of covenant renewal had definite political consequences.

---

21. Ray R. Sutton, *That You May Prosper: Dominion By Covenant* (Tyler, Texas: Institute for Christian Economics, 1987), Appendix 8.

In the New Testament, the mark of the covenant is also by birth, but only through personal profession of faith (self-acknowledged *new birth*) or by parental representation.[22] In both cases, the person so marked can lose his citizenship, and in the same way as in the Old Covenant: by breaking God's laws, by failing to repent and make restitution, and by failing to attend the required feast of covenant renewal: the Lord's Supper.

The Office of Civil Magistrate

The law of the mandatory feasts did not impose negative *civil* sanctions against those who refused to attend the required feasts, but it did remove a civil privilege: the right to serve as a civil officer. Every civil government in New Testament times is supposed to respect the Bible's definition of what constitutes a true citizen in the eyes of God: *a person under the covenantal discipline of a Trinitarian church.* A citizen today, as in ancient Israel, is one who eats God's communion feast. If he refuses, he thereby removes himself from the jurisdiction of the church's court, either through resigning church membership or through excommunication. He thereby redefines himself as no longer being a citizen, but rather a stranger in the land. The State acknowledges his renouncing of his citizenship. This is not a negative sanction; it is a judicial response to the former citizen's voluntarily chosen new covenantal status, namely, that of public covenant-breaker.

Covenant-keepers were the only ones who were entitled to exercise judicial authority in the land of Israel. They could legally serve as judges or as electors of judges (Deut. 1:13; 16:18). How do we know this? Because all men were under the protection of biblical civil law. There was no distinguishing mark based on differing degrees of protection from the civil law; one's presence in the land was a sufficient mark entitling one to full legal protection (Ex. 12:49). Thus, *circumcision had to be a mark of judicial authority as well as a mark of judicial subordination.* It was a mark of covenantal subordination under God, and therefore a mark of one's authority to be eligible to serve as a judge. This is why Paul could write to the Corinthians: "Do ye not know that the saints shall judge the world? And if the world shall be judged by you, are ye unworthy to judge the smallest matters? Know ye not that we shall judge angels? how much more

---

22. *Ibid.*, Appendix 9.

things that pertain to this life? If then ye have judgments of things pertaining to this life, set them to judge who are least esteemed in the church" (I Cor. 6:2-4).

Baptism and Civil Authority

Women were not absolutely required to go to these three feasts. They also did not normally serve as judges, although Deborah did (Jud. 4). Women were not to be kept away from these feasts, but they were not under judicial compulsion to attend. This is why the New Testament represents a major break with the Old Testament. *Females are baptized in the church; therefore, they are required to take communion.* Females (except infants) are not represented by a man — father or husband — in either baptism or the required ritual feast.

As was the case in the Old Covenant, they are not allowed to become priests, for they cannot lawfully speak judicially in church. God presents Himself to humanity as a Husband, and thus He cannot be lawfully represented in His role as the priestly Lawgiver and sacrificial lamb by women. Women cannot lawfully declare God's law in formal church worship ceremonies (I Cor. 14:34-35). In this sense, women are analogous to all those attendees at the required feasts of Israel who were also not authorized to become priests.[23]

Covenanted women were and still are eligible to become civil judges in the holy commonwealth. They did and still can lawfully represent God in declaring His judgments in civil courts. In ancient Israel, women did not bear the mark of circumcision, but their fathers, brothers, husbands, and sons did. Women were circumcised representatively. Thus, they had lawful access to the feasts, though not as actual household priests.[24] They could lawfully serve as civil judges,

---

23. Women, male children under age 20 (Ex. 30:14), castrated males (Deut. 23:1), plus: circumcised Moabites, Ammonites, and heirs of bastards to the tenth generation (Deut. 23:2-3), and circumcised Edomites and Egyptians to the third generation (Deut. 23:7-8).

24. It might be argued that a widow with no brothers and no adult son would have been allowed to participate in the required feasts as a recipient of the family's burned sacrifice. She was clearly the head of her household, and the priestly office was a household office. She could take a vow that was binding before God without having to wait a day for her husband or father to confirm it (Num. 30:9). This points to her position as a household priest. The response to this argument is that the importance of God's masculinity outweighs even the importance of the office as the head of the household. A Levite could have represented the widow at the actual ritual sacrifice.

although this was not common practice.[25] Deborah was breaking no
civil law when she served as a prophetess and judge. "And Deborah, a
prophetess, the wife of Lapidoth, she judged Israel at that time"
(Jud. 4:4). She could not serve as a sacrifice-offering priest in her
household, but she could serve as a public prophetess[26] and judge.
She could declare God's law outside the sanctuary of the temple.

There is no representation with respect to the woman's covenantal mark in the New Testament. There surely should be no question of the right of women to vote in elections, to serve on juries, and
to be elected to political and judicial office in a Christian social order.
Baptism is the mark of this judicial civil authority. Baptized women
possess the covenantal proof of judicial subordination to God that is
also a mark of civil authority in a Christian civil commonwealth.

This doctrine does not authorize universal women's suffrage,
however. Baptism as the basis of rulership is the mark of God's theocratic order. Nevertheless, there can be no lawful discrimination by
the State on the basis of differences in race, color, or sex. Why not?
Because of Exodus 12:49: "One law shall be to him that is homeborn,
and unto the stranger that sojourneth among you." *But there must
always be civil discrimination with respect to creed*, not in the sense of the
application of biblical civil law, but with respect to those who have
lawful access to the civil offices that apply it.

With respect to the right of baptized women to vote, to hold political office, and to sit on juries, it is clear that such rights were ignored
by Christian men from the days that Christians first gained access to
political power in Rome. This judicial blindness is analogous to the
refusal of Christians to liberate their permanent lifetime slaves, and
to refuse to pass civil laws liberating them. It took until the mid-
nineteenth century to persuade civil governments of the moral evil of
refusing to abolish slavery. It took another three-quarters of a century to persuade national governments that all women should have
the right to vote. In both cases, Christian scholars and leaders did
not take the lead. They followed the lead of the humanists.[27]

---

25. Those who argue that the Israelite women never ate the Passover must find
some way to explain the legitimacy of Deborah's office as civil judge. He will have to
separate citizenship from participation at the feasts. This will make citizenship in
Israel very difficult to explain.

26. Philip the evangelist had four daughters who prophesied (Acts 21:8-9).

27. The first women's rights meeting was held in 1848 in Seneca Falls, New York.
In 1861, the state of Kansas authorized women to vote in school board elections. In
1890, the state of Wyoming authorized general women's suffrage, the first general

Does this mean that the institutional church learns only slowly how to apply fundamental biblical principles as time goes on? Yes. Does this mean that basic biblical principles of justice have been ignored by the church for many centuries? Yes. Does this mean that if the church refuses to acknowledge the Bible's authority for law, politics, economics, education, and similar supposedly non-ecclesiastical topics that the enemies of God will take the lead in promoting such ideas, but only by universalizing these judicial principles and removing their biblical covenantal content? The historical testimony of the last two centuries certainly indicates that such is the case. For example, Christians in the era of the early American republic sold their birthright for a mess of judicial pottage in 1788 — an historical and judicial fact still vehemently denied by today's disinherited American Christians — and the Unitarian humanists immediately began to collect their newly purchased inheritance.[28] They were able to do this initially by deception: stealing the language of biblical civic and judicial righteousness by substituting the doctrine of Newtonian natural law.[29] They continued the transfer after 1788 by capturing Christianity's rhetoric of mission and its vision of victory.[30] The final transfer was made by Darwin: the destruction of natural law and the coming of the scientific planning elite.[31]

---

civil government to do so. In 1893, New Zealand granted the right to vote to women; in 1902, Australia followed New Zealand's lead. Norway was the first nation in Europe to do so, in 1907 on a limited basis, and full suffrage in 1913. The Nineteenth Amendment (1920) modified the U.S. Constitution to allow women full voting rights: "The right of citizens of the United States to vote shall not be denied or abridged by the United States or by any state on account of sex. Congress shall have power to enforce this article by appropriate legislation." Not until 1928 did English women gain full suffrage.

28. See Appendix H: "Selling the Birthright: The Ratification of the U.S. Constitution."

29. Keith Thomas, *Religion and the Decline of Magic* (New York: Scribner's, 1971); cf. Gary North, *Political Polytheism: The Myth of Pluralism* (Tyler, Texas: Institute for Christian Economics, 1989), Part 3.

30. If one event best captures the nature of the transfer it was the capture of Harvard College by the Unitarians in 1805, symbolized by Henry Ware's election to the chair of theology. On the transformation, see C. Gregg Singer, *A Theological Interpretation of American History* (Nutley, New Jersey: Craig Press, 1964), ch. 3; Alice Felt Tyler, *Freedom's Ferment* (New York: Harper Torchbook, [1944] 1965); Edward McNall Burns, *The American Ideal of Mission: Concepts of National Purpose and Destiny* (New Brunswick, New Jersey: Rutgers University Press, 1957); Albert K. Weinberg, *Manifest Destiny: A Study in Nationalist Expansion in American History* (Chicago: Quadrangle, [1935] 1963).

31. Gary North, *The Dominion Covenant: Genesis* (2nd ed.; Tyler, Texas: Institute for Christian Economics, 1987), Appendix A: "From Cosmic Purposelessness to Humanistic Sovereignty."

Humanist Citizenship

The modern humanist wants the political fruits of ritual subordination to God, namely, the right to exercise civil judgment in society, but without the roots: actual ritual subordination to God. He wants the judicial fruits of lawful access to God's required feasts without actually having to attend them. He wants universal suffrage: a guarantee of his continuing access to the office of judge, despite his public denial of God's authority over him. He insists on being allowed to serve as a civil judge despite the fact that he is not under ecclesiastical discipline. If this demand is biblically legitimate, it means one of two things: 1) that he can interpret and apply God's revealed civil law as well as a Christian can, despite the fact that he refuses to honor the counsel of church officers by affirming the church covenant and submitting to church discipline; or 2) that God's revealed civil law — if such even exists — is irrelevant to civil affairs.

We need to understand what this means judicially and politically. *The humanists want a different covenant*, with a different set of five points: sovereignty (the General Will, the People, The *Volk*, the proletariat, etc.), hierarchy-representation (the Party, the vanguard of the proletariat, the *Führer*, the Supreme Court, national plebiscites, etc.), law (majority rule, evolutionary forces, Marxism-Leninism, etc.), judgment (oaths to different sovereignties in order to gain citizenship, welfare rights and entitlements, etc.), and inheritance (political citizenship). They have been successful in persuading voters, including Christian voters, of the supposed judicial necessity of abandoning the biblical covenant model that long undergirded Europe's civil commonwealths.

Humanists have written civil covenants (constitutions) that make citizenship the product of physical birth or of State adoption ("naturalized citizenship") rather than citizenship by ritual subordination to the God of the Bible. In the twentieth century, for example, the suffragettes got their wish: the right to vote. But the suffragettes were radicals and humanists, not Christians. They wanted the right of all women to vote because of their supposed birthright as human beings. They saw political citizenship as a product of physical birth in a modern secular democracy. But the Bible does not teach that men and women have any birthrights, save one. They are born in sin and corruption, and what they are entitled to, apart from God's special grace, is *a legal right to eternal death*.

So, universal suffrage is the political demand of those who bear no marks of ritual subordination to God. Biblically, the right of all Christian women to vote is clear from the meaning of circumcision and baptism. The right of all women to vote is denied by the same law that denies the right of all men to vote: the law that authorized circumcised men to attend Passover. "A foreigner and an hired servant shall not eat thereof" (Ex. 12:45).

Conclusion

The Old Testament laws of the feasts specified that the judges of Israel in the broadest sense had to appear before the Lord in Jerusalem three times a year. This reminded them of the magnitude of their blessings: a court appearance in the presence of the King of heaven. It also reminded them that they were under this King's authority judicially. If they disobeyed this law, they were brought under condemnation: expulsion from the congregation of the Lord. This meant the removal of the condemned man's office of judge.

Regular rituals of covenant renewal in the house of God were basic to the exercise of citizenship in the Old Testament. This is equally true in the New Testament. The New Testament covenant mark of baptism and the New Testament feast of the Lord's Supper have replaced the Old Covenant's mark of circumcision and Passover.

Women now have the mark of the covenant placed directly on them. Because women receive the mark of the covenant in baptism, they are required to participate in the ritual meal of covenant renewal: the Lord's Supper. This becomes their legal title to access to the civil office of judge.[32] With respect to civil office, "There is neither Jew nor Greek, there is neither bond nor free, there is neither male nor female: for ye are all one in Christ Jesus" (Gal. 3:28). But this cannot mean that today there is no civil covenant. The civil covenant is an inescapable concept. It is never a question of "civil covenant vs. no civil covenant." It is always this question: "*Which* civil covenant, under *which* God?"

The Hebrews were required to give the firstfruits to God. He was the owner of the land. He was entitled to his percentage of the land's

---

32. Again, I am not arguing that women were not permitted to exercise judicial authority in Old Covenant Israel. I am making it clear, however, that there is still a covenant mark of judicial subordination, and this mark must be received by anyone who claims citizenship, meaning rulership, in a biblical commonwealth. It was received *representatively* by women in the Old Covenant through their male relatives.

output. The Hebrews were required to declare ritually and collectively that they were sharecroppers on God's property. Only those who acknowledged their position as economic sharecroppers were allowed to serve as judges. Without both ritual subordination and economic subordination to God, they were not allowed by God to exercise justice as officials in the civil commonwealth. *Those who are not formally under the ecclesiastical covenant may not bear the sword of judgment as officers of God's civil court.* Those who are not under the terms of God's "sharecropping" agreement are to be removed from the congregation, meaning from the list of those entitled by law to become candidates for civil office.

This indicates that those in a church who do not tithe should not become voting members. They may be communicant members, but not voting members. In a fully Christian social order, all churches would require tithing for voting membership. Only voting church members would be allowed to become voting members of civil government. The tithe, as the firstfruits of production, is basic to both social order and, ultimately, political order. But Christians do not believe this today, so we suffer great disorder.

29

THE CURSE OF ZERO GROWTH

And ye shall serve the LORD your God, and he shall bless thy bread, and thy water; and I will take sickness away from the midst of thee. There shall nothing cast their young, nor be barren, in thy land: the number of thy days I will fulfil (Ex. 23:25-26).

Given the nature of the announced blessings, there is only one possible source: God. The State is incapable of applying these positive biological sanctions in history.

God is the Judge, both in history and eternity. When God renders judgment, He does at least three things: 1) He evaluates a person's thoughts and actions in terms of the requirements of His law; 2) He pronounces judgment, either "guilty" or "not guilty"; and 3) He imposes the appropriate sanctions, either cursings or blessings.

What is not generally recognized or sufficiently emphasized is that *God does this in His capacity as Father.* He created man in His own image. It is the image of God in man that brings man under God's sanctions. This is what makes him judicially responsible before God. God puts the work of the law in each person's heart; each person is capable of understanding the ethical standards God lays down. Each person knows enough to condemn him on judgment day. "For when the Gentiles, which have not the law, do by nature the things contained in the law, these, having not the law, are a law unto themselves: Which shew the work of the law written in their hearts, their conscience also bearing witness, and their thoughts the mean while accusing or else excusing one another" (Rom. 2:14-15).

God the Father disinherited Adam, but He adopts those who have been elect by Him in Jesus Christ before the foundation of the world. "Blessed be the God and Father of our Lord Jesus Christ, who hath blessed us with all spiritual blessings in heavenly places in Christ: According as he hath chosen us in him before the foundation of the world, that we should be holy and without blame before him in love. Having predestinated us unto the adoption of children by Jesus Christ to himself, according to the good pleasure of his will" (Eph. 1:3-5). The two most fundamental sanctions in time and eternity—inheritance and disinheritance—are imposed by God in His office as the Head of the family. This is why it is the head of the earthly family who is most analogous judicially to God's role as Judge, not the civil magistrate or church officer.

Inheritance and Disinheritance

The exodus was based judicially on Israel's office as God's son. God had told Moses: "And thou shalt say unto Pharaoh, Thus saith the LORD, Israel is my son, even my firstborn: And I say unto thee, Let my son go, that he may serve me: and if thou refuse to let him go, behold, I will slay thy son, even thy firstborn" (Ex. 4:22-23). His ability to deliver His people from bondage in Egypt was the sign of His office as Father, and the sign of Israel's subordination to Him as a son. From that point on, the primary question for national Israel would be: "Am I the son who will inherit?" And the evidence, generation after generation, pointed to the answer: *no*. Israel was disinherited finally when the true Son, Jesus Christ, came to collect His inheritance, and the Jews refused to honor His claim:

They answered him, We be Abraham's seed, and were never in bondage to any man: how sayest thou, Ye shall be made free? Jesus answered them, Verily, verily, I say unto you, Whosoever committeth sin is the servant of sin. And the servant abideth not in the house for ever: but the Son abideth ever. If the Son therefore shall make you free, ye shall be free indeed. I know that ye are Abraham's seed; but ye seek to kill me, because my word hath no place in you. I speak that which I have seen with my Father: and ye do that which ye have seen with your father. They answered and said unto him, Abraham is our father. Jesus saith unto them, If ye were Abraham's children, ye would do the works of Abraham. But now ye seek to kill me, a man that hath told you the truth, which I have heard of God: this did not Abraham. Ye do the deeds of your father. Then said they to him, We be not born of fornication; we have one Father, even God. Jesus said unto them, If God were your Father, ye would love me: for I proceeded forth and came from God; neither came I of myself, but he sent me. Why do ye not understand my speech? even because ye cannot hear my word. Ye are of your father the devil, and the lusts of your father ye will do. He was a murderer from the beginning, and abode not in the truth, because there is no truth in him. When he speaketh a lie, he speaketh of his own: for he is a liar, and the father of it (John 8:33-44).

Jesus called the Jews bastards. Bastards were to be cut off from judicial office ("the congregation") in Israel for at least ten generations (Deut. 23:2).[1] This is why Jesus also announced: "Therefore say I unto you, The kingdom of God shall be taken from you, and given to a nation bringing forth the fruits thereof" (Matt. 21:43). The Father was about to cut off His son Israel for what Israel had done to His true Son, Jesus Christ.[2]

It is God in His office as heavenly Father who serves as the archetype of the earthly judge. It is the father as head of his household, rather than the church officer or the civil magistrate, who reveals God as Judge most accurately in history.

The Father as Rewarder

The human father hands out punishments and rewards to his children. He treats them as children during their period of dependency and hierarchical training. Jesus announced: "If a son shall ask bread of any of you that is a father, will he give him a stone? Or if he ask a fish, will he for a fish give him a serpent? Or if he shall ask an egg, will he offer him a scorpion? If ye then, being evil, know how to give good gifts unto your children: how much more shall your heavenly Father give the Holy Spirit to them that ask him?" (Luke 11:11-13). The author of the Epistle to the Hebrews wrote: "But with-

---

1. This means that genetic-covenant Israel can be adopted back into God's family. This is what Paul says will happen in the future: "I say then, Have they stumbled that they should fall? God forbid: but rather through their fall salvation is come unto the Gentiles, for to provoke them to jealousy. Now if the fall of them be the riches of the world, and the diminishing of them the riches of the Gentiles; how much more their fulness? For I speak to you Gentiles, inasmuch as I am the apostle of the Gentiles, I magnify mine office: If by any means I may provoke to emulation them which are my flesh, and might save some of them. For if the casting away of them be the reconciling of the world, what shall the receiving of them be, but life from the dead? For if the firstfruit be holy, the lump is also holy: and if the root be holy, so are the branches. And if some of the branches be broken off, and thou, being a wild olive tree, wert graffed in among them, and with them partakest of the root and fatness of the olive tree" (Rom. 11:11-17). That genetic-covenantal Israel will be brought back into the church is the position of such Presbyterian and Reformed commentators on Romans 11 as Charles Hodge, Robert Haldane, and John Murray. It is also the position of the Larger Catechism of the Westminster Confession of Faith: Question 191. See also Ray R. Sutton, "Does Israel Have a Future?" *Covenant Renewal* (Dec. 1988), published by the Institute for Christian Economics, P. O. Box 8000, Tyler, TX 75711.

2. David Chilton, *The Days of Vengeance: An Exposition of the Book of Revelation* (Ft. Worth: Dominion Press, 1987).

out faith it is impossible to please him: for he that cometh to God must believe that he is, and that he is a rewarder of them that diligently seek him" (Heb. 11:6). The judicial authority of the earthly father to issue rewards to those who diligently serve him is the primary mark of his unique covenantal authority.

God hands out rewards in history. So do earthly fathers. Neither the church nor the State is supposed to hand out rewards when it hands down formal judgments. The judges of these two God-ordained (but God-limited) covenant institutions are supposed to deal with people as adults. They are to settle disputes that arise between legal adults. They are to prepare people to serve as heads of their own households, not treat them as children. For this reason, neither church nor State is supposed to hand out earthly rewards at the end of a trial. They are to declare the legal status of the parties of the dispute — guilty or not guilty — impose negative sanctions on the guilty party, and release the innocent party from further obligations.

What this means is that *judges are not to offer positive sanctions from the government to those declared "not guilty."*[3] Why not? Because this would make the judges into tyrants and/or servants of sycophants. Judges would thereby become bribe-seekers: not necessarily seekers of monetary gifts, but seekers of toadies to make them feel important. They would move steadily from the dominion religion to the power religion. Judges are not supposed to issue orders and gain loyal followers; they are instead authorized to settle disputes. *The biblical commonwealth is not a top-down bureaucracy; it is a bottom-up appeals court.*

Judges are placed in the midst of a hierarchy. They are the legal servants of God, and they are also the servants of those who are under their judicial authority. They are servants upward to God and downward to men. In a biblical civil order, those who are under the judges are in fact the sovereign agents in the delegation of covenant authority. "Take you wise men, and understanding, and known among your tribes, and I will make them rulers over you" (Deut. 1:13). "Judges and officers shalt thou make thee in all thy gates, which the LORD thy God giveth thee, throughout thy tribes: and they shall judge the people with just judgment" (Deut. 16:18). Thus, there

---

3. This is not to say that judges are not to force the guilty parties to make restitution. Also, victims of unsolved crimes such as hit-and-run driving may be legitimately rewarded out of special trust funds administered by the civil government and financed by fines collected from those who commit "victimless crimes," such as speeding. But these rewards are not from the government; they are from convicted criminals.

is never to be a final single voice of human authority until Jesus Christ speaks His words of judgment at the final judgment. The Bible divides authority in a series of hierarchies that remove final authority from any single individual or group.

It is the dream of the covenant-breaker either to annul this system of divided authority, and replace it with a top-down centralized order (statism), or else annul all hierarchical order and gain autonomy for himself (anarchism).

Contrasting Supernatural Systems of Authority

The visible sign of God's authority is His ability to bring judgments in history: blessing and cursing. He is invisible; His blessings and cursings are visible. Israel was warned: "And thou shalt become an astonishment, a proverb, and a byword, among all nations whither the LORD shall lead thee" (Deut. 28:37). God can deliver His people; He can also lead them back into bondage to a foreign nation.

Satan imitates God when he promises his followers blessings and cursings. But he owns nothing of his own. He is a thief[4] and a squatter in history.[5] Neither his threats nor his gifts are to be taken very seriously. His promises and threats are all deceptions that are designed to deflect men's vision of God's true promises and the true threats. Jesus warned people to fear God, not Satan: "And fear not them which kill the body, but are not able to kill the soul: but rather fear him which is able to destroy both soul and body in hell" (Matt. 10:28).

God owns the world; thus, He has the power to distribute blessings out of his own capital. Satan can offer no blessings that he has not previously stolen. The mark of Satan's imitation sovereignty is his ability to deceive people into believing in *something for nothing* on any terms except God's grace. (And even God's free gift of grace to man was paid for by Jesus Christ.) God distributes true gifts; Satan creates the illusion of distributing rewards, net, but in fact he has to collect more than he gives. There is waste, confusion, and deception

---

4. Judas was representative of his covenantal master, Satan: "Then took Mary a pound of ointment of spikenard, very costly, and anointed the feet of Jesus, and wiped his feet with her hair: and the house was filled with the odour of the ointment. Then saith one of his disciples, Judas Iscariot, Simon's son, which should betray him, Why was not this ointment sold for three hundred pence, and given to the poor? This he said, not that he cared for the poor; but because he was a thief, and had the bag, and bare what was put therein" (John 12:3-6).

5. Gary North, *Inherit the Earth: Biblical Blueprints for Economics* (Ft. Worth, Texas: Dominion Press, 1987), p. 61.

in his world.[6] *Satan always runs a deficit.*

God is independent of His creation; Satan is dependent on God's creation and God's unmerited gift of time, knowledge, and power to Satan.[7] Satan can do only what God permits him to do (Job 1). God therefore tells His servants to serve others because He has the power to renew their strength and their economic resources. Satan tells his followers to compel service from others because he does not have the power to renew their strength and their economic resources. God gives; Satan steals. God's service moves from the center (productivity) to the periphery (the needy). Satan's service moves from the periphery (tax collections) to the center (centralized political power). God's blessings reflect the procession of the Holy Spirit. Satan's blessings reflect the contraction of his kingdom in history. God brings economic growth; Satan brings economic contraction. God expands society's capital; Satan consumes society's capital. These competing systems of *supernatural covenantal sanctions* are reflected in the rival economic systems that objectify their rival ethical and legal principles: free market capitalism vs. the welfare State, whether Keynesian, socialist, or Marxist.

Dominion Through Service

The biblical principle of authority in every area of life is this: the greater the *service to others*, the greater the *authority over others.* "And whosoever will be chief among you, let him be your servant" (Matt. 20:27). "But he that is greatest among you shall be your servant" (Matt 23:11). The servant does not take; the servant gives. This is why Jesus Christ is the greatest servant with the greatest authority: He laid down His life for mankind in general and for His followers in particular (I Tim. 4:10).[8] The satanic version of dominion is the reverse of this biblical principle. Satan teaches that the greater one's *authority over others*, the greater the *services extracted from others.*

It must be understood that the biblical principle of service is not to be manifested in the same way in every institution. What is ap-

---

6. In an otherwise unmemorable movie, *Time Bandits,* David Warner's portrayal of Satan is masterful. Satan is presented as a creature who cannot get decent help. His demonic subordinates are incompetents. He cannot get accurate information about what is going on or efficient compliance with his orders. "Computers!" he screams. "If only I had computers!"

7. Gary North, *Dominion and Common Grace: The Biblical Basis of Progress* (Tyler, Texas: Institute for Christian Economics, 1987), pp. 21, 35, 39-44.

8. *Ibid.*, ch. 2.

propriate service for a father is not always appropriate for a civil magistrate, and vice versa. Both are different from a church officer. Men are to serve and give; but the particular office determines what exactly is to be given and under what conditions.

It is the mark of authority of the messianic State that it hands out rewards to those who diligently serve it. It extracts capital from all groups, but returns the booty (minus at least 50 percent "for handling") to its supporters and clients. The State steadily converts its citizens into lifetime servants (who pay, and may or may not receive anything back) and children (who obey, but also receive something). The bureaucrats, as so-called "public servants," become the actual masters. (Tell the person who stands before the tax collector that the tax collector is a public servant, and that the U.S. Internal Revenue Service is in fact a service.) The messianic State converts its citizens into permanent servants and children, and then this pseudo-parent collects the inheritance for itself from society's true families.[9]

Because both church and State are agencies that are dependent on those under their jurisdiction for financial support, neither is supposed to hand out rewards to those declared judicially innocent in a trial. Guilty parties are supposed to pay their victims. The court restores the *status quo ante* as much as possible; this includes restitution. They are to administer justice, not administer rewards.

Productivity and Judicial Authority

The family, in contrast to both church and State, is an independently productive unit. It is not simply a necessary protective agency whose services make possible economic creativity and economic growth, as is the case with the State. It creates net wealth through the skills and talents of its members. The family's primary productivity stems generally from the father. The senior judge is usually also the primary breadwinner.[10] Fathers therefore can lawfully hand down rewards to those they declare "not guilty," as well as impose

---

9. Gary North, *The Sinai Strategy: Economics and the Ten Commandments* (Tyler, Texas: Institute for Christian Economics, 1986), pp. 103-14.

10. The confusion of office in the modern world is the result of a change in religion, but also a change in income sources. When mothers become secondary breadwinners, it is difficult for fathers to maintain comparable authority. Nevertheless, the judicial status of the office is primary, not the economic foundation of the office. The father still declares final judgment. But the more economically dependent the family is on the wife, the more he will have to listen to her counsel. She possesses a negative sanction: the authority to quit working.

sanctions on those they declare "guilty." They can use both the "carrot" and the "stick." Unlike the judges of both church and State, fathers earn wealth through their own labors; they do not rely on either tithe or taxes to fill the family's treasury. Thus, fathers are entitled to distribute rewards in their judicial capacity as judges. They are judges who in this sense are *uniquely analogous to God*, who also is not dependent on the productivity of those under His jurisdiction. "If I were hungry, I would not tell thee: for the world is mine, and the fulness thereof" (Ps. 50:12).

When the biblical civil government pronounces judgment through its authorized representatives, it can lawfully impose only negative sanctions. It does not reward those who are declared "not guilty." It simply releases them from bondage or the threat of bondage. It is prohibited from issuing positive injunctions, nor may it lawfully hand out positive rewards to those declared innocent. Why is the biblically mandated State to be a negative sanctioning agency only? Because the State's purpose is not to imitate God as a rewarder of those who diligently search Him and obey Him. It is also not supposed to make people righteous. Its purpose is to protect those under its lawful jurisdiction from the evil acts of others who are also under its jurisdiction. The civil government's functions are exclusively negative — prohibiting specified publicly evil acts — and therefore its sanctions are exclusively negative.

History: Cyclical or Linear?

We return now to the sanctions of Exodus 23:25-26: "I will take sickness away from the midst of thee. There shall nothing cast their young, nor be barren, in thy land: the number of thy days I will fulfil." These are positive sanctions in nature.

These sanctions presuppose that nature is not normative; rather, nature is under a curse as a result of man's ethical rebellion (Gen. 3:17-19). The so-called "balance of nature" hypothesis assumes either an autonomous process of temporary linear developments locally within an overall framework of decay (Darwinism and cosmic entropy), or else an eternal alternating process of development and cosmic decay (cosmic cycles). Both perspectives regarding nature are completely antithetical to the biblical viewpoint. The biblical scientific worldview is based on the theme of death and resurrection.[11]

---

11. Gary North, *Is the World Running Down? Crisis in the Christian Worldview* (Tyler, Texas: Institute for Christian Economics, 1988).

The growth of human population, if directed by God in response to the widespread honoring of God's law, is normative. So is economic growth (Deut. 8). Not cycles of nature or culture, but rather *linear development* is God's response in history to men's ethical conformity to His law-order. God's law-order is designed to promote the *rapid* fulfilling of the terms of the dominion covenant. God does not desire nature to remain governed by the law of the jungle, the desert, or the frozen wastes. He wants the *ethical obedience of mankind*. When they give Him obedience, He promises to extend their rule over nature in history.[12] The extension of man's rule over nature is delayed primarily by the ethics of rebellion, not by innate "limits to growth" in nature. Individual limits can be overcome in a few generations, though not at zero cost.

It was sin and rebellion that thwarted the Hebrews in the attainment of their assigned tasks. They turned to the gods of Canaan — gods of the chaos festivals, the eternal cycles, and the abolition of time.[13] It was not the hypothetical autonomous restraint of biological "negative feedback" which kept the Hebrews from multiplying and filling the earth; it was instead their adoption of Canaanitic religions of cyclical growth and decay. They began to work out the implications of these rival religions, and God permitted them to sink their culture into the paralyzing pessimism of pagan faiths. He gave them their request, but sent leanness into their souls (Ps. 106:15). Then He scattered them: by the Assyrians, the Babylonians, the Greeks, and finally the Romans. This was the fulfillment of the prophecy of God's negative covenantal sanctions on the nation in history: "And the LORD shall scatter thee among all people, from the one end of the earth even unto the other; and there thou shalt serve other gods, which neither thou nor thy fathers have known, even wood and stone. And among these nations shalt thou find no ease, neither shall the sole of thy foot have rest: but the LORD shall give thee there a trembling heart, and failing of eyes, and sorrow of mind" (Deut. 28:64-65).

Obedience and Biology

Is dominion essentially biological? Could the Israelites' growth of population have been even more rapid than it had been in Egypt? In Egypt there had been no guarantee against miscarriages. In short,

---

12. *Ibid.*, ch. 6.

13. Gary North, *Moses and Pharaoh: Dominion Religion vs. Power Religion* (Tyler, Texas: Institute for Christian Economics, 1985), ch. 17.

that which is *biologically abnormal* — no miscarriages — is declared by God to be *culturally and historically normative* for His redeemed people. Did God expect them to fill the earth in only a few centuries?

The rate of conception could have been reduced by God, either directly or, as in the modern world, through the development of the technology of contraception. Thus, the birth rate might have dropped in response to the increasing pressures of population growth. It is possible that God would have delayed the external fulfillment of the population aspect of the dominion covenant. We are not told, however, that any such delay was normative. There is no indication in the revelation of God to His Old Covenant people that they would experience anything except large families, zero miscarriages, and high rates of population growth, *if* they would conform themselves to His law. Certainly, the *biological option* of rapid population growth was offered to them by God.

Biological Blessings

Exodus 23:25-26 speaks of God's positive sanctions in history. These sanctions are biological. "And ye shall serve the LORD your God, and he shall bless thy bread, and thy water; and I will take sickness away from the midst of thee. There shall nothing cast their young, nor be barren, in thy land: the number of thy days I will fulfil." There is no question what the source of such positive sanctions must be: *God the Father.* The State is not capable of granting this kind of reward. Thus, by promising biological rewards, God announced His covenantal office of Father.

As slaves in Egypt, the Hebrews had already experienced what has to be the most rapid population growth on record. Using Donovan Courville's estimate of 215 years from Joseph to the exodus, a single family, plus bondservants, had grown in two centuries to as many as two million people (Ex. 12:37). Mathematically speaking, such an increase can be explained only by assuming that during the first century of Israel's residence in Egypt, other tribes and even Egyptians had voluntarily joined themselves with the Hebrews through conversion and circumcision during the era of prosperity in the land of Goshen.[14]

Even after the exodus, God told them that their numbers were insufficient to enable them to subdue the land of Canaan all at once.

---

14. *Ibid.*, ch. 1.

Speaking of the pagan cultures still in the land, God said: "I will not drive them out from before thee in one year; lest the land become desolate, and the beast of the field multiply against thee. By little and little I will drive them out from before thee, until thou be increased, and inherit the land" (Ex. 23:29-30).

This is an extremely important passage. *First*, it affirms man's authority over land and animals. Even the morally perverse Canaanite tribes possessed God-given authority over the works of nature. Men, not the beasts, are supposed to subdue the earth.[15] *Second*, this passage warns God's covenant people against attempting to achieve instant dominion. They must first build up their numbers, their skills, and their capital before they can expect to reign over the creation. Pagans possess skills and capital that are important to the continuity of human dominion. Pagans can be competent administrators. Their labor can be used by God and society until an era comes when God's people are ready to exercise primary leadership in terms of God's law. At that point, ethical rebels will either be regenerated through God's grace, or else steadily replaced by the new rulers of the land.[16] Until then, God's people must be content to wait patiently, improving their own administrative abilities and increasing their numbers. *Dominion is an ethical process*, a process of *self-government under God's law.*[17]

God promised His people a specific reward for covenantal faithfulness (23:25): *health*, including an absence of miscarriages among both humans and domesticated animals. This *conditional promise* would have enabled the Hebrews, had they remained faithful as a nation, to have achieved cultural dominion more rapidly. Ultimately, it would have led to the subduing of the whole earth, had the same rate of population growth which they had experienced in Egypt been sustained for a few more centuries.

---

15. The all-too-familiar statement of evolutionists that insects, especially cockroaches, are the true inheritors of the earth, the longest-lived of animals, the creatures that endure throughout history, is fully consistent with Darwinian history. It is also theologically perverse. I call it "cockroach eschatology": the bugs shall inherit the earth.

16. See Appendix A: "Common Grace, Eschatology, and Biblical Law." See also North, *Dominion and Common Grace.*

17. Ray R. Sutton, *That You May Prosper: Dominion By Covenant* (Tyler, Texas: Institute for Christian Economics, 1987), ch. 3.

Biological Cursings

God promised to heal them if they remained faithful to Him. But if they refused to obey Him, He promised to bring them under the negative biological sanctions that had plagued them in Egypt:

> If thou wilt not observe to do all the words of this law that are written in this book, that thou mayest fear this glorious and fearful name, THE LORD THY GOD; Then the LORD will make thy plagues wonderful, and the plagues of thy seed, even great plagues, and of long continuance, and sore sicknesses, and of long continuance. Moreover he will bring upon thee all the diseases of Egypt, which thou wast afraid of; and they shall cleave unto thee. Also every sickness, and every plague, which is not written in the book of this law, them will the LORD bring upon thee, until thou be destroyed. And ye shall be left few in number, whereas ye were as the stars of heaven for multitude; because thou wouldest not obey the voice of the LORD thy God (Deut. 28:58-62).

These negative national sanctions would be visible symbols of a return to Egypt, a reversal of the exodus, the transition from grace to wrath. *The God who brings health as a corporate covenantal blessing is also the God who brings sickness as a corporate covenantal cursing.* The text says specifically that plague is a negative sanction used by God to call His people back to Him as a covenant unit. This is why God judged Israel with a plague that killed 70,000 people when He punished David for illegally numbering the people. "So the LORD sent a pestilence upon Israel from the morning even to the time appointed: and there died of the people from Dan even to Beer-sheba seventy thousand men" (II Sam. 24:15). Sickness in general is also a negative covenant sanction. (That some Christians affirm the positive sanction of health as being from God but simultaneously deny the negative sanction of sickness testifies to their hostility to the biblical doctrine of covenantal judgment. We must positively confess Christ as Healer and negatively confess Christ as Plague-master. To refuse to do the latter is the equivalent of preaching heaven but denying hell.)[18]

---

18. I have in mind here the so-called "positive confession" charismatics who refuse to admit that God brings sickness and plagues as covenantal judgments. I suspect that they have analogous views regarding the inappropriateness of public church discipline. Televised Pentecostal healers of the 1980's also gained international reputations as the front-page adulterers of the 1980's. (One turned out to be a bi-sexual adulterer.) When ever-so-mild church discipline was imposed on two of the most notorious of them, they resigned their denominational membership, thereby removing themselves from further ecclesiastical sanctions. But not from God's sanctions.

What God did not promise was covenantal neutrality. He did not promise mere stagnation. These promised biological sanctions *take from*; they do not simply "fail to add to."

Covenantal Cause and Effect: Life Expectancy

A nation that is characterized by increasing longevity is clearly under the common-grace blessing of God. "Honour thy father and thy mother: that thy days may be long upon the land which the LORD thy God giveth thee" (Ex. 20:12). As Paul reminded his readers: "Honour thy father and mother; which is the first commandment with promise" (Eph. 6:2). Ultimately, as nations conform themselves to God covenantally, God promises to restore something analogous to people's pre-Flood longevity — a covenantal promise that is the greatest single stumbling stone in the Bible for amillennial eschatology: "There shall be no more thence an infant of days, nor an old man that hath not filled his days: for the child shall die an hundred years old; but the sinner being an hundred years old shall be accursed" (Isa. 65:20). This promise is found in the midst of a group of promises, mostly economic in scope:

> For, behold, I create new heavens and a new earth: and the former shall not be remembered, nor come into mind. But be ye glad and rejoice for ever in that which I create: for, behold, I create Jerusalem a rejoicing, and her people a joy. And I will rejoice in Jerusalem, and joy in my people: and the voice of weeping shall be no more heard in her, nor the voice of crying. There shall be no more thence an infant of days, nor an old man that hath not filled his days: for the child shall die an hundred years old; but the sinner being an hundred years old shall be accursed. And they shall build houses, and inhabit them; and they shall plant vineyards, and eat the fruit of them. They shall not build, and another inhabit; they shall not plant, and another eat: for as the days of a tree are the days of my people, and mine elect shall long enjoy the work of their hands. They shall not labour in vain, nor bring forth for trouble; for they are the seed of the blessed of the LORD, and their offspring with them (Isa. 65:17-23). [19]

---

19. Archibald Hughes, an amillennialist, wrote a book called *A New Heaven and a New Earth* (Philadelphia: Presbyterian & Reformed, 1958). He refused to comment on the meaning of this passage, one of only two in the Old Testament that refers to the New Heaven and New Earth, and one of only four in the Bible. The others are Isaiah 66:22, II Peter 3:13, and Revelation 21:1. I can understand his reluctance to do so; the passage has to be denied. There is a sinner mentioned in verse 20. This means that the verse cannot possibly refer to the post-final judgment world of the resurrection. Thus, the "new heaven and new earth" cannot possibly be relegated exclusively to the post-historical world.

A Map of Life Expectancy

If we look at a map of the world that compares life expectancy, we find that there are some three dozen nations that have life expectancies at age 70 or above. This matches the maximum average life expectancy of Moses' day (Ps. 90:10). These nations include the North American nations of the United States and Canada, Japan, Taiwan, New Zealand and Australia, the United Kingdom and Ireland, Norway and Sweden, Iceland, all continental European nations except Turkey (most of which is in Asia), Chile, Argentina, Uruguay, and the tiny oil kingdoms of Kuwait and the United Arab Emirates.[20] These high rates of life expectancy have come since the late nineteenth century. No major medical breakthroughs have been introduced since the mid-1940's, with the development of antibiotics and modern insecticides.[21]

The improvement in life expectancy has been the result of many factors, most notably rising per capita wealth, better personal hygiene, inoculation against smallpox, vaccines, better sanitation, improved public water treatment, and the development and marketing of the "super drugs" from the mid-1930's to the mid-1940's, including sulpha drugs and penicillin. Without modern technology and modern capital markets, none of these developments would have been likely.

The major extension of human life expectancy has come as a result of falling rates of infant mortality. One estimate calculates that in the sixteenth and seventeenth centuries, infant mortality among Europe's ruling families was over 200 per 1,000 live births.[22] This fell to 70 per 1,000 in the nineteenth century.[23] In the U.S. after 1900, the rate fell by 2.5 percent per annum to 65 in 1930, and similar declines were experienced by all nations undergoing rapid economic development.[24] By 1961, the rate was down to about 26 deaths per 1,000 in the first five years of life, and by 1980, to about 12.[25] Reduced

---

20. *Atlas of the United States* (New York: Macmillan, 1986), p. 119; data based on the *World Bank Atlas, 1985.*

21. William Peterson, *Population* (2nd ed.; New York: Macmillan, 1969), p. 576.

22. Sigismund Teller, "Birth and Death among Europe's Ruling Families since 1500," in D. V. Glass and D. E. C. Eversley (eds.), *Population in History* (London: Edward Arnold, 1965); cited by Victor Fuchs, *Who Shall Live? Health, Economics, and Social Choice* (New York:Basic Books, 1974), p. 32.

23. Fuchs, *idem.*

24. *Idem.*

25. William A. Knaus, *Inside Russian Medicine* (New York: Everest House, 1981), chart, p. 375.

infant mortality is why the statistics show that we live longer in this century. "Comparison of life tables from various countries at various times suggests that as life expectancy rises from 35 to 70, about four-fifths of the increase is contributed by reductions in death rates under 70. . . ."[26]

What has taken place in the industrializing nations during the last century is simply unprecedented in man's recorded history: babies who are allowed by their mothers to survive do survive. (Meanwhile, there are between 35 million and 55 million abortions performed worldwide each year.)[27] As population scholar George Stolnitz concluded in 1955, the rise in Western life expectancy during the past century has probably been more far-reaching than the gains of the previous two millennia.[28] In fact, it is even more remarkable than this: most of the improvement in Western Europe and English-speaking North America came between 1850 and 1900.[29] This is additional evidence that the bulk of the West's gain in life expectancy since 1900 has come through the reduction of infant mortality, since this period was marked by rapidly falling rates of infant mortality. There has been a sharp average rise in life expectancy within the West, meaning a remarkable decline of differences within the region.[30] Today, "West" primarily means high technology and low mortality rates, not geography, race, or religion.

Doesn't this deny the premise of Exodus 23:25-26, namely, that God rewards His covenant people with long life? No; it means that He rewards those *societies that obey His covenant's external ethical requirements* even if they do not adhere to the formal theological affirmation of Trinitarian faith. Like Nineveh, which avoided God's wrath by repenting of its external sins, despite the fact that it did not affirm the covenant,[31] the modern world has adopted the Protestant work ethic and the Puritan concept of time and thrift without accepting Protestantism.

---

26. Fuchs, *Who Shall Live?*, p. 40.

27. *World Population and Fertility Planning Techniques: The Next 20 Years* (Washington, D.C. Office of Technology and Assessment, 1982), p. 63.

28. George J. Stolnitz, "A Century of International Mortality Trends," *Population Studies* (July 1955); reprinted in Charles B. Nam (ed.), *Population and Society* (New York: Houghton Mifflin, 1968), p. 127.

29. Peterson, *Population*, p. 547.

30. Stolnitz, *op. cit.*, p. 132.

31. If it had been converted, there would have been signs of covenantal continuity: point five of the covenant. On the contrary, the Assyrian empire conquered Israel and carried the nation into captivity.

What about the third world? The introduction of DDT and antibiotics into third world nations has received considerable attention
from those who try to explain the post-World War II population explosion in these areas. Another reason is the increasing urbanization
of many areas and the introduction of modern agricultural techniques. The two most ignored major technological innovations that
have extended life expectancy in backward countries, according to
economist Peter Drucker, were the invention by an unknown American in the 1860's of wire mesh screens for doors and windows, which
poor families adopted to escape flying insects, and the separation of
drinking water supplies from latrine areas, a technique known before Alexander of Macedon. These two ignored developments are the
primary health care component of the third world's population explosion, he argues.[32]

The USSR: A Third-World Nation Medically

The Soviet Union is the great actuarial exception among major
industrial nations. Its reported life expectancy is no higher than
Communist China's, which is a vast underdeveloped nation.[33] In recent years, life expectancy has declined in the USSR. Reported infant mortality rose from 22 deaths per 1,000 live births in 1971 to over
31 in 1977. The reported data have declined to about 29 in 1980.[34]
The age-adjusted death rates of the USSR and the United States in-
tersected in 1966 at about 7.5 per 1,000. Since then, the Soviet death
rate has climbed to over 9 per 1,000, while the U.S. rate has fallen to
about 6 per 1,000.[35]

But the reported data probably understate the reality. On De-
cember 7, 1988, a massive earthquake struck the Armenian region of
the USSR. In less than one minute, 400,000 people were left homeless in the middle of winter. The death toll was initially estimated to
be as high as 100,000 (later revised by the Soviet government to
25,000). The Soviets then called for international aid to the victims,
a sign of its third-world status economically.

In the immediate aftermath of the tragedy, a *Los Angeles Times*
wire story revealed the fact that during the previous two years, as a

---

32. Peter Drucker, *Management: Tasks, Responsibilities, Practices* (New York: Harper
& Row, 1974), p. 330.
33. *Atlas of the United States*, p. 118.
34. Knaus, *Inside Russian Medicine*, chart, p. 375.
35. *Ibid.*, chart, p. 376.

result of Premier Gorbachev's loosening of controls on the Soviet press, the Soviets have admitted that their health care system is in shambles. Soviet medical authorities acknowledge that the quality of medical care has deteriorated since the 1960's, with male life expectancy dropping. The Soviet Union is now 51st in male life expectancy in the world, behind the Caribbean island of Barbados. Medical equipment is 1940's and 1950's vintage. "Soviet newspapers now write critically of dilapidated hospitals, corrupt and underpaid doctors who earn less than the average blue-collar worker, and nationwide shortages of antibiotics and other pharmaceuticals. . . ."[36] Yet the USSR has over twice the number of physicians as the United States for a population only slightly larger.[37]

William Knaus served as a Foreign Service Medical Officer for the United States Information Agency in 1973-74. In his book, *Inside Russian Medicine*, he offers an appendix: "Taking Care of Yourself in the USSR — An Informal Guide for Tourists." He warns tourists to take two sets of prescription drugs in two separate suitcases. "There is no way for you to have a prescription filled in the USSR."[38] If you get a toothache, learn to live with it. "Most Soviet dental care is crude and done without anesthetics." If there is a problem with a loose filling, the Soviet dentist will probably just extract the tooth.[39]

What is the secret of Soviet medicine? It is free of charge — *besplatno* — to all citizens. You get what you pay for unless the State pays for it, and the Soviet State since 1917 has been far more concerned about military expenditures than public health expenditures.

A Tale of Two States

Economist Victor Fuchs includes a fascinating section in his book, *Who Shall Live?* He compares two U.S. western states that border each other, Utah and Nevada. Utah is the state where the Mormons live. Nevada is the state where everyone comes to gamble and see the floorshows with the famous entertainers and the infamous seminude showgirls. Infant mortality is about 40 percent higher in Nevada than in Utah.[40] It is the same throughout Nevada, and not just in the large cities. Statistically, infant mortality or survival is heavily dependent on the physical and emotional condition of the mother.

---

36. "Soviet health system deteriorating," *Dallas Times Herald* (Dec. 10, 1988).
37. Knaus, *Inside Russian Medicine*, p. 378.
38. *Ibid.*, p. 362.
39. *Ibid.*, p. 363.
40. Fuchs, *Who Shall Live?*, p. 52.

The death rates for children ages 1-19 is 16 percent higher for males in Nevada; it is 26 percent higher for females. Then the disparity increases: 44 percent (males) and 42 percent (females), ages 20-39. It climbs to an astounding discrepancy of 54 percent (males) and 69 percent (females), ages 40-49. Then it drops to 20 percent (males) and 6 percent (females), ages 70-79.[41] Fuchs analyzes the differences.

The two states are very much alike with respect to income, schooling, degree of urbanization, climate, and many other variables that are frequently thought to be the cause of variations in mortality. (In fact, average family income is actually higher in Nevada than in Utah.) The numbers of physicians and of hospital beds per capita are also similar in the two states.

What, then, explains these huge differences in death rates? The answer almost surely lies in the different life-styles of the residents of the two states. Utah is inhabited primarily by Mormons, whose influence is strong throughout the state. Devout Mormons do not use tobacco or alcohol and in general lead stable, quiet lives. Nevada, on the other hand, is a state with high rates of cigarette and alcohol consumption and very high rates of marital and geographical instability. The contrast with Utah in these respects is extraordinary.

In 1970, 63 percent of Utah's residents 20 years of age and over had been born in the state; in Nevada the comparable figure was only 10 percent; for persons 35-64 the figures were 64 percent in Utah and 8 percent in Nevada. Not only were there more than nine of ten Nevadans of middle age born elsewhere, but more than 60 percent were not even born in the west. . . .

The differences in marital status between the two states are also significant in view of the association between marital status and mortality. . . . More than 20 percent of Nevada's males ages 35-64 are single, widowed, divorced, or not living with their spouses. Of those who are married with spouse present, more than one-third had been previously widowed or divorced. In Utah the comparable figures are only half as large.[42]

After studying the data, Fuchs concludes that rising income in the United States will make only marginal improvements in life expectancy. The great strides in life expectancy had little to do with improved medical care until the 1930's, and then only for one decade. Today, it is heart disease, cancer, and other degenerative diseases that kill us. He sees no major gains in life expectancy ahead based on

---

41. *Idem.*
42. *Ibid.*, p. 53.

improvements in public health or medical technology.[43] Effective medicine is widely distributed and widely available. Thus, he concludes, the greatest potential for improving the health of Americans is a change in their life-style: diet, smoking, drinking, marriage, and so forth. In short, the fundamental health issues are now ethical.

If he would define ethics as covenantal, and if he would link ethics to such matters as invention, capitalization, and the diffusion of technology to the masses, I would agree with him. Ethics has effects far beyond personal life-style. Covenant-keeping and covenant-breaking affect everything, including personal health.

Stagnation as Judgment

God's covenants are frequently familistic. So are His blessings: long life for honoring parents (Ex. 20:12), health for general obedience (Ex. 23:25), and large families (Ps. 127:5). Long-term stagnation—economically, demographically, intellectually—is a sign of God's displeasure. Growth must not be seen as inherently destructive. More than this: *a static culture cannot survive*. It has to change in order to survive. Population growth, like any kind of social growth, can be either a blessing or a curse (a prelude to disaster), depending on the character of the people who are experiencing the expansion.

---

43. I disagree with him here. My wife was healed in 1988 of a major viral disease, spreading with plague-like rapidity in the United States, Epstein-Barr Virus (also called Chronic Fatigue Syndrome), by a few days of painless treatment, hooked up to an electronic "black box." She had been suffering from a debilitating weakness for 18 months. The treatment is a repeatable phenomenon. Another friend of mine was cured of the same disease (and several other major physical defects) by the same technology after having one week of treatments. My wife met others at the clinic who were being cured of far worse diseases, including muscular dystrophy (two months later, the woman was cured, with full use of her formerly paralyzed arm). The machine can be operated effectively and safely by someone with a high school education and a few months of training.

Short of a medical collapse, however—AIDS-induced, perhaps—the medical community will resist to the death—yours, if necessary—any such innovation, as it has resisted others very similar to this one since the 1930's. Such treatments break with medical orthodoxy—drugs, surgery, and radiation—and much worse from the profession's viewpoint, this technology would not require medical licensure by the State, the economic basis of the medical profession's current monopoly. On the nature of this monopoly, see the classic study by Reuben Kessel, "Price Discrimination in Medicine," *Journal of Law and Economics*, I (1958), pp. 1-19. For a scientist-physician's cautious appraisal, after a lifetime of pioneering research, of the astounding effects of electricity on rates of body repair, see Robert O. Becker, M.D. and Gary Selden, *The Body Electric: Electromagnetism and the Foundation of Life* (New York: Morrow, 1985).

It is *ethics*, not growth as such, which determines the legitimacy or illegitimacy of any given social growth process in a particular period of history.

Greater numbers of people can and often do result in more efficient ways to fulfill the cultural mandate. The increasing division of labor permits greater specialization and greater output per unit of resource input.[44] Population growth is specifically stated to be a response of God to covenantal faithfulness, but it is also a tool of dominion. God's ethical universe is one of *positive feedback*: from victory unto victory. This ethical standard has visible effects in history. Ethical development, meaning progressive sanctification ("set-apartness") in terms of God's law, is eventually accompanied by the compound growth process, i.e., positive feedback, in human affairs.[45]

Entropy and Its Effects

Negative feedback is a limiting factor in a cursed world. The animals are not allowed to multiply and overcome the land. They are restrained by man or by "the forces of nature," meaning the environment's built-in limitations on the compound growth process. Negative feedback is *in part* the product of God's curse. There are indeed limits to growth. Growth is not automatic. Growth is not a zero-price process. But negative feedback—sometimes characterized as the so-called "law of entropy"—is not the characteristic feature of the universe. The grace of God through faith in Jesus Christ is the characteristic feature of the universe: *redemption, resurrection, and restoration.*

Entropy is a fundamental principle of physical science that states that the movement of molecules tends to become increasingly random over time. Less and less usable energy is available to perform work as time goes on. When the idea of entropy—a scientific phenomenon of hypothetically autonomous physical nature—begins to turn the faith of a particular civilization toward pessimism about mankind's long-term future, then that civilization has come under the judgment of God.[46] It was lack of faith in the future which brought down the ancient city-states, including Rome. When classical civili-

---

44. This does not mean that a growing population is always an economic blessing. Again, it is the ethical character of the people, not rates of biological reproduction, which determines the character of the growth process, either curse or blessing.

45. North, *Is the World Running Down?*, chaps. 7, 8.

46. See, for example, the book by Marxist critic and New Age commentator Jeremy Rifkin, *Entropy: A New World View* (New York: Bantam, [1980] 1981). For a detailed refutation, see my book, *Is the World Running Down?*.

zation finally capitulated to the inherent pessimism of all cyclical history, nothing could save it.[47] Rome fell: to Christianity in the East (Byzantium), and to the barbarians in the West.

Negative feedback in one's personal life is not necessarily a sign of God's curse. Positive feedback in life is not necessarily a sign of God's grace. There are cases where righteous individuals are judged (Job, for instance). It all depends on one's ethical standing before God. God sometimes "sets up" sinners for destruction — a kind of entrapment (the Pharaoh of the exodus, for instance). But generally, growth is a blessing, and contraction is a curse: "For whosoever hath, to him shall be given, and he shall have more abundance: but whosoever hath not, from him shall be taken away even that [which] he hath" (Matt. 13:12). The general rule is growth for the godly and contraction for the ungodly. In neither case can people preserve the status quo.

Humanism, Paganism, and the Status Quo

A zero-growth philosophy is the product of humanism, both secular and occult. It is a philosophy of the status quo — the preservation of the society of Satan, as if he had not been dealt a mortal wound at Calvary, as if he were not on the defensive internationally against the leaven of Christ's kingdom (Matt. 13:33). The universe is cursed; its resources are limited; but this reality is not evidence that favors a no-growth philosophy. The biblical doctrine of fallen man does not teach men to believe in a world that is cursed forever. Judgment and final restoration are coming. Time is bounded. Redeemed mankind must fulfill God's dominion assignment, in time and on earth, before Jesus returns in final judgment.[48]

Humanists and satanists wish to deny the sovereignty of God, and therefore virtually all of them affirm the sovereignty of the entropy process. They wish to escape the eternal judgment of God, so they affirm an impersonal finality for all biological life. Men have sometimes turned to a philosophy of historical cycles to help them avoid the testimony of God concerning linear history. Others have turned to the entropy process when they have adopted a Western

---

47. Charles Norris Cochrane, *Christianity and Classical Culture: A Study of Thought and Action from Augustus to Augustine* (New York: Oxford University Press, [1944] 1957).

48. Perfect fulfillment is impossible because of sin, but it can be approached as an ethical limit.

version of linear history. They settle for slow decay rather than cycles. The goal is to escape the judgment of God. All of them prefer to avoid the truth: for covenant-breakers, the growth process will be cut short. A new downward cycle will triumph, they argue. Entropy will triumph. Anyway, *something* will triumph, but not the God of the Bible.

In the 1960's and 1970's, a new phenomenon hit the academic and intellectual world: defenders of no-growth economics.[49] Prior to this, virtually all professional economists had been concerned with fostering economic growth.[50] This was part of an overall attack on growth in general.[51] Population growth was the primary target of these attacks.[52] From 1965 through 1976, governments had poured over a billion and a quarter dollars into programs promoting worldwide population control, and the Rockefeller Foundation and Ford Foundation added another $250 million.[53] All of this public concern over the population explosion was virtually an overnight phenomenon, beginning around 1965. All of it sprang from anti-Christian roots.[54]

Rushdoony's comments on pagan antiquity's hostility to change is applicable to the zero-growth movement of the modern humanist world: "The pagan hatred of *change* was also a form of asceticism, and it is present in virtually all anti-Christianity. The hatred of change leads to attempts to stop change, to stop history, and to create an end-of-history civilization, a final order which will end mutability and give man an unchanging world. Part of this order in-

---

49. The most prominent academic economist in the no-growth camp is E. J. Mishan: *The Costs of Economic Growth* (New York: Praeger, 1967); *The Economic Growth Debate: An Assessment* (London: George Allen & Unwin, 1977).

50. Bert F. Hoselitz (ed.), *Theories of Economic Growth* (New York: Free Press, 1960). This book traces economic theories on growth back to the seventeenth century.

51. Dennis Meadows, *et al.*, *The Limits to Growth* (New York: Universe Books, 1972). See also Mancur Olson and Hans H. Landsberg (eds.), *The No-Growth Society* (New York: Norton, 1973).

52. Paul Ehrlich, *The Population Bomb* (New York: Ballentine, 1968). This became a runaway best-seller. See also Gordon Rattray Taylor, *The Biological Time Bomb* (New York: World, 1968). These books are in contrast to an earlier, more restrained discussion of population issues: Philip M. Hauser, *The Population Dilemma* (Englewood Cliffs, New Jersey: Prentice-Hall, 1963). Then came a Presidential commission report, *Population and the American Future* (New York: Signet, 1972), a popular paperback version of a government report. The story was the same: the danger of population growth.

53. Julian Simon, *The Ultimate Resource* (Princeton, New Jersey: Princeton University Press, 1981), p. 292.

54. See my critique in *Moses and Pharaoh*, Appendix B: "The Demographics of Decline." See also James A. Weber, *Grow or Die!* (New Rochelle, New York: Arlington House, 1977).

volves also the scientific efforts to abolish death. This hatred of change is a hatred of creation, and of its movement in terms of God's purpose. Unlike the pagan and the humanist, the orthodox Christian is committed to a respect for creation. This respect for creation gave roots to science in the Christian west. It is not an accident of history that science in other cultures has had a limited growth and a quick withering. . . . The pagan perspective is one of a fundamental disrespect for creation, for the universe. The central problems for the Hellenic mind were *change* and *decay*. . . ."[55]

The religion of zero growth is a religion of *decay* and *delay*. It proclaims inescapable decay, and offers a short-term social program of delaying the effects on society of this supposedly inescapable decay. The proper response to this religion is to point to God, whose law-order, through grace, offers redeemed man an escape hatch from entropy. The godly response is to promote long-term growth by means of a proclamation and enforcement of biblical law. We must proclaim *dominion through long-term growth* — a growth process which is the product of *progressive ethical sanctification*.

Christianity is not a religion of decay, but of life and progress. It is not a religion of delay, but of the return of Christ in judgment, after He has delivered up a developed earthly kingdom to God the Father (I Cor. 15:24), and has put all His enemies under His feet (I Cor. 15:25). Christianity is not a religion of entropy, either cosmic or social; it is a religion of progress, both cosmic and social.

We must not promote growth for its own sake. "Growth for the sake of growth is the ideology of the cancer cell," Edward Abbey once remarked. We are not to pursue the fruits of Christian faith; we are to pursue the roots. We are to conform ourselves and our institutions to the requirements of biblical law. The result will be long-term growth. Growth is a reward for righteous living, not a goal to pursue at the expense of righteous living. But we must not be deluded into believing that the fruit of righteousness is zero growth. Far less are we to pursue zero growth as a way of life. Our obligation is to seek first the kingdom of God; all these other things will be added unto us (Matt. 6:33). *Added* — not subtracted, and not kept the same.

---

55. R. J. Rushdoony, *Foundations of Social Order: Studies in the Creeds and Councils of the Early Church* (Fairfax, Virginia: Thoburn Press, [1969] 1978), pp. 208-9.

Conclusion

God brings His sanctions in history: cursings and blessings. He delegates to heads of families the authority to dispense positive sanctions to covenant-keeping children. The family unit is the heart of all economic growth, and therefore the head of the family, as the one who lawfully allocates the family's assets, is entitled to grant positive sanctions to those under his authority.

Church and State are not originally creative economically, but only corrective and protective ethically. The State provides the institutional framework of property ownership, which in turn affects economic productivity. The church declares God's ethical standards, and it provides access to the sacraments which alone make possible God's common grace in history. Without common grace, there could be no economic growth for pagans, and there would be a drastically reduced division of labor, which would also reduce the wealth of Christians.[56] Both church and State are dependent economically on the blessings of God and the productivity of private citizens because these covenant institutions serve both God and private citizens. They possess lawful authority as derived sovereignties — derived from God and man — which means that they must derive their direct economic support from those over whom they rule and therefore also serve. Their authority cannot be separated from their economic dependence on those over whom they exercise authority.

This is one reason why both the tithe and civil taxes are supposed to be proportional to the net output and therefore the net income of those under their jurisdiction. Civil and ecclesiastical judges are supposed to declare and enforce God's law, so that the whole society can prosper. They should be able to expand their income and influence only to the extent that they serve God and man in a covenantally faithful way. The visible manifestation of their success or failure in this task is the performance of the economy, including the ability of the economy to deliver effective medical services.

Dominion requires the mastery of every area of life in terms of God's revealed laws. This in turn requires faithful preaching of the comprehensive effects of God's redemption. Christ bought back everything when He sacrificed Himself. What dominion produces is order and growth, as well as orderly growth.

---

56. North, *Dominion and Common Grace*, pp. 53, 58, 76, 245.

When God brings judgment on rebellious societies, He brings sickness, disorder, and economic stagnation. The modern no-growth humanists, including baptized humanists who call themselves Christians, are proclaiming a gospel of stagnation. They want order—a top-down, centrally planned order—but they do not want growth. The very complexity of a modern growing economy threatens their ability to promote a growing State-directed order.[57] Other critics of capitalism want decentralization, a "down on the farm" world of a minimal division of labor and zero growth.[58] Thus, their ideology is hostile to growth of most kinds.

God says that such a view of His kingdom is evil, although it is an accurate view of Satan's kingdom. To promote a zero-growth philosophy is to promote historical stalemate—a stalemate between God's kingdom and Satan's, between growth and decay, between good and evil. Satan wants a stalemate if he cannot get a victory. Long-term economic growth is a product of God's grace in response to covenantal faithfulness, itself a gift from God. Long-term economic growth is therefore a denial of stalemated kingdoms. It is a demonstration of God's victory over Satan, creativity over destruction, ethics over power.

---

57. See the anti-population growth arguments of socialist Bertrand Russell, *The Prospects of Industrial Civilization* (2nd ed.; London: George Allen & Unwin, 1959), p. 273. I have reproduced his arguments in *Moses and Pharaoh*, p. 27.

58. Art Gish, "Decentralist Economics," in Robert Clouse (ed.), *Wealth and Poverty: Four Christian Views of Economics* (Downers Grove, Illinois: InterVarsity Press, 1984), Pt. III.

30

GOD'S LIMITS ON SACRIFICE

And this is the offering which ye shall take of them; gold, and silver, and brass, And blue, and purple, and scarlet, and fine linen, and goats' hair, And rams' skins dyed red, and badgers' skins, and shittim wood, Oil for the light, spices for anointing oil, and for sweet incense, Onyx stones, and stones to be set in the ephod, and in the breastplate. And let them make me a sanctuary; that I may dwell among them (Ex. 25:3-8).

And they spake unto Moses, saying, The people bring much more than enough for the service of the work, which the LORD commanded to make. And Moses gave commandment, and they caused it to be proclaimed throughout the camp, saying, Let neither man nor woman make any more work for the offering of the sanctuary. So the people were restrained from bringing. For the stuff they had was sufficient for all the work to make it, and too much (Ex. 36:5-7).

God is the Creator of the world. He therefore owns it: "The earth is the LORD's, and the fulness thereof; the world, and they that dwell therein" (Ps. 24:1). As the cosmic Owner, God demands a percentage of the profits from His subordinates. We are all sharecroppers in God's world.

God is also the King of creation. Thus, as a reigning monarch, God is entitled to occasional public manifestations of loyalty from His people. At times of formal covenant renewal, His people are asked by God to bring offerings to Him. This is a continuing theme in the Bible. The word "offerings" appears 265 times in the King James Version. The word "offering" appears 724 times. "Sacrifice" appears 218 times.[1] When a man comes formally into the presence of God, he is expected to bring an offering.

---

1. I am using the handy tallies provided by the Godspeed electronic Bible search program.

God is present with His people at all times, but there are times of special covenantal presence with His people. There are also special times of God's covenantal departure from His people. Both instances are times of judgment. This is why God's presence is associated with peace offerings of various kinds. Man is not to come empty-handed into the presence of the King. A man who brings no offering or a cheap offering does not really expect judgment, either positive or negative. This was God's warning to Israel through Malachi:

Ye have wearied the LORD with your words. Yet ye say, Wherein have we wearied him? When ye say, Every one that doeth evil is good in the sight of the LORD, and he delighteth in them; or, Where is the God of judgment? Behold, I will send my messenger, and he shall prepare the way before me: and the Lord, whom ye seek, shall suddenly come to his temple, even the messenger of the covenant, whom ye delight in: behold, he shall come, saith the LORD of hosts. But who may abide the day of his coming? And who shall stand when he appeareth? For he is like a refiner's fire, and like fullers' soap: And he shall sit as a refiner and purifier of silver: and he shall purify the sons of Levi, and purge them as gold and silver, that they may offer unto the LORD an offering in righteousness. Then shall the offering of Judah and Jerusalem be pleasant unto the LORD, as in the days of old, and as in former years. And I will come near to you to judgment; and I will be a swift witness against the sorcerers, and against the adulterers, and against false swearers, and against those that oppress the hireling in his wages, the widow, and the fatherless, and that turn aside the stranger from his right, and fear not me, saith the LORD of hosts. For I am the LORD, I change not; therefore ye sons of Jacob are not consumed. Even from the days of your fathers ye are gone away from mine ordinances, and have not kept them. Return unto me, and I will return unto you, saith the LORD of hosts. But ye said, Wherein shall we return?

Will a man rob God? Yet ye have robbed me. But ye say, Wherein have we robbed thee? In tithes and offerings. Ye are cursed with a curse: for ye have robbed me, even this whole nation. Bring ye all the tithes into the storehouse, that there may be meat in mine house, and prove me now herewith, saith the LORD of hosts, if I will not open you the windows of heaven, and pour you out a blessing, that there shall not be room enough to receive it. And I will rebuke the devourer for your sakes, and he shall not destroy the fruits of your ground; neither shall your vine cast her fruit before the time in the field, saith the LORD of hosts. And all nations shall call you blessed: for ye shall be a delightsome land, saith the LORD of hosts (Mal. 2:17-3:12).

A Question of Subordination

God's intention is to gain loyalty from His subordinates. The visible sign of their continued subordination is their willingness to bring Him their tithes and offerings. But the ultimate offering is always ethical. "Will the LORD be pleased with thousands of rams, or with ten thousands of rivers of oil? shall I give my firstborn for my transgression, the fruit of my body for the sin of my soul? He hath shewed thee, O man, what is good; and what doth the LORD require of thee, but to do justly, and to love mercy, and to walk humbly with thy God?" (Mic. 6:7-8). The ultimate offering is man's own life: "I beseech you therefore, brethren, by the mercies of God, that ye present your bodies a living sacrifice, holy, acceptable unto God, which is your reasonable service" (Rom. 12:1).

In one sense, the sacrifices that men are required to bring are limited: the regular, disciplined tithe on all net increases. In another sense, the sacrifice is unlimited: a lifetime of perfect obedience. This points to the necessity of a substitute payment. Fallen man's gifts are insufficient to meet God's demands, and a man will destroy himself if he attempts to satisfy the perfect demands of God. No matter how hard he works, it is pointless. "But we are all as an unclean thing, and all our righteousnesses are as filthy rags; and we all do fade as a leaf; and our iniquities, like the wind, have taken us away" (Isa. 64:6). Yet at the same time, God does demand this total sacrifice. There seems to be a contradiction here, but it is resolved in history by Jesus Christ's sacrifice on Calvary, the only offering that pleases God perfectly, once and for all.

But Christ being come an high priest of good things to come, by a greater and more perfect tabernacle, not made with hands, that is to say, not of this building; Neither by the blood of goats and calves, but by his own blood he entered in once into the holy place, having obtained eternal redemption for us. For if the blood of bulls and of goats, and the ashes of an heifer sprinkling the unclean, sanctifieth to the purifying of the flesh: How much more shall the blood of Christ, who through the eternal Spirit offered himself without spot to God, purge your conscience from dead works to serve the living God? And for this cause he is the mediator of the new testament, that by means of death, for the redemption of the transgressions that were under the first testament, they which are called might receive the promise of eternal inheritance (Heb. 9:11-15).

The underlying ethical reason why God does not demand total sacrifice from men is that they do not have the means of placating

His wrath or meeting His demands. So, He is gracious to man. *He limits His demands on them as a testimony to His grace to them.* He calls them to slow, steady, faithful, lifetime service, and He restrains their orgies of self-justifying sacrifice that cannot be sustained emotionally or economically over a lifetime. He announced this to Israel at the beginning of their journey in the wilderness.

Covenant Law, Covenant Presence

God brought Moses to Mt. Sinai in the third month after He had brought the Israelites out of the land of Egypt (Ex. 19:1). He first instructed Moses to deliver His commandments and the case-law applications of these Ten Commandments to the people, and these laws fill chapters 20-23 of the Book of Exodus. The Israelites affirmed their allegiance to these laws, promising their obedience (Ex. 24:3). To seal this covenantal promise, Moses then subjected them to a rite of covenant creation:

> And Moses wrote all the words of the LORD, and rose up early in the morning, and builded an altar under the hill, and twelve pillars, according to the twelve tribes of Israel. And he sent young men of the children of Israel, which offered burnt offerings, and sacrificed peace offerings of oxen unto the LORD. And Moses took half of the blood, and put it in basins; and half of the blood he sprinkled on the altar. And he took the book of the covenant, and read in the audience of the people: and they said, All that the LORD hath said will we do, and be obedient. And Moses took the blood, and sprinkled it on the people, and said, Behold the blood of the covenant, which the LORD hath made with you concerning all these words (Ex. 24:4-9).

The ethical terms of this covenant are eternal and therefore still binding on all who desire to participate in God's covenant.[2] Half the blood he sprinkled on the altar, and half on the people (Ex. 24:6-8). This bloody sacrifice made by Moses pointed to *the necessity of the shedding of blood as the means of gaining God's protection*, the same message which had been proclaimed ritually to the Hebrews by the blood on the doorposts on the night of the death of Egypt's firstborn.[3]

Again, God called Moses to return to the mountain. He told Moses that once again, the people would be given His laws on tables

---

2. Greg L. Bahnsen, *Theonomy in Christian Ethics* (2nd ed.; Phillipsburg, New Jersey: Presbyterian & Reformed, [1977] 1984).

3. Gary North, "The Marriage Supper of the Lamb," *Christianity and Civilization*, 4 (1985).

of stone (Ex. 24:12). For six days, the glory of God shone on Mt. Sinai, and the cloud covered it. On the seventh day, God called out of the midst of the cloud to Moses, and Moses went into the cloud (Ex. 24:16-18). The symbolism should be obvious: God is transcendently distant from man for six days, imaging the original week of creation; then He calls man into His glorious presence on the seventh day, the day of the Lord. The transcendent God brings man into His presence. The day of the Lord is the archetypal day of judgment.[4]

Recapitulating the Creation

Meredith Kline says that the history of the exodus, which culminates in the building of the tabernacle, is presented to us in such a way that it brings out its character as a redemptive re-enactment of creation.[5] The building of the tabernacle was a microcosmic imitation of God's original creation week. Both were covenantal events, he says. There is a historical-literary parallelism between the original creation and the exodus re-creation.[6] In this re-creation event, the tabernacle is important as a visible manifestation of God's transcendence and also His presence in His glory-cloud. The cloud hovers over Mt. Sinai and reproduces its likeness below. "At the foot of Sinai the tabernacle appears, made according to the archetypal pattern seen on the mount, designed to be a replica of the Glory-Spirit-temple."[7]

The earth-cosmos was made after the archetypal pattern of the Glory-Spirit referred to in Genesis 1:2 and accordingly is viewed in Scripture as a cosmic royal residence or temple.[8] Heaven and earth were established as a holy palace of the Creator-King, with the heaven of heavens in particular corresponding to the Glory-cloud as the seat of his sovereignty.

Then, preparing a place for the man-priest who was to be created, the Lord God produced in Eden a microcosmic version of his cosmic sanctuary. The garden planted there was holy ground with guardianship of its sanctity

---

4. Christians bring sacrifices to God each Sunday on the Lord's Day: tithes and offerings. This is fitting and proper. It is a day of judgment because it is a day of the Lord's presence. But rarely do churches celebrate the Lord's Supper weekly. Why not? The presence of the Lord was manifested at his regular required feasts in Israel. Why is this not also the case in New Testament times?

5. Meredith G. Kline, *Images of the Spirit* (Grand Rapids, Michigan: Baker Book House, 1980), p. 37.

6. *Ibid.*, p. 39.

7. *Ibid.*, p. 37.

8. Rom. 13:14; I Cor. 15:53-54; II Cor. 5:2ff.; Gal. 3:27; Eph. 4:24; Col. 3:10.

committed in turn to men and to cherubim.[9] It was the temple-garden of God,[10] the place chosen by the Glory-Spirit who hovered over creation from the beginning to be the focal site of his throne-presence among men.[11]

The tabernacle would be God's place of residence within the nation of Israel. His transcendent glory, manifested in the glory-cloud, would reside in the tabernacle. Kline continues: "Thus, in producing the tabernacle as a symbolic image of his Glory-Spirit, the Creator Lord so designed it that it also recapitulated the macrocosmic and microcosmic versions of the Glory-temple which he fashioned in the original creation. And as God crowned the finished Genesis creation with his majestic Glory over Eden, so, when the tabernacle stood complete at Sinai, the Glory-cloud covered and filled it, sealing it as an authentic likeness of the Spirit-temple (Exod. 40:34ff.), the Alpha and Omega of all creation."[12]

The first instructions that God gave to Moses after his entrance into God's glory-cloud involved the plans of the proposed tabernacle. The plans for this structure were so detailed that the written account takes up more space in Exodus (chapters 25-28) than the laws that had just been delivered to the people. Then came the detailed instructions concerning the ceremonies to be conducted in the tabernacle (chapters 29-31). Nothing else is recorded about God's instructions to Moses during the forty days and nights that Moses spent with God on Mt. Sinai, except for God's warning to the Israelites to keep the sabbath (31:12-17).

Covenants and Sacrifice

The importance of sacrifice in all religion cannot be overemphasized. The sacrifices inaugurated by God in these chapters are contrasted with the sacrifice demanded by the Israelites during Moses' absence. *Both paganism and orthodoxy require sacrifices from the faithful.* Abel brought his sacrifice before God, and Cain brought his. God gave specific instructions to Moses concerning the kinds of sacrifices that He required, just as the people of Israel had instructed Aaron about the kind that their god required.

---

9. Gen. 2:15; 3:24.
10. Isa. 51:3; Ezek. 28:13, 16, 31:9.
11. *Ibid.*, pp. 35-36.
12. *Ibid.*, p. 42.

Recapitulating the Fall

The Israelites had "spoiled" the Egyptians before they left, taking with them gold and jewels that had belonged to their former masters. This had been God's gracious restoration to them of the lost capital that the Egyptians had extracted from them and their forefathers.[13] These goods offered them a new beginning economically. To this extent, the exodus was a restoration of Eden.

In Eden, God had departed from Adam and Eve for a while. During his absence, they sinned. Moses also departed, climbing the mountain of God. During Moses' initial absence, the Israelites had insisted to Aaron that they be allowed to sacrifice a portion of this wealth in order to construct gods to go before them (Ex. 32:1). Aaron used their gold to construct a calf, and the people then attributed their victory over the Egyptians to these new gods that were represented by the calf (Ex. 32:8). They re-enacted the fall of man.

It is not surprising that the Hebrews turned to the sculpture of a bull when they sought to represent polytheistic power. The Apis bull was the single most important religious animal in Egypt. The birth and death of each Apis bull were recorded in Egyptian records as faithfully as the ritual ordination and death of each Pharaoh. In fact, *only* these events were important enough in the eyes of the Egyptians to maintain in official records, dynasty after dynasty.[14] The Hebrews demonstrated by the construction of the calf that their world-and-life view was still dominated by the theology of Egypt. Though they had been delivered physically and geographically from Egypt, they had not yet been delivered spiritually. They still were under the influence of the religion of their former captors. They were still in spiritual bondage. For this reason, that first generation of the exodus did not enter the land of Canaan. They went out of Egypt, but they did not come into the promised land. They could not return to the sin-filled pseudo-garden of Egypt, just as Adam and Eve could not return to the garden. Yet they refused to go forward on God's terms, so they wandered until they died.

---

13. Gary North, *Moses and Pharaoh: Dominion Religion vs. Power Religion* (Tyler, Texas: Institute for Christian Economics, 1985), ch. 6: "Cumulative Transgression and Restitution."

14. George Rawlinson, *History of Ancient Egypt*, 2 vols. (New York: John B. Alden, 1886), II, p. 2.

The Works of Man's Hand

They had cried out to Aaron, "Up, make us gods, which shall go before us" (Ex. 32:1b). Why did they choose to worship *gods*? The calf represented the polytheistic gods of Egypt. They preferred to worship the defeated gods of their captors rather than worship the victorious God of the exodus. Had they been disciples of power as such, they would have worshipped God, but *the power religion necessarily is humanistic*: it worships only those gods who manifest themselves through man and the works of man's hand. This kind of hand-crafted god, they recognized clearly, was not the God of the Bible, who had brought judgment on Egypt despite their continual complaints and fears. He was a God who did not need their assistance or their sacrifices in order to manifest His consummate power in history. This God was not yet visibly manifested in their midst, and they were unwilling to wait for His presence — a familiar biblical theme (I Sam. 13:8-14). They had Aaron build a calf as their representative before the gods.

The Hebrews were not naive. They did not believe that the calf had delivered them. They wanted to worship an object that was symbolic of the supernatural powers that they now claimed had delivered them from the bondage of Egypt, and which supposedly communicated with men through the medium of man-created idols. Pagan religion is not the worship of sticks and stones. It is the worship of powerful occult forces that do the bidding of men, if men worship them in a rigorously prescribed manner. Man manipulates his world by manipulating these occult forces. Even the English word *man*ipulates testifies to the theology of idol worship: control is achieved manually, "by hand." This is the theology of magic: "As above, so below." Man believes that he can manipulate the creation in certain ways that force the gods of power to conform to his will. What he does on earth calls forth the man-directed power of the gods. The popular description of the occult voodoo religion is accurate: the person sticking pins into a doll. Sticking pins into a doll is a form of what is called sympathetic magic. What man does to the doll will then be reflected in what happens to the person who is represented by the doll. As below (pins in the doll), so above (power of the gods). As above (power of the gods), so below (the human victim suffers). Man calls down (or calls up) the gods to serve his purposes. He chooses ritual manipulation rather than covenantal faithfulness as his tool of dominion. This is also the theology of modern autonomous science.[15]

The Creator-Creature Distinction

"As above, so below" is not simply the basis of the power religion, both magic and science; it is also the basis of cause and effect in biblical religion. The error of power religion is to assume that the link is metaphysical rather than covenantal; that it is based on a chain of being between the gods, man, and the creation. The Bible rejects all versions of the religion of the chain of being.[16] The Creator-creature distinction is absolute. As Van Til says, "The entire Christian theistic position stands or falls with the concept of the nature of the relation of God to man."[17] "The idea of creation makes a distinction of being between God and man. Anyone holding to the idea of creation (we speak of temporal and not of logical creation) must also hold to the idea of a God who existed apart from the world and had meaning for himself apart from the world . . . If theism is right, all things are at bottom two, and not one."[18] God is not man, nor is God part of the creation.

---

15. Prior to the 1920's, Western scientists believed that the forces put into the service of man were strictly impersonal. A specially trained priesthood — pure scientists and technologists — was seen as the source of access to these generally unknown powers. The priesthood has not changed, but the theology has shifted. Something far closer to ancient magic now dominates modern thought. The sharp distinction between subject and object, between man and his environment, has become blurred. Simultaneously, man has become more impersonal, while the external world around us has become far more personal, a reflection of man, and even the creation of man.

Does this mean that modern humanist thought teaches that it is actually man who creates the orderliness of nature? Increasingly, this is exactly what is being said. Timothy Ferris writes of Sir Arthur Eddington, the brilliant British astronomer of the early twentieth century: "Eddington believed the laws of nature reside within our minds, are created not by the cosmos but by our perceptions of it, so that a visitor from another planet could deduce all our science simply by analyzing how our brains are wired. In Eddington's view, we know physical laws a priori, as [Immanuel] Kant maintained, although where Kant conceived part of our a priori knowledge as inborn, Eddington felt it was derived from experience in observation and reasoning." Ferris, *The Red Limit: The Search for the Edge of the Universe* (New York: William Morrow, 1977), p. 116. This is radical subjectivism, an obvious development of consistent humanism. See Gary North, *Is the World Running Down? Crisis in the Christian Worldview* (Tyler, Texas: Institute for Christian Economics, 1988), ch. 2.

16. Ray R. Sutton, *That You May Prosper: Dominion By Covenant* (Tyler, Texas: Institute for Christian Economics, 1987), pp. 33-39.

17. Cornelius Van Til, *A Survey of Christian Epistemology*, vol. II of *In Defense of Biblical Christianity* (den Dulk Foundation, 1969), p. 16.

18. *Ibid.*, pp. 18, 19.

The link between the two realms, natural and supernatural, is the covenant. Christ told the disciples to pray: "Thy kingdom come. Thy will be done in earth, as it is in heaven" (Matt. 6:10). The will of God, as revealed in His covenant law, is the standard of what should take place both above and below. Christ also told Peter, after Peter's confession of Jesus as the Son of God: "And I will give unto thee the keys of the kingdom of heaven: and whatsoever thou shalt bind on earth shall be bound in heaven: and whatsoever thou shalt loose on earth shall be loosed in heaven" (Matt. 16:19). It is the law of God which binds and looses; the keys of the kingdom are biblical law.[19] Men in their capacity as ordained officers, as God's representative covenantal agents, declare His law and enforce it. The will of God, not the will of man, is absolute. This is why the Creator-creature distinction must be at the foundation of all Christian philosophy, for without it, the chain-of-being theology of autonomous man undermines the revelation of God to man and the law of God for man. As Van Til says:

The Christian position maintains that man, as a creature of God, naturally would have to inquire of God what is right and wrong. Originally God spoke to man directly and man could speak to God directly. Since the entrance of sin man has to speak to God mediately. He has now to learn from Scriptures what is the acceptable will of God for him. In opposition to this the non-Christian position holds that man does not need Scripture as a final authority. And this is maintained because the non-Christian does not believe that man ever needed to be absolutely obedient to God. Non-Christian ethics maintains that it is of the nature of the ethical life that man must, in the last analysis, decide for himself what is right and what is wrong.[20]

Broken Tablets, Broken Covenant

Moses' dramatic response to the Hebrews' public demonstration of magical power religion — his response of symbolic ritual — was to break the stone tablets that had been delivered to him by God. These inscribed tablets were not the product of man's hand. God, not Moses, had written His ten laws on the tablets (Ex. 31:18). These laws set forth the basis of God's cooperation with man, a set of *ethical principles rather than prescribed rituals*. The ethical bond was based on a

---

19. R. J. Rushdoony, *Institutes of Biblical Law* (Nutley, New Jersey: Craig Press, 1973), p. 619.

20. Cornelius Van Til, *Christian Theistic Ethics*, vol. III of *In Defense of Biblical Christianity* (Phillipsburg, New Jersey: Presbyterian & Reformed, 1980), p. 33.

personal covenant between God and His people, a *law-covenant*.
Moses destroyed the tablets as a ritual response to the people because they had broken the ethical covenant (Ex. 19) by their rebellious ritual response to God. They had chosen to worship a god of
their own hands; Moses demonstrated ritually what this really
meant: their breaking of the covenant of God the Cosmic Potter,
who makes man as a potter forms the clay. They were not willing to
acknowledge, as Isaiah later acknowledged: "But now, O LORD, thou
art our father; we are the clay, and thou our potter; and we all are
the work of thy hand" (Isa. 64:8). God then smashes the rebellious
clay in judgment: "Behold, ye are of nothing, and your work of
nought: an abomination is he that chooseth you. I have raised up
one from the north, and he shall come: from the rising of the sun
shall he call upon my name: and he shall come upon princes as upon
morter, and as the potter treadeth the clay" (Isa. 41:24-25).

To dramatize the inevitable judgment of God, Moses then conducted another ritual—from a strictly economic standpoint, probably the most graphic ritual ever recorded in the Bible. He burned the
calf in the fire, smashed its remains to powder, put the powder in
water, and then commanded the people to drink the water (32:20).[21]
Biological processes then took over to produce the final, graphic, and
memorable ritual disposal of the religious symbol that had consumed
so much of their capital. They saw their capital go down the proverbial drain.

The people had demanded the right to sacrifice part of their
wealth to the god of their own hands. The calf had been made quickly
by amateur craftsmen working under Aaron, and had been put into
immediate service. They sacrificed joyfully, participating in sexual
debauchery (Ex. 32:25) as a religious affirmation of their faithfulness
to the gods of the chaos festival, the gods of cosmic renewal through
ritual lawlessness.[22] These were the gods that were familiar to them,
polytheistic gods like those of Egypt, from which they had been delivered, and also like those of Canaan, which they believed was
about to be delivered into their hands. *Here were gods that demanded sac-*

---

21. This was equivalent to the ordeal of jealousy which was required in the Old
Testament when a husband brought a charge of adultery against his wife (Num.
5:11-31).

22. Roger Caillois, *Man and the Sacred* (Glencoe, Illinois: The Free Press, 1959), p.
164. Cf. Thorkild Jacobsen, "Mesopotamia: The Function of the State," in H. and
H. A. Frankfort, et al., *The Intellectual Adventure of Ancient Man: An Essay on Speculative
Thought in the Ancient Near East* (University of Chicago Press, [1946] 1977), pp. 198-201.

rifice and ritual, but not ethical regeneration. Here were gods of their hearts and hands.

Pyramid and Tabernacle

In contrast to the calf that had been crafted by amateurs, with its religion of professional debauchery, God's tabernacle was detailed and magnificent, yet portable. It moved with the people because God moved before the people, guiding them. To build it, the people had to dig deeply once again into what remained of their treasure. It was to be a voluntary sacrifice. They responded enthusiastically (Ex. 35:21-22, 29). The craftswomen contributed the best that they had (35:25-26). Bezaleel, a craftsman, was given special knowledge from God to master the arts (35:31), as well as a special gift of teaching (35:34). He and Aholiab, who also had been given the gift of teaching, became the contractors who directed the building of the tabernacle (35:30-34). God imparted special skills to those who assisted them (35:35). The people brought in their offerings daily (36:3). In fact, they continued to bring in so much that there was an overflow of materials (36:5). Moses had to tell them to cease their labors and to stop bringing in their handicrafts (36:6-7).

A very different structure is the Cheops pyramid of Giza in Egypt. It remains an architectural and technological wonder. It is the last surviving edifice of the seven wonders of the ancient world. Scholars have studied it in great detail. There is even a school of arcane knowledge called "pyramidology," which attempts to find in its dimensions prophetic truths.[23]

No one knows how it was built, but the usual estimate is that 100,000 slaves and 40,000 skilled craftsmen had to work on it for 20 years.[24] Not only is the pyramid a technological wonder — we still have no clear idea of how it was built — it is a mathematical wonder. This has been recognized by Western scholars for over a century. John Taylor, editor of the *London Observer*, and a gifted mathematician, began playing with the measurements of the Great Pyramid reported by Col. Richard Howard-Vyse. This was in the 1850's. Taylor asked why only this pyramid had the angle of 51 degrees and 51 minutes. He found that each of the Pyramid's four faces had the

---

23. How it supposedly can do this by means of different measuring systems is indeed a wonder.

24. Peter Tomkins, *Secrets of the Great Pyramid* (New York: Harper Colophon, [1971] 1978), pp. 227-28. The figure of 20 years comes from Herodotus.

area of the square of its height.[25] No other pyramid was so constructed. Then he discovered that if he divided the perimeter of the Pyramid by twice its height, it gave him a quotient of 3.144, which is very close to *pi*: 3.14159 + . Peter Tomkins remarks in a footnote that not until the sixth century A.D. was *pi* correctly worked out to the fourth decimal point by a Hindu scholar, Arya-Bhata.[26]

This was only the beginning. He concluded that the Pyramid was a representation of the earth, with the perimeter as the circumference at the equator and the height as the distance from the earth's center to the pole. But what unit of measurement could they have used? He looked for a unit that would retain the *pi* proportion and fit the Pyramid in whole numbers

When he came to 366.116.5 he was struck by the similarity of 366 to the number of days in the year and wondered if the Egyptians might have intentionally divided the perimeter of the Pyramid into units of the solar year.

He then noticed that if he converted the perimeter into inches, it came very nearly to 100 times 366. Also he was surprised to see that if he divided the base by 25 inches, he obtained the same 366 result. Could the ancient Egyptians have used a unit so close to the British inch? And a cubit of 25 such inches?[27]

At the same time, the famed astronomer Sir John Herschel had postulated a unit of measurement half a hair's breadth longer than a British inch as the only sensible earth-commensurable unit based on the actual size of the earth. He was critical of the French meter derived from a curved meridian of the earth because of its erratic and variable nature from country to country because the earth is not a true sphere. Each meridian of longitude would be different. (One wonders if this may have been a bit of intellectual British imperialism, a reaction against the revolutionary French with their far more easily computed units of tenths, hundredths, and thousandths.) Herschel argued that the only reliable basis of a standard of measure is the polar axis of the earth—a straight line from pole to pole—which a recent British ordinance survey had set at 7898.78 miles, or

---

25. This fact later led to the discovery that the Pyramid was designed to incorporate not only *pi* but also the so-called Golden Section, or *phi*, or 1.618. *Phi* + 1 = *phi* square. Also, 1 + 1/*phi* leads to the additive series known as the Fibonacci series. *Ibid.*, pp. 190, 192. They had also figured out the relation between *pi* and *phi*: *pi* = *phi* × 6/5. *Ibid.*, p. 194.

26. *Ibid.*, p. 71n.

27. *Ibid.*, p. 72.

500,500,000 British inches, or an even 500 million inches if the unit was half a hair's breadth longer.[28] (Do we all have equally wide hairs?)

So what? Fifty of such modified inches would make a yard exactly one ten-millionth of the polar axis, and half that measure would make a useful cubit. This was the unit that Taylor had found to fit the Pyramid in multiples of 366. "To Taylor the inference was clear: the ancient Egyptians must have had a system of measurements based on the true spherical dimensions of the planet, which used a unit which was within a thousandth part of being equal to a British inch."[29]

These studies were followed by Charles Piazzi Smyth, the Astronomer Royal of Scotland, who went to Egypt, made many detailed measurements, and concluded that the Egyptians had computed *pi* down to 3.14159.[30]

Studies by British engineer David Davidson in the 1920's and 1930's revealed that the Pyramid measures all three types of the calendar year: solar, sidereal (star), and anomalistic (orbital-perihelion).[31]

The base of the Pyramid corresponds to the distance the earth rotates in half a second at the equator.[32]

The priests could have measured the length of the solar year within a minute, or four points of a decimal.[33]

I could go on, but it is not necessary. The Egyptian priests and architects were masters of mathematics and geography to a degree unknown in the textbooks. Why did they go to such an effort in building the Cheops Pyramid? Because the Cheops Pyramid served them well. It was a measuring device as well as a symbol of their mastery of science. But it no doubt also served them as a giant talisman. It was a microcosm of the earth. Magic proclaims: "As above, so below." Here was a device for initiations, for manipulating the world.

In contrast to the Pyramid stands — though it no longer stands — the tabernacle, and later the temple. The tabernacle did not rely on sophisticated measurements to put man in contact with cosmic forces. God's law did that, written on tablets at the center of the tabernacle and therefore at the center of society. God's presence with

---

28. *Ibid.*, p. 73.
29. *Ibid.*, p. 74.
30. *Ibid.*, p. 90.
31. *Ibid.*, p. 111.
32. *Ibid.*, p. 210.
33. *Ibid.*, p. 161.

man was not based on their ability to reproduce His world in a model. His presence or absence was established by their covenantal faithfulness. It was the law that was crucial, not measurements in stone. It was man's heart of stone that was his problem, not the design of the tabernacle. The temple no longer stands because God destroyed it when it no longer served His covenantal purposes. He would not tolerate those who treated His temple as a talisman.

> Thus saith the LORD of hosts, the God of Israel, Amend your ways and your doings, and I will cause you to dwell in this place. Trust ye not in lying words, saying, The temple of the LORD, The temple of the LORD, The temple of the LORD, are these. For if ye throughly amend your ways and your doings; if ye throughly execute judgment between a man and his neighbour; If ye oppress not the stranger, the fatherless, and the widow, and shed not innocent blood in this place, neither walk after other gods to your hurt: Then will I cause you to dwell in this place, in the land that I gave to your fathers, for ever and ever (Jer. 7:3-7).

The Renaissance, with its fatal attraction to magic, misunderstood this. Frances Yates, who more than anyone else has opened this academically closed door of the Renaissance,[34] notes that Isaac Newton, a dedicated alchemist, was fascinated with Solomon's temple. She says that he was "determined to unravel the exact plan and proportions of the Temple of Solomon. This was another Renaissance interest; the plan of the temple, laid down by God himself, was believed to reflect the divine plan of the universe. For Renaissance scholars, the theory of classical architecture was believed to derive from the Temple and, like it, to reflect the world in human proportions."[35] Newton even sketched the temple's dimensions.[36]

The Renaissance was treating the temple as if it were the Great Pyramid. It was not. The religion of the Bible is covenantal and ethical, not metaphysical and magical. God is not to be manipulated; He is to be obeyed.

Man's Need of Limits

Limits were placed by God on their sacrifices. Moses did not ask them to bring in all of their capital in a wave of sacrificial giving,

---

34. Frances A. Yates, *Giordano Bruno and the Hermetic Tradition* (New York: Vintage, [1964] 1969).

35. Frances A. Yates, *Ideas and Ideals in the North European Renaissance*, vol. III of *Collected Essays*, 3 vols. (London: Methuen, 1984), p. 270.

36. Frank E. Manuel, *Isaac Newton, Historian* (Cambridge, Massachusetts: Harvard University Press, 1963), plate facing p. 148.

despite their sin in building the calf. Their giving was voluntary, meaning *beyond the mandatory tithe*. These were what Protestants call "gifts and offerings." So powerful was the motivation for sacrificial giving that the people had to be restrained. They were not to make the same mistake again: believing that the work of their hands could save them from the wrath of God, believing that the greater their giving, the less the wrath. Furthermore, they were to preserve capital for future productive uses.

Men need to sacrifice to their gods. They insist on it. Their sacrifice links them to a source of power. But God warns men that He is not so concerned about men's material sacrifices; instead, He is concerned about justice, humility, and mercy (Deut. 10:12; I Sam. 15:22; Micah 6:8). He desires the sacrifice of a contrite heart: "For thou desirest not sacrifice; else would I give it: thou delightest not in burnt offering. The sacrifices of God are a broken spirit: a broken and a contrite heart, O God, thou wilt not despise" (Ps. 51:16-17). Only on these terms are burnt offerings acceptable to God. God grants wealth and power, not in terms of ritualistic precision, but in terms of conformity to an ethical law-order (Deut. 8). Righteousness is more important than ritual (II Chron. 30:13-20).

Early Protestantism, especially Puritan and Anabaptist Protestantism, criticized the cathedral builders. They argued that the money spent on cathedrals should have been given to the poor, or used for other purposes. As it has turned out historically, the great cathedrals have become tourist attractions, as the Christian faith of the public has waned. But these magnificent structures still stand as testimonies to the dedication, skill, and sacrifices of men for their God. The cathedrals reflect the builders' and worshippers' conception of the authority and majesty of God. The long-run perspective of the builders is still evident: they expected their work to survive. They expected it to glorify God for centuries. This long-run perspective is an important aspect of serious Christian faith. Men's time perspective is reflected in their architecture.[37] So is their view of God.[38]

---

37. The cathedral becomes a pyramid rather than a home for God if the faith of the builders has been transferred to another god. The cathedrals of Europe have become tourist attractions. The enormous, unfinished Episcopalian pyramid, the Church of St. John the Divine, is still being built in New York City after a century of labor and fund-raising. Meanwhile, the Harlem ghetto has moved almost to its borders, and it is unsafe to visit it at night.

38. Little that is orthodox remains in today's mainline Anglican and Roman Catholic churches, even in their liturgies, although there are pockets of orthodoxy. Nevertheless, their cathedrals have survived. What visible token remains of Cromwell's reign? A creed: the Westminster Confession of Faith. Almost nothing visible remains of Puritanism; its legacy was almost entirely ideological and theological.

Sacrificing to the State

Modern man worships the political order as the source of power and meaning. He shares this perspective with ancient man, both classical and Near Eastern.[39] Throughout the West, since the days of World War I, men have willingly sacrificed their capital, their lives, and their futures to the messianic State, whether democratic, fascist, or Communist. Like God, the State loves a cheerful giver. Unlike God, the statist managers do not tell the people to cease sacrificing when they have given too much. *God limits the sacrifices that men are required to offer to any human, earthly institution.* God, not institutions, is wholly sovereign. The sacrifice of Jesus Christ was the only sacrifice sufficient to meet God's ethical requirements. Man and his institutions are limited. But the modern salvationist political order places no limits on men's sacrifices, for it places no limits on its own sovereignty.

The universal grumbling about taxes that has shaken the revenue structures of every Western, industrial nation since 1970 (or earlier, in the case of European nations) indicates that men are increasingly distrustful about their god, the modern State. *A growing tax revolt indicates that a shift in faith is in progress.* Socialist humanism is cracking under the strain of increased spending on poverty programs and military hardware, as well as high unemployment and slower economic growth. The old statist faith is dying. Middle-class voters are at long last becoming aware that they have become the sacrificial lambs, not the elusive rich they sought for three or four generations to sacrifice on the altar of envy. They are still humanists, and their faith in individualism is inconsistent, but the ideological pendulum has unquestionably shifted away from the almost unquestioned monotheism of the State toward the mixed polytheism of hedonistic individualism and compulsory retirement subsidies.

Conclusion

Men want to sacrifice to something or some power higher than themselves. This act of sacrifice re-establishes their faith in some sort of cosmic order. The modern world has generally abandoned faith in a cosmic order, but it has affirmed faith in a man-directed earthly order. Thus, the most powerful agency of man, the State, has become the focus of modern man's sacrifice.

---

39. R. J. Rushdoony, *The One and the Many: Studies in the Philosophy of Order and Ultimacy* (Fairfax, Virginia: Thoburn Press, [1971] 1978), chaps. 3-5.

Man worships the creation of his own hands, just as Israel did in the wilderness rebellion. Men believe that they must sacrifice to mankind. Some men do this for profit, by serving consumers on a free market. Others serve the State. Others serve some other human institution. But the point is, they attempt to offer themselves as a living sacrifice (Rom. 12:1) to the gods of their choice.

God limits such sacrifice. A person is supposed to present himself as a living sacrifice to God, for God owns him and everything else (Ps. 50:10). He owes God everything. In baptism, man places himself and everything he owns at God's disposal. But then God returns 90 percent of whatever is offered. He keeps the tithe as a symbolic token of man's subordination. This is offered to Him through His monopolistic covenantal institution, the church. God limits men's required sacrifices. Men in general cannot be trusted to make such sacrifices, for they make them only to gods of their own hands and imaginations. Thus, God's Old Testament law of sacrifice required only the tithe and three feasts. Today, God requires only the tithe.

Those who deny this formal limit have two motives: 1) to place man under unbearable guilt for not having given enough — "the better to control you with, my dear" — and 2) to escape the sense of personal guilt when they fail to pay what they owe. *By refusing to honor the tithe as a minimum required sacrifice, antinomians place man under an open-ended maximum.* This is a denial of man's fallen condition. It is also a denial of man's creaturehood. It is a re-enactment of the golden calf incident.

Men are growing weary of the economics of perpetual sacrifice to the State at payment levels far above anything God has required. Today, all men pay at least 40 percent of their income to various branches of civil government — double the extraction imposed by ancient Egypt (Gen. 47:24-26), the most bureaucratic tyranny of the ancient world. But men must believe in a god, a source of power and meaning. They need to sacrifice to a god. What will they sacrifice next? And to which god? The answers to these two questions will determine the next phase of the history of Western civilization.

31

THE ECONOMICS OF THE TABERNACLE

*And let them make me a sanctuary; that I may dwell among them.
Accordingly to all that I shew thee, after the pattern of the tabernacle,
and the pattern of all the instruments thereof, even so shall ye make it
(Ex. 25:8-9).*

God had promised to provide Israel with a sanctuary, the land of
Canaan. This sanctuary would be both geographical and covenantal, an identifiable location where His covenant would be the law
of the land. God first required from them that they build Him a
place to serve as His personal sanctuary, which would be physical,
transportable, and covenantal. In this tabernacle, God would meet
with them in judgment. He would reward or curse them. Without
covenant renewal, they could not expect to gain His blessing, yet
with covenant renewal, they risked His wrath.

The tabernacle has been a familiar sermon topic for over a century in American fundamentalist circles. This theme allows a
preacher to fulfill his annual quota of Old Testament messages without ever coming to grips with the comprehensive ethical and social
requirements of Old Testament law. The tabernacle offers seemingly
endless opportunities for allegorizing, spiritualizing, internalizing,
and discovering secret meanings — all pointing to "great prophetic
truths." (Oddly, people who insist that "we should take Bible prophecy literally" also insist on deriving much of this supposedly literal
prophecy from highly symbolic sources.) The tabernacle is a popular
sermon topic, but only to the extent that the specific applications of
the sermon's message can be reduced to cultural irrelevance in New
Testament times.

The Tabernacle as the Place of Judgment

What the preachers seldom mention is that the tabernacle was a
place where the people came to God to receive judgment: blessing or

cursing. God's judgment was handed down in terms of the people's covenantal faithfulness to the revealed laws of God. Three times a year the citizens of Israel were required to come before God and offer sacrifices (Ex. 23:14-19). This meant that they would have to face God in judgment, as individuals and as a nation. *The tabernacle was God's place of judgment and sanctions in history.* To preach on the tabernacle is therefore risky business, for it leads straight to the doctrine of the covenant, with its five doctrines that so alienate modern evangelicalism: the absolute sovereignty of a predestinating God; the three hierarchical appeals courts: church, State, and family; the Bible-revealed law of God that is supposed to govern the decisions of the judges of all three courts; God's sanctions in history; and the disinheritance of covenant-breakers and the inheritance of covenant-keepers in history.[1] This also raises the question of the Lord's Supper as the church's covenant-renewing event that brings people into the presence of God to receive His judgments in history.[2]

The goal of modern sermons on the tabernacle is to make judicially irrelevant everything associated with the tabernacle in New Testament times. The discontinuity of the cross has supposedly made the tabernacle irrelevant today. As a building, this is unquestionably true, but this was true in Moses' day, too. The building was symbolic; what was symbolized was crucial. What was symbolized was Jesus Christ as the coming Judge in history. "But Christ being come an high priest of good things to come, by a greater and more perfect tabernacle, not made with hands, that is to say, not of this building; Neither by the blood of goats and calves, but by his own blood he entered in once into the holy place, having obtained eternal redemption for us" (Heb. 9:11-12). Thus, every sermon on the tabernacle is supposed to point to the relevance of Christ as Judge today.

Judgments in New Testament history? Ethical cause and effect in New Testament history? Covenantal sanctions in New Testament history? The authority of God's law in New Testament history? Such thoughts are not pleasant to shepherds who have denied all of this throughout their careers. They have dedicated their lives to the principle that Old Covenant history, with all its visible judgments, no longer operates today. The tabernacle is supposed to become a principle of the church's cultural irrelevance today, for ours is a world devoid of visible judgments based on covenantal cause and effect.

---

1. Ray R. Sutton, *That You May Prosper: Dominion By Covenant* (Tyler, Texas: Institute for Christian Economics, 1987).

2. *Ibid.*, pp. 304-13.

Kline as the Archetype

Professor Meredith Kline is representative of this ethereal approach to the tabernacle. Unlike the average pastor, he has the footnotes to prove that he has studied the tabernacle in depth, which he displays in his book *Images of the Spirit* (1980). Even earlier, in his *Structure of Biblical Authority* (1975), he argued that there is an architectural aspect of the Bible. The building of God's house, he says, "comes to the fore in the Book of Exodus." House-building is also a familiar theme in the Canaanitic epic poem, *Enuna Elish*, he adds.[3] First, God structured the people of Israel into His house by means of His covenant words spoken at Mt. Sinai. Then God told them to build Him a house. "Though a more literal house than the living house of Israel, the tabernacle-house was designed to function as symbolical of the other; the kingdom-people house was the true residence of God (a concept more fully explored and spiritualized in the New Testament)."[4] Spiritualized indeed!

Kline has devoted his academic career to two primary tasks: 1) exploring in great detail the covenantal evidence and implications in the Old Testament; and 2) doing whatever possible to persuade his readers that God has abandoned these implications in the New Testament.[5] He insists that any New Testament connection between visible blessings and covenant-keeping is, humanly speaking, random. "And meanwhile it [the common grace order] must run its course within the uncertainties of the mutually conditioning principles of common grace and common curse, prosperity and adversity being experienced in a manner largely unpredictable because of the inscrutable sovereignty of the divine will that dispenses them in mysterious ways."[6] Largely unpredictable? Dr. Kline has obviously never considered just why it is that life insurance premiums and health insurance premiums are cheaper in Christianity-influenced societies than in pagan societies. Apparently, the blessings of long life that are promised in the Bible are sufficiently non-random and predictable that statisticians who advise insurance companies can detect statistically relevant differences between societies.

---

3. Meredith G. Kline, *The Structure of Biblical Authority* (2nd ed.; Grand Rapids, Michigan: Eerdmans, 1975), p. 79.

4. *Ibid.*, p. 80.

5. Sutton, *That You May Prosper*, Appendix 7: "Meredith G. Kline: Yes and No."

6. Meredith G. Kline, "Comments on the Old-New Error," *Westminster Theological Journal*, XLI (Fall 1978), p. 184.

What Kline is arguing is that the testimony of God's covenant law and covenant sanctions in history was scrapped by God after Christ's resurrection from the dead. The visible sanctions of God do not operate in New Testament times. Ethical cause and effect in today's culture is random. Christianity is therefore culturally irrelevant and progressively impotent. The fact is, Kline's assertion that visible events are essentially random is a smokescreen that covers up his pessimistic eschatological views. What he really believes is that things will get worse for the church as time goes on. Ethical cause and effect in New Testament history is not merely random; it is positively perverse. This conclusion is basic to Kline's amillennial eschatology.[7] Once again, we see that covenantal neutrality is impossible.

It should be clear that the tabernacle was not culturally irrelevant or impotent in its day. It was basic to the religious life of Israel for almost half a millennium, until Solomon built the temple, 480 years after the Hebrews came out of Egypt (I Ki. 6:1). The tabernacle was the resting place of the Ark of the Covenant, which contained the tablets of the law (Ex. 25:10-22). God appeared at the tabernacle in the form of a cloud-pillar (Ex. 33:9-10; Num. 12:5; Deut. 31:15). The tabernacle was filled with gold, silver, jewels, and the finest artistic accomplishments of the people. It symbolized the majesty of the supernatural King who was in their midst.[8]

A Symbol of Covenantal Continuity

These pilgrims in the wilderness were given a symbol of the presence of God — a fundamental aspect of the biblical covenant.[9] They had a stake in a covenantal society. The tabernacle gave them *a place of sacrifice*. God is master of the universe, and men must acknowledge their subordination to Him through sacrifice.[10] The animal sacrifices would take place at a particular place. The tabernacle could therefore serve as a focus for the community's *sense of order and permanence*. The tribes would be drawn together, overcoming the potential fragmentation of tribal society.

---

7. Gary North, *Political Polytheism: The Myth of Pluralism* (Tyler, Texas: Institute for Christian Economics, 1989), ch. 3: "Halfway Covenant Ethics."

8. Meredith G. Kline, *Images of the Spirit* (Grand Rapids, Michigan: Baker Book House, 1980), pp. 35-42.

9. Sutton, *That You May Prosper*, ch. 1.

10. *Ibid.*, ch. 2.

The tabernacle was also a symbol of permanence, but only for as long as they honored the ethical terms of the covenant. While the building itself was portable, the ornaments were permanent and could be used by future generations in the promised land. The very portability of the tabernacle testified against the quest for man-made permanence — the kind of hoped-for stability that was reflected in Egypt's pyramids. *Permanence is ultimately covenantal, and therefore is governed by the ethical terms of the covenant.*[11] Permanence is mythical unless it is God-centered.

The tabernacle was evidence that they were pilgrims — people journeying toward a final destination — rather than nomads wandering in a circle. The Israelites never were nomads. Liberal theologians often refuse to accept this. The oft-repeated claim by liberal theologians that the Israelites were nomads is basic to most liberal studies of ancient Israel. Typical is Hans Jochen Boecker's statement that "The Israelites came basically from the eastern or southeastern and southern steppe countries and penetrated the cultivated areas of Palestine. They were not originally inhabitants of cultivated land; they were nomads, and their legal arrangements were typical of nomads."[12] He offers no evidence of these nomadic legal arrangements, for no such evidence exists. He goes on to say that "Unlike the CH [Code Hammurabi], for example, the OT laws are still strongly marked by the nomadic view of property, which is characterised by being centered on the group rather than on the individual and so pays less attention to the property of the individual."[13] The less intelligent liberal can then defend his antinomian rejection of Old Testament law by saying that Israel's law was nomadic, having nothing to do with the modern world. The more clever liberal is less direct in his defense of antinomianism. He can argue that the non-nomadic character of biblical law testifies to a much later date of the authorship of the Pentateuch, thereby denying the Mosaic authorship and calling into question the continuing authority of everything in it, including the law.[14]

---

11. *Ibid.*, ch. 3.

12. Hans Jochen Boecker, *Law and the Administration of Justice in the Old Testament and Ancient East*, translated by Jeremy Moiser (Minnesota, Minneapolis: Augsburg, [1976] 1980), p. 28.

13. *Ibid.*, p. 167.

14. Boecker cites Max Weber and a 1927 book by A. Jepsen, both of whom denied any significant nomadic influence in Old Testament law. *Ibid.*, pp. 141-43. Boecker never clearly states which view of "Israelite nomadism" he holds, pro or con, which

An Eschatology of Victory

The people's economic contributions in constructing the tabernacle served as a ritual means for them to testify to an eschatology of victory. First, their craftsmanship was an affirmation of permanence. Second, their labor on the tabernacle was an affirmation of history. Each man's contribution would be seen by later generations and be appreciated, so long as the community retained its covenantal faithfulness to God. Those who would come later would look back and be thankful to those who had gone before. Finally, the tabernacle would replace the places of worship in the various cities of Canaan. The Canaanites would surely be defeated — an affirmation of the coming military conquest of Canaan. God would bring judgment against their enemies. This pointed to God as cosmic Judge, the fourth aspect of the biblical covenant.[15]

The tabernacle was important in reinforcing the doctrine of the covenant. This covenant joined the tribes together into one people. The covenant also extended through time, linking the fathers in the wilderness with the sons who would occupy the promised land. The covenant meant *continuity over time*, point five of the biblical covenant,[16] and the tabernacle symbolized this future-orientation.

The importance of symbols for society should not be disregarded. Symbols will always exist; the issue is not "symbols vs. no symbols"; rather it is a question of *which* symbols and *whose* symbols. Symbols are an inescapable concept, whether linguistic, musical, architectural, or whatever. Men need to sacrifice something of value in order to affirm their deeply felt commitments. Men do not choose wedding rings made of iron or brass to give to their wives. If they are committed to orthodox worship, they should prefer beautiful buildings to churches that resemble large shoe boxes.

Architecture and Culture

Architecture is closely linked to culture. The tabernacle revealed the centrality of the covenant in Hebrew culture. It was in terms of

---

is typical of someone who has read far more than he can digest intellectually — to the extent that liberal Old Testament studies can be digested intellectually at all. Generally, they are fit only for ingestion and rapid regurgitation in doctoral dissertations and journal articles. It never ceases to amaze me how readily liberal theologians return to their regurgitations.

15. Sutton, *That You May Prosper*, ch. 4.

16. *Ibid.*, ch. 5.

their confidence in this covenant that they subsequently constructed the other institutions of godly culture. The Israelites began with the tabernacle, for it was the place of God's special presence.

In New Testament times, there is no need to build just one majestic structure as a central point of cultural focus. Since the time of Christ's resurrection, the law has been written on the hearts of the faithful (Heb. 8:10; 10:16-18). People no longer need to journey to Jerusalem in order to worship; they worship the Father in spirit and in truth (John 4:23). The law is not written on stone tablets, nor do copies rest in the Ark of the Covenant. There has been a permanent *decentralization of authority, worship, and culture* in New Testament times.

This requirement of ecclesiastical decentralization in the New Testament era was recognized by Protestants of the sixteenth century, but they did not fully comprehend the importance of the tabernacle principle for the emotional and spiritual life of the families that built churches in local communities. They did not understand how fundamental to every culture is an economics of sacrifice. Men need to affirm and symbolize the permanence of their religious vision of the present and its links to the future. One of the problems with Protestant architecture during the Reformation was the denial by Protestant leaders of the legitimacy of the cathedrals of Europe. The reformers often displayed a self-conscious rejection of the legitimacy of architectural beauty and community economic sacrifice. The drab surroundings of the Protestant churches, especially in the seventeenth century, denied the eschatology of victory held by many of them. The need for sacrifice was sublimated and transferred to business concerns, charity, and affairs external to the affairs of the institutional churches. This led to historically unprecedented economic growth, but also to social and political instability. The brief reign of Oliver Cromwell, after all, was followed by the restoration to the English throne of Charles II, not by some Puritan republic. Economic growth continued to disrupt traditional social class relationships in Puritan New England.[17]

The economic and geographical mobility of modern capitalist society has also worked against the classical ideal of aesthetic perma-

---

17. Gary North, "From Medieval Economics to Indecisive Pietism: Second-Generation Preaching in New England, 1661-1690," *Journal of Christian Reconstruction*, VI (Summer 1979), pp. 144-50: "Status and Social Mobility." North, "From Covenant to Contract: Pietism and Secularism in Puritan New England, 1691-1720," *ibid.*, VI (Winter 1979-80), pp. 175-77. For a summary, see Gary North, *Puritan Economic Experiments* (Tyler, Texas: Institute for Christian Economics, 1988), pp. 50-54.

nence. A cathedral is very expensive. If it is constructed in a central city, it will soon find itself surrounded by very a different economic and social environment. A cathedral could be constructed in some distant rural region, but that would not serve the needs of worshippers. Any site within a two-hours' drive or train ride from a central city could become surrounded by urban decay within two generations.[18] In this sense, the modern world has become a tabernacle society rather than a temple society. Cathedrals are not designed, as the tabernacle was, as a prefabricated mobile construction project.

Regional Splendor

The church is both local and international. It is bound to local historical circumstances at any stage in history, yet it is always international because it is linked to eternity. There is a tendency within Protestantism to ignore the international and eternal aspects of the church. Protestant pastors often enjoy building large, fancy places of worship, for these testify to the influence of the pastor as a builder. Seldom do these churches reflect long-lasting architectural standards. Architects display little concern with architectural manifestations of the church as a force to be reckoned with over long periods of time at every level of society. Too often the architects selected by churches are deeply humanistic and governed by aesthetic standards that are openly rebellious against beauty. They are committed to an architecture of self-conscious ugliness.[19] Beauty is far more objective than something in the eye of the human beholder; beauty is in the eye of the Cosmic Beholder. Architects symbolically deny the Cosmic Beholder by rebelling against all permanent standards of beauty.

Because of the fragmenting of religious denominations, the economic resources necessary for constructing great cathedrals have not appeared in the twentieth century. The large, mainline denominations that might be able to afford to build them no longer bother. Central denominational bureaucracies are far more likely to give money to revolutionary causes or bureaucracy-expanding causes. Meanwhile, the smaller denominations concentrate on missions or other spiritual ventures.

There is no architectural representation of the majesty of God that competes today with the majesty of the State. This statist majesty

---

18. This is exactly what happened to the most grandiose of all American cathedral projects, the Episcopalians' Church of St. John the Divine in New York City.

19. Tom Wolfe, *From Bauhaus to Our House* (New York: Farrar Straus Giroux, 1981).

is anything but beautiful. There is a grim, ugly architectural style that is common to government buildings throughout the West: huge stones, few windows, marble or imitation marble. These make men feel insignificant. The buildings dwarf people. This style was pioneered in ancient imperial Rome. A similar theology of Empire undergirds today's structures.

The Soviet Union is the most self-conscious empire we have seen in modern times. In the decades following the Revolution, the Soviets produced grand monuments to poor taste. Malcolm Muggeridge's autobiography recalls his stay in Moscow's National Hotel during the 1930's as a reporter for Britain's *Manchester Guardian*. "The decor was in heavy marble and gilt, rather like the stations in the Moscow underground [subway—G.N.], then under construction, and to become a tourist show-place. Once, sitting with Mirsky in the hotel lounge, I remarked upon its excruciating taste. Yes, he agreed, it was pretty ghastly, but it expressed the sense of what a luxury hotel should be like in the mind of someone who had only stared in at one through plate-glass windows from the cold, inhospitable street outside. This, he said, was the key to all the régime's artistic products — the long turgid novels, the lifeless portraits and landscapes in oils, the gruesome People's neo-Gothic architecture, the leaden conservatory concerts and creaking ballet. Culturally, it was all of a piece. There is no surer way of preserving the worst aspects of bourgeois style than liquidating the bourgeoisie. . . ."[20]

Restoring Cooperation

The theological and institutional fragmentation of the West's churches is visible today. The original ecumenical impulse of Christianity has dimmed. We should expect a future revival to bring new unity, for the church is now visibly at war with humanist empires, as it was from Christ's day to Constantine's. A revival is more likely to unify Christians than split them, for there is a visible, threatening common enemy. Thus, we should expect to see a new ecumenism of Bible-believing people to rival and offset the collectivist ecumenism of modernism. It will be a bottom-up ecumenicism, not a top-down bureaucratic ecumenism.[21]

---

20. Malcolm Muggeridge, *Chronicles of Wasted Time: The Green Stick* (New York: Morrow, 1973), p. 245.

21. Gary North, *Healer of the Nations: Biblical Blueprints for Foreign Relations* (Ft. Worth, Texas: Dominion Press, 1987), ch. 11.

Thus, rather than expecting huge national cathedrals (a symbol of nationalism) or international cathedrals (a symbol of ecclesiastical empire), we should expect to see new buildings that coordinate the activities of various regional Christian groups. They will have to be functional yet magisterial. Instead of the sports arenas — modern man's urban equivalent of the Roman arenas — we will see artistic, educational, and meeting centers. They will not be primarily denominational, but oriented toward dominion activities. They will represent the activism of Christian civilization, not of the church narrowly defined.

Churches may also build common structures in various regions, comparable in sacrifice to the Mormon temples we find in many cities throughout the world. They will reflect the "best" that a denomination's regional efforts can produce. We will also see national and international architectural efforts, both secular and ecclesiastical. There will be regional, national, and international architectural manifestations of the majesty of God on earth. But there will not be a single center, as there was in Israel, for God has decentralized sacrifice and therefore His kingdom.

Such is my prophecy. Yet the very decentralization of Christian culture is the would-be prophet's stumbling-stone. The freedom that Christianity provides invariably unleashes human creativity that defies categorization in advance. What is most significant architecturally is the stylistic freedom that Christian civilization offers within the overall constraints of finances and the restored image of God in redeemed man. What is far less important is the accuracy of the prophecy.

Conclusion

Local churches should embody visible elements of personal sacrifice. Modern concepts of long-term debt have reduced the psychological burden of present sacrifice, but long-term uncertainty and the threat of debt servitude have accompanied the increase in church indebtedness. The medieval churches sometimes took centuries to construct, calling forth the sacrifices and talents of many generations. Modern congregations build smaller, less beautiful, more efficient structures, borrow heavily from fractional reserve banks to do so, or sell usurious long-term bonds to church members,[22] and then

---

22. Gary North, "Stewardship, Investment, and Usury: Financing the Kingdom of God," Appendix 3 in R. J. Rushdoony, *Institutes of Biblical Law* (Nutley, New Jersey: Craig Press, 1973).

take a generation to pay off the debt. The medieval Christians were
closer to the truth in this area of worship. They understood what the
Old Testament Hebrews had been told by God: that *holy wastefulness*
has its place in godly worship, as the tithe of celebration indicates
(Deut. 14:23-29). Construction costs per square foot should not be
the primary factor in constructing every place of worship. An eschatology of victory should be reflected in an architecture of majesty and
permanence.

32

BLOOD MONEY, NOT HEAD TAX

And the LORD spake unto Moses, saying, When thou takest the sum of the children of Israel after their number, then shall they give every man a ransom for his soul unto the LORD, when thou numberest them; that there be no plague among them, when thou numberest them. This they shall give, every one that passeth among them that are numbered, half a shekel after the shekel of the sanctuary: (a shekel is twenty gerahs:) an half shekel shall be the offering of the LORD. Every one that passeth among them that are numbered, from twenty years old and above, shall give an offering unto the LORD. The rich shall not give more, and the poor shall not give less than half a shekel, when they give an offering unto the LORD, to make an atonement for your souls. And thou shalt take the atonement money of the children of Israel, and shalt appoint it for the service of the tabernacle of the congregation; that it may be a memorial unto the children of Israel before the LORD, to make an atonement for your souls (Ex. 30:11-16).

The people needed a covering, an atonement before God. Why? The text does not say, but other texts tell us. This was a mustering of the fighting men of Israel. Moses counted them as they left Egypt, on the assumption that they would soon enter into a war against Canaan. Israel had left Egypt as an army: "And it came to pass the selfsame day, that the LORD did bring the children of Israel out of the land of Egypt by their armies" (Ex. 12:51). So God told Moses to number this assembly of tribal armies: "Take ye the sum of all the congregation of the children of Israel, after their families, by the house of their fathers, with the number of their names, every male by their polls; From twenty years old and upward, all that are able to go forth to war in Israel: thou and Aaron shall number them by their armies" (Num. 1:2-3). After the plague that God brought on Israel for their fornication with the Midianite women, God ordered another census. "And it came to pass after the plague, that the LORD spake unto Moses and unto Eleazar the son of Aaron the priest, saying,

Take the sum of all the congregation of the children of Israel, from twenty years old and upward, throughout their fathers' house, all that are able to go to war in Israel" (Num. 26:1-2). Joshua numbered them again a generation later for the same reason (Josh. 8:10).

A nation has a legitimate need for statistics on its military capability. It must count the costs of war. "Or what king, going to make war against another king, sitteth not down first, and consulteth whether he be able with ten thousand to meet him that cometh against him with twenty thousand? Or else, while the other is yet a great way off, he sendeth an ambassage, and desireth conditions of peace" (Luke 14:31-32). This is why the military commander of Israel numbered the people before he took them into battle.

Bloodshed and Blood Covering

The people needed an atonement before they marched into battle. The shedding of man's blood must be placed under tight covenantal limits. This is why the numbering of the circumcised males of Israel required their payment of atonement money. This numbering was only to be done in preparation for a war.

One thing is certain about this passage: *it does not have anything to do with a civil tax.* The State is in no way responsible for taking money from anyone for the purpose of making an atonement for his soul. Making atonement as God's representative is a priestly function, not a kingly function. The recipient of the funds was to be the tabernacle, not the civil government.

The atonement or covering was required by God whenever the adult males were numbered prior to military conflict. If they refused to pay, God threatened them with a plague. When David decided to number the people of Israel despite the fact that no war was imminent, his advisor Joab warned him not to do it (II Sam. 24:3). David refused to listen, and insisted that the census be taken. When he realized that this assertion of his sovereignty was wrong, he admitted his sin to God. The seer Gad was told by God to inform David that he would be given three options: seven years of famine for the nation, three months of fleeing before his enemies, or a plague. David asked God to make the decision, and God sent the plague in which 70,000 people died (II Sam. 24:15).[1]

---

1. The passage says that God was angry with Israel, so He "moved David against them" by numbering them (II Sam. 24:1). David could have brought the judgment of God on himself had he been willing to accept the curse of fleeing three months from his enemies, but he left the judgment up to God.

If the census had been a normal source of revenue for the civil government, it would have been an annual event. It was not an annual event; taking the national census was strictly limited to wartime, and required an atonement payment to the tabernacle. By acting as though the State had the authority to take a census at any time, David sinned against God. To "number" (*paqad*) the army meant to muster the troops for battle. James Jordan comments: "The word is also used throughout the prophets to mean 'visit' or 'punish.' There are other words in Hebrew which refer to numbering in the sense of counting up or adding up, as Exodus 30:12 aptly illustrates ("When you take a *sum* . . . to *muster* them"). Thus, the numbering spoken of here in Exodus 30 is not a mere counting census, but *a visitation or judgment designed to see who is on the LORD's side*. Those who pass over into the camp of the mustered men are thereby declaring themselves to be in the army of God, as opposed to the army of Satan. When the LORD comes, he comes to visit and punish, to muster all men and see who has and who has not passed over into his army."[2] Jordan therefore concludes that this was not an annual census.

Jordan argues that it was *the presence of God in their midst* that threatened those who had not been covered by the payment of the atonement money. God walks in the midst of the army (Deut. 23:14), so the camp must be holy. "The fact that the money is used for the upkeep of the Tabernacle/Temple indicates a connection between the environment of the Temple (God's House) and that of the army camp (God's War Camp). Both are especially holy, and thus especially threatening to sinful man. Under the Old Covenant, each had to be especially sanctified, and the men who entered each had to be especially sanctified. . . ."[3]

Jordan also points out that in the Old Testament, *holy war was a priestly function*. Torched cities were called "whole burnt sacrifices" (Deut. 13:16; Jud. 1:17, in Hebrew). During a holy war, the soldiers became temporary priests by taking a Nazarite vow.[4] "This is all to say that the rendering of specific judgments is a sabbatical and priestly function, not a kingly one. The kingly function in the Bible is in the area of leading, cultivating, and shepherding, especially through the skillful serving of one's subordinates (Mark 10:42-45).

---

2. James B. Jordan, *The Law of the Covenant: An Exposition of Exodus 21-23* (Tyler, Texas: Institute for Christian Economics, 1984), p. 227.

3. *Ibid.*, p. 229.

4. *Ibid.*, p. 231.

The sword of the state executes according to the judgments rendered by the priests. (In the New Covenant age, every believer is a priest, just as the Old Covenant believers became priests by taking the Nazarite vow. In our system, the priests render judgment by sitting on a *jury*, and then the state executes the judgment.)"[5]

The point should be clear: the covering or atonement payment of Exodus 30 has nothing to do with the civil government. It is not a tax at all. "Thus, the military duty is priestly, and a duty of every believer-priest. Both Church and state are involved in it, since the Church must say whether the war is just and holy, and the state must organize the believer-priests for battle. The mustering of the host for a census is, then, not a 'civil' function as opposed to an ecclesiastical one, and the atonement money of Exodus 30 is not a poll tax, as some have alleged."[6]

Jordan is being polite (or cautious) by refraining from mentioning the target of his exposition, but readers may not fully understand the nature of the theological problem unless they know the specifics of the debate. Jordan's target is R. J. Rushdoony.

Rushdoony's Theory of the Civil Head Tax

There has been considerable confusion about this in recent years because of Rushdoony's insistence that this atonement payment became a civil head tax after the construction of the tabernacle. "It was used to maintain the civil order after the tabernacle (the throne room and palace of God's government) was built."[7] He offers no evidence for this assertion. On the face of it, it seems utterly implausible. How did such a shift in the locus of taxing sovereignty take place? How did the State become the recipient of an atonement payment, thereby converting a ransom paid to God through the priesthood into a head tax collected by the State? *This would implicitly transfer sovereignty from the church to the State*, a procedure totally at odds with everything else Rushdoony has written about illegitimate State power.

He correctly observes that this payment was an atonement payment to the tabernacle which was paid by those going into battle, and he cites other commentators to support his point — a relatively

---

5. *Ibid.*, pp. 231-32.
6. *Ibid.*, p. 232.
7. R. J. Rushdoony, *The Institutes of Biblical Law* (Nutley, New Jersey: Craig Press, 1973), p. 50.

noncontroversial point.[8] Problem number one: *On what basis did the State become the recipient of this atonement payment?* He tries to solve this problem by arguing that the tabernacle was as much a civil center as an ecclesiastical center. Civil taxes, he insists, were brought to God at His throne room, the tabernacle. "The sanctuary was thus the civil center of Israel and no less religious for that fact."[9] Thus, a "poll tax," as he calls it, was always brought to the tabernacle.[10] He then stretches the argument to conclude that in Israel, "The basic tax was the poll or head tax (Ex. 30:11-16), which had to be the same for all men."[11]

Thus, what is explicitly stated in the Bible to be an atonement payment made to the tabernacle, one which most commentators (including Rushdoony) believe was a payment associated with a military census taken immediately prior to a war, later became, in Rushdoony's interpretation, a normal revenue collection device for the State — indeed, the *only* source of legitimate revenue for the State. "*First*, the basic civil tax in Scripture, the only tax, is the poll or head tax, paid by every man twenty years of age and older (Ex. 30:11-16)."[12] "Its purpose was to provide for civil atonement, i.e., the covering or protection of civil government. Every male twenty years old or older was required to pay this tax to be protected by God the King in His theocratic government of Israel. This tax was thus a civil and religious duty (but not an ecclesiastical one)."[13]

Problem number two: *When did the State become the recipient of these atonement payments?* He argues that the head tax "was used originally for the construction of the tabernacle (Ex. 38:25-28)."[14] The key word here is *originally*. He implies that after the construction of the tabernacle, the money went to the State to finance its day-to-day operations. He does not explain anywhere in his writings just exactly how the day-to-day expenses of the entire civil government — local, tribal, and national — could have been financed by this one tax payment, one which could be legitimately collected only prior to a war. He does not explain this obvious difficulty because it obviously cannot be explained — not without concluding that Israel was a permanent warfare State. He does not want to make such a conclusion, so he simply ignores the problem.

---

8. *Ibid.*, p. 277.
9. *Ibid.*, p. 281.
10. *Idem.*
11. *Ibid.*, p. 492.
12. *Ibid.*, p. 510.
13. *Ibid.*, p. 719.
14. *Ibid.*, p. 50.

Why does Rushdoony make this unwarranted leap from an aton-ing tabernacle payment during wartime to a permanent payment to the tabernacle as a civil tax? Why doesn't he see the enormous threat to liberty involved in making the State a tax-collector in the name of atonement? Why does he fail to recognize that if this was the only le-gitimate tax in Old Testament Israel, that it would have created either an ecclesiocracy or a political tyranny? If the atonement pay-ment was in fact a tax, one collected by the tabernacle's agents, meaning Aaronic priests, to be doled out as they saw fit to the civil authorities, then the church would inevitably be at the top of a single civil pyramid. On the other hand, if the civil magistrates possessed the authority to enter the tabernacle and collect the atonement pay-ment, then the State would be at the top. Yet Rushdoony always argues that there is no single church-State pyramid of power in a biblical commonwealth; church and State are separate sovereign au-thorities under God and God's law.

Rushdoony's Unstated Problem

His unstated problem is that he does not want to face an unpleas-ant reality: the Old Testament never specifically says anything about what is proper for civil taxation, except in Samuel's warning against the king's collection of as great a percentage of a person's income as 10 percent (I Sam. 8). This is James Jordan's conclusion.[15] It is also mine. If defenders of biblical law cannot point to any specific biblical laws that govern civil taxation, an apparent gap in their whole her-meneutic is exposed for all to see.

Rushdoony prefers not to face this problem directly, although he clearly recognizes that it exists. "Commentaries and Bible dic-tionaries on the whole cite no law governing taxation. One would assume, from reading them, that no system of taxation existed in an-cient Israel, and that the Mosaic law did not speak on the subject."[16] If the Bible is truly silent here, then the theonomist is placed in the seemingly embarrassing position of claiming that the Old Testament's law-order has specific guidelines and answers for all so-cial and civil policy, yet he is unable to find explicit rules governing what has become the central issue of civil sovereignty in the twenti-eth century, namely, the legal sanction of tax collection. Yet apart from Samuel's critique of the king's collecting a tithe, the only

---

15. Jordan, *Law of the Covenant*, p. 239.
16. Rushdoony, *Institutes*, p. 281.

references to compulsory payments in ancient Israel are the various tithes and sacrifices — clearly ecclesiastical — and the census atonement money of Exodus 30.

To overcome this embarrassment, Rushdoony offers a unique theory of Old Testament civil order and its relation to the taxing authority. "This failure to discern any tax law is due to the failure to recognize the nature of Israel's civil order. God as King of Israel ruled from His throne room in the tabernacle, and to Him the taxes were brought. Because of the common error of viewing the tabernacle as an exclusively or essentially 'religious,' i.e., *ecclesiastical* center, there is a failure to recognize that it was indeed a *religious, civil* center. In terms of Biblical law, the state, home, school, and every other agency must be no less religious than the church. The sanctuary was thus the civil center of Israel and no less religious for that fact."[17]

A Question of Sovereignty

He systematically refuses to explore the startling implications of this theory of the tabernacle as the only place where the Israelites paid their taxes to God as King of Israel. The issue is clearly not the "religiousness" of the civil order, for as he correctly says, all of society's institutions are equally religious — State, home, school business, etc. But this is not to say that all institutions are equally covenantal, for only three institutions — family, church, and State — bear the marks of the covenant, namely, the legitimate imposition of a self-maledictory oath.[18]

Church and State collect their lawful payments from those who are covenanted to each institution, though not necessarily to both institutions: churches collect tithes from church members, and civil governments collect taxes from those under their jurisdiction. This has nothing to do with the question of the "religiousness" of either or both of these God-ordained covenant institutions. For example, private businesses are not entitled to collect taxes from anyone, except as agents of the civil government. Yet according to Rushdoony, businesses are inescapably religious institutions.

Rushdoony's argument throughout his career has been that all of life is inescapably religious. Following Van Til, he argues that all men are either covenant-keepers or covenant-breakers. "Neutral

---

17. *Idem.*

18. Gary North, *The Sinai Strategy: Economics and the Ten Commandments* (Tyler, Texas: Institute for Christian Economics, 1986), ch. 3.

man does not exist. Man is either a covenant-keeper or a covenant-breaker, either obeying God in faith, or in revolt against God as a would-be god."[19] Everything man does is therefore religious. This being the case, an appeal to religiousness as such cannot solve the crucial question he is dealing with: *To which institution or institutions has God delegated the lawful sovereignty to collect His taxes and His tithes?* God was surely both King and Priest in Israel, but that is not the issue here. The issue is: Did He delegate to a single institution the lawful sovereignty to collect payments owed to Him in His capacity as both King and Priest?

It is obvious that King Uzziah violated the temple by going into it to burn incense. God struck him down with Old Testament leprosy as a punishment (II Chron. 26:16-23). Rushdoony uses this example to defend the institutional separation of church and state.[20] Speaking of priest and king, he writes, "The two offices were not to have an immanent union but only a transcendental one."[21] But to allow one of these offices to collect payments owed by people to the other is un-questionably declaring an immanent (earthly) union of the two offices, as surely as Uzziah's attempt to offer incense in the temple was such a declaration.

The State is not to collect payments owed to the tabernacle for atonement purposes. Similarly, the priesthood is not to collect taxes owed to the civil government. The fact that the tabernacle, and later the temple, was the civil center of Israel was manifested symbolically by the fact that the Ark of the Covenant inside the holy of holies was the center of all Israel, and that inside the Ark were the two tablets (tables or copies)[22] of God's law. God's law was the center of life in Israel, and God was present with His law in the holy of holies. This has nothing to do with the institutional details of tax collecting or tithe collecting; it has everything to do with the inescapable religiousness of all life.

---

19. Rushdoony, "Implications for Psychology," in Gary North (ed.), *Foundations of Christian Scholarship: Essays in the Van Til Perspective* (Vallecito, California: Ross House Books, 1976), p. 43.

20. R. J. Rushdoony, *Foundations of Social Order: Studies in the Creeds and Councils of the Early Church* (Fairfax, Virginia: Thoburn Press, [1969] 1978), p. 70.

21. *Idem.*

22. Meredith G. Kline, *The Structure of Biblical Authority* (rev. ed.; Grand Rapids, Michigan: Eerdmans, 1972), pp. 123-24.

Ed Powell's Modification

Ed Powell's essay, "God's Plan of Taxation," is an extension of Rushdoony's position, which is why Rushdoony allowed it to appear in his only co-authored book. There is one interesting addition that Powell makes, however. He quite correctly points out that the Levites were not subject to military conscription (Num. 1:47-49), and therefore they were not required to pay the so-called poll tax. Rushdoony had insisted in the *Institutes*: "It was paid by Levites and all others."[23] Powell argues that the Levites were not part of the civil order, and so were not required to pay any tax to the State, and this was the only tax the State could lawfully collect, according to both Rushdoony and Powell. "This tax went solely for the purpose of supporting the state, and only those who were members of the civil order because of their military service paid it."[24] Thus, in Powell's version of political theory, civil citizenship is based on two things, the payment of taxes and participation in the military. He clearly recognizes the connection between the "tax" of Exodus 30:11-16 and military service. Would he conclude that in New Testament times, ordained ministers of the gospel should not be allowed to vote or be required to pay taxes? If he denies this, then would he then conclude that they should be subject to military conscription?

What Powell does not recognize is central to Jordan's argument and mine: *by becoming a Nazarite during a holy war, the soldier in Old Covenant Israel became a temporary priest.* It was the army's very position as a temporary priesthood that made the payment of blood money mandatory if the soldiers were to avoid the plague when God came into the camp. Thus, the requirement to pay blood money to the tabernacle had nothing to do with the supposed status of the Levites as being outside the civil order. It had everything to do with the need for atonement by those who were temporarily set aside (made holy) for God's special purposes during a war.

The Rushdoony-Powell position leads to innumerable problems, especially in extending into New Testament times the erroneous principle of the head tax as the sole means of State financing. I have dwelt at some length on this explanation of Exodus 30:11-16 only be-

---

23. Rushdoony, *Institutes*, p. 50.

24. Rushdoony and Powell, *Tithing and Dominion* (Fairfax, Virginia: Thoburn Press, 1979), p. 64. The irony here is that it was my "freewill" offering to Pastor Robert Thoburn's church in Fairfax, Virginia, that financed the publication of this book.

cause Rushdoony's *Institutes* presented the preliminary model of the Christian Reconstruction position. His few remarks on taxation are found in the sections of the *Institutes* that attempt to explain this passage. Thus, by systematically restricting any discussion of biblical taxation to the supposed civil head tax of the Old Testament, Rushdoony has eliminated the possibility of discussing such alternative tax policies as the gasoline tax used exclusively for local roadways, or income taxes lower than 10 percent, or sales taxes lower than 10 percent. He has made the head tax as the sole source of civic revenue, a conclusion unwarranted by the text and unworkable in practice.

Conclusion

The atonement money required from each adult male in Israel prior to a holy war had nothing to do with civil taxation. It was a unique assessment that took place only during the military census, and the taking of such a census was authorized by God only when war threatened the commonwealth. The State was not allowed to conduct such a census under any other circumstances (II Sam. 24). For the civil magistrate to have collected such a blood covering payment as a civil tax would have been an abomination. To have made it the only civil tax in Israel, to be collected on an annual or other regular basis, would have brought the wrath of God on the State. The collection of this mandatory payment was exclusively a priestly function. Thus, any discussion of the methods and limits of lawful civil taxation in Old Testament Israel must be based on passages other than Exodus 30:11-16.

R. J. Rushdoony's discussion of the atonement money as a civil head tax has been widely quoted by those who are not his followers on any other issue, especially those involved in the tax-rebellion movement, a movement which Rushdoony has repudiated. His work on biblical law has attracted British Israelites or "Identity" cultists who are the backbone of the tax rebellion movement. They seek a biblical argument to justify their refusal to pay the income tax. They argue that only a head tax is legitimate. But any appeal to Exodus 30:11-16 to defend such a position is illegitimate. This required payment was not a head tax or any other kind of tax; it was a blood covering for warriors-become-Nazarite priests who were about to go into battle.

33

SABBATH REST VS. AUTONOMY

Six days shall work be done, but on the seventh day there shall be to you an holy day, a sabbath of rest to the LORD: whosoever doeth work therein shall be put to death (Ex. 35:2).

God's work of creation is the archetype for man: six days of labor and a day of rest, or ceasing from our normal labors. If God rested the seventh day, then we must rest one day in seven. Originally, Adam's day of rest was his first full day of life. His firstday was God's seventhday. He was to have honored his position as a creature by resting the first day of the week, thereby acknowledging God's prior work as the foundation of his life and rest. Adam pretended that his autonomous labor would bring forth fruits. He pretended that he had not received everything as a gift from God. He therefore imitated God's week, beginning his rebellion on the first day of his week. Because of Adam's sin of autonomy—playing God—God imposed a temporary six-and-one pattern for man's week until the resurrection of Jesus Christ. We now are required as individuals to structure our work weeks in terms of a one-and-six resurrection pattern. God has restored to His church the original pattern.[1]

Sabbath and Sanctions

This chapter is really more of a summary of the material that I presented in Chapter 4 and Appendix A of *The Sinai Strategy*. This passage is an extension of Exodus 20:8-11, the law of the sabbath. It specifies the sanction: capital punishment.

God's designation of a specific sanction is crucial. Dispensationalist Roy Aldrich reminds us: "If the Ten Commandments of the law

---

1. Gary North, *The Dominion Covenant: Genesis* (2nd ed.; Tyler, Texas: Institute for Christian Economics, 1987), ch. 5: "God's Week and Man's Week."

are still binding then all of the penalties must remain the same. The death penalties should be imposed for Sabbath-breaking, idolatry, adultery, rebellion against parents, etc. To change the penalty of a law means to abolish that law. A law without a penalty is an anomaly. A law with its penalty abolished becomes only good advice."[2] The fourth commandment was basic to the Decalogue. Thus, this case law specified the appropriate sanction: *execution*. This was reaffirmed by God in His specially revealed requirement that the stick-gatherer be stoned to death (Num. 15).

What I have argued previously is that this capital sanction was removed from God's law when the locus of *this particular law's* enforcement shifted from the civil government to the individual conscience. This is not to say that sabbath rest was abolished by God. It was transformed by the resurrection of Jesus Christ, which is why Christians honor the principle by resting on the Lord's Day, the first day of the week. The *individual Christian* who operates as a covenantal agent *directly under God* becomes the sole earthly agent for enforcing the law of the sabbath. There is no longer any civil sanction attached to it. (There was never any ecclesiastical sanction mentioned in the Old Testament.) Paul writes that some men regard all days the same; other men regard one day as special; each individual is to obey his conscience in this matter (Rom. 14:5). Thus, the transfer of earthly sovereignty in enforcing the sabbath rest principle necessarily removed the capital sanction — the only sanction specified in the Old Testament. This is not to say that this law no longer holds. God will enforce whatever sanctions He believes are appropriate in history and on judgment day. But for all practical *judicial* purposes, the fourth commandment has been transformed from a civil law into good personal advice.

To argue otherwise is necessarily to call for the re-establishment of the death penalty for sabbath violators. To appeal to the Old Testament — meaning the fourth commandment — necessarily also involves an appeal to this passage, for it specifies the appropriate sanction. Again, let me repeat the theme of this entire book:

No sanctions, no laws; no laws, no social order; no social order, no civilization; no civilization, no kingdom of God in church history.

---

2. Roy L. Aldrich, "Causes for Confusion of Law and Grace," *Bibliotheca Sacra*, Vol. 116 (July 1959), p. 226.

Sanctions and Sanctification

Let me repeat what I said in the Introduction: "What I argue throughout this book is really quite simple: *we can legitimately assess the importance of any biblical law by examining its case-law sanction.* This simple and seemingly obvious principle of jurisprudence has been implicitly denied for almost two millennia by the church. There has been an ancient tradition on the part of Christian commentators of appealing selectively to Old Testament laws whenever convenient in moral arguments, but almost never to the God-specified sanctions." Exodus 35:2 seldom appears in any sabbatarian's discussion of how important the sabbath remains, and what we must do in order to honor it. This is wholly illegitimate exegetically, and it has led to the accusation by consistent critics that Christians who uphold "the moral law of God" apart from God's specified civil sanctions are hypocritical, that they want all the moral benefits of theocracy without any of the embarrassing theocratic sanctions.

The defenders of the "moral law only" approach inescapably have to agree in principle with dispensationalist Aldrich: "It should be remembered that the Ten Commandments were part of the legal system of Israel as a theocracy. In this Mosaic economy 'every transgression and disobedience received a just recompence of reward' (Heb. 2:2b). A law without a penalty is only good advice. The Mosaic penalty for violation of each of the first four commandments was death. For certain overt violations of all the other commandments the penalty was death. Only a theocracy could enforce such laws. No government, or denomination, or society even pretends to enforce them today. This is as it should be for they were given only to Israel and have long been abolished."[3] They are for the general law of God but not the specific sanctions. They argue for a *general theocracy* — a world controlled by God, who judges it continually and finally — yet they deny *specific theocracy,* meaning civil governments that are legitimately governed in terms of Old Testament laws and their God-revealed sanctions.

What I have argued for many years is this: *the covenantal standard of progressive sanctification applies to all human institutions,* not just to the hearts, minds, and actions of regenerate believers. The Bible unquestionably teaches the concept of progressive sanctification which operates in the lives of redeemed individuals. This doctrine informs

---

3. Aldrich, "Has the Mosaic Law Been Abolished?" *ibid.*, Vol. 116 (Oct. 1959), p. 332.

us that as redeemed people self-consciously conform themselves progressively to the requirement of God's law as they mature in the faith, they progressively approach (but never achieve in history) the perfect humanity (but never the divinity) of the incarnate Jesus Christ.[4] Because God brings historical judgment on collectives, meaning human institutions (Deut. 28), especially the three covenant institutions — church, State, and family — progressive sanctification also applies to groups. It is the basis of worldwide dominion.[5]

No Salvation by Works

God's grace is the only basis of man's salvation, in the sense of healing (salve) as well as personal regeneration. Men cannot legitimately expect to work their way back into favor with God. Eternal life is by God's sovereign act of adoption (John 1:12). We are made true sons of God by means of adoption. Apart from this act of adoption, we remain *disinherited sons* through our covenantal (representative) father Adam.

The sabbath law was designed to remind man that he cannot work his way into a position of authority. To think that the works of man's hand are the basis of success, power, and prosperity is to adopt the religion of humanism, the forbidden religion in the Bible. God warned the people of Israel through Moses against vain imaginations regarding the basis of their wealth: "And thou say in thine heart, My power and the might of mine hand hath gotten me this wealth" (Deut. 8:17). God then warned them about the sanctions He would bring against them in history if they forgot this warning against the concept of man's autonomy:

> And it shall be, if thou do at all forget the LORD thy God, and walk after other gods, and serve them, and worship them, I testify against you this day that ye shall surely perish. As the nations which the LORD destroyeth before your face, so shall ye perish; because ye would not be obedient unto the voice of the LORD your God (Deut. 8:19-20).

Man is told that he owes his success to God. God gives him the original capital base that man possesses. Then, in response to man's

---

4. Gary North, *Unconditional Surrender: God's Program for Victory* (3rd ed.; Tyler, Texas: Institute for Christian Economics, 1988), pp. 66-72.

5. *Ibid.*, pp. 111-15. Cf. Gary North, *Dominion and Common Grace: The Biblical Basis of Progress* (Tyler, Texas: Institute for Christian Economics, 1987), ch. 5.

covenantal faithfulness — outward conformity to God's revealed law — God showers man with external, visible blessings. These blessings are designed to become a means of evangelism, both to individuals within the commonwealth and foreigners abroad.

> Behold, I have taught you statutes and judgments, even as the LORD my God commanded me, that ye should do so in the land whither ye go to possess it. Keep therefore and do them; for this is your wisdom and your understanding in the sight of the nations, which shall hear all these statutes, and say, Surely this great nation is a wise and understanding people. For what nation is there so great, who hath God so nigh unto them, as the LORD our God is in all things that we call upon him for? And what nation is there so great, that hath statutes and judgments so righteous as all this law, which I set before you this day? (Deut. 4:5-8).

God gave them the law of the sabbath in order to spare them. It was to remind them that they had been hard-pressed servants in Egypt. In the recapitulation of the Ten Commandments in Deuteronomy, this is the reason given for the sabbath: "And remember that thou wast a servant in the land of Egypt, and that the LORD thy God brought thee out thence through a mighty hand and by a stretched out arm: therefore the LORD thy God commanded thee to keep the sabbath day" (Deut. 5:15). They must give their human and animal servants a day off each week (v. 14). God was gracious in delivering them from bondage; they must also be gracious to those under their authority. This is the *hierarchical principle of God's grace*. It is appropriate that we find this principle clearly displayed in the second book of the Pentateuch, Exodus, the book that deals with hierarchy, authority, and deliverance.

The man who honors the sabbath by refusing to work at his calling publicly admits to himself and to those around him that he cannot work his way into prosperity, that is, into the favor of God. God requires him to rest one day in seven if he expects to receive long-term external blessings from God. But Old Testament law went beyond the mere promise of external blessings; it required the State to impose the ultimate civil sanction: execution. Execution is what will happen to the whole society if it disobeys God (Deut. 8:19-20); this is what also happens to individuals now if they disobey Him (Ex. 35:2). The covenantal sanction that was attached to the microcosm (the individual) reflected the covenantal sanction that was attached to the macrocosm (society). Men are not to imagine that they owe their wealth to the work of their own hands. They are to understand that their wealth has come through God's covenant of grace, one which has both types of sanction: blessing and cursing.

Conclusion

Those who want a detailed account of this case law can read the sections in *The Sinai Strategy*. The basic point for this study is that the sanction attached to this law was a civil sanction, and it was the ultimate civil sanction. All discussions regarding the continuing legitimacy of the Old Testament sabbath must henceforth begin with a full discussion of Exodus 35:2, and how it applies in the New Testament era. The capital sanction was fundamental to the law as originally given. No appeal to the various Old Testament passages relating to the sabbath can be taken literally if this one is conveniently ignored. The discussion must begin with Exodus 35:2.

The meaning of the sabbath law is clear: man must rest one day in seven. In the Old Testament, it was the last day of the work week, for the day of rest was a national testimony to the sabbath rest to come, the fulfillment of God's covenant promise of salvation and deliverance. This deliverance is wholly the gift of God. Man cannot save himself. Thus, the sabbath law was a testimony to a theological truth: salvation by grace and not by works of the law. The work of autonomous man's hands brings only death, this law affirms. The same is equally true for societies.

34

THE ABILITY TO TEACH

And he hath filled him [Bezaleel] with the spirit of God, in wisdom, in understanding, and in knowledge, and in all manner of workmanship; . . . And he hath put in his heart that he may teach, both he, and Aholiab . . . (Ex. 35:31, 34a).

God is the source of all wisdom and all technical skills. Human civilization is the result of the procession of God's Holy Spirit in time. There is continuity in human culture, generation to generation, only because there is continuity of the work of God's Spirit in time. God uses human instruments in order to achieve the progressive establishment of His kingdom in history. The kingdom of God is best described as the civilization of God. It is both heavenly and earthly. Architecture is certainly a visible aspect of God's earthly kingdom, and it points to the architecture of heaven. This was understood far better by medieval Christians than it is today. They also understood the need of personal apprenticeship as the best means of training men in building skills. As Christians' time perspective has shortened, so has their sense of architectural aesthetics. The aesthetic link between earth and heaven is not taken seriously by most evangelical Christians, as their church buildings reveal.[1]

It is significant that almost nothing remains of Israelite architecture. Neither the first nor second temple survived the invasions of Israel's enemies, nor did the king's palace. God destroyed all traces of Israelite monumental architecture because of their repeated rebellion. The Israelites lost continuity architecturally because they did not maintain continuity ethically.

---

1. The aesthetic link between earth and hell has been taken very seriously by satanists, as their record album and audio disk covers and posters reveal so blatantly.

From Discontinuity to Continuity

This public announcement by Moses regarding the Spirit's connection to the two young architects is a repetition of the assignment given to the young men by God (Ex. 31:1-6). In this case, however, it is specifically stated that God gave Bezaleel and Aholiab the desire and capacity to teach. They became God's temporal intermediaries, as surely as Noah had been. In both instances, someone had to serve as God's aesthetic vessel after the ordeal of water passage — the flood and the Red Sea — from wrath to grace. The leaven of Egypt was not to be brought into the land.

The fact that God specifically intervened in history to give these two young men the ability to design and execute plans for the tabernacle points to the non-evolutionary nature of the Hebrew experience in the wilderness. The Israelites were former slaves. They had all been assigned construction tasks in Egypt that were far less skilled than the requirements of careful craftsmanship necessary to construct an intricate, aesthetically awesome place of religious worship. They were brick-makers, not skilled artisans. But God did not wait for several generations to see His tabernacle built. His people did not rely on the borrowed technologies of Egypt or the surrounding cultures of Canaan in order to design and construct God's tabernacle. It was not to be constructed by means of a slave people's skills and in terms of a slave culture's liturgical preferences. God performed yet another miracle by granting these young men His spirit of competence.

A radical error of all humanistic outlines of human history is their dependence on a view of man which presupposes man's autonomy from God. They also presuppose an evolutionary history. Because he erroneously assumes that man was not created "overnight," the evolutionist also assumes that man's culture must have developed over long periods of time. Mankind as a collective whole supposedly creates culture over great periods of time. That which is *undeveloped culturally* — by the standards of a later, presumably higher culture — is seen as being *chronologically prior*. Step by step, the theory goes, mankind learned the arts of civilization. Long eons of time were required for this slow process of cultural development, and humanistic scholars grant to primitive men all the time thought to be necessary for cultural and technological development. Such is the myth of cultural Darwinism.

The Bible teaches another view of human progress. Civilization develops in terms of *ethics*, not in terms of the advent of private property and alienation (Rousseau and Marx), or sexual sublimation (Freud), or "challenge and response" (Toynbee), or voluntary contracts (Maine), or the "cunning of history" (Hegel), or the survival of the fittest (Spencer), or planning by a scientific elite (Lester Frank Ward), or the development of the *volk* (Nazism), or the construction of democratic institutions (the "new" American historians), or psychological self-realization (just about everyone else). The story of the Tower of Babel and the continuing testimony of the Cheops pyramid indicate that the early history of man was marked by cultural and technological *devolution*. Mankind began with remarkable mathematical[2] and technological skills that were subsequently lost.

Educational Capital

Adam and Eve lost the bulk of their computational abilities after the Fall. Adam had named the animals in the garden in less than one day; only after this task was completed did God give Eve to him (Gen. 2:19-23).[3] The life of man was shortened, forcing more frequent gaps in human knowledge, as each generation died off. To extend knowledge, over time, each generation must devote considerable quantities of scarce economic resources to the training of the next generation. There is an economic incentive in this, of course: the provisioning of one's heirs with income-producing skills so that one might be provided for in old age.

The education of one's heirs is required for the expansion of family capital over time. The familistic focus of the Bible inescapably calls men to educate their children (Deut. 6:6-7).[4] The passing down of precepts and skills takes time and effort. This is an investment in the future that pays returns not only in one's own lifetime, but also down through history. But like any investment, it requires that we forfeit present consumption and alternative investment possibilities in order to educate our children.

---

2. Giorgio de Santillana and Hertha von Dechend, *Hamlet's Mill: An Essay on Myth and the Frame of Time* (New York: Gambit, 1969); Peter Tomkins, *Secrets of the Great Pyramid* (New York: Harper Colophon, [1971] 1978).

3. Gary North, *The Dominion Covenant: Genesis* (Tyler, Texas: Institute for Christian Economics, 1982), ch. 7.

4. Robert L. Thoburn, *The Children Trap: Biblical Blueprints for Economics* (Ft. Worth, Texas: Dominion Press, 1986).

God openly intervened in history to bring the Israelites out of Egypt. But leading them out of Egypt was only the first phase of God's program of dominion. He also intended that they learn the skills of building a civilization. The radical discontinuity of the exodus from Egypt was to be followed by a radical discontinuity of conquest. Then *a long-term continuity of dominion* was to begin.

The Hebrews possessed a minimal educational inheritance. They had learned some construction skills in Egypt. But this inheritance could easily become a snare to them. They needed an *infusion of educational capital* before they could hope to extend the dominion covenant. Like a parent who educates his children in order to extend his own name in history—the family name, the family vision, and the family power—so God had to educate His people in every area of life. This included architecture and aesthetics.

The Need for Aesthetic Discontinuity

The Hebrews had been in bondage in Egypt. They had served as construction workers for at least a generation. To the extent that they knew anything about architecture, they understood the architecture of the Egyptian State. The pyramids and the treasure cities were monuments to empire.

Egypt was a top-down civilization. The pyramids were the architectural representation of this society. The Pharaoh was the divine-human link who mediated between man and the gods. He was the high priest of the society.[5] The priests possessed specialized knowledge which gave them life-and-death power over the lives of the Egyptians: knowledge of the cycles of the flooding of the Nile. Egypt was the archetype of what Wittfogel has called the "hydraulic society"—a civilization built in terms of a water monopoly by the State or priesthood. Their knowledge of astronomy, the calendar, and the flooding of the Nile gave the priests an unchallenged authority. Without them, the nation starved. They did not rule Egypt, but they were powerful.[6]

The architecture of hydraulic societies is monumental. "The style is apparent in the fortress-like settlements of the Pueblo Indians. It is conspicuous in the palaces, temple cities, and fortresses of ancient Middle and South America. It characterizes the tombs, palace-

---

5. Karl Wittfogel, *Oriental Despotism: A Comparative Study of Total Power* (New Haven, Connecticut: Yale University Press, [1957] 1964), p. 93.

6. *Ibid.*, p. 88.

cities, temples, and royal monuments of Pharaonic Egypt and ancient Mesopotamia. No one who has ever observed the city gates and walls of a Chinese capital, such as Peking, or who has walked through the immense palace gates and squares of the Forbidden City to enter the equally immense court buildings, ancestral temples, and private residences can fail to be awed by their monumental design. Pyramids and dome-shaped tombs manifest most consistently the monumental style of hydraulic building. They achieve their aesthetic effect with a minimum of ideas and a maximum of material. The pyramid is little more than a huge pile of symmetrically arranged stones."[7]

In contrast to the pyramid was the tabernacle. It was ornate and magnificent inside (for the priests to view), but it was not monumental. It was transportable. Its builders were wilderness wanderers. There was no possibility of pyramid-building for the Hebrews in the wilderness. The tabernacle's grandeur was visual, but this grandeur was based upon the creation of a sense of subordination in those few who entered it. God taught the Hebrews a sense of awe, but this sense of awe was based on God's actual presence in the tabernacle, not on its shape. The closer they came to the center, the more awesome it became, and only priests were able to get close to the holy of holies, and only the high priest could enter it. Take away God's presence, and the tabernacle became a large, ornament-filled tent; it lost its awesome quality.

The great Cheops pyramid of Egypt is empty and awesome, but hardly beautiful. Its awesomeness is based on its height and immensity, not its communicated sense of God's presence. The tabernacle required constant care, meaning constant devotion; the pyramids stand unattended, monuments to the static civilization that they represented.[8] They have always served as giant graveyard monuments.

The massive, monumental architecture of Egypt had glorified the State and the static social pyramid. It had inspired the wrong kind of awe. It had been designed by tyrants and built by slaves. The rulers of Egypt paid for such architecture but had not participated in its construction.

The "empire" architecture of almost every national capital— Washington, D.C., the Kremlin, Nazi Berlin—is easily recog-

---

7. *Ibid.*, pp. 43-44.

8. Gary North, *Moses and Pharaoh: Dominion Religion vs. Power Religion* (Tyler, Texas: Institute for Christian Economics, 1985), ch. 2: "Imperial Bureaucracy."

nizable. Government buildings look alike: huge stones piled straight up to impress anyone who walks by or walks in. They are designed to dwarf men in the presence of the power State. They are also designed to produce massive cost overruns and therefore immense profits for the construction firms that build them. The State requires appropriate sacrifices.

The tabernacle was uniquely suited to the wilderness experience. It was also uniquely suited to the spiritual needs of the Hebrews. They had to develop a wholly new sense of aesthetics. The tabernacle was portable, not a huge imitation of timeless eternity. God's presence was made visible when Israel moved, in the pillar of fire and the cloud. God is a God of history, they learned.

The Hebrews could participate in the building of the tabernacle, if they were provided with teachers. This is precisely what God gave them. *The tabernacle was neither designed by tyrants nor built by slaves.* It inspired a sense of God's presence, not a sense of man's presence. It did not elevate an elite by humiliating the common man.

The construction of the tabernacle represented a definitive break with the architecture of empire. *The psychological and aesthetic discontinuity with Egypt reinforced the covenantal discontinuity with Egypt that God required of them.* They were not to bring the architectural leaven of Egypt into the promised land.

The Need for Aesthetic Continuity

The two senior craftsmen needed assistants. God gave them the ability to raise up apprentices who could multiply the skills of the masters. Instruction by masters led to an increase of productivity. The skills could be imparted, freeing up the time of the masters. Without this multiplication effect, it would have taken far longer to construct the tabernacle. The people would have been left in the wilderness for many years with memories of Egypt's awesomeness and confronted by the sight of the architectural greatness of their enemies across the Jordan River. Without a magnificent alternative which testified to God's ability as a designer, and which also testified to God's ability to endow His people with the skills to construct such a symbol of God's presence, the Hebrews would have suffered from an inferiority complex. The *splendor of the tabernacle* was clearly a *psychological implement of dominion.*

Who got inside to see it? The priests. They served as representatives of the people. They shared with God the splendor of the interior.

They experienced this splendor as *representative agents* of the nation. Nevertheless, everyone who read the account in Exodus knew what was inside. The people were called upon to visualize this splendor whenever they heard this section of the Word of God. They learned of a God who enjoys splendor for His own sake.

Man is made in God's image. Why, then, shouldn't a person enjoy the beauties of art for his own sake? Christian art and architecture do not have to serve the needs of State in order to be legitimate. Art must please God, but in a free society, God's delegated aesthetic agents are the patron and the artist, not anyone else. The very fact that the interior of the tabernacle had to be visualized by most Hebrews must have called forth the creative imaging process in the minds of artists.

They needed teachers. The students gained confidence in their ability to build. This gave them confidence concerning the future. They would not be dependent on the architectural capital of the Canaanites after the conquest. They would not be forced to live in the shadow of a rebellious culture's greatness. Apprentices now were present in the Hebrew commonwealth who had been given direction by master teachers who had been filled by God with the spirit of competence. *The nation would not be forever dependent on the continuing miracles of architectural revelation and Spirit-filled craftsmen.*

Men need self-confidence if they are to perform difficult tasks. If the two master craftsmen had been unable to impart their skills to others, then the society would have been aesthetically dependent on the one-time creation of two God-endowed men whose skills might not appear again. The Hebrews would then have lived in the fear of becoming aesthetic slaves to their experience in the wilderness, unable to take a progressive culture across the face of the globe in confidence.

Once the tabernacle was built, men who were recently trained in creative architecture could pass these skills down to their successors. This would not be easy in a wilderness. The locus of artistic creativity would have to be personal and local. Essentially, the source of demand must have been familial or tribal. The small scale of artistic creativity must have decentralized craftsmanship. This is one reason why we find no examples of magisterial artistry in the archeological digs of Israel.

Another reason was covenantal: they kept rebelling against God, and God kept delivering them into the hands of their enemies. There was a constant dispersion of Hebrew wealth out of the land. *The dis-*

continuities of Hebrew ethical life led to discontinuities in Hebrew artistic life.
The disastrous cultural effects of these discontinuities are what
Alfred Edersheim ignored when he wrote in the late-nineteenth century that "Israel, as a nation, was not intended to attain pre-
eminence either in art or science. If we may venture to pronounce on
such a matter, this was the part assigned, in the Providence of God,
to the Gentile world. To Israel was specially entrusted the guardianship of that spiritual truth, which in the course of ages would develop in all its proportions, till finally it became the common property of the whole world. On the other hand, it was the task assigned
to that world, to develop knowledge and thought so as to prepare a
fitting reception for the truth. . . ."[9] This dualism between Israel's
spirit and culture was never intended by God, nor did it ever exist.
There was a unity between Israel's spirit of rebellion and the continual uprootings that God imposed as His covenantal judgment.
There was a unity between these uprootings and the inability of the
Israelites to produce anything artistic that survived.

Finally, wood was used extensively both for the temple and Solomon's house. Wood does not survive for eons. Common people in
the ancient world used mud-based materials for their homes, or else
used animal skins or wood. Only the State could afford to use stone
extensively. The self-professed divine State had an incentive to build
stone monuments, then as now, as testimonies to their hypothetical
eternality. A handful of these monuments survived to become tomb-
stones to dead civilizations.

Conclusion

The teachers provided both *discontinuity and continuity.* They provided discontinuity with the pagan past by enabling the Hebrews to
break with Egypt and the surrounding Canaanite cultures. At the
same time, their ability to instruct others provided continuity into a
covenantal future, for the nation of Israel would not become stagnant architecturally. They could build a temple which would utilize
some of the implements of the tabernacle. They could take the land
of Canaan in the knowledge that what they might destroy in battle
could be rebuilt, and not through imitation. Architecturally speaking, they had abandoned the monumental leaven of Egypt and had

9. Alfred Edersheim, *Bible History: Old Testament*, 7 vols. (Grand Rapids, Michigan: Eerdmans, [1890] 1972), V, pp. 70-71.

been given a new leaven which would enable the cultural loaf to rise in the promised land. They had abandoned the pyramids.

The presence of teachers enabled the Israelites to make use of the division of labor principle, both in time and across time. Much of the artistry of the tabernacle was eventually transferred to the temple. Later generations continued the work in this way. The teachers brought God's presence to the people, not ritually but instead artistically. The artists were not God, but their skills manifested the instructions of God. There is a reason why artists have been regarded throughout history as special people, even mediatorial between man and God.

CONCLUSION

No sanctions, no laws; no laws, no social order; no social order, no civilization; no civilization, no kingdom of God in church history.

The Book of Exodus contains the book of the covenant: "And he [Moses] took the book of the covenant, and read in the audience of the people: and they said, All that the LORD hath said will we do, and be obedient" (Ex. 24:7). It therefore bears the marks of all five aspects of the biblical covenant model: transcendence/immanence, hierarchy/representation, ethics/dominion, oath/sanctions, and succession/inheritance.[1] The first chapter of Exodus indicates that a war between rival covenants was the heart of the dispute between God and Pharaoh. Pharaoh attempted to impose his own alternative covenant on the Hebrews. It, too, had the same five aspects, and this confrontation reveals all five. This covenant structure appears twice in the first chapter: a double witness.

The first presentation of the Pharaoh's covenant program appears in the Bible's description of his general rule over the Hebrews. First, transcendence/immanence: the book begins with the advent of a false god, the Pharaoh who had forgotten Joseph (Ex. 1:8). Second, hierarchy: this false god immediately established a tyrannical hierarchy over the people of Israel, with "taskmasters to afflict them with their burdens" (v. 11). Third, law: he forced them to build treasure cities for him (v. 11). But their afflictions led to even greater growth in their population (v. 12), threatening Pharaoh's program of dominion. Fourth, sanctions: he announced a program of infanticide (v. 16). Fifth, inheritance: he was seeking to destroy their inheritance in the land by killing their male children, but allowing the females to survive — an attempt to capture the inheritance of Israel through future

---

1. Acronym: THEOS. See above, p. 67. Cf. Ray R. Sutton, *That You May Prosper: Dominion By Covenant* (Tyler, Texas: Institute for Christian Economics, 1987).

concubinage. Egypt would marry Israel, God's bride, steal the bride's God-granted dowry, and declare her a concubine.[2]

The second presentation of the Pharaoh's covenant program appears in the Bible's description of his enforcement of the infanticide decree. To achieve this program of stealing the Hebrews' inheritance, Pharaoh (the self-proclaimed sovereign) assigned this task of infanticide to representative agents, the Hebrew midwives (hierarchy). He gave them a command: destroy the newborn males (law). They disobeyed the command, but instead of being punished by Pharaoh (negative sanction), God blessed them (positive sanction). And the people multiplied (inheritance).

In response to this false Egyptian covenant, the sovereign God of Israel announced to Moses that He was with His people, for He had seen their afflictions and had heard their cries (Ex. 3:7). He then raised up Moses, his representative agent, to serve as the earthly leader of the nation (hierarchy). He gave Moses His laws (law). The people made an oath to God, which they broke, and God brought sanctions against them (oath/sanctions). They then repented, renewed the covenant, and built the tabernacle, which their sons later carried into the Promised Land, the lawful inheritance which had been promised to Abraham (inheritance/continuity).[3]

The Doctrine of Covenantal Representation

The conflict between Moses and Pharaoh was a representative battle between God and Satan. It was a battle over the question of ultimate sovereignty. It was a battle over lawful representation. It was also a battle over the right to impose sanctions and the right to collect the inheritance. But primarily Exodus is a battle over representation: Moses vs. Pharaoh. Who would represent Israel in the court of the gods or God of history, Moses or Pharaoh? Which representative agent would manifest true covenantal authority in the midst of time? The answer of the Book of Exodus is clear: Moses. The Book of Exodus is, above all, a book about representative gov-

---

2. Gary North, *Moses and Pharaoh: Dominion Religion vs. Power Religion* (Tyler, Texas: Institute for Christian Economics, 1985), pp. 85-86, "The Slave Wife."

3. Critics of Ray Sutton's five-point covenant model can and do continue to deny the appearance of this outline again and again in the Bible. I believe that this blindness testifies to the inability of those who cling to an old paradigm to understand the evidence of the new one. They, of course, will reply that those of us who see the covenant structure clearly in the text are reading our invention into the text. Time and the final judgment will tell whose view is correct.

ernment in history. It is clearly a book about *hierarchy*, which all government structures must always be.

Exodus 18, 20, and 21

Exodus 18 is the best biblical example of a civil hierarchy. Moses'
father-in-law suggested that Moses establish a system of hierarchical
appeals courts, in order to lessen the load on Moses, and also to reduce the time that people had to wait in their quest for civil justice.[4]
Moses, a wise son-in-law, accepted his father-in-law's excellent advice, and he established just such an appeals court system. Having
established a bottom-up appeals court system, Moses then came before the people to proclaim the law, the Ten Commandments. Immediately after the words of the tenth commandment, we read:

> And all the people saw the thunderings, and the lightnings, and the noise
> of the trumpet, and the mountain smoking: and when the people saw it, they
> removed, and stood afar off. And they said unto Moses, Speak thou with us,
> and we will hear: but let not God speak with us, lest we die (Ex. 20:18-19).

They clearly understood the doctrine of representation, and they
affirmed it. More than this: they *insisted* on it. They did not want to
come into the presence of a holy God. They wanted another person
to go before God, to speak with Him, and to return to speak His
word to them. They promised to hear, which in the context of affirming a covenant with God meant that they promised to obey. They
would obey God by obeying Moses. They would obey the details of
the law that Moses brought from God.

Then God announced case laws to Moses, His hierarchical (mediatorial) representative: "Now these are the judgments which thou
shalt set before them" (Ex. 21:1). These laws began with the law governing Hebrew indentured servitude. The Hebrews broke these case
laws repeatedly. They did not take these laws seriously. God therefore placed them in bondage repeatedly: to the Moabites, Midianites, Philistines, Assyrians, Babylonians, Medo-Persians, Greeks,
and finally the Romans. This punishment fit the crime. *The sanction
against the crime of disobedience to God is bondage.* In the lake of fire, the
ultimate negative sanction, this bondage is personal, direct (unmediated), and eternal. The protective human and institutional hierarchy
is removed. When this non-hierarchical form of judgment comes,

---

4. North, *Moses and Pharaoh*, ch. 19: "Imperfect Justice."

unlike judgments in history (which are always mediated and hierarchical), no grace accompanies it. In short, *When God's grace is totally removed, all institutional hierarchies are removed.* The evidence of this lack of grace is the absence of any institutional hierarchy. *Without a mediator between God and man, covenant-breaking men inescapably die.* The Israelites fully understood this: ". . . let not God speak with us, lest we die."

The Doctrine of Covenantal Hierarchy

The case laws of Exodus reflect the position of Exodus as the second book in the Pentateuch. It corresponds to the second point of the biblical covenant model: hierarchy. Thus, the bulk of the case law section deals with God's civil appeals court. The book is related to all five points in the covenant, especially point three (the actual laws) and point four (judgment and sanctions), but the legitimate question of civil law and civil sanctions cannot be separated from the question of the institutional structure of God's civil courts. This structure is hierarchical: a bottom-up appeals court.

The message of the Book of Exodus is *deliverance*: from slavery to freedom, from Egypt to Sinai, from work to rest, from Pharaoh's kingdom to God's kingdom. Ultimately, it is the story of Israel's deliverance from wrath to grace. It is not, however, the story of Israel's deliverance from institutional hierarchy. There can be no deliverance from hierarchy in history. Hierarchy is an inescapable concept. It is never a question of hierarchy vs. no hierarchy; it is always a question of which hierarchy.

The case laws reflect this fact of institutional hierarchy. They begin with the laws of bondservice: masters and servants. They continue with laws governing fathers and daughters, bridegrooms and concubines, the stronger and the weaker, kidnappers and victims, parents and sons, fighters and bystanders, goring oxen and victims, thieves and victims, fire-starters and victims, safekeepers and victims, seducers and seduced, citizens and strangers, creditors and debtors, finders and keepers. All of these relationships are hierarchical. They all involve authority and subordination. They all involve the imposition of power, and power is inevitably imposed hierarchically. A humanist slogan such as "man must take control of man" really means that some men must take control over all the others.

Who Is Our God?

Rushdoony writes that "in any culture *the source of the law is the god of that society*."[5] The source of biblical law is the God of the Bible. His moral character is revealed in His laws — *all* His laws, not just the Ten Commandments. Without biblical law at the center of a society's legal order,[6] its legal order testifies falsely regarding the true source of all morally valid laws, namely, the God of the Bible. It testifies falsely regarding God. A society is in rebellion against God to the extent that its people refuse to acknowledge in the civil realm the Bible-mandated terms of the civil covenant. There is a specific legal order which God requires the State to uphold by force and the threat of force. God is totally sovereign, as manifested by the presence of His required laws and sanctions. A society that denies the continuing judicial validity of Old Testament civil law in general thereby refuses to acknowledge that this world was, is, and ever shall be a theocracy. *God rules*. How does a nation testify in history to this fact? *God's rules*. To the extent that the legal order does not conform to the legal standard that God announces in His Bible, to that extent is a society in rebellion against God.

Renouncing a Tool of Evangelism

This is denied by virtually all Christian denominations and congregations today. They deny that God reveals himself judicially to men in New Testament times as clearly as He did in the Old Testament. Christians should ask themselves: Why would God choose to reveal himself less clearly in the New Testament era by allowing every society except Puritan New England to adopt a law-order that is openly a renunciation of what He has revealed as judicially binding in the Old Testament? The theonomists have an answer to this intriguing question. God allows this in order to reveal the visible failure in history of all rival law-orders compared to the visible success of His revealed law-order. This necessarily implies that at some point in the future, there will be such a visible example. The visible failure of rival civil law-orders, meaning rival gods, can then become a worldwide tool of evangelism.

---

5. R. J. Rushdoony, *The Institutes of Biblical Law* (Nutley, New Jersey: Craig Press, 1973), p. 4.

6. At the center of Israel was the Ark of the Covenant. In the Ark was the law: the two tablets.

Behold, I have taught you statutes and judgments, even as the LORD my God commanded me, that ye should do so in the land whither ye go to possess it. Keep therefore and do them; for this is your wisdom and your understanding in the sight of the nations, which shall hear all these statutes, and say, Surely this great nation is a wise and understanding people. For what nation is there so great, who hath God so nigh unto them, as the LORD our God is in all things that we call upon him for? And what nation is there so great, that hath statutes and judgments so righteous as all this law, which I set before you this day? (Deut. 4:5-8).

Modern Christians do not take these words seriously. They believe that in this New Testament era of gospel deliverance, God has for some unstated reason removed this judicial tool of evangelism from the church's tool kit of legitimate missionary techniques. For some reason, in this New Testament "age of grace," God has removed a major Old Covenant means of grace, namely, the visible testimony of cultural success that a covenant-honoring society possesses. He supposedly has removed His positive visible sanctions from faithful covenant-keepers. Worse; God has supposedly reversed the Old Covenant order of visible sanctions. We are assured by premillennialists and amillennialists — but only when pressed very hard to explain their eschatological position — that *God in the "Church Age" rewards covenant-breakers with the earthly blessing of civil authority, and He places the church and individual Christians under this authority.* He does this as a witness to Himself. By placing His people under bondage to covenant-breakers, we are assured by pessimillennial theologians, God has not really reversed the exodus order of wrath to grace. It may look this way, of course. In fact, it *does* look this way. But looks are deceiving. Looks were not deceiving in the Old Covenant era (Deut. 4:4-8), but they are deceiving today. As to why this should be the case, no one wants to say for the public record.[7]

---

7. Except, of course, they *do* say, if pressed hard enough. Their answer is the supposedly legitimate and supposedly irresistible triumph of democracy in history. You know: *demos* (the people) and *kratos* (rule). This is not seen by non-theonomic Christians as the judicial substitution of a false god for the Bible's God. Somehow, the voice of the people has become the voice of God, the only legitimate mediatorial voice of God in the civil covenant. And when modern Christians say "the people," they mean a majority of voters, which at least so far has meant *covenant-breakers*. "The voice of covenant-breakers is the voice of God." Write this down. Put it on a note card. Keep repeating it over and over to yourself. If you do this long enough, you will be epistemologically ready to achieve academic success in a Christian college or seminary.

There are many reasons for this peculiar view of God's shrinking supply of the tools of grace in history, but the main reason, I suspect, is this: *the people of God do not regard God's Bible-revealed law as a true means of grace, even though Paul affirmed the opposite.*

What shall we say then? Is the law sin? God forbid. Nay, I had not known sin, but by the law: for I had not known lust, except the law had said, Thou shalt not covet. But sin, taking occasion by the commandment, wrought in me all manner of concupiscence. For without the law sin was dead. For I was alive without the law once: but when the commandment came, sin revived, and I died. And the commandment, which was ordained to life, I found to be unto death. For sin, taking occasion by the commandment, deceived me, and by it slew me. Wherefore the law is holy, and the commandment holy, and just, and good. Was then that which is good made death unto me? God forbid. But sin, that it might appear sin, working death in me by that which is good; that sin by the commandment might become exceeding sinful. For we know that the law is spiritual: but I am carnal, sold under sin (Rom. 7:7-14).

God has allowed this judicial evangelical testimony to fade time after time in the New Testament era because His people have so seldom maintained or enacted His revealed laws whenever they have gained political influence. This does not mean that He has abandoned His judicial standards, which are revealed in the Old Testament. It only means that so far in history, He has repeatedly allowed His people to depart from His law, just as Israel did, only to find themselves as subordinates to their God-hating enemies. God does not renounce His sanctions in history; He continues to enforce them. God still delivers His people from sociological grace to wrath in direct response to their covenant-breaking acceptance of the civil laws of rival gods. He did this in the Old Testament, and He does it in the New. But so thorough has been the training of Christians in the accredited schools of their cultural conquerors that *God's people have very seldom regarded this deliverance from civil grace to wrath as God's specific negative sanction for their specific sin of denying the legitimacy of the biblical civil covenant.* This punishment fits the crime.[8] They do yet not cry out to God in their bondage in the democratic West. They regard their own judicial bondage as true political freedom, as if this bond-

---

8. In the late 1960's, I saw a lapel button: "Chastity is its own punishment." I would alter that button as follows: "Pluralism is its own punishment."

age were both historically normal and historically normative.[9] Pagan taskmasters have done a far better job in educating modern Christians than the Babylonians did with the Hebrew youths (Dan. 1), and so have the ordained Christian collaborators who serve as the paid assistants of the taskmasters, collaborators whose name is legion.[10]

Christianity's historical failure to extend the gospel "as the waters cover the sea" (Hab. 2:14) is in part caused by Christians' systematic and self-assured unwillingness to make effective use of a biblical tool of evangelism, namely, the self-conscious construction of a civil law-order that honors God's revealed civil law by imposing the biblically mandated civil sanctions. They have left the gospel message without a visible witness in civil institutions. Worse; church leaders and theologians have again and again denied that such an institutional testimony is legitimate in the New Testament era. It is legitimate in church affairs, of course, they hasten to affirm; it is also legitimate with respect to the covenantal institution of the family. But God's Bible-revealed standards are not legitimate with respect to the civil government. So Christians have been told for well over a millennium.

The question of questions for Christian applied theology, ethics, and social theory is this one: Why should Christians accept as their long-term earthly goal the establishment of any system of civil law other than the one set forth in the Bible? In other words, why should Christians affirm *in principle* the acceptability of any law-order other than biblical law, in every area of life? Why should they enthusiastically choose second-best, third-best, or even a totalitarian civil order in preference to biblical law? Why is their last choice for civil judicial standards always God's Bible-revealed law? We could search for answers in psychology, sociology, education, and in any other academic specialties. I prefer to begin looking for the answer in the area of ethics: *Christians prefer irresponsibility.*

---

9. See, for example, Norman L. Geisler, "A Premillennial View of Law and Government," in J. I. Packer (ed.), *The Best in Theology* (Carol Stream, Illinois: Christianity Today/Word, 1986). Professor Geisler, then of Dallas Theological Seminary, now of Jerry Falwell's Liberty University, is a dispensationalist and a staunch defender of natural law theology. He received his Ph.D. in philosophy from a Jesuit university, back when Jesuit universities were scholastic rather than Marxist and "liberationist." At least he is consistent; few other opponents of theonomy are willing to admit that natural law is the only logical alternative to God's law on this side of total relativism or tyranny.

10. Gary North, *Political Polytheism: The Myth of Pluralism* (Tyler, Texas: Institute for Christian Economics, 1989), ch. 5. See also North, *Backward Christian Soldiers? An Action Manual for Christian Reconstruction* (Tyler, Texas: Institute for Christian Economics, 1984), Part II: "The Enemy."

A Preference for Irresponsibility

In the Northern Kingdom from the days of Jeroboam's revolt, there were only two publicly acceptable operating religious systems: the worship of Jehovah by means of Baalist icons and practices (the golden calves: I Ki. 12:28) and the worship of Baal by means of Baalist icons and practices (I Ki. 18). Elijah challenged the representatives of the people of Israel to choose between Baal and Jehovah, but they answered not a word (I Ki. 18:21). Even when they at last declared themselves in favor of God (I Ki. 18:39), it was only as a result of God's display of greater supernatural but highly visible power, and their commitment did not last longer than Elijah's ability to repeat such displays on a regular, invariable basis. In their deepest apostasy, they became disciples of the power religion. They had returned to Egypt spiritually.

The Northern Kingdom was worse in this regard than the Southern Kingdom was. Judah did have the temple. It had a ritually acceptable religion. It never adopted pure Baalism. God therefore delivered Israel into captivity to the Assyrians more than a century before He delivered Judah (and Assyria) to the Babylonians. Even so, He had graciously waited several centuries to deliver up Israel to her enemies. The Northern Kingdom's religious practices had been corrupt from the beginning, but there are degrees of corruption. For a time, God graciously delays bringing His negative sanctions in history. It is not that He honors corruption; instead, He honors the absence of fully developed corruption. But corruption, like "incorruption," does not remain idle. Corruption either grows or contracts. Both corruption and righteousness are kingdom principles. It depends upon which kingdom we are discussing: God's or Satan's. Each kingdom seeks extension geographically, temporally, institutionally, and psychologically. Each serves as leaven.[11] Each recognizes that, in principle, there can be no neutrality. Each therefore recognizes that as time goes on, there will be less and less cooperation possible between covenant-keepers and covenant-breakers.

Progressive Ethical Self-Consciousness

Covenant-breakers generally recognize the nature of this ethical and institutional conflict much earlier than covenant-keepers do.

---

11. Gary North, *Unconditional Surrender: God's Program for Victory* (3rd ed.; Tyler, Texas: Institute for Christian Economics, 1987), pp. 315-19, 325-26.

They see what will happen when covenant-keepers at last become self-conscious in their commitment to God's Bible-revealed kingdom principles. Like the leaders of the Jews who understood that Jesus had prophesied that He would rise again in three days, and so put a stone and guards at the tomb (Matt. 27:62-66), so are the covenant-breakers in history. Similarly, like the disciples who did not understand what Jesus had said, and who therefore departed in despair, so Christians have been in their misunderstanding of Christ's comprehensive challenge to non-Christian society. They have not understood the comprehensive challenge of the gospel.[12] Nevertheless, a few disciples eventually returned to the tomb, only to find it empty. As time went on, a few more recognized that Jesus' words were true. The word of His resurrection spread among the called-out *ekklesia*. Then the war between the kingdoms began in earnest — earnest in the sense of serious, and also earnest in the sense of God's down payment in history of a future fulfillment. When Christians at last begin to see the comprehensive implications of the resurrection, the war will escalate. (This escalation has been going on since the resurrection, but it has been a process marked by many historical discontinuities.)

Once a new phase of the war begins, both sides become increasingly consistent. This has been going on for centuries. The cultural advantage inevitably swings to the covenant-keepers *whenever they honor the external terms of God's covenant.* Their obedience brings visible, external blessings (Deut. 28:1-14), while the rebellious receive visible blessings more and more in terms of their public honoring of the kingdom principles announced by the covenant-keepers. If they refuse to adapt, covenant-breakers grow weak and eventually disappear in history.[13] Those who survive become increasingly dependent on the good behavior and good works of covenant-keepers. This dependence tends to persuade them to reduce their persecution of covenant-keepers. They hire them because covenant-keepers — *when the latter are adhering to the external terms of God's covenant* — are honest, effec-

---

12. Gary North, *Is the World Running Down? Crisis in the Christian Worldview* (Tyler, Texas: Institute for Christian Economics, 1988), Appendix C: "Comprehensive Redemption: A Theology for Social Action."

13. My favorite example is the disintegration of the culture of the Ik, a thoroughly perverse Kenyan tribal people. See Colin Turnbull, *The Mountain People* (New York: Touchstone, 1972). The author in the Preface attempts to deny that this society is inhuman, by denying the existence of common standards of what might be termed true humanity. Once you deny the image of God in man, as both Turnbull and the Ik do, anything goes. Eventually, civilization goes.

tive workers. They buy from them for the same reason. Service leads to dominion.

External Standards, External Sanctions

The law of God is the primary tool of dominion that God offers to all men, irrespective of their personal faith. He gives the Holy Spirit to His people, but if His people refuse for a season to honor the terms of the covenant, while God-rejecting men willingly adopt the external terms of the covenant, then the latter will prosper externally. The best example of this process in recent history is the reversal of economic power between Japan and the United States after 1945. The Japanese, not being Protestants, nevertheless adopted the Protestant ethic of their American conquerors. The Americans, having become the richest people on earth by their adherence to this ethic, steadily abandoned it in the post-War era. They concluded incorrectly that the might of their hands had gotten them this wealth (Deut. 8:17).

Long-term, it requires that God grant special grace (regeneration) to large numbers of people in order for a society to adhere to the external terms of the covenant.[14] But in the short run, which can last several generations, the appropriate visible blessings of the covenant can go to those who are committed only externally to particular terms of the covenant. Japan, for example, was the first nation to adopt abortion as a national policy after World War II. As of 1988, there were three abortions for every live birth in Japan. (Pornography also is widespread in Japan, including sado-masochistic literature.)[15] Why should the Japanese be uniquely blessed? It is a case of comparative obedience: the Soviet Union and the Chinese also began to promote abortions as national policy; the United States also accepted its legality nationally in 1973, and its intellectual leaders are overwhelmingly pro-abortion. So, God looks at other aspects of the covenant, those related to the economics of dominion: honesty, hard work, precise work, rigorous education, thrift, future-orientation, etc. In these areas, the Japanese excel. They therefore receive the lion's share of the external blessings. If they refuse to convert to faith in Jesus Christ, however, the Japanese will eventually find it impossible to adhere as a nation to the external terms of the covenant. God's negative sanctions will come.

---

14. Gary North, *Dominion and Common Grace: The Biblical Basis of Progress* (Tyler, Texas: Institute for Christian Economics, 1987), ch. 6.

15. "Women's Groups: Sayonara to Smut," *Insight* (March 23, 1987).

The modern church has abandoned faith in the covenantal cause-and-effect relationship between national external conformity to God's law and His external blessings. The church therefore does not believe in God's sanctions in history. In Old Testament times, yes, but not in New Testament times. *The church today implicitly believes that God gave a clearer revelation of His ethical standards before Jesus Christ came to redeem the world.* Christians implicitly assert with Van Til that God's system of visible sanctions in Old Covenant history was a mark of His condescension to His people in an earlier era.[16] In short, they conclude that Christians and non-Christians do not need visible manifestations of the ethical character of God, so He has removed this revelation of Himself by removing His historical sanctions. Covenant-breakers understandably rejoice at this thought, for this hypothetical removal of God's sanctions in history supposedly leaves Satan's sanctions intact: compound cursings in history for the righteous and compound blessings in history for the unrighteous. Unfortunately, Van Til did not believe that this removal is hypothetical.[17] Neither do non-theonomic pessimillennialists generally. Van Til never understood that *sanctions in history are an inescapable concept.* Since God's servants so far have chosen not to impose His civil sanctions in New Testament history, Satan's servants have imposed his.

Ethics and Eschatology

History is not visibly neutral in any eschatological system that is based on the Bible: *either the gospel message is blessed progressively over the ages or else humanism is.* The Bible is not a dualistic document. It does not teach of an endless conflict between good and evil, between God and Satan. This conflict is bounded by time. It will end at the final judgment. This is why neither ethical dualism nor some version of manichaeanism can be successfully defended by means of an appeal to the Bible. The two positions are inevitably connected: eschatology and ethics. The Bible denies both eschatological manichaeanism and ethical dualism.

---

16. He writes: "In the New Testament God expects his people to live more fully into the absolute future than in the Old Testament. He expects of them that they will be able to sustain the unevenness of the present revelation to the day of their death, since they have a clearer revelation of the new heavens and the new earth. In the Old Testament, on the contrary, God condescends to give an external manifestation of the principle that righteousness, holiness and blessedness belong together." Cornelius Van Til, *Christian Theistic Ethics*, vol. III of *In Defense of Biblical Christianity* (Phillipsburg, New Jersey: Presbyterian & Reformed, 1980), p. 104.

17. For a critique of this view, see North, *Political Polytheism*, ch. 3.

The debate within Christendom over eschatology and ethics has arisen because the majority of those who have ever called themselves Christians have accepted the assertion by the humanists—whether Greek, Newtonian, or Kantian—that there is an inherent ethical dualism in history. There is supposedly no progressive triumph of God's kingdom law over Satan's kingdom law. They have accepted the presupposition that there is a universal system of ethics that is independent of God's revelation of Himself in the Bible, and that it is this universal ethical system which God enforces by means of His sanctions in history. Thus, God's historical sanctions are supposedly not linked closely to the progressive improvements in the church's creeds and its improving methods of evangelism throughout history. History therefore is not a visible "earnest" (Eph. 1:14) or down payment on the eschatological triumph of God over Satan in eternity. History, the Greek-influenced church has affirmed, is not a tale told by an idiot, signifying nothing; it just looks like it. Or, to cite Meredith Kline: "And meanwhile it [the common grace order] must run its course within the uncertainties of the mutually conditioning principles of common grace and common curse, prosperity and adversity being experienced in a manner largely unpredictable because of the inscrutable sovereignty of the divine will that dispenses them in mysterious ways."[18]

Case Laws and Kingdom

Rarely in the history of the church have leaders or laymen taken the Old Testament case laws seriously. (Rarely also have they taken seriously the idea of "Thy kingdom come. Thy will be done in earth, as it is in heaven." Fully consistent dispensationalists refuse to pray this "Jewish kingdom" prayer in this, the "Church Age.") Christians have assumed that Jesus' earthly ministry, or at least Paul's, did away entirely with the case laws. Nevertheless, when pressed to defend some traditional practice of any particular denomination, the groups' in-house theologians usually turn to the Old Testament in search of a legal precedent. This is an aspect of what Rushdoony has called *smorgasbord religion*: selectively picking what you like out of a large selection of rules and doctrines. The best example of such selective New Testament shopping is the strict sabbatarian's appeal

---

18. Meredith G. Kline, "Comments on the Old-New Error," *Westminster Theological Journal*, XLI (Fall 1978), p. 184.

to every verse in the Old Testament regarding keeping holy the sabbath except one, Exodus 35:2: "Six days shall work be done, but on the seventh day there shall be to you an holy day, a sabbath of rest to the LORD: whosoever doeth work therein shall be put to death." When it comes to announcing the legitimate imposition of this most rigorous of Old Testament civil sanctions, capital punishment, the church flees in holy terror.

A biblically required sanction clearly identifies God's attitude toward a particular infraction. The severity of the sanction tells us just how important the infraction is in the overall operation of the kingdom of God. Without sanctions, there can be no civil law, and without civil law there can be no civilization, meaning no identifiable kingdom. But there is always some form of civilization. There are no historical vacuums. Thus, we ought to conclude that God has His required sanctions, while self-proclaimed autonomous man has his. God has revealed His required sanctions in His law; man has revealed his required sanctions in his legislation. For as long as there are infractions of a judicial standard, there will be sanctions. The question is: Whose? Whose standards and whose sanctions?

The church has not wanted to face the stark contrast between the two kingdoms. It has wanted to find some rationally acceptable position between theocracy and tyranny and also between theocracy and anarchy. Christian scholars have asserted the existence of neutral, "natural" laws that can serve as the church's earthly hope of the ages, an agreeable middle way that will mitigate the conflict in history between the Kingdom of God and the kingdom of man. The victor in such a naive quest will always be the kingdom of man. *Theoretical neutrality means practical autonomy*: men do not have to consider what God requires or threatens in history.

God brings His sanctions in history, both positive and negative. He can do this either through His people, who act representatively as His agents, or through pagan armies or seemingly impersonal environmental forces. He can choose war, pestilence, or famine. He can even choose "all of the above." But He does bring His sanctions in history. There is no escape from these historical sanctions, any more than there is an escape from His eternal sanctions. The former point to the latter. This is one of the primary functions of historical sanctions: as a witness to the holiness of God.

God's historical sanctions serve as public evidence of His theocratic sovereignty over the creation. This is why Christians who rebel at the idea of theocracy also are tempted to rebel against the idea of God's temporal sanctions.[19] The idea of the national covenant repels them, for such a covenant testifies to the existence of a Christian civil hierarchy, Christian civil laws, Christian civil sanctions, and Christian civil conquest in history by means of God's sanctions of blessings and cursings. Thus we find a trio of Christian historians, safe and tenured in their humanist-accredited colleges and universities, who insist on placing the word *Christian* in quotation marks when they speak of America's "Christian" origins or "Christian" cultures in general.[20] They reject the use of this adjective in describing America.

God as Cosmic Torturer

This is a grim concept, one which I have deliberately chosen as a means of shocking Christians and non-Christians alike into recognizing the key offense of the Bible: the assertion that God will torture His enemies without mercy forever if they do not submit to Him covenantally in history. It is the doctrine of God as the cosmic Judge which above all repels the covenant-breaker. Even Christians are today hesitant to say in public that the lake of fire is not a cosmic rehabilitation scheme. God is a cosmic torturer, but to say so in public or in print is regarded by Christians as a *faux pas* of the highest order. This testifies against them, not God.

It is because history is an earnest on eternity — simultaneously a promise and a warning — that Christians are required by God to affirm the biblical legitimacy of civil sanctions imposed by the State in the name of God, and therefore a State governed in its severity by His revealed law. The covenantally faithful State, as a hierarchical institution, is supposed to be limited by God's law in order for it lawfully to execute God's judgments. In order to establish a Christian culture, there have to be identifiably Christian laws — biblical blueprints, in other words — by which the national covenant could be judged by God and other nations. Only one idea is more repugnant to modern Christian intellectuals than the idea of judicially binding

---

19. They will also prefer to downplay or even deny God's eternal negative sanctions. Twentieth-century evangelism is notable for its reluctance to discuss hell and the lake of fire. "Fire and brimstone preaching" is mostly a figment of liberal imaginations in this century.

20. Mark A. Noll, Nathan O. Hatch, and George M. Marsden, *The Search for Christian America* (Westchester, Illinois: Crossway, 1983), p. 28. For a refutation, see North, *Political Polytheism*, ch. 5.

biblical civil blueprints.[21] That idea is the doctrine of an inescapably predestined eternity of personal negative sanctions that will be imposed on everyone God hates. These two hated ideas are linked judicially: *sanctions*. Men do not like to be reminded by Paul that "the scripture saith unto Pharaoh, Even for this same purpose have I raised thee up, that I might shew my power in thee, and that my name might be declared throughout all the earth. Therefore hath he mercy on whom he will have mercy, and whom he will he hardeneth" (Rom. 9:17-18). If God did this with Pharaoh, He can do it to anyone. *This means sanctions.*

The comparatively gentle negative civil sanctions of the Old Testament — whipping, restitution, slavery, banishment, and public execution — are light taps on the wrist when compared to an eternity of screaming agony in the lake of fire. Civil sanctions are limited by time; eternity is forever. Men easily understand this distinction. Thus, in order to banish from their consciousness the thought of eternal torture at the hand of an outraged, implacable, non-rehabilitating God, they feel compelled to banish also the idea that God has established civil covenants in history that authorize and require His lawful civil representatives to apply the Old Testament's minimal negative sanctions. Instead, they have implicitly adopted two other doctrines, the doctrine of autonomous man and the concomitant doctrine, the autonomous State.

The State becomes the sole agency authorized by autonomous man to impose compulsory sanctions. (The only alternative to this view is the doctrine of zero civil government, meaning zero compulsory sanctions, a consistent but seldom articulated viewpoint.) In order to assert his autonomy from God, the covenant-breaker places himself under the authority of a self-proclaimed autonomous State. He prefers to believe that the State's sanctions are final. The State's

---

21. That no such blueprints exist in the field of economics was the assertion of all three of the other authors in the book, *Wealth and Poverty: Four Christian Views*, edited by Robert G. Clouse (Downers Grove, Illinois: InterVarsity Press, 1984). The fourth view — the explicitly, self-consciously, blueprint-insistent Christian one — was mine. I, of course, challenged all three of the others, calling attention to their self-conscious rejection of any explicitly biblical standards in economic analysis. Not surprisingly, in less than a year, with the book selling well and our royalties adequate, the neo-evangelical liberals who run InterVarsity pulled the book off the market and sold my company the remaining 6,000 copies at 25 cents per copy, just to wash their hands of the whole project. That was when I knew who had won the debate. Liberals would never be so crass as to burn conservative books; they simply refuse to publish them or, once the mistake has been made, dump them.

sanctions must be seen as alternatives to God's final judgment, not evidence for it. He must assert this if God's final sanctions are to be denied effectively. In order to make such an assumption believable, the State must be given power to impose sanctions far worse than those authorized by the Old Testament.

You cannot beat something with nothing. A Christian who is unwilling to affirm publicly the inescapability of God's eternal negative covenant sanctions is also unlikely to insist on the *temporal* reality of God's negative covenant sanctions, for such temporal sanctions are an earnest — down payment — on His final sanctions. Such sanctions-denying Christians eventually find themselves under the civil (and also intellectual) authority of covenant-breakers who also deny the continuing validity of biblical law, meaning Old Testament sanctions. *You can't beat something with something less.* Those who assert their defiance of covenant law the most insistently are covenant-breakers who affirm the autonomy of man, or who at least deny the existence of the God of the Bible. Thus, in their quest to avoid thinking about God's eternal torture chamber beyond the grave, Christians have willingly submitted *in principle* to temporal rule by those covenant-breakers who deny the lake of fire with the greatest self-confidence.

On the other hand, those Christians who in history were most willing to affirm God's predestinated, inescapable, eternal sanctions were also the only ones ready to insist on the covenantal necessity of legislating the most feared of God's negative sanctions, public execution, for every crime identified as a capital crime in the Old Testament. I am speaking of the Puritans, who did exactly this when they were given the legal authority in history to do so, in New England: the Massachusetts Body of Liberties (1641). The Puritans understood that civil liberty begins with the civil government's enforcement of God's required sanctions.

Sanctions and Civilization

Kingdom means civilization. It means either the lawful or unlawful exercise of authority in history. In short, kingdom means sanctions. God's kingdom can operate with minimal sanctions in history, meaning a minimal State, only because it is authorized by God and accepted covenantally by people who believe in God's horrifying negative sanctions beyond the grave. The widespread belief in hell and the lake of fire is one of the foundations of Western liberty. It made less necessary for social order men's faith in a State that possesses imitation final sanctions.

What the case laws provide is an alternative to the messianic State. The case laws provide sanctions that match the magnitude of the crime. The basic penalty for crimes against property and body is some form of restitution. Crimes against the integrity of God are capital crimes: those convicted of such infractions are delivered into God's court for His direct judgment. As history moves closer to the day of judgment, society will progressively be conformed to these standards. Democratically, meaning a bottom-up movement of the Holy Spirit, voters will enact the whole law-order of God. Thus, what the Puritans attempted to do in England was wrong because it was a top-down imposition of God's law. What the New England Puritans attempted to do was valid; there was general agreement about biblical civil law. But immigration and defections within Puritanism after 1660 changed the circumstances.

What the critics of theocracy always assume is that it has to be anti-democratic. But if the Spirit of God moves a vast majority of men to confess Jesus Christ as Lord and Savior, and if they return to the Old Testament in search of biblical blueprints, then the resulting theocratic republic will be legitimate in terms of democratic standards, assuming that such standards refer simply and exclusively to techniques of campaigning and voting.[22]

When that theocratic majority appears, you can bet your life that the humanists will then try to subvert it by means of an elitist conspiracy. We read about such a revolt against Moses and Aaron in Numbers 16. It was done in the name of the People: "And they gathered themselves together against Moses and against Aaron, and said unto them, Ye take too much upon you, seeing all the congregation are holy, every one of them, and the LORD is among them: wherefore then lift ye up yourselves above the congregation of the LORD?" (v. 3). We read about the final such attempt in Revelation 20:8-9, at the very end of history. These voices of the People are in favor of democracy for only so long as they can control a majority of voters by means of a hierarchical elite that pretends to listen to the People—an elite far more subtle than the Communists' one-party dictatorship in the name of the people.

A sovereign agent always acts through spokesmen in a hierarchy. There will always be an elite: intellectual, educational, military, and

---

22. Modern democratic theory is far more than a theory of legitimate electoral techniques. It has the character of being a rival religion. Cf. Charles Fergusson, *The Religion of Democracy* (New York: Funk & Wagnalls, 1900).

so forth. The question is never elite or no elite. It is always a question of which elite. It is a question of which sovereign agent. The Bible is clear: God is completely, absolutely sovereign over the creation, and men are subordinately, inescapably responsible for their actions. Thus, the goal of covenant-keepers is to work toward a social order in which every institution reflects this dual sovereignty, absolute and delegated. It is the creation of an entire world order that prays, "Thy kingdom come. Thy will be done in earth, as it is in heaven" (Matt. 6:10).

A subset of this broad social goal is politics. Politically, the only legitimate long-term biblical goal is the creation of a worldwide theocratic republic.[23] It is the creation of a bottom-up political order whose civil courts enforce the law of God, and whose people rejoice, not because such a law-order is natural but because it is supernatural.

The Restoration of Covenant Order

The primary social function of civil law is to persuade God to withdraw His negative sanctions. The State acts as God's agent in imposing sanctions against sin. This is the biblical rationale of civil laws against so-called victimless crimes. Obviously, this purpose relates to the hierarchical nature of all society: the society is under God, meaning under His temporal sanctions.

There is also a secondary goal of civil law: the restoration of social order among men. This, too, is hierarchical. If a person owns a piece of property, then he exercises dominion over it in terms of his subordination to God. He acts as God's agent in a hierarchical system of ownership, which Christians call *stewardship*. When a criminal or negligent person invades this hierarchical system of ownership, God calls the civil magistrate to defend His interests, and therefore also His steward's interests. The system of justice in the Bible is geared to restoration of the original God-assigned hierarchical order.

The issues of crime and punishment are inescapably questions of the appropriate hierarchy. The victim has been victimized by someone who has asserted a judicially illegitimate authority over him. The criminal in some way invaded the victim's legitimate, God-given sphere of personal responsibility. The criminal subordinated

---

23. Gary DeMar, *Ruler of the Nations: Biblical Blueprints for Government* (Ft. Worth, Texas: Dominion Press, 1987); Gary North, *Healer of the Nations: Biblical Blueprints for International Relations* (Ft. Worth, Texas: Dominion Press, 1987).

the victim's goals and property to his own. He intervened in the hierarchy and placed himself between God and the lawful subordinate. He implicitly declared that God's assignment of property and lawful authority was illegitimate. In short, the criminal decided to play God.

This illegitimate assertion of covenantal authority must be punished by the State, which is required by God to act as His representative. The *status quo ante* must be re-established. The way that biblical civil law achieves this goal is to establish a system of economic restitution. The criminal pays double restitution or even more to the victim, depending on what biblical law has established as the maximum payment, and also in terms of victim's rights: the victim can lawfully reduce the payment. Multiple restitution marks criminal law in the Bible. The negligent caretaker or injurer pays only like-for-like restitution to the victim, what might be called civil law.

The modern messianic State has imitated the criminal. It, too, has disrupted the social hierarchy. It has placed itself between God and the criminal, as if God's sanctions were not binding. It has declared different sanctions. The State has attempted to become a healer of society and ultimately its savior, not by restoring the previous hierarchy and social order but rather by transforming the individual criminal through techniques of rehabilitation. The modern State has generally ignored the victim and his rights in its selection of appropriate sanctions. It has sought to play God as a savior of men. It has substituted a different set of sanctions from those required in the Bible. In doing this, it has received the tacit acquiescence of Christians, and even their public approval, for they self-consciously deny the legitimacy of God's Bible-revealed sanctions in civil government. They have therefore implicitly and even explicitly denied the judicial foundation of Christian civilization. In short:

> **No sanctions, no laws; no laws, no social order; no social order, no civilization; no civilization, no kingdom of God in church history.**

Final Comment

Having burdened the reader with an enormous amount of detailed biblical exegesis and specific applications based on it, it seems appropriate to end this book on a lighter note. It appears that a bank in Canada has intuitively grasped the logic of the biblical concept of restitution, much to the consternation of one malefactor, Mr. Brian

McNeilly. The case of Mr. McNeilly was summarized in the *Wall Street Journal* (Dec. 21, 1988), page B1, in the lower left-hand corner. This space is reserved daily for humorous economic oddities. I reprint it here without comment or alteration.

He Shouldn't Complain—
At Least They Didn't Charge Him Interest
By John Urquhart, Staff Reporter

OTTAWA—Brian McNeilly wants it known that when he holds up a bank, he is stealing money, not borrowing it.

Mr. McNeilly has had a problem getting this point across to the Canadian Imperial Bank of Commerce. Last month, he pleaded guilty to robbing a branch of that bank, as well as to nine other heists in the Ottawa area. Following the trial, Commerce decided to treat him like just another delinquent borrower. It deducted 1,500 Canadian dollars (US$1,246) from a savings account he had with the bank to make up for the like sum he'd stolen.

"I Won't Stand for It"

Commerce recovered its funds under a banking law known as "the right of offset," which allows banks to deduct money from accounts when the account holders have fallen behind on loan payments. This may be the first time it has been used to recover funds from a robber, bankers say.

Although he couldn't be reached for comment, Mr. McNeilly was recently interviewed on a radio show here and said he is consulting with his lawyer to see if the bank acted legally. "I don't feel the bank has the right to do that," he said. "I won't stand for it." The money in his Commerce savings account, he added, came from an inheritance, not from the robberies. Mr. McNeilly also noted that the court didn't order him to pay back the C$23,000 he had stolen from the banks. Instead, he was sentenced to six years in jail. So, if the bank had the right to take his funds, he said, "I want some time off my sentence."

The Commerce bank claims that a debt is a debt whether Mr. McNeilly borrowed the money or stole it. "It is just like recovering money owed on an overdue demand loan," says Dan Maceluch, a bank spokesman, who adds that just because Mr. McNeilly was sentenced to jail doesn't mean the debt was forgiven.

Account Closed

Mr. McNeilly has taken steps to ensure that the bank can't relieve him of any more money. He has had his girlfriend close his account at the branch where he banked for six years and where he still has a loan on the books. (According to Mr. McNeilly, the loan is in good standing.)

In the radio interview, Mr. McNeilly also said that since arriving in jail, other bank robbers have told him that they've never heard of banks dipping into robbers' accounts. Ottawa Police Inspector Steve Nadori isn't surprised. "Most bank robbers don't have bank accounts," he says.

Part III
APPENDIXES

Therefore thou shalt keep the commandments of the LORD thy God, to walk in his ways, and to fear him. For the LORD thy God bringeth thee into a good land, a land of brooks of water, of fountains and depths that spring out of valleys and hills; A land of wheat, and barley, and vines, and fig trees, and pomegranates; a land of oil olive, and honey; A land wherein thou shalt eat bread without scarceness, thou shalt not lack any thing in it; a land whose stones are iron, and out of whose hills thou mayest dig brass. When thou hast eaten and art full, then thou shalt bless the LORD thy God for the good land which he hath given thee. Beware that thou forget not the LORD thy God, in not keeping his commandments, and his judgments, and his statutes, which I command thee this day: Lest when thou hast eaten and art full, and hast built goodly houses, and dwelt therein; And when thy herds and thy flocks multiply, and thy silver and thy gold is multiplied, and all that thou hast is multiplied; Then thine heart be lifted up, and thou forget the LORD thy God, which brought thee forth out of the land of Egypt, from the house of bondage; Who led thee through that great and terrible wilderness, wherein were fiery serpents, and scorpions, and drought, where there was no water; who brought thee forth water out of the rock of flint; Who fed thee in the wilderness with manna, which thy fathers knew not, that he might humble thee, and that he might prove thee, to do thee good at thy latter end; And thou say in thine heart, My power and the might of mine hand hath gotten me this wealth. But thou shalt remember the LORD thy God: for it is he that giveth thee power to get wealth, that he may establish his covenant which he sware unto thy fathers, as it is this day. And it shall be, if thou do at all forget the LORD thy God, and walk after other gods, and serve them, and worship them, I testify against you this day that ye shall surely perish. As the nations which the Lord destroyeth before your face, so shall ye perish; because ye would not be obedient unto the voice of the LORD your God.

—Deuteronomy 8:6-20

For there is no respect of persons with God. For as many as have sinned without law shall also perish without law: and as many as have sinned in the law shall be judged by the law; (For not the hearers of the law are just before God, but the doers of the law shall be justified. For when the Gentiles, which have not the law, do by nature the things contained in the law, these, having not the law, are a law unto themselves: Which shew the work of the law written in their hearts, their conscience also bearing witness, and their thoughts the mean while accusing or else excusing one another;) In the day when God shall judge the secrets of men by Jesus Christ according to my gospel.

—Romans 2:11-16

Appendix A

COMMON GRACE, ESCHATOLOGY, AND BIBLICAL LAW

The concept of common grace is seldom discussed outside of Calvinistic circles, although all Christian theologies must come to grips eventually with the issues underlying the debate over common grace. The phrase itself was common in the days of colonial American Puritanism. I came across it on several occasions when I was doing research on the colonial Puritans' economic doctrines and experiments. The concept goes back at least to John Calvin's writings.[1]

Before venturing into the forest of theological debate, let me state what I believe is the meaning of the word "grace." The Bible uses the idea in several ways, but the central meaning of grace is this: a gift given to God's creatures on the basis, first, of His favor to His Son, Jesus Christ, the incarnation of the second person of the Trinity, and second, on the basis of Christ's atoning work on the cross. Grace is not strictly unmerited, for Christ merits every gift, but in terms of the merit of the creation — merit deserved by a creature because of its mere creaturehood — there is none. In short, when we speak of any aspect of the creation, other than the incarnate Jesus Christ, grace is defined as an *unmerited gift*. The essence of grace is conveyed in James 1:17: "Every good gift and every perfect gift is from above, and cometh down from the Father of lights, with whom is no variableness, neither shadow of turning."

Special grace is the phrase used by theologians to describe the gift of eternal salvation. Paul writes: "For by grace are ye saved through faith; and that not of yourselves: it is the gift of God: Not of works, lest any man should boast" (Eph. 2:8-9). He also writes: "But God

---

The original version of this essay appeared in the Winter, 1976-77 issue of *The Journal of Christian Reconstruction*, published by the Chalcedon Foundation, P.O. Box 158, Vallecito, California 95251.

1. John Calvin, *Institutes of the Christian Religion* (1559), Book II, Section II, chapter 16; II:III:3; III:XIV:2.

commendeth his love toward us, in that, while we were yet sinners, Christ died for us" (Rom. 5:8). God selects those on whom He will have mercy (Rom. 9:18). He has chosen these people to be recipients of His gift of eternal salvation, and He chose them before the foundation of the world (Eph. 1:4-6).

But there is another kind of grace, and it is misunderstood. *Common grace* is equally a gift of God to His creatures, but it is distinguished from special grace in a number of crucial ways. A debate has gone on for close to a century within Calvinistic circles concerning the nature and reality of common grace. I hope that this essay will contribute some acceptable answers to the people of God, though I have little hope of convincing those who have been involved in this debate for 60 years.

Because of the confusion associated with the term "common grace," let me offer James Jordan's description of it. Common grace is the equivalent of the crumbs that fall from the master's table that the dogs eat. This is how the Canaanite woman described her request of healing by Jesus, and Jesus healed her because of her understanding and faith (Matt. 15:27-28).[2]

Background of the Debate

In 1924, the Christian Reformed Church debated the subject, and the decision of the Synod led to a major and seemingly permanent division within the ranks of the denomination. The debate was of considerable interest to Dutch Calvinists on both sides of the Atlantic, although traditional American Calvinists were hardly aware of the issue, and Arminian churches were (and are still) completely unaware of it. Herman Hoeksema, who was perhaps the most brilliant systematic theologian in America in this century, left the Christian Reformed Church to form the Protestant Reformed Church. He and his followers were convinced that, contrary to the decision of the CRC, there is no such thing as common grace.

The doctrine of common grace, as formulated in the disputed "three points" of the Christian Reformed Church in 1924, asserts the following:

---

2. Dogs in Israel were not highly loved animals, so the analogy with common grace is biblically legitimate. "And ye shall be holy men unto me: neither shall ye eat any flesh that is torn of beasts in the field; ye shall cast it to the dogs" (Ex. 22:31). If we assume that God loves pagans the way that modern people love their dogs, then the analogy will not fit.

1. There is a "favorable attitude of God toward mankind in general, and not alone toward the elect, . . ." Furthermore, there is "also a certain favor or grace of God which he shows to his creatures in general."

2. God provides "restraint of sin in the life of the individual and in society, . . ."

3. With regard to *"the performance of so-called civic righteousness . . .* the unregenerate, though incapable of any saving good . . . can perform such civic good."[3]

These principles can serve as a starting point for a discussion of common grace. The serious Christian eventually will be faced with the problem of explaining the good once he faces the biblical doctrine of evil. James 1:17 informs us that all good gifts are from God. The same point is made in Deuteronomy, chapter 8, which is quoted as the introduction to this essay. It is clear that the unregenerate are the beneficiaries of God's gifts. None of the participants to the debate denies the existence of the gifts. What is denied by the Protestant Reformed critics is that these gifts imply the *favor of God* as far as the unregenerate are concerned. They categorically deny the first point of the original three points.

For the moment, let us refrain from using the word grace. Instead, let us limit ourselves to the word *gift*. The existence of gifts from God raises a whole series of questions:

Does a gift from God imply His favor?

Does an unregenerate man possess the power to do good?

Does the existence of good behavior on the part of the unbeliever deny the doctrine of total depravity?

Does history reveal a progressive separation between saved and lost?

Would such a separation necessarily lead to the triumph of the unregenerate?

Is there a common ground intellectually between Christians and non-Christians?

Can Christians and non-Christians cooperate successfully in certain areas?

Do God's gifts increase or decrease over time?

Will the cultural mandate (dominion covenant) of Genesis 1:28 be fulfilled?

---

3. Cornelius Van Til, *Common Grace* (Philadelphia: Presbyterian and Reformed Publishing Co., 1954), pp. 20-22. This essay was reprinted in Van Til, *Common Grace and the Gospel* (Nutley, New Jersey: Presbyterian & Reformed, 1974), same pagination.

The Favor of God

This is a key point of dispute between those who affirm and those who deny the existence of common grace. I wish to save time, if not trouble, so let me say from the outset that the Christian Reformed Church's 1924 formulation of the first point is defective. The Bible does not indicate that God in any way favors the unregenerate. The opposite is asserted: "He that believeth on the Son hath everlasting life: and he that believeth not the Son shall not see life; but the wrath of God abideth on him" (John 3:36). The prayer of Christ recorded in John 17 reveals His favor toward the redeemed and them alone. There is a fundamental ethical separation between the saved and the lost. God hated Esau and loved Jacob, before either was born (Rom. 9:10-13).

What are we to make of the Bible's passages that have been used to support the idea of limited favor toward creatures in general? Without exception, they refer to *gifts* of God to the unregenerate. They do not imply God's favor. For example, there is this affirmation: "The Lord is good to all: and his tender mercies are over all his works" (Ps. 145:9). The verse preceding this one tells us that God is compassionate, slow to anger, gracious. Romans 2:4 tells us He is longsuffering. Luke 6:35-36 says:

> But love ye your enemies, and do good, and lend, hoping for nothing again; and your reward shall be great, and ye shall be the children of the Highest: for he is kind unto the unthankful and to the evil. Be ye therefore merciful, as your Father also is merciful.

I Timothy 4:10 uses explicit language: "For therefore we both labour and suffer reproach, because we trust in the living God, who is the Saviour of all men, specially of those that believe." The Greek word here translated as "Saviour" is transliterated *sōtēr*: one who saves, heals, protects, or makes whole. God saves (heals) everyone, *especially* those who believe. Unquestionably, the salvation spoken of is universal — not in the sense of special grace, and therefore in the sense of common grace. This is probably the most difficult verse in the Bible for those who deny universal salvation from hell and who also deny common grace.[4]

---

4. Gary North, "Aren't There Two Kinds of Salvation?", Question 75 in North, *75 Bible Questions Your Instructors Pray You Won't Ask* (2nd ed.; Tyler, Texas: Institute for Christian Economics, [1984] 1988).

The most frequently cited passage used by those who defend the idea of God's favor to the unregenerate is Matthew 5:44-45:

> But I say unto you, Love your enemies, bless them that curse you, do good to them that hate you, and pray for them which despitefully use you, and persecute you; That ye may be the children of your Father which is in heaven: for he maketh his sun to rise on the evil and on the good, and sendeth rain on the just and on the unjust.

It is understandable how such verses, in the absence of other verses that more fully explain the nature and intent of God's gifts, could lead men to equate God's favor and gifts. Certainly it is true that God protects, heals, rewards, and cares for the unregenerate. But none of these verses indicates an attitude of favor toward the unregenerate beneficiaries of His gifts. Only in the use of the word "favor" in its slang form of "do me a favor" can we argue that a gift from God is the same as His favor. Favor, in the slang usage, simply means *gift* — an unmerited gift from the donor. But if favor is understood as an attitude favorable to the unregenerate, or an emotional commitment by God to the unregenerate for their sakes, then it must be said, God shows no favor to the unrighteous.

Coals of Fire

One verse in the Bible, above all others, informs us of the underlying attitude of God toward those who rebel against Him despite His gifts. This passage is the concomitant to the oft-quoted Luke 6:35-36 and Matthew 5:44-45. It is Proverbs 25:21-22, which Paul cites in Romans 12:20:

> **If thine enemy be hungry, give him bread to eat; and if he be thirsty, give him water to drink: For thou shalt heap coals of fire upon his head, and the Lord shall reward thee.**

Why are we to be kind to our enemies? First, because God instructs us to be kind. He is kind to them, and we are to imitate Him. Second, by showing mercy, we heap coals of fire on their rebellious heads. From him to whom much is given, much shall be required (Luke 12:47-48). Our enemy will receive greater punishment for all eternity because we have been merciful to him. Third, we are promised a reward from God, which is always a solid reason for being obedient to His commands. The language could not be any plainer. Any discussion of common grace which omits Proverbs 25:21-22 from consideration is not a serious discussion of the topic.

The Bible is very clear. The problem with the vast majority of interpreters is that they still are influenced by the standards of self-proclaimed autonomous humanism. Biblically, *love is the fulfilling of the law* (Rom. 13:8). Love thy neighbor, we are instructed. Treat him with respect. Do not oppress or cheat him. Do not covet his goods or his wife. Do not steal from him. In treating him lawfully, you have fulfilled the commandment to love him. In so doing, you have rendered him without excuse on the day of judgment. God's people are to become conduits of God's gifts to the unregenerate.

This is not to say that every gift that we give to the lost must be given in an attempt to heap coals of fire on their heads. We do not know God's plan for the ages, except in its broad outlines. We do not know who God intends to redeem. So we give freely, hoping that some might be redeemed and the others damned. We play our part in the salvation of some and the damnation of others. For example, regenerate marriage partners are explicitly instructed to treat their unregenerate partners lawfully and faithfully. "For what knowest thou, O wife, whether thou shalt save thy husband? or how knowest thou, O man, whether thou shalt save thy wife" (I Cor. 7:16)? We treat our friends and enemies lawfully, for they are made in the image of God. But we are to understand that our honest treatment does make it far worse on the day of judgment for those with whom we have dealt righteously than if we had disobeyed God and been poor testimonies to them, treating them unlawfully.

God gives rebels enough rope to hang themselves for all eternity. This is a fundamental implication of the doctrine of common grace. The law of God condemns some men, yet it simultaneously serves as a means of repentance and salvation for others (Rom. 5:19-20). The same law produces different results in different people. What separates men is the saving grace of God in election. The law of God serves as a tool of final *destruction* against the lost, yet it also serves as a tool of active *reconstruction* for the Christian. The law rips up the kingdom of Satan as it serves as the foundation for the kingdom of God on earth.

Christ is indeed the savior of all people prior to the day of judgment (I Tim. 4:10). Christ sustains the whole universe (Col. 1:17). Without Him, no living thing could survive. He grants to His creatures such gifts as *time, law, order, power,* and *knowledge.* He grants all of these gifts to Satan and his rebellious host. In answer to the question, "Does God show His grace and mercy to all creation?" the answer is emphatically yes. To the next question, "Does this mean that

God in some way demonstrates an attitude of favor toward Satan?" the answer is emphatically no. God is no more favorable toward Satan and his demons than He is to Satan's human followers. But this does not mean that He does not bestow gifts upon them — gifts that they in no way deserve.

Total Depravity and God's Restraining Hand

Law is a means of grace: common grace to those who are perishing, special grace to those who are elect. *Law is also a form of curse*: special curse to those who are perishing, common curse to those who are elect. We are all under law as creatures, and because of the curse of Adam and the creation, we suffer the *temporal* burdens of Adam's transgression. The whole world labors under this curse (Rom. 8:18-23). Nevertheless, "all things work together for good to them that love God, to them who are the called according to his purpose" (Rom. 8:28). As men, we are all under law and the restraint of law, both physical and moral law, and we can use this knowledge of law either to bring us external blessings or to rebel and bring destruction. But we know also that all things work together for evil for them that hate God, to them who are the rejected according to His purpose (Rom. 9:17-22). Common grace — common curse, special grace — special curse: we must affirm all four.

The transgression of the law brings a *special curse* to the unregenerate. It is a curse of eternal duration. But this same transgression brings only a *common curse* to the elect. A Christian gets sick, he suffers losses, he is blown about by the storm, he suffers sorrow, but he does not suffer the second death (Rev. 2:11; 20:6, 14). For the believer, the common curses of life are God's chastening, signs of God's favor (Heb. 12:6). The difference between common curse and special curse is not found in the intensity of human pain or the extent of the loss; the difference lies in God's *attitude* toward those who are laboring under the external and psychological burdens. There is an attitude of favor toward the elect, but none toward the unregenerate. The common curse of the unregenerate is, in fact, a part of the special curse under which he will labor forever. The common curse of the elect man is a part of the special grace in terms of which he finally prospers. The common curse is nonetheless common, despite its differing effects on the eternal state of men. The law of God is sure. God does not respect persons (Rom. 2:11), with one exception: the person of Jesus Christ. (Christ was perfect, yet He was punished.)

But if the effects of the law are common in cursing, then the effects of the law are also common in grace. This is why we need a doctrine of common grace. This doctrine gives meaning to the doctrine of common curse, and vice versa. The law of God restrains men in their evil ways, whether regenerate or unregenerate. The law of God restrains "the old man" or old sin nature in Christians. Law's restraint is a true blessing for all men. In fact, it is even a temporary blessing for Satan and his demons. All those who hate God love death (Prov. 8:36b). This hatred of God is restrained during history. Evil men are given power, life, and time that they do not deserve. So is Satan. They cannot fully work out the implications of their rebellious, suicidal faith, for God's restraint will not permit it.

The common grace which restrains the totally depraved character of Satan and all his followers is, in fact, part of God's *special curse* on them. Every gift returns to condemn them on the day of judgment, heaping coals of fire on their heads. On the other hand, the common grace of God in law also must be seen as a part of the program of special grace to His elect. God's special gifts to His elect, person by person, are the source of varying rewards on the day of judgment (I Cor. 3:11-15). Common grace serves to condemn the rebels proportionately to the benefits they have received on earth, and it serves as the operating backdrop for the special grace given to the elect. The laws of God offer a source of order, power, and dominion. Some men use this common grace to their ultimate destruction, while other use it to their eternal benefit. It is nonetheless common, despite its differing effects on the eternal state of men.

The Good That Men Do

The Bible teaches that there is no good thing inherent in fallen man; his heart is wicked and deceitful (Jer. 17:9). All our self-proclaimed righteousness is as filthy rags in the sight of God (Isa. 64:6). Nevertheless, we also know that history has meaning, that there are permanent standards that enable us to distinguish the life of Joseph Stalin from the life of Albert Schweitzer. There are different punishments for different unregenerate men (Luke 12:45-48). This does not mean that God in some way favors one lost soul more than another. It only means that in the eternal plan of God there must be an eternal affirmation of the validity and permanence of His law. It is worse to be a murderer than a liar or a thief. Not every sin is a sin unto death (I John 5:16-17). History is not some amorphous, undifferentiated mass. It is not an illusion. It has implications for eternity. Therefore, the law of God stands as a reminder to unregenerate men that it is better to conform in part than not to conform at all, even though the end result of rebellion is destruction. There are degrees of punishment (Luke 12:47-48).

But what is the source of the good that evil men do? It can be no other than God (James 1:17). He is the source of all good. He restrains men in different ways, and the effects of this restraint, person to person, demon to demon, can be seen throughout all eternity. Not favor toward the unregenerate, but rather perfect justice of law and total respect toward the law of God on the part of God Himself are the sources of the good deeds that men who are lost may accomplish in time and on earth. There are, to use the vernacular, "different strokes for different folks," not because God is a respecter of persons, but because the deeds of different men are different.

The Knowledge of the Law

The work of the law is written on every man's heart. There is no escape. No man can plead ignorance (Rom. 2:11-14). But each man's history does have meaning, and some men have been given clearer knowledge than others (Luke 12:47-48). There is a *common knowledge* of the law, yet there is also *special knowledge* of the law — historically unique in the life of each man. Each man will be judged by the deeds that he has done, by every word that he has uttered (Rom. 2:6; Matt. 12:36). God testifies to His faithfulness to His word by distinguishing every shade of evil and good in every man's life, saved or lost.

Perhaps a biblical example can clarify these issues. God gave the people who dwelt in the land of Canaan an extra generation of sovereignty over their land. The slave mentality of the Hebrews, with the exceptions of Joshua and Caleb, did not permit them to go in and conquer the land. Furthermore, God specifically revealed to them that He would drive the people out, city by city, year by year, so that the wild animals could not take over the land, leaving it desolate (Ex. 23:27-30). Did this reveal God's favor toward the Canaanites? Hardly. He instructed the Hebrews to destroy them, root and branch. They were to be driven out of their land forever (Ex. 23:32-33). Nevertheless, they did receive a temporal blessing: an extra generation or more of peace. This kept the beasts in their place. It allowed the Hebrews to mature under the law of God. It also allowed the Hebrews to heap coals of fire on the heads of their enemies, for as

God told Abraham, the Hebrews would not take control of the promised land in his day, "for the iniquity of the Amorites is not yet full" (Gen. 15:16). During that final generation, the iniquity of the Amorites was filled to the brim. Then came destruction.

The Canaanites did receive more than they deserved. They stayed in the land of their fathers for an extra generation. Were they beneficiaries? In the days of wandering for the Hebrews, the Canaanites were beneficiaries. Then the final payment, culturally speaking, came due, and it was exacted by God through His people, just as the Egyptians had learned to their woe. They cared for the land until the Hebrews were fit to take possession of it. As the Bible affirms, "the wealth of the sinner is laid up for the just" (Prov. 13:22b). But this in no way denies the value of the sinner's wealth during the period in which he controls it. It is a gift from God that he has anything at all. God has restrained the sinners from dispersing their wealth in a flurry of suicidal destruction. He lets them serve as caretakers until that day that it is transferred to the regenerate.

The Hivites of Gibeon did escape destruction. They were wise enough to see that God's people could not be beaten. They tricked Joshua into making a treaty with them. The result was their perpetual bondage as menial laborers, but they received life, and the right to pursue happiness, although they forfeited liberty. They were allowed to live under the restraints of God's law, a far better arrangement culturally than they had lived under before the arrival of the Hebrews. They became the recipients of the cultural blessings given to the Hebrews, and perhaps some of them became faithful to God. In that case, what had been a curse on all of them — servitude — became a means of special grace. Their deception paid off (Josh. 9). Only the Hivites escaped destruction (Josh. 11:20).

In the day that Adam and Eve ate of the tree of knowledge, they died spiritually. God had told them they would die on that very day. But they did not die physically. They may or may not have been individually regenerated by God's Spirit. But they were the beneficiaries of a promise (Gen. 3:15). They were to be allowed to have children. Before time began, God had ordained the crucifixion. Christ was in this sense slain from the very beginning (Rev. 13:8). God granted them time on earth. He extended their lease on life; had they not sinned, they would have been able to own eternal life. God greatly blessed them and their murderous son Cain with a stay of execution. God respected Christ's work on the cross. Christ became a savior to Cain—not a personal savior or regenerating savior, but a savior of his life. God granted Cain protection (Gen. 4:15), one of the tasks of a savior.

Meaning in History

Once again, we see that history has meaning. God has a purpose. He grants favors to rebels, but not because He is favorable to them. He respects His Son, and His Son died for the whole world (John 3:16). He died to save the world, meaning to give it time, life, and external blessings. He did not die to offer a hypothetical promise of regeneration to "vessels of wrath" (Rom. 9:22), but He died to become a savior in the same sense as that described in the first part of I Timothy 4:10—not a special savior, but a sustaining, restraining savior. God dealt mercifully with Adam and Adam's family because He had favor for His chosen people, those who receive the blessings of salvation. But this salvation is expressly *historical* in nature. Christ died in time and on earth for His people. They are regenerated in time and on earth. He therefore preserves the earth and gives all men, including rebels, time.

With respect to God's restraint of the total depravity of men, consider His curse of the ground (Gen. 3:17-19). Man must labor in the sweat of his brow in order to eat. The earth gives up her fruits, but only through labor. Still, this common curse also involves common grace. Men are compelled to cooperate with each other in a world of scarcity if they wish to increase their income. They may be murderers in their hearts, but they must restrain their emotions and cooperate. The division of labor makes possible the specialization of production. This, in turn, promotes increased wealth for all those who labor. Men are restrained by scarcity, which appears to be a one-sided curse. Not so; it is equally a blessing. This is the meaning of common grace; common curse and common grace go together.

The cross is the best example of the fusion of grace and curse. Christ was totally cursed on the cross. At the same time, this was God's act of incomparable grace. Justice and mercy are linked at the cross. Christ died, thereby experiencing the curse common to all men. Yet through that death, Christ propitiated God. That is the source of common grace on earth—life, law, order, power—as well as the source of special grace. The common curse of the cross— death—led to *special grace* for God's elect, yet it also is the source of that *common grace* which makes history possible. Christ suffered the

"first death," not to save His people from the first death, and not to
save the unregenerate from the second death of the lake of fire. He
suffered the first death to satisfy the penalty of sin — the first death
(which Adam did not immediately pay, since he did not die physically
on the day that he sinned) and the second death (God's elect will
never perish).

At some time in the future, God will cease to restrain men's evil
(II Thess. 2:6-12). As He gave up Israel to their lusts (Ps. 81:12;
106:15), so shall He give up on the unregenerate who are presently
held back from part of the evil that they would do. This does not
necessarily mean that the unregenerate will then crush the people of
God. In fact, it means precisely the opposite. When God ceased to
restrain Israel, Israel was scattered. (True, for a time things went
badly for God's prophets.) But the very act of releasing them from
His restraint allowed God to let them fill up their own cup of iniquity.
The end result of God's releasing Israel was their fall into iniquity,
rebellion, and impotence (Acts 7:42-43). They were scattered by the
Assyrians, the Babylonians, and finally the Romans. The Christian
church became the heir to God's kingdom (Matt. 21:43). The Romans,
too, were given up to their own lusts (Rom. 1:24, 26, 28). Though it
took three centuries, they were finally replaced by the Christians.
The empire collapsed. The Christians picked up the pieces.

When God ceases to restrain men from the evil that they are
capable of committing, it seals their doom. Separated from restraint,
they violate the work of the law written in their hearts. Separated
from God's law, men lose God's tool of cultural dominion. Men who
see themselves as being under law can then use the law to achieve
their ends. Antinomians rush headlong into impotence, for, denying
that they are under law and law's restraints, they throw away the
crucial tool of external conquest and external blessings. They rebel
and are destroyed.

Wheat and Tares

The parable of the tares is instructive in dealing with the question: Does history reveal a *progressive separation* between the saved and
the lost? The parable begins with the field which is planted with
wheat, but which is sown with tares by an enemy during the night
(Matt. 13:24-30, 36-43). The parable refers to the kingdom of God,
not to the institutional church. "The field is the world," Christ explained (Matt. 13:38). The good wheat, the children of God, now

must operate in a world in which the tares, the unregenerate, are operating. The servants (angels) instantly recognize the difference, but they are told not to yank up the tares yet. Such a violent act would destroy the wheat by plowing up the field. To preserve the growing wheat, the owner allows the tares to develop. What is preserved is *historical development.* Only at the end of the world is a final separation made. Until then, *for the sake of the wheat,* the tares are not ripped out.

The rain falls on both the wheat and the tares. The sun shines on both. The blight hits both, and so do the locusts. Common grace and common curse: the law of God brings both in history. An important part of historical development is man's fulfillment of the dominion covenant. New productive techniques can be implemented through the common grace of God, once the care of the field is entrusted to men. The regularities of nature still play a role, but increasingly fertilizers, irrigation systems, regular care, scientific management, and even satellite surveys are part of the life of the field. Men exercise increasing dominion over the world. A question then arises: If the devil's followers rule, will they care tenderly for the needs of the godly? Will they exercise dominion for the benefit of the wheat, so to speak? On the other hand, will the tares be cared for by the Christians? If Christians rule, what happens to the unrighteous?

This is the problem of *differentiation in history.* Men are not passive. They are commanded to be active, to seek dominion over nature (Gen. 1:28; 9:1-7). They are to manage the field. As both the good and the bad work out their God-ordained destinies, what kind of development can be expected? Who prospers most, the saved or the lost? Who becomes dominant?

The final separation comes at the end of time. Until then, the two groups must share the same world. If wheat and tares imply slow growth to maturity, then we have to conclude that the radically discontinuous event of separation will not mark the time of historical development. It is an event of the last day: the final judgment. It is a discontinuous event that is the capstone of historical continuity. The death, resurrection, and ascension of Christ was the last historically significant series of events that properly can be said to be radically discontinuous (possibly the day of Pentecost could serve as the last earth-shaking, kingdom-shaking event). The next major eschatological discontinuity is the day of judgment. So we should expect growth in our era, the kind of growth indicated by the agricultural parables.[5]

---

5. Gary North, *Moses and Pharaoh: Dominion Religion vs. Power Religion* (Tyler, Texas: Institute for Christian Economics, 1985), ch. 12: "Continuity and Revolution."

What must be stressed is the element of continuous development. "The kingdom of heaven is like to a grain of mustard seed, which a man took and sowed in his field: Which indeed is the least of all seeds: but when it is grown, it is the greatest among herbs, and becometh a tree, so that the birds of the air come and lodge in the branches thereof" (Matt. 13:31-32). As this kingdom comes into maturity, there is no physical separation between saved and lost. That total separation will come only at the end of time. There can be major changes, even as the seasons speed up or retard growth, but we should not expect a radical separation.

While I do not have the space to demonstrate the point, this means that the separation spoken of by premillennialists — the Rapture — is not in accord with the parables of the kingdom. The Rapture comes at the end of time. The "wheat" cannot be removed from the field until that final day, when we are caught up to meet Christ in the clouds (I Thess. 4:17). There is indeed a Rapture, but it comes at the end of time — when the reapers (angels) harvest the wheat and the tares. There is a Rapture, but it is a postmillennial Rapture.

Why a postmillennial Rapture, the amillennialist may say? Why not simply point out that the Rapture comes at the end of time and let matters drop? The answer is important: We must deal with the question of the development of the wheat and tares. We must see that this process of time leads to Christian victory on earth and in time.

Knowledge and Dominion

Isaiah 32 is a neglected portion of Scripture in our day. It informs us of a remarkable day that is coming. It is a day of "epistemological self-consciousness," to use Cornelius Van Til's phrase. It is a day when men will know God's standards and apply them accurately to the historical situation. It is not a day beyond the final judgment, for it speaks of churls as well as liberal people. Yet it cannot be a day inaugurated by a radical separation between saved and lost (the Rapture), for such a separation comes only at the end of time. This day will come before Christ returns physically to earth in judgment. We read in the first eight verses:

Behold, a king shall reign in righteousness, and princes shall rule in judgment. And a man shall be as an hiding place from the wind, and a covert from the tempest; as rivers of water in a dry place, as the shadow of a great rock in a weary land. And the eyes of them that see shall not be dim, and the ears of them that hear shall hearken. The heart also of the rash shall understand knowledge, and the tongue of the stammerers shall be ready to speak plainly. The vile person shall be no more called liberal, nor the churl said to be bountiful. For the vile person will speak villany, and his heart will work iniquity, to practise hypocrisy, and to utter error against the LORD, to make empty the soul of the hungry, and he will cause the drink of the thirsty to fail. The instruments also of the churl are evil; he deviseth wicked devices to destroy the poor with lying words, even when the needy speaketh right. But the liberal deviseth liberal things: and by liberal things shall he stand.

To repeat, "The vile person shall be no more called liberal, nor the churl said to be bountiful" (v. 5). Churls persist in their churlishness; liberal men continue to be gracious. It does not say that all churls will be converted, but it also does not say that the liberals shall be destroyed. The two exist together. But the language of promise indicates that Isaiah knew full well that in his day (and in our day), churls are called liberal and vice versa. Men refuse to apply their knowledge of God's standards to the world in which they live. But it shall not always be thus.

At this point, we face two crucial questions. The answers separate many Christian commentators. First, should we expect this knowledge to come instantaneously? Second, when this prophesied world of epistemological self-consciousness finally dawns, which group will be the earthly victors, churls or liberals?

The amillennialist must answer that this parallel development of knowledge is gradual. The postmillenialist agrees. The premillennialist must dissent. The premil position is that the day of self-awareness comes only after the Rapture and the establishment subsequently of the earthly kingdom, with Christ ruling on earth in person. The amil position sees no era of pre-consummation, pre-final judgment righteousness. Therefore, he must conclude that the growth in self-awareness does separate the saved from the lost culturally, but since there is no coming era of godly victory culturally, the amillennialist has to say that this ethical and epistemological separation leads to the defeat of Christians on the battlefields of culture. Evil will triumph before the final judgment, and since this process is continuous, the decline into darkness must be part of the process of differentiation over time. This increase in self-knowledge therefore leads to the victory of Satan's forces over the church.

The postmillennialist categorically rejects such a view of knowledge. As the ability of Christians to make accurate, God-honoring judgments in history increases over time, more authority is transferred to them. As pagans lose their ability to make such judgments, as a direct result of their denial of and war against biblical law, authority will be removed from them, just as it was removed from Israel in 70 A.D. True knowledge in the postmillennial framework leads to blessing in history, not a curse. It leads to the victory of God's people, not their defeat. But the amillennialist has to deny this. The increase of true self-knowledge is a curse for Christians in the amillennial system. Van Til makes this fundamental in his book on common grace —his only systematically erroneous and debilitating book.

Van Til's Amillennial Version of Common Grace

We now return to the question of common grace. The slow, downward drift of culture parallels the growth in self-awareness, says the amillennialist. This has to mean that common grace is to be withdrawn as time progresses. The restraining hand of God will be progressively removed. Since the amillennialist believes that things get worse before the final judgment, he has to see common grace as *earlier* grace (assuming he admits the existence of common grace at all). This has been stated most forcefully by Van Til, who holds a doctrine of common grace and who is an amillennialist:

> All common grace is earlier grace. Its commonness lies in its earliness. It pertains not merely to the lower dimensions of life. It pertains to all dimensions of life, but to all these dimensions ever decreasingly as the time of history goes on. At the very first stage of history there is much common grace. There is a common good nature under the common favor of God. But this creation-grace requires response. It cannot remain what it is. It is conditional. Differentiation must set in and does set in. It comes first in the form of a common rejection of God. Yet common grace continues; it is on a "lower" level now; it is long-suffering that men may be led to repentance. . . . Common grace will diminish still more in the further course of history. With every conditional act the remaining significance of the conditional is reduced. God allows men to follow the path of their self-chosen rejection of Him more rapidly than ever toward the final consummation. God increases His attitude of wrath upon the reprobate as time goes on, until at the end of time, at the great consummation of history, their condition has caught up with their state.[6]

Van Til affirms the reality of history, yet it is the history of continuous decline. The unregenerate become increasingly powerful as

---

6. Van Til, *Common Grace*, pp. 82-83.

common grace declines. But why? Why should the epistemological self-awareness described in Isaiah 32 necessarily lead to defeat for the Christians? By holding to a doctrine of common grace which involves the idea of the common favor of God toward all creatures (except Satan, says Van Til), he then argues that this favor is withdrawn, leaving the unregenerate a free hand to attack God's elect. If common grace is linked with God's favor, and God's favor steadily declines, then that other aspect of common grace, namely, God's restraint, must also be withdrawn. Furthermore, the third feature of common grace, civic righteousness, must also disappear. Van Til's words are quite powerful:

> But when all the reprobate are epistemologically self-conscious, the crack of doom has come. The fully self-conscious reprobate will do all he can in every dimension to destroy the people of God. So while we seek with all our power to hasten the process of differentiation in every dimension we are yet thankful, on the other hand, for "the day of grace," the day of undeveloped differentiation. Such tolerance as we receive on the part of the world is due to this fact that we live in the earlier, rather than in the later, stage of history. And such influence on the public situation as we can effect, whether in society or in state, presupposes this undifferentiated stage of development.[7]

Consider the implications of what Van Til is saying. *History is an earthly threat to Christian man.* Why? His amil argument is that common grace is earlier grace. It declines over time. Why? Because God's attitude of favor declines over time with respect to the unregenerate. With the decline of God's favor, the other benefits of common grace are lost. Evil men become more thoroughly evil.

Van Til's argument is the generally accepted one in Reformed circles. His is the standard statement of the common grace position. Yet as the reader should grasp by now, it is deeply flawed. It begins with *false assumptions*: 1) that common grace implies common favor; 2) that this common grace-favor is reduced over time; 3) that this loss of favor necessarily tears down the foundations of civic righteousness within the general culture; 4) that the amillennial vision of the future is accurate. Thus, he concludes that the process of differentiation is leading to the impotence of Christians in every sphere of life, and that we can be thankful for having lived in the period of "earlier" grace, meaning greater common grace.

---

7. *Ibid.*, p. 85.

It is ironic that Van Til's view of common grace is implicitly opposed to the postmillennialism of R. J. Rushdoony, yet his view is equally opposed to the amillennialism of the anti-Chalcedon amillennial theologian (and former colleague of Van Til's), Meredith G. Kline, who openly rejects Rushdoony's postmillennial eschatology.[8] It is doubly ironic that Rushdoony has adopted Van Til's anti-postmillennial version of common grace, meaning "earlier grace."[9]

Van Til's amillennism colors his whole doctrine of common grace. Perhaps unconsciously, he selectively structured the biblical evidence on this question in order to make it conform with his Netherlands amillennial heritage. This is why his entire concept of common grace is incorrect. It is imperative that we scrap the concept of "earlier grace" and adopt a doctrine of common (crumbs for the dogs) grace.

---

8. Kline rejects Van Til's assertion that common grace declines over time. Kline says that this is what the Chalcedon postmillennialists teach — which simply is not true, nor even implied by their eschatology — and in doing so Kline breaks radically with Van Til. It is unlikely that Kline even recognizes the anti-Van Til implications of what he has written. "Along with the hermeneutical deficiencies of Chalcedon's millennialism there is a fundamental theological problem that besets it. And here we come around again to Chalcedon's confounding the biblical concepts of the holy and the common. As we have seen, Chalcedon's brand of postmillennialism envisages as the climax of the millennium something more than a high degree of success in the church's evangelistic mission to the world. An additional millennial prospect (one which they particularly relish) is that of a material prosperity and a world-wide eminence and dominance of Christ's established kingdom on earth, with a divinely enforced submission of the nations to the world government of the Christocracy. . . . The insuperable theological objection to any and every such chiliastic construction is that it entails the assumption of a premature eclipse of the order of common grace. . . . In thus postulating the termination of the common grace order before the consummation, Chalcedon's postmillennialism in effect attributes unfaithfulness to God, for God committed himself in his ancient covenant to maintain that order for as long as the earth endures." Meredith G. Kline, "Comments on an Old-New Error," *Westminster Theological Journal*, XLI (Fall 1978), pp. 183, 184.

9. It is one of the oddities in the Christian reconstruction movement that R. J. Rushdoony categorically rejects amillennialism, calling it "impotent religion" and "blasphemy," and yet he affirms the validity of Van Til's common grace position, calling for the substitution of Van Til's "earlier grace" concept for "common grace." Rushdoony's anti-amillennial (and therefore by implication anti-Van Til) essay appeared in *The Journal of Christian Reconstruction*, III (Winter 1976-77): "Postmillennialism versus Impotent Religion." His pro-"earlier grace" statement appeared in his review of E. L. Hebden Taylor's book, *The Christian Philosophy of Law, Politics and the State*, in *The Westminster Theological Journal*, XXX (Nov. 1967): "A concept of 'earlier grace' makes remnants of justice, right, and community tenable; a concept of 'common grace' does not" (p. 100). "The term 'common grace' has become a shibboleth of Dutch theology and a passageway across the Jordan and into Reformed territory of those who can feign the required accent. Has not the time come to drop the whole concept and start afresh?" (p. 101).

A Postmillennial Response

In response to Van Til, I offer three criticisms. First, God does not favor the unregenerate at any time after the rebellion of man. Man is totally depraved, and there is nothing in him deserving praise or favor, nor does God look favorably on him. God grants the unregenerate man favors (not favor) in order to heap coals of fire on his head (if he is not part of the elect) or else to call him to repentance (which God's special grace accomplishes). Thus, God is uniformly hostile to the rebel throughout history. God hates unregenerate men with a holy hatred from beginning to end. "Earlier" has nothing to do with it.

Second, once the excess theological baggage of God's supposed favor toward the unregenerate is removed, the other two issues can be discussed: God's restraint and man's civic righteousness. The activity of God's Spirit is important in understanding the nature of God's restraint, but we are told virtually nothing of the operation of the Spirit. What we *are* told is that *the law of God restrains men.* They do the work of the law written on their hearts. This law is the primary means of God's external blessings (Deut. 28:1-14); rebellion against His law brings destruction (Deut. 28:15-68). Therefore, as the reign of biblical law is extended by means of the preaching of the whole counsel of God, as the law is written in the hearts of men (Jer. 31:33-34; Heb. 8:10-11; 10:16), and as the unregenerate come under the sway and influence of the law, common grace must *increase*, not decrease. The central issue is the restraint by God inherent in the work of the law. This work is in every man's heart.

Remember, this has nothing to do with the supposed favor of God toward mankind in general. It is simply that as Christians become more faithful to biblical law, they receive more bread from the hand of God. As they increase the amount of bread on their tables, more crumbs fall to the dogs beneath.

Third, the amillennial view of the process of separation or differentiation is seriously flawed by a lack of understanding of the power which biblical law confers on those who seek to abide by its standards. Again, we must look at Deuteronomy, chapter eight. Conformity to the precepts of the law brings external blessings. The blessings can (though need not) serve as a snare and a temptation, for men may forget the source of their blessings. They can forget God, claim autonomy, and turn away from the law. This leads to destruction. The formerly faithful people are scattered. Thus, the paradox of Deuteronomy 8: covenantal faithfulness to the law—external blessings by God in response to faithfulness—temptation to rely on the blessings as if they were the product of man's hands—judgment. The blessings can lead to disaster and impotence. Therefore, *adherence to the terms of biblical law is basic for external success.*

Ethics and Dominion

As men become epistemologically self-conscious, they must face up to reality—God's reality. Ours is a moral universe. It is governed by a law-order which reflects the very being of God. When men finally realize who the churls are and who the liberals are, they have made a significant discovery. They recognize the relationship between God's standards and the ethical decisions of men. In short, they come to grips with the law of God. The *law* is written in the hearts of Christians. The *work of the law* is written in the hearts of all men. The Christians are therefore increasingly in touch with the source of earthly power: biblical law. To match the power of the Christians, the unregenerate must conform their actions externally to the law of God as preached by Christians, the work of which they already have in their hearts. The unregenerate are therefore made far more responsible before God, simply because they have more knowledge. They desire power. Christians will some day possess cultural power through their adherence to biblical law. Therefore, unregenerate men will have to imitate special covenantal faithfulness by adhering to the demands of God's external covenants. The unregenerate will thereby bring down the final wrath of God upon their heads, even as they gain external blessings due to their increased conformity to the *external requirements* of biblical law. At the end of time, they revolt.

The unregenerate have two choices: Conform themselves to biblical law, or at least to the work of the law written on their hearts, or, second, abandon law and thereby abandon power. They can gain power only on God's terms: acknowledgement of and conformity to God's law. There is no other way. Any turning from the law brings impotence, fragmentation, and despair. Furthermore, it leaves those with a commitment to law in the driver's seat. Increasing differentiation over time, therefore, does not lead to the impotence of the Christians. It leads to their victory culturally. They see the implications of the law more clearly. So do their enemies. The unrighteous can gain access to the blessings only by accepting God's moral universe as it is.

The Hebrews were told to separate themselves from the people and the gods of the land. Those gods were the gods of Satan, the gods of chaos, dissolution, and cyclical history. The pagan world was faithful to the doctrine of cycles: there can be no straight-line progress. But the Hebrews were told differently. If they were faithful, God said, they would not suffer the burdens of sickness, and no one and no animal would suffer miscarriages (Ex. 23:24-26). Special grace leads to a commitment to the law; the commitment to God's law permits God to reduce the common curse element of natural law, leaving proportionately more common grace — the reign of *beneficent common law*. The curse of nature can be steadily reduced, but only if men conform themselves to revealed law or to the works of the law in their hearts. The blessing comes in the form of a more productive, less scarcity-dominated nature. There can be *positive feedback* in the relation between law and blessing: the blessings will confirm God's faithfulness to His law, which in turn will lead to greater convenantal faithfulness (Deut. 8:18). This is the answer to the paradox of Deuteronomy 8: it need not become a cyclical spiral. Of course, special grace is required to keep a people faithful in the long run. Without special grace, the temptation to forget the source of wealth takes over, and the end result is destruction. This is why, at the end of the millennial age, the unregenerate try once again to assert their autonomy from God. They attack the church of the faithful. They exercise power. And the crack of doom sounds — for the unregenerate.

Differentiation and Progress

The process of differentiation is not constant over time. It ebbs and flows. Its general direction is toward epistemological and ethical self-consciousness. But Christians are not always faithful, any more than the Hebrews were in the days of the judges. The early church defeated Rome, and then the secular remnants of Rome compromised the church. The Reformation launched a new era of cultural growth, the Counter-Reformation struck back, and the secularism of the Renaissance swallowed up both — for a time. This is not cyclical history, for history is linear. There was a creation, a fall, a people called out of bondage, an incarnation, a resurrection, Pentecost. There will be a day of epistemological self-consciousness, as promised in Isaiah 32. There will be a final rebellion and judgment. There has been a

Christian nation called the United States. There has been a secular
nation called the United States. (The dividing line was the Civil
War, or War of Southern Secession, or War between the States, or
War of Northern Aggression—take your pick.) Back and forth, ebb
and flow, but with a long-range goal.

There has been progress. Look at the Apostles' Creed. Then look
at the Westminster Confession of Faith. Only a fool could deny progress. There has been a growth in wealth, in knowledge, and culture.
What are we to say, that technology as such is the devil's, that since
common grace has been steadily withdrawn, the modern world's development is the creative work of Satan (since God's common grace
cannot account for this progress)? Is Satan creative—autonomously
creative? If not, from whence comes our wealth, our knowledge, and
our power? Is it not from God? Is not Satan the great imitator? But
whose progress has he imitated? Whose cultural development has he
attempted to borrow, twist, and destroy? There has been progress
since the days of Noah—not straight-line progress, not pure compound
growth, but progress nonetheless. Christianity produced it, secularism
borrowed it, and today we seem to be at another crossroad: Can the
Christians sustain what they began, given their compromises with
secularism? And can the secularists sustain what they and the Christians have constructed, now that their spiritual capital is running
low, and the Christians' cultural bank account is close to empty?

Christians and secularists today are, in the field of education and
other "secular" realms, like a pair of drunks who lean on each other
in order not to fall down. We seem to be in the "blessings unto temptation" stage, with "rebellion unto destruction" looming ahead. It has
happened before. It can happen again. In this sense, it is the *lack* of
epistemological self-consciousness that seems to be responsible for
the *reduction* of common grace. Yet it is Van Til's view that the increase of epistemological self-consciousness is responsible for, or at
least parallels, the reduction of common grace. Amillennialism has
crippled his analysis of common grace. So has his equation of God's
gifts and God's supposed favor to mankind in general.

The separation between the wheat and the tares is progressive. It
is not a straight-line progression. Blight hits one and then the other.
Sometimes it hits both at once. Sometimes the sun and rain help
both to grow at the same time. But there is maturity. The tares grow
unto final destruction, and the wheat grows unto final blessing. In
the meantime, both have roles to play in God's plan for the ages. At

least the tares help keep the soil from eroding. Better tares than the destruction of the field, at least for the present. They serve God, despite themselves. There has been progress for both wheat and tares. Greek and Roman science became static; Christian concepts of optimism and an orderly universe created modern science. Now the tares run the scientific world, but for how long? Until a war? Until the concepts of meaningless Darwinian evolution and modern indeterminate physics destroy the concept of regular law — the foundation of all science?

How long can we go on like this? Answer: until epistemological self-consciousness brings Christians back to the law of God. Then the pagans must imitate them or quit. Obedience to God alone brings long-term dominion.

Law and Grace

The dual relationship between common law and common curse is a necessary backdrop for God's plan of the ages. Take, for example, the curse of Adam. Adam and his heirs are burdened with frail bodies that grow sick and die. Initially, there was a longer life expectancy for mankind. The longest life recorded in the Bible, that given to Methuselah, Noah's grandfather, was 969 years. Methuselah died in the year that the great flood began.[10] Thus, as far as human life is concerned, the greatest sign of God's common grace was given to men just before the greatest removal of common grace recorded in history.

This is extremely significant for the thesis of this essay. The *extension of common grace to man* — the external blessings of God that are given to mankind in general — is a *prelude to a great curse for the unregenerate*. As we read in the eighth chapter of Deuteronomy, as well as in the twenty-eighth chapter, men can be and are lured into a snare by looking upon the external gifts from God while forgetting the heavenly source of the gifts and the *covenantal terms* under which the gifts

---

10. Methuselah was 969 years old when he died (Gen. 5:27). He was 187 years old when his son Lamech was born (5:25) and 369 years old when Lamech's son Noah was born (5:28-29). Noah was 600 years old at the time of the great flood (7:6). Therefore, from the birth of Noah, when Methuselah was 369, until the flood, 600 years later, Methuselah lived out his years (369 + 600 = 969). The Bible does not say that Methuselah perished in the flood, but only that he died in the year of the flood. This is such a remarkable chronology that the burden of proof is on those who deny the father-to-son relationship in these three generations, arguing instead for an unstated gap in the chronology.

were given. The gift of long life was given to mankind in general, not as a sign of God's favor, but as a prelude to His almost total destruction of the seed of Adam. Only His special grace to Noah and his family preserved mankind.

Thus, the mere existence of external blessing is no proof of a favorable attitude toward man on the part of God. In the first stage, that of *covenantal faithfulness*, God's special grace is extended widely within a culture. The second state, that of *external blessings* in response to covenantal faithfulness, is intended to reinforce men's faith in the reality and validity of God's covenants (Deut. 8:18). But that second stage can lead to a third stage, covenantal or ethical *forgetfulness*. The key fact which must be borne in mind is that this third stage cannot be distinguished from the second stage in terms of measurements of the blessings (economic growth indicators, for example). An increase of external blessings should lead to the positive feedback of a faithful culture: victory unto victory. But it can lead to stage three, namely, forgetfulness. This leads to stage four, *destruction*. It therefore requires *special* grace to maintain the "faithfulness-blessing-faithfulness-blessing . . ." relationship of positive feedback and compound growth. But common grace plays a definite role in reinforcing men's commitment to the law-order of God.

Everyone in the Hebrew commonwealth, including the stranger who was within the gates, could benefit from the increase in external blessings. Therefore, the curse aspect of the "common grace-common curse" relationship can be progressively removed, and common grace either increases, or else the mere removal of common cursing makes it appear that common grace is increasing. (Better theologians than I can debate this point.)

The Reinforcement of Special Grace

Nevertheless, without special grace being extended by God—without continual conversions of men—the positive feedback of Deuteronomy 8 cannot be maintained. A disastrous reduction of blessings can be counted on by those who are not regenerate if their numbers are becoming dominant in the community. When regenerate Lot was removed from Sodom, and the unregenerate men who had been set up for destruction by God no longer were protected by Lot's presence among them, *their* crack of doom sounded (Gen. 18, 19). And the effects were felt in Lot's family, for his wife looked back and suffered the consequences of her disobedience (19:26), and his daughters committed sin (19:30-38). But it had been Lot's presence among them that had held off destruction (19:21-22).

The same was true of Noah. Until the ark was completed, the world was safe from the great flood. The people seemed to be prospering. Methuselah lived a long life, but after him, the lifespan of mankind steadily declined. Aaron died at age 123 (Num. 33:39). Moses died at age 120 (Deut. 31:2). But this longevity was not normal, even in their day. In a psalm of Moses, he said that "The days of our years are threescore years and ten; and if by reason of strength they be fourscore years, yet is their strength labour and sorrow; for it is soon cut off, and we fly away" (Ps. 90:10). The common curse of God could be seen even in the blessing of extra years, but long life, which is a blessing (Ex. 20:12), was being removed by God from mankind in general.

The Book of Isaiah tells us of a future restoration of long life. This blessing shall be given to all men, saints and sinners. It is therefore a sign of extended common grace. It is a gift to mankind in general. Isaiah 65:20 tells us: "There shall be no more thence an infant of days, nor an old man that hath not filled his days: for the child shall die an hundred years old; but the sinner being an hundred years old shall be accursed." The gift of long life shall come, though the common curse of long life shall extend to the sinner, whose long life is simply extra time for him to fill up his days of iniquity. Nevertheless, the infants will not die, which is a fulfillment of God's promise to Israel, namely, the absence of miscarriages (Ex. 23:26). If there is any passage in Scripture that absolutely refutes the amillennial position, it is this one. This is not a prophecy of the New Heavens and New Earth in their post-judgment form, but it is a prophecy of the pre-judgment manifestation of the preliminary stages of the New Heavens and New Earth — an earnest (down payment) of our expectations. There are still sinners in the world, and they receive long life. But to them it is an ultimate curse, meaning a *special curse*. It is a special curse because this exceptionally long life is a common blessing — the reduction of the *common curse*. Again, we need the concept of common grace to give significance to both special grace and common curse. Common grace (reduced common curse) brings special curses to the rebels.

There will be peace on earth extended to men of good will (Luke 2:14). But this means that there will also be peace on earth extended to evil men. Peace is given to the just as a reward for their covenantal faithfulness. It is given to the unregenerate in order to heap coals of fire on their heads, and also in order to lure rebels living in the very last days into a final rebellion against God.

Final Judgment and Common Grace

An understanding of common grace is essential for an understanding of the final act of human history before the judgment of God. To the extent that this essay contributes anything new to Christian theology, it is its contribution to an understanding of the final rebellion of the unregenerate. The final rebellion has been used by those opposing postmillennialism as final proof that there will be no faith on earth among the masses of men when Christ returns. The devil shall be loosed for a little season at the end of time, meaning his power over the nations returns to him in full strength (Rev. 20:3). However, this rebellion is short-lived. He surrounds the holy city (meaning the church of the faithful), only to be cut down in final judgment (Rev. 20:7-15). Therefore, conclude the critics of postmillennialism, there is a resounding negative answer to Christ's question: "Nevertheless when the Son of man cometh, shall he find faith on earth" (Luke 18:8)? Where, then, is the supposed victory?

The doctrine of common grace provides us with the biblical answer. *God's law is the main form of common grace.* It is written in the hearts of believers, we read in Hebrews, chapters eight and ten, but the work of the law is written in the heart of every man. Thus, the work of the law is universal—common. This access to God's law is the foundation of the fulfilling of the dominion covenant to subdue the earth (Gen. 1:28). The command was given to all men through Adam; it was reaffirmed by God with the family of Noah (Gen. 9:1-7). God's promises of external blessings are conditional to man's fulfillment of external laws. The reason why men can gain the blessings is because the knowledge of the work of the law is common. This is why there can be outward cooperation between Christians and non-Christians for certain earthly ends.

From time to time, unbelievers are enabled by God to adhere more closely to the work of the law that is written in their hearts. These periods of cultural adherence can last for centuries, at least with respect to some aspects of human culture (the arts, science, philosophy). The Greeks maintained a high level of culture inside the limited confines of the Greek city-states for a few centuries. The Chinese maintained their culture until it grew stagnant, in response to Confucian philosophy, in what we call the Middle Ages. But in the West, the ability of the unregenerate to act in closer conformity to the work of the law written in their hearts has been the result of the historical leadership provided by the cultural triumph of Christianity. In short, special grace increased, leading to an extension of common grace throughout Western culture. Economic growth has increased; indeed, the concept of linear, compound growth is unique to the West, and the foundations of this belief were laid by the Reformers who held to the eschatology known as postmillennialism. Longer lifespans have also appeared in the West, primarily due to the application of technology to living conditions. Applied technology is, in turn, a product of Christianity[11] and especially Protestant Christianity.[12]

In the era prophesied by Isaiah, unbelievers will once again come to know the benefits of God's law. No longer shall they twist God's revelation to them. *The churl shall no longer be called liberal.* Law will be respected by unbelievers. This means that they will turn away from an open, consistent worship of the gods of chaos and the philosophy of ultimate randomness, including evolutionary randomness. They will participate in the blessings brought to them by the preaching of the whole counsel of God, including His law. The earth will be subdued to the glory of God, including the cultural world. Unbelievers will fulfil their roles in the achievement of the terms of the dominion covenant.

This is why a theology that is orthodox must include a doctrine of common grace that is intimately related to biblical law. Law does not save men's souls, but *it does save their bodies and their culture.* Christ is the savior of all, especially those who are the elect (I Tim. 4:10).

Antinomian Revivalism vs. Reconstruction

The blessings and cultural victory taught by the Bible (and adequately commented upon by postmillennialists) will not be the products of some form of pietistic, semi-monastic revivalism. The "merely

---

11. Stanley Jaki, *The Road of Science and the Ways to God* (Chicago: University of Chicago Press, 1978); *Science and Creation: From eternal cycles to an oscillating universe* (Edinburgh and London: Scottish Academic Press, [1974] 1980).

12. Robert K. Merton, *Social Theory and Social Structure* (rev. ed.; New York: Free Press of Glencoe, 1957), ch. 18: "Puritanism, Pietism, and Science"; E. L. Hebden Taylor, "The Role of Puritanism-Calvinism in the Rise of Modern Science," *The Journal of Christian Reconstruction*, VI (Summer 1979); Charles Dykes, "Medieval Speculation, Puritanism, and Modern Science," *ibid.*

soteriological" preaching of pietism — the salvation of souls by special grace — is not sufficient to bring the victories foretold in the Bible. The whole counsel of God must and will be preached. This means that the law of God will be preached. The external blessings will come in response to the covenantal faithfulness of God's people. The majority of men will be converted. The unconverted will not follow their philosophy of chaos to logical conclusions, for such a philosophy leads to ultimate impotence. It throws away the tool of reconstruction, biblical law.

The great defect with the postmillennial revival inaugurated by Jonathan Edwards and his followers in the eighteenth century was their neglect of biblical law. They expected to see the blessings of God come as a result of merely soteriological preaching. Look at Edwards' *Treatise on the Religious Affections*. There is nothing on the law of God in culture. Page after page is filled with the words "sweet" and "sweetness." A diabetic reader is almost risking a relapse by reading this book in one sitting. The words sometimes appear four or five times on a page. And while Edwards was preaching the sweetness of God, Arminian semi-literates were "hot-gospeling" the Holy Commonwealth of Connecticut into political antinomianism.[13] Where sweetness and emotional hot flashes are concerned, Calvinistic preaching is no match for antinomian sermons. The hoped-for revival of the 1700's became the Arminian revivals of the early 1800's, leaving emotionally burned-over districts, cults, and the abolitionist movement as their devastating legacy. Because the postmillennial preaching of the Edwardians was culturally antinomian and pietistic, it crippled the remnants of Calvinistic political order in the New England colonies, helping to produce a vacuum that Arminianism and then Unitarianism filled.

Progress culturally, economically, and politically is intimately linked to the extension and application of biblical law. The blessings promised in Romans, chapter eleven, concerning the effects of the promised conversion of Israel (not necessarily the state of Israel) to

---

13. On the opposition to Edwards' toleration of revivalism, not from theological liberals but from orthodox Calvinistic pastors, see Richard L. Bushman, *From Puritan to Yankee* (Cambridge, Massachusetts: Harvard University Press, 1967). Bushman also explains how the Great Awakening was a disaster for the legal remnants of biblical law in the colony of Connecticut. The political order was forced into theological neutralism, which in turn aided the rise of Deism and liberalism.

the gospel, will be in part the product of biblical law.[14] But these blessings do not necessarily include universal regeneration. The blessings only require the extension of Christian culture. For the long-term progress of culture, of course, this increase of common grace (or reduction of the common curse) must be reinforced (rejuvenated and renewed) by special grace — conversions. But the blessings can remain for a generation or more after special grace has been removed, and as far as the external benefits can be measured, it will not be possible to tell whether the blessings are part of the *positive feedback program* (Deut. 8:18) or a *prelude to God's judgment* (Deut. 8:19-20). God respects His conditional, external covenants. External conformity to His law gains external blessings. These, in the last analysis (and at the last judgment), produce coals for unregenerate heads.

Universal Regeneration?

The postmillennial system requires a doctrine of common grace and common curse. It does not require a doctrine of universal regeneration during the period of millennial blessings. In fact, no postmillennial Calvinist can afford to be without a doctrine of common grace — one which links *external* blessings to the fulfillment of *external* covenants. There has to be a period of external blessings during the final generation. Something must hold that culture together so that Satan can once again go forth and deceive the nations. The Calvinist

---

14. John Murray's excellent commentary, *The Epistle to the Romans* (Grand Rapids, Michigan: Eerdmans, 1965), contains an extensive analysis of Romans 11, the section dealing with the future conversion of the Jews. Murray stresses that God's regrafting in of Israel leads to covenantal blessings unparalleled in human history. But the Israel referred to in Romans 11, argues Murray, is not national or political Israel, but the natural seed of Abraham. This seems to mean genetic Israel.

A major historical problem appears at this point. There is some evidence (though not conclusive) that the bulk of those known today as Ashkenazi Jews are the heirs of a converted tribe of Turkish people, the Khazars. It is well-known among European history scholars that such a conversion took place around 740 A.D. The Eastern European and Russian Jews may have come from this stock. They have married other Jews, however: the Sephardic or diaspora Jews who fled primarily to western Europe. The Yemenite Jews, who stayed in the land of Palestine, also are descendants of Abraham. The counter-evidence against this thesis of the Khazars as modern Jews is primarily linguistic: Yiddish does not bear traces of any Turkic language. On the kingdom of the Khazars, see Arthur Koestler, *The Thirteenth Tribe: The Khazar Empire and Its Heritage* (New York: Random House, 1976).

If the Israel referred to in Romans 11 is primarily genetic, then it may not be necessary that all Jews be converted. What, then, is the Jew in Romans 11? Covenantal? I wrote to Murray in the late 1960s to get his opinion on the implications of the Khazars for his exegesis of Romans 11, but he did not respond.

denies that men can "lose their salvation," meaning their regenerate status. The rebels are not "formerly regenerate" men. But they are men with power, or at least the trappings of power. They are powerful enough to delude themselves that they can destroy the people of God. And power, as I have tried to emphasize throughout this essay, is not the product of antinomian or chaos-oriented philosophy. The very existence of a military chain of command demands a concept of law and order. Satan commands an army on that final day.

The postmillennial vision of the future paints a picture of historically incomparable blessings. It also tells of a final rebellion that leads to God's total and final judgment. Like the long-lived men in the days of Methuselah, judgment comes upon them in the midst of power, prosperity, and external blessings. God has been gracious to them all to the utmost of His common grace. He has been gracious in response to their covenantal faithfulness to His *civil* law-order, and He has been gracious in order to pile the maximum possible pile of coals on their heads. In contrast to Van Til's amillennialist vision of the future, we must say: *When common grace is extended to its maximum limits possible in history, then the crack of doom has come—doom for the rebels.*

Epistemological Self-Consciousness and Cooperation

Van Til writes: "But when all the reprobate are epistemologically self-conscious, the crack of doom has come. The fully self-conscious reprobate will do all he can in every dimension to destroy the people of God." Yet Van Til has written in another place that the rebel against God is like a little child who has to sit on his father's lap in order to slap his face. What, then, can be meant by the concept of increasing epistemological self-consciousness?

As the wheat and tares grow to maturity, the amillennialist argues, the tares become stronger and stronger culturally, while the wheat becomes weaker and weaker. Consider what is being said. As Christians work out their own salvation with fear and trembling, improving their creeds, improving their cooperation with each other on the basis of agreement about the creeds, as they learn about the law of God as it applies in their own era, as they become skilled in applying the law of God that they have learned about, they become culturally impotent. They become infertile, also, it would seem. They do not become fruitful and multiply. Or if they do their best to follow this commandment, they are left without the blessing of God—a blessing which He has promised to those who follow the laws He has established. In short, the increase of epistemological self-consciousness on the part of Christians leads to cultural impotence.

I am faced with an unpleasant conclusion: *the amillennialist version of the common grace doctrine is inescapably antinomian.* It argues that God no longer respects His covenantal law-order, that Deuteronomy's teaching about covenantal law is invalid in New Testament times. The only way for the amillennialist to avoid the charge of antinomianism is for him to abandon the concept of increasing epistemological self-consciousness. He must face the fact that to achieve cultural impotence, Christians therefore must not increase in knowledge and covenantal faithfulness. (Admittedly, the condition of twentieth-century Christianity does appear to enforce this attitude about epistemological self-consciousness among Christians.)

Consider the other half of Van Til's dictum. As the epistemological self-consciousness of the unregenerate increases, and they adhere more and more to their epistemological premises of the origins of matter out of chaos, and the ultimate return of all matter into pure randomness, this chaos philosophy makes them confident. The Christian is humble before God, but confident before the creation which he is to subdue. This confidence leads the Christian into defeat and ultimate disaster, say amillennialists, who believe in increasing epistemological self-consciousness. On the other hand, the rebel is arrogant before God and claims that all nature is ruled by the meaningless laws of probability—ultimate chaos. By immersing themselves in the philosophy of chaos, the unbelievers are able to emerge totally victorious across the whole face of the earth, says the amillennialist, a victory which is called to a halt only by the physical intervention of Jesus Christ at the final judgment. A commitment to lawlessness, in the amillennial version of common grace, leads to external victory. How can these things be?

Amillennialism Has Things Backwards

It should be clear by now that the amillennialist version of the relationship between biblical law and the creation is completely backwards. No doubt Satan wishes it were a true version. He wants his followers to believe it. But how can a consistent Christian believe it? How can a Christian believe that adherence to biblical law produces cultural impotence, while commitment to philosophical chaos —the religion of satanic revolution—leads to cultural victory? There is no doubt in my mind that the amillennialists do not want to teach such a doctrine, yet that is where their amillennial pessimism inevitably leads. Dutch Calvinists preach the cultural mandate (dominion covenant), but they simultaneously preach that it cannot be fulfilled. But biblical law is basic to the fulfillment of the cultural mandate. Therefore, the amillennialist who preaches the obligation of trying to fulfil the cultural mandate without biblical law thereby plunges himself either into the camp of the chaos cults (mystics, revolutionaries) or into the camp of the natural-law, common-ground philosophers. There are only four possibilities: revealed law, natural law, chaos, or a mixture.

This leads me to my next point. It is somewhat speculative and may not be completely accurate. It is an idea which ought to be pursued, however, to see if it is accurate. I think that the reason why the philosophy of Herman Dooyeweerd, the Dutch philosopher of law, had some temporary impact in Dutch Calvinist intellectual circles in the late 1960s and early 1970s is that Dooyeweerd's theory of sphere sovereignty—sphere laws that are *not* to be filled in by means of revealed, Old Testament law—is consistent with the amillennial (Dutch) version of the cultural mandate. Dooyeweerd's system and Dutch amillennialism are essentially antinomian. This is why I wrote my 1967 essay, "Social Antinomianism," in response to the Dooyeweerdian professor at the Free University of Amsterdam, A. Troost.[15]

Either the Dooyeweerdians wind up as mystics, or else they try to create a new kind of "common-ground philosophy" to link believers and unbelievers. It is Dooyeweerd's outspoken resistance to Old Testament and New Testament authority over the *content* of his hypothesized sphere laws that has led his increasingly radical, increasingly antinomian followers into anti-Christian paths. You cannot preach the dominion covenant and then turn around and deny the efficacy of biblical law in culture. Yet this is what all the Dutch adherents to common grace have done. They deny the cultural efficacy of biblical law, by necessity, because their eschatological interpretations have led them to conclude that there can be no external, cultural victory in time and on earth by faithful Christians. Epistemological self-consciousness will increase, but things only get worse over time.

If you preach that biblical law produces "positive feedback," both personally and culturally—that God rewards covenant-keepers and

---

15. Gary North, *The Sinai Strategy: Economics and the Ten Commandments* (Tyler, Texas: Institute for Christian Economics, 1986), Appendix C: "Social Antinomianism."

punishes covenant-breakers in time and on earth — then you are preaching a system of positive growth. You are preaching the dominion covenant. Only if you deny that there is any relationship between covenant-keeping and external success in life — a denial made explicit by Meredith G. Kline[16] — can you escape from the postmillennial implications of biblical law. This is why it is odd that Greg Bahnsen insists — perhaps for tactical reasons — on presenting his defense of biblical law apart from his well-known postmillennialism.[17] Kline attacked both of Bahnsen's doctrines in his critique of *Theonomy*,[18] and Bahnsen in his rebuttal essay did respond to Kline's criticisms of his postmillennial eschatology, but he again denies that eschatology has anything logically to do with biblical ethics.[19] But Kline was correct: there is unquestionably a necessary connection between a *covenantal* concept of biblical law and eschatology. Kline rejects the idea of a New Testament covenantal law-order, and he also rejects postmillennialism.

Amillennial Calvinists will continue to be plagued by Dooyeweerdians, mystics, natural-law compromisers, and antinomians of all sorts until they finally abandon their amillennial eschatology. Furthermore, biblical law must be preached. It must be seen as the tool of cultural reconstruction. It must be seen as operating *now*, in New Testament times. It must be seen that there is a relationship between covenantal faithfulness and obedience to law — that without

---

16. Kline says that any connection between blessings and covenant-keeping is, humanly speaking, random. "And meanwhile it [the common grace order] must run its course within the uncertainties of the mutually conditioning principles of common grace and common curse, prosperity and adversity being experienced in a manner largely unpredictable because of the inscrutable sovereignty of the divine will that dispenses them in mysterious ways." Kline, *op. cit.*, p. 184. Dr. Kline has obviously never considered just why it is that life insurance premiums and health insurance premiums are cheaper in Christian-influenced societies than in pagan societies. Apparently, the blessings of long life that are promised in the Bible are sufficiently non-random and "scrutable" that statisticians who advise insurance companies can detect statistically relevant differences between societies.

17. "What these studies present is a position in Christian (normative) *ethics*. They do *not* logically commit those who agree with them to any particular school of *eschatological* interpretation." Greg L. Bahnsen, *By This Standard: The Authority of God's Law Today* (Tyler, Texas: Institute for Christian Economics, 1985), p. 8. He is correct: *logically*, there is no connection. *Covenantally*, the two doctrines are inescapable: when the law is preached, there are blessings; blessings lead inescapably to victory.

18. Kline, *op. cit.*

19. Greg L. Bahnsen, "M. G. Kline on Theonomic Politics: An Evaluation of His Reply," *Journal of Christian Reconstruction*, VI (Winter, 1979-80), No. 2, especially p. 215.

obedience there is no faithfulness, no matter how emotional believers may become, or how sweet the gospel tastes (for a while). And there are blessings that follow obedience to God's law-order. Amillennialists, by preaching eschatological impotence culturally, thereby immerse themselves in quicksand — the quicksand of antinomianism. Some sands are quicker than others. Eventually, they swallow up anyone so foolish as to try to walk through them. Antinomianism leads into the pits of impotence and retreat.

Epistemological Self-Consciousness

What is meant by epistemological self-consciousness? It means a greater understanding over time of what one's presuppositions are, and a greater willingness to put these presuppositions into action. It affects both wheat and tares.

In what ways does the wheat resemble the tares? In what ways are they different? The angels saw the differences immediately. God therefore restrained them from ripping up the tares. He wanted to preserve the soil — the historical process. Therefore, the full development of both wheat and tares is permitted by God.

What must be understood here is that *the doctrine of special grace in history necessarily involves the doctrine of common grace.* As the Christians develop to maturity, they become more powerful. This is not a straight-line development. There are times of locusts and blight and drought, both for Christians and for satanists (humanists). There is ebb and flow, but always there is direction to the movement. There is maturity. The creeds are improved. This, in turn, gives Christians cultural power. Is it any wonder that the Westminster Confession of Faith was drawn up at the high point of the Puritans' control of England? Are improvements in the creeds useless culturally? Do improvements in creeds and theological understanding necessarily lead to impotence culturally? Nonsense! It was the Reformation that made possible modern science and technology.

On the other side of the field — indeed, right next to the wheat — self-awareness by unbelievers also increases. But they do not always become more convinced of their roots in chaos. The Renaissance was successful in swallowing up the fruits of the Reformation only to the extent that it was a pale reflection of the Reformation. The Renaissance leaders rapidly abandoned the magic-charged, demonically inspired magicians like Giordano Bruno.[20] They may have kept the

---

20. On the magic of the early Renaissance, see Frances Yates, *Giordano Bruno and the Hermetic Tradition* (New York: Vintage, [1964] 1969).

humanism of a Bruno, but after 1600, the open commitment to the demonic receded. In its place came rationalism, Deism, and the logic of an orderly world. They used stolen premises and gained power. So compelling was this vision of mathematically autonomous reality that Christians like Cotton Mather hailed the new science of Newtonian mechanics as essentially Christian. It was so close to Christian views of God's orderly being and the creation's reflection of His orderliness, that the Christians unhesitatingly embraced the new science.

What we see, then, is that the Christians were not fully self-conscious epistemologically, and neither were the pagans. In the time of the apostles, there was greater epistemological awareness among the leaders of both sides. The church was persecuted, and it won. Then there was a lapse into muddled thinking on both sides. The attempt, for example, of Julian the Apostate to revive paganism late in the fourth century was ludicrous — it was half-hearted paganism, at best. Two centuries earlier, Marcus Aurelius, a true philosopher-king in the tradition of Plato, had been a major persecutor of Christians; Justin Martyr died under his years as emperor. But his debauched son, Commodus, was too busy with his 300 female concubines and 300 males[21] to bother about systematic persecutions. Who was more self-conscious, epistemologically speaking? Aurelius still had the light of reason before him; his son was immersed in the religion of revolution — culturally impotent. He was more willing than his philosopher-persecutor father to follow the logic of his satanic faith. He preferred debauchery to power. Commodus was assassinated 13 years after he became Emperor. The Senate resolved that his name be execrated.[22]

If a modern investigator would like to see as fully consistent a pagan culture as one might imagine, he could visit the African tribe, the Ik. Colin Turnbull did, and his book, *The Mountain People* (1973), is a classic. He found almost total rebellion against law — family law, civic law, all law. Yet he also found a totally impotent, beaten people who were rapidly becoming extinct. They were harmless to the West because they were more self-consistent than the West's satanists.

---

21. Edward Gibbon, *The History of the Decline and Fall of the Roman Empire*, Milman edition, 5 Vols. (Philadelphia: Porter & Coates, [1776]), I, p. 144.

22. Ethelbert Stauffer, *Christ and the Caesars* (Philadelphia: Westminster Press, 1955), p. 223.

The Marxist Challenge

Marxists, on the other hand, *are* a threat. They believe in linear history (officially, anyway — their system is at bottom cyclical, however).[23] They believe in law. They believe in destiny. They believe in historical meaning. They believe in historical stages, though not ethically determined stages such as we find in Deuteronomy. They believe in science. They believe in literature, propaganda, and the power of the written word. They believe in higher education. In short, they have a philosophy which is a kind of perverse mirror image of Christian orthodoxy. They are dangerous, not because they are acting consistently with their ultimate philosophy of chaos, but because they limit the function of chaos to one area alone: the revolutionary transformation of bourgeois culture. (I am speaking here primarily of Soviet Marxists.) And where are they winning converts? In the increasingly impotent, increasingly existentialist, increasingly antinomian West. Until the West abandoned its remnant of Christian culture, Marxism could flourish only in the underdeveloped, basically pagan areas of the world. An essentially Western philosophy of optimism found converts among the intellectuals of the Far East, Africa, and Latin America, who saw the fruitlessness of Confucian stagnation and relativism, the impotence of demonic ritual, or the dead-end nature of demon worship. Marxism is powerful only to the extent that it has the trappings of Augustinianism, coupled with subsidies, especially technological subsidies and long-term credit, from Western industry.

There is irony here. Marx believed that "scientific socialism" would triumph only in those nations that had experienced the full development of capitalism. He believed that in most cases (possibly excepting Russia), rural areas had to abandon feudalism and develop a fully capitalist culture before the socialist revolution would be successful. Yet it was primarily in the rural regions of the world that Marxist ideas and groups were first successful. The industrialized West was still too Christian or too pragmatic (recognizing that "honesty is the best policy") to capitulate to the Marxists, except immediately following a lost war.

Marxists have long dominated the faculties of Latin American universities, but not U.S. universities. In 1964, for example, there

---

23. Gary North, *Marx's Religion of Revolution: Regeneration Through Chaos* (Tyler, Texas: Institute for Christian Economics, [1968] 1989), pp. 100-1.

were not half a dozen outspoken Marxist economists teaching in American universities (and possibly as few as one, Stanford's Paul Baran). Since 1965, however, New Left scholars of a Marxist persuasion have become a force to be reckoned with in all the social sciences, including economics.[24] The skepticism, pessimism, relativism, and irrelevance of modern "neutral" education have left faculties without an adequate defense against confident, shrill, vociferous Marxists, primarily young Marxists, who began to appear on the campuses after 1964. Epistemological rot has left the establishment campus liberals with little more than tenure to protect them.[25]

Since 1965, however, Marxism has made more inroads among the young intellectuals of the industrialized West than at any time since the 1930s — an earlier era of pessimism and skepticism about established values and traditions. Marxists are successful among savages, whether in Africa or at Harvard — epistemological savages. Marxism offers an alternative to despair. It has the trappings of optimism. It has the trappings of Christianity. It is still a nineteenth-century system, drawing on the intellectual capital of a more Christian intellectual universe. These trappings of Christian order are the source of Marxism's influence in an increasingly relativistic world.

Satan's Final Rebellion

In the last days of this final era in human history, the satanists will still have the trappings of Christian order about them. Satan has to sit on God's lap, so to speak, in order to slap His face — or try to. Satan cannot be consistent to his own philosophy of autonomous order and still be a threat to God. An autonomous order leads to chaos and impotence. He knows that there is no neutral ground in philosophy. He knew Adam and Eve would die spiritually on the day that they ate the fruit. He is a good enough theologian to know that there is one God, and he and his host tremble at the thought (James 2:19). When demonic men take seriously his lies about the nature of reality, they become impotent, sliding off (or nearly off) God's lap. It is when satanists realize that Satan's official philosophy of chaos and antinomian lawlessness is a *lie* that they become dangerous. (Marx-

---

24. Martin Bronfenbrenner, "Radical Economics in America: A 1970 Survey," *Journal of Economic Literature*, VIII (Sept. 1970).

25. Gary North, "The Epistemological Crisis of American Universities," in Gary North (ed.), *Foundations of Christian Scholarship: Essays in the Van Til Perspective* (Vallecito, California: Ross House Books, 1976).

ists, once again, are more dangerous to America than are the Ik.) They learn more of the truth, but they pervert it and try to use it against God's people.

Thus, the biblical meaning of epistemological self-consciousness is not that the satanist becomes consistent with Satan's official philosophy (chaos), but rather that Satan's host becomes consistent with what Satan really believes: that order, law, power are the product of God's hated order. They learn to use law and order to build an army of conquest. In short, *they use common grace* — knowledge of the truth — *to pervert the truth and to attack God's people*. They turn from a false knowledge offered to them by Satan, and they adopt a perverted form of truth to use in their rebellious plans. They *mature*, in other words. Or, as C. S. Lewis has put into the mouth of his fictitious character, the senior devil Screwtape, when materialists finally believe in Satan but not in God, then the war is over.[26] Not quite; when they believe in God, know He is going to win, and nevertheless strike out in fury — not blind fury, but *fully self-conscious fury* — at the works of God, *then* the war is over.

Cooperation

How, then, can we cooperate with such men? Simply on the basis of common grace. *Common grace has not yet fully developed.* But this cooperation must be in the interests of God's kingdom. Whether or not a particular *ad hoc* association is beneficial must be made in terms of standards set forth in biblical law. Common grace is not common ground; there is no common ground uniting men except for the image of God in every man.

Because external conformity to the terms of biblical law does produce visibly good results — contrary to Prof. Kline's theory of God's mysterious will in history — unbelievers for a time are willing to adopt these principles, since they seek the fruits of Christian culture. In short, some ethical satanists respond to the knowledge of God's law written in their hearts. They have a large degree of knowledge about God's creation, but they are not yet willing to attack that world. They have knowledge through common grace, but they do not yet see what this means for their own actions. (To some extent, the Communists see, but they have not yet followed through; they have not launched a final assault against the West.)

---

26. C. S. Lewis, *The Screwtape Letters* (New York: Macmillan, 1969), Letter 7.

The essence of Adam's rebellion was not intellectual; it was *ethical*. No one has argued this more forcefully than Van Til. The mere addition of knowledge to or by the unregenerate man does not alter the essence of his status before God. He is still a rebel, but he may possess knowledge. Knowledge can be applied to God's creation and produce beneficial results. Knowledge can also produce a holocaust. The issue is ethics, not knowledge. Thus, men can cooperate in terms of mutually shared knowledge; ultimately, they cannot cooperate in terms of a mutually shared ethics.

What of the *special curse*? What is the ethical rebel's ethical relation to God? Common grace increases the unregenerate man's special curse. When common grace increases to its maximum, the special curse of God is revealed: total rebellion of man against the *truth* of God and *in terms of the common grace*—knowledge, power, wealth, prestige, etc.—of God, leading to final judgment. God does remove part of His restraint at the very end: the restraint on suicidal destruction. He allows them to achieve that death which they love (Prov. 8:36b). But they still have power and wealth, as in the Babylonian Empire the night it fell.

Pagans can teach us about physics, mathematics, chemistry, and many other topics. How is this possible? Because common grace has increased. They had several centuries of leadership from Christians, as well as Enlightenment figures who adopted a philosophy of coherence that at least resembled the Christian doctrine of providence. They cannot hold the culture together in terms of their philosophy of chaos—Satan's official viewpoint—but they still can make important discoveries. They use stolen capital, in every sense.

Christians Must Lead

When there is Christian revival and the preaching and application of the whole counsel of God, then Christians can once again take the position of real leadership. The unbelievers also can make contributions to the subduing of the earth because they will be called back to the work of the law written in their hearts. Common grace will increase throughout the world. But Christians must be extremely careful to watch for signs of ethical deviation from those who seemingly are useful co-workers in the kingdom. There can be cooperation for external goals—the fulfilling of the dominion covenant which was given to all men—but not in the realm of ethics. We must watch the Soviets to see how *not* to build a society. We must construct countermeasures to their military offenses. We must not adopt their view of proletarian ethics, even though their chess players or mathematicians may show us a great deal. The law of God as revealed in the Bible must be dominant, not the work of the law written in the hearts of the unrighteous. The way to cooperate is on the basis of biblical law. The law tells us of the limitations on man. It keeps us humble before God and dominant over nature. We shall determine the accuracy and usefulness of the works of unregenerate men who are exercising their God-given talents, working out their damnation with fear and trembling.

Strangers within the gates were given many of the benefits of common grace — God's response to the conversion of the Hebrews. They received full legal protection in Hebrew courts (Ex. 22:21; 23:9; Deut. 24:17). They were not permitted to eat special holy foods (Ex. 29:33; Lev. 22:10), thereby sealing them off from the religious celebrations of the temple. But they were part of the feast of the tithe, a celebration before the Lord (Deut. 14:22-29). Thus, they were beneficiaries of the civil order that God established for His people. They also could produce goods and services in confidence that the fruits of their labor would not be confiscated from them by a lawless civil government. This made everyone richer, for all men in the community could work out the terms of the dominion covenant.

We are told that the natural man does not receive the things of the Spirit (I Cor. 2:14-16). We are told that God's wisdom is seen as foolishness by the unregenerate (I Cor. 1:18-21). We are told to beware, "lest any man spoil you through philosophy and vain deceit, after the tradition of men, after the rudiments of the world, and not after Christ" (Col. 2:8). There is an unbridgeable separation philosophically between unbelievers and believers. They begin with different starting points: chaos vs. creation, God vs. man. Only common grace can reduce the conflict *in application* between pagan and Christian philosophy. The ethical rebellion of the unregenerate lies beneath the surface, smoldering, ready to flare up in wrath, but he is restrained by God and God's law. He needs the power that law provides. Therefore, he assents to some of the principles of applied biblical law and conforms himself to part of the work of the law that is written on his heart. But on first principles, he cannot agree. And even near the end, when men may confess the existence of one God and tremble at the thought, they will not submit their egos to that God. They will fight to the death — to the second death — to deny the claims that the God of the Bible has over every part of their being.

Thus, there can be cooperation in the subduing of the earth. But Christians must set forth the strategy and the tactics. The unregenerate man will be like a paid consultant; he will provide his talents, but the Lord will build the culture.

Common Grace vs. Common Ground

We must not argue from common grace to common ground. We cannot do so because with the increase of common grace we come closer to that final rebellion in all its satanic might. Common grace combines the efforts of men in the subduing of the earth, but Christians work for the glory of God openly, while the unregenerate work (officially) for the glory of man or the glory of Satan. They do, in fact, work to the glory of God, for on that last day every knee shall bow to Him (Phil. 2:10). The wealth of the wicked is laid up for the just (Prov. 13:22). So there are no common facts, ethically speaking.

At that final day, when their rebellion begins, all of Satan's host will know about the facts of God's world, for common grace will be at its peak. Nevertheless, they turn their backs on God and rebel. All facts are interpreted facts, and the *interpretation*, not the facts as such — there are no "facts as such" — is what separates the lost from the elect. Inevitably, the natural man holds *back* (actively suppresses) the truth in unrighteousness (Rom. 1:18).[27] No philosophical "proofs" of God (other than a proof which begins by assuming the existence of the God revealed in the Bible) are valid, and even the assumption of the existence of the God of the Bible is not sufficient to save a man's soul.[28] Only God can do that (John 6:44). There is no common ground philosophically, only metaphysically. We are made in God's image by a common Creator (Acts 17:24-31). Every man knows this. We can, as men, only remind all men of what they know. God uses that knowledge to redeem men.

The unbeliever uses *stolen intellectual capital* to reason correctly — correctly in the sense of being able to use that knowledge as a tool to subdue the earth, not in the sense of knowing God as an adopted son knows Him. His conclusions can correspond to external reality sufficiently to allow him to work out his rebellious faith to even greater destruction than if he had not had accurate knowledge (Luke 12:47-48). He "knows" somehow that "2 plus 2 equals 4," and also

---

27. Murray, *Romans*, commenting on Romans 1:18.

28. Van Til, *The Defense of the Faith* (Philadelphia: Presbyterian and Reformed, 1963), attacks the traditional Roman Catholic and Arminian proofs of God. They do not prove the God of the Bible, he argues, only a finite god of the human mind.

that this fact of mental symmetry can be used to cause desired effects in the external realm of nature. Why this mental symmetry should exist, and why it should bear any relation to the external realm of nature, is unexplainable by the knowledge of natural man, a fact admitted by Nobel prize-winning physicist, Eugene Wigner.[29]

Christians, because they have a proper doctrine of creation, can explain both. So the unbeliever uses borrowed intellectual capital at every step. Christians can use some of his work (by checking his findings against the revelation in the Bible), and the unbeliever can use the work of Christians. The earth will be subdued. The closer the unbeliever's presuppositions are to those revealed in the Bible (such as the conservative economist's assumption of the fact of economic scarcity, corresponding to Gen. 3:17-19), the more likely that the discoveries made in terms of that assumption will be useful. By useful, I mean useful in the common task of all men, subduing the earth. Thus, there can be cooperation between Christians and non-Christians.

Conclusion

Unbelievers appear to be culturally dominant today. Believers have retreated into antinomian pietism and pessimism, for they have abandoned faith in the two features of Christian social philosophy that make progress possible: 1) the dynamic of *eschatological optimism*, and 2) the tool of the dominion covenant, *biblical law*. We should conclude, then, that either the dissolution of culture is at hand (for the common grace of the unregenerate cannot long be sustained without leadership in the realm of culture from the regenerate), or else the regenerate must regain sight of their lost truths: postmillennialism and biblical law. For common grace to continue, and for external cooperation between believers and unbelievers to be fruitful or even possible, Christians must call the external culture's guidelines back to God's law. They must regain the leadership they forfeited to the speculations of self-proclaimed "reasonable" apostates. If this is not done, then we will slide back once more, until the unbelievers resemble the Ik and the Christians can begin the process of cultural

---

29. Eugene Wigner, "The Unreasonable Effectiveness of Mathematics in the Natural Sciences," *Communications on Pure and Applied Mathematics* XIII (1960), pp. 1-14. See also Vern Poythress, "A Biblical View of Mathematics," in Gary North (ed.), *Foundations of Christian Scholarship, op. cit.,* ch. 9. See also his essay in *The Journal of Christian Reconstruction*, I (Summer 1974).

domination once more. For common grace to continue to increase, it must be sustained by special grace. Either unbelievers will be converted, or leadership will flow back toward the Christians. If neither happens, we will return eventually to barbarism.

Understandably, I pray for the regeneration of the ungodly *and* the rediscovery of biblical law and accurate biblical eschatology on the part of present Christians and future converts. Whether we will see such a revival in our day is unknown to me. There are reasons to believe that it can and will happen. There are also reasons to doubt such optimism. The Lord knows.

We must abandon antinomianism and eschatologies that are inherently antinomian. We must call men back to faith in the God of the whole Bible. We must affirm that in the plan of God there will come a day of increased self-awareness, when men will call churls churlish and liberal men gracious (Isa. 32). This will be a day of great external blessings — the greatest in history. Long ages of such self-awareness unfold before us. And at the end of time comes a generation of rebels who know churls from liberals and strike out against the godly. They will lose the war.

Therefore, *common grace* is essentially *future grace*. There is an ebb and flow throughout history, but essentially it is future grace. It must not be seen as essentially prior or earlier grace. Only amillennialists can hold to such a position — antinomian amillennialists at that. The final judgment appears at the end of time against the backdrop of common grace. The *common curse* will be at its *lowest* point, the prelude to *special cursing* of eternal duration. The final judgment comes, just as the great flood came, against a background of God's external benefits to mankind in general. The iniquity of the Amorites will at last be full.

Does the postmillennialist believe that there will be faith in general on the earth when Christ appears? Not if he understands the implications of the doctrine of common grace. Does he expect the whole earth to be destroyed by the unbelieving rebels before Christ strikes them dead — doubly dead? No. The judgment comes before they can do their work. Common grace is extended to allow unbelievers to fill up their cup of wrath. They are vessels of wrath. Therefore, the fulfilling of the terms of the dominion covenant through common grace is the final step in the process of filling up these vessels of wrath. The vessels of grace, believers, will also be filled. Everything is full. Will God destroy His preliminary down payment on the New Heavens and the New Earth? Will God erase the sign that His word has been obeyed, that the dominion covenant has been fulfilled? Will Satan, that great destroyer, have the joy of seeing God's word thwarted, his handiwork torn down by Satan's very hordes? The amillennialist answers yes. The postmillennialist must deny it with all his strength.

There is continuity in life, despite discontinuities. The wealth of the sinner is laid up for the just. Satan would like to burn up God's field, but he cannot. The tares and wheat grow to maturity, and then the reapers go out to harvest the wheat, cutting away the chaff and tossing chaff into the fire. Satan would like to turn back the crack of doom, return to ground zero, return to the garden of Eden, when the dominion covenant was first given. The fulfillment of the dominion covenant is the final act of Satan that is positive — an extension of common grace. After that, common grace becomes malevolent — absolutely malevolent — as Satan uses the last of his time and the last of his power to strike out against God's people. When he uses his gifts to become finally, totally destructive, he is cut down from above. *This final culmination of common grace is Satan's crack of doom.*

And the meek — meek before God, active toward His creation — shall at last inherit the earth. A renewed earth and renewed heaven is the final payment by God the Father to His Son and to those He has given to His Son. This is the postmillennial hope.

Postscript

By now, I have alienated every known Christian group. I have alienated the remaining Christian Reformed Church members who are orthodox by siding with the Protestant Reformed Church against Point 1 of the 1924 Synod. There is no favor in God's common grace. I have alienated the Protestant Reformed Church by arguing for postmillennialism. I have alienated the premillennialists by arguing that the separation between wheat and tares must come at the end of history, not a thousand years before the end (or, in the dispensational, pretribulational premillennial framework, 1007 years before). I have alienated postmillennial pietists who read and delight in the works of Jonathan Edwards by arguing that Edwards' tradition was destructive to biblical law in 1740 and still is. It leads nowhere unless it matures and adopts the concept of biblical law as a tool of victory. I have alienated the Bible Presbyterian Church, since its leaders deny the dominion covenant. Have I missed anyone? Oh, yes, I have alienated postmillennial Arminians ("positive confession" charismatics) by arguing that the rebels in the last day are not backslidden Christians.

Having accomplished this, I hope that others will follow through on the outline I have sketched relating common grace, eschatology, and biblical law. Let those few who take this essay seriously avoid the theological land mines that still clutter up the landscape. There are refinements that must be made, implications that must be discovered and then worked out. I hope that my contribution will make other men's tasks that much easier.

Appendix B

MAIMONIDES' *CODE*: IS IT BIBLICAL?

*A heathen who busies himself with the study of the Law deserves
death. He should occupy himself with the (study) of the seven commandments only. So too, a heathen who keeps a day of rest, even if it be on a
weekday, if he has set it apart as his Sabbath, is deserving of death. It is
needless to state that he merits death if he makes a new festival for himself. The general principle is: none is permitted to introduce innovations
into religion or devise new commandments. The heathen has the choice
between becoming a true proselyte by accepting all the commandments,
and adhering to his own religion, neither adding to it nor subtracting
anything from it. If therefore he occupies himself with the study of the
Law, or observes a day of rest, or makes any innovation, he is flogged, or
otherwise punished and advised that he is deserving of death, but he is not
put to death.*

Moses Maimonides (1180)[1]

The typical non-Jew would imagine that Jews throughout history
would have rejoiced whenever gentiles[2] read the Old Testament in

---

1. Moses Maimonides, *The Book of Judges*, Book 14 of *The Code of Maimonides*, 14
vols. (New Haven, Connecticut: Yale University Press, 1949), "Laws Concerning
Kings and Wars," Chapter Ten, Section Nine, p. 237.

2. I do not capitalize "gentile," although the King James translators did, and it is
still common for writers to do so. I do not view the gentiles as a separate people in
the ethnic or national way that Americans, Mexicans, Chinese, and Jews are. To
capitalize the word would imply that gentiles are a separate people, meaning a separate people as contrasted to Jews, who alone are "not gentiles." Such ethnic separation no longer exists in principle: "That at that time ye were without Christ, being
aliens from the commonwealth of Israel, and strangers from the covenants of promise, having no hope, and without God in the world: But now in Christ Jesus ye who
sometimes were far off are made nigh by the blood of Christ. For he is our peace,
who hath made both one, and hath broken down the middle wall of partition between us" (Eph. 2:12-13). Jews equate gentiles with heathen, yet they do not capitalize "heathen," for they correctly understand "heathenism" as a spiritual condition
rather than an ethnic or national condition. I use "gentiles" in the sense of "not
Jews," but not in the sense of a separate ethnic or national group.

998

search of God's permanent moral and civil standards of righteousness. After all, this would tend to bridge the cultural and judicial gap between Jews and non-Jews. This, however, was precisely the problem in the minds of the rabbis for at least 1,700 years. The rabbis did not want this gap bridged; at most, they wanted external peace and quiet for Jews, meaning they wanted social order in the midst of gentile culture. Sufficient social order within the gentile world is supposedly achieved through their adherence to the seven commandments specifically given to the heathen, meaning gentiles. Six of these laws were first given to Adam, according to Jewish law: the prohibitions against idolatry, blasphemy, murder, adultery, and robbery, plus the command to establish courts of justice. A seventh law was also supposedly given to Noah: the prohibition against eating the limb of a living animal.[3] Beyond this minimal list of seven laws, the gentiles — "Noahides" or "Noahites," the descendants of Noah[4] — are not supposed to go in their inquiry into the ethical requirements of Old Testament law, which belongs exclusively to the Jews.

In making this assertion, Maimonides was faithfully following the teaching of the Talmud. He was taking Rabbi Johanan at his word: "R. [Rabbi — G.N.][5] Johanan said: A heathen who studies the Torah deserves death, for it is written, *Moses commanded* us *a law for an inheritance*; it is *our* inheritance, not theirs."[6] Resh Lakish (third century, A.D.) said that a gentile who observes the Sabbath deserves death.[7] Why should God have forbidden the gentiles to study His law? The Talmud offers this answer:

R. Abbahu thereupon said: The Writ says, *He stood and measured the earth; he beheld and drove asunder the nations*, [which may be taken to imply that] God beheld the seven commandments which were accepted by all the descendants of Noah, but since they did not observe them, He rose up and declared them to be outside the protection of the civil law of Israel [with reference to damage done to cattle by cattle].[8]

Lest this position seem utterly outrageous to Christian readers, I need to point out that a similar view of the sufficiency of Noah's cov-

---

3. Maimonides, *Judges*, "Laws Concerning Kings and Wars," Chapter Nine, Section One, pp. 230-31.

4. *Ibid.*, Chapter Nine, Section Two, p. 231

5. When you see brackets inside a direct quotation from the Talmud, they appeared in the Soncino Press edition. I will note any brackets of my own with my initials.

6. Babylonian Talmud, *Sanhedrin* 59a. I am using the Soncino Press edition.

7. *Sanhedrin* 59b.

8. *Baba Kamma* 38a. Bracketed comments are by the editor.

enant for non-Israelite civil law has been offered by Calvinist theologian John Murray and also by neo-dispensational theologians H. Wayne House and Thomas D. Ice. In fact, all three of them conclude that there is only one biblically required sanction in Noah's covenant, capital punishment for murder. This, they believe, is the only biblical law that God has required all men to obey throughout mankind's post-flood history.[9] The Talmud at least adds an additional six laws that God specifically established through Adam and Noah that gentiles are supposed to honor throughout history.

How Little Most People Know About Judaism

Maimonides' opinion regarding the immorality of non-Jews who read the Old Testament would probably come as a shock to most Christians, assuming they had ever heard of Maimonides and his *Mishneh Torah*. It might even come as a shock to most contemporary Jews. The average Bible-believing Christian in the United States knows very little about post-New Testament Judaism. He may be vaguely aware that American Judaism is divided into three theological wings: Reform (liberal), Conservative, and Orthodox. He may also be aware that European Judaism has two great ethnic branches: the Sephardim[10] (those whose ancestors once lived in Spain, Portugal, or the Eastern Mediterranean) and the Ashkenazic Jews[11] (those who came west from Russia and Poland), who were the Yiddish-speaking Jews in the late 1800's and early 1900's, prior to their linguistic assimilation into American culture. But as to how these Jewish groups overlap,[12] or which group dominates Judaism

---

9. John Murray, *Principles of Conduct: Aspects of Biblical Ethics* (Grand Rapids, Michigan: Eerdmans, 1957), pp. 118-19; House and Ice, *Dominion Theology: Curse or Blessing?* (Portland, Oregon: Multnomah, 1988), p. 130.

10. Heinrich Graetz, *History of the Jews*, 6 vols. (Philadelphia: Jewish Publication Society of America, [1893] 1945), IV, chaps. 10-13. On the influence of the Sephardic Jews in the U.S., see Stephen Birmingham, *The Grandees: America's Sephardic Elite* (New York: Harper & Row, 1971).

11. Graetz, *History*, IV, ch. 14; V, chaps. 6, 18; V, ch. 1. See also Bernard D. Weinryb, *The Jews of Poland: A Social and Economic History of the Jewish Community in Poland from 1100 to 1880* (Philadelphia: Jewish Publication Society, 1972). On their influence in the U.S., see Stephen Birmingham, *"Our Crowd": The Great Jewish Families of New York* (New York: Harper & Row, 1967); Irving Howe, *World of Our Fathers* (New York: Simon & Schuster, [1976] 1983); Irving Howe and Kenneth Libo, *How We Lived: A Documentary History of Immigrant Jews in America, 1880-1930* (New York: Richard Marek, 1979).

12. Thomas Sowell, *Ethnic America: A History* (New York: Basic Books, 1981), ch. 4: "The Jews."

either in the U.S. or in the state of Israel today,[13] the average Christian has no idea. Few Christians have heard that there is a third branch, Oriental or Yemenite Judaism (North African), members of which have long complained that they are discriminated against politically in the state of Israel.

Christians are unaware that the medieval Jewish body of literature known as the Kabbalah ("tradition") is not only mystical but closely tied to numerology and occultism.[14] They do not know that the mystical-magical tradition of the Kabbalah had its roots in the Talmud.[15] They have never read anything about the history of Zionism, either pro[16] or con.[17]

To the extent that the Bible-believing Christian thinks about Reform Jews generally, he assumes that they are something like Unitarians: politically liberal, skeptical about the Bible, and essentially humanistic. (Orthodox Jews also view Reform Jews in much the same way.) Christians, however, tend to think of almost all Jews in this way, which turns out to be a statistically correct political

---

13. I refer to the "state of Israel" rather than "Israel" out of respect for the terminology of Orthodox Jews, who sharply distinguish the two.

14. "Kabalah," in Lewis Spence (ed.), *An Encyclopaedia of Occultism* (New Hyde Park, New York: University Books, [1920] 1960). An example of popular (though underground) magical literature based on the Kabbalah, which has been reprinted generation after generation, is *The Sixth and Seventh Books of Moses*. See also Arthur Edward Waite, *The Holy Kabbalah: A Study of the Secret Tradition of Israel* (New Hyde Park, New York: University Books, 1960 reprint); Denis Saurat, *Literature and Occult Tradition*, trans. Dorothy Bolton (Port Washington, New York: Kennikat, [1930] 1966), Pt. III, ch. 2. The pioneering modern Jewish studies of the Kabbalah are by Gershom G. Scholem: *Major Trends in Jewish Mysticism* (3rd ed; New York: Schocken, 1961) and *On the Kabbalah and Its Symbolism* (New York: Schocken, [1960] 1965). The primary source of Kabbalah is *The Zohar*, 5 vols. (London: Soncino Press, 1934). On the influence of the Kabbalah on the gentile world, see Frances A. Yates, *The Occult Philosophy in the Elizabethan Age* (London: ARK, [1979] 1983) and A. E. Waite, *The Brotherhood of the Rosy Cross* (New Hyde Park, New York: University Books, 1961 reprint).

15. Gershom G. Scholem, *Jewish Gnosticism, Merkabah Mysticism, and Talmudic Tradition* (2nd ed.; New York: Bloch, 1965).

16. Walter Laqueur, *A History of Zionism* (New York: Holt, Rinehart & Winston, 1972); Ronald Sanders, *The High Walls of Jerusalem: A History of the Balfour Declaration and the Birth of British Mandate for Palestine* (New York: Holt, Rinehart & Winston, 1983).

17. Gary V. Smith (ed.), *Zionism: The Dream and the Reality, A Jewish Critique* (New York: Barnes & Noble, 1974); Rabbi Elmer Berger, *The Jewish Dilemma: The Case Against Zionist Nationalism* (New York: Devin-Adair, 1945). The major published English-speaking critic of Zionism is Alfred M. Lilienthal: *What Price Israel?* (Chicago: Regnery, 1953); *There Goes the Middle East* (New York: Devin-Adair, 1957); *The Zionist Connection: What Price Peace?* (New York: Dodd, Mead, 1978).

assumption; American Jews are consistently liberal in their voting behavior.[18] Conservative Jews are seen by Christians as being somewhere in between Reform and Orthodox: they do not eat pork, but they wear normal clothes; other than this, Christians know little about them.

The Orthodox Jew, in contrast, is assumed by the Bible-believing Christian to be rather like the Christian: he has minority status within the larger Jewish community, he tends to be more conservative politically, pro-family in outlook, and probably anti-abortion. He is in conflict with the Reform Jews, just as the Bible-believing Christian is at war with the liberal defenders of biblical higher criticism. Thus, the Orthodox Jew is assumed to be a kind of Old Testament Christian who wears black clothing and a beard — a quaint, Amish-like figure[19] — and who avoids pork. This perception is incorrect. The Orthodox Jew is in fact a self-conscious, self-professed spiritual heir of the Pharisees. His book is the Talmud, the written version of Judaism's oral law, far more than it is the Old Testament.

The "Star of David"

Very few people know much about the history of Judaism, including those who identify themselves as Jews. This may seem like an outrageous statement. You can test its accuracy by asking the average gentile or average Jew what the most important symbol of modern Judaism is. He probably will say either the scroll of the Torah or "the star of David," also known as the Mogen David or Magen David. After all, it appears on the state of Israel's national flag. Ask him where the latter symbol originated, and you will get a blank stare. He has no idea.

The fact is, the so-called star of David is a universal pagan symbol, long pre-dating Judaism. It was adopted by Zionists in the late nineteenth century. Before then, it was used as a decoration by Jews, Muslims, and Christians. It was long called the Seal of Solomon.

---

18. ". . . Jews in this country have the economic status of white Anglo-Saxon Episcopalians but vote more like low-income Hispanics." Milton Himmelfarb, cited by Irving Kristol, "Liberalism & American Jews," *Commentary* (Oct. 1988), p. 19; cf. Peter Steinfels, "American Jews Stand Firmly to the Left," *New York Times* (Jan. 8, 1989). Steinfels reports that recent polls reveal that four times as many Jews belong to the Democratic Party as belong to the Republican Party, compared to about equal numbers of other white voting groups. Almost two to one, Jews believe in the legal right to abortion.

19. This link is featured in a scene in a movie about a mid-nineteenth century Jew, *The Frisco Kid*, and in a scene in a movie about a modern Amish family, *Witness*.

How many Jews, let alone Christians, have ever been informed of the following information, presented by Jewish scholar and art historian Joseph Gutmann?

The Magen David is a hexagram or six-pointed star. It appears as early as the Bronze Age and is at home in cultures and civilizations widely removed in time and geographic area. Mesopotamia, India, Greece, and Etruria are among the places where it has been found — but without any discoverable meaning. Possibly it was an ornament or had magical connotations. Only occasionally before the 1890's is it found in a Jewish context; the oldest Jewish example is from seventh-century B.C.E. [B.C.] Sidon, a seal belonging to one Joshua ben Asayahu. In the synagogue at Capernaum, Galilee, a synagogue which may date from the fourth century C.E. [A.D.], the Magen David is found alongside the pentagram and the swastika, but there is no reason to assume that the Magen David or the other signs on the synagogue stone frieze served any but decorative purposes.

In the Middle Ages, the Magen David appears quite frequently in the decorations of European and Islamic Hebrew manuscripts and even on some synagogues, but appears to have no distinct Jewish symbolic connotation; it is also found on the seals of the Christian kings of Navarre, on mediaeval church objects, and on cathedrals. As a matter of fact, what is today called Magen David was generally known as the Seal of Solomon in the Middle Ages, especially in Jewish, Christian and Islamic magical texts. In the medieval Islamic world the hexagram was popular and was widely used. Generally known, especially in Arab sources, as the Seal of Solomon, it gradually became linked with a magic ring or seal believed to give King Solomon control over demons. An early Jewish source in the Babylonian Talmud (*Gittin* 68a-b) already mentions it.

The hexagram and pentagram, it should be pointed out, both carried the designation "Seal of Solomon" and were employed in both Christianity and Islam as symbols with magical or amuletic power. On the parchment of many medieval *mezuzot* (capsules placed on the doorposts of every Jewish home) the hexagram and pentagram (Seal of Solomon) were written out and also served as a talisman or had magical powers to ward off evil spirits.[20]

The point is, few Jews or gentiles are aware of any of this. That the flag of the state of Israel bears an ancient pagan symbol is not a well-known fact either to those who respect it or who resent it. In short, the vast majority of Christians and many Jews know very little about the history of Judaism. Jews and Christians are aware that

---

20. Joseph Gutmann, *The Jewish Sanctuary* (Leiden: E. J. Brill, 1983), p. 21. This study is Section XXIII: Judaism, of the Iconography of Religions, produced by the Institute of Religious Iconography of the State University Gronigen, Netherlands.

their respective religious practices are quite different, yet not many of them know why, and to what extent, their religions differ. People speak of "the Judeo-Christian tradition," yet they are not quite sure what this tradition is, or if it even exists.[21]

Rival Religions

I agree with the astoundingly prolific Orthodox Jew, Jacob Neusner, whose studies on Jewish law are as close to definitive as the writings of any one person can be.[22] He writes: "Judaism and Christianity are completely different religions, not different versions of one religion (that of the 'Old Testament,' or 'the written Torah,' as Jews call it). The two faiths stand for different people talking about different things to different people."[23] He argues that the key differences center on the two rival programs: salvation (Christianity) vs. sanctification (Pharaiseeism). It is therefore also a debate over the issue of eschatology: God's kingdom manifested in world history. Christianity is inherently universalistic; Judaism is inherently particularistic. Neusner writes:

> Salvation, in the nature of things, concerned the whole of humanity; sanctification, equally characteristic of its category, spoke of a single nation, Israel. To save, the messiah saves Israel amid all nations, because salvation characteristically entails the eschatological dimension and so encompasses all history. No salvation, after all, can last only for a little while or leave space for time beyond itself. To sanctify, by contrast, the sage sanctifies Israel in particular. Sanctification categorically requires the designation of what is holy against what is not holy. To sanctify is to set apart. No sanctification can encompass everyone or leave no room for someone in particular to be holy. One need not be "holier than thou," but the *holy* requires the contrary category, the *not holy.* So, once more, how can two religious communities understand one another when one raises the issue of the sanctification of Israel, and the other the salvation of the world?[24]

Christianity, by adopting a view of salvation that necessarily encompasses all the nations of the earth, broke forever with rabbinic

---

21. Arthur A. Cohen, *The Myth of the Judeo-Christian Tradition* (New York: Schocken, 1971); J. H. Hexter, *The Judeo-Christian Tradition* (New York: Harper & Row, 1966).

22. Jacob Neusner, *History of the Mishna Laws*, 5 parts, 43 volumes (Leiden, Netherlands: E. J. Brill). He has written many other books.

23. Jacob Neusner, "Two Faiths Talking about Different Things," *The World & I* (Nov. 1987), p. 679.

24. *Ibid.*, p. 683.

Judaism. This was the meaning of Jesus' analogy of new wine. "Neither do men put new wine into old bottles: else the bottles break, and the wine runneth out, and the bottles perish: but they put new wine into new bottles, and both are preserved" (Matt. 9:17). Neusner is correct: Christianity is universalistic in scope and vision; Judaism is particularistic.

Neusner also contrasts sanctification with salvation. This is fundamentally incorrect. He misses what should be obvious: *the Bible presents salvation as a process that necessarily involves both progressive personal sanctification and progressive institutional sanctification as history unfolds.*[25] Biblical salvation is a comprehensive process.[26] This is a major aspect of its universalism. Christianity's doctrine of salvation (soteriology) is inescapably tied to its doctrine of progressive sanctification. This was especially true of Anglo-American Protestant missionary activity until the late nineteenth century.[27] Neusner is not alone in this error, however. The institutional-historical aspect of salvation has also been generally ignored by most Bible-believing Christian theologians in the twentieth century. They have not recognized the extent to which biblical soteriology, ethics, and eschatology are intertwined. By failing to grasp this fact, both rabbinic Judaism and modern fundamentalism have adopted ghetto mentalities.[28]

If the debate between Jews and Christians with regard to the nature of covenantal society is inherently an ethical debate — ethics' sources and applications in history — then the key book in the history of Judaism is the Talmud. Christians need to be aware of it, but very few are. It is not sufficient to go to the Old Testament to learn about Judaism. Judaism and Christianity both claim to go to the Old Testament; so does Islam. These three religions — not to mention their factions, sects, splinter groups, and offshoots — offer radically different interpretations of the Old Testament. We must therefore look

---

25. Gary North, *Dominion and Common Grace: The Biblical Basis of Progress* (Tyler, Texas: Institute for Christian Economics, 1987).

26. Gary North, *Is the World Running Down? Crisis in the Christian Worldview* (Tyler, Texas: Institute for Christian Economics, 1988), Appendix C: "Comprehensive Redemption: A Theology for Social Action."

27. J. A. De Jong, *As the Waters Cover the Sea: Millennial Expectations in the rise of Anglo-American missions, 1640-1810* (Kampen, Netherlands: J. H. Kok, 1970).

28. Modern intellectual evangelicalism has generally adopted the prevailing humanist worldview. It has adopted a "we, too" view of social theory. See James Davison Hunter, *Evangelicalism: The Coming Generation* (University of Chicago Press, 1987).

briefly at the Talmud in order to get the sense of the theological and historical differences separating Orthodox Judaism and biblical Christianity.

The Talmud: A Closed Book, Even When Open[29]

Most Christians have never heard of the Talmud. I have never met a Christian who claims to have read all of it, all 34 fat volumes. The Christian who may have heard of it but who has never read in it probably believes that it is a large Bible commentary on the Old Testament. I hope to show here that this assumption is incorrect.

The problem Christians face is that there is no work of serious yet forthright scholarship on the Talmud that is written by a trinitarian, Bible-believing Christian. Alfred Edersheim, the mid-nineteenth-century convert from Judaism who taught at Oxford and who wrote *The Life and Times of Jesus the Messiah* and *Old Testament History*, could have written such a work, but he chose not to, although his *History of the Jewish Nation* does include a 21-page section on Jewish law in the Talmud and Mishnah.[30] (Under the section, "Jewish Theology," he admitted: "In attempting to arrange the doctrinal views of the Rabbins, we are bewildered by a mass of erroneous, blasphemous, and even contradictory statements."[31] I would add: *especially* we find contradictory statements, for dialecticism is the reasoning process of the Talmud. Solomon Schechter's restrained comment in 1901 is accurate: "This indifference to logic and insensibility to theological consistency seems to be a vice from which not even the later successors of the Rabbis — the commentators of the Talmud — emancipated themselves entirely."[32] Or more impishly, "Whatever the faults of the

---

29. Israel Shenker refers to David Weiss' leisurely reading of it on vacations, without Weiss' normal line-by-line analysis, "as though it were an open book." Shenker, "A Life in the Talmud," *New York Times Magazine* (Sept. 11, 1977). Professor Robert L. Wilken of the University of Virginia calls the Soncino edition of the Talmud a closed book: *Insight* (May 16, 1988). A more readable translation, but probably with modifications, by Rabbi Adin Steinsaltz, is scheduled for publication, beginning in 1990.

30. Alfred Edersheim, *History of the Jewish Nation After the Destruction of Jerusalem Under Titus* (Grand Rapids, Michigan: Baker Book House, [1856] n.d.), pp. 361-81. Edersheim was ordained at age 21 in the Scottish Presbyterian Church and was later ordained an Anglican. He wrote this book at age 30.

31. *Ibid.*, p. 424.

32. Solomon Schechter, *Aspects of Rabbinic Theology* (New York: Schocken, [1901] 1961), p. 15.

Rabbis were, consistency was not one of them."[33]) Even today, there are remarkably few serious works on the Talmud in English written by Jews, and none of them that I have read even mentions the disturbing material that I will briefly refer to in this appendix.

What Is the Talmud?

The Babylonian Talmud is an immense compilation.[34] It has been well described by Jews as "the sea of the Talmud." (Sargasso Sea is closer to it.) Jews have called it "the Great Labyrinth" and "Sphinx-like,"[35] which is getting even closer, given the occult roots of the labyrinth and its connection with the Sphinx.[36] R. Travers Herford, the Unitarian master (yet concealer) of the Talmud, described it as "a great wilderness."[37] Few Christians have ever seen a set; almost no one reads it today, Christians or Jews. An unabridged version of the Talmud became available in English only in the early 1950's — about two generations after the vast majority of English-speaking Jews had ceased to pay any attention to it. It is 34 volumes long, plus a large index volume. Prior to the mid-twentieth century, it had been a hidden book to the English-speaking gentile world. As England's chief rabbi, J. H. Hertz mentions in his Foreword, "All the censored passages reappear in the Text or in the Notes."[38] Earlier editions, most notably Michael Rodkinson's (1903), had been voluntarily censored by their editors.

The Talmud is a compilation of the oral teachings of the rabbis from perhaps 200 years before Christ until the end of the second century, A.D. (Mishnah), plus an additional three hundred years of commentary (Gemara). The total is almost seven (possibly eight)

---

33. *Ibid.*, p. 46. Schechter was a leader in the Conservative movement of Judaism: Joseph Gaer and Rabbi Alfred Wolf, *Our Jewish Heritage* (Hollywood, California: Wilshire Book Co., 1957), p. 24.

34. The Jerusalem Talmud is much smaller and has never had impact on Judaism comparable to the Babylonian Talmud.

35. Jacob Schachter, "Talmudical Introductions Down to the Time of Chajes," in Z. H. Chajes, *The Student's Guide Through the Talmud* (London: East and West Library, 1952), p. xvi.

36. Gary North, *Moses and Pharaoh: Dominion Religion vs. Power Religion* (Tyler, Texas: Institute for Christian Economics, 1985), Appendix C: "The Labyrinth and the Garden."

37. R. Travers Herford, *Christianity in Talmud and Midrash* (London: Williams and Norgate, 1903), p. 1.

38. Hertz, Foreword, *Baba Kamma*, *The Babylonian Talmud* (London: Soncino Press, 1935), p. xxvii.

centuries.[39] Those who adhere to the Talmud claim that this oral tradition extends back to Moses. They cite Exodus 24 as proof: "And Moses came and told the people all the words of the LORD, and all the judgments" (3a). Then we read, "And Moses wrote all the words of the LORD" (4a). But he did not write the judgments, they say; instead, the judgments became the oral law, taught from rabbi to rabbi down through the ages. An Orthodox Jewish rabbi believes that he can trace his line of teachers back to Moses.

What eventually became the authoritative version of this oral tradition was compiled by several Jewish authorities, but especially by Rabbi Judah, "the Prince," "the patriarch," HaNasi,[40] or just "Rabbi" (135-210 A.D.). He completed what later became known as the Mishnah sometime around 189.[41] The word "completed" is somewhat misleading. Completed what? Some Jews have insisted that it was not written down in his day because it was considered by the Jews as a crime to do so. Writes the Jewish historian Graetz: "Christendom had taken possession of the Holy Scriptures as its own spiritual property, and considered itself as the chosen part of Israel. According to the views of the times, Judaism was now possessed of no distinguishing feature, except the Oral Law."[42] There is obviously some debate about this, however. Hermann Strack, a highly respected gentile German scholar of the Talmud, writes: "Just how much of it was written by Rabbi himself is a subject of debate."[43] He uses the verb "written," but he is judicious about referring directly to the writing down of the Mishnah, for that would mean coming to a conclusion, and Prof. Strack avoids conclusions like the plague.[44] He says that

---

39. Schachter, "Talmudical Introductions," in Chajes, *Student's Guide Through the Talmud*, p. xvi (footnote).

40. The Nasi or Prince was the head of the Sanhedrin. George Horowitz, *The Spirit of Jewish Law* (New York: Central Book Co., [1953] 1963), p. 628.

41. Graetz, *History of the Jews*, II, p. 460.

42. *Ibid.*, II, p. 608.

43. Hermann Strack, *Introduction to the Talmud and Midrash* (New York: Atheneum, [1931] 1983), p. 20. This book was first published in English by the Jewish Publication Society of America.

44. Anyone trying to read Strack's book will find how useless it is as an introduction. Only the most skilled Talmudic scholar could follow its reams of names without dates or summaries of their thought (ch. XIII), bibliography without evaluation (ch. XIV), and its lack of conclusions about anything. Here was a man who compiled a mountain of notes, and in five editions achieved little more than pasting this mass of notes together. There is hardly a glimmer of insight in any of it. This is Germanic scholarship at its worst: massive scholarly paraphernalia, little substance, and no conclusions. He labored mightily all his life, and brought forth a mouse. If you think

portions of the Mishnah had been written down both by Rabbi Akiba and his pupil Rabbi Meir in the early second century A.D., but not everything had been written down: "Great stress was laid on memorizing and retaining in memory the enormous material; witness the remark of Dosthai ben Jannai in the name of Meir: 'When a scholar forgets a single word of his Mishna, they account it to him as if he forfeited his life.' "[45] He says that there had been earlier codifications than Akiba's. Graetz did not exaggerate when he wrote that "Concurrently with the Bible, the Mishna was the principal source of intellectual activity and research; it sometimes even succeeded in entirely supplanting the Scripture, and in asserting its claim to sole authority. It was the intellectual bond which held together the scattered members of the Jewish nation."[46] I can think of another criticism of Judaism even more devastating than Graetz's: the Jews later chose the Talmud over the Mishnah, which at least had been vastly shorter.

Pharisees vs. Sadducees

The Pharisees were the Jewish rabbis who embraced the oral tradition as equal to the Old Testament; the Sadducees were priests who accepted the oral law's traditions but rejected the Pharisees' claim that the oral law is equally as binding as Scripture.[47] The Jewish historian and former priest Josephus, who was alive at the fall of Jerusalem in A.D. 70, summarized the differences between the two, and his summary makes it clear why Jesus rejected both groups:

I am exaggerating, you owe it to yourself to sit down and read it. I warn you: you won't make it through the first four chapters—not if you have any sense. You will never make it past the chapter on the Mishna. I prefer to play the role of the little boy who announced that the emperor had no clothes. Prof. Strack had no ideas. That a man's life could be wasted on such a project as futile as this one is pathetic. Hermann Strack is one of the few scholars about whose book I can honestly say: "It is less useful than biblical higher criticism."

45. *Ibid.*, p. 22.
46. Graetz, *History*, II, p. 462.
47. Jacob Z. Lauterbach, "The Sadducees and Pharisees" (1913); reprinted in Lauterbach, *Rabbinic Essays* (Cincinnati, Ohio: Hebrew Union College Press, 1951); J. H. Hertz, Foreword, *The Babylonian Talmud, Seder Nezikin* (London: Soncino Press, 1935), p. xiv. Unitarian scholar R. Travers Herford has written several sympathetic accounts of the tradition of the Pharisees, most notably *The Pharisees* (London: George Allen & Unwin, 1924); *The Ethics of the Talmud: Sayings of the Fathers* (New York: Schocken, [1945] 1962). The standard Jewish work on the Pharisees is Rabbi Louis Finkelstein's study, *The Pharisees*, 2 vols (3rd ed.; Philadelphia: Jewish Publication Society of America, 1963).

What I would now explain is this, that the Pharisees have delivered to the people a great many observances by succession from their fathers, which are not written in the law of Moses; and for that reason it is that the Sadducees reject them, and say that we are to esteem those observances to be obligatory which are in the written word, but are not to observe what are derived from the tradition of our forefathers. . . .[48]

. . . the Pharisees are those who are esteemed most skillful in the exact explication of their laws, and introduce the first sect. They ascribe all to fate [or providence,] and to God, and yet allow, that to act what is right, or the contrary, is principally in the power of men, although fate does co-operate in every action. They say that all souls are incorruptible; but that the souls of good men are only removed into other bodies, — but that the souls of bad men are subject to eternal punishment. But the Sadducees are those who compose the second order, and take away fate entirely, and suppose that God is not concerned in our doing or not doing what is evil; and they say, that to act what is good, or what is evil, is at men's own choice, and that the one or the other belongs so to every one, that they may act as they please. They also take away the belief of the immortal duration of the soul, and the punishments and rewards in Hades.[49]

The Sadducees' influence faded rapidly after the destruction of the temple in A.D. 70. Herbert Danby, whose English translation of the Mishnah is still considered authoritative by the scholarly world, both Jewish[50] and gentile, commented on the undisputed triumph of the Pharisees after the fall of Jerusalem (which lives on as Orthodox Judaism): "Until the destruction of the Second Temple in A.D. 70 they had counted as one only among the schools of thought which played a part in Jewish national and religious life; after the Destruction they took the position, naturally and almost immediately, of sole and undisputed leaders of such Jewish life as survived. Judaism as it has continued since is, if not their creation, at least a faith and a religious institution largely of their fashioning; and the Mishnah is the authoritative record of their labour. Thus it comes about that while

---

48. Josephus, *Antiquities of the Jews*, Bk. XIII, Ch. X, Sect. 6. William Whiston translation, 1737.

49. Josephus, *Wars of the Jews*, Bk. II, Ch. VIII, Sect. 14.

50. I do not understand why it is polite to say "Jewish" and frequently impolite to say "Jew." The suffix "ish" means "sort of." Surely, Christians would take offense if they were referred to as "Christianish." I should think that a Jew, if asked by someone, "Are you Jewish," would reply, "No. I'm a Jew." Anyway, an Orthodox Jew might respond this way. An Orthodox Jew regards Reform Jews as Jewish, i.e., sort of Jews.

Judaism and Christianity alike venerate the Old Testament as canonical Scripture, the Mishnah marks the passage to Judaism as definitely as the New Testament marks the passage to Christianity."[51] Neusner is correct when he observes that "the rabbis of late antiquity rewrote in their own image and likeness the entire Scripture and history of Israel, dropping whole eras as though they had never been, ignoring vast bodies of old Jewish writing, inventing whole new books for the canon of Judaism. . . ."[52]

The supremacy of the Mishnah after A.D. 70 meant the triumph of the Pharisees. Similarly, in the modern era, the waning of the Mishnah in Judaism has meant the waning of the Pharisees' spiritual heirs, Orthodox Jews.

Again, the Mishnah is the written version of the Jews' oral tradition, while the rabbis' comments on it are called Gemara. The Talmud contains both Mishnah and Gemara. The rabbinical comments comprise the bulk of the Talmud. Danby's standard translation of the Mishnah is one long volume. The Soncino Press edition of the Talmud is 34 volumes, plus the index.

The Torah

When Jews speak of "Torah,"[53] they do not always mean the Old Testament or even the Pentateuch. Sometimes they mean something much broader. Christians are generally unaware of this broader usage, which leads them to believe that Orthodox Jews are somehow Christians without Christ, or Unitarians who believe in miracles and angels, i.e., people who believe in the Old Testament by itself. They think of Orthodox Jews as undeveloped Christians, theological first cousins who were publicly disinherited in A.D. 70. They have missed the point of Jesus' absolute challenge to the Pharisees.

Orthodox Judaism constitutes a rival religion that developed alongside the early church. The Pharisees insisted that the oral law is equal to the written law, as surely as Christians insist that the New Testament is as authoritative as the Old Testament, the Muslims insist that the Koran is as authoritative as the Old Testament, and the Mormons insist that the Book of Mormon is as authoritative as the Old Testament. Each group really means that its unique post-Old

---

51. Herbert Danby, Introduction, *The Mishnah* (New York: Oxford University Press, [1933] 1987), p. xiii.

52. Neusner, "Two Faiths Talking," *World & I, op. cit.*, p. 690.

53. "Direction, instruction, doctrine, law": *Oxford English Dictionary*.

Testament document is *more* authoritative now than the Old Testament is. No major religion since the fall of Jerusalem has taken the Old Testament as its sole or even primary authoritative document. Only the Karaite sect of Judaism has pretended to.[54]

The rabbinic Torah is very different from the Old Testament. Danby comments: "It includes the Written Law, the laws explicitly recorded in the Five Books of Moses; it includes also 'the traditions of the elders' or the Oral Law, namely, such beliefs and religious practices as piety and custom had in the course of centuries, consciously or unconsciously, grafted on to or developed out of the Written Law; and it includes yet a third, less tangible element, a spirit of development, whereby Written Law and Oral Law, in spite of seeming differences, are brought into a unity and interpreted and reinterpreted to meet the needs of changed conditions."[55] In short, there are three elements that comprise the Torah: the Old Testament, the oral law, and casuistry.[56]

The two primary questions that I am raising in this appendix are these: 1) Is traditional Judaism's casuistry even remotely biblical? 2) Is it the product of an anti-Old Testament perspective?

Dialecticism and Dualism

Dialecticism is that approach to human knowledge which insists that all truths are inherently opposed to each other. Dialecticism is to human logic what Manichaeanism is to cosmology: the assertion of the eternal struggle of opposites. Whenever we discover dialecticism in questions regarding epistemology — "What can man know, and

---

54. The tiny Karaite sect, begun in the mid-eighth century, openly opposed the oral law until the nineteenth century, when Reform Judaism began to take hold of Judaism. The Karaites never became influential. For this entire period, Rabbi Chajes' mid-nineteenth-century assessment is representative of the preceding seventeen centuries of Judaism: "Allegiance to the authority of the said rabbinic tradition is binding upon all sons of Israel, since these explanations and interpretations have come down to us by word of mouth from generation to generation, right from the time of Moses. They have been transmitted to us precise, correct, and unadulterated, and he who does not give his adherence to the unwritten law and the rabbinic tradition has no right to share the heritage of Israel; he belongs to the Sadducees or the Karaites who severed connection to us long ago." Chajes, *Student's Guide Through the Talmud*, p. 4.

55. Danby, Introduction, *Mishnah*, pp. xiii-xiv.

56. For a detailed discussion of these additions to the written law of the Old Testament, see R. Travers Herford, *Talmud and Apocrypha* (London: Soncino, 1933), pp. 66-69. Herford was a Unitarian scholar; Soncino Press is the Jewish publishing house that published the official and unabridged English-language Talmud.

how can he know it?"—we should also begin our search for traces of ethical dualism, the idea that there is one set of ethical standards for the elite, and another set for those on the outside, the "uninitiated." Exodus 12:49 denies the legitimacy of judicial dualism: "One law shall be to him that is homeborn, and unto the stranger that sojourneth among you." The Old Testament placed everyone in Israel under the same law. God required all the people to assemble one year in seven and listen to a public reading of the whole law: "Gather the people together, men, and women, and children, and thy stranger that is within thy gates, that they may hear, and that they may learn, and fear the LORD your God, and observe to do all the words of this law: And that their children, which have not known any thing, may hear, and learn to fear the LORD your God, as long as ye live in the land whither ye go over Jordan to possess it" (Deuteronomy 31:12-13). All people were expected to be able to understand the specifics and the principles of God's law, "the letter and the spirit." All residents were equal under God's law.

The judicial principle of equality before the civil law made Israel unique in ancient history. Other nations, including Greece and Rome, did not grant non-citizens equal status under the law. Foreigners and resident aliens were not members of the families and clans that alone could lawfully participate in the rites of the city; therefore, they were not entitled to protection by the civil law.[57] Not so in ancient Israel.

This judicial principle of equality before the law is basic to the Bible's *lex talionis* principle of "eye for eye." Rabbinic Judaism denies it. For example, a gentile who so much as strikes a Jew is worthy of death. "R. Hanina said: If a heathen smites a Jew, he is worthy of death, for it is written, *And he looked this way and that way, and when he saw that there was no man, he slew the Egyptian.* R. Hanina also said: He who smites an Israelite on the jaw, is as though he had thus assaulted the Divine Presence; for it is written, *One who smiteth man* [i.e. an Israelite] *attacketh the Holy One.*"[58]

This view of the inherent inequality of all men before God's law is a denial of God's command not to respect persons:

---

57. Numa Denis Fustel de Coulanges, *The Ancient City* (Garden City, New York: Anchor, [1864] 1955).

58. *Sanhedrin* 58b.

Ye shall not respect persons in judgment; but ye shall hear the small as well as the great; ye shall not be afraid of the face of man; for the judgment is God's: and the cause that is too hard for you, bring it unto me, and I will hear it (Deut. 1:17).

Thou shalt not wrest judgment; thou shalt not respect persons, neither take a gift: for a gift doth blind the eyes of the wise, and pervert the words of the righteous (Deut. 16:19).

To distinguish different proper penalties for striking Jews as opposed to striking gentiles elevates the Jews to a position of an international elite. This is in accord with Talmudic reasoning. The Talmud offers this doctrine of God's common grace to all men: "*All the families of the earth*, even the other families who live on the earth are blessed only for Israel's sake. *All the nations of the earth*, even the ships that go down from Gaul to Spain are blessed only for Israel's sake."[59]

Dialecticism vs. Casuistry

The Talmud is just about useless for writing a Bible commentary, not simply because it is such a difficult set of books to use by Jews or gentiles, but also because the large number of comments by the rabbis are so often very brief, and so often contradictory to each other. A self-conscious dialecticism underlies the Talmud: endless debate without authoritative or logical reconciliation. Dialecticism is one aspect of Judaism's tradition of deliberate secrecy, a tradition adopted by Maimonides in the style of his *Guide of the Perplexed*.[60]

A good example of this Talmudic dialecticism is the debate over whether gentiles should be allowed to read the Torah (the five books of Moses). Consider the saying of Rabbi Johanan, on which Maimonides' assertion cited at the beginning of this appendix is based: "R. [Rabbi] Johanan said: A heathen who studies the Torah deserves death, for it is written, *Moses commanded* us *a law for an inheritance*; it is *our* inheritance, not theirs." Johanan was one of the most prestigious of the rabbis, a disciple of Hillel (late first century B.C.).[61] Yet in the same paragraph is recorded the saying of Rabbi Meir, an equally

---

59. *Yebamoth* 63a.

60. ". . . Maimonides deliberately contradicts himself, and if a man declares both that *a* is *b* and that *a* is not *b*, he cannot be said to declare anything." Leo Strauss, "How to Read The Guide of the Perplexed," in Moses Maimonides, *The Guide of the Perplexed*, 2 vols., trans. Shlomo Pines (University of Chicago Press, 1963), p. xv.

61. *Sanhedrin* 59a.

prestigious authority, both jurist and preacher, from the second century A.D.: ". . . even a heathen who studies the Torah is as a High
Priest!" So, which is it? Maimonides sided with Johanan, but he
could as easily have sided with Meir. This is the main problem in
assessing the ethical pronouncements of the Talmud. There is
seldom any effective resolution of conflicting viewpoints. This is the
characteristic feature of the Talmud: a mountain of brief, sometimes
outlandish statements, without any coherent resolution. Paul, a former Pharisee (Phil. 3:5), warned Titus regarding such speculation:
"But avoid foolish questions, and genealogies, and contentions, and
strivings about the law; for they are unprofitable and vain" (Titus
3:9). Thirty-four fat volumes of this material is wearying to the soul.

The rabbis were often incredibly obscure, in stark contrast to the
clear statements of the biblical texts. This was a major point of conflict between Sadducees and Pharisees before the destruction of Jerusalem: the Sadducees believed that the texts of the Torah are clear.[62]
Writes Lauterbach of the Sadducees: "They would not devise ingenious methods to explain away a written law or give it a new
meaning not warranted by the plain sense of the words."[63] The
Pharisees disagreed with the Sadducees on this method of interpretation, and the Talmud is the book of the Pharisees. Its comments are
often contrary to the biblical text. For example, what are we to make
of this comment, obviously an application of Leviticus 18:23 and
21:7, the prohibition on bestiality? "R. [Rabbi] Shimi b. [son of]
Hiyya stated: A woman who had intercourse with a beast is eligible
to marry a priest."[64] The footnote by the modern Soncino Press commentator makes it even worse: "Even a High Priest." The Old Testament sets forth this rule for the high priest: "And he shall take a wife
in her virginity. A widow, or a divorced woman, or profane, or an
harlot, these shall he not take: but he shall take a virgin of his own
people to wife" (Lev. 21:13-14). Are we being asked by the rabbis to
regard as a virgin a woman who has committed bestiality?

Major university libraries will generally have a complete set of
the Soncino Press Babylonian Talmud. Because very few English-

---

62. Lauterbach, "Sadducees and Pharisees," *Rabbinical Essays*, p. 31.
63. *Ibid.*, p. 32. The Sadducees were not "proto-Christians," however. They did
not believe in the resurrection of the dead, for example, which is why Paul successfully divided the crowd of hostile Jews by claiming that he was being persecuted simply because he accepted the idea of the resurrection (Acts 23:6-10).
64. Babylonian Talmud, *Yebamoth* 59b.

speaking Christians or Jews have ever even seen a set of the Talmud, let alone read in it, they owe it to themselves to locate a set, open at random in any volume, and carefully read five consecutive pages. Just five pages; that will be sufficient. As they read, they will repeatedly ask themselves this question: "What in the world is this all about?" Then will come a second question: "How can anyone make sense of this?" Most of all, this question: "What has any of this got to do with the Old Testament?"

"You Have Heard It Said"

Orthodox Judaism is not simply "Old Testament theology without Jesus." It is the religion of "You have heard it said." This was Jesus' repeated response to the erroneous oral teachings of the Pharisees. We can do the same as we read the Talmud. For example:

"You have heard it said that gentiles who oppose Israel spend eternity in the nether world being boiled in semen, while Christians spend eternity with Jesus in boiling excrement,[65] but I say unto you that the New Testament teaches of a far worse eternity for covenant-breakers."

Or: "You have heard it said that Adam had intercourse with every beast of the field before cohabiting with Eve,[66] but I tell you that bestiality is a great sin before God."

---

65. Babylonian Talmud, *Gittin* 56b-57a. The text tells a story of a sorcerer, Onkelos son of Kolonikos: "He then went and raised Balaam by incantations. He asked him: Who is in repute in the other world? He replied: Israel. What then, he said, about joining them? He replied: *Thou shalt not seek their peace nor their prosperity all thy days for ever.* He then asked: What is your punishment? He replied: With boiling hot semen. He then went and raised by incantations the sinners of Israel. He asked them: Who is in repute in the other world? They replied: Israel. What about joining them? They replied: Seek their welfare, seek not their harm. Whoever touches them touches the apple of his eye. He said: What is your punishment? They replied: With boiling hot excrement, since a Master has said: Whoever mocks at the words of the Sages is punished with boiling hot excrement."

What has all this got to do with Christ and Christians? Everything. The entry for "Jesus" in *The Jewish Encyclopedia* says that the name of Balaam refers to Jesus, who was "the prototype of Jesus." It specifically cites this passage in the Talmud, *Gittin* 56a-57b, and it equates "the sinners of Israel" with Jesus. It says of Onkelos, "He asked Jesus: 'Who is esteemed in that world?' Jesus said: 'Israel.' 'Shall one join them?' Jesus said to him: 'Further their well-being; do nothing to their detriment; whoever touches them touches even the apple of His eye.'" *Jewish Encyclopedia*, 12 vols. (New York: Funk & Wagnalls, 1904), VII, p. 172.

66. "R. [Rabbi] Eleazar further stated: What is meant by the Scriptural text, *This is now bone of my bones, and flesh of my flesh?* This teaches that Adam had intercourse with every beast and animal but found no satisfaction until he cohabited with Eve." Babylonian Talmud, *Yebamoth* 63a. Eleazar was an important scholar of the oral law in the years immediately following the fall of Jerusalem in A.D. 70.

Or: "You have heard it said that a homosexual who seduces a boy under the age of nine need have no guilt, while others have argued that age three is the minimum,[67] but I say unto you that anyone who does this should be executed, as required by biblical law."

Did you read the footnotes? This is only the beginning, but it should be sufficient. You now recognize that the Talmud is not a conventional commentary on the Old Testament, although with certain key New Testament concepts missing. On the contrary, the Talmud's contents are only peripherally related to the Old Testament. The Talmud is a giant exercise in finding ways to escape the Old Testament texts. The Pharisees were in rebellion against God's law, all in the name of God's law. This was Jesus' assertion from the beginning:

Woe unto you, scribes and Pharisees, hypocrites! for ye compass sea and land to make one proselyte, and when he is made, ye make him twofold more the child of hell than yourselves. Woe unto you, ye blind guides, which say, Whosoever shall swear by the temple, it is nothing; but whosoever shall swear by the gold of the temple, he is a debtor! Ye fools and blind: for whether is greater, the gold, or the temple that sanctifieth the gold? And, Whosoever shall swear by the altar, it is nothing; but whosoever sweareth by the gift that is upon it, he is guilty. Ye fools and blind: for whether is greater, the gift, or the altar that sanctifieth the gift? Whoso therefore shall swear by the altar, sweareth by it, and by all things thereon. And whoso shall swear by the temple, sweareth by it, and by him that dwelleth therein. And he that shall swear by heaven, sweareth by the throne of God, and by him that sitteth thereon. Woe unto you, scribes and Pharisees, hypocrites! for ye pay tithe of mint and anise and cummin, and have omitted the weightier matters of the law, judgment, mercy, and faith: these ought ye to have done, and not to leave the other undone. Ye blind guides, which strain at a gnat, and swallow a camel. Woe unto you, scribes and Pharisees, hypocrites! for ye make clean the outside of the cup and of the platter, but within they are full of extortion and excess. Thou blind Pharisee, cleanse first that which is within the cup and platter, that the outside of them may be clean also. Woe

---

67. "Rab said: Pederasty with a child below nine years of age is not deemed as pederasty with a child above that. Samuel said: Pederasty with a child below three years is not treated as with a child above that." Babylonian Talmud, *Sanhedrin* 54b. The modern commentator's note explains: "Rab makes nine years the minimum; but if one committed sodomy with a child of lesser age, no guilt is incurred. Samuel makes three the minimum." Rab is the nickname of Rabbi Abba Arika (175?-247 A.D.), the founder of the Jewish academy in the Persian city of Sura [Sora], one of the three great Jewish academies in Persia. Samuel was Mar-Samuel (180-257 A.D.), Rab's contemporary and fellow teacher at Sura, a master of Jewish civil law. See Heinrich Graetz, *History of the Jews*, II, pp. 512-22.

unto you, scribes and Pharisees, hypocrites! for ye are like unto whited sepulchres, which indeed appear beautiful outward, but are within full of dead men's bones, and of all uncleanness (Matthew 23:24-27).

What the average Christian does not suspect is that modern Orthodox Jews are the self-conscious and self-proclaimed spiritual heirs of the Pharisees. This is what distinguishes them in their own eyes from Conservative Jews and Reform Jews.

Departing From the Old Testament Texts

This tradition of departing from the biblical text was maintained by medieval Jewish commentators. S. M. Lehrman is quite forthright about this: "To the rabbis, it was a trivial criticism that at times their explanations were somewhat remote from the actual literary meaning (*peshat*) of the text they sought to illuminate. Surely, the thing that mattered most was to make the Scriptures a living book with a message for all times."[68] If this really is what matters most, then the Talmud failed. Men cannot depart from the original meaning of the text without killing the Torah.[69]

David Weiss, formerly an Orthodox Jew but now a professor at the Conservative Jewish Theological Seminary,[70] is a master of the Talmud, the model for the character David Malter in Chaim Potok's novel, *The Promise*. He has devoted his academic career to a detailed study of the various versions of the Talmud in an attempt to piece together the true text. This discipline is what Christians call "lower criticism" when applied to biblical texts. Here is how Weiss describes the effective use of the Talmud: "With one hand you acknowledge God's existence. At the same time, you want to have some maneuverability. Studying critically is contending with God's writ — acknowledging it but using criticism to alter it. Man is powerless vis-à-vis God and powerful vis-à-vis His Torah. *There* he can assert his independence by offering an interpretation different from the one God intended."[71]

---

68. S. M. Lehrman, *The World of the Midrash* (London: Thomas Yoseloff, 1961), p. 11.

69. What makes the Bible unique among all books is its permanent ethical applicability within a world of historical change. This is because it is the Word of God. It applies perpetually because it is valid eternally. No other document in man's history has possessed or can possess this characteristic.

70. "Like the Orthodox, the Conservatives accept the Torah; but, unlike the Orthodox, they do not necessarily accept it as of divine origin." Gaer and Wolf, *Our Jewish Heritage*, p. 25.

71. Israel Shenker, "A Life in the Talmud," *New York Times Magazine* (Sept. 11, 1977).

It was this approach to Old Testament law that Jesus publicly challenged. This is the heart and soul of Phariseeism. The rabbinic compilers of Jewish oral law or "Unwritten Torah" (Mishnah) understood what they were doing: substituting the speculations of men for the "low maneuverability" biblical texts. The compilers of the rabbis' comments on the Mishnah (Gemara) also understood what they were doing. The Talmud is the product of their compiling of Mishnah and Gemara. The fundamental premise of the Talmud is incorrect: that it is more meritorious to read the Mishnah and Talmud than to read the Old Testament. "Our rabbis taught: They who occupy themselves with the Bible [alone] are but of indifferent merit; with Mishnah, are indeed meritorious, and are rewarded for it; with Gemara — there can be nothing more meritorious; yet run always to the Mishnah more than to the Gemara. Now, this is self-contradictory."[72] This, by the way, is an example of the dialecticism that is basic to the Talmud.

A Most Peculiar Book

Orthodox Jews believe that the Talmud is an inspired book. They do not treat is as "folklore." They treat it as authoritative.

The Old Testament forbade Molech worship. "And thou shalt not let any of thy seed pass through the fire to Molech, neither shalt thou profane the name of thy God: I am the LORD" (Leviticus 18:21). This is repeated in Leviticus 20:2-5. What does the Talmud say about this practice?

MISHNAH. HE WHO GIVES OF HIS SEED TO MOLECH INCURS NO PUNISHMENT UNLESS HE DELIVERS IT TO MOLECH AND CAUSES IT TO PASS THROUGH THE FIRE. IF HE GAVE IT TO MOLECH BUT DID NOT CAUSE IT TO PASS THROUGH THE FIRE, OR THE REVERSE, HE INCURS NO PENALTY, UNLESS HE DOES BOTH. [The Mishnah is always in capital letters in the Talmud — G.N.]

GEMARA. The Mishnah teaches idolatry and giving to Molech. R. Abin said: Our Mishnah is in accordance with the view that Molech worship is not idolatry. . . . R. Simeon said: If to Molech, he is liable; if to another idol, he is not.[73]

R. Aha the son of Raba said: If one caused all his seed to pass through [the fire] to Molech, he is exempt from punishment, because it is written, of *thy seed* implying, but not all thy seed.[74]

---

72. *Baba Mezia* 33a.
73. *Sanhedrin* 64a.
74. *Sanhedrin* 64b.

This approach to ethics and civil law has become known as "Talmudic reasoning."

Much of the Talmud's space is devoted to diet. For example, it says that eating dates makes a person ineligible to render a legal decision. "Rab said: If one has eaten dates, he should not give a legal decision. An objection was raised. Dates are wholesome morning and evening, in the afternoon they are bad, at noon they are incomparable. . . ."[75] To cure swollen glands, eat the dust from the shadow of a privy. "To make the flesh close he should bring dust from the shadow of a privy and knead it with honey and eat. This is effective."[76] Bladder stones are dealt with as follows: "For stone in the bladder let him take three drops of tar and three drops of leek juice and three drops of clear wine and pour it on the membrum of a man or on the corresponding place in a woman. Alternatively he can take the ear of a bottle and hang it on the membrum of a man or on the breasts of a woman. Or again he can take a purple thread which has been spun by a woman of ill repute or the daughter of a woman of ill repute and hang it on the membrum of a man or the breasts of a woman. Or again he can take a louse from a man and a woman and hang it on the membrum of a man and the corresponding place in a woman; and when he makes water he should do so on dry thorns near the socket of the door, and he should preserve the stone that issues, as it is good for all fevers."[77]

It offers very specific explanations of the origins of specific diseases. Consider the causes of epilepsy: "And do not stand naked in front of a lamp, for it was taught: He who stands naked in front of a lamp will be an epileptic, and he who cohabits by the light of a lamp will have epileptic children."[78] It offers comments on such seemingly trivial topics as the proper disposal of fingernails, and the consequences of ignoring this advice. "Three things were said in reference to nails: One who buries them is righteous; one who burns them is pious and one who throws them away is a villain! What is the reason? Lest a pregnant woman should step over them and miscarry."[79]

The Old Testament's teaching on how people should deal with sin is very clear: "He that covereth his sins shall not prosper: but

75. *Kethuboth* 11a.
76. *Gittin* 69a.
77. *Gittin* 69b.
78. *Peshaim* 112b.
79. *Mo'ed Katan* 18a.

whoso confesseth and forsaketh them shall have mercy" (Proverbs 28:13). "Wash you, make you clean; put away the evil of your doings from before mine eyes; cease to do evil" (Isaiah 1:16). There is no second strategy. The Talmud suggests a second strategy: "For R. Ilài says, If one sees that his [evil] *yezer* is gaining sway over him, let him go away where he is not known; let him put on sordid clothes, don a sordid wrap and do the sordid deed that his heart desires rather than profane the name of Heaven openly."

The wages of sins not recorded in the Book of Judges: "That wicked wretch [Sisera] had sevenfold intercourse [with Jael] at that time, as it says, *At her feet he sunk, he fell, he lay;* etc."[81]

A way to get even with one's enemies: "In R. Judah's opinion the snake's poison is lodged in its fangs; therefore, one who causes it to bite [by placing its fangs against the victim's flesh] is decapitated, whilst the snake itself is exempt. But in the view of the Sages the snake emits the poison of its own accord; therefore the snake is stoned, whilst he who caused it to bite is exempt."[82]

Binding, you may bind: "Raba said: If one bound his neighbor and he died of starvation, he is not liable to execution. . . . Raba also said: If he bound him before a lion, he is not liable. . . ."[83]

Their view of women: "ENGAGE NOT IN TOO MUCH CONVERSATION WITH WOMEN. THEY SAID THIS WITH REGARD TO ONE'S OWN WIFE, HOW MUCH MORE [DOES THE RULE APPLY] WITH REGARD TO ANOTHER MAN'S WIFE."[84] Maimonides' comments do not make the passage any more acceptable: "It is a known thing that for the most part conversation with women has to do with sexual matters."[85] This view is consistent with the Talmud's general view of women: "The world cannot do without either males or females. Yet happy is he whose children are males, and alas for him whose children are females."[86] At least one section of the Talmud questions the wisdom of instructing women in the law: "How then do we know that others are not

80. *Mo'ed Katan* 17a.
81. *Nazir* 23b.
82. *Sanhedrin* 78a.
83. *Sanhedrin* 77a.
84. *Aboth*, Chap. I. This is the famous *Pierke Aboth*, or "Sayings of the Fathers."
85. Cited by Judah Goldin, *The Living Talmud* (University of Chicago Press, 1957), p. 55.
86. *Baba Bathra* 16b.

commanded to teach her? — Because it is written, *'And ye shall teach them your* sons' — but not your daughters."[87]

The Question of Circumcision

Most important of all is circumcision, the Talmud says.

It was taught: Rabbi said, Great is circumcision, for none so ardently busied himself with [God's] precepts as our Father Abraham, yet he was called perfect only in virtue of circumcision, as it is written, *Walk before me and be thou perfect*, and it is written, *And I will make my covenant between me and thee*. Another version [of Rabbi's teaching] is this: Great is circumcision, for it counter-balances all the [other] precepts of the Torah, as it is written, *For after the tenor of these words I have made a covenant with thee and with Israel*. Another version is: Great is circumcision, since but for it heaven and earth would not endure, as it is written, *[Thus saith the Lord,] But for my covenant by day and night, I would not have appointed the ordinances of Heaven and earth.*[88]

Contrast these words with Paul's: "But as God hath distributed to every man, as the Lord hath called every one, so let him walk. And so ordain I in all churches. Is any man called being circumcised? let him not become uncircumcised. Is any called in uncircumcision? let him not be circumcised. Circumcision is nothing, and uncircumcision is nothing, but the keeping of the commandments of God" (I Cor. 7:17-19). He warned all men that the issue of life and death is obedience to the God who imposed the requirement of circumcision on the Jews.

For circumcision verily profiteth, if thou keep the law: but if thou be a breaker of the law, thy circumcision is made uncircumcision. Therefore if the uncircumcision keep the righteousness of the law, shall not his uncircumcision be counted for circumcision? And shall not uncircumcision which is by nature, if it fulfil the law, judge thee, who by the letter and circumcision dost transgress the law? For he is not a Jew, which is one outwardly; neither is that circumcision, which is outward in the flesh: But he is a Jew, which is one inwardly; and circumcision is that of the heart, in the spirit, and not in the letter; whose praise is not of men, but of God (Rom. 2:25-29).

This is why he could write of Christians: "For we are the circumcision, which worship God in the spirit, and rejoice in Christ Jesus, and have no confidence in the flesh" (Phil. 3:3).

---

87. *Kiddushin* 29b.
88. *Nedarim* 32a.

It should not be surprising that there has been a conflict of views for almost two millennia between Talmudic Jews and Christians. The two religions are very different. Jesus summarized these irreconcilable differences with His words, "you have heard it said . . . but I say unto you."[89] Paul, a former Pharisee, was even more blunt:

> For there are many unruly and vain talkers and deceivers, specially they of the circumcision: Whose mouths must be stopped, who subvert whole houses, teaching things which they ought not, for filthy lucre's sake. One of themselves, even a prophet of their own, said, The Cretians are alway liars, evil beasts, slow bellies. This witness is true. Wherefore rebuke them sharply, that they may be sound in the faith; Not giving heed to Jewish fables, and commandments of men, that turn from the truth. Unto the pure all things are pure: but unto them that are defiled and unbelieving is nothing pure; but even their mind and conscience is defiled. They profess that they know God; but in works they deny him, being abominable, and disobedient, and unto every good work reprobate (Titus 1:10-16).

Printing Makes a Difference

When a gentile reads the Talmud or Talmud-related writings, he necessarily enters into Talmud-forbidden ground. If study by gentiles of the written Torah itself is forbidden by Talmudic law, then surely the once-secret Jewish oral tradition of the Torah is prohibited. But when the Talmud is made available in vernacular languages by those who are still believers in its sacred character, as has been done in this century, the traditional criticisms against gentiles who read it necessarily fade. Perhaps even more obviously to those who have struggled through as few as three consecutive pages of the Talmud, by making available a comprehensive index, its defenders in principle thereby "opened the book." Its English-language translators, editors, and publisher have moved the Talmud from the world of religion exclusively to the world of open scholarship. This has clearly modified the ancient rules.

Of course, this has always been the dilemma of Talmudic Judaism. Maimonides faced it when he wrote *A Guide of the Perplexed* (1190). Leo Strauss is correct: the *Guide* is devoted to "the difficulties of the Law" or to "the secrets of the law": "Yet the Law whose secrets

---

89. I have relied in this section on the summaries and photocopies of 163 passages in the English-language Talmud which was published in *Christian News* (July 25, 1988 and August 1, 1988), a conservative Lutheran tabloid: P.O. Box 168, New Haven, Missouri.

Maimonides intends to explain forbids that they be explained in public, or to the public; they may only be explained in private and only to such individuals as possess both theoretical and political wisdom as well as the capacity of both understanding and using allusive speech; for only 'the chapter headings' of the secret teaching may be transmitted even to those who belong to the natural elite. Since every explanation given in writing, at any rate in a book, is a public explanation, Maimonides seems to be compelled by his intention to transgress the Law."[90] Maimonides was quite forthright about this need for secrecy:

For my purpose is that the truths be glimpsed and then again be concealed, so as not to oppose that divine purpose which one cannot possibly oppose and which has concealed from the vulgar among the people those truths especially requisite for His apprehension. As He has said: *The secret of the Lord is with them that fear Him* [Ps. 25:14]. Know that with regard to natural matters as well, it is impossible to give a clear exposition when teaching some of their principles as they are. For you know the saying of [the Sages], *may their memory be blessed: The Account of the Beginning ought not to be taught in the presence of two men* [Babylonian Talmud, *Hagigah*, 11b]. Now if someone explained all those matters in a book, he in effect would be *teaching* them to thousands of men. Hence these matters too occur in parables in the books of prophecy. The *Sages, may their memory be blessed*, following the train of these books, likewise have spoken of them in riddles and parables, for there is a close connection between these matters and the divine science, and they too are secrets of that divine science.[91]

In speaking about very obscure matters it is necessary to conceal some parts and to disclose others. Sometimes in the case of certain dicta this necessity requires that the discussion proceed on the basis of a certain premise, whereas in another place necessity requires that the discussion proceed on the basis of another premise contradicting the first one. In such cases the

---

90. Strauss, "How to Begin to Study The Guide of the Perplexed," in Maimonides, *Guide of the Perplexed*, p. xiv. Strauss argues that Maimonides overcame this restriction by adopting literary techniques that made the *Guide* itself a secret writing: p. vx. It was Maimonides' emphasis on secrecy and rigorous writing that influenced the Jewish political theorist Strauss and his followers, of whom Pines is one. Political philosopher and former U.S. Senator John P. East insisted that Strauss "cast himself in the role of a modern Maimonides"; this can be seen in Strauss' book, *Persecution in the Art of Writing* (Westport, Connecticut: Greenwood, [1952] 1973). Cf. John P. East, "Leo Strauss and American Conservatism," *Modern Age*, XXI (Winter 1977), p. 7; Archie P. Jones, "Apologists of Classical Tyranny: An Introductory Critique of Straussianism," *Journal of Christian Reconstruction*, V (Summer 1978), pp. 112-14.

91. Maimonides, *Guide* 3b-4a; pp. 6-7.

vulgar must in no way be aware of the contradiction; the author accordingly uses some device to conceal it by all means.[92]

There may be Orthodox Jews who will criticize me for going to the Talmud and extracting these embarrassing passages for the purpose of public disclosure and debate. They may say that I am misinterpreting these passages because I am not familiar with another oral teaching tradition that somehow explains away these passages. This would imply that there is a still more secret tradition. Even if this criticism is correct — that a consistent, universally agreed-upon secondary secret oral teaching does exist which explains the primary oral (now translated and printed) once-secret tradition — and even if this additional secret oral teaching does offer interpretations that somehow make these passages in the Talmud appear morally acceptable, all of which I sincerely doubt, Orthodox Jews must then face the reality of any appeal to yet another oral tradition. A tradition of secondary oral explanations and glosses on a 1500-year-old written version (the Talmud) of an authoritative ancient oral tradition is not going to be regarded by outsiders (or even Orthodox Jewish insiders, I suspect) as equally authoritative. What is printed eventually becomes authoritative, especially in the field of civil and criminal law. Lawyers and casuists appeal to known written sources. The Talmud stands as written.

Orthodox Judaism by 1952 had at long last provided the English-speaking public with an officially sanctioned, expensively published version of the Talmud: seemingly unexpurgated, fully annotated, and professionally edited. Until the era of the Industrial Revolution, the Talmud was regarded by all Jews except a handful of Karaites as the sacred oral tradition of Judaism. Orthodox Jews should therefore not object when a gentile reads the Talmud, cites it verbatim, and criticizes it whenever he can demonstrate that it is obviously at odds with non-Talmudic morality. What else did they expect when they published it? They should refrain from criticizing gentiles who are critical of the Talmud's ethics unless they are prepared to discuss these issues in public without appealing to the escape hatch of an even more authoritative secret oral tradition which cannot lawfully be revealed.

---

92. *Guide* 10b; p. 18.

Debating Ethical Standards

Why should Orthodox Jews be surprised or even upset when non-Jews react strongly against the Talmud's teaching, for example, that it is legitimate for a man to have sexual relations with a little girl, just so long as she is under the age of three? The Mishnah says: "WHEN A GROWN-UP MAN HAS HAD SEXUAL INTERCOURSE WITH A LITTLE GIRL, OR WHEN A SMALL BOY HAS HAD INTERCOURSE WITH A GROWN-UP WOMAN, OR [WHEN A GIRL WAS ACCIDENTALLY] INJURED BY A PIECE OF WOOD [IN ALL CASES] THEIR KETHUBAH IS TWO HUNDRED [ZUZ]; SO ACCORDING TO R. MEIR."[93] Then the Gemara explains: "It means this: When a grown-up man has intercourse with a little girl it is nothing, for when the girl is less than this [annotation: "Lit., 'here', that is, less than three years old"] it is as if one puts a finger into the eye; . . ."[94] Should Orthodox Jews really expect Christians to accept the moral validity of such a teaching? Surely the vast majority of Jews today would reject it if they knew about it, which they do not.

As I said earlier, it might be argued that the rabbis were not really arguing for such a seemingly grotesque ethical principle, that it was all some sort of hypothetical debate. This particular debate in the Talmud concerned the kethubah. The kethubah was a deed given by a husband to his bride which specified that if he divorced her, she would receive a monetary payment. The minimum payment was 200 zuzim[95] for virgins, but only 100 zuzim for non-virgins.[96] A defender of the Talmud might argue that what the Mishnah really teaches is the perfectly reasonable principle that very young girls who are subjected to the kinds of intercourse described in the text are to be considered as virgins. While it would be possible to argue that this law's ethical concern focuses only on the innocence of the girl under three year old who is sexually abused, and that the words "it is nothing" refer only to her, and not to her abuser, then the question inevitably arises: What about the girl aged three years and older? Why treat a four-year-old sexually abused girl as a willing fornicator for the purposes of establishing her kethubah price? Furthermore, why treat as a virgin an adult woman who deliberately has had sex-

---

93. *Kethuboth* 11a.
94. *Kethuboth* 11b.
95. The smallest Jewish coin was the zuz.
96. Cf. "Ketubbah," in *The Principles of Jewish Law*, edited by Menachem Elon (Jerusalem: Keter, [1975?]), col. 387.

ual relations with a small boy who is "less than nine years of age,"[97] as the annotator says?

Christians do not ask such questions today. Therefore, Jews do not answer them. The fact is, virtually all modern Christian scholars — at least those who publish — are completely unfamiliar with the passages in the Talmud that I have cited in this essay, and Jews do not try to defend such passages; they remain discreetly silent. There has been a kind of implicit cease-fire agreement regarding the ethical details of the Talmud, and a willingness on both sides to limit all discussions of the ethics of traditional Judaism and especially the Talmud to general ethical principles that have been derived from the less controversial passages. So, over the years, the Talmud has fallen into the shadows. Most Jews do not read it any more. Yet it is only here that we find a detailed account of what Paul calls "the traditions of my fathers" (Gal. 1:14).

Concealment and Initiation

Jews for many centuries hid the Talmud from the eyes of gentiles. They correctly surmised that Christian leaders would be shocked and outraged if they thought that such teachings were the basis of the autonomous civil legal order that Jews enjoyed through most of medieval history. From time to time, the authorities ordered the confiscation and burning of copies of the Talmud. Rabbi Trattner provides a list of about two dozen of these edicts, from 1240 to 1757.[98] But he misleads his Christian audience (his publisher, Thomas Nelson, published and still publishes predominantly Christian books) when he offers these three reasons why Christian magistrates have been so hostile to the Talmud in the past:

1. Since it forms the main teaching of the Jewish religion, it has been regarded as the supreme obstacle in preventing Jews from being converted to Christianity.

2. Since the *Talmud* interprets the Old Testament by reshaping ancient Biblical laws to meet the needs of post-Biblical times, it has been charged with the falsification of Scripture.

3. Since the *Talmud* is a non-Christian production, it has been accused of harboring an evil and irreverent attitude towards Christ and the Church.[99]

---

97. *Kethuboth* 11a.

98. Ernest R. Trattner, *Understanding the Talmud* (New York: Thomas Nelson & Sons, 1955), pp. 200-1.

99. *Ibid.*, p. 198.

Would he say that teaching that Jesus Christ and His followers will be boiled in hot semen and hot excrement for eternity constitutes a reverent attitude? Are Christians supposed to believe that this is a reverent "attitude toward Christ and the Church"?

He goes on: "For many centuries the *Talmud* was regarded as mysterious and a source of blasphemous statements against Christianity. This suspicion was not only grossly untrue but it was magnified and distorted by ignorance of the *Talmud*. The inability of Christian scholars to read the *Talmud* made matters worse."[100] An uncensored (as far as we gentiles know) version of the Talmud is now in English. Those few of us who bother to consult it still do not find that these ancient suspicions have been calmed. They have in fact been confirmed.

I do not think that Michael Rodkinson was being any more honest that Rabbi Trattner when he wrote these words in the Preface to his expurgated version of the Talmud: "The Talmud is free from the narrowness and bigotry with which it is usually charged, and if phrases used out of their context, and in a sense the very reverse from that which their author intended, are quoted against it, we may be sure that those phrases never existed in the original Talmud, but are the later additions of its enemies and such as never studied it."[101] Then came the Soncino edition.

It is my belief that mandatory training in the oral law served covenant-breaking Judaism for at least two millennia as a means of initiating its religious leaders into what was basically a secret society. By requiring its brightest adolescent males to go through long hours of memorization and discussion of such material, year after year, if they wanted to become rabbis, Judaism for almost two millennia sidetracked its best and brightest young men into some very peculiar ethical avenues — peculiar at least to the outlook of Christians.

It is also my contention that the unprecedented economic, intellectual, and cultural strides made by Jews in the West could begin, and did begin, only when their young men at last were allowed to become rabbis and leaders within the community without being required to go though this initiatory process. But a price has been extracted by Western society for this advancement. The price has been the steady secularization of the vast majority of Jews, just as Orthodox rabbis have warned their upwardly mobile brethren from the early decades of the nineteenth century until today. Most Western Jews

---

100. *Idem.*
101. Michael L. Rodkinson, Editor's Preface, *New Edition of the Babylonian Talmud* (Boston: New Talmud Pub. Co., 1903), I, p. xi.

today have become little more than Karaites without the Pentateuch, or even like Unitarians, though with better business connections.

The Erosion of Orthodox Judaism

The heart and soul of Orthodox Judaism is its evolutionary ethical character, not its explicit theology. It is the world's most detailed and self-conscious example of process theology — dialectical, evolutionary, and ultimately open-ended. So radical is this process theology that Orthodox Jews believe that God Himself is continually engaged in a study of His own law, in association with the souls of deceased Jews. This goes on in the Academy on High — a concept so preposterous that modern Jewish scholars downplay it, describe it as merely a metaphor, and refuse to consider the possibility that Jews once took the Talmud and the Old Testament as literally inspired. (Literalism of ancient texts and ancient religious beliefs is simply not permitted to the founders of still-existing Western religions by those who still want the prestige, communal stability, and tenured security provided by the skeptical heirs of these still-literalistic religions.) The uninitiate — a very important word — cannot easily understand this commitment to process. Rabbi Louis Finkelstein was the head of the Jewish Theological Society of America. In his introduction to the reprint of Solomon Schechter's *Aspects of Rabbinic Theology* (1901), he writes:

> The view that inquiry into the nature and requirements of Torah is more than a human need, being a cosmic process, is even more difficult to communicate to the uninitiate. Doubtless that is why Schechter did not include in his book any discussion of the fundamental Rabbinic concept of the Academy on High. The belief that study of the Torah is one of the Deity's main concerns, and that God Himself is each day expanding the scope and insight of Torah, engaging in this labor in association with the souls of the saints who have departed mortal life, is a theological metaphor; but for the Rabbinic scholars the metaphor represented reality — the profoundest of all realities.
>
> That the Torah is at once perfect and perpetually incomplete; that like the Universe itself it was created to be a process, rather than a system — a method of inquiry into the right, rather than a codified collection of answers; that to discover possible situations with which it might deal and to analyze their moral implications in the light of its teachings is to share the labor of Divinity — these are inherent elements of Rabbinic thought, dominating the manner of life it recommends.[102]

---

102. Louis Finkelstein, Introduction to New Edition (1961), in Schechter, *Aspects of Rabbinic Theology*, pp. xix-xx.

Judaism is a religion that historically has spent very little time on systematic theology and philosophy. "Inherent logical unity can be forced on Judaism only at the cost of distortion," writes Finkelstein.[103] Maimonides in this sense was a self-conscious exception to this tradition. This is one reason why Orthodox Jewish scholars have been nervous about Maimonides from the beginning: *Guide of the Perplexed* has always been perceived as just too philosophical for comfort, too Aristotelian for reliability, however tight a grip his *Strong Hand* has maintained on their thinking.[104] This, despite the fact that he warned the reader, "I adjure — by God, may he be exalted! — every reader of this Treatise of mine not to comment upon a single word of it and not to explain to another anything in it save that which has been explained and commented upon in the words of the famous Sages of our Law who preceded me."[105]

Judaism is overwhelmingly a religion defined by a system of evolving rules of conduct. Again, Christians have not understood this, for they mistakenly equate Judaism with the fixed rules of the Old Testament. Danby is correct in his evaluation: "The Mishnah is not a finally authoritative corpus of the beliefs and practices of Judaism: it is of the nature of Judaism that it can have no such thing. 'The Law', which alone is Jewish doctrine, has in it an inherent principle of development which, while holding fast to the foundations laid down in the Mosaic legislation, makes it intolerant of dogmatic definition or set credal forms."[106]

Evolving Ethics and Cultural Suicide

It is this anti-dogmatism and anti-credalism that is the inescapable fact of Judaism's history, which today threatens to overwhelm mainstream Judaism, just as a very similar theological relativism has very nearly overwhelmed mainstream Christianity. But Christianity has always had an institutional advantage over Orthodox Judaism: it is both credal and judicial, both dogmatic and ethical. Its doctrine of the covenant proclaims fixed biblical laws at its third point.[107]

---

103. *Ibid.*, p. xiii.

104. For example, Maimonides insisted that "this divine science cannot become actual except after a study of natural science." *Guide* 5a; p. 9.

105. *Guide* 9a; p. 15.

106. Danby, Introduction, *Mishnah*, pp. xv-xvi.

107. Ray R. Sutton, *That You May Prosper: Dominion By Covenant* (Tyler, Texas: Institute for Christian Economics, 1987), ch. 3.

The revival of Christian casuistry that is presently taking place[108] proclaims self-consciously the authoritative character of the Old Testament's ethical principles and, as my economic commentary indicates, the contemporary applicability of the letter of Old Testament law as well.

The evolutionary judicial character of Judaism has led to the near-destruction of Orthodoxy's influence in Western Judaism. The dual social forces of Western capitalism and secularism established institutional and philosophical foundations that have steadily undermined Talmudic religion and culture. The more ethically evolutionary any particular worldview has been, the more rapidly it has succumbed to this powerful pair of social forces. Judaism was especially vulnerable.

The factor that most threatened Orthodox Judaism was industrial society's growing toleration. In the mid-nineteenth century, when Jews in Western Europe and the United States began to enter the new industrial capitalist world, they found that the older discriminatory legal barriers had been progressively weakened by the new forces of economic competition. An individual's economic productivity in an open ("impersonal")[109] competitive market is judged apart from considerations of his religious affiliation. To the extent that non-market forms of racial or religious discrimination persist, those who discriminate against economically efficient employees or suppliers (or—much more rare—buyers) must pay a price for their actions: reduced income because of reduced efficiency.[110] The free market penalizes economically all those who discriminate on any basis except price and quality of output. Price competition has always been fundamental to the spread of free market capitalism,[111] and Jews became masters of competitive pricing.[112] Jews began to

---

108. I refer here to Christian Reconstruction or theonomy.

109. On the proper and improper use of the term "impersonal" to describe market economies, see Gary North, *The Dominion Covenant: Genesis* (2nd ed.; Tyler, Texas: Institute for Christian Economics, 1987), pp. 9-11.

110. "The least prejudiced sellers will come to dominate the market in much the same way as people who are least afraid of heights come to dominate occupations that require working at heights: They demand a smaller premium." Richard A. Posner, *Economic Analysis of Law* (Boston: Little, Brown, 1986), p. 616.

111. Max Weber, *General Economic History*, trans. Frank H. Knight (New York: Collier, [1920] 1966), p. 230.

112. The common phrase, "he Jewed me down," points to this phenomenon of the Jew as a price-cutter. If one were to say, "he Jewed me up," it would make no sense. The Jew as the price-cutting haggler is universally recognizable, but not the Jew as the price-gouger. He is resented by people in their capacity as producers and retail

move out of the ghetto. The ghetto's walls, both literal and figurative, came tumbling down.

Jewish legal scholar Menachem Elon has argued that it was the Jews' system of separate civil courts that was crucial to the maintenance of the autonomy of Jews as a people. When judicial emancipation began in eighteenth-century Western Europe, this autonomous character of Judaism began to erode. Jews were increasingly entitled to civil justice in secular civil courts, and they took advantage of this revolutionary development. Jewish commercial law and other areas of "secular world" law began to atrophy. This secularism began to undermine the foundations of Orthodox Judaism[113] — a term which itself was the product of the process of change.[114] Rabbi Samson Raphael Hirsch asked the key question which most Jews have refused to face: "What would you have achieved if you became *free* Jews, and you ceased to be *Jews*?"[115] Nevertheless, his own efforts to integrate the techniques and findings of modern science and philosophy with Judaism eventually led to a reduced resistance of Orthodox Judaism to secularism, as surely as Aquinas' analogous efforts had done for Christianity seven centuries earlier.

The Faustian Bargain

From the New Testament period to the present, the lure of pagan philosophy has proven irresistible to Jews, as it has also for Christians. Out of Greek philosophy came Hellenism, and Hellenism's influence on early rabbinic Judaism was very great.[116] Nevertheless, the impact of pagan philosophy in Judaism was less direct in the Middle Ages, probably due to the isolation of Jews from the sur-

---

sellers, not as consumers. Gentiles are always looking for the elusive "Jewish brother-in-law deal."

It is not random that the four ethnic groups that are thought of as price-cutters have had decidedly biblical backgrounds: the Dutch ("Dutch treat" dates are those in which the girl pays), the Scots, the Armenians, and the Jews.

113. Menachem Elon, "Introduction," in Elon (ed.), *The Principles of Jewish Law* (Jerusalem: Keter, 1975), col. 35.

114. It was Rabbi Samson R. Hirsch who accepted the term "Orthodox" which had been used as an epithet by secular Jews in the mid-nineteenth century. I. Grunfeld, "Samson Raphael Hirsch—The Man and His Mission," in *Judaism Eternal: Selected Essays from the Writings of Samson Raphael Hirsch* (London: Soncino Press, 1956), p. xlvii.

115. *Ibid.*, p. xxxix.

116. Martin Hengel, *Judaism and Hellenism: Studies in their Encounter in Palestine during the Early Hellenic Period*, 2 vols. (Philadelphia: Fortress Press, 1974). Cf. W. D. Davies, *Paul and Rabbinic Judaism: Some Rabbinic Elemenys in Pauline Theology* (4th ed.; Philadelphia: Fortress Press, 1980), ch. 1.

rounding gentile Christian culture. It is not surprising that the path of Greek philosophy into late medieval Judaism, and then into Christianity, was by way of Islam, especially through Maimonides. Aristotelian Athens came to Paris through Cairo and Spain.

For centuries, Talmudic Judaism resisted the rational categories of pagan wisdom, despite *The Guide of the Perplexed*. But with Rabbi Samson Raphael Hirsch in the mid-nineteenth century, the epistemological barriers began to break down.[117] This process of cultural and intellectual assimilation accelerated rapidly in twentieth-century America, especially after the Second World War. The most prestigious American universities opened their doors to all those who could compete academically, and Jews surely could compete. They at last gained equal access to the professional schools—law, medicine, architecture—as well as to the Ph.D-granting graduate schools. The price they were asked to pay, however, was very high. Too high. The universities offered a Faustian bargain to Jews (and also to Bible-believing Christians): "You may go as high as your brains can carry you, just so long as you leave your religion off campus." Most academically oriented Jews could not resist this offer.[118] Intermarriage with the gentiles whom they met on campus was also nearly inevitable. Cohen's remarks are on target: "The Jew, in joining the West, no longer joined a Christian West, for he did not join a church wedded to a society. . . . The Jew joined an already de-Christianizing West, and as part of the bargain he agreed—foolishly—to de-Judaize."[119] What Nazi Germany's politics had not achieved in the 1930's, Prussia's earlier export of the academic state certification system did achieve: the suppression of traditional religion through the enthusiastic cooperation of the suppressed. Secular education is the humanist world's hoped-for "final solution" for both orthodox Christianity and Orthodox Judaism.

In the twentieth century, the tide has rapidly flowed against Talmudic Judaism; first the Nazis and then secularism uprooted Orthodox Judaism. Higher criticism of the Bible has produced the

---

117. I. Grunfeld, "Samson Raphael Hirsch—The Man and His Mission," in *Judaism Eternal*.

118. A very effective presentation of this post-1940 transformation of Judaism is found in Chaim Potok's novel and the movie based on it, *The Chosen*. In the early 1960's, Potok served as editor of the Jewish Publication Society of America's translation of the Hebrew Bible. Potok, "The Bible's Inspired Art," *New York Times Magazine* (Oct. 3, 1982), p. 63.

119. Cohen, *Myth of the Judeo-Christian Tradition*, p. 186.

same bitter fruit of skepticism and liberalism in Jewish circles that it
has produced in Christian circles.[120] There was not only bitter fruit
but also forbidden fruit to be eaten. By the millions, they have
feasted on this forbidden fruit. Solomon Schechter is correct: biblical
higher criticism was in fact the "higher anti-Semitism," for it obliter-
ated the official foundation of the Jewish experience.[121] But this was
a case of the hermeneutical chickens coming home to roost, for Judaism had long undermined this original foundation through its ever-
evolving traditionalism.

Traditional Judaism's ethical rules began to change, and therefore the whole religion had to change. Reform Judaism launched a
successful intellectual attack on Orthodox Judaism in the early decades of the nineteenth century, leading to the steady isolation of the
defenders of old Pharisee tradition, and in the twentieth century, secular Judaism and Conservative Judaism have become the dominant
traditions. Orthodox Judaism today retains very little influence outside of the state of Israel. Reform Judaism and conservative Judaism
are overwhelmingly dominant in the West. Secular Jews seem to be
the norm today, as far as gentiles can discern. (The most memorable
description I have ever read regarding the outlook of secular Jews regarding Judaism is Lis Harris' description of her family, "fans whose
home team was the Jews.")[122] Anti-credalism giveth, and anti-
credalism taketh away.

---

120. The Jewish scholar most responsible for the introduction of higher criticism
into Jewish curricula was the extraordinary linguist, Julian Morgenstern, who also
served as president of Hebrew Union College in Cincinnati, Ohio, after 1921. Born
in 1881, he was still writing scholarly essays in the mid-1960's in the *Hebrew Union College Annual*. ("The *Hasidim* — Who Were They?" *HUCA*, XXXVIII, 1967.) Indicative
of the extent of his life's work was his four-part study, "The Book of the Covenant."
Part I appeared in the 1928 issue; Part II appeared in 1930; Part III in 1931-32; and
Part IV in 1962. He was elected president of the American Oriental Society in
1928-29 and president of the Society of Biblical Literature in 1941. "Morgenstern
assumed a position of pre-eminence as a philosopher and theoretician of Reform
Judaism. . . . Modern developments, he showed convincingly, are only the latest
manifestations of the adjustments that have taken place over and over whenever
Judaism has come into contact with a superior culture." Morris Lieberman, "Julian
Morgenstern — Scholar, Teacher and Leader," *Hebrew Union College Annual*, XXXII
(1962), p. 6. Morgenstern was a dedicated humanist and internationalist. Cf. Mor-
genstern, "Nationalism, Universalism, and World Religion," in Charles Frederick
Walker (ed.), *World Fellowship, Addresses and Messages by Leading Statesmen of All Faiths,
Races and Countries* (New York: Liveright, 1935). This was his address to the second
Parliament of Religions, held in Chicago in 1933.
121. Cited in Cohen, *Myth of Judeo-Christian Tradition*, p. xviii.
122. Lis Harris, *Holy Days: The World of a Hasidic Family* (New York: Summit
Books, 1985), p. 17.

Hermeneutics: An Inescapable Concept

Commenting on anything requires a principle of interpretation. This is true of Bible commentaries. Principles of interpretation differ, and sometimes very sharply. This means that rival hermeneutical principles can and do become divisive. That, too, is the price of open inquiry. It is a price that must be paid on both sides. There is no way to reconcile these rival principles of biblical interpretation: 1) Jesus as the sole fulfillment of Old Testament messianic prophecies vs. Jesus as a false prophet and blasphemer, for which He was lawfully executed; 2) the New Testament as the sole authoritative commentary on the Old Testament vs. the New Testament as false prophecy; 3) Christians as the only true covenantal heirs of Abraham vs. Jews as the only true covenantal heirs of Abraham. It is the ancient debate, recently revived politically in the state of Israel, over the question, "Who is a Jew?"[123] It is a debate over the truth of Paul's assertion: "For we are the circumcision, which worship God in the spirit, and rejoice in Christ Jesus, and have no confidence in the flesh" (Phil. 3:3). Only theological liberals on both sides of the debate can sensibly play down these differences, since liberals do not accept the truth of either religion's set of hermeneutical principles.

This essay deals with Orthodox Judaism and its relation with orthodox Christianity. Orthodox Christianity is no longer the dominant stream of Christianity in the West, just as Orthodox Judaism is no longer the dominant stream of Judaism outside of the state of Israel, and which is in sharp political conflict with secular Judaism inside that nation. Always in the background of the life of the orthodox Christian and the Orthodox Jew are the liberals "within the camp." The Orthodox Christian does not believe that liberal, mainstream Christianity is *really* Christianity, just as the Orthodox Jew does not believe that mainstream Judaism is *really* Judaism.[124] Van Til is correct in his assessment of the theological unity of the liberal Jew and the liberal Christian:

---

123. In Judaism, this question is really, "Who is the rabbi?" The rabbi sanctions marriages and therefore the legitimacy of the children.

124. There is a problem here for Bible-affirming Christians. They normally do accept as valid the baptisms of converts out of mainstream churches. They would not accept Mormon baptism as valid. So, to some degree, they do accept mainstream churches as still Christian. For the Orthodox Jew, the determination of who is a Jew is established by examining the training of the Rabbi who circumcised him or circumcised her father or husband.

When Jesus says that all power is given to him by the Father in view of his death and resurrection, and that he will vanquish the last enemy which is death, the modern Jew and the modern Protestant consider this mythology. The modern Jew will gladly join the modern Protestant in speaking of Christ as a Messiah if only the messianic idea be demythologized by means of the self-sufficient ethical consciousness. The modern Protestant theologian is ready and eager to oblige the modern Jew.[125]

The implicit theological unity that modernism creates between mainstream Christians and Jews — the many shades of Unitarianism — in no way reduces the explicit theological disunity between orthodox Christians and Orthodox Jews. The battle over the proper interpretation of the Old Testament still divides the orthodox Christian and the Orthodox Jew, even as it divides Jews from liberal Jews and Christians from liberal Christians. At best, the common "battle for the Text" of Torah-affirming Christians and Jews against the higher critics of the Bible within their respective camps has created pressure for a temporary cease-fire between the besieged camps of the Bible-affirmers. But a temporary cease-fire is not a permanent peace treaty. The war over interpretation is great because of the commitment of both sides to the divine origin of the Old Testament. Again, citing Van Til: "When a Christian worships Christ as the Son of God, he is, says the Jew, an idolater. And he sees his mission as that of bringing such an idol-worshiper back to the God of Abraham and of Moses. In seeking to fulfill his mission in relation to Christian idolaters the Jew must, of course, *oppose* the claims of Christ."[126]

Is There a Judeo-Christian Tradition?

The battle over hermeneutics is inescapable. The question then must be raised: If Western civilization was Christian in the era of the exclusion of the Jews, and today is humanist to the exclusion of Torah-believing Christians and Jews, to what extent is it valid to speak of a Judeo-Christian tradition? This leads immediately to a second question: To what extent are the respective commitments to the divine origin of the Old Testament a unified commitment, and therefore the basis of the Judeo-Christian tradition in Western history? If the two hermeneutics are permanently divided, how can there be a unified tradition?

---

125. Cornelius Van Til, *Christ and the Jews* (Philadelphia: Presbyterian & Reformed, 1968), p. 97.
126. *Ibid.*, p. 1.

It is one of the oddest facts of modern Bible-affirming Christianity that the dispensationalist fundamentalists, who categorically deny the continuing authority of Old Testament law in New Testament times, see themselves as the "soul cousins" if not "soul brothers" of Orthodox Jews. They regard any deviation from the West's support of the state of Israel as a theological deviation, not just bad foreign policy.[127] Yet the only possible basis of a supposed Judeo-Christian tradition would be a mutual commitment to Old Testament legal norms. Yet dispensationalist leaders make statements such as this:

At the heart of the problem of legalism is pride, a pride that refuses to admit spiritual bankruptcy. That is why the doctrines of grace stir up so much animosity. Donald Grey Barnhouse, a giant of a man in free grace, wrote: "It was a tragic hour when the Reformation churches wrote the Ten Commandments into their creeds and catechisms and sought to bring Gentile believers into bondage to Jewish law, which was never intended either for the Gentile nations or for the church."[128] He was right, too.[129]

Thus, to the extent that there has been a Judeo-Christian tradition in the West, the *consistent, well-informed* dispensationalist is forced by his theology to deny that such a tradition is judicially valid. It has to be seen as the product of a spurious, deviant form of Christianity.

The question that the defender of Old Testament judicial standards must then ask himself is this: Has there been a sufficient unanimity between orthodox Christians and Orthodox Jews over the interpretation and application of Old Testament legal norms to have constituted a Judeo-Christian tradition? This is the question that I am attempting to answer in this essay.

Before dealing with this issue, let me ask a question: Is there a Moslem-Christian tradition? The Moslems claim to believe in both the Old and the New Testaments as God-inspired. If the Christian answers that the Koran (which he has not read) overthrows both the Old and New Testaments, no matter what the Moslem says he believes about the Bible—which in fact is the case—then what about the Mishnah and the Talmud?

---

127. See, for example, Hal Lindsey, *The Road to Holocaust* (New York: Bantam, 1989).

128. He cites Barnhouse, *God's Freedom*, p. 134.

129. S. Lewis Johnson, "The Paralysis of Legalism," *Bibliotheca Sacra*, Vol. 120 (April/June, 1963), p. 109.

An Invention of Modernism

Arthur A. Cohen, in his provocatively titled book, *The Myth of the Judeo-Christian Tradition*, which was published by a respected publishing house that specializes in scholarly Jewish studies, denies that this tradition ever existed. It is an intellectual fabrication, he argues. He has identified the origins of this myth: the Enlightenment and, later, German liberal Protestant scholarship of the late-nineteenth century.[130] Protestant "higher critics" of the Old Testament were implacably hostile to Old Testament law, so they attempted to disengage the New Testament from the Old. The Jew of the Old Testament was described as being "in bondage to a hopeless legalism. On the one hand the genius of the Hebrew Bible is commended; on the other hand Christianity is set in superior condescension to the traditions of Judaism which survive, like ruins, the advent of Jesus Christ, the new architect of mankind. . . . The Judaism which survives the onslaught of Protestant Higher Criticism is buried under a mountain of historicist formulations, while a pure, virtuous Kantian Christianity — freed from Jewish accretion — is defined. Once more, almost in recapitulation of the Gnostic tendencies of the early Church (though turned this time to a different task), a 'Christo-Jewish' tradition was defined."[131]

This implicit antinomianism of the higher critics was indeed quite similar to the anti-Old Testament perspective of the gnostics. Gnosticism and antinomianism are two sides of the same counterfeit coin. Denying mankind's access in history to a permanent higher law above existing humanist culture, critics of the existing culture face a grim choice: either their absorption into the prevailing culture or their removal from influence, i.e., either assimilation or confinement to a cultural ghetto.[132] The prevailing culture is seen as the equivalent of ethical quicksand; one should not seek to walk through it in the pilgrimage of life. But if men dwell in a self-imposed cultural

---

130. Cohen, *Myth of the Judeo-Christian Tradition*, pp. xviii, 196-200.
131. *Ibid.*, p. 199.
132. This dualism between the individual and society is a manifestation of autonomous man's philosophical dualism between the one and the many. If autonomous man is part of the one (unity), he in principle loses himself, his personality, and his individuality. But if he maintains his independence (autonomy), he loses any point of contact with any other individual. To use one of Cornelius Van Til's analogies, he is like a bead with no hole that seeks attachment to an infinitely long string. Philosophically speaking, without God's higher law and without man as the created image of God, individuals have no logical point of contact with each other.

ghetto, they will be tempted to create a psychological zone of internal retreat in their quest for meaning and significance as they wait for death or eschatological deliverance. What else can they do? They see no way to transform the world, for they have no point of ethical or judicial contact with the world. They do not regard biblical law as a tool of dominion, as a lengthy lever capable of moving the general civilization in the direction of God's permanent standards. On the contrary, they see themselves on the short end of this lever: it is the general culture that threatens to move them by law, not the other way around. Their antinomianism — their lack of faith in permanent biblical standards and the empowering of the Holy Spirit[133] — inevitably produces cultural impotence. This is the legacy of gnosticism, and it is still influential in modern Christianity.[134]

Talmud or New Testament?

The conflict between Bible-believing Christians and Orthodox Jews today has not changed in principle since A.D. 30. It is a conflict over the proper interpretation of the Old Testament. Jesus said to the Jewish leaders: "Do not think that I will accuse you to the Father: there is one that accuseth you, even Moses, in whom ye trust. For had ye believed Moses, ye would have believed me: for he wrote of me. But if ye believe not his writings, how shall ye believe my words?" (John 5:45-47). Because contemporary Christians cannot seem to make up their minds about contemporary Jews — whether they are demonic international conspirators or economic and academic supermen who somehow have the favor of God — they have been ineffective witnesses to Christ when in the presence of Jews. Once Christians recognize what Judaism offers to its adherents — the Talmud, or the mystical-magical Kabbalah,[135] or the steady erosion of modern secularization — they will better understand the words of Robert L. Reymond: "The Christian should love the Jew, certainly. But the sooner the Christian realizes that the Jew is as hopelessly lost and as hopelessly blind, if not more so (Rom. 11:6-11), than the Gen-

---

133. Greg L. Bahnsen, *By This Standard: The Authority of God's Law Today* (Tyler, Texas: Institute for Christian Economics, 1985), pp. 185-86.

134. Philip J. Lee, *Against the Protestant Gnostics* (New York: Oxford University Press, 1987), Pt. III.

135. Scholem, *On the Kabbalah and Its Symbolism*; Jacob Z. Lauterbach, "The Belief in the Power of the Word," *Hebrew Union College Annual*, XIV (1949). See also Joshua Trachtenberg, *Jewish Magic and Superstition* (New York: Atheneum, [1939] 1970).

tile, and that to win the Jew to Christ he must crush any and every hope for salvation which is related in any way to the fact that he is a Jew and a 'son of Torah,' the sooner the Christian will honor his Lord by his witness to the Jew and the more effective will his witness become."[136] There is no valid message of salvation in the Talmud. This was Peter's message to Israel:

Be it known unto you all, and to all the people of Israel, that by the name of Jesus Christ of Nazareth, whom ye crucified, whom God raised from the dead, even by him doth this man stand here before you whole. This is the stone which was set at nought of you builders, which is become the head of the corner. Neither is there salvation in any other: for there is none other name under heaven given among men, whereby we must be saved (Acts 4:10-13).

Orthodox Judaism is at war with the Old Testament. This is the primary thesis of this essay. But, unlike Reform Judaism, which is infected with the same biblical higher criticism that has undermined mainstream Christianity, Orthodox Judaism claims to accept the Old Testament as the inspired Word of God. How, then, can anyone rightfully say that Orthodox Judaism is at war with the Old Testament? Only by accepting Jesus' words literally:

I am come in my Father's name, and ye receive me not: if another shall come in his own name, him ye will receive. How can ye believe, which receive honour one of another, and seek not the honour that cometh from God only? Do not think that I will accuse you to the Father: there is one that accuseth you, even Moses, in whom ye trust. For had ye believed Moses, ye would have believed me: for he wrote of me. But if ye believe not his writings, how shall ye believe my words? (John 5:43-47).

To demonstrate the accuracy of Jesus' words, I here present a summary of the exegetical methodology of the judicial writings of the most famous and most respected master of the Talmud in the history of Judaism: Moses Maimonides.

Rabbi Moshe ben Maimon, The Rambam

Few gentile scholars have ever heard of the *Mishneh Torah*, but all medieval historians and specialists in the history of Western philosophy know of Maimonides. Moshe, the son of Maimon, better known as Maimonides (1134-1204), is by far the most famous Jew in medieval

---

136. Robert L. Reymond, Editor's Preface, to Van Til, *Christ and the Jews*, p. v.

history. He was the Rambam (Rabbi Moshe ben Maimon: RMBM). He lived in Spain and later in Cairo, where he served as the Sultan's physician. He became world-famous as a physician. Copies of at least ten of his medical treatises still survive.[137] He is best known for his theological-philosophical treatise, *The Guide of the Perplexed* (a better translation than "guide *to* the perplexed"), completed in 1190. His native tongue was Arabic. He was familiar with the Arabic translations of Aristotle, and he became a major conduit of the flow of Aristotelian philosophy into the Jewish community in Europe, as well as into the Christian community.

What very few non-Jewish scholars are aware of is that he also became the chief classifier of an immense body of Jewish law, which included the Talmud ("study" or "learning"). He wrote a 14-volume study that systematically arranged the teachings of the Jewish rabbis on every aspect of Talmudic law. It was called the *Mishneh Torah* (1180), also known as Maimonides' *Code*.[138] (It is less well known as "The Strong Hand.")[139] It has for centuries remained the definitive summary of the commands of Talmudic law.

The words *mishneh Torah* mean "repetition of the Torah" or law. It is the phrase by which Jews have traditionally identified the Book of Deuteronomy. Deuteronomy restated the Mosaic law for the sake of the children of the generation that had died in the wilderness. Their days of wandering were about to end; they would now face the problems of running God's earthly commonwealth. Lerner writes: "Maimonides' *Code* has a similar character; in it he restates the laws of the Torah and of the Talmud without limiting himself to those laws that are applicable to life in the Diaspora. Maimonides' *Mishneh Torah*, like Moses', is concerned with the practical needs of an actual state, that is, the Jewish state prior to the Diaspora and after the coming of the Messiah."[140] The influence of this work on medieval and subsequent Judaism was very great, beginning almost from the day he wrote it.

Jewish legal scholar George Horowitz writes: "The restatement of Maimonides, the *Mishneh Torah* is still the most orderly and logical classification of the Halakah [Jewish law—G.N.] in existence."[141]

---

137. Paul Johnson, *A History of the Jews* (New York: Harper & Row, 1987), p. 186.

138. Paul Johnson mentions it, but does not cite it directly.

139. Schachter, Talmudical Introductions, in Chajes, *Student's Guide Through the Talmud*, p. 3n.

140. Ralph Lerner, "Moses Maimonides," in Leo Strauss and Joseph Cropsey (eds.), *History of Political Philosophy* (Chicago: Rand McNally, 1963), p. 193.

141. Horowitz, *Spirit of Jewish Law*, p. 16.

He is not alone in his assessment of Maimonides' *Code*. Maimonides specialist Isadore Twersky says that "The *Mishneh Torah*, which was to change the entire landscape of Rabbinic literature, also pushed back the frontiers of Maimonides' sphere of influence and made his fame global as well as imperishable. It transformed him, in the course of a few decades, from the 'light of the East' to 'the light of the [entire] exile.' He almost literally became a major Jewish luminary. . . . In one broad generalization, we may say that the *Mishneh Torah* became a prism through which reflection and analysis of virtually all subsequent Talmud study had to pass. There is hardly a book in the broad field of Rabbinic literature that does not relate in some way to the *Mishneh Torah*."[142] Furthermore, "The *Mishneh Torah* is reputedly second only to the Bible in the number of commentaries and studies it has elicited."[143]

An incomplete list of 220 major commentaries on the *Mishneh Torah* was made in 1893.[144] Michael Guttman has written: "The *Mishneh Torah* became the center of the whole halachic literature. It acquired the place of a new code of general esteem and acknowledgment, like the Mishna a thousand years before, and the greatest halakhic scholars entered into competition with each other in composing commentaries to Maimonides and settling the difficulties, which the lack of indicating sources left to them."[145] His fame throughout Europe spread even faster than copies of the *Code*.[146]

Why should the *Code* have had such an impact? For one thing, because copies of any book as massive as the Talmud were scarce in the era before modern printing. Maimonides' 14 relatively compact volumes were minuscule when compared to the gigantic Talmud. Furthermore, the *Code* is structured by judicial topics; the Talmud's structure is highly complex and intimidating.

---

142. Isadore Twersky, *Introduction to the Code of Maimonides (Mishneh Torah)* (New Haven, Connecticut: Yale University Press, 1980), pp. 19-20; cf. 516-18.

143. *Ibid.*, p. 526. Nevertheless, for generations Talmudists refused to mention the *Mishneh Torah* by name: p. 527. This may have been because it enabled laymen to check the decisions of the judges: Johnson, *History*, p. 191.

144. Alexander Marx, *Studies in Jewish History and Booklore* (New York, 1969), pp. 38-41; cited by Johnson, *History*, p. 191.

145. Michael Guttman, "The Decisions of Maimonides in His Commentary on the Mishna," *Hebrew Union College Annual*, II (1925), p. 229.

146. Alexander Marx, "The Correspondence Between the Rabbis of Southern France and Maimonides About Astrology," *ibid.*, III (1926), pp. 325-26.

Maimonides' Use of the Old Testament

I have interacted repeatedly with Maimonides' *Code* in the foot-notes of the text of *Tools of Dominion*. Sometimes he got things correctly, and sometimes he did not. It is my task here to deal with the ways that he got things wrong rather than right, as well as the reasons why. I suppose I would have a much more difficult task in writing a chapter analyzing S. R. Hirsch's commentary on Exodus. I find so often that he got things right. [147] How was this possible, when he, like most Orthodox Jews of his day and earlier, must have relied heavily on Maimonides — not Maimonides the Aristotelian philosopher, who was regarded with suspicion by Jewish scholars from the beginning, but Maimonides the Talmudist?

So, I find that I am critical of many of Maimonides' economic and judicial opinions, and through him, of the Talmud. But how does a gentile scholar say this politely yet effectively, and also avoid the counter-charge of anti-Semitism? I suppose he does this in the same way that a Jewish scholar would discuss Martin Luther's notoriously anti-Semitic book on the Jews, [148] yet remain free of "anti-gentilism." All I can say is this: what we have here is more than a

---

147. Again and again as I wrote this commentary, I found myself turning to Hirsch and citing him. James Jordan has been working on his study of the dietary laws during the period that I have been working on the case laws. He also has noticed this phenomenon: Hirsch frequently makes sense, while the observations in Maimonides' *Code* often seem archaic, superstitious, and irrational. Hirsch sticks to the biblical text far more closely than Maimonides does. Yet he also cites the Talmud, and the conclusions he draws from these citations seem sensible, whereas Maimonides, if he is in fact being faithful to the Talmud (and I find that he seems to be faithful in the cases that I have studied), frequently makes the Talmud seem unreliable. I leave it to Orthodox Jewish scholars to sort out the discrepancies between these two giants of Jewish thought. I have run out of time to pursue the matter.

148. *On the Jews and Their Lies* (1543), published over the years in cheap, poorly printed paperback editions for the anti-Semitic masses, as well as in an expensive hardback collectors' edition by Revisionist Press, 1982. It appears as volume 47 of *Luther's Works* (Philadelphia: Fortress, 1971), pp. 137-306. Luther was not alone in his hostility to Judaism. Two years prior to the publication of his book, his arch-rival, Catholic theologian John Eck, published *Refutation of a Jew-Book*, and two years before this, Calvinist Martin Bucer published *On the Jews*. Luther, however, was typically extreme. He recommended seven steps to be taken by the civil government: 1) burn down every synagogue until not a cinder remains; 2) raze the homes of all Jews; 3) confiscate and destroy their books and the Talmud; 4) forbid rabbis to teach on the threat of execution; 5) revoke all safe-conduct passes on the highways; 6) forbid them to loan money at interest; and 7) require them to work at manual labor. *Luther's Works*, vol. 47, pp. 268-72. For a study of European life for Jews in the sixteenth century, see Selma Stern, *Josel of Rosheim* (Philadelphia: Jewish Publication Society, 1965).

failure to communicate. It is more than a difference over semantics or semitics. *It is a fundamental debate over biblical hermeneutics*, and both Orthodox Judaism and orthodox Christianity teach that this ultimate division cannot be overcome in principle. It divides Christians from Jews, and has from the first century, whether A.D. or C.E. Cohen is correct: "I suggest in part, therefore, that the Judeo-Christian tradition is a construct, an artificial gloss of reason over the swarm of fedeist passion. . . . What is omitted is the sinew and bone of actuality, for where Jews and Christians divide, divide irreparably, divide finally . . . is that for Jews the Messiah is to come and for Christians he has already come. That is irreparable."[149]

From the day that the English-language translation of Maimonides' *Code* was completed, the terms of this division came to the surface of the academic waters, and have drifted along ever since. That this debate has not previously broken out stems mainly from the fact that the two sides that presumably care one way or the other about the underlying religious issues and therefore the hermeneutical questions — Orthodox Jews and orthodox Christians — have not debated publicly, primarily because the Christians have never heard of the *Mishneh Torah*. Very few have read any of the Talmud, either. Maimonides' *Code* is an unknown book that comments on a closed book.

Talmud vs. Torah

Maimonides' *Code* does represent both the letter and spirit of the Talmud. This is not simply my opinion. Orthodox Jews have long believed that the *Code* is faithful to the Talmud. The translator of his introduction to the Talmud, which he wrote at the age of 23, is adamant on this point: "Although he utilized the fruits of his time's researches, *every statement of Maimonides is securely grounded and borne from the Torah literature*. It is extremely important to bear this in mind. The Torah is the means by which the Rambam saw and explained everything."[150]

Horowitz begins his detailed, readable, and nearly indispensable study of Jewish law with this assertion: "Though there are in the laws of Moses not a few specific and literal commands which give emphatic expression to the spirit of that legislation, it is the gradual changes against the letter of Scripture which came about in the

---

149. Cohen, *Myth of the Judeo-Christian Tradition*, p. xii.

150. Zvi L. Lampel, *Maimonides' Introduction to the Talmud* (New York: Judaica Press, 1975), p. 9.

course of centuries, that offer the most striking manifestation of the true, the humane spirit of Jewish law."[151] But is this really true? Was the "humaneness" of the Jewish legal order truly increased when the rabbis departed from the letter of Old Testament law? I argue that the self-conscious departure on the part of both Christians and Jews from the revealed law of God has decreased the West's humaneness.

The question I am raising in this essay is this: Does the *Code* represent the spirit of the Old Testament? As we shall see, it clearly does not represent the letter of the Old Testament. But were Maimonides and the Talmudic scholars whose conclusions he summarized and classified able to retain and make practical the spirit of the Mosaic law? My answer is simple: *no.* But I must prove my case. To provide evidence of my assertion regarding Jewish law, I have decided to provide a kind of lawyer's brief against Moses Maimonides — specifically, against his views of restitution to gentile victims by Jewish criminals.

The Double Standard

Maimonides insisted that biblical law's general requirement that the thief make two-fold restitution to his victim (Ex. 22:7) applies only in the case of Jews who steal from Jews. It does not apply if a Jew steals from a heathen (gentile). Incredibly, it also does not apply in the case of sacrilege: stealing an animal from a Jewish household if the animal has been set aside for sacrifice to God; the thief is exempted from making two-fold, four-fold, or five-fold restitution, "For Scripture says, *And it be stolen from the house of the man* (Ex. 22:6), but not from the house of the sanctuary."[152] This means that it is less of a crime to steal from God than to steal from man — a strange system of ethics on which to build an explicitly theocentric civilization.

A convicted Jew need not pay double restitution to a gentile, either: "If one steals from a heathen, or if one steals sacred property, he need pay only its capital value, for Scripture says, *Shall pay double to his neighbor* (Ex. 22:8) — *to his neighbor*, but not to the sanctuary; *to his neighbor*, but not to a heathen."[153]

---

151. Horowitz, *Spirit of Jewish Law*, pp. 1-2. This reflects a view quite similar to that expressed by Lauterbach in his criticism of Sadduceeism because of its having become "blind slaves of the law without regard for its spirit. It divorced the law from life, in that it made the two absolutely independent of each other." *Jewish Essays*, p. 38.

152. Moses Maimonides, *The Book of Torts*, Book 11 of *The Code of Maimonides*, 14 vols. (New Haven, Connecticut: Yale University Press, 1954), "Laws Concerning Theft," Chapter Two, Section One, p. 64.

153. *Idem.*

This is an ethical and judicial system based on a double standard. The Talmud is clear on this point: "Where a suit arises between an Israelite and a heathen, if you can justify the former according to the laws of Israel, justify him and say: 'This is *our* law'; so also if you can justify him by the laws of the heathens justify him and say [to the other party:] 'This is *your* law'; but if this can not be done, we use subterfuges to circumvent him."[154] In short, the Jewish lawyer must do whatever he can to keep his guilty Jewish client from being convicted. (In this sense, Jewish jurisprudence serves as the model for all modern jurisprudence: the lawyer's primary task is supposedly to use the law in order to see his client go free, guilty or not.)

A dual standard of justice applies to lost property:

R. Bibi b. Giddal said that R. Simeon the Pious stated: The robbery of a heathen is prohibited, though an article lost by him is permissible. . . . His lost article is permissible, for R. Hama b. Guria said that Rab stated: Whence can we learn that the lost article of a heathen is permissible? Because it says: *And with all lost thing of thy brother's:* it is to your brother that you make restoration, but you need not make restoration to a heathen.[155]

Come and hear: If one finds therein [Soncino Press editor's footnote: "In a city inhabited by Jews and heathens"] a lost object, then if the majority are Israelites it has to be announced, but if the majority are heathens it has not to be announced.[156]

WHERE AN OX BELONGING TO AN ISRAELITE HAS GORED AN OX BELONGING TO A CANAANITE, THERE IS NO LIABILITY. WHEREAS WHERE AN OX BELONGING TO A CANAANITE GORES AN OX BELONGING TO AN ISRAELITE . . . THE COMPENSATION IS TO BE MADE IN FULL."[157]

In response to such judicial standards, gentiles in the late medieval period over-reacted by forcing Jews into urban ghettos that were surrounded by high walls and locked at night. They did not want to live as geographical neighbors to people who held such a double standard.[158]

---

154. *Baba Kamma* 113a.

155. *Baba Kamma* 113b.

156. *Baba Mezia* 24a.

157. *Baba Kamma* 37b. Cf. 38a. Reproductions of these passages appear in *Christian News* (Aug. 1, 1988).

158. The social and political results of this policy were evil: forced urbanization, the creation of a permanently alienated political element within the towns, and the eventual subsidizing of nineteenth-century Jewish radicalism, which was far more common in urban settings than in rural ones.

They chose instead to allow Jews to be governed by their own courts in most matters that involved disputes between Jews. Of course, when it came to Christian rulers (and presumably also private citizens) who defaulted on loans, the Jews may also have occasionally appreciated the walls that protected them from excessive contact with gentiles.[159] (It is also interesting that in the twelfth century, the walled-in Jewish community of Constantinople also had its own wall that separated the 2,000 Talmudic Jews from the 500 anti-Talmudic, "Torah-only" Karaites.)[160]

Forced social division is inevitably the curse of a double legal standard in a single society. Neither group trusts the other; both groups seek to exploit the other, or at least tolerate those within their midst who do. This is why the Bible says, "One law shall be to him that is homeborn, and unto the stranger that sojourneth among you" (Ex. 12:49). This case law appears in the section on the laws regarding strangers and the Passover; it was given to Israel immediately after the exodus itself. This indicates how emphatically God demands that men observe it: even their oppressors, the Egyptians, are entitled to equal treatment before the law.

"For the Sake of the Peace"

The rabbis were not fools, of course. They modified this judicial double standard for practical purposes, namely, "for the sake of the peace." Horowitz explains: "Halakot [law] and customs which discriminated against Gentiles and which might, therefore, appear unjust in the eyes of the world, were not to be enforced or practiced though perhaps 'legally' valid, because it might reflect unfavorably on the Jewish people, its morals and its religion. 'For the Sake of Peace' was in effect an equitable principle which modified the strict law, with regard to treatment of Gentiles."[161] This was a belated recognition of the need for a unified legal standard in civil justice and economic dealings. He offers several examples, including this one: "The Talmud seemed definitely to countenance the over-reaching of

---

159. In 1306, Philip IV of France evicted the Jews, repudiated his debts to them, and confiscated their property. England drove them out in 1290, after having taxed them heavily and soaked up their capital with forced loans that were then repudiated. In 1370, they were driven from the low countries. Herbert Heaton, *Economic History of Europe* (New York: Harper & Row, 1948), p. 184.

160. This was recorded by Benjamin of Tudela in his *Book of Travels* (1168); cited in Johnson, *History of the Jews*, p. 169.

161. Horowitz, *Spirit of Jewish Law*, p. 100.

heathens by Jews in business transactions (*Bava Kamma* 113b). But later authorities held otherwise. 'It is forbidden,' says Maimonides, 'to defraud or deceive any person in business—Jew and non-Jew are to be treated alike. . . . It is wrong to deceive any person in words even without causing him any pecuniary loss (*M. T. Sale*, XVIII, i).[162] Centuries later with respect to an error of a Gentile in overpaying eighteen ducats, R. Benjamin b. Mattathiah declared, 'For the sake of sanctifying the Holy Name a Jew should correct and make good the mistake of the Gentile.' "[163]

Maimonides put it this way: "The lost property of a heathen may be kept, for Scripture says, *Lost thing of thy brother's* (Deut. 22:3). Furthermore, if one returns it, he commits a transgression, for he is supporting the wicked of the world. But if one returns it in order to sanctify God's name, thereby causing persons to praise the Israelites and realize that they are honest, he is deemed praiseworthy."[164] It is revealing that he cited Deuteronomy 22:3, which refers to the lost property of one's brother, but he made no mention of Exodus 23:4-5, which explicitly deals with the lost property of enemies: "If thou meet thine enemy's ox or his ass going astray, thou shalt surely bring it back to him again. If thou see the ass of him that hateth thee lying under his burden, and wouldest forbear to help him, thou shalt surely help with him."

Obviously, when the legal system allows a Jew to discriminate ethically and judicially in terms of religion, and when it also repeatedly requires Jews to ignore this principle of judicial dualism, it becomes almost impossible for the individual Jew to know what to do in specific cases. He is to be guided by his conscience, of course, but a conscience informed by which principle, the principle of discrimination or the principle of preserving the peace?

This is the fundamental problem for all casuists: the application of fixed laws to specific circumstances. Horowitz is aware of the problem, at least with respect to biblical law, a problem for which the rabbis have offered no solution: "Thus, paradoxical as it may seem the Rabbis believed that it was their right and duty to make changes in the Biblical law if imperatively required, while maintaining,

---

162. See Maimonides, *The Book of Acquisition*, Book 12 of *The Code of Maimonides*, 14 vols. (New Haven, Connecticut: Yale University Press, 1951), "Laws Concerning Sales," pp. 63-64.

163. *Ibid.*, p. 101.

164. Maimonides, *Torts*, "Laws Concerning Robbery and Lost Property," Chapter Eleven, Section Three, p. 128.

nevertheless, that the commands of the Torah were unchangeable and might not be added to or diminished."[165] This is also true with respect to Talmudic law. The key question is this: Which principle of application is dominant in any given case, preserving the peace or allowing a Jewish thief to escape the restitution penalty specified by the Torah? The individual Jew is left without clear ethical guidelines. The rabbis will decide after the fact whether an act is immoral, illegal, or just good business, but that knowledge is of little help to the Jewish decision-maker at the "moment of truth." The predictability of the law and its sanctions—indispensable to social order and also to freedom[166]—is thereby drastically reduced.

Nowhere is the double standard more visible than in Maimonides' handling of the crime of murder. He stated categorically in Section One of Chapter One of "Laws Concerning Murder and the Preservation of Life" that "If one slays a human being, he transgresses a negative commandment, for Scripture says, *Thou shalt not murder* (Exod. 20:13). If one murders wilfully in the presence of witnesses, he is put to death by the sword, for when Scripture says, *He shall surely be punished* (Exod. 21:20), we have learned from tradition that this means death by the sword."[167] Well and good. But then comes the double standard: "If an Israelite kills a resident alien, he does not suffer capital punishment at the hands of the court, because Scripture says, *And if a man come presumptuously upon his neighbor* (Exod. 21:12). Needless to say, one is not put to death if he kills a heathen."[168] I do not think any additional comment is needed at this point.

Escaping Restitution

Horowitz asserts that the spirit of Jewish law has been humane because the rabbis have departed from the letter of Mosaic law. (Implicitly or explicitly, this is the same defense offered by Christian theologians when they also depart from the letter of the Mosaic law without specific New Testament authorizations.) One problem with Horowitz's argument is that Maimonides' interpretations are frequently opposed to the spirit of biblical justice precisely because he ignored the letter of biblical law.

---

165. Horowitz, *Spirit of Jewish Law*, p. 94.
166. F. A. Hayek, *The Constitution of Liberty* (University of Chicago Press, 1960).
167. Maimonides, *Torts*, "Laws Concerning Murder and the Preservation of Life," Chapter One, Section One, p. 195.
168. *Ibid.*, Chapter Two, Section Eleven, p. 201.

For example, Maimonides discussed the case of a thief who stole an animal or a vessel, and who then immediately slaughtered the animal or deliberately broke the vessel—perhaps to conceal the evidence of the crime?—and later is convicted of the theft. What if, in the meantime, the market value of the stolen object has doubled? Does the thief pay double restitution based on the value of the item at the time of the theft or based on its market value at the time of the trial? If he has profited from the transaction, Maimonides said, he must pay restitution based on the stolen object's value at the time of the trial. But what if the thief accidentally lost the animal or accidentally broke the vessel? Maimonides stated, though without presenting any justifying argument, that the negligent thief owes restitution only on the value of the object at the time of the theft.[169]

Undermining Justice

Such a legal principle would undermine biblical civil justice. First, how is the court to determine whether the loss was accidental? The thief obviously has a financial incentive to lie, since the burden of his repayment will be lighter. Second, what of the victim's added economic loss? Who protects the victim's interests? Why should his loss as a result of the time delay between the theft and the trial not be fully compensated by the thief, irrespective of the latter's quality of stewardship over the stolen goods? What Maimonides should have concluded was that the thief must provide multiple restitution to a victim based on the *replacement cost at the time of his conviction* for the crime. If the animal were still alive, he would be required to return that animal, and the animal would obviously be worth today's market value. Thus, the replacement value for a slaughtered animal is also to be worth today's market value, and so is the equivalent proportional restitution payment. This is obvious, this is fair, and Maimonides ignored it. He departed from both the letter of biblical law and its spirit.

He concluded all this by stating that two-fold restitution is not required from any thief who is convicted of stealing bonds, land, or slaves, "because Scripture has imposed the liability for double payment only on movable things that have an intrinsic value, for it says, *On an ox or an ass or a sheep or a garment* (Ex. 22:8)." But aren't slaves mov-

---

169. ". . . if, however, the animal dies or the vessel is lost, he need pay only double its value at the time of the theft." *Ibid.*, "Laws Concerning Theft," Chapter One, Section Fourteen, p. 63.

able? Physically, yes, but not legally, he said. "Now slaves are legally regarded the same as land, for Scripture says of them, *And you shall bequeath them to your sons* (Lev. 25:46). . . . ." But aren't bonds as valuable as movable stolen goods? No; "bonds have no intrinsic value."[170]

Committing Crimes Rationally

Furthermore, if a person is subject to flogging for a crime involving the theft of money, Maimonides insisted that he need not make any monetary penalty payment whatsoever to the victim, "because one is not subjected to both flogging and paying."[171] Why would a thief be subject to flogging in the first place? Possibly because he had stolen for a second or third time. We would imagine that the victim would receive compensation in the form of a monetary penalty payment, and the civil authorities would also flog the thief as a warning. Not in Maimonides' system. But he did make this clarification: the criminal must become subject to the monetary penalty and the flogging at the same time; if he commits two separate offenses, he can be required to suffer both penalties.[172]

What, then, is the economically rational conclusion for thieves? *Steal money, not goods*, and be sure you commit a trespass at the same time that will involve flogging if you are convicted.[173] Habitual thieves should steal only money, if the automatic added penalty is a flogging.

Along this same line is his insistence that thefts committed on the Sabbath are exempt from the requirement of restitution, since work-

---

170. *Ibid.*, Chapter Two, Section Two, p. 64. Yet he admits elsewhere that "if one burns a creditor's bonds, he must pay the full debt recorded in the bond — for although the bond is not intrinsically money, he has caused the loss of money. . . ." *Ibid.*, "Laws Concerning Wounding and Damage," Chapter Seven, Section Nine, p. 185.

171. *Ibid.*, "Laws Concerning Theft," Chapter Three, Section One, p. 67. He made this one exception: injuring someone, who then becomes eligible for compensation: *ibid.*, "Laws Concerning Wounding and Damaging," Chapter Four, Section Nine, p. 173.

172. In the case of robbery — stealing openly by threatening the victim — he said that the restitution payment is mandatory, so there can be no flogging, because "any prohibition the transgression of which may be repaired by restitution does not entail flogging." *Ibid.*, "Laws Concerning Robbery and Lost Property," Chapter One, Section One, p. 90. If we are to accept this explanation at face value, then why did he ever bring up the parallel issue of crimes that require monetary penalties in relation to flogging? Shouldn't the requirement of restitution always eliminate the possibility of flogging? There is an inconsistency here.

173. Maimonides did not say what kind of crime would bring a person under both penalties simultaneously. This makes it difficult to know what he had in mind.

ing on the Sabbath was a capital offense in the Old Testament, and
he insisted that "if one commits a transgression entailing capital punishment and also a monetary penalty, he need not pay even if he has
acted through error."[174] But the two crimes must occur at the same
time.[175] "If one steals an animal and butchers it on the Sabbath or
kills it as a heathen sacrifice, even through error, he need not pay
fourfold or fivefold, as we have explained."[176] "If one borrows a cow
and then butchers it on the Sabbath in an act of theft, he is exempt
even from paying double, because the breach of the Sabbath and the
theft are done at the same time, and where there is no payment for
theft, there can be no penalty for butchering or selling."[177] Who then
protects the innocent victim from doubly perverse thieves, who are
Sabbath-breakers, too? The more corrupt the criminal, the more judicially vulnerable becomes the innocent victim in Maimonides' system.

We see this especially in his treatment of the thief who is sold into
slavery to compensate his victim. Biblical law requires that a thief be
sold into slavery if he does not have enough money or assets to compensate his victim: ". . . if he have nothing, then he shall be sold for
his theft" (Ex. 22:3b). Scripture protects the victim, not the thief.
Maimonides said that if the thief steals a second time, and from a different victim, he may be sold into slavery again, as many times as he
steals from a new victim, even a hundred times. "But if he steals a second time from the first person, he may not be sold again, rather whatever he has stolen is counted as a debt against him."[178] A truly vicious
criminal who repeatedly steals from a truly victimized citizen does not
suffer the required biblical penalty, said Maimonides. Once again,
the interests of the victim are sacrificed for the benefit of the criminal.

He wrote that a thief who improves a stolen good, such as fattening a stolen animal, needs to make double restitution only of the
value of the item at the time of the theft. He gets to keep any of the
improvements. If the owner had abandoned hope of ever having his
goods returned to him, the thief even gets to keep any resulting productivity, such as the offspring of a stolen female animal. Thus, the
longer the anguish of the innocent, and the greater his loss of hope,
the more likely the thief will profit from his crime.[179]

---

174. *Ibid.*, "Laws Concerning Theft," Chapter Three, Section One, p. 67.
175. *Ibid.*, Chapter Three, Section One, p. 68.
176. *Ibid.*, Chapter Three, Section Two, p. 68.
177. *Ibid.*, Chapter Three, Section Four, pp. 68-69.
178. *Ibid.*, Chapter Three, Section Fifteen, p. 71.
179. *Ibid.*, Chapter One, Sections Eleven and Twelve, pp. 61-62.

There should be no double restitution penalty imposed on those who use false weights and measures, Maimonides insisted. It is unquestionably theft, as he recognized. Why no penalty payment? He never said. "Although one who measures or weighs falsely steals thereby, he need not pay double but need only pay for the deficiency in measure or weight. Nor is flogging inflicted for breach of this prohibition, since there is a liability to pay."[180] Here is another loophole for thieves: *judicially risk-free theft.* If a man steals and is not caught, he keeps what he has stolen; if he gets caught, he is required to give back only what he stole. Worse: it is risk-free for a form of theft which is extremely difficult for the victims to detect, false weights and measures. In short, the more self-conscious the criminal, and the more vulnerable his intended victims, the less the penalty.

The crime of robbery — theft by force[181] — is clearly worse than theft by stealth. The robber steals the object, and he also inflicts fear. True to form, Maimonides exempted the robber from the requirement of making double restitution, which is required from the thief: "If one commits robbery, he must return the very object he robbed, for Scripture says, *He shall restore that which he took by robbery* (Lev. 5:23). If, however, the object is lost or altered, he must pay its value. But he is liable for the repayment of its capital value only, whether he confesses of his own accord or whether witnesses testify that he took it by robbery."[182] Furthermore, "If the owner has abandoned hope of recovery but the property is unchanged, the robber acquires title to any improvement that takes place after hope is abandoned, and he need pay only its value as of the time of the robbery. This rule is on the authority of the Scribes, enacted for the benefit of penitents."[183] If the owner has given up hope of ever recovering it, he forfeits both the earnings the property might have produced for him and any improvements made by the robber.[184] In short, *the worse the crime, the less the penalty; the greater the suffering by the victim, the less the compensation due to him.*

---

180. *Ibid.*, Chapter Seven, Section Two, p. 80.

181. "Who is deemed a robber? One who takes another's property by force." *Ibid.*, Chapter One, Section Three, p. 90.

182. *Ibid.*, Chapter One, Section Five, p. 91.

183. *Ibid.*, Chapter Two, Section Two, p. 94.

184. Maimonides cites the anonymous sages to prove that the victim is entitled to the increased market value of the stolen object, if this increase has not come as a result of improvements made by the robber: *ibid.*, Chapter Two, Section Sixteen, p. 97.

Kidnapping

If any crime sends fear into the hearts of parents, it is this one. God's law makes the penalty clear: "And he that stealeth a man, and selleth him, or if he be found in his hand, he shall surely be put to death" (Ex. 21:16). But the rabbis could not tolerate this law, so they created a system of judicial requirements that made it virtually impossible to convict anyone. Horowitz writes: "The crime consisted of four elements: carrying off, detention, enslavement, and selling, which must occur in the order named."[185] The prisoner must be taken completely from his home. He must be detained on the offender's premises. "If the victim is detained anywhere else, even though he be locked up and completely under the abductor's control, the crime is not made out."[186] He must be made a slave by means of "any service or use however slight which the victim was compelled to render or submit to, e.g. to be leaned on or to be used as a screen against the draft even while he was asleep or unconscious."[187] He must then be sold as a slave, and to strangers rather than kinsmen. He cites *Sanhedrin* 85b. On this basis, none of the sons of Jacob could have been convicted of kidnapping Joseph, for they did not take Joseph from his home, nor did they use him as a slave.

The term "Talmudic reasoning" is attached to logic like that employed by Maimonides — the splitting of hairs in order to make impossible any judicial sanctions against an offender. Maimonides wrote: "If one abducts another and uses him and sells him, but the kidnapped person is still on his own premises and has not been taken onto the premises of the kidnapper, the kidnapper is exempt. If one abducts another and takes him onto his premises and uses him but does not sell him, or sells him before using him, or uses him and sells him to one of the kidnapped person's relatives — for example, if he sells him to his father or his brother — the kidnapper is exempt, for Scripture says, *Stealing any of his brethren . . . and sell him*, implying that he must separate him from his brethren and kinsfolk by the sale. Similarly, if one abducts a person who is asleep, uses him asleep, and sells him while he is still asleep, the kidnapper is exempt."[188]

---

185. Horowitz, *Spirit of Jewish Law*, p. 196.
186. *Ibid.*, p. 197.
187. *Idem.*
188. Maimonides, *Torts*, "Laws Concerning Theft," Chapter Nine, Section Three, p. 86.

Horowitz's concluding remarks are appropriate: "That the Rabbis considered the death penalty too severe for this wrong to society and the individual, seems quite plain from the foregoing rules. But they were bound by the express command of Scripture; hence they devised such requirements as made conviction virtually impossible. There is no record, moreover, that a regular court ever convicted a person of Manstealing."[189] Lest this claim be thought unrepresentative because of a presumed lack of data, bear in mind that the Jewish rabbis from all over the world saved records of their court decisions since the tenth century. Something in the range of 3,000 volumes of these records, with at least 300,000 judgments, have been compiled.[190] While these records until recently were unindexed (they are now being put on computer in Israel),[191] and therefore were usable only by highly trained specialists who possessed astounding memories, the basic conclusions are known. Thus, Horowitz's statement is probably representative of the history of Jewish decisions regarding kidnapping: not one conviction.

Michael Guttman made a similar assessment: "The general principle upon which the Mishnah has to be valued juridically is the endeavor to restrict death punishment to a minimum. The Talmud could not flatly annul the death penalty since a Pentateuchal law could not be abrogated; therefore the requirements pertaining to the giving of evidence and the proof of premeditation were made so severe that a death verdict was almost impossible."[192]

One reason for this reticence to impose the penalties established in the Old Testament was that the Jews believed that every Jewish court had to have at least one judge who had been appointed by the laying on of hands (*semikah*) by a preceding judge. Like the rabbi who supposedly could trace his teachers back to Moses, so was the judge. But there was a problem. This laying on of hands could take place only in the Holy Land. "A court not thus qualified," writes Horowitz, "had no jurisdiction to impose the punishments prescribed in the Torah."[193]

After the Bar Kochba revolt ended in 135, the Romans scattered the Jews throughout the Empire; the Diaspora began in earnest.

---

189. Horowitz, *Spirit*, pp. 197-98.

190. Elon, Introduction, in Elon (ed.), *Principles of Jewish Law*, col. 13.

191. "Computer Digests the Talmud to Help Rabbis," *New York Times* (Nov. 24, 1984).

192. Michael Guttman, "The Term 'Foreigner' Historically Considered," *Hebrew Union College Annual*, III (1926), p. 17.

193. Horowitz, *Spirit of Jewish Law*, p. 93.

This loss of residence was used as an excuse by the rabbis to abandon the required sanctions of the Old Covenant:

The Rabbis were compelled, therefore, in order to preserve the Torah and to maintain law and order, to enlarge the authority of Rabbinical tribunals. This they accomplished by emphasizing the distinction between Biblical penalties and Rabbinical penalties. Rabbinical courts after the second century had no authority to impose Biblical punishments since they lacked *semikah;* but as regards penalties created by Rabbinical legislation, the Rabbis had of necessity, the widest powers of enforcement. They instituted, accordingly, a whole series of sanctions and penalties: excommunication, fines, physical punishment, use of the "secular arm" in imitation of the Church, etc."[194]

Thus ended, formally, the Old Covenant. It had ended judicially in God's eyes in A.D. 70, but now there could be no mistaking what had happened. *Judaism officially became rabbinic rather than Mosaic.* To "preserve the Torah," the rabbis decided to abandon it. That Rabbi Akiba, one of the early compilers of the oral law, had joined with Bar Kochba and died in this revolt,[195] was fitting; the defeat of Bar Kochba was to make possible the triumph of the Talmud over the Old Testament and its required sanctions.

Without sanctions, there can be no covenant.[196] Without God's specified sanctions, there can be no covenant under Him, except as a broken covenant. This is the dilemma of Judaism. The specified sanctions in the Old Testament are no longer applicable, Orthodox Jews believe, because they are outside the land. The specified sanctions of animal sacrifices are also gone. The temple was destroyed in A.D. 70. Yet without these sanctions — against criminals and against animal representatives — there cannot be Old Covenant religion. There can only be a broken covenant.

---

194. *Idem.* So serious was being outside the land that one rabbi cited in the Talmud taught that those Jews buried outside the land will not be resurrected. "R. Eleazar stated: The dead outside the Land will not be resurrected; for it is said in Scripture, *And I will set glory in the land of the living,* [implying] the dead of the land in which I have my *desire* will be resurrected, but the dead [of the land] in which I have no desire will not be resurrected." *Kethuboth* 111a.

195. Supposedly he died on the very day of the birth of Judah HaNasi, the compiler of the Mishnah: J. H. Hertz, Foreword, *Babylonian Talmud, Baba Kamma* (London: Soncino Press, 1935), p. xv.

196. Sutton, *That You May Prosper,* ch. 4.

Mastering a Book

There is no doubt in my mind that opening the Talmud does not really open it. Opening Maimonides' *Code*, however, does begin to get the Talmud's conclusions into the open, though not its various modes of reasoning. When Jewish scholars co-operated a generation ago in making available an English-language translation of the *Code*, they performed a service analogous to the translating of the Talmud. But this service, being intellectual in nature, opened the formerly linguistically locked gates. Inquirers today are free to enter the gateway and snoop around at their leisure. They may not do justice to everything they find. Or, from a different critic's perspective, they may do greater justice than some would prefer. But this is the cost of intellectual progress. Debates arise, and they sometimes continue for centuries without resolution. This is especially true of religious debates.

My part-time odyssey through Jewish literature has led me to things that I appreciate (e.g., the exegetical insights of U. Cassuto and S. R. Hirsch) and things that I do not appreciate (e.g., various teachings regarding Jesus and Christians in general that are found in the Talmud). The economic teachings of the Pentateuch are not all that easy to decipher at first glance. I am sure that Jewish commentators have had the same sorts of problems that I have encountered. They have come to their share of inaccurate conclusions. Who is to challenge these conclusions? Jews only? Then are Christians' conclusions equally immune from challenges by Jews? The answer is clear, I think. Anyway, it should be. We must all deal with the texts. If God spoke them, as I believe He did, then we must all seek to understand precisely what He said. Sometimes even higher critics can pinpoint a truth. Surely if they can, then those of us who take the texts seriously as the word of God can comment on them, as well as on each other's comments.

In the Preface to a book on the ethics of Judaism by Unitarian scholar R. Travers Herford, John J. Tepfer laments: "Over the centuries the many-tomed Talmud, and kindred products of the early Rabbinic mind such as the Midrash, have been subjected to keen scrutiny by numerous learned Christians, mainly, however, with an eye to their value for Christian faith and dogma. The aims of these men being largely apologetic, they drew invidious comparisons between the two faiths, pointing up what they considered to be the absurdities of Rabbinic law and lore, and demonstrating the superior spiritual worth of the authoritative writings of the Church."[197] I clearly would choose to be numbered among these unnamed Christian critics.

The more I read in Maimonides' *Code*, the more I detect a tendency on his part to give the benefit of the doubt to the thief or the cheat, and therefore to sacrifice the interests of the innocent victim. Consider this example: stealing an animal from a fellow Israelite who has set it aside for a priest. "If one steals heave offering from a (lay) Israelite who has designated it (to be given to a priest), he is not obliged to pay double, for the owner's only right in it is the pleasure of giving it to whom he pleases, and such a right has no monetary value."[198] I should think that any self-respecting Jew would hope that Maimonides was not a faithful compiler and summarizer of traditional rabbinic opinion, for the sake of the reputation of the rabbis, but his defenders insist that he was, and there have been few traditional Jewish detractors of Maimonides who have been visible to gentiles, from his day to the present.

By departing from the letter of the Mosaic law, time after time, the rabbis abandoned the spirit of Mosaic law as well. This is why Jesus began so many of His public lessons with the phrase, "You have heard it said . . . but I say unto you." He was waging war with both the spirit and the letter of Talmudic law, for it violates both the spirit and the letter of biblical law.

This is not to say that Talmudic laws are all corrupt or that the *responsa* (post-Talmudic case law decisions) based on the Talmud are all corrupt. The Jews at least attempted very early to create a unique, distinctly Jewish, systematic body of laws. By viewing their world in terms of law, they involved themselves and their culture in the task of casuistry: applying fixed laws to specific circumstances. They began this process nearly a millennium before the Christians did, and the Christian law codes (Theodosian's, Justinian's) after the sixth century fell into disuse in the West as feudal society steadily replaced Christian Roman rule.

The huge body of materials that their judges had to master required feats of memory that are astounding to gentiles of this day. Few of us can imagine the ability of the contemporary Talmud scholar David Weiss, who memorized 200 pages of the Talmud at

---

197. John J. Tepfer, Preface (1962) to R. Travers Herford, *The Ethics of the Talmud*, p. vii.
198. *Torts*, "Laws Concerning Theft," Chapter Two, Section Five, p. 64.

age five, and who earned money by answering such questions as this one: "If I put a pin through word X on page Y, what words would it pierce on the pages beneath?"[199] Yet there have been many Jews with David Weiss' training and abilities over the centuries. The production of such prodigies has been a Jewish academic specialty for at least two millennia.

Because they had to master "a book," and an immense one, Jewish scholars had to discipline themselves intellectually. They set the example for their followers. Because rabbis were frequently involved in business trades, this led to a unique attribute of Jewish culture. Writes Paul Johnson: "Rabbinical Judaism is essentially a method whereby ancient laws are adapted to modern and differing conditions by a process of rationalization. The Jews were the first great rationalizers in world history. This had all kinds of consequences as we shall see, but one of its earliest, in a worldly sense, was to turn Jews into methodical, problem-solving businessmen. A great deal of Jewish legal scholarship in the Dark and Middle Ages was devoted to making business dealings fair, honest and efficient."[200] But what if they had concentrated their efforts exclusively on the task of explaining the Old Testament without any of the excess baggage of fables, occultism, and judicial interpretations specifically designed to allow criminals to escape the full consequences of their actions? Think of the commentaries they would have produced! Christians could have learned from them (and they from Christians) the things I am spending my life trying to research from scratch. The modern world would be a very different and far more productive place. But they could not do it and still remain Jews, for Jesus had made their dilemma plain: "For had ye believed Moses, ye would have believed me: for he wrote of me. But if ye believe not his writings, how shall ye believe my words?" (John 5:46-47). The Mishnah and the Talmud are not what we Christians might have hoped for, and what some Christians have mistakenly believed that they are: commentaries on the Old Testament, but with no mention of the Trinity.

---

199. Israel Shenker, "A Life in the Talmud," *New York Times Magazine* (Sept. 11, 1977).

200. Johnson, *History*, p. 172. Quite properly, he cites Irving Agus' remarkable two-volume study of medieval *responsa* or legal decisions: *Urban Civilization in Pre-Crusade Europe* (New York: Yeshiva University Press, 1968), a book I stumbled across in the library in the late 1960's, and recommended to R. J. Rushdoony. He used it in his *Institutes of Biblical Law* (Nutley, New Jersey: Craig Press, 1973), p. 788.

Conclusion

If Christians and Jews do not agree about the nature of law and the proper approach to and interpretation of biblical legal texts, even when they officially appeal to the same legal sources, then the Judeo-Christian tradition is a myth. There would have to be a common legal tradition, yet such a tradition does not exist. Modern Christians and Jews, because they are modern, do not recognize the hypothetical nature of this academic construct; they no longer take law or religion seriously enough, especially law. The two religions are no longer viewed by their adherents as being inherently judicial in nature. Thus, the two religions have changed radically, yet this change has been disguised by the self-conscious triumphant humanism of modern culture. Both Jews and Christians have enthusiastically sent their children into tax-financed secular schools, and their common enemies have transformed the worldview of their children. The covenantal heirs no longer recognize the extent of the former division between the Christian and Jewish legal traditions because they no longer are aware of the legal revolution that has captured the West over the last century. This revolution, legal scholar Harold Berman argues, now threatens our freedom as no other revolution ever has: the rise of secular, bureaucratic, administrative law.[201]

Berman makes another important observation: law has broken down in the West because religion has been privatized. "The traditional symbols of community in the West, the traditional images and metaphors, have been above all religious and legal. In the twentieth century, however, for the first time, religion has become largely a private affair, while law has become largely a matter of practical expediency. The connection between the religious metaphor and the legal metaphor has been broken. Neither expresses any longer the community's vision of its future and its past; neither commands any longer its passionate loyalty."[202]

If there were a Judeo-Christian tradition, there would be a common legal order. What this essay has shown is that there has not been since A.D. 70 any common legal order uniting Bible-believing Christians and Talmud-believing Jews, which is why there were Jewish ghettos in medieval European cities and separate Jewish

---

201. Harold J. Berman, *Law and Revolution: The Formation of the Western Legal Tradition* (Cambridge, Massachusetts: Harvard University Press, 1983), pp. 33-41.
202. *Ibid.*, p. vi.

rural communities, especially in Russia. Jews insisted on these separate communities because they insisted on being ruled by their own courts, and Christian rulers gave them their request.[203] Jews recognized clearly that if they subordinated themselves under the civil laws of Christian states they would lose their covenantal autonomy. In the nineteenth century, they steadily abandoned this view, but only after the gentiles' civil orders ceased being Christian and became secular humanist.

If there were a Judeo-Christian tradition, there would be evidence of a shared legal tradition, especially in the formative years of the Western legal tradition: the eleventh through thirteenth centuries. Berman summarizes: ". . . neither Jewish thought nor Jewish law seems to have had any substantial influence on the legal systems of the West, at least so far as the surviving literature shows."[204] One reason for this, he speculates (I think correctly), is what he calls the casuistry of the Talmud. I would call it the dialecticism: ". . . the intense casuistry of the Talmud may have helped to make it seem alien to Western legal thought, which stressed the systematization of legal principles."[205]

We needed to examine some of the legal sources of the Jewish legal tradition in order to determine to what extent there has been or can be a Judeo-Christian tradition. Christian scholars have seldom done this in the past, and the result has been a major intellectual gap and therefore major blind spot in the thinking of modern Bible-believing Christians. But blind spots are not perceived by those who suffer from them unless they are shown to the victims. This essay, I trust, has made this blind spot visible.[206]

Because I am a Christian Reconstructionist, I am deeply interested in law, specifically biblical law. I am interested in the effects that biblical law and its specific applications have had on Christian civilization. I believe, as Berman does, that there can be no true so-

---

203. Louis Finkelstein, *Jewish Self-Government in the Middle Ages* (Westport, Connecticut: Greenwood, [1924] 1972).

204. Berman, *Law and Revolution*, p. 589.

205. *Idem.*

206. The physical blind spot in each eye exists because of the structure of the eye. Discover it for yourself. Get a piece of blank paper, and put an X in the middle of the paper and a dot about two inches to the left. Close your right eye. Keeping your left eye focused on the X, move the paper slowly toward your eye. At some point, the dot will disappear from view. Your brain will continue to "cover" for your eye's failure by filling the visual gap with the color of the paper. The dot disappears.

cial revolution without a change in a particular society's legal order; without such a transformation, a so-called revolution is merely a *coup d'état*. It takes more than one generation to consolidate a revolution, and the primary manifestation of this consolidation is always legal. [207] If it is true, as Berman believes, that we are approaching the end of an era, [208] then it is incumbent on Christians to begin to rethink their covenantal heritage. They must begin to offer an alternative to the present collapsing social order, and this alternative must be self-consciously judicial. Christians must become judicial revolutionaries, not simply defenders of the present legal order. [209] If we remain on the deck of this sinking ship, claiming that it is in principle conformable with biblical principles, we shall go down with it. [210] Sticking with the status quo means sure death by drowning.

---

207. *Ibid.*, p. 20.

208. *Ibid.* p. v.

209. Gary North, *When Justice Is Aborted: Biblical Standards for Non-Violent Resistance* (Ft. Worth, Texas: Dominion Press, 1989).

210. Gary North, *Political Polytheism: The Myth of Pluralism* (Tyler, Texas: Institute for Christian Economics, 1989).

Appendix C

THE HOAX OF HIGHER CRITICISM

For had ye believed Moses, ye would have believed me, for he wrote of me. But if ye believe not his writings, how shall ye believe my words? (John 5:46-47).

It is not just Jews who refuse to take these words seriously; it is also the vast majority of those who graduate from theological seminaries today. With few exceptions, seminaries are staffed by professors of literature rather than professors of Christ. They have adopted a view of the Bible which says that the biblical texts reveal gross errors on the part of the Bible's writers and editors. The critics refer to the Bible as a myth-filled book. These classroom skeptics and their intellectual predecessors have labored for over a century to remove Christians' confidence in the accuracy of the Bible. Their personal goal, above all other goals, is to escape the final judgment of the God who has revealed Himself clearly. They comfort themselves while discomforting their Bible-believing students with this syllogism: "No permanent Bible, no permanent law; no permanent law, no permanent judgment." But this absence of God's judgment must also be asserted with respect to history; higher criticism of the Bible plays a role in this dogma, too.

There is little doubt that the successful assault on Christianity in the late-nineteenth century came from two sources: Darwinism and higher criticism of the Bible. The latter was exported primarily from German universities. The Christian West has been under guerilla attack by German scholarship for about two centuries. Prussians invented the government-supported kindergarten and the Ph.D degree, two of the most insidious inventions of the modern world. (I have long appreciated the observation by literary critic Edmund Wilson regarding the absurdity of the oppressive Ph.D system. The world would be far better off today "if, at the time of the First World

War, when we were renaming our hamburgers Salisbury Steak and our sauerkraut Liberty Cabbage, we had decided to scrap it as a German atrocity.")[1]

Academic higher criticism of the Bible was nourished in its maturity in the same European corner of the academic world. It was promoted most successfully by intellectually disciplined German scholars in the nineteenth century. These men were dedicated to the destruction of orthodox Christianity. Their primary goal was to discover defects in the existing texts of Scripture, as well as to discover internal inconsistencies in the Bible's overall message. This strategy was designed to discredit the Christian world's faith in a permanent standard of righteousness. Higher criticism was the spiritual legacy of the Enlightenment, as one of its spiritual heirs frankly admits: "The rationalist Enlightenment radicalized the claim of reason and history; as a result it placed the claims of religion outside the realm of reason. In this division Orthodox theology lost its foundations in history. The cleft between reason and history triumphed among the learned — including theologians — and removed the basis of orthodoxy's epistemology."[2]

A War for English Civilization

What is not generally recognized, however, is that biblical higher criticism had its origin in the English-speaking world. It was English Deism rather than German scholarship that laid the intellectual foundation of modern higher criticism. Even before Deism, certain aspects of the critical attack on the Bible, especially the Old Testament, had begun with Renaissance humanism.[3] R. K. Harrison traces back to mid-seventeenth-century rationalist political philosopher Thomas Hobbes the idea that the Pentateuch was compiled from much earlier sources written by Moses.[4]

Edgar Krentz is an enthusiastic defender of higher criticism against what he describes as the dogmatic church's "fear of change,

1. Edmund Wilson, *The Fruits of the MLA* (New York: New York Review Book, 1968), p. 20. The MLA is the Modern Language Association.

2. Edgar Krentz, *The Historical-Critical Method* (Philadelphia: Fortress Press, [1975] 1977), p. 21.

3. A little-known and unfortunately neglected study of the history of higher criticism is Henning Graf Reventlow, *The Authority of the Bible and the Rise of the Modern World* (London: SCM Press, [1980] 1984), Pt. I.

4. Roland Kenneth Harrison, *Introduction to the Old Testament* (Grand Rapids, Michigan: Eerdmans, [1969] 1974), pp. 9-10.

fear of losing the basis for certainty of faith, and fear of posing questions in the area of authority."[5] He, too, identifies English Deism as the source of this intellectual development. "The eighteenth-century Deists treated the Bible with freedom when it did not, in their lights, accord with reason. For example, they argued that Isaiah was composite, the Gospels contradictory, and the apostles often unreliable."[6]

The Deist's attack on the divine authority of the Bible was not simply a product of the scholar's dusty study. It was closely associated with warring social and intellectual movements of the day. James Barr's observations are very important in understanding the roots of higher criticism and also in understanding the revival of biblical literalism as a social force in the United States, especially after 1960. The link between social action and biblical hermeneutics has been missed by most historians. Barr, following Reventlow's lead, does not make this mistake:

Church and state formed a single continuum, and political and theological questions were seen as interdependent. Questions about power and legitimacy rested in a high degree upon exegetical and interpretative ideas. In this the Old Testament — Reventlow's own specialism — was of primary importance. Even if the New Testament was the document of the earliest Christianity, the way in which the other collection of books form a yet older age, the Old Testament, was related to it. For it was the Old Testament, as it seemed, that offered guidance about king and state, about a commonwealth organized under divine statutes, about law and property, about war, about ritual and ceremony, about priesthood, continuity and succession. All of this was a disputed area from the Reformation onwards: because these were controversial matters in church and state, they generated deep differences in biblical interpretation. It was precisely because the Bible was assumed on all hands to be authoritative that it stimulated new notions about its own nature. It was because men sought answers to problems of life and society, as well as of thought and belief, that the Bible stimulated 'critical' modes of understanding itself.[7]

The heart of English Deism's attack on Christian orthodoxy was its faith in Newtonian natural law and hostility to Old Testament law and Old Testament prophecy. "If one could write off the Old Testament as testimony to a pre-Christian religion and vindicate the New Testament in another way (e.g. through its accord with the law

---

5. Krentz, *op. cit.*, p. 15.
6. *Ibid.*, p. 16.
7. James Barr, Foreword, in Reventlow, *Authority of the Bible*, p. xiii.

of nature) Christianity could still be defended, albeit as a pedagogical means to the moral illumination of mankind."[8] Once the denial of the indissoluble unity of the Bible became common, the next step was easy: the denial of the need for an infallible New Testament in Christianity.

Reventlow has provided evidence of the political aspects of the war for and against the infallibility of the Bible. He provides over 400 pages of text and 200 pages of endnotes to demonstrate, among related themes, that "the political thought of the sixteenth, seventeenth and eighteenth centuries continually sought its models and arguments within the Bible, and the approach of each particular thinker in question provided the real criterion for the analogies drawn between the reconstructed biblical model and the principles which were normative for shaping the society of his time."[9] The Deists launched their war on the Old Testament in an attempt to substitute natural law for biblical law. Anyone who fails to understand the ethical nature of this intellectual conflict does not understand the history of biblical higher criticism. The attack on the Old Testament was a fundamental aspect of the coming of modern humanist civilization.

Only as a result of the attack by Deists on the authority of Scripture (preparations for which were made, against their own intentions, by Latitudinarians, Locke and Newton), an attack which they made step by step, did the legacy of antiquity in the form of natural law and Stoic thought, which since the late Middle Ages had formed the common basis for thought despite all the changes of theological and philosophical direction, remain the one undisputed criterion. This produced a basically new stage both in the history of ideas and in the English constitution. This position already contains the roots of its own failure, in that the consistent development of the epistemological principles of Locke and Berkely [sic] by Hume soon showed that its basic presuppositions were untenable. However, two irreversible and definitive developments remained, which had made an appearance with it: the Bible lost its significance for philosophical thought and for the theoretical foundations of political ideals, and ethical rationalism (with a new foundation in Kant's critique) proved to be one of the forces shaping the modern period, which only now can really be said to have begun.[10]

Reventlow has pointed out that higher criticism has faded in importance since the end of the Second World War. In the immediate

8. Reventlow, *ibid.*, p. 398.
9. *Ibid.*, p. 413.
10. *Ibid.*, pp. 413-14.

post-war era, biblical criticism was an important aspect of Protestant colleges and seminaries. No longer. "Given a predominant concern with the present and its seemingly urgent practical problems, which claim almost exclusive attention," he writes, "historical criticism and exegesis have come to take very much a back place."[11]

Burying the Dead

Why, then, should I devote an appendix to this topic? Because of a parallel process: while modern humanism has visibly begun to fragment, taking with it modern liberal theology, there has been a recovery of interest within the evangelical world of real-world questions that are best summarized under the general heading, "Christian worldview." The implicit dualisms of modern fundamentalism — Old Testament vs. New Testament, law vs. grace, letter vs. spirit, church vs. state, Israel vs. the church, eternity vs. history, heart vs. mind, dominion vs. rapture, culture vs. kingdom — have begun to be either discarded or at least seriously criticized from within the camp.[12] The Christian world's recovery of a vision of ethical unity, of a comprehensive world-and-life view, is basic to any workable strategy of Christian reconstruction. In this intellectual and emotional process of recovering Christianity's lost unity of vision, we are required to return to the original source of the problem: men's loss of faith in the unity of God's Word.

There is an old political slogan, "You can't beat something with nothing." Throughout the twentieth century, the Christian world has found itself in the position of battling something — self-confident humanism — with nothing: a philosophy of ethical dualism, a kind of Christian gnosticism.[13] This was obvious to everyone after the Scopes' "monkey" trial of 1925.[14] (In the early church, this dualistic philoso-

---

11. *Ibid.*, p. 1.

12. On the Israel-church dichotomy, see William E. Bell, A Critical Evaluation of the Pretribulation Rapture Doctrine in Christian Eschatology (Ph.D dissertation, New York University, 1968). See also John F. MacArthur, *The Gospel According to Jesus* (Grand Rapids, Michigan: Zondervan Academie, 1988). This book sold over 100,000 copies in hardback within a year of its publication. The survival of the older dualism is best represented by Dave Hunt, *Whatever Happened to Heaven?* (Eugene, Oregon: Harvest House, 1988).

13. Douglas W. Frank, *Less Than Conquerors: How Evangelicals Entered the Twentieth Century* (Grand Rapids, Michigan: Eerdmans, 1986).

14. George Marsden, *Fundamentalism and American Culture: The Shaping of Twentieth-Century Evangelicalism, 1870-1925* (New York: Oxford University Press, 1980), ch. 10: "The Great Reversal."

phy which pitted the Old Testament against the New Testament was correctly identified by the church as heretical: Marcionism.) But the roles are now being reversed. Ever since the assassination of John F. Kennedy in November of 1963, Western humanism has steadily lost both its vision and its "can-do" confidence.[15] A similar loss of confidence also appeared in the mid-1980's behind the Iron and Bamboo Curtains. The implicit and inescapable dualism of all post-Kantian thought—fact vs. meaning, science vs. ethics, *phenomenal* vs. *noumenal*[16] —became a growing intellectual problem after the 1880's, and it could not, like Humpty Dumpty, be put back together again.[17] The social and political effects of this accelerating intellectual disorientation became clear to most social observers after 1963. Meanwhile, the appearance of Van Til's presuppositional apologetics in the mid-1940's,[18] the revival of biblical creationism after 1960,[19] and the preliminary recovery of the Puritan vision of the earthly victory of God's kingdom have combined to produce a new intellectual perspective: Christian reconstruction.

Basic to this reversal has been the recovery of confidence by Christians in the reliability of the whole Bible. They have been presented with a growing body of evidence that Darwinism is a hoax. It is time for them to recognize that biblical higher criticism is an even older hoax, though related philosophically to Darwinism.

Techniques of Higher Criticism

"Lower criticism" is the technical literary exercise of determining which of the existent ancient manuscripts of the Bible are authoritative and therefore belong in the canon of Scripture. Higher criticism, using similar techniques of analysis, and going mad in the process, argues that nothing in the canon of the Bible is what it appears to be, that the Creator God did not directly or uniquely inspire any of it, and that the scribes who assembled its component parts

---

15. Gary North, *Unholy Spirits: Occultism and New Age Humanism* (Ft. Worth, Texas: Dominion Press, 1986), Introduction.

16. Richard Kroner, *Kant's Weltanschauung* (University of Chicago Press, [1914] 1956).

17. H. Stuart Hughes, *Consciousness and Society: The Reorientation of European Social Thought, 1890-1930* (New York: Knopf, 1958).

18. Cornelius Van Til, *The New Modernism: An Appraisal of the Theology of Barth and Brunner* (Philadelphia: Presbyterian & Reformed, 1946).

19. Henry M. Morris and John C. Whitcomb, Jr., *The Genesis Flood: The Biblical Record and Its Scientific Implications* (Philadelphia: Presbyterian & Reformed, 1961).

centuries after the fact were pathetic louts who were unable to follow the logic of any argument, or keep names straight for three consecutive pages, or even imitate the style of the previous lout who first made up some imaginary story and included it in an earlier manuscript. All of these "discoveries" are reached by means of supposedly precise literary techniques.

These textual critics regard the Bible as a kind of novel, so they apply to the study of the Bible techniques that are used in the literary criticism of fiction. Again, let me cite Wilson's comments on the absurdity of these techniques when applied to novels, let alone the Bible. He refers to an edition of Hawthorne's *Marble Faun*, edited by the University of Virginia's specialist in Elizabethan bibliography, Fredson Bowers. He does not spare Mr. Bowers.

But the fourth volume of the Centenary Edition of the works of Nathaniel Hawthorne, which contains only *The Marble Faun*, is the masterpiece of MLA bad bookmaking. I have weighed it, and it weighs nine pounds. It is $9 \times 6\frac{1}{8}$ inches, and $2\frac{3}{8}$ inches thick. . . . *The Marble Faun*, since it is mainly Mr. Bowers's work, embodies the spirit of Mr. Bowers as no other of these volumes does. Of its 610 pages, the 467 of Hawthorne are weighed down by 89 pages of "Textual Introduction" and 143 pages of "Textual Notes." There are 44 pages of historical introduction preceding the textual introduction. We are told in these introductions, in accordance with the MLA formula, that, in the course of writing the book, the author, as novelists often do, changed the names of certain of the characters; and that many of the descriptions in it—as has been noted, also a common practice—have been taken from his Italian notebooks. This information is of no interest whatever. Nor is it of any interest to be told that Hawthorne's wife corrected certain inaccuracies in the Roman descriptions and otherwise made occasional suggestions, which Hawthorne did not always accept. It has evidently been trying for Mr. Bowers to find that, in the original manuscript, the author had been so inconsiderate as usually to make his changes "by wiping out with a finger while the ink was still wet and writing over the same space." But the places where these smudges occur have been carefully noted and listed. (It seems to me that this whole procedure meets an insurmountable obstacle when no corrected proofs survive that show the revisions of the author.)[20]

Wilson then asks the obvious question: "Now, what conceivable value have 276 pages of all this? Surely only that of gratifying the very small group of monomaniac bibliographers." He concludes,

20. Wilson, *Fruits of the MLA*, pp. 18-19.

"The indiscriminate greed for this literary garbage on the part of universities is a sign of the academic pedantry on which American Lit. has been stranded."[21]

All of this is both accurate and amusing. But these same techniques of literary and textual criticism, when applied to biblical texts by monomaniacal German pedants and their epigone Anglo-American imitators, have for over a century undermined people's faith in the integrity of the Bible all over the world.[22]

Criticizing Textual Criticism

The methods used by higher critics are circular: they use their colleagues' reconstructed literary texts to reconstruct the biblical past, and they use their own newly reconstructed biblical past to further reconstruct the biblical texts. On and on the academic game goes, signifying nothing except the futile purposes to which very dull people's minds can be put.

These literary techniques are highly complex, yet amazingly shoddy. The practitioners agree on very little; they reach no testable conclusions; and their required techniques absorb inordinate quantities of time to master. Liberal Bible scholar Calum Carmichael puts it mildly when he warns his readers: "Historical and literary criticism is undeniably useful when working with ancient sources, but not only has it limitations, it sometimes leads nowhere. One manifest restriction in its application to most biblical material is that the historical results hypothesized cannot be corroborated. The speculative character of most such results is easily overlooked because the historical method is so deeply entrenched in scholarly approaches. With a little distance, we can see just how shaky the historical method is. . . . The procedure is a dispiriting one, dull to read, difficult to follow, and largely illusory given the paucity of the results and the conjectured historical realities dotted here and there over a vast span of time. Its most depressing aspect is the no doubt unintentional demeaning of the intelligence of the lawgiver who was

---

21. *Ibid.*, p. 20.

22. Krentz freely admits of literary criticism that "The four-source theory of Pentateuchal origins and the two-source theory of the Synoptic interrelationships are its major results. Literary (source) criticism has achieved a more sharply contoured profile of the various sources and books, and the authors who stand behind them. It is indispensable for any responsible interpretation of the Bible." Krentz, *Historical-Critical Method*, p. 50.

responsible for the presentation of the material available to us. E. M. Forster, struck by the cavalier way in which we treat the past, attributed the attitude to the fact that those who lived then are all dead and cannot rise up and protest."[23]

He is being much too kind. The scholars' "demeaning of the intelligence of the lawgiver who was responsible for the presentation of the material available to us" is all too intentional, for that Lawgiver is God Almighty, who will judge every man on judgment day. Higher critics are determined to deny that such a cosmic Lawgiver exists, and they do their best to make His laws seem like an incoherent collection of disjointed and self-contradictory pronouncements, a judicial jumble compiled by a series of editors who apparently could not keep clear in their minds anything that was written in the text in front of them that was farther back or farther forward than three lines. Somehow, these deceptive ancient masters of language and textual subtleties could not keep any argument straight, or remember the plot line of even a one-page story. Their heavy-handed attempts to revise the ancient texts for their own contemporary purposes were so badly bungled that they succeeded only in so distorting the text that no careful reader could possibly believe that God had revealed the Pentateuch to one man, Moses.

It is not the Pentateuch that is disjointed. It was not the hypothetical "later editors" who could not keep things straight in their minds. Rather, it is the paid professional army of higher critics. I appreciate C. S. Lewis' comments, as a master of medieval and early modern English literature, regarding the ability of textual critics to understand their texts: "These men ask me to believe they can read between the lines of old texts; the evidence is their obvious inability to read (in any sense worth discussing) the lines themselves. They claim to see fern-seed and can't see an elephant ten yards away in broad daylight."[24]

Apostate Deceivers

The higher critics present the Bible as a poorly assembled patchwork of lies and myths, and then they add insult to injury by arguing

---

23. Calum M. Carmichael, *Law and Narrative in the Bible: The Evidence of the Deuteronomic Laws and the Decalogue* (Ithaca, New York: Cornell University Press, 1985), p. 14.

24. C. S. Lewis, *Christian Reflections*, edited by Walter Hooper (London: Geoffrey Bles, 1967), p. 157. The essay is titled, "Modern Thought and Biblical Criticism."

that their debunking operation somehow elevates our view of the
Bible. For example, the internationally respected (unfortunately) Bible
scholar G. Ernest Wright and his co-author argue that in the Bible,
"What is important is what this great Lord has done."[25] But as soon
as anyone raises the obvious question, "What exactly has God done?"
the authors run for the cover of symbolism and supposed myth, in
order to escape the Bible's detailed account of what God has done:

> This furnishes a clue to our understanding of the prehistoric material
> preserved in Genesis 1-11. These traditions go far back into the dim and un-
> recoverable history of Israel; they are the popular traditions of a people,
> traditions which in part go back to a pre-Canaanite and North Mesopotamian
> background. For this reason there is little question of objective history here.
> We are instead faced with the question of why the old traditions were written
> down. What was the purpose of the writers who preserved them for us?[26]

Notice the shift in their argument. They tell us on the one hand
that the Bible is a historical book, unique in the ancient world. The
Bible's view of God rests squarely on what God has done in history.
But when the key chapters that describe the creation of the universe
and the Fall of man are brought up, as well as the Noachic flood and
the tower of Babel, the authors immediately shift their focus away
from what the Bible says about God; they shift their concern to what
the Hebrews came later to *believe* about God. Their focus shifts from
God to man. This is the essence of humanism. The fact is, their
focus *began* with man rather than God — autonomous man.

The humanist scholar insists that we cannot deal with God, who
is not an objective fact of history that can be studied. We can only
deal with *men's recorded thoughts about God*, which are objective facts of
history that can be studied. Van Til has summarized this humanistic
impulse: "Men hope to find in a study of the *religious consciousness*
something that has never been found before. They hope to find out
what religion really is. The claim is made that now for the first time
religion is really being studied from the inside."[27] Man's religious
consciousness becomes determinative in history, not the acts of God.
Wright and Fuller should have titled their book, *The Book of the Sur-*

---

25. G. Ernest Wright and Reginald H. Fuller, *The Book of the Acts of God: Christian
Scholarship Interprets the Bible* (Garden City, New York: Doubleday, 1957), p. 36.

26. *Ibid.*, p. 24.

27. Cornelius Van Til, *Psychology of Religion*, vol. IV of *In Defense of Biblical Christianity* (Phillipsburg, New Jersey: Presbyterian & Reformed, 1971), p. 7.

viving Early Writings of Two Religious Groups, Judaism and Christianity, Regarding the Acts of a God Who Does Not Really Interact With History. Had they done so, of course, their academic charade would have been obvious from the beginning.

Historical Resurrection and Final Judgment

It is not only the creation of man and his subsequent fall from grace that must be discreetly covered up by the blanket of hypothetically objective history; it is also the resurrection of Christ. Both sin and redemption must be discussed apart from biblical revelation, for if the Bible's account of sin and redemption is taken seriously, then the issue of God's final judgment once again becomes a fundamental problem. This is the problem that autonomous man wishes most of all to avoid. So, the resurrection is relegated to the mythic past, and once again the authors focus on what a small group of people have thought about this non-historical event.

Finally, what shall we say about the resurrection of Christ, as understood in the New Testament? This cannot be an objective fact of history in the same sense as was the crucifixion of Christ. The latter was a fact available to all men as a real happening, and pagan writers like Tacitus and Josephus can speak of it. But in the New Testament itself the Easter faith-event of the resurrection is perceived only by the people of the faith. Christ as risen was not seen by everyone, but only by the few. Easter was thus a reality for those in the inner circle of the disciples and apostles. That is not an arena where a historian can operate. Facts available to all men are the only data with which he can work, the facts available to the consciousness of a few are not objective history in the historian's sense.[28]

They distinguish the "real happening" of the crucifixion from the "faith-event" of the resurrection, which was an event of a very different character. Only "facts available to all men"—meaning facts that are implicitly possible for all men to have seen—are "real happenings." This means that the resurrection was somehow not a fact that in principle all men might have seen and verified, in the same way that they could have seen and verified the crucifixion. In other words, the resurrection was not a "real happening," although the calculating deceivers who wrote *The Book of the Acts of God* are too wise to say this blatantly, for fear of tipping their hand. They argue that the

---

28. Wright and Fuller, *Acts of God*, p. 25.

resurrection was therefore not an objective historical event, not "an objective fact of history."[29]

The Bible tells a very different story. The fact of Christ's resurrection was sufficiently objective that Paul appealed to it as a commonly known fact when he defended himself in King Agrippa's court: "Why should it be thought a thing incredible with you, that God should raise the dead?" (Acts 26:8). He went on to remind skeptical Festus: "For the king knoweth of these things, before whom also I speak freely: for I am persuaded that none of these things are hidden from him; for this thing was not done in a corner" (Acts 26:26). And when Paul finished, Agrippa said to him: "Almost thou persuadest me to be a Christian" (Acts 26:28). But the higher critics are not even remotely persuaded. They see their man-appointed task to confuse Christians about the reliability of the orthodox faith, as well as to confuse non-Christians who might otherwise be persuaded.

A New Terminology

So, the critics have invented new terminology, the better to muddle the perceptions of their readers. For example, following the lead of Immanuel Kant's Protestant prophet Karl Barth, they substitute a grotesque hyphenated word like *faith-event* for the decisive and incriminating word, *fact*. "Hence we have to view the resurrection in the New Testament as a faith-event, unlike other events, which is nevertheless real to the Christian community. It testifies to the knowledge that Christ is alive, not dead. The living Christ was known to be the head of the Church; and his power was real. The process, the how of Christ's transition from death to the living head of the new community, and the language used to describe that transition ('raised the third day,' 'Ascension,' 'going up,' 'sitting on the right hand of God') — these are products of the situation. They are the temporal language of the first-century Christians. To us, they are symbols of deep truth and nothing more, though they are symbols that are difficult to translate."[30]

Of course these are difficult symbols to translate, meaning *difficult to translate into historical categories that are acceptable to liberal humanism*, because "raised the third day" and "going up" meant exactly the same

---

29. On the anti-historical concept of the resurrection-event or faith-event in modern neo-orthodox theology, see Cornelius Van Til, *Christianity and Barthianism* (Philadelphia: Presbyterian & Reformed, 1962), pp. 92-113.

30. Wright and Fuller, *Acts of God*, p. 25.

thing to a first-century Christian as they mean today. These hell-bound apostate scholars suffer from the problem Felix suffered when he heard the gospel from Paul, *fear*, for Felix trembled (Acts 24:25). They want to avoid thinking about the Bible's message of salvation, for it is also the message of God's inevitable final judgment. The biblical message of salvation is the only alternative to the biblical message of eternal torment.[31]

The higher critics have become the ultimate myth-makers by proclaiming the existence of a set of high ideals that are somehow associated with biblical myths (i.e., hoaxes). After telling the reader that the early chapters of Genesis are not historical, but simply symbolic, the authors assure us concerning the story of Adam's fall: "But let us not be deceived by the simple story form of presentation. The greatness of this story is its insight into the inner nature of man and the simple manner in which it presents that insight."[32] They first present evidence that, if true, any sensible reader—i.e., any non-Ph.D-holding higher critic—would recognize clearly as evidence that the Bible is a gigantic hoax, and then they speak as though this "new, improved" understanding of the Bible will lead society to higher ideals and moral righteousness. They are classic examples of C. S. Lewis' description of modern humanist culture: "In a sort of ghastly simplicity we remove the organ and demand the function. We make men without chests and expect of them virtue and enterprise. We laugh at honour and are shocked to find traitors in our midst. We castrate and bid the geldings be fruitful."[33]

What the higher critics want us to believe in is the world according to Immanuel Kant, a dialectical realm composed of two utterly separate worlds: the phenomenal world of historical facts—meaningless historical facts apart from man's interpretations of them—and the trans-historical noumenal world of human meaning—utterly timeless, non-cognitive meaning—that is completely distinct from the phenomenal world of measurable cause and effect.[34] Autonomous man stands at the intersection of these two dialectical realms, and somehow creates meaning for himself. God is given homage only as the unknown god of the Greeks (Acts 17:23), and even worse, as the

---

31. Gary North, Publisher's Epilogue, in David Chilton, *The Great Tribulation* (Ft. Worth, Texas: Dominion Press, 1987).

32. Wright and Fuller, *Acts of God*, p. 61.

33. C. S. Lewis, *The Abolition of Man* (New York: Macmillan, [1947] 1965), p. 35.

34. Kroner, *Kant's Weltanschauung*.

inherently *unknowable* god. An unknowable god is the only god who is acceptable to modern autonomous man, for an unknowable god presumably will not bring final judgment to inherently uninformed and uninformable finite mankind. We must never forget: *the primary goal of self-proclaimed autonomous man is to escape God's final judgment.* So, in order to escape this judgment, the higher critics spin a web of pompous verbiage that they hope and pray — well, at least they hope — will protect them from the eternal consequences of their God-defying rebellion.

Who Is the Hoaxer?

Our authors ask three rhetorical questions, and then give their hapless readers a bowl of lukewarm mental mush in reply. First, the questions: "Yet there is always the final lurking question: Is the Bible true? What is truth and what is just symbolic? Cannot I have anything that is absolutely certain?" Then the mush: "The answer must be that the symbol *is* the truth. We have no other truth. We know it is not literal truth, but we know that the biblical portrayal is the relationship between the unknown infinite and ourselves here and now. No precise dividing line can be drawn between the ultimately real and the poetic symbol, because God has not made us infinite."[35] In short, they argue that because I am not infinite, and therefore not God, I need not fear an infinite God, for my very finitude keeps me from knowing God. To which Paul answered many centuries ago:

> For the wrath of God is revealed from heaven against all ungodliness and unrighteousness of men, who hold [back] the truth in unrighteousness; because that which may be known of God is manifest in them; for God hath shewed it unto them. For the invisible things of him from the creation of the world are clearly seen, being understood by the things that are made, even his eternal power and Godhead; so that they are without excuse (Rom. 1:18-20).

The Bible of the higher critics cannot possibly be what it says clearly that it is: the revealed Word of the Creator and Judge of the universe. Now, if the Bible really isn't what it says it is, then it must be a hoax. Once the implicit though politely unstated accusation of hoaxing is made, the question then arises: Who is the true hoaxer, God or the higher critic? There should be no doubt in our minds: the literary critic is the myth-maker. Literary higher criticism of the

---

35. Wright and Fuller, *Acts of God*, p. 37.

Bible is a hoax. No other word does it justice. It is a fraud, a lie, a denial that God's revealed Word is what it says it is.[36] Wright and Fuller made a classic Freudian slip when they used the word *forged* for "hammered out" (as in "crucible"), when it is far easier to interpret *forged* as "falsified" (as in "forged signature"): "It is quite legitimate to use the methods of historical and literary criticism which were forged during the liberal period in order to reconstruct the underlying history."[37] Forged indeed! Higher criticism rests on the presupposition that all morality is relative to historical time and place, and that the laws of the Bible, a strictly historical human document, are also relative. It denies the unity and moral integrity of the Bible.

Textual Indeterminacy Equals Ethical Indeterminacy

The real motive of higher criticism is ethical. This, too, has been Van Til's assertion: covenant-breaking man's problem is not a lack of knowledge about God; rather, it is his *lack of obedience* to God. The higher critics seek to confuse men by blurring the universal ethical requirements of God's holy Word. If they were correct, then there could be no final judgment, for God's sanctions require God's permanent stipulations. To deny God's judgment, His stipulations must be presumed to be incoherent, unclear, and limited to the individual conscience, rather than coherent, clear, and universal in every human conscience.

Karl Barth was a defender of just such a radically individual ethics, an ethics which matched his thesis of a radically dialectical, incoherent, creed-denying, God-man encounter — a noumenal encounter beyond nature and history. He denied as "untenable" the assumption of the universality of God's ethical commands, for "the command of God . . . is always an individual command for the conduct of this man, at this moment and in this situation. . . ."[38] In short, on

---

36. Oswald T. Allis, *The Five Books of Moses* (Philadelphia: Presbyterian & Reformed, [1943] 1949). I appreciate the book's subtitle, reminiscent of the nineteenth century: *A Reexamination of the Modern Theory that the Pentateuch Is a Late Compilation from Diverse and Conflicting Sources by Authors and Editors Whose Identity Is Completely Unknown.* See also Allis, *The Old Testament: Its Claims and Its Critics* (Nutley, New Jersey: Presbyterian & Reformed, 1972); Robert Dick Wilson, *A Scientific Investigation of the Old Testament*, with revisions by Edward J. Young (Chicago, Illinois: Moody Press, 1959); Edward J. Young, *Thy Word Is Truth* (Grand Rapids, Michigan: Eerdmans, 1957).

37. Wright and Fuller, *Acts of God*, p. 237.

38. Karl Barth, *Church Dogmatics*, translated by A. T. Mackay (Edinburgh: T. & T. Clark, 1961), Vol. 3, Part 4, p. 11; cited by Walter Kaiser, Jr., *Toward Old Testament Ethics* (Grand Rapids, Michigan: Zondervan Academie, 1983), p. 25.

Barth's basis there cannot be a God-revealed permanent Christian ethics, nor civil statutes that conform to fixed biblical principles. Statutes
and creeds are supposedly only the inventions of men, not the appropriate human responses to God's fixed and reliable revelation of Himself in a God-inspired historical document. Barth thereby proclaimed
the triumph of Kant's noumenal trans-historical realm of randomness
over Kant's phenomenal historical realm of scientifically predictable
cause and effect, all in the name of higher ethics and higher critical
insights. This was Barth's assertion of the triumph of historical and
ethical relativism over the Bible. This was his announcement of the
triumph of covenant-breaking man over God, and above all, over
the final judgment. Autonomous man seeks to impose his temporal
judgments on God by denying the historic validity of God's revelation
of Himself. This, of course, was precisely what Adam attempted to
do in the garden by eating the forbidden fruit in defiance of God's explicit revelation. The results are equally predictable.

Permanent Standards for Eternal Judgment

A righteous God who judges men eternally does so only on the
basis of a *unified ethical system.* Only because the ethical standards
never change could the punishment never change. If the texts are
not ethically unified, then there is no threat to man from the God of
the Bible. Thus, the "prime directive" of higher criticism is to affirm
the lack of unity in the Bible. This is the "higher" critic's operating
presupposition when he begins to study the Bible.

He adopts a five-step process. First, he *assumes* that the books of
the Bible are textually jumbled. Second, he tries to *prove* that the
books of the Bible are textually jumbled. Third, he *assumes* that
through creative myth-making, he himself can produce a meaningful reconstruction of what the ancient authors ("redactors") really
wanted to convey to all mankind, despite each one's short-term goals
of political or bureaucratic manipulation. Fourth, he tries to present
a *"deeper" message* for modern man that transcends the Bible's unfortunately jumbled texts. Finally, the higher critic offers *his version of the
Bible's true transcendent ethical unity.* Somehow, this newly discovered
transcendent ethical unity always winds up sounding like the last
decade's political manifesto for social democracy, or else it sounds
like Marxism.

A good statement of this operating presupposition of textual disunity is J. L. Houlden's remark that "There is, strictly speaking, no

such thing as 'the X of the New Testament'. . . . It is only at the cost of ignoring the individuality of each, in thought and expression, that the unified account can emerge. . . . There can be no initial assumption of harmony."[39] So, it is supposedly illegitimate to speak of "the X of the New Testament." Well, how about a *heavenly Author* of the New Testament? How about solving the equation as "X = God." Sorry, says Houlden implicitly, we cannot begin with any such assumption. Well, then, how about "the *grammar* of the New Testament"? We will posit "X = grammar." Houlden is then silent, as befits a man who has implicitly denied the grammatical coherence of New Testament Greek. If he follows the logic of his statement, Greek grammar disappears, and with it, grammar in general. The coherence of the universe of rational discourse disappears, not to mention coherence of the universe itself. Once you play these sorts of verbal games, their self-contradictory nature swallows up your vaunted neutral scholarship.

Contrary to Mr. Houlden, we must begin our Bible studies (and every other kind of study) with the presupposition of the self-contained ontological Trinity and His creation of the universe out of nothing. We must begin with the Creator-creature distinction, as Van Til affirmed throughout his career. We must begin with the assumption of the unity and harmony of God's expression of Himself in the Word of God, the Bible. If we do not begin with this set of presuppositions, we will find ourselves as intellectually impotent as the scholarly higher critics of the Bible, who find it difficult to make sense of anything.

The higher critics are always alert to any hint of defection from the Party's line concerning ethical relativism. Hans Jochen Boecker criticizes the Postscript of another German scholar, H. -D. Bracker. Herr Doctor Bracker made an academic gaffe by concluding in 1962 that "Israel's law by far surpassed the other three [Babylonian, Hittite and Assyrian] in its ethical purity and in its humanity." Such a conclusion is "highly suspect," Herr Doctor Boecker assures his readers.[40] Why is this conclusion "highly suspect"? Because it breaks with the supposed academic neutrality and ethical relativism of modern scholarship, especially modern biblical scholarship.

---

39. J. L. Houlden, *Ethics and the New Testament* (Middlesex, England: Penguin, 1973), p. 2; cited by Kaiser, *ibid.*, p. 13.

40. Hans Jochen Boecker, *Law and the Administration of Justice in the Old Testament and Ancient East*, translated by Jeremy Moiser (Minneapolis, Minnesota: Augsburg, [1976] 1980), p. 16.

Young scholars are informed subtly from the outset of their careers as undergraduates that they must always begin with the assumption that all religious faiths are equal (except for fundamentalism, which preaches an infallible Bible), all political systems are equal (except for Nazi Germany's, of course, mainly because the Nazis lost the war, and South Africa's, which is not based on the politics of black Africa: "one man, one vote, one time only"), and all nations are equal (except for the United States, which occasionally dares to call the Soviet Union into question). What this kind of worldview produces is men without spines who cannot distinguish truth from falsehood, righteousness from perversion, or a cause worth dying for from the latest political slogan. It is only by the common grace of God that they can distinguish AIDS from scarlet fever, except that they probably think that people with scarlet fever should be quarantined.

So, in order to prove all this, higher critics self-consciously spend their myopia-inducing lives searching for internal evidence that denies the unity of that historical document. I agree with Walter Kaiser's observation of the crucial link between higher criticism and men's loss of faith in the unity of the biblical message (including its ethical requirements): "For many it is too much to assume that there is consistency within one book or even a series of books alleged to have been written by the same author, for many contend that various forms of literary criticism have suggested composite documents often traditionally posing under one single author. This argument, more than any other argument in the last two hundred years, has been responsible for cutting the main nerve of the case for the unity and authority of the biblical message."[41]

Higher Criticism and Evolution

Higher criticism is based on an evolutionary model of human morality and human history. It assumes, and then seeks to prove, that the texts of the Bible, and especially the Old Testament, were self-consciously altered by later scribes and "redactors" in order to make the Bible's message conform to the latest ethical and economic principles of the day. It helped to create the early nineteenth century's intellectual climate of opinion that was so favorable to Darwinism after 1859. Ethical relativism is an idea that has had pernicious consequences. Someday, some enterprising scholar is going

---

41. Kaiser, *Toward Old Testament Ethics*, p. 26.

to write a monograph tracing at least one of the historic roots of Nazism back to German higher criticism. Nazism has been traced back to just about everything else in German history, but this possibility has been regarded as off-limits by secular historians; it comes too close to home, theologically speaking. D. F. Strauss' *Life of Jesus* could easily serve as a starting point in such an investigation. Arthur Cohen has suggested this historical connection, and it deserves a detailed study.[42] Cohen's warning should be taken seriously: it is dangerous to separate ethics from faith, which is what higher criticism did. "Nineteenth-century theologians had, indeed, succeeded: the ethics of the Hebrew Bible were winnowed by the Gospels and the ethics restored to Christian conscience were ethics for the 'between time,' when history awaited the return of Christ. The purge of Christianity of its Jewish elements was disastrous."[43]

A representative academic example of the spoiled fruits of higher criticism is presented by the economic historian Morris Silver, who spends an entire volume painstakingly trying to collate and make coherent an immense body of archeological, economic, and higher critical textual evidence in order to prove what higher critics assume, namely, that the Book of Deuteronomy was written many centuries after the exodus. "A central hypothesis of this book is that Deuteronomy represents an attempt to revise and expand the old divine-law code *and thereby the legal practices of the Israelite state* in the light of the circumstances of a much more affluent society."[44] That his presentation of the evidence is painful to follow, let alone remember, should come as no surprise: he combines a false initial hypothesis with hundreds of disjointed citations from far too disjointed a body of scholarship.

There is another major intellectual goal of higher criticism besides re-dating the giving of God's laws in order to relativize them: re-dating every document in which a specific prophecy later came true. The author of the prophecy must have written it after the prophesied event took place. Thus, the so-called prophecy is regarded as merely a convenient lie on the part of a redactor, i.e., a myth. Even when this tactic of re-dating is not invoked, higher

---

42. Arthur A. Cohen, *The Myth of the Judeo-Christian Tradition* (New York: Schocken, 1971), pp. 199-200.

43. *Ibid.*, p. 200.

44. Morris Silver, *Prophets and Markets: The Political Economy of Ancient Israel* (Boston: Kluwer-Nijhoff, 1983), p. 230.

critics remain skeptical of all future-predicting prophecies. Jeremiah prophesied the death of the false prophet Hananiah, and Hananiah died later that year (Jer. 28:15-17). Silver asks rhetorically: "Does this story represent myth, hypnotic suggestion, coincidence, or political assassination?"[45] What it could not possibly represent, in his worldview, is a fulfilled prophecy.

If a person derives ethics from history, and then scrambles the historical data by means of an erroneous chronological scheme, both his ethics and his historiography will flounder.[46] He will write such nonsense as this: ". . . the indispensable agricultural-fertility aspect of Baalism[47] had long ago become a traditional part of Yahweh worship, taken for granted even by Amos and Hosea. It is a naive misconception to suppose that the latter had achieved its final form even at the time of Moses and the Exodus. As Morgenstern[48] well notes, the Jewish religion is the product of historical evolution to meet the needs of the Jewish people 'from the remote desert period to the present day.' The only 'pure Yahwism' is a dead Yahwism."[49] The book's bibliography is impressive, but its conclusions are trivial on those occasions when they are correct. Such is the endlessly repeated fate of two centuries of higher critical scholarship and historical studies based on higher criticism: the academic trumpets sound, and a mouse marches out, dragging behind him a mountain of jumbled chronologies and footnotes to obscure, unread, and unreadable journal articles, leaving behind him a trail of droppings for other busy mice to follow.[50]

---

45. *Ibid.*, p. 140.

46. There are few intellectual tasks more pressing on Christian historians of the ancient Near East and classical Greece and Rome than to rethink the various chronologies prior to about 750 B.C. Cf. Gary North, *Moses and Pharaoh: Dominion Religion vs. Power Religion* (Tyler, Texas: Institute for Christian Economics, 1985), Appendix A: "The Reconstruction of Egypt's Chronology."

47. Citing Ivan Engnell, *Studies in Divine Kingship in the Near East* (Oxford: Basil Blackwell, [1943] 1967), p. 172.

48. Julian Morgenstern, *Rites of Birth, Marriage, Death and Kindred Occasions Among the Semites* (Cincinnati, Ohio: Hebrew Union College Press, 1966), p. 64. If any single individual was most responsible for corrupting American Judaism by means of higher criticism, it was the remarkable, long-lived Julian Morgenstern. For a summary of his life, see Morris Lieberman, "Julian Morgenstern — Scholar, Teacher and Leader," *Hebrew Union College Annual*, XXXII (1961), pp. 1-9.

49. Silver, *Prophets and Markets*, p. 124.

50. The best definition of modern theology that I have come across is the one given by David Chilton to his seminary professor, Greg L. Bahnsen, when Prof. Bahnsen asked him why he was not taking his class on the theology of Pannenberg: "Modern theologians are like a pack of dogs who spend most of their time sniffing each other's behinds."

Higher criticism is today a backwater academic discipline that serves the needs of humanism by keeping linguistically skilled but stylistically handicapped scholars fully employed. It also serves to keep educated Christians confused about the legitimacy of their God-given marching orders. Christian scholars pay a great deal of attention to the latest findings of higher critics, filling their own unread academic journals with vaguely conservative modifications of, and an occasional refutation of, some unread essay in a higher critical academic journal. In contrast, secular scholars today pay very little attention to higher criticism's methods or its findings. This speaks far better of secular scholars than for neo-evangelical scholars who have succumbed to the siren song of certified academic respectability, and who have adopted an attitude of "me, too, but not quite so radical, at least not yet."[51]

Conclusion

Christians have made the mistake of regarding the debates over higher criticism as being the peculiar habit of linguistic specialists and theologians. The fact is, from the very beginning of the rise of humanism, there has been a war between those who defend the Bible, especially the Old Testament, and those who reject this testimony. This debate throughout most of its history involved all of culture, what we call today a conflict between comprehensive world-and-life views. It is only in the hands of modern scholars that the debate has been narrowly focused on the technical issues of textual analysis. Earlier generations recognized that the debate was far more important than modern scholars are willing to admit.

The task of the Christian scholar in defending the Bible as the Word of God must not be narrowly focused. The debate did not originate in the university library; it originated in the social conflicts of the day. The participants understood that the outcome of this academic debate over the textual integrity of the Bible would determine who would gain and retain control of the seats of power. This conflict was a life-and-death matter for English culture in the early modern period, and it was recognized as such by the participants.

---

51. I do not deny that an occasional linguistically gifted scholar such as Robert Dick Wilson, O. T. Allis, or Edward J. Young should devote a lifetime to refuting the best and most influential of the higher critics' presentations. This is a subdivision of apologetics — the intellectual defense of the faith. But surely there is little need for Christians to subsidize the bulk of what passes for academic Old Testament studies today: narrowly focused essays that prove or disprove theses that no one considers relevant, theses that will almost surely be abandoned in less than five years, in those rare instances that anyone adopts them in the first place.

This perception of the magnitude of the debate has been lost on modern Bible scholars. Humanists have rewritten history in order to downplay the importance of the Bible in Western thought and culture. Evangelical Christians have generally agreed to this view of Western history, almost by default. Members of the evangelical scholarly world have been trained by the humanists who control access to the major institutions of higher learning (i.e., trade union certification). At the same time, laymen in the pews have also accepted the humanists' view of the peripheral nature of the Bible's influence in the early modern history because such a view of the Bible's lack of relevance in history conforms to the mind-set of what has been called the left wing of the Reformation: Anabaptist pietism. This tradition has been at war with Old Testament law from the beginning. Indeed, this movement was one of the forerunners of higher criticism, for it contrasted the Bible with the inner testimony of man's spirit, and elevated the latter over the former.[52] This legacy of the internalization of the Word of God triumphed in the modern church through the influence of twentieth-century fundamentalism: grace over law.[53] Once again, we see evidence of the implicit alliance between the power religion and the escape religion.

It is time for Christian scholars of the Old Testament to stop their fruitless shadow-boxing with higher critics who will no more listen to Bible-defending scholars than they have listened to Moses and Christ. It is time for orthodox Bible scholars to go to the Pentateuch to find out what it says, not to discover some new bit of evidence that Moses really and truly did say it. There is no doubt a place in the division of intellectual labor for linguistically skilled Christians to defend the integrity of the Bible against the incoherent slanders of higher critics, but this technical task should be put on a low-priority basis. What we do need is a great deal of research on the chronology of the Pentateuch — not on when Moses wrote the Pentateuch, but on what was going on in the surrounding nations at the time of the exodus. We need a reconstruction of ancient chronology, one based on the presupposition that the Bible gives us the authoritative primary source documents, not Egypt or Babylon. Such a project would keep a lot of linguistically skilled scholars productively busy for several generations.

Meanwhile, let the higher critics drown in their own footnotes, the way that Arius died by falling head-first into a privy.[54] Let the dead bury the dead, preferably face down in a scholarly journal.

---

52. Reventlow, *Authority of the Bible*, ch. 3.
53. Frank, *Less Than Conquerors*.
54. R. J. Rushdoony, *Foundations of Social Order: Studies in the Creeds and Councils of the Early Church* (Fairfax, Virginia: Thoburn Press, [1969] 1978), p. 17.

Appendix D

THE EPISTEMOLOGICAL
PROBLEM OF SOCIAL COST

Costs and benefits cannot be compared across individuals, even when monetary sums are involved, because of the impossibility of interpersonal utility comparison. This insight is a straightforward application of the defining principle of the Austrian school: radical subjectivism. [1]

Since all costs and benefits are subjective, no government can accurately identify, much less establish, the optimum quantity of anything. But even the tort [private law suit over wrongs — G.N.] approach runs up against the immeasurability of costs and benefits: how are damages to be determined? [2]

Another problem is the lack of a method for calculating the effect of a decision or policy on the total happiness of the relevant population. Even within just the human population, there is no reliable technique for measuring a change in the level of satisfaction of one individual relative to a change in the level of satisfaction of another. [3]

Economists are a cynical bunch. What is a cynic? I do not mean the Greek definition. The cynic Diogenes' search for an honest man — a man whose support could not be purchased — would be regarded as a wasteful expenditure of scarce economic resources by any self-respecting economist. Economists know before they begin — begin anything — that "every person has his price." There is no more cen-

---

1. John B. Egger, "Comment: Efficiency Is Not a Substitute for Ethics," in Mario J. Rizzo (ed.), *Time, Uncertainty, and Disequilibrium* (Lexington, Massachusetts: Lexington Books, 1979), p. 121. Italics not in original.

2. Charles W. Baird, "The Philosophy and Ideology of Pollution Regulation," *Cato Journal*, II (Spring 1982), p. 303. Italics not in original.

3. Richard A. Posner, *The Economics of Justice* (Cambridge, Massachusetts, 1983), p. 54. Italics not in original.

tral statement of their operational faith. No, I have in mind the definition of a cynic offered by Oscar Wilde in *Lady Windermere's Fan*: "A man who knows the price of everything and the value of nothing."

Value and Price

This dilemma is in fact the central dilemma of the academic discipline known as economics, the search for an answer to one question, above all other questions: "What is the verifiable relationship between value and price?" For over two centuries, generations of economists have attempted to discover the answer, and it eludes them today as much as it did in the days of Adam Smith. The difference is, today the lack of any internally consistent answer is covered by far more layers of dead ends that were and are described as successful solutions to the problem.

Let us begin the search. Assume that you are interrogating a humanistic economist. You ask: If all value is objective, then why do prices keep changing? What is it that makes them change? *Supply and demand change.* But why does supply change? *In response to changes in demand.* But why does demand change? *Because people change their minds.* Why? *Because prices change.* Why do prices change? *Changing supply and demand.*

Wait a minute. We are going in circles. We had better talk about demand apart from price. *Sorry, you are not allowed to talk about demand apart from price, or price apart from demand.* All right, let me ask this: If the changing of people's minds is the source of the changes in demand, then isn't the price of anything really based on subjective value? *Yes, that is correct.* Personal subjective value? *Yes, that is correct.* But how is personal subjective value translated into objective value? *It isn't; there is no objective value.* Well, then, how is personal subjective value translated into objective prices? *Through competitive bidding.*

But how can we be sure that the outcome of the objective individual bids reflects the true value to society? *By denying that there is any true value to society apart from the outcome of the objective individual bids.* But what if society disagrees? *There is no such thing as society; there are only individuals.* But what if individuals vote to change the outcome? *That is their legal privilege in a democracy.* Are you saying that democracy is a valid way to achieve social goals? *I am an economist; I can only tell you the outcome of events, given certain causes.* Should democracies vote to change the outcome of the bids? *I am an economist; there is no ultimate "should" for an economist.*

That reminds me: What is the value of economics? *Sorry; economics does not objectively exist; only economists exist.* What is an economist? *An economist is someone who does economics.* I see. Well, then, what is the value of an economist? *That must be determined subjectively.* All right, what is the price of an economist? *All the market will bear.* Are we paying economists too much? *The free market will decide that.* Do we have a free market in economists today? *I'd prefer not to say; I might get fired. I work for a state university. It is not in my self-interest to answer your question.*

In my view, the answer is clear: yes, we are paying economists too much. Is my view correct? That *is* the question.

In this essay, I intend to show that all of modern economics is a gigantic intellectual fraud, an illusion so successful that its practitioners are not aware of the fraud which they are perpetrating. I will show that the procedures that economists say they use are not the ones they actually use, that the presuppositions they say they have adopted are not actually the ones they have adopted, and that their ability to make economic judgments is in fact denied by their very methodology. All you have to do is read the entire essay, paying attention to my arguments as you read.

Am I overstating my case? *You cannot know for sure until you read it.* Is it worth the risk—the time, energy, and mental effort—to find out? *Only you can say.*

And therein lies the problem of modern economics.

To Read or Not to Read

What will it cost you to read this essay? You will never know for sure. It is analogous to a far more important question in life, "What will it cost me to marry this person?" Both questions really mean: "What will I have to give up forever?" While the "foreverness" of the marriage decision is more obvious to us—"till death do us part" is a graphic covenant phrase—the "foreverness" of every decision is analogous, though not of the same order of magnitude.

When I choose *this* rather than *that*, I forever forfeit *that*, as well as all the little thats which might have been born later on. Perhaps I can change my mind later on, and buy *that*, but it will not be the same *that* which I choose not to buy today. It is a later *that*. Like a high school sweetheart whom you marry only after your first spouse dies, time has worked its changes on both of you. Everything a person might have accomplished with *that* during the period of *"this rather than that"* is gone forever.

A Fork in the Road

We know that in making any decision, we must forfeit many things that might have been but will never be — indeed, a whole lifetime of things that might have been — but we never know exactly what. Every decision, moment by moment, is to some extent the proverbial fork in the road. We cannot predict the next twenty moves and counter-moves in a chess game — moves that will become reality *in part* because of the next move — so it is safe to say that we cannot know what life has in store for us because we do one thing today rather than another.

If you read this essay, it is because you think it will be "worth your time." But what is your time worth? What is your time worth right now? It is worth whatever is the most valuable use to which you can put it. What is the cost of spending your time one way rather than another? The most valuable use foregone. So, what is your decision? "To read or not to read, that is the question!"

Decisions, decisions. Once our decision is made, we put the past irrevocably behind us. "The moving finger writes, and having written, moves on." We then face the consequences of our decision. But these consequences — these *costs* — are imposed on us after the decision, not before. They are costs, but they are not costs that affected the original action. *Expected* costs affected the original action, not the actual costs that we in fact subsequently experience. Is this unclear? Ask the person who married the "wrong" spouse to explain the difference between expected costs and resulting costs. Economist James Buchanan distinguishes between two kinds of costs: choice-*influencing* costs and choice-*influenced* costs.[4]

Unmeasurable Costs

Choice-influencing costs are inherently unmeasurable by any scientific standard. The economist insists that, like beauty in the eyes of the beholder, these economic costs exist only in the mind of the decision-maker. They are subjectively perceived, and *only* subjectively perceived. And yet, and yet . . . there really are beautiful women and ugly women, and just about everyone can discern the difference, including the respective women (*especially* the women).

---

4. James Buchanan, *Cost and Choice: An Inquiry in Economic Theory* (University of Chicago Press, 1969), pp. 44-45. Buchanan won the Nobel Prize in economics in 1986.

But how is this possible? How can we deny the objective reality of beauty in the name of a "higher" subjective reality, when we know that in order for our subjective appraisals to have meaning, there had better be an objective reality undergirding them? After all, two and two make four. Or do they? Does the objective answer depend on the subjective evaluator? The modern mathematician is not really sure.[5]

The costs that influence our decisions are always subjective evaluations of future potential consequences. This is Buchanan's argument. Once we act, however, objective reality takes over, replacing our mental forecasts with cold, hard facts. (And yet, and yet . . . in order to be perceived by us, these cold, hard facts must first be warmed in the microwave ovens of our minds.) Thus, concludes Buchanan: "Costs that are influential for behavior do not exist; they are never realized; they cannot be measured after the fact."[6] The dream becomes reality, but the reality is always different from the dream, at least to this extent: the dream could not be measured; the reality can be. Supposedly.

Buchanan argues that the choice-influenced costs that are subsequently imposed on people as a result of some previous decision are in some sense objective and measurable — so many forfeited dollars of income, for example[7] — but these real-world costs did not affect the original decision in any way. Yet even this doffing of the economist's cap to objective cost theory may be overly respectful, given the presuppositions of modern subjectivist economics. The *meaning* of these objective, choice-influenced costs — e.g., accounting costs — must be *subjectively evaluated* by the person who personally bears them. A number in a ledger is supposed to convey accurate and *economically relevant* information in order for it to be effective as a summary of past events. The individual who pays an accountant thinks he is getting something for his money. What is he getting? A bunch of numbers on a page? Or information? The individual must interpret the significance of this information. There is no escape from subjectivism.

---

5. Vern Poythress, "A Biblical View of Mathematics," in Gary North (ed.), *Foundations of Christian Scholarship: Essays in the Van Til Perspective* (Vallecito, California: Ross House Books, 1976), pp. 159-88.

6. *Ibid.*, p. vii.

7. Even here, who can be sure just how many dollars were actually forfeited as a result of the decision? Would the person's *perceived* alternative use of his money have been as wise (high return) as the best opportunity the market *objectively* offered at the time?

The Roads Untravelled

Consider your own situation. You are still reading this essay. You still have faith. Let us consider a hypothetical possibility. With the time you spend reading this essay (assuming you stick with it to the bitter end), you might be able to think of an investment strategy that would make you rich, but because of something you will read here, you will never think of it or have the courage to risk it. On the other hand, you may also avoid an investment that really would bankrupt you. Unlike the man in the story of the lady and the tiger, you have the option of ignoring both doors; instead, you choose to read this essay. But you could have opened a door. Which would it have been, the lady or the tiger? You cannot know for sure. You will never know. You can only guess. So, what is the true cost of reading this essay? Life with the lady or a brief but colorful encounter with the tiger?

If we take seriously the modern economist's discussion of costs and choices, we may find our world disturbing. We never really know what our actions are costing us, assuming that it is true that there is no way to relate our subjective evaluations before we act with objective costs after we act. This disturbing lack of certainty can be relieved, however: "And we know that all things work together for good to them that love God, to them who are the called according to his purpose" (Rom. 8:28). But this suggestion is hardly helpful to the modern humanistic economist.

We can of course sit around moaning and groaning about a past cost: the abandoned dream that might have come true. We can worry retroactively about what our decision has cost us. But the cost that really counted — "counted" is in fact misleading, since there was nothing objective to count — at the moment of our decision was imposed at that moment. What is past is past. Paul wrote: ". . . forgetting those things which are behind, and reaching forth unto those things which are before" (Phil. 3:13). This is what the economist says of all decisions. Decision-makers are necessarily forward-looking. The past is gone forever. We must do the best we can with whatever we have today. This is the doctrine of *sunk costs*.[8]

This is not to say that we do not bear the objective costs that are imposed by a previous decision. We do. Even if we do not perceive

---

8. Gary North, *An Introduction to Christian Economics* (Nutley, New Jersey: Craig Press, 1973), ch. 26: "Urban Renewal and the Doctrine of Sunk Costs."

these costs, we bear them. A madman may not understand that he is not Napoleon, but he bears the social costs of his delusion when he is placed in an insane asylum. This is why there can be no escape from objective costs, any more than from subjective costs. But whether we accurately foresaw these costs or not, they are the *result* of that action, not its cause. These costs are borne by us objectively in history, yet they are always subjectively borne. One person may bear his burden in good cheer; another is utterly oppressed by what objectively (i.e., to an outside evaluator) appears to be the same magnitude of burden. Who is to say whose evaluation is correct? Only the omniscient God can do this, and His evaluation is not objectively measurable by the economist.

Some Odd Conclusions

An exclusively subjectivist view of cost and choice can lead to some very odd conclusions. (So, for that matter, can any other exclusive line of human reasoning.) G. F. Thirlby follows the logic of the one-time decision and concludes: "Cost is ephemeral. The cost involved in a particular decision loses its significance with the making of a decision because the decision displaces the alternative course of action."[9] He says emphatically that "the cost figure will never become objective; *i.e.*, it will never be possible to check whether the forecast of the alternative revenue was correct, because the alternative undertaking will never come into existence to produce the actual alternative revenue."[10]

Should You Fire Your Accountant?

What does this mean for the accounting profession? What does it do to the very concept of personal or corporate budgeting? He does not say, but he does not stop, either. Following the persuasive logic of subjectivism, Thirlby concludes that "The cost is not the things — *e.g., money — which will flow along certain channels* as a result of the decision; it is a loss, prospective or otherwise, to the person making the

---

9. G. F. Thirlby, "The Subjective Theory of Value and Accounting Cost," *Economica*, XII (Feb. 1946), p. 34; cited by Buchanan, *Cost and Choice*, p. 31. This essay is reprinted in James Buchanan and G. F. Thirlby (eds.), *L.S.E. Essays on Cost* (New York: New York University Press, 1981). L.S.E. stands for London School of Economics.

10. Thirlby, "The Ruler," *South African Journal of Economics*, XIV (Dec. 1946), p. 264; *ibid.*, p. 33.

decision. . . . cost *cannot be discovered by another person who eventually watches and records the flow of those things along those channels.*[11] Then of what objective use are accountants? Why was the advent of double-entry bookkeeping such a revolutionary event in the history of civilization?[12] He does not say.

Furthermore, what does such a view of budgeting do to the idea of the free market as a social institution for producing economic order — objective economic order? What does such a view do to the idea of the stock market, since money prices for shares are the means by which decision-makers evaluate the past performance of all other participants in the market? What does the price of a share of corporate stock have to do with expected future performance of that corporation's management? What is the link, if any, between present share prices and future economic performance? How do we get from subjective value to objective share prices and back again? How do we preserve our capital? For that matter, how do we measure our capital? How can we bridge the gap between the world of purely subjective costs and objective market prices? Buchanan insists: *"Only prices have objective, empirical content. . . ."*[13] Then precisely what empirical content does a price possess or reveal, and how do we discover it or make effective use of it — subjectively and objectively, personally and socially?

In short, what does an objective price have to do with individual subjective value? What is the *economic meaning* of a price — individually and socially, subjectively and objectively? (This is the number-one epistemological problem that has beset modern economics since the 1870's.)

The Realm of Possibility

Another example: Buchanan makes this statement: "Any profit opportunity that is within the realm of possibility but which is rejected becomes a cost of undertaking the preferred course of action."[14] But Buchanan neglects any consideration of the economics of a rejected opportunity that is not in fact — *objective* fact — within the realm of possibility. We normally call such an opportunity a *loss*. Wouldn't avoid-

---

11. Thirlby, "Subjective Theory," *ibid.*, p. 31.
12. Ludwig von Mises, *Human Action: A Treatise on Economics* (3rd ed.; Chicago: Regnery, 1966), p. 230.
13. Buchanan, *Cost and Choice*, p. 85.
14. *Ibid.*, p. 28.

ing it be a *benefit* of undertaking the preferred course of action? If the decision-maker's first choice is to reject the objectively impossible (i.e., unprofitable) course of action for whatever reason, and also to reject the second, objectively possible, course of action for whatever reason, won't he remain in the profit column overall? I do not want to press this line of reasoning too hard because it bogs us down too deeply in the philosophical problem of available and unavailable information, but we need to recognize at least the nature of the epistemological problem: *If everything is completely subjective at the moment of decision, what does "the realm of possibility" have to do with anything?* Maybe the decision-maker believes that could achieve something great if he just had the courage of his convictions, when in fact he would have gone bankrupt. Is his true cost the forfeited unattainable greatness or the forfeited inevitable bankruptcy? If all costs at the time of his decision are purely subjective, then his cost must be the forfeited greatness. This, clearly, is nutty—logical but nutty. So is any theory of cost and choice that is exclusively subjective.

The economist, no matter how hard he tries to tie human decisions exclusively to the action-taker's subjective evaluations, cannot escape the bedrock realm of possibility. It is his measuring rod for discussing cost, a "ruler" without which all economic discussion becomes theoretically impossible. On the other hand, no matter how hard he tries to make objective that realm of possibility, through probability theory and other statistical techniques, he cannot escape the inherent subjectivity of the decision of the acting individual who is responsible for his actions. The economist needs—yes, *needs*[15]—a scientific theory of cost that is both subjective and objective without being eternally dialectical. Such a theory does not exist. This is the heart of my critique of all previous discussions of the problem of social cost.

The Persistent Problem of Value

Economists, as self-consciously humanistic social scientists, claim to be defenders of a rational academic discipline. Most of them defend their methodology in terms of the assertion that it allows them to make accurate predictions of human actions under limited,

---

15. Few concepts are less acceptable to an economist that the concept of *need*. A need is something which is not negotiable, and for an economist, everything economic is defined as negotiable.

specified conditions.[16] These predictions are supposed to enable people to make economic decisions that are more profitable than decisions made by flipping a coin, consulting a fortune teller, or throwing darts at a wall covered with slips of paper, with each slip containing a different suggested course of action.

To make their claim believable, economists have to make a myriad of assumptions about reason, the human mind, the powers of observation, the external world, and the interrelationships between the mind and matter. These assumptions are very seldom spelled out by economists.[17] Epistemology, the fundamental question of all philosophy — "What can man know, and how can he know it?" — is not a popular topic within the economics profession.[18]

The Problem of Measurement

The advent of modern economics is generally dated from the early 1870's, when three scholars independently came to the same conclusion, namely, that economic value is *imputed*: the concept of *subjective* value.[19] Value, they concluded, is subjectively determined. It is not an objective quantity. The key unit of value is the value (subjective) of the marginal unit. The decision-maker asks himself: How much (objective) of *this* must I give up in order to obtain *that*? By 1900, virtually all non-Marxist economists had broken with the older objective value theories of the classical economists, such as the labor theory of value or the cost-of-production theory of value. By grounding economics on the subjective valuations of individual decision-makers, economists today believe that they have escaped from the intellectual dilemmas that had arisen as a result of classical economics' objective value theory. (The most famous one was Adam Smith's "water-diamond paradox.")[20]

16. Milton Friedman, *Essays in Positive Economics* (University of Chicago Press, 1953), ch. 1: "The Methodology of Positive Economics."

17. Gary North, "Economics: From Reason to Intuition," in North, *Foundations of Christian Scholarship*.

18. Fritz Machlup, "Introductory Remarks," *American Economic Review, Papers and Proceedings*, XLII (May 1952), p. 34.

19. The three scholars were William Stanley Jevons (England), Carl Menger (Austria), and Leon Walras (Switzerland). See R. S. Hovey, *The Rise of the Marginal Utility School, 1870-1889* (Lawrence: University of Kansas Press, 1960); Emil Kauder, *A History of Marginal Utility* (Princeton, New Jersey: Princeton University Press, 1965).

20. "The things which have the greatest value in use have frequently little or no value in exchange. . . . Nothing is more useful than water: . . . A diamond, on the

They are self-deluded. They have not escaped such problems. They have merely created new intellectual problems for themselves — problems that are inescapable, given their commitment to the ancient ideal of humanism: "man as the measure of all things" (Protagoras).[21] (The careful economist would add this cautious corollary, "assuming for the sake of argument that there can be such a thing as a measure in economics.")

If man is the measure of all things, and man himself is a subjective, changing, and ultimately "free spirit," then man cannot serve as a measure of anything. Measures must be fixed, but there are no remaining fixed measures in modern thought — not even the speed of light (at least in quantum physics).[22] They are no longer fixed in biology: Darwinism's world of process has triumphed over fixed measures.[23] Measures are no longer fixed in morals.[24] They are no longer fixed in epistemology.[25] They do not exist in economics.[26]

---

contrary, has scarce any value in use; . . ." Adam Smith, *Wealth of Nations* (1776), end of Chapter IV. The paradox: Why is it that something as valuable to human life as water is worth so little in comparison to diamonds, which are not really crucial to mankind? The marginalist-subjectivist's solution: "We never choose between water in general and diamonds in general. We choose between a specific amount of water and a specific amount of diamonds at a specific point in time. In the middle of a desert, someone might choose a drink of water over a bag of diamonds. Normally he wouldn't. Water is abundant compared to diamonds most of the time. Thus, the decision-maker's subjective evaluation at a particular moment of time is crucial, not the hypothetical (and non-existent) objective value of water in general vs. the objective value of diamonds in general."

21. Assertion 5 of Humanist Manifesto I (1933) states: "Humanism asserts that the nature of the universe depicted by modern science makes unacceptable any supernatural or cosmic guarantees of human values." *Humanist Manifestos I and II* (Buffalo, New York: Prometheus Press, 1973), p. 8.

22. I refer here to the startling theory of subatomic physics, verified by numerous experiments, known as Bell's Theorem, which states that at the subatomic level, all events must be simultaneously related to each other across the entire universe. See Nick Herbert, *Quantum Reality: Beyond the New Physics* (Garden City, New York: Anchor Press/Doubleday, 1985), p. 214.

23. Assertion 2 of Humanist Manifesto I states: "Humanism believes that man is a part of nature and that he has emerged as the result of a continuous process." *Idem.*

24. Forty years later, Humanist Manifesto II stated: "Ethics is *autonomous* and *situational*, needing no theological or ideological sanction. Ethics stems from human need and interest." *Ibid.*, p. 17.

25. Delwin Brown, Ralph E. James, and Gene Reeves (eds.), *Process Philosophy and Christian Thought* (Indianapolis: Bobbs-Merrill, 1971).

26. Ludwig von Mises writes: "The truth is that there are only variables and no constants. It is pointless to talk of variables where there are no invariables." Mises, *Theory and History: An Interpretation of Social and Economic Evolution* (New Haven, Connecticut: Yale University Press, 1957), p. 13. This was reprinted by the Mises Institute in 1985.

There are no measures at all. There may be discrete, permanent numbers — even this is highly speculative[27] — but there are no measures. Everything is on a continuum, nothing is discrete.[28] This absence of measures leads, step by step, to radical subjectivism and radical relativism. Heraclitus' river of flux is at last definitively eroding Parmenides' fixed shore line. Chaos looms.[29]

Having said this, the economist nevertheless resists making the obvious conclusion regarding the relativity of all measurement: *the denial of the possibility of relevant scientific precision.* Vainly, he protests: "There are economists who have propounded the relativity of measure. Apparently, they failed to see that this view saps the entire foundation upon which the economic science rests."[30] Sap! He, too, is inescapably one of these epistemologically short-sighted economists.

Consider the question of environmental pollution. The consistent economist — an exceedingly rare creature — must conclude: "One man's polluted stream is another man's profit for the fiscal year, and there is no conceivable scientific way to say which is better for society in general, for there is no scientific way of identifying such an entity as society in general." To admit this, however, would be to commit methodological suicide in public. Modern economics has in fact committed suicide, but it has done so in private. Economists do not leap from tall buildings during the lunch hour. They much prefer to do away with themselves in private — through an overdose of qualifications.

The Great Debate

In *The Dominion Covenant: Genesis,* I discussed the problem of objective and subjective value at considerable length. I analyzed the important critique of Cambridge Professor A. C. Pigou by London School of Economics Professor Lionel Robbins, and then the subsequent debate between Robbins and Roy Harrod.[31] To review very briefly, Pigou, in his pioneering study of welfare economics, had argued that since each additional monetary unit's worth of income is worth less to a man than the previous unit, the value of one additional unit of income to a millionaire will necessarily be less than its

---

27. Poythress, "A Biblical View of Mathematics," *op. cit.*
28. Nicholas Georgescu-Roegen, *The Entropy Law and the Economic Process* (Cambridge, Massachusetts: Harvard University Press, 1971), ch. 3.
29. James Gleick, *Chaos: Making a New Science* (New York: Viking, 1987).
30. Georgescu-Roegen, *Entropy Law,* p. 111.
31. Gary North, *The Dominion Covenant: Genesis* (Tyler, Texas: Institute for Christian Economics, 1982), ch. 4.

value to a poverty-stricken man. Thus, Pigou concluded, the State can increase the aggregate social welfare of the community by taking a portion of the rich man's income in the high income brackets and transferring this money to the poor man. This tax will not hurt the rich man very much (he puts so little value on the last bit of money he receives), while the marginal income will greatly benefit the poor man (who has so little income to begin with).

Robbins replied in 1932 that the argument is invalid as a scientific statement. Since all value is subjective, we cannot, as scientists, make interpersonal comparisons of subjective utility. There is no objective column of figures to add up when we are talking about subjective value. (If true, then the science of accounting has no logical connection with either the science of economics or the vocation of business. This obvious conclusion, however, is too radical for most economists even to discuss.)[32] Therefore, economists cannot legitimately say anything about the increase or decrease of "social value" which is produced by taking a percentage of the rich man's income in the higher brackets and giving this money to the poor man.[33] No one in the economics profession has ever proposed a rational answer to Robbins' argument, yet hardly any economist — I would say no economist — has been able to develop a comprehensive economic theory in terms of this argument, including Robbins.[34]

Roy Harrod[35] complained in his rejoinder in 1938 that if Robbins

---

32. Gary North, "There's No (Autonomous) Accounting for Taste," *Biblical Economics Today*, XI (June/July 1988).

33. Lionel Robbins, *An Essay on the Nature and Significance of Economic Science* (2nd ed.; New York: St. Martins, [1935]).

34. Writes Richard Posner: "The 'interpersonal comparison of utilities' is anathema to the modern economist, and rightly so, because there is no metric for making such a comparison." Had he let it go at that, he would have been honest. But he knows what this would mean: the impossibility of formulating any social policy based on truly scientific economics, so he illegitimately adds the following unproven and unprovable statement: "But the interpersonal comparison of values, in the economic sense, is feasible, although difficult, even when the values are not being compared in an explicit market." Posner, *Economics of Justice*, p. 79. Apparently, all the economist needs to do is change the word "utility" to "values," and he goes from the impossible to the merely difficult. Let me tell you something about humanistic economists: *they cheat.* Maybe not self-consciously, but the resulting confusion is the same. At the very least, the economics profession is self-deceived.

35. Harrod later became Sir Roy Harrod. He was John Maynard Keynes' hand-picked successor as editor of *The Economic Journal*. Together, they controlled access to England's most prestigious academic economics journal for half a century. Like Keynes, he never received an academic degree in economics. He did study economics with Keynes for one year, 1922-23. Neither of them ever earned a degree above

were really serious about this argument, then he would have to abandon the idea that it is possible for the economist, as a scientist, to make *any* recommendations concerning proper economic policy, since any State-imposed policy always hurts some participants and benefits others. If it is impossible to make interpersonal comparisons of subjective utility, then economists must remain forever silent about the aggregate (social) economic benefits and costs of any decision by an individual or the State.[36]

Robbins was correct in his criticism of Pigou, given the presuppositions of modern, subjectivist economics. Harrod was equally correct in his criticism of Robbins, namely, that *his conclusion would destroy all applied economic science.* Robbins subsequently backed away from this conclusion concerning the inability of economists to say anything about social welfare or the benefits of social policies in general.[37] But he never explained how he could logically back away from this conclusion, and he lived until 1985. Even more inconsistently, he also never backed away from his critique of Pigou's argument in favor of graduated ("progressive") income taxation.

The implications of Robbins' position are radical, and economists have long been unwilling to face them, including Robbins. Buchanan once wrote that "it is precisely the problems posed in modern welfare economics that force the economist to come to grips with the basic issues of political and legal philosophy."[38] These issues also force the more astute economist to come to grips with the fundamental issue of all philosophy: epistemology. But the ranks of the economics profession are filled with men and women who have no training in epistemology and care nothing about it.[39] They never answer by means of modern subjectivism the fundamental philosophical question: "What can men know, and how can they know it?" They operate in

---

the bachelor's degree: Keynes' was in mathematics and Harrod's was in the humanities. See Don Patinkin, *Anticipations of the General Theory? And Other Essays on Keynes* (University of Chicago Press, 1982), pp. xv, xvi. John Neville Keynes, Maynard's father, and Pigou personally paid for young Maynard's salary when they hired him to teach economics at King's College, Cambridge in 1908. Keynes, Sr. was chairman of the department for many years.

36. R. F. Harrod, "Scope and Method of Economics," *Economic Journal*, XLVIII (1938), p. 397.

37. Lionel Robbins, "Interpersonal Comparisons of Utility: A Comment," *ibid.*, pp. 635-37.

38. James Buchanan, "Good Economics — Bad Law," *Virginia Law Review*, LX (1974), p. 488.

39. An exception is the Austrian School.

terms of an implicit though hidden dialecticism between objective and subjective value theory.

Social Cost

Pigou also raised another issue concerning welfare economics. It is a variant of the earlier problem of wealth redistribution. It has become known in the economics profession as "the problem of social cost." Pigou argued that there are cases of market failure[40] in which private benefits from a particular activity impose costs on third parties. Pollution is the obvious example, although there are many others, he said. The benefits to the polluter are immediate and direct, but there is no market-produced incentive for him to cease polluting as long as his costs of operation are less than expected revenues.[41] Part of these costs are borne by someone else. At most, the polluter bears only part of the costs (stinging eyes, for example), but he reaps all of the rewards (lower production costs). He continues to pollute the environment. Total costs in the community — *social* costs — are therefore greater than his personal private costs. Followers of Pigou's analysis frequently argue that the State should redistribute this "stolen" wealth back to the original owners, perhaps through a tax on polluters and tax reductions for victims, so as to balance total social benefits (from production) and total social costs.

There is a hidden problem with this line of reasoning, one which was not discovered for almost half a century. Buchanan points to it: "The Pigouvian norm aims at bringing marginal private costs, *as these influence choice,* into line with social costs, *as these are objectively measured.* Only with objective measurability can the proper corrective devices be introduced."[42] The problem is this: choice-influencing costs are exclusively subjective, according to modern economic theory. Only choice-influenced costs can be "objectively measured" (maybe). How can the judges impose objective costs that will be appropriate — scientifically appropriate — to reduce the existing level of pollution to a socially appropriate level?

This raises many other questions. How can the civil judges know what is the socially appropriate level of pollution? How can they pre-

---

40. Tyler Cowen (ed.), *The Theory of Market Failure: A Critical Examination* (Fairfax, Virginia: George Mason University Press, 1988).

41. Yes, yes, I know: "the present value of an expected future stream of income, discounted by the prevailing rate of interest." But sometimes I prefer to write in English.

42. Buchanan, *Cost and Choice,* p. 74.

serve the legal predictability of the courts if they cannot specify in advance the appropriate penalties? How can they be even vaguely confident that "the punishment fits the crime" of polluting? But these questions did not get asked for half a century, although they were implied by Robbins' original critique. What finally got scholars to start asking them was an essay by R. H. Coase.

The Coase Theorem[43]

Economists today freely acknowledge that this was one of the most important scholarly essays in the profession written during the 1960's.[44] Without warning, it hit both the economics profession and the world of legal theory. Coase had been the author of an important study of the firm, published a generation earlier in 1937.[45] For the next two decades, he published very little in professional scholarly journals.[46] In 1959, he published a significant article on the Federal Communications Commission.[47] Then, like a bombshell, came his essay on social cost. It has become a standard in modern economics, still found in other scholars' footnotes two decades after its publication. (Few essays that appear in scholarly economics journals ever get cited by anyone else, and certainly not by numerous economists. After five years, a scholarly essay in economics, assuming it ever was noticed, ceases to be cited, except for those regarded as classics.)[48]

Richard Posner goes so far as to argue in his widely read textbook on law and economics that Coase's essay and one by Guido Calabresi[49]

---

43. I am including this section as an example of the sort of reasoning that is common among free-market economists. I am not suggesting that non-economists need to master the details of Coase's arguments.

44. R. H. Coase, "The Problem of Social Cost," *Journal of Law and Economics*, III (1960), pp. 1-44.

45. Coase, "The Nature of the Firm," *Economica*, IV (1937), pp. 386-405.

46. Coase, "Business Organization and the Accountant," *The Accountant* (Oct.-Dec. 1938), a series of a dozen brief essays written for non-economists; a shortened version is reprinted by Buchanan and Thirlby in *L.S.E. Essays on Cost*; Coase, "The Marginal Cost Controversy," *Economica*, XIII (Aug. 1946). A bibliography of Coase's works appears in "On the Resignation of Ronald H. Coase," *Journal of Law and Economics*, XXVI (April 1983). The bulk of his academic articles came after 1960.

47. Coase, "The Federal Communications Commission," *The Journal of Law and Economics*, II (1959). This essay is reprinted in Eirik G. Furubotn and Svetozar Pejovich (eds.), *The Economics of Property Rights* (Cambridge, Massachusetts: Ballinger, 1974).

48. A. W. Coats, "The Role of Scholarly Journals in the History of Economics: An Essay," *Journal of Economic Literature*, X (1972), p. 42.

49. Guido Calabresi, "Some Thoughts on Risk Distribution and the Law of Torts," *Yale Law Journal*, vol. 70 (1961), pp. 499ff.

were instrumental in launching an entire academic discipline, law and economics,[50] "the application of the theories and empirical methods of economics to the legal system across the boards."[51] The Coase Theorem (he capitalizes it, indicating his respect for it) "established a framework for analyzing the assignment of property rights and liability in economic terms. This opened a vast field of legal doctrine to fruitful economic analysis."[52] Two scholarly journals, both published by the University of Chicago, have been heavily influenced by the Coase theorem: *The Journal of Law and Economics* and *The Journal of Legal Studies.* (This is understandable, given the fact that Coase edited the *Journal of Law and Economics* for 19 years, 1965-1983, and the *Journal of Legal Studies* is a sister publication.)[53] As Posner wrote in 1981, "Until recently, then, utilitarianism held sway in legal theory, but overt economic analysis was rare. The position is now reversed."[54]

Coase's essay was perhaps the key one in the revival of interest in the question of pollution and economics, as well as a crucially important contribution to a free market theory of property rights. And, let me say from the outset, it is a dangerously flawed essay. Few economists have seen its flaws. The first professional economist I ever heard even mention a really critical comment against it — essentially, the same criticism I had also come up with — could not get it published in a conventional professional economics journal, and he had to wait three years after he discussed his criticism with me before he saw it in print.[55]

Coase vs. Pigou

Coase summarized the state of the debate — it had long ceased to be debated very much — as of 1960. Pigou's statement of the problem

---

50. A. Mitchell Polinsky, *Introduction to Law and Economics* (Boston: Little, Brown, 1983).

51. Richard A. Posner, *Economic Analysis of Law* (Boston: Little, Brown, 1986), p. 19.

52. *Ibid.*, p. 20.

53. For a survey of this literature, see the footnotes in the article by Elizabeth Hoffman and Matthew Spitzer, "The Coase Theorem: Some Experimental Tests," *Journal of Law and Economics*, XXV (April 1982), pp. 73-98. The rigor of the limiting assumptions made by the authors of this article is much greater than Coase's own formulation; the article is also far less readable or usable.

54. Posner, *Economics of Justice*, p. 51.

55. Walter Block, "Coase and Demsetz on Private Property Rights," *Journal of Libertarian Studies*, I, No. 2 (1977), pp. 111-15. Dr. Block is presently the director of the Fraser Institute in British Columbia, Canada.

had given the problem of social cost its traditional framework. This discussion was categorized under the general rubric of "externalities." The term refers to the imposition of a firm's costs of operation on those who are not owners of the stream of future income generated by the production process. In other words, these victims are *external* to the firm or production unit, but not external to its costs of operation. Almost without exception, the economists' discussion of externalities ended with a consideration of what government measures are appropriate to reduce or eliminate these externalities. The conclusions reached by most economists, based on Pigou's analysis in *The Economics of Welfare* (4th ed., 1932; originally published in 1920), were as follows, Coase summarized: the producer of pollution (smoke, noise, etc.) should 1) pay damages to those injured, or 2) have a tax imposed on his production by the civil government, or 3) have his factory excluded from residential districts.[56] Coase's article broke with this tradition.

Aaron Levine summarizes Coase's theoretical breakthrough: "Assuming zero transaction costs and economic rationality, Coase, in his seminal work, demonstrated that the market mechanism is capable of eliminating negative externalities without the necessity of governmentally imposed liability rules."[57] Furthermore, the theorem leads to the conclusion that "if transactions are costless, the initial assignment of a property right will not determine the ultimate use of the property."[58] Free market economists of the "Chicago School" have increasingly sided with Coase. (What is also rather startling is that traditional Jewish law had adopted the basic features of the Coase theorem many centuries earlier; English law had not.)[59]

The problem is, of course, that *there are and always will be transaction costs.*[60] Or, I should say, this is *a* problem. The major problem is that this theorem assigns zero economic value — and therefore zero relevance — to the sense of moral and legal right associated with a willful violation of private ownership. It ignores the economic rele-

---

56. Coase, "Social Cost," p. 1.

57. Aaron Levine, *Free Enterprise and Jewish Law: Aspects of Jewish Business Ethics* (New York: Ktav Publishing House, Yeshiva University Press, 1980), p. 59.

58. Posner, *Economic Analysis of Law*, p. 7.

59. Yehoshua Liebermann, "The Coase Theorem in Jewish Law," *Journal of Legal Studies*, X (June 1981), pp. 293-303.

60. For a brief introduction to the question of transaction costs, see Oliver E. Williamson, "Transaction-Cost Economics: The Governance of Contractual Relations," *Journal of Law and Economics*, XXII (October 1979), pp. 233-61.

vance of the public's sense of moral outrage when there is no enforcement by the civil government of owners' legal immunities from invasion, even if done in the name of some "more efficient" social good or social goal. This is why I conclude that the Coase theorem is one of the most morally insidious pieces of academic nonsense ever to hit the economics profession; worse, it has infected — and I do mean *infected* — the thinking of a generation of very bright and very glib free market economists and legal theorists. Coase has served as the Typhoid Mary of Chicago School economists for about three decades. His essay has drastically compromised the academic case for liberty. It has imposed private costs on those of us who are attempting to make a case for free market economics. In this sense, Coase's theorem is a form of pollution. But because it is intellectual pollution, those injured cannot take him to court and sue for damages. The best we can do is offer a pollution-control system: proof that his whole argument is specious.

Coase fully recognized from the beginning the nature of the technical economic problem he had raised, namely, *the impossibility of a world in which there are no transaction costs.* (The moral issues related to property rights he dismissed without a moment's public hesitation as irrelevant to economic analysis.) Therefore, he allows civil judges to intervene to settle disputes. But there is a problem here: Coase cannot escape that nagging problem ignored by Pigou and all welfare economists, namely, *the problem of interpersonal comparisons of subjective utility.* Coase's "scientific" case against Pigou rests on the implicit assertion that men, especially judges, can make such comparisons in their act of formulating social policy. The only professional response deeply critical of Coase has been made by "Austrian School" economists, who recognize the weakness of Chicago School presuppositions concerning interpersonal comparisons. Still, their criticism leaves much to be desired, for if taken seriously, it would become impossible to defend the idea of government penalties against polluters.

The Ethical Pea Beneath the Neutral Shell

The astounding fact about the Coase theorem is that every economist knows that there are no cases of exchanges in which there are zero transaction costs. They also know that the Coase theorem applies *only* where there are zero transaction costs. Yet they do not identify the Coase theorem as an instance of curious but utterly irrelevant academic speculation. Instead, they try to work with his theorem. Richard Posner, an economist and a judge in the U.S. Appeals Court (Seventh Circuit), admits that the Coase theorem applies only to zero transaction cost situations, yet he has devoted much of his academic career to pursuing the economic implications of the Coase theorem in the field of law. He knows that Coase's initial assumption — that transaction costs are zero — cannot be true in the real world. Posner writes:

> The economist does not merely decree that absolute rights [of ownership — G.N.] be created and then fall silent as to where they should be vested. To be sure, if market transactions were costless, the economist would not care where a right was initially vested. The process of voluntary exchange would costlessly reallocate it to whoever valued it the most. But once the unrealistic assumption of zero transaction costs is abandoned, the assignment of rights becomes determinate. If transaction costs are positive (though presumably low, for otherwise it would be inefficient to create an absolute right), the wealth-maximization principle requires the initial vesting of rights in those who are likely to value them most, so as to minimize transaction costs. This is the economic reason for giving a worker the right to sell his labor and a woman the right to determine her sexual partners. If assigned randomly to strangers, these rights would generally (not invariably) be repurchased by the worker and the woman; the costs of the rectifying transaction can be avoided if the right is assigned at the outset to the user who values it most.[61]

Posner openly admits that in some cases, even where transaction costs are low, the worker or the woman in his example would not (i.e., could not afford to) repurchase these rights of ownership. This follows from his definition of value: "The most important thing to bear in mind about the concept of value is that it is based on what people are willing to pay for something rather than on the happiness they would derive from having it. . . . The individual who would like very much to have some good but is unwilling or unable to pay anything for it — perhaps because he is destitute — does not value the good in the sense in which I am using the term 'value.' "[62] The conclusion is obvious, and he does not hesitate to draw it: "Equivalently, the wealth of society is the aggregate satisfaction of those preferences

61. Posner, *Economics of Justice*, p. 71. For a critique of Posner's approach to the law, see Buchanan, "Good Economics — Bad Law," *Virginia Law Review, op. cit.* See also the biting and incisive essay by Arthur Allen Leff, "Economic Analysis of Law: Some Realism About Nominalism," *ibid.*, pp. 451-82.

62. *Ibid.*, pp. 60, 61.

(the only ones that have ethical weight in a system of wealth maximization) that are backed up by money, that is, that are registered in a market." In short, people's demonstrated preferences — money on the line — are the only ones that possess "ethical weight" in his definition of wealth-maximization. Does this include marriage? Of course. Does this include games of chance? Of course. "Much of economic life is still organized on barter principles. The 'marriage market,' child rearing, and a friendly game of bridge are examples. These services have value which could be monetized by reference to substitute services sold in explicit markets or in other ways."[63]

Question: Who makes the initial distribution of an ownership right to whomever "values it the most"? How does this sovereign agent know scientifically which potential owners "are likely to value them [ownership rights] the most"? In short: *By what standard of value does he make the initial distribution?* Dead silence from Chicago School economists. To say anything at this point would be a public admission that economic science is no longer value-free. The Coase theorem must be seen for what it is: an important component in a giant academic shell game. The ethical pea is always concealed beneath the seemingly neutral scientific shell of cost-benefit analysis. Watch what the economist does, not what he says he is doing. He is invariably making interpersonal comparisons of subjective utility every time he recommends a policy decision.

The debate over social costs raises once again the ancient debate between objective and subjective knowledge. It is one of the persistent antinomies in all humanist thought. The epistemological problem of social cost is an *ethical* problem, and as such, humanists cannot solve it "scientifically."

Reciprocal Harm

Coase reformulated the terms of the debate over externalities. "The question is commonly thought of as one in which A inflicts harm on B and what has been decided is: how should we restrain A? But this is wrong. We are dealing with a problem of a reciprocal nature. To avoid the harm to B would inflict harm on A. The real question that has to be decided is: should A be allowed to harm B or should B be allowed to harm A? The problem is to avoid the more serious harm."[64]

---

63. *Ibid.*, p. 61.
64. Coase, "Social Cost," p. 2.

To begin with, such reasoning is perverse, if accepted as a methodological standard governing economic analysis in all instances involving economic action. It would be just as easy to say of kidnapping that any restrictions on kidnapping by the State harm the kidnapper, and that a lack of restrictions harms the victims. If we are going to build an economic system in terms of the supposedly "reciprocal nature of harm" — that each economic actor suffers harm when he is restricted from acting according to his immediate whim — then economics becomes positively wicked, not value-free, in its attempt to sort out just how much harm the courts will allow each party to impose on the other.

There are some areas of life — areas governed by biblical morality — in which such "cost-benefit analyses" must not even be contemplated. For example, any attempt to impose cost-benefit analyses on competing techniques of mass genocide, including abortion, is demonic, not scientifically neutral. Whether a genocidal society should adopt either gas chambers or lethal injections for adults, or either saline solutions or suction devices for unborn infants, cannot be solved in terms of comparative rates of cost-efficiency, for the economist always ignores a major "exogenous variable": the wrath of God. God will efficiently judge those individuals who promote all such cost-efficient systems, as well as societies that adopt them. If legal restrictions against mass genocide harm the potential mass murderers, this is all to the good. Society faces no "reduction in social benefits" whatsoever. Justice does cost something, but the net economic effect is positive, whether the economist sees this or not. There is no reduction in net social benefits as a result of the thwarted goals of the now-restricted (or previously executed) genocidal technocrats.

Coase offered the following example of reciprocal harm. What about cattle that stray onto another man's property and destroy crops? This, it should be noted, is precisely the issue dealt with by Exodus 22:5. Coase writes: "If it is inevitable that some cattle will stray, an increase in the supply of meat can only be obtained at the expense of a decrease in the supply of crops. The nature of the choice is clear: meat or crops?"[65]

This appears to be correct economic analysis, as far as it goes. It forces us to think about the problem in terms of what members of the society must give up, meat vs. crops. But his next sentence is the

---

65. *Idem.*

very heart of the problem, and he never shows how economists — or anyone else, for that matter — can, as scientists, make an economically rational (i.e., neutral) choice in the name of society: crops vs. meat. Indeed, humanistic economics cannot possibly answer this question because of the inability of economists, as scientists, to make interpersonal comparisons of subjective utility.[66]

Subjective Value vs. Social Policy

Coase never comes to grips with this problem. "What answer should be given is, of course, not clear until we know the value of what is obtained as well as the value of what is sacrificed to attain it."[67] *Value?* As economists, we need to ask ourselves several questions: Value to whom? Society as a whole? The value to the cattle owner? The value to the farmer? Also, how can we make such estimates of economic value, since economic value is subjective? Questions of economic value are the main problems raised by his paper, yet he cannot answer them by means of the "scientific economics" he proclaims. No economist can. Economist Peter Lewin has gone to the heart of the matter when he writes in a withering critique of Coase that

costs are individual and private and cannot be "social." The social-cost concept requires the summation of individual costs, which is impossible if costs are seen in utility terms. The notion of social cost as reflected by market prices (or even more problematically by hypothetical prices in the absence of a market for the item) has validity only in conditions so far removed from reality as to make its use as a general tool of policy analysis highly suspect. . . .

The foregoing suggests that any perception of efficiency at the social level is illusory. And the essential thread in all the objections to the efficiency concept, be it wealth effects, distortions, or technological changes, is the refusal by economists to make interpersonal comparisons of utility. Social cost falls to the ground precisely because individual evaluations of the sacrifice involved in choosing among options cannot be compared.[68]

---

66. In other words, we cannot make scientific comparisons of the utility gained by one person vs. the utility thereby forfeited by another man. There is no unit of "utility measurement" which is common to both men. We cannot as neutral scientists legitimately say that one man has gained greater utility (a subjective evaluation on his part) than another man has lost (another subjective evaluation). I discuss this problem in *Dominion Covenant: Genesis*, ch. 4.

67. Coase, "Social Cost," p. 2.

68. Peter Lewin, "Pollution Externalities: Social Cost and Strict Liability," *Cato Journal*, II (Spring 1982), pp. 220, 222.

The inability of anyone to make scientifically valid interpersonal comparisons of subjective utility has once again smashed all the hopes of the free market's humanist defenders to deal "scientifically" with a problem of social policy. The more astute "anarcho-capitalists" have understood this, and have thereby abandoned the very idea of social utility and social costs. They have also abandoned the idea of civil government.[69] They have not been able to demonstrate how people can deal successfully with the problems created by such technological developments as the internal combustion engine. But at least they are consistent. They do not search for "fools gold" intellectual solutions to "scientifically" insoluble problems. They do not search for pseudo-market solutions — "What would the correct market price be in the absence of a market?" — or solutions involving the hypothetical (and scientifically impossible) ability of judges to make scientifically valid social cost-benefit analyses in settling disputes. *There can be no scientifically valid answers to such social problems, given the presuppositions of modern, subjectivistic, individualistic economic theory.* Yet the approach used by Coase and his academic followers to deal with these questions assumes that there *are* scientifically valid answers to them.

Since there are no "neutral, scientific" answers, Coase's whole essay is an exercise in intellectual gymnastics — an illusion of scientific precision.[70] Nevertheless, it is considered a classic essay — a pioneering work which literally created a new approach in both economics and legal theory. What is revealing is that the economics profession as a whole has refused to face up to this problem, and it took over two decades for a critical analysis based on a 45-year-old observation by Lionel Robbins to be applied to the Coase theorem by an assistant professor (untenured) at an obscure university to be published in a new intellectual journal that has no following within the academic community.[71] Such is academia: academia nuts.

---

69. "There is no government solution to pollution or to the common-pool problem because government is the problem." Gerald P. O'Driscoll, Jr., "Pollution, Libertarianism, and the Law," *ibid,* p. 50.

70. This same illusion of scientific precision is at the heart of virtually every professional journal in economics, every mathematical equation, and every call for scientific policy-making issued by members of the economists' guild. The day an economist admits to himself that no economist can make interpersonal comparisons of subjective utility is the day that his public claims of economics' objective, scientific precision make him a charlatan. The day before, he was simply ignorant.

71. I came across Lewin's article only after the bulk of this chapter was written. In my 1973 book, *An Introduction to Christian Economics,* I briefly referred to "R. H. Coase's clever sophistry," (p. 94n), but did not have space to pursue his arguments in detail. Some readers may think I should have let it go at that, or devoted the necessary space in some place other than here.

Property Rights

The meaning of "property rights" is this: individuals or associations represented by individuals possess a legal right to prevent others from stealing, invading, destroying, or otherwise interfering with their property. Owners therefore possess a legal right *to exclude others* from the use of specified property. This is analogous to covenantal forms of exclusion: the State's right to exclude non-citizens from voting; the married person's right to exclude others from sexual access to the partner; and the church's right to exclude non-members or non-Christians from the communion table. The phrase "property rights" means that there is a legally enforceable "bundle of rights" that is associated with specific forms of property.

Coase's essay undermines the very concept of private property rights. He offers a detailed, carefully constructed argument concerning the marginal gains to the cattleman vs. the marginal losses to the farmer from a roaming steer. What the essay demonstrates, *assuming that the psychological costs to the farmer of the cattleman's violation of his property rights are never taken into consideration*, is this: excluding transaction costs and information costs,[72] as well as assuming perfect competition (omniscience), *the gain or loss to society is the same*, whether the cattleman compensates the farmer for the value of the lost crops, should the cattle be left to roam, or the farmer compensates the cattleman for the higher costs of meat production, if the cattle are kept away from the farmer's crops (higher feed costs, costs of fencing, etc.). Again, assuming "conditions of perfect competition," Coase concludes: "Whether the cattle-raiser pays the farmer to leave the land uncultivated or himself rents the land by paying the land-owner an amount slightly greater than the farmer would pay (if the farmer was himself renting the land), the final result would be the same and would maximize the value of production."[73]

Given his initial, unrealistic hypothetical assumptions about free goods — transaction costs, information costs, and perfect competition — this conclusion initially appears to be correct, *assuming that farmers have no commitment to a sense of justice concerning property rights*. It also assumes that *members of such a society do not and will not suffer any addi-*

---

72. ". . . when the damaging business has to pay for all damage caused *and* the pricing system works smoothly (strictly this means that the operation of the pricing system is without cost)." Coase, "Social Cost," p. 2.

73. *Ibid.*, p. 6.

tional economic losses when the civil government refuses to make cattle owners responsible for the damage their animals cause. Both assumptions are implicit to Coase's thesis, and both are categorically incorrect. Coase begins with an unreal world in which transaction costs are defined away, and from this he draws his equally unrealistic conclusions.[74]

I say that his conclusion initially appears to be correct — that in a zero-cost world, the outcome of the bargaining process would be the same, the value of cattle vs. the value of crops. Yet in a perceptive essay by Donald Regan, we learn that Coase has no warrant for making this conclusion. Coase assumes that the bargaining process will produce the same economic results, but why should he? Regan says that Coase offers no model of how this bargaining process would inevitably produce such identical results in the absence of specified and enforceable property rights. For example, sometimes a bargainer makes economic threats of non-cooperation that must be occasionally enforced in order to persuade the other party that he should take such threats seriously, even if the actual carrying out of the threat may injure the threat-maker in the short run. How does Coase know what the short-run or long-run outcome of a bargaining process will be? He doesn't.[75] This is simply another way of saying that we cannot confidently make social and economic evaluations of real-world events by abstracting economic theory from temporal reality — i.e., by creating a mental world in which there are no costs, no ignorance of present or future opportunities, and no need of threats to achieve our goals.

Coase states clearly what he thinks the economic problem is. "The economic problem in all cases of harmful effects is how to maximize the value of production."[76] Furthermore, he is no fool. Later in the essay, he drops his essay's initial assumption of zero transaction

---

74. Writes Jules L. Coleman: "No term in the philosopher's lexicon is more imprecisely defined than is the economist's term 'transaction costs.' Almost anything counts as a transaction cost. But if we are to count the failure to reach agreement on the division of surplus as necessarily resulting from transaction costs (I have no doubt that sometimes it does), then by 'transaction cost' we must mean literally anything that threatens the efficiency of market exchange. In that case, it could hardly come as a surprise that, in the absence of transaction costs so conceived, market exchange is efficient." Coleman, "Economics and the Law: A Critical Review of the Foundations of the Economic Approach to Law," *Ethics*, 94 (July 1984), p. 666.

75. Donald H. Regan, "The Problem of Social Cost Revisited," *Journal of Law and Economics*, XV (October 1972), pp. 428-32.

76. Coase, "Social Cost," p. 15.

costs, perfect competition, and zero information costs.[77] Of course in real life there are transaction costs to settle disputes. For this reason, there is a role for civil government in settling costly disputes.[78] "All solutions have costs," including solutions imposed by the civil government.[79] But one underlying presupposition distorts all of Coase's analysis — a presupposition which is all too common (and unstated) in Chicago School economic analysis: the legitimacy of leaving aside issues of right and wrong, of justice, of *equity.* "Of course, if market transactions were costless, all that matters (questions of equity apart) is that the rights of the various parties should be well-defined and the results of legal actions easy to forecast."[80] Problem: How can we discuss "the rights of the various parties" if we leave aside questions of equity — questions of right and wrong? In short, how can we discuss "rights" apart from what is *right*?

Discounting Moral Outrage to Zero

Questions of equity apart: here is a continuing assumption in the "value-free, morally neutral" economic hypotheses of modern free market economists. They apparently think that questions of equity, being questions of opinion and morality, cannot be dealt with scientifically, nor can economists, as scientists, put a price tag on violations of moral principle. They conveniently ignore the inescapable conclusion of subjectivist economics and methodological individualism, namely, that there is no scientific way to "measure" costs and benefits of any kind, since interpersonal comparisons of subjective utility are impossible for mortals to make. They naively believe that there is a neutral, value-free science of economics, but not of morality. They are correct about the impossibility of neutral morality; they are incorrect about the existence of a value-free economics. Economics deals with value, and there is no value-free value. The moment

---

77. There is always the nagging suspicion that once these formal theoretical assumptions are dropped, the whole intellectual performance becomes nothing more than a scholarly puzzle game. Will any of the conclusions concerning the world of the theoretical model still remain accurate, let alone applicable, once we begin to discuss the empirical world? And how can we know for sure? Only through intuition — a nonrational, nonlogical category. See Gary North, "Economics: From Reason to Intuition," in North (ed.), *Foundations of Christian Scholarship, op. cit.* See also North, *Dominion Covenant: Genesis*, pp. 350-53.
78. Coase, "Social Cost," pp. 15-19.
79. *Ibid.*, p. 18.
80. *Ibid.*, p. 19.

an economist raises the question of value — social value, personal value, value of Gross National Product — he has left the hypothetical world of value-free science. Such a world is mythical anyway. But economists have invested so much of their intellectual and professional capital in this myth for so long that they find it difficult to abandon it. If they were to abandon this myth, their peers would not take them seriously, and they would not get their unreadable and unread essays into professional journals any more.

One of Coase's academic defenders, Yale Law School's Guido Calabresi, carries the Coase theorem to distant shores of speculation and social unreality. He says that the Coase theorem demonstrates that "the same allocation of resources will come about regardless of which of two joint cost causers is initially charged with the cost, in other words, regardless of liability rules."[81] He repeats Coase's example of the smoke-producing factory that damages the wheat crop of local farmers. "For example, if we assume that the cost of factory smoke which destroys neighboring farmers' wheat can be avoided more cheaply by a smoke control device than by growing a smoke resistant wheat, then, even if the loss is left on the farmers they will, under the assumptions made, pay the factory to install the smoke control device. This would, in the short run, result in more factories relative to farmers and lower relative farm output than if the liability rule had been reversed. But if, as a result of this liability rule, farm output is too low relative to factory output those who lose from this 'misallocation' would have every reason to bribe farmers to produce more and factories to produce less. The process would continue until no bargain could improve the allocation of resources."[82]

A Response to Calabresi

It sounds so precise, so logical. It also sounds crazy. Here is why it really is crazy. *First*, there are always transaction costs in life. To begin with any other assumption is to begin with utopianism. It makes as much sense as beginning with the assumption of the omniscience of the participants in exchange, which is another familiar assumption in almost all modern economic thought, especially in the journals. Without this theoretical ideal of omniscience, economic theory would have no formulas and equations, and professional econ-

---

81. Guido Calabresi, "Transaction Costs, Resource Allocation and Liability Rules — A Comment," *Journal of Law and Economics*, XI (April 1968), p. 67.
82. *Ibid.*, pp. 67-68.

omists would rather die than give up their formulas and equations. The epistemological problem is this: once the theoretical model is formulated in terms of a hypothetical set of assumptions that cannot exist in the real world, it takes an act of will for the economist to bring the model to bear on real-world problems without importing radical utopianism into his analysis. The debate over the Coase theorem is in my view the classic recent example of an unsuccessful attempt by economists to discard an economic model's utopian initial assumptions, yet still retain it for analytic purposes.[83] That it should be taken seriously by most economists is evidence of the theoretical bankruptcy of modern economics.

Second, the allocation problem and its solutions are not primarily technical and empirical problems but rather ethical and epistemological. Calabresi poses the problem, and then answers it (as Chicago School economists usually do) in terms of the least costly solution technically, not in terms of any visible ethical principle. "The primary implication is that problems of misallocation of resources and externalities are not theoretical but empirical ones. The resource allocation aim is to approximate, both closely and cheaply, the result the market would bring about if bargaining actually were costless."[84] In other words, the civil judge is to pretend that he can approximate the allocation that a free market would produce, if free markets were costless. This, it should be mentioned, is a denial of the most important of all theorems in economics: scarcity. A civil judge capable of completing this assigned task would be a scarce resource indeed! Of course, he would possess this advantage: since the

---

83. Calabresi writes: "Thus, if one assumes rationality, no transaction costs, and no legal impediments to bargaining, *all* misallocations of resources would be fully cured in the market by bargains. Far from being surprising, this statement is tautological, at least if one accepts any of the various classic definitions of misallocation. These ultimately come down to a statement akin to the following: A misallocation exists when there is available a possible reallocation in which all those who would lose from the reallocation could be fully compensated by those who would gain, and, at the end of this compensation process, there would still be some who would be better off than before." *Ibid.*, p. 68. This is one more application of Pareto's optimality theorem, perhaps the most non-optimal and misleading idea ever to get into the literature of economics. It is conceptually a dead end; it is also quite popular. I agree with Lutz and Lux: if it were buried forever, we could place a tombstone over it bearing these words: "Everybody has been made better off and nobody worse off." Mark A. Lutz and Kenneth Lux, *The Challenge of Humanistic Economics* (Menlo Park, California: Benjamin/Cummings, 1979), p. 101. Chapter 5 of their book is delightful: "The New Welfare Economics: Value-Free or Value-Less?"

84. Calabresi, *op. cit.*, p. 69.

initial limiting condition is impossible—zero transaction costs—
nobody could produce a model that could prove that his allocation is
off the mark.

How would this utopian task best be accomplished? Calabresi
combines the false precision of the economist with the real obfusca-
tion of the lawyer to produce this problematical conclusion: "This
question depends in large part on the relative *cost* of reaching the correct result by each of these means (an empirical problem which
probably could be resolved, at least approximately, in most instances), and the relative *chances* of reaching a widely *wrong* result
depending on the method used (also an empirical problem but one as
to which it is hard to get other than 'guess' type data). The resolution
of these two problems and their interplay is *the* problem of accom-
plishing optimal resource allocations."[85] It surely is!

So, the allocation problem for welfare economics is merely an
empirical problem. But this so-called empirical problem cannot be
solved scientifically, logically, or technically, for there is no way for
the scientific economist to deal with the key epistemological problem: the impossibility of making scientific interpersonal comparisons
of subjective utility. Yet the Chicago School economists babble on in
their journals as if more precise measurements could somehow solve
what they admit is *the* allocation problem. It is as if a gunnery sergeant
were attempting to hit a target at the edge of the universe by adding
just a bit more gunpowder to the load. It is simply a technical problem, you understand. It is as if a sprinter were trying to reduce his
time in the hundred meter race to one second flat by shaving a tenth
of a second off his time in each preliminary heat. It is an empirical
problem, you understand. If he could just get better shoes or a track
with better traction!

Calabresi knows all this. He acknowledges that the decision
which would be reached if the transactions were costless is an "un-
reachable goal."[86] He also acknowledges that "the gains which reaching nearer the goal would bring are not usually subject to precise definition or quantification. They are, in fact, largely defined by
guesses. As a result, the question of whether a given law is worth its
costs (in terms of better resource allocation) is rarely susceptible to
empirical proof . . . It is precisely the province of good government

85. *Idem.*
86. *Idem.*

to make guesses as to what laws are likely to be worth their costs. Hopefully it will use what empirical information is available and seek to develop empirical information which is not currently available (how much information is worth *its* costs is also a question, however). But there is no reason to assume that in the absence of conclusive information no government action is better than some action."[87]

Please get his argument clear in your mind: welfare economics is essentially an empirical science, except that empiricism cannot really solve the issues of welfare economics, so the State will have to decide what is the appropriate allocation of resources, but economists nevertheless hope that the bureaucrats will use empiricism as the means of finding solutions to the specific allocation problems, though only an economically efficient quantity and quality of empiricism should be purchased. In any case, the State's decision will necessarily be based primarily on guesswork. If this explanation resembles a walk through a hall of mirrors, it is because it *is* a hall of mirrors. Yet virtually all essays in welfare economics are little more than guided tours through this conceptual hall of mirrors. The allocation problem of welfare economics cannot be solved by humanist economics, for the economists are overcome by a series of antinomies: the subjective-objective dualism, the individual-society dualism, the problem of fixed law and the endless flux of circumstances, and the overwhelming and unanswered problem of interpersonal comparisons of subjective utility. It is all premised on this formula: *dialectics plus intuition equals cost-effective justice.* This formula does not produce anything except additional scholarly articles for professors' vitae — in short, negative returns.

Third, and far more important for social analysis, there would be a sense of outrage among the victims of the polluting factory if there were no State-enforced liability rules. The initial reaction of any one of the victims, if he knows that the civil law does not protect his ownership rights automatically, may be to blow up the factory or murder its owner. The multiplication of acts of violence would be assured under such a non-liability legal order. *The issue of economic efficiency therefore cannot be separated from the issue of judicial equity.* This is what Chicago School economists and legal theorists never show any signs of having understood. When righteous men are thwarted in their cause by seekers of local "efficiency" who care nothing about the eth-

---

87. *Ibid.*, pp. 69-70.

ics of the solution, there will be serious social consequences. To discuss the efficiency of any given transaction without also discussing the equity of it is to begin to deliver the society into the hands of socialist revolutionaries. Or, to put it in language more familiar to Chicago School economists, *penalizing righteousness in the name of economic efficiency is not a zero-cost decision.*

Micro-Efficiency and Macro-Revolution

It is not possible to discover an economically efficient solution to just one transaction. We cannot be efficient in just one thing. The question of efficiency is not simply a microeconomic issue; it is also macroeconomic. We cannot discover an efficient solution to any economic problem that does not in some way affect the whole social order. In short, *we cannot do just one thing efficiently.* The system of justice that governs any social order is itself a producer or reducer of both macro-efficiency and micro-efficiency. Equity cannot be segregated from efficiency. If our supposedly economically efficient decision at the micro level calls into question the moral integrity of the prevailing legal system, we have not in fact reached an efficient solution to our micro problem. This is why it is astonishing to find economist and Talmudist Aaron Levine siding with Coase: "While the principle of equity is promoted by the selection of appropriate liability rules, economic efficiency is realized when the negative externality is eliminated by the *least-cost* method. Hence, should it be less costly to avoid crop damage by growing smoke-resistant wheat than by installing a smoke-control device, the former method should be adopted. Whether the farmer or the factory-owner should bear the additional expense of eliminating the negative externality is entirely irrelevant as far as the efficiency question is concerned."[88] Charge the farmers for the cost of the factory's smoke abatement, and you have violated the principle of justice that governs Exodus 22:5-6. There will eventually be negative repercussions, whether economists believe in God or not.

These certified economists are certifiable idiots; they are anarchists who are brandishing equations rather than bombs. The reductionism of economic logic, even without the equations, has become so great that it has just about eliminated the real-world relevance of the academic discipline of economics, especially its academic journals. That which is obvious escapes these people. They speak of a

---

88. Levine, *Free Enterprise and Jewish Law*, p. 59.

world of zero transaction costs and zero rules establishing legal liability as if it would not be a world of turmoil, unpredictability, and
violence. It is the establishment of liability rules that makes civil order possible. Social order is clearly too important a matter to be left
in the hands of economists, even Chicago School economists.

Rothbard's Critique: Pure Subjectivism

One economist who has seen at least some of the implications of
Coase's position is Murray Rothbard. Rothbard very early recognized the reality of Robbins' complaint against Pigou, namely, that
there can be no scientifically valid interpersonal comparisons of subjective utility.[89] He has written a critique of the Coase theorem
which underscores some of the points I raised in the original draft of
this essay before I discovered Rothbard's 1982 essay. But he goes to
the full logical conclusion of the subjectivist school, namely, that *there
can be no such thing as social cost* — not simply that economists cannot
measure it, but that it does not exist as a category of economics.[90] He
discusses the case of the farmer whose orchard is burned by sparks
emitted by a passing train. His analysis focuses on the farmer's subjective costs that are imposed by the railroad's aggression. Should
the State solve this dispute by forcing the railroad to pay the farmer
the market value of the lost trees?

There are many problems with this [Coase's] theory. First, income and
wealth are important *to the parties involved*, although they might not be to uninvolved economists. It makes a great deal of difference to both of them
who has to pay whom. Second, this thesis works only if we deliberately ignore psychological factors. Costs are not only monetary. The farmer might
well have an attachment to the orchard far beyond the monetary damage.

---

89. Rothbard, "Toward a Reconstruction of Utility and Welfare Economics," in
Mary Sennholz (ed.), *On Freedom and Free Enterprise: Essays in Honor of Ludwig von
Mises* (Princeton, New Jersey: Van Nostrand, 1956). This has been reprinted by
Liberty Press, Indianapolis, Indiana.

90. The Christian economist must reject this thesis. There are indeed social costs
and social benefits. This is one reason why the Bible can and does specify certain social policies. They are beneficial for the covenanted community. But Rothbard's
logic is correct: in terms of the presuppositions of modern, subjectivist economics,
there is no way to add up subjective costs or benefits. In fact, if he were really rigorous, he would admit that this conclusion applies even to the measurement of *intra*-
personal subjective utilities, since such measurements takes place over time, and
therefore we again confront that old nemesis, the index number of satisfaction — an
impossibility, given the premises of subjective utility.

Therefore, the orchard might be worth far more to him than the $100,000 in damages. . . .

The love of the farmer for his orchard is part of a larger difficulty for the Coase-Demsetz doctrine: Costs are purely subjective and not measurable in monetary terms. Coase and Demsetz have a proviso in their indifference thesis that all "transaction costs" be zero. If they are not, then they advocate allocating the property rights to whichever route entails minimum social transaction costs. But once we understand that costs are subjective to each individual and therefore unmeasurable, we see that costs cannot be added up. But if all costs, including transaction costs, cannot be added, then there is no such thing as "social transaction costs," and they cannot be compared. . . .

Another serious problem with the Coase-Demsetz approach is that pretending to be value-free, they in reality import the ethical norm of "efficiency," and assert that property rights should be assigned on the basis of such efficiency. But even if the concept of social efficiency were meaningful, they don't answer the questions of why efficiency should be the overriding consideration in establishing legal principles or why externalities should be internalized above all other considerations.[91]

In an earlier essay, Rothbard presents perhaps the most comprehensive challenge to the whole economics profession that has ever been written. The reason why I quote him at length is that he is a very clear writer, and he is willing to follow the logic of subjectivist economics to great lengths — not to a biblical reconciliation of objective and subjective value, but at least to the far extremes of subjectivism. In a remarkable essay, "The Myth of Efficiency," Rothbard rejects not only social costs but the idea of efficiency:

. . . there are several layers of grave fallacy involved in the very concept of efficiency as applied to social institutions or policies: (1) the problem is not only in specifying ends but also in deciding *whose* ends are to be pursued; (2) individual ends are bound to conflict, and therefore any additive concept of social efficiency is meaningless; and (3) even each individual's actions cannot be assumed to be "efficient"; indeed, they undoubtedly will not be. Hence, efficiency is an erroneous concept even when applied to each individual's actions directed toward his ends; it is a fortiori a meaningless concept when it includes more than one individual, let alone an entire society.

Let us take a given individual. Since his own ends are clearly given and he acts to pursue them, surely at least *his* actions can be considered efficient? But no, they may not, for in order for him to act efficiently, he would

---

91. Rothbard, "Law, Property Rights, and Air Pollution," *Cato Journal*, II (Spring 1982), pp. 58-59.

have to possess perfect knowledge — perfect knowledge of the best technology, of future actions and reactions by other people, and of future natural events. But since no one can ever have perfect knowledge of the future, no one's action can be called "efficient." We live in a world of uncertainty. Efficiency is therefore a chimera.

Put another way, action is a learning process. As the individual acts to achieve his ends, he learns and becomes more proficient about how to pursue them. But in that case, of course, his actions cannot have been efficient from the start — or even from the end — of his actions, since perfect knowledge is never achieved, and there is always more to learn.

Moreover, the individual's ends are not *really* given, for there is no reason to assume that they are set in concrete for all time. As the individual learns more about the world, about nature and about other people, his values and goals are bound to change. The individual's ends will change as he learns from other people; they may also change out of sheer caprice. But if ends change in the course of an action, the concept of efficiency — which can only be defined as the best combination of means in pursuit of given ends — again becomes meaningless.[92]

Two comments are in order. *First*, we can perceive the whole corpus of economics steadily slipping through our fingers. If the question of efficiency is meaningless, what have economists been arguing about over the last three centuries? An illusion? The answer must be *yes*, if we hold to a rigorously subjectivist epistemology. "Not only is 'efficiency' a myth, then, but so too is any concept of social or additive cost, or even an objectively determinable cost for each individual. But if cost is individual, ephemeral, and purely subjective, then it follows that no policy conclusions, including conclusions about law, can be derived from or even make use of such a concept. There can be no valid or meaningful cost-benefit analysis of political or legal decisions or institutions."[93] Rothbard has shown the intellectual courage to affirm the validity of the implications that Roy Harrod used to frighten Lionel Robbins away from his own denial of the possibility of making interpersonal comparisons of subjective utility. He denies the possibility of policy-making based on economics.

The Problem of Exhaustive Knowledge

Second, we discover in Rothbard's arguments against the concept of efficiency, an argument based on the impossibility of using a concept

---

92. Murray N. Rothbard, "Comment: The Myth of Efficiency," in Mario J. Rizzo (ed.), *Time, Uncertainty, and Disequilibrium*, p. 90.

93. *Ibid.*, p. 94.

which is only meaningful in an imaginary changeless world. This is a variation of an antinomy (logical contradiction) of humanism which Van Til points to in several contexts, namely, that for the anti-theist, it is necessary to know everything exhaustively in order to know anything specifically. The heart of the problem, Van Til says, is that *there is no way for the anti-theist to integrate his timeless model of reality to the ceaseless flux of historical change.*

In contrast to the humanists, Van Til argues, Christians have God's revelation of Himself and His creation to guide them in making sense of this world, and "it is only by stressing the comprehensiveness and the inexhaustible character of the idea of revelation that the process of learning can have meaning and history have genuine significance. If man is made the final reference point in predication, knowledge cannot get under way, and if it could get under way it could not move forward. That is to say, in all non-Christian forms of epistemology there is first the idea that to be understood a fact must be understood exhaustively. It must be reducible to a part of a system of timeless logic. But man himself and the facts of his experience are subject to change. How is he ever to find within himself an a priori resting point? He himself is on the move. . . . Every effort of man to find one spot that he can exhaustively understand either in the world of fact about him or in the world of experience within, is doomed to failure. If we do not with Calvin presuppose the self-contained God back of the self-conscious act of the knowing mind of man, we are doomed to be lost in an endless and bottomless flux."[94]

The economist faces this problem continually; it cannot be overcome logically. Because the Austrian School of economics focuses above all on two fundamental questions — subjective knowledge (e.g., valuations) and purposeful human action (e.g., the market process over time) — "Austrians" have devoted more space than most economists to discussions of the interrelations between historical change and economic knowledge. Members of the Austrian School understand that the model used to undergird all modern economic theory, namely, the general equilibrium model, hypothesizes a world of perfect foreknowledge, and therefore zero uncertainty, a world in which human action cannot even be conceived.[95] As Mario Rizzo

---

94. Cornelius Van Til, *An Introduction to Systematic Theology*, vol. V of *In Defense of Biblical Christianity* (Phillipsburg, New Jersey: Presbyterian & Reformed, 1978), pp. 166-67.

95. Mises, *Human Action*, p. 248. For my comments on Mises, see *Dominion Covenant: Genesis*, p. 352.

puts it, "general equilibrium exists in the mind of the economist and not in the real world."[96] Rothbard agrees: ". . . not only has it never existed, and is not an operational concept, but also it could not conceivably exist. For we cannot really conceive of a world where every person has perfect foresight, and where no data ever change. . . ."[97]

This raises a crucial problem for the economist: the problem of objective cost. Buchanan summarizes this problem: "One of the central confusions leading to the false objectification of costs has been the extension of the perfect knowledge assumption of competitive equilibrium theory to the analysis of nonequilibrium choices, whether made in a market or nonmarket process. Genuine choice is confronted only in a world of uncertainty, and, of course, all economic choices are made in this context."[98] Take away equilibrium — from men's thinking, that is; it never has existed in the real world — and you thereby eliminate the economist's concept of objective cost. Eliminate the concept of objective cost, and you eliminate the possibility of scientifically valid policy-making by economists. Eliminate the concept of objective cost, and you also eliminate that trusty ideological weapon of all free market economists: the idea of the objective efficiency of the free market.

Efficiency for Whose Ends?

Here is the problem Rothbard is struggling with: How can we discuss the question of efficiency — the coherence of planning and action — in a context of *change*, both with respect to a man's plans and his environment which he attempts to change and yet also must respond to. Rothbard wants to believe that he can appeal to what he calls "proficiency" in learning, but his critique of efficiency applies equally well to proficiency. Why is human action a learning process? Why does anything we learned a decade, a year, or a moment ago still apply in the now-changed world of the present? Humanists have no answer to this fundamental question, at least none which is consistent with their epistemology of autonomous man.

Rothbard argues correctly that "efficiency only makes sense in regard to people's ends, and individuals' ends differ, clash, and conflict. The central question of politics then becomes: *whose* ends shall

---

96. Mario J. Rizzo, "Uncertainty, Subjectivity, and the Economic Analysis of the Law," in Rizzo (ed.), *Time, Uncertainty*, p. 82.

97. *Ibid.*, p. 93. Cf. Buchanan, *Cost and Choice*, p. 98.

98. Buchanan, *Cost and Choice*, p. 98; cf. pp. 49-50.

rule?"[99] He attacks modern economics because it is based on *utilitarianism* — "the greatest good for the greatest number" — a system of ethics which assumes that it is possible to make interpersonal comparisons of subjective utility. Utilitarianism ultimately asserts that there is a *universal common ethical system* and a *universal hierarchy of values*, for if there weren't, it would be impossible for social planners to devise and enforce social policies. "For utilitarianism holds that everyone's ends are *really* the same, and that therefore all social conflict is merely technical and pragmatic, and can be resolved once the appropriate means for the common ends are discovered and adopted. It is the myth of the common universal end that allows economists to believe that they can 'scientifically' and in a supposedly value-free manner prescribe what political policies should be adopted. By taking this alleged common universal end as an unquestioned given, the economist allows himself the delusion that he is not at all a moralist but only a strictly value-free and professional technician."[100]

Rothbard gives an example of the problem of social efficiency. What if one group in society wishes to exterminate all members of a rival group? "In these cases of conflicting ends, furthermore, one group's 'efficiency' becomes another group's detriment. So that the advocates of a program — whether of compulsory uniformity or of slaughtering a defined social group — would want their proposals carried out as efficiently as possible; whereas, on the other hand, the oppressed group would hope for as *in*efficient a pursuit of the hated goal as possible. Efficiency, as Rizzo points out, can only be meaningful relative to a given goal. But if ends clash, the opposing group will favor maximum *in*efficiency in pursuit of the disliked goal. Efficiency, therefore, can never serve as a utilitarian touchstone for law or public policy."[101]

Rothbard's conclusion is extremely important for a study of Christian economics. By systematically destroying the epistemological foundation for efficiency as a concept of subjectivist economics, he is then faced with a major question: What is the proper foundation for social policy? As an anarchist, he does not believe in social policy, meaning a State-enforced policy. He wants the market's forces to arbitrate in deciding whose plans become dominant at any point in time. But even these plans cannot be based on questions of

---

99. Rothbard, "Comment," *Time, Uncertainty*, p. 91.
100. *Idem.*
101. *Ibid.*, pp. 91-92.

efficiency, as he well knows. He then calls for a restructuring of economic thought — a reformation based on *ethics*.

> I conclude that we cannot decide on public policy, tort law, rights, or liabilities on the basis of efficiencies or minimizing of costs. But if not costs or efficiency, then what? The answer is that only *ethical principles* can serve as criteria for our decisions. Efficiency can never serve as the basis for ethics; on the contrary, ethics must be the guide and touchstone for any consideration of efficiency. Ethics is the primary. . . .
>
> One group of people will inevitably balk at our conclusion; I speak, of course, of the economists. For in this area economists have been long engaged in what George Stigler, in another context, has called "intellectual imperialism."[102] Economists will have to get used to the idea that not all of life can be encompassed by our own discipline. A painful lesson no doubt, but compensated by the knowledge that it may be good for our souls to realize our own limits — and, just perhaps, to learn about ethics and about justice.[103]

This represents a major break from contemporary economics, even from Austrian School economics. Rothbard is no longer willing to affirm, as Mises the utilitarian affirmed, that "when the superior efficiency of economic freedom could no longer be questioned, social philosophy entered the scene and demolished the ideology of the status system."[104]

Methodology: Ethics vs. Efficiency

Rothbard's straightforward abandonment of the concept of efficiency, and his call to economists to examine ethics as the source of their policy judgments, are significant intellectual developments. They constitute an admission that there is something dangerously

---

102. Rothbard attributes the phrase to George Stigler, but Kenneth Boulding is better known for its use, by which he means "an attempt on the part of economics to take over all the other social sciences." Boulding, "Economics As A Moral Science," *American Economic Review*, LIX (March 1969), p. 8.

103. *Ibid.*, p. 95. Rothbard is an advocate of a universal ethics based on natural rights. See *For a New Liberty: The Libertarian Manifesto* (rev. ed.; New York: Collier, 1978), pp. 15, 26-28, 134, 239. Not all "Austrians" share his confidence in natural rights and natural law as the basis of a universal ethics, as John Eggar points out: "Comment: Efficiency Is Not a Substitute for Ethics," in Rizzo (ed), *Time, Uncertainty*, p. 119. For critiques of natural law doctrines from a biblical viewpoint, see the essays by John Robbins, Rex Downie, and Archie Jones in *Journal of Christian Reconstruction*, V (Summer 1978): "Symposium on Politics."

104. Mises, *The Ultimate Foundation of Economic Science* (Princeton, New Jersey: Van Nostrand, 1962), p. 109.

wrong with the economists' reliance on the rational model of equilibrium. If the idea of economic equilibrium cannot be relied upon to illuminate questions of economic efficiency, then in what way can it safely be used by economists? Rothbard is calling into question the most important intellectual and technical tool that the economist has at his disposal, the "ideal type" of the perfectly competitive economy.[105] Challenge this, and you challenge the epistemological foundation of economic science.

Yet it must be challenged. More than this: *it must be scrapped.* If economics is to be reconstructed in terms of biblical revelation, economists must at last see the implications of Van Til's rejection of metaphysics in favor of ethics. The search for a timeless rational mental construct as the basis of a science of human action is fruitless. Even the great Mises was partially sidetracked by this quest. What confidence can we legitimately have in an explanation of market processes which argues that as entrepreneurship becomes successful, it "tends toward" the creation of a world in which human action and human choice is impossible, a world of automatons rather than people? Yet this is precisely the explanatory model used by Mises (and most other economists). As he says in *Human Action* concerning his theoretical construct, the Evenly Rotating Economy: "Action is change, and change is the temporal sequence. But in the evenly rotating economy change and succession of events are eliminated. Action is to make choices and to cope with an uncertain future. But in the evenly rotating economy there is no choosing and the future is not uncertain as it does not differ from the present known state. Such a rigid system is not peopled with living men making choices and liable to error; it is a world of soulless unthinking automatons; it is not a human society, it is an ant hill."[106] Nevertheless, he states flatly: "The theorems implied in the notion of the plain state of rest are

---

105. Perhaps the most influential explanation of the use of "ideal types" or hypothetical abstract models in the social sciences was offered by Max Weber. See Weber's book, *The Methodology of the Social Sciences*, translated and edited by Edward A. Shils and Henry A. Finch (New York: Free Press, 1949), pp. 43-45, 87-105. See also Thomas Burger, *Max Weber's Theory of Concept Formation: History, Laws and Ideal Types* (Durham, North Carolina: Duke University Press, 1976); Rolf E. Rogers, *Max Weber's Ideal Type Theory* (New York: Philosophical Library, 1969); Julien Freund, *The Sociology of Max Weber* (New York: Pantheon, 1968), pp. 59-70; Raymond Aron, "The Logic of the Social Sciences," in Denis Wrong (ed.), *Max Weber* (Englewood Cliffs, New Jersey: Prentice-Hall, 1970), pp. 80-89.

106. Mises, *Human Action*, p. 248.

valid with regard to all transactions without exception."[107] For the modern economist, all human action tends toward a final state in which human beings become omniscient and therefore take on one of the attributes of God.[108] The problem is, their view of God is that He could not possibly act if He existed. He would be a "rule-following automaton,"[109] because "A perfect being would not act."[110]

Timeless Metaphysical Models

Mises relies on this limiting concept of a hypothetical economy filled with soulless people in order to explain the operations of real world market forces. "This final state of rest is an imaginary construction, not a description of reality. For the final state of rest will never be attained. New disturbing factors will emerge before it will be realized. What makes it necessary to take recourse to this imaginary construction is the fact that the market at every instant is moving toward a final state of rest."[111] He calls this movement toward (or "tendency toward") a final state of rest a *fact*. But this "fact" is precisely what must be demonstrated. It is the same old pre-Socratic contradiction between Parmenides' changeless logic and Heraclitus' ceaseless flow. These two worlds cannot be shown to be connected; they are, however, correlative in the thinking of humanistic scholars.

To explain this intellectual dilemma, Van Til uses the delightful analogy of someone who is trying to put together a string of beads, but the string is infinitely long, and the beads have no holes. The imaginary world of timeless logic (Van Til's "string") which cannot possibly exist serves as the *limiting concept* (to use Kant's terminology for the "noumenal"),[112] or *limiting notion* (to use Mises' term)[113] for our understanding of the world which does exist — the world of ceaseless flux (Van Til's "beads"). This world of timeless logic is, in short, a logical backdrop which cannot ever exist in the real world — and

---

107. *Ibid.*, p. 245.

108. Mises writes: "No matter whether this thirsting after omniscience can ever be fully gratified or not, man will not cease to strive after it passionately." Mises, *Ultimate Foundation*, p. 120.

109. Buchanan, *Cost and Choice*, p. 96.

110. Mises, *Epistemological Problems of Economics* (Princeton, New Jersey: Van Nostrand, 1960), p. 24. Cf. Mises, *Ultimate Foundations*, p. 3.

111. *Idem.*

112. Immanuel Kant, *Critique of Pure Reason*, translated by Norman Kemp Smith (New York: St. Martin's, [1929] 1965), B311, p. 272.

113. *Human Action*, p. 249.

which really cannot even be mentally conceived[114] — which is used to explain the world inhabited by men.

Nevertheless, with absolute confidence (even "apodictic certainty," one of Mises' favorite terms), Mises proclaims that "These insoluble contradictions, however, do not affect the service which this imaginary construction renders. . . ."[115] Or even more forcefully: "Even imaginary constructions which are inconceivable, self-contradictory, or unrealizable can render useful, even indispensable services in the comprehension of reality, provided the economist knows how to use them properly."[116] That word, "provided," covers a multitude of epistemological sins. So does the word "properly."

Anyone who has ever tried to read an article in such journals as *Econometrica* and *The Review of Economics and Statistics* knows how rarified economic logic can become.[117] It reminds me of what little I know about the formal academic debates carried on by the late medieval scholastics. The number of angels dancing on the point of a needle is a down-to-earth problem compared to stochastic analysis applied to a world of perfect foreknowledge. The *sophistication* of modern econometric analysis is matched ("correlation of at least .9") only by the *irrelevance* of its conclusions.

The Mathematical Games Economists Play

The non-mathematical economist John Kenneth Galbraith, formerly the President of the American Economics Association, has exposed the way the game is played, at least in the so-called "general"

---

114. How can we imagine a world in which every actor has perfect foreknowledge? Try to explain the meaning of human choice in a world in which everyone knows in advance precisely what the others will inevitably do in the future. We may take such a world on faith; we cannot explain it.

115. *Ibid.*, p. 248. He writes: "The method of imaginary constructions is indispensable for praxeology [the science of human action — G.N.]; it is the only method of praxeological and economic inquiry. It is, to be sure, a method difficult to handle because it can easily result in fallacious syllogisms. It leads along a sharp edge; on both sides yawns the chasm of absurdity and nonsense. Only merciless self-criticism can prevent a man from falling headlong into these abysmal depths." *Ibid.*, p. 237. Question: Self-criticism in terms of what truth, or by what standard? For a critique of this position, see North, *Dominion Covenant: Genesis*, pp. 352-53.

116. *Ibid.*, p. 236.

117. I do not have in mind merely the writings of Nobel Prize-winning economist Gerard Debreu, which do not pretend to deal with the real world. I have in mind investigations into the operation of real-world institutions, such as William S. Landes, "An Economic Analysis of the Courts," *Journal of Law and Economics*, XIV (April 1971), pp. 61-107.

economics scholarly journals, which are very nearly as unreadable as *Econometrica*. The fact is, hardly anyone in the profession actually reads the highly mathematical essays. "The layman may take comfort from the fact that the most esoteric of this material is not read by other economists or even by the editors who publish it. In the economics profession the editorship of a learned journal not specialized to econometrics or mathematical statistics is a position of only moderate prestige. It is accepted, moreover, that the editor must have a certain measure of practical judgment. This means that he is usually unable to read the most prestigious contributions which, nonetheless, he must publish. So it is the practice of the editor to associate with himself a mathematical curate who passes on this part of the work and whose word he takes. A certain embarrassed silence covers the arrangement."[118]

From time to time, prestige economists protest. Paul Samuelson, perhaps the most prestigious of all American economists, 1950-80, and a founder of the highly mathematical "neo-Keynesian synthesis," remarked in his presidential address to the American Economics Association that the three previous presidents had all criticized the excessive use of mathematical economics, and that the most hostile remarks had elicited a standing ovation of the audience.[119] But applause is one thing, and a change in habits is another. The professional journals are still mostly exercises in mathematics. Why?

One reason is the success of mathematics in the natural sciences — a correlation which, it should be noted, is so remarkable that there is no rational explanation for it, as one Nobel Prize-winner in physics has noted.[120] There is also the quest for elegance. There is no doubt about it: a mathematical proof appears to be elegant in its precision and sparseness. The problem is, however, that this elegance has a high price attached to it: irrelevance in the real world. The greater the precision, the greater the irrelevance. Furthermore, most of the major advances in economic science since World War II have owed little to mathematical economics, including the Coase theorem.[121]

---

118. John Kenneth Galbraith, *Economics Peace and Laughter* (New York: New American Library, 1972), p. 44n.

119. *Ibid.*, p. 40.

120. Eugene P. Wigner, "The Unreasonable Effectiveness of Mathematics in the Natural Sciences," *Communications in Pure and Applied Mathematics*, XIII (1960), pp. 1-14.

121. Alan Walters, "Frameworks for Thinking About Reality," *Cato Journal*, VII (Spring-Summer 1987), p. 72.

Galbraith offers another explanation: considerations of academic prestige.[122] Then, too, mathematical ability is used as a screening device within the profession, as Galbraith observes.[123] Screening by mathematics was actually recommended as a legitimate professional goal by Fritz Machlup, an economist who had been greatly influenced early in his career by Mises, and who was never known as a mathematical economist. He argued that proficiency in mathematics could overcome the inferiority complex of the social sciences.[124] Yet he also called the overuse of mathematics "mathematosis," and the assumption that science is primarily a matter of measurement, "metromania."[125]

The widespread use of mathematics is more than just a quest for prestige or a graduate school screening device. It is a *religious commitment* to the idea that metaphysics is more important than ethics. The use of mathematics in the development of the theoretical propositions of economics is an elegant, seemingly rigorous assertion of scientific man's neutrality, his "escape from ethics." God is to be banished from man's economic thinking through the use of simultaneous equations.[126]

---

122. Galbraith, *op. cit.*, pp. 41-42.

123. *Ibid.*, p. 43.

124. Machlup recommended requiring higher mathematics for all economics students as a screening device. "Even if some of us think that one can study social sciences without knowing higher mathematics, we should insist on making calculus and mathematical statistics absolute requirements — as a device for keeping away the weakest students." Machlup, "Are the Social Sciences Really Inferior?" *Southern Economic Journal*, XXVII (Jan. 1961), p. 182. This was Machlup's presidential address.

125. Machlup, "The Inferiority Complex of the Social Sciences," in Mary Sennholz (ed.), *On Freedom and Free Enterprise*, p. 169.

126. Leon Walras, the Swiss economist, was the first economist to offer a comprehensive analysis of economic theory in terms of simultaneous equations (general equilibrium). He did so in 1871. Writing of the simultaneous discovery of subjective value by Walras, William Stanley Jevons (England), and Carl Menger (Austria), Paul Samuelson writes: "Jevons, Walras, and Menger each independently arrived at the so-called 'theory of subjective value.' And I consider it a lucky bonus for my present thesis that Menger did arrive at his formulation without the use of mathematics. But, in all fairness, I should point out that a recent rereading of the excellent English translation of Menger's 1871 work convinces me that it is the least important of the three works cited; and that its relative neglect by modern writers was not simply the result of bad luck or scholarly negligence. I should also add that the important revolution of the 1870's had little really to do with either subjective value and utility or with marginalism; rather it consisted of the perfecting of the general relations of supply and demand. It culminated in Walrasian general equilibrium. And we are forced to agree with Schumpeter's appraisal of Walras as the greatest of theorists — not because he used mathematics, since the methods used are really quite elementary — but because of the key importance of the concept of general equilibrium

From the very beginning of modern economics in the seventeenth century, the use of hypothetically value-free arguments by economists has been viewed by them as a way to escape questions of right and wrong, of ethics. William Letwin, historian of this early period of economic thought, is correct when he says that "there can be no doubt that economic theory owes its present development to the fact that some men, in thinking of economic phenomena, forcefully suspended all judgments of theology, morality, and justice, were willing to consider the economy as nothing more than an intricate mechanism, refraining for the while from asking whether the mechanism worked for good or evil. . . . The economist's view of the world, which the public cannot yet comfortably stomach, was introduced by a remarkable *tour de force*, an intellectual revolution brought off in the seventeenth century."[127]

The problem with this reliance upon mathematics is that in removing ethics, it removes responsibility. It removes choice. This has been the complaint of the Austrian School for many decades. Buchanan, more an Austrian than a Chicagoan on this point, argues that the reduction of economics to mathematics is the reduction of man to an automaton. For the Austrian, cost is subjective. "This genuine opportunity cost vanishes once a decision is taken. By relatively sharp contrast with this, in the pure science of economic behavior choice is itself illusory. In the abstract model, the behavior of the actor is predictable by an outside observer. This requires that some criteria be objectively measurable, and this objectivity is supplied when the motivational postulate is plugged into the model."[128] The scientific ideal of prediction runs head-on into the voluntarist's case for freedom. As Van Til describes it, this is the Kantian ideal of

---

itself. We may say of Walras what Lagrange ironically said in praise of Newton: 'Newton was assuredly the man of genius *par excellence*, but we must agree that he was also the luckiest: one finds only once the system of the world to be established!' And how lucky he was that 'in his time the system of the world still remained to be discovered.' Substitute 'system of equilibrium' for 'system of the world' and Walras for Newton and the equation remains valid." Samuelson, "Economic Theory and Mathematics — An Appraisal," *American Economic Review*, XLII (May 1952), p. 61. Samuelson's appraisal concerning the importance of Walras vs. Menger is exactly the reverse of mine, and so is his appraisal of the comparative advantages of subjective value theory and marginalism vs. the concept of general equilibrium.

127. William Letwin, *The Origins of Scientific Economics* (Garden City, New York: Doubleday Anchor, [1963] 1965), pp. 158-59.

128. James Buchanan, *What Should Economists Do?* (Indianapolis, Indiana: Liberty Press, 1979), p. 46.

science against the Kantian ideal of personality.[129] It is the mathematical ideal against the freedom ideal. It is the world of science
against the world of purpose.[130] It is Kant's phenomenal against
Kant's noumenal.[131] Ethical dualism once again raises its ugly,
Janus-faced head.[132]

The Christian economist who acknowledges the validity of Van
Til's epistemology (and who also understands its application)[133] sees
no hope in the quest either for a rational ethics—an ethics supposedly derived from value-free presuppositions (which are mythical
anyway)—or the quest for a reliable hypothetical mental construct
which in any way relies on the idea of man, the omniscient. A wholly
rational methodological construct along the lines of Parmenides' unchanging logic—with or without mathematics—is apostate man's attempt to find coherence in a changing world apart from God. General equilibrium theory cannot serve as a reliable "limiting concept"
that will serve as a basis for judging the performance of a real-world
economy of change, responsible decision-making, and uncertainty.
But it is understandable that apostate men wish to believe in the
potency of such an intellectual tool. As Ludwig Lachmann wrote as
early as 1943: "Economists, not unnaturally, prefer to do their field-
work in a pleasant green valley where the population register is exhaustive and everybody is known to live on either the right or the left
side of an equation. Only on rare occasions—and scarcely ever of
their own free will—do they embark on excursions into the rough
uplands of the World of Change to chart the country and to record
the folkways of its savage inhabitants; whence they return with grim

---

129. Van Til, *The Doctrine of Scripture*, vol. 1 of *In Defense of Biblical Christianity* (den
Dulk Foundation, 1967), pp. 97-98.

130. Van Til, *The Case for Calvinism* (Nutley, New Jersey: Craig Press, 1964), p. 81.

131. *Ibid.*, p. 89.

132. Writes philosopher Richard Kroner: "The mutual dependence of subjectivity and objectivity rests upon the split of man's consciousness into the consciousness
of nature, i.e., the objective world and the consciousness of his own self and the
realm of persons. It is because of morality and freedom that this split cannot and must
not be overcome. The duality of science and action must be preserved at all costs."
Kroner, *Kant's Weltanschauung* (University of Chicago Press, [1914] 1956), p. 75.

133. I do not think that Douglas Vickers, a Keynesian economist who claims to
follow Van Til's epistemology, fully understands Van Til's writings or their proper
application in the discipline of economics. See his book, *A Christian Approach to Economics and the Cultural Tradition* (New York: Exposition Press, 1982), which is a follow-
up to his earlier book, *Economics and Man* (Nutley, New Jersey: Craig Press, 1976).
For a critique of Vickers, see Ian Hodge, *Baptized Inflation: A Critique of "Christian"
Keynesianism* (Tyler, Texas: Institute for Christian Economics, 1986).

tales of horror and frustration."[134]

A Permanent Ethical Model

In contrast to economic models that are supposedly timeless abstractions from the flux of human existence, God offers His law. This ethical law-order was designed by God to govern His creation. His ethical precepts were given to man as a means of subduing reality, including man himself. A perfect man, Jesus Christ, walked the earth and lived His life in terms of this revealed law. God's law is therefore not strictly "otherworldly," in the sense of applying only to a world beyond the human action, nor is it strictly "this-worldly," in the sense of being the product of human speculation. It is supernatural, yet delivered through revelation by God to mankind. It stands as both an ethical foundation of human action and as a tool of dominion. It explains the operations of the world to us, and it gives us power to exercise dominion over the creation.

Sanctification: Three Steps

We say that an individual is saved through God's imputation (judicial declaration) of Christ's righteousness to a sinner. This is called *justification*. It is a judicial act, God's declaration of "not guilty" by reason of the penalty which was paid by Jesus Christ. But this judicial act also has moral effects. God simultaneously *sanctifies* a person — sets him apart ethically or morally — in a *definitive* way at the moment

---

134. L. M. Lachmann, "The Role of Expectations in Economics as a Social Science," *Economica*, New Series, Vol. X (February 1943), p. 16. Lachmann is the "Austrian School" economist who has been insistent on the danger of relying heavily on general equilibrium models. "Such smooth transition from one equilibrium (long-run or short-run) to another virtually bars not only discussion of the process in which we are interested here, but of all true economic processes. . . . And all too soon we shall also allow ourselves to forget that what is of real economic interest are not the equilibria, even if they exist, which is in any case doubtful, but what happens between them." Lachmann, "The Market Economy and the Distribution of Wealth," in Mary Sennholz (ed.), *On Freedom and Free Enterprise*, p. 186. Lachmann's expressed hope in 1956 has not come true — in fact, the reverse has taken place: "It is very much to be hoped that economists in the future will show themselves less inclined than they have been in the past to look for ready-made, but spurious, coherence, and that they will take a greater interest in the variety of ways in which the human mind in action produces coherence out of an initially incoherent situation" (p. 187). Nevertheless, his Kantian individualism, with the human mind serving as the entrepreneurial provider of coherence to an incoherent world, is as impotent to deal epistemologically with the realities of God's creation as are the defenders of general equilibrium theory.

of his regeneration. Christ's righteousness is attributed to him as a whole, perfectly. But this definitive sanctification is to serve as the foundation of his *progressive* sanctification over time. He is to conform himself to Christ's perfect humanity through progressively adhering to God's law (through God's grace, of course). Then, on the day of final judgment, redeemed man will attain *final* sanctification — the perfect overcoming of evil. Each redeemed man finally attains the status of perfection which was implicit at the moment of his regeneration. This threefold aspect of moral sanctification — definitive, progressive, and final — is the basis of ethical progress of both the individual and of a civilization.[135]

What has not been understood by Christian social thinkers in the past, or at least not explicitly discussed, is that this same pattern of personal sanctification — definitive, progressive, and final — also applies to social organizations whose members have covenanted with God. There is the inescapable original covenant between God and Adam and Eve, which all institutions have violated in the original rebellion of Adam. There are also explicitly covenanted institutions that have been established by self-consciously regenerate believers. The most common examples are the family and the historical church. The same analysis applies also to contractual (though not covenantal)[136] institutions such as schools, businesses, and all other institutions that have been explicitly begun in terms of biblical morality. The perfection of Christ is *comprehensive perfection*. The salvation which He offers is *comprehensive salvation*.[137] It affects every institution. In other words, it affects every area of life in which men have responsibility.

Institutions such as churches and nations are definitively, progressively, and finally *judged* in history. On what basis? On the basis of God's law. Societies sometimes refuse to adopt an explicit covenant with God, or if they do, they later break it and fail to ask for its restoration. In both cases, they are judged in history. But if some so-

---

135. Gary North, *Unconditional Surrender: God's Program for Victory* (3rd ed.; Tyler, Texas: Institute for Christian Economics, 1988), pp. 66-72, 101-15.

136. On the distinction between covenants and contracts, see Gary North, *The Sinai Strategy: Economics and the Ten Commandments* (Tyler, Texas: Institute for Christian Economics, 1986), ch. 3. The presence of a self-maledictory oath identifies a covenantal institution: church, State, or family.

137. Gary North, "Comprehensive Redemption: A Theology of Social Action," in *Journal of Christian Reconstruction*, VIII (Summer 1981). Reprinted in Gary North, *Is the World Running Down? Crisis in the Christian Worldview* (Tyler, Texas: Institute for Christian Economics, 1988), Appendix C.

cial organizations are judged in history, isn't it equally true that others are blessed by God in history? The obvious example is the historical church. Isn't it blessed in history? Of course. On what basis? On the basis of its covenant with God, which includes permanent standards of ethical performance: biblical law. The church historical has been sanctified by God, i.e., set apart morally for His purposes. Therefore, we conclude that certain social institutions in history have also been definitively sanctified, progressively sanctified, and will be finally sanctified at the day of judgment. Without this threefold model of sanctification, how else could we argue for the continuing and guaranteed existence of the institutional church as a covenantal institution throughout history?

Jesus' perfect fulfilling of the law has effects in history. These effects are personal, but they are also institutional, since institutions are under the terms of the covenant as well as individuals. They develop or contract, are blessed or cursed, in terms of the specific terms of God's covenant, which are revealed in biblical law. Institutions, like individuals, cannot "earn" their salvation. They are granted their salvation, or healing, by the grace of God. Men covenant together to perform certain works, and God imputes the moral perfection and moral *accomplishments* of Jesus Christ to these newly covenanted institutions. How else can we explain the success or failure of families? How else can we explain why God visits the iniquity of certain families onto the members of the third and fourth generations (Ex. 20:5)? People make explicit covenants with God or rebel against His implicit covenants, such as the dominion covenant given to all men through our parents, Adam and Eve, and again with our other parents, Noah and his family. They succeed or fail in terms of *covenantal moral standards*. They advance or fall away in time, they grow or decay, *progressively* over time. This process is *ethical* and *covenantal*, not biological.

Providential Covenantalism

Here is the biblical solution of the question of social change. Here also is the biblical solution to the dualisms of metaphysical speculation: statics vs. dynamics. It is the 28th chapter of Deuteronomy, with its covenantal structure of social blessings and cursings, which is the *ethical* standard for social science, including economics. This is the biblical alternative to the timeless world of general equilibrium theory, "peopled" with inhuman omniscient beings, passively responding to their nearly infinite number of simultaneous equations. The real world of scarcity, uncertainty, and time is not a world of meaningless flux, but is instead a *providential world*, personally governed by a changeless God who has issued His sovereign decree.[138] The operational link between ethics and social change is *biblical law*. The personal link is Jesus Christ, the perfect man and simultaneously the divine Person who created this world.

Man, created in God's image, has access to knowledge, including economic knowledge, through revelation, both "natural" and "personally revealed." Both kinds of revelation are inescapably personal. Van Til calls this Christian-theistic ethics. Correct knowledge of the way the world works comes only from God's revelation of Himself and His law in the Bible. "The distinction between revealed and natural theology as ordinarily understood readily gives rise to a misunderstanding. It seems to indicate that man, though he is a sinner, can have certain true knowledge of God from nature but that for higher things he requires revelation. This is incorrect. It is true that we should make our theology and our ethics wide enough to include man's moral relationship to the whole universe. But it is not true that any ethical question that deals with man's place in nature can be interpreted rightly without the light of Scripture. For these reasons we prefer the name Christian-theistic ethics."[139]

It is this view of man's knowledge that is denied by all humanistic scholarship, and also by most forms of Christian scholarship. Christian apologetics has been corrupted by a Greek concept of autonomous knowledge from the days of the early church fathers.[140] When Christians at last abandon such a view of natural revelation, a paradigm shift of monumental proportions will take place that will transform the church, and then will transform the world.

Inefficient Humanism

The humanistic economist, like scientists of all kinds, rejects a biblical resolution of the "law-flux" problem. Most economists appeal "scientifically" to mechanistic explanations of human action. There are a few notable exceptions, but they are humanistic John

---

138. North, *Dominion Covenant: Genesis*, ch. 1: "Cosmic Personalism."
139. Van Til, *Christian Theistic Ethics*, p. 16.
140. Van Til, *Christianity in Conflict* (Philadelphia: Westminster Seminary, 1962).

the Baptists, crying in the epistemological wilderness.[141] Far more typical is Stephen Cheung, a rigorously empirical economist, and rigorously naive technician, who has titled his book, *The Myth of Social Cost*. The book is almost as mythical epistemologically as Coase's original essay. He argues that there is no theoretical barrier against making scientifically valid economic settlements where pollution is involved. He admits that abstracting from transaction costs does lead to problems. "The important conclusion is that the *solution becomes mechanical once the nature and magnitude of transaction costs, together with other constraints, are sufficiently specified.*"[142] He italicized his words, so he must have regarded them as significant.

What we can and must say, contrary to Professor Cheung, is that *no solution in economics is ever mechanical* because all solutions involve comparisons of subjective value — *inter*personal in the same period of time or across time, or *intra*personal across time.[143] Admit this, and Galbraith's conclusion is inescapable: "In the name of good scientific method he [the economist] is prevented from saying anything."[144] Thus, the economist is living in an epistemological dream world, a world of hypothetical scientific neutrality, complex formulas, mathematics, and (usually) taxpayer-financed tenure.

Neutrality is the essence of what we might call "economic formalism." Pro-free market economists continually appeal to *efficiency apart from equity*. How can we maximize value, they ask, *questions of equity apart*? This is the perhaps the major problem that pro-free market defenders have: How to overcome the objections of socialists

---

141. For example, Prof. Kenneth Boulding. See his presidential address to the American Economics Association, "Economics As A Moral Science," *American Economic Review*, LIX (March 1969).

142. Steven N. S. Cheung, *The Myth of Social Cost* (San Francisco: Cato Institute, [1978] 1980), p. 31.

143. On this point — which utterly devastates all humanistic economics, including Austrian subjectivism — see G. L. S. Shackle, *Time in Economics* (Amsterdam: North Holland Pub. Co., 1958), lecture 1; cf. "The Complex Nature of Time as a Concept in Economics," *Economica Internazionale*, VIII, No. 4. Shackle has pushed the logic of pure subjectivism, pure solipsism, and pure autonomy to a preposterous but consistent conclusion: every point in time is unique, incomparable, and autonomous. He calls it the "moment-in-being." For an attempted refutation which fails, see Ludwig Lachmann, *Capital, Expectations, and the Market Process* (Kansas City, Kansas: Sheed Andrews and McMeel, 1977), pp. 81-86. Lachmann falls back on the epistemologically hopeless concept of "common experience" to escape Shackle's logic: p. 86.

144. John Kenneth Galbraith, *The Affluent Society* (Boston: Houghton Mifflin, 1958), p. 150.

and other critics of the free market, who point to questions of equity and fairness as the crucial ones, rather than questions of efficiency? Throughout the twentieth century, the market's defenders have generally failed to convince the socialists and ethicists that the benefits of economic efficiency are greater than the social and personal costs of competition's "heartlessness," and "economic oppression." Inescapably, the decision as to which is more important — efficiency or morality — is a question of value (subjective and objective), a moral question. But free-market economists have so downplayed moral questions in their "scientific" discussions that they are not skilled competitors in any intellectual marketplace of moral ideas. Unfortunately for them, that is the only marketplace of ideas there is. *Because they have emphasized efficiency and have excluded or downplayed questions of morality and value, value-free economists have not been efficient competitors in the intellectual marketplace.* The religion of economic efficiency turns out to be woefully inefficient.

Weber's Critique: Dialecticism

Max Weber, the great German social scientist (d. 1920), recognized the tension — a permanent tension, he argued — in all humanistic economic systems between what he called "formal rationality" and "substantive rationality." It is the heart of the debate between capitalism and socialism. It is the question of efficiency vs. ethics.[145] With

---

145. Weber wrote: "A system of economic activity will be called 'formally' rational according to the degree in which the provision for needs, which is essential to every rational economy, is capable of being expressed in numerical, calculable terms, and is so expressed. . . . The concept is thus unambiguous, at least in the sense that expression in money terms yields the highest degree of formal calculability. . . . The concept of 'substantive rationality,' on the other hand, is full of ambiguities. It conveys only one element common to all 'substantive' analyses: namely, that they do not restrict themselves to note the purely formal and (relatively) unambiguous fact that action is based on 'goal-oriented' rational calculation with the technically most adequate available methods, but apply certain criteria of ultimate ends, whether they be ethical, political, utilitarian, hedonistic, feudal (*ständisch*), egalitarian, or whatever, and measure the results of the economic action, however formally 'rational' in the sense of correct calculation they may be, against these scales of 'value rationality' or '*substantive* goal rationality.' There is an infinite number of possible value scales for this type of rationality, of which the socialist and communist standards constitute only one group. The latter, although by no means unambiguous in themselves, always involve elements of social justice and equality." Weber, *Economy and Society: An Outline of Interpretive Sociology*, edited by Guenther Roth and Claus Wittich (New York: Bedminster Press, 1968), pp. 85-86. This is a translation of Weber's posthumous *Wirtschaft und Gesellschaft*, 4th German edition, 1956.

respect to economic efficiency (formal rationality), Weber argued, capitalism's critics very often take offense: "All of these [substantively rational, ethical—G.N.] approaches may consider the 'purely formal' rationality of calculation in monetary terms as of quite secondary importance or even as fundamentally inimical to their respective ultimate ends, even before anything has been said about the consequences of the specifically modern calculating attitude."[146] In short, Weber concluded, "Formal and substantive rationality, no matter by what standard the latter is measured, are always in principle separate things, no matter that in many (and under certain very artificial assumptions even in all) cases they may coincide empirically."[147] This dialectical tension is basic to Weber's sociological analysis.[148]

Economists who defend the free market seldom acknowledge the nature of this fundamental debate between the free market's intellectual defenders and the free market's critics. Their "value-free" methodology and their methodological individualism blind them to the realities of the debate—a debate over morality, values, and the effects of voluntary economic transactions on social aggregates. Free market economists cannot seem to understand those scholars and critics who raise the question of individual morality, let alone social consequences and social values, and who then ignore questions of economic efficiency for the attainment of the economic goals of individuals. The economists dismiss such criticisms as amateurish and irrational; the fact that most people accept the perspective of the critics does not faze the economists, most of whom see this battle as a technical academic debate rather than a life-and-death war for Western civilization. They see all conflicts as in principle resolvable "at the margin, at some price." They prefer not to discuss the Gulag.

Anti-capitalist critics, of course, really do tend to ignore questions of efficiency, a concept which does have to be considered carefully in any relevant discussion of men's economic ability to pursue moral goals, both personal and social. Weber recognized this: "Where a planned economy is radically carried out, it must further accept the inevitable reduction in formal, calculatory rationality

---

146. *Ibid.*, p. 86. See a slightly different translation of this passage and the one in the preceding footnote in Weber, *The Theory of Social and Economic Organization*, edited by Talcott Parsons (New York: The Free Press, [1947] 1964), pp. 185-86.

147. *Ibid.*, p. 108. [*Theory*, p. 212.]

148. Gary North, "Max Weber: Rationalism, Irrationalism, and the Bureaucratic Cage," in North (ed.), *Foundations of Christian Scholarship*, pp. 141-46.

which would result from the elimination of money and capital accounting. Substantive and formal (in the sense of exact *calculation*) rationality are, it should be stated again, after all largely distinct problems. This fundamental and, in the last analysis, unavoidable element of irrationality in economic systems is one of the important sources of all 'social' problems, and above all, of the problems of socialism."[149] Thus, Weber pointed to a dialectical tension in all humanistic discussions of social systems. Free market economists and capitalism's critics cannot come to grips with each other's arguments.

The free market economist does have one thing working for him: socialism really is inefficient. People around the globe want the fruits of free market capitalism, which are only too visible on television and in imported media, and steadily national leaders are drastically modifying socialist ownership in order to provide access to these fruits. There is a humorous definition in the late 1980's that describes the situation in Europe: "Socialist, noun: a capitalist who, for political reasons, cannot admit it publicly." Nevertheless, economic pragmatism is not sufficient to serve as the foundation for an entire civilization. Envy still has a large political constituency.[150] There is a desperate need today for a moral and ultimately religious defense of capitalism.[151] It will not suffice to defend the formal efficiency of the free market by means of an appeal to the formal political techniques of democracy. An appeal to formal rationalism from the market to the election booth and back again is little more than the proverbial pair of drunks who lean on each other in order to stay on their feet. Eventually, they tumble together. Weber's dualism between substantive rationalism and formal rationalism is as applicable to democratic theory as to market theory. The spirit of democratic capitalism needs moral content derived from outside market theory and democratic theory.[152] The naked public square needs more than the fig leaf of political and religious pluralism to protect it from the socially destructive elements of revolutionary violence and moral erosion.[153]

---

149. *Ibid.*, p. 111. [*Theory*, pp. 214-15.]

150. Gonzalo Fernández de la Mora, *Egalitarian Envy: The Political Foundations of Social Justice*, translated by Antonio T. de Nicholas (New York: Paragon House, 1987), Part B.

151. Paul Johnson, "The moral dilemma confronting capitalism," *Washington Times* (Feb. 21, 1989).

152. Michael Novak, *The Spirit of Democratic Capitalism* (New York: Touchstone, 1982).

153. Richard John Neuhaus, *The Naked Public Square: Religion and Democracy in America* (Grand Rapids, Michigan: Eerdmans, 1984). Cf. Gary North, *Political Polytheism: The Myth of Pluralism* (Tyler, Texas: Institute for Christian Economics, 1989).

"Weighing Up the Gains and Losses"

Let us return to Coase's arguments — arguments that deliberately ignore the ethical question of private property rights and the losses to those whose rights are violated. "It is all a question of weighing up the gains that would accrue from eliminating these harmful effects against the gains that accrue from allowing them to continue."[154] But here is the *real* "problem of social costs": *the economist, as a scientist, has no way to "weigh up" economic gains and losses.*[155]

Coase and all of his followers go on blithely as if all this talk about tallying up costs and benefits — social or individual — had any epistemologically valid theoretical meaning for a methodological individualist, let alone any scientific application. "The problem which we face in dealing with actions which have harmful effects is not simply one of restraining those responsible for them. What has to be decided is whether the gain from preventing the harm is greater than the loss which would be suffered elsewhere as a result of stopping the action which produces the harm."[156] *But economists cannot measure social costs and benefits, according to the logic of modern economics, since costs and benefits are exclusively subjective categories.*

Humanistic economists go about their business as if "equilibrium analysis" were anything more than a teaching device, and very often a misleading one.[157] The assumptions of equilibrium analysis deny the possibility of human action in a world in which these equilibrium conditions exist. There is perfect knowledge for market participants in such a universe, and therefore neither profits nor losses. (Yet even in equilibrium, there would be transaction costs. There are no free lunches in the land of equilibrium; it is just that everyone knows exactly how much lunch will cost.) It is a world of automatons, not humans, as Mises wrote. Yet all of the "rigorously scientific" discussions of economic efficiency and optimal distribution are based on the trans-historical model of equilibrium. Peter Lewin has seen this more clearly than most economists have: "The other important as-

---

154. Coase, "Social Cost," p. 26.

155. North, *Dominion Covenant: Genesis*, ch. 4.

156. Coase, "Social Cost," p. 27.

157. Debreau's mathematical analysis of free market equilibrium may have won him the 1983 Nobel Prize in economics, but it tells us little about how the real world of supply and demand really works. Gerard Debreau, *Theory of Price: An Axiomatic Analysis of Equilibrium* (New Haven, Connecticut: Yale University Press, 1959). This is wood, hay, and stubble.

sumption underlying the efficiency approach is the absence of significant distortions elsewhere in the economy. The calculation of social costs and benefits is profoundly affected if this assumption is violated. In a world of distortions, where prices are not general equilibrium competitive prices that reflect marginal costs, the imposition of a Pigouvian tax or a liability that would achieve efficiency if distortions were absent may *reduce* efficiency. . . . In more general terms, outside of equilibrium there is no way to know if any move is efficiency-enhancing or not."[158] He goes so far as to say — quite accurately with respect to a methodology devoid of the concept of God, revelation, and absolute objective values — that "the notion of efficiency makes little sense outside of general equilibrium."[159]

Coase is unquestionably correct that "In a world in which there are costs of rearranging the rights established by the legal system, the courts, in cases relating to nuisance, are, in effect, making a decision on the economic problem and determining how resources are to be employed."[160] To the extent that Coase's article helps judges or others to become more aware of this inescapable reality of economic allocation, it is a useful essay. But how useful is a rarified academic exercise which overlooks that most fundamental of economic costs: *the cost of suffering a violation of justice*? Never forget: he wants to limit his discussion to costs and benefits, "questions of equity apart."

Optimal Crime and Optimal Punishment

We see the same sort of "add it up" reasoning in a subdivision of law and economics: crime and punishment. Ever since Gary S. Becker's pioneering article in 1968, University of Chicago-type economists have been analyzing crime and law enforcement in terms of a model that minimizes social losses from crime. This model treats social costs and optimal social solutions as if such concepts had scientific validity in a world of subjectivist economic analysis. Please forgive the following; it was written by an economist:

Optimal policies are defined as those that minimize the social loss from crime. That loss depends upon the net damage to victims; the resource costs of discovering, apprehending, and convicting offenders; and the costs

---

158. Peter Lewin, "Pollution Externalities: Social Cost and Strict Liability," *Cato Journal*, II (Spring 1982), pp. 216-17.

159. *Ibid.*, p. 217.

160. Coase, "Social Cost," p. 27.

of punishment itself. These components of the loss, in turn, depend upon the number of criminal offenders, the probability of apprehending and convicting offenders, the size and form of punishments, the potential legal incomes of offenders, and several other variables. The optimal supply of criminal offenses — in essence, the amount of crime — is then determined by selecting values for the probability of conviction, the penalty, and other variables determined by society that minimize the social loss from crime. Within this framework, theorems are derived that relate the optimal probability of conviction, the optimal punishments, and the optimal supply of criminal offenses to such factors as the size of the damages from various types of crimes, changes in the overall costs of apprehending and convicting offenders, and differences in the relative responsiveness of offenders to conviction probabilities and to penalties.[161]

This all sounds so scientific, but it is all spurious if economics does not allow the interpersonal comparison of subjective utilities or the aggregating of interpersonal utilities, which it doesn't. But sophisticated, intellectually rigorous analyses such as this certainly do increase the likelihood of academic tenure and personal career advancement — an employment guarantee that some people (myself included) regard as less than socially optimal.[162]

What the reader should be aware of is that the practitioners of economics are unhappy with the public's perception of their trade. One the one hand, the economist as rigorous scientist cannot do without the concept of equilibrium to build his theories, and this concept begins with the presupposition of perfect, zero-cost knowledge. Then the economist attempts to fit this model onto the error-filled real world, "making appropriate modifications," of course. Problem: the moment you make any modification, the model disintegrates. At best, the equilibrium model is useful as a platform for making intuitive leaps of faith. Intuitive leaps of faith are inescapable aspects of all economic thought, but something which economists prefer not to discuss.[163]

---

161. William M. Landes, in Gary S. Becker and William M. Landes (eds.), *Essays in the Economics of Crime and Punishment* (New York: National Bureau of Economic Research, 1974), p. xiv. Each of the five authors who contributed the book's six essays was at the time a professor at the University of Chicago.

162. Cf. Robert A. Nisbet, "The Permanent Professors: A Modest Proposal," *Public Interest* (Fall 1965); reprinted in Nisbet, *Tradition and Revolt: Historical and Sociological Essays* (New York: Random House, 1968), ch. 12.

163. North, "Economics: From Reason to Intuition," in North (ed.), *Foundations of Christian Scholarship*, ch. 5.

Becker's Breakthrough

Gary Becker insists that his approach to crime and punishment does not "assume perfect knowledge, lightning-fast calculation, or any of the other caricatures of economic theory."[164] Dr. Becker is self-deceived; this is exactly what all discussions of socially optimum decision-making must assume. This so-called caricature is in fact the heart, mind, and soul of modern economics as an academic discipline. Without it, there could be no mathematics or equations in economic analysis, and without mathematics, one rarely gets into print in the prestigious scholarly economics journals.[165] Certainly, Dr. Becker's essay is made nearly unreadable by page after page of pseudo-scientific equations, as are most of his other essays. (I have decided to coin a new adjective that describes this pseudo-scientific approach to economic reasoning: *psientific*.)

Becker insists that "This essay concentrates almost entirely on determining optimal policies to combat illegal behavior and pays little attention to actual policies."[166] In this regard, the essay is representative of virtually the whole field of law and economics. Becker prefers equations and equilibrium to personal responsibility when it comes to suggesting what should be done about crime. He and his colleagues refuse to honor Baird's warning: "Since all costs and benefits are subjective, no government can accurately identify, much less establish, the optimum quantity of anything."[167] Admit this, and 90 percent of what gets published in the professional academic journals would have to be rejected by the editors. Where, under such academically sub-optimal circumstances, would a career economist publish an essay such as Isaac Ehrlich's representative example, "Optimal Participation in Illegitimate Market Activities: A One-Period Uncertainty Model"?[168]

Biblical law is the foundation of optimal social and economic policies — the *only* foundation that honors God and can therefore produce long-term benefits: covenantal blessings. This is why we need

---

164. Gary S. Becker, "Crime and Punishment: an Economic Approach" (1968), in *Essays in the Economics of Crime and Punishment*, p. 9.

165. Galbraith, *Economics Peace and Laughter*, ch. 2.

166. *Essays in the Economics of Crime and Punishment*, p. 44.

167. Charles W. Baird, "The Philosophy and Ideology of Pollution Regulation," *Cato Journal*, II (Spring 1982), p. 303.

168. Actually, this was only a subsection in his influential and equation-filled article, "Participation in Illegitimate Activities: An Economic Analysis," in *Essays in the Economics of Crime and Punishment*.

to adhere to the Bible's system of penalties to be imposed by the civil government; without this, we are flying blind. We are flying as blind as Gary Becker is when he writes: "A wise use of fines requires knowledge of marginal gains and harm and of marginal apprehension and conviction costs; admittedly, such knowledge is not easily attained."[169] *Not easily attained!* In terms of the logic of subjective economics, such knowledge cannot be attained at all. We cannot make scientific interpersonal comparisons of subjective utility or disutility. Professional economists may shudder at the thought of restructuring civil sanctions to make civil law conform more closely to God's revealed law, but they have nothing to offer in its place except endless self-deception regarding the scientific possibility of discovering socially optimal levels of crime and punishment.[170]

That Becker's essay does not even consider the possibility of restitution payments by criminals to their victims, but instead focuses on the social benefits of fines paid to the State, indicates how far from common sense these psientific economists are. What mainly disturbs Becker is that with imprisonment, "some of the payment 'by' offenders would not be received by the rest of society, and a net social loss would result."[171] He is so concerned with questions of "net social loss" that he neglects the crucial question of the net *personal* loss suffered by the victim.[172] The word "restitution" does not appear in the index of *Essays in the Economics of Crime and Punishment.* (The book has approximately 170 pages of equations or parts of equations in its 273 pages, with most of the remainder devoted to charts, graphs, statistical regression analysis, brief bibliographies, and the five and a half page index in which the word "restitution" does not appear.)[173] Two dec-

---

169. Becker, in *ibid.*, p. 28.

170. For example, Nobel Prize-winning University of Chicago economist George Stigler's essay, "The Optimum Enforcement of Laws," *ibid*, pp. 55-67.

171. *Ibid.*, pp. 24-25.

172. He says that criminal law should deal only with crimes in which victims cannot be compensated. "Thus an action would be 'criminal' precisely because it results in uncompensated 'harm' to others." *Ibid.*, p. 33. I have some questions. First, if someone can serve a prison term or pay a fine to the State, why can't he compensate victims instead? Second, why does Becker refuse to discuss the overwhelming majority of crimes in which there are identifiable victims, preferring instead to fill up pages with equations? Is he conveniently defining away the problem of crime and punishment for the vast majority of crimes? Third, why does he feel it necessary to put quotation marks around *criminal* and *harm*? Is it because such language smacks too much of objective moral norms?

173. For an equally arcane academic treatment, see David J. Pyle, *The Economics of Crime and Law Enforcement* (New York: St. Martin's, 1983).

ades later, Becker is still humming the same old tune: "deterrence, not vengeance," fines, not restitution to victims. And he still has discovered no objective answer to the problem he raises: making the punishment fit the crime: "Obviously, it is hard to estimate damages for many company crimes and even harder to determine the probability of conviction."[174] Hard? By the standards of subjective value theory, it is theoretically impossible.

Buchanan is correct in his discussion of the economics of crime: ". . . any costs which the economist may objectify need bear little relation to those costs which serve as actual obstacles to decisions." He is not correct, however, in his next sentence: "Recognition of this fact need not destroy the usefulness of the economic analysis."[175] Without a scientifically verifiable link between subjective decision-making and objective fines, the economist cannot make a coherent case for any outcome other than judicial chaos. (It should not be surprising that Becker has argued that the free market would bring economic order even if all men's decisions were irrational.)[176] The economist needs a ruler, as Thirlby has so accurately identified it. In fact, he capitalizes it.[177] The economist does indeed need a Ruler, an "omniscient observer who can read all preference functions," as Buchanan so professionally describes Him.[178] But economists have denied His relevance from the beginning of the profession; economics was the first scientific guild to do so. It was this self-conscious separation of economics from both theology and morality that economist William Letwin praises as "the greatest accomplishment of the seventeenth century."[179] (It apparently overshadowed the less significant work of Director of the Mint Mr. Newton.)

This digression has been necessary in order to demonstrate what the academic field of economics and law is really all about. It is all about making scholarly reputations and making preposterous assumptions. The more preposterous the assumptions, the more schol-

---

174. Gary Becker, "Make the Punishment Fit the Corporate Crime," *Business Week* (March 13, 1989).

175. Buchanan, *Cost and Choice*, p. 93.

176. Gary Becker, "Irrational Behavior and Economic Theory," *Journal of Political Economy*, LXX (Feb. 1962). For my critique of his position, as well as Israel Kirzner's very different critique, see North, *Dominion Covenant*, pp. 347-53.

177. Thirlby, "The Ruler," *South African Journal of Economics*, XIV (Dec. 1946), reprinted in *L.S.E. Essays on Cost.*

178. Buchanan, *Cost and Choice*, p. 95.

179. Letwin, *Origins of Scientific Economics*, p. 159.

arly the reputation. And it is all done in the name of optimality: "The main contribution of this essay, as I see it, is to demonstrate that optimal policies to combat illegal behavior are part of an optimal allocation of resources."[180]

The Social Benefits of Criminal Behavior

A unique component of the Becker thesis on criminal behavior is his thesis that the concern of society in prohibiting criminal behavior ought to be the reduction of *net* social cost. This is a very important qualification. In calculating the net cost to society of any criminal act, *Becker insists that we must count as a positive benefit the gains made by the criminal by committing the crime.* "The net cost or damage to society is simply the difference between the harm and gain," he writes.[181] How can he say this? Because of his thesis — the one which undergirds this whole subdivision of economics — that *criminal behavior is no different from any other profit-seeking behavior.* Ethics has no role to play in distinguishing crime from other profit-seeking activities. "The approach taken here follows the economists' usual analysis of choice and assumes that a person commits an offense if the expected utility to him exceeds the utility he could get by using his time and other resources at other activities. Some persons become 'criminals,' therefore, not because their basic motivation differs from that of other persons, but because their benefits and costs differ."[182]

Notice, first, that he puts the word *criminals* in quotation marks, indicating his fear of making an ethical judgment in a scholarly journal. Second, he hesitates to follow what economists sometimes call the pure logic of choice.[183] He says that *some* persons become criminals "because their benefits and costs differ" from law-abiding persons. Why not use cost-benefit analysis to explain the actions of *all* criminals? Why limit it to only *some*? Why bother to distinguish the non-economic motives of criminals from those of non-criminals? The logic of his argument is that non-economic motives and personal tastes are irrelevant for economic analysis; only costs and benefits are relevant for making predictions regarding people's economic

---

180. *Ibid.*, p. 45.
181. Becker, "Crime and Punishment," *op. cit.*, p. 6.
182. *Ibid.*, p. 9.
183. F. A. Hayek, "Economics and Knowledge," *Economica*, IV (1937), reprinted in Hayek, *Individualism and Economic Order* (University of Chicago Press, 1948), pp. 35, 39, 46-47. See also Richard Fuerle, *The Pure Logic of Choice* (New York: Vantage, 1986).

behavior.[184] Why not follow the logic of the argument? Why not conclude in print that there is no theoretically valid economic difference between profit-seeking activities and criminal acts; there are only differences in net social utility? But he does not go this far. It is almost as if some last remaining trace of common sense and moral values has kept Dr. Becker from pursuing the logic of his position.

His followers have not been so reticent: "An individual decision to commit a crime (or not to commit a crime) is simply an application of the economist's theory of choice. If the benefits of the illegal action exceed the costs, the crime is committed, and it is not if costs exceed benefits. Offenders are not pictured as 'sick' or 'irrational,' but merely as engaging in activities that yield the most satisfaction, given their available alternatives."[185] Then what of the warning of God in Proverbs? "All they that hate me love death" (8:36b). Of course: just redefine suicidal criminal behavior in terms of the criminal's subjective preference for death, assume the existence of subjective ordinal (or even cardinal) utility in his subjective value preference scale, and economic analysis still holds! Common sense disappears, but economic analysis, like the smile of the cheshire cat, remains. (In all honesty, this kind of economic analysis goes back to the mid-nineteenth century. Jeremy Bentham used a very similar approach based on net pleasure or pain. Mercifully, the academic world had not yet discovered either econometrics or multivariate regression analysis, so his essays were literate and coherent.)

---

184. This is how professional economists assess Becker's argument. Writes Paul H. Rubin: "Becker essentially argued that criminals are about like anyone else — that is, they rationally maximize their own self-interest (utility) subject to the constraints (prices, incomes) that they face in the marketplace and elsewhere. Thus the decision to become a criminal is in principle no different from the decision to become a bricklayer or a carpenter, or, indeed, an economist. The individual considers the net costs and benefits of each alternative and makes his decision on this basis. If we then want to explain changes in criminal behavior over time or space, we examine changes in these constraints. The basic assumption in this type of research is that tastes are constant and that changes in behavior can be explained by changes in prices." But we all know that tastes do change. This is economically irrelevant, say the economists. Why? Because economics cannot yet deal with changes in taste. "Tastes are assumed to be constant because we have absolutely no theory of changes in tastes. . . ." Rubin, "The Economics of Crime," in Ralph Andreano and John J. Siegfried (eds.), *The Economics of Crime* (New York: Wiley, 1980), p. 15.

185. Morgan O. Reynolds, "The Economics of Criminal Activity" (1973), reprinted in Ralph Andreano and John J. Siegfried (eds.), *The Economics of Crime* (New York: Wiley, 1980), p. 34.

Becker was too timid to pursue his remarkable thesis very far. Let me show you where it leads. What about the net social cost or net social benefit of murder? He writes that "the cost of murder is measured by the loss of earnings of victims and excludes, among other things, the value placed by society on life itself. . . ."[186] But this is insufficiently rigorous by the standards of Chicago School economics. He forgot that the victim's ability to earn a living also involves costs. The producer must eat, use public facilities of various kinds, and be a life-long absorber of resources. So, what Becker really meant to say is that the cost of murder is the net loss — discounted by the prevailing rate of long-term interest, of course[187] — of the late victim's lifetime earning potential, *minus* net lifetime expenditures (also discounted). This raises a key question in our era of legalized abortion, which may be a preliminary to legalized euthanasia (as it has been in the Netherlands): *What if the dead victim had been sick, dying, mentally retarded, or in some other way is a net absorber of society's scarce economic resources?* Must we not conclude that the murderer has in fact increased the net wealth of society? Remember Becker's rule: "society's" estimation of net social costs or benefits "excludes, among other things, the value placed by society on life itself." On what economic grounds could a legislator oppose the concept of selective murder, with criminal indictments to be handed down in specific cases only after a retrospective evaluation (by some committee or other) of net costs and benefits?[188] Who is to say? After all, as he says, "Reasonable men will often differ on the amount of damages or benefits caused by different activities."[189]

---

186. Becker, "Crime and Punishment," p. 9.

187. See Posner's discussion: *Economic Analysis of Law*, pp. 170-81.

188. Becker also fails to mention the value of life to the late victim, which seems a bit odd, given the fact that Becker also pioneered a subdivision in the economics profession called human capital: Gary S. Becker, *Human Capital* (New York: National Bureau of Economic Research, 1964). Fortunately, Richard Posner has attempted to rectify this gaping hole in Becker's analysis. He does try to make an objective estimation of the economic value of life to the victim, which he concludes is nearly infinite. He uses a hypothetical example of rising economic payment that someone would demand to induce him to get involved in death-producing activities: the more likely death becomes, the higher the pay demanded. If death is sure, the price demanded will approach infinity. (Why, then, do men volunteer for suicide missions in wartime?) This is his surrogate for making a subjective posthumous estimation of life's monetary value to the late victim: Posner, *Economic Analysis of Law*, pp. 182-86. He draws no important conclusions from this analysis, however, and does not include it in his book's index under "death" or "death," for which there are no entries, or under the entries for "murder."

189. Becker, "Crime and Punishment," p. 45.

If all this begins to sound like the work of a madman, this is only because it is the work of a technically skilled University of Chicago economist who follows the logic of his position.[190] Bear in mind that Becker's essay on crime is regarded by his peers as a classic in the field, one comparable to (and written with the same presuppositions as) Coase's essay on social cost. One European economist has called Becker's work truly revolutionary. Even more: ". . . Gary Becker is classed among the greatest living American economists."[191]

Pin-Stickers and Their Victims

Becker has returned us to the age-old question of the pin-sticker and his victim.[192] If a person enjoys sticking pins into other people, and if other people resent this, what should society do? Construct a measuring device to record the joy of the pin-sticker and then compare it to the pain of his victim? Should society base the decision of whether to identify this act as a crime in terms of the pin-sticker's pleasure minus his victim's pain — "net social utility"? And if so, what do we do about the masochist who enjoys being stuck? (Yes, I know: sticking him is a victimless crime, and therefore outside economic policy analysis.)

The biblical view of man rests on the presupposition that there are two kinds of people: covenant-breakers and covenant-keepers. There is also such a thing as common grace.[193] When God removes it, people become more consistent with their own ethical presuppositions. Increasing numbers of covenant-breakers turn to crime as an expression of their ethical rebellion against God. The economics of crime and punishment no doubt can be discussed *in part* in terms of criminals' expected costs and benefits, but equally important, if not

---

190. For a brief, intelligent, and methodologically rigorous response to Becker, see G. Warren Nutter, "On Economism," *Journal of Law and Economics*, XXII (October 1979), pp. 263-68. It was in response to Becker's methodology that I wrote my tongue-in-cheek piece, "A Note on the Opportunity Cost of Marriage," *Journal of Political Economy* (April 1968), in which I concluded that male Ph.D-holding scholars cannot afford to marry women who are not high school drop-outs. Astoundingly, George Stigler (seemingly straight-faced) replied in a subsequent issue that I had not dealt with Adam Smith accurately.

191. Henri Lepage, *Tomorrow, Capitalism: The Economics of Economic Freedom* (La Salle, Illinois: Open Court, [1978] 1982), p. 161. The chapter is titled, "The Gary Becker Revolution."

192. North, *Dominion Covenant: Genesis*, pp. 44-45.

193. Gary North, *Dominion and Common Grace: The Biblical Basis of Progress* (Tyler, Texas: Institute for Christian Economics, 1987).

more important, is the psychological link between crime and certain forms of addiction, especially the addiction to illicit thrills and danger. People's tastes are not stable, contrary to Chicago School economists; people can and do develop an addiction to criminal behavior. They need ever-increasing doses of crime to satisfy their habit. Thus, to analyze all economic actors in terms of the pure logic of expected profit and loss is a fundamental error of modern economic analysis.

Becker disagrees. He wants to consider only people's perceived costs and benefits, risks and rewards, *net*. The logic of Becker's position seems to infer the right of a criminal to inflict damage as heavy as murder so long as he can demonstrate in court through cost-benefit analysis that the particular murder produced net social utility. Coase, writing eight years earlier, was more judicious in his conclusions. He wanted only to assert the right *at some price* of an individual to inflict on other people less permanent forms of damage than murder.

The "Right to Inflict Damage"

Coase considers an example taken from Pigou's *Economics of Welfare*. Suppose that it would pay a railroad firm to run a train faster than normal, thereby throwing off more sparks. (The example applies to railroads before the era of diesel engines, but it is still valid as an example.) Suppose also that the sparks set a fire that burns a farmer's crop. Pigou said that the railroad company should reimburse the farmer for the loss of his crops by paying him the crop's market value. This, it should be pointed out, is also what Exodus 22:6 says. Coase denies Pigou's conclusion. "The conclusion that it is desirable that the railway should be made liable for the damage it causes is wrong."[194] Why? Because *the economic gains to the total economy*, as revealed by the value of the crops lost vs. the cost of installing spark-arresters on the engine, or the losses to the railroad company if the train was not run at all, *might be greater by allowing the train to emit sparks*. (Might be, might be, might be: How can anyone *know*, given the intellectual tools of modern, subjectivist economics?) The judge should consider the monetary value of the burned crops in relation to the cost of installing a spark-arrester or the monetary losses to the company of running the train more slowly, and then make a decision as to what each party owes the other. In other words, he must consider

---

194. Coase, "Social Cost," p. 32.

the *value of total production.* "This question can be resolved by considering what would happen to the value of total production if it were decided to exempt the railway from liability from fire-damage. . . ."[195] Coase argues that it might be better for society in general if the farmer's property rights are ignored, leaving him free to pay the railroad company sufficient money to install the spark-arrester. After all, the value of the crop may be greater than the cost of the spark-arrester.[196]

What if the farmer had worked for years to build up the soil or build his family's dream home? This labor was unquestionably a manifestation of the dominion covenant. Perhaps he dimly understood that his labor to build the house was in a unique way a moral act under God, meaning his personal conformity to God's injunction to subdue the earth to His glory. His home is not simply a manifestation of his technical competence as a builder; it may also be a manifestation of his self-conscious fulfillment of the dominion covenant. In other words, this house may be in a very real sense a holy thing — a thing set apart for God by the very act of constructing it. This is why people are sometimes "irrationally" committed to a piece of ground. A spark-emitting train is threatening his home's existence, meaning the work of his hands, meaning his dream or vision. Is he entitled to no compensation? Isn't the railway *always* liable for damages? Furthermore, if the court decides that the railway is liable — and Coase denies that the court should automatically decide that it is — is the man's shattered dream worth only monetary compensation for the market value of his crops? Maybe he resents the fact that the railway is reducing to mere dollars his right to safety from fire, and market-determined dollars at that? Shouldn't the engines be fitted with a spark retarder, by law? After all, this is not an accidental, occasional incident; this is a daily threat of fire that is a statistically probable event because of the technology involved in running the trains. In

---

195. *Ibid.*, p. 33.

196. Clearly, the damage inflicted on the crops planted close to the tracks by numerous farmers could be high. The costs would be high to organize the farmers together in order to contribute money to finance the installation of the spark arrester. Each farmer would tend to wait for the others to put up the money. Each would prefer to become a "free rider" in the transaction: paying nothing, but benefitting from the spark arrester. The payment to the railroad firm probably would not be made apart from intervention by the civil government to compel all farmers who are benefitted by the spark arrester to pay their proportional share. The civil government eventually must decide who pays whom: the railroad firm paying damages to the farmers, or the farmers paying "protection money" to the railroad company.

short, what about the *psychic costs* to the victim? Coase's analysis completely ignores this fundamental issue.[197]

"Coase, Get Your Cattle Off My Land!"

Or what about the farmer who sees the cattleman move in next door? Or the cattleman who sees the sheepherder move in next door to him? If the other man's animals come roaming into his garden or into his pasture, isn't the victim entitled to compensation? What if the "accident" of wandering animals is not an accident, but a regular way of doing business? Shouldn't the offender be required to put a fence around the wandering beasts? Why should the injured party be required by the court to share the costs of fencing? *Are the victim's property rights of undisturbed ownership not to receive predictable compensation?* What I am arguing, in short, is that the victimized property owner has the right to announce: "Coase, get your cattle off my land!"

My land: there is greater value to me in my right to enjoy my land undisturbed than Coase's reductionist economic analysis indicates. To count the market value of the crops that the cattle trampled, and then to compare that value to society with the meat that someone will put on his table, is *to reduce the value of a man's right of undisturbed ownership to zero*. Coase's concept of social costs ignores one of the most valuable assets offered to men by a free market social order: *the right of the owner to determine who will and who will not have legal access to his property, and on what terms*. To think that monetary compensation for damaged goods at a market price is all that matters to an owner is ridiculous. Rothbard is correct, and I cite his statement again: "There are many problems with this theory. First, income and wealth are important *to the parties involved*, although they might not be to uninvolved economists. It makes a great deal of difference to both of them who has to pay whom. Second, this thesis works only if we deliberately ignore psychological factors. Costs are not only monetary. The farmer might well have an attachment to the orchard far beyond monetary damage. . . . But then the supposed indifference totally breaks down."[198]

Even more important, there must also be compensation for the loss of security that is necessarily involved in every willful violation

---

197. This is Walter Block's main criticism: "Coase and Demsetz on Private Property Rights," *Journal of Libertarian Studies*, I, No. 2 (1977).

198. Rothbard, "Law, Property Rights, and Air Pollution," *Cato Journal*, II (Spring 1982), p. 58.

of another man's property rights. The Bible says plainly that restitution shall be paid with "the best" of the violator's field, "and of the best of his own vineyard." To argue, as Coase does, that as far as society is concerned, it is economically irrelevant to the total economic value accruing to society whether the victim (farmer) builds the fence at his expense or the cattleman (violator) does at his expense is to place zero price on the rights of ownership. *When free market economists place zero economic value on the rights of ownership, they have given away the case for the free market.* This is precisely what Coase and the many academic "economics of law" specialists have done. They have preferred the illusion of value-free economics to the ideal of private property — our legal right to exclude others from using our property.

Theft as a Factor of Production

Coase explicitly argues that the *ability to cause economic injury* is a *factor of production*. Therefore, the State's decision to deny a person the *right* to exercise this ability involves a social cost: the loss of a factor of production. "If factors of production are thought of as rights, it becomes easier to understand that the right to do something which has a harmful effect (such as the creation of smoke, noise, smells, etc.) is also a factor of production. Just as we may use a piece of land in such a way as to prevent someone else from crossing it, or parking his car, or building his house upon it, so we may use it in such a way as to deny him a view or quiet or unpolluted air. The cost of exercising a right (of using a factor of production) is always the loss which is suffered elsewhere in consequence of the exercise of that right — the inability to cross land, to park a car, to build a house, to enjoy a view, to have peace and quiet or to breathe clean air."[199] Coase simply ignores the crucial free market concept that *legal right to exclude others* from invading your property is *a far more crucial factor of production* — the factor of personal confidence in the honesty and reliability of the civil government. Without this confidence, the free market is steadily reduced to little more than black market operations.

Coase wants us to "have regard for the total effect" of such uses of our so-called capital, namely, the right to pollute the environment.[200] But "total costs" are precisely what he has deliberately chosen to ignore: *the right to determine whether or not another person can invade my*

---

199. Coase, "Social Cost," p. 44.
200. *Idem.*

privacy, wake me up at 2:00 A.M., set fire to my crops, send his cattle to eat in my fields, or, ultimately, sell tickets to people to peek through my window at 3:00 A.M. The economic value of my right to say "Keep your cattle off my land!"—and my right to demand restitution for the violation of this right—is simply ignored by Coase and all those economists who take seriously his economic analysis of social costs. *He offers economic analysis of the right to inflict damage, but he ignores any economic analysis of the right to deny the damage-producer his so-called right.* More than this: *Coase explicitly denies the right of property owners to have their property defended by predictable law, for he says that any consideration of the right to demand compensation depends on "circumstances."*[201] If the right of collecting compensation is not predictable, the right of private property loses its status as a right.

By elevating the "right to inflict damage" to the same level as the right to demand compensation for a violation of a property right, Coase has effectively compromised the latter right by making a potential right out of the ability to inflict damage. *The application of Coase's argument would destroy property rights by attempting to extend the status of property right to a man's ability to damage his neighbor's property.* He does not discuss anywhere in the essay *the economic costs to society of compromising the injured party's right to demand and receive by law economic restitution from the offending party.* He does not even seem to understand the implications of his own argument. Most astounding of all, his arguments have been taken seriously by economists who see themselves as defenders of the free market order. Economic reductionism is a kind of occupational affliction for the Chicago School economists.

Transaction Costs at the O.K. Corral

Coase's academic colleague at the University of Chicago, Nobel Prize-winning economist George Stigler, has extended the Coase theorem. Coase argues that in the absence of transaction costs, different initial assignments of property rights will lead to the same economic output. In his authoritative textbook, *The Theory of Price*, Stigler takes this thesis one step farther. He concludes that if there is perfect competition, meaning perfect foreknowledge, market transactions between the polluter and his victim will lead to the production of exactly the same economic output as would have been produced if one firm had owned both the source of pollution and its sink.[202] In other

---

201. *Ibid.*, p. 21.
202. George Stigler, *The Theory of Price* (3rd ed.; New York: Macmillan, 1966), p. 113.

words, the rights of private ownership—the legal right to exclude—
and the sense of outrage at an invasion of one's property are economically irrelevant. In a world of perfect competition, amazing things
happen. The economic significance of the theft involved in polluting
a neighbor's environment is zero.[203]

All we need is to reduce transaction costs. That should not be too
difficult. The polluter can pick up a gun, walk over to his neighbor,
put the gun to his head, and force him to deed over his property.
Presto: the "internalization" of pollution costs! It will not alter economic output one little bit, Stigler assures us. This surely is a cost-
effective way to reduce transaction costs. Unless, of course, one's
neighbor also has a gun. That, of course, is the whole point.

What possible objection can a self-proclaimed ethically neutral
economist offer to this sort of wealth-transfer? This is the question
Leff asks is a perceptive critique of the "economics and law" approach to social theory:

Let us say I am naturally superior to a rich man in taking things, either by
my own strength or by organizing aggregations of others (call them governments) to do my will. I am not much of a trader, but I'm one hell of a grabber.
That's just the way things are. Is there any way to criticize my activities except from the standpoint of taste (or some other normative proposition)? It
would be inefficient to allow violent acquisitions? How can one know that?
All of Posner's arguments about the efficiency-inducing effects of private
property assume only that someone has the right to use and exclude, not that
it be any particular person. If force, organized or not, were admissible as a
method of acquisition there is no reason to assume that eventual equilibrium
would not be reached, albeit in different hands than it presently rests. After
all, as Posner would be the first to tell you, "force" is just an expenditure. If
a man is "willing" to pay that price, and the other party is "unwilling" to pay
the price of successful counterforce, we have an "efficient" solution.[204]

One Nobel Prize-winning economist who does not ignore the transaction costs of an economic approach to law that elevates efficiency
over all other considerations is James Buchanan. In a perceptive law
review article, he warned the practitioners of both economics and
law that the great benefit which the free market offers society is not
its efficiency or its maximizing of economic value. What the free

---

203. In complete agreement is Warren G. Nutter, "The Coase Theorem on Social
Cost: A Footnote," *Journal of Law and Economics*, XI (Oct. 1968).

204. Leff, "Economic Analysis of Law: Some Realism About Nominalism,"
Virginia Law Review (1974), *op. cit.*, p. 454.

market offers is its support for "institutional alternatives which generate less social tension, less evasion of postulated standards of conduct, more general adherence to legal norms."[205] Yet economists and legal theorists argue that free market economic processes that exist only in an imaginary zero-cost world can and do offer us a cost-effective real-world model: just substitute voluntary market exchanges for enforcement by the State of legal titles. Those who argue this way are not only utopians, they are intellectual arsonists.[206] This is the mid-1960's social philosophy of "Burn, baby, burn!" applied not only to the adjacent field but to society itself.

The Social Costs of the Coase Theorem

There may be an essay by a professional economist that has inflicted more damage on the case for economic freedom than Coase's "Problem of Social Cost." There may be a scholarly essay that has polluted the moral environment of market choice more than Coase's. I cannot imagine what that essay might be. (Becker's 1968 essay on "Crime and Punishment: an Economic Approach" comes close, but it is really only an application of Coase's approach to law.) Coase can always argue that his right to inflict such moral damage is merely a factor of academic production. No doubt this essay advanced his academic reputation after 1960. But for every benefit there is a cost: it surely has inflicted and will continue to inflict damage on human freedom, for it assailed the moral case for private property as no article "within the camp" ever had. It created an intellectually and morally bogus concept of the supposed social economic efficiency of production costs that remain the same irrespective of any initial distribution of ownership. With that seemingly scientific and academically irresistible conclusion, Coase seduced some of the brightest economists and legal theorists of the next generation. Without a moral case for private property, private property will not survive the attacks, political and intellectual, of its ever-present, ever-envious enemies.

---

205. Buchanan, "Good Economics — Bad Law," *ibid.*, p. 486.

206. Dahlman is overstating the case against traditional welfare economics when he says that transction costs "are at the heart of the matter of what prevents Pareto optimal bliss from ruling sublime. For if we could only eliminate transaction costs, externalities would be of no consequence. . . ." Carl J. Dahlman, "The Problem of Externality," *Journal of Law and Economics*, XXII (April 1979), p. 161.

The Biblical Response

It may seem odd that I have devoted so much space to the obvious. Unfortunately, economists quite frequently spin complex theories and arguments that are internally consistent — to the extent that arguments are capable of internal consistency[207] — but to perform these mental gymnastics, they must ignore, or define away, the obvious. Coase's essay is regarded by many economists as a classic. It is a classic all right — a classic exercise in rarified and misleading sophistry. Yet it is taken very seriously by some of those Chicago School economists who have developed the subdiscipline, "the economics of property rights." What we have to say is that the Bible declares exactly who must pay damages: *the initiator of the damage.* If one man sets a fire, and it spreads to his neighbor's field, he must compensate the neighbor for the accident. If he is an outright arsonist, he is a criminal, and he must pay double restitution — double the market value of the lost crop and equipment. It is not a matter of indifference to the legal system as to who initiated the "nuisance." The Bible does not teach that "from an economic point of view, a situation in which there is 'uncompensated damage done to surrounding woods by sparks from railway engines' is not necessarily undesirable. Whether it is desirable or not depends on the particular circumstances."[208] What the Bible teaches is that the victims of accidental fires must be compensated for their loss. It also teaches that a deliberate violation of another man's property rights is a crime. This is where we must begin any discussion of social costs.

Social costs and social benefits cannot be calculated precisely by means of scientific economics. The economist cannot make interpersonal comparisons of subjective utility. We need the Bible to tell us what is right and what is wrong, who pays whom, and whose property should be protected. Society is required by God to adhere to this general principle of justice. The economist has nothing to offer in its place except epistemologically blind intuition.[209] Neither, for that matter, does the modern legal theorist. Intuition is undefined and undefinable. As the old political slogan says, "you can't beat some-

---

207. I have in mind the layman's understanding of Gödel's theorem on the impossibility of arguing both completely and consistently.

208. Coase, "Social Cost," p. 34.

209. North, "Economics: From Reason to Intuition," in North (ed.), *Foundations of Christian Scholarship*.

thing with nothing." Men cannot legitimately fight the Bible's definition of property rights with an appeal to circumstances, or to the intuitive ability of men to assess total social costs and total social benefits — especially a total cost package that ignores the right, meaning *legal predictability*, of compensation to the victims.

In the case of the problem of social costs, Pigou's analysis of pollution and restitution was generally in accord with the Bible's discussion of the problem of social cost. The railroad has the legal responsibility to compensate the farmer for any fire it sets. There will undoubtedly be problems for a jury or arbitrator in assessing exactly what the losses were. If the fires continue, then the railroad's officers can be sued for criminal misconduct. Like the man whose ox gains a reputation for goring, but is not penned up by its owner, so are the railroad officers who do not take care to protect people from an identified physical hazard. The formerly docile ox that gores someone to death must be killed (Ex. 21:28). (The engine would at that point be fitted with a spark-arrester or prohibited from the tracks.) But the ox with a bad reputation that kills a man must die, and so must its owner, unless he makes restitution to the heirs of the victim (Ex. 21:29-30). (The directors of the railroad could be held responsible in a court of law for criminal actions for not taking care to install safety equipment after the fire threat had been pointed out to them by the authorities.) Biblical case laws are to govern the courts, not the speculative conclusions of economists that are opposed to the Bible's explicit statements. Sometimes very bright economists can come up with outrageous hypotheses. The public adopts these "logical discoveries" at its peril. Coase's essay is regarded by academic economists — at least non-Keynesian and non-mathematical economists — as a landmark essay. What it is, on the contrary, is clever sophistry: a land mine essay.

Conclusion

In a brilliant yet almost despairing essay, Arthur Allen Leff has described the development of modern legal theory: a war between legal formalism (the "logic of the law") and legal empiricism or positivism ("man announces the law"). The fact is, this debate goes back at least to the Socratic revolution in Greek political thought: the debate over *physis* (nature) and *nomos* (convention).[210] Writes Leff: "While all this

---

210. On the rival conceptions of law, see Sheldon Wolin, *Politics and Vision: Continuity and Innovation in Western Political Thought* (Boston: Little, Brown, 1960), pp. 29-34. On *physis*, see Robert A. Nisbet, *Social Change and History: Aspects of the Western Theory of Development* (New York: Oxford University Press, 1969), pp. 21-29.

was going on, most likely conditioning it in fact, the knowledge of good and evil, as an intellectual subject, was being systematically and effectively destroyed." What he calls the swamp of historical legal studies was replaced by the desert of legal positivism: the "normative thought crawled out of the swamp and died in the desert."

There arose a great number of schools of ethics — axiological, materialistic, evolutionary, intuitionist, situational, existentialist, and so on — but they all suffered the same fate: either they were seen to be ultimately premised on some intuition (buttressed or not by nosecounts of those seemingly having the same intuitions) or they were even more arbitrary than that, based solely on some "for the sake of argument" premises. I will put the current situation as sharply and nastily as possible: there is today no way of "proving" that napalming babies is bad except by asserting it (in a louder and louder voice) or by defining it as so, early in one's game, and then later slipping it through, in a whisper, as a conclusion.[211]

There is no way for either law or economics to be conducted without an appeal to good and evil, yet it is this appeal, above all, which is prohibited by the methodological standards of modern academic scholarship. The appeal to efficiency by the legal theorists is simply another example of seeking meaningful content for the ethically empty box of legal formalism. When the search for meaning turns to the criteria of economic efficiency, the searchers are being lured down one more dead-end trail. As Leff says, "while you are now working with *is*-terms only (you have escaped the dreaded *ought*), they are, as a matter of fact, very different matters of fact: what indeed *is* of 'value' must be known before one rates the 'efficiency' of getting there. Thus it is possible that all you have ended up doing is substituting for the arbitrariness of ethics the impossibilities of epistemology."[212]

This is the heart of the problem. Without ethics, there can be no epistemology. This assertion — which is also a dreaded but inescapable conclusion of modern economics — was the theme that Van Til worked with throughout his career. Economics is a blind science. So is its subdivision, law and economics. Again, Leff zeroes in on the problem faced by the law schools:

---

211. Leff, "Economic Analysis of Law: Some Realism About Nominalism," *Virginia Law Review* (1974), *op. cit.*, p. 454.
212. *Ibid.*, p. 456.

It is a most common experience in law schools to have someone say, of some action or state of events, "how awful," with the clear implication that reversing it will de-awfulize the world to the full extent of the initial awfulness. But the true situation, of course, is that eliminating the "bad" state of affairs will not lead to the opposite of that bad state, but to a third state, neither the bad nor its opposite. That is, before agreeing with any "how awful" critic, one must always ask him the really nasty question, "compared to what?" Moreover, it should be, but often is not, apparent to everyone that the process of moving the world from one state to another is itself costly. If one were not doing *that* with those resources (money, energy, attention), one could be doing something else, perhaps righting a few different wrongs, a separate pile of "how ghastly's."[213]

Coase himself has admitted as much, though he confines this admission to the narrow confines of the question of transaction costs. "Since property rights can be changed in such a way as to raise as well as lower the costs of transactions, how can one say that a move from regulation to a private property rights system, the use of the market, will necessarily represent an improvement? If the question is put in such a general form, one cannot say that it will."[214]

Christian economists must therefore enter the debate regarding costs, whether social or personal. There is no intellectually consistent way that the humanist economist can legitimately keep Christian economics out of the arena. He has adopted a position of intuitional and arbitrary ethics in the name of value-free methodology. It is all a sham. The more loudly the economist insists that ethics should be left outside the temple of economics, almost as one leaves one's shoes outside a Moslem mosque, the more irrelevant his findings and concealed his own system's ethics. It is better to be open about one's ethics, and the source of one's ethics. The reduction of self-deception is clearly a legitimate intellectual end. The problem is, neither the embarrassed Christian economist nor the self-deceived humanist economist is willing to pay the methodological price. But we should have expected this; it is an ancient problem: "Beware lest any man spoil you through philosophy and vain deceit, after the tradition of men, after the rudiments of the world, and not after Christ" (Col. 2:7).

---

213. *Ibid.*, p. 460.
214. Coase, "The Choice of the Institutional Framework: A Comment," *Journal of Law and Economics*, XVII (October 1974), p. 493.

Appendix E

POLLUTION IN THE SOVIET UNION

Fyodor Morgun, head of the State Committee for Environmental Protection, revealed last year [1988] that air pollution in all Soviet industrial centers now exceeds Soviet safety limits and is more than ten times the permitted level in 102 Soviet cities. He also revealed (at the 19th special Communist Party conference last June) that water from the great rivers of Russia, including the fabled Volga and the Don, is now almost unusable for drinking or irrigation. [1]

Until the Chernobyl nuclear power plant accident in 1986, the assumption of many anti-capitalist critics of modern pollution had been that socialist societies, especially the Soviet Union, had somehow avoided the social costs of pollution. This belief was always entirely mythical. What is different today is that *glasnost* has opened up the outlets for complaints within the U.S.S.R.

For example, Western reporters have now learned of the story of the Aral Sea. This sea in northwest Uzbekistan is steadily disappearing. At one time, it was the fourth-largest inland body of water on earth. It has shrunk by 40 percent since 1960, leaving behind 10,000 square miles of salty desert. Soviet developers have siphoned off into the cotton fields of Uzbekistan and neighboring Turkmenia the waters of the two rivers that feed the Aral Sea, leaving these rivers little more than slow-moving sewers. The fish cannery at Muinak which had been built on the southern shore is now landlocked, 30 miles from the water. No matter: the sea's commercial fishing catch has now fallen to zero because of the high concentration of salt, fertilizers, and pesticides. The Muinak area remains off-limits to foreigners, including reporters. Reports the *New York Times*, "The high concentration of salt and farm chemicals in the rivers and under-

---

1. "The Ecology Crisis," *National Review* (April 7, 1989), p. 28.

ground water are blamed for universally high rates of stomach and liver disease, throat cancer and birth defects."[2]

Free Pebbles

Almost two decades before this information began leaking out of the Soviet Union, Marshall Goldman, in a book-length study of pollution in the Soviet Union, detailed the devastation of the Soviet Union's environment produced by Soviet managers. Consider the Black Sea. It is the nation's prime tourist region, the warmest region of the Soviet Union, and a region close to a large body of water. There is little room for construction in the narrow coastal area, and few construction materials. "To provide the concrete and other materials needed for construction, the contractors used the pebbles and sand located along the beach. Like the Riviera coastline, much of the Black Sea shore consists of small pebbles which would whet any cement maker's appetite. Because they were free for the taking and easily accessible and because obtaining other construction materials would necessitate the extra expense of transport over the mountains, local contractors used the beach materials."[3] When men are given the use of a "free good," they are going to waste it. They have mined the beach area since 1930.

What did they build? Seaports, dams, and resort buildings. The beaches began to erode after 1940. For centuries, the pebbles on the beach had acted as buffers to the power of the waves, Goldman points out. Now the waves crash against the shoreline, carrying away parts of the beach. The dams cut the supply of new pebbles that had come in from the mountains. In 1967, a crisis occurred near Adler, when "resort hotels, port structures, hospitals and (of all things) the sanitarium of the Ministry of Defense collapsed as the shoreline gave way. . . . Elsewhere along the eastern shore in places such as Krinshch at the mouth of the Pshad River, the beach which was 100 meters (109 yards) wide in 1950 had shrunk to 15-20 meters (16-22 yards) by 1960."[4] Hotels in Pitsunda almost washed out to sea in 1970. "Only by mobilizing all the trucks in the Autonomous Republic of Abkhazia in which Pitsunda is located and diverting them to the task of carrying

2. "Developers Turn Aral Sea Into a Catastrophe," *New York Times* (Dec. 20, 1988).

3. Marshall I. Goldman, *The Spoils of Progress: Environmental Pollution in the Soviet Union* (Cambridge, Massachusetts: M.I.T. Press, 1972), p. 156.

4. *Ibid.*, pp. 158-59.

in rocks and other solid fill were the hotels able to survive the inundation."[5] Even some streets at Yalta are threatened.[6]

"Belatedly," Goldman writes, "large sums of money are being spent in an effort to restore a semblance of the natural balance to the area. From 1945 to 1960, the Ministry of Transportation spent 40 million rubles to strengthen the coastline, but to no avail. Some specialists have insisted that as much as three times that amount is needed. Gravel is being hauled in from inland mountains, giant cement slabs are being embedded in the sea coast, walls are being built, and man-sized cement blocks are being dumped along the beach to replace with a buffer what has been washed away. Invariably the waves tear such fortifications apart in six to eight years."[7]

The Hole in the Mountain

High in the Caucasus mountains lies one of the Soviet Union's most famed resorts, Kislovodsk. Because it is sheltered on three sides by mountains, it escapes the continental weather of the Russian land mass. It is a warm-weather oasis, according to Goldman. The city has 311 days a year of sun, while another city on the other side of the mountain has only 122.[8] "Sometime after World War II, an unknown but enterprising bureaucrat from the railroad ministry strode into this idyllic scene. His mission was to increase the volume of railroad freight shipments in the area. He discovered that the mountains and hills in the area were rich in limestone. Without asking anyone, he arranged for the construction of a lime kiln at the Podkumok railroad station near the narrow gorge. 'It was a small operation and in the beginning nobody paid any attention to it. When people finally did ask what was going on, it already appeared to be too late to do anything about it. The railroad and kiln operators met all arguments with, "We are a productive enterprise. Our product is sent all over. We have an assignment and we are fulfilling our plan." ' (*Izvestia*, 7/3/66, p. 5.)"[9] Result: the gorge widened, and the winter weather of the north hit Kislovodsk. The dust level has risen drastically: one and a half times the allowable limit in a *non-resort* city. "On the one hand the state invests millions of rubles in new tourist facilities in

5. *Ibid.*, p. 159.
6. *Ibid.*, p. 160.
7. *Ibid.*, pp. 161-62.
8. *Ibid.*, pp. 163-64.
9. *Ibid.*, p. 164.

Kislovodsk, while on the other hand the state destroys the very thing that makes it attractive. Moreover the destroyers are not only being paid a good salary for their vandalism but they are winning premiums for doing so in the name of 'socialist competition.' "[10]

Lake Baikal

Lake Baikal is the largest fresh water lake in the world, holding about one-sixth of all the fresh water in the world. It is 45 miles wide and 385 miles long. Until the early 1970's, socialist enterprises used it as a free disposal unit for effluents of all kinds, including human sewage. The fish catch dropped 55 percent from 1945 until 1957.[11] In 1958, a plan to industrialize the Lake Baikal region with pulp and cellulose mills became official. There were a few sporadic pamphlet protests, to no avail. Only in 1962 did these plans become public. Several official agencies protested over the next few years, but the plans went forward. The plants were built, redesigned, and were found uneconomical. They had been built because the lake's water was pure; steadily, this purity dropped. A water treatment facility was built. Costs of construction doubled. The process did not work. Islands of alkaline sewage have been observed floating near the lake's surface—one of them 18 miles long and 3 miles wide.[12] Russian timber trusts stripped parts of the region bare. Soil washed away. Silt now flows into the lake. No one knows now if this ecological devastation will be reversed. And Lake Baikal's crisis was matched by the crisis of the Baltic Sea.[13]

About the time that Goldman's book was published, a serious effort was begun to clean up Lake Baikal. A ban was placed on fishing certain rare fish in the lake, the golomyanka. The result was that two-thirds of the human population around the lake had to move. The fishermen could no longer make a living.[14] The trade-off between employment and ecology is as inescapable in the Soviet Union as it is in a free market economy.

Bureaucracy vs. Bureaucracy

Protests against ecologically disrupting practices are almost always made by a government or government-run agency. "When a

10. *Ibid.*, p. 165.
11. *Ibid.*, p. 182.
12. *Ibid.*, pp. 200-1.
13. *Ibid.*, p. 285.
14. Associated Press story, *Tyler Courier-Times* (Feb. 10, 1985).

government newspaper decides to publish a letter to the editor or it commissions a writer to publish such an attack, this usually indicates the existence of an interagency squabble." Goldman says these attacks are quite common, but no one is clear about how officials make a decision to protest.[15] "Moreover, there are no independent conservation groups like the Sierra Club or the League of Women Voters, which scrutinize the country like watchdogs looking for such abuses." When a debate emerges publicly, the bureaucratic feuding must already be intense, or else the consequences must be far-reaching.[16]

Goldman's summary of the differences between ownership in the two societies is very important. *Private ownership is the first line of defense against pollution.* "In a socialist society it would seem that it would be more difficult to stimulate preventive action in both the case of public and private social costs. Because private land ownership is prohibited in the USSR, the individual has less of a vested interest in fighting the construction of a new factory in his neighborhood or the mining of some raw material in the area. Except when a state-owned factory finds that its operating costs are substantially and directly altered by another factory's pollution, protest must depend on social consciousness, and not on the actions of private property holders who respond out of the fear of a private loss. Of course, social consciousness can be very effective, as has been demonstrated by the success of such groups as the Sierra Club and the League of Women Voters. Nevertheless, the elimination of the private property holder and his accumulating instincts often means the elimination of the first line of defense against the expansion of environmental disruption."[17]

Geographer Philip Pryde's assessment of the Soviet Union's antipollution program is less critical than Goldman's, but it still makes the fundamental point: Soviet attempts to clean up the environment have been late and discoordinated at best, half-hearted generally, and deliberately reactionary in far too many cases.

First, there is only one effective lobby in the Soviet Union, and that is the fully understood and immutable emphasis on industrial expansion. The voices of conservationists, while present, are weak by comparison, and certainly hold no threat of voting an unreceptive Central Committee out of office.

---

15. Goldman, *Spoils*, pp. 185-86.
16. *Ibid.*, p. 186.
17. *Ibid.*, pp. 74-75.

This represents an important distinction between the United States and the U.S.S.R. If, in the United States, private enterprise displays poor conservation practices, there are still two avenues of recourse open for correcting the situation—public opinion and government regulation. But if the Soviet central planning mechanism is lax in these regards, there is no effective avenue of recourse. The Party-government supervision of both resource exploitation and environmental conservation has strong built-in conflicts of interest, and brings to mind the analogy directed by some toward our own Atomic Energy Commission of 'foxes guarding henhouses.'[18]

The sheer size of the Soviet planning bureaucracy has inhibited the implementation of new, pollution-control technologies, he concludes.[19] Furthermore, Marxist ideology sees pollution as a problem only of capitalist societies. "On the other hand, it is believed that a socialist economy, faced with the obligation to plan centrally the use of all its resource wealth, will necessarily do so in the wisest possible manner."[20] This attitude, coupled with the Marxist emphasis on economic growth, has led to a lack of interest in creating institutional mechanisms—economic, legal, or political—to reduce pollution.

The Poverty Factor

Goldman does not mention it, but by keeping people poor, socialist societies create an atmosphere that is more favorable to pollution, for it is only as men's wealth increases that they believe that they can afford the reduction in per capita output that pollution-control usually involves. Are the Soviets really that poor? Yes. Goldman's statistics on the availability of running water in homes gives us an indication of the tremendous discrepancy between the productivity of the respective economic systems. In 1960, only about 38 percent of city housing in the Soviet Union had running water, and 35 percent had sewers.[21] By the late 1960's, only 50 percent of the Soviet Union's urban homes had running water that was supplied by a central community source, as compared to 70-75 percent of U.S. citizens. Most other Americans had electrically operated water pumps for their homes' running water; these are unheard of in the USSR.[22]

---

18. Philip R. Pryde, *Conservation in the Soviet Union* (Cambridge: At the University Press, 1972), pp. 162-63.
19. *Ibid.*, p. 163.
20. *Ibid.*, p. 165.
21. Goldman, *Spoils*, p. 106.
22. *Ibid.*, p. 107.

The newer apartments in the USSR have running water, which indicates the existence of a policy to force people into apartments — a housing policy that is common in socialist nations.[23] If we include apartment buildings in the "urban housing fund," then 73 percent of the residential units had running water, and approximately 70 percent were connected to sewers in the late 1960's.[24] On the collective farms, under 3 percent had running water, and under 2 percent on the State farms.[25]

By the end of the 1980's, the Western press began to report on the sorry condition of the Soviet economy. The Soviet economy is much weaker than Western experts had estimated.[26] It has run massive budget deficits that had not shown up in official figures or in Western estimates (with a few exceptions).[27] The Soviet economy may even be facing something like a crash.[28] Richard Grenier's description of the USSR hits home: "Bangladesh with missiles."

Conclusion

The modern socialist State has not demonstrated that it is capable of dealing with the growing problem of pollution in a technological society. The free market creates incentives for people to protest against those who are transferring part of their production costs to private citizens who do not share in the benefits. It allows the creation of independent knowledge-distribution media that can mobilize people. It allows private citizens to challenge polluters. Socialist monopolies are not so easily challenged by private citizens or associations in socialist commonwealths.

---

23. On this policy in Sweden, see Roland Huntford, *The New Totalitarians* (New York: Stein & Day, 1972), ch. 12.

24. Goldman, *Spoils*, pp. 107-8.

25. *Ibid.*, p. 108.

26. Nichaolas Eberstadt, "The Soviet Economy: Worse Than We Thought," *New York Times* (Nov. 23, 1988).

27. Igor Birman, "Kremlin Red Ink (And You Thought We Had a Deficit Problem)," *Wall Street Journal* (Nov. 15, 1988).

28. Judy Shelton, *The Coming Soviet Crash: Gorbachev's Desperate Pursuit of Credit in Western Financial Markets* (New York: Free Press, 1989).

Appendix F

VIOLENT CRIME IN THE UNITED STATES, 1980

The Model Penal Code [of the American Law Institute, 1962] requires the judge to employ "generally accepted scientific methods." Until at least 1978, the consensus of the criminology establishment was that offenders could be rehabilitated in prisons and also in the community under the tutelage of probation officers. This opinion prevailed even though irrefutable statistics revealed that at least two thirds of all offenders upon release from prison or discharge from probation commit other offenses.

The goals and standards embodied in the Model Penal Code are really little more than vague concepts which at one time were found palatable by the criminology and jurisprudence establishments. They do not provide precise modalities of treatment or clear instructions to the sentencing judge. It is interesting and significant that the word "punishment" is not used nor is the concept of making whole the victims of crime any part of the purposes of sentencing. Indeed, the victim of crime is not even mentioned except in a passing reference in Section 7 that a fine should not be imposed if it would prevent restitution. Neither restitution nor reparation is included in the purposes of sentencing.[1]

This short appendix focuses on violent crime in the United States. Three observations are necessary. First, the year 1980 seems to have been a peak year for violent crime in the U.S. Subsequent data indicate that rates dropped in many areas. This may be due to the aging of the U.S. population, since young unmarried men commit the largest proportion of crimes. Second, the rates for murder began to rise in the mid-1980's, probably because of drug-related criminal behavior. Third, the growth in criminal activity is a Western phenomenon, not just national. In Canada between 1970 and

---

1. Lois G. Forer, *Criminals and Victims: A Trial Judge Reflects on Crime and Punishment* (New York: Norton, 1980), pp. 77-78.

1167

1974, the number of recorded crimes rose by over 30%. In England and Wales, crime also rose by 30 percent, 1974-78. Substantial increases also took place in France, Sweden, the Netherlands, West Germany, Denmark, Austria, and Italy.[2] This indicates the direction of the growth in the 1970's. Of great concern is the fact that actual crimes seem to have exceeded reported crimes by many times. In the U.S., actual crimes were as high as three times those reported; in England and Wales, it was closer to ten times higher.[3]

There is no doubt that there is a still major crime problem today in the U.S. Reports one article on the economics of prisons: "Every week, like clockwork, the total number of prison inmates in the U.S. grows by 1,000 people. That's two big prisons worth of lawbreakers, most of whom cost between $14,000 and $30,000 a year to feed, house and guard. With 605,000 men and women behind bars in state and federal prisons, the U.S. already has the highest incarceration rate in the Western world; about four times that of the U.K or France on a per capita basis. And that's not even counting the 300,000 or so in county jails across America. . . . With 37 states under court orders to reduce overcrowding, the U.S. has embarked on a prison-building program unparalleled in history."[4] The primary response of the authorities to crime has been prison-building. The rate of incarceration has grown every year from 1972: from slightly under 100 per 100,000 population to over 220.[5] "Just as rehabilitation was the byword of the 1960s, in the late 1980s a crime-weary citizenry wants to lock the bad guys up and throw away the keys."[6]

The Explosion in Crime, 1960-80

In the United States, from 1960 to 1980, reported violent crimes skyrocketed in the United States and Western Europe, although not in Japan.[7] The major increase in the United States took place in the

2. David J. Pyle, *The Economics of Crime and Law Enforcement* (New York: St. Martin's, 1983), pp. 1-2.

3. *Ibid.*, p. 2; citing H. J. Schneider, "Crime and Criminal Policy in some Western European and North American Countries," *International Review of Criminal Policy*, (1979), pp. 55-65.

4. Katherine Barrett and Richard Greene, "Prisons: The Punishing Cost," *Financial World* (April 18, 1989), p. 18. (Gold's price was about $385 per ounce.)

5. *Ibid.*, p. 21.

6. *Ibid.*, p. 18.

7. "Social Scientists Say U.S. Crime Has Leveled Off," *New York Times* (Feb. 2, 1982). On Japan, see "Tokyo, Where Law Means Order," *Wall Street Journal* (Nov. 29, 1973).

periods 1964-73 and 1976-80. (Part of this reported increase in the 1960's was the result of improvements in the statistics of several large cities.)[8] Between 1963 and 1973, violent crimes rose 174 percent, while population increased by 11 percent, a 16-to-one ratio. Local public spending on police forces increased from less than $1 billion in 1964 — an incredibly low figure, given the enormous size of tax expenditures on public schools, welfare, streets, and buildings — to $7 billion in 1974.[9] In 1960, there were about 3.4 million serious crimes committed in the United States. By 1974, there were over 10 million.[10] Violent crimes increased by 47 percent, 1969-74, from 659,000 to 970,000.[11]

Scholars debate furiously as to the causes of crime, and why rates of violent crime change.[12] Such factors as urbanization, the growing proportion of young unmarried males in a society, and the absence of wars — outlets for violent behavior — have all been used to explain the increase. Since 1968, economists have entered the debate; they tend to focus on the costs and rewards of crime and crime prevention, on the assumption that crime is just another form of profit-seeking, risk-avoiding behavior.[13] One scholar even argues that on the whole, over the last seven centuries, homicides as a proportion of total population have declined by a factor of 10 in Britain.[14] But the American public is aware of the fact of violent crime, whatever the causes.[15] The March 23, 1981 issues of both Time and *Newsweek*, the two most widely read U.S. news magazines, ran articles on violent

8. James Q. Wilson and Richard J. Herrnstein, *Crime and Human Nature* (New York: Touchstone, 1985), p. 32.

9. *U.S. News and World Report* (June 10, 1974).

10. *Ibid.* (April 7, 1975).

11. *Ibid.* (Nov. 24, 1975).

12. One source of information on these scholarly debates is the university of Chicago publication, *Crime and Justice: An Annual Review of Research.*

13. Between 1968 and 1979, about 250 articles on crime by economists appeared; before that, there had been only a handful. D. J. Pyle, *The Economics of Crime and Law Enforcement: A Selected Bibliography* (New York: Rand Institute, 1979). Most economists believe that the key essay that launched the field was Gary Becker's "Crime and Punishment: an Economic Approach," *Journal of Political Economy*, LXXVI (1968), pp. 169-217; reprinted in Gary S. Becker and William M. Landes (eds.), *Essays in the Economics of Crime and Punishment* (New York: National Bureau of Economic Research, 1974), ch. 1.

14. Ted Robert Gurr, *Crime and Justice: An Annual Review of Research*, Vol. III.

15. On crime rates, see Donald J. Mulvihill and Melvin M. Tumin (eds.), *Crimes of Violence*, Vol. 11 of the staff report to the National Commission of the Causes and Prevention of Violence (Washington, D.C.: Government Printing Office, 1969), p. 54.

crime: "The Plague of Violent Crime" (*Newsweek*) and "The Curse of Violent Crime" (*Time*). (We might also consider conducting a research project on "spying and petty theft in the news magazine publishing industry.")

In the United States between the periods 1930-34 and 1975-79, population grew by 84 percent, 123 million to 226 million. Homicides went up by almost 600 percent, from 14,618 to 101,044. Homicides per 100,000 population climbed from 11.9 to 44.7. Interestingly, the number of civil executions per homicide dropped by over 99 percent, from one per 18.8 to one per 33,681. The growth in homicides was relatively low from the 1935-39 era until 1945-49. But the curious fact is that homicides per 100,000 of population dropped from 1946 until 1962, from 6.9 murders per 100,000 to 4.5. By 1972, it had climbed to 9.4.[16] Homicides went from 44,000 in 1960-64 to 101,000 in the 1975-79 period.[17] In Los Angeles, the increases were comparable: population increase was 142 percent, homicides were up 686 percent, and homicides per 100,000 of population tripled.

As evil as the crime of murder is, however, it must be understood that many of the victims are far from innocent victims. A study of murder victims in New York City made in 1977 found that half of 1,622 victims in 1976 had police records. Thirty-five had been arrested on murder charges themselves. Young men were the most vulnerable single group, constituting about a third of the victims. Youths between the ages of 16 and 20 accounted for over a quarter of those arrested for murder. Almost half of the victims were black, and 30 percent were hispanic. But 124 of the victims were elderly people who were probably killed during robberies.[18]

James Q. Wilson points out that the number of robberies per 100,000 dropped from 1946 until 1959. Then, in 1960, it increased sharply, remained stable for two years, and then jumped again in 1963, 1964, and 1965. In 1959, the rate had been 51.2 per 100,000; in 1968, it was 131. Auto theft had increased from 1949 until 1963, when it rose dramatically.[19] He writes, "It all began in about 1963. That

---

16. James Q. Wilson, *Thinking About Crime* (New York: Basic Books, 1975), pp. 5-6.

17. Statistics compiled by the staff of California State Senator H. L. Richardson, based on the Federal Bureau of investigation's *Uniform Crime Reports* and the U. S. Department of Justice's *Sourcebook of Criminal Justice Statistics, 1979.*

18. *New York Times* (August 28, 1977).

19. Wilson, *Thinking About Crime*, p. 6.

was the year to overdramatize a bit, that a decade began to fall apart."[20]

The 1970's brought no relief. The combined rate of three violent crimes — murder, rape, and robbery — in the United States increased from slightly over 350 per 100,000 of population in 1970 to just under 600 per 100,000 in 1979. The rate had peaked in 1975, dropped with the recession of 1975-76, and then began increasing again during the Carter Administration.[21]

"Fear of Crime Leads in Survey on Reasons to Leave Big Cities" announced a *New York Times* headline (May 16, 1981). The poll was conducted by the Gallup organization. In the 1970's there was no prominent cause of the migration out of the cities. In cities of one million residents or more, half of those who left cited a high crime rate. The article goes on to say that the Federal Bureau of Investigation's *Uniform Crime Reports* on the number of crimes reported to the police show that violent crimes of murder, rape, robbery, and assault rose 31 percent from 1976-80, while crimes against property — larceny, burglary, and theft — rose by 16 percent in the same period. The biggest increase for both categories came in 1980. "For cities over one million population, violent crime was up 17 percent and property crime 13 percent. Also, suburban and rural crime have been increasing in all regions of the country at a rate not far behind that of the big cities."

Juvenile Crime

Juvenile crime has accelerated since the end of World War II. Arrests for violent crimes by juveniles increased by 98 percent from 1967-76, and arrests of those 18 and older increased by 65 percent.[22]

---

20. *Ibid.*, p. 5. As I point out in my book, *Unholy Spirits: Occultism and New Age Humanism* (Ft. Worth, Texas: Dominion Press, 1986), the period beginning with the assassination of President John F. Kennedy brought radical changes to the culture of the West: a rise in revolutionary activity, beginning with the campus violence of the fall of 1964; the escalation of the Vietnam war and the protests against that war; a radical change in culture, especially music, beginning with the Beatles in late 1963 and 1964; and a tremendous shift in the theory of knowledge (epistemology) on the campus: from empiricism and liberalism's optimistic "can-do" pragmatism to subjectivism, relativism, and mysticism. This shift was accompanied by a huge increase in the use of drugs and hallucinogens, and also a tremendous increase in the extent of visible occult activity, especially among those who had received college educations.

21. *Time* (March 23, 1981).

22. *U.S News and World Report* (July 17, 1978). Wilson cites Prof. Norman Ryder, a demographer at Princeton University, concerning children: "There is a perennial invasion of barbarians who must somehow be civilized and turned into contributors to fulfillment of the various functions requisite to societal survival." Wilson, *Thinking About Crime*, p. 12. The increasing failure of humanist society to effect this transformation of its children is the source of endless crises. Wilson lays much of the blame for rising crime on family disorganization: p. 206.

A study released by the Ford Foundation in 1978, *Violent Delinquents*, reveals that a hard core of 3 percent to 5 percent of those arrested account for more than half of the violent crimes perpetrated by juveniles —in effect, a hard-core criminal class. According to Prof. Marvin Wolfgang of the University of Pennsylvania, who has conducted studies of delinquent youths in Philadelphia since 1945, over one-third of the youths were picked up by the police for something more serious than a traffic offense, but 46 percent of these delinquents had no further police contact after the first offense. Concludes Wilson: "Though a third started on crime, nearly half seemed to stop spontaneously. . . . Out of the ten thousand boys, however, there were six hundred twenty-seven—only 6 per cent—who committed five or more offenses before they were eighteen. Yet these few chronic offenders accounted for *over half* of all the recorded delinquencies and about *two-thirds* of all the violent crimes committed by the entire cohort."[23] Wolfgang's research also indicates that the degree of injury inflicted by youths on their victims has increased. "People are getting their heads bashed in and seriously hurt in ways that didn't happen before."[24]

A Loss of Confidence

The result of this visible failure of the criminal justice system has been a growing distrust of the police and the courts by the public. A poll taken by *Newsweek* magazine in 1981 and published in the March 23 issue asked: "How much confidence do you have in the *police* to protect you from violent crime?" The responses:

A great deal 15%
Quite a bit 34%
Not very much. 42%
None at all 8%
Don't know 1%

Second question: "How much confidence do you have in the *courts* to sentence and convict criminals?" The responses:

A great deal 5%
Quite a bit 23%
Not very much. 59%
None at all 11%
Don't know 2%

---

23. Wilson, *Thinking About Crime*, p. 200.
24. *New York Times* (Feb. 2, 1982).

When 70 percent of those surveyed have very little or no confidence in the court system, there has been a massive failure on the part of those high officials who are entrusted with the responsibility of providing justice and safety for the public.

On Average, Crimes Pays

It is a well-known fact that very few crimes result in an arrest. This does not tell the whole story. Most crimes are committed by a handful of professional criminals. By arresting, convicting, and eliminating the activities of one burglar or rapist, the law-enforcement system drastically reduces crime on the streets. One estimate says that if all people convicted of a serious crime in New York State were given prison sentences of at least three years, the rate of serious crime would be reduced by two-thirds.[25]

The U.S. Department of Justice's National Institute of Justice in 1987 released the results of a study of 2,190 inmates in California, Michigan, and Texas. It concluded that when a repeat offender is released from prison, he commits an average of 187 crimes per year until he is again imprisoned. The cost to victims of crimes committed by these people is an estimated $430,000 per year. (Warning: this assumes that the 187 crimes a year are on average expensive crimes, rather than shoplifting, which involves large numbers of less expensive crimes. This does not appear to be the case. The reliability of the statistics have been challenged by academic professionals, as statistics so often are.)[26] The cost of building a new cell and maintaining it for a year is $25,000 per prisoner, the study estimated. (This can be seen in a different way: the construction cost is between $50,000 and $100,000 per bed, with the amortized cost at $25,000 a year per prisoner.[27] Actual operating costs run about $15,000 per prisoner.[28]) The study concluded that the $8.6 billion cost of operating the nation's prisons and jails was about one-tenth of the cost to society if the institutions were shut down.[29] This conclusion appears to be self-serving on the part of the corrections bureaucracy, but the public sees no other alternative.

---

25. Wilson, *Thinking About Crime*, p. 201.
26. Barrett and Greene *op. cit.*, p. 19.
27. "Passing through for lack of cells," *Washington Times* (Jan. 27, 1989).
28. "The Success of Authority in Prison Management," *Insight* (Feb. 13, 1989), p. 15.
29. Associated Press story, *Dallas Times Herald* (July 4, 1988), p. A-3.

In any case, it needs to be recognized that the total expenditures of civil government at all levels in the U.S. is today in the range of $1.5 trillion per year. Thus, the cost of prisons, or even the law enforcement system as a whole, is a tiny fraction of total government expenditures.

Arrest and Conviction

Nevertheless, the issue is not simply the cost of maintaining prisons. The issue is the effectiveness of this particular sanction. Does this threatened sanction reduce crime more effectively than some other sanction would? Are actual victims better off? Are potential victims more secure in the long run? The threat of imprisonment is no better than the likelihood of a sentence being imposed and carried out. The question must be asked: What is the relationship between arrest and conviction? According to the headline of a *New York Times* article (Jan. 4, 1981), "99% of Felony Arrests in the City Fail to Bring Terms in State Prison." About 80 percent are not even prosecuted as felons. About one in six serves time in a city jail for under one year. "At a time of rising concern about crime, the police, prosecutors, city officials and research specialists say that law enforcement officials have decided to treat all but the most serious offenses as misdemeanors, more often than not by a plea agreement reached during arraignment."

The process by which felonious crimes are dealt with in New York City — and, by implication and statistics, most other major American cities — is revealing. Consider statistics for 1979. Officially, 539,102 felonies were reported to the police. This, of course, is only a fraction of the felonies committed, although no one is sure just how large a fraction.[30] The police arrested 104,413 persons on felony charges. This cleared up about 63,000 of the reported crimes, or only about 12 percent. Grand juries charged 16,318 of these arrested people with felony crimes. The cases against the other 88,095 were dismissed by the district attorneys or treated as misdemeanors. Of the 16,318, 56 percent resulted in felony pleas by the defendants of guilty; 16 percent resulted in misdemeanor pleas; 13 percent in trials leading to a verdict; and 12 percent in dismissals.[31] In short, criminals are rarely

---

30. Some national estimates of the ratio between crimes committed and crimes reported run as high as five to one: "Study Finds Crime Rates Far Higher than Reports," *New York Times* (April 27, 1973).

31. These statistics appear to be precise. This is an illusion. The confusion in New York City police and court records is legendary. See the article, "Police in New

sent to prison for any particular criminal act.

The criminals know for certain what the public suspects: crime *does* pay.[32] The risks of being caught for one crime are low. The risks of a repeater's being caught are high. The risks of being convicted and serving a lengthy period in prison are minimal. Prof. Walter Burns, a political scientist at the University of Toronto, has summarized the problem: "Between 1966 and 1971 the U.S. murder rate increased by 52%, and the crime rate as a whole rose by 74%, as reported in *Crime in the United States: Uniform Crime Reports, 1971.* Crimes of violence (murder, forcible rape, robbery and aggravated assault) went up 80%. In 1971 there were 5,995,200 index crimes (crimes catalogued by the FBI) reported to the police, and everyone knows that a large number of crimes are never reported to the police. The proportion of arrests to crimes reported was only 19%, persons charged 17%, persons convicted as charged 5%, and persons convicted of lesser offenses .9%. All of which means that punishment was meted out in only 5.7% of the *known* cases of crime. The conclusion is inescapable: *crime pays.* Moreover, some authorities insist that most crimes are not reported to the police and that only 1½% of all crimes are unpunished, which is to say that 98½% of the crimes committed go unpunished."[33]

Aging and Crime

The rate of crime began to drop in the early 1980's in the United States. The only reasonable hope that citizens of the United States

---

York City Turning to Computers to Untangle Records," *New York Times* (Feb. 27, 1982). For every arrest, 15 different forms have to be filled out, and paper work is scattered throughout the city. "According to the police, about 2,000 of the 100,000 or so persons arrested on felony charges last year will have been tried. They say they want to know what happened to the other 98,000 cases. . . ." This raises another problem: Who will have access to the computerized files? Will the security system resist intrusion? No such system has been devised so far.

32. Economists and economics-influenced legal scholars, especially those of the so-called "Chicago School," have used economic theory to produce some remarkable conclusions in this regard, especially Gary Becker, Richard Posner, and Gordon Tullock. For an introduction to this literature, see Posner's speech, *The Economic Approach to Law*, published in 1976 by the Law and Economics Center of the University of Miami, Coral Gables, Florida. Posner's textbook is also important, *Economic Aspects of Law* (Boston: Little, Brown, 1986). *The Journal of Law and Economics* and *The Journal of Legal Studies*, published by the University of Chicago, are important outlets for this research.

33. Walter Burns, "Justified Anger: Just Retribution," *Imprimis*, III (June 1974), published by Hillsdale College, Hillsdale, Michigan.

seem to have for continuing this reduction in crime in the near future, apart from a religious revival, is that with a falling birth rate, the number of young men, especially unmarried young men, ages 18-24, as a percentage of population, will fall. Older men commit fewer crimes. They get married, and marriage reduces crime. Gilder points out that about 3 percent of criminals are women; only 33 percent are married men. "Although single men number 13 percent of the population over age fourteen, they comprise 60 percent of the criminals and commit 90 percent of major and violent crimes."[34] In short, there is little evidence that tinkering with the criminal-investigation system will bring relief to the victims. The causes of crime are too complex.

By the late 1980's, major U.S. cities began to experience a rapid escalation of violent crime, especially murder, as the drug culture began to be organized on a highly businesslike basis.[35] An estimated 50,000[36] to 80,000[37] youths in the Los Angeles area now belong to gangs. Homicides per year peaked in Los Angeles County at 350 in 1980, fell to about 200 in 1982, and then rose again, beginning in 1984, to about 400.[38]

Biblical Law and Social Order

Modern criminology is a recent and very inexact science. It has been dominated by the ideology of political liberalism, which in turn is deeply committed to environmental determinism. Criminologists have had very few scientific studies available to support their opinions concerning the relationship between poverty and crime, or overcrowded urban life and crime. As Harvard University political scientist James Q. Wilson has pointed out: "It was not until 1966, fifty years after criminology began as a discipline in this country and after seven editions of the leading text on crime had appeared, that there began to be a serious and sustained inquiry into the consequences for crime rates of differences in the certainty and severity of penalties. Now, to an increasing extent, that inquiry is being fur-

---

34. George Gilder, *Naked Nomads: Unmarried Men in America* (New York: Quadrangle/New York Times Book Co., 1974), p. 20.

35. "Dead Zones," *U.S. News & World Report* (April 10, 1989).

36. "Los Angeles Seeks Ultimate Weapon in Gang War," *Wall Street Journal* (March 30, 1988).

37. "Turf Wars," *ibid.* (Dec 29, 1988).

38. *Idem.*

thered by economists rather than sociologists."[39] It is not surprising that criminology has not been influenced much by the concept of biblical law.

The legal standards found in the Bible provide society with a means of establishing social order. Biblical law works because it is comprehensive, and it deals with men as they are, yet in terms of an ethical code that tells us what we should attempt to become. When those who would shatter the foundations of social order openly disrupt the lives of law-abiding citizens, then the civil government is required to step in and restore order. This may involve the permanent elimination of the criminal. Biblical law imposes conditions which make crime expensive.

Thus, biblical law imposes the death penalty for certain classes of crimes that involve an intolerable attack on the foundations of social order. The biblical social order must be preserved. Courts make mistakes, justice is not perfect, and the innocent defendant may sometimes see his hopes crushed by a miscarriage of justice. *But an occasional miscarriage of justice is preferable to the advent of a permanent criminal class.* There will always be miscarriages of justice; the question is: In what direction is the criminal code headed? Toward the Bible or toward humanism?

There is a slogan in American jurisprudence: "Better that a hundred guilty men go free than one innocent victim be punished." This implies that it is legitimate to require standards of evidence so rigorous that only criminals are ever convicted. But the price of earthly perfect justice is the destruction of the legal system which attempts to provide such justice, as Moses discovered (Ex. 18). Such a quest for perfect earthly justice would subject a law-abiding society to waves of criminals who could not be convicted in terms of the standards of the perfection-seeking criminal justice system. The justice system would bankrupt the treasury by attempting to deliver perfect justice. The delay in punishment would increase the likelihood of crimes committed by present-oriented criminals, who tend to ignore the long-run consequences of their acts. The courts would be jammed with appeals, delays, and unpunished criminals waiting to be sentenced. The judges would tend to issue milder sentences, in order to speed up the wheels of justice. Plea bargaining by lawyers would get

---

39. Wilson, *Thinking About Crime*, pp. 54-55.

sentences reduced by getting criminals to plead guilty to lesser crimes. "The bigger the backlog, the lighter the sentence."[40]

There will be no plea bargaining on the day of final judgment. Justice will be perfect then. We must content ourselves with imperfect justice until then.[41]

---

40. Former New York City District Attorney Robert Morgenthau; quoted by U.S. Senator James Buckley, "Foreword," to Frank Carrington, *The Victims* (New Rochelle, New York: Arlington House, 1975), p. xv.

41. Gary North, *Moses and Pharaoh: Dominion Religion vs. Power Religion* (Tyler, Texas: Institute for Christian Economics, 1985), ch. 19: "Imperfect Justice."

Appendix G

LOTS OF FREE TIME: THE EXISTENTIALIST UTOPIA OF S. C. MOONEY

Another popular excuse for usury is that it is no different than rent. It is said that "interest" is merely rent on "money", and that if rent is assumed to be legitimate, then usury would have to be considered legitimate as well. . . . The economic similarity between usury and the rent of property readily is admitted. However, this close connection does not serve to legitimize usury, as Locke et al suppose; but to condemn rents. . . . [I]t is not lawful for one to sell the use of his property (rent).

S. C. Mooney[1]

Consider the economic logic offered by any promoter of a zero-interest economy. As I have argued in Chapter 23, he is the economic world's equivalent of the self-proclaimed scientist who insists that a perpetual motion machine is legal. But the promoter of a zero-interest economy is really far worse: he is like a crackpot physicist who insists that *only* perpetual motion machines should be legal. He is the classic defender of something (the use of an asset over time) for nothing (no rental fee). He says that you can construct an honest, fair, and productive economy by making interest payments illegal.

Again, let me apologize in advance for filling up space in this commentary with arguments against nonsense. If this nonsense, or nonsense quite similar to it, had not been offered in the name of the Bible for about a millennium and a half, I would not bother to comment on it. Life is too short, and this book is too long. But the lure of crackpot theories of interest has been with us for a long, long time; first, under the authoritarian rule of clerics in an era before economics was an intellectual discipline, and second, under the hoped-for

---

1. S. C. Mooney, *Usury: Destroyer of Nations* (Warsaw, Ohio: Thopolis, 1988), pp. 172, 173.

rule of amateurs who resent the very thought of economics as an intellectual discipline, and who have therefore never taken an economics course in their lives.[2]

Before I begin my analysis, let me also say that in one sense, it is legitimate to call for a restructuring of economics by revising interest theory. In fact, it is imperative. Böhm-Bawerk's path-breaking *History and Critique of Interest Theories* (1884) certainly set forth economic principles that were instrumental in making possible a major revision of economics. But let me also say that it is insufficient to offer a new theory of interest—or even a revived version of Aristotle's theory, dressed in swaddling clothes—without restructuring all of economics. Like value theory and price theory, interest theory is at the heart of economics. In fact, price theory apart from a theory of interest is dead before it begins. It does no good for a self-proclaimed economic revolutionary to offer a wholly new theory of interest and then not explain exactly how his interest theory is to be integrated into the whole of economics. The economist must show that economic reasoning as such is still possible in terms of his proposed interest theory. This is what Böhm-Bawerk did a century ago. This is what not even one of the zero-interest theorists has ever attempted.

I do not believe that a person has to earn a Ph.D in a particular field in order for him to have an academic impact in that field. I do believe that a person needs to demonstrate the same degree of intellectual self-discipline and accomplishment that a Ph.D degree requires before he thinks himself competent to restructure the whole world from behind his computer. It is not the formal degree that counts; it is the years of thankless work in the shadows that are required to produce a successful paradigm shift. It is this price that the monetary cranks are not willing to pay. They offer us half-finished blueprints for 80-story skyscrapers, before they have built a tree house, and then demand that the world's architects give them a polite hearing.

And Christians wonder why we are not taken seriously.

Mooney on Money

I have in my possession a first edition paperback book by a self-identified Christian Reconstructionist, Mr. S. C. Mooney. It is his

---

2. I suggested to Mr. Mooney in a letter that he had never taken a course in economics in college, and he admitted to me in his written reply that he had not. Some things are obvious on first reading.

first book. (If he does not change his views, I pray it is his last.) It was financed by Mr. David Wiley, who calls his publishing company Theopolis. You know: God's city, as in city of God, I imagine. The book, however, is not Augustinian in either grandeur or scope. (Neither is its typography or cartoons.)

I offer my comments for your consideration not because there is a groundswell of interest (pun intended) in Mr. Mooney's book, nor because it is coherent in its analysis, but because it is one more primary source documenting a very strange phenomenon: Christians who think they are ready to overturn the modern intellectual world with their very first book by announcing undeveloped theories for their shock value. They offer "fringe" theories, but without any suggestion about how these theories might become the foundation for governing at the center of a society. They offer fringe theories that are destined to keep their disciples — if any — forever on the cultural, intellectual, and perhaps even emotional fringe. They offer preliminary findings that would require a lifetime of disciplined effort in order to make their conclusions even vaguely plausible, and then they stand back and announce: "The world now must refute me, or else I win by default." Well, the world does not have to refute them; they will not win by default; but for the sake of argument — and for the sake of intellectually immunizing the reader, who may have a fondness for fringe hypotheses (a weakness I occasionally share) — I will offer a few observations.

Mr. Mooney calls for an economically just world which is devoid of both rents and interest payments, just as John Maynard Keynes did. Since I have responded to the main thrust of his arguments in Chapter 23, there is no need of going over the same material.[3] We need to go right to the "soft underbelly" of his critique of interest. Mooney insists that from a biblical perspective, "it is not lawful for one to sell the use of his property (rent)."[4]

Rental Income and Interest Income

If a person has money at his disposal, he faces a decision: What is the most productive use of this capital? Say that he does not want to manage his investments actively. He wants to spend his life doing other things. He therefore decides to buy an economic asset which he expects will produce a stream of future income. He could buy a

---

3. See above, pp. 734-36.
4. Mooney, *Usury*, p. 173.

piece of real estate that he expects will give him a return of 5% per annum ("net, net, net") after he delegates management responsibilities to a professional. He could also deposit the money in a bank. How much will the bank have to offer him in order to persuade him to make the deposit? Assuming that he expects no entrepreneurial profits from the appreciation of the real estate, the bank will have to offer him something in the range of 5%. Why? Because in each case, the bidders—the property seller and the banker—are in the market for his money. They must offer competitive bids, as with any auction. They bid in terms of a promise: so much future income per annum. This competitive bidding process is why the economists have long concluded that the rate of interest on a money loan produces a percentage rate of return that will be competitive with a comparably risky investment in income-producing real estate. In short, *interest income equals rental income on a competitive free market.* So, Mr. Mooney's argument against the biblical legitimacy of interest income lives or dies with his conclusion that income from rental property is also prohibited by the Bible. If rental income is allowed, then there seems to be no economic reason why interest income from a collateral-secured loan is not also allowed.

Mr. Mooney's conclusion is in direct opposition to the economic terms of the jubilee year, which specified that anyone could lawfully rent his life and his property to another person for a period of time. In other words, a buyer could lawfully contract with a seller for the latter to supply him with a stream of income—labor income or agricultural income. In either case, when a kinsman bought the land or the person out of bondage (the contract), he had to pay the lease-holder a *pro-rated price* based on the number of years remaining until the jubilee year. This, it should be obvious, was a rental contract. Not only was it legal, it was legal even for unbelieving resident aliens to buy up to 49 years of future labor services from poverty-stricken Hebrews or 49 years worth of agricultural income.

If thy brother be waxen poor, and hath sold away some of his possession, and if any of his kin come to redeem it, then shall he redeem that which his brother sold. And if the man have none to redeem it, and himself be able to redeem it; Then let him count the years of the sale thereof, and restore the overplus unto the man to whom he sold it; that he may return unto his possession. But if he be not able to restore it to him, then that which is sold shall remain in the hand of him that hath bought it until the year of jubilee: and in the jubilee it shall go out, and he shall return unto his possession (Lev. 25:25-28).

And if a sojourner or stranger wax rich by thee, and thy brother that dwelleth by him wax poor, and sell himself unto the stranger or sojourner by thee, or to the stock of the stranger's family: After that he is sold he may be redeemed again; one of his brethren may redeem him: Either his uncle, or his uncle's son, may redeem him, or any that is nigh of kin unto him of his family may redeem him; or if he be able, he may redeem himself. And he shall reckon with him that bought him from the year that he was sold to him unto the year of jubilee: and the price of his sale shall be according unto the number of years, according to the time of an hired servant shall it be with him. If there be yet many years behind, according unto them he shall give again the price of his redemption out of the money that he was bought for (Lev. 25:47-51).

Mooney's Strategy of Avoidance

It is worth pointing out that Mr. Mooney's book includes comments on Leviticus 25, but only on verses 2-7, 15-16, 35-37, and 39-45. He scrupulously avoids mentioning verses 25-28 and 47-51— verses that absolutely refute his conclusion regarding the supposedly biblically illegitimate nature of rental income. He freely admits that the economists are correct, that rental income is the same as interest income—a payment for the use of an asset over time, said Böhm-Bawerk, whom he quotes favorably on the question of the equivalence of rental income and interest income[5]—and then he tries to justify his universal condemnation of interest income by laying down an equally universal condemnation of rental income. The problem is, the Bible clearly honors the legitimacy of rental income: a stream of income, either labor income or land income, which one receives when he purchases an income-producing asset for cash (i.e., capitalization). Mr. Mooney's answer to this dilemma is simple and direct: he refuses to cite that portion of the Bible that categorically destroys his argument.

So, he says, it is immoral to collect income from any form of property. While Mr. Mooney is sufficiently astute tactically not to spell out the implications of this statement—in this regard, he follows the lead of his predecessor, Mr. Keynes—what he really means is that it is illegal biblically to seek a positive rate of return by loaning someone money to buy a house, and it is also illegal biblically to rent

---

5. *Ibid.*, p. 172.

him a house. You are morally obligated to give him the use of the loan, interest-free, or the use of the house, rent-free. This is the economics of love.[6] It is also a classic crank prescription for creating a society of homeless people. Sadly, this book is being read by otherwise intelligent Christians who are not used to following a complex chain of economic reasoning, so this broken chain of economic error impresses them.

He wrote the book specifically to refute me, as his footnotes and text reveal. He has read (but has not understood) my view of time-preference as the true origin of interest. He recognizes that I am following Böhm-Bawerk and Mises on this point: that there is always a *discount for cash* when you purchase an expected stream of future services. People discount the present value of expected future goods in comparison to the same goods in the present. Because of this, no rational person will pay a thousand ounces of gold, cash, for that hypothetical gold mine.

The "Present" Is Mostly in the Future

Mr. Mooney argues that there are no future goods but only present goods. In one sense, he is correct. I would put it this way: "The present is all that any man can be certain he has, moment by present moment." He puts it this way: "*Future goods do not exist.* There are only present goods in external reality."[7] The author believes that he has somehow refuted the concept of the inescapable discount applied to future goods. He has not.

Future goods are not real in the present, he says, so therefore they do not command a cash price. He does not recognize, for one thing (among many, many others), that this non-existence of future goods is a very good reason why there is always a *risk premium* in free market interest rates: the promised future goods may not actually be returned to the lender. Instead of acknowledging this obvious fact, the author concludes: "Since the contemplation of 'future goods' is characterized by idealism, one may not actually compare 'present goods' and 'future goods' for purposes of economic calculation. The preference that is dictated by the discount of the 'future goods' can-

---

6. This is the assertion of Mr. Mooney and his publisher, Mr. Wiley: *ibid.*, pp. iii, 231-34.

7. *Ibid.*, p. 207.

not be avoided because one cannot possibly call upon an idea in his mind to serve a purpose that only a concrete object can serve."[8] This is the economics of love. It is also the economics of incoherence.

To the extent that I can make any sense of this argument, I think he is saying that future goods, not being *physically* present, are therefore irrelevant for present decisions. So much for the biblical doctrine of eternal judgment in the afterlife! Mr. Mooney regards the concept of future goods in much the same way as the covenant-breaker regards the concept of eternal punishment. "If it ain't here now, it ain't relevant now." This is a fanatical form of *present-orientation*, the outlook of the lower-class individual.[9] He makes himself as clear as he can on this point: "The point is that 'future goods' vs. 'present goods' presents no *real* choice. The two cannot be compared in value as though they were different quantities of the same class of goods. In truth, the choice of goods for meeting one's needs is a choice of presently available goods. One present good compares only to other present goods."[10] The clearer he becomes, the more preposterous he sounds.

What's the Point?

Fact: the present moment — a "point in time" — is as philosophically and operationally undefinable a phenomenon as a Euclidian point (an infinitesimal, no-dimensional section of a sequential phenomenon, a line). The fact is, we really cannot fully describe the pure instant in time that we call "the present." Anyway, I cannot, and surely Mr. Mooney does not attempt to do so in his book. What we call "the present" is in fact the *relatively more immediate future*. I cannot do everything I would like to do right now, including offering you a precise working definition of "right now." I have to pick and choose my decisions through time. I must order my choices: first, second, and third in the future, and even this ordering process takes time.

Therefore, when I make a decision regarding the present cash value of any good, I make this evaluation moment by moment as I move through time. I make it in terms of whatever value I place on a future stream of services or pleasures that I expect to receive from

---

8. *Idem.*

9. See Edward C. Banfield, *The Unheavenly City* (Boston: Little, Brown, 1970), pp. 53-54.

10. Mooney, p. 207.

the physical or the contractual item.[11] The "front end" of this stream of future services is close at hand; how long it will continue to flow is guesswork. The initial flow of services may in fact be somewhat removed, as indicated by the warning in the fine print on the side of the box, "some assembly required." The beginning of that expected flow of services may be a day away or a week away or a year away. The point is, *there is just barely a "now" in any economic decision.* There are only present expectations of varying degrees of the future. So, contrary to Mr. Mooney, who insists that there are no future goods in the present, I insist that from a rational decision-maker's point of view, there are *mostly* future goods in the present — and this "mostly" is very, very close to *only.*

Infinite Interest Rates

If everyone were to conclude that the expected future stream of services provided by physical goods is irrelevant for present economic calculation, as Mr. Mooney insists that it is, then *free market interest rates would approach infinity,* for no one would voluntarily give up present goods for the sake of receiving economically "irrelevant" future goods. Also, the price of durable capital goods and durable consumer goods would fall almost to zero, for no one would value them for the sake of their expected future productivity, meaning any expected value three seconds away. Or two seconds away. Or a split second away. In short, we would say goodbye to civilization. This is the "economics of love." It is also the economics of existentialism: the philosophy of the autonomous moment.

Decapitalization

I single out Mr. Mooney's analysis because he is the only person I have ever seen who so forthrightly confronts the issue of time-preference in his denial of the moral legitimacy of interest. He offers

---

11. Mr. Mooney tries to argue exclusively from the physical. But I as a lender may not want to own the physical object, such as a farm. I may prefer to own a promise to pay (mortgage) made by the owner of the farm, with the farm serving as legal collateral should he default on his promise. If he defaults, I will probably try to get someone else to buy the farm and make me another promise. Yes, the contract may be based on the productivity of the farm, as administered by someone, but the focus of my concern may be the promise, not the physical asset itself. Perhaps the person decides to get out of farming and use the property as a resort, or as a consumer good. I care only about the promised payment, so long as his decision regarding the use of the land does not reduce its collateralized market value.

economic nonsense—incredibly naive nonsense—in his attempted denial of time-preference in human action; to oppose the Fetter-Mises view of interest is necessarily to argue nonsense. It is the stark reality of Mr. Mooney's nonsense that is so impressive. He makes it clear that if you refuse to go with Mises on the question of time-preference, you logically must wind up with Mooney's view regarding the economic irrelevance of the future. If society were to adopt Mr. Mooney's view, and then attempt to enforce it by civil law, it would decapitalize itself. Rushdoony's eloquent explanation of capitalization and his warnings regarding decapitalization should be taken seriously: we must choose between Christianity and existentialism.

Capitalization is the product of work and thrift, the accumulation of wealth and the wise use of accumulated wealth. This accumulated wealth is invested in effect in progress, because it is made available for the development of natural resources and the marketing of goods and produce. The thrift which leads to the savings or accumulation of wealth, to capitalization, is a product of character. Capitalization is a product in every era of the Puritan disposition, of the willingness to forego present pleasures to accumulate some wealth for future purposes. Without character, there is no capitalization but rather decapitalization, the steady depletion of wealth. As a result, capitalism is supremely a product of Christianity, and, in particular, of Puritanism, which, more than any other faith, has furthered capitalization.[12]

Today, however, the mood of modern Western man can best be described as existentialist. It subscribes to a philosophy in which the "moment" is decisive. It is not future oriented in that it does not plan, save, and act with the future in mind. The existentialist demands the future now.[13] Some of the causes which concern student rebels may be valid, but their existentialist demand that the future arrive today make them incapable of capitalizing a culture. Existentialism requires that a man act undetermined by standards from the past or plans for the future; the biology of the moment must determine man's acts.

Very briefly stated, existentialism is basically lower class living converted into a philosophy. It is, moreover, the philosophy which governs church, state, school, and society today. The "silent majority" has perhaps never heard of existentialism, but it has been thoroughly bred into it by the American pragmatic tradition of the "public" or state schools.

Our basic problem today, all over the Western world, is that Western civilization no longer has a true upper class at the helm. Future-oriented

---

12. *Chalcedon Report* (April 1967).

13. There is no better explanation for why the West has fallen behind Asia in productivity.

men no longer dominate society, politically, economically, religiously, educationally, or in any other way. Instead, dreamers who are basically lower class, who believe that political power can convert today into tomorrow, are in charge. The result is the domination of our politics by an economic policy which is the essence of the lower class mind and which leads to radical inflation. Spending today with no thought of tomorrow is a lower class standard, and this is the essence of our modern scene. The vocal minority and silent majority are both deeply in debt, and they create national economies which are deeply in debt. The growing anarchism of our social life is a product of this same lower class mentality. This popular anarchism is a refusal to submit to law and discipline, and unwillingness to accept any postponement of hopes and dreams. It is closely related to tantrums of a child who demands his will be done now. Every major social agency today, church, state, school, and home is dedicated to creating this anarchistic, lower class mentality.[14]

Mr. Mooney's view of time-preference is existentialist and lower class to the core. He no doubt fails to understand this. His recommended policies would destroy civilization. He no doubt fails to understand this, too. Such is the fate of the compulsory economics of love. The road to economic hell is paved with good intentions.

He says that my views are incorrect because I rely on the Austrian School economists for insights into time-preference. Were he more familiar with the history of economic thought, he would recognize the origin of his own ideas: the worst of Aristotle and the worst — economically, I mean — of John Maynard Keynes.

Conclusion

Every new movement that calls for a transformation of thought or culture will attract its share of fringe figures. The more publishing-oriented it is, the more it will attract people looking for the bogus immortality that the printing press appears to provide. I call this phenomenon the graffiti syndrome. It is the same temptation that persuades people of more limited literary aspirations to carve "John loves Mary" on public school desks, or limericks on the inside of lavatory doors. The Fabian movement in England is a good example of the sometimes fatal attractiveness of publishing: occultists, vegetarians, free love advocates, feminists, and screwballs of all varieties were drawn to the Webbs like midnight moths to a candle.[15] All of

---

14. *Chalcedon Report* (August 1970).

15. The most uproarious descriptions of the pontificating Webbs are found in Malcolm Muggeridge's two-volume autobiography, *Chronicles of Wasted Time* (New York: Morrow, 1973-74). He was married to Beatrice Webb's niece.

them were looking to become part of the "wave of the future." Only a few of them survived the test of time, to become remembered as the founders of yet another failed social religion.

Anyone can hang out a sign which announces that he is a Christian Reconstructionist. There is no licensing required. Not very many people choose to do this, since to join the tiny band of theonomists today is to become a modern-day John the Baptist, typing in the wilderness. But what should make a reader more than a little suspicious of anyone who claims to be a theonomist is the promoter's narrow range of concern. Specialization is legitimate, but anyone who claims that he is offering a revolutionary blueprint for this or that aspect of society had better also offer at least a first draft of the overall integrated plan. The old rule of ecology is true: *you cannot change just one thing*. You cannot reconstruct just one aspect of society, or just one aspect of an economy. For example, if you suggest a zoning code that makes sewers illegal, you had better strongly recommend the installation of septic tanks; otherwise, you can expect considerable overflow problems. I perceive that Mr. Mooney is drowning in overflow.

Again, I do not expect any society to adopt Mr. Mooney's baptized Aristotelianism. If it does, it will not remain productive very long. What does concern me is that a lot of well-meaning Christians will take such nonsense seriously, assume that it is "truly biblical" economics, and then try to "spread the gospel" of crackpottery in the name of Jesus. This would be an embarrassment to the kingdom of God generally and Christian Reconstruction specifically. We Christians are already regarded as otherworldly dreamers. Let us not provide additional ammunition to our enemies.

But if you're not convinced by the logic of my presentation, I'd like to borrow a few ounces of gold from you, interest-free, for ten years. Drop me a letter.

Appendix H

SELLING THE BIRTHRIGHT: THE RATIFICATION
OF THE U.S. CONSTITUTION[1]

And Jacob sod pottage: and Esau came from the field, and he was faint: And Esau said to Jacob, Feed me, I pray thee, with that same red pottage; for I am faint: therefore was his name called Edom. And Jacob said, Sell me this day thy birthright. And Esau said, Behold, I am at the point to die: and what profit shall this birthright do to me? And Jacob said, Swear to me this day; and he sware unto him: and he sold his birthright unto Jacob. Then Jacob gave Esau bread and pottage of lentiles; and he did eat and drink, and rose up, and went his way: thus Esau despised his birthright (Gen. 25:29-34).

The church . . . was thrown out into the street by the lawyers of Philadelphia, who decided not to have a Christian country. . . . [I]n effect, they took all the promises of religion, the pursuit of happiness, safety, security, all kinds of things, and they set up a lawyers' paradise, and the church was disenfranchised totally.

Otto Scott (1988)[2]

Otto Scott, in a perceptive essay on the ever-changing U.S. Constitution, warns us against becoming deluded by "a sloganized history" of this nation and its Constitution. He traces the history of growing tyranny in the United States in terms of the steady transformation and reinterpretation of the Constitution. "The history of the Constitution of the United States, like all other aspects of our national history, reflects the changes in American society and government through the years. To understand these changes it is essential

---

1. A more developed version of this thesis is presented in my book, *Political Polytheism: The Myth of Pluralism* (Tyler, Texas: Institute for Christian Economics, 1989), Part 3.

2. "Easy Chair" audiotape #165 (March 10, 1988), distributed by the Chalcedon Foundation, P. O. Box 158, Vallecito, California 95251.

to understand that history as it was, and ourselves as we are. Yet we have as a nation failed to confront the truth of our history in many important respects."[3] He then calls for the restoration of Christianity to "its early prominence among us. Let us, therefore, abandon the legend that the Constitution is intact, and set about the task of Christian Reconstruction — and Constitutional restoration."[4]

Stirring words, indeed! But what he fails to note in this perceptive essay is something he called to R. J. Rushdoony's attention during a taped discussion they had regarding the theological foundation of the Constitution. Scott, over Rushdoony's protest, identified the Constitutional Convention accurately: a successful effort by lawyers to overcome Christianity.[5] Thus, if we are to achieve Scott's two-fold goal — the restoration of Christianity as it once prevailed in this nation and Constitutional restoration — we must return to the expressly Christian oaths of the state constitutions of 1787, the constitutions that prevailed before the Philadelphia lawyers displaced them by means of a new national oath, an oath that refused to acknowledge the sovereign God of history who had made possible this nation's experiment in freedom. We must no longer ignore Scott's analysis: "The United States is the only government in the history of the world that has been established without a god . . . without specifically acknowledging any definition of any religion. The Constitution of 1789 was unique in that respect. No society had ever done that."[6]

Beginning in the eighteenth century in Northern Europe, anti-Trinitarian humanists combined with dissenting (non-State-established) churchmen[7] to restructure the existing basis of citizenship, which had previously been explicitly Christian. The two wings of the Enlightenment, Scottish empiricism and French *a priori* rationalism, both proclaimed a new concept of citizenship: citizenship without a required profession of faith in the God of the Bible.

We can see in the U.S. Constitutional Convention of 1787 an example of how theological Socinians (Unitarians) and dissenting Prot-

---

3. Otto Scott, "The Legend of the Constitution," *Journal of Christian Reconstruction*, XII (1988), p. 59.

4. *Ibid.*, p. 59.

5. "Easy Chair" audiotape #165.

6. Otto Scott, question and answer session, message on Leviticus 8:1-13 by R. J. Rushdoony (Jan. 30, 1987).

7. A detailed study of their movement is found in Caroline Robbins, *The Eighteenth-Century Commonwealthman* (Cambridge, Massachusetts: Harvard University Press, 1959).

estants worked together politically to overturn the existing Trinitarian judicial foundations of colonial citizenship. The Federalists (nationalists) persuaded the electorate in 1788 to ratify the proposed Constitution which substituted *a new concept of judicial office, one based on the presupposition of a universal humanity.* The key provision of the U.S. Constitution that made this transformation possible, long ignored by the history textbooks, is Article VI, Section 3:

> The Senators and Representatives before mentioned, and the Members of the several State Legislatures, and all the executive and judicial Officers, both of the United States and of the several States, shall be bound by Oath or Affirmation, to support this constitution; but no religious Test shall ever be required as a Qualification to any Office or public Trust under the United States.

This was the section of the Constitution that established the required judicial oath for the new government. It was a new oath, and therefore it was a new covenant. But this would not be an act of covenant renewal with the God of the Bible, under whom the state constitutions had been legally constituted. It instead was an act of covenantal apostasy.

Citizenship Under the State Constitutions

Prior to this, the states had generally required Christian professions of faith of voters. The colonies' state constitutions were explicitly religious. This was especially true of the New England constitutions. The old Puritan rigor was still noticeable. Vermont's 1777 constitution begins with the natural rights of man (Section I), goes to a defense of private property (Section II), and then sets forth the right of religious conscience, "regulated by the word of GOD. . . ." There is religious freedom for anyone to worship any way he chooses, just so long as he is a Protestant: ". . . nor can any man who professes the protestant religion, be justly deprived or abridged of any civil right, as a citizen, on account of his religious sentiment. . . ." The public authorities have no authorization to interfere with people's rights of conscience; "nevertheless, every sect or denomination of people ought to observe the Sabbath, or the Lord's day, and keep up, and support, some sort of religious worship, which to them shall seem most agreeable to the revealed will of GOD."[8] (Not reproduced in the A.B.A.

---

8. Richard L. Perry and John C. Cooper, *The Sources of Our Liberties* (American Bar Association, 1952), p. 365.

compilation are the crucial clauses regarding the required confessional oath administered to state officers, reprinted below.)

The 1780 Massachusetts constitution and the 1784 New Hampshire constitution had almost identical passages requiring public worship. Section I of the Massachusetts document affirms that "All men are born free and equal, and have natural, essential, and unalienable rights," and then lists them: life, liberty, and property ownership. Section II says: "It is the right as well as the duty of all men in society, publicly, and at stated seasons, to worship the SUPREME BEING, the great Creator and Preserver of the universe." This sounds universalistic and even Masonic. But Section III establishes the right of the state to support the building of churches and the payment of ministers' salaries. All the denominations were placed on equal status. Section III ends with these words: "And every denomination of Christians, demeaning themselves peaceably, and as good subjects of the commonwealth, shall be equally under the protection of the law. . . ."⁹ The same religious provisions are found in Sections I-VI of the New Hampshire constitution, and Section VI repeats verbatim the statement from Massachusetts' constitution: "And every denomination of christians. . . ."¹⁰ In short, the commonwealths were explicitly designated as Christian.

The Virginia constitution of 1776 was less specific. It affirmed freedom of conscience, and recommended "Christian forbearance, love, and charity towards each other."¹¹ Virginia had a state-supported church. Pennsylvania's 1776 constitution specified that a man's civil rights could not be abridged if he "acknowledges the being of a God."¹² Delaware in 1776 was more explicit. "That all persons professing the Christian religion ought forever to enjoy equal rights and privileges in this state, unless, under color of religion, any man disturb the peace, the happiness or safety of society."¹³ Maryland's 1776 constitution was similar: ". . . all persons, professing the Christian religion, are equally entitled to protection in their religious liberty. . . ." Furthermore, "the Legislature may, in their discretion, lay a general and equal tax, for the support of the Christian religion. . . ."¹⁴ North

---

9. *Ibid.*, p. 375.
10. *Ibid.*, p. 383.
11. *Ibid.*, p. 312.
12. *Ibid.*, p. 329.
13. *Ibid.*, p. 338.
14. *Ibid.*, p. 349.

Carolina simply affirmed liberty of conscience.[15] North Carolina's Assembly in 1703 passed a rigorous law against blasphemy. Anyone who had once confessed Christianity could not publicly deny its truth. Violators could not hold political office. Virginia removed test oaths after the Revolutionary War, which had long been James Madison's dream.[16] So did Pennsylvania.

Confessional Oaths for State Officers

All states except New York had special confessional oaths for state officials. It was this explicitly Christian character of the state constitutions that became the target of the handful of anti-Trinitarian delegates to the Constitutional Convention in Philadelphia.

To serve in Congress under the Articles, a man had to be appointed by his state legislature. He could be recalled at any time. He could serve in only three years out of every six. He was under public scrutiny continually. And to exercise the authority entrusted to him by his state legislature, he had to take an oath. These oaths (except in New York) were both political and religious. The officer of the state had to swear allegiance to the state constitution and also allegiance to God. Consider Delaware's required oath:

Art. 22. Every person who shall be chosen a member of either house, or appointed to any office or place of trust, before taking his seat, or entering upon the execution of his office, shall take the following oath, or affirmation, if conscientiously scrupulous of taking an oath, to wit:

"I, A B, will bear true allegiance to the Delaware State, submit to its constitution and laws, and do no act wittingly whereby the freedom thereof may be prejudiced."

And also make and subscribe the following declaration, to wit:

"I, A B, do profess faith in God the Father, and in Jesus Christ His only Son, and in the Holy Ghost, one God, blessed for evermore; and I do acknowledge the holy scriptures of the Old and New Testament to be given by divine inspiration."

And all officers shall also take an oath of office.[17]

The Constitution of Vermont in 1777 was not much different:

---

15. *Ibid.*, p. 356.

16. Robert A. Rutland, "James Madison's Dream: A Secular Republic," *Free Inquiry* (Sept. 1983), pp. 8-11.

17. *The Founders' Constitution*, edited by Philip B. Kurland and Ralph Lerner, 5 vols. (University of Chicago Press, 1987), V, p. 634.

Section IX. A quorum of the house of representatives shall consist of two-thirds of the whole number of members elected and having met and chosen their speaker, shall, each of them, before they proceed to business, take and subscribe, as well the oath of fidelity and allegiance herein after directed, as the following oath or affirmation, viz.

I _____ do solemnly swear, by the ever living God, (or, I do solemnly affirm in the presence of Almighty God) that as a member of this assembly, I will not propose or assent to any bill, vote, or resolution, which shall appear to me injurious to the people; nor do or consent to any act or thing whatever, that shall have a tendency to lessen or abridge their rights and privileges, as declared in the Constitution of this State; but will, in all things, conduct myself as a faithful, honest representative and guardian of the people, according to the best of my judgment and abilities.

And each member, before he takes his seat, shall make and subscribe the following declaration, viz.

I do believe in one God, the Creator and Governor of the universe, the rewarder of the good and punisher of the wicked. And I do acknowledge the scriptures of the old and new testament to be given by divine inspiration, and own and profess the protestant religion.

And no further or other religious test shall ever, hereafter, be required of any civil officer or magistrate in this State.[18]

The Constitutional Convention's Judicial Revolution

At the Constitutional Convention of 1787, Edmund Randolph defended a national oath of allegiance. He said that the officers of the states were already bound by oath to the states. "To preserve a due impartiality they ought to be equally bound by the Natl. Govt. The Natl. needs every support we can give it. The Executive & Judiciary of the States, notwithstanding their national independence on the State Legislatures are in fact, so dependent on them, that unless they be brought under some tie to the Natl. system, they will always lean too much to the State systems, whenever a contest arises between the two."[19] He added this comment as debate progressed: "We are erecting a supreme national government; ought it not be supported, and can we give it too many sinews?"[20]

A Loyalty Oath for U.S. Officials

It is to Hamilton's explanation on the need for this loyalty oath that we must turn in order to see what was really involved. He was

---

18. *Idem.*
19. Max Farrand (ed.), *Records of the Federal Convention*, I, p. 203; extract in *The Founders' Constitution*, IV, p. 637.
20. *Records*, I, p. 207; *idem.*

the most eloquent defender of the strongest possible national government. In *Federalist No. 27*, he stated plainly what was being done by means of this required oath. A new judicial relationship was being created by the Constitution: *a direct covenant between the new national civil government with the individual citizen, without any intermediary civil government.* (This alteration is generally regarded by legal theorists as the most important single innovation that the Constitution imposed.)

The lack of intermediate governments, social and civil, between the individual and the national civil government, was the heart of Rousseau's concept of the General Will, meaning the heart of Rousseau's totalitarianism, as Robert Nisbet and many other scholars have argued.[21] Because the colonial political and social traditions were Christian, and therefore decentralist and *institutionally* pluralist (though not ethically pluralist), the Constitution could not have been ratified, had any comparable degree of monolithic sovereignty been passed to the national government. But Hamilton made it clear that the Constitution, when ratified, would take a major step forward in the direction of Rousseau's General Will ideal or weakening intermediary civil governments. He wrote:

> The plan reported by the Convention, by extending the authority of the foederal head to the individual citizens of the several States, will enable the government to employ the ordinary magistry of each in the execution of its laws. It is easy to perceive that this will tend to destroy, in the common apprehension, all distinction between the sources from which they might proceed; and will give the Foederal Government the same advantage for securing a due obedience to its authority, which is enjoyed by the government of each State; in addition to the influence on public opinion, which will result from the important consideration of its having power to call to its assistance and support the resources of the whole Union. It merits particular attention in this place, that the laws of the confederacy, as to the *enumerated* and *legitimate* objects of its jurisdiction, will become the SUPREME LAW of the land; to the observance of which, all officers legislative, executive and judicial in each State, will be bound by the sanctity of an oath. Thus the Legislatures, Courts and Magistrates of the respective members will be incorporated into the operations of the national government, *as far as its just and constitutional authority extends;* and will be rendered auxiliary to the enforcement of its laws."[22]

---

21. Robert A. Nisbet, *Tradition and Revolt: Historical and Sociological Essays* (New York: Random House, 1968), ch. 1: "Rousseau and the Political Community." J. L. Talmon, *The Origins of Totalitarian Democracy* (New York: Praeger, 1960).

22. Hamilton, Federalist 27, *The Federalist*, edited by Jacob E. Cook (Middletown, Connecticut: Wesleyan University Press, 1961), pp. 174-75; extract in *Founders' Constitution*, IV, p. 641.

Hamilton did not consider the loyalty oath irrelevant. He understood very well the important role it would play judicially and also in public opinion.

Objections to it were raised at the Convention. James Wilson of Virginia said "A good Govt. did not need them, and a bad one could not or ought not to be supported."[23] His objection was voted down. The delegates to the Convention knew the importance of oaths, public and secret, especially secret.

Religious Tests

Now we come to the second part of Article VI's provisions on a *religious* loyalty oath. That meant, in the context of the required state oaths, a *Christian* loyalty oath. At this point, the arguments for and against oaths were reversed. There is no need for such an oath, a majority of the Convention's delegates insisted. Echoing Wilson's comments on the uselessness of a federal oath, Madison later wrote to Edmund Pendelton: "Is not a religious test as far as it is necessary, or would be operate, involved in the oath itself? If the person swearing believes in the supreme Being who is invoked, and in the penal consequences of offending him, either in this or a future world or both, he will be under the same restraint from perjury as if he had previously subscribed to a test requiring this belief. If the person in question be an unbeliever in these points and would notwithstanding take an oath, a previous test could have no effect. He would subscribe to it as he would take the oath, without any principle that could be affected by either."[24] In short, a believer already believes; a liar will subscribe; so why bother with an oath? This argument was used by other defenders of the abolition of a religious oath.[25]

But the argument misses a key point: What about *honest* Deists who would not want to betray their principles by taking a false oath? A Christian oath would bar them from serving as covenantal agents of the ultimate sovereign, the God of the Bible. By removing the requirement of the oath, the Convention's delegates were in fact opening up the door to federal office-holding that would otherwise be

---

23. *Records*, II, p. 87; in *ibid.*, IV, p. 638.

24. *Founders' Constitution*, IV, p. 639. Cf. Mr. Spencer, North Carolina ratifying convention, in *The Debates in the Several State Conventions on the Adoption of the Federal Constitution*, edited by Jonathan Elliot, 5 vols. (Philadelphia: Lippencott, [1836] 1907), IV, p. 200.

25. Cf. Mr. Shute in the debate in Massachusetts' ratifying convention: *ibid.*, IV, p. 642; Mr. Iredell of North Carolina: Elliot, *Debates*, IV, p. 193.

closed to *honest* non-Christians, a point observed by some of the defenders of the removal of the religious test.[26] It would also open up
offices of authority to *men who had taken other binding oaths that were
hostile to Christianity — men who had taken these rival oaths in good faith.*
That possibility was never openly discussed, but it was a possibility
which lay silently in the background of the closed Convention in
Philadelphia. By closing the literal doors in Philadelphia the delegates were opening the judicial door to a new group of officials. They
were therefore closing the judicial door to the original authorizing
Sovereign Agent under whom almost all officials had been serving
from the very beginning of the country.

Greco-Roman Models

The fact remains that John Locke, a private and cautious Trinitarian, made no mention of Christianity in presenting the case for
political liberty in his *Second Treatise of Government* (1690). It was to the
Second Treatise that literate defenders of English liberties appealed in
the eighteenth century, not to his *Paraphrase and Notes on the Epistles of
St. Paul*, which were non-political.[27] We find few references to the
Christian religion in *Cato's Letters* and *The Independent Whig*, the anti-
clerical and libertarian English newspapers of the 1720's that became
popular reading in the colonies in the 1770's, according to John
Adams[28] and patriot historian David Ramsey.[29] If one were to trace
the political thought of John Adams back to anyone, it would have to
be James Harrington, the author of *The Commonwealth of Oceana*
(1656), a secular, aristocratic document that is concerned with questions of property and political power, not covenants and dominion.[30]

---

26. Trench Coxe, Oliver Ellsworth, Mr. Shute, Edmund Randolph: *Founders'
Constitution*, IV, pp. 639, 643, 644.

27. Locke wrote manuscripts that were published posthumously in 1704-7, and
have been ignored by historians: *A Paraphrase and Notes on the Epistles of St. Paul* (5th
ed.; London, 1751). Locke, in discussing chapter 2 of Galatians, affirms both God's
revelation to Paul and the miracles Paul performed (p. 10, note 2). He speaks of the
Holy Ghost and His bestowal of the office of apostle on Peter and Paul, "whereby
they were enabled to do Miracles for the Confirmation of their Doctrine" (p. 14,
note 8).

28. David L. Jacobson (ed.), *The English Libertarian Heritage* (Indianapolis, Indiana:
Bobbs-Merrill, 1965). Adams' remark is reproduced in the Introduction, p. xvii.

29. David Ramsey, *History of the United States* (1816), I; extract in Verna M. Hall
(ed.), *The Christian History of the American Revolution: Consider and Ponder* (San Francisco: Foundation for American Christian Education, 1976), p. 435.

30. Zoltan Harasti, *John Adams and the Prophets of Progress* (New York: Grosset and
Dunlap, [1952] 1964), pp. 34-35.

Harrington explained so Puritan a conflict as the English Civil War of the 1640's in terms of social forces, not religion, a secular tradition of historiography to which Marxist historian Christopher Hill appeals.[31] The textbook histories of the American Revolution from the earliest days have been far closer to Harrington's view of historical causation than to R. J. Rushdoony's.

We do not find authoritative references to the Bible or church history in either *The Federalist Papers* or the Anti-Federalist tracts. Adrienne Koch's compilation of primary source documents, *The American Enlightenment*, is not mythological, even though it is self-consciously selective.[32] There was an American Enlightenment, though subdued in its hostility to Christianity.[33] Jefferson, after all, kept hidden his cut up, re-pasted New Testament, purged of the miraculous and supernatural; he knew what his constituents would have thought of such a theology.[34] He refused to publish this book, he told his friend, Christian physician Benjamin Rush, because he was "averse to the communication of my religious tenets to the public, because it would countenance the presumption of those who have endeavored to draw them before that tribunal, and to seduce public opinion to erect itself into that inquest over the rights of conscience, which the laws have so justly proscribed."[35] That is, if word got out to the American voters, who were overwhelmingly Christian in their views, regarding what he really believed about religion, he and his party might lose the next election, despite a generation of systematic planning by him and his Deistic Virginia associates to get Christianity removed from the political arena in both Virginia and in national elections.[36] (The book was not made public until 1902. In 1904, the 57th Congress reprinted 9,000 copies, 3,000 for use by Senators and 6,000 for the House.[37] It was a very different America in 1904.)

---

31. Christopher Hill, *Puritanism and Revolution: Studies in Interpretation of the English Revolution of the 17th Century* (New York: Schoken, [1958] 1964), p. 5.

32. Adrienne Koch (ed.), *The American Enlightenment: The Shaping of the American Experiment and a Free Society* (New York: Braziller, 1965).

33. Henry F. May, *The Enlightenment in America* (New York: Oxford University Press, 1976).

34. *The Life and Morals of Jesus of Nazareth Extracted textually from the Gospels.* Reprinted as *An American Christian Bible Extracted by Thomas Jefferson* (Rochester, Washington: Sovereign Press, 1982).

35. Cited by Russell Kirk, *The Roots of American Order* (LaSalle, Illinois: Open Court, 1974), pp. 342-43.

36. *Ibid.*, p. 343.

37. Introduction, *American Christian Bible*, p. 4.

The Founding Fathers self-consciously appealed back to Roman law and classical political models in their defense of the Constitution. Madison, Jay, and Hamilton used the Roman name "Publius" in signing the *Federalist Papers*. The anti-Federalists responded with pseudo-Roman names. The political discourse of the age was dominated by classical models, not by the Bible. The classical education model of Oxford and Cambridge did its work of secularization in the English-speaking world (even in Puritan Harvard and Yale, which is why neither university remained Christian) until the post-Darwinian worldview and modern specialization led to the elective system. What we must understand from the beginning is that the U.S. Constitution is a product of a self-conscious Enlightenment appeal back to the Greco-Roman world.

The Fourteenth Amendment

Then came the Civil War (1861-65) and the unconstitutionally ratified Fourteenth Amendment (1868).[38] It is with the Fourteenth Amendment, as Harvard legal historian Raoul Berger has so conclusively demonstrated, that we find the origins of what he calls government by judiciary.[39]

We need to consider the Fourteenth Amendment in relation to citizenship. The first sentence of Section 1 reads:

All persons born or naturalized in the United States, and subject to the jurisdiction thereof, are citizens of the United States and the State wherein they reside.

The Constitution had not previously defined "citizen." Citizenship had been left to the individual states to define. After the Civil War, freed slaves needed legal protection. Thus, they were made full citizens under the protection of the law. They had not been protected as citizens prior to the war. This was one reason why the Constitution had been silent regarding citizenship: to avoid a walk-out by Southern delegates to the Convention. The other reason was religious: the states in 1787 had made Christian faith the basis of citizenship. To have admitted this judicially at the national level, the

---

38. Walter J. Suthon, Jr., "The Dubious Origin of the Fourteenth Amendment," *Tulane Law Review*, XXVIII (1953), pp. 22-44.

39. Raoul Berger, *Government by Judiciary: The Transformation of the Fourteenth Amendment* (Cambridge, Massachusetts: Harvard University Press, 1977).

Framers would have had to abandon their judicial confrontation against Christianity.

American citizens now take this inherently atheistic national oath of citizenship. They take it at birth. It is taken *implicitly* and *representatively.* They are citizens by birth. This concept — citizenship by physical birth and geography — is absolutely crucial in understanding the transformation of the American covenant. In the Massachusetts Bay Colony in the seventeenth century, an adult male became a citizen by formal church covenant. Without formal church membership, he was merely a town resident, not a citizen. This system began to break down almost from the beginning; becoming a property holder made you eligible to vote in town elections, though not always in colony-wide elections. Steadily, the possession of capital replaced the oath as the basis of political citizenship. Later, the formal development of this principle of civil contract became John Locke's intellectual legacy to political thought.[40]

Nevertheless, there was always the oath taken in a civil court. God's name was brought into the proceedings. Locke was aware of the binding nature of an oath, and its religious foundations. In his *Essay on Toleration* (1685), he specifically exempted the atheist from the civil protection of toleration: "Lastly, those are not all to be tolerated who deny the being of God. Promises, covenants, and oaths, which are the bonds of human society, can have no hold upon an atheist. The taking away of God, though but even in thought, dissolves all; besides also, those that by their atheism undermine and destroy all religion, can have no pretence of religion whereupon to challenge the privilege of toleration."[41] The oath to God reminded a citizen of the Sovereign who would impose sanctions on courtroom liars, so men were required to swear with one hand on a Bible and the other one raised toward heaven. Presidents still do this when they have the Constitutional oath administered to them. This rite is not required by law. It is an empty formal rite in the eyes of most

---

40. I do not wish to overemphasize Locke's impact on American political thinking. An American edition of his *Treatise on Civil Government* did not appear until 1773. Of far greater influence were the writings of the 1720's by John Trenchard and Thomas Gordon in *Cato's Letters* and *The Independent Whig*. See Bernard Bailyn, *The Ideological Origins of the American Revolution* (Cambridge, Massachusetts: Harvard University Press, 1967), pp. 25-36, 43-45. See also Robbins, *Eighteenth-Century Commonwealthman, op. cit.*

41. Locke, *Treatise of Civil Government and A Letter Concerning Toleration*, edited by Charles L. Sherman (New York: Appleton-Century Co., 1937), pp. 212-13.

people, yet rites are never entirely empty. There is always some mysterious element in a rite, some degree of foreboding if the proper traditional formulas are not observed. The shell of the original civil covenant still perseveres.

The Fourteenth Amendment completed the work begun by the anti-Trinitarian Founding Fathers who led the Constitutional ratification movement, men committed to an anti-Trinitarian concept of political citizenship: Washington, Madison, Jefferson, Hamilton, John Adams, and Franklin.[42]

Those hostile to Article VI, Clause 3 suspected what might happen. Criticisms of this provision were offered in several of the state ratifying conventions. Henry Abbot of North Carolina was especially prophetic: ". . . if there be no religious test required, pagans, deists, and Mahometans might obtain offices among us, and that the senators and representatives might all be pagans."[43] His warning was not heeded. But this objection was more distinctively political and practical. The more important issue was covenantal, but the opponents of the Constitution did not fully understand this. (Surely today's textbook commentators do not.) The officers of the U.S. government are not to be subjected to a religious test for holding office.

We must understand what this means. It means that *civil officers are not under an oath administered by the God of the Bible.* It means that in the exercise of their various offices, civil magistrates are bound by an oath to a different god. That god is the People, considered as an autonomous sovereign who possesses original *and final* earthly jurisdiction. This view of the sovereign People is radically different from anything formally stated or publicly assumed by all previous Christian political philosophers. The People are no longer acting as God's delegated judicial agents but as their own agent. This same view of political sovereignty undergirded Rousseau's political theory, and also the various constitutions of the French Revolution. The ratification of the U.S. Constitution was therefore a formal covenantal step toward the left-wing Enlightenment and away from the halfway covenant political philosophy of Christianity combined with right-wing

---

42. That these men were Enlightenment figures is obvious from their writings — the right-wing Scottish Enlightenment. See Adrienne Koch (ed.), *The American Enlightenment: The Shaping of the American Experiment and a Free Society* (New York: Braziller, 1965). This book is a compilation of writings from five of the six; only Washington is excluded.

43. Henry Abbot, North Carolina ratifying convention: Elliot's *Debates*, IV, p. 192.

Scottish Enlightenment rationalism. It would take the rise of Darwinism and the victory of the North in the Civil War to make clear the definitive nature of this definitive step toward Rousseau.[44]

The Framers knew that religious oaths were required for testifying in local and state courts. They knew that religious oaths were sometimes required for exercising the franchise in state elections. But they made it clear: *Federal jurisdiction is governed by another covenant, and therefore by another god.* It is therefore a rival system of hierarchy. It is not a complementary system of courts; it is rival system, *for an oath to the God of the Bible is prohibited by law in one of those hierarchies.*

Rushdoony's Rewriting of Constitutional History

It is this covenantal fact which Rushdoony, in his 30-year defense of the Constitution as an implicitly Christian document, has refused to face. Indeed, he has created a whole mythology regarding the oath in order to buttress his case. To an audience of Australian Christians, who could not be expected to be familiar with the U.S. Constitution, he said in 1983: "In every country where an oath of office is required, as is required in the United States by the Constitution, the oath has reference to swearing to almighty God to abide by His covenant, invoking the cursings and blessings of God for obedience and disobedience."[45] But what does the Constitution actually say? Exactly the opposite: "no religious Test shall ever be required as a Qualification to any Office or public Trust under the United States." To his own American audiotape audience, he insisted: "The Constitution required an oath of office. To us this doesn't mean much. Then it meant that you swore to Almighty God and involved all the curses and blessings of Deuteronomy 28 and Leviticus 26 for obedience and disobedience. Nobody knows that anymore."[46] Nobody knew it then, either; it did not happen. Rushdoony has never offered so much as a footnote supporting such a claim *with respect to the U.S. Constitution.* The story is mythical. What he has done is to pretend

---

44. I am not arguing that this was a self-conscious step toward Rousseau. Rousseau's influence in colonial America was minimal, limited mainly to his educational theories in *Emile.* See Paul M. Spyrlin, *Rousseau in America, 1760-1809* (University, Alabama: University of Alabama Press, 1969).

45. Rushdoony, *The "Atheism" of the Early Church* (Blackheath, New South Wales: Logos Foundation, 1983), p. 77.

46. Rushdoony, question and answer session at the end of his message on Leviticus 8:1-13 (Jan. 30, 1987).

that the oath-taking that did take place at the state level became a Christian oath-taking ceremony at the Federal level.

How, in good conscience, could he announce this to his followers? "An oath to the men who wrote the Constitution was a Biblical fact and a social necessity."[47] If this was true, then why did they exclude God from the mandatory oath? They well understood the importance of oaths.[48] They insisted on a required oath as the judicial (and psychological) foundation of a Federal officer's allegiance to the U.S. Constitution. They well knew the importance of oaths. It was not because they were all Christians; it was because so many of the leaders were Freemasons.[49] They had all sworn to a Masonic self-maledictory blood oath, for there was no other way to become a Mason. This is the most crucial neglected topic in the historiography of the Revolutionary War era, and especially the Constitutional Convention, which Rushdoony has known about from the beginning of his published career,[50] but which he has categorically refused

---

47. Rushdoony, "The United States Constitution," *Journal of Christian Reconstruction*, XII, No. 1 (1988), pp. 28-29.

48. Writes Albert G. Mackey, the Masonic historian: "It is objected that the oath is attended with a penalty of a serious or capital nature. If this be the case, it does not appear that the expression of a penalty of any nature whatever can affect the purport or augment the solemnity of an oath, which is, in fact, an attestation of God to the truth of a declaration, as a witness and avenger; and hence every oath includes in itself, and as its very essence, the covenant of God's wrath, the heaviest of all penalties, as the necessary consequence of its violation." Albert G. Mackey (ed.), *An Encyclopaedia of Freemasonry and Its Kindred Sciences*, 2 vols. (New York: Masonic History Co., [1873] 1925), II, p. 523. On the illegitimacy of such self-maledictory oaths except in church, State, or family, see Gary North, *The Sinai Strategy: Economics and the Ten Commandments* (Tyler, Texas: Institute for Christian Economics, 1986), ch. 3.

49. James D. Carter, *Masonry in Texas: Background, History, and Influence to 1846* (Austin: University of Texas Press, 1955), chaps. 2,3, Appendix 2; Dorothy Ann Lipson, *Freemasonry in Federalist Connecticut* (Princeton, New Jersey : Princeton University Press, 1977), ch. 1; Sidney Morse, *Freemasonry in the American Revolution* (Washington, D.C.: Masonic Service Association, 1924); J. Hugo Tatsch, *Freemasonry in the Thirteen Colonies* (New York: Macoy, 1929); Tatsch, *The Facts About George Washington as a Freemason* (New York: Macoy, 1931); Philip A. Roth, *Masonry in the Formation of our Government, 1761-1799* (Wisconsin: Masonic Service Bureau, 1927). A comparative study of freemasonry in both the American and French revolutions is Bernard Faÿ, *Freemasonry and Revolution, 1680-1800* (Boston: Little, Brown, 1935). A non-Masonic historian who is familiar with Masonic historical records needs to produce a detailed study of the lodge membership of signers of both the Declaration of Independence and the Constitution. William J. Whalen says that a certain Gen. John C. Smith discovered that only six signers of the Declaration were lodge members, rather than the 55 claimed by Masons, but Whalen does not footnote this source nor mention it in his bibliography. William J. Whalen, *Christianity and American Freemasonry* (Milwaukee: Bruce, 1958), p. 6.

50. See his reference to Faÿ in his book, *The Nature of American History* (Fairfax, Virginia: Thoburn Press, [1965] 1978), p. 143n.

to discuss publicly. The reader must search his footnotes for the appropriate bibliographical leads, and very few readers do this. He only discusses freemasonry in relation to the French Revolution, which he knows was pagan to the core, and in relation to New England in the nineteenth century. He insists that "This decline came later. At the time of the Revolution and much later, New England and the rest of the country shared a common faith and experience."[51] Absolutely crucial to his interpretation of Constitutional history is what he never mentions: the legally secular ("neutral") character of Article VI, Section 3. He pretends that it does not says what it says, and it does not mean what it has always meant: a legal barrier to Christian theocracy. Instead, he rewrites history:

> Forces for secularization were present in Washington's day and later, French sympathizers and Jacobins, deists, Illuminati, Freemasons, and soon the Unitarians. But the legal steps towards secularization were only taken in the 1950's and 1960's by the U.S. Supreme Court. For the sake of argument [!!!!!—G.N.], we may concede to the liberal, and to some orthodox Christian scholars,[52] that Deism had made extensive inroads into America by 1776, and 1787, and that the men of the Constitutional Convention, and Washington, were influenced by it. The fact still remains that they did not attempt to create a secular state. The states were Christian states, and the federal union, while barred from intervention in this area, was not itself secular. The citizens were citizens of their respective states and of the United States simultaneously. They could not be under two sets of religious law.[53]

This is mytho-history designed to calm the fears of Bible-believing Christians as they look back to the origin of the Constitution. Of course the Framers created a secular state. The secular character of the Federal union was established by the oath of office. Politically, the Framers could not in one fell swoop create a secular state in a Christian country; judicially and covenantally, they surely did. Hamilton made it clear in *Federalist 27* that the oath of allegiance to the Constitution superseded all state oaths. That was why he insisted on it. Yet Rushdoony substitutes the language of church worship

---

51. Rushdoony, *This Independent Republic: Studies in the Nature and Meaning of American History* (Fairfax, Virginia: Thoburn Press, [1964] 1978), p. 60.

52. He seems to have in mind here C. Gregg Singer's *A Theological Interpretation of American History* (Nutley, New Jersey: Craig Press, 1964), ch. 2: "Deism in Colonial Life."

53. Rushdoony, *Nature of American History*, p. 48.

when speaking of early American politics: "Officers of the federal government, president and congress, worshipped as an official body, but without preference extended to a single church."[54] In February, 1860, the House of Representatives invited the first rabbi to give the invocation, only a few years after the first synagogue was established in Washington, using a New York rabbi, since no officially ordained rabbi was yet in Washington.[55] It took no Supreme Court decision to make this covenantal denial of a judicially Christian culture a reality. It was not the product of nineteenth-century freemasonry. It was the product of late-eighteenth-century freemasonry. It was an outworking of Article VI, Section 3.

That a President might, as Washington did (and George Bush did two centuries later) swear his non-religious oath of office with his hand on a Masonic Bible, is legally and covenantally irrelevant. (That this same copy of the Bible was used by four other Presidents at their inaugurations is surely symbolically significant.)[56] An oath, to be judicially binding, must be *verbal*. It must call down God's sanctions on the oath-taker. This is what is specifically made illegal by the U.S. constitution. Any implied sanctions are secular, not divine. Without this self-maledictory aspect, a symbolic gesture is not a valid biblical oath. Rushdoony knows this, which is why he has invented the myth of the Levitical and Deuteronomic "almost-oath." The Presidents have thrown a sop of a symbol to the Christians — one hand on a Bible while taking an explicitly and legally non-Christian oath — and the Christians have accepted this as being somehow pleasing in God's eyes.

Covenants and Sanctions

Every covenant has sanctions. Without sanctions, there is no covenant. Rushdoony knows this, which is why he invokes Leviticus 26 and Deuteronomy 28: they set forth God's sanctions in history. The Constitution is a covenant document. He writes that "the Con-

---

54. *Idem.*

55. Bertram W. Korn, "Rabbis, Prayers, and Legislatures," *Hebrew Union College Annual*, XXIII, Part II (1950-51), pp. 95-108. Part of the reason for this delay was that there had not been a Jewish congregation in Washington, D.C. until 1852, and they worshipped in homes until 1855. Those pastors asked to pray before Congress were usually local pastors (p. 109). The rabbi who gave the prayer was Dr. Morris J. Raphall of New York City.

56. *Life* (Feb. 1989), p. 8.

stitution is not only a law but also a contract or covenant."[57] The question is: Whose sanctions are invoked by this covenant document? Clearly, autonomous man's sanctions. Rushdoony knows this. So he has restructured all political theory to create a justification of this absence of any reference to God's law or God's sanctions: "*Second*, we must remember that the Constitution can make no man nor nation good; it is not a moral code. It does not give us a substantive morality, but it does reflect a procedural morality."[58]

Notice the shift in the argument: the Constitution cannot make anyone good. This is the standard humanist line against all Christian legislation: "You can't legislate morality!" What Rushdoony has always maintained is that you can't legislate *anything except* morality. As he wrote in the *Institutes of Biblical Law* (1973), "But, it must be noted, *coercion against evil-doers is the required and inescapable duty of the civil authority*."[59] Again, "law is a form of warfare. By law, certain acts are abolished, and the persons committing those acts either executed or brought into conformity to law."[60]

Of course the Constitution cannot make anyone good; the function of biblical civil law is not to make anyone good; it is *to suppress public evil*. For 30 years, Rushdoony previously had argued that any other view of civil law is the "work's doctrine" of all non-Christian religion: *salvation by law*. This is humanism's view, he always insisted: "Man finds salvation through political programs, through legislation, so that *salvation is an enactment of the state*."[61] What is the Christian alternative? To enforce God's law and God's sanctions in history, and *only* God's law and God's sanctions.

The second aspect of *man under law* is that man's relationship to law becomes *ministerial, not legislative*, that is, man does not create law, does not decree what shall be right and wrong simply in terms of his will. Instead, man seeks, in his law-making, to approximate and administer fundamental

---

57. Rushdoony, "U.S. Constitution," p. 21.

58. *Ibid.*, p. 22.

59. Rushdoony, *The Institutes of Biblical Law* (Nutley, New Jersey: Craig Press, 1973), p. 292. Contrast this statement with the following position taken in the *Journal of Christian Reconstruction*: "God did not make salvation coercive. Neither is morality coercive. . . . Punishing sin is *not* a role delegated to civil government." Tommy W. Rogers, "Federalism and Republican Government: An Application of Biblically Derived Cultural Ethos to Political Economy," vol. XII, No. 1 (1988), p. 95.

60. *Ibid.*, p. 191. See also pp. 92-95.

61. Rushdoony, *Politics of Guilt and Pity* (Fairfax, Virginia: Thoburn Press, [1970] 1978), p. 145.

law, law in terms of God's law, absolute right and wrong. Neither majority nor minority wishes are of themselves right or wrong; both are subject to judgment in terms of the absolute law of God, and the largest majority cannot make valid and true a law contrary to the word of God. All man's lawmaking must be in conformity to the higher law of God, or it is false.[62]

A fourth aspect of man under law is that *law means true order as justice.* The law is justice, and it is order, godly order, and there can be neither true order nor true law apart from justice, and justice is defined in terms of Scripture and its revelation of God's law and righteousness. The law cannot be made more than justice. It cannot be made into an instrument of salvation without destruction to justice. Salvation is not by law but by the grace of God through Jesus Christ.[63]

The issue is *justice, not salvation.* So, why does he now raise the spurious issue that the Constitution "can make no man nor nation good; it is not a moral code"? This is utter nonsense; *every law-order is a moral code.* This had been Rushdoony's refrain for 30 years! As he wrote in the *Institutes,* there is "an absolute moral order to which man must conform."[64] He insisted therefore that "there can be no tolerance in a law-system for another religion. Toleration is a device used to introduce a new law-system as a prelude to a new intolerance."[65] In this sentence, he laid the theological foundation for a biblical critique of the U.S. Constitution as a gigantic religious fraud, a rival covenant, "a device used to introduce a new law-system as a prelude to a new intolerance," which it surely was and has become. But he has been blinded for 30 years by his love of the Constitution. In a showdown between his theocratic theology and the U.S. Constitution, he chose the Constitution.

He says that it will do no good for Christians to appeal to the Constitution. "The Constitution can restore nothing, nor can it make the courts or the people just."[66] The courts are the enforcing arm of the Constitution, yet it supposedly cannot make the courts good. Of course it cannot; but a Constitution can and must *prohibit evil, lawless decisions by lower courts.* It must reverse all lower court decisions that are not in conformity to the fundamental law of the land. This is the doctrine of judicial review. This is the whole idea of

---

62. *Ibid.,* p. 143.
63. *Ibid.,* p. 144.
64. Rushdoony, *Institutes,* p. 18.
65. *Ibid.,* p. 5.
66. Rushdoony, "U.S. Constitution," p. 39.

American Constitutional law. Rushdoony knows this. In 1973, he appealed to that crucial covenantal and legal concept: *sanctions*. He warned Christians that the concept of treason is inescapably religious:

> But no law-order can survive if it does not defend its core faith by rigorous sanctions. The law-order of humanism leads only to anarchy. Lacking absolutes, a humanistic law-order tolerates everything which denies absolutes while warring against Biblical faith. The only law of humanism is ultimately this, that there is no law except self-assertion. It is "Do what thou wilt.". . . To tolerate an alien law-order is a very real subsidy of it: it is a warrant for life to that alien law-order, and a sentence of death against the established law-order. [67]

The Founding Fathers issued a death warrant against Christianity, but for tactical reasons, they and their spiritual heirs refused for several generations to deliver it. They covered this covenantal death sentence with a lot of platitudes about the hand of Providence, the need for Morality, the grand design of the universe, and similar Masonic shibboleths. The death sentence was delivered by the Fourteenth Amendment. It has been carried out since the 1950's. But Rushdoony dares not admit this chain of covenantal events. He writes as though everything bad leaped full-blown from the head of Chief Justice Earl Warren, a *Zeus ex machina* of American Constitutional law. To admit the historical truth would mean that a restoration of so-called "original American Constitutionalism" would change nothing covenantally.

The Constitution must prevent treason. Every constitution must. Treason is always a religious issue. The question must be raised: In terms of the U.S. Constitution, what constitutes treason, Christianity or pluralism (secular humanism)? If you want to see the change in his thinking, consider these observations:

> [1973:] The question thus is a basic one: what constitutes treason in a culture? Idolatry, i.e., treason to God, or treason to the state? [68]

> [1973:] Because for Biblical law the foundation is the one true God, the central offense is therefore treason to that God by idolatry. Every law-order has its concept of treason. . . . Basic to the health of a society is the integrity of its foundation. To allow tampering with its foundation is to allow its total subversion. Biblical law can no more permit the propagation of idolatry

---

67. Rushdoony, *Institutes*, pp. 66, 67.
68. *Ibid.*, p. 68.

than Marxism can permit counter-revolution, or monarchy a move to execute the king, or a republic an attempt to destroy the republic and create a dictatorship.[69]

[1973:] The commandment is, "Thou shalt have no other gods before me." In our polytheistic world, the many other gods are the many peoples, every man his own god. Every man under humanism is his own law, and his own universe.[70]

[1988:] The Constitution is no defense against idolatry; . . .[71]

Substantive vs. Procedural Justice

This is a basic dualism of all humanistic thought: ethics vs. procedure in the judicial system. Max Weber, the great German sociologist, spent considerable space dealing with this dualism, and I devoted a section of my essay on Weber to just this topic in Chalcedon's book of essays honoring Van Til.[72] I concluded that discussion with this warning: "Weber's vision of the increasingly bureaucratic, rationalized society hinged on the very real probability of such a subordination of substantive law to formal law. . . . He hated what he saw, but he saw no escape. Bureaucracy, whether socialistic or capitalistic, is here."[73]

Today, reversing his entire intellectual career (except for his view on the Constitution as somehow an implicitly Christian document) — including his commitment to Van Til's presuppositional apologetics, as well as his commitment to biblical law — Rushdoony says that the Constitution's procedural morality can be *and is* legitimately religiously neutral, and that any interest group can adopt the Constitution's procedural morality to create whatever law-order they choose, without violating the text of the nation's covenanting document. *But the text is all there is of the underlying religious foundation.* If the text were silent, then there would be no formal underpinning. But the text is not silent. The text categorically prohibits the imposition of the biblical covenant oath in civil law. Let us put it covenantally: *what the text of the U.S. Constitution prohibits is Christianity.*

---

69. *Ibid.*, pp. 38-39.

70. *Ibid.*, p. 40.

71. Rushdoony, "U.S. Constitution," p. 43.

72. Gary North (ed.), *Foundations of Christian Scholarship: Essays in the Van Til Perspective* (Vallecito, California: Ross House Books, 1976), pp. 141-46.

73. *Ibid.*, p. 146.

There can be no dualism in a covenantal document. It either serves the God of the Bible or some other God. There can be no neutrality. Constitutions are inherently substantive, but this ethical foundation is manifested in its procedural stipulations. Rushdoony built the case for biblical law in society by arguing that every covenant requires a unique law that reflects its concept of ultimate authority, i.e., *sovereignty.* He even rejected Calvin's affirmation of a universal law of nations in preference to Mosaic law as "heretical nonsense."[74] (That Calvin was no theonomist is clear; that he was no defender of secular natural law theory is also clear. The *Institutes* are misleading if read apart from his other writings on civil law.)[75]

So, following his lead, I cannot but conclude that his distinction — indeed, dualism — between the Constitution's supposedly neutral procedural law and the supposedly implicit Christian religious foundations of America is simply nonsense. It is an affirmation of neutrality that cannot possibly exist, if Van Til is correct. Constitutional procedure is the covenantal development of the religious foundation of that covenant: in church, state, and family. To argue that a system of covenantal procedural sanctions is anything but a judicial development of the underlying covenantal law-order is to adopt a domestic version of Calvin's theory of a universal law of nations . . . and we know what Rushdoony thinks of that idea!

Rushdoony now admits that there is nothing in the U.S. Constitution to protect itself from the transformation from substantive (ethical) law to procedural (bureaucratic) law. "The U.S. Constitution gives us no substantive morality, only a procedural one."[76] This worldwide legal transformation is the crisis of Western civilization, writes Harvard legal historian Harold J. Berman,[77] yet Rushdoony says that the U.S. Constitution is inherently powerless to do anything about it. His view of the U.S. Constitution — that it is only a procedural document — is the same as saying that logic is only procedural or liturgy is only procedural, or that church government is

---

74. Rushdoony, *Institutes*, p. 9.

75. In his sermons on Deuteronomy 28, he reaffirmed the Old Testament's penal sanctions: *The Covenant Enforced: Sermons on Deuteronomy 27 and 28*, edited by James B. Jordan (Tyler, Texas: Institute for Christian Economics, 1990).

76. Rushdoony, "U.S. Constitution," p. 36.

77. Harold J. Berman, *Law and Revolution: The Formation of the Western Legal Tradition* (Cambridge, Massachusetts: Harvard University Press, 1983), Introduction.

only procedural, or that family government is only procedural. In short, he is saying what Van Til denied: that form can be segregated from content, ethically speaking. Rushdoony wrote in the *Institutes* that "The basic premise of the modern doctrine of toleration is that all religious and moral positions are equally true and equally false."[78] This is exactly the worldview which the Framers wrote into the Constitution when they abolished state religious tests for holding Federal office.

I cannot avoid the obvious conclusion: if a defense of the U.S. Constitution as being somehow inherently Christian, or in some way fundamentally conformable to Christianity, is the position of the Christian Reconstruction movement, this means the suicide of Christian Reconstructionism. Rushdoony said it best: "The modern concept of total toleration is not a valid legal principle but an advocacy of anarchism. Shall all religions be tolerated? But, as we have seen, every religion is a concept of law-order. Total toleration means total permissiveness for every kind of practice: idolatry, adultery, cannibalism, human sacrifice, perversion, and all things else. Such total toleration is neither possible nor desirable. . . . And for a law-order to forsake its self-protection is both wicked and suicidal."[79]

The Question of Sovereignty

His rewriting of U.S. history has gone on from the beginning. In the *Institutes*, he says that "The presidential oath of office, and every other oath of office in the United States, was in earlier years recognized precisely as coming under the third commandment, and, in fact, invoking it. By taking the oath, a man promised to abide by his word and his obligations even as God is faithful to His word. If he failed, by his oath of office, the public official invoked divine judgement and the curse of the law upon himself."[80] This is Presidential mytho-history.

Rushdoony's view of U.S. political history is heavily influenced by a bizarre idea that he picked up in a speech by President John Quincey Adams,[81] who shared his President father's Unitarian theology. So far as I know, no one else has maintained the following interpretation: the U.S. Constitution rests on no concept of God because

---

78. Rushdoony, *Institutes*, p. 295.
79. *Ibid.*, p. 89.
80. *Ibid.*, p. 111.
81. Cited in Rushdoony, *This Independent Republic*, p. 38.

the Framers believed that only God has legal sovereignty. In a brief and highly confusing (I would even say "confused") chapter, "Sovereignty," Rushdoony writes of American thought in the 1780's, "*Legal sovereignty was definitely denied. . . .*"[82] He says this distrust of legal sovereignty "was both early medieval and Calvinist." He offers no evidence for this statement. The thesis is sufficiently peculiar that some reference to primary source documentation is mandatory, but none is offered. He refuses to define what he means by "legal sovereignty," which makes things even more difficult. He cites some historians on Americans' opposition to the sovereign State, but it is clear from the context that their hostility was to a centralized, monopolistic sovereignty, which is not the point Rushdoony is trying to make.

The question Rushdoony has been attempting for three decades to avoid answering from the historical record is this one: Why did the Framers refuse to include a Trinitarian oath? If the states had such oaths—and they did—and the Patriot party regarded the colonies as legal, sovereign civil governments under the king, which is the thesis of *This Independent Republic*, then why not impose the oath requirement nationally? The presence of an oath is basic to any covenant, as Rushdoony knows. The question is: Who is the identifiable sovereign in the Federal covenant? And the answer of the Framers was clear, "We the People." Not we the states, but "We the people." It is right there in the Preamble.

Patrick Henry had been invited to attend the Philadelphia convention, but he had refused. He recognized what was implicitly being asserted in the Preamble. In the Virginia debate over ratification in 1788, he spoke out against ratification. He warned against the implications of "We the People": "Give me leave to demand, what right had they to say, 'We the People,' instead of 'We the States'? States are the characteristics, and the soul of a confederation. If the States be not the agents of this compact, it must be one great consolidated national government of the people of all the States . . . Had the delegates, who were sent to Philadelphia a power to propose a consolidated government instead of a confederacy? Were they not deputed by States, and not by the people? The assent of the people, in their collective capacity, is not necessary to the formation of a federal government. The people have no right to enter into leagues, alliances, or confederations: they are not the proper agents for this

---

82. *Ibid.*, p. 33.

purpose: States and sovereign powers are the only proper agents for this kind of government. Show me an instance where the people have exercised this business: has it not always gone through the legislatures?. . . . This, therefore, ought to depend on the consent of the legislatures." He said emphatically of the delegates, "The people gave them no power to use their name. That they exceeded their power is perfectly clear."[83] Rushdoony, for all his praise of Henry's Christianity, has steadfastly refused to discuss the religious and judicial foundation of Henry's opposition to ratification. This is not an oversight on Rushdoony's part. He knows exactly why Henry objected. Henry knew where this new government was headed. And so it has.

The Constitution was ratified under the presumption of the sovereignty of the people. But it was more than mere presumption: it is right there at the beginning of the document. Here is why there is no Trinitarian oath in the Constitution: the Framers were operating under the legal fiction that the sovereign People, not the God of the Bible, had authorized the new national covenant.[84] "We the People" were not the vassals of the Great King in this treaty; "We the People" *were* the great king, and there shall be no other gods beside "We the People." Thus, the Framers outlawed religious oaths. *Outlawed*!

It is hardly the case that the Framers had no concept of earthly legal sovereignty. It was that they had *only* a concept of earthly legal sovereignty. They wanted divine rights — not of kings, not of legislatures, but of the People. The divine right of kings doctrine meant that no one and no institution could appeal any decision of the king; he was *exclusively* sovereign under God. This was exactly what the oath of Article VI, Section 3 was intended to convey: *no appeal*. The national government was the final voice of the people, for it operated under the treaty of the great collective king: the Constitution. This was why the Framers insisted on requiring an oath of allegiance to the Constitution that made illegal any judicial allegiance to God by Federal officers. The oath made the Federal government sovereign. This is exactly what Hamilton announced in *Federalist 27*.[85] Yet

---

83. I am using the version in Norine Dickson Campbell, *Patrick Henry: Patriot and Statesman* (Old Greenwich, Connecticut: Devin-Adair, 1969), p. 338. This statement appears in Elliot's *Debates*, IV, p. 200. III, p. 22.

84. Edmund S. Morgan, *Inventing the People: The Rise of Popular Sovereignty in England and America* (New York: Norton, 1988).

85. Rushdoony has invented another historical myth: that Hamilton was ready to launch a new Christian Constitutional political party just before he was killed. He relates this legend in his taped lecture on Leviticus 8:1-13. Hamilton was the man

Rushdoony is still using this bit of mytho-history regarding the idea of sovereignty in the early American period in order to justify his defense of the Constitution. "The Constitution is unique in world history in that there is no mention of sovereignty, because sovereignty was recognized as being an attribute of God."[86] Indeed, it truly was seen as an attribute of God, and the Framers identified this god: the People.

The transformation of Rushdoony's biblical judicial theology of the early 1970's into a theological defense of judicial neutrality in the late 1980's was accurately predicted . . . by Rushdoony: "If a doctrine of authority embodies contradictions within itself, then it is eventually bound to fall apart as the diverse strains war against one another. This has been a continuing part of the various crises of Western civilization. Because the Biblical doctrine of authority has been compromised by Greco-Roman humanism, the tensions of authority have been sharp and bitter."[87] No sharper and no more bitter than in the remarkable case of *Rushdoony v. Rushdoony.*

Conclusion

The ratification of the U.S. Constitution in 1788 created a new nation based on a new covenant. The nation had broken with its Christian judicial roots by covenanting with a new god, the sovereign People. There would be no other God tolerated in the political order. There would be no appeal beyond this sovereign god. That collective god, speaking through the Federal government, began its

---

who engineered the acceptance of a privately owned central bank, the Bank of the United States, the forerunner of the modern Federal Reserve System. But he had apparently repented. The story of Hamilton's plans is Rushdoony's version of the familiar story of the death-bed conversions of atheists.

In response, let me cite Rushdoony's June, 1968 *Chalcedon Report*: "Why am I quoting this story? Because it illustrates so well the desire of many people for a happy ending, for fairy tales. A few years ago when I spoke in one city, a woman told me (the entire group knew the story from her) that Charles Darwin had renounced evolution in his old age and died a Christian. Also, she claimed this could be found in a book she had seen, of Darwin's letters, and the book had since disappeared from the public library. I stated that I owned the book, and it contained no such statement. The result: no one in that group wanted to hear me again!" He has said it best. Christians want to believe that enemies of the faith who are famous eventually convert to Christianity.

86. This was his reply to Otto Scott's comment about the U.S. being the first nation to establish itself without reference to God. Q & A, Leviticus sermon, Jan. 30, 1987.

87. Rushdoony, *Institutes*, p. 213.

inevitable expansion, predicted by the Anti-Federalists, most notably Patrick Henry. The secularization of the republic began in earnest. This process has not yet ceased.

Nevertheless, the surrender to secular humanism was not an overnight process. The rise of abolitionism, the coming of the Civil War, the advent of Darwinism, the growth of immigration, the development of the public school system, and a host of other social and political influences have all worked to transform the interdenominational American civil religion into a religion not fundamentally different from the one that Jeroboam set up, so that the people of the Northern Kingdom might not journey to Jerusalem in Judah to offer sacrifices (I Ki. 12:26-31). The golden calves may not be on the hilltops, but the theology is the same: religion exists to serve the needs of the State, and the State is sovereign over the material things of this world. There are many forms of idol worship. The worship of the U.S. Constitution has been a popular form of this ancient practice, especially in conservative Christian circles.

The sanctions of the pre-Constitutional colonial covenants are still in force. One cannot break covenant with the Great King. He will bring additional negative sanctions unless those original covenants are renewed. This, however, requires that we break covenant with the present god of this age, the People. The People are under God as legally protected vassals. If this is not acknowledged covenantally and formally, then the common people eventually will find themselves under tyrants as legally unprotected vassals.

SCRIPTURE INDEX

OLD TESTAMENT

NEW TESTAMENT

INDEX

If my time is worth what a plumber's is, then this index cost me about \$4,500 in forefeited earnings. The worst aspect of writing non-fiction is not "dry spells" — I've never had one, however — or the pain of creativity, or the pain in one's lower back, or the research effort. It is indexing. I hate to index.